Civilizations Past & Present

Twelfth Edition

Volume II: From 1300

Robert R. Edgar
Howard University

George F. Jewsbury
Centre d'études des mondes Russe, Caucasien, et Centre Européen. École des hautes études en sciences sociales

Neil J. Hackett
St. Louis University

Barbara Molony
Santa Clara University

Matthew S. Gordon
Miami University

This book has benefited from the contribution over many editions of the following authors:

T. Walter Wallbank (Late)
Alastair M. Taylor (Late)
Nels M. Bailkey
Clyde J. Lewis (Late)
Palmira Brummett

New York Boston San Francisco
London Toronto Sydney Tokyo Singapore Madrid
Mexico City Munich Paris Cape Town Hong Kong Montréal

Senior Acquisitions Editor: Janet Lanphier
Assistant Development Manager: David B. Kear
Development Editor: Adam Beroud
Executive Marketing Manager: Sue Westmoreland
Supplements Editor: Brian Belardi
Media Editor: Melissa Edwards
Production Manager: Eric Jorgensen
Project Coordination and Electronic Page Makeup: Electronic Publishing Services Inc., New York City
Text Design: Pre-press PMG
Senior Cover Design Manager: Nancy Danahy
Cover Image: Kuban Mask of Ngaddy aMwaash, Congo, © The Bridgeman Art Library/Getty Images, Inc.
Senior Manufacturing Buyer: Roy L. Pickering, Jr.
Printer and Binder: Courier Corporation
Cover Printer: Phoenix Color Corporation

Library of Congress Cataloging-in-Publication Data
Civilizations : past and present / Robert R. Edgar ... [et al.]. -- 12th ed.
p. cm.
Revision of: Civilization past & present. 11th ed.
Includes bibliographical references and index.
ISBN 978-0-205-57430-8 (combined vol. : alk. paper) -- ISBN 978-0-205-57375-2 (v. 1 : alk. paper) -- ISBN 978-0-205-57431-5 (v. 2 : alk. paper)
I. Edgar, Robert R. II. Civilization past & present.
CB69.C57 2008
930--dc22
2007038549

Please visit us at http://www.ablongman.com.

ISBN-13: 978-0-205-57430-8 (Combined Volume)
ISBN-10: 0-205-57430-0 (Combined Volume)
ISBN-13: 978-0-205-57375-2 (Volume One)
ISBN-10: 0-205-57375-4 (Volume One)
ISBN-13: 978-0-205-57431-5 (Volume Two)
ISBN-10: 0-205-57431-9 (Volume Two)

1 2 3 4 5 6 7 8 9 10—CRK—10 09 08 07

Brief Contents

Detailed Contents

Each chapter ends with a Conclusion, Suggestions for Web Browsing, Literature and Film, and Suggestions for Reading.

Chapter 15

State Development in Europe

Chapter 16

Global Encounters

Chapter 17

Absolutism and Limited Central Power in Europe, 1650–1774 Politics During the First Age of Capitalism 511

Chapter 18

New Ideas and Their Political Consequences The Scientific Revolution, the Enlightenment, and the French Revolutions 547

Chapter 19

Africa in the World Economy, 1650–1850 581

Chapter 20

Asian and Middle Eastern Empires and Nations, 1650–1815 607

Chapter 21

The Americas, 1650–1825

From European Dominance to Independence 639

Chapter 35

Asia and the South Pacific Since 1945

Political, Economic, and Social Revolutions 1047

Chapter 36

Into the Twenty-first Century

An Uncertain Future 1079

FEATURES

Documents

Maps

Global Issues

Discovery Through Maps

Seeing Connections

To the Instructor

The twelfth edition of *Civilizations Past & Present* continues to present a survey of world history, treating the development and growth of civilization as a global phenomenon involving the interaction of all of the world's cultures. This new edition, like its predecessors, includes all the elements of history—social, economic, political, military, religious, aesthetic, legal, and technological—to illustrate this global interaction.

Because economic and political events that happen in even the most remote corners of the earth affect each of us individually, an appreciation for all the civilizations of the world must be an essential aim of education. Thus, the twelfth edition of *Civilizations Past & Present* emphasizes world trends and carefully avoids placing these trends within a Western conceptual basis.

New to This Edition

The twelfth edition maintains the many strengths that have made *Civilizations Past & Present* a highly respected textbook throughout its many editions. As the authors revised the text, they relied on the latest historical scholarship and profited from suggestions from the book's users and reviewers. Throughout, they have sought to maintain the fluid writing style and consistent level of presentation—traits often lacking in multiauthored texts.

One of the most significant changes in the twelfth edition is the addition of a **new co-author,** Matthew Gordon. Matthew is a professor of Middle Eastern history at Miami University. Well versed in Islam and the Arab world of Late Antiquity, he has rewritten the chapters on the eastern Mediterranean and Islamic worlds.

This edition also benefits from the addition of **two new chapters:** "Latin America Since 1910: Reform, Repression, and Revolution" (Chapter 34) and a new final chapter, "Into the Twenty-first Century: An Uncertain Future" (Chapter 36). The new chapter on Latin America provides detailed coverage of the region, including the political, social, and economic challenges confronting its many nations from World War I into the twenty-first century. The new final chapter uses a worldwide perspective to examine the pressing issues of our times and the coming decades, including globalization, technology, migration, cultural conflict, and the environment.

Other chapter changes are as follow:

- **Chapter 1:** "Stone Age Societies and the Earliest Civilizations of the Near East" provides coverage of human prehistory, Mesopotamian and Egyptian civilizations, and the development of the smaller states and regional empires. This chapter now includes more on women in the ancient Near East.
- **Chapter 2:** "Early Chinese Civilization: From Neolithic Origins to 220 C.E." and **Chapter 3:** "Early Indian Civilizations: From Neolithic Origins to 300 C.E." explore the foundation of East Asian and South Asian civilizations, including expanded coverage of their cultural and economic linkages to other civilizations of Eurasia.
- **Chapter 6:** "The Eastern Mediterranean World, 300–750 C.E." has been completely rewritten by new co-author Matthew Gordon, and it now examines the three great Eastern Mediterranean/ Near Eastern states of Late Antiquity: the Sasanid, the Byzantine, and the Umayyad empires. The chapter examines the role that universalist faiths played in these three imperial states, giving special emphasis to Muhammad and the early development of Islam.
- **Chapter 7:** "The Islamic World, 800–1300 C.E." has also been rewritten by Matthew Gordon. This chapter picks up where Chapter 6 leaves off, examining the rise and fall of the Abbasid dynasty and other regional Islamic states, the further development of Islam, the arrival of Turkic peoples in the Near East, and Arab-Islamic responses to the Latin Crusades.
- **Chapter 8:** "African Beginnings: African Civilizations to 1500 C.E." contains new coverage of African cultural practices, religion, social institutions, family patterns, and art.
- **Chapter 9:** "The Formation of Christian Europe: 476–1300 C.E." now offers a more complete story by adding material on medieval Russia, Eastern Europe, and Byzantium that appeared in Chapter 6 of the eleventh edition.
- **Chapter 10:** "Culture, Power, and Trade in the Era of Asian Hegemony, 220–1350" now includes new material on the Srivijayan maritime empire of Southeast Asia and the early peoples and cultures of Oceania.
- **Chapter 15:** "State Development in Europe: Western and Central Europe, Russia, and the Balkans to 1650" has been enhanced by late medieval and early modern material about Russia and the Balkans that formerly appeared in Chapter 6 of the eleventh edition.
- **Chapter 16:** "Global Encounters: Europe and the New World Economy, 1400–1650" includes new material on women and social history.

- **Chapter 18:** "New Ideas and Their Political Consequences: The Scientific Revolution, the Enlightenment, and the French Revolutions" includes new material on the artistic movements of the era.
- **Chapter 19:** "Africa in the World Economy, 1650–1850" contains new coverage of African responses and resistance to the slave trade and Africa's role in the new world economy.
- **Chapter 20:** "Asian and Middle Eastern Empires and Nations, 1650–1815" includes new content about Australia and Oceania.
- **Chapter 23:** "Europe, 1815–1914: Political Change and Diplomatic Failure" was formerly Chapter 26 of the eleventh edition. The chapter adds new material on Russia in the first half of the nineteenth century, and the discussion of the United States during this same period has been moved to Chapter 26, providing sharper focus to both chapters.
- **Chapter 24:** "Africa and the Middle East During the Age of European Imperialism" has undergone structural refinement and contains new material on women in Africa and the German colonization of Namibia.
- **Chapter 25:** "Imperialism and Modernity in Asia and the Pacific, 1815–1914: India, Southeast Asia, China, Japan, and Oceania" provides expanded coverage of technology, modernity, and Social Darwinism in Japan and contains new material about Australia, New Zealand, and the Pacific Islands.
- **Chapter 26:** "The Americas, 1825–1914: The Challenges of Independence" adds material about the United States that formerly appeared in the chapter on nineteenth-century European politics and diplomacy (now Chapter 23).
- **Chapter 28:** "The Failure of the Liberal Model and the Rise of Authoritarianism: Japan, Italy, Germany, and the USSR, 1917–1940" has undergone structural refinement and provides new material on women and the development of liberal democracy in Japan prior to World War II.
- **Chapter 32:** "Europe and the United States Since 1945: The Cold War and After" brings together topics that formerly appeared in chapters 32 and 33 of the eleventh edition. The chapter examines the competing economic systems of the U.S. and the USSR, the Cold War, the collapse of communism in Soviet Union and Eastern Europe, and the role of technology and social change in modern Europe and the United States.
- **Chapter 33:** "The Middle East and Africa Since 1945: The Struggle for Survival" now restricts its focus to the Middle East and Africa; Latin American coverage that had formerly appeared in this chapter is now covered in the new chapter **34:** "Latin America Since 1910: Reform, Repression, and Revolution."

Features and Pedagogy

The text has been developed with the dual purpose of helping students acquire a solid knowledge of past events and, equally important, of helping them think more constructively about the significance of those events for the complex times in which we now live. A number of pedagogical features will assist students in achieving these goals.

New! Seeing Connections boxes These new features, one of which appears in each of the book's 36 chapters, visually illustrate the diverse links among the world's civilizations, religions, ideologies, arts, and social movements. As pedagogical tools, the photographs and their extended captions seek to promote deeper student understanding of world history by depicting and explaining the web of interconnections that tie our planet's many civilizations together.

Global Issues Essays These essays—all of which have been updated and four of which are entirely new—explore ten topics of unique transcultural and transhistorical significance: **Migration, Church and State, Technological Exchange, Location and Identity, Disease and Civilization (new), Slavery, War and International Law, The Environment (new), Terrorism (new),** and **Marriage (new).** Each essay employs examples that span both time and the world's many civilizations. As pedagogical tools, the essays are intended to do more than just inform students about global topics. They also reveal challenges that have confronted and still confront civilizations the world over. The essays carefully avoid discussing their topics from a Western conceptual basis and instead strive to examine them using a global framework. Each essay contains an image that illustrates its ideas and ends with critical thinking questions. The essays appear in chapters 3, 6, 10, 14, 19, 22, 27, 32, 33, and 36.

Pronunciation Guide This feature helps students correctly pronounce key foreign words and names. Pronunciations appear in parentheses immediately after the first use of a key foreign term or name in the text.

On-page Glossary This feature provides students with concise definitions of key historical terms. Glossary definitions appear at the bottom of the page in which they are discussed.

Chapter Opening Pages Newly designed chapter opening pages feature an illustration and accompanying caption, a chapter outline, and a short chapter introduction. They are followed by an easy-to-read chronology of the chapter's key political, social, religious, and cultural events. The introduction previews the chapter's themes, while the chronology sets its major topics within a framework easy for students to comprehend at a glance. Students can easily refer back to the chronology as they read the chapter. Chapter opening images reflect a wide range of genres, including sculpture, painting, mosaics, tapestries, and illuminated manuscripts.

Chronology Tables Brief chronology tables throughout each chapter highlight the major events occurring within a text section. Whether focusing on broad movements, as does "African Societies and European Imperialism" (Chapter 24), or on a single country, as does "Qing China" (Chapter 20), the chronology tables give the student an immediate summary view of a topic, at its point of discussion.

Discovery Through Maps This special feature focusing on primary maps offers a unique historical view—local, urban, civilizational, global, or imagined—of the way a particular culture looked at the world at a particular time. Students tend to take the orientation of a map for granted; however, "An Islamic Map of the World" (Chapter 7) makes clear that not all peoples make the same assumptions. The world map of the famous Arab cartographer al-Idrisi is oriented, as was common at the time, with south at the top. The "Myth of the Empty Land" in Chapter 19 shows how European settlers of South Africa laid claim to the South African interior by asserting that they were moving into an unpopulated area. Review questions help students better understand the concepts presented by the maps.

Excerpts from Primary Source Documents Nineteen of the 81 primary source documents are new. "In The First Crusade Takes Jerusalem" (Chapter 9), for example, a priest accompanying the First Crusade recounts the bloody fall of Jerusalem with cultural superiority and the certainty of religious justification for the cause. Simón Bolívar, in his powerful "Proclamation to the People of Venezuela" (Chapter 21), addresses his fellow countrymen and encourages them to reestablish a republican form of government in the state.

Almost every chapter includes a document concerning the status of women during a particular era or one that details the accomplishments of a specific woman. In Chapter 35, for example, Benazir Bhutto, Pakistan's first female prime minister, relates the dilemma of being a "foreign" student at Harvard during an era of political turmoil for both Pakistan and the United States. Several discussion questions now follow each excerpt.

Additional Resources To give the student an additional view of world cultures and timeframes, a **Literature and Films** section at the end of each chapter offers a listing of novels, poetry, films, and videos. **Suggestions for Reading** have been updated and carefully trimmed of dated entries. Students can consult these general interpretations, monographs, and collections of traditional source materials to expand their understanding of a particular topic or to prepare reports and papers. **Suggestions for Web Browsing** have also been updated throughout the book.

Maps Of the more than 100 maps in the text, some make clear the nature of a single distinctive event, others illustrate larger trends. For example, "Trade and Cultural Interchange," c. 50 B.C.E. (Chapter 2), makes clear that an interconnected world economy existed long before the advent of modern communication and technology. The specific focus of the "Persian Gulf Region, c. 1900" (Chapter 24), foretells some of today's complexities in this area of the world. A caption accompanying each map highlights the significance of the map and its relevance to a specific text topic. Many of the maps have been revised, updated, and/or increased in size. Most of the maps also include insets that show where their territory fits within a larger hemisphere or the globe.

Supplements

For Qualified College Adopters

- **Instructor's Manual:** This collection of resources prepared by Rick D. Whisonant of York Technical College includes chapter outlines, definitions, discussion suggestions, critical thinking exercises, term paper and essay topics, and audiovisual suggestions.
- **Test Bank:** Prepared by Susan Hellert of the University of Wisconsin at Platteville, this resource contains thousands of objective, conceptual, and essay questions.
- **Computerized Test Bank:** This flexible, easy-to-master computerized test bank includes all of the items found in the printed test bank. Instructors can edit existing questions, create their own questions, and print tests in several different formats.
- **Instructor Resource Center (IRC) (www.ablongman.com/irc):** Text-specific materials such as instructor's manuals, test banks, and PowerPoint™ presentations are available for download from the Instructor Resource Center.
- **Research Navigator and Research Guide:** Research Navigator is a comprehensive website offering EBSCO's ContentSelect Academic Journal & Abstract Database, the *New York Times* Search-by-Subject Archive, *Financial Times* Article Archive and Company Financials, and "Best of the Web" Link Library.
- **PowerPoint™ Presentations:** These customizable slides outline key points of each chapter of the text and contain full-color images of maps, tables, and figures. Available exclusively on the IRC (www.ablongman.com/irc).
- **Digital Transparency Masters:** These text-specific digital transparency masters include full-color representations of maps, tables, and figures found in the text. Available exclusively on the IRC (www.ablongman.com/irc).
- **Discovering World History Through Maps and Views Digital Transparency Masters:** This unique resource prepared by Gerald Danzer of the University of Illinois at Chicago contains more than 100 full-color digital masters of beautiful reference maps, source maps, urban plans, views, photos, art, and building diagrams. Available exclusively on the IRC (www.ablongman.com/irc).
- **World History Study Site (www.longmanworldhistory.com):** This open-access online course companion provides a wealth of course-based resources for both students and professors. Students will find test questions, flashcards, links for further research, and Web-based assignments.
- **The History Digital Media Archive on CD-ROM:** This resource contains hundreds of images, maps, interactive maps, and audio/video clips ready for classroom presentation or for downloading into PowerPoint™.
- **Guide to Teaching World History:** This guide by Palmira Brummett of the University of Tennessee at Knoxville offers explanations of major issues and themes in world history, sample syllabi, ideas for cross-cultural and cross-temporal connections, a pronunciation guide, and tips for getting through all of the material.
- **Historical Newsreel Video:** This 90-minute video contains newsreel excerpts that examine U.S. involvement in world affairs over the past 60 years.

For Students

- **Study Guide:** This two-volume guide, prepared by Norman Love of El Paso Community College, includes chapter overviews, lists of themes and concepts, map exercises, multiple-choice practice tests, and critical thinking and essay questions.
- **Study Card for World History:** Colorful, affordable, and packed with useful information, this study card makes studying easier, more efficient, and more enjoyable.
- **World History Study Site (www.longmanworldhistory.com):** This course-based, open-access online companion provides a wealth of resources for both students and professors. Students will find test questions, flashcards, links for further research, and Web-based assignments.
- **World History Map Workbooks, Second Edition, Volumes I and II:** These workbooks, created by Glee Wilson of Kent State University, are designed to explain the correlations between historical events and geography through assignments that involve reading and interpreting maps.
- **Longman World History Atlas:** A comprehensive collection of historical maps that reflects truly global coverage of world history. Each of the atlas's 56 maps are designed to be readable and informative, as well as beautiful.

MyHistoryLab (www.MyHistoryLab.com)

With the best of Longman's multimedia solutions for history in one easy-to-use place, MyHistoryLab offers students and instructors a state-of-the-art interactive instructional solution for the World History survey course. MyHistoryLab is offered both as an easy-to-use website and with course management capabilities hosted by Pearson. MyHistoryLab can also be provided in a course management system used locally on your campus, such as Blackboard and WebCT. MyHistoryLab is designed to be used as a supplement to a traditional lecture course or to administer a completely online course. MyHistoryLab provides helpful tips, review materials, and activities to make the study of history an enjoyable learning experience. Icons in the e-book, an electronic version of the textbook, link directly to relevant materials in context, many of which are assignable. Please check with your Pearson sales representative for further details.

MyHistoryKit (www.MyHistoryKit.com)

This website offers many of the best features of MyHistoryLab without course management or the online e-book. This access-protected site is course-based and contains primary sources, quizzes, Research Navigator, and more.

Acknowledgments

We are most grateful to the following reviewers who gave generously of their time and knowledge to provide thoughtful evaluations and many helpful suggestions for the revision of this edition. They include:

Wayne Ackerson, Salisbury State University
Maurice Amutabi, Washington University
Milan Andrejevich, Ivy Tech Community College, South Bend, IN
Gene Barnett, Calhoun Community College
Otto B. Burianek, Georgia Perimeter College
Gary G. Gibbs, Roanoke College
William S. McDonald, Mid-America Christian University
Margaret Sankey, Minnesota State University, Moorhead
Nancy L. Stockdale, University of Central Florida
Fred Witzig, Franklin College

We also thank the many conscientious reviewers who reviewed previous editions of this book: Henry Abramson, Florida Atlantic University; Wayne Ackerson, Salisbury State University; Jay Pascal Anglin, University of Southern Mississippi; Lee Annis, Montgomery County Community College–Maryland; Joseph Appiah, J. Sargeant Reynolds Community College; Michael Auslin, Yale University; Daniel Ayana, Youngstown State University; Mark C. Bartusis, Northern State University; Charlotte Beahan, Murray State University; Martin Berger, Youngstown State University; Joel Berlatsky, Wilkes College; Jackie R. Booker, Kent State University; Mauricio Borrero, St. John's University; Darwin F. Bostwick, Old Dominion University; Robert F. Brinson Jr., Santa Fe Community College; James W. Brodman, University of Central Arkansas; Robert H. Buchanan, Adams State College; Nancy Cade, Pikeville College; Michael L. Carrafiello, East Carolina University; Thomas Cary, City University; James O. Catron Jr., North Florida Junior College; Mark Chavalas, University of Wisconsin; William H. Cobb, East Carolina University; J. L. Collins, Allan Hancock College; J. R. Crawford, Montreat-Anderson College; Edward R. Crowther, Adams State College; Lawrence J. Daly, Bowling Green State University; Demoral Davis, Jackson State University; Cole P. Dawson, Warner Pacific College; Dr. Michael de Nie, State University of West Georgia; Anne Dorazio, Westchester Community College; Dawn Duensing, Maui Community College; Shannon L. Duffy, Loyola University New Orleans; Ellen Emerick, Georgetown College; Charles T. Evans, Northern Virginia Community College; William Edward Ezzell, Georgia Perimeter College; John D. Fair, Auburn University at Montgomery; Nancy Fitch, California State University; Robert B. Florian, Salem-Teikyo University; Nels W. Forde, University of Nebraska; Ronald Fritze, University of Central Arkansas; Joseph T. Fuhrmann, Murray State University; Lydia Garner, Southwest Texas State University; Robert J. Gentry; University of Southwestern Louisiana; Paul George, Miami Community College, Dade; David Gleason, Armstrong Atlantic State University; Richard M. Golden, University of North Texas; Oliver Griffin, Weber State University; Michael Hall, Armstrong Atlantic State University; Paul Halsall, University of North Florida; Jeffrey S. Hamilton, Old Dominion University; Elizabeth P. Hancock, Gainesville College; Eric J. Hanne, Florida Atlantic University; Donald E. Harpster, College of St. Joseph; Gordon K. Harrington, Weber State University; J. Drew Harrington, Western Kentucky University; Janine Hartman, University of Cincinnati; Geoff Haywood, Beaver College; Thomas Hegarty, University of Tampa; Madonna Hettinger, McHenry County College; David Hill, McHenry County College; Caroline Hoefferle, Wingate University; Conrad C. Holcomb, Jr., Surry Community College; Thomas Howell, Louisiana College; Clark Hultquist, University of Montevallo; Scott Jessee, Appalachian State University; Roger L. Jungmeyer, Lincoln University of Missouri; Daniel R. Kazmer, Georgetown University; Bernard Kiernan, Concord College; David Koeller, North Park University; Michael L. Krenn, University of Miami; Teresa Lafer, Pennsylvania State University; Harral E. Landry, Texas Women's University; George Longenecker, Norwich University; Norman Love, El Paso Community College; Marsha K. Marks, Alabama A&M University; Caroline T. Marshall, James Madison University; Eleanor McCluskey, Broward Community College; Robert McCormick, Newman University; Christopher McKay, University of Alberta; David A. Meier, Dickinson State University; Arlin Migliazzo, Whitworth College; William C. Moose, Mitchell Community College; Zachary Morgan, William Patterson University; Wayne Morris, Lees-McRae College; John G. Muncie, East Stroudsburg University; Justin Murphy, Howard Payne University; Jeffrey W. Myers, Avila University; David Owusu-Ansah, James Madison University; George Pesely, Austin-Peay State; Al Pilant, Cumberland College; Jana Pisani, Texas A&M International University; Sr. Jeannette Plante, CSC, Notre Dame College; Norman Pollock, Old Dominion University; J. Graham Provan, Millikin University; George B. Pruden Jr., Armstrong State College; John D. Ramsbottom, Northeast

Missouri State University; Ruth Richard, College of Lake County; Charles Risher, Montreat College; Hugh I. Rodgers, Columbus College; Ruth Rogaski, Princeton University; William R. Rogers, Isothermal Community College; Patrick J. Rollins, Old Dominion University; Chad Ronnander, University of Minnesota; R. A. Rotz, Indiana University; Robert Rowland, Loyola University; Barry T. Ryan, Westmont College; Daniel E. Schafer, Belmont University; Bill Schell, Murray State University; Roger Schlesinger, Washington State University ; Louis E. Schmier, Valdosta State College; William Seavey, East Carolina University; William M. Simpson, Louisiana College; Paul J. Smith, Haverford College; Barbara G. Sniffen, University of Wisconsin—Oshkosh; Lawrence Squeri, East Stroudsburg University; Lawrence Stanley, McHenry County College; Terrence S. Sullivan, University of Nebraska at Omaha; John Swanson, Utica College of Syracuse; Deborah A. Symonds, Drake University; Edward Tabri, Columbus State Community College; Mark B. Tauger, West Virginia University; Gordon L. Teffeteller, Valdosta State College; Malcolm R. Thorp, Brigham Young University; Helen M. Tierney, University of Wisconsin—Platteville; Leslie Tischauser, Prairie State College; Arthur L. Tolson, Southern University; Joseph A. Tomberlin, Valdosta State University; Marcia Vaughan, Murray State University; Thomas Dwight Veve, Dalton College; Chris Warren, Copiah-Lincoln Community College; Mary Watrous, Washington State University; Ted Weeks, Southern Illinois University; Rick Whisonant, Winthrop University; David L. White, Appalachian State University; Thomas Whigham, University of Georgia; and John R. Willertz, Saginaw Valley State University.

ROBERT R. EDGAR
GEORGE F. JEWSBURY
NEIL J. HACKETT
BARBARA MOLONY
MATTHEW S. GORDON

ARCTIC OCEAN
GREENLAND
ICELAND
Arctic Circle
Yukon R.
BERING SEA
GULF OF ALASKA
ALEUTIAN ISLANDS
HUDSON BAY
NORTH AMERICA
PACIFIC OCEAN
Mississippi R.
Rio Grande
GULF OF MEXICO
ATLANTIC OCEAN
Tropic of Cancer
WEST INDIES
HAWAIIAN ISLANDS
CARIBBEAN SEA
GUIANA HIGHLANDS
Equator
Amazon R.
SOUTH AMERICA
ANDES MOUNTAINS
BRAZILIAN HIGHLANDS
ATACAMA DESERT
Tropic of Capricorn
Paraná
PACIFIC OCEAN
Antarctic Circle

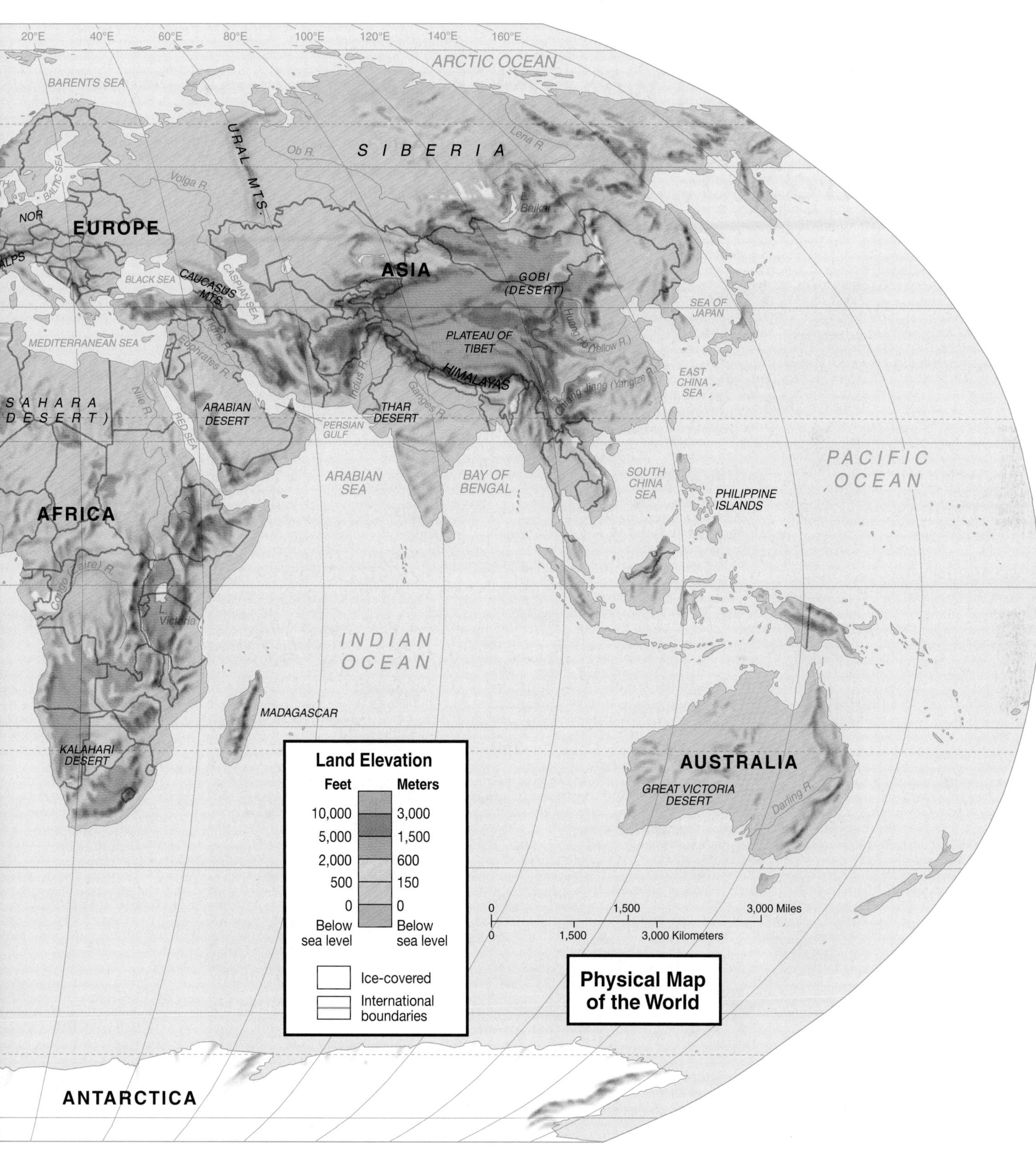

Physical Map of the World

CHAPTER 12

The Great Dynastic Empires of Eurasia, 1300–1650

Outline

- New Polities in Eurasia
- The Ottoman Empire
- The Safavid Empire in Iran
- The Mughal Empire in South Asia
- Networks of Trade and Communication

Features

DISCOVERY THROUGH MAPS **The World Map of Piri Reis**

DOCUMENT **The Coming of Ismail Safavi Foretold**

SEEING CONNECTIONS **Religious Tolerance Under Akbar**

DOCUMENT **The Idea of Seclusion and Lady Nurjahan**

◄ This eighteenth century painting of a seventeenth century miniature brings together the founders of Mughal rule in India: Timur (1336–1405), his great-grandson Babur (1483–1530), and Babur's son Humayan (1508–1556). Timur had brutally sacked Delhi in 1398, but his empire fell apart after his death. Babur returned in 1525, and that time the Mughal empire was established. Humayun, a learned man, was exiled in Persia for much of his adult life, but he left a legacy for his son, Akbar, whose religious tolerance stabilized Muslim control over India's majority Hindu population.

BY THE FOURTEENTH century, the waves of migration and conquest out of Central Asia that had established the Mongol Empire and altered the political configurations of the Islamic world had mostly ceased. Late in that century, a new Turco-Mongol conqueror named Timur began a campaign that ravaged northern India, Iran, Iraq, and Anatolia. His empire was not to endure. In the fifteenth and sixteenth centuries, however, three great Turkic empires gained preeminence in the old Mongol and Byzantine domains. The Ottoman, Safavid, and Mughal empires flourished on the bases of preexisting civilizations, Turco-Mongol military organization, and enhanced firepower; in the process they also crafted a new cultural synthesis. Historians nicknamed the three states "the gunpowder empires" because, like their European counterparts, they incorporated gunpowder weaponry into their traditional military systems. All three formed parts of a vast trading network reaching from the Pacific to the Atlantic Ocean. At the same time that the Ming Chinese were launching voyages that reached the East African coast, the Ottoman Turks were building an empire in the eastern Mediterranean that, in the sixteenth century, would dominate the region and challenge the Portuguese in the Indian Ocean.

Europeans were active in Asia during this period but exerted relatively little influence. Awed by the wealth and power of Muslim empires, they were generally held in disdain by Asian elites, who considered their own cultures superior. Akbar, the great Mughal emperor, referred to the "savage Portuguese" at his court,[1] Ottoman sultans regarded European envoys as supplicants, and the Safavid shah kept English merchants waiting for weeks while he attended to more important matters.

New Polities in Eurasia

How did political conditions in Central Asia influence the rise of the Ottoman, Safavid, and Mughal empires?

For the kingdoms of Europe, the Ottoman conquest of Constantinople in 1453 signaled a catastrophe: the end of the Eastern Roman Empire and a disruption in established commercial patterns. Preachers and writers in Europe depicted the Ottoman victories as a type of divine punishment for the sins of Christendom. Even more significant, the Ottomans symbolized a new Muslim world emerging between the eastern Mediterranean and Southeast Asia. In that expansive territory, the three new Turkic empires would hold sway for centuries. Geographically, this world was centered in Iran, under its Shi'ite Safavid (sah-fa-wid) dynasty. Culturally, it was influenced by Iranian, Arab, and Byzantine courtly traditions. To the east, the magnificent Mughal (moo-GUL) Empire emerged at a crucial crossroads of the east-west and north-south trade. Militarily, this Muslim world was dominated by the forces of the Ottoman Empire, which were far more formidable than those of any country in Europe at the time. War often raged among these contending

▼ The so-called "gunpowder empires" dominated South and West Asia, North Africa, and Southeastern Europe in the sixteenth century.

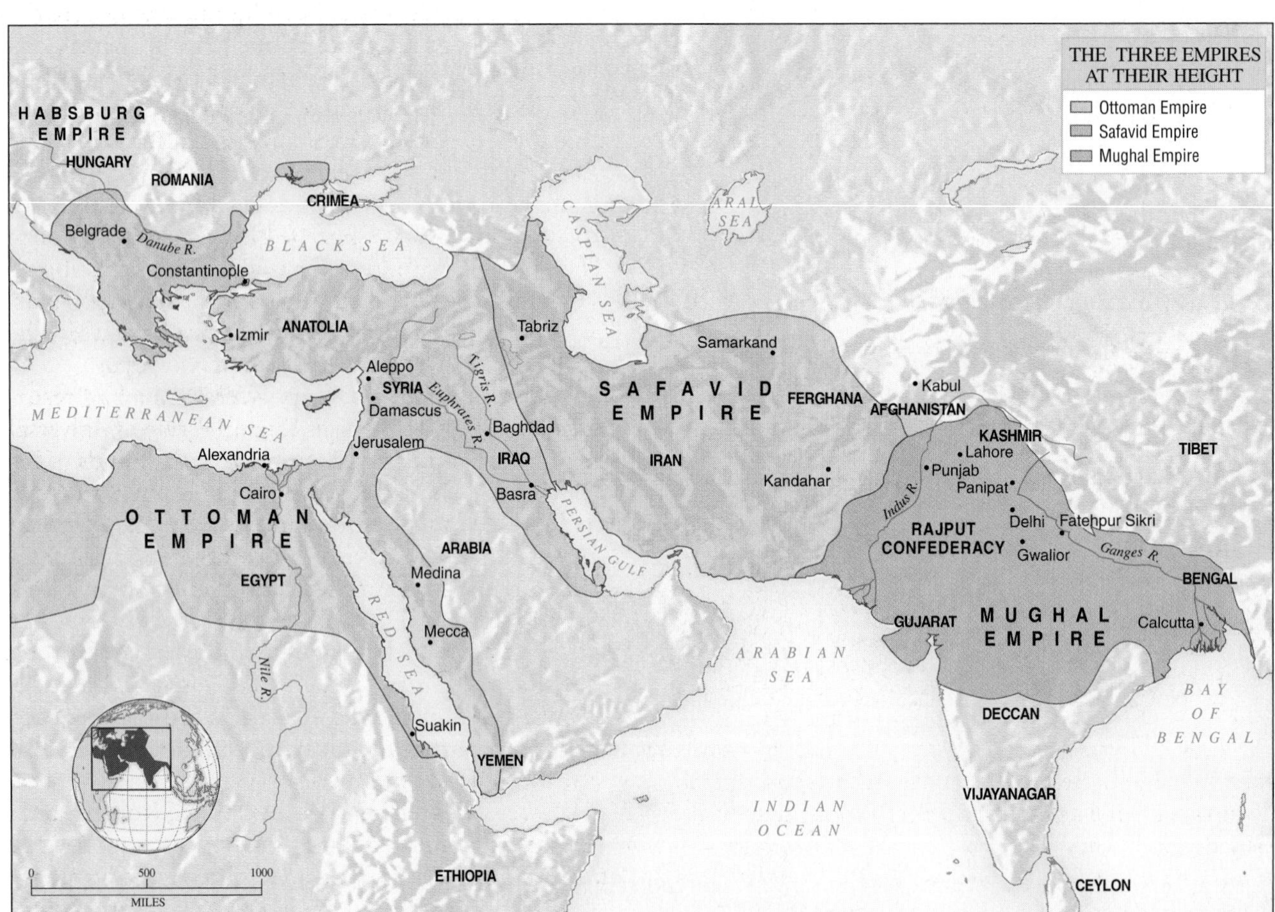

Chronology

1300	1400	1500			1600
1324 End of the reign of Osman, first Ottoman ruler **1398–1402** Timur invades India and Anatolia	**1453** Mehmed II conquers Constantinople	**1501** Ismail Safavi establishes the Safavid dynasty **1517** Ottomans conquer Cairo and gain control of Mecca **1517** Piri Reis world map	**1520–1566** Reign of Ottoman Suleiman the Magnificent **1525** Babur, first Mughal emperor, invades India **1538–1588** Sinan Pasha, Ottoman royal architect	**1556–1605** Reign of Akbar over the Mughal domains **1588–1629** Reign of Shah Abbas in Iran **1597** Shah Abbas founds his imperial center at Isfahan	**1634–1654** Taj Mahal built **1658–1707** Reign of Mughal emperor Aurangzeb in India

◀ This miniature painting depicts the envoy of Timur at the court of the Ottoman sultan Bayezid I. The sultan is surrounded by his courtiers, with pages to his right and janissaries and officials in the foreground. Bayezid looks imposing, but he was defeated and killed by Timur. Note the fine carpets around the sultan's throne and the soldiers armed with gunpowder weapons in the foreground.

states. Nevertheless, they shared the Islamic faith, common steppe antecedents, and Iranian artistic and literary traditions.

Background: The Steppe Frontier

Relations between the Near East, including Iran, and the Central Asian steppe dated back centuries (see Chapter 7). After the mid-fourteenth century, tumultuous conditions in Central Asia helped generate the Muslim empires to the south. The fragmented Mongol Empire left the steppe politically divided into states that dissolved and re-formed in new combinations. Although the old **khanates** survived for a while, war was almost continuous along the southern steppe frontier, from the Crimea to China.

The continuing steppe influence was well illustrated by the quick rise and collapse of the Timurid (ti-MOR-id) Empire at the close of the fourteenth century. Timur the Lame, the "Tamerlane" celebrated in Western literature, who claimed descent from Chinggis (Genghis) Khan, rose to power during the 1370s as an *emir* ("commander") in the Chaghatai (chagh-HAH-tai) khanate of Central Asia. In his quest to restore the original Mongol Empire, Timur led whirlwind campaigns through the western steppe, the Crimea, Iran, and Anatolia. He crushed Ottoman resistance and carted the defeated Ottoman sultan, Bayezid I, off across Anatolia in a cage, subjecting him to ridicule. Timur terrorized northern India and was planning to invade Ming China when he died in 1405. But once Timur's army withdrew, the leaders who had submitted to him were less likely to comply with his demands. A conqueror's real domains were those from which he could effectively collect taxes and levy troops.

For more than a century after Timur had resurrected the spirit of Chinggis Khan, a dream of universal empire—real or imagined—lingered in the minds of his descendants, among the many Turco-Mongol rulers in northern Iran and Transoxiana to its east. The Ottoman sultans, who had established their hegemony in Anatolia before Timur's time and only barely survived his onslaught, were not direct heirs of his traditions, but they too aspired to the conquests and prestige of Chinggis Khan and Alexander the Great. Russia and particularly northern India, where Muslim regimes took hold after Timur's armies devastated Delhi in 1398, were also sites of a renewed struggle for power.

Drastic change marked the steppe frontier after the late fifteenth century, as populations settled around cities and firearms moderated the advantages of tribal cavalry. Indeed, the Uzbeks, who seized most of Transoxiana in this era, were among the last steppe conquerors. Like their predecessors, they were integrated into the courtly cultures of the lands they conquered. But long after the Uzbek conquest, old nomadic traditions continued to shape the rituals and military ethos of Turco-Mongol dynasties.

The Ottoman Empire

How did the Ottoman Turks create and sustain their empire?

The most powerful of the new Muslim empires was that of the Ottoman Turks. Ottoman rule, from the

khanate—A Turkic state ruled by a khan.

CASE STUDY
The Ottoman Empire in the Late Sixteenth Century

start, would have as profound an impact on the history of premodern Europe as it would upon that of the eastern Mediterranean and North Africa. By the middle of the sixteenth century, the Ottoman patrimony stretched from Hungary to Ethiopia and from the borders of Morocco to Arabia and Iraq.

The origin myth of the Ottomans suggests the unique role played by Central Asian warrior traditions and sufi Islam in the legitimization of kingship. The founder of the Ottoman line was Osman. According to legend, he was a valiant young warrior, fighting as a Seljuk subordinate on the frontiers of the Byzantine Empire in the late thirteenth century (see Chapter 7). Osman had, as a warrior must, a good horse, a strong arm, and a loyal companion. He fell in love with the daughter of a revered sufi ***shaykh*** and asked for her hand in marriage. Her father refused, but that night the *shaykh* dreamed that he saw the moon descending on his sleeping daughter, merging into her breast. From this union grew a huge and imposing tree that spread its branches over many lands and many flowing streams. When he awoke, the *shaykh* decided to approve the marriage.

Dreams play an important role in Middle Eastern literatures, and many kings took the interpretation of dreams seriously. The legend of the *shaykh*'s dream linked the warrior tradition to the mystical religious authority of sufi masters, thus legitimizing Osman's rule. His dynasty, like the tree, would endure, expanding its reach over numerous and prosperous territories. As the dynasty grew more powerful, the Ottomans also falsified a genealogy linking them to the prophet Muhammad. This Ottoman claim, like Timur's claim to be a descendant of Chinggis Khan, also lent an aura of legitimacy to their rule. The Ottomans were not the first or the last family to imagine illustrious ancestors for themselves. Osman's line was spectacularly successful; it ruled for over six centuries, from the late thirteenth century until World War I.

Osman's successors won independence from their Seljuk Turk overlords and gradually conquered the surrounding principalities. They had gained control over most of Asia Minor when Timur's army invaded Anatolia, defeated the Ottomans, and forced a half century of internal restoration. Two remarkable sultans then resumed the Ottoman conquests. The first, Mehmed II (second reign 1451–1481), took Constantinople, Romania, and the Crimea. The second, Selim I (1512–1520), annexed Kurdistan, northern Iraq, Syria, and Egypt. Mehmed's conquests alarmed European Christendom and brought the Ottoman state considerable wealth and prestige. The sultan repopulated Constantinople, renamed Istanbul in the nineteenth century, using a combination of tax breaks and forced population transfers. The declining but intrepid old warrior was planning new campaigns when he died.

DOCUMENT
Mehmed II

IMAGE
Mehmed II

shaykh—An Arabic term for a tribal chief or religious master.

	The Ottomans
c. 1281	Osman establishes the Ottoman dynasty
1453	Ottomans capture Constantinople
1517	Sultan Selim conquers Cairo, becomes Protector of the Holy Cities
1520–1566	Reign of Suleiman the Magnificent, Ottoman Golden Age

Mehmed's son, Bayezid II, acquired further territories and established a powerful fleet. Selim's conquest of Egypt and Arabia only added to the dynasty's prestige: control of another great imperial capital, Cairo, and claim to the title Protector of the Holy Cities (Mecca and Medina), coveted by all Muslim monarchs. It also gave him control over the wealth and grain of Egypt and all the Mediterranean outlets of the eastern trade in spices, textiles, and jewels. Under Selim, the Ottoman navy dominated the eastern Mediterranean.

Ottoman power increased under Selim's only son, Suleiman (SU-lay-mahn; 1520–1566). This determined campaigner soon became the most feared ruler among a generation of monarchs that included Henry VIII of England, Francis I of France, and Charles V of Spain. Suleiman's estimation of his own supremacy is illustrated in a letter to the French monarch in which Suleiman claimed glorious and elaborate titles but addressed Francis simply as "King."

Suleiman extended all his borders, particularly those touching Habsburg lands in Europe. After taking Belgrade in 1521 and the island of Rhodes from the Knights of St. John in 1522, he invaded Hungary in 1526 with 100,000 men and 300 artillery pieces. At Mohacs (mo-hach), Ottoman forces achieved an overwhelming victory. Hungary was then integrated into the Ottoman Empire. Although many leading Hungarians were slaughtered in the war, Suleiman continued the Ottoman practice of integrating local nobles and military men into the Ottoman administrative system. If a governor submitted, he was often allowed to retain his post; this pragmatic administrative flexibility helped ensure the success of Ottoman conquests.

Suleiman aspired to the conquest of even further territory, aiming particularly at the rich agricultural lands, timber sources, and mines of eastern Europe; he also proposed to control the rich commerce of the

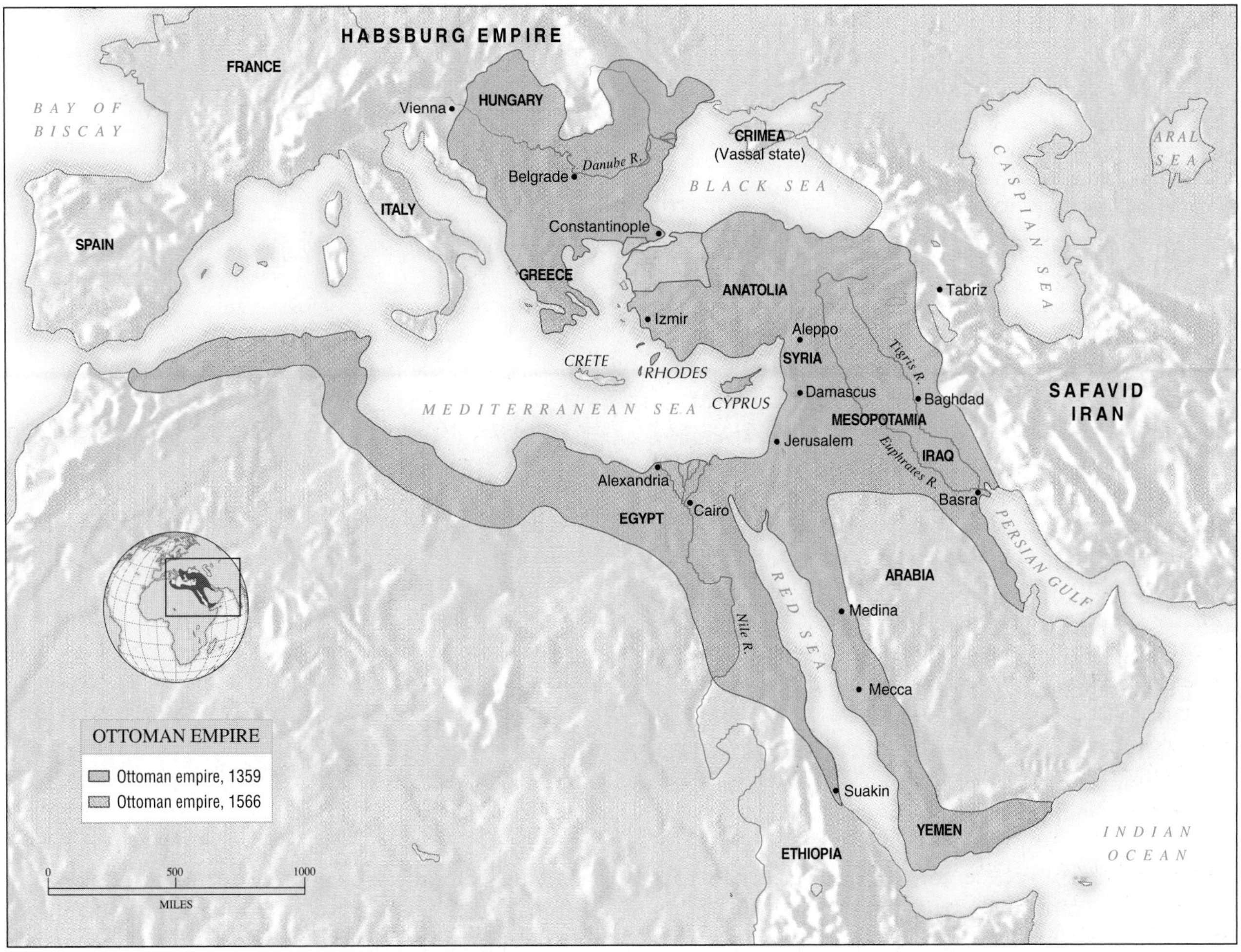

▲ By the mid-sixteenth century, the Ottoman Empire encompassed much of the Mediterranean. It included the core territories (excluding Iran) of the Middle East and extended across North Africa and into Europe.

The Islamic World: The Ottoman Empire

Mediterranean. Meanwhile, his forces took Iraq from the Safavids, thus acquiring access to the Persian Gulf. This monarch, who built the great wall around Jerusalem that remains in place today, claimed to be "Lord of the two lands and two seas." His conquests provoked conflicts with the Portuguese in the Red Sea and Indian Ocean. The Portuguese imagined taking Mecca to chastise the "heathen" Ottomans, but no such attack ever materialized.

Suleiman responded harshly to challenges to his authority. He executed his own favorite son and a grandson who rebelled against him. His palace life was marked by pomp and splendor exceeding that of Louis XIV's France. An army of servants attended him, and those men who worked in his palace inner service gained prestige and status because of their proximity to the sultan. The sultan's banquets were served on elaborate tableware of gold, silver, and an expanding collection of fine Chinese porcelain. In the hours between waking and sleeping, Suleiman met with advisers and petitioners, read, or listened to music. For amusement he watched wrestling matches and listened to court poets and jesters. He was trained in the fine art of goldsmithing, also wrote poetry, and had a keen interest in maps. Foreign ambassadors, such as those from the French king or Habsburg emperor, were forced to prostrate themselves before the sultan, an indication of the perceived balance of power. European observers commented on the intimidating nature of a visit to Suleiman's court, where thousands of massed troops would stand for hours in absolute silence. In Europe, he was known as Suleiman the Magnificent; in the Ottoman Empire he was called Suleiman the Lawgiver.

The sultan's rule was based on an ideal of Iranian origin called the "circle of justice." This ideal stated that in order for the kingdom to be prosperous and secure, the sultan required a strong army. To provide for this army, the state needed tax revenues from its citizens, and in order for the citizens to pay their taxes they had to receive in return security and justice from the sultan. Although there were many abuses at various levels of

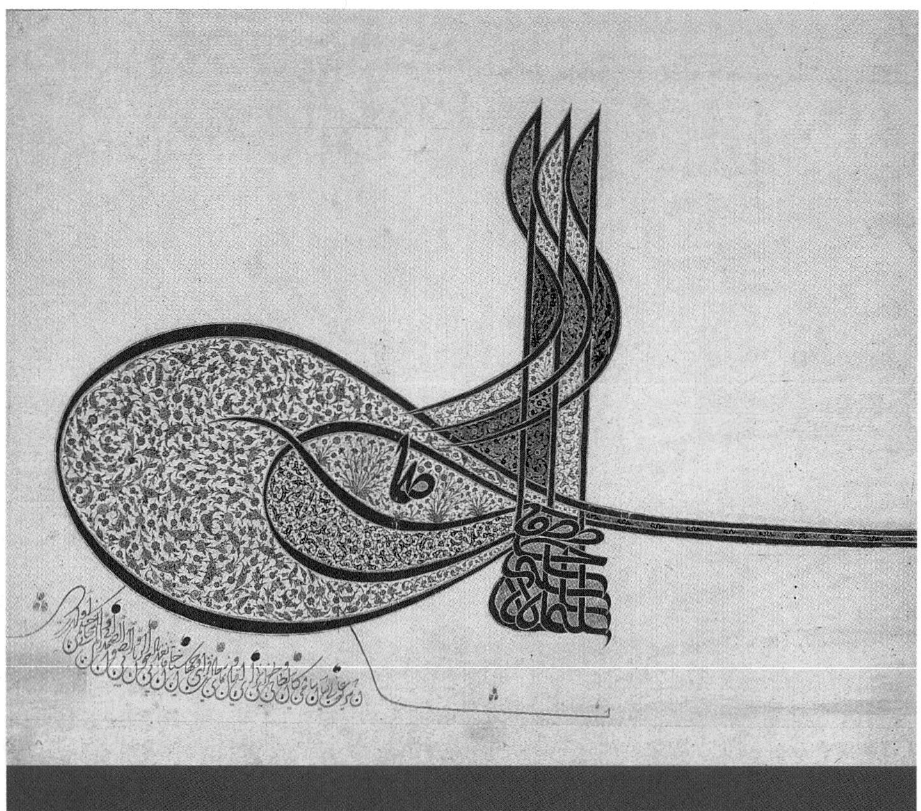

An illuminated *tughra* of Sultan Suleiman. The *tughra* was the sultan's signature, used to validate imperial documents and mark coinage. It included the sultan's name and his father's name and designated the sultan as "eternally victorious." The palace employed hundreds of artists, including the designers who fashioned and illuminated such beautiful *tughras.*

government, the Ottoman sultans did adhere to this ideal. Any of the sultan's subjects could submit a petition to the palace asking redress of wrongs—sometimes the sultan rode out into the streets while his attendants gathered petitions from the crowd. Ottoman court records show many instances in which peasants complained to the local judge (*kadi*) that officials were extracting extra taxes or labor from them. These complaints were then forwarded to the central government, which punished or replaced the offenders.

The Empire Under Suleiman

Suleiman governed the mightiest state of his day. Extending from Poland to Yemen and from Persia to Tripoli, it included 21 provinces and many linguistic and ethnic groups, such as Magyars, Armenians, Bosnians, Albanians, Greeks, Tartars, Kurds, Arabs, Copts, and Jews. "Multiculturalism," often thought of as a twentieth-century concept, was in fact typical of many large agrarian empires of this age.

Economically, Suleiman's empire was nearly self-sufficient, with expanding production and flourishing trade. The Ottoman dominions produced annual revenues greater than those available to any contemporary European monarch and grain surpluses that gave the Ottomans considerable leverage in the Mediterranean region, where grain shortages were endemic. Merchants smuggled grain out despite government attempts to control them, and Ottoman rivals like Venice often purchased grain supplies from the sultan's **pashas.** Indeed, food has been, and still is, one of the most powerful motivating forces in history.

DOCUMENT An Ambassador's Report on the Ottoman Empire

pasha—Top military-administrative official (governor) in the Ottoman Empire.

Power in such a far-flung empire could never be absolute. The sultan delegated authority to local governors and to pashas. Rule in distant provinces, like Egypt, was more flexible and less direct. Conquered lands closer to the capital were given to Ottoman *sipahis* (se-PAH-hees) or "fief" holders, who were expected to bring cavalry contingents for military campaigns. At other times, *sipahis* lived on their lands (*timars*), administering local affairs, collecting taxes, and keeping order. Unlike European feudal lords, they were not usually local residents and were often away in distant wars. Provincial governors (*pashas* or *beys*) were drawn from the higher-ranking Ottoman commanders. All members of this governing class were thus heavily dependent on the sultan, who might suddenly change their assignments or revoke their land holdings. By Suleiman's reign, the political power of the *sipahis* over their *timars* had been partly usurped by the sultan's central bureaucracy. It functioned under a **vizir,** or chief minister, with a host of subordinate officials. The top officials met regularly as the sultan's **divan** or council to advise the ruler, but his word was law (although top officials and religious authorities—the **ulama**—might use their authority to challenge or moderate his decrees).

vizir—A chief minister or comparable high-ranking government official in the Muslim world, but most particularly in the Ottoman Empire.

divan—A council or place of administrative assembly within the Ottoman Empire.

ulama—Muslim religious authorities; men versed in Islamic sciences and law.

Discovery Through Maps

The World Map of Piri Reis

Western historiography has highlighted Europeans' "discovery" of the New World. But the Age of Discovery produced many visions of the world, only some of which were preoccupied with the Americas. Ottoman cartographers were interested in the Americas, although Ottoman ambitions for conquest were directed primarily eastward to Asia. Mapping in this era was intimately associated with the objectives of merchants and sailors, and the most famous of Ottoman cartographers was a skilled sea captain named Piri Reis. Like other members of the Ottoman military-administrative class, Piri Reis was a man of diverse talents. In 1517, when his sovereign, Sultan Selim, conquered Cairo, Piri Reis presented him with a parchment map of the world, only part of which survives. The segment reproduced here shows the Atlantic Ocean, the western shores of Africa and Europe, and the eastern shores of South and Central America. Piri Reis's map incorporates elaborate illustrations of ships, kings, wildlife, and mythical creatures. It depicts strange tales (like the sailors who landed on a whale's back, mistaking it for an island, at top left) and gives nautical distances. The cartographer provided a list of 20 Western and Islamic sources he consulted, including a map that had belonged to Christopher Columbus. Piri Reis's map suggests the currents of shared knowledge that linked the scholars, merchants, and sailors of Asia, Africa, and Europe at this time. The boundaries of scholarship were fluid, and learned men eagerly sought out new information. Cartographers like Piri Reis benefited from and contributed to the knowledge assembled by peoples of many nations and religions.

For the sailor or merchant, any map that was more accurate, regardless of its provenance (Portuguese, Ottoman, Christian, Muslim), was a tool for ensuring a more successful and safer journey.

Questions to Consider

1. In the sixteenth century, why would a sea captain be a good mapmaker?
2. Think about the different kinds of maps you have seen in this text and elsewhere. How does the way a map is constructed and illustrated tell us something about the beliefs and objectives of the mapmaker and the people for whom he makes the map?
3. Why do you think there are figures of people and animals on this map?

The Ottomans developed a unique "slave" (*kul*) system that was a major factor in their success. The system was based on the *devshirme* (dev-SHEHR-me), a levy of boys from the non-Muslim subjects of the empire, which functioned as a special type of "human tax" on the Balkan provinces. These boys were brought to the capital, converted to Islam, and taught Turkish. Most of them went to the **janissaries** (JAN-i-sehr-ees), the famed elite Ottoman infantry corps that was armed with gunpowder weapons. They formed the backbone of the formidable Ottoman armies. The

janissaries—An elite Ottoman infantry corps armed with gunpowder weapons and composed mostly of converted Balkan slaves.

smartest and most talented of the boys, however, were sent to the palace to be educated in literature, science, the arts, religion, and military skills. These boys, when they reached maturity, were given the highest military and administrative posts in the state. Ideally, the *kul* system provided the state with a group of expert administrators who, because they had been separated from their families and homes, would remain loyal to the sultan, to whom they owed everything. These "slaves," rather than occupying the lowest level of the social order, controlled much of the wealth and power in Ottoman society. Many of the buildings they endowed are still standing today. The more common type of domestic or agricultural slave did, of course, also exist in Ottoman society. Slavery and slave markets were scattered throughout the Afro-Eurasian world, although Islamic law prohibited the enslaving of fellow Muslims.

▼ European writers and their audiences were fascinated by the Ottoman harem and often depicted it in exaggerated erotic terms. This engraving from a seventeenth-century French history of the Ottoman palace imagines the sultan taking his bath attended by naked harem women. In fact, this image is pure fantasy; both sexuality and reproduction in the harem were tightly controlled, and the sultan's attendants were male, not female.

Western literature has produced an exotic, erotic image of the Ottoman sultan's **harem** (the sacred area of the palace, or of any home, forbidden to outsiders). But much of this image is a myth produced by the overactive imaginations or hostile sentiments of European men inspired by the prospect of several hundred women in one household. In fact, sexuality in the palace was tightly controlled. Like women in other traditional patriarchal societies, most Ottoman women had to work in the fields and towns. Only the women of the elite classes could be fully veiled and secluded. In the palace, the harem women were arranged in a rigid hierarchy much like that of the men; each was paid according to her rank. Most of the women were not destined for the sultan's bed; instead they were married to the sultan's officers to create further ties of loyalty to the palace. A select few were chosen to bear the sultan's heirs.

The harem women wielded power because of their wealth, their connections, and their proximity to the sultan. The most powerful among them was the sultan's mother (the ***valide sultan***), not his wife. The *valide sultans* participated actively (although behind the scenes) in court politics. Petitioners, including pashas, applied to these high-ranking women to intercede on their behalf with the sultan. Some *valide sultans* even served a diplomatic function, corresponding with European rulers like the Venetian doge, Catherine de' Medici in France, and Queen Elizabeth in England.

In the Ottoman system, proximity to the sultan was the primary avenue to power, and membership in the royal household or military class brought with it the highest status in society. But pashas, palace women, religious officials, and members of the palace staff jockeyed for positions of power and formed alliances to advance their own inter-

harem—In Arabic, literally "forbidden." A sacred area of palace or home forbidden to outsiders, often but not always used to protect and sequester women.

valide sultan—The mother of the Ottoman sultan; generally the most powerful and influential woman in the empire.

ests. Harem politics, illustrated in Suleiman's reign by the contending influences of his mother and his wife, have often been blamed for weakening the Ottoman state. In fact, however, the factors that compromised Ottoman power were much more complex. Continued conquests produced serious communication and transportation problems, and long wars and failure to pay the troops on time caused rebellions in the ranks. Religious contention, provoked by the rise of the Shi'ite Safavids in Iran, also threatened the empire.

Another important factor in Ottoman politics was the fact that the eldest son had no automatic claim to the throne. The sultan's sons thus contended to succeed him, sometimes producing extended periods of interregnum. That was the case with Bayezid II, whose sons got tired of waiting for him to die and launched a civil war to determine who would sit on the throne in his stead. Once a prince established himself as sultan, he would often have his brothers executed, a grim task designed to ensure the stability of the state and avoid further struggles. A wise prince would try to gain the favor of the janissary corps, for their support might make or break him.

Religion was an integral part of government and society. But as in other Muslim lands, the religious authorities (*ulama*) did not run the government; they were subordinated to the state and the sultan. The grand **mufti,** as head of the Islamic establishment, was also the chief religious and legal adviser to the sultan. The sultan approved religious appointments and might dismiss any religious officer, including the grand mufti. A corps of learned religious scholars represented the sultan as judges (*kadis*), dispensers of charities, and teachers. Non-Muslim subjects or ***dhimmis*** were regarded as inferior but were granted a significant degree of legal and religious toleration through government arrangements with their religious leaders (rabbis and priests, for example), who were responsible for their civil obedience. Non-Muslim subjects lived under their own laws and customs, pursuing their private interests within limits imposed by Islamic law and Ottoman economic needs. As in other Islamic lands, they had to pay the ***jizya,*** an additional head tax.

Ottoman society, like other societies, can be divided along different types of lines based on gender, occupation, class, religion, or race. For tax purposes, Ottoman society was divided roughly between taxpaying subjects (*reaya,* or flock) and the military-administrative class (*askeri*). This division between *askeri* and *reaya* was the primary determinant of status, crossing lines of gender, race, and sometimes religion. A woman of the *askeri* class could command authority over a man of lesser status. People of various races could be members of the *askeri* class; the chief black eunuch, for example, was one of the most powerful men in the state. Although merchants and members of the *ulama* might achieve considerable wealth and authority, they did not have access to the same type of power and status as the military administrative class.

▲ *Portrait of a Sufi,* c. 1535, was attributed to the painter Shaykh-Zadeh who studied in Herat and then painted and instructed disciples at the Safavid Court in Tabriz. Talented painters were in great demand in the courts of the Islamic dynastic empires. Sufi *shaykhs* often served as influential advisors to the sultans and shahs.

mufti—A high-ranking Muslim religious and legal adviser.

dhimmis—Non-Muslim subjects of an Islamic state.

jizya—An additional head tax imposed on non-Muslims living under Islamic rule.

Artistic Production

Ottoman success resulted in a vigorous cultural renaissance, most evident in monumental architecture and

IMAGE
The Suleymaniye Mosque

decorative tile work. Mehmed II rebuilt his decaying capital, from sewers to palaces. His monumental Fatih Mosque and splendid Topkapi Palace, with its fortress walls, fountains, and courtyards, were models of the new Ottoman style, which was influenced by the Byzantine artistic tradition. The palace was divided into three courts that reflected Ottoman concepts of power and space. The outer court was for public affairs, as well as stable and kitchen facilities. The second court provided a dividing line between the public and private life of the sultan. There the sultan met with diplomats and built his library. The inner court was reserved for the sultan and his intimates, a place for relaxation and privacy. Suleiman surpassed Topkapi's splendor with the beautiful and elegant Suleimaniye, his own mosque and mausoleum. These were but three architectural wonders among thousands scattered throughout the empire, many of which remain today.

In addition, the period was marked by wondrous productions in the realms of decorative arts. Calligraphy could take the form of birds or boats in official documents. Elaborate calligraphy and stunning painted tiles decorated Ottoman mosques and buildings. For example, Suleiman added luminous tiles to the Dome of the Rock in Jerusalem. Ottoman high culture also produced a great outpouring of scholarship and literature, mostly following Persian traditions but also reflecting a unique Ottoman synthesis. Poets, artists, and historians vied for the attentions—and rewards (silver, sable furs, robes of honor, even houses)—of the sultan. Some achieved remarkable rank and success; others left the palace disheartened and poor. The great majority of artisans, however, held relatively low status. They lived and worked in the palace or in the cities, grouped often according to their occupations on "the street of the gold-thread makers" or "the street of the coppersmiths."

Challenges to Ottoman Supremacy

Beginning in Suleiman's reign, cheap silver from the Americas and a population increase led to rising inflation, rebellions, and military mutinies, all of which weakened the government. None of the eight sultans who followed Suleiman before 1648 could duplicate his successes. Selim II was known as "the drunkard"; another sultan gained notoriety by having 19 of his brothers killed on his accession. Increasingly, the sultans did not themselves lead their troops into battle. Other problems plaguing Suleiman's successors were the rising power of the Russians and Habsburgs in Europe, stalemated wars with Iran, and the end of Ottoman naval supremacy in the Red Sea. Nonetheless, the period between 1566 and 1650 should be viewed as one of reorganization and retrenchment rather than decline. The Ottoman Empire was adjusting to newly emerging global configurations of power and commerce, and Ottoman armies still managed to gain important victories in this era, notably the reconquest of Iraq by Murad IV (1623–1640) in 1638.

With Suleiman's death, the Ottoman Empire passed its zenith, but it remained a significant contender for power in the Afro-Eurasian sphere well into the eighteenth century. It continued to dominate the overland trade with Asia. Moreover, the sultans moderated Portuguese domination of the Indian Ocean, ultimately aiding the Dutch and English seaborne empires in the East while humbling their Habsburg rivals in Europe.

DOCUMENT
The Decline of the Ottomans

The Safavid Empire in Iran

What role did Shi'ism play in the Safavid Empire?

In the beginning of the sixteenth century, a new Turkic dynasty came to power in Iran, led by a charismatic, red-headed, adolescent sufi *shaykh*. This dynasty, emerging out of the Safavid sufi religious order, would unite Iran, challenge the Ottoman empire, and convert Iran's predominantly Sunni population to Shi'ism. The Safavid dynasty had its origins in an Islamic religious order founded by Safi al-Din (c. 1252–1334). One of his descendants, Ismail (1501–1524), gathered an army of devoted followers and began a series of lightning campaigns that united Iran, conquered Iraq, and posed a formidable challenge to the Ottomans on their eastern frontiers. Ismail was only 14 when he seized his first territories. Although such precocity may seem unusual today, it was common enough in this era for the sons of powerful men to be trained to fight and rule while still boys.

Ismail was not only a successful military commander; he was also the head of a Shi'ite Muslim sect. Contemporary accounts portray him as a charismatic leader whose army thought him invincible. They followed him into battle crying *"Shaykh, Shaykh!"* The Safavid troops wore red headgear with 12 folds to com-

	The Safavids
1501	Ismail Safavi establishes the Safavid dynasty
1524–1576	Reign of Tahmasp
1588–1629	Reign of Shah Abbas
1597	Shah Abbas founds his imperial center at Isfahan

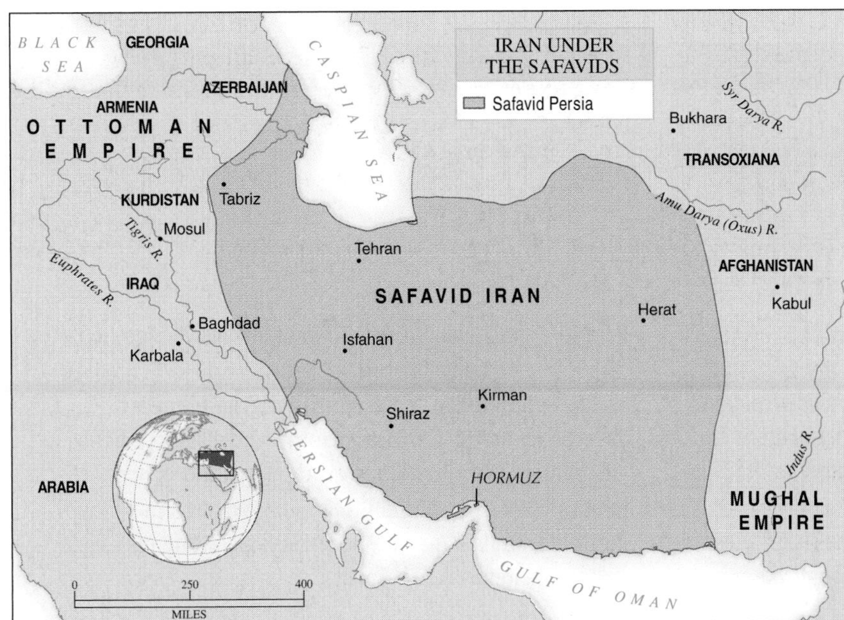

The Safavid Empire was based on the broad, semiarid Iranian plateau. The Safavids and Ottomans contended for control of Iraq and Azerbaijan.

memorate the 12 Shi'ite *imams* (descendants of the prophet Muhammad; see Chapter 7). Their signature headgear earned them the nickname "redheads."

Ismail angered the Ottoman sultan by sending missionaries and agitators to stir up the sultan's subjects on the Ottoman Empire's eastern frontiers. He also launched a sometimes violent campaign to convert the Sunni Muslims of his domain to Twelver Shi'ism. Because Persia had been predominantly Sunni, he had to import Shi'ite scholars and jurists from the Arab lands, such as Syria and Iraq. Under the Safavid *shahs* (monarchs), Iran became overwhelmingly Twelver Shi'ite, as it is today.

Power is acquired not only on the field of battle but also in the arenas of reputation and diplomacy. Legends arose around the youthful leader Ismail because of his many and rapid conquests. He was also supposed to have received the secret knowledge of the Safavi religious order, passed down from his brother as he lay dying. Hence he had a powerful aura of both political and religious legitimacy. European rulers, including the Portuguese king and the pope, were inspired by the accounts of Ismail's victories and the rumors of his quasi-divine prowess. Hoping that the Safavids would help them defeat the Ottomans, who were Sunni Muslims, these rulers sent envoys to the young shah. Ismail had some interest in exploring possibilities with European powers, but he was apparently more interested in acquiring European artillery and defeating the Ottomans than in a Christian-Shi'ite alliance.

Given that transport and communication technology were so primitive in the sixteenth century, rulers often knew little about their rivals. Diplomatic missions were thus crucially important as a means by which a ruler might establish his reputation and gain information about foreign powers. The Portuguese, for example, thought of the Safavids as uncivilized, but they were interested in securing an ally against the Ottomans. Their envoy to Ismail was instructed to brag to the Safavids about the fine quality of Portuguese horses, table service, and women (all considered prize possessions). Envoys were also used to send messages of intimidation. When, in 1510, Ismail defeated Shaibani Khan, the Uzbek ruler in Central Asia, he had the Khan's skull gilded and made into a drinking cup. He sent an envoy with the grisly trophy, along with a taunting message, to the Ottoman sultan, Bayezid II. Of course, being an envoy in this era was dangerous, especially for the bearers of rude messages. The Ottoman sultans often imprisoned Safavid envoys, and messengers to the Safavid court were sometimes detained or abused. When Ismail sent another arrogant message to the Mamluk sultan in Egypt, the latter was so enraged that he sponsored a poetry contest to see which of his poets could write the most insulting reply in verse. But he did not harm Ismail's messenger because he was afraid of a Safavid invasion.

The Ottomans were intimidated by Ismail's early successes. In 1514, however, they soundly defeated Ismail's forces on the frontier between Anatolia and Iran. This victory is often attributed to the fact that the Ottomans had more and better gunpowder weaponry. Demoralized, Ismail withdrew to his palace, having lost his reputation for invincibility. After his death, the Safavids fought a series of long wars against the Ottomans to the west and the Uzbeks to the east.

None of his successors wielded the same charismatic religious power as Ismail. They were kings, not *shaykhs* (holy men), even though Ismail's son Tahmasp still claimed the headship of the Safavid sufi order.

Document

The Coming of Ismail Safavi Foretold

Histories and legends of famous leaders and religious figures often recount the ways in which the coming of these men was predicted or foretold. In this selection, from an anonymous Persian manuscript, the story is told of a sufi mystic named Dede Mohammad. This sufi, or *darwish,* returning from a pilgrimage to Mecca, becomes separated from his caravan in the desert. Dying of thirst, he is rescued by a mysterious youth who takes him to a magnificent encampment in a flowering plain. There he sees a veiled prince, whom he does not realize is the Twelfth *Imam,* a descendant of the Prophet revered by the Shi'ite Muslims who is believed to be in occultation (that is, he has disappeared but is not dead). In this vision, the Twelfth *Imam* girds and sends forth the young Ismail Safavi, thus legitimizing his reign to the Shi'ites.

After his rescue, Dede Mohammad... walked by the young man's side, until they came to a palace, whose cupola outrivaled the sun and moon.... Golden thrones were arranged side by side, and on one of the thrones a person was seated whose face was covered by a veil. Dede Mohammad, placing his hand on his breast, made a salutation, whereupon an answer to his salutation came from the veiled one, who having bidden him be seated, ordered food to be brought for him. The like of this food he had never seen in his life before.... As soon as he had finished his repast, he saw that a party of men had entered, bringing a boy of about fourteen years of age, with red hair, a white face, and dark grey eyes; on his head was a scarlet cap.... The veiled youth then said to him, "Oh! Ismail, the hour of your 'coming' has now arrived." The other replied: "It is for your Holiness to command."... His Holiness, taking his belt three times lifted it up and placed it on the ground again. He then, with his own blessed hands, fastened on the girdle and taking [Ismail's] cap from his head, raised it and then replaced it.... His Holiness then told his servants to bring his own sword which, when brought, he fastened with his own hands on the girdle of the child. Then he said, "You may now depart." [The Arab youth then guided Dede Mohammad back to his caravan, and the sufi asked his guide to reveal the identity of the veiled prince.] He replied, "Did you not know that the prince you saw was no other than the Lord of the Age?" When Dede Mohammad heard this name he stood up and said: "Oh! youth, for the love of God take me back again that I may once more kiss the feet of His Holiness [the Twelfth *Imam*], and ask a blessing of him, perchance I might be allowed to wait on him." But the youth replied: "It is impossible. You should have made your request at first. You cannot return. But you can make your request where you will, for His Holiness is everywhere present and will hear your prayers."

Questions to Consider

1. This manuscript apparently dates from the seventeenth century. Why was it important for the Safavids to relate in this way such stories of the predicted coming of Ismail?
2. The Twelfth *Imam* tied a belt or sash around Ismail's waist, placed his cap on his head, and gave him his own sword. What is the significance of this ceremony? Can you think of similar rituals that take place today?
3. What is the significance of the flowering plain in the middle of a desert and of the miraculous food?

From E. Dennison Ross, "The Early Years of Shah Ismail," *Journal of the Royal Asiatic Society* (1896), pp. 328-331.

The Middle East

Still, the next hundred years of Safavid rule were characterized by a consolidation of state power, lavish patronage of the arts, and an exploration of diplomatic and commercial relations with Europe. European merchants visited the shah's court, trying to gain access to the coveted Iranian silk trade, but they met with little success. Tahmasp ruled for half a century (1524–1576), despite having to contend with foreign invasions, religious factionalism, and power struggles among the tribal leaders. The Safavids, with the aid of European renegades, developed their gunpowder weaponry but never to the same extent as the Ottomans. Nor did they imitate the elaborate "slave"-based hierarchy and infantry corps (janissaries) that became the basis for Ottoman success. In Iran, the tribal leaders and their cavalry-based militaries retained their position of power.

The Reign of Abbas the Great

The reign of Shah Abbas (1588–1629) is considered a "golden age" of Safavid power, comparable to that of Suleiman in the Ottoman Empire. Ascending the throne at the age of 17, Abbas ultimately became a pragmatic politician, a wise statesman, a brilliant strategist, and a generous patron of the arts. During his reign, Iran acquired security, stability, and a reputation for cultural creativity, symbolized by the shah's splendid new capital at Isfahan.

Abbas directed much of his attention to the threat posed by an Ottoman-Uzbek alliance, which had almost destroyed his country. He held his holy men in political check but labored to project an image of Shi'ite piety. He reorganized his government and army, creating a personal force of "slaves" of the royal household. This force acted as a counterweight to the ambitious and often unruly tribal chiefs. Within the army, Abbas increased his artillery and musket forces, relying less on traditional cavalry. During the 1590s, he slowly recovered territory lost by his less adept predecessors.

Iran prospered under Abbas, and Isfahan was a great center of trade, production, and consumption. The government employed thousands of workers, and the shah, his family, and retainers consumed great quantities of luxury textiles, jade vessels, jeweled weapons, and exotic food items. Government monopolies, particularly in silk, promoted various crafts such as weaving and dying. Hundreds of new roads, bridges, hostels, and irrigation projects promoted agriculture, encouraged trade, and swelled urban populations. These projects also enhanced the prestige of the ruler. Contemporaries noted that a person could travel from one end of the empire to another in safety, without fear of bandits. That was a significant claim in an age when bandits roamed the countryside and merchants traveled at their own risk, often with large retinues of armed guards.

The silk trade was so lucrative that merchants on both sides conspired to get the shipments through, even when the Safavids and the Ottomans were at war.

▼ The image shows the domes of the great Safavid mosque of Isfahan. Known once as the Masjid-i Shah mosque, and today as the Imam mosque, this magnificent structure was built between 1612 and 1638 under Shah Abbas (1588–1629). The mosque is known for its twin minarets and its innovative and lush decorative patterns of tilework and mosaics.

Nominally, this image illustrates a story about an elderly dervish who is in love with a handsome young man. But miniatures often depicted scenes of everyday life like this sixteenth-century Safavid scene of a bath house. On the roof, servants shake out towels. In the dressing room, men are shown changing their clothes and an attendant brings a man who appears to be the bathkeeper some food. A father carries his son into the bath while outside, a servant takes care of a horse with rich saddle cloths. Inside the bath (*hammam*), assisted by bath attendants, men of various ages wash, get their hair trimmed, or enjoy a massage. The bath was a place for socializing, relaxing, and conducting business. Bathing was a same-sex activity. Women, who either attended separate baths or attended on different days, might bring their children or use the bath as an opportunity to evaluate potential brides for their sons.

Iran was an important center in the networks of East–West trade. Its silk was in such demand in Europe that Venetian, French, and other traders would wait in the Syrian entrepots for the caravans of Iranian silk to come in. They negotiated with local agents, trying to outbid each other for the rights to purchase each incoming load. One Venetian observer stated that a merchant would willingly pluck out his own eye to triumph over a competitor. The British tried for years to gain concessions from the Safavids on Iranian silk. Ultimately, the shah signed a commercial agreement with the British, and the Portuguese were forcibly ejected from Hormuz in the Persian Gulf, moves that allowed direct shipment of Iranian silk to Europe by sea, thus avoiding Ottoman tolls on the overland routes.

Iran at this time was one of the primary cultural centers of the world. It was a conduit to the West not only for the goods but also for the spiritual and literary influences of India. Meanwhile, sufi missionaries traveled across South and Southeast Asia, transmitting their own ideas and bringing a synthesis of mystical ideas and practices back to the Islamic heartlands. Iran's fine arts—ceramics, tapestries, and carpets—were eagerly sought from Alexandria to Calcutta. Iranian literary forms, particularly the exquisite imagery of Iranian poetry, were imitated at both the Ottoman and Mughal courts, even by the rulers themselves. Iranian painters explored realist styles and erotic themes. They were recruited from abroad, as were two émigrés, Khwaja Abdus Samad and Mir Sayyid Ali, who founded the famous Mughal school of painting in India.

Major Middle Eastern courts housed large workshops of artists, sometimes numbering in the hundreds. The Safavid shahs paid their painters to produce lavish manuscripts. Ismail commissioned a wondrous illustrated version of the *Epic of Kings (Shahnamah),* a long rhyming poem by Firdawsi, that was not finished in the shah's lifetime. Five court calligraphers spent 9 years transcribing a single edition of the poet Jami's *Seven Thrones,* for Prince Ibrahim Mirza; it was then turned over to a group of painters who produced its lavish illustrations. When the Ottomans conquered the Iranian capital of Tabriz, they carried back many of the Safavid artists and their works as a valuable part of the booty.

Iranian architecture, with its jewel-like colors, intricate geometric and floral patterns, luxurious gardens, and artificial streams, exerted considerable influence on the architecture of the Islamic world. Abbas made the capital at Isfahan a showcase for these artistic and architectural talents. One of the largest cities of its time, Isfahan had a million inhabitants. Its public life centered around a broad square (used for assemblies and polo matches), the palace compound, a huge bazaar, and the main mosque. Five hundred years later, the beauty of Abbas's surviving monuments still inspires awe in visitors. As one Persian writer put it in his boyhood memoirs, "Isfahan is half the world."

The Mughal Empire in South Asia

How did the Turco-Islamic Mughals modify their rule to accommodate a Hindu majority population?

The Safavid and Ottoman states were contemporaries of the mighty Mughal Empire in India. It too was ruled by a Turkic dynasty. But unlike the Ottoman sultans and Safavid shahs, the Mughals ruled a population that was predominantly Hindu rather than Muslim. That fact marked the Mughal Empire indelibly and helped craft its distinctive character.

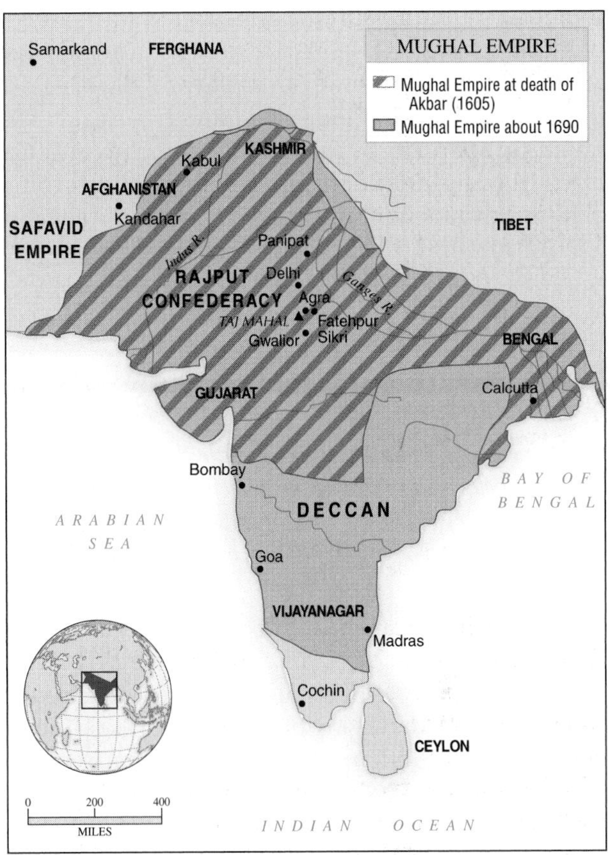

▲ At its height, the Mughal Empire comprised most of the Indian subcontinent.

Origins

The Ottoman Empire emerged out of a warrior principality in what is now Turkey, and the Safavid Empire was established by a sufi boy-king who commanded both political and religious authority in Iran. The origin of the Mughal Empire was different from each of these; one might say it was founded by a determined prince in search of a kingdom.

The establishment of the Mughal Empire was not the first instance of Muslim contact with the diverse, but predominantly Hindu, population of India. Muslim merchants and sufi mystics had traveled to India from the Islamic heartlands for many centuries. From the seventh century on, Muslim rulers extended the frontiers of Islam eastward to the borders of South Asia. Then a Turkic warrior, Mahmud of Ghazna (c. 971–1030), gained control of Khurasan province in eastern Iran and Afghanistan and seized control of northern India. Muslim sultanates were also established on the west coast of India, and the Muslim Delhi Sultanate ruled in the thirteenth and fourteenth centuries until Timur's invasion. Thus, by the sixteenth century, much of South Asian society had had some contact with Islamic culture and political power.

	The Mughals
1525	Babur invades India
1556–1605	Reign of Akbar, Mughal Golden Age
1632	Shah Jahan commissions the Taj Mahal
1658–1707	Reign of Aurangzeb, reasserts Islamic orthodoxy

India is a land of many peoples, many languages, and diverse terrain. At the beginning of the sixteenth century, it was politically fragmented. The Delhi Sultanate, having spawned a number of independent contending Muslim states, had been partially resurrected under the Lodi Afghan dynasty. The Rajput Confederacy held sway in the northwest, the Vijayangar Empire controlled much of southern India, and a string of commercial city-states held sway along the southwestern coast. Although many rulers had aspired to unite the entire subcontinent, that goal remained daunting.

Early in the sixteenth century, a new conqueror cast his eye on India. The adventurous Turco-Mongol ruler of Kabul, Babur ("The Tiger"; 1483–1530), was a descendant of both Timur and Chinggis Khan. Babur did not begin his career in India. He inherited the Afghan principality of Ferghana and twice conquered the Timurid capital at Samarkand before losing everything to the Uzbeks. He and his troops finally seized the throne of Kabul in 1504. Babur is a striking historical figure because, unlike many rulers of his time, he compiled his memoirs. They are a tale of triumphs and losses that reveal Babur as a straightforward narrator who built gardens wherever he went, paid careful attention to geography, was solicitous of his mother, and seemed to enjoy good wine and a good fight. He also loved to compose and recite poetry. Babur's memoirs tell of rhinoceros hunts and military relations. He notes, rather ruefully, that he had sworn to give up drink when he reached the age of 40 but now felt compelled to drink out of anxiety because he was already 39. Armed with Turkish artillery, this intrepid warrior mobilized an invasion in 1525, winning decisive battles against the Afghan Sultanate at Delhi and the Rajput Confederacy. Babur was not impressed with Indian culture. He criticized native dress, religion, and the failure of Indians to have running water in their gardens.

> *Hindustan [India] is a place of little charm. There is no beauty in its people, no graceful social intercourse, no poetic talent or understanding, no etiquette, nobility or manliness....There are no good horses, meat, grapes, melons, or other fruit. There is no ice, cold water, good food or bread in the markets.*[2]

Like many travelers, Babur tended to find his own culture superior to those of other peoples. He did, however, admire the Indian systems of numbers, weights, and measures and the country's vast array of craftsmen. Speaking as a prospective ruler, he could not help but remark that "the one nice aspect of Hindustan is that it is a large country with lots of gold and money."[3] When Babur died, soon after the conquest, the hard-living and thoughtful ruler had laid the foundations for a Mughal empire that would dominate most of the subcontinent and endure into the eighteenth century.

Babur was succeeded by his able but erratic son, Humayun (hu-MAH-yoon). After 10 years of rule during which he expanded Mughal domains, Humayun was overthrown by his vassal Sher Khan. He then fled to the Safavid court of Tahmasp in Iran. The Safavid shah welcomed Humayun. It was always useful for monarchs of the time to shelter in their courts the sons or rivals of neighboring kings, as such refugees gave rulers leverage against their enemies. Rulers also demanded that vassals send their sons to reside at court; it was a practical way to ensure the loyalty of subordinates.

In 1555, Shah Tahmasp helped Humayun regain his kingdom, no doubt presuming that Humayun would prove a significant ally on the Safavids' eastern frontiers. But Humayun died shortly thereafter in a fall down his library steps—perhaps a fitting end for a learned man, but a rather ignominious one for a warrior.

The Reign of Akbar

Humayun's son Akbar (r. 1556–1605) was 14 years old when he succeeded his father, about the same age as Shah Ismail when he commenced his reign. During a half century of rule, Akbar united northern India, advanced against the sultanates in the south of the subcontinent, and presided over a glorious courtly culture. Akbar ruled an empire more populous than those of the Ottoman sultan and the Iranian shah; Mughal subjects numbered between 100 and 150 million.

Unlike Ismail, Akbar did not immediately consolidate his power. Initially, he was controlled by a regent. As often happens when a prince comes to power at an early age, powerful men in the court used the prince's youth to advance their own influence and objectives. By the age of 20, however, Akbar took charge and began a determined campaign of conquest that would continue into his old age.

This Mughal potentate was the counterpart of Suleiman in the Ottoman Empire and Shah Abbas in Safavid Iran. His reign is associated with military might, prosperity, and patronage of the arts at a spectacular level. At 13, Akbar led troops in battle; in his thirties, he challenged an enemy commander to personal combat; in late middle age, he still hunted wild animals with sword and lance. Akbar's concern for morality and social justice was indicated by his advice to a son: "Avoid religious persecution; be strong but magnanimous; accept apologies, sincerely given."[4]

A significant aspect of Akbar's reign is that he adapted the Islamic state to the conditions of ruling a non-Muslim population. In so doing, he promoted cultural synthesis, incorporated Hindus and others into the inner workings of government, and showed himself to be a pragmatic monarch. He married a number of Rajput princesses and made alliances with Hindu families, taking the men into his service. The mother of his heir, Jahangir, was a Hindu. He also abolished the *jizya,* the head tax on non-Muslims. This decision may seem like a simple matter, but the *jizya* was a standard of Islamic rule and had been institutionalized in the Sharia (Islamic law). By abolishing it, Akbar gave notice to his Hindu subjects that they were granted a more equitable position vis-à-vis the Muslims, who constituted the ruling class.

Akbar also stopped taxing Hindu pilgrims, financed the construction of Hindu temples, and forbade Muslims to kill or eat the cow, which was sacred to Hindus. These measures alienated the *ulama* and the diverse Muslim elite of Turks, Afghans, Mongols, and Iranians but won new support among the majority. Akbar, however, also initiated certain measures designed to force Hindu practice into compliance with Islamic law; he issued decrees outlawing Hindu child marriages and ***sati*** (the self-burning of widows), two reforms that violated Hindu traditions.

Akbar's tolerance in public administration was matched by his pursuit of knowledge and personal

sati—The practice by Hindu widows of self-immolation on their husbands' funeral pyres.

Seeing Connections

Religious Tolerance Under Akbar

The Mughal emperor Akbar (1542–1605) was militarily powerful, uniting all of north India and ruling as a great cultural leader over Muslims and Hindus alike. Akbar promoted a cultural synthesis through his policies of religious tolerance, alliances with powerful Hindu families, and adoption of Hindu practices such as the prohibition of eating beef. At the same time, he required Hindus to accept certain Islamic laws and forbade the practice of *sati*. Akbar was fascinated by world religions and established a forum for religious discussions among Muslims, Jews, Christians, Jains, Hindus, and Zoroastrians. Here, a Mughal portrait depicts a Jesuit priest in India around 1600.

explorations of various religious faiths. He was devoted to certain sufi *shaykhs* and launched at his court a "house of worship," a forum for religious discussion to which he invited Muslims, Christians, Jews, Jains, Hindus, and Zoroastrians. In 1582, Akbar proclaimed a new cult, the *Din-i-Ilahi* (deen-i-eel-AH-hee), or "Divine Faith," which centered on Akbar himself and was highly influenced by **Zoroastrianism.** The new creed gained few adherents, but it further antagonized the *ulama* and demonstrated Akbar's religious eclecticism.

Akbar and the Jesuits

The Mughal State and Its Culture

St. Francis Xavier, Jesuit in India

One of the great accomplishments of the Mughal Empire was its establishment of a highly organized and intrusive central administration. In many ways like that of the Ottomans, it was designed to produce a consistent supply of taxes and troops for the government and to manage distant provinces. Akbar's military administrators, about two-thirds of whom were foreign-born Muslims, were organized in military ranks and paid salaries according to the number of soldiers

Zoroastrianism—A religion founded by the Iranian prophet and mystic Zoroaster in the fifth century; initially monotheistic, it evolved into a dualistic faith in which the gods of light and good, led by Ahura-Mazda, opposed the gods of darkness and evil, led by Ahriman; influenced the development of Judaism and Christianity; Zoroastrians who migrated to India are known as Parsees.

they commanded. Promotion for these military administrators, who were called ***mansabdars*** (mahn-SAHB-dahrs), was, ideally, based on merit. Their ranks were open to Hindus, and their positions were not hereditary, like those of European nobles. Like the Ottoman *kul* system, the *mansabdar* system was designed to produce loyalty to the state. Officials, in turn, were now made more dependent on the emperor. Like the Ottomans and Safavids, Akbar drew conquered foes into his service as long as they offered their submission. In this way, he took advantage of the military expertise of defeated commanders.

In the early seventeenth century, the Mughal Empire was one of the wealthiest states in the world, with revenues ten times greater than those of France. Cities were numerous and large by European standards. Akbar's capital at Agra, for example, housed 200,000 people—twice the population of contemporary London. In the towns and villages, many industries flourished, particularly cotton textiles, which were exported to most of Asia and Africa. The majority of subjects were Hindu peasants. One-third to one-half of their produce, paid in land taxes, supported the army and kept the administrative elite in considerable luxury.

The early Mughal period saw a new Hindu-Muslim cultural synthesis, well illustrated in literature. Beginning with Babur, each emperor considered himself a poet, a scholar, and a collector of books. Akbar himself could not read, but he founded a great library

mansabdars—Mughal military-administrative official.

▼ In 1632, the Mughal emperor, Shah Jahan, commissioned the building of the resplendent Taj Mahal as a memorial to his late wife. Tall minarets surround a central dome, and a reflecting pool perfectly mirrors the white marble building, one of the glories of Mughal architecture. The Taj Mahal is one of the more spectacular examples of the ways in which various peoples commemorate their dead.

housing over 20,000 illustrated manuscripts. The Mughals used their wealth to patronize the arts. Their literature was cosmopolitan, reflected a fresh originality, and was expressed in a variety of languages, including Turkish, Persian, Hindi, Arabic, and Urdu (an Indo-Persian fusion).

Despite the Muslim prohibition of representational figures, human or animal, painting developed rapidly as an art in the early Mughal period. Akbar had studied art as a child under Abdus Samad and Mir Sayyid Ali, two Safavid court painters whom Humayan brought to Kabul and later took to India. Akbar's royal studio employed over a hundred artists, mostly Hindus, who created works of great variety including miniatures of courtly life and large murals for Akbar's palaces.

The royal studio produced beautifully illustrated manuscripts requiring many painters and many years to complete. Foremost among these is the spectacular *Hamzanamah* (hahm-ZAHN-ah-mah), which includes 1400 illustrations on cloth. Akbar also sponsored illustrated versions of Babur's memoirs and of the great Sanskrit epics the *Mahabharata* (MAH-he-BAH-re-te) and the *Ramayana* (rah-MAI-yah-nah). The Mughal school of painters under Jahangir, Akbar's son, produced wonderful animal and bird imagery, developed new strains of sensual and realist representation, and expertly incorporated motifs of European painting into Mughal art.

The most imposing symbols of Mughal glory are to be seen in architecture. Fusing Iranian and Indic styles, it featured the lavish use of mosaics, bulbous domes, cupolas, slender spires, lofty vaulted gateways, and formal gardens, all carefully harmonized. Akbar's major building project was his palace complex at Fatehpur Sikri (fe-te-POOR SIK-ree). Akbar wanted to build his new palace on a site dedicated to a famous sufi holy man, *Shaykh* Salim Chishti. But Fatehpur Sikri became a monument to man's vanity and lack of planning. Akbar's court abandoned the complex (which took 15 years to build) after only 14 years because the water supply was inadequate. But visitors still marvel at the red sandstone blocks of the monumental fortress, which were hewn so precisely that they needed no fasteners or mortar.

Akbar's son Jahangir and his grandson Shah Jahan continued the tradition of monumental building. The latter replaced Akbar's sandstone buildings at Delhi with new ones of marble. At Agra, Shah Jahan erected the famous Taj Mahal, a tomb for his favorite wife, Mumtaz Mahal, who died while giving birth to her fifteenth child. This elaborate tomb, set in beautiful gardens, took over 20 years to build. Its luminous white marble, beautiful tracery of semiprecious stones, and elegant lines make the Taj Mahal one of the best-known buildings in the world today.

▲ Miniatures were not painted solely for artistic expression; they also suggested relationships. In this Mughal painting of Shah Jahangir and the Safavid Shah Abbas, Jahangir's artist portrayed his master as big and powerful, dominating his rather puny-looking Safavid rival. The monarchs both stand on the globe, but Jahangir's lion is much more imposing than Abbas' lamb. The angels supporting the rulers' halo show the influence of European art motifs on Mughal imagery. According to the inscription on this miniature, Jahangir commissioned the painting after having a dream about Shah Abbas.

Akbar's Successors: Contesting the Hindu-Muslim Synthesis

Like most empires, the Mughal polity fared best when its administration was relatively tolerant, its treasury full, and its military successful. Jahangir (1605–1627) and Shah Jahan (1628–1658) continued Akbar's policies of relative tolerance. Jahangir was learned and artistically sensitive (as demonstrated in his memoirs), but he was also a drunkard and a drug addict, often lacking the strength to act decisively and conduct policy. He lost Kandahar to the Iranians. Shah Jahan launched three costly and unsuccessful campaigns to retake Kandahar, a disastrous thrust into Central Asia, four costly invasions of the Deccan, and an extravagant expedition to oust a Portuguese enclave on the Indian coast. To compensate for these military expeditions, he had to raise land taxes, thus oppressing the peasantry.

Document

The Idea of Seclusion and Lady Nurjahan

The idea of seclusion (being hidden away from view) is often associated with women in Muslim societies. But historically, we find that women in all Muslim households were clearly not secluded and that "seclusion" itself is a notion that varies over time, place, class, status, and culture. Even when women were considered to be "secluded," they might have been engaged in a variety of activities that we don't ordinarily associate with seclusion. So, one question for historians, of any time, place, and group of women is: "What were those women doing?" Some examples of what elite, secluded women were doing are found in the memoirs of the Mughal emperor Jahangir. Like those of his forefather, Babur, Jahangir's memoirs are full of minute and interesting details, including discussion of the affairs of his principal wife Nurjahan (1577–1645). Nurjahan was the daughter of a Mughal vizir, and, at the end of Jahangir's reign, she, along with her brother, took over effective control of the empire. In her husband's account, we find Nurjahan portrayed as an avid hunter, an owner of estates, and a mover-and-shaker in political affairs. She engaged in all these activities while "secluded." These selections from Jahangir's memoirs (and an appendix by his historian Muhammad-Hadi) give some idea of Nurjahan's activities.

On April 16 [1617]...the scouts had cornered four lions. I [Jahangir] set out with the ladies of the harem to hunt them. When the lions came into view, Nurjahan Begam said, "If so commanded, I will shoot the lions." I said, "Let it be so." She hit two of them with one shot each and the other two with two shots, and in the twinkling of an eye the four lions were deprived of life with six shots. Until now such marksmanship has not been seen—from atop an elephant and from inside a howdah [covered seat] she had fired six shots, none of which missed.... As a reward for such marksmanship I scattered a thousand ashrafis [coins] over her head and gave her a pair of pearls and a diamond worth a lac [100,000] of rupees.

When Jahangir was suffering from chest pain and shortness of breath, his physicians could not ease his discomfort, so he committed himself to his wife's care:

Nurjahan Begam's remedies and experience were greater than any of the physicians', especially since she treated me with affection and sympathy. She made me drink less and applied remedies that were suitable and efficacious. Although the treatments the physicians had prescribed before were done with her approval, I now relied on her affection, gradually reduced my intake of wine, and avoided unsuitable things and disagreeable food. It is hoped that the True Physician will grant me a complete recovery from the other world.

When Nurjahan's father died, Jahangir awarded his estate to her:

I awarded I'timaduddawla's jagir [a type of fief, revenue from land], household, and paraphernalia of chieftainship and amirship to Nurjahan Begam, and I ordered that her drums should be sounded after the imperial ones.

When Mahabat Khan mounted a rebellion against Jahangir, Nurjahan escaped and mobilized for the emperor's defense:

[She] convened the grandees of the empire and addressed them in rebuke, saying, "It was through your negligence that things have gone so far and the unimaginable has happened. You have been disgraced before God and the people by your own actions. Now it must be made up for. Tell each other what the best thing to do is."

Questions to Consider

1. Nurjahan was a royal woman. What do these stories suggest about class and gender as determinants of women's activities?
2. What do these excerpts suggest about the relationship between Jahangir and his wife?
3. If royal women routinely went on hunting expeditions with the emperor, how could they still be secluded?

From Wheeler Thackston, ed. and trans., *The Jahangirnama: Memoirs of Jahangir, Emperor of India* (New York: Oxford University Press, 1999), pp. xx–xxi, 219, 368, 376, 441.

The tension between Mughal tolerance and Muslim rule culminated in the seventeenth century with Akbar's great-grandsons, Dara Shikoh and Aurangzeb (1658–1707). Dara Shikoh took Akbar's tolerance one step further. He was a devoted sufi and wrote his own mystical works; he also studied Hindu mysticism. In the end, this prince's attempt to find a middle ground between Islam and Hinduism provoked a violent response from the empire's Muslims and from his brother, Aurangzeb (OR-ang-zeb). Dara Shikoh was his father's favorite, but in the battle to succeed Shah Jahan, Aurangzeb was victorious. Charging his brother with apostasy (renunciation of his religion), Aurangzeb marched him through the streets of Delhi in humiliation and had him executed.

Both sufi orders and the *ulama* opposed the ecumenicalism of Akbar and Dara Shikoh. With their support, Aurangzeb, having gained the throne, was

▲ The birth of a prince in the Mughal harem. This unusual scene shows the numerous female attendants of the princely court and suggests the ceremonial significance of such an event. Note the varying dress styles of the women and the rich textiles surrounding the princess.

determined to restore Sunni orthodoxy to the Mughal dominions. He reimposed the *jizya* and enforced Sharia law more stringently. Many Hindu temples were destroyed during his reign, and his intolerance and rigid orthodoxy weakened the Mughal hold on its diverse Hindu populations.

The Mughal Social Order

As already noted, Mughal society comprised a series of hierarchies based on a Hindu majority and a predominantly Muslim ruling class. The vast majority of the populace, as in China, the Middle East, and Europe, consisted of illiterate peasants who provided the bulk of the empire's revenue through agricultural taxes. Wealth was an important factor in determining status, but it was not the primary factor. A merchant could be very wealthy but could not achieve the same status as a member of the elite military-administrative class. Among Hindus, status was intimately linked to caste.

Mughal society, like most societies, was also patriarchal; it allocated family, religious, and political dominance to men. This system of male dominance is often attributed to Islam, but patriarchy predated Islam in India, as it did in the Middle East. In general, it would be more accurate to say that Islam both reinforced preexisting patriarchal structures and improved the position of women by forbidding female infanticide and granting women inheritance rights. In India under Islamic rule, the position of women derived from a synthesis of Hindu custom and Islamic law. Despite Akbar's reform-minded decrees, *sati* and child marriages continued. Formal education of females, as in most societies, was practically nonexistent, except in a few affluent or learned families.

These practices must, of course, be understood in their temporal and social contexts. In Hindu society, as in Muslim society, in which marriage is considered a preferred state (especially for women), early marriage age acted to prevent the girl's sexual purity from being compromised or questioned. By social convention, women were deemed to need male protectors, and when a woman married, she left the protection of her father or brother and became part of her husband's household. By immolating herself on her husband's funeral pyre, a widow prevented herself from becoming a social burden on her husband's family or the family she was born into.

As for female education, we should remember that the overwhelming majority of people, in all the world civilizations of this era, were illiterate. Only certain of the elites could read, and even many people of rank, like Akbar, were illiterate. Men's and women's roles were considered complementary, not equal. Because men were expected to perform the political, religious, and administrative tasks that required literacy, formal education tended to be reserved for them.

Networks of Trade and Communication

What role do trade and communication play in the maintenance of the Ottoman, Safavid, and Mughal empires?

The Islamic dynastic empires emerged in a set of interconnected regions that were in turn embedded in even more extensive networks of trade and communication. The primitive nature of transport and communication technology limited the flow of goods, knowledge, and information. But all three circulated in ways that might seem surprising, given that the only ways to get from one place to another were on foot, on animalback, or aboard oared and sailing vessels. Despite these limitations, scholars traveled from one court to another, enjoying the patronage of Ottoman, Safavid, or Mughal emperors and sharing literary, artistic, and legal traditions. The royal courts consumed prodigiously and supported the exchange of goods and culture on a grand scale. Mehmed II had his portrait painted by the famous Italian painter Bellini. Babur brought Iranian artists into India, and the Safavid court imported Arab jurists. Rulers in all three empires drank from Chinese porcelain cups.

The Ottoman, Safavid, and Mughal empires derived most of their income from agriculture. But trade was their second source of wealth. None of these empires invented the trading routes. Rather, these routes emerged and expanded across a set of well-established commercial networks linking urban centers. They inherited these networks from their predecessors and competed with rival kingdoms to monopolize goods and collect commercial taxes. To understand how these empires worked, we must abandon the notion of modern boundaries that are marked, fixed, and defended. Rulers could not control frontiers absolutely; instead they defended and taxed key routes, fortresses, and cities. The porous nature of borders encouraged tax evaders. If officials demanded high taxes along one route, merchants might shift to another route. If taxes were collected by the camel-load, merchants stopped their beasts outside of town and repacked in order to have fewer loads.

In this context of flexible boundaries, trading communities developed that facilitated the flow of goods from one place to another. Although the Ottomans fought long wars with both Christian states in Europe and Muslim competitors in Iran and Egypt, trade among these regions was seldom squelched for long. The furs of Muscovy flowed south into the empire and the gold of Africa came north. Armenian merchants played a prominent role in the Iranian silk trade, which drew European silver in large quantities into the Safavid Empire. Jewish merchants traded copper to Arab merchants, who sold it to South Asian traders in return for cotton, jewels, and spices.

Many great trading centers were scattered throughout the territories of the Islamic dynastic empires. Babur described the emporium of Kabul, located between Iran and India, as receiving merchant caravans of 15,000 or 20,000 pack animals carrying slaves, textiles, sugar, and spices. Kabul channeled the trade of China and India westward in exchange for goods coming eastward from the Ottoman and Safavid realms.

The merchants in turn served an information function. Because communication technologies were so limited, rulers used travelers of all sorts to gain knowledge about the rest of the world. Scholars, sufis, traders, envoys, and spies all served this purpose. Monarchs used envoys as spies, and their rivals tried to control information by keeping visiting envoys sequestered and by intimidating them with military displays. Response to another ruler's challenge could never be swift because it was often months or years before a monarch received a reply or news about his envoy's fate.

Outside these channels of communication, relations between the Islamic empires and European or East Asian states were still quite limited. Only the Ottomans had resident consuls from some of the European states in their capital. In this era, the balance of trade was tipped very much in favor of the East, with eastern goods flowing into Europe and cash flowing back. European imports, with the exception of certain kinds of textiles, were negligible by comparison.

DOCUMENT
The English in South Asia

Conclusion

In the three and a half centuries before 1650, Europe still lagged behind Asia in many respects. No European state, not even the polyglot empire of Charles V, could compare in manpower and resources with the realms of Suleiman or Akbar. Europeans were impressed by the resources and taxation capabilities of the Ottoman governing system. Opportunities for minorities and toleration for dissenting religions were greater in the Muslim countries than in Europe. Asian cities were usually better planned, more tastefully adorned with works of art, and even better supplied with water and with sewage disposal.

Europe's advantages, which began to be more apparent after the beginning of the seventeenth century, were most evident in the realm of technology, specifically in the production of field artillery and oceangoing ships. These technical assets helped certain of the European states gain leverage in a new age, when powerful states would depend on strategic control of sea lanes and world markets. But in the period from 1300 to 1650, it was the Islamic dynastic empires that tended to dominate, using their resources and militaries to become the great imperial powers of that age.

Suggestions for Web Browsing

You can obtain more information about topics included in this chapter at the websites listed below. See also the companion website that accompanies this text, http://www.ablongman.com/brummett, which contains an online study guide and additional resources.

Ottoman Pages
http://www.theottomans.org
A site dedicated to Ottoman society, culture, and history, with many excellent images and maps. Free membership signup required.

Istanbul
http://www.istanbul.com/splash.html
The official website of the city of Istanbul, an excellent source of images of major Ottoman mosques and other monuments.

Topkapi Palace
http://www.ee.bilkent.edu.tr/~history/topkapi.html
A guide to Topkapi Palace, with numerous images of the palace rooms and grounds and its phenomenal artifacts, including portraits of the sultans, manuscripts, clothing, porcelains, and armaments.

Internet Islamic History Sourcebook: The Iranians
http://www.fordham.edu/halsall/islam/islamsbook.html
Links to a variety of documents detailing the rise and spread of the Safavid Empire.

Internet Indian History Sourcebook
http://www.fordham.edu/halsall/india/indiasbook.html
http://www.lib.berkeley.edu/SSEAL/SouthAsia/wsaonlin.html
Extensive indexed sites of sources for India.

Mughal Monarchs
http://www.wsu.edu/~dee/MUGHAL/THREE.HTM
http://www.es.flinders.edu.au/~mattom/science+society/lectures/illustrations/lecture14/akbar.html
Biographical material on the last three great Mughal monarchs.

BBC World Religions Series
http://www.bbc.co.uk/religion/religions/islam/history/mughalempire_1.shtml
Features an excellent summary of the great Mughal kings and their eras.

Literature and Film

A short primary source on Jahangir, available in paperback, is Mutribi al-Asamm, *Conversations with Emperor Jahangir,* trans. Richard Foltz (Mazda, 1998). *The Intimate Life of an Ottoman Statesman: Melek Ahmed Pasha (1588–1662),* trans. Robert Dankoff (SUNY Press, 1991), is a wonderful portrayal of the realities of Ottoman administration. An excellent selection of Ottoman poetry can be found in *Ottoman Lyric Poetry: An Anthology,* eds. Walter Andrews, Najaat Black, and Mehmet Kalpakli (University of Texas Press, 1997).

The University of North Carolina library (Chapel Hill) has a large collection of films on the Islamic world which are cataloged by topic. These include films on the Ottoman Empire and the Modern Middle East. See listings on their website at http://www.lib.unc.edu/house/nonprint.

Suleiman the Magnificent depicts the life, accomplishments and regional significance of this Ottoman sultan.

Isfahan: A City Known as "Half the World" is a great video, in Farsi and English, about Isfahan and its historic sites. For additional information, see http://www.iranianmovies.com/reviews/isfahan.html.

Suggestions for Reading

On inner Asia and Turkic groups, see Peter Golden, *An Introduction to the History of the Turkic Peoples* (Harassowitz, 1992). Luc Kwanten, *Imperial Nomads, a History of Central Asia, 500–1500* (University of Pennsylvania Press, 1979), is an illuminating study of a subject long neglected in standard texts.

The Ottoman Golden Age is ably depicted in Halil Inalcik, *Phoenix: The Ottoman Empire, the Classical Age 1300–1600* (Phoenix Press, 2001); Norman Itzkowitz, *The Ottoman Empire and the Islamic Tradition* (University of Oklahoma Press, 1980); and Stanford Shaw, *A History of the Ottoman Empire and Modern Turkey,* 2 vols. (Cambridge University Press, 1976–1977). On Sultan Suleiman, see Metin Kunt and Christine Woodhead, eds., *Süleyman the Magnificent and His Age* (Longman, 1995). The harem is covered in Leslie P. Peirce, *The Imperial Harem* (Oxford University Press, 1993).

On medieval Iran (Persia), see Ann Lambton, *Continuity and Change in Medieval Persia* (Persian Heritage Foundation, 1988), and David Morgan, *Medieval Persia, 1040–1797* (Longman, 1988). See also Roger Savory, *Iran Under the Safavids* (Cambridge University Press, 1980). Coverage in English of the Safavid period is still limited; an old standard is Percy M. Sykes, *A History of Persia* (Routledge/Curzon, 2003), first published in 1938 and now in its third edition. On Safavid trade, see Rudolph Matthee, *The Politics of Trade in Safavid Iran: Silk for Silver, 1600–1730* (Cambridge University Press, 1999).

The Mughal system is ably described in Annemarie Schimmel, *The Empire of the Great Mughals: History, Art and Culture* (London: Reaktion Books, 2004); Douglas E. Streusand, *The Formation of the Mughal Empire* (Oxford University Press, 1990); and Neelam Chaudhary, *Socio-Economic History of Mughal India* (Discovery, 1987). For collections of articles on a variety of topics by top Mughal scholars, see John F. Richards, Gordon Johnson, and C. A. Bayly, eds., *The Mughal Empire* (Cambridge University Press, 1996); and Zeenut Ziad, *The Magnificent Mughals* (Oxford University Press, 2002).

CHAPTER 13

East Asian Cultural and Political Systems, 1300–1650

Outline

- China: The Ming Dynasty
- Korea: The Making of a Confucian Society
- Japan: The Era of Shōguns and Warring States
- Southeast Asia: States Within a Region

Features

DISCOVERY THROUGH MAPS **Map of China's Ancient Heartland, circa 1500 C.E.**

SEEING CONNECTIONS **A Giraffe in the Ming Court**

DOCUMENT **Zhang Han's Essay on Merchants**

DOCUMENT ***Sotoba Komachi,* a Fourteenth-Century Japanese Nō Play**

DOCUMENT **A Traveller's Account of Siam**

◀ The Temple of the Golden Pavilion was commissioned by the Japanese shōgun Ashikawa Yoshimitsu in 1397. The building was intimate in scale and designed as part of a garden in which the shōgun could meditate. The building, destroyed by an arsonist in 1950, was rebuilt exactly as the original.

FROM THE FOURTEENTH to the seventeenth centuries, China, Korea, Japan, and the countries of Southeast Asia continued to share many ideologies, religions, and cultural traditions. The early Ming dynasty launched the world's largest maritime explorations, dominated world trade, and was deeply connected to the world's silver-based economy. Regional trade was maintained until the seventeenth century, when it was changed by the introduction of new players and products from Europe and the Americas and by restrictions in Japan's international commerce. China was still the dominant actor in East Asia, but individual societies were forming their own political and cultural traditions and identities.

In Korea, the Koryŏ dynasty, struggling with slave-owning landholders who had been allied with the Mongols in China, was overturned by a reformist faction in 1392. King T'aejo (1335–1408), founder of the new Chosŏn dynasty, sent tribute missions to the Ming, cut all ties to the Mongols, and blended Chinese and Korean culture.

In Japan, turmoil and civil war beginning at the end of the fifteenth century and the coming of Iberian missionaries—who brought guns along with religion—in the sixteenth, radically altered Japan's history. In 1600, Japan was once again unified, and by 1640, it restricted its trade to just three partners—China, Korea, and Holland. The lands and islands southeast of China, today called Southeast Asia, were long influenced by Indian culture and religions. Chinese culture deeply influenced Vietnam as well. In the fourteenth and fifteenth centuries, Islam spread to maritime Southeast Asia—today's Philippines, Malaysia, and Indonesia—as merchants recognized the benefit of Muslim ties in expediting trade in the Indian Ocean. Chinese and Indian traders continued to operate throughout Southeast Asia, while Western merchants and missionaries began to influence Southeast Asian life in the seventeenth century.

China: The Ming Dynasty

In what ways can Ming China be considered an early modern state?

Before the modern period, Chinese historians wrote the history of their country as a series of consecutive dynastic waves—as one dynasty declined after a period of growth, another would rise and receive Heaven's mandate (see Chapter 2). The struggle to overthrow the Yuan in the fourteenth century was brutal, but it contained many of the elements of dynastic change identified by contemporaries in China. That is, natural disasters and disease accompanied by religious uprisings suggested Heaven was shifting its support from the Yuan emperor to new rulers. The traditional dynastic cycle model downplays change over time. The Yuan dynasty's brevity gave it little opportunity to change China in lasting ways, and this seemed to confirm the dynastic cycle's validity. Yet, as we have seen in Chapter 10, the Yuan was at the center of a cosmopolitan Eurasian commercial world which influenced culture far beyond China's borders.

The Yuan dynasty declined after Khubilai's death in 1294. The north of China began to decline economically, and southerners suffered discriminatory treatment. Everywhere, the pre-Yuan power structure had been challenged, as the Mongols had altered civil service recruitment policies. Many peasants were brought to the brink of despair in the face of natural disasters in the fourteenth century, especially the Huanghe River's change in course, the outbreak of the bubonic plague in 1331, and a "little ice age" that undermined the agricultural economy and weakened people's resistance to disease in the early fourteenth century. China's population plummeted to 85 million; it had been as high as 120 million in 1200. Further, the traditionally nomadic Mongol soldiers, now serving in permanent posts, lost some of their toughness and discipline. In the 39 years after Khubilai's death and the installation of the last Mongol sovereign in 1333, disorder also prevailed at the highest level of government. The Mongol royal clan had no orderly method for determining succession, and eight of the nine emperors were either overthrown or killed. Bureaucratic breakdown weakened the base of Yuan power at a time when the Mongols were severely challenged. Religious rebellions sparked by peasant discontent spread throughout southern China in the 1350s.

In 1356, a former Buddhist monk, Zhu Yuanzhang (JOO yoo-ahn-JAHNG), who had taken over the leadership of a religious-based rebel group, the **Red Turbans,** captured Nanjing. Using that city as his capital, Zhu—better known by his reign name, Ming Hongwu (HONG-woo)—conquered other warlords until he was able to march on the Yuan capital at Beijing. The Mongol emperor fled with his court to Mongolia. Hongwu thus founded a new dynasty, the Ming, without actually conquering the old. Hongwu (r. 1368–1398) attempted to assert strong imperial control, even killing thousands of scholars whom he believed were scheming against him or ridiculing him. Neither he nor his successors were model rulers, and the last decades of Ming rule were marked by administrative failure and corruption. The strength of the Ming era lay less in its monarchs and more in the contributions of its artisans, scholars, and philosophers to a Chinese society increasingly claimed by people of all walks of life as their own.

After a period of expansion, the Ming ruled over China until factionalism, corruption, and natural disasters again led to popular uprisings, a symbol of the passage of the Mandate of Heaven, in the middle of the seventeenth century. Although modern historians often judge the Ming a failure, the three centuries were, in fact, an era of population growth, commercial expansion, and a broadening of average people's participation in the culture of the country. The negative judgment of history may be the result of China's falling behind Europe in global exploration in the fifteenth century.

Red Turbans—A branch of White Lotus Society, a millenarian Buddhist group that used Confucian and Daoist ideas as well. One of several anti-Yuan religious groups.

Chronology

1300	1400		1500	1600
1283–1317 Rama Khamheng, Thai king who established independent Thai state, created Thai alphabet **1338** Ashikaga Shogunate succeeds Kamakura Shogunate in Japan **1368–1644** Ming dynasty rules China **1392–1910** Chosŏn dynasty rules Korea	**1400s** Islam spreads in Indonesia **1400s** Nō plays flourish in Japan **1400s** Vietnam and Thailand control mainland Southeast Asia **1402** Malacca founded **1403–1424** Reign of Yongle, emperor of China; Forbidden City built	**1405–1433** Chinese maritime expeditions by Zheng He **1418–1450** Reign of King Sejong of Chosŏn dynasty, creator of han'gul alphabet **1467–1600** Warring States Period in Japan	**1500s** Era of Chinese popular novels such as *The Water Margin, Journey to the West* **1557** Ming grants Portuguese traders limited operations in Macao **1592–1598** Korea repulses invasions by Japan	**1603** Tokugawa Shogunate in Japan begins **1627, 1636** Korea invaded by Manchus **1639** Japanese restriction of trade to Chinese, Koreans, and Dutch

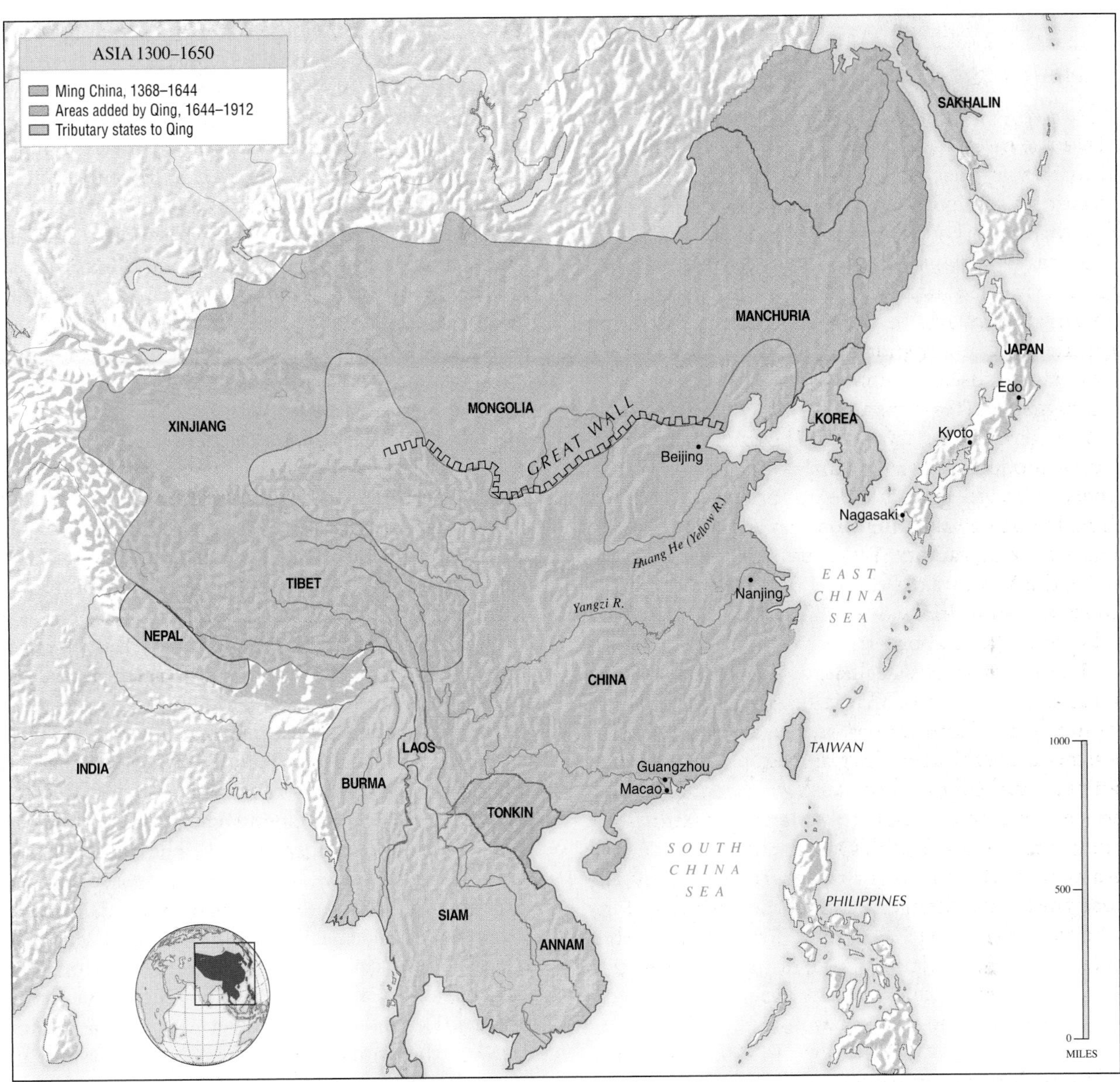

▲ After the first two Ming emperors consolidated and expanded their rule, the rest of the dynasty remained content with the extent of their realm. The Chinese realm was greatly expanded under the Qing, who took power in the second half of the seventeenth century.

To be sure, the imperative to seek trade routes was less urgent for China than for Europe. Compared to China, Europe had few resources. In addition, the fall of the Mongol Empire led to more difficult and therefore more expensive transit across Eurasia. China, with its larger market and higher productivity, seemed at the time to have less need to seek trade routes. The last decades of the Ming dynasty were also characterized by government corruption. While the second half of the Ming dynasty was wracked by problems, however, the first half was a period of growth.

The Early Ming Era

Hongwu was a rather brutal and paranoid emperor, although he tried to govern effectively. He believed that people should be self-sufficient and motivated to serve their community without having to be paid. He sought to lighten the tax burden of the poor and gave the families of China's 2 million soldiers plots to farm themselves to be self-supporting. More successful villagers were to look out for their less fortunate neighbors, collect village taxes, and serve their communities essentially as administrators but without formal government appointment or pay. At the level of the court, Hongwu tried to cut back the power of the **eunuchs** by forbidding them a role in politics. All these policies failed, however. Village leaders were overworked and

eunuchs–Castrated males who served as palace attendants and administrators for the emperor.

▲ Portrait of Hongwu, the first emperor of the Ming dynasty.

undercompensated for their work, soldiers who were unable to support themselves absconded, and eunuchs became more powerful than ever over the next two centuries. The third Ming emperor, Hongwu's son Yongle (YAWNG-luh; r. 1403–1424), moved the capital to Beijing and transformed it into a grand city. He also undertook massive engineering projects, especially the enlarging of the Grand Canal including the construction of 15 locks, and the expansion of the protective northern wall into the Great Wall of China we know today.

Policy in the first century of the Ming reflected a definite interest in border areas and beyond. Non-Chinese tribes, especially the Miao (mee-OW) and the Yao (YOW) in the southwest, were brought under Ming control, engendering a discussion about Chinese identity and cultural blending. The conquest of the Miao was accomplished in several ways. Perhaps the most successful was the intentional destruction of Miao culture and its replacement with Han Chinese culture. The government did this by deforesting Miao lands and opening up those lands to agriculture, thereby dispossessing the Miao of their traditional means of survival and shifting the land use to one employed by Han Chinese. This environmental transformation was done for political reasons, but it ultimately had significant environmental implications as well.

Cultural blending could, of course, also be a two-way street. For example, in the fourteenth century, the Bai people taught the Han Chinese living among them in Yunnan that malaria was linked to the anopheles mosquito, some 500 years before Europeans were aware of that connection.

The expansive early Ming invaded Vietnam in 1407, but popular resistance there soon forced them out. The early Ming government, unlike its sixteenth-century successors, encouraged foreign trade with Japan, Southeast Asia, and India. European and South American products also were acquired through trade with Spain's colony in the Philippines. Private trade surpassed the official trade permitted under the tribute system. Yongle regularly sent diplomatic and commercial missions to neighboring states and encouraged Chinese migration south into the Malay Archipelago and north into Mongolia. In 1405, Yongle sponsored a series of naval expeditions to potential tributary states. The greatest were led by Zheng He (JUHNG HUH), a trusted eunuch (see pp. 393–394). The Chinese flotilla of 62 large and 225 small ships (with some ships exceeding 500 tons and carrying crews of 700) visited Sumatra, India, the Persian Gulf, Aden, and East Africa. There they exchanged porcelain for ivory, ostrich feathers, and exotic animals such as zebras and giraffes. These fancy goods were a source of fascination, but the primary purpose of the voyages was neither conquest nor trade but rather the expansion of the tribute system at the heart of Ming foreign relations. China had already penetrated the Indian Ocean while Portuguese captains were just beginning to explore the Atlantic coast of Morocco.

A Ming Naval Expedition

The voyages ended in 1433. They were considered too expensive compared to the potential gains of enrolling additional countries in the tribute system. China maintained a powerful, dominant position in that system with its closest neighbors. These neighbors received Chinese support and reciprocal gifts but were also subjected to Chinese domination—at times even invasion—and to the requirement that they humbly present gifts to the Son of Heaven, the Chinese emperor, as a sign of subordination in an almost parent-child relationship. People in distant lands were far less likely to comprehend that particular Confucian proprieties were at the heart of Chinese identity, and enrolling distant people in a tribute relationship was much less useful

MAP

Voyages of Zheng He

Discovery Through Maps

Map of China's Ancient Heartland, Circa 1500 C.E.

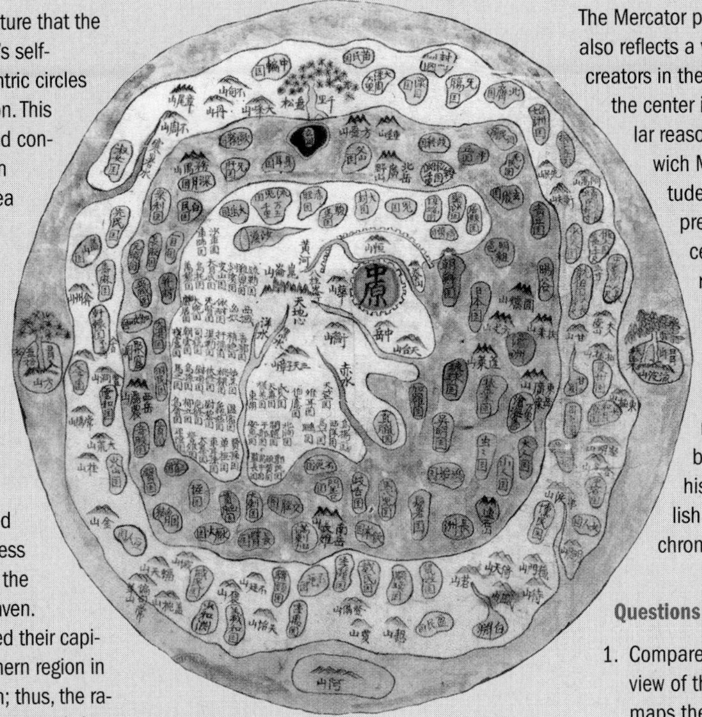

It is one of the marks of human nature that the center of the world is found in one's self-consciousness, and then in concentric circles in the family, community, and nation. This trait extends across civilizations and continents and can be seen not only in this Chinese map depicting the area known as the *Zhongyuan* (JONG-yoo-AHN) or heartland of ancient China, but also in maps created around the same time by Europeans as they made their voyages of discovery. The Chinese map is particularly informative because it reminds its viewers that even within China itself, the heartland was the repository of culture and power, and the farther one ventured from the center of that circle, the less likely one was to be influenced by the virtue embodied in the Son of Heaven.

By 1500, the Ming had moved their capital to Beijing, which lay in the northern region in which Chinese civilization was born; thus, the radiance of the Ming emperor was fortuitously in the same region as the birthplace of the culture he represented. In concentric circles around the Central Plain were other areas of China or countries involved in tributary relations with China. The term *central* may also be seen in a common name for China, *Zhongguo* (JONG-gwaw), meaning "Central Kingdom." The Chinese worldview placed it at the center of the world, and it was very much part of the world in terms of cultural and commercial interactions.

The map has political implications, in that it shows its viewers that the original heartland of China was the same place as the home of the Ming. This portrayal is difficult, however, for those trained to see geography in terms of a Mercator projection (see, for example, p. 485).

The Mercator projection, like the Ming map, also reflects a worldview that places the map's creators in the center—in the Mercator case, the center is in Europe. Is there any particular reason, for example, why the Greenwich Meridian (from which all longitudes on the surface of the earth are presently measured) should be the central point of the world's geography and Greenwich Mean Time should be the standard by which most clocks of the world are presently set? English dominance in the eighteenth and nineteenth centuries proved to be only a temporary moment in history, but it was enough to establish at least a cartographic and chronological centrality.

Questions to Consider

1. Compare and contrast this map with the view of the world on p. 485. How are the maps the same? How are they different?
2. Given the particular approach of the China map, draw a simple circular map of the United States. Would Washington, D.C., or some other city be appropriately located at the center of your map? Is the Mercator projection that is generally used today (see, for example, p. 485) necessarily better in portraying sense and relationship?

than demanding the subordination of a neighbor. In time, maritime exploration came to be seen as an unwise investment when costly defense against land-based border tribes was more crucial. Chinese emperors never again sponsored such pathbreaking journeys.

Administration of the realm was seen as central to Ming power throughout the period. While foreign adventures could be curtailed, good government demanded that emperors lead by example and that the examination system bring in loyal and honest bureaucrats.

Yet despite their attempts at eliminating past problems, the Ming emperors perpetuated many of the corrupt and weak practices they wanted to reform. The excesses of court eunuchs—male children sold by their parents to be castrated for court service—continued. At the beginning of the Ming dynasty only 100 eunuchs were employed, and not in direct government posts, but by the end of the dynasty 300 years later, 100,000 were working for the throne. Eunuchs had served as court advisers and servants since the Zhou dynasty; under the Ming, they included men from Annam and Korea, some brought as tribute, and some captured in war. Under the Ming, 28 Korean-born eunuchs served as leaders of missions to Seoul. Although eunuchs served as generals, admirals, explorers, diplomats,

Seeing Connections

A Giraffe in the Ming Court

Shen Du (1357–1434), a Ming court artist, was delighted to paint this new animal brought back from Africa by the explorer Zheng He. He had never seen a giraffe, so he was sure it was a mythical animal that was a harbinger of good fortune. The animal was one of many exotic creatures the great eunuch explorer brought to the court of the emperor Yongle.

Zheng He's voyages were massive in scale, with huge armed crews, intended to bring the states in the Indian Ocean world into the Chinese tributary system. At times, he used force to subdue local princes, like the ruler of Ceylon, who preferred to avoid the linkage with China. The boats probably hugged the coast, as they were massive wooden vessels and would have broken up in storms. Zheng He sailed as far as East Africa before the Ming court abandoned their support for the voyages. As a consequence of the voyages, China gained better knowledge of the Indian Ocean and Africa.

architects, secret police, and hydraulic engineers, the majority of them were servants of low and even slave status. The increased number of eunuchs was due not only to the expansion of the imperial family under the Ming but also to the influx of men, many self-castrated, who poured into Beijing, hoping to find a secure livelihood after escaping from poverty or famine in the countryside.

The growth in the number and influence of eunuchs was paralleled by an expansion of Confucian scholarship and scholars. Preparing for a career as a bureaucrat became increasingly attractive despite the danger of repression by paranoid emperors like Hongwu. The Ming decreed that the examinations for entering the civil service be written in a strict, formal style, but at the same time they opened opportunities for students from less advanced regions of the country to pass the exams. A new lower level category was created, permitting locally successful exam candidates to become local leaders even if they were not eligible for

	Ming China
1368–1398	Reign of Hongwu
1403–1424	Reign of Yongle, sponsor of encyclopedia
1405–1433	Naval expeditions led by Zheng He
1472–1529	Wang Yangming, philosopher
1583–1610	Matteo Ricci at Ming court
1644	Founding of Qing dynasty

a better government post. In time, wealthy families perpetuated their status by their sons' success in the examination system. Poor boys, whose work was needed on their parents' farms, were far less likely to devote years to exam preparation. In spite of the system's theoretical openness to boys of all backgrounds, in reality only the rich had the chance to study and enter government service. By the sixteenth century, there were approximately 100,000 students preparing for exams at any given time.

As time passed, Ming rulers became resistant to innovation. Yet even this resistance had a positive aspect, in that it generated an aura of stability through most of the 1500s, when Chinese culture was a model for East Asia. Sixteenth-century European visitors were impressed by Chinese courtesy, respect for law, confidence, and stately ceremonies. They saw material prosperity in the bustling markets, stone-paved roads, and beautiful homes of Ming officials. They noted with awe the breadth of literacy and the availability of books written in vernacular language comprehensible to many readers. The elaborate Ming examination system, with its proclaimed principle of advancement on merit, often evoked favorable surprise. European commentators were lavish in their praise of Chinese justice, an attitude that would change greatly several centuries later.

Ming Society, Scholarship, and Culture

Market towns and commercial networks had been growing in China since the Song dynasty (see Chapter 10). As the post-plague population rebounded following its decline during the Yuan dynasty, market towns expanded. The distance between market towns shortened, and commercial links were improved. At the same time, other forms of social interaction developed, especially kinship (lineage) groups and community associations pledging to do good deeds and lead moral lives. Community orientation did not necessarily require that all people be treated equally, but rather humanely. During the Ming era, for instance, women became less visible to the larger society. They were to stay inside the house; widows were not supposed to remarry but rather continue to live with the family of their deceased husband; and the practice of foot binding spread throughout the country, even among commoners. The ideal of the exemplary Confucian woman was institutionalized in the form of written accounts of virtuous widows and arches built in front of the homes of women widowed before they were 30 who reached the age of 60 without remarrying. Though Ming law, ironically, offered a financial incentive to widows' families to marry them off—if she remarried, a widow's dowry could be kept by her late husband's family, who would also earn a "bride price" from her next husband's family—widows deemed virtuous did not remarry. Morality tales written during the Ming, although likely exaggerated for didactic effect, portrayed virtuous widows as committing suicide or self-mutilation to show grief or prove their loyalty to dead husbands.

Under Ming rule, legal recognition of **concubinage** also encouraged the sale of young virgins from poor families to families of generally higher status. Although women's official legal status, especially that of widows, was lowered because of stricter adherence to Confucian norms, it also can be said that women's independence was encouraged by the same ideology. New Confucian regulations and standards encouraged education for girls as well as boys. Young women, who read the more than 50 works extolling female obedience through accounts of the lives of virtuous women, were also given access to other reading material that easily could have challenged the official vision of a woman as a person confined to a household.

Even foot binding can be seen from several perspectives. The practice mutilated the foot in order to enhance a woman's desirability; mothers bound their daughters' feet to improve their marriage prospects and thus, perhaps, spare their daughters a life of hard physical labor. Farm women often did not have bound feet, as their labor was needed. On the one hand, it could be said that a life of field work liberated a woman from bound feet; on the other, bound feet usually freed a woman from backbreaking field work. Nowhere else in Asia was foot binding practiced, and yet women had subordinate status there as in most parts of the world. Thus, foot binding was a painful, mutilating practice but was itself not a cause of women's second-class status.

The Ming respect for learning and literacy was evident in officially commissioned works as well as popular works. Numerous official works were published, including vast multivolume collections, 1500 local histories, and famous medical works like *The Outline of*

concubinage—A legal relationship of a man and a secondary wife, who usually did not have the rights and protection of a primary wife. Concubines were often obtained by rich men to produce sons.

Shen Zhou's *Mountain Scene* from his *Album of Eight Landscape Paintings* embodies the artistic values of Ming literati painting.

Herb Medicine, which took 30 years to complete. The Yongle emperor ordered the compilation of all existing literature, that is, an encyclopedia of all knowledge. It has been surmised that these works added up to more printed works than all the manuscript books throughout the world at that time. (This was also, of course, a half century before Gutenberg printed his first book.) The ***Yongle Encyclopedia*** was produced by over 2,000 scholars, who arranged material taken from more than 7,000 works, by subject, into over 22,000 chapters bound into half that number of volumes. Although the encyclopedia was too unwieldy to print and distribute, more accessible intellectual developments—not only for the use of the emperor and his officials—were encouraged by the increased printing of books and by the growth of education in private academies that prepared students for public examinations.

During the first half of the Ming, the state considered Zhu Xi (JOO SHEE) Confucianism (see Chapter 10) as orthodox. Zhu Xi's interpretations were reflected in the exam system. Other scholars' views became increasingly important in the sixteenth century, the most important of which was that of the soldier, poet, and philosopher Wang Yangming (WAHNG yahng-MING; 1472–1528), who taught that knowledge is intuitive and inseparable from experience. Wang believed anyone could be a sage and could practice self-cultivation even while doing other tasks. In later centuries, Wang Yangming's ideas inspired reformers and revolutionaries in China, Japan, and Korea.

Yongle Encyclopedia—Compilation of all known scholarship by Yongle emperor's team of scholars in the fifteenth century.

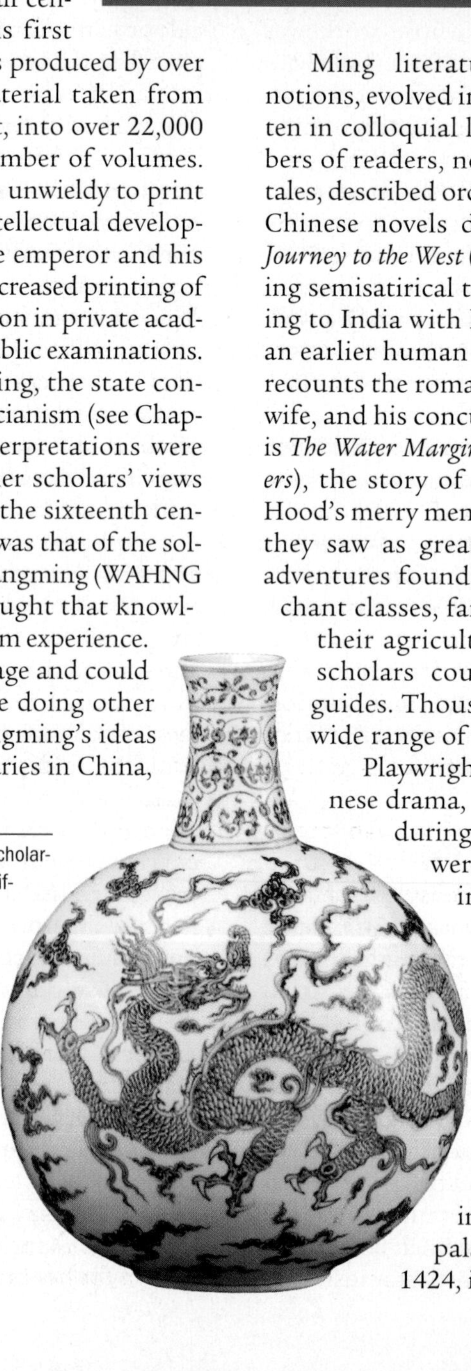

The blue-and-white pattern on the Ming jar (sixteenth century) is usually associated with the era, but red was an equally vivid color in Ming culture.

Ming literature, which embraced romantic notions, evolved in ways similar to scholarship. Written in colloquial language accessible to larger numbers of readers, novels, based on orally transmitted tales, described ordinary life. Three of the best-known Chinese novels date from the sixteenth century. *Journey to the West* (also known as *Monkey*) is a rollicking semisatirical tale about a Buddhist monk traveling to India with his pig and a monkey that had led an earlier human life. The erotic novel *Golden Lotus* recounts the romantic adventures of a merchant, his wife, and his concubines. Perhaps the best-read work is *The Water Margin* (also known as *All Men Are Brothers*), the story of an outlaw band who, like Robin Hood's merry men, broke the law in the name of what they saw as greater justice. Travel literature and adventures found great acceptance among the merchant classes, farmers read treatises on improving their agricultural practices, and students and scholars could cram for exams with study guides. Thousands of titles were available for a wide range of tastes.

Playwrights from the south dominated Chinese drama, which had a golden age of its own during the Ming period. Plays sometimes were as long as ten acts, developing intricate plots and subplots with unexpected endings. Music became more prominent on the stage as solos, duets, and even entire choirs alternated with the spoken word in performances.

Ming artists and architects produced great quantities of high-quality works. The horizontal lines of the Forbidden City, the imperial family's area of temples and palaces constructed from 1403 to 1424, illustrate the period's values of balance and formalism. In Ming painting, naturalistic landscapes were a favorite topic of literati painters Shen Zhou (SHEN JOH; 1427–1509) and his most talented pupil, Wen Zhengming (WEN juhng-MING; 1470–1559). The great later Ming painter Dong Qichang (DONG chee-CHAHNG; 1555–1636) was noted for the formal discipline of his brush strokes. The period's major artistic achievement was its porcelains, mostly produced at the Ming imperial kilns at Jingdezhen (JING-duh-JEN). Although blue pottery had been produced earlier, it so characterized these kilns that Ming pottery is often assumed (incorrectly) to all be blue. Ming porcelain was emulated in Japan and Holland (where it was named Delft pottery), and it was a major Chinese export item.

The Ming and the Sixteenth-Century World

The Ming's great voyages of exploration and its expansion toward the southwest were completed by the end of the fifteenth century. Although official maritime trade was limited to the ports of Ningbo for Japan, Fuzhou (foo-JOH) for the Philippines, and Guangzhou (gwahng-JOH) for Indonesia, extralegal trade carried on by Japanese, Chinese, Korean, Dutch, Portuguese and Spanish "pirates" enriched Chinese consumers' access to exotic goods. China exported mainly pottery and silk, importing Southeast Asian woods, spices, and food; New World foods like corn, sweet potatoes, and peanuts; and silver from both Mexico and, especially, Japan. The Ming economy became monetized with the huge influx of silver.

DOCUMENT
A European View of Asia

DOCUMENT
Matteo Ricci's Journals

DOCUMENT
A Chinese View of Ricci

The population had expanded from 85 million in 1400 to 310 million by 1650, fueling a rise in the number and size of market towns, particularly in the heavily populated south. Crowded conditions led many to emigrate to Indonesia and the Philippines, where they functioned as cultural and commercial intermediaries. Domestic trade grew alongside foreign trade. Portuguese traders, banned in 1517, were permitted to operate from Macao after 1557. Soon, other European traders were knocking on China's door. They were accompanied by missionaries, at first mostly Jesuits who impressed the Ming imperial court with their scholarly ways and technical expertise in science, medicine, shipbuilding, calendar-making, and mathematics. The primary goal of the Jesuits and other Christian missionaries was to convert the Chinese to their religion, but the court was most impressed by their secular knowledge. Jesuits hoped to influence the top rulers by wearing the clothes of Confucian gentlemen and by speaking Chinese. Matteo Ricci, the best known among them, was extraordinarily erudite, but neither he nor other Christians won many converts.

Exciting new ideas and products were entering China, while much of the world looked to China as the source of both luxuries and everyday items. China continued to be the center of trade in Eurasia and was one leg of a triangle of trade whose other two legs were the Spanish colonies in the Philippines and in the Western Hemisphere (the trans-Pacific vessels were called "Manila Galleons"). Other sixteenth-century successes were in the area of food production. Effective hydraulic engineering by Pan Jixun (PAHN jee-SHOON) kept the Huanghe River under control and facilitated irrigation. Together with the extensive use of fertilizers, this water control allowed the Ming—and their successors, the Qing—to have much higher grain productivity than Europeans until the nineteenth century. But governance began to fall apart at the end of the sixteenth century, and the Ming's sophisticated global commerce and hydrology projects could not save it from the effects of its shoddy economic mismanagement at home.

Corruption, waste, bureaucratic inertia, and conservatism prevailed at every level of government at the end of the Ming. The emperor Wanli (wahn-LEE; r. 1573–1619) was known as particularly ineffective, especially in the last decades of his reign. Thousands of his imperial family members lived off the revenues paid by a decreasing number of tax-paying peasants (rich landowners managed to remove themselves from the tax rolls). Peasant discontent with these injustices, combined with the imperial government's inability to respond to weather catastrophes in the 1620s (another "little ice age"), led to tenant uprisings and urban riots. Foreign issues exacerbated the Ming's economic worries at home. In the 1630s, Japan severely restricted its foreign trade, and Japanese silver supplies were rapidly being depleted. Struggles between Chinese and Spanish immigrants in the Philippines cut off access to China's other source of silver, which was brought to Asia from South America by the Manila Galleons.

The decline of the military also undermined the Ming. It was badly equipped and, in general, poorly led. The army suffered a serious drop in morale as disorder increased throughout the country: pirates ravaged the coasts, and Mongol attacks brought near-anarchy along the Great Wall. The Chinese helped defend the Koreans against Japanese attacks in the 1590s, but that was the Ming army's last major stand against an outside threat.

Local governors and commanders, rather than the imperial government, had some success in dealing with these threats. There were even some women among these local leaders. The famous female general Qin Liangyu (CHIN lee-ahng-YOO; 1574–1648) put down local rebellions in southwestern China and later fought the Manchus at the end of the Ming dynasty. Known for her bravery and strength of character, she

Document

Zhang Han's Essay on Merchants

Zhang Han (1511–1593) was an important Ming trade official whose family had made its fortune in business. Although Confucian attitudes officially scorned business, Chinese society was thoroughly commercialized by the Ming dynasty, and merchants were, in fact, generally respected. Merchants' sons could take the examinations that led to entrance into the ruling scholarly class. Scholars, especially those who rose from the merchant class as did Zhang Han, came to see merit in trade and commerce, even with foreigners.

Money and profit are of great importance to men. They seek profit, then suffer by it, yet they cannot forget it. They exhaust their bodies and spirits, run day and night, yet they still regard what they have gained as insufficient.

Those who become merchants eat fine food and wear elegant clothes. They ride on beautifully caparisoned, double-harnessed horses.... Opportunistic persons attracted by their wealth offer to serve them. Pretty girls in beautiful long-sleeved dresses and delicate slippers play stringed and wind instruments for them and compete to please them....

Because I have traveled to many places during my career as an official, I am familiar with commercial activities and business conditions in various places. The capital is located in an area with mountains at its back and a great plain stretching in front. The region is rich in millet, grain, donkeys, horses, fruit, and vegetables, and has become a center where goods from distant places are brought. Those who engage in commerce, including the foot peddler, the cart peddler, and the shopkeeper, display not only clothing and fresh foods, but also numerous luxury items such as precious jade from Kunlun, pearls from the island of Hainan, gold from Yunnan, and coral from Vietnam. Those precious items, coming from the mountain or the sea, are not found in central China....

South of the capital is the province of Henan, the center of the empire. Going from Kaifeng, its capital, to Weizhong, one can reach the Yangzi and Han rivers. Thus, Kaifeng is a great transportation center; one can travel by either boat or carriage from this spot to all other places, which makes it a favorite gathering place for merchants. The area is rich in lacquer, hemp, sackcloth, fine linen, fine gloss silk, wax, and leather. In antiquity, the Zhou dynasty had its capital here.... In general, in the southeast area the greatest profits are to be had from fine gauze, thin silk, cheap silk, and sackcloth.... My ancestors' fortunes were based solely on such textile businesses....

As to the foreigners in the southeast, their goods are useful to us just as ours are to them. To use what one has to exchange for what one does not is what trade is all about. Moreover, these foreigners trade with China under the name of tributary contributions. That means China's authority is established and the foreigners are submissive.... The southeast sea foreigners are more concerned with trading with China than with gaining gifts from China.... Trading with them can enrich our people. So why should we refrain from the trade?

Questions to Consider

1. How did Zhang Han explain foreign trade in a way that could be acceptable to his follow government officials?
2. Did he seem to be bothered that some people fawned over merchants?
3. Confucian scholars viewed business as less cultivated and less noble than government service. Do you think they thought that business was, as a result, less important?

From Patricia Buckley Ebrey, ed., *Chinese Civilization: A Sourcebook* (Free Press, 1993), pp. 216–218.

was also a refined woman who wrote elegant poetry. Meanwhile, the central administration nearly ceased to function. The highly formalized system was insufficiently flexible to deal with new challenges. Moreover, some emperors were puppets of eunuch ministers who pursued policies that were increasingly frivolous and unrealistic.

In the summer of 1644, after attempting to kill his oldest daughter to prevent her inevitable rape, mutilation, and death at the hands of rebels, the last Ming emperor, Chongzheng (chong-JUHNG; r. 1627–1644), hanged himself in his imperial garden, leaving a pitiful note to indicate his shame in meeting his ancestors. An insurgent government had already formed to the west in Sichuan, another rebel army was approaching Beijing, and only a few Portuguese mercenaries and some imperial guards remained nominally loyal. But neither of the Chinese countermovements would succeed. As the Ming regime collapsed, Manchu forces crossed the northern border into Ming territories and began the Qing (Ching) dynasty in 1664.

Korea: The Making of a Confucian Society

How were Confucian ideas adopted and modified in the early Chosŏn dynasty?

For fifteen centuries, kingdoms on the Korean peninsula had produced a blend of indigenous and Chinese culture, arts, religions, and statecraft. At the end of the fourteenth century, King T'aejo (TAI-joh), founder of the Chosŏn dynasty, and his successors, especially the fourth Chosŏn king, the brilliant King Sejong (SEH-jong; r. 1418–1450), both enhanced Korean culture and effectively used Chinese governance and political theory. T'aejo continued the practice of sending tribute missions to China, adopted Chinese-style state ministries, and made Confucian learning the basis for government and hence for the exams taken by many candidates for bureaucratic posts. In spite of T'aejo's respect for the Ming, the Ming refused to recognize the Korean dynasty as legitimate until the third Chosŏn king, T'aejong (TAI-jong; r. 1400–1418).

Unlike in China, in Korea only the sons of the hereditarily elite class, the *yangban* (YAHNG-bahn), undertook Confucian study and self-cultivation in preparation for a prestigious government post. (The term *yangban* meant "of the two branches," the branches being civil and military.) Other talented young men interested in technical positions as medical doctors, law clerks, scribes, astronomers, and translators came from the hereditary *chung'in* (CHOONG-een) or middle class and took different types of technical exams. In addition, there were nonexam routes to official jobs in Korea. As in China, a comprehensive history of the preceding dynasty was commissioned as a way of asserting one's own dynasty's legitimacy. Although Chosŏn Korea became as Confucianized as China, Koreans were also interested in preserving their own culture, arts, religion, and language. Diverging from China in the fifteenth century, they devised a new syllabary (a set of written symbols that represent syllables rather than letters) called **han'gul** (HAHN-gool) to better represent Korean literature.

Chosŏn Korea	
1392–1910	Chosŏn dynasty
1418–1450	Reign of King Sejong
1501–1570	Yi T'oegye, Confucian scholar
1592, 1598	Invasions by Japan
1627, 1630	Invasions by Manchus

The Early Years of the Chosŏn Dynasty

In addition to setting up Chinese-style government ministries, King T'aejo made a number of other changes when he came to power. He created a capital with a Chinese-style palace at Hanyang, now the modern city of Seoul. He set up a military controlled by the throne, replacing the armed militias of powerful families. He handed out **Rank Lands** to officials recruited from the yangban class through Confucian examinations. These Rank Lands were intended to be used as pay during the lifetime of the official, but because the lands tended to become hereditary, they were replaced in the 1450s with salaries. T'aejo also made permanent grants of land to "merit subjects," people who had helped him in his rise to power. Merit lands and the power that went with them were often resented, however, by other yangban without such privileges.

Free and unfree farmers lived on the lands granted to officials or merit subjects. As many as one-third of the farmers were slaves in the Chosŏn period. Actors and entertainers, butchers and hide tanners, and women entertainers called *kisaeng* (kee-SENG)—a Korean version of the Japanese *geisha* (GAY-shah)—were considered to be "lowborn" people as well. Free peasants paid a very low tax on their output (just one-tenth and later one-twentieth of their harvest), but together with local tribute taxes, labor service, military duty, and other requirements, the total tax burden was heavy. Nevertheless, some free but not initially rich peasants eventually became wealthy landholders called commoner-landlords. By the beginning of the seventeenth century, new crops were grown for the expanding urban market. Improved farming technology and irrigation were used by some farmers involved in the production of these commercial crops, and in time, some became wealthy enough to get out of debt and buy enough land to be landlords themselves. The demographic structure of the countryside shifted from one with rich, elite people on top and poor commoners or slaves on the bottom to a more complicated structure that had some yangban, some rich commoner-landlords, some small peasants, some tenants, and some unemployed homeless people. Although the development of the countryside was good for overall economic growth in Korea, the resulting rural stratification would eventually lead to peasant discontent and uprisings.

Chosŏn society was officially divided into four groups, roughly equivalent to the Chinese status

---

han'gul—Indigenous Korean script, invented by King Sejong.

Rank Lands—Lands granted to yangban officials as pay. They became hereditary, thereby making yangban hereditary aristocracy.

groups (scholars, farmers, artisans, and merchants). In Korea, the yangban were at the top of the social hierarchy, followed by farmers, artisans, and the lowborn. In effect, the biggest divide was between the yangban and everyone else. Artisans were, at first, either government employees or government slaves. About 2800 lived in Seoul and 3500 elsewhere in Korea. In addition to doing work for the state, they also took private orders, and in time, these private commissions played a more important role in their professions. Eventually, most artisans became independent. Merchants, too, were more restricted than elsewhere in Asia in the early Chosŏn era. Money was used less commonly, and cotton cloth was a major unit of exchange. By the seventeenth century, however, merchants developed a lively commercial scene. They sold new commercial products produced by artisans and farmers—ginseng, cotton, and tobacco, the latter a New World product, were the most common cash crops—and increasing quantities of imported goods. Rows of shops selling a variety of products joined the official Six Licensed Stores that had been permitted since the early years of the dynasty.

In addition to divisions by class and status, Koreans were divided by gender. Women were subordinate to men, and this was particularly true in family law. Inheritance and succession were in the male line, so men with land or any valuables would often have a secondary wife or concubine, believing that could enhance their chances of having a son. Sons of concubines, though educated alongside their "legitimate" brothers, were barred from taking the civil service exams; they could, however, take the specialized exams for the *chung'in.*

Yangban women were more restricted than women of other classes in this period, though no women had rights of inheritance or the ability to decide such family matters as where they would live. Wives had to go along with their husbands and their parents-in-law. Women's most important virtue was preservation of their "chastity." This led to the prohibition of premarital contact with one's fiancée, of a woman having sexual relations with any man other than her husband, and of the remarriage of widows. Some impoverished widows were unable to avoid remarriage, but as in China, it was strongly discouraged. Also, as in China, chastity was encouraged through didactic writings and laws and with rewards. In 1152, *The Register of Licentious Women* stated that when a married woman did some "lustful deed," her position in society should be demoted to that of a sewing woman, a sort of servant. Moreover, her children were to be barred from office. During the Chosŏn dynasty, this sentiment intensified. By the end of the dynasty, yangban women were confined to their homes, had lost ritual duties in ancestral rites, and were not allowed to inherit property. The emphasis on chastity was to have repressive effects on women in Korean society until the end of the twentieth century.

The most effective king of the Chosŏn dynasty was Sejong. Under his rule, Korean borders were extended northward to the present borders. Although Korea was itself in the subordinate position to China in its tribute system, Sejong established a parallel system with the ruler of the Japanese island of Tsu from whom he required tribute (this relationship eventually played a very significant role in Japanese international trade). A great patron of scholarship, Sejong embodied the **Neo-Confucian** (see Chapter 10) ideal of the scholar-king. He gathered the top scholars of his day in a "Hall of Worthies" and commissioned them to create a Korean writing system because, as he wisely noted, the Chinese characters Koreans had been using did not fit the Korean language. Their efforts produced *han'gul,* which Sejong called "proper sounds to instruct the people." The king then established an Office for Publication, which put out numerous Buddhist texts, geographies, histories, and didactic works of various kinds, including books on medical science and farming. The publication office occasionally used movable copper type, and a number of books were printed with it between 1403 and 1484. Other "Worthies" made advances in mathematics and invented musical instruments, a rain gauge, clocks, and military weapons.

The new han'gul alphabet stimulated cultural expression, particularly in literature and philosophy. Some of these works were prose compositions on simple subjects, but poetry, stressing love of nature, personal grief, and romantic love, was especially popular. Many of the Chosŏn lyric poets were women. The government also sponsored professional painters, most of whom painted landscapes. Confucian gentlemen—often referred to as *literati*—also painted, did calligraphy, and wrote poetry, but always as amateurs. Since artisans were professional artists, it was less appropriate for a gentleman of the yangban class to be a professional artist; it was expected, however, that he would cultivate his skills at the same level as a professional. As in China and Japan, skilled amateurs of this era preferred black ink paintings, sometimes with subdued colors. Other aspects of Korean painting differentiated it from Chinese styles, including humor that made use of bold calligraphy, chromatic contrasts, and an emphasis on vertical expressions rather than on depth.

Among all of the arts, the Chosŏn era is best known for its ceramics. The early Chosŏn blue-green pottery contrasted with the white porcelain produced by the government by the middle of the fifteenth century. The difference was not only one of color. The

---

Neo-Confucianism—Chinese Confucian school of thought, originated in eleventh century; adopted throughout East Asia; focus on *li* ("principle") and *qi* ("matter" or "energy").

▲ King Sejong of Korea (1418–1450), a member of the Chosŏn dynasty. During his reign, Korea reached the height of cultural achievements, and the modern boundaries of the country were fixed. Sejong is also credited with the creation of the Korean phonetic, or han'gul, alphabet.

blue-green ceramics were simple but imaginative and intended for commoners. The white porcelain was made for the aristocratic yangban class.

The sixteenth century was a time of great growth in scholarship as well. One of Korea's best-known philosophers of Neo-Confucianism, Yi T'oegye (YEE TO-eh-ghee-EH; 1501–1570) was a strong supporter of Zhu Xi's learning. Yi T'oegye launched a debate about the relative importance of *i* (EE; Chinese *li,* meaning "principle") and *ki* (KEE; Chinese *qi,* "material force" or "energy"), and other philosophers weighed in. Neo-Confucian scholars have debated this point since the twelfth century. What is interesting about this debate is that many of the philosophers involved went on to establish their own schools. The boys in those schools were fiercely loyal to their teachers. Eventually, this loyalty led to intense school rivalry and the development of factions. The early sixteenth century saw a proliferation of private academies and the increasing role—and factionalism—of men educated in those academies who were advising rulers at the national level.

Korea faced a serious crisis at the hands of Japan in the 1590s. In 1592, soon after consolidating his control over a previously divided Japan, Toyotomi Hideyoshi (TOH-yoh-TOH-mee HEE-deh-YO-shi), Japan's hegemonic military overlord at the time, extended his ambitions to a desire for continental conquest. He took his soldiers, well trained though exhausted from years of conflict in Japan, and invaded Korea with a force of 200,000 soldiers supported by 9,000 sailors. Hideyoshi hoped to use Korea as the first stage of his ultimate conquest of Ming China. The official Chosŏn military was no longer effective, and peasants, merchants, yangban, and other ordinary Koreans rose up to defend Korea against an invader armed with guns that the Koreans did not possess. The Chosŏn king was useless, and after he and his high officials fled Seoul, that city's slaves set fire to many government buildings, especially the one where the lists of slaves were kept. The Ming sent soldiers in support of their tributary partner, but it was naval warfare that saved Korea. The hero of the Korean defense was Admiral Yi Sunsin (YEE soon-SHEEN; 1545–1598) who maneuvered his copper-clad ships into narrow waterways where he trapped the invading forces and cut their supply lines. The odd appearance of Yi's armored boats, used almost 300 years before armored vessels were used in the American Civil War, earned them the name "turtle boats." Hideyoshi's forces retreated, but when the terms of the peace treaty were not carried out, the war began again. Again Admiral Yi was called into action. The war was going well for the Koreans, and the Japanese forces withdrew as soon as Hideyoshi died in Japan (of natural causes). The impact on Korea, in spite of its victory, was enormous. The 7 years of war diminished Korea's wealth and inflicted terrible hardships on its people. There are few buildings in Korea dating from before the 1590s; unlike other parts of Asia, few ancient Buddhist temples remain.

King Kwanghaegun (gwahng-HAI-goon; r. 1608–1623) made determined efforts to rebuild the country, but he was also concerned about maintaining careful foreign relations with new rival continental forces—the Ming dynasty in

◄ This Chosŏn era bottle is *punchŏng* ware. The attention to detail on an object of daily use indicates the level of Korean cultural sophistication.

China and the rising Manchus north of Korea in Manchuria. His successors were not so fortunate or skillful at negotiating. Twice, in 1627 and again in 1636, the Manchus invaded Korea when it appeared that the Chosŏn king would side with the Ming. Thousands of Koreans, held hostage by the Manchus, suffered great cruelty and privation before they could be ransomed. Many Korean families rejected female members who had been sexually violated and therefore dishonored. This attitude reflected the intensification of a Neo-Confucian emphasis on female chastity in Chosŏn Korea. When the Manchus conquered China and established the Qing dynasty in 1644, the Koreans had to submit to them until the 1890s. For a long time, Koreans, who had favored the Ming, resented being in a tributary relationship with the Qing.

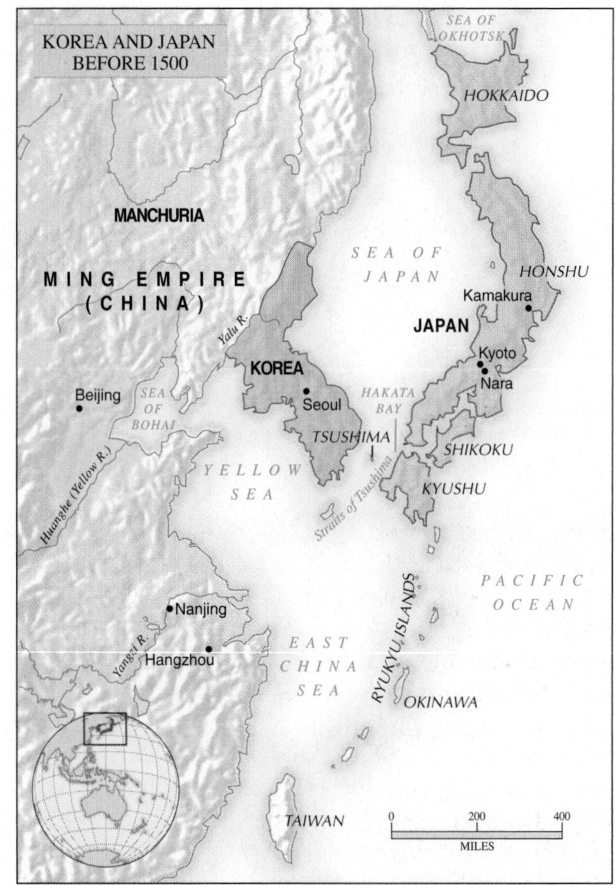

▲ Korea was part of the Chinese tribute system throughout the Chosŏn dynasty. Japan also traded with China and Korea, but was able to circumvent the more restricted measures of the tribute system because of its maritime separation from the continent.

Japan: The Era of Shōguns and Warring States

How were art, culture, and religion central to the creation of Japanese identity?

Like Korea and China, Japan had a monarch, the *tennō* (TEN-noh), or emperor, whose dynasty had already reigned for almost a millennium by the fourteenth century. But the emperor's court had not held real power since the late twelfth century, although it had twice attempted in the thirteenth and fourteenth centuries to reassert its authority in the political and economic realms. Instead, military lords and their samurai supporters had created a political system in the eastern town of Kamakura that in many ways resembled medieval European feudalism (see Chapter 10). The Kamakura system was not entirely stable, and internal and external pressures, including the Mongol invasions in the late thirteenth century, undermined the dominance of the shōgun's government.

Renewed warfare in the fourteenth century ended in 1336 with a shaky balance of power among dozens of provincial lords and a new overlord, Ashikaga Takauji (ah-shee-KAH-gah tah-kah-OO-jee), invested with the title of **shōgun** in 1338. Because the Ashikaga set up their shogunal court in the Muromachi (MOO-roh-MAH-chee) section of Kyoto (kee-OH-toh), the period from 1338 to 1568 is called the Muromachi period. The balance of power had actually ended before the end of the Muromachi period, when succession disputes and a struggle for power among newly emerging provincial forces began a 130-year-long Warring States period in 1467. During this period, coalitions of samurai with initially tiny landholdings, supported by villagers whose crops they used to support their troops, fought their samurai neighbors for increasingly larger areas of control. By the mid-sixteenth century, the largest of these warrior lords came to be known as *sengoku daimyō* (SEN-goh-koo DAI-mee-oh) or Warring States lords, and it is from those ranks that three powerful warriors, Oda Nobunaga (OH-dah NOH-boo-NAH-gah; 1534–1582), Toyotomi Hideyoshi (1536–1598), and Tokugawa Ieyasu (toh-koo-GAH-wah EE-eh-YAH-soo; 1544–1616), brought Japan under unified control.

Villages and Towns: The Base of Samurai Power

Villages provided most of the wealth for the rise of these powerful ***daimyō*** from among the hundreds of small-scale samurai lords. Not all samurai lords survived the warfare of the fifteenth and sixteenth centuries. Those who enjoyed good relations with villagers, often by being part-time samurai-farmers themselves, were more likely to mobilize the villages'

shōgun—The supreme military overlord in Japan from 1185 to 1868.

daimyō—A military lord, served by samurai.

	Japan
1338–1568	Muromachi period
c. 1368–1443	Zeami Motokiyo, playwright
1467–1600	Warring States period
1568–1582	Oda Nobunaga begins unification, attacks Buddhists
1588	Toyotomi Hideyoshi's Sword Hunt
1600	Tokugawa victory at Sekigahara
1637–1638	Shimabara revolt

output for their own benefit. Oppressed villagers could run away from their land, and land was worthless without peasants to farm it. Thus, in many areas of Japan, villagers were granted a large degree of autonomy and gradually developed methods of self-government. This does not mean, however, that sixteenth-century villages were democratic entities. Local government varied from village to village; some allowed all families a voice in a village council, whereas others had a hereditary village headman. Still others were run from the local Shintō shrine or Buddhist temple association.

Just as villages were not run democratically despite their freedom from constant control by warriors or aristocrats, so, too, families were not run democratically. Although women had been able to inherit and make important personal decisions in earlier centuries, inheritance was increasingly in male hands. Village men and women all participated in festivals, and women were responsible for spring planting and often for marketing products. No farm could run without both men and women, as each had necessary chores. But by the Muromachi and Warring States eras, even farm women had to take a back seat to their husbands in ceremonial and political participation in village associations. Wives and daughters of samurai and *daimyō* in the Warring States era had a much more dangerous life than farm women. They were expected to be skilled at defending themselves and their families' interests, but they were also frequently married off by powerful fathers and other relatives in order to cement alliances with other warlords. In those treacherous times, when military alliances shifted frequently, marriage was often not a safe haven for samurai-class women; husbands wondered if their wives were spies on behalf of their fathers or brothers, and many wives were involuntarily divorced, used as hostages, or in a few cases, even executed. Of course, life was hard for male samurai warriors, too; but the decline in the official status of elite women from the early medieval era was quite clear.

The heads of the largest extended families in the villages (families with multiple generations and married cousins or siblings living under one roof) were often samurai-farmers, serving as local notables who settled village disputes and oversaw some of the farming activities of their less fortunate neighbors. Some villages were more independent and powerful than others, particularly those villages, organized around Pure Land (see Chapter 10) temples, which became increasingly militant in the defense of both their faith and their livelihoods during the Warring States period. The first of the "three great unifiers," Oda Nobunaga, found these villages to be one of the greatest challenges to his rise to dominance. After ending the Muromachi **Shogunate** in 1568, he conquered and forced the submission of other *daimyō* lords. But the Pure Land villagers refused to surrender, believing their faith would keep them strong against their enemies' military power. Oda Nobunaga attacked the Buddhists with extreme violence. His forces killed 20,000 men, women, and children in one brutal struggle in 1574. Three years earlier, he had attacked the 700-year-old temple community at Mt. Hiei (HEE-ay), founded by Saichō, burning 300 monastic buildings, including residences, libraries with irreplaceable treasures, and prayer halls.

As a symbol of his power, Oda Nobunaga built the enormous Azuchi (ah-ZOO-chee) Castle (1576–1579). He filled it with art intended to glorify his rule. It was lavishly painted by the great master Kanō Eitoku (KAH-noh AY-to-koo; 1543–1590), using fine colors and gold leaf. Despite his self-aggrandizement, however, Oda Nobunaga was cut down in a most ordinary way—he was assassinated by one of his subordinates in 1582. Nobunaga's assassination afforded Hideyoshi (a man of humble origins who had not yet been awarded the surname Toyotomi at that time) the opportunity to seize power. Intercepting a message not meant for him, Hideyoshi learned that Nobunaga had been killed. Hideyoshi mobilized his forces secretly to attack the perpetrator. This began Hideyoshi's march to power throughout Japan. He conquered rival military leaders and, recognizing that other rural samurai-farmers might become great leaders as he had, decided to neutralize their potential power. In 1588, he issued the famous "Sword Hunt" edict, disarming all villagers and, in the process, gaining them merit in the afterlife:

> *The farmers of the various provinces are strictly forbidden to possess long swords, short swords, bows, spears, muskets, or any form of weapon.... So that the...swords collected shall not be wasted, they shall be [melted down and] used...in the forthcoming construction of the Great Buddha. This will be an act by which the farmers will be*

shogunate—The government headed by the shōgun.

> *saved in this life, needless to say, and in the life to come.... If farmers possess agricultural tools alone and engage [themselves] completely in cultivation, they shall [prosper] unto eternity.*[1]

In 1591, Hideyoshi followed up with the Edict on Changing Status, which stipulated that samurai, farmers, and merchants all must remain in the status group into which they were born. The same year he carried out surveys of land and its productivity so that he could tax his own lands and gain information about the wealth of other *daimyō* lords. The growth of cities and towns in the seventeenth century shows that the prohibition on mobility was never as rigidly applied as Hideyoshi and his successors in the Tokugawa Shogunate intended. He got the emperor to name him "regent," an old title from the Heian period, which had no meaning except as a sign of the emperor's recognition. Hideyoshi was never shōgun.

Although Hideyoshi's edicts applied only to lands under his own direct control, they were copied by other *daimyō*. Hideyoshi and the *daimyō* lords moved the samurai from the countryside and housed them in barracks around their castles. Merchants and artisans moved nearby to supply the samurai and their lords. In time, these towns, called "castle-towns," became Japan's main cities. Hideyoshi and the *daimyō* built castles, roads, drainage ditches, bridges, port facilities, temples, and countless other structures. Most of the labor force came from the countryside. *Daimyō* ordered farmers to work on their own urban construction projects and on those demanded by Hideyoshi. For example, Hideyoshi requisitioned from his *daimyō* approximately 250,000 workers to build his grand castle at Fushimi (foo-SHEE-mee). After completing their projects, many of these workers settled in the new castle-towns, in spite of Hideyoshi's edict forbidding farmers to permanently change their status.

Art and Culture in Medieval Japan

Hideyoshi's period was an era of grand and colorful art. Like Oda Nobunaga, Hideyoshi used architectural monuments as symbols of his power. Castles and temples, decorated in the most ornate and at times even ostentatious styles, were built by legions of conscripted laborers. The bold and lavish paintings of Kanō Eitoku and his followers, patronized by the rich and powerful, continued to dominate painting for several decades into the next century. The Europeans, with their exotic clothing, appearance, and strange objects of daily life, were another popular theme in artwork patronized by urban connoisseurs.

Townsfolk, whether merchants, samurai, or the highest level elite, were not the only ones to patronize and enjoy artistic production. From the fourteenth to the sixteenth centuries, itinerant storytellers, many of them originally monks and nuns, traveled throughout Japan, to villages and mansions alike, creating what one historian has called a "national literature" that transcended regional and class boundaries. These performances included song, dance, recitation, the playing of stringed instruments, the use of puppets, and the showing of pictures to accompany the text or songs.

Urban elites built permanent theaters to present plays with human actors or puppets. In the Muromachi period, **Nō** (NOH) plays, which had religious and often historical themes and the refined, spare sensibility of Zen, were created by master playwrights like the actor-playwright-critic Zeami Motokiyo (zeh-AH-mee MOH-toh-KEE-yo; c. 1363–1443). Nō developed from thirteenth-century religious rites into a sophisticated theatrical form by the fourteenth century. In the seventeenth century, new forms like puppet plays and kabuki (kah-BOO-kee) plays with human actors emerged (see Chapter 20).

The tea ceremony, intended to be refined, intimate, and meditative, was another artistic form that became more popular in the harsh times of the Warring States period. Beautiful teapots and cups were manufactured in Japan or imported as luxury items from China or Korea. Hideyoshi had studied with the greatest tea master of his day, Sen no Rikyō (SEN no REE-kee-oh), but for reasons historians still cannot understand, ordered this important artist to commit suicide in 1591.

Architecture was another art that developed during the three centuries of the Muromachi period and Warring States period. Ashikaga shōguns, especially the third, Yoshimitsu (YOH-shee-MEE-tsoo), and sixth, Yoshimasa (YOH-shee-MAH-sah), built remarkable religious retreats of a modest size which blended with their surroundings. The Temple of the Golden Pavilion (see p. 388), though rebuilt following a fire after World War II, and the Temple of the Silver Pavilion, which still stands, are the finest examples of Muromachi architecture. Later buildings might be grandiose, as were the castles of Oda Nobunaga and Toyotomi Hideyoshi, or beautiful as well as functional, like Himeji (Hee-MAY-jee) castle, built by *daimyō* during the Warring States period.

Japan was very much part of the international commercial world during the Muromachi and Warring States periods. Arts were freely imported and exported to the rest of Asia. As we have seen, the Ming tried to control the volume of trade, but freebooting merchants from China, Japan and Korea, called "Japanese pirates" by the Ming, got around the Ming restrictions. Hideyoshi imposed some restrictions of his own. In 1587, attempting to allay Ming concerns about piracy, Hideyoshi suppressed many of the Japanese who had

---

Nō—A dramatic form developed in Japan in the fourteenth century; inspired by Buddhist themes.

Document

Sotoba Komachi, a Fourteenth-Century Japanese Nō Play

Kan'ami (1333–1384), father of the great playwright Zeami, pioneered the transformation of simple plays and complex court dances into the sophisticated dramatic form of the Nō. Zen aesthetics, Pure Land salvation, and shamanistic spirit possession come together in these dramas. The spare stage and tranquility of action of most of a Nō play culminates in a wild dance, as the main actor is transformed into the tormented soul of another. In this play, Komachi, a poet who had actually lived in the Heian period, is an old woman, no longer the famous beauty of her day. She comes upon two priests who inform her she is sitting on a stupa (*sotoba* in Japanese), whereupon she is possessed by the spirit of a man whose soul cannot cease to be reborn in worldly torment because it is consumed by desire due to the young Komachi's toying with his love. She had told him that if he called on her 100 times, she would consent to see him, but he died after 99 visits, unrequited. The excerpts here are from her conversation with the Buddhist priests at the beginning of the play and from her frenzied comments, as well as those of the Chorus which advances the action of the play, at the end.

KOMACHI: How sad that once I was proud....
Golden birds in my raven hair
When I walked like willows nodding, charming
As the breeze in spring.
The voice of the nightingale
The petals of the rosewood, wide stretched...
I was lovelier than these.
Now I am foul in the eyes of the humblest creature
...The wreck of a hundred years...

FIRST PRIEST: ...That old beggar woman sitting on a sacred stupa. We should warn her to come away.

Following some discussion between the priests and the old woman about Buddhist spiritual matters, the priests ask the old woman her name. All three, as well as the Chorus, lament the evanescence of life. Suddenly, Komachi turns into her spurned lover. At times, she speaks as though she is the lover, at other times as herself. The Chorus also speaks as the lover.

KOMACHI: An awful madness seizes me
And my voice is no longer the same.
Hey! Give me something you priests!

FIRST PRIEST: What do you want?

KOMACHI: To go to Komachi!

FIRST PRIEST: What are you saying? You are Komachi!

KOMACHI: No. Komachi was beautiful.
Many letters came, many messages
But she made no answer, even once...
Age is her retribution now
Oh, I love her!...

CHORUS: I came and went, came and went
One night, two nights, three...
I came and carved my mark upon the pillar.
I was to come a hundred nights,
I lacked but one...

KOMACHI: It was his unsatisfied love possessed me so...
In the face of this I will pray
For life in the worlds to come
Before the golden, gentle Buddha I will lay
Poems as my flowers
Entering in the Way...

Questions to Consider

1. Nō plays were intended as entertainment for samurai and *daimyō*. Why do you think their content was so strongly religious?
2. What Buddhist principles are evident in this excerpt?
3. Why do you think a fourteenth-century playwright would use a tenth-century event as the theme of his play?

From Kan'ami Kiyotsugu, "Sotoba Komachi," in Donald Keene, ed., *Anthology of Japanese Literature* (New York: Grove Press, 1955).

been involved in uncontrolled trade. But Hideyoshi's other foreign policy initiatives were decidedly a failure. His invasions of Korea were disastrous not only for Korea but also for his own ability to establish long-lasting rule by his family in Japan. Indeed, though the invasions were immediately terminated when he died in 1598, he had so weakened his closest supporters by sending them to war in Korea that other powerful men, rivals to his child heir Hideyori (HEE-deh-YOH-ree), were able to defeat the boy's supporters and take over Japan in 1600. An additional result of Hideyoshi's disastrous foreign adventurism was the policy of the Tokugawa shōguns to minimize and strictly control foreign relations.

Christians presented a related problem. Europeans had been arriving in the islands since a shipwreck in 1543 in which three Portuguese came ashore with arquebuses. These early muskets would soon alter the course of warfare, for Nobunaga and a few other *daimyō* used firearms to great tactical advantage. Thereafter, Portuguese ships began arriving in greater numbers, bringing not only new products, as noted

Himeji Castle, completed in the early seventeenth century, is the finest extant example of late Warring States era castle construction. Like other such castles, it sits atop a hill and its stone base is capable of defending against the cannons that began to be used in the late sixteenth century. The lovely living quarters at the top were vulnerable to fire, but manifested the glory of the *daimyō* who commanded the castle.

above, but also Jesuit missionaries, starting in 1549. Some *daimyō* converted to Christianity to facilitate trade and often forced their samurai to convert as well. By the 1580s, as many as 200,000 residents of the island of Kyūshū had adopted the foreign faith. Hideyoshi first noticed the divisive role played by Christians in 1586 while fighting his rivals on that island. He issued two edicts, one to expel missionaries and one to limit the propagation of Christianity, but neither edict was effectively carried out. A few years later, Hideyoshi treated Jesuits cordially and offered land in Kyoto to the rival order of Franciscans. Hideyoshi's first expulsion and limitation edicts were apparently not intended to be applied generally but rather were directed at a small group of troublesome Jesuits in Nagasaki who encouraged destruction of Shintō shrines and Buddhist temples and served as currency brokers. Later, however, Hideyoshi became convinced that missionaries were the leading edge of Iberian colonialism and executed several missionaries and converts. But few other actions were taken, as trade was too valuable to jeopardize by offending the Iberians at that time. The systematic expulsion of Christians would come later, under the Tokugawa.

The Road to Sekigahara

In 1590, Tokugawa Ieyasu received a highly productive territory, the Kantō plain in eastern Japan, in exchange for his military assistance to Hideyoshi. The Kantō, which had been the home of the Minamoto shōguns in the Kamakura period (see Chapter 10) and is today the heartland of Japan, was Japan's most productive rice-producing area. Tokugawa Ieyasu selected a tiny farming village along Edo creek to build a castle-town, which he called Edo. By 1610, Edo had 5,000 houses; by 1620, it had 150,000 residents; and by 1700, with over a million inhabitants, the little fishing village had become the world's largest city. As Hideyoshi and Nobunaga had done, in the 1590s Ieyasu mobilized peasants to clear forests; to cut timber to construct castles, barracks, temples, and buildings for mercantile activities; to lay out roads and canals; and to build bridges and docks. He needed skilled workers of all kinds. He exhausted natural resources, especially lumber, an environmental problem that would have be dealt with later in the Tokugawa period.

Ieyasu was one of five regents appointed by Hideyoshi on his deathbed to administer the realm until his son Hideyori came of age. Soon, tensions among the five erupted into a renewal of warfare. Ieyasu and his allies created an army of 80,000 men and challenged the supporters of Hideyori at the battle of Sekigahara (SEH-kee-gah-HAH-rah) in the fall of 1600. Victory in this battle established Tokugawa hegemony and allowed Tokugawa Ieyasu to reward his followers and punish his opponents by either eliminating or reducing their domains. Hideyori and his family were moved to one of the Toyotomi castles, at Osaka, where they remained until the Tokugawa eliminated them in 1615. Tokugawa Ieyasu asked the emperor to declare him shōgun, which he did in 1603. His wealthy domain in the Kantō, his use of natural and human resources, and his military effectiveness led to his victory.

Tokugawa Ieyasu was not known for his kindness, though he was a strong leader. Like his predecessors, Ieyasu manipulated the marriages of women in his family for his own ends. As we have seen, *daimyō* women were expected to act as spies for their fathers or brothers, leading to their husbands' distrust of them. Ieyasu himself was the victim of manipulation at the hands of Nobunaga, whose daughter he married. Hideyoshi forced his sister to divorce her first husband to marry Ieyasu, whereupon the sister's distraught first husband committed suicide. Ieyasu married his granddaughter to Hideyori, son of Hideyoshi; Ieyasu's forces went on to execute the granddaughter's little son (and Ieyasu's own great-grandson) in 1615. The status of women was entirely dependent on their social status, with *daimyō* women the only ones used as marriage pawns. Fortunately, though women's status would remain low during the Tokugawa period, women of other classes were not placed in that kind of jeopardy, and the worst excesses, the use of women as hostages through forced marriages, were terminated with the end of the battles for unification in Japan.

The Early Tokugawa Years

Ieyasu faced some difficult problems in the first years of the Tokugawa Shogunate (1600–1868). Even simple public safety was an early problem, as samurai whose *daimyō* had been defeated at the battle of Sekigahara in 1600 roamed the streets of Japan's towns with little to do but make trouble. These masterless samurai, called rōnin (ROH-neen), continued to emerge in times of turmoil in the next several hundred years. For the most part, however, the Tokugawa managed to control them within a few years by offering them alternate forms of employment and amusement. Another problem concerned the shogunate's relationship to the loyal *daimyō*. What Ieyasu and his next two successors, his son Hidetada (HEE-deh-TAH-dah; r. 1606–1623) and grandson Iemitsu (EE-eh-MEE-tsoo; r. 1623–1651), did was to move the *daimyō* around the country to form layers of protection from those they believed least trustworthy; to proclaim a code of conduct for the *daimyō* in 1615; to take over control of roads, mines, ports, and international relations; and to set up a control system called the "alternate attendance system."

DOCUMENT

Edicts by Tokugawa Ieyasu

MAP

Tokugawa Japan, 1600-1800

The shrine at Nikko is one of several built after the death of Tokugawa Ieyasu to legitimize the shogunate's power by designating its founder as a Shintō deity. The ornate construction contrasts with the simplicity of medieval architecture.

The alternate attendance system had many unanticipated effects, which are discussed in Chapter 20, but it also achieved its primary goal of controlling the *daimyō*. To be a *daimyō* in the Tokugawa era, a lord had to possess a domain that produced at least 10,000 *koku* of rice (a *koku* is a unit of measurement; one *koku* fed approximately one person for one year). Each *daimyō* had to maintain a mansion in the shōgun's capital at Edo in addition to his castle in his home domain. He had to live in the mansion every other year (hence, he *attended* the shōgun in *alternate* years), and his wife and children had to live permanently in Edo, thus making sure he would not raise the banner of rebellion while back at home in his own castle. The alternate attendance system, requiring the movement across the whole country of vast numbers of samurai in the retinues of the *daimyō*, was extremely expensive, as was the maintenance of two homes and two staffs. The impoverishing of the *daimyō* also kept them from rising up against the Tokugawa.

A Japanese View of European Missionaries

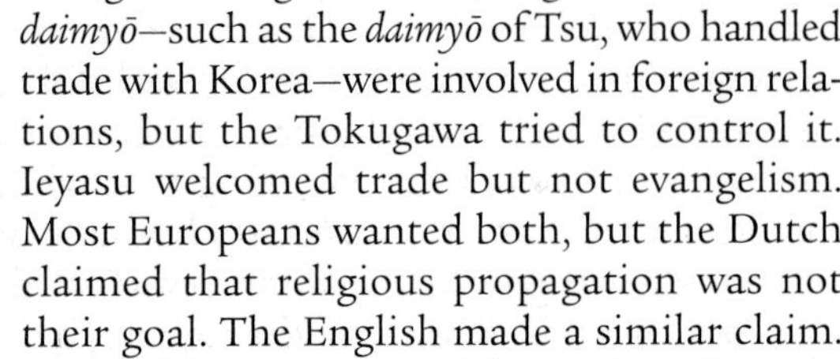

Another area brought under regulation by the first three Tokugawa shōguns was foreign affairs. Some *daimyō*—such as the *daimyō* of Tsu, who handled trade with Korea—were involved in foreign relations, but the Tokugawa tried to control it. Ieyasu welcomed trade but not evangelism. Most Europeans wanted both, but the Dutch claimed that religious propagation was not their goal. The English made a similar claim. But unable to compete with Dutch traders, the English abandoned Japan by 1623. The Japanese were finding it more difficult to conduct business as silver supplies began to run low, but trade continued for many years into the seventeenth century. Evangelism was another story. Ieyasu's son Hidetada increased pressure to suppress the Christians in Japan. The end of all missionary activity, and indeed, the closing of Japan to all international contacts except those by the Chinese, the Koreans, and the Dutch, was precipitated by a revolt at Shimabara in which Christian banners were raised in 1637–1638, reminding the fearful Tokugawa of the Buddhist-inspired village revolts of the Warring States period.

By the end of the 1630s, peasant starvation and overwork, exacerbated by poor weather due to a devastating El Niño pattern, were at the heart of a movement of peasants who joined rōnin in demands against the state. Revolts broke out in many places, but the most severe was the Shimabara (SHEE-mah-BAH-rah) revolt. Laying siege to the peasants and rōnin holed up at Shimabara, the Tokugawa starved out 37,000 villagers. The stringent regulation of foreign trade began after this revolt. Japan continued to have a high volume of trade through the rest of the seventeenth century, but its trading partners were limited to the three it could be confident would not try to smuggle in forbidden Christian texts. Japan's foreign policy was then called a **sakoku** (SAH-koh-koo) or closed-country policy, but it would be more accurate to call it a strictly regulated foreign policy.

By 1650, the Tokugawa had established control of Japan's foreign policy, brought the *daimyō* under their control, and created a regulated society. They continued their control of Japanese politics—the emperor was honored by the Tokugawa but had no power—until the middle of the nineteenth century (see Chapter 25). For the next 200 years, Japan was at peace, and the arts, commerce, scholarship, and the people's livelihood flourished.

Southeast Asia: States Within a Region

How did cultural blending influence Southeast Asian civilizations?

Situated on the main sea route between East Asia and the Indian Ocean and divided geographically into diverse subregions, Southeast Asia had long been an area of contending states. Although each of these regions had been influenced for centuries by the cultures of India and China, they developed a strong sense of separate cultural identities and statehood. Wars in defense of independence or attempted conquest of neighboring states were, as a result, fairly common.

In the thirteenth century, the powerful land-based Khmer (KMEHR) state, which had dominated southern and central mainland Southeast Asia for four centuries, began to decline. Its very wealth and power were, ironically, factors leading to its decline. With great agricultural wealth derived from its sophisticated irrigation system, Khmer built 20,000 shrines, 102 hospitals, and other monuments. The state supported 300,000 priests and monks. These expenditures sapped the state, as did wars against the neighboring Chams and the encroaching Thais. In the fourteenth century, the Mongols in China encouraged the Thais to move into Khmer territory. The Mongols, who temporarily received tribute from mainland Southeast Asia and parts of Java, seriously disrupted all existing governments. Throughout Southeast Asia, there were ruinous petty wars, often based on Hindu-Buddhist conflicts, each side of which suffered individually under Muslim expansion. Finally, Muslim regimes replaced many traditional Hindu states in Indonesia, which also felt the effects of European empire building, first by the Portuguese and then by the Dutch. Before 1650, however, the total European impact on the mainland was negligible.

Tracing the political interactions among the nations and empires making up the region we now know as Southeast Asia may often seem confusing.

sakoku—Policy of limiting Japan's foreign and trade relations to China, Korea, and the Netherlands from 1640 to 1853. Literally, "closed country."

◄ Cambodia's Angkor Wat, built in the early twelfth century, first as a temple to the god Vishnu and later converted to a Buddhist temple in the fourteenth century, is the epitome of classical Cambodian architecture. These towers are just one small part of this massive edifice, filled with intricate sculpture. By the end of the nineteenth century, it had fallen into poor repair. Restoration began in the early twentieth century but was often postponed due to war.

Here, what is most significant is that we recognize the important regional influences, such as the roles of religion and trade networks.

Burma and the Thais

In the first millennium C.E., the region of present-day Burma remained an ethnically diverse region, divided into a number of small principalities. Around 1050, a process of political unification began under the Burmese, a group of people who moved to the south from the Tibetan frontier about nine hundred years earlier. This movement was shattered by the Mongol invasions of the 1280s. The process of unification recommenced after the invasions, but it took until the sixteenth and seventeenth centuries for the Tongoo kingdom to unify most of Burma.

Advancing to the south during the Mongol invasions were the Thais, a group of people from Yunnan, in China. The Mongols' destruction of Burma and the threat to the Khmer helped the expansion of Ayuthaya (AH-yoo-TAI-ya), the Thai state, but it was not the only reason for the rise of the Thais. The weakening of these two other states offered opportunities for expansion to the Thais, who had already begun to penetrate the region centuries earlier. Arriving in Khmer and Burma, the Thais—whose name *Thai* meant "free"—also absorbed the richness of the Indian civilization that had for centuries influenced Southeast Asia. In the late thirteenth century, the Thai monarch Rama Khamheng (RAH-mah KAHM-heng; r. 1283–1317), the head of the small Thai principality of Sukhothai (SOO-koh-THAI), extended Thai power after deciding to establish an independent Thai state. Under Sukhothai rule, the Thai people were given a cultural and political identity derived from several sources in the region. The idea of a divine monarch was borrowed from the Khmer. Burma provided principles of law and Theravada Buddhism. The Thai alphabet was created by Rama Khamheng, based on South Indian script. In the fifteenth century, the Thai kingdom moved its capital to the agricultural center of the country and brought the various Thai principalities under the king's control. This centralized monarchical system lasted into the nineteenth century.

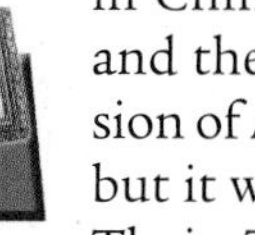

Thai Statue

	Southeast Asia
1050	Beginnings of Burmese unification
1283–1317	Rama Khamheng, king of Thailand
1280s	Mongol invasions
1402	Founding of Malacca
1407–1418	Ming invasion of Vietnam
1418	Founding of Le dynasty in Vietnam

Under the Tongoo King Bayinnaung (BAI-in-NOWNG; r. 1551–1581) in the 1550s and 1560s, Burma briefly absorbed Laos (LAH-ohs) and conquered Siam (now Thailand) with an army estimated at 500,000, the largest ever assembled in Southeast Asia. Bayinnaung's capital at Pegu was a nucleus of Buddhist culture, a thriving commercial center, and the site of his wondrous palace, which was roofed in solid gold. But his successor wasted resources in unsuccessful wars on its neighbors. Later, the Thai state gained supremacy, humbling Cambodia and Burma after 1595 and profiting from a commercial alliance with the Dutch.

Vietnam

Under Chinese rule for a millennium, Vietnam was the Southeast Asian country that was, at the same time, most sinified and most ardently committed to

Document

A Traveller's Account of Siam

This description is by Ma Huan, a translator and interpreter for the fourth expedition of eunuch maritime navigator Zheng He, from 1413 to 1415. The account tells us as much about Chinese attitudes as about "Xian Luo," known to Europeans as Siam, and now known as Thailand.

...Travelling from Chan city towards the south-west for several days and nights with a fair wind, the ship comes to the estuary at New Street Tower and enters the anchorage; then you reach the capital.

The country is a thousand *li* in circumference, the outer mountains [being] steep and rugged, [and] the inner land wet and swampy. The soil is barren and little of it is suitable for cultivation. The climate varies—sometimes cold, sometimes hot.

The house in which the king resides is rather elegant, neat, and clean. The houses of the populace are constructed in storeyed form; in the upper [part of the house] they do not join planks together [to make a floor], but they use the wood of the areca-palm, which they cleave into strips resembling bamboo splits; [these strips] are laid close together and bound very securely with rattans; on [this platform] they spread rattan mats and bamboo matting, and on these they do all their sitting, sleeping, eating, and resting.

As to the king's dress: he uses a white cloth to wind round his head; on the upper [part of his body] he wears no garment; [and] round the lower [part he wears] a silk-embroidered kerchief, adding a waist-band of brocaded silk-gauze. When going about he mounts an elephant or else rides in a sedan-chair, while a man holds [over him] a gold-handled umbrella... [which is] very elegant. The king is a man of the So-li race, and a firm believer in the Buddhist religion.

In this country the people who become priests or become nuns are exceedingly numerous; the habit of the priests and nuns is somewhat the same as in the Central Country; and they, too, live in nunneries and monasteries, fasting and doing penance....

It is their custom that all affairs are managed by their wives; both the [illegible text] of the country and the common people, if they have matters which require thought and deliberation—punishments light and heavy, all trading transactions great and small—they all follow the decisions of their wives, [for] the mental capacity of the wives certainly exceeds that of the men.

If a married woman is very intimate with one of our men from the Central Country, wine and food are provided, and they drink and sit and sleep together. The husband is quite calm and takes no exception to it; indeed he says "My wife is beautiful and the man from the Central Country is delighted with her." The men dress the hair in a chignon, and use a white headcloth to bind round the head [and] on the body they wear a long gown. The women also pin up the hair in a chignon, and wear a long gown.

Questions to Consider

1. Would the role of Thai women in decision-making have been surprising to a Chinese observer of the Ming dynasty?
2. Did Ma Huan find Thailand exotic? What kinds of exchanges do you think the Ming and Thailand would have made under the tribute system? In this description of Thailand in the fifteenth century can you see cultural or social similarities with any other parts of East Asia during approximately the same time period?

From Ma Huan, *Ying-yai Sheng-lai: The Overall Survey of the Ocean's Shores (1433)*, trans. Feng Ch'eng Chun, intro. by J. V. G. Mills (Cambridge: Cambridge University Press, 1970).

independence from China. Vietnam used Chinese script, borrowed institutions of government, and adopted Buddhism from Chinese missionaries. Political independence from China was followed by the two countries' continuing tributary relationship and Vietnam's careful study of Confucian scholarship. The Mongol attacks were repulsed by the Vietnamese, but the Ming, who invaded in 1407, did briefly rule Vietnam early in the fifteenth century. In 1418, Le Loi (LEH LO-ee), an aristocratic landholder, led an army to push out the Ming. A decade of warfare finally succeeded in 1428, and Le Loi founded the Le dynasty, which reigned in name until 1788—though effectively only until the 1520s. Le and his successors in the Le dynasty adopted Chinese methods; they then succeeded in dominating their Southeast Asian neighbors. These nations were all in decline; indeed, Burma was still broken into a number of principalities. An exception was the Thai polity under King Trailok (1448–1488), who was more successful in creating an efficient army and establishing a civil administration. By the end of the fifteenth century, the Vietnamese, along with the Thais, momentarily controlled the mainland region of Southeast Asia. Rather than encouraging trade, however, Vietnam's ruling dynasty based its rule on a Confucian approach to national wealth. Stating that commerce was "peripheral," the powerful monarch Le Thanh Tong (LEH TAHNG TONG; r. 1460–1497) focused on agriculture, stating: "Concentrate all our forces on agriculture, expand our potential." Le Thanh Tong was the Le dynasty's most prominent monarch, having installed an effective examination system, rooted out aristocratic corruption, and instituted a variety of governmental reforms.

Early in the sixteenth century, tensions between powerful aristocratic families burst into open warfare between a faction headed by Mac Dang Dong and supporters of the Le monarchs, the Nguyen and Trinh families. Mac Dang Dong temporarily usurped the throne, killing the Le monarch in 1524, but the Nguyen (NWEN) and Trinh (TRIHN) fought back. By 1533, they had recaptured the Winter Palace. Although the loyalists proclaimed a restoration of Le authority, the Mac were not driven out of Hanoi until 1592. After that, Trinh lords held sway over the north while Nguyen lords ruled in the south—with the Le as nominal kings. The Trinh opened commercial contacts with the Dutch and later the English, but those trade ties lasted only till 1700. The Nguyen acquired cannons from the Portuguese, but the Portuguese were soon kicked out. The Nguyen also accepted numerous Chinese refugees, Ming loyalists fleeing the Manchus in the seventeenth century. The Trinh, more leery of the colossus directly to their north, refused to accept Ming refugees.

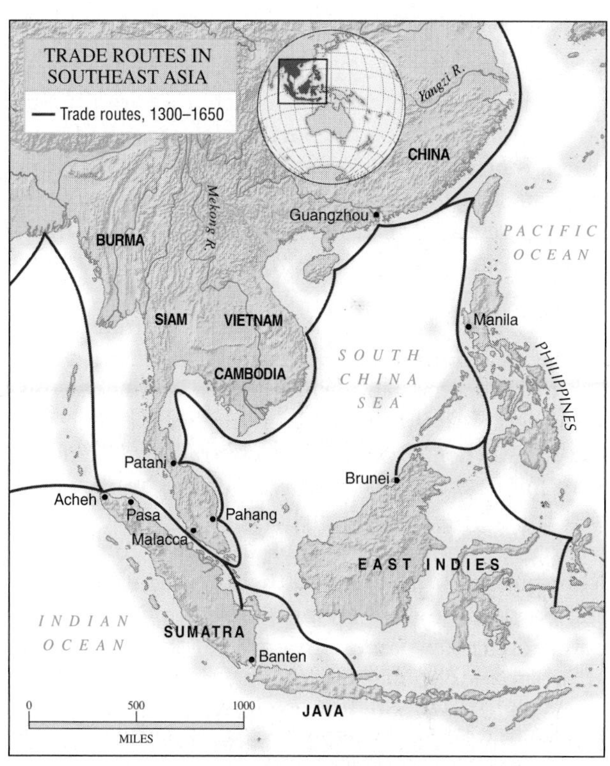

▲ The trade routes across the Indian Ocean served as an arena for the interaction of Chinese, Indian, Arab, and Southeast Asian cultures as well as Hindu, Buddhist, and Muslim religions and eastern and western goods and products.

Maritime Southeast Asia

The kingdom of Majapahit (MAH-jah-pah-HEET), like the Thai state, was able to consolidate its position on the Indonesian island of Java due to Mongol pressure on its neighbors. From the late thirteenth century, Majapahit extended its hegemony over most of the islands of Indonesia, dominating the trade controlled earlier by Srivijaya and developing a sophisticated and artistic culture. In 1402, Malacca (mah-LAH-ka) declared itself an independent sultanate, and one by one, other Indonesian rulers involved in maritime trade converted to Islam and abandoned Majapahit. Expanding into Indonesia in a gradual and generally peaceful manner, Islam achieved a great success in the fourteenth and fifteenth centuries. Sufi Muslim missionaries were drawn to the area by the expanding India-China trade, particularly when Chinese interests waned in the decade after 1424. Many local rulers embraced Islam to gain independence from the great Hindu state of Majapahit; others sought a share of Indian commerce. The Muslims were tolerant of the Hindu-Buddhist culture of the new converts, and daily practices, rituals, arts, and music, even those contrary to Muslim rules, were allowed to continue. Foreigners, among them the large number of immigrant Chinese and merchants from Egypt, Persia, Arabia, and western India, were accepted. The Muslims mixed easily with the populations of the port cities. As the power of the Majapahit Empire weakened, the influence of Islam grew. Muslim sailors—either pirates or traders, depending on the circumstances—came to control the various straits between the islands and set up their own states.

The indigenous population adopted Islam, as the local princely families intermarried with Muslims in alliances uniting the power and legitimacy of the local nobility with the wealth of the Muslim merchants. From this base in Indonesia, Islam spread throughout present-day Malaysia, the Molucca Islands, and some of the islands of the Philippines. Only Bali remained relatively untouched by the Islamic advance.

The rising Muslim commercial center of Malacca, on the Malay coast opposite Sumatra, best illustrates the entry of Islam into Southeast Asia. Founded in 1402 and by 1404 part of the Ming tribute system, its rulers converted to Islam and built an empire of commercial vassal states in the region. Despite the sultan's profession of Islam, Malacca continued to use the structure of Hindu-Buddhist princely courts. Malacca was multicultural. For example, in 1462, the Arab navigator Ibn Majid described the people of Melaka (Malacca) as follows:

> *They have no culture at all. The infidel marries Muslim women while the Muslim takes pagans to wife. You do not know whether they are Muslims or not. They are thieves for theft is rife among them and they do not mind.*
>
> *The Muslim eats dogs for meat for there are no food laws.*
>
> *They drink wine in the markets and do not treat divorce as a religious act.*[2]

Malacca was the busiest port in Asia, linking China and the Moluccas with India and Africa. Its growing success paralleled Muslim expansion through western Indonesia to the Philippines in the sixteenth century.

Arrival of the Europeans

The Portuguese arrived in maritime Southeast Asia in the early sixteenth century. Butchering its Muslim population, they took the port of Malacca in 1511 and held it for the next 130 years. By 1550, the profits from the trade through Malacca were four times Portugal's internal revenues. But Portuguese rule was arbitrary and cruel and turned increasing numbers of Southeast Asians to convert to Islam to facilitate joining a trade network apart from the Portuguese. Mainland governments in Southeast Asia generally maintained their independence against the Europeans. Portuguese missionaries, at first active in Vietnam, were expelled by the end of the period. Portuguese traders and mercenary soldiers served everywhere, but they were usually controlled. Some were enslaved in Burma; only in weakened Cambodia and Laos did they acquire significant political influence. By the seventeenth century, the Portuguese were giving way to the Dutch, who courted the Vietnamese in only partially successful efforts to monopolize trade with Siam and Burma.

Well before 1650, Europeans were becoming very active in Indonesia. The Portuguese used Malacca as a base for dominating trade in the region, but Muslim rulers in nearby states forcefully ejected them from Java and Sumatra and limited their operations in the Molucca Islands. In the late 1500s, Spain acquired a foothold in the Philippines. The Spanish established a colonial capital at Manila in 1571 and sent in missionaries to convert the country to Christianity. The missionaries eventually exerted even greater control over people's daily lives than the Spanish colonial officials in Manila. With the creation of the colony of the Philippines, the triangular trade of the Manila Galleons embraced Mexico, Peru, the Philippines, Japan, and China. This trade constituted the world's first true "globalization." Expansive linkages had been created 1500 years earlier with the first Silk Roads and Zheng He's and Columbus's voyages of exploration in the early and late fifteenth century, respectively, have been cited by numerous historians as world-changing moments of globalization. The late sixteenth-century development of the Pacific Ocean trade route, however, was the final link that created truly global exchange. The mineral wealth of the New World, exploited through the use of slaves from Africa and the Americas, was shipped by Europeans to feed the demand for silver of China, the world's greatest producer and consumer at the time. All parts of the world were now linked across the Atlantic and the Pacific.

Dutch trading companies merged into the United East India Company in 1602, and initially sought trade, not territory or the conversion of souls, in Southeast Asia. They took control of the Moluccas and expelled the Portuguese in 1641. Soon after that, the Dutch concluded a long war in Java by forcing upon the sultans a treaty that guaranteed a Dutch commercial monopoly in return for native political autonomy. Thereafter, however, Dutch plantation agriculture began undermining Indonesian economies. By the second half of the century, the Dutch had replaced the Muslims as the most powerful merchants in the region. From then on, Europe's demands for the spices and riches of the region would be satisfied by the merchants of Amsterdam. Later, the Dutch would take complete political control of Indonesia.

Conclusion

The years after the Mongol conquest of China, which had created a massive Eurasian commercial network, saw the development of diverse nations and cultures. Yet each was tied in some important ways to the others. In China, the tribute system tried to arrange states hierarchically by their proximity and conformity to China's Confucian order. The Confucian emphasis on hierarchy moderated by benevolence (see Chapter 2) was replicated in the obeisance of subordinate states in return for China's protection. The Ming rulers began by trying to expand the tribute system but ended up increasingly inward-directed. At the same time, the people of China began to lay claim to a national culture that defined their identity as Chinese. In Korea, the Chosŏn dynasty rested under the immediate gaze of its immense neighbor and struggled, in the middle of the period, with calamitous foreign invasions. But, just as the Chinese during the Ming dynasty, the Korean people as a whole gradually laid claim to Korean culture. Japan was part of the East Asian commercial world but, unlike Korea, was only tangentially part of the China-centered tribute system, and even that involvement continued for only part of the late medieval period. Japan was further differentiated from Korea and Vietnam by being relatively uninfluenced by Confucianism in this period; Buddhism dominated both the popular and the elite culture in medieval Japan.

Southeast Asia, both maritime and mainland, was part of international trading networks. These networks attracted many religions and cultures to the region. For hundreds of years, Southeast Asians have borrowed eclectically from many traditions, enhancing the multicultural nature of the region. This period was one of the pivotal eras in world history, with an economic engine driven by East Asia though dependent on world trade in commodities from the Americas and dominated by European merchants and fleets.

Suggestions for Web Browsing

You can obtain more information about topics included in this chapter at the websites listed below. See also the companion website that accompanies this text, http://www.ablongman.com/brummett, which contains an online study guide and additional resources.

Imperial China: The Ming
http://www.fordham.edu/halsall/eastasia/eastasiasbook.html#Imperial%20China
This site features maps and images pertaining to the Ming dynasty, 1368–1644; it is part of the Internet East Asian History Sourcebook.

Chinese History
http://sun.sino.uni-heidelberg.de/igcs
This Internet guide to Chinese studies covers all periods and all topics in Chinese history.

Japanese Samurai
http://www.samurai-archives.com
An extensive collection of biographies of important samurai and daimyō *in medieval and early modern Japan.*

Masterpieces of the Kyoto National Museum
http://www.kyohaku.go.jp/
Numerous images, with descriptions, of the artworks of Japan, Korea, and China.

History of Korea
http://www.lifeinkorea.com/Information/history1.cfm
Text and images documenting the Koryŏ and Chosŏn dynasties of Korea.

Literature and Film

An abridged version of the Chinese classic *Monkey, Journey to the West,* trans. David Kherdian (Shambhala, 2000), offers students a chance to think about Ming era popular beliefs. For a translation of *The Romance of the Three Kingdoms* see *Three Kingdoms: A Historical Novel,* trans. Moss Roberts (University of California Press, 1991).

Films include *China's Forbidden City,* produced for the History Channel, A&E TV Network (1997); *Rise of the Dragon: The Genius That Was China, Part One,* produced by John Merson and David Roberts (1990; Coronet Film & Video); and *Japan: Memoirs of a Secret Empire, The Way of the Samurai,* the first of a four-part series on the Tokugawa period produced by Lyn Goldfarb for PBS (2004).

Classic movies by some of Japan's premier filmmakers deal with the Warring States period. See, for example, *Kagemusha,* by Akira Kurosawa (1980; 20th Century Fox) and *Ugetsu Monogatari,* by Kenzo Mizoguchi (1953; Daiei Studios).

Suggestions for Reading

Fine general histories of early modern China include Charles O. Hucker, *China's Imperial Past* (Stanford University Press, 1975), and the *Cambridge History of China*, Vol. 7 (Cambridge University Press, 1988) and Vol. 8 (Cambridge University Press, 1998), which cover the Ming. Ray Huang, *1587, A Year of No Significance* (Yale University Press, 1981), is noteworthy for its penetrating case study of late Ming weaknesses. For complete coverage of Chinese technology and engineering, see Joseph Needham, *Clerks and Craftsmen in China and the West* (Cambridge University Press, 1970). Dorothy Ko's *Teachers of the Inner Chambers* (Stanford University Press, 1994) is an excellent treatment of women.

On Korea, see Carter J. Eckert et al., *Korea Old and New* (Harvard University Press, 1990); Andrew C. Nahm, *Introduction to Korean History and Culture* (Holly International, 1993); and James Palais, *Politics and Policy in Traditional Korea* (Council of East Asian Studies, 1991). Yung-Chung Kim, *Women of Korea* (Ewha Women's University, 1982), provides a readable and informative treatment of women of the period.

A wealth of material on medieval and early modern Japan has come out in the last several decades. Among these fine studies are Conrad Totman, *Early Modern Japan* (University of California Press, 1993); Jeffrey P. Mass, *Origins of Japan's Medieval World* (Stanford University Press, 1997); Hitomi Tonomura, *Community and Commerce in Late Medieval Japan* (Stanford University Press, 1992); Andrew Goble, *Kenmu: Go-Daigo's Revolution* (Harvard University Press, 1996); and Hitomi Tonomura, Anne Walthall, and Wakita Haruko, eds., *Women and Class in Japanese History* (University of Michigan, 1999). These are also fine studies: John W. Hall et al., *Japan Before Tokugawa* (Yale University Press, 1981), and John W. Hall and Takeshi Toyoda, *Japan in the Muromachi Age* (Cornell University Press, 2001). Two excellent biographies that mirror the time are Mary Elizabeth Berry, *Hideyoshi* (Harvard University Press, 1989), and Conrad Totman, *Tokugawa Ieyasu: Shogun* (Heian International, 1983).

The most comprehensive treatment of Southeast Asia may be found in Nicholas Tarling, ed., *Cambridge History of Southeast Asia,* 2 vols. (Cambridge University Press, 1992). Anthony Reid, *Southeast Asia in the Age of Commerce, 1450–1680* (Yale University Press, 1995), covers separate cultures and attempts a synthesis of the whole region in terms of commerce. Fine general works include D. R. Sardesai, *Southeast Asia: Past and Present* (Westview Press, 2003), and George Coedes, *The Making of Southeast Asia,* 2nd ed. (Allen & Unwin, 1983). Treatments of individual countries may be found in Michael Aung-Thwin, *Pagan: The Origins of Modern Burma* (University of Hawaii Press, 1985); David K. Wyatt, *Thailand: A Short History,* 2nd ed. (Yale University Press, 2003); David P. Chandler, *A History of Cambodia,* 3rd ed. (Westview, 2000); Barbara W. Andaya and Leonard Y. Andaya, eds., *A History of Malaysia,* 2nd ed. (Macmillan, 2000); and John David Legge, *Indonesia,* 3rd ed. (Prentice Hall, 1980). Barbara W. Andaya, *Other Pasts: Women, Gender and History in Early Modern Southeast Asia* (University of Hawaii Press, 2001) is excellent.

CHAPTER 14

European Cultural and Religious Transformations

The Renaissance and the Reformation 1300–1600

Outline

- An Era of General Crisis
- The Italian Renaissance
- Italian Renaissance Art
- The Northern Renaissance
- The Crisis in the Catholic Church: 1300–1517
- Luther and the German Reformation
- Henry VIII and the Anglican Reformation
- Protestantism from Switzerland to Holland
- Reform in the Catholic Church

Features

GLOBAL ISSUES **Disease and Civilization**

DISCOVERY THROUGH MAPS **The Lagoon of Venice**

DOCUMENT **Machiavelli, *The Prince: On Cruelty and Mercy***

SEEING CONNECTIONS **Marco Polo's *Book of Wonders***

DOCUMENT **Anne Ayscough (Mrs. Thomas Kyme), English Protestant Martyr**

◄ *The Creation of Adam,* part of Michelangelo's remarkable painting that decorates the entire ceiling of the Vatican's Sistine Chapel.

MOST OF THE WORLD'S great civilizations have experienced a period of unprecedented stability, wealth, and confidence that encouraged its thinkers, artists, and artisans to create expressions of that civilization's values that not only appealed to their contemporaries, but served as models for future generations. These rare periods are sometimes called "Golden Ages." The reign of the Han dynasty in China, the era of Classical Mayan civilization in Mesoamerica, and the florescence of Benin and Mali in Africa all set standards of excellence for their citizens.

In the Mediterranean world, the Golden Ages of Greece and Rome produced cultural achievements that formed the classical basis of European civilization. That legacy was enriched by the accomplishments of the Islamic world from 900 to 1100. The work of Arab thinkers, artists, and scientists made its way, through translations, into Spain and Italy and thence became integrated into the Western heritage.

In most of the Golden Ages cited above, a certain atmosphere of confidence and security existed, in which philosophical and artistic creation took place. But this was not the case for the Italian and Northern Renaissance during the fifteenth and sixteenth century. This Golden Age of European history began in crisis: recession, famine, plague, and war; and it ended amid similar crises: war, revolutionary economic change, and religious ferment. In spite of, but also in part because of these crises, Europe during the centuries of Renaissance and Reformation developed a unique individualism that distinguished this period of European history from the Golden Ages of other civilizations and eras.

An Era of General Crisis

What were the most significant effects of the Black Death on European society in the fourteenth and fifteenth centuries?

The period from 1300 to 1600 was one of the most disruptive in European history. France and England engaged in a long and extremely destructive conflict known as the Hundred Years' War from 1337 to 1453 (see Chapter 15). The Catholic Church was subjected to unprecedented criticism for corruption, and the split between its leaders eventually led to a rivalry between three popes for control of the Church. Among these significant challenges to European stability were widespread famine and economic depression, and the devastation caused by the **Bubonic Plague.** The combination of these two destructive forces provoked an upheaval that changed the nature of European society.

Economic Depression and Bubonic Plague

In the three centuries preceding 1300, European agricultural methods had improved, crops were more productive, arable land increased, and the population probably doubled between 1000 and 1300. But the beginning of the fourteenth century saw changing weather patterns bring drought, famine, and widespread starvation and unemployment. Overpopulation and unsanitary lifestyles contributed to the factors that made Europe more vulnerable to a plague that killed probably one-third of the continent's population—around 25 million people—between 1347 to 1350 and continued to reappear sporadically until the seventeenth century.

Called the Black Death because of the discoloring effects it had on the body (especially the lymph nodes), the plague was carried by fleas on infected rats and had worked its way through the trade routes of Asia and India to Europe. Cities were particularly devastated; Florence's population fell from 114,000 to 50,000, London's from 60,000 to 40,000. The outbreak of the Hundred Years' War between France and England in 1337 (see Chapter 15) added to the destruction in both those nations. (See *Global Issues—Disease and Civilization* on page 418 for more on the influence of pandemic diseases in world history from ancient times up until present day.)

Many looked for spiritual explanations for the plague's devastation: that God was punishing a sinful humanity, or perhaps that there was no God at all. Many blamed the Jews for the plague and sought their expulsion from cities throughout Europe. Some found other scapegoats for their miseries—ranging from the plague, crop failures, economic crises, and religious uncertainty—in their searches for witches over the next two centuries. Over 100,000 of these unfortunate victims were prosecuted during this period, and many were executed by strangling, drowning, burning, or beheading. Seventy percent of those killed were women, nearly half of whom were older single women or widows.

Bubonic Plague—An infectious and usually fatal disease caused by the bacterium *Yersinia pestis,* which is carried and spread by the rat flea. Characteristics include high fever and swollen lymph nodes (buboes).

The Plague's Effect on European Society

By devastating the population of Europe, the Bubonic Plague fundamentally changed traditional social patterns. A lack of rural workers effectively ended the remnants of the feudal structure in many places on the continent. Wage payments replaced the centuries-old payments in kind. In the cities in the late fourteenth and early fifteenth century, skilled craftsmen and the guilds that gave them security in an earlier age now became beneficiaries of higher prices paid for their goods, and their economic good fortune resulted in increased power and new opportunities to participate in urban politics. The church was also an economic beneficiary of the devastation; despite the decline of its revenues from its agricultural holdings, its wealth was vastly increased from donations and bequests from those wishing to increase their possibilities for a heavenly reward. But for those who were not cared for either in the guilds or in the clergy, life in the cities and the countryside became increasingly difficult.

The beginning of the sixteenth century marked the beginning of another economic downturn that spread suffering throughout Europe. Economic dislocation accompanying the early development of capitalism added to the strains of transitioning between medieval

Chronology

1300

1300s Classical revival, humanism (Petrarch, Boccaccio)

1305–1377 Babylonian Captivity of the church; papacy under French influence

1320–1384 John Wycliffe

1348 Black Death begins to devastate Europe

1350

1378–1417 Great Schism of the Catholic Church

1400

1400s *Quattrocento,* Italian Renaissance (Donatello, Masaccio, Botticelli)

1414 Council of Constance

1415 John Hus, Bohemian reformer, burned at the stake

1434–1494 Medici family rules Florence

and modern times, especially for the peasantry. The sixteenth century also marked the end of the relatively favorable situation women had enjoyed in the Middle Ages. The new emphasis on wage labor and competition from men limited their opportunities for outside work. Although women could find some part-time employment as field laborers, this type of work paid very little.

A newly developing global economy brought high rates of inflation to Europe, as well as shifting trade routes. The decline of the importance of the Hanseatic League in the Baltic and North Seas, the Mediterranean, and the routes connecting the two hurt the economy of central Europe. The shifting of work to laborers in the smaller villages surrounding older towns—the cottage industry—ruined many old guild trades while swelling the ranks of the urban unemployed. Large-market agriculture weakened the peasants' traditional rights, subjected them to rents beyond their resources, and drove them from the land into the towns, where they joined the unemployed and impoverished.

The poor and those who were out of work often directed their anger increasingly against the Church because it was a visible source of authority, and it was rich. For society at large, the profit motive overshadowed the church's canon law, which called for compassion for the weak and the poor and a **"just price."**

In the midst of this widespread economic and social upheaval, a cultural movement began in Italy that initially touched only the elites but eventually had consequences that would affect the further development of Western civilization. It would come to be called the Renaissance, or the "rebirth."

The Italian Renaissance

Why is this period in Europe's history called a Renaissance—a "rebirth"?

This cultural rebirth or Renaissance did not take place in a vacuum. Prior to the twelfth century, almost all learning in Europe was under the control of the church, and medieval art and literature reflected the church's influence. Latin was the European language of diplomacy, scholarship, and serious literature. But in the later medieval period, the number of literate men and women in secular society began to increase, and the popularity of literature written in the vernacular, or commonly spoken languages of Europe, gained more and more acclaim and acceptance, especially in the forms of poetry and song.

Literary Precedents

Dante and Chaucer provided a transition between the medieval and Renaissance worlds. Dante Alighieri (DAHN-teh ah-lig-hi-EH-ree; 1265–1321) was the author of the *Divine Comedy*, one of the great masterpieces of world literature. Combining a deep religious impulse with a thorough knowledge of classical and medieval literature, Dante composed an allegory of medieval man (Dante) journeying through earthly existence (hell) through conversion (purgatory) to a spiritual union with God (paradise). Dante's work is regarded both as a culmination of the medieval intellectual tradition and at the same time as a composition of such unique brilliance that it should be considered one of the first creative works of the Renaissance.

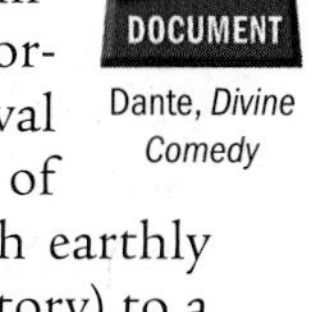

Dante, *Divine Comedy*

Geoffrey Chaucer (c. 1340–1400), the author of *Canterbury Tales,* wrote an English vernacular account of the journey of 29 pilgrims to the shrine of St. Thomas á Becket at Canterbury. His personality profiles and stories satirized contemporary English customs and lifestyles, and his work solidly established the vernacular as a legitimate literary form of expression in England.

Another voice reflective of the transition to a new age was one of the most gifted vernacular poets of the fourteenth century, Christine de Pizan (pi-ZAHN; 1365–c. 1430), who wrote to support her children after her husband's death. She authored more than ten volumes of poetry and prose, and her allegorical work—*The Book of the City of Ladies*—presented a defense of women's significance in society and a plea for greater compassion for their burdens.

"just price"—A medieval theory of economics supported by the Christian church. The church maintained that a just price should set the standards of fairness in all financial transactions. According to this theory, making interest on any loans was considered improper and labeled as *usury.*

1450

1450s Movable type used in printing

1453 Constantinople falls to Turks

1483–1546 Martin Luther

1500

c. 1500 Northern Renaissance begins (Erasmus, More, Rabelais, von Hutten, Montaigne, Cervantes, Shakespeare, van Eyck, Dürer, Bosch, Holbein, Brueghel)

c. 1500–1530 High Renaissance in Italy (da Vinci, Raphael, Michelangelo, Castiglione)

1509–1564 John Calvin, leader of Reformation in Geneva

1517 Luther issues Ninety-Five Theses

1524–1525 German Peasant Revolt

1527 Sack of Rome; Venice becomes center of Renaissance art (Titian)

1545–1563 Council of Trent

c. 1530–1600 Mannerist style popular (Parmigianino, Cellini)

Global Issues

Disease and Civilization

What is the relationship between disease and civilization?

Disease has always afflicted humans but its impact has varied throughout history. Prior to the Neolithic Revolution, it is likely that disease played a less significant role in the lives of our distant ancestors. Archaeology indicates that early hunter-gatherers experienced relatively disease-free lives. The small size of hunter-gatherer communities, their isolation from one another, their nomadic lifestyle, and their omnivorous, varied diet all contributed to limiting the contraction and spread of diseases. In a worst-case scenario, even if a single community were to be afflicted by an epidemic, the disease, however many individual lives it might claim, would likely run its course before it could be passed onto other communities.

Starting around 8000 B.C.E., humans began to practice agriculture and domesticate animals. Farming provided humans with larger and more reliable food supplies and kept them settled in fixed dwellings near their crops, trends that eventually led to larger populations and the rise of urban civilization. Densely populated towns and cities were unsanitary places, serving as ideal environments for the transmission of diseases. In such urban settings, people lived among human waste, consumed contaminated food and water, suffered dietary deficiencies due to over reliance on individual cereal grains like wheat or rice, and were exposed to illnesses transported by travelers and merchants. Worst of all, close proximity to livestock and vermin such as mice and rats meant that many animal diseases were able to bridge species and jump to human populations. Animals, in fact, have been the source of the majority of the epidemic diseases that have afflicted humanity, including influenza (pigs and poultry), measles (pigs), smallpox (cows), and, more recently, HIV/AIDS (monkeys). Even when animals weren't the immediate source of disease, they often served as vectors of transmission, which was the case with the Bubonic Plague or Black Death (carried by the fleas living on rats) and typhus (carried by the lice and fleas on livestock and vermin).

▲ Japanese woodblock print of the heroic archer, Tametomo, driving away smallpox demons.

In time, the growth of empires, improved transportation technology, and development of long-distance trade created far-flung networks by which diseases could develop and spread quickly. Many diseases then became endemic, embedded within human populations. Wherever people, goods, technologies, religions, and arts traveled, so too did bacteria and viruses. Eventually, trade routes spanned continents and crossed oceans, making possible pandemics—epidemic disease that swept through entire civilizations.

Prior to the rise of modern medicine and the acceptance of the germ theory of disease in the nineteenth century, human responses to epidemic disease were often more informed by superstition than an accurate understanding of what was making people sick. These responses ranged from theological conceptions about the origin of disease to attempts to prevent disease through quarantine—the segregation of the diseased. Medieval European Christians thought disease—like war, famine, and death—was a divinely willed punishment for sin and a stern call to repentance. The Chinese concept of the Mandate of Heaven suggested that pestilence, along with natural and human-made disasters, was a sign that Heaven had judged the reigning dynasty unfit to rule.

The historical impact of disease on civilization cannot be understated. At its worst, pandemic disease led to the collapse of complex communities, leaving them so depopulated that they could no longer maintain their economic and political structures. The survivors of such calamitous disease events had to adapt to new cultural circumstances, usually by making profound shifts in religious beliefs and social attitudes. The series of infectious diseases that struck the Roman Empire between 150 and 800 C.E. may have played a significant role in convincing people to abandon their old gods and accept Christianity. The Mongols' control of China and central Asia collapsed alongside the spread of Bubonic Plague throughout Eurasia in the mid-fourteenth century.

Disease could, conversely, aid states attempting to extend their political authority. The Spaniards conquered Central and South America in the early sixteenth century with invisible allies of enormous strength: smallpox and other diseases they unwittingly introduced to the Americas. These Old World diseases devastated indigenous populations who had never been exposed to diseases common in Europe, Asia, and Africa and thus had no built up resistance. Almost immediately, smallpox and other Eurasian diseases like measles compromised the capacity of the Aztec, Maya, and Inca to resist the Spanish. Over the first half of the sixteenth century it is estimated that these diseases killed the majority of the indigenous population in these civilizations.

But disease did not always aid conquerors. It could just as easily thwart them. From the fifteenth through nineteenth centuries, lethal diseases like malaria, yellow fever, dengue fever and sleeping sickness that were indigenous to sub-Saharan Africa greatly assisted African societies in staving off, at least for several centuries, European colonization. In the Americas, the Haitian Revolution was in part successful because half of the invading French army perished from yellow fever.

Attempts to control disease have varied. The earliest efforts relied on religious practices, ceremonies, and taboos. The latter were sometimes quite effective, as in the case of Manchurian nomads, who traditionally avoided marmots because they believed they were inhabited by the spirits of dead ancestors. This avoidance served a kind of "barrier," as the marmots and the fleas they carried harbored the Bubonic Plague. Traditionally, the most common effort to control disease was simply to segregate the sick from the healthy. While action of this sort might offer some protection, because of the prevalence of ignorance, prejudice, and hysteria, the aim of locking disease out of a community was often extended beyond those who were already ill to those who were deemed responsible for spreading of disease. In such instances, people might blame epidemic disease on specific ethnic groups; for example, during the Black Death in the fourteenth century, European Christians persecuted Jews because they believed them to be malevolent spreaders of the disease. In other instances, they blamed disease on individuals they considered witches. In rural parts of the developing world today, sorcerers and witches are still seen as a cause and potential cure for many diseases.

By far the most effective means to prevent disease has been the scientific approach to identifying and understanding diseases. Although medical knowledge has exploded during the past century, ancient societies also applied scientific study to fight disease. Greek physicians of the fifth century B.C.E. developed methods that continued into Roman times and that were passed down to Islamic and European societies in later centuries. Physicians in China and India developed similar medical traditions, producing notable works like "The Yellow Emperor's Classic of Medicine" and the compilation of *vedic* medical practices called the "Ayurveda" (Science of Life). These collections produced a fund of technical descriptions that diagnosed influenza, pneumonia, malaria, and tuberculosis, and led to an increasing understanding of how diseases worked. By the end of the nineteenth century, with the emergence of germ theory, the identification of microbes and viruses, and the development of vaccines and modern inoculation techniques (early forms of inoculation had originated in India and Africa centuries before), it became possible to control and even to eradicate diseases.

During the twentieth century, especially after the perfection of antibiotics in the 1940s, disease control entered a new era as cures or vaccines were developed for syphilis, cholera, yellow fever, polio, Bubonic Plague, leprosy, and rickets. Smallpox was even declared eradicated from the planet in 1980 (although Russia and the United States both keep stockpiles of the disease). But the emergence in the later decades of the twentieth century of resistant strains of several diseases such as syphilis and tuberculosis has led medical experts to wonder if the future of medicine will be a continuing struggle to keep the old diseases at bay. At the same time, new viruses like HIV/AIDS and avian flu threaten to mutate faster than medical science can respond. Until avian flu mutates into a form which can easily be passed from human to human, like common influenza, it only represents a potential threat to become a pandemic, although if this were to happen it would likely prove as deadly as the Spanish Flu of 1918–1919, which worldwide claimed between 50 and 100 million lives in just 18 months. HIV/AIDS, on the other hand, has already attained pandemic status. Since its identification in 1981, it has killed more than 25 million people around the world, most of them in Africa. Hopes for a vaccine against HIV/AIDS, and the more traditional killer malaria, have not yet been realized. Because the rise of air transportation has made it possible for any disease to move around the globe in hours, many experts feel that it is a question of *when,* not *if,* the next great pandemic will sweep the world.

Questions

1. Have humans always suffered from epidemics? Why and when did these begin to attack human populations?
2. What impact did epidemic diseases have on the societies they attacked?
3. What techniques have people used to control disease? How effective have these techniques been?

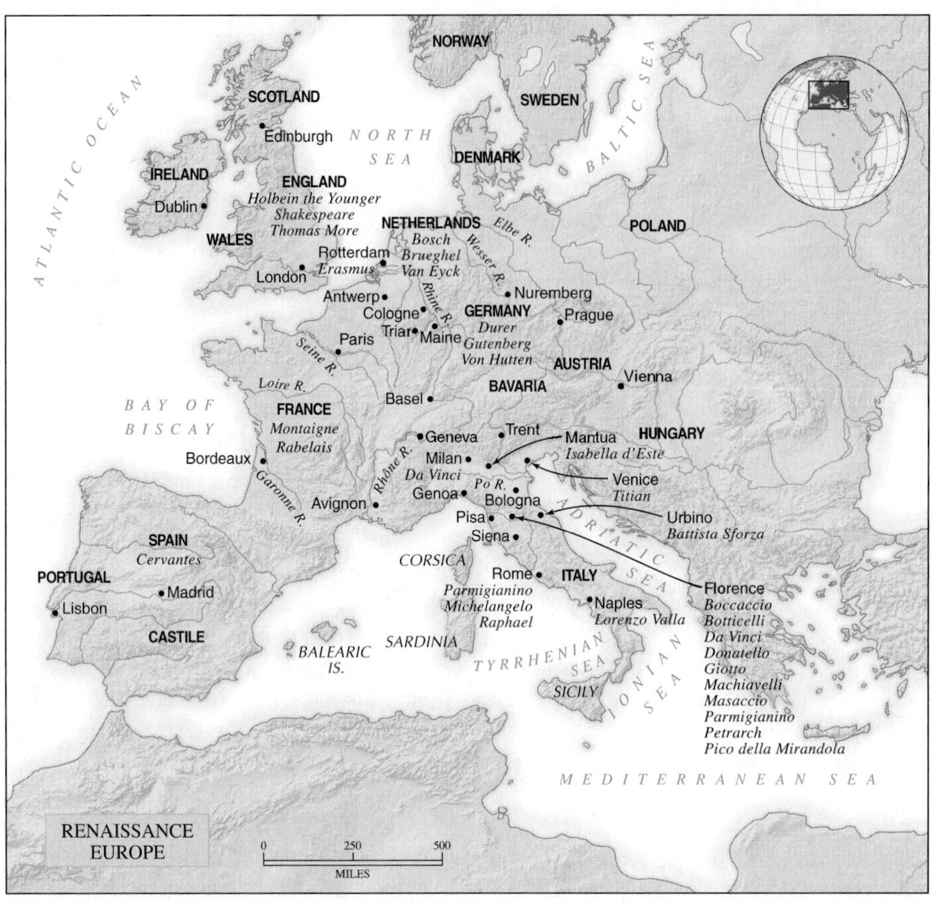

▲ This map illustrates Europe in the time of the Italian and Northern Renaissance, as well as some of the cities that served as centers for artistic and humanist activities during the period.

The Italian Setting for the Development of Humanism

In Italy during the fourteenth century, a growing number of literate and artistic individuals began to call themselves *humanists*—citizens of a modern world that would perfect itself through the recovery, study, and transmission of the cultural heritage of Greece and Rome. They believed themselves to be the initiators of a new era—a renaissance (rebirth) of the culture and values of classical antiquity. But this culture that historians now call the Italian Renaissance did not come into being without tremendous influence from its medieval past—in fact, many historians consider the Renaissance to be more of a natural maturation of medieval society than a radical break with traditional culture. Yet most students of the period agree that the heritage of the past, in combination with a newly found passionate concern with Greece and Rome and newly emerging political and economic patterns, produced a distinctly different culture.

During the fourteenth and fifteenth centuries, after recovering from the effects of the Black Death, the city-states of northern and central Italy experienced a tremendous growth in population and expanded to become small territorial states. Eventually five such states emerged: the duchy of Milan; the Papal States, in which the restored authority of the popes crushed the independence of many smaller city-states in central Italy; the republics of Florence and Venice; and the kingdom of Naples. Selling or leasing their country holdings, Italian nobles moved to the cities and joined with the rich merchants to form an urban ruling class. By 1300, nearly all the land of northern and central Italy was owned by profit-seeking urban citizens who produced their goods for city markets. In the large export industries, such as woolen cloth (the industry employed 30,000 in Florence), a capitalistic system of production, in which the merchants retained ownership of the raw material and paid others to finish the product, brought great profits. More great wealth was gained from commerce, particularly the import-export trade in luxury goods from the East.

So much wealth was accumulated by these merchant-capitalists that they turned to money-lending

Discovery Through Maps
The Lagoon of Venice

Maps can be designed to illustrate much more than merely the physical features of a geographical area. They may also be designed to serve as vehicles to enhance the image of a particular state—to serve as propaganda. For instance, examine this cartographic rendering of the Lagoon of Venice and the neighboring regions of Friulli and Istria, one of a series of magnificently designed maps painted by Ignazio Danti (1536–1586), a mathematician, astronomer, geographer, and Dominican priest and bishop—another example of the idealized "Renaissance man." Danti was commissioned by Pope Gregory XIII to make a number of maps of ancient and modern Italy, many of which are presently on display in the Vatican Museum in Rome. Danti's map of the Lagoon of Venice depicts an idealized land and seascape that features a bustling harbor, replete with sailing vessels both mythical and contemporary to the sixteenth century. Over the harbor the sun radiates its glory on the land and sea, and a formal inscription in Latin gives testimony to the ancient significance of the harbor and past glories.

The primary purpose of this map was certainly not to provide geographical assistance, but rather to promote the power and glory of the Republic of Venice. Such a map provided its observers with a sense of the historic significance of the Lagoon, its almost mythical role in the history of the Italian peninsula, and the opulence and splendor of one of the most significant republics of Renaissance Italy.

Questions to Consider

1. What seem to be the most significant features emphasized in this map of the Lagoon of Venice? Why does the artist appear to focus most of his attention on the sea rather than the land itself?
2. What effects do you think this map would have had on its viewers in the sixteenth century? What impressions do you believe Danti wanted to impart to his contemporaries who studied this map?
3. Why do you think Danti portrayed such a variety of vessels from different eras and subjects drawn from both pagan mythology and Christian tradition in the harbor?

The classic example of the Renaissance nobleman, statesman, and patron of the arts was the Florentine Lorenzo de' Medici, known as Lorenzo the Magnificent. Under his patronage and guidance, Florence became the leading city of the Italian Renaissance, renowned for the splendor of its buildings and lavish support for the arts.

and banking. From the thirteenth to the fifteenth centuries, Italians monopolized European banking (Florence alone had 80 banking houses by 1300). These economic and political successes made the Italian upper-class groups strongly assertive, self-confident, and passionately attached to their city-states. Even literature and art reflected their self-confidence.

Political leaders and the wealthy merchants, bankers, and manufacturers conspicuously displayed their wealth and that of their cities by patronizing the arts and literature. Artists and scholars were provided with governmental, academic, and tutorial positions and enjoyed the security and protection offered by their patrons and the advantage of working exclusively on commission. Among the most famous patrons were members of the Medici family, who ruled Florence for 60 years (1434–1494). Renaissance popes also were lavish patrons who made Rome the foremost center of art and learning by 1500.

Humanism and the Classical Revival: Petrarch and Boccaccio

Historians are not able to agree on an exact meaning of the Renaissance term *humanism*. But they generally agree that humanism consisted of the study and popularization of the Greek and Latin classics and the culture those classics described. The humanists, students of the classics as well as advocates of the Roman concept of a liberal education (or *studia humanitatis*), promoted an education in "humanistic studies," but also advocated civic patriotism and social betterment.

The humanists were also the founders of modern historical research and linguistics. Humanism was not an anti-Christian movement, and most humanists remained religious, but the church bureaucracy and the extreme authority claimed by the popes received their strongest criticism.

"Father of humanism" is a title given to Francesco Petrarca (frahn-CHEHS-koh peh-TRAHR-kah), better known as Petrarch (1304–1374), by later Italian humanists because he was the first to play a major role in making people conscious of the attractions of classical literature. He wrote Latin epic poetry and biography in addition to his famous and innovative love sonnets to a married woman named Laura, whom Petrarch admired romantically. Petrarch's works held to his Christian values, but displayed much more of a secular orientation and an involvement with the society and social issues of his day.

Petrarch, *Letter to Cicero*

Another celebrated early humanist was the Florentine Giovanni Boccaccio (gee-oh-VAH-nee boh-KAH-chee-oh; 1313–1375), a student and friend of Petrarch who began his career as a writer of poetry and romances. But his masterpiece was the *Decameron,* a collection of 100 stories told by three young men and seven young women as they attempted to avoid the Black Death in the seclusion of a country villa. The *Decameron* offers a wealth of anecdotes, portraits of flesh-and-blood characters, and vivid glimpses of Renaissance life.

The *Decameron* was both the high point and the end of Boccaccio's career as a creative artist. Largely through the influence of Petrarch, whom he met in 1350, Boccaccio gave up writing in Italian and turned to the study of antiquity. He began to learn Greek, composed an encyclopedia of classical mythology, and visited monasteries in search of manuscripts. By the time Petrarch and Boccaccio died, the study of the literature and learning of antiquity was growing rapidly throughout Italy.

Classical Revival and Philosophy

The recovery and absorption of Greek and Roman learning was a consuming passion of the humanists.

Document

Machiavelli, *The Prince*: On Cruelty and Mercy

Niccoló Machiavelli, born into an impoverished branch of a noble family of Florence, began his pubic life as a diplomat in the service of the Florentine republic. When the Medici family returned to dominate Florence in 1512, Machiavelli was imprisoned and tortured for his supposed plot against the Medici family. He then retired to the countryside to write his most famous works. Machiavelli's best known work is *The Prince* (1532), which presents a description of how a prince might best gain control and maintain power. His ideal prince is calculating and ruthless in his quest to best those who would destroy him in his effort to establish a unified Italian state. The following excerpts from this famous work describe how a prince must decide how, when, and if a prince should use cruelty or mercy to accomplish his aims:

From this arises an argument: whether it is better to be loved than to be feared, or the contrary. I reply that one should like to be both one and the other: but since it is difficult to join them together, it is much safer to be feared than to be loved when one of the two must be lacking. For one can generally say that about men: that they are ungrateful, fickle, simulators and deceivers, avoiders of danger, greedy for gain; and while you work for their good they are completely yours, offering you their blood, their property, their lives, and their sons, as I said earlier, when danger is far away; but when it comes nearer to you they turn away. And that prince who bases his power entirely on their works, finding himself stripped of other preparations, comes to ruin; for friendships that are acquired by a price and not by greatness and nobility of character are purchases but are not owned, and at the proper moment they cannot be spent. And men are less hesitant about harming someone who makes himself loved than one who makes himself feared because love is held together by a chain of obligation which, since men are a sorry lot, is broken on every occasion in which their own self-interest is concerned; but fear is held together by a dread of punishment which will never abandon you.

A prince must nevertheless make himself feared in such a manner that he will avoid hatred, even if he does not acquire love: since to be feared and not hated can very well be combined; and this will always be so when he keeps his hands off the property and the women of his citizens and his subjects. And if he must take someone's life, he should do so when there is proper justification and manifest cause; but, above all, he should avoid the property of others; for men forget more quickly the death of their father than the loss of their patrimony. Moreover, the reasons for seizing their property are never lacking; and he who begins to live by stealing always finds a reason for taking what belongs to others; on the contrary, reasons for taking a life are rarer and disappear sooner.... I conclude, therefore, returning to the problem of being feared and loved, that since men love at their own pleasure and fear at the pleasure of the prince, a wise prince should build his foundation upon that which belongs to him, and not upon that which belongs to others: he must strive only to avoid hatred, as has been said.

Questions to Consider

1. Comment on Machiavelli's speculations about the nature of man, and the ways in which a prince should capitalize on the reality of human character as he analyzes it. Is he overly cynical, or is he a realist?
2. Does Machiavelli's advice seem out of date given the realities of politics and the quest for power in the modern world?
3. What principles of conduct does Machiavelli advise a prince to cultivate? Is his prince a complete despot, or a more crafty and manipulative, yet ethical, student of man's nature?

From Peter Bondanella and Mark Musa, eds., *The Portable Machiavelli* (New York: Viking Press, 1979), pp. 135–136.

The search for manuscripts became a mania, and before the middle of the fifteenth century, original works, unedited by the church, of most of the important Latin authors had been found. In addition to these Latin works, precious Greek manuscripts were brought to Italy from Constantinople after it fell to the Turks in 1453, and many Greek scholars were welcomed to Italy, in particular to Florence, where the Medici gave their support to a gathering of Florentine humanists that came to be called the Academy. Under the leadership of the humanists Marsilio Ficino (mar-SEE-lee-oh fee-CHEE-noh; 1433–1499) and Pico della Mirandola (PEE-koh de-lah mee-RAHN-doh-lah; 1463–1494), the Academy focused its study on the works of Plato, and placed particular emphasis on Plato's admiration of human reason and free will. The influence of Aristotle still remained strong among Scholastic thinkers during the Renaissance, especially at the University of Padua, where the study of natural science, logic, and metaphysics continued to be emphasized. Scholasticism remained the dominant school of thought in the West from the ninth through seventeenth centuries, drawing its inspiration from Aristotle, St. Augustine, and the declared truths of the church (see Chapter 9).

A growing number of women were well educated, read the classics, and wrote during the Renaissance. Most of these women were daughters or wives of wealthy aristocrats who could afford private tutoring in liberal studies, since the universities were for the most part still inaccessible to females. But in the works of most humanists—echoing their classical precedents—there is little that supports the participation of women on equal footing with males in scholarly or civic activities. Some historians even maintain that Renaissance women were more restricted in their intellectual pursuits than they had been in the late Middle Ages. Still, some noble women gained great reputation and respect for their political wisdom and intelligence. Battista Sforza (SFOHR-zah), wife of the Duke of Urbino in the fifteenth century, was well known for her knowledge of Greek and Latin and admired for her ability to govern in the absence of her husband. Her contemporary, Isabella d'Este, wife of the Duke of Mantua, was renowned for her education and support of the arts, and for assembling one of the finest libraries in Italy.

	Major Artists of the Italian Renaissance and Their Works
c. 1266–1337	Giotto: *Life of the Virgin, Life of St. Francis, Life of St. John the Baptist*
1401–1428	Masaccio: *Tribute Money, Trinity, St. Peter*
1447–1510	Botticelli: *Judith and Holofernes, St. Sebastian, The Birth of Venus*
1452–1519	Da Vinci: *Adoration of the Magi, The Last Supper, La Gioconda* (Mona Lisa)
1475–1564	Michelangelo: Ceiling of the Sistine Chapel, *Moses, Pietá, David*
c. 1477–1576	Titian: *The Venus of Zerbine, The Allegory of Marriage, Venus and Adonis*

Italian Renaissance Art

How did Italian Renaissance artists differ from their medieval predecessors?

Fourteenth- and fifteenth-century Italian artists produced innovations that culminated in the classic High Renaissance style of the early sixteenth century. These innovations were the products of a new society centered in rich cities, the humanistic and more secular spirit of the times, a revived interest in the classical art of Greece and Rome, and the creativity of some of the world's most gifted artists.

From Giotto to Donatello

The new approach in painting was first evident in the work of the Florentine painter Giotto (JOT-toh; c. 1266–1337). Earlier Italian painters had copied the stylized, flat, and rigid images of Byzantine paintings and mosaics; Giotto observed from life and painted a three-dimensional world portraying believable human beings moved by deep emotion. He humanized painting much as Petrarch humanized thought and St. Francis, whose life was one of his favorite subjects, humanized religion. Giotto initiated a new era in the

▼ Giotto, *St. Francis Receiving the Stigmata* (c. 1295). Both a painter and architect, Giotto is credited as the first great genius of Italian Renaissance art. Like his medieval predecessors, his subjects were mainly religious, but his human subjects were portrayed as full of life and emotion. One of his favorite subjects was St. Francis of Assisi, who here receives the wounds of Jesus's crucifixion—the stigmata.

Masaccio, *Expulsion from Eden*. Masaccio's mastery of perspective creates the illusion of movement as the angel drives Adam and Eve from Paradise.

history of painting, one that expressed the religious piety of his secular patrons, but also his own delight in the images of everyday life.

In his brief lifetime, the Florentine Masaccio (mah-SAH-chee-oh; 1401–1428) completed the revolution in technique begun by Giotto. Masaccio was concerned with the problems of perspective, and the modeling of figures in light and shade (*chiaroscuro;* CHAH-roh-SKOO-roh). He was also the first Renaissance artist to paint nude figures (Adam and Eve, in his *Expulsion from Eden*), reversing the tradition of earlier Christian art.

Inspired by Masaccio's achievement, most *quattrocento* (quah-troh-CHEN-toh; Italian for "the 1400s" or "fifteenth century") painters constantly sought to improve technique. But the Florentine Sandro Botticelli (sahn-DROH boh-tah-CHEH-lee; 1447–1510) proceeded in a different direction, abandoning the techniques of straightforward representation of people and objects and trying instead to inspire the viewer's imagination and emotion through close attention to strikingly beautiful portraiture and decorative backdrop landscapes.

New directions were also being taken in sculpture, and like painting, it reached stylistic maturity at the beginning of the *quattrocento*. The Florentine Donatello (1386–1466) produced truly freestanding statues based on the realization of the human body as a coordinated mechanism of bones and muscles; his *David* was the first bronze nude made since antiquity.

Botticelli, *The Birth of Venus*. The last great Florentine painter of the early Renaissance, Botticelli did most of his best work for Lorenzo de' Medici and his court. In *The Birth of Venus,* Botticelli blends ancient mythology, Christian faith, and voluptuous representation.

The High Renaissance, 1500–1530: Leonardo da Vinci, Raphael, and Michelangelo

The painters of the High Renaissance had learned the solutions to such technical problems as perspective space from the *quattrocento* artists. The artists of the earlier period had been concerned with movement, color, and narrative detail, but painters in the High Renaissance attempted to eliminate nonessentials and concentrated on the central theme of a picture and its basic human implications.

The three greatest High Renaissance painters were Leonardo da Vinci, Raphael, and Michelangelo. Leonardo da Vinci (1452–1519) was brilliant in a variety of fields: engineering, mathematics, architecture, geology, botany, physiology, anatomy, sculpture, painting, music, and poetry. Because he loved the process of experimentation more than seeing all his projects through to completion, few of the projects da Vinci started were ever finished. He was a master of soft modeling in light and shade and of creating groups of figures perfectly balanced in a given space. One of his most famous paintings is *La Gioconda,* known as the Mona Lisa, a portrait of a woman whose enigmatic smile captures an air of tenderness and humility. Another is *The Last Supper,* which he painted on the walls of the refectory of Santa Maria delle Grazie in Milan. In this painting, da Vinci experimented with the use of an oil medium combined with plaster, which unfortunately was unsuccessful. The painting quickly began to disintegrate and has been restored several times.

Raphael (1483–1520) was summoned to Rome in 1508 by Pope Julius II to aid in the decoration of the Vatican. His **frescoes** there display a magnificent blending of classical and Christian subject matter and

fresco—A type of wall painting in which water-based pigments are applied to wet, freshly laid lime plaster. The dry-powder colors, when mixed with water, penetrate the surface and become a permanent part of the wall. The Italian Renaissance was the greatest period of fresco painting.

▼ Leonardo da Vinci, *Drawing of a Flying Machine*. One of the artist's later designs for a flying machine, which modern engineers speculate could have worked, although it was much too heavy. Da Vinci was convinced that a successful flying machine had to be modeled after the wings of bats and birds, as his numerous sketches of these animals show.

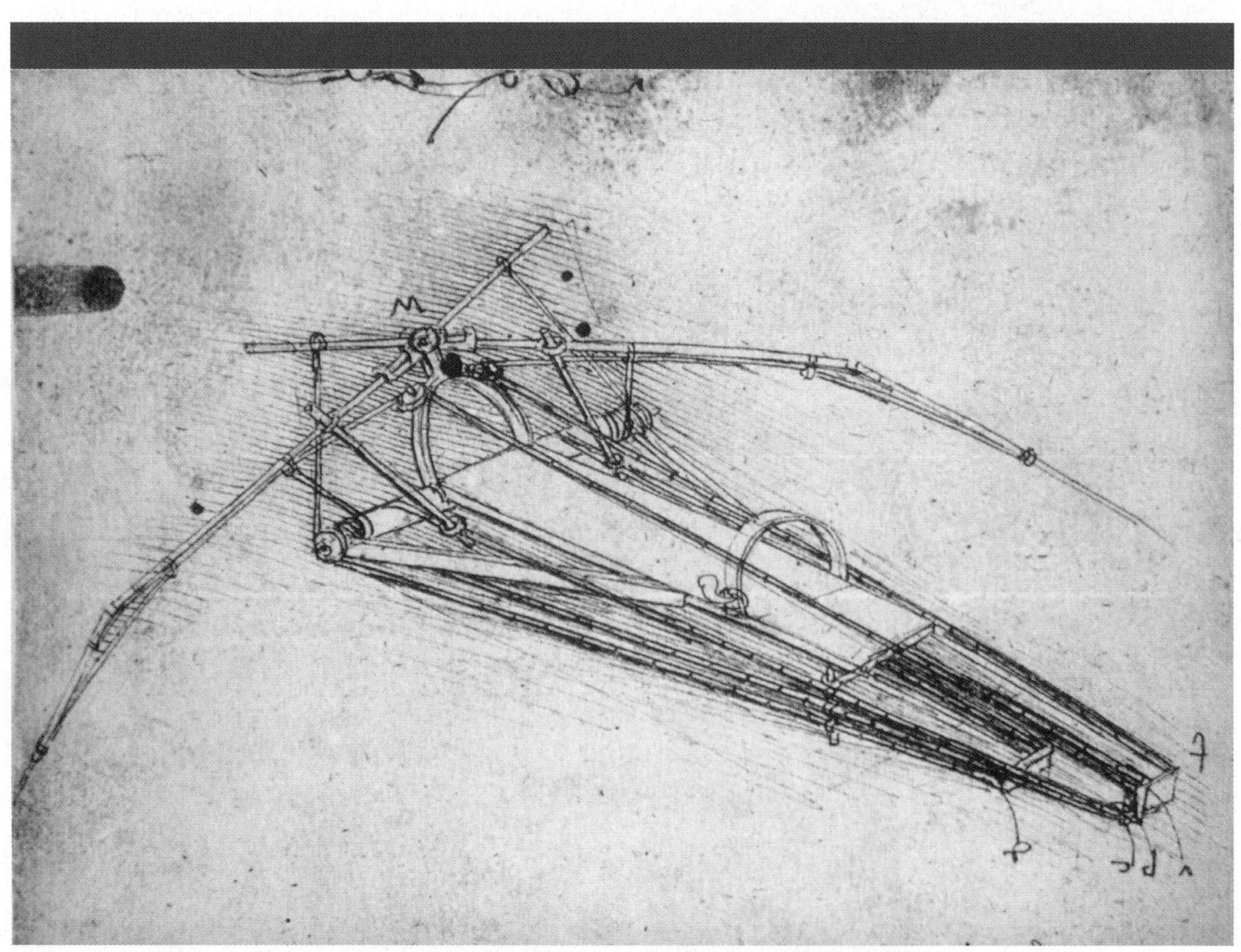

are the fruit of careful planning and immense artistic knowledge. Critics consider him the master of perfect design and balanced composition.

The individualism and idealism of the High Renaissance have no greater representative than Michelangelo Buonarroti (MEE-kel-AHN-je-loh boo-na-ROH-ti; 1475–1564). Stories of this stormy and temperamental personality have helped shape our definition of a genius. His great energy enabled him to paint the entire ceiling of the Vatican's Sistine Chapel for Julius II in 4 years. The ceiling covers an area of several thousand square yards, and his art embodies a

Raphael, *Madonna of the Meadow* (c. 1505/1506). Raphael's painting in oil on canvas is a classic example of a composition based on the figure of a pyramid. The scene is formally balanced yet features the interaction of the figures. The infants portrayed are John the Baptist (*left*) and Jesus.

superhuman ideal. With his unrivaled genius for portraying the human form, he devised a wealth of expressive positions and attitudes for his figures in scenes from Genesis. Michelangelo also excelled as poet, engineer, and architect and was undoubtedly the greatest sculptor of the Renaissance. The glorification of the human body was his great achievement. His statue of *David,* commissioned in 1501 when he was 26, expressed his idealized view of human dignity and majesty. He also became chief architect of St. Peter's in 1546, designed the great dome, and was still actively creative as a sculptor when he died, almost in his ninetieth year, in 1564.

From about 1530 to the end of the sixteenth century, Italian artists responded to the stresses of the age with a new style called *Mannerism*. Reacting against the classical balance and simplicity of High Renaissance art, Mannerist artists sought to express their own inner vision in a manner that evoked shock in the viewer. Typical are the paintings of Parmigianino (par-me-zhian-NI-no), whose *Madonna with the Long Neck* (1535) purposely shows no logic of structure.

▲ *The Madonna with the Long Neck* by Girolamo Parmigianino (1503–1540), one of the founders of the Mannerist school of painting. Rejecting conventional artistic forms, Parmigianino unnaturally elongated the Madonna's features to promote a new and purposefully shocking artistic effect.

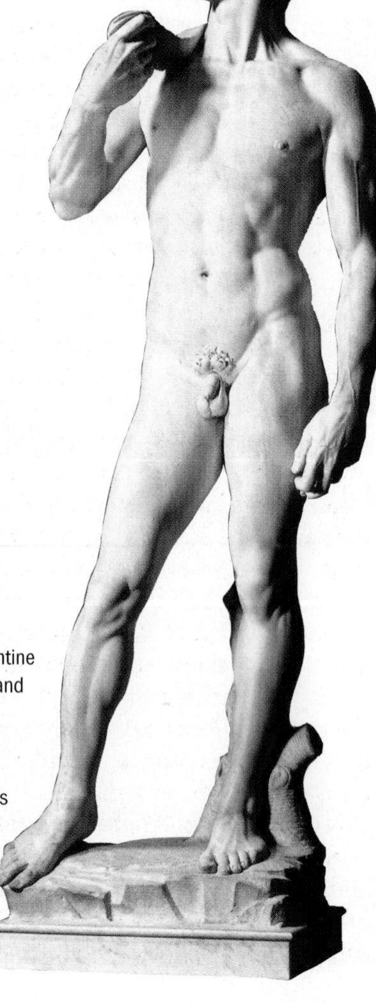

► Michelangelo, *David.* To Michelangelo, the Florentine painter, sculptor, poet, and architect, sculpture was the noblest of the arts. The large marble statue of the biblical David was commissioned in 1501 to stand in Florence as a symbol of the city, its government, and its culture.

The Northern Renaissance

How did the Northern Renaissance differ from the Italian Renaissance?

The Italian Renaissance, by seeking a rebirth in the classical world, had placed human beings once more in the center of life's stage and infused thought and art with humanistic values. These stimulating ideas spread north to inspire other humanists, who absorbed and adapted the Italian achievement to their own particular national and social circumstances.

Throughout the fifteenth century, hundreds of northern European students studied in Italy. Though the chief interest of most was the study of law and medicine, many were influenced by the intellectual climate of Italy with its new enthusiasm for the classics. When these students returned home, they often carried manuscripts—and later printed editions—produced by classical and humanist writers. Both literate laymen and clergy in the north were ready to welcome the new outlook of humanism, although these northern humanists were more interested in religious reform than were their Italian counterparts.

The Influence of Printing

Very important in the diffusion of the Renaissance and later in the success of the Reformation was the invention of printing with movable type in Europe. The essential elements—paper and block printing—had been known in China since the eighth century. During the twelfth century, the Spanish Muslims introduced papermaking to Europe; in the thirteenth century, Europeans in close contact with China, such as Marco Polo (see Chapter 10) brought knowledge of block printing to the West. The crucial step was taken in the 1440s at Mainz, Germany, where Johann Gutenberg (YOH-hahn GOOT-en-berg) and other printers invented movable type by cutting up old printing blocks to form individual letters. Gutenberg used movable type for papal documents and for the first printed version of the Bible (1454).

	Major Figures of the Northern Renaissance and Their Works
c. 1395–1441	Jan van Eyck (painter): *Man with the Red Turban, The Wedding Portrait*
c. 1466–1536	Desiderius Erasmus (humanist and scholar): *The Praise of Folly, Handbook of the Christian Knight*
1471–1528	Albrecht Dürer (painter): *Adam and Eve, The Four Apostles, Self-Portrait*
1478–1535	Sir Thomas More (humanist and diplomat): *Utopia*
c. 1483–1553	François Rabelais (writer): *Gargantua and Pantagruel*
1488–1523	Ulrich von Hutten (humanist and poet)
1547–1616	Miguel de Cervantes (writer): *Don Quixote*
1564–1616	William Shakespeare (playwright and poet): *Julius Caesar, Romeo and Juliet, King Lear*

Soon all the major countries of Europe possessed the means for printing books. Throughout Europe, the price of books sank to one-eighth of their former cost and came within the reach of many people who formerly had been unable to buy them. In addition, pamphlets and controversial tracts soon began to circulate, and new ideas reached thousands more people in a relatively short span of time. In the quickening of Europe's intellectual life, it is difficult to overestimate the effects of the printing press.

Humanism in France, Germany, Spain, and England

One of the best-known French humanists was François Rabelais (frahn-SWAH RAH-be-lay; c. 1483–1553), who is best remembered for his novel *Gargantua and Pantagruel*. Centering on figures from French folklore, this work relates the adventures of Gargantua and his son Pantagruel, genial giants of tremendous stature and appetite. Rabelais satirized his society while putting forth his humanist views on educational reform and inherent human goodness. He made powerful attacks on the abuses of the church and the hypocrisy and repression he found in contemporary political and religious practice.

Another notable northern humanist was the French skeptic Michel de Montaigne (mee-SHEL de mohn-TENYE; 1533–1592). At age 38, he gave up the practice of law and retired to his country estate and well-stocked library, where he studied and wrote. Montaigne developed a new literary form and gave it its name—the *essay*. In 94 essays he set forth his personal views on many subjects: leisure, friendship, education, philosophy, religion, old age, death. He advocated open-mindedness and tolerance—rare qualities in the sixteenth century, when France was racked by religious and civil strife.

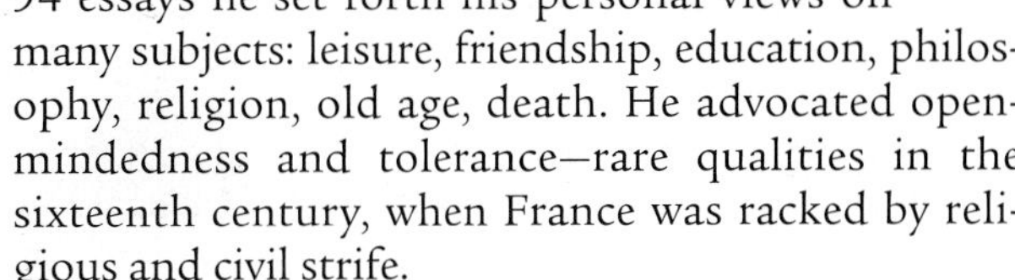

Montaigne, *Essays*

One of the most outstanding German humanists was Ulrich von Hutten (HOO-ten; 1488–1523). His idealism combined a zeal for religious reform and German nationalist feelings. This member of an aristocratic family, who wanted to unite Germany under the emperor, supported Martin Luther as a rallying point for German unity against the papacy, to which he attributed most of his country's problems.

In the national literatures that matured during the northern Renaissance, the transition from feudal knight to Renaissance courtier finds its greatest literary expression in a masterpiece of Spanish satire, *Don Quixote de la Mancha,* the work of Miguel de Cervantes (1547–1616). By Cervantes's time, knighthood and ideals of chivalry had become valueless in a world of practical concerns. Cervantes describes the adventures of Don Quixote (ki-HOH-te), a knight who is a

Seeing Connections

Marco Polo's *Book of Wonders*

This miniature painting is found in a circa 1410 copy of Marco Polo's *Book of Wonders* and depicts a hunting scene in Asia, along with an inset commemorating the meeting of that famous European traveler with Kublai Khan, the Mongol emperor of Yuan dynasty China. The fabulous tales recorded by Polo after his return from 17 years of service to the great Khan became the most popular travelogue in Europe for centuries.

Marco Polo (1254-1324) was a Venetian born into a family of wealthy traders. At the age of 17, young Marco accompanied his father and two uncles on a 3-year, 5600-mile-long journey through Armenia, Persia, Afghanistan, and then on the Silk Road to the court of the Great Khan in Cambaluc (Beijing). Marco stayed to serve his friend the Khan for the next 17 years, traveling extensively in Asia, observing cultures and customs never imagined by Europeans. A harrowing return by sea to Europe forced him to spend months in India and Africa. He arrived in Venice in 1295, and in the next few years began to record his observations and experiences. He called his account *The Description of the World,* and immediately copies were in great demand. Soon the work became known as *Il Milione* (The Million)—a disparaging label given to the work by his critics, who held that the traveler was presenting his readers with a million lies.

Polo's adventures and observations fascinated Europeans—his description of Mongol and Chinese culture and history, the geography of much India and Asia, innovations unknown in the West—Polo was particularly impressed with asbestos, the Chinese paper currency, and the government-run postal system. Many of his geographical observations were confirmed by European travelers in India and Asia in the eighteenth and nineteenth centuries. Christopher Columbus found the account inspirational, and kept a thoroughly annotated copy with him on his voyages to the New World.

Marco Polo died at 70 in Venice, believed by many, yet criticized as fanciful liar by others. He is said to have commented in his last moments that "I have only told the half of what I saw!" His place in history is assured not so much as a historian or geographer, but as an inspirational figure—an adventurer who stirred the imagination of many Europeans about exotic lands and cultures of high achievement and sophistication very different than their own.

representative of an earlier age. Don Quixote appears to be a ridiculous old man who desires the great days of the past and has a series of misadventures in his attempts to recapture past glories. But Cervantes's real objective was to expose the inadequacies of chivalry's ideals in a world that valued new and very practical aims. He did so by creating a sad but appealing character to serve as the personification of an outmoded way of life.

The reign of Queen Elizabeth I (1558–1603) was the high point of the English Renaissance and produced an astonishing number of gifted writers. Strongly influenced by the royal court, which served as the busy center of intellectual and artistic life, these writers produced works that were intensely emotional, richly romantic, and often wildly creative in combination with traditional poetic allusions to classical times.

The dominant figure in Elizabethan literature is William Shakespeare (1564–1616). His rich vocabulary and poetic imagery were matched by his turbulent imagination. He was a superb lyric poet, and numerous critics have judged him the foremost sonnet writer in the English language.

Shakespeare wrote 37 plays—comedies, histories, tragedies, and romances. His historical plays reflected the patriotic upsurge experienced by the English after the defeat of the Spanish Armada in 1588. For his comedies, tragedies, and romances, Shakespeare in most instances borrowed plots from earlier works. His great strength lay in his creation of characters and in

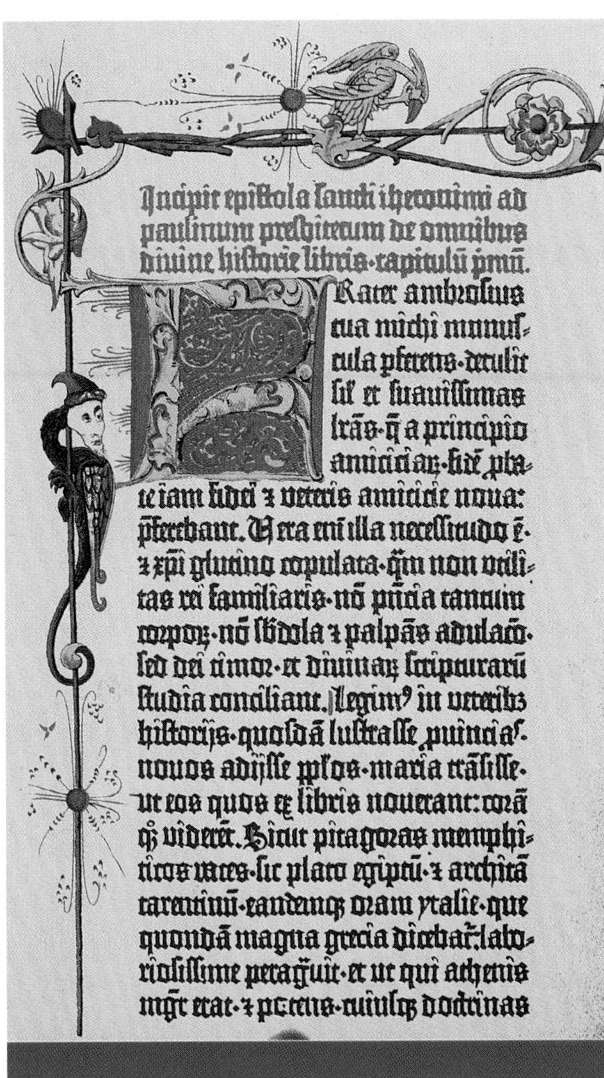

Incipit epistola sancti ieronimi ad
paulinum presbiterum de omnibus
diuine historie libris·capitulū pmū.
Frater ambrosius
tua michi munus-
cula pferens·detulit
sil et suauissimas
lrãs·q̃ a principio
amicicíar·fidé pba-
te iam fidei ⁊ ueteris amicicie noua:
pferebant. Uera enim illa necessitudo ē·
⁊ xpi glutino copulata·q̃m non utili-
tas rei familiaris·nõ p̃ncia tantum
corpoꝝ·nõ subdola ⁊ palpãs adulacō·
sed dei timor·et diuinaꝝ scripturarū
studia conciliant. Legim⁹ in ueteribꝫ
historiis·quosdã lustrasse puincias·
nouos adiisse ppłos·maria trãsisse·
ut eos quos ex libris nouerant: corã
q̃ uiderent. Sicut pitagoras memphi-
ticos uates·sic plato egiptū·⁊ architã
tarentinū·eandemq; oram ytalie·que
quondã magna grecia dicebatr: labo-
riosissime peragrauit·et ut qui athenis
mgr̃ erat·⁊ potens·cuiusq; doctrinas

◀ Facsimile copy of a page from the Gutenberg Bible, the Book of Genesis. With the development of printing, learning was no longer the private domain of the church and those few persons wealthy enough to own hand-copied volumes.

his ability to translate his knowledge of human nature into dramatic speech and action. Today his comedies still play to enthusiastic audiences, but it is in his tragedies that the poet-dramatist runs the gamut of human emotion and experience.

Northern Painting

Before the Italian Renaissance began to influence the artistic circles of northern Europe, the painters of the Low Countries—modern Belgium, Luxembourg, and the Netherlands—had been making significant advances on their own. Outstanding was the Fleming Jan van Eyck (YAHN van AIK; c. 1395–1441), who painted in the realistic manner developed by medieval miniaturists. Van Eyck also perfected the technique of oil painting, which enabled him to paint with greater realism and attention to detail. In his painting of the merchant Arnolfini and his wife, for example, he painstakingly gives extraordinary reality to every detail, from his own image reflected in the mirror in the background to individual hairs on the little dog in the foreground.

The first German painter to be influenced deeply by Italian art was Albrecht Dürer (1471–1528) of Nuremberg. Dürer made several journeys to Italy, where he was impressed both with the painting of the Renaissance Italians and with the artists' high social status—a contrast with northern Europe, where artists were still treated as craftsmen, not men of genius. His

▼ Jan van Eyck, *The Wedding Portrait*. The painting of a merchant named Arnolfini and his pregnant bride is extraordinary for its meticulously rendered realistic detail. Van Eyck painted exactly what he saw—he "was there," as his signature on the painting says (*Johannes de Eyck fuit hic*). The painting is also filled with symbolism; the dog, for instance, stands for marital fidelity.
Jan van Eyck, *The Wedding Portrait*, 1434. NG 186. © National Gallery, London.

▲ *St. Jerome in His Study,* one of the most popular engravings by the prolific German master Albrecht Dürer (1503–1540). The engraving depicts the scholarly Jerome working at his desk, surrounded by animals and objects of symbolic and allegorical significance.

own work is a blend of the old and the new and fuses the realism and symbolism of Gothic art with the style and passion of the Italian artists. In his own lifetime and after, Dürer became better known for his numerous engravings and woodcuts, produced for a mass market, than for his paintings.

Another famous German painter, Hans Holbein the Younger (1497–1543), chiefly painted portraits and worked abroad, especially in England. His memorable portraits blend the realism and concern for detail characteristic of all northern painting with Italian dignity.

Two northern painters who remained completely isolated from Italian influences were Hieronymus Bosch (hai-ROH-ni-muhs BAHSH; 1480–1516) and Pieter Brueghel (BROI-gel) the Elder (c. 1525–1569). Brueghel retained a strong Flemish flavor in his portrayal of the faces and scenes of his native land. He painted village squares, landscapes, skating scenes, and peasants at work and at leisure just as he saw them, with an expert eye for detail.

▼ Hieronymous Bosch, *Hell,* from *The Garden of Earthly Delights* (1503/1504). Part of a three-paneled altarpiece (a triptych) depicting the dreams that affect people in a pleasure-seeking world. The panel pictured here displays the horrors that await those sent to hell, where they spend their days tortured by half-human monsters, devils, and demons in a fantastic landscape.

Very little is known about the Dutch master Bosch other than that he belonged to one of the many puritanical religious sects that were becoming popular at the time. This accounts for his most famous painting, *The Garden of Earthly Delights,* a triptych whose main panel is filled with large numbers of naked men and women partaking in the sins of the flesh. The smaller left panel, by contrast, depicts an idealized Garden of Eden, and the right panel portrays a nightmarish hell filled with desperate sinners undergoing punishment. Bosch was a stern moralist whose obsession with sin and hell reflects the fears of many of his contemporaries—concerns that contributed to the religious movement known as the Reformation.

Erasmus, Thomas More, and Northern Humanism

The most influential of the northern humanists was Desiderius Erasmus (c. 1466–1536). Dutch by birth, he passed most of his life elsewhere—in Germany, France, England, Italy, and especially Switzerland. He corresponded with nearly every prominent writer and thinker in Europe and personally knew popes, emperors, and kings. He was *the* scholar of Europe, and his writings, translations of the classics and the works of the church fathers, as well as a new Latin translation of the New Testament, were eagerly read everywhere.

Perhaps the most famous and influential work by Erasmus was *The Praise of Folly,* a satire written in 1511 at the house of the English humanist Sir Thomas More. This influential work poked fun at and ridiculed a broad range of political, social, economic, and religious evils of the day. Erasmus's scholarship and the objects of his literary satire typify the central concerns of the northern humanists. They were interested not only in the classics, but in the Bible and early Christian writings. Their primary focus of reform was not civil society and the state, but morality and a return to the simplicity of early Christianity.

The most significant figure in English humanism was Sir Thomas More (1478–1535), a good friend of Erasmus. More is best known for his *Utopia.* In this work, More criticized his age through the portrayal of a fictitious sailor who contrasts the ideal life he has seen in Utopia (the "Land of Nowhere") with the harsh conditions of life in England. In Utopia, the evils brought on by political and social injustice were overcome by the holding of all property and goods in common. More's economic outlook was a legacy from the Middle Ages, and his preference for medieval collectivism over modern economic individualism was consistent with his preference for a church headed, in medieval tradition, by popes rather than kings. This view prompted Henry VIII, who had appropriated the pope's position as head of the Church of England, to execute More, who had been one of Henry's most trusted advisers and officials, for treason.

More, *Utopia*

▲ *Portrait of Erasmus* by Hans Holbein the Younger. Erasmus's scholarly achievements include a Greek edition of the New Testament and editions of the writings of St. Jerome and other early church fathers. Erasmus is best known, however, for his popular works, especially *The Praise of Folly.*

Erasmus and More transmitted humanist values and literary research skills throughout Northern Europe. Through their writings they contributed to the increasing demand for reform of the Catholic Church; however, neither man sought the Church's breakup. But the humanist's call for critical examination of texts and proof of literary authenticity resulted in a questioning of authoritative documents. **Polyglot** versions of the Bible were produced in printed form and quickly made available to literate laymen. Careful study of documents sometimes resulted in the discovery of inconsistencies and errors, some intentional. The Italian humanist Lorenzo Valla's study of the so-called Donation of

polyglot—A book, usually a Bible, containing the same text in several languages.

Constantine, a document in which the emperor supposedly granted the pope rule over Italy and the entire Western empire, found it to be a medieval forgery. Instances of such mistranslations and errors encouraged the church's critics to press for reform.

The Crisis in the Catholic Church: 1300–1517

What factors led to the erosion of church authority from 1300 to 1517?

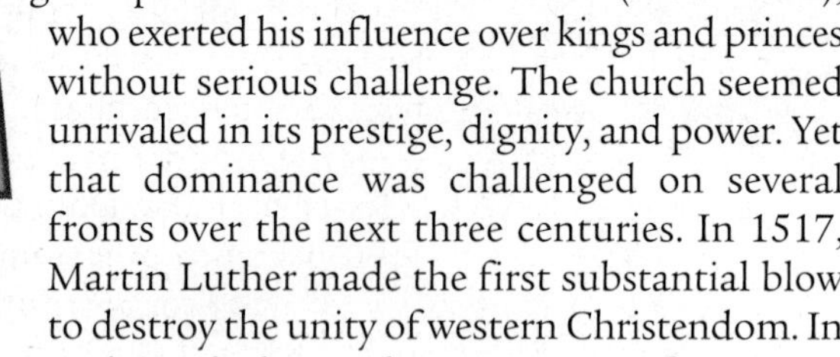

Religious Diversity in the Western World

The power of the medieval papacy reached its height during the pontificate of Innocent III (1198–1216), who exerted his influence over kings and princes without serious challenge. The church seemed unrivaled in its prestige, dignity, and power. Yet that dominance was challenged on several fronts over the next three centuries. In 1517, Martin Luther made the first substantial blow to destroy the unity of western Christendom. In so doing, he began the Protestant Reformation.

Boniface VIII

During the thirteenth century, papal supremacy came to be threatened by the growth of nation-states, whose monarchs challenged the church's legal and financial powers within their realms. Political leaders at all levels did not like to see the **tithes** and other fees collected in their lands going off to Rome. In addition, the papacy became regularly criticized by reformers who questioned the legitimacy of papal authority and the church's secular power and corruption. They believed the church had departed from the biblical examples of simplicity and piety. The bourgeoisie, the middle-class workers and craftsmen of the towns, were much more pragmatic and questioning than had been the rural peasantry of an earlier age. City people were more independent in their notions of religion, more skeptical about the church, and more patriotic in their loyalties to their king or country.

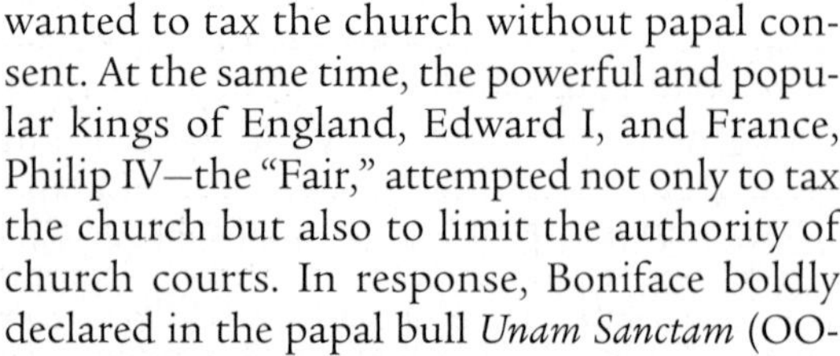

Boniface VIII, *Unam Sanctum*

Pope Boniface VIII (1294–1303) believed strongly in papal superiority and opposed any monarch who wanted to tax the church without papal consent. At the same time, the powerful and popular kings of England, Edward I, and France, Philip IV—the "Fair," attempted not only to tax the church but also to limit the authority of church courts. In response, Boniface boldly declared in the papal bull *Unam Sanctam* (OO-nam SANK-tam; 1302) that all temporal matters, and even rulers, were ultimately subject to the spiritual power wielded by the pope. Philip was not impressed. He demanded that the pope be brought to trial by a general church council. When this did not happen, in 1303, French officials and their allies broke into Boniface's summer home at Anagni, roughed the old man up, and attempted to arrest him and take him to France to stand trial. The pope was rescued by his supporters, but he died a month later, perhaps from the shock and physical abuse he suffered during the attack.

Role and Authority of the Pope

tithes—Contribution of a tenth of one's income to the Church. Tithing dates to the Old Testament and was adopted by the Western Christian church in the sixth century and enforced in Europe by secular law from the eighth century.

The Avignon Papacy

Philip's success was as complete as if Boniface had actually been dragged before the king to stand trial. Two years after Boniface's death, a French archbishop was chosen pope; he never went to Rome but instead moved the papal headquarters to Avignon (AH-vin-yahn), a city on the southern border of France, on land technically owned by the papacy. From 1305 to 1377, the popes and the papal court remained under strong French influence. During this Avignon papacy, also called the Babylonian Captivity of the church by those not pleased with French dominance, papal prestige suffered enormously. Most Europeans believed that Rome was the only proper capital for the church. Moreover, France's enemies—among them the English, Germans, and Italians—accused the popes and the cardinals, the majority of whom now were also French, of being instruments of the French king.

The Avignon papacy's abuses gave evidence to support the arguments of the critics and reformers who had already attacked the financial and moral corruption of the church. The Avignon popes increased their demands for more money from England, Germany, and Italy to finance their splendid lives in the newly built fortress-palace. To that end, they expanded the papal bureaucracy, added new church taxes, and collected the old fees more efficiently.

Wycliffe and Hus

With the abuses of the church at Avignon all too obvious, reformers across Europe began to call for not only an end to corruption, but also a change in church teaching and structure. In England, a professor of philosophy and theology at Oxford, John Wycliffe (WIK-lif; c. 1320–1384), attacked church abuses and some of the church's doctrines. He also worked for the English royal government of Richard II as a cleric attached to foreign missions and was employed to write pamphlets justifying the crown's seizure of church property.

Wycliffe was strongly influenced by the writings of St. Augustine and emphasized the primacy of the

Bible in the life of a Christian. He believed that God directly touched each person and that the role of the popes was of minor importance. In fact, he asserted, the kings had a higher claim on their subjects' loyalty, and the monarchs themselves were accountable only to God, not the pope. Wycliffe believed that the church is the community of believers, and not the Catholic hierarchy. He even went so far as to question the validity of some of the sacraments. Toward the end of his life, the Roman Church launched a counterattack, and after his death he was declared a heretic. In 1428, his corpse was taken from consecrated ground and burned, and his ashes were thrown into a river. In the church's eyes, this act condemned his soul to perpetual wandering and suffering and destroyed the possibility that Wycliffe's followers could preserve any parts of his body as relics. But the influence of his writings had already taken root in England through a group he helped organize called the "poor priests," later known as the Lollards, who were likewise condemned and outlawed, but they continued an underground church that surfaced in the sixteenth century.

In Bohemia, where a strong reform movement linked with the resentment of the Czechs toward their German overlords was under way, Wycliffe's opinions were popularized by Czech students who had studied with him at Oxford. In particular, his beliefs influenced John Hus (c. 1369–1415), a teacher in Prague and later rector of the university there. Hus's attacks on the abuses of clerical power led him to conclude that the true church was composed of a universal priesthood of believers and that Christ alone was its head. In 1402, after becoming the dominant figure at his university, he started to give sermons in the Czech language that soon attracted congregations as large as 3000 people. He preached that the Bible is the only source of faith and that every person has the right to read it in his own language. Like Wycliffe, Hus preached against clerical abuses and the claim of the church to guarantee salvation. This message became more explosive because it was linked with his criticism of the excesses of the German-dominated church at a time of a growing Czech nationalist movement.

In his preaching, he openly acknowledged his debt to Wycliffe and refused to join in condemning him in 1410. Hus was later excommunicated and called to account for himself at the Council of Constance in 1415. Even though he had been given the assurance of safe passage, he was seized and burned at the stake as a heretic, and his ashes were thrown into the Rhine. His death led to the Hussite wars (1419–1437), in which the Czechs withstood a series of crusades against them. They maintained their religious reforms until their defeat by the Habsburgs in the Thirty Years' War.

The Great Schism and the Conciliar Movement

In response to pressure from churchmen, rulers, scholars, and commoners throughout Europe, the papacy returned to Rome in 1377, and it seemed for a time that its credibility would be regained. However, the reverse proved true. In the papal election held the following year, the **College of Cardinals** elected an Italian pope. A few months later, the French cardinals declared the election invalid and elected a French pope, who returned to Avignon. During the Great **Schism** (1378–1417), as the split of the church into two allegiances was called, there were two popes, each with his college of cardinals and capital city, each claiming complete authority, each sending out papal administrators and collecting taxes, and each excommunicating the other. The nations of Europe gave allegiance as their individual political interests influenced them. The Great Schism continued after the original rival popes died, and each group elected a replacement. Doubt and confusion caused many Europeans to question the legitimacy and holiness of the church as an institution.

Positive action came in the form of the Conciliar Movement. In 1395, the professors at the University of Paris proposed that a general council, representing the entire church, should meet to heal the schism. A majority of the cardinals of both factions accepted this solution, and in 1409 they met at the Council of Pisa, deposed both popes, and elected a new one. But neither of the two deposed popes would give up his office, and the papal throne now, temporarily, had three claimants.

The intolerable situation necessitated another church council. In 1414, the Holy Roman Emperor assembled at Constance (discussed previously) the most impressive church gathering of the period. By deposing the various papal claimants and electing Martin V as pope in 1417, the Great Schism was ended and a single papacy was restored at Rome.

The Conciliar Movement represented a reforming and democratizing influence in the church. But the movement was not to endure, even though the Council of Constance had decreed that general councils were superior to popes and that they should meet at regular intervals in the future. Taking steps to preserve his authority, the pope announced that to appeal to a church council without having first obtained papal consent was heretical. Together with the inability of

---

College of Cardinals—Cardinals are the highest-ranking churchmen serving under the pope in the Catholic Church. Collectively, they constitute the Sacred College of Cardinals, and their duties include electing the pope, acting as his principal counselors, and aiding in governing the church.

schism—Literally a split or division (from the Greek *schizein,* to split). The word is usually used in reference to the Great Schism (1378–1417), when there were two, and later three, rival popes, each with his own College of Cardinals.

	Religious Reforms and Reactions
1415	John Hus, Bohemian reformer, burned at the stake
1437–1517	Cardinal Ximenes carried out reforms of Spanish Catholic Church
c. 1450	Revival of witchcraft mania in Europe
1452–1498	Savonarola attempted religious purification of Florence
1483–1546	Martin Luther
1484–1531	Ulrich Zwingli, leader of Swiss Reformation
1491–1556	Ignatius Loyola, founder of Society of Jesus (Jesuits)
1509–1564	John Calvin, leader of Reformation in Geneva
1515–1582	St. Teresa of Avila, founder of Carmelite religious order
1517	Luther issues Ninety-Five Theses
1521	Luther declared an outcast by the Imperial Diet at Worms
1534–1549	Pontificate of Paul III
1545–1563	Council of Trent
1561–1593	Religious wars in France

later councils to bring about much-needed reform and with lack of support for such councils by secular rulers, the restoration of a single head of the church enabled the popes to discredit the Conciliar Movement by 1450. Not until almost a century later, when the Council of Trent convened in 1545, did a great council meet to reform the church. But by that time the church had already irreparably lost many countries to Protestantism.

Although the popes refused to call councils to effect reform, they also failed to bring about reform themselves. Rather than address internal church problems, the popes instead busied themselves with Italian politics and the patronage of the arts. The issues of church reform and revitalization were largely ignored, as the church struggled to defend itself against the rising European political powers over issues such as control of taxes and fees, the courts, the law, and trade. The Catholic Church owned vast properties and collected fortunes in tithes, fees, and religious gifts, controlling, by some estimates, between a fifth and a fourth of Europe's total wealth. Impoverished secular rulers looked enviously at the church's wealth. Because the Atlantic states of England, France, and Spain were more unified, they were better able to deal with Rome than the states of the fragmented Holy Roman Empire.

No longer able to prevail over secular rulers by its religious authority alone after 1300, the papacy fared badly in an era of power politics in foreign relations. Free Italian cities, such as Venice and Florence, had helped build a new balance-of-power diplomacy after the 1450s. But the French invasion at the end of the fifteenth century made the peninsula an arena for desperate struggle between the Habsburg and French Valois (Val-WAH) dynasties that would last until 1559. The Papal States became a political pawn. The papacy's weaknesses were exploited by the troops of Charles V when they sacked Rome in 1527.

Spiritual and Intellectual Developments

The Roman Catholic Church faced more than just social and political challenges by 1500. At the lowest level, popular religion remained based on illiterate believers who worshipped for the magical or practical earthly benefits of the sacraments and the cults of the saints. In their short and grim lives, they were far from the political intrigue and sophisticated theological disputes that would trigger the Reformations and much closer to beliefs in the existence of ghosts, phantom grunting swine, and demons who might lurk around the next corner. Arguments between Augustinian and Dominican monks meant little, and dedication to the opinions of the pope in faraway Rome was weak. Of much greater concern was how to avoid going to hell, a possibility that was constantly in evidence during this time of fragile life and early death.

An increased belief in the existence of witches indicated the fear and superstition that dominated European life at the time. In response, in 1484, Pope Innocent VIII issued a *bull* dealing with the problem. Referring particularly to Germany, the pope stated that "it has recently come to our ears, not without great pain to us...[that] many persons of both sexes heedless of their own salvation and forsaking the catholic faith, give themselves over to devils male and female." The results of their evil works were "[to] ruin and cause to perish the offspring of women, the foal of animals, the products of the earth," among other disasters. The inquisitors Jacobus Sprenger and Henricus Institoris were ordered to go out with full powers to "exercise their office of inquisition and to proceed to the correction, imprisonment, and punishment" of witches. As spelled out in 1486 in the *Malleus maleficarum,* "The Hammer of Witches," the inquisitors had the full range of instruments of torture at their disposition.[1]

At the elite levels, during the fifteenth century, humanist reformers asserted that abuses in the

Catholic Church resulted largely from misinterpretation of Scripture by late medieval Scholastic philosophers and theologians (see p. 281). Northern humanists such as Sir Thomas More ridiculed later Scholastics as pedantic (see p. 433). Erasmus scathingly discussed the monks allied to the Scholastics in his *The Praise of Folly:*

> *Those who are the closest to these [the theologians] in happiness are generally called "the religious" or "monks," both of which are deceiving names, since for the most part they stay as far away from religion as possible and frequent every sort of place.... Though most people detest these men that accidentally meeting one is considered to be bad luck, the monks believe that they are magnificent creatures.... Many of them work so hard at protocol and at traditional fastidiousness that they think that one heaven hardly a suitable reward for their labor; never recalling, however, that the time will come when Christ will demand a reckoning of that which he had prescribed, namely charity, and that he will hold their deeds of little account.*[2]

Intellectual conflict was not new in Europe. But the means of communicating the nature and extent of the disagreements after the 1450s was new. The printing presses, after their European introduction in the 1350s, produced 6 million publications in more than two hundred European towns by 1500. There was a growing number of literate people with a thirst to read these books, most of which dealt with religious themes, and the result was the force of mobilized public opinion.

Some of these readers responded to critics, such as the Augustinian monks, who saw the Scholastics as presumptuous and worldly. Following the teachings of St. Augustine, they believed humans to be such depraved sinners that they could be saved not through "good works," as the Church taught, but only through personal repentance and faith in God's mercy. **Augustinians** accepted only Scripture as religious truth; they believed that faith was more important than the Scholastics' manipulated power of reason. And it was to the Augustinians that Martin Luther would turn to pursue his search for understanding.

Luther and the German Reformation

Why did the most important fracture in Christendom occur in Germany?

Martin Luther had no intention of striking the spark that launched the Protestant Reformation and more than a century of European conflict. Born in 1483, the son of an ambitious and tough Thuringian peasant turned miner and small businessman, he was raised by his parents, who in the name of Christian love, often punished him severely when he misbehaved. This contradictory upbringing of love and violence shaped his way of dealing with the world. Like many young boys of his time, he enjoyed the sometimes earthy and profane humor of his peasant society. Unlike many of his friends, he, as did St. Augustine 1200 years earlier, suffered guilt because of his own lustful passions and he became obsessed with fear of the devil and an eternity in hell. His parents wanted him to become a lawyer, and he did study law for 4 years. But Martin Luther was more concerned with his immortal soul. He became a monk following what was to him a miraculous survival in a violent thunderstorm. Until 1517, Luther's pursuit of his salvation was an intensely personal one, with little regard to the religious controversies of the time.

Martin Luther

The Search for Salvation

After he became an Augustinian at the age of 22, Martin Luther found comfort in being in a monastic community. But, even as a monk, Luther continued to be tormented by what he saw as his sinful nature and his fear of damnation. Then, in his mid-thirties, he read St. Paul's "Epistle to the Romans" and found freedom from despair in the notion of justification by faith: "Then I grasped that the justice of God is that righteousness by which through grace and sheer mercy God justifies us through faith. Thereupon, I felt myself to be reborn and to have gone through open doors into paradise."[3]

Luther entered into the religious debates of the age that became more spirited because of the widespread problems of the church in central Europe. He disagreed with the prevailing practices of buying and selling church offices and charging fees to give comfort through a variety of services to superstitious and sinful parishioners. But the practice that outraged Luther the most and brought him openly to oppose the Roman Catholic Church was the sale of indulgences. Theologically considered, indulgences were shares of surplus grace, earned by Christ and the saints and available for papal dispensation to worthy souls after death. Originally, they were not sold or described as tickets to heaven. By the sixteenth century, however, papal salesmen regularly peddled them as guarantees of early release from purgatory. It was one such salesman, a **Dominican** monk named Johan Tetzel (TET-zel) who infuriated Luther and drove him openly to oppose church practices.

Augustinians–Founded in 1256, a religious order dedicated to following of St. Augustine's life and teaching.

Dominicans–St. Dominic established this religious order in 1215 to go out into the world to teach and preach the word of God.

▲ Lucas Cranach, *Martin Luther and His Friends*. That Martin Luther (*left*) and other Protestant reformers did not suffer the same fate as John Hus a century earlier was largely due to the political support of rulers such as the Elector Frederick of Saxony (*center*).

Tetzel had been commissioned by Pope Leo X and Archbishop Albert of Mainz. At the papal level, the sale of indulgences was part of a large undertaking by which Pope Leo X hoped to finance completion of St. Peter's Basilica in Rome. The Archbishop of Mainz received 50 percent of the money from the sale of Tetzel's indulgences for his own purposes. Tetzel used every appeal to crowds of the country people around Wittenberg (vit-en-BERG), begging them to aid their deceased loved ones and repeating the slogan "A penny in the box, a soul out of purgatory."[4] Luther and many other Germans detested Tetzel's methods and his Roman connections. He also rejected Tetzel's Dominican theology, which differed from his own Augustinian beliefs.

There are moments in history when the actions of a single person will link all of the prevailing and contrasting currents of an era into an explosive mixture. In Wittenberg on October 31, 1517, Martin Luther issued his Ninety-Five Theses, calling for public debate—mainly with the Dominicans—on issues involving indulgences and basic church doctrines. This document was soon translated from Latin into German and published in all major German cities. The Theses denied the pope's power to give salvation and declared that indulgences were not necessary for a contrite and repentant Christian. Number 62, for example, stated that the "true treasure" of the Church was the "Holy Gospel of the Glory and Grace of God," and number 36 indicated that Christians truly desiring forgiveness could gain it without "letters of pardon." The resulting popular outcry forced Tetzel to leave Saxony, and Luther was almost immediately hailed as a prophet, directed by God to expose the pope and a corrupt clergy.

His message was so well received because it satisfied those who wanted a return to simple faith; it also appealed to those, like the humanists, who fought church abuses and irrational authority. Luther's message provided an outlet for German resentment against Rome, and it gave encouragement to princes seeking political independence. The ensuing controversy, which soon raged far beyond Wittenberg, split all of western Christendom and focused and strengthened the social, economic, and political contradictions of the time.

Luther's message and its wide acceptance made him a public figure, and the Roman Catholic church hierarchy began to attack him. Although Pope Leo X (1513–1521) was not immediately alarmed, the Dominicans levied charges of heresy against their Augustinian competitor. Having already begun his defense in a series of pamphlets, Luther continued in 1519 by debating the eminent theologian John Eck (1486–1543) at Leipzig (LEIP-zig). There Luther denied the **infallibility of the pope** and church councils, declared the Scriptures to be the sole legitimate doc-

infallibility of the pope—The belief that popes cannot be wrong in matters of faith and doctrine.

trinal authority, and proclaimed that salvation could be gained only by faith. That same year, a last effort at reconciliation failed completely, and in June 1520 Luther was excommunicated by the pope.

Charles V, only recently crowned emperor and aware of Luther's increased following among the princes, afforded the rebellious monk an audience before the **Imperial Diet** at Worms in 1521 to hear his defense of statements against church teachings and papal authority. If Luther recanted, he could perhaps escape his excommunication and execution. After much discussion, when the Orator of the Empire finally asked if he was prepared to recant, Luther responded:

> *Your Lordships demand a simple answer. Here it is, plain and unvarnished. Unless I am convicted of error by the testimony of Scripture or (since I put no trust in the unsupported authority of Pope or of councils, since it is plain that they have often erred and often contradicted themselves) by manifest reasoning I stand convicted by the Scriptures to which I have appealed, and my conscience is taken captive by God's word, I cannot and will not recant anything, for to act against our conscience is neither safe for us, nor open to us. On this I take my stand, I can do no other. God help me. Amen."*[5]

The Diet finally declared him an outcast. Soon afterward, as he left Worms, Luther was taken for his own protection to Wartburg (VART-burg) Castle by Elector Frederick of Saxony, his secular lord. He would not burn at the stake, as did John Hus, because he enjoyed substantial political and popular support. His message had been spread by the 300,000 copies of his 30 works printed between 1517 and 1520. He was now a German hero.

The Two Kingdoms: God and the State

At Wartburg, Luther organized an evangelical church, separate and distinct from Rome. Although he denounced much of the structure, formality, and ritual of the Catholic Church, Luther spent much of his time after the Diet of Worms building a new structured, formal church with new rituals for his followers.

The church he built reflected his main theological differences with Rome, while keeping most traditional Christian ideas and practices. The fundamental principle of the Lutheran creed was that salvation occurred *only* through faith that Christ's sacrifice alone could wash away sin. Luther rejected the Catholic doctrine that salvation could be gained only by faith, good works, and following Roman Catholic prescribed dogmas and rituals.

Another major change instituted by Luther touched the most essential part of the Christian ritual, the commemoration of the Last Supper. Luther rejected the notion that at communion a priest performed a ritual that transformed the bread and wine into Christ's actual body and blood. He instead believed that the divine presence automatically "coexisted" with the wafer and the wine, and the Lutheran Communion involved all baptized people who attended services. Other changes included church services in German instead of Latin, an emphasis on preaching, the abolition of monasteries, and the curtailment of formal ceremonies foreign to the personal experiences of ordinary people. The Lutheran Church claimed to be a "priesthood of all believers" in which each person could receive God directly or through the Scriptures. To that end, Luther translated the Bible from Latin into German and composed the sermons that would be repeated in hundreds of Lutheran pulpits all over Germany and Scandinavia.

During the 1520s, his views drew numerous women to Wittenberg, where they found refuge from convents or their Catholic husbands. Among them was the former nun Katherine von Bora. Luther's final break with his Catholic past came when he took off his clerical habit in 1523 and 2 years later married her. She bore him six children—two died in their infancy—raised his nieces and nephews, managed his household, secured his income, entertained his colleagues, and served as his supportive—if argumentative—companion. He stressed the importance of wives as marriage partners for both the clergy and the **laity**. Contrary to Catholic doctrine, he even condoned divorce in cases of adultery and desertion.

Luther's ideas on marriage and Christian equality promised women new opportunities, which were only partly realized. Some Lutheran women became wandering preachers, but they evoked protests from male ministers and legal prohibitions from many German municipal councils, including those of Nuremberg and Augsburg. Although first teaching that women were equal to men in opportunities for salvation and in their family roles, in his later writings, Luther described them as subordinate to their husbands and not meant for the pulpit. A religious revolutionary in so many ways, Luther was unable to shed the Christian church's 1500-year-old view—dating back to the writings of St. Paul (see p. 149)—that women were sources of temptation and not capable of serious thought.

Luther brought major changes in more than theological concerns. In worldly affairs, he recognized two

Imperial Diet—A meeting of the political and religious leaders of the various member states of the Holy Roman Empire.

laity—The community of believers in the Christian Church, served by the clergy, the trained and specialized leaders of the community.

DOCUMENT
Sermon at the Castle Pleissenberg

main human spheres of human obligation: the first and highest duty was to God. The next duty involved a loyalty to earthly governments, which also existed in accordance with God's will. Luther's idea of "two kingdoms," one of God and one of the world, helped kings and princes wanting to be free of Rome's domination, and won him support from German and Scandinavian rulers who connected his church to their own dynasties. Luther's political orientation was clearly revealed in 1522 and 1523 during a rebellion of German knights. When Lutheran support was not forthcoming, the rebellion was quickly crushed. Luther took no part in the struggle but was embarrassed by opponents who claimed his religion threatened law and order.

Another example of Luther's political and social conservatism was provided by a general revolt of peasants and discontented townsmen in 1524 and 1525. Encouraged by Lutheran appeals for Christian freedom, the rebels drew up petitions asking for religious autonomy. At first Luther expressed sympathy for the requests, particularly for each congregation's right to select its own pastor. Then, one of the movement's leaders, Thomas Muentzer, radicalized the movement by calling for an end to earthly authority, however constituted, and the creation of a primitive communist society of equality and shared goods, governed under Christian principles. In response to the violent uprisings that erupted throughout central Germany in April and May 1525, imperial and princely troops crushed the rebel armies, killing an estimated 90,000 insurgents. Luther had advised rebel leaders to obey their rulers' law as God's will; when they turned to war, he penned a virulent pamphlet, *Against the Thievish and Murderous...Peasants.* In it he called on the princes to "knock down, strangle,...stab,...and think nothing so venomous, pernicious, or Satanic as an insurgent."[6]

There was soon a struggle for religious control in Germany between the Holy Roman Emperor—the defender of the Catholic church—and the Lutheran princes. When Catholics sought to impose conformity in Imperial Diets during the late 1520s, Lutheran leaders drew up a formal protest (hence the title *Protestant*). After this Augsburg Confession (1530) was rejected, the Lutheran princes organized for defense in the Schmalkaldic League. Because Charles V was preoccupied with the French and the Turks, open hostilities were minimized, but a sporadic civil war dragged on until after Luther's death in 1546. It ended with the Peace of Augsburg in 1555, when the imperial princes were permitted to choose between Lutheranism and Catholicism in their state churches, thus increasing their independence from the emperor. In addition, Catholic properties confiscated before 1552 were retained by Lutheran principalities, which provided a means for financing their policies. Although no concessions were made to other Protestant groups, such as the Calvinists, this treaty shifted the European political balance against the empire and the church.

Outside Germany, Lutheranism furnished a religious stimulus for developing national monarchies in Scandinavia. There, as in Germany, rulers welcomed not only Lutheran religious ideas but also the chance to acquire confiscated Catholic properties. They appreciated having ministers who preached obedience to constituted secular authority. In Sweden, Gustavus Vasa (goos-TA-vus VAH-sah; 1523–1560) used Lutheranism to lead a successful struggle for Swedish independence from Denmark. In turn, the Danish king, who also ruled Norway, issued an ordinance in 1537 establishing the national Lutheran Church, with its bishops as salaried officials of the state. Throughout eastern Europe, wherever there was a German-speaking community, the Lutheran church spread—for a brief time even threatening the supremacy of the Catholic Church in Poland and Lithuania.

Henry VIII and the Anglican Reformation

What were the political considerations impelling Henry VIII to create the Anglican Church?

In the fourteenth and fifteenth centuries, England suffered under the same economic and social crises and changes that the rest of Europe did. But unlike in the Germanies, England was one of the new Atlantic states characterized by national monarchies, centralized authority, and greater independence from the papacy. The Tudor dynasty's (1485–1603) rise to power following the Hundred Years' War (see p. 454) and the devastating War of the Roses (see p. 455) had destroyed much of the traditional nobility.

Legitimate Heirs and the True Church

In a monarchy, one of the prime duties of a king and his queen was to produce and raise a strong and healthy heir—preferably male—to ensure the continuity of the dynasty. Henry VII found himself in the fortunate position of having two strong heirs to further the Tudor line and increase the strength of England. The first son, Arthur, died in 1502 at the age of 16, 1 year after his dynastic marriage to Catherine of Aragon of Spain. Henry VIII (1509–1547)—5 years younger—then became the heir to the English throne. It had not been expected that he would be king, and his education ran to that of a true Renaissance man. He showed talent in music, literature, philosophy, jousting, hunting, and theology. However, not only did he become the king of England on his father's

◀ The Dutch artist Michael Sittow served as the official court painter for the English king Henry VII, and in that capacity he created this portrait of Catherine of Aragon shortly after the death of her husband, the heir apparent Prince Arthur Tudor, in 1502. Sittow captured the grace and strength of the Spanish princess during her time of mourning, and the beauty and intelligence that would captivate Arthur's brother, Henry VIII, when he married Catherine to cement the Anglo-Spanish alliance.

death in 1509, but he also married the woman who had been his brother's wife, Catherine of Aragon (1485–1536), thus continuing the dynastic alliance with Spain. Catherine was a cultured, strong, respected woman and devoted wife: she successfully oversaw a war against Scotland when Henry was campaigning in France. She and her husband immediately turned to their duty to produce an heir: the first effort ended in a miscarriage in early 1510; on January 1, 1511, she carried to term and produced a son, who died in February.

Henry was both an active player in diplomacy on the continent and a devout Roman Catholic who gained the title "Defender of the Faith" from Pope Leo X for a pamphlet he wrote denouncing Luther and his theology. However, his immediate problem in the 1520s was the lack of a male heir. After 11 years of marriage, he had only a sickly daughter and an illegitimate son. His queen, after four earlier pregnancies, gave birth to a stillborn son in 1518: by 1527, when she was 42, Henry had concluded that she could have no more children. His only hope for the future of his dynasty seemed to be a new marriage and a new queen. This, of course, would require the end of his marriage to Catherine. In 1527, he appealed to the Pope Clement VII (1523–1534), asking for an **annulment** stating that the marriage itself was invalid and had never taken place.

Normally, the request would probably have been granted; the situation at that time, however, was not normal. Because she had been the wife of Henry's brother, Catherine's marriage to Henry had necessitated a papal dispensation, based on her oath that the first marriage had never been consummated. Now Henry professed concern for his soul, tainted by "living in sin" with Catherine. He also claimed that he was being punished, citing a passage in the Book of Leviticus that predicted childlessness for the man who married his dead brother's wife. The pope was sympathetic and certainly aware of an obligation to the king, who had strongly supported the church. However, granting the annulment would have been admission of papal error, perhaps even corruption, in issuing the earlier dispensation. Added to the Lutheran problem, this would have doubly damaged the papacy. A more immediate concern for Henry was Catherine's nephew. As the aunt of Charles V, whose armies occupied Rome in 1527, she was able to indirectly exert considerable pressure on the pope to refuse an annulment.

When Pope Clement delayed a decision, Henry began to rally his support at home. During the 3 years after 1531, when Catherine saw him for the last time, Henry took control of affairs. Sequestering his daughter Mary (1516–1558) and his banished wife in separate castles, he forbade them from seeing each other. The king forced the English clergy into proclaiming him head of a separate, English church "as far as the law of Christ allows." Clergymen or any others who refused to recognize Henry's new religious authority found themselves hanged or executed, which was the fate that befell Sir Thomas More in 1535. Henry then extracted from Parliament the authority to appoint bishops, and designated his willing tool Thomas Cranmer (1489–1556) as archbishop of Canterbury. In 1533, Cranmer pronounced Henry's marriage to Catherine invalid; at the same time, he legalized his union with Anne Boleyn (bo-LIN), a lady of the court who was carrying his unborn child, the future Elizabeth I. Henry even forced his daughter Mary to accept

---

annulment–A religious or political judgment that a marriage was/is not valid and hence no longer existed/exists.

Document

Anne Ayscough (Mrs. Thomas Kyme), English Protestant Martyr

Anne Ayscough, the daughter of Sir William Ayscough, received a good education and became remarkably independent at a time when the normal expectation was that a woman's role was to look after the house and be able to entertain guests. She read voraciously, especially Tyndale's version of the New Testament, and participated vigorously in the theological controversies of her time. She did not like the papacy, nor did she much like Henry's VIII's pet theologians and their version of English Catholicism—the Anglican Church. Duty to her family forced her to marry a Catholic husband, but soon he was not pleased when she set out to spread the Gospels by reading from the Bible to the peasants—a practice later forbidden by the law of 1543. For Anne the issues were quite clear: "[T]he papists were the agents of Antichrist and would always be opposed to the Saints of God...." In standing upon her own righteousness and excluding from her heart all love of her enemies, Anne Ayscough was very much a child of her age. In 1545, she was called to London to face charges of heresy. She was then tortured—the only woman in English history put on the rack, tried, and found guilty for her refusal to believe that the wafer literally becomes the body of Christ in the communion, a process called transubstantiation.

On the eve of her execution, she wrote: "O friend most dearly beloved in God, I marvel not a little what should move you to judge in me so slender a faith as to fear death, which is the end of all misery. In the Lord I desire you not believe of me such weakness. For I doubt it not but God will perform his work in me, like as he hath begun. I understand the Council is not a little displeased, that it should be reported abroad that I was racked in the Tower. They say now that what they did there was but to frighten me; whereby I perceive they are ashamed of their uncomely doings and fear much lest the King's majesty should have information thereof. Wherefore they do not want any man to tell it abroad. Well, their cruelty God forgive them."

At the same time, she wrote Henry VIII: "I Anne Ayscough, of good memory, although God hath given me the bread of adversity and the water of trouble (yet not so much as my sins have deserved), desire this to be known unto your Grace. Forasmuch as I am by the law condemned for an evil-doer, here I take heaven and earth to record that I shall die in my innocence. And according to what I have said first and will say last, I utterly abhor and detest all heresies. And as concerning the Supper of the Lord, I believe so much as Christ hath said, therein, which he confirmed with his most blessed blood, I believe so much as he willed me to follow, and I believe so much as the Catholic church of him doth teach. For I will not forsake the commandment of his holy lips...."

And as she was taken out to be executed, her final prayer was written down: "O Lord, I have more enemies now than there be hairs on my head. Yet, Lord, let them never overcome me with vain words, but fight thus, Lord, in my stead, for on thee cast I my care. With all the spite they can imagine they fall upon me, which am thy poor creature. Yet, sweet Lord, let me pay no heed to them which are against me, for in thee is my whole delight. And, Lord, I heartily desire of thee, that thou wilt of thy most merciful goodness forgive them that violence which they do and have done unto me. Open also thou their blind hearts, that they may hereafter do that thing in thy sight, which is only acceptable before thee, and to set forth thy verity aright, without all vain fantasy of sinful men. So be it, O Lord, so be it."

Anne Ayscough was burned at the stake with four companions on July 16 1546. Already viewed as a heroine by many in England, she became the best known English martyr.

Questions to Consider

1. What was there in Anne Ayscough's views that provoked such a harsh response from the leaders of the English Church, such as putting her on the rack?
2. Why were heretics burned at the stake and not, for example, hanged, or decapitated?
3. What qualities earn a person such as Anne Ayscough the accolade of being a "martyr"? What is a martyr? Whom would you consider to be martyrs during the twentieth century?

From Derek Wilson, *A Tudor Tapestry: Men, Women and Society in Reformation England* (London: Heinemann, 1972), pp. 164, 229-232.

him as head of the church and to admit the illegality of her mother's marriage—by implication acknowledging her own illegitimacy. Parliament also ended all payment of revenues to Rome.

Now, having little other choice, the pope excommunicated Henry, making the breach official on both sides. On his side, Henry divided up the Church's properties—an estimated 25 percent of the wealth of the realm—to distribute to the gentry to consolidate his domestic support. In 1539, Parliament completed its seizure of monastery lands and the wealth of pilgrimage sites such as Canterbury Cathedral. Meanwhile, in the north of England, there were mass uprisings against Henry's decisions to shut down the monasteries: the king bloodily stopped these and imposed his control.

There had already been a strong religious resistance movement present in England even before Henry came to power. English theologians, beginning with John Wycliffe and his followers, played an active role in the intellectual and theological debates of the High Middle Ages. During the fifteenth and first part of the sixteenth centuries, there was an active underground church, the Lollards, in which lay people—especially women—played an important role. William Tyndale's (1494–1536) skillful translation of the New Testament, a work marked by Lutheran influences, served as the basis for the English Bible published in 1537, which made scripture available to all literate English-speaking people. This popular Protestantism was not at all close to the new Anglican Church, which brought about little change in doctrine or ritual. The Six Articles, Parliament's declaration of the new creed and ceremonies in 1539, reaffirmed most Catholic theology except papal supremacy. Because of the king's need for a fertile wife, and for no other reason, a new English church was created.

Radical Protestants and Renewed Catholics

In his later years, after the decapitation of Anne Boleyn on charges of adultery in 1536 (the year that Catherine of Aragon also died), Henry grew increasingly suspicious of popular Protestantism, which grew rapidly, supported as it was by reformist movements spreading into England and Scotland from the Continent. Further, he refused to legalize clerical marriage and lashed out indiscriminately at those people such as the Protestant Anne Ayscough (1521–1546), whom he had tortured on the rack and burned at the stake for daring to question him.

In the decade after Henry's death in 1547, religious fanaticism brought social and political upheaval. For 6 years, during growing political corruption, radical Protestants ruled the country and dominated the frail young king, Edward VI (1547–1553), born of Henry's third wife Jane Seymour—who died in childbirth. His government was controlled by the Regency Council, dominated first by the duke of Somerset and then, after 1549, by his rival, the duke of Northumberland. The same mix of political opportunism and religious change continued as the council members enriched themselves and pursued their ambitions. At the same time, a radical form of Protestantism swept through many parishes. The government sought political support by courting the religious radicals: it repealed the Six Articles, permitted priests to marry, replaced the Latin service with Cranmer's English version, and adopted the Forty-Two Articles, an expression of radical Protestantism.

When Edward died in 1553, Mary Tudor came to the throne and tried to restore Catholicism through harsh persecutions, which earned her the name "Bloody Mary" from Protestant historians. The new queen possessed many of the same admirable qualities of her mother, Catherine of Aragon: dignity, intelligence, compassion, and a strong moral sense. Her religious obsession, however, eventually cost her the support of a substantial number of her subjects. Her hopeless love for her Catholic husband, Philip II of Spain—who married her in 1554—led to her being seen as a puppet of Spanish diplomacy. She restored the Catholic Church service, proclaimed papal authority in her realm, and forged an alliance with Spain. In putting down the Protestants, she burned 300 of them at the stake—among whom were Cranmer, two other bishops, and 55 women. Mary died pitifully, rejected by her husband and people, but steadfast in her hope to save English Catholicism. Leaving no heir, she was compelled to name Elizabeth, her half-sister, as her successor.

Protestantism from Switzerland to Holland

Why was Protestantism in the Rhine valley so much more radical than Lutheranism and Anglicanism?

A very different kind of church reforms took place in Switzerland and France. The leaders of these reforms were aware of the state but not dominated by it, as the Anglicans were. Like the Lutherans, they were also concerned for the salvation of their souls, but in a much more doctrinal and often vindictive way. Calvinism was the most popular and the most conservative of the reforms.

Ulrich Zwingli

During the late medieval period, Swiss craftsmen and merchants in Zurich, Bern, Basel, and Geneva prospered as part of the growing trade between Italy and Northern Europe. However, in the latter part of the fifteenth century, they suffered from policies imposed on them by their Habsburg overlords and by papal policies—particularly the church's financial demands and the sale of indulgences. In 1499, the Confederation of Swiss Cantons won independence from the Holy Roman Empire and the Habsburgs. To many Swiss, this was also the first step in repudiating outside authority. At the same time, Protestantism grew rapidly in northern Switzerland.

The Swiss Reformation began in Zurich, shortly after Luther published his Theses at Wittenberg. It was led by Ulrich Zwingli (OOL-rikh ZWING-lee; 1484–1531), a scholar, priest, and former military chaplain who persuaded the city council to create a regime of clergymen and magistrates to supervise government, religion, and individual morality. Zwingli agreed with Luther in repudiating papal in favor of scriptural authority. He simplified services, preached justification by faith, attacked monasticism, and opposed clerical celibacy. More rational and less emotional than Luther, he was also more interested in practical reforms. He went beyond the German reformer in advocating additional grounds for divorce and in denying any mystical conveyance of grace by baptism or communion; both, to Zwingli, were only symbols. These differences proved irreconcilable when Luther and Zwingli met to consider merging their movements in 1529.

Zwingli's influence spread rapidly among the northern cantons. However, the linguistic, cultural, national, and economic diversity of Switzerland worked against him. Religious controversy separated northerners from southerners, rural areas from urban, and feudal overlords—both lay and ecclesiastical—from towns within their dominions. When, in the 1520s, Geneva repudiated its ancient obligations and declared its independence from the local bishop and the count of Savoy, the city became a hotbed of Protestantism, with preachers streaming in from Zurich. Switzerland entered an intense period of cantonal wars, and Zwingli was killed in a battle in 1531. Rather than continue to weaken themselves, the practical Swiss decided in the Second Peace of Kappel that each Swiss canton could choose its own religion.

John Calvin

Hoping to ensure the dominance of Protestantism in Geneva after the religious wars, local reformers invited John Calvin (1509–1564) to Geneva. Calvin arrived from Basel in 1536. He was an uncompromising French reformer and a formidable foe of the ungodly, but a caring colleague and minister to humble believers. His preaching, based on his study of theology in Paris and law in Orleans, ultimately won enough followers to make his church the official religion. From Geneva, the faith spread to Scotland, Hungary, France, Italy, and other parts of Europe after the early 1540s.

In Basel, he had published the first edition of his *Institutes of the Christian Religion* (1536), a theological work that transformed the general Lutheran doctrines into a more logical system based around the concept of predestination. It also earned Calvin his invitation to Geneva. His original plan for a city government there called for domination by the clergy and banishment of all dissidents. This aroused a storm of opposition from Anabaptists—who believed in adult baptism and separation of church and state—and from the more worldly portion of the population, and Calvin was forced into exile. He moved north to Strasbourg, where he associated with other reformers who helped him refine his ideas. Calvin's second regime at Geneva after 1541 involved a long struggle with the city council. His proposed ordinances for the Genevan Church gave the clergy full control over moral and religious behavior, but the council modified the document, placing all appointments and enforcement of law under its jurisdiction.

Although recognizing the Bible as supreme law and the *Institutes* as a model for behavior, the Geneva city council did not always act on recommendations from the Consistory, Calvin's supreme church committee. For the next 14 years, Calvin fought against public criticism and opposition in the council. He gradually increased his power, however, through support from the Protestant refugees who poured into the city. His influence climaxed after a failed "revolt of the godless" in 1555. From that year until his death in 1564, he dominated the council, ruling Geneva with an iron hand, within the letter, but not the spirit, of the original ordinances.

Particularly in the later period, the Consistory apprehended violators of religious and moral law, sending its members into households to check every detail of private life. Offenders were reported to secular magistrates for punishment. Relatively light penalties were imposed for missing church, laughing during the service, wearing bright colors, dancing, playing cards, or swearing. Religious dissent, blasphemy, mild heresies, and adultery received heavier punishments, including banishment. Witchcraft and serious cases of heresy led to torture, and then execution—sometimes as many as a dozen or more a year. Michael Servetus (SEHR-vee-tus; 1511–1553), a Spanish theologian–philosopher and refugee from the Catholic Inquisition, was burned for heresy in Calvin's Geneva because he had denied the doctrine of the Trinity.

Calvin accepted Luther's insistence on justification by faith; like Luther, he saw Christian life as a constant struggle against the devil, and he expected a coming divine retribution, an end-time, when God would redress the evils that were increasing on every side. Calvin also agreed with Luther in seeing God's power as a relief for human anxiety and a source of inner peace. Both reformers believed man to be totally depraved, but Calvin placed greater emphasis on this point, at the same time emphasizing God's immutable will and purpose. If Calvinism, to human minds, seemed contradictory in affirming man's sinful nature and his creation in God's image, this connection only proved that God's purposes were absolutely beyond human understanding. For depraved humans, God required faith and obedience, not understanding.

God's omnipotence was Calvin's cardinal principle. He saw all of nature as governed by a divinely ordained order, discernible to man but governed by laws that God could set aside in effecting miracles as he willed. Carried to its logical conclusion, such ideas produced Calvin's doctrine of predestination.

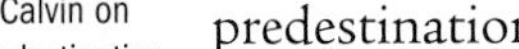

Calvin on Predestination

By predestination we mean the eternal decree of God, by which he determined with himself whatever he wished to happen with regard to every man. All are not created on equal terms, but some are preordained to eternal life, others to eternal damnation; and, accordingly, as each has been created for one or other of these ends, we say that he has been predestined to life or to death....[7]

In Calvin's grand scheme, as laid out precisely in the *Institutes,* his church served to aid the elect in honoring God. The human purpose was not to win salvation—for this had already been determined—but to honor God and prepare the elect for salvation. As communities of believers, congregations were committed to constant war against Satan. They also functioned to spread the Word (Scripture), educate youth, and alleviate suffering among the destitute.

Calvin was particularly vague in his views on government. Ministers of the church were responsible for advising secular authorities on religious policies and resisting governments that violated God's laws. He believed that all rulers were responsible to God and subject to God's vengeance. But throughout the 1540s, when he was hoping to gain the support of monarchs, he emphasized the Christian duty of obedience to secular authorities. Even then, however, he advised rulers to seek counsel from church leaders, and he ordered the faithful, among both the clergy and the laity, to disregard any government that denied them freedom in following Christ. Although willing to support any political system that furthered the true faith, Calvin always preferred representative government.

Another ambiguity in Calvin's social thought involved his attitude toward women. Unlike Catholic theologians, he did not cast women in an inferior light. In his mind, men and women were equally full of sin, but they were also equal in their chance for salvation. As he sought recruits, he stressed women's right to read the Bible and participate in church services. During his residence in Strasbourg, Calvin married Idelette de Bure, a widow of a converted Anabaptist with three children to support. She became, as Calvin noted with great sadness after her death in 1549, "a faithful helper of my ministry." At the same time, he saw women as naturally subordinate to their husbands in practical affairs, including the conduct of church business.

Before the Peace of Augsburg, Calvinism was strongest in France, the reformer's own homeland, where the believers were known as *Huguenots.* Calvinism made gains elsewhere but did not win political power. In Italy, the duchess of Ferrara installed the Calvinist church service in her private chapel and protected Calvinist refugees. Strasbourg in the 1530s was a free center for Protestant reformers such as Matthew Zell and his wife Katherine, who befriended many Calvinist preachers, including Martin Bucer (BOOT-sur), a missionary to England during the reign of Edward VI. In the same period, John Knox spread the Calvinist message in Scotland.

Anabaptists and Other Radicals

Along the Rhine River to its mouth in Holland, there were many other reform movements, including different versions of **Anabaptism**—that is, the baptism of those who had studied the texts of Christianity and made a conscious decision to be Christians. This was a controversial position and those believing in the need for another baptism after that given to infants were viewed as heretics by church authorities after the sixth century and after 1517 by the Lutherans, Calvinists, and Anglicans. These movements went farther than Lutheranism and Anglicanism in rejecting Catholic dogma and ritual. Generally, they were opposed to monarchy, but their position did not become very apparent until they were deeply involved in religious wars after 1560, when they often found themselves under attack by both the Catholics and the Lutherans.

Each of these divergent Protestant splinter groups pursued its own "inner lights." Some saw visions of the world's end, some advocated a Christian community of shared wealth, some opposed social distinctions and economic inequalities, and some denied the need for any clergy. Most of the sects emphasized biblical literalism

Anabaptism—A Protestant faith that holds that baptism and church membership come only when one is an adult. Anabaptists also tend to believe in a strict separation of church and state.

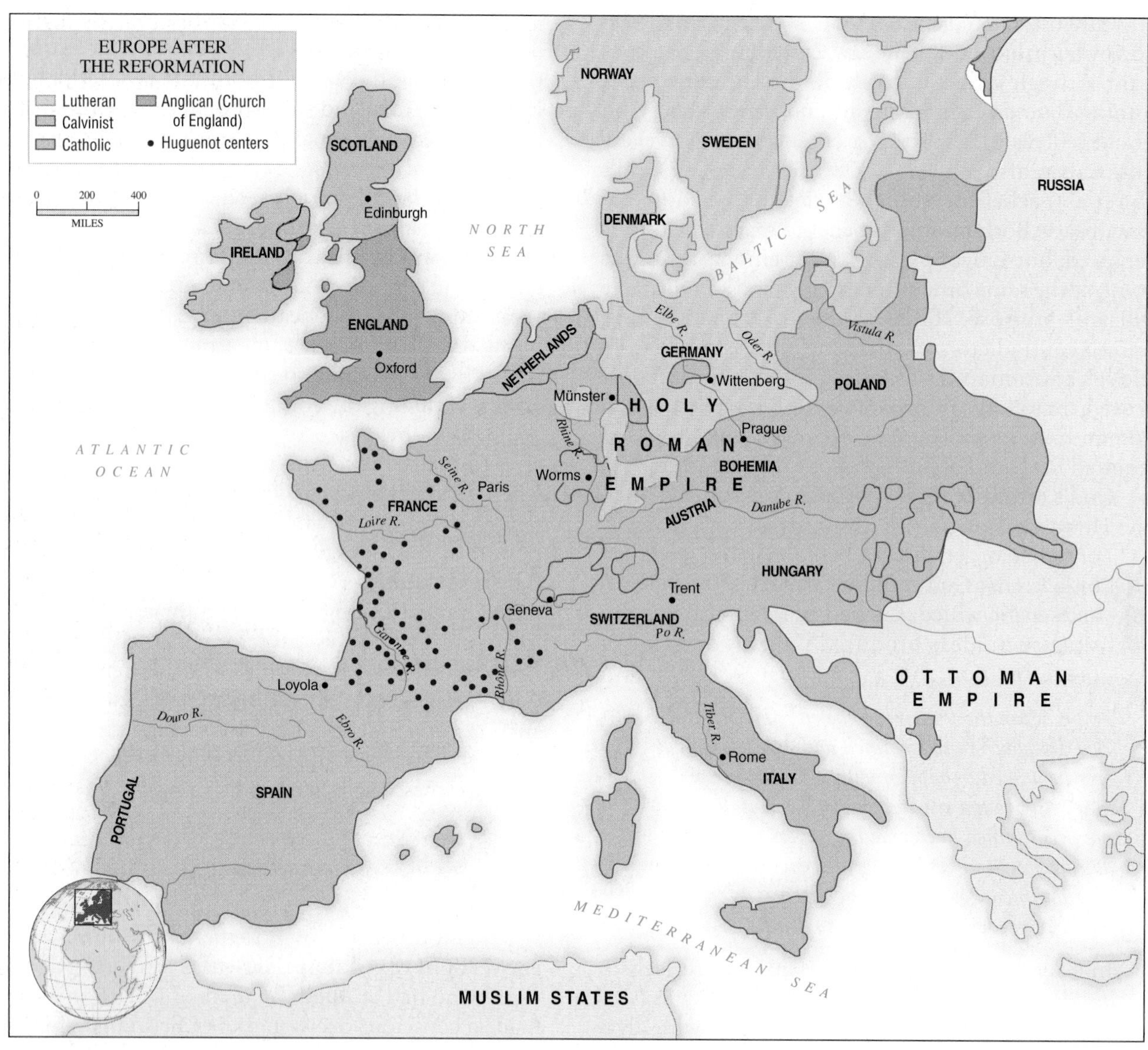

▲ This map illustrates the geographical patterns of the Protestant Reformation. Lutheranism spread through German-speaking areas along the Baltic Sea but rarely crossed the Rhine River. The spread of Calvinism defies linguistic explanation.

and direct, emotional communion between the individual and God. The majority of them were indifferent or antagonistic to state governments and courts; many favored pacifism and substitution of the church for the state.

Women were prominent among the sects, although they were usually outnumbered by men. These women were known for their biblical knowledge, faith, courage, and independence. They helped found religious communities, wrote hymns and religious tracts, debated theology, and publicly challenged the authorities. Some preached and delivered prophecies, although such activities were suppressed by male ministers by the end of the century. More women than men endured torture and suffered martyrdom. Their leadership opportunities and relative freedoms in marriage, compared to women of other religions, were bought at the high price of hardship and danger.

Persecution of the sects arose largely because of their radical ideas. But Catholics and other Protestants who opposed them usually cited two revolutionary actions. The first came when some radical preachers took part in the German peasants' revolt of the 1520s and shared in the savage punishments that followed. The second came in 1534, when a Catholic army besieged Münster (MIUN-ster).

Thousands of recently arrived Anabaptist extremists had seized control and expelled dissenters from this German city near the southern Netherlands. Following their radical theology, the "regime of saints" took private property, allowed polygamy, and planned to convert the world. John of Leyden (LI-den), a former

Dutch tailor who claimed divine authority, headed a terrorist regime during the final weeks before the city fell. Those who survived the fall of the city suffered horrible tortures and then execution.

Among the most damaging charges against the Münster rebels were their alleged sexual excesses and the dominant role played by women in this immorality. Such charges were mostly distortions. The initiation of **polygamy,** justified by references to the Old Testament, was a response to problems arising from a shortage of men, hundreds of whom had fled the city. Many other men were killed or injured in the fighting. Thus, the city leaders required women to marry so that they could be protected and controlled by husbands. Most Anabaptist women accepted the requirement as a religious duty. Although some paraded through the streets, shouting religious slogans, the majority prepared meals, did manual labor on the defenses, fought beside their men, and died in the fighting or at the stake. Most of the original, Catholic, Münster women, however, fiercely resisted forced marriage, choosing instead jail or execution.

Like Calvin later in Geneva, the Anabaptist regime of John of Leyden closely monitored and controlled private life and public behavior. Their theocratic state found its laws in Scripture. In looking at the laws of the city, capital punishment was applied in the following cases:

> *Whoever curses God and his holy Name or his Word shall be killed (Lev. 24).*
>
> *No one shall curse governmental authority (Ex. 22, Deut. 17), on pain of death.*
>
> *Both parties who commit adultery shall die (Ex. 20, Lev. 20, Matt. 5).*
>
> *...Whoever disobeys these commandments and does not truly repent, shall be rooted out of the people of God, with ban and sword, through the divinely ordained governmental authority.*[8]

For more than a century, memories of Münster plagued the Protestant sects in general. Although most did not go to the extremes of "the saints," they were almost immediately driven underground throughout Europe, and their persecution continued long after they had abandoned violence. In time, they dispersed over the Continent and to North America as the Amish, Mennonites, Quakers, and Baptists, to name only a few denominations. Given their suffering and oppression, voices of the radicals were among the first raised for religious liberty. Their negative experience with governments made them even more suspicious of authority than the Calvinists were. In both the Netherlands and England, they participated in political revolutions and helped frame the earliest demands for constitutional government, representative institutions, and civil liberties.

With the exception of Henry VIII's political reformation, the reformers, going back to Wycliffe and Hus and moving on through Luther and Calvin and the Anabaptists, did not believe that they were creating something new. Instead, they were trying to reclaim the purity of the early church.

polygamy—A type of marriage in which a husband has more than one wife.

Reform in the Catholic Church

How successful was the Catholic Church in dealing with the problems that faced it?

The era of the Protestant Reformation was also a time of rejuvenation for the Roman Catholic Church. This revival was largely caused by the same conditions that had sparked Protestantism. Throughout the fifteenth century, many sincere and devout Catholics had recognized a need for reform, and they had begun responding to the abuses in their church long before Luther acted at Wittenberg. Almost every variety of

▼ Pope Paul III, also known as Alessandro Farnese, was the last of the Renaissance popes—men who lived full lives of intellectual, political, and physical passion (he had three legitimate sons). He served as pope between 1534-1549 and shepherded the Church through the opening salvos of the Protestant Reformation and strengthened it by arranging the Council of Trent.

reform opinion developed within the Catholic Church. Erasmus, More, and other Christian humanists provided precedents for Luther, but none followed him out of the Catholic Church. In a category of his own was Savonarola (sa-vo-na-RO-la; 1452–1498), a Dominican friar, puritan, and mystic who ruled Florence during the last 4 years before his death. This "Catholic Calvin" consistently railed against the worldly living and sinful luxuries he found: his criticisms of the pope and the clergy were much more severe than Luther's grievances. At the other extreme of the Church was Cardinal Ximenes (hee-MAY-neth; 1437–1517) in Spain, who carried out his own Reformation by disciplining the clergy, compiling the Complutensian Bible—eliminating many of the errors made by medieval copyists and instilling a new spirit of dedication into the monastic orders.

After the Protestant revolt began, the primary Catholic reformer was Alessandro Farnese (far-NAY-se), Pope Paul III (1534–1549). Coming into office at a time when the church appeared ready to collapse, Paul struggled to overcome the troubled legacy of his Renaissance predecessors and restore integrity to the papacy. Realizing that issues raised by the Protestants would have to be resolved and problems within the church corrected, he attacked the indifference, corruption, and vested interests of the clerical organization. In pursuing these reforms, he appointed a commission, which reported the need for correcting such abuses as the worldliness of bishops, the traffic in benefices (church appointments with guaranteed incomes), and the transgressions of some cardinals. Their recommendations led Paul to call a church council, an idea that he continued to press against stubborn opposition for more than ten years.

When Paul died in 1549, he had already set the Roman Church on a new path, although his proposed church council, the Council of Trent, had only begun its deliberations. Perhaps his greatest contribution was his appointment of worthy members to the College of Cardinals, filling that body with eminent scholars and devout stewards of the church. As a result of his labors, the cardinals elected a succession of later popes who were prepared, intellectually and spiritually, to continue the process of regeneration.

The spirit of reform was reflected in a number of new Catholic clerical orders that sprang up in the early sixteenth century. Some of these worked with the poor, ministered to the sick, and taught. Among the better known were the Carmelites founded by St. Teresa of Avila (1515–1582), whose determination and selfless devotion became legendary. She inspired mystical faith and reforming zeal in written works such as *Interior Castle* and *The Ladder of Perfection*.

DOCUMENT
Rules for Thinking with the Church

The most significant of the new orders was the Society of Jesus, whose members are known as Jesuits.

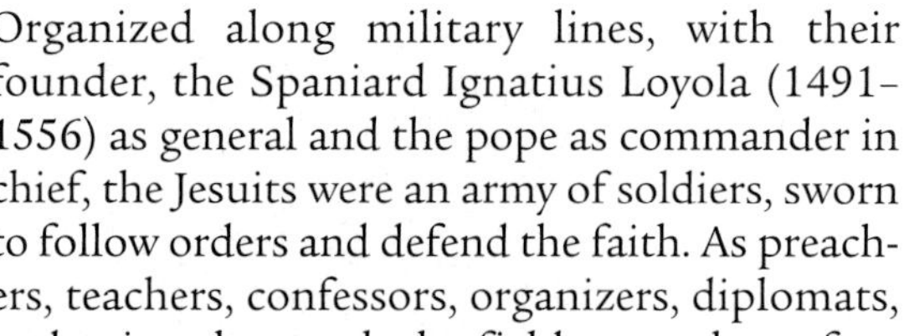

IMAGE
Ignatius of Loyola

Organized along military lines, with their founder, the Spaniard Ignatius Loyola (1491–1556) as general and the pope as commander in chief, the Jesuits were an army of soldiers, sworn to follow orders and defend the faith. As preachers, teachers, confessors, organizers, diplomats, and spies, they took the field everywhere, founding schools and colleges, serving as missionaries on every continent, and working their way into government wherever possible. Their efforts were probably most responsible for the decided check that Protestantism received after the 1560s, as they zealously defended Catholicism in France, pushed the Protestants out of Poland, and reclaimed southern Germany. Jesuit missions also helped Spain and Portugal develop their global empires.

Pope Paul's reform initiatives were given form by the great multinational church council, the first since 1415, which met in three sessions between 1545 and 1563 in the northern Italian city of Trent. Devoting much attention to the external struggle against Protestantism, the council also sought to eliminate internal abuses by ordering changes in church discipline and administration. It strictly forbade absenteeism, false indulgences, selling church offices, and secular pursuits by the clergy. Bishops were ordered to supervise their clergies—priests as well as monks and nuns—and to fill church positions with competent people. The Council of Trent also provided that more seminaries be established for educating priests, while instructing the clergy to set examples and preach frequently to their flocks.

Rejecting all compromise, the Council of Trent retained the basic tenets of Catholic doctrine, including the necessity of good works as well as faith for salvation, the authority of church law and traditions, the sanctity of all seven sacraments, the use of only Latin in the Mass, and the spiritual value of indulgences, pilgrimages, veneration of saints, and the cult of the Virgin. The council also strengthened the power of the papacy. It defeated all attempts to place supreme church authority in any general council. When the final session voted that none of its decrees were valid without papal approval, the church became more than ever an absolute monarchy.

The full significance of Trent became evident after the 1560s when the Catholic reaction to Protestantism acquired a new vigor and militancy. Having steeled itself from within, the church and its shock troops, the Jesuits, went to war against Protestants and other heretics. The new crusade was both open and secret. In Spain, Italy, and the Netherlands, the Inquisition more than ever before became the dreaded scourge of Protestants and other heretics. Jesuit universities, armed with the *Index of Forbidden Works,* trained scholars and missionaries who would serve as priests and organizers in Protestant countries such as England. Many died as

▲ The devotional works and personal example of St. Teresa of Avila, mystic and visionary, inspired the rebirth of Spanish Catholicism. In 1970, she was proclaimed a doctor of the church, the first woman to be so honored. The sculpture here, *The Ecstasy of St. Teresa* (1645–1652), is by the Italian Baroque artist Giovanni Bernini.

martyrs, condemned by Protestant tribunals, while others suffered similar fates meted out by the pagans whom they sought to convert in America and Asia. But Protestantism made no more significant gains in Catholic lands after Trent. Indeed, after Trent, the Catholic Church became a global church.

Conclusion

It could be argued that Europe's Golden Age of the Renaissance was no more than a recapitulation of that which had gone before. By resurrecting the gifts of the Greeks and Romans and learning from the science and history of the Arabs, the elites who participated in the movement were, in fact, reactionaries. But in looking back, they invented new and demanding methods of research, and the most important legacy they revived was the old Greek message that "Man Can Know." This individual liberation could be seen immediately in the artistic and architectural works as well as in the writings of Lorenzo Valla and Machiavelli. The new humanism was not necessarily intellectually superior to the best of the scholastic thinking. However, it allowed new questions to be posed in critical ways.

Christianity had always been a religion in ferment, and, after the Seventh Ecumenical Council, the religious authorities in Rome and Constantinople had sought to stamp out any heretical views not in accord with orthodoxy. Luther, in many ways, echoed the thoughts of earlier figures like John Wycliffe and John Hus. He succeeded where they failed because of the more favorable political context he found himself in.

In many ways, the Protestant Reformation and Catholic Counter-Reformation helped create the modern world. By breaking the religious monopoly of European Catholicism, Lutheranism and Anglicanism assisted the growth of northern European national monarchies. Later, the Puritan values and "work ethic" of Calvinism helped justify the profit-seeking activities of the middle classes. The Catholic Church itself was transformed by the various Protestant challenges. After the Council of Trent, the Catholic Counter-Reformation checked the spread of Protestantism, and the Roman Church emerged strengthened to protect and advance itself. Because the Reformation and Counter-Reformation coincided with the development of the state system (see Chapter 15), faith came to play an integral, and often dangerous, role in politics until 1648.

Because these momentous changes occurred at the same time the Europeans were beginning their maritime exploration and colonization of the world, Protestant and Catholic missionaries were able to spread their messages around the globe. Political and economic imperialism were accompanied by a religious imperialism. The Christians had no doubt they were saving the heathen from hell, but this well-intentioned zealousness had mixed, and often destructive, results to the peoples of Asia, Africa, and the Americas touched by European expansion.

Suggestions for Web Browsing

You can obtain more information about topics included in this chapter at the websites listed below. See also the companion website that accompanies this text, http://www.ablongman.com/brummett, which contains an online study guide and additional resources.

Italian Renaissance Art Project
http://www.italian-art.org
One of the very best and most comprehensive sites for reproductions of the major paintings, works of sculpture, and architecture from the Renaissance. An amazing resource of the study of Renaissance art.

Florence in the Renaissance
http://www.mega.it/eng/egui/epo/secrepu.htm
A history of the Florentine Republic, with details about the city's influence on Renaissance culture.

Sistine Chapel and St. Peter's Cathedral
http://www.christusrex.org/www1/sistine/0-Tour.html
Photo collection depicting all facets of the Sistine Chapel, including images of Michelangelo's ceiling, and detailed description of St. Peter's.

Michelangelo
http://www.michelangelo.com/buonarroti.html
Featuring the works of the artist beautifully illustrated and annotated.

The Louvre
http://www.paris.org/Musees/Louvre
Website for one of the world's greatest museums offers many paths to some of the most beautiful Renaissance art in existence.

Medieval and Renaissance Women's History
http://womenshistory.about.com/od/medieval/
Site serves as a directory for a wide variety of discussions and references about Renaissance women painters, writers, and women of social standing.

Northern Renaissance ArtWeb
http://www.msu.edu/~cloudsar/nrweb.htm
A collection of links for exploring the artists and literature of the Northern Renaissance.

Internet Medieval History Sourcebook: Protestant and Catholic Reformations
http://www.fordham.edu/halsall/sbook1y.html
Extensive online source for links about the Protestant and Catholic Reformations, including primary documents by or about precursors and papal critics, Luther, and Calvin, as well as details about the Reformations themselves.

Martin Luther
http://www.wittenberg.de/e/seiten/personen/luther.html
This brief biography of Martin Luther includes links to his Ninety-Five Theses and images of related historical sites.

Tudor England
http://englishhistory.net/tudor.html/
Site detailing life in Tudor England includes biographies, maps, important dates, architecture, and music, including sound files.

Lady Jane Grey
http://www.ladyjanegrey.org/
A biography of the woman who would be queen of England for nine days, and a general history of the time.

Literature and Film

One of the best novels dealing with the Renaissance is Irving Stone, *The Agony and the Ecstasy: A Biographical Novel of Michelangelo* (New American Library, 1996). An outstanding account of the past and present of Florence is given by Mary McCarthy in *The Stones of Florence* (Harvest Books, 2002). Mark Twain recreated the time of Edward VI in *The Prince and the Pauper*, and more recently, Robin Maxwell sheds some light on the reign of Henry VIII in *The Secret Diary of Anne Boleyn: A Novel* (Scribner, 1998).

There are also many excellent videos available, especially on the art and architecture of the Renaissance. Some of the more notable are *Landmarks of Western Art: The Renaissance* (2006; Kultur Video); *Empires—The Medici: Godfathers of the Renaissance* (2005; PBS Paramount); *Florence: Birthplace of the Renaissance* (2004; Educational Video Network); and *The Forbidden Book—The History of the English Bible* (2006; New Liberty Videos).

Filmmakers have been equally attracted to the period, especially to the English Renaissance. *A Man for All Seasons* (1966; Columbia/Tristar), directed by Fred Zinnemann, is an excellent interpretation of the story of Sir Thomas More. Queen Elizabeth has been the subject of a number of films including *Elizabeth* (1998; Umvd), indirectly in Academy Award winner *Shakespeare in Love* (1998; Miramax), and in the award-winning *Elizabeth I* (2006; HBO) with Helen Mirren. A film dealing with the period after Henry VIII is *Lady Jane* (1985; Paramount), directed by Trevor Nunn. *Luther* (2003; MGM) stars Joseph Fiennes as the religious reformer.

Suggestions for Reading

Johnathan Zophy, *A Short History of Renaissance and Reformation Europe,* 2nd ed. (Prentice Hall, 1998), and J. H. Plumb, *The Renaissance* (Mariner Books, 2001), are both excellent introductions to the period. Jacob Burckhardt, The *Civilization of the Renaissance in Italy,* 2 vols. (Torchbooks, 1958), first published in 1860, inaugurated the view that the Italian Renaissance of the fourteenth and fifteenth centuries was a momentous turning point in the history of Western civilization. Donald R. Kelley, *Renaissance Humanism* (Twayne, 1991) and Brian P. Copenhaver, *Renaissance Philosophy* (Oxford University Press, 1992) are excellent surveys. Katharina M. Wilson, ed., *Women Writers of the Renaissance and Reformation* (University of Georgia Press, 1987), is an excellent study. D. G. Wilkins and D. Wilkins, A *History of Italian Renaissance Art,* 6th ed. (Prentice Hall, 2006), is an excellent standard work. Ross King, *Brunelleschi's Dome* (Walker, 2000), is an excellent account of the construction of the famous Florentine's work. Also, Silvio Bedini, *The Pope's Elephant* (Penguin, 2000), is a delightful account of Pope Leo X and his court. Also excellent is James Snyder, *The Northern Renaissance,* 2nd ed. (Prentice Hall, 2004).

A fascinating study of the attitudes of the Christian laity during the Reformation period can be found in Keith Thomas, *Religion and the Decline of Magic: Studies in Popular Beliefs in Sixteenth and Seventeenth Century England* (Oxford University Press, 1997). A useful context to the religious upheavals of the time is given by John Bossy, *Christianity in the West, 1400–1700* (Oxford University Press, 1985). On the impact of John Hus, see Thomas A. Fudge, *The Magnificent Ride: The First Reformation in Hussite Bohemia* (Ashgate Publishing, 1998). The general background of the Reformation is covered well in Steven E. Ozment, *Protestants: The Birth of a Revolution* (Doubleday, 1992). Brad S. Gregory, *Salvation at Stake: Christian Martyrdom in Early Modern Europe* (Harvard University Press, 2000), is a distinguished work of scholarship that takes the martyrs of the time at their word. Richard Marius, *Martin Luther: The Christian Between God and Death* (Belknap Press of Harvard University Press, 1999), is a superb new study of Luther to 1526. The context for the English Reformation is provided in Richard H. Britnell, *The Closing of the Middle Ages: England, 1471–1529* (Blackwell, 1997), and G. W. Bernard, *The King's Reformation: Henry VIII and the Remaking of the English Church* (Yale University Press, 2005). Ulrich Gabler gives a thorough background of Ulrich Zwingli's place in history in his *Huldrych Zwingli: His Life and Work* (Clark, 1995). William J. Bouwsma, *John Calvin* (Oxford University Press, 1988), is a scholarly portrayal of Calvin's human side, emphasizing his inner conflict against the humanistic trend of his time. On the "left wing" of Protestantism, Anthony Arthur's *The Tailor-King: The Rise and Fall of the Anabaptist Kingdom of Münster* (St. Martin's Press, 1999) is a first-rate history of the radical Reformation city-state in northern Germany. John C. Olin places the Catholic response in perspective in *The Catholic Reformation: From Savonarola to Ignatius Loyola* (Fordham University Press, 1993). R. Po-chia Hsia, *The World of Catholic Renewal 1540–1770* (Cambridge University Press, 1998), is an innovative study of the history of the Catholic Church from the run-up to the Council of Trent to the suppression of the Jesuits.

CHAPTER 15

State Development in Europe

Western and Central Europe, Russia, and the Balkans to 1650

Outline

Features

◀ In her short life (December 8, 1542–February 8, 1587), Mary was buffeted by the tumultuous political and religious waves of her time. She was baptized a Catholic and became Queen of Scotland before she was one year old. Later she was Queen of France for a year and a half during the beginning of the French wars of religion. Thereafter she returned to Scotland where she reigned again until she was forced from her throne by Protestants in 1568. She spent the next nineteen years as more or less a prisoner in England, implicated in alleged Spanish and Catholic plots against Queen Elizabeth. Finally she was condemned to death and clumsily decapitated.

STATES HAVE BEEN the primary political unit of urban civilization since its birth in the wake of the Neolithic Revolution. Whether the city-state, federation, empire, or some other political entity, states all share the same qualities: they have defined boundaries, possess the power to tax, and monopolize force. By 1650, the most successful European political unit was the nation-state, made up in large part by people of a similar ethnic and linguistic background (the nation) and led by a king or queen who embodied the state.[1] In this chapter we will see that many countries of Europe successfully formed nation-states. Because of Ottoman domination, the countries in southeastern Europe could not.

Political developments in medieval and early modern Europe proceeded at different paces and in different ways in each of the three zones of Europe. Politics in western and central Europe, the first two zones, developed within the cultural and religious context of the Roman Catholic Church and the political ambitions of national monarchs. States became established based on cities, middle classes, a society held together by contract, and after 1517, conflicting religious movements. In this *multicentered society,* there was a real competition of classes and ideas that limited central power.

Russia—in east Europe—and the Balkan states—south of a line formed by the Sava and Danube rivers—emerged within the context of Orthodox Christianity. In this third European zone, politics developed in a context of a peasant-dominated society with few cities, the absence of a middle class, and the religious-political precedent of *caesaropapism,* in which the political leader is head of both state and church. The subsequent influence of the Mongols on Russia and the Ottoman Turks in the Balkans reinforced the tendency toward a *single-centered society* dominated by an overwhelmingly powerful ruler.

Western and Central Europe, 1300–1500

What factors influenced the development of nation-states in western and central Europe?

Europe saw many changes during the final two centuries of the late Middle Ages, some disastrous, some constructive. The suffering produced by the Black Death (Bubonic Plague), famine, and economic depression took a massive toll on the population (see Chapter 14) and was compounded by a number of destructive wars. At the same time, however, political changes were under way that would have lasting effects on the growth and expansion of European power.

▲ A fifteenth-century portrait of Joan of Arc in battle dress. After leading the French to victory at Orléans in 1429, she was captured by the English, tried and convicted of witchcraft and heresy, and burned at the stake in 1431. The French king, Charles VII, whose kingdom she had helped save, did nothing to rescue her.

England and France: The Hundred Years' War

Nation-making in both England and France was greatly affected by the long conflict that colored much of both nations' history during the fourteenth and fifteenth centuries. The Hundred Years' War (1337–1453) had its origins in a fundamental conflict between the English kings, who claimed much of French territory as theirs, and the French monarchs, whose ultimate goal was a centralized France under the direct rule of the monarchy at Paris.

Another cause was the clash of French and English economic interests in Flanders. This region was falling more and more under French control, to the frustration of both the English wool-growers, who supplied the great Flemish woolen industry, and the English king, whose income came in great part from duties on wool.

The first years of warfare witnessed impressive English victories. With no thought of strategy, the French knights charged the enemy and then engaged in hand-to-hand fighting. But the English had learned more effective methods. Their greatest weapon was the longbow. Six feet long and made of yew wood, the longbow shot steel-tipped arrows that were dangerous at 400 yards and deadly at 100. The usual English plan

Chronology

1300	1400	1500		1600
1305–1377 Babylonian Captivity of the church; papacy under French influence **1337–1453** Hundred Years' War between England and France **1354** Ottoman Turks begin to settle in southeastern Europe **1356** Golden Bull regulates the election of German emperors **1380** Battle of Kulikovo **1389** Battle of Kosovo	**1455–1485** Wars of the Roses in England **1453** Fall of Constantinople, end of East Roman Empire **1462–1505** Reign of Ivan III, the Great **1479** Ferdinand and Isabella begin joint rule in Spain **1492** Spain conquers Granada, unifies Spanish nation	**1526** Ottomans defeat Hungarians at Mohacs **1556–1598** Reign of Philip II of Spain **1560s** Ivan the Terrible wages war against disobedient boyars **1561–1593** Religious wars in France **1564** Start of Dutch Revolt	**1571** Spanish and Venetian navy defeat Ottomans at Lepanto **1587** Dutch Republic formed **1588** English defeat Spanish Armada	**1613** Beginning of Romanov Dynasty (1613–1917) **1618–1648** Thirty Years' War **1648** Peace of Westphalia

of battle called for the knights to fight dismounted. Protecting them was a forward wall of bowmen just behind a barricade of iron stakes planted in the ground to slow the enemy's cavalry charge. By the time the French cavalry reached the dismounted knights, the remaining few French were easily killed.

The revival of the French military effort and a rebirth of national spirit is associated with Joan of Arc, who inspired a series of French victories. Moved by inner voices that she believed divine, Joan persuaded the French ruler to allow her to lead an army to relieve the besieged city of Orléans. Clad in white armor and riding a white horse, she inspired confidence and a feeling of invincibility in her followers, and in 1429 Orléans was rescued from what had seemed certain conquest. Joan was captured by the enemy, found guilty of bewitching the English soldiers, and burned at the stake. But her martyrdom seemed a turning point in the long struggle.

France's development of a permanent standing army and the greater use of gunpowder also began to transform the art of war. English resistance crumbled as military superiority now turned full circle; the English longbow was outmatched by French artillery. Of the vast territories they had once controlled in France, the English retained only Calais when the war ended in 1453.

The Hundred Years' War exhausted England and fueled discontent with the monarchy in Parliament and among the common people. Baronial rivalry to control both Parliament and the crown erupted into full-scale civil war known as the Wars of the Roses (1455–1485); the white rose was the symbol of the Yorkists, and the red rose the House of Lancaster. Thirty years of bloody civil war ended in 1485 with the victory of Henry Tudor over his rivals. His victory at Bosworth Field enabled him to become Henry VII, the first of the Tudor dynasty. Henry VII (1485–1509) proved to be a popular and effective monarch, bringing national unity and security to the English people.

The Hundred Years' War left France with a new national consciousness and royal power that was stronger than ever. Shortly after the war, Louis XI (1461–1483) continued the process of consolidating royal power. Astute and tireless, yet completely lacking in scruples, Louis XI earned himself the epithet the "universal spider" because of his constant intrigues. In his pursuit of power he used any weapon—violence, bribery, treachery—to obtain his ends. The "spider king" devoted his reign to restoring prosperity to his nation and to reducing the powers of the noble families still active and ambitious after the long war. Like Henry VII in England, Louis XI was one of the "new monarchs" who worked for the creation of a subject-sovereign relationship in their kingdoms, replacing the old feudal ties of personal fidelity.

	Western and Central Europe, 1300–1500
1337–1453	Hundred Years' War between France and England
1356	Golden Bull regulates the election of German emperors
1386	Unification of Poland and Lithuania
1454	Treaty of Lodi brings peace to Italian city-states
1455–1485	Wars of the Roses: civil war in England
1479	Marriage of Ferdinand of Aragon and Isabella of Castile
1492	Spain conquers Granada, unifies Spanish nation
1494	France invades Italy

Spain: Ferdinand and Isabella and the Reconquista

Spain became strongly centralized under an assertive and aggressive monarchy in 1479, when Isabella of Castile and Ferdinand of Aragon began a joint rule that united the Iberian peninsula except for Navarre, Portugal, and Granada. The "Catholic Majesties," the title the pope conferred on Ferdinand and Isabella, set out to establish effective royal control in all of Spain.

Ferdinand and Isabella believed that the church should be subordinate to royal government. By tactful negotiations, the Spanish sovereigns induced the pope to give them the right to make church appointments in Spain and to establish a Spanish court of **Inquisition** largely free of papal control. The Spanish Inquisition confiscated the property of many conversos (Jews and Muslims who had converted to Christianity to avoid persecution) and terrified the Christian clergy and laity into accepting royal absolutism as well as religious orthodoxy. Although the Inquisition greatly enhanced the power of the Spanish crown, it also caused many people to flee Spain and the threat of persecution. About 150,000 Spanish Jews, mainly merchants and professional people, fled to the Netherlands, England, North Africa, and the Ottoman Empire. Calling themselves Sephardim (su-faer-DUIM), many of these exiles retained their Spanish language and culture into the twentieth century.

Another manifestation of Spanish absolutism, defined by Isabella herself as "one king, one law, one faith," was the intentional neglect of the Cortes of

Inquisition—A special Roman Catholic court directed to search out and punish heretics, believers in doctrines other than those prescribed by the Church.

▲ The uniting of Castile and Aragon, represented here by Isabella and Ferdinand, provided the foundation for the dominant Spanish state in the sixteenth century.

Castile and Aragon. These representative assemblies, having emerged in the twelfth century, never were allowed by the monarchy to take an effective position as legislative bodies.

One of the most dramatic achievements of the Catholic Majesties was the completion of the Reconquista in 1492 with the defeat of Granada, the last Muslim state on the Iberian Peninsula. This occurred in same year that Columbus claimed the New World for Spain. Before Ferdinand died in 1516, a dozen years after Isabella, he seized the part of Navarre that lay south of the Pyrenees. This acquisition, together with the conquest of Granada, completed the unification of the Spanish nation-state.

Portugal

The western part of the Iberian Peninsula, Portugal, had a different historical evolution than did Spain. There was never a classic feudal tradition in the country, in which kings gave grants of land and positions to their vassals; rather the country was dominated by strong regional barons against whom the kings would struggle during the thirteenth century. But during the fourteenth century, the centralizing power of monarchy began to impose its will over the country, and the Avis dynasty would rule Portugal from 1384 to 1580.

As will be shown in Chapter 16, the Portuguese were the first Europeans to venture out into the Atlantic in search of new business and resources. The person most known for this adventure was Prince Henry (1394–1460), the Navigator. He established an observatory where advances in navigation and ship making were made. In 1411, he crossed the Straits of Gibraltar and captured the Moroccan city of Ceuta (SIU-ta). During his life, his sailors took the Azores and penetrated as far south as Senegal. In response to the economic stimulus of new markets and resources, Portugal doubled its population between 1400 and 1600 and established a global trading empire, however briefly. Then in 1580, during the reign of the Spanish Habsburg, Philip II, Spain incorporated Portugal into its realm.

Central Europe 1300–1521

Central Europe at this time included the Holy Roman Empire, Italy, and the Catholic nations of Poland, the Czech lands of Bohemia and Moravia, and Hungary. The history of this region was largely one of conflict: political (Empire-Papacy), ethnic (German-Slav), or religious (Orthodox-Catholic). The region was, however, tied together by economics. It comprised an economic zone anchored on the west by the Rhine river, the primary route of the overland trade from the Mediterranean to the North Sea and beyond to the Baltic Sea and Russia. The cities of the **Hanseatic League** dominated the northern portions of this trade route, trading primarily in beer, wool, wood, and grain. Until the opening of the Atlantic trade routes in the sixteenth century, this zone experienced comparative economic well-being and important cultural exchange, despite the plague and wars.

The Holy Roman Empire

In the late Middle Ages, the Holy Roman Empire lapsed progressively into political disunity. In 1273, the imperial crown was given to the weak Count Rudolf of the House of Habsburg. During the remainder of the Middle Ages, the Habsburgs had amazing success in territorial acquisition; Rudolf himself acquired Austria through marriage, and, thereafter, the Habsburgs ruled their holdings from Vienna.

While the empire grew, however, its authority over its constituent states weakened. In 1356, the German

Hanseatic League—A commercial league of mostly German cities extending from the English Channel to the eastern end of the Baltic Sea that was active between the thirteenth and seventeenth centuries.

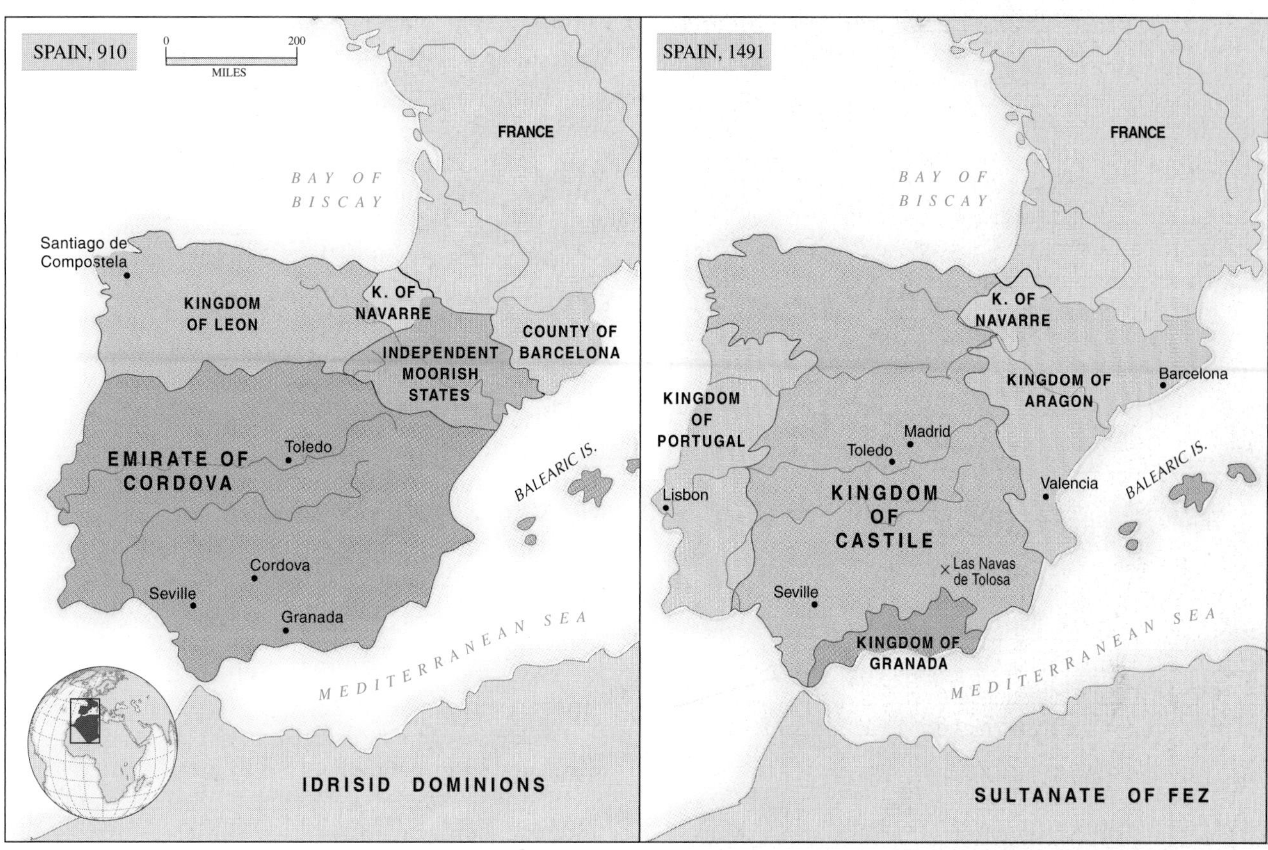

▲ The progress of nation-building in Spain was linked to the Reconquista, the effort to expel the Muslims from the peninsula—in 1492, the kingdom of Granada, the last Muslim stronghold in Spain, fell to the Spanish.

nobility won significant victory in their efforts to avoid the creation of a powerful monarchy. The **Golden Bull,** a document that served as the political constitution of Germany until early in the nineteenth century, established a procedure by which seven German electors—three archbishops and four lay princes—chose the emperor. The electors and other important princes were given rights that made them virtually independent rulers, and the emperor could take no important action without the consent of the imperial feudal assembly, the Diet, which met infrequently. The empire, including 2000 independent lesser nobles, 66 autonomous cities, over 100 imperial counts, 30 secular princes, and 70 quasi-independent bishoprics, was loosely governed by the Imperial Diet.

Despite the absence of political unity with the Empire, the Habsburg family managed to vastly expand its power in the fifteenth century. They achieved this power primarily through successful marriage alliances and not by battle. Most marriage contracts among royal families involved a clause in which, in the case of the death of one of the participants in the marriage, all of the holdings of that person would pass to the survivor. The Habsburgs started this period of marital expansion in 1477 when Frederick III, largely ineffectual in the face of attacks by the Hungarians, arranged the marriage of his son Maximilian I to Maria of Burgundy—whose family laid claim to the lands of northeastern France and the Low Countries. Their marriage produced one son, Philip.

When Frederick died, Maximilian picked up his deceased father's Austrian lands, and then put together a marriage alliance between his son Philip and the daughter of the Spanish king, Juana. Although their marriage ended sadly, they produced a number of children, three of whom became important: Charles, Ferdinand, and Maria. Charles (1516–1556) became Holy Roman Emperor in 1519 and controlled the family's central and western holdings—including Spain and its world empire. Ferdinand headed the eastern part of the Empire, and Maria was married off to the king of Hungary, Louis II. When Louis was killed by the Turks at Mohacs in 1526, Maria Habsburg received her late husband's holdings.

The Hapsburgs' rise to power was not unnoticed at the time, as a phrase that made the rounds at the time indicates: *Bella gerant alii, tu felix Austria nube* ("Let the others fight wars; you lucky Austria, marry").[2]

Golden Bull—A document issued from the Holy Roman Emperor King Charles IV in 1356 that served as the political constitution of the German-speaking lands until the nineteenth century.

▲ Because of his long reign and political skill, the Austrian monarch Frederick III (r. 1440–1493) started the successful policy of favorable marriage alliances that led to the Habsburgs ruling over a world empire in the sixteenth century.

Switzerland

In 1291, citizens in the German-speaking parts of the Alps began the drive to separate themselves from the Habsburg-dominated Empire. In 1291, the three cantons that controlled the access to Italy through the Saint Gothard Pass made an alliance to protect their independence. Fourteen years later, they fought off the Habsburgs at the battle of Mortgaten, thus beginning the history of the country of Switzerland.

Because of its location on the overland route between the Mediterranean and the Rhine road to the North Sea, the region became rich. In addition, the Swiss artisans became known throughout Europe for the quality of their weapons. As we saw in Chapter 14, the region became touched by the currents of the Reformation during the career of Ulrich Zwingli.

Italy

After 1300, the middle and southern parts of the Italian peninsula gained a bit of distance from the Germans. In southern Italy, the Angevin dynasty asserted itself. In the center of the country, the papacy worked to extend its holdings. Between Rome and the Alps, the rich and powerful city-states of Genoa, Milan, and Florence joined with Venice to construct their own diplomatic and political structures.

The years between 1300 and 1500 were not stable: as one authority notes, it was a time of threatened cities, kingdoms without kings, and feudal holdings in transition to becoming principalities. Throughout the fourteenth and early fifteenth centuries, the area was marked by intra-city conflicts fought using mercenary forces known as the ***condotierri*** (kon-do-TIER-ree). These mercenaries, many of them Spanish, fought for pay and would change sides in mid-battle if a better offer was made by their opponents. Economic developments shifted the political center of gravity during the 1400s to the northern cities from the Kingdom of Sicily and the Papal States.

As we saw in Chapter 14, in the northern Italian cities, new, bourgeois elites led by families such as the Medici accumulated great wealth from the wool business and banking to sponsor the great artists and thinkers of the middle classes. In 1454, they tired of their ongoing conflicts and at the Treaty of Lodi worked out a way of getting along, including exchanges of ambassadors with extraterritoriality. Unfortunately, all of the new peace was destroyed when the French invaded in 1494, and Italy became an object of and no longer a subject in European diplomacy. Incipient steps toward some sort of Italian sovereignty would have to wait nearly four centuries before being realized.

The Catholic Frontier: Poland, Bohemia, and Hungary after 1300

This region did not suffer as heavily from the Black Death as western Europe, and as a result Poland, Bohemia, and Hungary experienced a golden age of cultural and economic development in the fourteenth century. There were universities established at Prague (1348), Krakow (1364), and Pecs (1369), and scholars from those schools participated in the humanist movement in the fifteenth century. Even with their economic and cultural progress, the three states argued over a number of issues as their respective kings sought to expand their influences and fought over regions such as Silesia.

condotierri—Mercenaries employed by the Italian city-states during the conflicts of the fourteenth and fifteenth centuries.

During that fourteenth century, the originating dynasties died out in Hungary and Bohemia. Foreign kings such as the Angevin Louis the Great of Hungary (1342–1382), and the Luxembourger Charles the Great of Bohemia (1333–1378) were elected by the powerful nobles and bourgeoisie of the area. The last Piast, Casimir the Great of Poland (1333–1370) led his country through its golden age, but after his death the Poles resorted to a system of elective kingship.

This well-being of the fourteenth century, however, would not last long because of the expansion of Russia to the east, Sweden to the north, and the Ottoman Empire to the south. Internal problems also would lead to a weakening of the realms. Elective kings in Poland and Hungary frittered away their central powers to satisfy the demands of the nobles who elected them. The weakening of central power hit its peak in Poland, where successive royal elections cut the powers of the monarchy until the installation of the ***Liberum* Veto,** an act that allowed one member of the nobility, the *szlachta* (SCHLOK-tah), to block a king's program by his negative vote.

In 1386, Poland united with Lithuania—the last pagan country in Europe—and became the largest state in Europe. Invasions from the east and the west, however, eroded the strength of this state. The Poles had earlier added to their own problems in 1225 when they invited the crusading order of the Teutonic knights into Poland to aid in the combat against the indigenous Baltic peoples to the north, the Prus. The Teutonic knights, out of work after failed crusades in the Eastern Mediterranean, slaughtered the Prus, established their own state based around present-day Kaliningrad (Koenigsberg), and called it Prussia. They proved a considerable threat to the Poles and were not defeated until the battle of Tannenberg in 1410. Later the Teutons would turn their territory of West Prussia over to the Poles and keep East Prussia as a fief of the Polish crown. Poland would face competition and eventual destruction by Russia, Prussia, Sweden, and Austria in the seventeenth and eighteenth centuries.

The Bohemians became the richest part of the Catholic orbit and went on to challenge the Germans politically, economically, and religiously. The Golden Bull of 1356 made the Bohemian king one of the seven electors of the Holy Roman Empire. We have already discussed the religious controversy between the Czechs and the Germans during the late fourteenth century. The creation of the Hussite Church after Jan Hus's immolation led to four crusades preached by the Catholic Church against the forces at Prague. The Czechs

***Liberum* Veto**—In order to guard against the potential power of a strong central monarchy, the Polish nobles in 1652 installed the *Liberum* Veto, an act that allowed one member of the nobility to block the king's program by his single negative vote in the noble assembly.

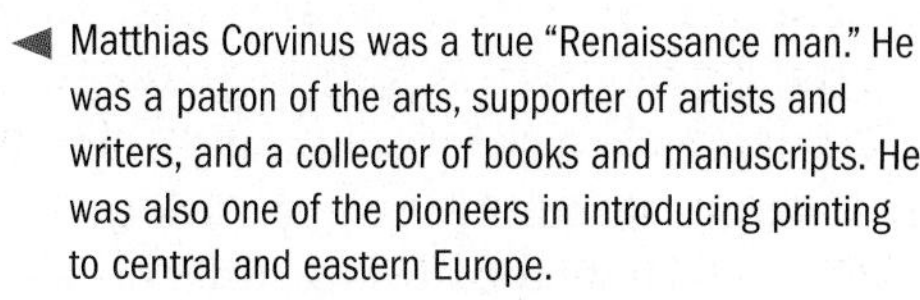

◄ Matthias Corvinus was a true "Renaissance man." He was a patron of the arts, supporter of artists and writers, and a collector of books and manuscripts. He was also one of the pioneers in introducing printing to central and eastern Europe.

successfully defended themselves under leaders such as John Žižka (ZHISH-kah), and they would continue to progress, growing economically and politically until the seventeenth century—when they were defeated in the first phase of the Thirty Years' War.

The Hungarians experienced a brilliant fifteenth century under János Hunyadi (YAWN-nosh HOON-ia-dee) and his son and successor Mathias Corvinus. As Magyar aristocrats, they ended the period of foreign kings. János Hunyadi, by his wealth and military prowess, paved the way for his son Mathias to be elected king in 1458, who came to be known as Mathias Corvinus. During his 32-year reign, Mathias established close ties with the Italian Renaissance cities, especially Florence. Scholars and artists at his court participated fully in the cultural movements of the time. He founded a printing press and had one of the most important libraries in Europe. Although he was unable to increase his central power in competition with the Czechs and the Poles, he did manage to capture Vienna. After he died in 1490 from unknown causes, the Hungarian magnates went back to electing foreign kings. The Hungarians became disunited and were finally defeated by the Ottoman Turks at the battle of Mohacs (1526). Hungary was divided into three zones, the larger part controlled directly by the Ottomans.

Politics, Diplomacy, and the Wars of Religions, 1556–1598

What role did religion play in the use of state power by Spain's Phillip II?

After the 1560s, religious fanaticism, both Protestant and Catholic, combined with pragmatic politics to form a combustible mixture. Sometimes religious conflict caused the reshaping of the old political system to justify movements against royal authority. More often, it popularized centralized monarchies, whose rulers promised to restore order by wielding power. Despite pious declarations, kings and generals in this period conducted war with little regard for moral principles; indeed, as time passed they steadily subordinated religious concerns to dynastic ambitions or national interests. This change, however, came slowly and was completed only in 1648, after Europe was thoroughly exhausted by the human suffering and material destruction of religious wars.

Religious Diversity in Western Europe

Until the end of the sixteenth century, Spain, led by Philip II, attempted to impose its will over the Continent. When he took power in 1556, he looked across the Pyrenees and across the Mediterranean and saw a Europe split by religious strife and still threatened by the presence of the Ottoman Empire. In central Europe, the Peace of Augsburg ended a short war in Germany and sought to bring an accord between the Catholics and Lutherans. Even before Calvin died in 1564, however, his movement was spreading rapidly throughout the Continent. The Council of Trent launched a formidable counteroffensive, led by the Jesuits and supported by the Spanish and Austrian Habsburgs, against all Protestants. England remained on the verge of religious civil war after the death of Queen Mary, while France plunged into three decades of conflict after the extinction of the Valois line to the throne in 1559. Religious conflict broke out in the Spanish Netherlands, and in eastern Europe, militant Catholicism reversed the gains made by Protestants in the previous half-century. Philip saw opportunity in this tumultuous setting, where the politics of religion dominated the scene in Europe.

The Era of Spanish Habsburg Dominance

Although it was a relatively underdeveloped and sparsely populated country of 8 million people, Spain, under Philip II (1556–1598), was the strongest military power in Europe. Seven centuries of resistance against Islamic forces (see Chapter 9) had formed a chivalric nobility that excelled in the military arts, if not also in business. This tradition, in addition to the promise of empire, saw the rigidly disciplined Spanish infantry absorb neighboring Portugal and fan out around the world as *conquistadors,* bringing back silver in seemingly unlimited quantities from the Americas. Working in tandem with the army was the Spanish Church, whose

	War and Politics in the Age of Philip II
1556–1598	Reign of Philip II of Spain
1558–1603	Reign of Elizabeth I of England
1561–1593	Religious wars in France
1566	Revolt in the Netherlands
1571	European forces defeat Turks at Lepanto
1572	Massacre of St. Bartholomew's Eve in Paris
1581	Dutch United Provinces declare independence from Spain
1587	Dutch Republic formed
1588	English defeat Spanish Armada

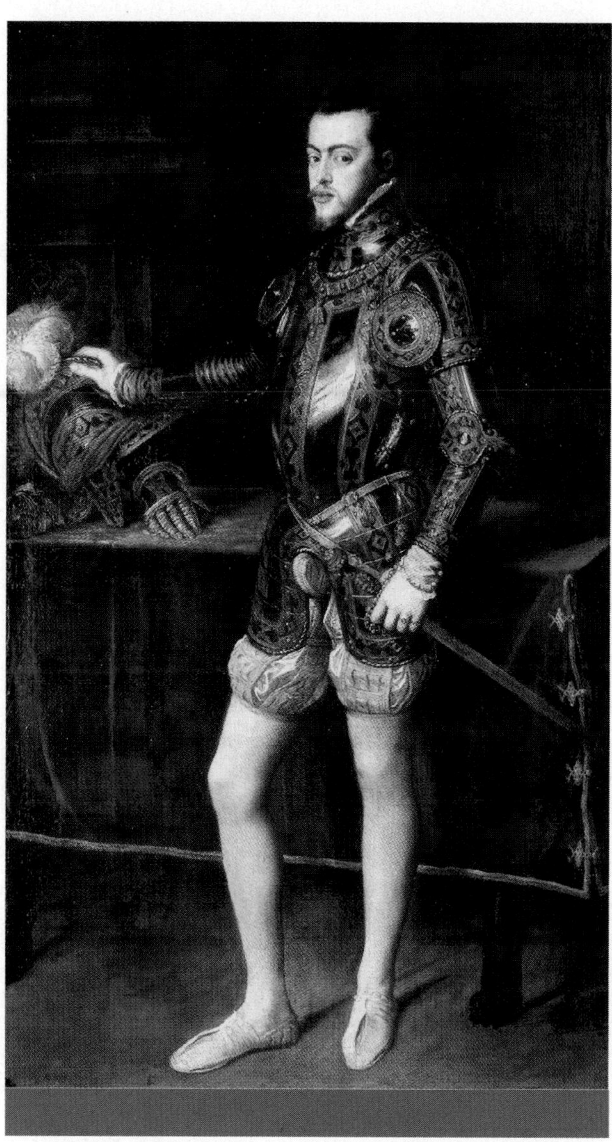

◄ Philip II dominated the European scene during the second half of the sixteenth century. Even though he worked hard to assure Spanish Habsburg dominance, he failed to defeat the Dutch and the British and left Spain in an exhausted condition.

courts of the Inquisition, which had earlier banished the Jews, were now being used to eliminate the few remaining Moors and Spanish Protestants.

Philip willingly took on the Habsburgs' global burdens of maintaining Catholic orthodoxy, fighting the Turks, and imposing his will on his troublesome European neighbors. He considered this responsibility a part of his inheritance from his father, Charles V, whose long reign ended in 1556 when he abdicated his imperial throne and entered a monastery. At that time, Charles split his Habsburg holdings. His brother Ferdinand acquired control of Austria, Bohemia, and Hungary and became Holy Roman Emperor in 1556. Philip received Naples, Sicily, Milan, the Netherlands, Spain, and a vast overseas empire, which was much more lucrative than the traditional imperial domain in central and eastern Europe. Indeed, the division of Habsburg lands appeared to be a blessing for Philip, allowing him to shed his father's worrisome "German problem" and concentrate more effectively on his Spanish realm.

Philip was a slightly built, somber, hardworking man. He was totally absorbed by the tasks of running a worldwide empire and rarely broke away to enjoy the luxurious life offered by his position. He seldom delegated authority, and his councilors served more as advisers than as administrators. Philip labored endlessly, reading and annotating official documents and dominating the Cortes (the traditional assembly of estates) of Castile. He married each of his four wives—Maria of Portugal, Mary of England, Elizabeth of France, and Anne of Austria, his niece—for political reasons; except for Mary, they bore his children but ate at his table only during official banquets. Elizabeth was his favorite, as were her daughters, who received some of his few open shows of tenderness and loving concern.

Philip took advantage of his role as defender of the Catholic faith. Although the church was wealthy and had unleashed the Inquisition to wipe out dissent, Philip used it to enforce Spanish traditions, arouse patriotism, and increase his popularity to strengthen the state. He was by no means a tool of the papacy: indeed, he defied more than one pope by denying jurisdiction over Spanish ecclesiastical courts, opposing the Council of Trent on clerical appointments, and fighting the Jesuits when they challenged his authority. He saw the Catholic Church as an arm of his government, and not vice versa.

Throughout his long reign, Philip continually encountered limitations to his authority. Spain had only recently been unified, and powerful nobles opposed him and his viceroys in their local councils. An overworked and overextended bureaucracy and a weak financial, communications, and industrial infrastructure placed the victories gained by the army and the state on a weak foundation. The backward Spanish sociopolitical system caused Philip many economic problems. Tax-exempt nobilities, comprising under 2 percent of the people, owned 95 percent of nonchurch land; the middle classes, overtaxed and depleted by purges of Jews and Moriscos (Spanish Muslims), were diminished; and the peasants were so exploited that production of food, particularly grains, was insufficient to feed the population. State regulation of industry and trade further limited revenues and forced

▲ The inherent logic of balance-of-power politics is readily evident in this map showing the extent of Habsburg—both Spanish and Austrian—holdings.

primary reliance on precious metals from the Americas to fill the treasury, which ultimately produced a ruinous inflation. When his income failed to meet expenses, Philip borrowed at rising interest rates from Italian and Dutch banks. In 1557 and 1575, Philip had to suspend payments, effectively declaring national bankruptcy.

Revolt in the Netherlands

Philip's centralized rule encouraged some unity in Spain; the Netherlands, however, with its own traditions, was immediately suspicious of its foreign king, who tried to enforce Catholic conformity. The Netherlands ("Low Countries") at the time also included modern Belgium, Luxembourg, and small holdings along 200 miles of marshy northern coast, an area not open to easy conquest. The geographical setting promoted strong local nobilities but also relatively independent peasants and townsmen. Even in medieval times, cities were centers of rapidly expanding commerce: of the 300 walled towns in 1560, some nineteen had populations of over 10,000. (At the same time, England had only three or four of that size.) Antwerp was the commercial hub of northern Europe, serving as the crossroads of the Hanseatic League and the Italian-English trade axis. The combination of geography and wealth created a spirit of independence in religious affairs, as Lutherans, Calvinists, and Anabaptists were found in great numbers. Charles V had attempted sporadically to suppress the Protestants and had even burned a few notable heretics. But his status as a native son allowed him to maintain a tenuous stability in the region.

Anabaptist Torture in Muenster

Charles's daughter, Margaret of Parma (1522–1586) served as Philip's first regent for the Netherlands. She was sensitive to the religious complexities of her task; Philip, however, ordered a crackdown on the Protestants. Margaret introduced the Inquisition to fight heresy, a policy that forced leading nobles to leave her council and provoked vocal protests from her subjects. As the Inquisition did its work and executed prominent Protestants, the protests became loud and violent. Finally, the so-called Calvinist Fury erupted in 1566, terrorizing Catholics and desecrating 400 churches. Most of the people in the Netherlands were shocked by the excesses of the radicals and voiced their support for Margaret.

Philip's response was to send the duke of Alva to the Netherlands with 10,000 Spanish troops, a great baggage train, and 2,000 camp followers to establish order. Alva removed Margaret from her regency and clamped a brutal military dictatorship on the country. By decree, he centralized church administration, imposed new taxes, and established a special tribunal, soon dubbed the Council of Blood, to stamp out treason and heresy. During Alva's regime, between 1567 and 1573, at least 8,000 people were killed, including the powerful counts of Egmont and Horne. In addition, the Catholic terror deprived 30,000 people of their property and forced 100,000 to flee the country.

By 1568, Alva's excesses had provoked open rebellion—the first national liberation struggle, led by William of Orange (1533–1584), nicknamed William the Silent. Constant early defeats left him impoverished and nearly disgraced, but in 1572 the port of Brielle fell to his privateers, the "sea beggars," an event that triggered revolts throughout the north. Soon thereafter, William cut the dikes near Zeeland and mired down a weary Spanish army. The continuing war was marked by savage ferocity, such as the sack of Antwerp by mutinous Spanish soldiers (1576). At the Spanish siege of Maestricht (MICE-treeschte) in 1579, women fought beside their men on the walls, and Spanish soldiers massacred the population, raping women first before tearing some limb from limb in the streets. That same year, in the Pacification of Ghent, Catholics and Protestants from the 17 provinces united to defy Philip, demand the recall of his army, and proclaim the authority of their traditional assembly, the States General.

Unfortunately for the rebel cause, this unity was soon destroyed by religious differences between militant northern Calvinists and Catholic southerners, particularly the many powerful nobles. The Spanish commander Alessandro Farnese exploited these differences by restoring lands and privileges to the southern nobles. He was then able to win victories that induced the ten southern provinces to make peace with Spain in 1579. The Dutch, now alone, proclaimed their continued resistance to Spanish persecution and, in 1581, declared their independence from Spain. They persisted after William of Orange was assassinated in 1584, but meanwhile, the Spanish continued their war on heresy, butchering, burning, and burying alive Protestants who would not renounce their faith. The conflict lasted until a truce was negotiated in 1609.

Religious Wars in France

Although frustrated in the Netherlands, Philip did not face his father's French problem. According to the Treaty of Cateau-Cambrésis (KA-tow kam-BRAY-sees) in 1559, France gave up claims in Italy and the Netherlands. This humiliating surrender to the Habsburgs marked a definite turning point in French history. With its government bankrupt, its economy nearly prostrate, and its people disillusioned, France lost its leverage in foreign affairs as civil wars encouraged by Philip wasted the country during the next four decades.

Beneath the prevailing religious contention was another bitter struggle between the haves and have-nots. High prices, high rents, and high taxes drove the lower classes to riot and rebel against urban oligarchies, noble landlords, and government tax collectors. The social unrest continued sporadically throughout the sixteenth century. It brought no improvement of conditions for suffering peasants and town artisans, but it did frighten the wealthy nobles, merchants, and bankers, whose mildly divergent interests were unified by threats from below.

By the 1560s, Calvinism had become a major outlet for the frustrations of the discontented. Although outlawed and persecuted earlier, the movement grew rapidly during the decade. It converted approximately 15 percent of the population, most of whom were of the lower urban middle class; however, the leadership came mainly from the nobility, 40 to 50 percent of whom accepted Calvinism. Their motives varied—although many were sincerely religious, most pursued political ends. Even among the lesser nobles, the Calvinist side promised military employment, political prominence, and a way for taking advantage of popular discontent. The movement's potential popular support was particularly appealing to contenders for the throne among the high nobility. In 1559, the Huguenots held a secret synod in Paris that drew representatives from 72 congregations and a million members. A distinct minority, they were nevertheless well-placed and well organized with articulate spokesmen and competent military leaders.

Religious, political, and social forces combined when France suffered the loss of King Henry II in 1559, who left his crown to his sickly 15-year-old son, Francis II. His young queen was Mary Stuart (later Mary, Queen of Scots), whose uncles, the brothers Guise, took actual control of the government. They were opposed by noble families from the Huguenot camp. Francis II died in 1560, and the crown passed to his 9-year-old brother

Charles. At that time, however, the real power behind the throne was Charles's mother, Catherine de Medici. Single-minded, crafty, and ready to use any means, she was determined to save the throne for one of her three sons, none of whom had produced a male heir. Exploiting the split between the Guises—the champions of the Catholic cause—and their enemies, she assumed the regency for Charles. She then attempted, through reforms of the church, to reconcile the differences between Catholics and Protestants. In this endeavor, she was unsuccessful, but she kept her tenuous control, using every political strategy, including a squadron of noble women who solicited information by seducing powerful nobles.

Religious war erupted in 1561; supported by substantial Spanish financial and military interventions, it lasted through eight uneasy truces until 1593. Fanaticism evoked the most violent and inhumane acts on both sides, as destructive raids, assassinations, and torturous atrocities became commonplace. Catherine maneuvered through war and uneasy peace, first favoring the Guises and then the Bourbons. In 1572, fearing that the Huguenots were gaining supremacy, she joined a Guise plot that resulted in the murder of some 10,000 Huguenots in Paris. This Massacre of St. Bartholomew's Eve was a turning point in decisively dividing the country. The final "war of the three Henries" in the 1580s involved Catherine's third son, Henry III, who became king upon the death of Charles in 1574. The king's rivals were Henry of Guise and the Protestant Henry of Navarre. When the other two Henries were assassinated, Henry of Navarre proclaimed himself king of France in 1589. Spain would have little to fear from France for the next half-century.

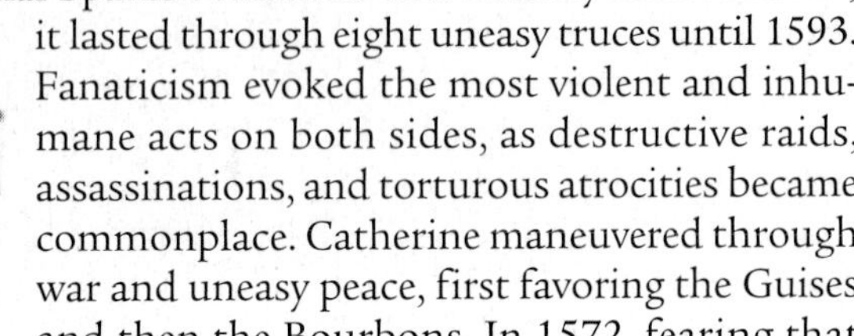

Massacre of St. Bartholomew

England 1509–1603

The Tudor dynasty, begun by Henry VII in 1485, adapted itself to the new conditions apparent in Europe after the Hundred Years' War and the Wars of the Roses. Among its most important tasks was the need to insure continuity by producing male heirs. After the heir apparent of Henry VII, Arthur, died in 1502, Henry's second son Henry VIII married his brother's widow, Catherine of Aragon, as England's sign of its desire to continue to participate in the Anglo-Spanish alliance. After many attempts, Henry and Catherine were unable to produce a male heir, and in order to obtain a divorce—refused by the pope—the British king created his own church to grant him a divorce. In his new marriage with Anne Boleyn, a daughter, later to become Elizabeth I was born. After executing Anne Boleyn on charges of adultery, Henry continually attempted to produce a male heir, finally succeeding with the birth of the weak and sickly Edward I (r. 1547–1553).

Throughout, the English attempted to maintain the Spanish alliance, which became stronger when the daughter of Catherine and Henry, Mary Tudor (r. 1553–1558) married the Spanish king Philip II. Spain continued to build its European foreign policies on the base of an English alliance. For the better part of his reign, Philip had to deal with England's most outstanding monarch, Elizabeth I, who ruled a country that was, as the earl of Essex put it, "little in territory, not extraordinarily rich and defended only by itself."[3]

Elizabeth, a superb image maker, projected the picture of a country united behind a national church, even as her government suppressed Catholicism, put down a northern rebellion, and avoided serious troubles with Scotland and Ireland. Elizabeth dealt with potential dangers from the great Catholic powers by playing them against each other. Such successes were seen as the natural result of her brilliance and courage. This image only partly reflected reality. The "Protestant Queen" detested most of the Protestants, especially those founded on the heretical traditions of the **Lollards.** Her support for Scottish and Dutch rebels went against her fervent belief in absolute monarchy. Her celebrated coy approach in encouraging but ultimately denying prospective royal suitors, despite the diplomatic advantages of the practice, often ran counter to her emotional inclinations, throwing her into momentary rages against her advisers.

But she had learned her lesson well from Tudor politics—to compromise and discount personal feelings for the larger interests of her realm. Consequently, England became her family and her primary interest. She was especially skilled at judging people, dealing with foreign diplomats in their own languages, and projecting her charisma in public speeches. With these notable talents, she brought the English people a new sense of national pride, often expressed in Shakespeare's plays. In the second half of the sixteenth century—in contrast to France—England gave the impression of having achieved relative peace and prosperity.

Elizabeth's earliest immediate danger emerged in Scotland, where Mary of Guise was regent for her daughter Mary Stuart, queen of both France and Scotland. French troops in Scotland supported this Catholic regime. Because Mary Stuart was also a direct descendant of Henry VII of England, she was a leading claimant for the English throne and a potential rallying symbol for Catholics who hoped to reestablish

---

Lollards—Followers of John Wycliffe who spread his doctrines both openly and secretly throughout England in the fifteenth and sixteenth centuries.

their faith in England. These expectations were diminished in 1559 when a zealous Calvinist named John Knox (1505–1572), fresh from Geneva, led a revolt of Scottish nobles. Aided by English naval forces, the Scots broke religious ties with Rome, established a Presbyterian (Calvinist) state church, and, with Elizabeth's help, drove out the French soldiers.

Another serious problem loomed in Ireland, where Spanish and papal emissaries used old grievances over taxes and religion to arouse uprisings against English rule. James Maurice, an Irish leader in the southwest, began a series of revolts in 1569. Eight years later, the pope helped raise troops and money for him on the Continent. An expedition in 1579 to aid the Irish rebels was ruthlessly suppressed, but fighting dragged on for 4 more years. In 1601, a more serious Irish rebellion aided by 3000 Spanish troops cost Elizabeth a third of her revenues. Although never directing a successful Irish policy, as has been true of all of her successors up to the present, she managed to escape catastrophe by her stubborn persistence.

Her innate pragmatism was most beneficial in quieting English sectarian strife. She despised **Puritans** and favored rich vestments for the clergy, but she thoroughly understood the practical necessity of securing Protestant political support. Moving firmly but slowly, Elizabeth re-created a nominal Protestant national church, but one similar to her father's. The queen's policy lessened religious controversy and persecution but failed to end either completely.

Elizabeth also faced a serious danger from abroad. In 1568, after Mary Stuart was forced into exile by her Protestant subjects, she was received in England by her royal cousin. Although kept, for all intents and purposes, a prisoner, she became involved in a series of Catholic plots, which appeared even more dangerous after the pope excommunicated Elizabeth in 1570. Philip of Spain aided the plotters but still hoped to enlist Elizabeth's cooperation in creating a Catholic hegemony in Europe.

Despite all her troubles, Elizabeth's reign showed marked economic improvement. By careful—some said stingy—financial management, her government reduced debt and improved national credit. A new coinage helped make London the financial center of Europe, especially after the Spanish destruction of Antwerp. Monopolies granted to joint stock companies promoted foreign trade and brought wealth into the country. By the end of her reign in 1603, England, despite festering social and religious problems, was the most prosperous state in Europe.[4]

Puritans—Those English Protestants in the 1500s and 1600s who found the theology and worship services of the Church of England to be not in accord with Holy Scripture.

Lepanto and the Armada

Philip's wars against Turkey—including the destruction of the Turkish fleet at Lepanto off the western coast of Greece—promoted his image as the Catholic champion, boosted Spanish morale, and revived the traditional national pride in defending the faith. When Cyprus, the last Christian stronghold in the eastern Mediterranean, fell to the Turks in 1570, Philip responded to the pope's pleas and formed a Holy League to destroy Turkish naval power. Spanish and Venetian warships, together with smaller squadrons from Genoa and the Papal States, made up a fleet of over 200 vessels that drew recruits from all over Europe. In 1571, the Holy League's fleet and the Turkish navy clashed at Lepanto, off the western coast of Greece. Christian Europe scored a major victory over the Ottoman Empire, which would never pose a naval threat again. The Spanish king could bring all of his resources to bear in northwest Europe.

Philip's diplomatic efforts, particularly his marriage to Mary Tudor in 1558, his next marriage to Elizabeth of Valois in 1560, and his clumsy efforts to court Queen Elizabeth, brought no lasting influence over English or French policies. Indeed, English captains were preying on Spanish shipping in the Atlantic, and Dutch privateers, with English and Huguenot support, were diminishing the flow of vital supplies to northern Europe. In 1580, after 9 years of frustration in the Netherlands, Philip launched the first phase of his new offensive policy, using military force to validate his claim to the Portuguese throne. As king of Portugal, he gained control of the Portuguese navy and Atlantic ports, where he began assembling an oceangoing fleet, capable of operations against the Dutch and English in their home waters.

Philip's last hope for an easy solution to his problems was dashed in 1587. Pressed by the pope and the English Catholic exiles, he had tried for years to use Mary Stuart to overthrow Elizabeth, regain England for Catholicism, and seize control of the country. But Mary's complicity in a plot against the English queen's life was discovered, and Elizabeth finally signed a death warrant. Mary's execution confirmed Philip's earlier decision that England had to be conquered militarily. In pursuing this end, Philip planned a "great enterprise," an invasion of England blessed by the pope.

The Spanish strategy depended on a massive fleet, known as the Invincible Armada. It was ordered to meet a large Spanish army in the southern Netherlands and land this force on the English coast. But in 1588, when the Armada sailed for Flanders, Dutch ships blocked the main ports, preventing the Spanish galleons from entering the shallow waters. Philip's project was then completely ruined when the smaller and

DOCUMENT
John Hawkins Reports on the Spanish Armada

more maneuverable English ships, commanded by Charles Howard and captained by privateers such Sir Francis Drake and Sir John Hawkins, scattered the Armada in the English Channel. Retreating through the North Sea, the Spanish fleet was then battered by a severe storm, called the "Protestant wind," and forced to make a miserable return to Spain.

Philip II's Failure in Europe

Contrary to English expectations, the defeat of the Armada brought no immediate shift in the international balance of power. Spain retained its military might, built new ships, and defended its sea-lanes. On the ground, the Spanish infantry would not suffer defeat until 1643 at the battle of Rocroi (ruh-KWAH). In fact, all the major combatants were exhausted, a factor that largely explains the Bourbons' acquisition of the French crown and continued Dutch independence. Lingering wars brought new opportunities for France and the Netherlands, but only more exhaustion for England and Spain.

During the last decade of Philip's life, his multiple failures foreshadowed the decline of his country. He encountered rebellion in Aragon, quarreled with Pope Clement VIII over recognizing the Bourbons, and sent two more naval expeditions against England, both of which were scattered by storms. Before he died in 1598, he turned over the Netherlands to his favorite daughter Clara Isabella Eugenia and her husband, Archduke Albert, an Austrian Habsburg. He had also made peace with France. He left Spain bankrupt for the third time during his reign, having wasted the country's considerable resources and sacrificed its future to his dynastic pride. His son Philip III (r. 1598–1621), no match for his father, presided in a lazy, extravagant, and frivolous way over the beginning of the long decline of the Spanish Empire.

England experienced similar difficulties. Though sea raids on Spanish shipping continued and brought in badly needed money, all of Elizabeth's grand projects failed, such as in 1596, when the earl of Essex plundered Cadiz but missed the Spanish treasure fleet. Conflicts in France, the Netherlands, and Ireland drained her treasury, and Parliament delayed in granting her funds to continue fighting. Social and religious tensions surfaced at the turn of the seventeenth century, and the Puritans proved to be an especially irritating group for the aging queen. At her death in 1603, she left no successors, and the Stuarts took the English throne.

The Dutch declaration of independence in 1581 reflected more concern for aristocratic privilege and national survival than democratic principles, but it served as a basis for holding the northern Netherlands together. After finding no acceptable French or English person to be their king, the Dutch created a republic in 1587 and tenaciously persevered to sign a truce with Spain in 1609. As time passed, their growing maritime trade and naval power guaranteed their security.

The post-Armada stalemate most benefited the French. With the death of the last Valois claimant in 1589, the Bourbon Protestant king of Navarre was proclaimed king of France as Henry IV. This act threw the Catholic Holy League into a fanatical antiroyalist frenzy and encouraged Philip's military intervention in France to support his daughter's claim to the throne. But English aid and Henry's willingness to turn Catholic—he is said to have claimed that "Paris is worth a mass"—led to Philip's withdrawal and the Peace of Vervins in 1598. To pacify his Huguenot allies, Henry issued the Edict of Nantes, which guaranteed them some civil and religious rights and permitted them to continue holding more than a hundred fortified towns. Henry had at last gained peace for his exhausted country.

The Austrian Hapsburgs and the Thirty Years' War, 1618–1648

What made the Thirty Years' War the most destructive military conflict in Europe until the twentieth century?

By 1600, the Spanish Habsburgs' golden age had ended, but the potent mixture of religious and political competition among dynasties and nations would continue with even greater intensity. Philip had taken on too much and had failed to impose his will. Now, in their turn, his cousins in central Europe—the Austrian Habsburgs—would attempt to impose their dominance in Europe. Religious passions remained at a high pitch as increasing numbers of Calvinists and Lutherans on one side and proponents of the Catholic Counter-Reformation on the other still dreamed of the complete victory of their faith and their realms. It was a dangerous time of disruption, frustration, and fanaticism.

Europeans faced severe economic depression, along with intensified conflict in every sphere of human relations. The first few decades of the seventeenth century brought a marked decline to the European economy, even before the advent of open warfare. Prices continued to fall until about 1660, reversing the inflation of the 1500s. International trade declined, as did Spanish bullion imports from Central and South America. Heavy risks on a falling market caused failures among many foreign trading companies; only the larger houses, organized as joint-stock companies, were able to survive. A climate change, bringing on

	War and Politics in the Age of Austrian Habsburg Dominance
1589–1610	Reign of Henry IV of France, beginning of Bourbon dynasty
1598	Edict of Nantes guarantees Protestant rights in France
1611–1632	Reign of Gustavus Adolphus in Sweden
1618–1648	Thirty Years' War
1624–1642	Cardinal Richelieu holds power in France
1643	Spanish infantry suffers first defeat at battle of Rocroi
1648	Peace of Westphalia

colder weather, reduced the growing season and agricultural production, and the hard times in the countryside were felt in the cities, where urban craftspeople saw their wages drop.

Tensions accompanying economic depression added to those arising from continuing religious differences. The most dangerous area for religious conflict was in central Europe, which had directly experienced an increasingly militant Counter-Reformation since the Peace of Augsburg. Although the European power balance in 1618 resembled that of the 1500s, it was much less fixed. The power of the Habsburgs of Vienna drove even normally competitive states to come together in alliances. Underneath the facade of their sixteenth-century dominance there was a sense of vulnerability. Spain was weakening and there were other states—France, the Netherlands, and Sweden—that were growing more powerful. Under these circumstances European opposition against Austrian Habsburg dominance became almost inevitable.

The Bohemian and Danish Phases of the Thirty Years' War

The Thirty Years' War, fought between 1618 and 1648, was a culmination of all these related religious and political conflicts. Almost all of western Europe except England was directly involved and suffered accordingly. Central Europe was hit particularly hard, as can be seen in an account by a soldier writing under the name Simplicissimus, suffering population declines that would take two centuries to replace.

Despite the devastation, neither Protestantism nor Catholicism won decisively. What began as a religious war in Bohemia and the German principalities turned into a complex political struggle involving the ambitions of northern German rulers, the expansionist ambitions of Sweden, and the efforts of Catholic France to break the "Habsburg ring."

Despite the general decline of Habsburg supremacy in Spain, the early years of the war before 1629, usually cited as the Bohemian (1618–1625) and Danish (1625–1629) phases, brought a last brief revival of Habsburg prospects. The new Habsburg emperor, Ferdinand II, a fanatical Catholic, was determined to intensify the Counter-Reformation, set aside the Peace of Augsburg, and literally wipe out Protestantism in central Europe. For a time he almost succeeded.

Ferdinand's succession came amid severe political tension. Spreading Calvinism, in addition to the aggressive crusading of the Jesuits, had earlier led to the formation of a Protestant league of German princes in 1608 and a Catholic league to counter it the next year. The two alliances had almost clashed in 1610. Meanwhile, the Bohemian Protestants had extracted a promise of toleration from their Catholic king, Rudolf II (1576–1612). In 1618, the Bohemian leaders, fearing that Ferdinand would not honor that promise, threw two of his officials out a window after heated discussions—an incident known as the **defenestration of Prague.** When Ferdinand mobilized troops, the Bohemians refused to recognize him and gave their throne to Frederick, the Protestant elector of the Palatinate, in western Germany.

In the short Bohemian war that followed, Frederick was quickly overwhelmed. In 1620, Ferdinand deployed two strong armies, one from Spain and the other from Catholic Bavaria, and scattered the Bohemian forces at the battle of the White Mountain, near Prague. Ferdinand gave the Bohemian lands to Maximillian of Bavaria, distributed the holdings of Bohemian Protestant nobles among Catholic aristocrats, and proceeded to stamp out Protestantism in Bohemia. Of the some 3.2 million Bohemians in 1618, mostly Protestants, all that remained 30 years later were less than 1 million people, all Catholics.

War began again in 1625 when Christian IV (r. 1588–1648), the Lutheran king of Denmark, invaded Germany. As duke of Holstein and thus a prince of the empire, he hoped to revive Protestantism and win a kingdom in Germany for his youngest son. Unlike Frederick in Bohemia, Christian had support from the English, the Dutch, and the North German princes. Their help was not enough. Ferdinand dispatched his new general, Albert von Wallenstein, to crush the Protestants in a series of overpowering campaigns. By 1629, Christian had to admit defeat and withdraw his forces, thus ending the Danish conflict with another

defenestration of Prague—The end of negotiations between Bohemia and the Holy Roman Empire in 1618; the Bohemian representatives were so angry with the representatives of the Holy Roman Emperor that they threw them out the window.

▲ By the simplicity and starkness of his portrayal, the French artist Jacques Callot captured, in a series of 24 etchings, the senseless tragedy of the Thirty Years' War (1633). The dangling bodies in this plate dramatize the tenuousness of life in turbulent times.

Protestant debacle. Their successful campaigns of the 1620s gave the Habsburgs almost complete domination in Germany. In 1629, Ferdinand issued his Edict of Restitution, restoring to the Catholics all properties lost since 1552. This step seemed to be only the first step toward eliminating Protestantism completely and creating a centralized Habsburg empire in central Europe.

The Swedish and French Phases and the Balance of Power, 1630–1648

Fearing the Counter-Reformation and the growing Habsburg power behind it, threatened European states resumed the war in 1630. As the war rapidly spread and intensified, religious issues were steadily subordinated to power politics. This transformation could be seen in the phases of the conflict usually designated as the Swedish (1630–1635) and the French (1635–1648) because these two countries led successive and ultimately successful anti-Habsburg coalitions. By 1648, the Dutch Republic had replaced Spain as the leading maritime state, and Bourbon France had become the dominant European land power.

Protestant Swedes and French Catholics challenged Ferdinand's imperial ambitions for similar political reasons. Although Gustavus Adolphus (r. 1611–1632), the Swedish king, wanted to save German Lutheranism, he was also determined to prevent a strong Habsburg state on the Baltic from restricting his own expansion and interfering with Swedish trade. A similar desire to liberate France from Habsburg encirclement motivated Cardinal Richelieu, the powerful minister of Louis XIII. Richelieu offered Gustavus French subsidies, for which the Swedish monarch promised to invade Germany and permit Catholic worship in any lands he might conquer. Thus, the Catholic cardinal and the Protestant king compromised their religious differences in the hope of achieving mutual political benefits.

Gustavus invaded Germany in 1630, while the Dutch attacked the Spanish Netherlands. With his superior muskets, mobile cannons, and his hymn-singing Swedish veterans, Gustavus and his German allies won a series of smashing victories, climaxed in November 1632 at Lützen, near Leipzig, where Wallenstein was decisively defeated. Unfortunately for the Protestant cause, Gustavus died in the battle. A stalemate for the next 3 years led to the 1635 Peace of Prague and a momentary compromise between the emperor and the German Protestant states.

The situation now demanded that France act directly to further its dynastic interests. Thus, a final

Document

Simplicissimus on the Horrors of the Thirty Years' War

The Protestant and Catholic armies that ranged throughout central Europe destroyed entire villages, cities, and districts. Battles were the least of the problems for the unfortunate peasants caught in the way. Accompanying the armies were thousands of camp followers who took what they wanted and destroyed the rest. In some instances, it took two centuries for the devastated regions to regain their population levels and recover from the damage done by the competing forces. This account of disaster and suffering by Hans von Grimmelshausen (c. 1622–1676), the son of a German innkeeper who was left an orphan and carried away by soldiers during the Thirty Year's War, gives vivid testimony to the horrors of war. Writing under the name of Simplicissimus, he describes the arrival of an army in his home and the activities of the invaders. These ring as true for his day as they do for recent wars such as those in the Balkans, where destruction for destruction's sake and rape are common fare.

The first thing that the riders did was to stable their horses. After that, each one started to his own business which indicated nothing but ruin and destruction. While some started to slaughter, cook and fry, so that it looked as though they wished to prepare a gay feast, others stormed through the house from top to bottom as if the golden fleece of Colchis were hidden there. Others again took linen, clothing and other goods, making them into bundles as if they intended on going to market; what they did not want was broken up and destroyed. Some stabbed their swords through hay and straw as if they had not enough pigs to stab. Some shook the feathers out of the beds and filled the ticks with ham and dried meat as if they could sleep more comfortably in these. Others smashed the ovens and windows as if to announce an eternal summer. They beat copper and pewter vessels into lumps and packed the mangled pieces away. Bedsteads, tables, chairs, and benches were burned, although many stacks of dried wood stood in the yard. Earthenware pots and pans were all broken, perhaps because our guests preferred roasted meats, or perhaps they intended to eat only one meal with us. Our maid had been treated in the stable in such a way that she could not leave it any more—a shameful thing to tell! They bound the farm-hand and laid him on the earth, put a clamp of wood in his mouth and emptied a milking churn full of horrid dung water into his belly. This they called the Swedish drink, and they forced him to lead a party of soldiers to another place, where they looted men and cattle and brought them back to our yard. Among them were my dad, my mum and Ursula.

The soldiers now started to take the flints out of their pistols and in their stead screwed the thumbs of the peasants, and they tortured the poor wretches as if they were burning witches. They put one captive peasant into the bake-oven and put fire on him. Then they tied a rope around the head of another one, and twisted it with the help of a stick so tightly that blood gushed out through his mouth, nose and ears. In short everybody had his own invention to torture the peasants, and each peasant suffered his own martyrdom.... What happened to the captive women, maids and daughters I do not know as the soldiers would not let me watch how they dealt with them. I only very well remember that I heard them miserably crying in corners here and there, and I believe that my mum and Ursula had no better fate than the others.

In the midst of this misery I turned the spit and did not worry as I hardly understood what all this meant. In the afternoon I helped to water the horses and found our maid in the stable looking amazingly dishevelled. I did not recognize her but she spoke to me with pitiful voice:

"Oh, run away, boy, or the soldiers will take you with them. Look out, escape! Can't you see how evil..."

More she could not say.

Questions to Consider

1. What military roles do the physical abuse and rape mentioned by Simplicissimus play in the securing of an area? Are they just instances of bestial behavior or do they reflect military strategy?
2. In considering recent instances of conflict—for example, Yugoslavia, the Palestinian conflict, and Indonesia—do you find that the nature of warfare has changed significantly in the past four centuries?
3. Do you believe that if the local peasantry in the account you have just read had had their own weapons against the occupying army that their villages and property would have been saved?

Mark A. Kishlansky, ed., *Sources of the West: Readings in Western Civilization,* 4th ed., Longman Publishers, New York, 2001, pp. 15–18.

◀ Sweden's warrior-king Gustavus Adolphus is portrayed here at the battle of Breitenfeld in 1631.

French phase of the war began when French troops moved into Germany and toward the Spanish borders. The French also subsidized the Dutch and Swedes and an army of German Protestant mercenaries. The Paris government continued limiting Protestantism within its borders but gladly allied with Protestant states against Spain, Austria, Bavaria, and their Catholic allies. The war that had begun in religious controversy had now become pure power politics, completing the long political transition from medieval to modern times.

For 13 more years, the seemingly endless conflict wore on. France's allies, the Swedes and northern Germans, kept Habsburg armies engaged in Germany, while French armies and the Dutch navy concentrated on Spain. In 1643, the French beat the Spaniards in the decisive battle at Rocroi, in the southern Netherlands. Next they moved into Germany, defeating the imperial forces and, with the Swedes, ravaging Bavaria.

▼ Exhausted Europeans finally agreed to put an end to the Thirty Years' War with the Treaty of Westphalia. This agreement put an end to Habsburg ambitions in central Europe, marked the emergence of France as the major continental power, and removed religion as a factor in interstate relations. It also laid the foundations for modern international law.

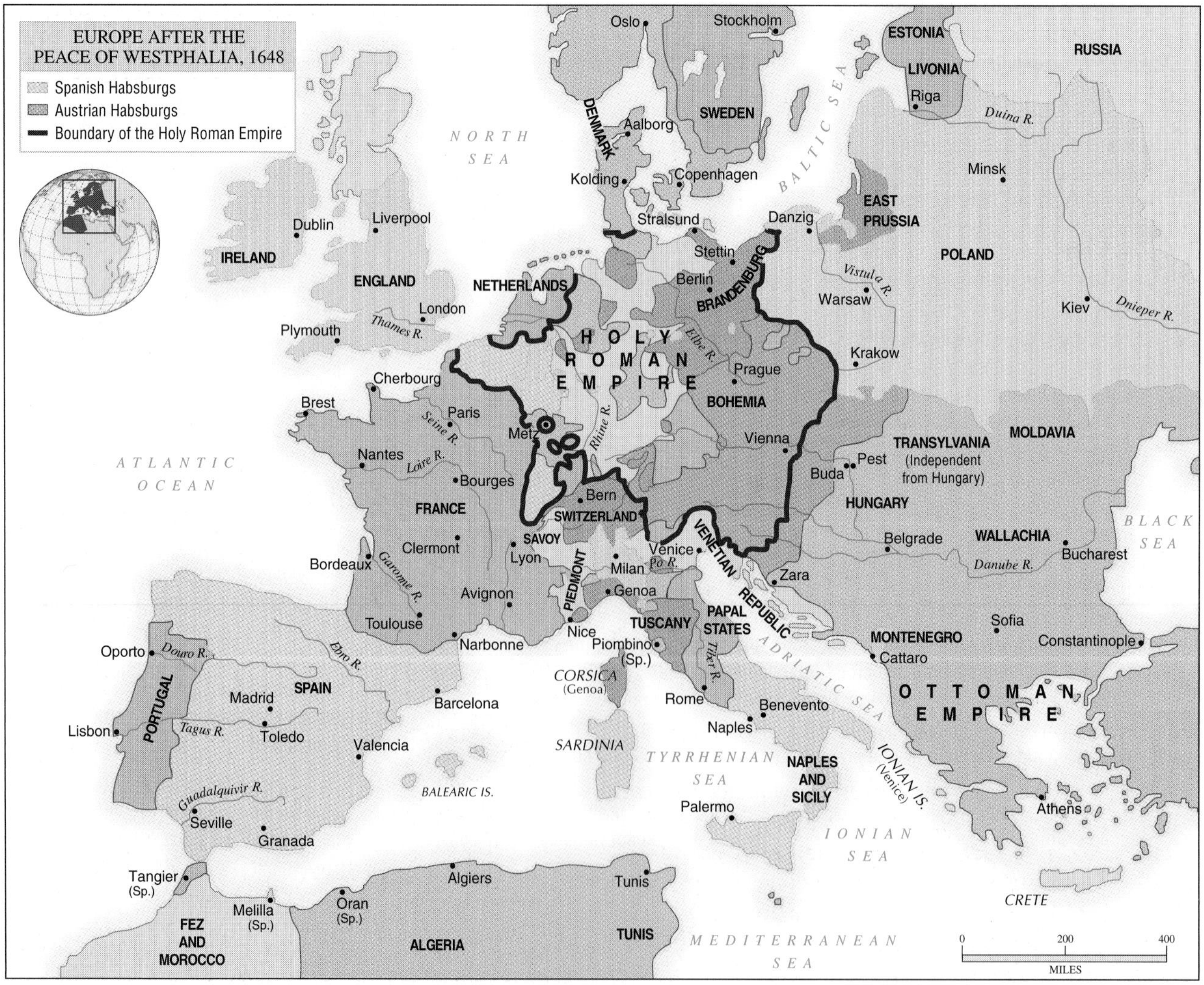

EUROPE AFTER THE PEACE OF WESTPHALIA, 1648

Spanish Habsburgs
Austrian Habsburgs
Boundary of the Holy Roman Empire

For all practical purposes, the war was over, but years of indecisive campaigning and tortuous negotiations delayed the peace. Finally, a horde of diplomats met at Westphalia in 1644. Even then, Spain and France could reach no agreement for 4 years, but a settlement for the empire, the Treaty of Westphalia, was finally completed in 1648.

The Peace of Westphalia

The peace agreement at Westphalia signaled a victory for Protestantism and the German princes while almost dooming Habsburg imperial ambitions: France moved closer to the Rhine by acquiring Alsatian territory; Sweden and Brandenburg acquired lands on the Baltic; and the Netherlands and Switzerland gained recognition of their independence. The emperor was required to obtain approval from the Imperial Diet for any laws, taxes, military levies, and foreign agreements—provisions that nearly nullified imperial power and afforded the German states practical control of their foreign relations. German religious autonomy, as declared at Augsburg, was also reconfirmed, with Calvinism now permitted along with Lutheranism. In addition, Protestant states were conceded all Catholic properties taken before 1624.

In its religious terms, the treaty ended the dream of reuniting Christendom. Catholics and Protestants now realized that major faiths could not be destroyed. With this admission, a spirit of toleration would gradually emerge. Although religious uniformity could be imposed within states for another century, it would not again be a serious issue in foreign affairs until the end of the twentieth century.

The Peace of Westphalia is particularly notable for confirming the new European state system. Henceforth states would customarily shape their policies in accordance with the power of their neighbors, seeking to expand at the expense of the weaker and to protect themselves—not by religion, law, or morality, but by alliances against their stronger adversaries. Based on the works of the Dutch jurist Grotius, the treaty also instituted the international conference as a means for registering power relationships among contending states, instituted the principle of the equality of all sovereign states—as seen today in the General Assembly of the United Nations—and put into practice the tools of modern diplomacy such as extraterritoriality and diplomatic immunities.

Both Spain and Austria were weakened, and the Austrian Habsburgs shifted their primary attention from central to southeastern Europe. German disunity was perpetuated by the autonomy of so many of the microstates. France emerged from this time as the clear winner, the potential master of the Continent. The war also helped England and the Netherlands. No matter the condition of the surviving states, their future relations would be based on the pure calculus of power, both military and economic.

Russia: From the Tatar Yoke to the Romanovs

How did the Russians free themselves from Mongol domination and create their own independent and expansive nation?

As we saw in Chapter 9, the center of Russian civilization moved from Kiev to Moscow during the period of the Mongol domination (1240–1480). While under the Tatar Yoke, as Mongol rule came to be called, Russia was cut off from contact with Europe and the small principality of Muscovy emerged to serve as collector of tribute for the Mongol court. New internal markets developed, and the Orthodox Church, left unhampered by the Mongols, grew in strength and influence.

▼ Beginning as a small fortress town, first mentioned in the chronicles in the mid-twelfth century, Moscow grew rapidly by 1500.

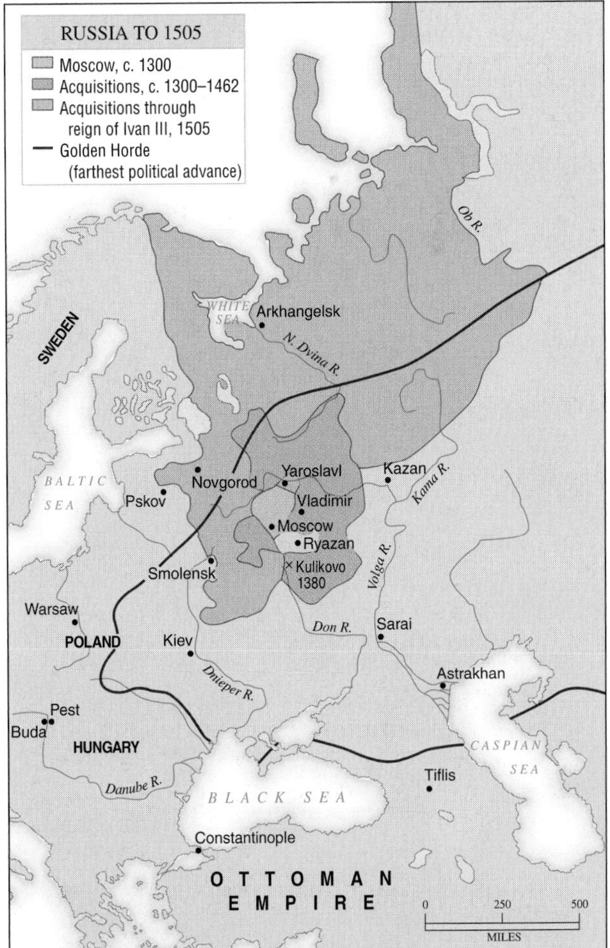

	Russia, 1300 to 1650
1380	Russians defeat the Mongols at battle of Kulikovo
1462–1505	Reign of Tsar Ivan III, the Great
1480	Mongol domination of Russia ends
1533–1584	Reign of Tsar Ivan IV, the Terrible
1613	Romanov dynasty begins (to 1917)
1649	Serfdom formally established

Moscow: Working For and Against the Mongols

In the first century after the Mongol invasion, the Muscovite princes showed a great deal of ambition and ability, albeit in a sometimes unattractive way. For example, the Muscovite leader Ivan I Kalita (r. 1328–1341), whose surname means "moneybags," greatly increased the wealth and power of his city through aggressive tax collection practices in the service of the Mongols.

On the surface, the fourteenth century appeared to be a time of decline for the Russians, who chafed under the Tatar Yoke and lost territory to European states to the west. Russia, however, was laying foundations for its future, with Moscow growing in stature to become the region's religious and political center. Indeed, by the close of the fourteenth century, Moscow grew so powerful that it stopped paying tribute to the Mongols. In 1380, when the Mongols came to punish the rebellious city, the Muscovite prince Dmitri Donskoi (r. 1359–1389) led combined Russian forces against their overlords, defeating the renowned Tatar horsemen at Kulikovo. The victory had great symbolic significance for the future Russian nation even though Mongol power was hardly broken. A Mongol army returned the next year and burned the wooden city of Moscow in retribution for its defiance. The Russians would have to endure another century under the Tatar Yoke.

Ivan III and the Third Rome

Moscow was rebuilt and continued to gain in stature in fifteenth century, but the nation that was growing up around it was continually threatened by civil war and invasions. Finally, Ivan III (r. 1462–1505) made major strides to build the modern Russian state. He conquered Novgorod and 2 years later ceased acknowledging Mongol domination. He then began to advance toward the south and east against the Tatars, setting in motion a drive of expansion that lasted for centuries.

In developments of considerable symbolic importance, the Russians embraced many elements of the Roman tradition. Ivan III married the niece of the last East Roman emperor, an alliance arranged by the pope. Russians espoused the theory that Moscow was the Third Rome, the logical successor to Constantinople as the center of Christianity. In 1492 (the year 7000 in the Orthodox calendar and the beginning of a new millennium), the Muscovite metropolitan, Zosima, stated that Ivan III was "the new Emperor Constantine of the new Constantinople Moscow." Zosima for the first time called Moscow an imperial city. Philotheus of Pskov (SKOV) expounded the theory of Third Rome in full detail in the 1520s. Ivan began to use the title *tsar* ("caesar") and adopted the Roman two-headed eagle as the symbol of the Russian throne.

DOCUMENT

Filofei and the Christian Role of Moscow

Ivan opened the doors to the West ever so slightly. He established diplomatic relations with a number of European powers. He brought in Italian technicians and architects such as Aristotele Fieravanti and Pietro Antonio Solari to work on the churches, palaces, and walls of the Kremlin: the vastly expanded site of the original fortress that was the center of the town three

◀ Ivan III understood the importance of symbolic affirmations of Russia's independent existence, free of Mongol domination. He claimed for Moscow the status of the "Third Rome," negotiated a marriage alliance with the family of the last Byzantine emperor, and asked leading Italian architects such as Aristotle Fioraventi to design and construct the Kremlin churches in 1475–1479. Shown here are the domes of the cathedrals of Annunciation and Assumption.

centuries earlier. The Italian artistic tradition had no lasting cultural impact on Russia, but use of Italian artists nonetheless signified an awareness of the West. In recognition of the need to establish a standing army, Ivan began the difficult process of building up a modern state structure and increased restrictions on the Russian peasants. During the fifteenth century, Ivan was the equal of his western European colleagues Henry VII of England and Louis XI of France. After three centuries of isolation under the Mongols, the Russians were again interacting with Europe.

Russian Autocracy Threatened

Ivan III's grandson, Ivan IV (1533–1584), later surnamed "the Terrible," tried to take the next step toward the imposition of a truly imperial, autocratic rule. Ivan was 3 years old when his father died, and during the next decade he learned to distrust the aristocratic boyars, who showed him, his mother, and his tutors no respect as they took advantage of his youth. Once he took power in the late 1540s, he began a series of reforms to put the Russian state on a modern footing. He published a new law code, brought together representatives of the Russian population—the ***Zemski Sobor*** (ZIEM-ski so-BOR)—to reform the administration of the land, saw his forces take Kazan and Astrakhan, and opened trade with the West.

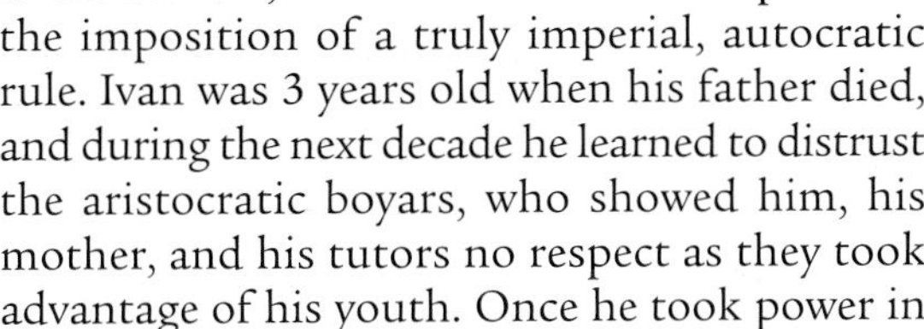

Ivan "the Terrible"

Zemski Sobor—A meeting of representatives of the Russian population—an assembly of the land—to reform the state in the 1550s and then to approve the choice of the Romanovs as the ruling family in 1613.

As would be the case with the monarchies in western and central Europe, Ivan faced the opposition of his nobles, the boyars, to his plans to strengthen the state. After 1560, he launched a full-scale war against them. He declared most of Russia, including Moscow, to be under a martial law, enforced by a group of special forces called the *oprichniki* (oh-PREACH-nee-kee), masked men of legendary cruelty dressed in black, riding black horses, carrying broomsticks topped with dog skulls. Ivan wanted to replace the old independent boyar class with a service nobility loyal only to him. To that end, he and the *oprichniki* drove 12,000 families from their lands in the dead of winter. To those who opposed him, Ivan responded with an inventive cruelty that gained him his name. As the terror increased, he lost control of himself, accidentally killing his beloved son and heir to the throne. Finally he achieved his goals, and the terror diminished. When he died in 1584, he was succeeded by another son, Fedor, who was totally unequipped to face the challenge of a devastated and discontented land.

Initially, Fedor ruled with the advice of his brother-in-law, Boris Godunov, a competent and ambitious boyar. For 7 years the country recovered from the trauma through which it had been put by Ivan IV; however, in 1591 Ivan's last son, Dmitri, died under mysterious circumstances, and when Fedor died in 1598 without an heir, the Rurik line of rulers came to an end. Boris presented himself as the next tsar and received the acclaim of the nobles and church. However, Russia felt the effects of the same famine, economic failure, and discontent that preceded the Thirty Years' War in central Europe. Boris's policies

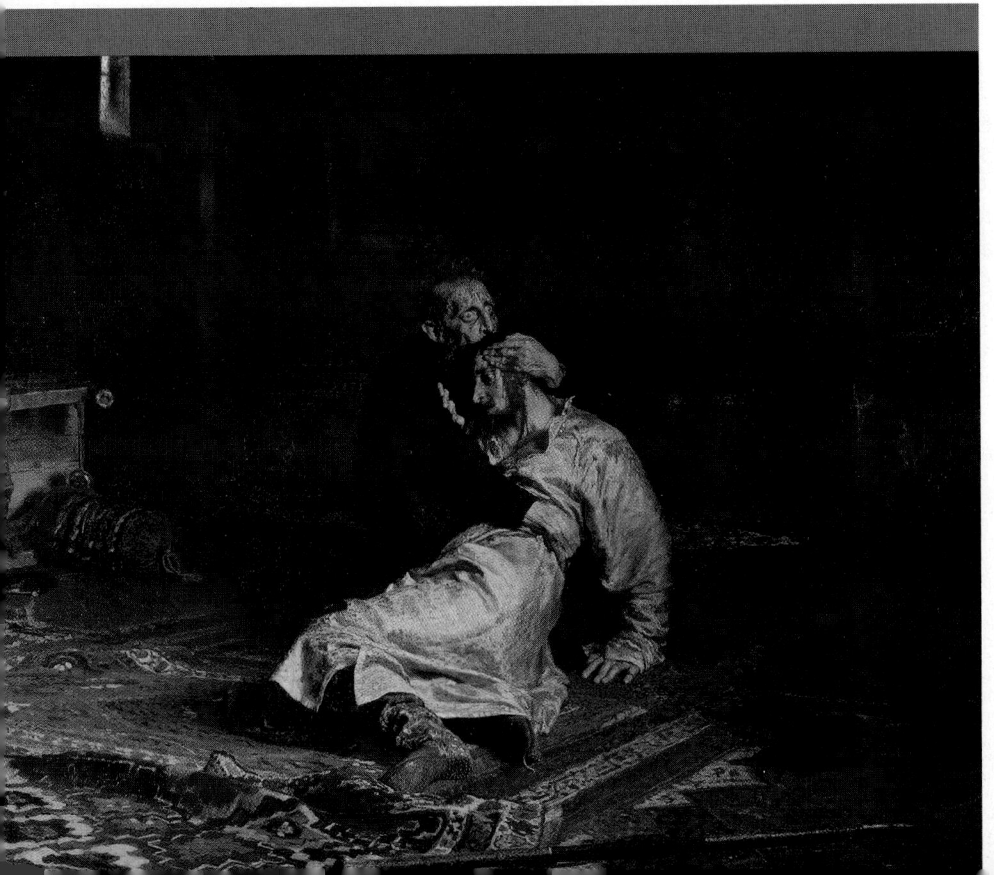

◄ In the second part of his reign, Ivan the Terrible lapsed into periods of insanity from time to time. In one of these periods he killed his favorite son and heir. Il'ya Repin captured this tragedy in a nineteenth-century painting.

failed to bring the country back to even minimal prosperity. At the same time, plots against him spread throughout the country, and when he died in 1605, there was no agreed-on successor. Eight years of civil war and Polish intervention, known as the "time of troubles," devastated Russia. Finally, the Russians reunited to drive the Poles out and call a *Zemski Sobor* in 1613 to choose a new ruling family, the Romanovs.

Between 1613 and 1676, the first two Romanov tsars, Michael and Alexis, integrated most aristocrats into the state nobility and achieved some degree of stability. As in Prussia, the nobles and the government were reconciled in their common exploitation of the serfs through the Code of 1649, which established serfdom, and the primitive agricultural economy encouraged aristocratic independence. Russian ignorance and technical deficiencies, along with a conservative-minded nobility, made the country stagnant in comparison with Western states.

Adan Olearius: A Foreign Traveler in Early Russia

The Balkans: Byzantine Collapse and Ottoman Rule

What were the factors that allowed the Ottoman Turks to conquer and rule the Balkans for 500 years?

Byzantium's last two centuries under its final dynasty, the Paleologus (1261–1453), saw the formerly glorious realm become a pawn in a new game. Having thrown off the Latin rule of the Crusaders in 1261 (see Chapter 9), the Greeks regained control of the church and the state, but there was precious little strength to carry on the ancient traditions. Byzantine coinage, which had retained its value from the fourth through the eleventh centuries, fell victim to inflation and weakness. The church, once a major pillar to help the state, became embroiled in continual doctrinal disputes. Slavic peoples such as the Bulgarians and the Serbs, who had posed no danger to the empire in its former strength, became threats. After Mongol invasions of the Middle East destroyed the exhausted Seljuq Turks in the thirteenth century, a new more formidable foe, the Ottoman or Osmanli Turks, appeared.

	The Balkans, 1300 to 1650
1261–1453	Paleologus dynasty rules Byzantium
1389	Ottomans defeat Serbs and Bosnians at battle of Kosovo, beginning domination of the Balkans
1396	Ottomans defeat Crusaders at Nicopolis
1453	Fall of Constantinople to the Ottomans

The Fall of Constantinople

The Ottomans (see Chapter 12) emerged from the groups of elite Turkish warriors, the *ghazis,* which came together on the northwestern frontier of Anatolia. They participated in the complex political and diplomatic relations in the Aegean area in the wake of the Fourth Crusade and were ready to take advantage of the weakened Byzantine Empire. Blessed after 1296 with a strong line of male successors and good fortune, the Ottomans rapidly expanded their power through the Balkans.

It was the Byzantines themselves who had invited the Turks to cross the Dardanelles during one of their periodic dynastic disputes. But after 1345, the Ottoman Turks began their biannual incursions into Europe. Three hundred years later, the Ottomans would be at the gates of Vienna. In a time of economic difficulties and religious controversies, there was a considerable degree of class conflict in the area. In addition, instead of uniting against the Ottomans, the various Slavic princes squabbled with each other, mirroring the civil wars in the Byzantine world, until it was too late.

The Ottomans were nothing if not patient, and they took advantage of the conflicts within the Balkans. They understood that they did not have enough troops in the 1350s and 1360s to take the area by force, so they proceeded forward diplomatically, signing treaties, establishing tribute payments, and then rearming for the next advance.

They crossed the Darndanelles into Europe in 1354 and moved up the Vardar and Morava valleys to take Adrianopole, the present day Edirne, in 1362, and from there they proceeded in a measured matter through Macedonia, taking Serres (1383), Sofia (1385), Nis (1386), Thessalonica (1387).

Finally on June 15, 1389, Sultan Murad I defeated the Serbian and Bosnian forces at Kosovo and effectively sealed Ottoman control over the Balkans for the next 500 years. Of all of the Balkan nations, only Montenegro would be able to escape Ottoman rule.

The Ottoman Turks' overwhelming infantry and cavalry superiority gave them their military victories. But their administrative effectiveness, which combined strength and flexibility, solidified their rule in areas they conquered. In contrast to the Christians, both Roman and Byzantine, who were intolerant of theological differences, the Turks allowed monotheists or any believers in a "religion of the book" (the Bible, Torah, or Qur'an) to retain their faith and be ruled by their own religious superior through the **millet system,** a network of religious ghettos.

---

millet system—The Ottoman Turks ruled in accord with religious law and governed their holdings as a theocratic state. Non-Turks were ruled according to their religious faith, and responsibilities for governance were handed over to the chief figures of each religious area, or millet.

Seeing Connections

The Fall of Constantinople

Constantinople, as befits a rich and powerful city at the crossroads between Europe and Asia, had been besieged a number of times since its dedication in 325 C.E. Excepting the Latin conquest of 1204, the city's magnificent defensive site and imposing walls repelled all attackers for more than a thousand years. In 1453, the city again faced a besieging force, this time the Ottoman Turks led by Sultan Mehmed II. The 7,000 or so Byzantine forces defending the city included some 2,000 Italian mercenaries led by the Genoese general Giovanni Giustiani. Among the vastly more numerous Ottoman forces—estimates range between 80,000 and 150,000 men—was a Catholic Hungarian artillery engineer named Urban. Urban had offered his services to the Byzantines first, but the emperor Constantine XI did not want to pay the demanded price or acquire the bronze needed to cast Urban's artillery pieces. Motivated more by money than culture or faith, Urban then went to the Ottomans in Adrianople, who hired him. The Turks began their attack on the city on April 2, 1453. Despite the vast disparity in forces, the city walls held for 57 days. Finally, a combination of Urban's cannons and the numerical superiority of their forces allowed the Turks to breach the walls and take the city on Tuesday, May 29. Urban was not the only Christian who fought alongside the Muslim Ottomans, who centuries earlier had themselves fought as mercenaries in the pay of the Byzantines. Under the Turks, Constantinople, renamed Istanbul in 1922, remained—and remains to this day—a rich and powerful city at the crossroads between Europe and Asia, a meeting place for the cultures, economies, ideologies, and religions of Eurasia.

In response to the Ottoman advance, the West mounted a poorly conceived and ill-fated crusade against them. The confrontation at Nicopolis on the Danube in 1396 resulted in the capture and slaughter of 10,000 knights and their attendants. Only the overwhelming force of Tamerlane (Timur the Magnificent), a Turco-Mongol ruler who invaded from the east and defeated the Ottoman army in 1402, gave Constantinople and Europe some breathing space.

DOCUMENT

Kritovoulos on the Fall of Constantinople

The end for Constantinople came in May 1453. The last emperor, Constantine XI, and his force of 9,000, half of whom were Genoese, held off 160,000 Ottomans for seven weeks. Finally, with the help of Hungarian artillerymen, the Turks breached the once impenetrable walls of the depopulated city. After 1123 years, the shining fortress fell.

DOCUMENT

Nestor-Iskander on the Fall of Constantinople

▼ By the mid-sixteenth century, the Ottoman Empire encompassed the entire Balkan peninsula.

The Balkans Under Ottoman Rule

After the Ottoman conquest, the Balkans would experience a different historical development from the rest

Discovery Through Maps

The Battle of Kahlenberg

The expansion of the Ottomans into eastern and central Europe brought them to the gates of Vienna more than once. They first besieged the city in 1529 and, having failed to conquer it then, attempted to take it again a second time in 1683. In the 150 years since the first attack, the Habsburg emperors had grown stronger, but Vienna remained a goal for the Ottomans: control of the town would offer them a strategic advantage for a push deeper into central Europe.

On September 11 and 12, 1683, the invading Ottomans fought an alliance of Polish, Austrian, and German defenders. The outcome of the battle of Kahlenberg would either be the Turkish conquest of Vienna, which had been under siege since July 14, or the breach of the siege and a retreat of the Ottoman forces. The Ottoman forces commanded by Grand Vizier Merzifonlu Kara Mustafa Pasha numbered 140,000; those of the combined European forces, led by Poland's King Jan Sobieski III, numbered only 70,000. After savage fighting, however, the Polish forces carried the day, and the Turks retreated in disarray.

The second siege of Vienna in 1683 marked high tide of the Turkish advance into Europe, and although the Ottomans remained formidable into the eighteenth century, the battle of Kahlenberg generally marks the beginning of their long decline.

Franz Geffels's painting of the battle shown here renders Vienna and its environs with maplike detail. Set above and behind the fighting in the foreground, the painting offers a view of Vienna from the hills to the west, the *Wienerwald,* and clearly shows Stephen's Church and other smaller churches set within the city's circular defensive walls. Vienna survived the battle and prospered, as the Habsburg moved on to consolidate their control of large parts of central and eastern Europe. Seen from a distance, the city remains today, if one allows for a little imagination, not much changed from Geffels's painting.

Questions to Consider

1. How does the artist portray the Turks in their assembled might? As an organized, or as a slightly disordered force?
2. Why do you think the city of Vienna developed in a circular layout?
3. Why was this attack in 1683 historically significant?

of Europe. The Ottomans ruled through a theocratic model—all were slaves of the sultan who was, himself, the shadow of God. Sharia law was to be followed by Muslims, based on the Koran and other religious writings. There was no secular state.

The nations of the Balkans were ruled either as core provinces or as vassal states. In the core, the different regions were under the command of a governor—who had his miniature version of the Istanbul government. He delegated power to various regional and district authorities, while combining military and civilian authority. Then there were the vassal states—Moldavia, Wallachia, Transylvania, and Ragusa-Dubrovnik (ra-GOOZ-a dew-

An Ambassador's Report on the Ottoman Empire

BROV-nik)—who were allowed to rule themselves in return for loyalty to the sultan and extensive payments in money and grain.

In the core provinces, those who were not Muslims, but followers of a religion of the book—the Bible or the Torah—were governed theocratically, also, through the millet system. As Peter Sugar noted, "These were parallel organizations, and each was independent within the limits of its own competence. The Ottomans had no concept corresponding to national lines of differentiation ... but of religions....The purpose of the ... system was simply to create a secondary imperial administrative and primary legal structure for the *dhimmis* (non-Muslims in a protected position)."[5] The chief rabbi in Istanbul had his own courts and law enforcers for Jews, as did the leaders of each Christian division—Armenian Catholics, Roman Catholics, and Orthodox Christians. The Phanariote Greeks who dominated the Orthodox structure became extremely powerful in the Balkans during Ottoman rule.

The Ottoman armies remained the most important part of the sultan's government. Before going into Europe, the military was characterized by valiant, independent volunteer horsemen, who fought when there was a war and went home when there was none. Once the empire began to expand in Europe, Sultan Orkhan began to divide the new land among his soldiers, to be given to them for their lifetime. This rewarded the forces for their work but did not create, for the moment, a hereditary service nobility. Orkhan also created a new, slave-based army, the janissaries.

As the empire grew larger, the Ottomans needed more fighters and bureaucrats. They instituted in the core area an arrangement to supply soldiers and bureaucrats, the **devshirme** (dev-SHIR-ma) system. Ottoman officials would go to villages throughout the Balkans and select male children whom they would take from their families and enroll in Ottoman service. The boys thus chosen would be given examinations to determine where they would serve the sultan, whether as janissaries or officials at the highest levels. This levy of Christian male children was carried on between the end of the fourteenth century and the beginning of the seventeenth system, and historians estimate that around 200,000 sons were taken from their families during that time. Most of the boys taken came from the Slavic Orthodox populations.

The Balkans participated in none of the formative developments of modern European civilization. They did not experience the Renaissance nor the Reformation, the Capitalist and Scientific Revolutions, nor the Enlightenment and Industrialization. The splendor of Ottoman-controlled Constantinople was paid for by the exactions—human and materials—taken from the Balkans peoples. When the region reentered European affairs in the nineteenth century, it lagged behind central and western Europe.[6]

Conclusion

On a global scale, the nations of Europe in the fourteenth century were a diverse group of conflicting states that were poor in comparison to China, weak in comparison with the Ottomans, disorganized in comparison with the Incas, and uncultured when compared to the peoples of the Indian subcontinent. Four centuries later, the Europeans had passed from a underdeveloped fringe of the Eurasian land mass to imposing themselves on the rest of the world. One of the key factors influencing this change of fortune was the formation of the nation-state. Despite almost constant military, political, and religious conflict, the years between 1300 and 1650 saw the nation-state system firmly established in western and central Europe, particularly in the Atlantic states of Spain, France, and England.

The 130 years after Luther's stand at Wittenberg in 1517 was an era of decisive change for Europe. At the opening of the period, most people in their villages were still imbued with the individual, medieval concern for salvation, which gave meaning to the religious issues of the Protestant Reformation and Catholic Counter-Reformation. In the century after the Peace of Augsburg (1555), the nature of state and society changed. Initially, long and exhaustive religious wars and civil wars dominated the Continent. Later, secular political concerns became increasingly evident. But whether the wars were for faith or for state, or a combination of the two, the period until the Treaty of Westphalia ended the Thirty Years' War was the bloodiest century Europe would endure until the twentieth. Finally, in 1648, the modern state structure emerged. Western and central Europeans now lived, for better or worse, in a world of nation-states dominated by secular concerns.

In Russia and the Balkans, state building proceeded in vastly different ways. The leaders of Kiev Rus' chose to be converted by the Orthodox Church of Constantinople, and accepted the major elements of the Byzantine civilization. The Balkan states came into existence under the political, religious, and cultural dominance of the Byzantine Empire: the Bulgarians and Serbs, directly, and the Albanians and Romanians, indirectly. In Eastern Europe, the Russians under Ivan III finally broke 300 years of Mongol rule and attempted to construct a strong central state. The early Russian attempts consolidating state power were only

devshirme—The Ottoman levy of Christian male children in the Balkans. More than 200,000 young boys were taken from their families to serve in the Ottoman army or bureaucracy.

partially successful in the face of numerous internal and external challenges until the Romanovs finally brought some stability to the nation. To the southwest of Russia, the Balkan nations fell under the domination of the Ottoman Turks during the fourteenth and fifteenth centuries, which delayed state development in this region until the nineteenth century.

Suggestions for Web Browsing

You can obtain more information about topics included in this chapter at the websites listed below. See also the companion website that accompanies this text, http://www.ablongman.com/brummett, which contains an online study guide and additional resources.

End of Europe's Middle Ages
http://www.ucalgary.ca/applied_history/tutor/endmiddle/
This site is developed to aid students of the late Middle Ages by providing collected links and access to primary sources.

Tudor England
http://tudor.simplenet.com/
Site detailing life in Tudor England includes biographies, maps, important dates, architecture, and music, including sound files.

The Thirty Years' War
http://www.pipeline.com/~cwa/TYWHome.htm
http://en.wikipedia.org/wiki/Thirty_Years'_War
http://www.historylearningsite.co.uk/thirty_years_war.htm
Images and explanations of Europe's bloodiest conflict until 1914.

Peace of Westphalia
http://www.yale.edu/lawweb/avalon/westphal.htm
Complete text of the peace treaties that together made up the Treaty of Westphalia (1648), which ended the Thirty Years' War.

Byzantium Studies on the Internet
http://www.fordham.edu/halsall/byzantium/
A collection of the more significant documents relating to the evolution of Byzantine institutions.

Ottoman Page
http://ottoman.home.mindspring.com/
Site dedicated to classical Ottoman history, 1300–1600, offering numerous links to other sites.

Literature and Film

Several recent and outstanding translations and/or editions of later medieval literature are available: Geoffrey Chaucer, *The Canterbury Tales in Modern English,* ed. Neville Coghill (Penguin, 2000); Dante Alighieri, *The Divine Comedy,* trans. Allen Mandelbaum (Knopf, 1995); and Giovanni Boccaccio, *Decameron,* trans. G. H. McWilliam (Penguin, 1996) are outstanding presentations.

This is a rich period for novels. The activities of this time attracted the best attentions of Alexandre Dumas. Writing about events in France, he produced *The Two Dianas* (dealing with the time of Francis I), *The Page of the Duke of Savoy* (touching the time of the emperor Charles V), *Ascanio* (France in the middle of the century), and *Marguerite de Valois* (touching the civil wars), and this is only an incomplete list. Mark Twain wrote about the time of Edward VI in *The Prince and the Pauper* (1881). More recently, Robin Maxwell sheds some light on the reign of Henry VIII in *The Secret Diary of Anne Boleyn: A Novel* (Scribner, 1998), and Reay Tannahill's *Fatal Majesty: A Novel of Mary Queen of Scots* (Griffin, 2000) offers another recent discussion of the tragic queen.

Some excellent video explorations of the late medieval period are *Siena: Chronicle of a Medieval Commune* (Metropolitan Museum of Art, 1988); *Landmarks of Western Art: The Medieval World* (Kultur Video, 1999); *Living in the Past: Life in Medieval Times* (Kultur Video, 1998); and *Medieval Warfare* (Kultur Video, 3 tapes; 1997).

Filmmakers have been equally attracted to the period, especially the English scene. (All of the following are available in VHS.) Fred Zinnemann's *A Man for all Seasons* (1966; Columbia) is a fine telling of the story of Sir Thomas More. Queen Elizabeth has been the subject of films throughout the twentieth century, including Shekhar Kapur's *Elizabeth* (1998; Channel Four Films), and indirectly in *Shakespeare in Love* (1998; Miramax). A film dealing with the period after Henry VIII is Trevor Nunn's *Lady Jane* (1986; Paramount). A 1933 film, Alexander Korda's *The Private Life of Henry VIII* (London Film Productions) is worth seeing, as is *Mary Queen of Scots* (Charles Jarrett, director; 1971; Universal Pictures). On the Continent, *The Return of Martin Guerre* (Daniel Vigne, director; 1982; European International) does justice to Natalie Zemon Davis's fine monograph. *Martin Luther* (1953; Louis de Rochemont Associates) is a revealing look at the reformer.

Suggestions for Reading

Daniel Herlihy, *The Black Death and the Transformation of the West* (Harvard University Press, 1997), is a fine introduction to western and central European events. For English history see Nigel Saul, ed., *The Oxford History of Medieval England* (Oxford, 2001) and P. S. P. Goldberg, ed., *Women in Medieval English Society* (Sutton, 1997). See also Bernard T. Reilly, *The Medieval Spains* (Cambridge University Press, 1993) and Jonathan Sumpton, *The Hundred Years' War: Trial by Battle* (University of Pennsylvania Press, 1999). Geoffrey Parker, *The Grand Strategy of Philip II* (Yale University Press, 1998), is the best study of the construction of the Spanish world empire.

For the Dutch rebellion, see James D. Tracy's *Holland Under Habsburg Rule* (University of California Press, 1990). See also Charles R. Boxer, *The Dutch Seaborne Empire* (Penguin, 1989), for a depiction of the republic at the apex of its struggle for power and wealth.

French society and politics during the whole era are ably treated in Mack P. Holt, *The French Wars of Religion, 1562–1629* (Cambridge University Press, 1995). A good survey of the reign of the Virgin Queen is Wallace T. MacCaffrey, *Elizabeth I, War and Politics 1588–1603* (Princeton University Press, 1992).

See Lonnie R. Johnson, *Central Europe: Enemies, Neighbors, Friends* (Oxford University Press, 1996) for a good survey of the region's history. On the less-developed absolutism in eastern Europe, see Robert James Weston Evans, *The Mak-*

ing of the Habsburg Monarchy, 1550–1700 (Oxford University Press, 1984); see also Norman Davies, *A History of Poland,* Vol. 1 (Columbia University Press, 1981. Ronald G. Asch, *The Thirty Years' War, the Holy Roman Empire and Europe, 1618–1648* (St. Martin's Press, 1997), is a brief up-to-date survey with a good appreciation of the historiographical conflicts surrounding this event.

Robert O. Crummey, *The Formation of Muscovy, 1304–1613* (Longman, 1987), is a first-rate survey of the early phases of Russian history. See also W. Bruce Lincoln, *The Romanovs* (Dial, 1981). Oscar Halecki, *Borderlands of Western Civilization* (Random House, 1984), gives the outlines of eastern European history, especially the northern region.

Donald Nicol, *The Last Centuries of Byzantium,* 2nd ed. (Cambridge University Press, 1993), discusses the empire in its state of weakness. The Ottoman Golden Age is ably depicted in Halil Inalcik, *Phoenix: The Ottoman Empire, the Classical Age 1300–1600* (Phoenix Press, 2001).

CHAPTER 16

Global Encounters

Europe and the New World Economy, 1400–1650

Outline

- The Iberian Golden Age
- The Portuguese and Africa
- The Growth of New Spain
- Iberian Systems in the New World
- Beginnings of Northern European Expansion

Features

SEEING CONNECTIONS **The Portuguese in Benin**

DISCOVERY THROUGH MAPS **Savage Pictures: Sebastian Munster's Map of Africa**

DOCUMENT **Portuguese Encounters with Africans**

DOCUMENT **Disease and the Spanish Conquest**

◀ This ivory saltcellar, with its carved figure of a Portuguese sailor in the crow's nest, makes clear the European influence on the artists of Benin.

During the fifteenth century, European nations began a process of exploration, conquest, and trade, affecting almost all areas of the world. Their activities were mirrored in other parts of the world as Asian and Arab states took the lead in expanding their trading networks and their connections with each other. The processes were furthered by improved navigational technology and the resulting expansion of trade that encouraged long sea voyages by Arabs, Japanese, and Chinese. Likewise, sea power, rather than land-based armies, was the key to Europe's becoming a significant force in various parts of the world.

European endeavors overseas were obviously related—both as cause and as effect—to trends set in motion as Europe emerged from the medieval era. The Crusades and the Renaissance stimulated European curiosity; the Reformation produced thousands of zealous missionaries seeking converts in foreign lands and refugees searching for religious freedom; and the monarchs of emerging sovereign states sought revenues, first by trading in the Indian Ocean and later by exploiting new worlds. Perhaps the most critical influence was the rise of European capitalism, with its monetary values, profit-seeking motivations, investment institutions, and consistent impulses toward economic expansion. Some historians have labeled this whole economic transformation the Commercial Revolution. Others have used the phrase to refer to the shift in trade routes from the Mediterranean to the Atlantic. Interpreted either way, the Commercial Revolution and its accompanying European expansion helped lay the foundation for the emergence of a global economy.

Europe's Commercial Revolution developed in two quite distinct phases. The first phase involved Portugal and Spain; the second phase, after 1600, was led by the Netherlands, England, and to some extent France.

The Iberian Golden Age

What motivated the Portuguese and Spanish to develop global commercial networks?

Portugal and Spain, the two Iberian states, launched the new era in competition with each other, although neither was able to maintain initial advantages over the long term. Portugal lacked the manpower and resources required by an empire spread over three continents. Spain wasted its new wealth in waging continuous wars while neglecting to develop its own economy. In 1503, Portuguese pepper cost only one-fifth as much as pepper coming through Venice and the eastern Mediterranean. Within decades, gold and silver from the New World poured into Spain. Iberian bullion and exotic commodities, flowing into northern banks and markets, provided a major stimulus to European capitalism. This early European impact abroad also generated great cultural diffusion, promoting an intercontinental spread of peoples, plants, animals, and knowledge that the world had never seen before. But it also destroyed states in the Americas and weakened societies in Africa.

Conditions Favoring Iberian Expansion

A number of conditions invited Iberian maritime expansion in the fifteenth century. Muslim control over the eastern caravan routes, particularly after the Turks took Constantinople in 1453, brought rising prices in Europe. At the same time, the sprawling Islamic world lacked both unity and intimidating sea power, and China, after 1440, had abandoned its extensive naval forays into the Indian Ocean. Because Muslim and Italian rivals prevented the Iberian states from tapping into the spice trade in the eastern Mediterranean and the gold trade in West Africa, Portugal and Spain sought alternative sea routes to the East, where their centuries-old struggle with Muslims in the Mediterranean might be continued on the ocean shores of sub-Saharan Africa and Asia.

During the 1400s, Iberian navigators became proficient in new naval technology and tactics. They adopted the compass (which came from China through the Middle East), the **astrolabe,** the portolan map that made it possible to plot courses across open seas, and the triangular **lateen sail** that gave their ships the ability to take advantage of winds coming from oblique angles and cut weeks off longer voyages. They also learned to tack against the wind, thus partly freeing them from hugging the coast on long voyages. This skill was important because prevailing winds and ocean currents made it impossible for Portuguese sailors to go farther south than Cape Bojador (bo-hyah-DOR) and still return home. Beyond that point, the sailors believed there was an impenetrable "Green Sea of Darkness," but in 1434, a Portuguese seafarer learned that it was possible to sail west toward the Canary Islands and catch trade winds that allowed ships to proceed home. This discovery opened up a new era of exploration.

The Iberians, especially the Portuguese, were also skilled cartographers and chartmakers. But their main advantages lay with their ships and naval guns. The stormy Atlantic required broad bows, deep keels, and complex square rigging for driving and maneuvering fighting ships. Armed with brass cannons, such ships could sink enemy vessels without ramming or boarding at close range, which were the traditional means of fighting at sea. They could also bombard coastal defenses. Even the much larger Chinese junks were no match for the European ships' maneuverability and firepower.

A strong religious motivation augmented Iberian naval efficiency. Long and bitter wars with the Muslim Moors had left the Portuguese and Spanish with an obsessive drive to convert non-Christians or destroy them in the name of Christ. Sailors with Columbus recited prayers every night, and Portuguese seamen were equally devout. Every maritime mission was regarded as a holy crusade.

For two centuries, Iberians had hoped to expand their influence in Muslim lands by launching a new

astrolabe—An instrument used in navigation for calculating latitude.

lateen sail—A triangular sail that is set at a 45-degree angle to the mast and takes advantage of winds coming from oblique angles.

Chronology

1300	1400		1500	1600	
1394–1460 Prince Henry the Navigator	**1400s** Iberian navigators develop new naval technology; Spain and Portugal stake claims in Asia, Africa, and the Americas; Atlantic slave trade begins	**1492** Christopher Columbus reaches San Salvador **1498** Vasco da Gama rounds Cape of Good Hope, reaches India	**1513** Vasco de Balboa reaches Pacific Ocean **1519** Hernando Cortés arrives in Mexico, defeats Aztecs **1520** Ferdinand Magellan rounds South America	**c. 1600** Second phase of European overseas expansion begins **1609** Henry Hudson establishes Dutch claims in North America; English East India Company chartered	**1620** Pilgrims land at Plymouth

Christian crusade in concert with Ethiopia. The idea originated with twelfth-century crusaders in the Holy Land; it gained strength later with Ethiopian migrants at Rhodes, who boasted of their king's prowess against the infidels. Thus arose the myth of "Prester John," a mighty Ethiopian monarch and potential European ally against Mongols, Turks, and Muslims. In response to a delegation from Zar'a Ya'kob, the reigning emperor, a few Europeans visited Ethiopia after 1450. These and other similar contacts greatly stimulated the determination to find a new sea route to the East that might link the Iberians with the legendary Ethiopian king and bring Islam under attack from two sides.

"The Land of Prester John"

This dream of war for the cross was sincere, but it also served to rationalize more worldly concerns. Both Spain and Portugal experienced dramatic population growth between 1400 and 1600. The Spanish population increased from 5 to 8.5 million; the Portuguese population more than doubled, from 900,000 to 2 million, despite a manpower loss of 125,000 in the sixteenth century. Hard times in rural areas prompted migration to cities, where dreams of wealth in foreign lands encouraged fortune seeking overseas. Despite the obvious religious zeal of many Iberians, particularly among those in holy orders, a fervent desire for gain was the driving motivation for most migrants.

The structures of the Iberian states provided further support for overseas expansion. In both, the powers of the monarchs had been recently expanded and were oriented toward maritime adventure as a means to raise revenues, divert the Turkish menace, spread Catholic Christianity, and increase national unity. The Avis dynasty in Portugal, after usurping the throne and alienating the great nobles in 1385, made common cause with the gentry and middle classes, who prospered in commercial partnership with the government. In contrast, Spanish nobles, particularly the Castilians, were very much like Turkish aristocrats, who regarded conquest and plunder as their normal functions and sources of income. Thus, the Portuguese and Spanish political systems worked in different ways toward similar imperial ends.

Staking Claims

During the late fifteenth century, both Portugal and Spain staked claims abroad. Portugal gained a long lead over Spain in Africa and Asia. But after conquering Granada, the last Moorish state on the Iberian peninsula, and completely uniting the country, the Spanish monarchs turned their attention overseas. The resulting historic voyage of Christopher Columbus established Spanish claims to most of the Western Hemisphere.

The man most responsible for Portugal's ambitious exploits was Prince Henry (1394–1460), known as "the Navigator" because of his famous observatory

▼ Using ships like these broad-beamed carracks, the Portuguese controlled much of the carrying trade with the East in the fifteenth and sixteenth centuries.

at Sagres (SAH-greesh), where skilled mariners and mapmakers gathered to plot voyages and record their results. As a young man in 1415, Henry directed the Portuguese conquest of Ceuta (see-YOO-tah), a Muslim port on the Moroccan coast, at the western entrance to the Mediterranean. This experience imbued him with a lifelong desire to divert the West African gold trade from Muslim caravans to Portuguese ships. He also shared the common dream of winning Ethiopian Christian allies against the Turks. Such ideas motivated him for 40 years as he sent expeditions down the West African coast, steadily charting and learning from unknown waters.

Before other European states began extensive explorations, the Portuguese had navigated the West African coast to its southern tip. Henry's captains claimed the Madeira Islands in 1418 and the Azores in 1421. A thousand miles to the west of Portugal, these uninhabited islands were settled to produce, among other things, wheat for bread-starved Lisbon.

	Portuguese and Spanish Exploration and Expansion
1470–1541	Francisco Pizarro
1474–1566	Bartolomé de Las Casas
1479	Treaty of Alcacovas
1494	Treaty of Tordesillas
1509–1515	Alfonso de Albuquerque serves as eastern viceroy of Portugal
1510–1554	Francisco de Coronado
1510	Portuguese acquire Goa, in India
1531	Pizarro defeats Incas in Peru
c. 1550	Spanish introduce plantation system to Brazil
1565	St. Augustine founded; first European colony in North America

▼ Motivated by a desire to find a sea route to India that bypassed the overland caravan routes controlled by Muslim states, Prince Henry the Navigator was a leading figure in promoting Portuguese explorations down the West African coast. Ironically he seldom left Portugal himself. When he died in 1460, his sailors had reached the Canary Islands, but by the end of that century, Vasco da Gama had sailed from Portugal to India.

By 1450, the Portuguese had explored the Senegal River and then traced the Guinea coast during the next decade. After Henry's death in 1460, they pushed south, reaching Benin in the decade after 1470 and Kongo, on the southwest coast, in 1482. Six years later, Bartolomeu Dias rounded southern Africa, but his disgruntled crew forced him to turn back. Nevertheless, King John II of Portugal (1481–1495) was so excited by the prospect of a direct route to India that he named Dias's discovery the "Cape of Good Hope."

Spain soon challenged Portuguese supremacy. The specific controversy was over the Canary Islands, some of which were occupied by Castilians in 1344 and others by Portuguese after the 1440s. The issue, which produced repeated incidents, was ultimately settled in 1479 by the Treaty of Alcacovas (ahl-KAHS-ko-vahsh), which recognized exclusive Spanish rights in the Canaries but banned Spain from the Madeiras, the Azores, the Cape Verdes, and West Africa. Spanish ambitions were thus temporarily frustrated until Christopher Columbus provided new hope.

Columbus (1451–1506), a Genoese sailor with an impossible dream, had been influenced by Marco Polo's journal to believe that Japan could be reached by a short sail directly westward. Although he underestimated the distance by some 7000 miles and was totally ignorant of the intervening continents, Columbus persistently urged his proposals on King John of Portugal

Christopher Columbus and the Round World

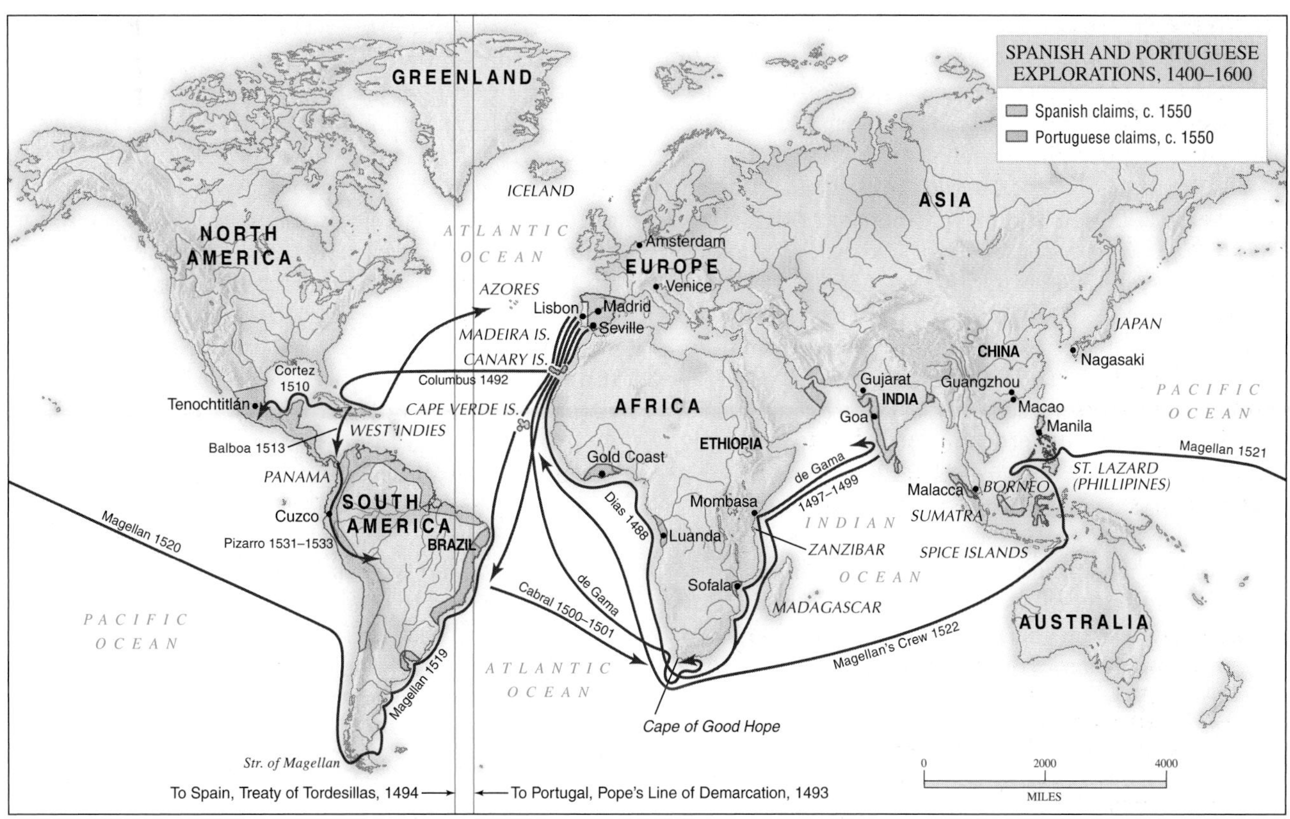

▲ From the mid-fifteenth to the mid-sixteenth centuries, Portugal and Spain took advantage of new naval technology and tactics to become the leading seafaring nations in the world.

and Queen Isabella of Spain, who was captivated by Columbus's dream and became his most steadfast sponsor of his voyages until her death in 1504.

The year 1492 was a momentous one for the Spanish crown. It finally took Granada, the last Muslim state in Iberia, expelled Jews from the country for refusing to convert to Christianity, and backed Columbus's voyage. Columbus sailed from Palos, Spain, with 90 men in three small ships on August 3, 1492, and landed at San Salvador in the West Indies on October 12, thinking he had reached the islands of Japan. In three more attempts, he continued his search for a passage to China. His voyages touched the major Caribbean islands, Honduras, the Isthmus of Panama, and Venezuela. Although he continued to believe that he had reached Asia until his death, he had instead claimed a new world for Spain.

Columbus's first voyage posed threats to Portuguese interests in the Atlantic and called for compromise if war was to be averted. At Spain's invitation, the pope issued a "bull of demarcation," establishing a north-south line about three hundred miles west of the Azores. Beyond this line all lands were opened to Spanish claims. The Portuguese protested, forcing direct negotiations, which produced the Treaty of Tordesillas (tor-dhai-SEE-lyahs) in 1494. It moved the line some 500 miles farther west. Later explorations showed that the last agreement gave Spain most of the New World but left eastern Brazil to Portugal.

The Developing Portuguese Empire

Through the first half of the sixteenth century, the Portuguese developed a world maritime empire while maintaining commercial supremacy. They established trading posts around both African coasts and a faltering colony in Brazil, but their most extensive operations were in southern Asia, where they gained control of shipping routes and dominated the Indian Ocean spice trade.

Two voyages at the turn of the sixteenth century laid the foundations for the Portuguese interests in the Americas and the Orient. In 1497, Vasco da Gama (1469–1524) left Lisbon, Portugal, in four ships, rounding the Cape of Good Hope after 93 days on the open sea. While visiting and raiding the East African ports, da Gama picked up an Arab pilot, who brought the fleet across the Indian Ocean to Calicut (KAL-i-kut), on the western coast of India. When he returned to Lisbon in 1499, da Gama's voyage had spanned 27,000 miles and taken four times as long as Columbus's first voyage. Da Gama had lost two ships and a third of his men, but his cargo of pepper and cinnamon returned the cost of the expedition 60 times over.

Shortly afterward, Pedro Cabral (1468–1520), commanding a large fleet on a second voyage to India, bore too far west and sighted the east coast of Brazil. The new western territory was so unpromising that it was left unoccupied until 1532, when a small settlement was established at São Vicente. In the 1540s, it had attracted only some 2000 settlers, mostly men, although a few Portuguese women came after the arrival of the lord protector's wife and her retinue in 1535. By 1600, the colony had only 25,000 European residents.

Brazil was neglected in favor of extensive operations in the Indian Ocean and Southeast Asia, where the Portuguese sought to gain control of the spice trade by taking over flourishing port cities, places strategically located on established trade routes. The most striking successes were achieved under Alfonso de Albuquerque, eastern viceroy from 1509 to 1515. He completed subjugation of the Swahili city-states and established fortified trading posts in Mozambique and Zanzibar. By mounting guns and galleons, Albuquerque's force won a decisive naval victory over an Arab fleet (1509).

In 1510, the Portuguese acquired Goa on the west coast of India; it became a base for aiding Hindus against Indian Muslims and conducting trade with Gujerat (goo-ja-RAHT), a major producer of cloth. The next year, a Portuguese force took Malacca, a Muslim stronghold in Malaya, which controlled trade with China and the Spice Islands through the narrow straits opposite Sumatra (soo-MAH-trah). Although a Portuguese goal was to spread the Christian faith at the expense of Islam, the expulsion of Muslim traders had the opposite effect. These traders moved to the Malaysian peninsula and founded new Muslim states. In 1515, the Portuguese captured Hormuz (hor-MOOZ), thus disrupting Arab passage from the Persian Gulf.

The Indian Ocean had previously been open to all traders, but the Portuguese network left no room for competitors, and rival traders, especially Muslims, were squeezed out of their previous settlements. Portuguese officials financed their operations from two sources, customs duties and a tax levied on ships trading in the Indian Ocean. All ships were required to stop at Portuguese ports and take a **cartaz.**

The Portuguese presence was largely felt on the ocean; it had very little impact on the land-based empires and trading networks of the Ottomans, the Safavids, the Mughuls, and the Chinese. On the Asian mainland, for instance, the Portuguese were mostly supplicants because they had to interact with well-established and more powerful states. They acquired temporary influence in Laos and Cambodia but were expelled from Vietnam and enslaved in Burma. In China, their diplomatic blunders and breaches of etiquette offended Ming officials, who regarded the Portuguese as cannibals. In 1519, a Portuguese representative angered the Chinese by, among other things, starting to erect a fort in Canton harbor without permission and buying Chinese children

cartaz–A license issued by the Portuguese that permitted non-Portuguese traders to operate in areas of the Indian Ocean controlled by the Portuguese.

► In the sixteenth century, a Japanese artist depicted the Portuguese as "Southern Barbarians" in a decorative screen.

as slaves. Chinese officials responded by jailing and executing a group of Portuguese emissaries who had been visiting Beijing. After being banished from Chinese ports in 1522 and 1544, the Portuguese cooperated with Chinese smuggling rings off South China before Chinese officials granted them strictly regulated trading rights in Macao (mah-KOU) in 1554. Although the Chinese generally had little interest in European goods, the Portuguese served a useful purpose by supplying the Chinese economy with Indian manufactures such as cloth, Indonesian spices, and silver from the Americas reexported through Europe.

The Portuguese developed an extensive relationship with Japan. The connection was established accidentally in 1542 when three Portuguese traders landed off southern Japan after a storm blew their ship off course. At the time, Japanese *daimyō* (feudal lords) were contending with each other for power, and Portuguese traders prospered initially by selling matchlock muskets to rival factions and then by trading Chinese silk for Japanese gold.

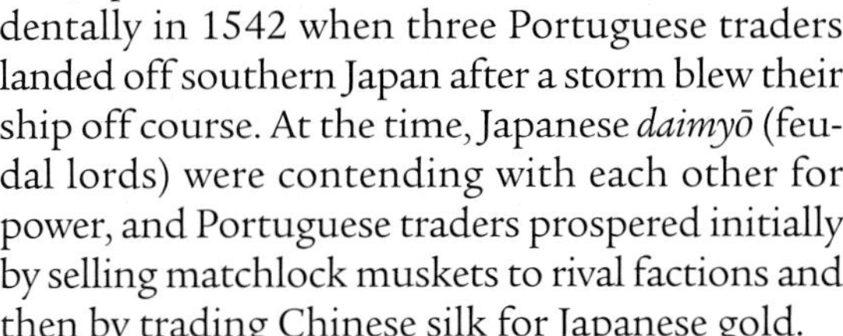

A Japanese View of European Missionaries

The Jesuit priests who followed the merchants in 1549 had great success in winning converts. While the *daimyō* Nobunaga was gaining mastery over his opponents, he encouraged the Catholics because they were useful allies against Buddhist sects opposing him. By the 1580s, the Catholics were claiming as many as 150,000 adherents, but the relationship soured over time, and in the late 1630s, the Japanese government expelled all Europeans except for a small contingent of Dutch traders who were confined to a small island in the Nagasaki harbor.

Long before this expulsion, the Portuguese Empire had begun to decline. It did not have the special skills or fluid capital required by a global empire and had become dependent on the bankers and spice brokers of northern Europe for financing. To make matters worse, the home population dropped steadily after 1600. Thus, the relatively few Portuguese men overseas mated with local women. Most were concubines, prostitutes, or slaves. These conditions contributed to a decided weakening of morale, economic efficiency, and military power. After the turn of the seventeenth century, the Portuguese lost ground to the Omani Arabs in East Africa, the Spanish in the Philippines, and the Dutch in both hemispheres. Despite a mild later revival, their empire never regained its former glory.

The Portuguese and Africa

How did Africans respond to the opportunities offered by trade with the Portuguese?

The Portuguese came to Africa as traders rather than settlers. Their original goal was to find a way around Muslim middlemen who controlled the trans-Saharan caravan trade and to gain direct access to the fabled gold fields of West Africa. Muslim kingdoms of the Sudan, such as Mali, Kanem-Bornu, and the Hausa states, dominated trade in the West African interior and were reluctant to open up their trade to Europeans. Therefore, the Portuguese concentrated their efforts on establishing commercial bases along the West African coast.

Africa, Europe, and the World

The Portuguese in West Africa

Africa was not of primary importance to the Portuguese, especially after they opened up sea routes to Asia. Thus, they selectively established links with African states where they could trade for goods of value such as gold, which could be traded anywhere in the world, and slaves, which were initially taken to southern Portugal as laborers. The first bases of operation for Portuguese seafarers were at Cape Verde, Arguin (ahr-GWEEN), and Senegambia.

Portuguese Travelers in Africa

Although the Portuguese conducted hit-and-run raids for slaves and plunder, they soon learned that if they expected to sustain a profitable trade in gold, they could not afford to alienate African rulers. When the Portuguese arrived on the Gold Coast (present-day Ghana) in 1471, they found Akan states carrying on a vigorous trade to the north through Muslim Dyula traders. Still hoping to develop trade links with the kingdom of Mali, the Portuguese sent several envoys with Dyula traders to Mali in the late fifteenth century. However, Mali's king sent a clear signal about his lack of interest in ties with Portugal by informing the envoy that he recognized only three kings beside himself—the rulers of Yemen, Cairo, and Baghdad.

From that point on, the Portuguese concentrated on establishing a profitable relationship with the Akan kingdom, exchanging firearms (that could not be obtained through Mali), copper and brass objects, textiles, slaves, and later cowrie shells for gold. Akan's

	The Portuguese and Africa
1482	Portuguese establish Fort Elmina on Gold Coast; Portuguese reach kingdom of Kongo
1506	Portuguese seize Sofala
1506–1543	Reign of Nzinga Mbemba, king of Kongo
1571	Portuguese establish colony of Angola
1607	King of Mutapa signs treaty with Portugal
1698	Portuguese driven from East African coast by Omani Arabs

Seeing Connections

The Portuguese in Benin

The Portuguese trading with the Kingdom of Benin began in the 1480s, exchanging cloth, cowrie shells, coral, brass, and weapons for ivory, spices, and later, slaves. Benin valued the Portuguese visitors so highly that its artists began representing them as lifelike figures in art forms such as brass, ivory and wood plaques, regalia, and even statues placed on altars. One explanation of why the Yoruba portrayed the Portuguese this way was because they came to regard the fair-skinned Portuguese as relatives of their god of the sea, Olokun. Benin's artists usually depicted important events in their kingdom's history in plaques—in this one, the Portuguese stand out in the scene, identifiable by their long wavy hair and military uniforms.

ruler warned the Portuguese that if they were dishonest, he would withhold the gold. So from their fort at São Jorge de Mina ("St. George of the Mine"), established in 1482, the Portuguese received 20,000 ounces of gold annually for the next half century. Because the Akan required slave labor to clear forests for arable agricultural land, the Portuguese brought slaves from the region of Benin and Kongo. It took several more centuries before Akan states actively participated in selling rather than buying slaves.

The Portuguese also initiated contacts with the kingdom of Benin, located in the forests of southwestern Nigeria. The kings of Benin, called *obas,* had governed their land since the eleventh century. When the Portuguese arrived, Benin possessed a formidable army and was at the peak of its power. Edo, the walled capital, was a bustling metropolis with wide streets, markets, and an efficient municipal government. The huge royal palace awed Europeans who chanced to see it, although the Portuguese—and later the Dutch—were generally prohibited from living in the city. The few European visitors who gained entrance were amazed by Benin's metalwork, such as copper birds on towers, copper snakes coiled around doorways, and beautifully cast bronze statues.

The first Portuguese emissary who arrived at oba Ozuola's court in 1486 was sent back to Lisbon with gifts, including a Maltese-type cross. The cross excited the Portuguese who interpreted it as a sign that Benin was near Prester John's kingdom and that its inhabitants would be receptive to conversion to Christianity. However, when Ozuola admitted Catholic missionaries to his kingdom in the early 1500s in the hope of securing Portuguese muskets, the Portuguese made acceptance of Christianity a precondition for receiving arms. Although the missionaries converted several of Ozuola's sons and high-ranking officials, their influence ended at Ozuola's death.

Portugal believed that it could manipulate Benin's rulers to extend Portuguese trade over a much wider area, but the *obas* did not regard trade with the Portuguese as a vital necessity and did not allow them to establish a sizable presence in the kingdom. The *obas* controlled all transactions, and Portuguese traders duly paid taxes, observed official regulations, and conducted business only with the *obas'* representatives.

Discovery Through Maps

Savage Pictures: Sebastian Munster's Map of Africa

Voyages of exploration in the fifteenth and sixteenth centuries greatly expanded European knowledge of the rest of the world. However, mapmakers who knew little about the geography and peoples of continents such as Africa still tended to rely on outdated information or stereotypical representations. Thus, when Sebastian Munster (1489–1552 C.E.), a professor of Hebrew and mathematics at Basel, the home of Switzerland's oldest university, developed an interest in maps, he turned to Ptolemy (90–168 C.E.), a celebrated astronomer, geographer, and mathematician of Alexandria, Egypt, whose theories about the universe influenced the European and Arab worlds for many centuries. When Ptolemy's *Guide to Geography* was published in Florence around 1400, it was the first atlas of the world.

Ptolemy's view of the world heavily influenced Munster when he began drawing his own world atlas. First published in 1544, Munster's *Cosmographia Universalis* went through 46 editions and was translated into six languages. It was the first collection to feature individual maps of Europe, Asia, the Americas, and Africa.

Munster's map of Africa relied not only on Ptolemy but also on Portuguese and Arab sources. However, it still contained many errors. The map identified the source of the Nile far to the south and, based on the assumption that the Senegal was connected to the Niger River in West Africa, showed a river flowing westward to the Atlantic.

The *Cosmographia* was also a descriptive geography, providing an accompanying narrative and drawings of prominent figures, the customs and manners of societies, and the products, animals, and plants of regions. Munster's Africa map depicted a lone human figure that bore no resemblance to Africans and a large elephant at the southern end of the continent. His rendering of Africa conformed to Jonathan Swift's satirical lines:

> *So Geographers in Africa-Maps*
> *With Savage-Pictures fill their Gaps;*
> *And o'er unhabitable Downs*
> *Place Elephants for want of Towns.*

Questions to Consider

1. Why do you think Muster chose to rely on Ptolemy's views rather than on more recent information?
2. Compare the portrayal of Africa in Munster's map with that in Abraham Cresque's Catalan map (see p. 251). Why does Cresque's map contain so much more detail than Munster's?

The Portuguese traded brass and copper items, textiles, and cowrie shells for pepper, ivory, cloth, beads, and slaves. Because Benin did not have access to sources of gold, the Portuguese took the slaves from Benin and traded them for gold with the Akan states, which needed laborers for clearing forests for farmland. Although Benin decided to curtail the slave trade in 1516 and offered only female slaves for purchase, even its rulers eventually came to rely on the slave trade in order to control Benin's tributaries and hold their own against Europeans.

The Portuguese and the Kongo Kingdom

Farther south, near the mouth of the Congo River, the Portuguese experienced their most intensive involvement in Africa. There, Portuguese seafarers found the recently established Kongo kingdom of several million people, ruled by a king who was heavily influenced by the queen mother and other women on his royal council. Although the Kongo initially perceived the Europeans as water or earth spirits, Kongo's king, Nzinga Nkuwu, soon came to regard them as a potential ally against neighboring African states. In the 1480s, he invited the Portuguese to send teachers, technicians, missionaries, and soldiers. His son, Nzinga Mbemba (1506–1543), who converted to Catholicism in 1491, consolidated the control of the Catholic faction at his court, making Portuguese the official language and Catholicism the state religion. He encouraged his court to adopt European dress and manners while changing his own name to Don Afonso. Many friendly letters subsequently passed between him and King Manuel of Portugal.

Loango, Capital of the Kingdom of the Congo

This mutual cooperation did not last long, as the Portuguese desire for profits won out over their humanitarian impulses. When the trade in a cloth woven from raffia palms did not satisfy Portuguese traders, they ranged over Kongo seeking slaves for their sugar plantations at São Tomé (SAH-o TO-mai) and Principe (PRIN-si-peh). By 1530, some 4000 to 5000 slaves were being taken from Kongo annually. No longer satisfied with treaty terms that gave them prisoners of war and criminals, the traders ignored the laws and bought everyone they could get, thus creating dissension and weakening the country. Driven to despair, Afonso wrote to his friend and ally Manuel: "There are many traders in all corners of the country. They bring ruin.... Every day, people are enslaved and kidnapped, even nobles, even members of the King's own family."[1] Such pleas brought no satisfactory responses. Although Afonso tried to curb the slave trade for a while, disgruntled Portuguese slavers shot him while he was attending Mass in 1430. Afonso's successors were no more successful, and Portuguese slavers continued to operate with impunity throughout Kongo and in neighboring areas.

In 1520, the Portuguese crown also established ties with Ngola, the king of the Mbundu kingdom to the south of Kongo, and São Tomé slavers were given a free hand to join with Mbundu's rulers to attack neighboring states. Using African mercenaries known as *pombeiros* equipped with firearms and sometimes allied with feared Imbangala warriors, the slavers and their allies began a long war of conquest. For Kongo's rulers, the price for Portuguese protection from Imbangala attacks was to give the slave traders free rein.

In 1571, the Portuguese crown issued a royal charter to establish the colony of Angola, situated on the Atlantic coast south of the Kongo kingdom. Although Portugal had ambitious plans to create an agricultural colony for white settlement and to gain control over a silver mine and the salt trade in the interior, Angola was never a successful venture. Few settlers immigrated, and Angola remained a sleepy outpost, consisting of a handful of Portuguese men, even fewer Portuguese women, a growing population of Afro-Portuguese, and a majority of Africans. The colony functioned primarily as a haven for slavers. By the end of the sixteenth century, 10,000 slaves were flowing annually through Luanda (loo-AHN-dah), Angola's capital.

The Portuguese in East Africa

Portuguese exploits in East Africa were similar to those in Kongo and Angola. The Swahili city-states along the coast north of the Zambezi (zam-BEE-zee) River were tempting targets for Portuguese intervention because they were strategically well located for trade with Asia. Because they rarely engaged in wars with each other or supported sizable militaries, they could not effectively defend themselves against a ruthless Portuguese naval force that sacked and plundered city-states from Kilwa to Mombasa. At Mombasa, Portuguese sailors broke into houses with axes, looted, and killed before setting the town afire. The sultan of Mombasa wrote to the sultan of Malindi: "[They] raged in our town with such might and terror that no one, neither man nor woman, neither the old or the young, nor even the children, however small, was spared to live."[2]

"Off the Coasts of East Africa and Malabar"

Although a few city-states such as Malindi (mah-LEEN-dee) escaped the wrath of the Portuguese by becoming allies, the Portuguese usually relied on coercion to keep the city-states in line. They constructed fortified stations from which they attempted to collect tribute and maintain trade with the interior. In the 1590s, the Portuguese built a fort at Mombasa, hoping to intimidate other cities and support naval operations against Turks and Arabs in the Red Sea. Although the Portuguese dominated trade in gold and ivory along

Document

Portuguese Encounters with Africans

The Portuguese had very specific objectives in Africa. They usually established amicable relations with stronger states, although they were more likely to coerce weaker states such as the Swahili city-states in East Africa. When Vasco da Gama dealt with the ruler of Kilwa, an island off the East African coast, he showed little patience for the subtleties of diplomacy and quickly resorted to threats to achieve his aims. This document records an exchange between da Gama and the King of Kilwa.

In the case of the Kingdom of the Kongo, the Portuguese were dealing with a state that clearly defined its interests and did not regard Portugal as a superior nation. Kongo's king, Don Afonso, who converted to Catholicism, wrote a series of letters to the king of Portugal in 1526. These letters demonstrate the complex relationship between the Kongolese leadership and the Portuguese. Afonso complains about Portuguese involvement in the slave trade but also conveys a request for doctors and apothecaries to treat illnesses.

King Ibrahim of Kilwa: Good friendship was to friends like brothers are and that he would shelter the Portuguese in his city and harbor ... to pay tribute each year in money or jewelry was not a way to a good friendship, it was tributary subjugation ... to pay tribute was dishonor ... it would be like to be a captive ... such friendship he did not want with subjugation ... because even the sons did not want to have that kind of subjugation with their own parents.

Vasco da Gama: Take it for certain that if I so decide your city would be grounded by fire in one single hour and if your people wanted to extinguish the fire in town, they would all be burned and when you see all this happen, you will regret all you are telling me now and you will give much more than what I am asking you now, it will be too late for you. If you are still in doubt, it is up to you to see it.

King Ibrahim: Sir, if I had known that you wanted to enslave me, I would not have come and I would have fled into the forest, for it is better for me to be a fox but free, than a dog locked up in a golden chain.

From Chapurukha M. Kusimba, *The Rise and Fall of Swahili States* (Walnut Creek: AltaMira Press, 1999), pp. 161–162.

Moreover, Sir, in our Kingdom there is another great inconvenience which is of little service to God, and this is that many of our people [*naturaes*], keenly desirous as they are of the wares and things of your Kingdoms, which are brought here by your people, freed and exempt men; and very often it happens that they kidnap even noblemen and the sons of noblemen, and our relatives, and take them to be sold to the white men who are in our Kingdoms; and for this purpose they have concealed them, and others are brought during the night so that they might not be recognized.

And as soon as they are taken by the white men they are immediately ironed and branded with fire, and when they are carried to be embarked, if they are caught by our guards' men the whites allege that they have brought them but they cannot say from whom, so that it is our duty to do justice and to restore to the freemen their freedom, but it cannot be done if your subjects feel offended, as they claim to be.

And to avoid such a great evil we passed a law so that any white man living in our Kingdoms and wanting to purchase goods in any way should first inform three of our noblemen and officials of our court ... who should investigate if the mentioned goods are captives or freemen, and if cleared by them there will be no further doubt nor embargo for them to be taken and embarked. But if the white men do not comply with it they will lose the aforementioned goods....

[1526] Sir, Your Highness has been kind enough to write to us saying that we should ask in our letters for anything we need, and that we shall be provided with everything, and as the peace and health of our Kingdom depend on us ... it happens that we have continuously many and different diseases which put us very often in such a weakness that we reach almost the last extreme; and the same happens to our children, relatives and natives owing to the lack in this country of physicians and surgeons who might know how to cure properly such diseases.

And to avoid such a great error and inconvenience, since it is from God in the first place and then from your Kingdoms and from Your Highness that all the good and drugs and medicines have come to save us, we beg of you to be agreeable and kind enough to send us two physicians and two apothecaries and all the necessary things to stay in our kingdoms....

From Basil Davidson, *African Past* (Boston: Little, Brown and Co., 1964), pp. 192–194.

Questions to Consider

1. Why did the Portuguese treat the kings of Kongo and Kilwa in different ways?
2. What do the letters from the King of the Kongo reveal about the involvement of his people and the Portuguese in the slave trade?

the East African coast, they could not control the whole coastline, and Swahili merchants continued to trade with their traditional partners. However, local industries such as ironworking and weaving virtually disappeared under Portuguese rule. When Omani Arabs expelled the Portuguese from the Swahili coast in 1698, the Swahili did not lament their departure. A Swahili proverb captured Swahili sentiment: "Go away, Manuel [the king of Portugal], you have made us hate you; go, and carry your cross with you."[3]

On the southeast coast, the Portuguese were drawn to the Zimbabwe Plateau by reports of huge gold mines. The Portuguese needed gold to finance their trade for spices in the Indian Ocean, and Shona kingdoms desired beads and cotton cloth from India. The Portuguese seized Sofala in 1506, diminishing the role of Muslim traders and positioning themselves as the middlemen for the gold trade with the coast. After establishing trading settlements along the Zambezi River at Sena and Tete, the Portuguese developed a close relationship with the Karanga kingdom of Mutapa, which received Portuguese tribute as well as traders and Catholic missionaries. This relationship soured when Mutapa's king ordered the death of a Jesuit missionary in 1560. In the 1570s, the Portuguese retaliated by sending several expeditionary forces up the Zambezi to seize control over the gold-producing areas. The Portuguese believed that the gold came from rich mines, when, in reality, African peasants recovered most of the gold from riverbeds during the winter months. In any event, these adventures ended disastrously as drought, disease (especially malaria), and African resisters decimated the Portuguese forces.

A series of internal rebellions and wars with neighboring states, however, forced Mutapa's rulers to turn to the Portuguese for assistance. In 1607, they signed a treaty that ceded control of gold production to the Portuguese. For the rest of the century, the Portuguese regularly intervened in Mutapa's affairs until the forces of Mutapa and a rising power, Changamire, combined to expel the Portuguese from the Zimbabwe Plateau. Along the Zambezi River, the Portuguese crown granted huge land concessions (***prazos***) to Portuguese settlers (*prazeros*) who ruled them as feudal estates. Over time, the *prazeros* loosened their ties with Portugal's officials and became virtually independent. In the absence of Portuguese women, *prazeros* intermarried with Africans and adopted African culture.

The tale of Prester John, the mythical Ethiopian Christian monarch who held the Muslims at bay, had long captivated Portugal's monarchs. Thus, they initially responded positively when the astute Ethiopian empress Eleni made diplomatic overtures. Eleni, the daughter of a Muslim king, had married the Ethiopian emperor Baeda Maryam and converted to Christianity. After his death in 1478, she remained an influential figure as regent during the reigns of two of her sons and two grandsons. Recognizing that the interests of both Ethiopia and Portugal would be served by defeating Muslim states on the Red Sea coast, she wrote Portugal's king in 1509 proposing an alliance against the Ottoman Turks. She reasoned that the combination of Ethiopia's army and Portugal's sea forces would be very potent. However, the Portuguese, disappointed that Ethiopia did not meet their grand expectations of a kingdom ruled by Prester John, were reluctant to sign a pact.

After Eleni's death in 1522, her projected alliance was not completed for several decades. In 1541, the army of Muslim leader Ahmad Gran of the kingdom of Adal had come close to conquering Ethiopia. This time, the Portuguese responded to Ethiopian appeals by dispatching 400 Portuguese musketeers who helped to defeat the Muslims. The following year, however, Muslim forces, augmented by Turkish soldiers, rallied and defeated the Portuguese contingent, killing its commander, Christopher da Gama, Vasco's son. When the Ethiopians eventually pushed the Muslims out, they enticed some of the Portuguese soldiers to stay on by granting them large estates in the countryside. Subsequent Ethiopian rulers called on descendants of the Portuguese in their conflicts with the Turks.

The Portuguese impact on Africa was not as immediately disastrous as Spanish effects on the New World. The Portuguese did not have the manpower or arms to dictate the terms of trade with most African states. However, they did inflict severe damage in Kongo, Angola, Zimbabwe, and the Swahili city-states. Their most destructive involvement was the slave trade.

By the end of the sixteenth century, the Portuguese had moved an estimated 240,000 slaves from West and Central Africa; 80 percent were transported after 1575. These trends foreshadowed much greater disasters for African societies in the seventeenth and eighteenth centuries as the Atlantic slave trade expanded (see Chapter 19).

The Growth of New Spain

What factors contributed to the Spanish conquest of the Americas?

While Portugal concentrated on Asian and African trade, Spain won a vast empire in America. Soon after 1492, Spanish settlements were established in the West Indies, most notably on Hispaniola (ees-pah-nee-O-lah) and Cuba. By 1500, as the American continents were recognized and the passage to Asia remained undiscovered, a host of Spanish adventurers—the ***conquistadora***—set out for the New World with dreams

---

prazo—A land grant from the Portuguese crown to a Portuguese settler (*prazero*) in the Zambezi River valley in Mozambique that gave the settler control over tribute and labor service from local residents.

conquistadora—The Spanish soldiers who conquered Mexico and Peru.

◀ An illustration from the *Codex Azacatitlán* of the Spanish arriving in Mexico. Standing next to Cortés is Malintzin, the Aztec woman who served as his interpreter.

of acquiring riches. From the West Indies, they crossed the Caribbean to eastern Mexico, fanning out from there in all directions, toward Central America, the Pacific, and the vast North American hinterlands.

In Mexico, the Spaniards profited from internal problems within the Aztec Empire. By the early 1500s, the Aztecs ruled over several million people in a vast kingdom that stretched from the Gulf of Mexico to the Pacific Ocean and from present-day central Mexico to Guatemala. However, unrest ran rampant among many recently conquered peoples, who were forced to pay tribute and taxes and furnish sacrificial victims to their Aztec overlords.

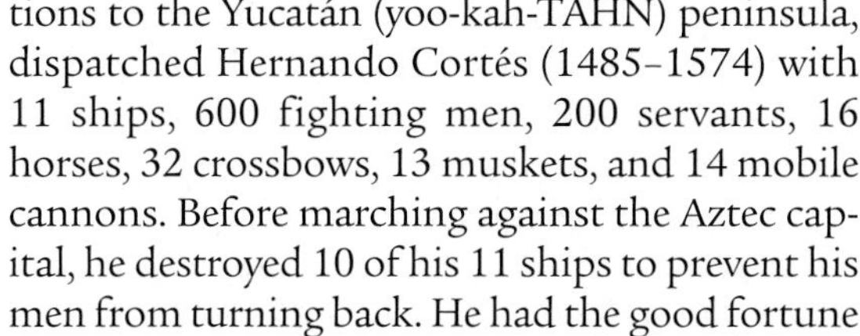

Cortés to King Charles V of Spain

In 1519, Spanish officials in Cuba, excited by reports of a wealthy indigenous civilization from two expeditions to the Yucatán (yoo-kah-TAHN) peninsula, dispatched Hernando Cortés (1485–1574) with 11 ships, 600 fighting men, 200 servants, 16 horses, 32 crossbows, 13 muskets, and 14 mobile cannons. Before marching against the Aztec capital, he destroyed 10 of his 11 ships to prevent his men from turning back. He had the good fortune to secure the services of two people familiar with indigenous languages. One was a Spaniard who had learned the Mayan language after being shipwrecked in the Yucatán, and the other was an indigenous woman, Malintzin, later christened Doña Marina, who spoke both Mayan and the Aztec language, Nahuatl (nah-WAHT-ul). Using these two, Cortés could communicate with the Aztecs. Later, Malintzin learned Spanish and became Cortés's personal interpreter, intelligence-gatherer, and lover, bearing him a son.

As Cortés's band marched inland, he added thousands of Indian warriors to his small force. He easily enlisted allies, such as the Cempoala, who had suffered under Aztec rule. By contrast, the loyalty of the Tlaxcalan (tlash-KAH-lahn) was secured only after Cortez's force demonstrated the superiority of its firearms, steel swords and armor, and crossbows and horses (that the Aztecs initially thought were deer) and coerced them into cooperating.

The Aztec emperor Moctezuma II closely observed Cortés's actions as his force approached the Aztec capital, Tenochtitlán (te-noch-teet-lahn), a city with an estimated population of between 250,000 and 400,000 people. Moctezuma warily welcomed Cortés and housed him in his father's palace. Although surrounded by a host of armed Aztecs, Cortés seized the ruler and informed him that he must cooperate or die. The bold scheme worked temporarily, even though tension between the two sides was growing toward a breaking point. When Cortés left the capital to head off a Spanish force sent from Cuba to relieve him of his command, his lieutenant, fearing a plot against his men, attacked unarmed Aztec nobles performing at a religious festival, killing many. The massacre touched off an uprising. After Cortés returned with reinforcements, he placed Moctezuma on the palace roof to pacify the Aztecs. Spanish accounts claim that the Aztecs renounced their former ruler as a traitor and stoned him to death, but Aztec sources place responsibility for his murder on the Spaniards. What is certain is that neither the Aztecs nor the Spaniards showed any mercy in the fierce fighting that followed. Besieged in the palace compound, vastly outnumbered, with the city's close quarters neutralizing their military superiority, the Spanish were in a desperate

From the "Account of Alva Ixtlilxochiltl"

situation. On June 30, 1520, they attempted to flee Tenochtitlán under the cover of darkness, but the Aztecs discovered their plans and attacked them. Although Cortés narrowly escaped, more than half of his men were slaughtered on what became known as the *noche triste* or "night of tears."

Moctezuma's successor attempted to win back support of the conquered peoples aiding the Spanish by abolishing all tribute for a year. But Cortés and his force regrouped and, with their Indian allies, laid siege to the Aztecs' capital. What tipped the balance in the Spaniard's favor was "the big rash," a devastating smallpox epidemic that ravaged Tenochtitlán for 70 days in late 1520, killing many thousands of Aztecs. Finally, on August 13, 1521, after four months of fierce fighting, some 60,000 exhausted and half-starved defenders surrendered.

Once the Spaniards had seized control of the Aztec empire, they found the Aztecs' hierarchical system suited to their needs. They replaced an urbanized Aztec elite with their own and gave privileged positions to Indian allies such as the Tlaxcalans, who were exempted from annual tribute. The Spanish built the capital of their expanding empire, Mexico City, on the ruins of Tenochtitlán. Because the climate of their new capital so closely resembled Spain's, they called their new province *Nueva Espana* (New Spain).

Although *conquistadora* steadily penetrated the interior, the Mayas of Yucatán and Guatemala put up a determined resistance until the 1540s. By then, Spanish settlements had been established throughout Central America. The first colony in North America was founded at St. Augustine, on Florida's east coast, in 1565. Meanwhile, numerous expeditions, including those of Hernando de Soto (1500–1542) and Francisco de Coronado (1510–1554), explored what is now California, Arizona, New Mexico, Colorado, Texas, Missouri, Louisiana, and Alabama. Spanish friars established a mission at Santa Fe in 1610, providing a base for later missions. All these new territories were administered from Mexico City after 1542.

The viceroyalty of Mexico later sponsored colonization of the Philippines, a project justified by the historic voyage of Ferdinand Magellan (1480–1521). Encouraged by the exploits of Vasco de Balboa (1479–1519), who had crossed Panama and discovered the Pacific Ocean in 1513, Magellan sailed from Spain in 1520, steered past the ice-encrusted straits at the tip of South America, and endured a 99-day voyage to the Philippines. He made an unwise choice by intervening in a conflict between two sheikdoms, and he lost his life in a battle with the inhabitants of Mactan Island. Many of Magellan's crew died after terrible suffering from **scurvy.** This illness explains why only one of Magellan's five ships completed this first circumnavigation of the world. However, the feat established a Spanish claim to the Philippines. It also prepared the way for the first tiny settlement of 400 Mexicans at Cebu in 1571. By 1580, when the Philippine capital at Manila had been secured against attacking Portuguese, Chinese, and Moro fleets, the friars were beginning conversions that would reach half a million by 1622. The colony prospered in trade with Asia but remained economically dependent on annual galleons bearing silver from Mexico and Peru. Because the Spanish were excluded from China, they relied on a community of Chinese merchants in Manila to trade the silver in the Chinese market for luxury items such as porcelain, silk, and lacquerware.

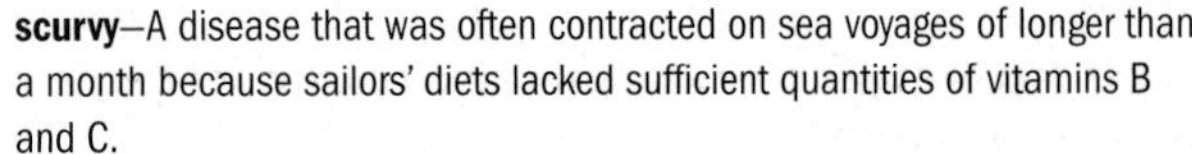

scurvy—A disease that was often contracted on sea voyages of longer than a month because sailors' diets lacked sufficient quantities of vitamins B and C.

The Development of Spanish South America

As in Mexico, the Spanish exploited unique opportunities as well as epidemics in their process of empire building in Peru. Just before they arrived, the recently formed Inca state had been torn apart by a succession crisis. When the emperor Huayna Capac and his heir apparent suddenly died of smallpox in 1526, the claim of his son Huascar (was-KAR) to the throne was contested by Atahualpa (AH-teh-WAL-peh), a half-royal son who had been Huayna Capac's favorite. This succession struggle, which soon destroyed nearly every semblance of imperial unity, was a major factor in the surprisingly easy triumph of a handful of Spanish freebooters over an empire of more than 13 million people, scattered through Peru and Ecuador in hundreds of mountain towns and coastal cities.

Francisco Pizarro (1470–1541), the illegitimate son of a minor Spanish noble and a landholder in the Isthmus of Panama, was the conqueror of the Incas. Partnered by Diego de Almagro, Pizarro made two exploratory visits to South America before landing on the northern coast of what is now Peru in January 1531. He had with him a privately financed army of 207 men and 27 horses. For more than a year, they moved south, receiving some reinforcements as they plundered towns and villages. Leaving a garrison of 60 soldiers in a coastal base, Pizarro's tiny force started inland in September 1532. About the same time, word reached the party that Atahualpa's forces had defeated Huascar's in battle and were poised to capture the imperial capital, Cuzco. At nearby Cajamarca, Pizarro and his advisers decided to rely on the tested Spanish tactic of capturing an opposing ruler. After luring Atahualpa into a meeting, Pizarro's small force attacked and slaughtered some 6000 lightly armed retainers and servants and seized the Inca monarch. In November, Pizarro's forces agreed to Atahualpa's boastful offer to raise a ransom. However, after a room was filled with 26,000 pounds of pure silver and over 13,000 pounds of gold, Pizarro ordered the execution of his royal prisoner in July 1533 and installed Manco, Atahualpa's half-brother, as emperor.

Thus, upon arriving in Cuzco with their puppet ruler, the Spaniards secured tentative control of the country. Manco, after suffering terrible indignities from the Spaniards, organized a rebellion in 1536. Although his army of 60,000 heavily outnumbered Pizarro's 200 Spaniards, whose horses and armor were ineffective in the narrow mountain passes of the Andes, they still could not score a decisive victory. Manco and his supporters retreated to the northwest to a mountain outpost at Vilacamba where an independent Inca kingdom survived until the Spanish captured and executed the last Incan emperor, Tupac Amaru, in 1572.

Although the *conquistadors* had triumphed over the Incas, political anarchy still reigned in Peru as the Pizarro and Almagro families fell out over how to divide the spoils of conquest. When Almagro family members assassinated Pizarro in his palace in 1542, it touched off a bloody civil war that raged until the Spanish crown asserted its authority in 1549. Marauding Spanish expeditions also moved south into Chile and north through Ecuador into Colombia. Expeditions from Chile and Peru settled in Argentina, founding Buenos Aires. Some indigenous tribes continued resistance against Spanish conquest. In Yucatán and Guatemala, Mayan rebellions lasted until the 1540s. About that time, the Spanish put down a revolt on the Mexican Pacific coast with great difficulty. As the silver mines opened in northern Mexico into the 1590s, the Chichimecs, relatives of the Apaches of North America, conducted a border war, using horses and captured muskets. The most stubborn resistance came from the Araucanians of southern Chile, who fought the Spaniards successfully until the close of the sixteenth century.

The arrival of the Spanish and Portuguese in America led to a mixing of three cultures: European, African, and Amerindian. This painted wooden bottle, done in Inca style and dating from about 1650, shows the mix. The three figures are an African drummer, a Spanish trumpeter, and an Amerindian official.

Iberian Systems in the New World

What role did forced Indian and African labor play in the Spanish and Portuguese colonial empires?

European expansion overseas after the fifteenth century brought revolutionary change to all the world's peoples and laid the foundation for an emerging global economy, but the Iberian impact on its colonies in the New World in the period before 1600 stood out for its violence and ruthless exploitation. Not only were highly organized states destroyed, but whole populations were traumatized by European diseases, conquest and enslavement, and inhumane treatment.

European Empires in Latin America, 1660

The General Nature of Regimes

Iberian regimes in America faced serious problems in creating a colonial administration. They had to oversee vast territories, far greater than the homelands, and they had to move supplies thousands of miles, often across open seas. Communications were difficult, wars with indigenous peoples were frequent, and disease was often rampant.

With all their unique features, Iberian overseas empires were similar to Roman or Turkish provinces: they were meant to produce revenues. In theory, all Spanish lands were the king's personal property, but the crown had to assert its authority in colonies in which the *conquistadors* had already taken on enormous power. To govern Mexico and Peru, the Spanish established two viceroyalties that by 1600 contained over 200 towns with a Spanish and **mestizo** (mehs-TEE-soh) population of 200,000. The Council of the Indies, which directed the viceroys in Mexico City and Lima, offered advice on colonial policies. The backbone of colonial administration was a system of councils (*audiencias*; ow-dee-EHN-see-ahs), made up of aristocratic lawyers from Spain, that served as regional legislative and judicial tribunals. Local governors, responsible to the viceroys, functioned with the assistance of town councils (**cabildos**; kah-BEEL-dohs). Only persons of influence—first conquistadors and later merchants—dominated the cabildos. Poor Spaniards and mestizos had little voice, even in their own taxation. At the village level, Indian nobles (**caciques**; kah-SEE-kay),

New Laws for the Treatment and Preservation of the Indians

mestizo—A person of Spanish and Indian descent.

cabildos—Town councils whose members were usually appointed by the governor.

cacique—An Amerindian chief who assisted the Spanish in collecting taxes from his subjects.

still acting as local rulers, maintained order and collected taxes and tribute for the Spanish.

Ninety-six times the size of Portugal, Brazil was at first less directly controlled than the Spanish colonies. For years, Brazil fell under the almost unrestricted domination of 15 aristocratic "captains" who held hereditary rights of taxing, disposing lands, making laws, and administering justice. In return, they sponsored settlement and paid stipulated sums to the king. Responding to French threats to Portugal's control, the Portuguese appointed a royal governor-general in the 1540s, but his powers never approached those of the viceroys in Mexico and Peru.

Iberian Economies in America

The Spanish monarch owned all resources below the surface of the earth, so when precious metals such as gold and silver were mined, the crown dispensed permits to companies in exchange for 10 to 20 percent of the returns. The mining revenues financed colonial administration as well as filled the royal treasury. Extracted largely from riverbeds, gold at first was the primary source of mining revenues, but after strikes in Mexico and Peru, silver became far more important. Because it was usually found in less-populated areas, silver required more capital to pay for wage laborers and processing the silver using a mercury amalgamation process. Silver poured a steady stream of wealth back to Spain in the annual treasure fleets, convoyed by warships from Havana to Seville. However, much wealth was siphoned off by pirates as well as Portuguese, French, and English traders who attacked Spanish ships or dealt in contraband.

Merchant wholesalers in Seville controlled most of the Atlantic trade in grain, wine, olive oil, and textiles that the fleets brought over twice a year. Asian porcelains and silks also found their way across the Pacific from Manila. Once the goods reached America, they were distributed through agents to smaller towns or by itinerant peddlers. Regional transport systems developed with wagons carrying the bulk of the goods. In rough mountain terrain, however, the best way of conveying goods was on pack animals such as mules and llamas. Mulattoes, mestizos, and Indians often found employment opportunities as carters and mule-drivers.

Besides mining, agriculture and ranching were the main economic pursuits of the Spaniards. In Mexico, Spanish officials allowed Indians to retain their lands as long as they occupied or cultivated them, but as the Indian population declined because of diseases, the Spanish either seized or bought up Indian lands and allocated huge estates to officials and military officers. Traditionally, Indians had farmed without domesticated animals, but after the Spanish settlers introduced new animals such as sheep, goats, cattle, horses, and burros and crops such as wheat, the land was

The peoples of the Andes domesticated llamas for meat and transport. Under Spanish rule, they were used as pack animals for transporting silver from mines.

intensively farmed. As a consequence, the ecological balance was upset as cattle, goats, and sheep overgrazed grasslands. In Brazil, Portuguese settlers developed enterprises in brazilwood (for which the country was given its name), sugar, livestock, and coffee.

Before 1660, plantations (large estates that used servile labor to grow crops) were not typical for agriculture in Iberian America, although they were developing in certain areas. The Spanish tried plantations in the Canaries, later establishing them in the West Indies, the Mexican lowlands, Central America, and along the northern coasts of South America. Even in such areas, which were environmentally suited for intensive single-crop cultivation, it was not easy to raise the capital and obtain the workers the plantation system required.

A common labor system in the Spanish colonies was the ***encomienda*** (ehn-koh-mee-EHN-dah). This system was instituted in Mexico by Cortés as a way of using Indian caciques to collect revenues and provide labor. It was similar to European feudalism and manorialism, involving a royal grant that permitted the holder (*encomendero;* ehn-koh-mehn-DAY-roh) to take income or labor from specified lands and the people living on them. Many *encomenderos* lashed and starved their Indian laborers, working men and women to exhaustion or renting them to other equally brutal masters. Indian women on the *encomiendas* were generally used as wet nurses, cooks, or maids or as sex slaves by the owners and the caciques, who served as overseers.

The *encomienda* system was slowly but steadily abandoned after the 1550s, largely because of the campaigning of a former conquistador and *encomendero*, Bartolomé de Las Casas (1474–1566). A Dominican friar, he protested the cruel treatment of indigenous peoples of the Americas and persuaded Charles V that if Indians could become Christians like Spaniards, they should hold the same rights as other subjects. However, his humanitarian ideals did not extend to Africans. He maintained that since Africans were not subjects of any Christian nation, it was permissible to utilize them as slaves on plantations and mines. Las Casas recanted this position late in his life.

Las Casas and others persuaded Charles to enact the New Laws of 1542–1543, which ended existing *encomiendas* upon the death of their holders, prohibited Indian slavery, and gave Indians full protection under Spanish law. Spanish officials, however, did not implement most of these provisions because they needed the support of *encomenderos* for their administration. In Peru, the laws were openly resisted, and alternative regulations were introduced to draft Indian labor.

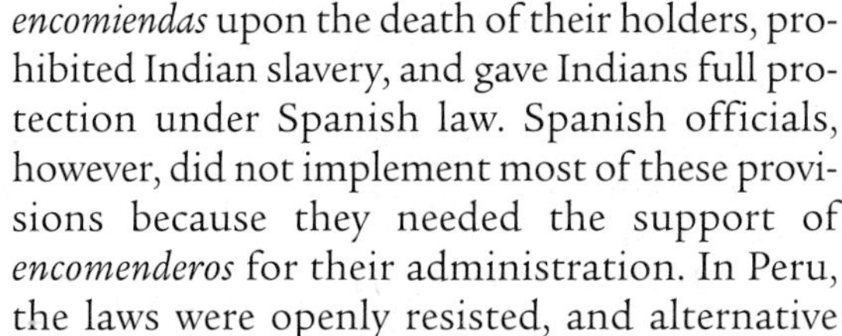

DOCUMENT

From "In Defense of the Indians"

encomienda—A system of control over land and Indian labor granted to a Spanish colonist (*encomendero*).

▲ Moved by the simplicity and gentle nature of the Amerindians, Bartolomé de Las Casas launched a vigorous campaign to ensure their protection. His *Apologetic History of the Indies* (1566) is an indictment of the Spaniards' harsh treatment of the Amerindians.

Although *encomiendas* were gradually eliminated, many Indians were put on reservations and hired out as contract laborers under the direction of their caciques and local officials (*corrigodores;* koh-ray-hee-DOR-ays). This practice eliminated some of the worst excesses of the *encomiendas,* but corrupt officials often exploited their wards, particularly in Peru.

The Spanish initially dealt with the labor problem in Mexico and Peru by taxing the indigenous population. In order to earn the wages necessary to pay the tax, the natives were forced to enter the labor market. Many died because of the harsh work conditions, but many more died because they had no immunity from the devastating impact of European diseases such as smallpox, measles, yellow fever, mumps, influenza, and

Document

Disease and the Spanish Conquest

Diseases introduced by Europeans had a devastating impact on indigenous societies in the New World. This account of the impact of a smallpox epidemic among the Aztecs appeared in the *Florentine Codex,* an invaluable history of the Aztecs published in the mid-sixteenth century. Written in Nahuatl, the Aztec language, and translated into Spanish, the books were based on information gathered by Aztec scribes under the supervision of a Franciscan priest Bernadino de Sahagún. This story of the smallpox epidemic drew on eyewitness accounts of individuals who lived through the Spanish conquest.

Before the Spanish appeared to us, first an epidemic broke out, a sickness of pustules.... Large bumps spread on people, some were entirely covered. They spread everywhere, on the face, the head, the chest, etc. The disease brought great desolation; a great many died of it. They could no longer walk about, but lay in their dwellings and sleeping places, no longer able to move or stir. They were unable to change position, to stretch out on their sides or face down, or raise their heads. And when they made a motion, they called out loudly. The pustules that covered people caused that covered people caused great desolation. Very many people died of them, and many just starved to death; starvation reigned, and no one took care of others any longer.

On some people, the pustules appeared only far apart, and they did not suffer greatly, nor did many of them die of it. But many people's faces were spoiled by it, their faces and noses were made rough. Some lost an eye or were blinded.

This disease of pustules lasted a full sixty days; after sixty days it abated and ended. When people were convalescing and reviving, the pustules disease began to move in the direction of Chalco. And many were disabled or paralyzed by it, but they were not disabled forever.... The Mexica warriors were greatly weakened by it.

And when things were in this state, the Spaniards came, moving toward us from Tetzcoco.

Questions to Consider

1. What was more responsible for the Spanish conquest of the Aztecs—Spanish weapons, armor, horses, or the diseases that accompanied the Spanish?
2. What was the overall impact of diseases such as smallpox on the indigenous populations of the Americas?

From James Lockhart, *We People Here: Nahuatl Accounts of the Conquest of Mexico* (Berkeley: University of California Press, 1993), pp. 180–182.

the plague. By 1600, the indigenous populations of the Spanish-held regions of the Americas had dramatically declined—in the Caribbean by as much as 90 percent, in Mexico from an estimated 30 million in 1519 to 3 million, and in the former Inca Empire from an estimated 13 million in 1492 to 2 million. In the 1600s, indigenous populations in the Americas began to stabilize and increase somewhat.

To make up for the lack of Indian labor, the Spanish imported huge numbers of African slaves. Despite the added costs of buying slaves and transporting them from their home countries across the Atlantic, there were a number of factors that made the use of African slaves more advantageous than Indian labor. Africans were less susceptible to European diseases than natives and so generally survived much longer under harsh working conditions. Moreover, the Spanish maritime empire was already connected to an established trade in African slaves and possessed the capital and trade goods needed to conduct business in this system on favorable terms. Finally, African slaves, once transported to the Americas and separated from their families and home societies, were isolated, making escape harder and facilitating their use as a mobile labor force (see p. 586).

In 1518, Charles I decreed that the Spanish crown would oversee and directly profit from the transport of African slaves to the Spanish colonies. Between 1519 and 1650, the Spanish brought in about 120,000 African slaves into Mexico primarily to labor in mines. By the 1550s, some 3,000 African slaves were in Peru, working in gold mines and on cattle ranches and participating in a variety of unskilled and skilled occupations in the capital, Lima. At the end of the century, Africans, although replaced in the mines by Indians, continued to labor on coastal plantations and serve in elite households.

Although Spanish officials attempted to maintain distinct identities among Indians, Africans, and Spaniards, they found it impossible to control sexual relations between different racial and ethnic groups. There was a bewildering array of racial mixtures in colonial society, and one of the most important new social categories was that of the **castas** (KAHS-tahs), free men and women of mixed ancestry. The two main groups, mestizos and **mulattoes,** served as intermediate groups between Europeans and Indians and Africans. Since there were not enough Spaniards to take up all jobs, they were allowed to hold positions as skilled laborers and artisans. What distinguished them was the degree to which they absorbed the Spanish language and culture and adopted Christianity and western technical skills.

Another mixed-race group was the **zambos,** typically a mixture of Indian women and African men. Zambo communities were formed in several ways—in urban areas where Africans and Indians mingled together and in situations where black slaves escaped from plantations or were shipwrecked and found sanctuary among Indians. Those zambo communities usually isolated themselves from contact with Spanish settlements.

Indians generally fared poorly under Spanish rule. By creating a new racial identity, Indian, the Spanish erased the separate identities among pre-Hispanic Indian societies. Some Indians who lived in areas outside Spanish control maintained their identities, languages, and communal lifestyles. But most Indians had to adapt to the new colonial order and Spanish culture out of necessity. Many went from their rural homes to labor in the towns, mines, or **haciendas** (ah-see-EHN-dahs); some caciques enjoyed wealth and privilege; and a few established Indian families retained their nobility as early Spanish allies.

Africans generally were at the bottom of the social hierarchy, but there were exceptions. In Spain, a small black population, whether free or slave, had assimilated into Spanish culture but were still treated as second-class citizens. Some free blacks served as soldiers in the conquest of Mexico and Peru and were rewarded with *encomiendas* or worked as supervisors over Indian laborers. They and their descendants enjoyed an intermediate position between Spaniards and Indians. African slaves who came to the New World as soldiers or as servants were often granted freedom as a reward for their service.

Although African slaves were generally consigned to the lowest rung of society, the status of slaves varied from colony to colony. Where slave labor was most in demand, restrictive racial laws were rigidly enforced. But in some areas such as Peru, Argentina, and eastern Cuba, where plantations were scarce, there were possibilities for upward mobility, especially in urban areas, where black slaves could be apprenticed as shoemakers, tailors, carpenters, bricklayers, and blacksmiths. In Lima, Peru, white masters sometimes gave their artisan slaves time off during the day to earn extra money, which they used to purchase their freedom and that of family members.

casta—free men and women of mixed racial ancestry in colonial Latin America.

mulatto—A person of European and African descent.

zambo—A person of African and Indian descent.

hacienda—An estate or plantation belonging to elite families.

Beginnings of Northern European Expansion

How did Dutch, French, and British colonial expansion get started?

European overseas expansion after 1600 entered a second phase, comparable to developments at home. As Spain declined, so did the Spanish Empire and that of Portugal, which was unified with Spain by a Habsburg king after 1580 and plagued with its own developing imperial problems. These conditions afforded opportunities for the northern European states. The Dutch between 1630 and 1650 almost cleared the Atlantic of Spanish warships while taking over most of the Portuguese posts in Brazil, Africa, and Asia. The French and English also became involved on a smaller scale, setting up a global duel for empire in the eighteenth century.

The Shifting Commercial Revolution

Along with this second phase of expansion came a decisive shift in Europe's Commercial Revolution. Expanding foreign trade, new products, an increasing supply of bullion, and rising commercial risks created new problems, calling for energetic initiatives. Because the Spanish and Portuguese during the sixteenth century had depended on quick profits, weak home industries, and poor management, wealth flowed through their hands to northern Europe, where it was invested in productive enterprises. Later it generated a new imperial age.

European markets after the sixteenth century were swamped with a bewildering array of hitherto rare or unknown goods from around the world. New foods from the Americas included potatoes, sweet potatoes, peanuts, maize (corn), tomatoes, cassava, and fish from Newfoundland's Grand Banks. In an era without refrigeration, imported spices—such as pepper, cloves, and cinnamon—were valued for making spoiled foods palatable. Sugar became a common substitute for honey, and the use of cocoa, the Aztec sacred beverage, spread throughout Europe. Coffee and tea from the New World and Asia would also soon change European social habits. Similarly, North American furs,

Europe's commercial expansion during the fifteenth and sixteenth centuries was based on its dominance of ocean trade. As depicted in this drawing, a typical scene in a busy European port included dockworkers unloading goods from ships that were trading in many parts of the world.

Chinese silks, and cottons from India and Mexico revolutionized clothing fashions. Furnishings of rare woods and ivory and luxurious oriental carpets appeared more frequently in the homes of the wealthy. The use of American tobacco became almost a mania among all classes, further contributing to the booming European market.

Imported gold and, even more significant, silver probably affected the European economy more than all other foreign goods. After the Spaniards had looted Aztec and Inca treasure rooms, the gold flowing from America and Africa subsided to a respectable trickle, but 7 million tons of silver poured into Europe before 1660. Spanish prices quadrupled, and because most new bullion went to pay for imports, prices more than tripled in northern Europe. Rising inflation hurt landlords who depended on fixed rents and creditors who were paid in cheap money, but the bullion bonanza ended a centuries-long gold drain to the East, with its attendant money shortage. It also increased the profits of merchants selling on a rising market, thus greatly stimulating northern European capitalism.

At the opening of the sixteenth century, Italian merchants and moneylenders, mainly Florentines, Venetians, and Genoese, dominated the rising Atlantic economy. The German Fugger banking house at Augsburg also provided substantial financing. European bankers, particularly the Fuggers and the Genoese, suffered heavily from the Spanish economic debacles under Charles V and Philip II, however. As the century passed, Antwerp, in the southern Netherlands, became the economic hub of Europe. It was the center for the English wool trade as well as a transfer station, drawing southbound goods such as wheat and herring from the Baltic and Portuguese goods from Asia. It was also a great financial market, dealing in commercial and investment instruments. The Spanish sack of the city in 1576 ended Antwerp's supremacy, which passed to Amsterdam and furthered Dutch imperial ventures. Amsterdam became a center for currency exchanges in Europe as well as commercial banking. In 1609, a stock exchange was founded.

Meanwhile, northern European capitalism flourished in nearly every category. Portuguese trade in Africa and Asia was matched by that of the Baltic and the North Atlantic. Northern joint-stock companies pooled capital for privateering, exploring, and commercial venturing. The Dutch and English East India companies, founded early in the seventeenth century, were but two of the better-known stock companies. In England, common fields were enclosed for capitalistic sheep runs. Throughout western Europe, domestic manufacturing, in homes or workshops, was competing with the guilds. Large industrial enterprises, notably in mining, shipbuilding, and cannon casting, were becoming common. Indeed, the superiority of English and Swedish cannons caused the defeat of the Spanish Armada and Catholic armies in the Thirty Years' War.

The Dutch Empire

By 1650, the Dutch were supreme in both southern Asia and the South Atlantic. Their empire, like that of the Portuguese earlier, was primarily commercial; even their North American settlements specialized in fur trading with the Indians. They acquired territory where necessary to further their commerce but tried to act

	Dutch Exploration and Expansion
1576	Sack of Antwerp; Amsterdam becomes commercial hub of Europe
1595	First Dutch fleet enters East Indies
1609	Henry Hudson explores Hudson River
1621	Dutch form West India Company
1624	Dutch found New Amsterdam on Manhattan Island
1641	Dutch drive Portuguese out of Malacca

pragmatically in accordance with Asian cultures rather than expanding by conquest. An exception was their colony in Java, where the Dutch drive for monopolizing the spice trade led them to take direct control of the island. Unlike the Spanish and the Portuguese, the Dutch made little attempt to spread Christianity.

Dutch involvement in the Indian Ocean was the direct result of the Spanish absorption of Portugal in 1580. The Spanish restricted the flow of spices, especially pepper, to northern Europe, and Dutch seafarers set out to control the sources of the trade. Systematic Dutch naval operations commenced in 1595 when the first Dutch fleet entered the East Indies. Dutch captains soon drove the Portuguese from the Spice Islands. Malacca, the Portuguese bastion, fell after a long siege in 1641. The Dutch also occupied Sri Lanka (SHREE-lahn-KAH) and blockaded Goa, thus limiting Portuguese operations in the Indian Ocean. Although largely neglecting East Africa, they seized all Portuguese posts on the west coast north of Angola. Across the Atlantic, they conquered and held part of Brazil for a few decades, drove Spain from the Caribbean, and captured a Spanish treasure fleet. Decisive battles off the English Channel coast near Kent (1639) and off Brazil (1640) delivered final blows to the Spanish navy. What the English began in 1588, the Dutch completed 50 years later.

Five Dutch trading companies initially conducted trade with Asia, but the Dutch state decided their competition with each other cut into profits and established the Dutch East India Company. Chartered in 1602 and given a monopoly over all operations between the Cape of Good Hope in South Africa and the Strait of Magellan, it conserved resources and cut costs. In addition to its trade and diplomacy, the company sponsored explorations of Australia, Tasmania, New Guinea, and the South Pacific.

The Dutch Empire in the East was established primarily by Jan Pieterszoon Coen, governor-general of the Indies for two periods between 1619 and 1629 and founder of the company capital at Batavia in northwestern Java. At first he cooperated with local rulers in return for a monopoly over the spice trade. When this involved him in costly wars against local sultans as well as their Portuguese and English customers, Coen determined to control the trade at its sources. In the ensuing numerous conflicts and negotiations, which outlasted Coen, the Dutch acquired all of Java, most of Sumatra, the spice-growing Moluccas (mol-U-kuz), and part of Sri Lanka. They began operating their own plantations, overseen by Dutch settlers and worked by thousands of slaves brought in from such diverse areas as East Africa, Bengal, Persia, and Japan. The plantations produced cinnamon, nutmeg, cloves, sugar, tea, tobacco, and coffee, but it was pepper that reaped the highest profits. In the seventeenth century, 7 million pounds of pepper were shipped to Europe annually.

Although commercially successful in Asia, the Dutch were not able to found flourishing colonial settlements. Many Dutchmen who went to the East wanted to make their fortunes and return home; those willing to stay were usually mavericks, uninterested in establishing families but instead pursuing temporary sexual liaisons with female slaves or servants. For a while after 1620, the company recruited "eligible virgins" from orphanages in the Netherlands and placed them on "maiden ships" to the Indies, but such efforts were abandoned when the venture failed to enlist much interest at home or in the foreign stations. Consequently, the Dutch colonies in Asia, as well as those in Africa, the Caribbean, and Brazil, remained primarily business ventures with less racial mixing than in the Iberian areas.

After resuming war with Spain in 1621, the Dutch chartered the Dutch West India Company, charged with overtaking the diminishing Spanish and Portuguese holdings in West Africa and America. The company wasted no time. It soon supplanted the Portuguese in West Africa; by 1630, it had taken over the slave trade with America. After driving the Spanish from the Caribbean, the Dutch invited other European planters to the West Indies as customers, keeping only a few bases for themselves. The company then launched a successful naval conquest of Brazil, from the mouth of the Amazon south to the San Francisco River. In Brazil, the Dutch learned sugar planting, and after being expelled in 1654, passed on their knowledge to the Caribbean and applied it directly in the East Indies.

Dutch settlements in North America never amounted to much because of the company's commercial orientation. In 1609, Henry Hudson (d. 1611), an Englishman sailing for the Dutch, explored the river (ultimately named for him) and established Dutch claims while looking for a northwest passage.

Fifteen years later, the company founded New Amsterdam on Manhattan Island; over the next few years it built a number of frontier trading posts in the Hudson valley and on the nearby Connecticut and Delaware rivers. Some attempts were made to encourage planting by selling large tracts to wealthy proprietors (**patroons**). Agriculture, however, remained secondary to the fur trade, which the company developed in alliance with the Iroquois tribes. This arrangement hindered settlement; in 1660, only 5000 Europeans were in the colony.

The French Empire

French exploration began early, but no permanent colonies were established abroad until the start of the seventeenth century. The country was so weakened by religious wars that most of its efforts, beyond fishing, privateering, and a few failed attempts at settlement, had to be directed toward internal stability. While the Dutch were winning their empire, France was involved in the land campaigns of the Thirty Years' War. Serious French empire building thus had to be delayed until after 1650, during the reign of Louis XIV.

Early French colonization in North America was based on claims made by Giovanni da Verrazzano (1485–1528) and Jacques Cartier (1491–1557). The first, a Florentine mariner commissioned by Francis I in 1523, traced the Atlantic coast from North Carolina to Newfoundland. Eleven years later, Cartier made one of two voyages exploring the St. Lawrence River. These French expeditions duplicated England's claim to eastern North America.

French colonial efforts during the sixteenth century were dismal failures. They resulted partly from French experiences in exploiting the Newfoundland fishing banks and conducting an undeclared naval war in the Atlantic against Iberian treasure ships and trading vessels after 1520. In 1543, Cartier tried unsuccessfully to establish a colony in the St. Lawrence valley. No more serious efforts were made until 1605, when a French base was established at Port Royal, on Nova Scotia. It was meant to be a fur-trading center and capital for the whole St. Lawrence region. In 1608, Samuel de Champlain (1567–1635), who had been an aide to the governor of the Nova Scotia colony, acted for a French-chartered company in founding Quebec on the St. Lawrence. The company brought in colonists, but the little community was disrupted in 1627 when British troops took the town and forced Champlain's surrender. Although when Champlain came back as governor, the fort was returned to France by a treaty in 1629, growth was slowed by the company's emphasis on fur trading, the bitterly cold winters, and skirmishes with Indians. Only a few settlers had arrived by Champlain's death in 1635, and just 2500 Europeans were in Quebec as late as 1663. Nevertheless, Montreal was established in 1642, after which French trapper-explorers began penetrating the region around the headwaters of the Mississippi.

	British and French Exploration and Colonization
1485–1528	Giovanni da Verrazzano
1491–1557	Jacques Cartier
1497–1498	John Cabot establishes English claims in North America
1567–1635	Samuel de Champlain
1605	French establish base at Port Royal, in Nova Scotia
1607	First English colony in North America founded at Jamestown
1627	British conquer Quebec
1629	Puritans settle near Boston
1632–1635	English Catholics found colony of Maryland
1642	Montreal established

Elsewhere, the French seized opportunities afforded by the decline of Iberian sea power. They acquired the Isle of Bourbon (BOOR-bon), later known as Réunion, in the Indian Ocean (1642) for use as a commercial base. In West Africa, they created a sphere of commercial interest at the mouth of the Senegal River, where they became involved in the slave trade with only slight opposition from the Dutch. Even more significant was the appearance of the French in the West Indies. They occupied part of St. Kitts in 1625 and later acquired Martinique, Guadeloupe, and Santo Domingo. Fierce attacks by the indigenous Caribs limited economic development before 1650. However, by the late eighteenth century, Santo Domingo had become the crown jewel of France's Caribbean possessions. Possessing half of the Caribbean's slave population, the island was the largest producer of sugar in America, and—after coffee was introduced in 1723—the world's largest coffee producer until the Haitian revolution of 1791.

The English Empire

In terms of power and profit, English foreign expansion before 1650 was not impressive. Like French colo-

patroon—An owner of a landed estate granted by the Dutch West India Company in New York and New Jersey.

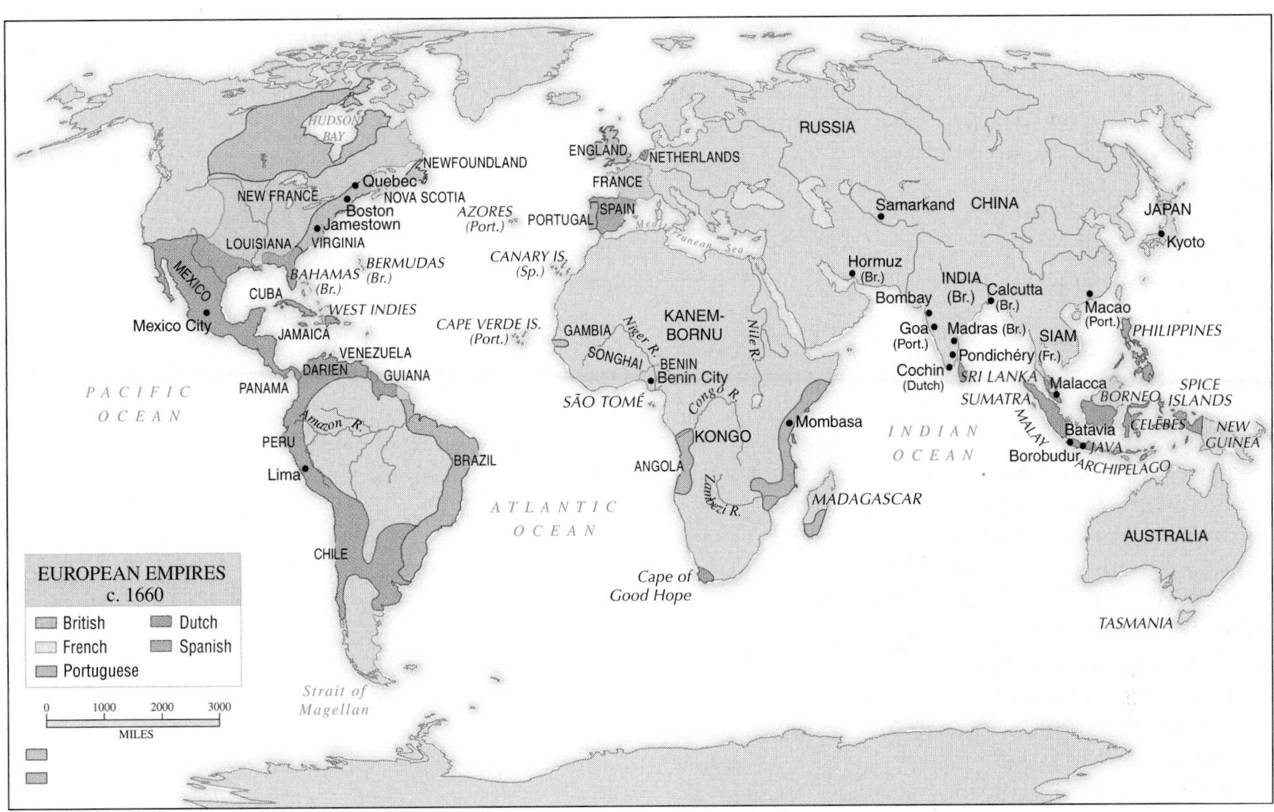

▲ By the late 1600s, the Portuguese and Spanish, the pioneers in global exploration, had been displaced in many regions by the English, French, and Dutch.

nialism, it was somewhat restricted by internal political conditions, particularly the poor management and restrictive policies of the early Stuart kings, which led to civil war in the 1640s. A number of circumstances, however, promoted foreign ventures. The population increased from 3 to 4 million between 1530 and 1600, providing a large reservoir of potential indentured labor; religious persecution encouraged migration of nonconformists; and holders of surplus capital were seeking opportunities for investment. Such conditions ultimately produced a unique explosion of English settlement overseas.

During the sixteenth century, English maritime operations were confined primarily to exploring, fishing, smuggling, and plundering. English claims to North America were registered in 1497 and 1498 by two voyages of John Cabot, who explored the coast of North America from Newfoundland to Virginia but found no passage to Asia. For the next century, English expeditions sought such a northern passage, both in the East and in the West. All of them failed, but they resulted in explorations of Hudson Bay and the opening of a northeastern trade route to Russia. From the 1540s, English captains, including the famous John Hawkins of Plymouth, indulged in sporadic slave trading in Africa and the West Indies, despite Spanish restrictions.

After failures in Newfoundland and on the Carolina coast, the first permanent English colony in America was founded in 1607 at Jamestown, Virginia. For a number of years, the colonists suffered from lack of food and other privations, but they were saved by their leader, Captain John Smith (1580–1631), whose romantic rescue by the native princess Pocahontas (1595–1617) is an American legend. Jamestown set a significant precedent for all English colonies in North America. By the terms of its original charter, the London Company, which founded the settlement, was authorized to supervise government for the colonists, but they were to enjoy all the rights of native Englishmen. Consequently, in 1619 the governor called an assembly to assist in governing. This body would later become the Virginia House of Burgesses, one of the oldest representative legislatures still operating.

Shortly after the founding of Jamestown, large-scale colonization began elsewhere. In 1620, a group of English protestants, known as Pilgrims, landed at Plymouth. Despite severe hardships, they survived, and their experiences inspired other religious dissenters against the policies of Charles I. In 1629, a number of English Puritans formed the Massachusetts Bay Company and settled near Boston, where their charter gave

▲ This is an anonymous engraving made around 1776 of the Mohawk chief and diplomat Tiyanoga (TEE-yah-HOH-gah). He was an ally for the British and known to them as "King Hendrick." In this portrait, one can see the influence of European trade goods in Tiyanoga's dress. His shirt is made of linen or calico, and his mantle and breechcloth are made of English wool duffels.

them the rights to virtual self-government. From this first enclave, emigrants moved out to other areas in present-day Maine, Rhode Island, and Connecticut. By 1642, more than 25,000 people had migrated to New England, laying the foundations for a number of future colonies. Around the same time (1632–1635), a group of English Catholics, fleeing Stuart persecution, founded the Maryland colony. These enterprises firmly planted English culture and political institutions in North America.

Life in the English settlements was hard during those first decades, but a pioneering spirit and native colonial pride was already evident. Food was scarce, disease was ever present, and conflicts with indigenous tribes were not uncommon. Yet from the beginning, and more than in other European colonies, settlers looked to their future in the new land because they had left so little behind in Europe. Most were expecting to stay, establish homes, make their fortunes, and raise families. The first Puritans included both men and women; a shipload of "purchase brides" arrived in 1619 at Jamestown to lend stability to that colony. This was but the first of many such contingents, all eagerly welcomed by prospective husbands. In addition, many women came on their own as indentured servants.

Anglo-American colonial women faced discrimination but managed to cope with it pragmatically. They were legally dependent on their husbands, who controlled property and children; a widow acquired these rights, but it was not easy to outlive a husband. Hard work and frequent pregnancies—mothers with a dozen children were not uncommon—reduced female life expectancies. Nevertheless, many women developed a rough endurance, using their social value to gain confidence and practical equality with their husbands, although some did this more obviously than others. This independent spirit was exemplified by Anne Hutchinson (1591–1643), who was banished from Massachusetts for her heretical views and founded a dissenting religious settlement in Rhode Island. Another freethinker was Anne Bradstreet (c. 1612–1672), who, although painfully aware that men considered her presumptuous, wrote thoughtful poetry.

The English government considered the rough coasts and wild forests of North America less important in this period than footholds in the West Indies and Africa, where profits were expected in planting and slave trading. Therefore, a wave of English migrants descended on the West Indies after the Dutch opened the Caribbean. In 1613, English settlers invaded Bermuda, and by the 1620s, others had planted colonies on St. Kitts, Barbados, Nevis, Montserrat (mawn-suh-RAHT), Antigua (ahn-TEE-gwah), and the Bahamas. Tobacco planting was at first the major enterprise, bringing some prosperity and the promise of more. The white population expanded dramatically, especially on Barbados, which was not subject to Carib attacks. There, the English population increased from 7,000 to 37,000 in 7 years. As yet, there were few African slaves on the English islands, although some were already being imported for the sugar plantations.

Meanwhile, English slaving posts in West Africa were beginning to flourish, and English adventurers were starting operations in Asia. Captain John Lancaster took four ships to Sumatra and Java in 1601, returning with a profitable cargo of spices. But expansion outside of the Caribbean was difficult because the Dutch were uncooperative. In the Moluccas, for example, they drove out the English in the 1620s, after repeated clashes. The English fared better in India. By 1622, the British East India Company, which had been

This drawing shows Anne Hutchinson on trial before a Puritan court in Boston in 1638 for violating the sect's moral and legal codes and challenging the male hierarchy by inviting men and women into her home at the same time for Bible study. Found guilty, she was banished from the colony and founded another religious community in Rhode Island.

chartered in 1600, had put the Portuguese out of business in the Persian Gulf. Subsequently, the English established trading posts on the west coast of India at Agra, Bombay, Masulipatam, Balasore, and Surat. The station at Madras, destined to become the English bastion on the east coast of the Indian subcontinent, was founded in 1639. The East India Company prospered from the trade in Indian cotton and silk cloth for the English and European markets.

Conclusion

Between 1450 and 1650, the era of the early Commercial Revolution, Europeans faced outward toward a new world and, following precedents set by earlier Eurasian empires, initiated their own age of oceanic expansion that laid the foundation for the first truly global economy. In the process, they stimulated capitalistic development, found a sea route to Asia, became more familiar with Africa, began colonizing America, and proved that the world had a spherical surface. The key to Europe's political and economic strength was its control over sea routes. For most of the period, Spain and Portugal dominated the new ocean trade. Spain profited most from exploiting American gold and silver, which they utilized to develop transatlantic trade and finance trade with Asia. After 1600, leadership shifted to the Dutch, French, and English.

Overseas expansion exerted a tremendous effect on European culture and institutions. Spain's political predominance in the sixteenth century was largely bought with New World treasure, and Spain's eventual decline was mainly caused by the squandering of wealth on war rather than on investment, and the influx of American bullion, which inflated Spanish money and discouraged Spanish economic development. Northern European capitalism, developing in financial organization, shipbuilding, metalworking, manufacturing, and agriculture, brought a new vitality to northern economies in response to Spanish and Portuguese purchasing power. Economic advantages also contributed to Protestant victories in the Thirty Years' War.

By the late seventeenth century, the Europeans were exerting influence in Asia, Africa, and the Americas, but they experienced mixed results in their encounters with societies around the world. In Asia, where they engaged well-established states, such as China, Japan, and India, they usually had to respect their laws and authority and even do their bidding and had little impact on land-based trading networks. The Portuguese were run out of China twice before they came to respect Chinese law, and other Europeans fared worse. All were ultimately excluded from Japan. Southern India was not entirely open, as the Portuguese found by the end of the period. In the main, Turks, Arabs, Chinese, Japanese, Thais, and Vietnamese felt superior to Europeans and were usually able to defend their interests with effective action.

Where they dealt with smaller states and city-states, such as in Indonesia and East Africa, Europeans were more likely to directly intervene or dominate their affairs. Sri Lanka and the Spice Islands of the Malay archipelago, which were vulnerable to sea attack, came under domination, directly or indirectly, and were exploited by the Portuguese and the Dutch.

In the New World, the European presence led to the increased exploitation of natural resources. Portuguese captains and Spanish conquistadors, as well as diseases such as smallpox and measles, nearly destroyed indigenous peoples and subjected most of the survivors to terrible hardships, indignities, cultural deprivations, and psychological injuries. However, the Portuguese and Spanish contact with the Americas also sparked exchanges in plants, animals, and peoples that eventually reached societies around the world.

The European impact on Africa was less apparent at the time but perhaps more damaging in the long run. When the Portuguese began exploring the African coastline, they were more concerned with scoring quick profits through gold exports than with establishing stable, long-term relationships with African states. Moreover, with the exception of Angola or landed estates along the Zambezi River, the Portuguese did not have the manpower or resources to conquer or influence the political affairs of African states. However, as the Atlantic slave trade expanded, the Portuguese and African states, especially along the Atlantic and Indian Ocean coasts, became bound up in a destructive process that would run its tragic course over the next few centuries.

Suggestions for Web Browsing

You can obtain more information about topics included in this chapter at the websites listed below. See also the companion website that accompanies this text, http://www.ablongman.com/brummett, which contains an online study guide and additional resources.

Age of Discovery
http://www.win.tue.nl/cs/fm/engels/discovery/#age
An excellent collection of resources that includes text, images, and maps relating to the early years of European expansion.

Internet Medieval History Sourcebook: Exploration and Expansion
http://www.fordham.edu/halsall/sbook1z.html
An extensive online source for links about Western exploration and expansion, including primary documents by or about da Gama, Columbus, Drake, and Magellan.

Columbus Navigation Home Page
http://www1.minn.net/~keithp/
This site provides extensive information regarding the life and voyages of Christopher Columbus.

Internet African History Sourcebook
http://www.fordham.edu/halsall/africa/africasbook.html
An extensive online source for links about African history, including primary documents about the slave trade and by people who opposed it, supported it, and were its victims.

Literature and Film

Two major documentary series marked the quincentennial of Columbus's 1492 voyage in different ways. *Columbus and the Age of Discovery* (1991) is a seven-part series that primarily treats European exploration and expansion in the New World, whereas *500 Nations* (1995) is an eight-part series that examines Native American history before and after the arrival of Europeans. *Conquistadores* (2001) is Michael Wood's presentation of European explorers/conquerors such as Cortés and Pizarro.

Mexican writer Carlos Fuentes has written a major epic, *Terra Nostra*, trans. Margaret Peden (Farrar, Straus, and Giroux, 1976), and a collection of short stories and novellas, *The Orange Tree*, trans. Alfred MacAdam (Farrar, Straus, and Giroux, 1994), with Spanish exploration and conquest of the New World as their backdrop. James Lackhart's *We People Here: Nahuatl Accounts of the Conquest of Mexico* (University of California Press, 1993) presents indigenous narratives of the Spanish conquest compiled by a Franciscan priest in the sixteenth century.

Suggestions for Reading

Several excellent works, which cover the subject of European exploration and colonization, are Geoffrey V. Scammell, *The First Imperial Age: European Overseas Expansion, 1400–1700* (Unwin Hyman, 1989); Anthony Pagden, ed., *European Encounters with the New World* (Yale University Press, 1993); and Nicholas Canny and Anthony Pagden, *Colonial Identity in the Atlantic World* (Princeton University Press, 1989). European encounters with other peoples are treated in Urs Bitterli, *Cultures in Conflict: Encounters Between European and Non-European Cultures, 1492–1800* (Stanford University Press, 1989), and Stuart Schwartz, ed., *Implicit Understandings: Observing, Reporting, and Reflecting on the Encounters between Europeans and Other Peoples in the Early Modern Era* (Cambridge University Press, 1994).

For more information about the Iberian New World, see Cheryl Martin and Mark Wasserman, *Latin America and its People* (Pearson, 2005), and Mark A. Burkholder and Lyman Johnson, *Colonial Latin America*, 4th ed. (Oxford University Press, 2001). Works on Columbus include Felipe Fernandez-Armesto, *Columbus* (Oxford University Press, 1992), and John

Yewell, Chris Dodge, and Jan De Surey, *Confronting Columbus: An Anthology* (McFarland, 1992).

The consequences of European diseases on the indigenous cultures of the Americas are examined in Noble David Cook, *Born to Die: Disease and the New World Conquest, 1517–1570* (Cambridge University Press, 1998). The impact of colonization on ecology is highlighted in Alfred Crosby, *The Columbian Exchange: Biological Consequences of 1492* (Praeger Publishers, 2003).

Luis Martin, *Daughters of the Conquistadores* (Southern Methodist University Press, 1989), documents the significant role of women in the grueling process of colonization. The Spanish campaigns in Peru are assessed in Susan Ramirez, *The World Upside Down: Cross-Cultural Contact and Conflict in Sixteenth-Century Peru* (Stanford University Press, 1996).

On political, economic, and social conditions, see Leslie B. Simpson, *The Encomienda in New Spain,* 3rd ed. (University of California Press, 1982). Edward Murguca, *Assimilation, Colonialism, and the Mexican American People* (University Press of America, 1989), depicts the racial and cultural synthesis in colonial Mexico.

A respected work on Portuguese exploration and colonization is A. J. R. Russell-Wood, *A World on the Move: The Portuguese in Africa, Asia and America, 1415–1808* (St. Martin's Press, 1992). On the Portuguese in Asia, see Michael Pearson, *The Indian Ocean* (Routledge, 2003).

A sound treatment of Dutch imperial development is Charles R. Boxer, *The Dutch Seaborne Empire* (Penguin, 1989). French colonialism in America is covered in William J. Eccles, *France in America* (Michigan State University Press, 1990), and the British Empire in William R. Lewis, Nicholas Canny, P. J. Marshall, and Alaine Low, eds., *The Origins of Empire: British Overseas Enterprise to the Close of the Seventeenth Century* (Oxford University Press, 1998).

CHAPTER 17

Absolutism and Limited Central Power in Europe, 1650–1774

Politics During the First Age of Capitalism

Outline

- Louis XIV, the Sun King: The Model for European Absolutism
- The Gravitational Pull of French Absolutism
- Holland and England: Limited Central Power
- Breaking the Bank: Diplomacy and War in the Age of Absolutism: 1650–1774
- The Decline of European Absolutism, the Example of Louis XV: 1715–1774
- Capitalism and the Forces of Change
- Social Crises During the Capitalist Revolution

Features

DOCUMENT **Catherine II on Life in St. Petersburg in 1750**

DISCOVERY THROUGH MAPS **The Elegant Destruction of Poland**

SEEING CONNECTIONS **A New Product from the New World: Tobacco**

DOCUMENT **Conditions Among Eighteenth-Century French Peasants**

◄ Maria Theresa is known as one of the more progressive rulers of the eighteenth century. She sponsored a number of reforms—ranging from strengthening the military forces of the Hapsburg Monarchy to implementing important economic changes. At the same time she and her husband created one of the largest families in European history, producing 16 children, including Marie Antoinette.

IN 1648, a century and a half of religious wars in Europe finally came to an end. As we saw in Chapter 15, the new European political system that arose after the Treaty of Westphalia derived from political calculation, *raison d'état.* Kings ruled through one of two political systems. Most followed the absolutist model in which all power was vested in the person of the monarch, who in turned received his right to rule—his legitimacy—from God. France's Louis XIV served as the exemplar of this model for other European monarchs. In contrast to absolutism, the Netherlands and England chose the approach of limited central power. In these two countries, the rulers exercised their power under the limitations of precedents, laws, and legislatures that came to be increasingly influenced by merchants and other members of the growing middle class.

In the period between the Treaty of Westphalia and the outbreak of the French Revolution 150 years later, however, politics and diplomacy—including numerous "balance of power wars"—were not the most important developments in Europe.

Capitalism—an economic system based on private ownership of property, individual risk taking, and market determination of the prices of goods—would grow to extend beyond Europe and became the basis of a global economy. Rich European states such as England, with access to great resources and comparatively efficient bureaucracies, grew stronger while poor nations such as Poland, which remained mired in its medieval political and economic structure, literally disappeared from the map.

Louis XIV, the Sun King: The Model for European Absolutism

What were the advantages and disadvantages of French absolutism?

The term **absolutism,** which is applied to regimes such as that of Louis XIV (1638–1715, r. 1643–1715), is somewhat misleading. The French king never had total control over his realm. Despite his grandiose role-playing, Louis faced problems arising from preindustrial technology, diverse ethnic groups, local customs, traditional rights, and nobles who still commanded formidable followings, both regionally and nationally.

Absolutism: France, England, and Russia, 1600–1700

Foundations of Absolutism

Europeans, especially those on the Continent, had suffered greatly, in both loss of life and material and economic costs, during the long wars of religion. Not surprisingly, they desired order and stability, social and political conditions that served as theoretical justifications for absolute monarchy. Some justifications, such as the arguments advanced by the French Bishop Jacques Bossuet (BOS-siu-ay), relied on the older idea of "divine right," claiming that rulers were agents of God's will, and thus were His representatives on earth whose orders were to be followed unquestioningly. The most influential nonreligious justification for absolutism came from the English philosopher Thomas Hobbes (1588–1679), whose political treatise, *Leviathan,* appeared in 1651. Unlike Bossuet, he did not see God as the sole source of political authority. According to Hobbes, people created governments as a protection against their self-destructive tendencies: he wrote that human life was "poor, nasty, brutish, and short." Forced by their depraved human nature to surrender their freedoms to the state in order to survive, people have no rights under government except obedience. Monarchs were therefore legitimately entitled to absolute authority for the sake of maintaining order and stability and were limited only by their own weaknesses and by the power of other states.

Neither Hobbes' nor Bossuet's views, however, described the workings of the monarchy of Louis XIV. Louis and other monarchs functioned within institutional systems carried over from the medieval past. Their success or failure depended on their ability to shape old feudal structures into centralized states. In this process, none succeeded completely in eliminating aristocratic influence and local tradition as limits to royal authority. Their proclaimed absolutism reflected a trend and a hope, rather than an accomplished fact.

One primary goal that Louis and other monarchs across Europe shared was a desire to dominate and control their nobles, many of whom came from families with far more distinguished lineages than those of the kings. To these nobles, the king was simply *primus inter pares* (PREE-moos in-ter pa-REES) or "first among equals." Centralizing kings could not tolerate such familiarity.

Louis XIV's version of absolutism followed a long monarchical tradition of French kings trying to centralize power. Francis I in the early sixteenth century had increasingly subordinated the feudal nobility, decimated after the wars of the fourteenth and fifteenth centuries, and created a centralized administration. Henry IV and his chief minister, the duke of Sully (suil-EE; 1560–1641) ended the nobles' control of hereditary offices and council seats. At the same time, the two produced a balanced budget and a treasury surplus in little more than a decade. This centralization was temporarily disrupted in 1610 when François Ravaillac, a mentally unstable religious fanatic, assassinated Henry.

Marie de' Medici (MEH-de-chee; 1573–1642), Henry's wife, served as a regent for her young son Louis XIII until 1617 when he, at the age of 15, seized power to rule for himself. For the next 13 years, son and mother continued their duel for power. Marie favored a pro-Spanish and Catholic policy, whereas Louis—following

absolutism—The political system in which the ruler has total power, with no limitations.

Chronology

1550	1600		1650	1700
1587 Dutch Republic formed **1588–1679** Thomas Hobbes, author of *Leviathan* (1651), which provided secular, contractual justification for absolutism	**1603–1625** Reign of James I of England, beginning of Stuart dynasty **1619–1683** Jean Baptiste Colbert, finance minister for Louis XIV **1640–1688** Reign of Frederick William, the Great Elector of Prussia	**1642–1649** English Civil War **1643–1715** Reign of Louis XIV of France, the Sun King **1648** Peace of Westphalia **1649–1653** French Civil War, the *Fronde,* revolt of the nobility against absolutism	**1688** Glorious Revolution in England **1689–1725** Reign of Peter the Great of Russia	**1707** Act of Union between England and Scotland **1713** Peace of Utrecht **1713–1740** Reign of Frederick William I of Prussia **1715–1774** Reign of Louis XV of France

◄ Not only did Louis XIV take the title of the "Sun King," theologians such as Jacques Bossuet stated that he was king by "Divine Right," as suggested by this image.

the advice of the Cardinal Richelieu (REESH-e-lieu; 1585–1642)—saw the Habsburgs and the papacy as the main threats to French interests. Cardinal Richelieu finally came out the winner in this contest for power, and Marie de' Medici was banished from France in 1631.

Richelieu worked ceaselessly for the next decade to increase the king's powers over the nobles: he organized a royal civil service, restricted the traditional local courts and *parlements,* brought local government under central control, outlawed dueling, prohibited fortified castles, stripped the Huguenots of their military defenses, and developed strong military and naval forces loyal only to the king. His policies were carried on after his death by his colleague, Cardinal Mazarin (1602–1661), who, for all intents and purposes, ran the government until his death, when the 23-year-old Louis XIV could finally take direct control of the state. These two politically astute cardinals laid the final stones of the foundations for the absolutist state of Louis XIV.

During the time of Mazarin's supervision, a civil war, the *Fronde* (1649–1653), was waged by some of the highest-ranking French nobles in one last desperate outburst to regain their old powers lost in the previous century. A demand for increased taxes to pay for the expenses of the French phase of the Thirty Years' War sparked the noble uprising. During this civil war, Louis barely escaped being captured by the rebel forces more than once. Eventually, a combination of lack of unity among the nobles and increased support for the king led to the destruction of the *Fronde* and the subjugation of the nobles. As France became more centralized, the nobles were forced to pay court to the king at Versailles, but they and their descendants never forgot their loss of power at the hands of Richelieu and others. When France fell into a financial crisis in the 1780s, the nobles would move again to reclaim lost power.

The memories of the *Fronde* and the impact of the lessons he received from Mazarin prepared Louis well to be king. His personal political convictions were clearly revealed in a characteristic statement: "All power, all authority resides in the hands of the king, and there can be no other in his kingdom than that which he establishes. The nation does not form a body in France. It resides entirely in the person of the king."[1] Louis also claimed authority over the French church and the religion of his subjects, enforcing that authority in conflicts with both Protestants and the papacy. In 1685 he revoked the Edict of Nantes, by which in 1598 Henry IV had granted freedom of worship to Protestant Huguenots. The new law subjected Protestants to torture or imprisonment. Luckily for them, but not for France, some 300,000 escaped to other lands, taking with them valuable skills and knowledge. Throughout his reign, he was involved in a long struggle with Rome over revenues claimed by the church.

The Functioning of French Absolutism

During his reign, Louis projected an image of himself to France and Europe as a "Grand Monarch," a figure worthy of fear as well as worship. He constantly worked to inspire awe of the monarchy as something above and apart from the rest of society, especially the nobles. To symbolize his life-giving presence in the council chamber, Louis had a rising sun painted on his official chair, signifying that he was the center of France just as the sun was the center of the planetary system. A person could exist politically only in the presence of the king at Versailles.

Louis XIV moved his residence from Paris to the magnificent palace at Versailles, 16 miles away, in 1682. It was set in 17,000 beautifully landscaped acres. The parks and buildings, surrounded by a 40-mile wall, contained 1400 fountains, 2000 statues, and innumerable rooms decorated with marble columns, painted ceilings, costly draperies, mirrored walls, and handcrafted furniture. Historians debate the cost of building and maintaining Versailles, with an average figure of approximately 10 percent of the total production of the French economy.

The most striking characteristic of the government of Louis XIV was the decided contrast between local and central functions. In the provinces, he had to contend with entrenched local authorities and legal structures, which remained despite his attempts at centralization. They constituted an obstacle that hindered the enforcement of royal edicts and the collection of revenues. At Versailles, the situation was quite different. There, Louis was the final authority and arbiter of policy and fashion. Theoretically, he made all major decisions. He was the supreme lawgiver, the chief judge, the commander of all military forces, and the head of all administration.

The aristocracy through which Louis funneled his power dominated France with clear distinctions precisely defined by law. The rest of French society consisted of unprivileged taxpaying commoners, including merchants, craftsmen, and, above all, peasants. Many peasants owed dues and services to their landlords, although most were no longer bound to the soil as serfs. Commoners, including middle-class townspeople, paid most of the taxes, which were used to finance frequent wars and extravagant royal courts.

	The Reign of Louis XIV
1638	Birth of Louis XIV
1643	Louis ascends to the throne under the aegis of Cardinal Mazarin
1649–1653	Revolt of the nobles in the *Fronde*
1661	Death of Mazarin: Louis takes personal control
1661–1685	First phase of rule: Colbert installs mercantilism, Louvois reforms army
1670–1713	Four wars of Louis XIV
1685	Revocation of Edict of Nantes
1715	Death of Louis XIV

In France during the reign of Louis XIV, an alliance paired royal government with wealthy merchant-bankers in the king's attempt to gain the most money he could from the capitalists to support his ambitious plans. This was part of a of national economic regulations known as **mercantilism,** which had originated earlier but was adopted generally by European governments through the late seventeenth century. This system gained strength through the expansion of overseas trade, the expenses incurred in wars, and the economic depression of the middle 1600s.

Louis's comptroller of finance, Jean-Baptiste Colbert (1619–1683), installed mercantilism at the expense of Dutch overseas commerce. He created a comprehensive system of tariffs and trade prohibitions, levied against foreign imports. French luxury industries—silks, laces, fine woolens, and glass—were subsidized or developed in government shops. The state imported skilled workers and prescribed the most specific regulations for each industry. Colbert also improved internal transportation by building roads and canals that allowed commerce to pass between the Mediterranean, the Atlantic Ocean, the North Sea, the English Channel, and the Rhine River. He chartered overseas trading companies, granting them monopolies on commerce with North America, the West Indies, India, Southeast Asia, and the Middle East. In all of this, he tried to harness the energies of **capitalism**—but ultimately failed.

Bullionism was one of the system's basic principles. It sought to increase precious metals within a country by achieving a "favorable balance of trade," in which the monetary value of exports exceeded the value of imports. The result was, in a sense, a national profit. This became purchasing power in the world market, an advantage shared most directly by the government and favored merchants. Louis's advisers believed state economic regulation to be absolutely necessary for gaining a favorable balance. They used subsidies, chartered monopolies, taxes, tariffs, harbor tolls, and direct legal prohibitions to encourage exports and limit imports. For the same purpose,

---

mercantilism—Governmental regulation of all aspects of the economy.

capitalism—An economic system based on private ownership of property, individual risk taking, and market determination of the price of goods.

bullionism—A theory that states that wealth is to be found only in precious metals, and trade policy should guarantee a favorable balance of trade to insure a continuous increase in the amount of precious metals held by the state.

◀ Madame de Maintenon, shown here with her niece, exercised considerable influence in the court of Louis XIV.

French state enterprises received advantages over private competitors. Because Colbert viewed the world market in terms of competing states, he emphasized the importance of aggressive colonial expansion. He regarded colonies as favored markets for French products and as sources of cheap raw materials.

Louis's able minister of war, the Marquis de Louvois (lou-VWAH; 1641–1691), revolutionized the French army. In addition to the infantry and cavalry, he organized special units of supply, ordnance, artillery, engineers, and inspectors. Command ranks, combat units, drills, uniforms, and weapons were standardized for the first time in Europe. Louvois also improved weaponry by such innovations as the bayonet, which permitted a musket to be fired while the blade was attached. By raising military pay, providing benefits, and improving conditions of service, the war minister increased the size of the army from 72,000 to 400,000, a force larger than all belligerents put together at any one time during the Thirty Years' War. Louvois also improved and expanded the navy. In addition to a Mediterranean galley fleet based at Toulon, the overseas forces by 1683 consisted of 217 warships, operating from Atlantic ports and served by numerous shipyards. The new navy was also part of Colbert's grand strategy for building an enormous overseas dominion. In the last decades of the seventeenth century, the French Empire extended to North America, Africa, and Asia.

The Gravitational Pull of French Absolutism

Why did most European states admire and try to imitate French absolutism?

The popular image of Louis XIV as the Sun King symbolized his position in France but also implied that the French system exerted an influence on other European states. Like all such symbolism, the idea was only partly true. As much as it was a response to the French example, royal authority was accepted because it promised efficiency and security, the greatest needs of the time. Yet, French wealth and power certainly generated European admiration and imitation. Countries across the Continent imitated various aspects of the political theater created by Louis in Versailles and also copied the economic and military policies of the Sun King.

Absolutism in Prussia

The rise of the Hohenzollerns (HO-hen-zol-lerns) was among the most important political developments of the era. These relatively unimportant nobles, who once occupied a castle on Mount Zollern in southern Germany, pursued their ambitious policies through marriage, intrigue, religious factionalism, and war. By the early seventeenth century, they held lands scattered across northern Germany. The Thirty Years' War was almost disastrous for the Hohenzollerns but conditioned them to austerity, perseverance, and iron discipline.

Two reigns laid permanent foundations for the later monarchy. Frederick William (r. 1640–1688),

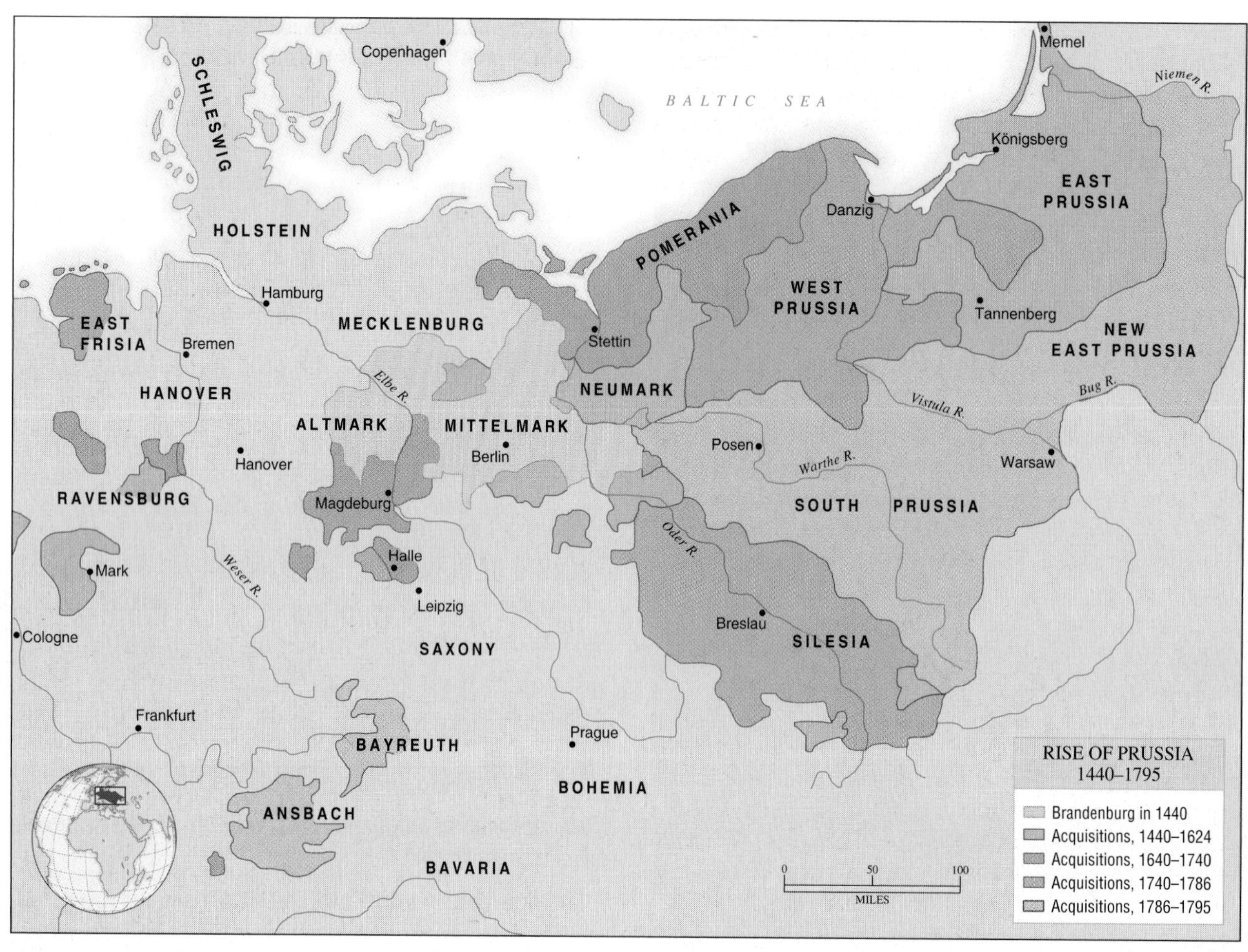

▲ Unlike most of their colleagues in the Holy Roman Empire, the electors of Brandenburg showed a single-minded drive over the centuries to expand from their bases in Berlin and Königsberg to become a major European power at the end of the eighteenth century.

called "the Great Elector," used his small but well-trained army to win eastern Pomerania (see map above) at the end of the Thirty Years' War. In the near-anarchy that prevailed in Germany immediately after Westphalia, he reformed the administration in Brandenburg, created a strong army of 30,000 soldiers, intimidated the nobles in Prussia and Cleves, and won central control over all three areas. His son Frederick I (r. 1688–1713) exploited Russia's victory over Sweden to annex western Pomerania. As a reward for fighting France, he was also recognized as "King in Prussia" by the Peace of Utrecht in 1713.

After Utrecht, Prussia became a military camp, with the monarch Frederick William I (r. 1713–1740) as drillmaster. This crusty soldier-king demanded hard work and absolute obedience from his subjects. He once told a group of them, "We are king and master and can do what we like." On another occasion he proclaimed as a good absolutist, "I need render account to no one as to the matter in which I conduct ... affairs."[2] He reorganized the government under the so-called **General Directory,** established a civil service for local administration, created a royal supreme court, taxed the nobles, required the nobles to train for professional military careers, and built an army of 80,000, considered the best trained and best equipped in Europe. At the end of his reign, the Hohenzollern monarchy was ready for military expansion.

Frederick William I held high hopes for his son Frederick II (r. 1740–1786). The young prince, however, reacted against his Spartan training, secretly seeking escape in music, art, and philosophy. When caught after attempting to run away to France, he was forced to witness the beheading of his accomplice and best friend. More years of severe training and discipline brought him in line with his father's wishes. In later years, while retaining his cultural interests and mingling freely with writers and artists, he developed no lasting relationships. He married early to escape his father's household, but as a homosexual he

General Directory—The efficient, centralized organization of the Prussian state in 1722.

ignored his wife, Elizabeth, subjecting her to a courteous but cold formality. Neither she nor any of his frequent but temporary lovers could influence his judgment. Neither did he confide in his family after the old king died. Wilhelmina, the sister who had shared his youthful enmity against their father, lost his confidence as they both matured. Such was the price he paid to become a superb administrator, a master of Machiavellian diplomacy, and—as we shall see—the greatest soldier of his day.

In 1780, the Prussia of Frederick II, called "the Great," was regarded as a perfectly functioning absolute monarchy. Stretching some 500 miles across northern Germany between the Elbe and Niemen rivers, its flourishing population had grown from 750,000 in 1648 to 5 million. For 23 years, between 1740 and 1763, it had waged nearly continuous war, with 200,000 men often in the field. Consequently, the government ran as precisely as an efficient army. Like any good commander, Frederick claimed all ultimate authority. He required rigid discipline and deference to superiors from civilian officials as well as from military officers. Prussian nobles were honored over merchants or nonnoble officials and were permitted complete mastery over their serfs. Frederick's mercantilism stressed tariff protection for agriculture, encouraged industry with government subsidies, imported artisans, and sought economic self-sufficiency as a means of achieving military superiority.

Russian Absolutism

A new era in Russian history began with Peter I, "the Great" (r. 1682–1725). When he was 10 years old, Peter's half-sister Sophia staged a palace coup, in which her troops looted the palace, killing many of Peter's maternal uncles. For 7 years, while Sophia ruled as regent for Peter and his handicapped half-brother, Ivan, the young co-tsar lived in fear and insecurity. Later, Peter roamed the part of Moscow reserved for foreigners, without discipline or much formal education. He recruited and drilled his own guard regiments and learned about boats and Western ways. When he was 16, his mother arranged his marriage to a young noblewoman. From the beginning this was a mismatch; after impregnating his wife, Peter abandoned her within three months.

CASE STUDY: Reflections on the Accomplishments of Peter the Great

He was now a young giant, weighing 230 pounds and standing 6 feet 8 inches tall, with a temper to match. Fortunately, he also had a sharp mind and boundless energy. Perhaps unfortunately for Russia, he despised Moscow, the traditions of the Russian court, the Orthodox Church, the Byzantine autocracy, and the culture of his country. In his efforts to westernize Russia, he would drive a wedge between the elites of the country and the masses that would last through the twentieth century.

After 1689, Peter took control of the country and his life; although his brother Ivan remained co-tsar until his death in 1696, he had no effect on affairs of state. When Sophia failed in an attempt to become sole ruler, he forced her into a convent to become a nun. Peter amused himself with mistresses and epic, wild drinking parties, but at the same time, he continued his pursuit of Western knowledge. His difficulties in wars with the Turks convinced him that he must modernize his army and build a navy. In 1697, he traveled incognito as a member of a great embassy to Poland, Germany, the Netherlands, and England. He worked as a common ship carpenter in the Netherlands, learning Dutch methods firsthand.

DOCUMENT: Lomonosov to Peter the Great

Returning to Moscow, Peter crushed a rebellion of his palace guards with savage cruelty. At the same time, he renewed his war against the Turks and attacked Sweden in an effort to gain "a window on the sea." He achieved this goal in 1703 when he founded St. Petersburg as his future capital on the Baltic Sea. That same year Peter met Marfa Skavronska (ska-vron-SKA), a

DOCUMENT: Winter Palace at St. Petersburg

▼ Kings rarely fought in the front lines of eighteenth-century wars. But this image presents the fatigue and stress felt by Frederick after he suffered his first defeat, against the Austrians, at the battle of Kolin, 1757.

▲ Larger than life for the era in which he lived, 6-foot, 8-inch Tsar Peter the Great remains one of the most controversial figures in Russian history. Liberals see him as a positive force for opening his country to the West. Conservatives see him as a negative factor in Russian history for the same reason.

Lithuanian peasant girl who became his mistress, campaign companion, and, after the tsarina's death in a convent, his wife.

Peter began to implement a series of reforms to place his country on a more Western footing and to enforce his absolute power. He centralized the government, replacing all representative bodies with an appointed council and appointed ministries. Royal military governors assumed local authority. The Chancery of Police maintained order and collected information from an elaborate spy network. By forcing his nobles to shave their beards and don European-style attire, he conditioned them to accept change and become living symbols of his power over them. They were now required to serve Russia in the army, the government, or industry. Peter also abolished the office of patriarch as head of the state church, substituting a synod of bishops on a Lutheran model, dominated by a secular official, the procurator, who represented the tsar. In copying European mercantilism, Peter established factories, mines, and shipyards, importing technical experts along with thousands of laborers. He levied tariffs to protect native industries and taxed almost everything, including births, marriages, and caskets. As revenues increased, he improved the army and navy, both of which were expanded, professionalized, and equipped with efficient Western weapons. In all of this, he borrowed no money from abroad.

DOCUMENT On the Corruption of Morals in Russia

Before and after Peter's time, Russian absolutism reached into the forested wastes of Siberia. Russian

▼ From 1696 to 1725, Peter the Great allowed his country only 1 year of peace. During the rest of his rule, he radically changed the form and nature of his government in order to pursue war. At the end he had achieved his much desired "Window on the West" on the Baltic.

Document

Catherine II on Life in St. Petersburg in 1750

Marriage alliances always played a key role in the monarchical politics between 1648 and 1789, and after. Sons and daughters, or—in the case of Russia in 1742—nephews, were married off to cement alliances and provided heirs to the various thrones. When Peter the Great's younger daughter, Elizabeth, took the throne in that year she was not married and showed little interest in that institution. But she knew that continuity in the dynasty had to be maintained so she chose Peter—her sister Anne's son—to be her successor to the throne, and set off immediately to find him a suitable wife. Tsarist diplomats subtly sought the advice of neighboring states, including Prussia. There were candidates to be found from among the numerous German principalities at that time, and Frederick the Great indicated that a 15-year-old Lutheran girl, Sophie of Anhalt-Zerbst, would be a suitable candidate.

Sophie, or Catherine as she soon become known, learned Russian, converted to Orthodoxy in 1744, and celebrated her ceremonial marriage to Peter in 1745. As was often the case with royal marriages, the resulting union was not a happy one. Quite soon each person found affection and joy with others, while maintaining appearances at court. Catherine would later go on to oversee the assassination of her husband and become one of the most important and well-known Russian monarchs, as we will see in Chapter 18. Catherine's memoirs, which are excerpted below, tell of life in the new capital of St. Petersburg in 1750, offering a vision of a nation just emerging into European mores and manners and also of the intrigue and gossip that lay behind all of the facades of European courts.

On New Year's Day, 1750, I called for my Kalmuk hairdresser and saw that he was very red in the face and that his eyes were swollen. He admitted that he had a fever and a headache. I sent him to bed and learnt in the evening that he was ill with the pox. I escaped, though he had dressed my hair that very day.

After the New Year the Empress left for Tsarskoe Selo and we remained in town. Petersburg was almost deserted, grass grew in the streets. Only a few courtiers had arrived from Moscow by then. At that time, much more so than now, most of the nobility were reluctant to leave Moscow, a place they all cherished, and where idleness and sloth were the chief vices they indulged in. In Moscow one quite often sees a lady covered with jewels and elegantly dressed, emerging from an immense yard, filled with all possible refuse and mud, adjoining a decrepit hut, in a magnificent carriage, drawn by six horrible hacks, shabbily harnessed, with unkempt grooms wearing handsome liveries which they disgrace by their uncouth appearance. In general, both men and women grow spineless in this large town, busying themselves with trifles, a habit which can destroy the greatest intelligence. Governed only by their whims and fancies, they set aside or largely ignore the laws, and thus never learn to command or else turn into tyrants. The inclination to tyrannize is cultivated here more than in any other inhabited part of the world; it is inculcated at the tenderest age by the cruelty which children observe in their parents behavior towards servants, for where is the home that has no traps, chains, whips, and other instruments to penalize the smallest mistake on the part of those whom nature has placed in this unfortunate class which cannot break its chains without committing violence. One is barely allowed to admit that they are men like ourselves and when I say it I risk having stones flung at me....

In Tsarskoe we tried to entertain ourselves as best we could; in the daytime we strolled about or went hunting. The swing was also a great resource. It was on the swing that Mlle Balk, lady in waiting to the Empress, won the heart of M. Serge Saltikov, the Grand Duke's chamberlain. He proposed marriage to her the next day. She accepted and they were married soon afterwards. In the evenings we played cards; after that there was supper.

One evening I was overcome by a bad headache. I was forced to leave the table and go to bed. The Grand Duke (Peter) had paid more attention than usual to the Princess Kurland that night, which Mme Vladislavov has observed through some chink or keyhole (for she had the admirable habit of constantly satisfying her curiosity by this means), and as soon as I got to my room to undress, Mme Vladislavov instantly attributed my indisposition to the jealousy I appeared to have conceived against the Prince....

Hardly had I fallen asleep than the Grand Duke also came to bed. As he was tipsy and not quite aware of what he was doing, he started to speak to me, enumerating all the eminent qualities of his lady love. I pretended to be fast asleep to stop him talking, but after talking more and more loudly to wake me up and seeing that I gave no sign of awakening, he gave me two or three rather violent punches on the side, grumbling about me sleeping so soundly, and then turned over and went off to sleep himself.

I cried a lot that night because of all this and because of his having hurt me, also because of my whole position, which was as unpleasant in every way as it was tiresome.

Questions to Consider

1. What is Catherine's attitude toward the Muscovite nobility?
2. Characterize the relationship between Catherine and Peter.
3. Would you have liked to live at court in St. Petersburg in those days?

The Memoirs of Catherine the Great, translated from the French by Moura Budberg (Collier Books, New York, N.Y. 1961), pp. 136-140.

Cossacks and fur traders explored this enormous territory between 1580 and 1651. During the seventeenth century, it remained a vast game preserve, exploited by the Russian government for its fur. Agents responsible to the Siberian Bureau in Moscow or St. Petersburg governed the relatively peaceful native peoples, collecting tribute from them in furs and a percentage from the profits of chartered companies. Given the financial succession of the tightly regulated fur trade, the government discouraged settlement in Siberia. In the eighteenth century, however, restrictions were lightened and western Siberia, between the Ob and Yenesei rivers, began attracting colonists; convicts and political prisoners were transported there as well. Some 400,000 settlers had arrived by 1763, but Siberia was largely undeveloped until the late nineteenth century.

After his death in 1725, Peter's policies continued to affect Russian politics through the eighteenth century. In reaction, the nobles worked constantly to regain their former freedom from the state, while the "old believers," Orthodox Christians who refused to recognize seventeenth-century religious reforms, maintained an underground existence. Another striking characteristic of the period was the prominence of female rulers. Of the seven monarchs between 1725 and 1801, only three were men, and they reigned for just six and a half disastrous years. The four tsarinas were Catherine I (r. 1725–1727), Peter's camp-following second wife and the first Russian empress; Anna Ivanovna (r. 1730–1740), daughter of Peter's half-brother, Ivan; Elizabeth (r. 1741–1762), daughter of Peter and Catherine I; and Catherine II (r. 1762–1796), known as "the Great." All tried to continue Peter's policies of turning his country away from its roots toward western Europe. Anna Ivanovna allowed the Baltic Germans too much power, thus alienating their Russian subjects. Elizabeth avoided this mistake while further consolidating the central government and winning new respect in western Europe for Russian military power. She laid the foundations for the long and successful reign of Catherine the Great, whose role as an "enlightened despot" will be discussed in Chapter 18.

The Habsburgs

Aristocratic limits on absolutism, so evident in the declining kingdoms of Portugal and Spain, were even more typical of the Habsburg monarchy in eastern Europe. The Thirty Years' War had diverted Habsburg attention from the Holy Roman Empire to lands under the family's direct control. By 1700, the Habsburgs held the archduchy of Austria, a few adjacent German areas, the kingdom of Bohemia, and the kingdom of Hungary, recently conquered from the Turks. This was a very large domain, stretching from Saxony in the north to the Ottoman Empire in the southeast. It played a leading role in the continental wars against Louis XIV after the 1670s.

Leopold I (r. 1657–1705) was primarily responsible for strengthening the Austrian imperial monarchy during this period. In long wars with the French and the Turks, Leopold modernized the army, not only increasing its numbers but also instilling professionalism and loyalty in its officers. He created central administrative councils, giving each responsibility for an arm of the imperial government or a local area. He staffed these high administrative positions with court nobles, rewarded and honored like those in France. Other new nobles, given lands in the home provinces, became political tools for subordinating the local estates. Leopold suppressed Protestantism in Bohemia and Austria while keeping his own Catholic Church under firm control. In 1687 the Habsburgs were accepted as hereditary monarchs in Hungary, a status they had already achieved in Austria and Bohemia.

In the eighteenth century, Maria Theresa (r. 1740–1780) confronted Leopold's problems all over again. When she inherited her throne at the age of 22, her realm, lacking both money and military forces, faced threats from Prussia. In the years after Leopold's time, the nobles had regained much of their former power and were rebuilding their dominions at the expense of the monarchy. Known as "Her Motherly Majesty," Maria was a religious and compassionate woman, but she put aside this gentle image to hasten much needed internal reforms. Count Haugwitz (HOG-vitz), her reforming minister, rigidly enforced new laws that brought provincial areas under more effective royal control.

Despite its glitter and outward trappings, the Habsburg Empire was not a good example of absolutism. Its economy was almost entirely agricultural and, therefore, dependent on serf labor. This situation perpetuated the power of the nobles and diminished revenues available to the crown. In addition, subjects of the monarchy comprised a mixture of nationalities and languages—German, Czech, Magyar, Croatian, and Italian, to name only a few. Lacking ethnic unity, the various areas persisted in their localism. Even the reforms of Leopold and Maria Theresa left royal authority existing more in name than in fact. Imposed on still functioning medieval institutions, the Habsburg regime was a strange combination of absolutist theory and feudal fact.

The Germanies, the Scandinavian States, and the Iberian Peninsula

Among the most obvious satellites of the French sun were the numerous German principalities of the Holy Roman Empire. The 1648 Treaty of Westphalia

Discovery Through Maps

The Elegant Destruction of Poland

After the century and a half of continent-wide upheaval caused by the Reformation, Counter-Reformation, wars of religion, and Thirty Years' War, Europeans sought to impose stability through international law and absolutism. Concepts like "balance of power," *"raison d'état,"* and reason replaced the passions of the religious wars of the sixteenth and the first half of the seventeenth centuries.

This did not mean that peace came to Europe—far from it. War came to be more organized, professional, and limited as state competition took on not only a military but also an economic dimension. In the new arena of 1648 politics, state relations were conducted with almost mathematical precision. States took stock of their strength in terms of population, economic strength, and military power. They ranked themselves and their neighbors and then attacked when it seemed possible, in search of national interest, not religious truth. The wars of Louis XIV sought to gain France its "natural boundaries" of the Pyrenees and the Rhine. The Prussians sought to unify their diverse holdings in north-central Europe. Peter the Great led Russia into war against its neighbors in search of a "Window on the West."

In the last third of the eighteenth century, Poland paid the price for its inability to adapt to the modern world. Since the fourteenth century, the Polish nobility had tenaciously fought the attempts by their kings to assemble a strong army, preferring often to lose the first battle against invaders while waiting for the nobles to come to the country's defense. Poland after the seventeenth century fell under the influence of the Russians and the Prussians, and not until the 1770s did the Poles try to reform their institutions. It was too late. National interests led Prussia, Russia, and Austria to partition the country in 1772. After the French Revolution broke out, the Russians and Prussians partitioned the country again in 1793 and then, after a doomed national resistance, they removed Poland as a state from the map of Europe. The Polish nation remained divided among the three partitioning powers until 1918.

This engraving by Le Mire is a rather caustic commentary on what was, after all, the murder of a nation-state. Here we have the monarchs of Russia, Prussia, and Austria regally carving up Poland while the Polish king, Stanislaus Poniatowski, grabs his crown to keep from losing that too. Le Mire captures the "civilized" nature of post-1648 state relations, in which *raison d'état* imposed no moral or ethical limits.

Questions to Consider

1. What had Poland done to deserve being carved up by these monarchs?
2. Do you think the artist is celebrating the occasion he portrays, or is he being sarcastic?
3. What role does the angel play in this scene? What were the religious faiths of the Prussians, Russians, and Austrians?

recognized more than 300 sovereign states in the empire. Without serious responsibilities to the emperor and, in Protestant states, with treasuries filled with the proceeds of confiscated church properties, their rulers struggled to increase their prerogatives and dabble in international diplomacy. Many sought French alliances against the Habsburg emperor; those who could traveled to France and attended Louis's court. Subsequently, many a German palace became a miniature Versailles. Even the tiniest states were likely to have standing armies, state churches, court officials, and economic regulations. The elector of Brandenburg demonstrated the ultimate deference to the French model. Although sincerely loyal to his wife, he copied Louis XIV by taking an official mistress and displaying her at court without requiring her to perform the duty usually associated with the position.

The era of the Sun King also witnessed an upsurge of royal authority in Scandinavia. After an earlier aristocratic reaction against both monarchies, Frederick III (r. 1648–1670) in Denmark and Charles XI (r. 1660–1697) in Sweden broke the power of the nobles and created structures similar to the French model. Frederick in 1661 forced the assembled high nobility to accept him as their hereditary king. Later royal edicts proclaimed the king's right to issue laws and impose taxes. A similar upheaval in Sweden (1680) allowed Charles to achieve financial independence by seizing the nobles' lands. Both kingdoms developed thoroughly centralized administrations. Sweden, particularly, resembled France with its professional army, navy, national church, and mercantilist economy. Although Swedish royal absolutism was limited by the nobles in 1718, the Danish system remained into the nineteenth century.

Unlike the Scandinavian and German states, other European governments followed Louis's system more in their direction of development than in their specific institutions. The process is well illustrated by a time lag in the Spanish and Portuguese monarchies. United by Spanish force in 1580 and divided again by a Portuguese revolt in 1640, the two kingdoms were first weakened by economic decay and then nearly destroyed by the costs of the Thirty Years' War and their own mutual conflicts, which lasted until Spain accepted Portuguese independence in 1668. Conditions deteriorated further under the half-mad King Alfonso VI (r. 1656–1668) in Portugal and the feebleminded Charles II (r. 1665–1700) in Spain.

The nobilities, having exploited these misfortunes to regain their dominant position in both countries, could not be easily dislodged. Not until the 1680s did Pedro II (r. 1683–1706) in Portugal restore a semblance of royal authority. His successor, John V (r. 1706–1750), aided by new wealth from Brazilian gold and diamond strikes, centralized the administration, perfected mercantilism, and extended control over the church. In Spain, similar developments followed the War of the Spanish Succession and the granting of the Spanish crown to Louis XIV's Bourbon grandson, Philip V (r. 1700–1746). Philip brought to Spain a corps of French advisers, including the Princesse des Ursins (pran-SESS days ur-SAN), a spy for Louis XIV. Philip then followed French precedents by imposing centralized ministries, local **intendants,** and economic regulations.

Poland: The Tragic Exception to the Rule

Poland stood completely outside of the France-centered political and economic system. Local trade and industry were even more insignificant in its economy, the peasants were more depressed, and land-controlling lesser nobles—some 10 percent of the population—grew wealthy by supplying grain for Western merchants. Nobles avoided military service and most taxes; they were lords and masters of their lands. More than fifty local assemblies dominated their areas, admitting no outside jurisdiction. The national diet (council), which was elected by the local bodies, chose a king who had no real authority.

In effect, Poland in the middle of the seventeenth century was a patchwork of small and independent feudal estates that was unwilling and unable to compete with the neighboring centralizing states of Prussia, Russia, Sweden, and Austria. By the time Polish leaders awoke to the danger they faced in the 1770s, it was too late. The leaders in Berlin, St. Petersburg, and Vienna partitioned Poland in 1774, 1792, and finally in 1795 when it disappeared from the map of Europe, not to reappear until 1919.

Holland and England: Limited Central Power

Why did the Netherlands and England pursue the political model of limited central power?

In the century between the Dutch rebellion and the British **Glorious Revolution,** constitutional government took root in the Netherlands and survived and prospered in England. The Dutch profited from the declining fortunes of the Spaniards and established global trading dominance. Protected by its island geography and strengthened by its traditions, England carried on a sometimes bloody argument about its political structure. In both countries, rapidly develop-

intendants—Officials working for the king.

Glorious Revolution—A political uprising in 1688 that ended the Stuart dynasty's rule in England.

Emmanuel de Witte graphically portrayed daily life in seventeenth-century Holland with his rendering of *The New Fish Market in Amsterdam* (1679).

ing commerce and increasing social mobility encouraged a direct transition from feudalism to constitutional government, without a prolonged intermediate stage of centralized monarchy.

The Dutch Experiment

The Dutch blazed the trail to modernity in Europe in the first half of the seventeenth century, a period described by the historian Simon Schama as an *Embarrassment of Riches.*[3] They staged the first modern national liberation struggle; conducted the first modern guerrilla war; set up the first modern republic; established the first modern banks, insurance companies, and stock markets; created the first modern capitalist agriculture; and were among the first to practice the recycling of resources. After a long and tenacious struggle against the Spaniards, they went on to establish a global trading network (see Chapter 16) that gave them the highest quality of life in Europe. Unfortunately, their lack of military power led to their being dominated by the English in the 1660s. But their precedent-setting contributions established the foundations of modern political and economic life in the West.

The internal Dutch power balance shifted during the early seventeenth century. Republicans, representing the great urban merchants, supported religious toleration, limited central authority, and peace. The monarchists, representing a majority of the urban lower classes and the nobles, especially the House of Orange, wanted a Calvinist state church, strong stadtholders (provincial governors), a large army, and an aggressive foreign policy against the Habsburgs. Until 1619, the republicans held power, but their leader, John Oldenbarnveldt (OL-den-barn-feldt; 1547–1619), was ultimately overthrown and executed after a royalist uprising. Between 1619 and the Peace of Westphalia, the country was ruled by domineering stadtholders, who conducted the war against Spain and acquired a status approaching that of European kings.

In the mid-seventeenth century, the Dutch enjoyed prosperity and power far beyond their limited population base and territory. During the interval between the decline of Spain and the rise to dominance of modern France and England, the Dutch enjoyed naval, commercial, and colonial supremacy. This predominance, of course, could only be temporary. The Netherlands had not enough people nor defensible boundaries to afford long-term competition with France in Europe or with England overseas. But even as a secondary power, which it was destined to become after 1650, it remained economically progressive, culturally advanced, and a pioneer in developing constitutional government. Because of its liberal system, it became the refuge for many of Europe's finest scientists and philosophers, especially the Huguenots after 1685.

The English Debate: Crown vs. Parliament

Between the death of Queen Elizabeth in 1603 and the Glorious Revolution in 1688, the English carried on a fundamental debate about the nature of government. At its base were the questions of the control of property, the role of law, the nature of the state, and the notion of sovereignty. The Stuart dynasty and its allies upheld the divine rights centrality of the monarch as the fundamental principle of government. Arrayed against them were individuals who saw the nation's will as expressed through Parliament as the primary principle of government. The Stuarts saw their legitimacy in birth and "the natural order of things," whereas the parliamentary forces referred to four centuries of legal traditions and practices.

James, a cousin of Elizabeth and the son of Mary Stuart, had learned his lessons well in 36 years as king of Scotland. He was rational and learned and a fervent believer in monarchical divine right. He also hated parliaments and Presbyterians but recognized the need for taking what "can be" over what "should be" in political affairs. During his English reign (1603–1625), James maintained a shaky stability while tentatively pursuing unpopular policies that led to his being not very successful with Parliament. The problems here were mostly financial, involving rejection of his revenue proposals. Outside the political arena in the first part of the seventeenth century, the religious climate became more radical. English Protestants suspected first James and then his successor, Charles, of being pro-Catholic.

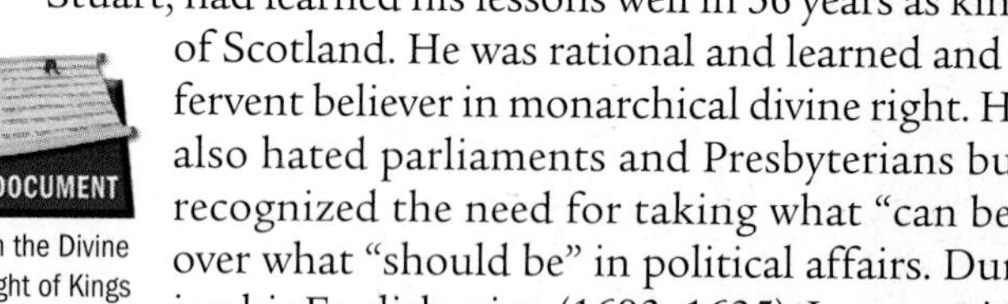

On the Divine Right of Kings

James's political skills were not to be found in his successor, Charles. After enduring many stormy debates with Parliament, he accepted the Petition of Right in 1628. This document affirmed ancient English rights by securing parliamentary approval of taxes, abolishing arbitrary imprisonment, ending the quartering of soldiers with citizens, and prohibiting martial law in peacetime. But Charles's cooperative attitude was only temporary. From 1629 to 1640, he ruled without Parliament, alienating much of English society, particularly the Puritan church reformers and the gentry. The king's personal rule cut him off from an understanding of what the parliamentary forces really wanted and deepened the suspicions of Charles's opponents. When his archbishop tried to force the Anglican prayer book on the Scottish kirk ("church"), the Scots rebelled and invaded England in 1640. Charles was forced to conclude a humiliating peace by paying the invaders to withdraw.

After agreeing to buy off the Scots, Charles called Parliament to raise the money and secure his future finances. When it insisted on debating other issues, this "Short Parliament" was dismissed after it sat for little more than three weeks. The government then resorted to forceful measures: it imprisoned dissidents, imposed more illegal taxes, forced loans from merchants, and conscripted men into the army— measures that made the situation only worse. Desperate for funds and facing mounting public hostility, the king called what would become known as the "Long Parliament," because it sat through 20 years of constitutional debate and civil war. Finally, in January 1642, he left the capital for York, and Parliament took the unprecedented action of declaring, without royal approval, its legal authority over national military forces.

The English Civil War

The ensuing civil war between Parliament and its supporters in London and the south and east of the country and the king and his cavaliers in the north and west of England would last seven years. In the first 2 years of the conflict, the king's armies were generally victorious. Then, Parliament organized its forces into a national army—the New Model Army, enlisted popular support by appeals to radical Protestantism, and made an alliance with the Scots. After defeating the royalists decisively at Marston Moor (1644) and Naseby (1645), they received Charles from the Scots,

	England: From Stuart Ambition to Parliamentary Power
1603	James VI of Scotland becomes James I of England
1625	Charles I becomes king of England
1628	Petition of Right
1629	Charles I dissolves Parliament
1640	Short Parliament; Long Parliament convenes
1642–1648	Civil war
1649	Charles I executed
1649–1660	Various attempts at a Puritan commonwealth
1660	Charles II restored to the English throne
1670	Secret Treaty of Dover between France and England
1685	James II becomes king of England
1688	Glorious Revolution
1689	William II and Mary II come to the throne of England
1702–1714	Queen Anne, the last of the Stuarts
1714	George I of Hanover becomes king of England

▲ The English Civil War led to the beheading of a monarch, seen by the parliamentary forces as guilty of exercising extra-constitutional powers. Ironically, Oliver Cromwell—shown here dissolving the Long Parliament—in his role as Lord Protector generated heated opposition to his rule from people who believed him also to be overreaching his authority.

who had taken him prisoner in 1646. After 4 long years, the war now seemed to be over.

Almost immediately, however, new conflicts arose between Parliament and its army. Conservative Presbyterians in Parliament, fearful of populist Protestantism in the army's ranks, were anxious to demobilize it. The conservatives feared some of the radicals in the army who advocated a truly democratic government and society. Their most striking proposals originated with the supporters of a civilian group known as **"Levellers"** who advocated reforms to favor the common people. They were led by the former army officer "honest John Lilburne" (1614–1657). Most officers, including the leading commanders Oliver Cromwell (1599–1658) and Lord Fairfax (1612–1671) insisted on maintaining the army and supporting the soldiers—including their demands for back pay. As it turned out, the radical program was only one issue in maneuvers for power among the Presbyterian Parliament, the conservative army officers, and some radical soldiers who mutinied when their demands were not met.

During this internal argument on the Parliament side, Charles managed to renew the war after escaping. He tried to reestablish his authority in the Midlands of England, but his forces were much reduced and he lost his last battle at Preston in August 1648. By this time, Oliver Cromwell had emerged as the most powerful person on the parliamentary side.

The key question facing the victors was what to do with the king. He had clearly violated 400 years of legal precedent by his actions in 1642. Despite that, a majority of the parliamentarians wanted a compromise in which peace would be established, the armies demobilized, concessions would come from the king, and Charles would be re-installed as the monarch. Oliver Cromwell and his allies did not agree. Finally resorting to force, they outlawed the Levellers and other radicals while purging Parliament of 143 Presbyterian opponents. The remaining "Rump Parliament"—containing less than half of the members of the original Long Parliament—abolished the House of Lords and brought Charles up for trial on charges of treason. Cromwell and his allies executed him by decapitation on January 30, 1649. Kings and nobles had killed kings before. This is the first time that a people, however represented, rose up and killed a king. England became a republic.

For the next 11 years, Cromwell's military regime was able to perpetuate itself in different forms. At first, the Rump and a Council of State, dominated by Cromwell, governed the country while crushing all

levellers—A group that advocated total economic, social, political, and religious equality during the English civil war.

DOCUMENT

Cromwell Abolishes the English Monarchy

resistance in Scotland and Ireland. In 1653 more contention between Rump politicians and the council resulted in dissolution of the token Parliament and creation of a thinly veiled dictatorship. A new constitution, the Instrument of Government, written by Cromwell's henchmen, assigned him extensive powers as Lord Protector. Two years later, Cromwell finally dismissed the Instrument's impotent Parliament and instead ruled through military governors. His regimes during the **interregnum** were able to increase trade and raise respect for England abroad, but they were never popular, a fact attested to by the continued life of the radical movements, which enlisted popular support and required government countermeasures until after the mid-1650s. Despite ultimate radical failures, the period of the civil war and the interregnum, which ended 2 years after Cromwell's death in 1658, brought significant changes to England.

Restoration and "Glorious" Revolution

The period from 1660 to 1688 was marked by increasingly severe struggles between the Stuarts and Parliament. Initially, almost everyone welcomed the new ruler, Charles II (1660–1685), called back from exile in France and restored to the throne, with his lavish court and his mistresses. Charles, the cleverest politician of the Stuart line, exploited this shared desire for normality to avoid the terms of his restoration, which bound him to rule in cooperation with Parliament. He cleverly manipulated the English political system to get what he wanted in the first, comparatively relaxed, years of the Restoration. By the secret Treaty of Dover with Louis XIV in 1670, he gained financial independence from Parliament in return for working to restore the Catholic Church in England and aiding France in its wars against the Dutch.

However, political opposition against him began to harden, precipitating a crisis by 1681. In the last part of his reign, he dismissed four Parliaments and governed without the legislative branch, taking advantage of the strong desire among the propertied classes to avoid another civil war. The Whig opposition, however, which represented the desires of the lesser landowners and their business allies in the cities, had forced a resignation from Charles II's first minister, imprisoned the second, excluded the king's Catholic supporters from public office, and provided individuals with legal security against arbitrary arrest and imprisonment.

Charles's brother James II (1685–1688) proved to be an even more determined—and less subtle—absolutist. Like Charles, he was an admirer of Louis XIV. Although Charles concealed his Catholic sympathies, his brother was openly Catholic. When James' wife gave birth to a prince who was widely regarded as a potential Catholic king, parliamentary leaders and Protestant aristocrats met and offered the crown to the former heir Mary Stuart, the Protestant daughter of James by an earlier marriage. Mary accepted the offer with the provision that her husband, William of Orange, be co-ruler. William landed at Dover with an efficient Dutch army and helped to force James to flee into exile in France. This "Glorious Revolution" marked the end of attempts to impose absolutist government in England and ensured the continuity of limited monarchy.

After William forced James into exile in France, he accepted Parliament's conditions for his kingship, enacted as the Bill of Rights. This declaration provided that the king could not suspend laws; no taxes would be levied or standing army maintained in peacetime without the consent of Parliament; sessions of Parliament would be held frequently; freedom of speech in Parliament would be assured; subjects would have the right of petition and be free of excessive fines, bail, or cruel punishments; the king would be a Protestant.

DOCUMENT

The English Bill of Rights

Other parliamentary acts supplemented the Bill of Rights and consolidated the Revolution. In 1689, the Mutiny Act required parliamentary approval for extending martial law more than one year. In 1693, when Parliament failed to renew the customary Licensing Act, the country achieved practical freedom of the press. Finally, in the Act of Settlement in 1701, Parliament prescribed a Protestant succession to the throne and barred the monarch from declaring war, removing judges, or even leaving the country without parliamentary consent. The Glorious Revolution permanently limited the English monarchy, guaranteed important legal rights, and helped popularize the ideal, if not the practice, of popular sovereignty.

Whigs and Tories

After 1688, the landed gentry—functionally a lower aristocracy of landed capitalists with a variety of economic interests—gained almost complete control of the House of Commons. From their base in the Whig alliance, they shaped state policy through a prime minister and a cabinet system that became responsible to Parliament, not the king. The gentry made government a closed system, putting members of their class into most of the public offices, lucrative positions in the Anglican Church, and commissioned ranks in the army and navy. These privileges were shared only with the few remaining nobles (220 in 1790) who sat in the House of Lords.

After the reign of William and Mary, English leaders looked to the German principality of Hanover

---

interregnum—The period of time between kings.

for the next monarchs. The first two Hanoverian kings, George I (r. 1714–1727) and George II (r. 1727–1760), relied on their chief advisers (prime ministers) to work with Parliament. Sir Robert Walpole (1676–1745) first held this post, managing a Whig political machine. Walpole insisted that the entire ministry (cabinet) should act as a body; single members who could not agree were expected to resign. Later he learned the practicality of resigning with his whole cabinet when they could not command a parliamentary majority. This pragmatically developed system of cabinet government and ministerial responsibility provided the constitutional machinery needed to apply the principles of the Glorious Revolution while permitting Parliament to avoid awkward conflicts with royal authority.

English politics became stagnant by the end of George II's reign in 1760. The next Hanoverian king, George III (r. 1760–1820), imposed his personality and policies more directly on British politics than did his predecessors. First, he alienated many commercial and colonial interests by opposing an aggressive policy toward France. Then, he began implementing powers never claimed by his Hanoverian predecessors, who had been virtual captives of Whig politicians. In only a few years, using lavish bribes and patronage (methods developed earlier by Walpole), George's ministers eroded Whig influence and gained control of Parliament. By 1770, they had filled the House of Commons with their supporters, known as "the King's Friends" (Tories). During George's first 12 years as king, his policies made domestic enemies and produced a determined opposition party. This trouble at home was less serious, in the long run, than that provoked in the American colonies. George Grenville (1712–1770), the king's chief minister after 1763, devised a comprehensive plan to settle problems in North America left after the Seven Years' War, which sparked the movement leading to the American Revolution.

Breaking the Bank: Diplomacy and War in the Age of Absolutism: 1650–1774

Why did European states fight so many wars with one another during the Age of Absolutism?

Because of dynastic and colonial rivalries, Europeans were constantly involved in conflicts during the age of absolutism. Fighting took place overseas in America, Africa, and Asia—not only against non-Europeans but also in global wars among European colonial powers. At the same time, wars raged on the Continent as dynastic states competed for predominance. As Spain, Sweden, and Poland were declining, Prussia, Russia, and Austria were becoming first-class powers. Along with England and its dominance overseas, the last three exerted major influences on the European balance of power.

From Westphalia to Utrecht: The Dominance of France

France was the strongest and most threatening military power in Europe from the Peace of Westphalia (1648) to the Treaty of Utrecht (1713). Louis XIV first dreamed of expanding French frontiers to the Rhine; later, he coveted the Spanish crown. Colbert also helped him plan the conquest of a large overseas empire in America, Africa, and Asia. The diplomacy of other European states in the era centered largely on their common efforts to unite against French expansion.

Russian policy was one important exception to this general trend. In early wars with the Turks, Peter the Great took Azov, on the Black Sea. His main target in the later Great Northern War (1700–1721) was Sweden, but his campaign began badly when his allies, Denmark and Poland, were quickly defeated by the Swedish warrior-king Charles XII (r. 1697–1712). The Swedes next invaded Russia. They were met with a "scorched earth" withdrawal before being annihilated at Poltava (1709). The war ended in 1721 with Sweden exhausted and Peter gaining a section of the Baltic coast, where he had already begun building his new capital at St. Petersburg.

The three Anglo-Dutch naval wars between 1652 and 1674 showed the balance-of-power principle in one of its more intricate applications. Conflicting commercial and colonial interests of the two maritime states were the immediate issues. At the same time, both belligerents were increasingly aware of danger from a powerful and aggressive France. The Dutch were most directly affected because French expansion toward the northern Rhine threatened the survival of the Netherlands as a nation. To deal with this problem, the Dutch tacitly accepted English maritime supremacy while preparing for an Anglo-Dutch alignment against Louis XIV. Ultimately, the French menace was more decisive than naval action in ending Anglo-Dutch hostilities.

After 1670, Louis was the prime mover in European diplomacy. He fought four major wars, each with overseas campaigns. In the first, Louis claimed the Spanish Netherlands (Belgium). Thwarted by the Dutch and their allies, he next bought off Charles II of England in the Treaty of Dover and attacked the Dutch directly. Frustrated again by a combination of enemies, he tried in the 1690s to annex certain Rhineland districts. This time, almost all of Europe allied against him and forced him to back down. The climax to these repeated French efforts came between 1701 and 1713, in the War of the Spanish Succession, when Louis sought to secure the Spanish throne for his grandson Philip. Although he finally succeeded in this project, the victory was a hollow one.

In this most destructive of Louis's wars, women played a major part behind the scenes. In England during the early years, Sarah Churchill, wife of the English supreme commander, the duke of Marlborough, consistently pressured Queen Anne (r. 1702–1714) and members of Parliament for vigorous prosecution of the war. On the other side, at the Spanish court and elsewhere on the continent, Mary of Modena, in exile with her husband, the deposed James II of England, exerted all of her influence to bolster support for France. Other women were most instrumental in bringing peace. Among them were Madame de Maintenon (men-te-NON) and Princesse des Ursins, who helped persuade Louis to drop the idea of uniting the French and Spanish Bourbon monarchies. In England after about 1709, Anne, a patient and plodding monarch, but one with at least some common sense, freed herself from Sarah Churchill's influence and guided her ministers toward the Peace of Utrecht.

Louis could not overcome all of the power balanced against him. As France became stronger, it invariably provoked more formidable counter-alliances. At first, Louis faced Spain, the Netherlands, Sweden, and some German states. In the last two wars, England led an alliance that included almost all of western Europe. In this anti-French alignment, Anglo-Dutch commercial rivalry and other traditional prejudices, such as Anglo-Dutch hatred of Spain, were subordinated to the balance-of-power principle.

The Treaty of Utrecht (1713) ushered in a period of general peace, lasting some 30 years. Philip V, Louis's grandson, was confirmed as king of Spain, with the provision that the thrones of France and Spain would never be united. Since Spain had been declining for a century and France was drained financially, the Bourbon succession promised little for French ambitions in Europe. In fact, Spain had surrendered the southern Netherlands (Belgium) and its Italian holdings (Naples, Milan, and Sardinia) to the Austrian Habsburgs. In addition, Savoy was ceded to Sicily, which was subse-

▼ The Treaty of Utrecht confirmed the expansion of French power in Europe after the half century of wars of Louis XIV, the increased strength of Brandenburg Prussia, and the decline of the Habsburg Empire.

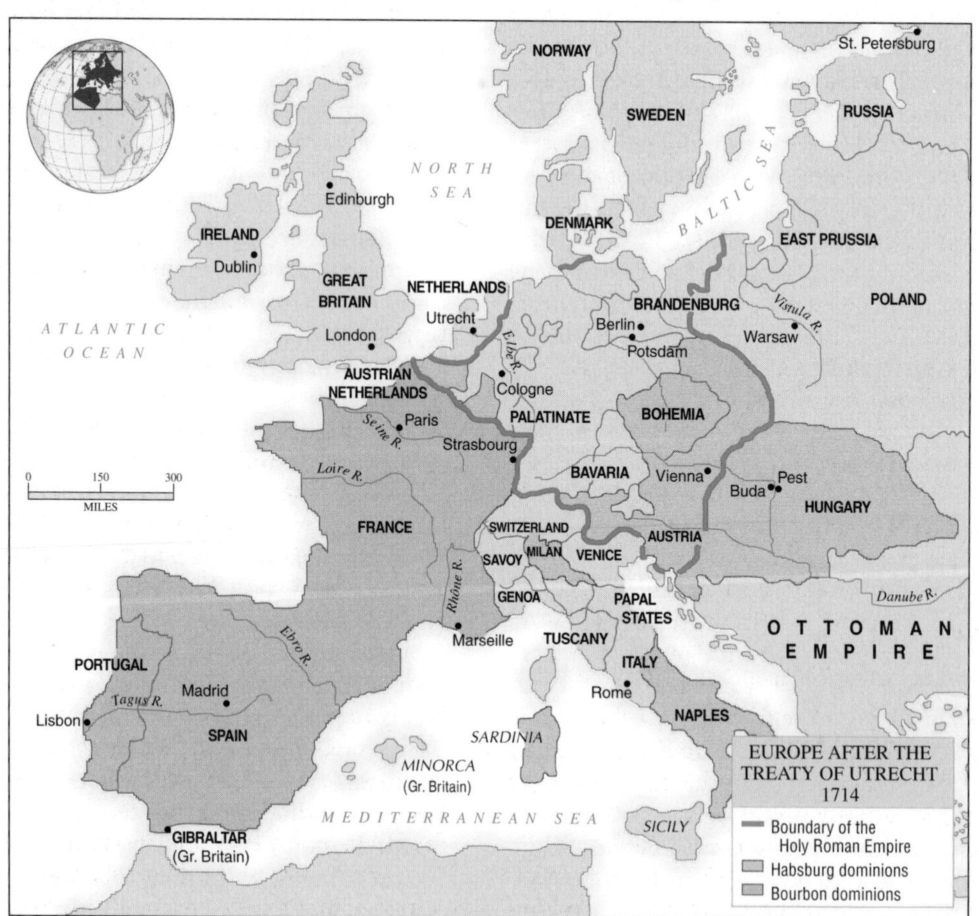

quently traded (in 1720) to Austria for Sardinia. The duke of Savoy was also recognized as king, as was Frederick I of Prussia. The House of Savoy would unify Italy in the nineteenth century, and the Hohenzollerns would accomplish the same for Germany.

By the Treaty of Utrecht, almost all the participants except Britain lost more in the wars than they gained. The Dutch had borne the cost of most land fighting against the French; France had been demoralized by a three-front war and a Huguenot uprising, for which it received no tangible compensation except the retention of Alsace; and Spain lost heavily to the Austrian Habsburgs. Britain, by contrast, received the North American properties of Newfoundland and Nova Scotia from France in addition to French acceptance of British claims to the Hudson Bay area. Britain also retained the Mediterranean naval bases at Gibraltar and Minorca it had taken from Spain. Even more important commercially were the concessions permitting Britain to supply Spanish America with slaves and to land one shipload of goods each year at Porto Bello in Panama. These stipulations helped Britain become the leading colonial power in Europe.

From Utrecht to Paris: An Unstable Balance

The balance of European power wavered dangerously in the eighteenth century. Prussia and Russia—and even Habsburg Austria—attained great military potential, and each was tempted by power vacuums in Poland and the Ottoman Empire. The situation was complicated by the difficulty in determining which of the Eastern states was the most serious threat and therefore the logical object of counteralliances. To confuse matters further, both Britain and France were absorbed in their growing colonial rivalry, in which Britain was the obvious frontrunner. Major conflicts were on the way.

By 1730, it was apparent that France and Britain would soon clash over their conflicting colonial ambitions. Both empires were rapidly increasing their wealth and populations. In the Caribbean, French sugar production had surpassed that of the British, while French slavers were not only supplying their own islands but also challenging British trading privileges in Spanish America, as defined at Utrecht. On the other side of the world, the British and French were also scrambling to obtain influence among the petty rulers of southern India. The two powers, each with Native American allies, were fighting sporadic little wars in North America. In the preliminary diplomatic testing, French size and military force in Europe were balanced against British financial resources, naval power, and a larger American colonial population.

The next wave of conflict began in 1739 over the question of British trade in Spanish America. An English captain testified before Parliament in 1738 that Spanish authorities had boarded his vessel 7 years earlier and had cut off his ear, which he displayed wrapped in cotton. This served as the pretext for the "War of Jenkins's Ear" which soon spread, with France immediately offering support to Spain. Frederick of Prussia, meanwhile, seized Silesia, part of the family holdings of the Habsburg heiress Maria Theresa, who had just succeeded to the Austrian throne. France and Spain now aligned with Frederick, along with the German states of Saxony and Bavaria. Fearful of France, Britain, and the Netherlands, now allied with Hanover, joined Austria in 1742 in the War of the Austrian Succession. By 1745, Prussia had almost knocked Austria out of the war, but fighting dragged on overseas in North America and India until 1748. The resulting Peace of Aix-la-Chapelle (ex la sha-PELLE) left Frederick with Silesia and the colonial positions of Britain and France about the same as they had been in 1739.

The agreements at Aix-la-Chapelle brought no peace but only a short truce of 8 years. During the cessation of hostilities, France and Britain prepared to renew their global conflict. At the same time, Maria Theresa, having learned some lessons in international politics and having introduced some necessary internal reforms, joined with Tsarina Elizabeth of Russia to negotiate an alliance against Frederick. The Austro-Russian alliance also included Sweden and some German states. Maria Theresa's greatest coup, however, was recruiting France, the old Habsburg enemy, possibly with help from Madame de Pompadour, Louis XV's mistress, who despised Frederick. Prussia was now effectively isolated, but so was Britain, which was more concerned about colonial issues than aggression on the Continent. Britain, therefore, formed a new alliance with Prussia against France, Russia, and Austria. This swapping of alliances, the famous diplomatic revolution of the 1750s, was another notable attempt at balance-of-power politics in both the European and world theaters.

Beginning in 1756, war raged relentlessly on three continents—Europe, North America, and Asia (India). Known in American history as the French and Indian War, the conflict in Europe is called the Seven Years' War. Attacked on all sides by three major powers, Frederick marched and wheeled his limited forces, winning battles but seeing little prospect for ultimate victory. He tried without success to buy Madame de Pompadour's influence for peace. Later he described his nearly hopeless predicament, comparing himself to a man assaulted by flies: "When one flies off my cheek, another comes and sits on my nose, and scarcely has it been brushed off then another flies up and sits on my forehead, on my eyes, and everywhere else."[4]

Frederick was saved and the war won by the narrowest of margins when a new pro-Prussian tsar, Peter

III, recalled the Russian armies from the gates of Berlin and withdrew from the war. Austria then sued for peace, leaving Frederick with Silesia.

The end of the Seven Years' War in 1763 confirmed the status of Prussia and Russia as great powers and prepared for a new diplomatic order in eastern Europe. Despite its great losses, Prussia gained enormously in prestige—its internal damage would not be revealed until the nineteenth century— and Russia regained the military reputation it had achieved under Peter I without winning any striking victories. Austria lost prestige and military strength but managed to retain its respectability. The Ottoman Empire and Poland were the real losers in the postwar decades. In 1772, Poland lost half its territory to the Russians, Prussians, and Austrians in a three-way partition, despite Maria Theresa's protestations of remorse. In 1793 and 1795, Poland was eliminated entirely in two final partitions. The Ottoman Empire, meanwhile, lost the Crimea and most of the Ukraine to the aggressive expansionist policies of Catherine the Great of Russia.

Much more significant than the war's effects on eastern Europe was its impact on Anglo-French colonial rivalry. Britain gained even more than it had at Utrecht, whereas French colonial hopes were all but destroyed. By the Peace of Paris (1763), France lost to Britain the St. Lawrence valley and the trans-Appalachian area east of the Mississippi. Spain also ceded Florida to Britain, receiving Louisiana west of the Mississippi from France as compensation. In the West Indies, France gave up Grenada, Dominica, and St. Lucia. The French kept their main trading stations in India but were not permitted to fortify them or continue their political ties with local rulers. Meanwhile, the British East India Company not only extended its political influence but also acquired Bengal. The Peace of Paris made Britain's empire the largest, wealthiest, and most powerful in the world. At the end of the last round of warfare, however, all of Europe's governments were economically exhausted.

The Economic Consequences of Warfare

Under the mercantile system devised by Colbert (see p. 514), the expenses of adding new markets through wars was supposed to be repaid by increased profits. In Prussia and Russia, state control of the economy worked well. Habsburg efforts met with less success because the empire was unable to impose regulations effectively on the aristocracy and the minority nationalities. France during the eighteenth century could not pay the bills for global competition.

The European states could, for the most part, solve the difficulties in regulating their domestic economies. Controlling the market forces in foreign trade was impossible. France and England invested heavily in money and manpower to regulate external commerce, but the increased volume and consequent promise of rich profits from such enterprise encouraged widespread smuggling. No government of a coastal state was sufficiently wealthy to police a long and irregular coastline. Moreover, the coast guards, port authorities, and customs officials charged with enforcing trade restrictions were usually so corrupt that they were ineffective. Thus, despite major efforts to stop it, illegal trade flowed with growing pressure through rotten and fragile mercantilist sieves, violating increasingly complicated commercial laws. To meet this problem, governments resorted to private contractors, often granting immunity from the laws as payment for enforcing the regulations. The resulting monopolies assumed and usually abused government authority.

Smuggling was big business in the colonies, where it exceeded legal trade in the 1700s. West Indian planters of all nationalities conducted illicit commerce with English colonial merchants. New England timber and manufactures were regularly exchanged for French molasses, which was then made into rum and smuggled into Europe. Half the trade of Boston in 1750 violated British laws; Rhode Island and Pennsylvania merchants grew rich supplying the French during the Seven Years' War; and 80 percent of all tea used in the English colonies before 1770 came in free of duties. In addition, large quantities of tobacco were landed illegally in England with the connivance of Virginia and Carolina planters.

Smuggling cut deeply into state revenues for Britain, the most commercially advanced state in Europe. In 1700, after war with France, the English state debt reached 13 million pounds sterling and was secured by the Bank of England. The public debt continued to rise, despite the government's efforts in the 1720s to eliminate it with profits from its overseas trading monopoly, the South Sea Company. Unfortunately, following a wild speculation in South Sea stock, the venture failed. Succeeding colonial wars with France drove the debt still higher. By 1782, it had risen to 232 million pounds. Britain was very wealthy with a sound banking system and, therefore, could easily carry this tremendous burden, but the debt nevertheless contributed to internal political unrest.

For France, where the economy was less expansive and commanded less foreign credit, the problem was more serious. Badly weakened by Louis XIV's wars, France averted financial disaster in the 1720s and 1730s only because of a time of peace and reduced military spending. After 1742, however, deficits mounted steadily while France fought three major wars. In 1780, the French debt was so large that interest payments absorbed over half the annual state revenues. Admittedly, the French debt was not excessive in

Necker Concealing the Deficit (Cartoon, 1789)

comparison with Britain's. What the French lacked, however, was the Dutch capital that poured into England. Without adequate foreign credit, France was thrown back on its own resources, which caused a tripling of taxes between 1715 and 1785. The ensuing tax burden, in addition to the growing anxiety of wealthy government creditors, created the most serious threat to the Old Regime in France.

The Decline of European Absolutism, the Example of Louis XV: 1715–1774

Why did French absolutism become the ancien régime, *an ineffective and corrupt form of government?*

The absolutists and their supporters in France—perhaps 2 percent of the population—made an inadequate response to the challenges of the time. After his death in 1715, Louis XIV was succeeded by his 5-year-old great-grandson. Known as "the Well-Beloved," the new king reigned as Louis XV until 1774, but never ruled as a Sun King, partly because of his personal weaknesses, but largely because the inflexible institutions of absolutism could not contain or direct the dynamic changes of the eighteenth-century world. In middle age, with most of his royal prerogatives still intact, Louis was openly pessimistic about the future of his dynasty. It is easy to believe that he might have delivered the famous prophecy, stated by his mistress Madame de Pompadour (1721–1764), but usually attributed to him: *"Après moi, le déluge"* (a-pre mwa le DAY-loozh; "After me, the flood"). France, the model of absolutist government for Europe, faced a severe crisis, as did the other governments that imitated the French example.

Such royal cynicism reflected the old regime's knowledge that it could do little to control the revolutionary developments of the time. Two centuries of war and foreign expansion had changed the basic way of life for most people and generated high expectations, particularly among the expanding urban middle classes—around 8 percent of the population—who benefited most by the worldwide explosion of foreign trade. Encouraged by the philosophies of the Enlightenment (see Chapter 18), they became more aggressive in improving their position, gaining social recognition, and demanding personal happiness outside the limits imposed by typical monarchical states and their privileged social orders.

Facing such challenges, those states could not respond effectively. They had earlier promised pragmatic compromise, whereby centralized government would maintain the interests of wealthy merchant-bankers and landed aristocrats. By the mid-eighteenth century, the system could no longer satisfy its supporters, nor could it absorb any more of the lesser nobles or the excluded middle class as each group grew more numerous. Indeed, with their expensive wars, ballooning debts, outmoded laws, passive bureaucrats, and corrupt officials, the absolute monarchies generally displayed striking political weaknesses and obvious misuses of the powers they managed to wield.

Despite all efforts at centralization, Louis XIV left a chaotic system of councils and committees, each with its own expanding network of officials and clerks, whose conflicting claims to authority were barely less perplexing than their complicated procedures. During the next reign, the selling of offices became a main source of revenue and patronage. There was no body comparable to the English Parliament for registering public opinion; the French **Estates-General** was last called in 1614. Government was most deficient in handling revenues,

Old Regime Monarchs

France	
1715–1774	Louis XV
1774–1792	Louis XVI
Habsburgs	
1711–1740	Charles VI
1740–1780	Maria Theresa
1780–1790	Joseph II
Prussia	
1713–1740	Frederick William I
1740–1786	Frederick the Great
1786–1797	Frederick William II
Russia	
1730–1740	Anna
1741–1762	Elizabeth
1762	Peter III
1762–1796	Catherine II
Great Britain	
1714–1727	George I
1727–1760	George II
1760–1820	George III

Estates-General—A national meeting in France of representatives of the three estates to present petitions to the king.

which it attempted to do without budgets, precise accounting, or standard assessments. French local government was even more chaotic. Late medieval districts, with their bailiffs and seneschals, coexisted with largely ceremonial provincial governors and royal intendants who struggled to placate other officials and influence local government after the seventeenth century. Some 360 different legal codes and 200 customs schedules applied in different parts of the country. Attempts to achieve uniformity invariably provoked strong reactions from local interests.

The French government, like some others, was severely damaged by the laziness of King Louis XV, who hated the tedium of governing and was more interested in beautiful women. Well into the 1740s, he left most power in the hands of an able minister, Cardinal Fleury (fleu-REE), who had maintained peace and reasonable stability since Louis was a boy. Even in his early reign, however, "mistress power" enlisted the king's fancy; later it influenced his policies. Louis's Polish queen endured a series of rivals who were installed in the palace near the king's bedchamber, granted titles, showered with costly gifts, and paraded by Louis in public. The best known of them was Jeanne-Antoinette Poisson (PWA-sohn), of nonnoble parentage, who became Madame de Pompadour. She received 17 estates, had a personal staff of 50 attendants, enjoyed nearly unlimited access to the royal treasury, and advised Louis effectively on public policy, particularly during the Seven Years' War. A later famous royal mistress, Madame Du Barry (1743–1793), was another woman of nonnoble origin who played the palace game better than the noble ladies at court, whom she overcame in a series of backbiting struggles for Louis's favor. Until he died in 1774, she reveled in her power, jewels, and luxurious houses. Such behavior earned France a reputation for "petticoat governance."

Other European kings squandered fortunes on mistresses, palaces, courts, and idle aristocrats, thus contributing to their common problem of rising public debt. Their financial difficulties also arose from their military expenses in attempting to protect colonial possessions and play the game of dynastic power politics in Europe. In the late 1700s, each of the great continental powers (France, Russia, and Austria) kept standing armies of 250,000 men. Rulers might have borne such heavy expenses if they could have governed by brute force, as former emperors had done, but they were prevented from doing so by their dependence on an international market, which supplied their vital material needs only in exchange for goods, bullion, or credit. Ultimately, they were forced to borrow, putting their states at the mercy of bankers and their own credit ratings. Such financial accountability, almost unknown in the ancient world, placed a serious restriction on monarchical policies in this era.

Capitalism and the Forces of Change

What role do economics and politics play in determining the success or failure of a state?

Dynamic economic and social forces challenged all European governments, no matter what their form, in the seventeenth and eighteenth centuries. Every part of Europe, from Britain to Russia, to the colonies around the world, and every social class, from peasants to the most tradition-bound nobles, felt the insecurity and restlessness inherent in the economic and social transformation. Governments with sufficient flexibility survived and profited from these changes; those that could not adapt were weakened or destroyed.

Expanding Capitalism

The primary force driving change was an energetic capitalistic economy developing so rapidly that it could hardly be controlled or even predicted. Capitalism generated new economic pursuits that developed almost spontaneously outside established institutions. It also created unprecedented increases in the volume of trade by dealing both in precious goods and in bulk commodities. Eastern Europe and the Baltic supplied grains, timber, fish, and naval stores, while western Europe supplied manufactures for its outlying regions and overseas trade. Dutch, English, and French merchant-bankers controlled shipping and credit. Plantation agriculture in the tropics, particularly the cultivation of Caribbean sugar, produced the greatest profits for overseas commerce. The African slave trade, along with its many supporting industries, also became an integral part of the intercontinental economic system. The New World economy widened European horizons while contributing to European wealth. New foods such as potatoes, yams, lima beans, tapioca, and peanuts became part of the European diet. Tropical

	The Rise of Capitalism
1600	English East India companies formed
1602	Dutch East India Company
1609	Bank of Amsterdam opens
c. 1688	Lloyds of London begins operation
1694	Bank of England is chartered
1698	London Stock Exchange opens
1724	Paris Bourse is established

plantation crops such as rice, coffee, tea, cocoa, and sugar ceased to be luxuries.

These new markets and resources contributed greatly to the development of modern capitalistic institutions. As the volume rose, great public banks chartered by governments replaced earlier family banks such as the Fuggers of Augsburg. The Bank of Amsterdam (1609) and the Bank of England (1694) are typical examples. Such banks, holding public revenues and creating credit by issuing notes, made large amounts of capital available for favored enterprises and the state.

Building on this seventeenth-century foundation, four new conditions produced the commercial boom in the century and a half after Westphalia. First, government demand for goods reached astronomical heights as huge standing armies and navies required mountains of food, clothing, arms, and ammunition. Second, a rising European population created another expanding market, demanding bulk commodities, while the increasing average life span allowed businessmen to amass more profits for investment over the course of their lives. Developing plantation agriculture in tropical colonies provided a third stimulus to foreign trade. Finally, Brazilian gold and diamond strikes stimulated the growth of capitalistic enterprises after the 1730s by driving up prices and creating greater profits.

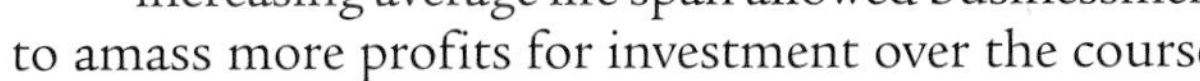

MAP

European Population Density, c. 1600

The resulting economic changes brought promising but sometimes disturbing results. As wealth increased beyond all expectations, investment and production rose accordingly in textiles, coal, iron, and shipbuilding. With enterprises growing larger, partnerships and **joint-stock companies** began replacing individually owned companies, as

joint-stock companies—A business or other enterprise in which the ownership is divided among a number of stock holders who jointly share the profits and the risks.

▼ That the small country of Holland became the richest country in Europe during the seventeenth century is a result of the hard and serious work of a diverse population, including people such as those shown in this detail from Rembrandt's *The Syndics of the Cloth Guild* (1662).

Seeing Connections

A New Product from the New World: Tobacco

The expanding capitalism of seventeenth- and eighteenth-century Europe produced a globalized economy of constantly circulating capital, raw materials, and finished goods. Some of the products sent from the "New World" to the "Old," such as maize and potatoes, enhanced the diet and life span of Europeans. Others, such as tobacco, shown here in an illustration from the book *Hortus Eystettensis,* circa 1613, initially met resistance from kings and popes. Tobacco had played an important role in Native American religious and social ceremonies for millennia before the arrival of the Europeans, who initially found the tobacco plant varieties used by native tribes to be too potent for everyday consumption. This changed after the English colonist John Rolfe, the husband of the fabled Pocahontas, developed a hybrid variety of tobacco that was more palatable to European tastes. Eventually, despite the powerful early opposition to its use, Europeans would become great consumers of tobacco. Some historians have even suggested that the intellectual ferment of the Enlightenment (see Chapter 18) was in part fueled by the two stimulants of nicotine and caffeine—the first being the active ingredient of tobacco and the second that of tea and coffee, two other products that by the late seventeenth century were also being imported into Europe in large quantities. The smoking of tobacco would become an entrenched feature of European culture for the next 300 years. In fact, it is only within the last decade that the nations making up the European Union have begun to restrict smoking in public places.

had happened earlier in foreign trade. At the same time, specialization became common in new phases of wholesaling and retailing operations.

Expansion and increasing complexity were accompanied by a steady monetary inflation. Wages, for example, increased far less than food prices, thus depressing the condition of workers. Nobles on the Continent who received fixed fees from their peasants and English landlords who had leased their fields on long-term contracts were hurt badly. Conversely, landowners who rented to short-term tenants or received payment in kind, profited, as did other capitalistic investors, who became wealthy from the general increase in the cost of goods. At times, their profits soared in a wildly speculative "boom-and-bust" market.

International trade was the most obvious indicator of European business prosperity. An even larger trade with overseas areas encouraged the formation of East India Companies in Austria and Prussia as clones of their older and better-known English, Dutch, and French counterparts. The resulting trade in sugar, silk, cotton, tobacco, and various luxury products generated whole new European industries. Perhaps more of an impact came from the African slave trade, centered in Liverpool and Bordeaux (bor-doh), which reached its peak during the eighteenth century. Altogether, the total foreign trade of Britain and France increased by some 450 percent. The Dutch, in imperial decline, experienced a notable decrease.

The Growth of Free Enterprise

Prosperity threatened government attempts to control the economy. As opportunities for profit increased, capitalists searched for profits outside state-sponsored enterprises and even beyond the legal limits set by governments and traditions. Some of these endeavors were deliberate efforts to evade the law; others—perhaps most—were responses to opportunity. This rising free enterprise capitalism, as distinct from mercantilist state capitalism, was evident in every phase of the pre-1789 economy.

A growing demand for food encouraged the trend in capitalist agriculture: the large-scale trading of agricultural goods as commodities in national and international markets. Soaring food prices lured surplus capital into land and improvements. This trend was most typical of England, but the agricultural boom, on a slightly smaller scale, extended to France, the Dutch Republic, the Low Countries, Prussia, and even the wine producers of Italy and Spanish Catalonia. Wherever it developed, capitalistic agriculture emphasized efficiency and profits, which usually required procedures that did not fit in with the traditional cooperative methods and servile labor of rural villages.

Four Englishmen pioneered the movement. Jethro Tull (1674–1741) carefully plowed the land planted in neat rows using a drill he invented and kept the plants well cultivated as they grew to maturity. Viscount Charles Townshend (1674–1738), nicknamed "Turnip Townshend," specialized in restoring soil fertility by such methods as applying clay-lime mixtures and planting turnips in **crop rotation.** Robert Bakewell (1725–1795) attacked the problem of scrawny cattle. Through selective breeding, he was able to increase the size of meat animals and also the milk yields from dairy cows. Another Englishman, Arthur Young (1741–1820), an ardent advocate for the new agriculture, made lecture tours throughout Europe and recorded his observations. He popularized the advantages of well-equipped farms and economical agricultural techniques and did much to free European agriculture from the less productive methods of the past.

New agricultural techniques demanded large capital investment and complete control of the land. Common fields, where villagers shared customary rights, could not be cultivated with the new methods. The land needed to be drained, irrigated, fertilized, and cultivated by scientific methods. Selective stockbreeding could not be practiced with an unregulated community herd. Landlords and investors who wanted to use the new methods brought about a devastating destruction of traditional society by trying to fence or enclose their acres. By outright purchase, foreclosure, suit, fraud, or even legislation, they tried to free their lands from old manorial restrictions, particularly from traditional rights to community use of the commons.

The gentry used their political dominance to improve their economic position, especially in the countryside. Although English manorial fees and services were abolished in the seventeenth century, many villages had retained their medieval rights to pasturage and fuel gathering on the commons. These rights were lost to enclosures. From 1750 until the end of the century, 40,000 to 50,000 small farms disappeared into large estates under the **Enclosure Acts.** Some of the peasants forced from the land went to the cities, some became agricultural laborers at pitifully poor wages, and others went into parish poorhouses, which were soon overflowing. This movement was strongest in England, but it also was seen on the Continent. Inflation and buyouts in France, particularly in the north, drove many peasants from the land, but they were so important as taxpayers that the government managed to restrict the movement. Consequently, French landlords were still complaining about manorial restrictions until 1789. But in England, the gentry—unlike many of their colleagues on the Continent—had

crop rotation—The practice of planting different crops in successive seasons on the same plot of land to preserve the soil's fertility. Otherwise, if the same crop is planted year after year on the same plot of land, the soil will become exhausted, and the land will have to lie fallow for at least a year to recover its fertility.

Enclosure Acts—A series of laws passed after 1760 that favored capitalist agriculture. Common lands were divided up, farming plots were combined, poor peasants lost the right to scavenge in the former common lands, and gates had to be installed at the boundaries around farms. The end result was to drive poor peasants off the land.

▼ As the English gentry rose to political dominance after 1685, they used their strength in Parliament to push through the Enclosure Acts, shutting the peasantry out from access to common lands.

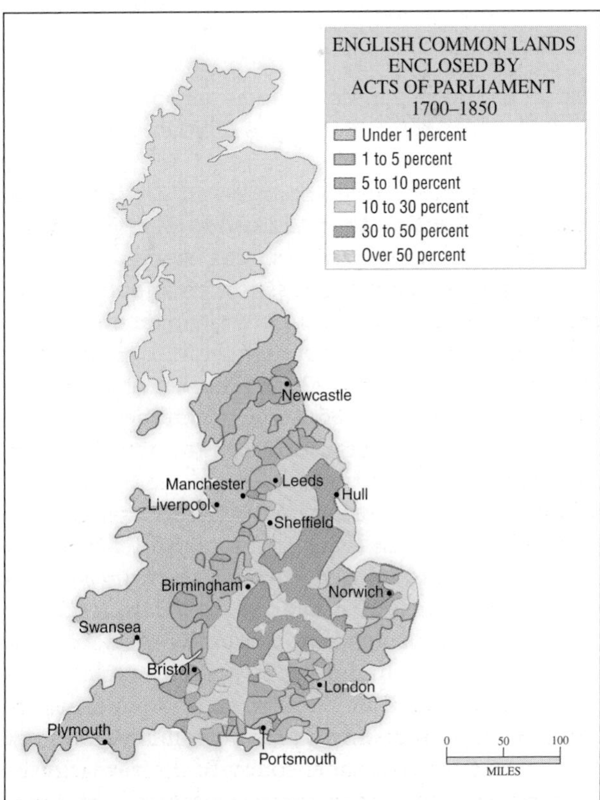

▲ The individual, human skills needed to perform the art of stocking frame work knitting were replaced by machines by the beginning of the nineteenth century.

already embraced capitalism and were powerful in Parliament: they were able to pass 2000 enclosure laws between 1760 and 1800.

In industry, the movement toward free enterprise produced the so-called domestic system, which involved contractual arrangements between capitalistic brokers and handworkers. Brokers supplied materials to the workers in their homes and later collected the products, to be sent through another stage of finishing or sold directly on the market. The system became common in industries where demand was high, profits were large, and capital was available. Domestic manufacturing moved early to the country, away from the regulations imposed by city guilds. The advantages and disadvantages were those associated with unregulated industry. Contracts were freely negotiated and prices were usually low, but capitalists and consumers faced considerable risks. Workers, particularly women and children, were easier to exploit than the guilds were.

Domestic industry was common all over western Europe after 1500, reaching a climax of growth in the eighteenth century. Although most typical of England, it also developed rapidly in northern France, the Low Countries, and southern Germany. It was involved in all essential processes of the woolen industries, notably spinning, weaving, fulling, and dyeing. The system also spread among other textile industries, such as linens and cottons, which provided a decided stimulus to the trend in the 1700s. Other affected industries were silk, lace, leather, paper, glass, pottery, and metals. By 1750, English domestic manufacturing employed over 4 million workers.

The career of Ambrose Crowley illustrates the domestic system in the infant English iron industry. Crowley started as a blacksmith who worked as a guildsman in Greenwich, where he accumulated a little capital. Around 1680, he moved to a small Durham village and built a domestic organization for the large-scale production of hardware. By 1700, the village had become a thriving town of 1500 workers. Crowley, who rented them their houses and supplied some of their tools as well as ore and fuel, employed most of them. The village produced nails, locks, bolts, hammers, spades, and other tools, which Crowley marketed elsewhere. A wealthy and respected citizen, he was knighted in 1706.

British industry benefited from the political system in place. Because most guild monopolies had passed with the seventeenth century, domestic industry faced few legal obstacles, but it did experience frequent functional crises. Despite widespread business prosperity, wages failed to keep up with the steady inflation. Between 1756 and 1786, wages rose by 35 percent but food prices increased by more than 60 percent. Workers also had to accept periodic unemployment, even in good times. They were thus inclined to resist the wage system and agitate for state intervention against low wages and high prices. Their bitter discontent was expressed in violent riots, most notably in 1765 and 1780.

Joint-stock companies were drastically reoriented in the late seventeenth century. Companies such as the Dutch and English East India Companies pooled the resources of many investors. In the late seventeenth century, exchanges for buying and selling stock—or **stock exchanges**—were becoming common, as were maritime insurance companies such as Lloyds of London, which began operations about 1688. Originally, joint-stock companies were exclusive monopolies, both in their areas of operation and in their limited number of stockholders. They were generally criticized, and their trading rights were regularly violated by competitors and smugglers. Under pressure, the British East India Company and similar firms steadily liberalized their policies until ultimately most stocks were sold on the open market. Sales of stock greatly increased opportunities for investment and multiplied the number of joint-stock companies. By 1715, more than 140 existed in England. This situation also encouraged a huge, speculative bull market on stock exchanges, which sprang up in taverns and coffeehouses all over western Europe. The London Stock Exchange opened in 1698 and the Paris Bourse in 1724; both were involved in the mania of speculation that collapsed the South Sea and Mississippi Companies in 1719–1720. Despite these disasters, such institutions became necessary to the private sector of Europe's economy in the early 1700s.

Banking performed a similarly necessary role. In a sense, the banks of Sweden, Amsterdam, and London were examples of state operations; their directors were often government advisers, authorized to perform semiofficial functions such as issuing notes and financing public debts. In another sense, however, these institutions became integral parts of the free market economy, providing the necessary credit for business enterprise while creating their own nonofficial commercial methods and institutions. Moreover, smaller banks developed within the private monetary and credit systems. The first English country bank was founded as a private enterprise in 1716 at Bristol; by 1780, there were 300 in the country.

Major insurance companies, banks, and stock exchanges formed an integrated institutional system, functioning in a free international market. Their standardized procedures became so complicated that ordinary people could not understand them. That strange new world of business enterprise, unlike the political world, was not controlled directly by anyone, not even by the power of concentrated capital. Goods and credit, commodity prices and wages, monetary values and stock quotations all interacted according to their own laws, which could be studied but not accurately predicted. Participants in this system learned that the number of losers could and often did outnumber the winners.

stock exchanges—Places where stocks—certificates representing the ownership of a part of a company or enterprise—were bought and sold.

Social Crises During the Capitalist Revolution

What happened to those people—noble and peasant—who were unable to compete in the capitalist market?

Ignoring the mass discontent and middle-class frustrations, the old regimes of Europe continued to depend largely on local authorities, military officers, and bureaucrats, drawn almost exclusively from nobilities and wealthy commoners. France provides a good illustration of the system. There the church owned 20 percent of the land and collected returns equal to half those from royal estates. Some of the monies supported education, social work, and charities, but most went to 11,000 of the 130,000 members of the clergy, particularly to 123 bishops and 28 archbishops. Some of their annual incomes exceeded the equivalent of $1 million—the equal of what top-ranking CEOs earn today—but many of the overworked lower clergy existed on $100 a year. Among the 400,000 nobles, only 1,000 families were represented at Versailles, where their members held numerous honorific appointments requiring no work. Titled nobles held 20 percent of the land, most by feudal tenures, which permitted them to collect numerous customary fees from their peasants. From all such sources, high French nobles probably averaged an annual equivalent of well over $100,000. Many, including some of the royal intendants, were former wealthy nonnobles who had bought their titles or offices.

The Few Rich and the Many Poor

Conspicuous consumption was typical of the high European nobility, such as the Fitzwilliamses in Ireland, the Newcastles in England, the Schonbrüns

▲ Fantastic hairstyles, such as the one shown in this engraving, were one of the ways in which members of the French upper class displayed their extravagance.

(SHOUN-brun) in Bohemia, the Radziwills (RODZH-veel) in Poland, and the Esterhazys (ES-ter-haz-ee) in Hungary. Prince Esterhazy owned about 10,000 acres, including 29 estates, 160 market towns, and 414 villages; his annual revenues exceeded the equivalent of $400,000. With such wealth, the magnates built elaborate city dwellings and sumptuous country retreats, filling them with priceless handcrafted furniture, rich tapestries, and fine works of art. While most people scratched for food, the high nobles enjoyed meats, fruits, and rare delicacies that were literally unknown among common people. Generally, the top aristocrats lived lavishly in a fantasy world, marred only by the dull ceremonies accompanying their brilliant but busy social activities.

Beneath this aristocratic superstructure lived millions of European commoners, 80 percent of whom were peasants. Except in Sweden, where they could protest to the parliament, they were unrepresented in government. Three-fourths were landless, and many were serfs, bound to their villages, not only in Russia, Poland, and Prussia, but also in Denmark. Among city-dwellers, only 11 percent were merchants, shopkeepers, artisans, and professionals. This proportion was higher in the Netherlands, England, and northern Italy, but generally lower elsewhere, particularly in eastern Europe. At the bottom of urban society was the mass of indigent poor, barely able to survive. Commoners of all economic levels paid most of the taxes. They were subject to legal discrimination in favor of the nobility, from whom they were also separated by differences in education, speech, manners, dress, and social customs.

This general pattern was evident in the French **Third Estate.** Including some 26 million people, it was more varied in its extremes than the first two estates, the clergy and nobles. At the top were about 75,000 wealthy bankers and merchants who had not bothered to buy titles. Another 3 million urban dwellers consisted largely of shopkeepers, lawyers, doctors, craftsmen, and street people, these last being most prevalent in Paris and port cities. Most of the commoners in France, as in Europe generally, were among the 23 million rural peasants. The greatest number of these peasants held some property rights to their lands, but many were tenants, and about a million were still serfs in 1789. Almost all peasants, serf or free, paid fees to their local nobles. Government taxes were irregular but heavy everywhere; the *taille* (TIE-yeh), or main land tax, fell heaviest on the class that was least able to pay. French peasants lived better than serfs in eastern Europe or the starving farm laborers of England, but life in a French village was a constant struggle for survival.

The Challenge of Population Growth

Europe experienced a population explosion in the eighteenth century. The number of people there increased more than 58 percent, from about 118 million in 1700 to 185 million a century later; some 50 million of this increase came after 1750. Population growth during the era was much higher in Europe than in Asia or Africa; in fact, in percentage terms it had never been as rapid before and has never been exceeded since. In the past, historians have emphasized rising life expectancy (falling death rates) as the cause. They have attributed this lower mortality to an improved social environment, involving such conditions as cleaner clothes and dishes, made possible by the new textile and pottery industries; better water and

Third Estate—Under the social system of pre-1789 France, society was divided by function: The First Estate—the clergy—prayed; the Second Estate—the nobles—fought; and the Third Estate—the rest of society—worked. Established in the tenth century, the Estate System was an anachronism by the eighteenth century.

sewage facilities, following wider use of iron piping; and better medical treatment, particularly in reducing infant mortality. However, other recent studies have suggested that a major cause for population growth was rising fertility in response to more productive agriculture and increasing food supplies, which also encouraged rural people to marry earlier and have more children to work the land. Whatever the cause, population expansion triggered major social changes, including rising economic demand, the growth of cities, an increasing labor surplus, vagabondage, and extensive migration.

Nearly every part of Europe experienced this tremendous expansion between 1650 and 1800. The English population rose from 5 million to over 9 million; that of Russia increased from 17 to 36 million; and the French population rose from 21 to 28 million. Other areas, which had earlier seen declines, posted gains: the Spanish population rose from 7.5 million to 11 million, and that of Italy expanded from 11 to 19 million. The increased number of people who could not afford to remain in their ancestral homes either migrated overseas or moved to urban areas, where 10 percent of Europe's population lived by 1800.

People moved in all directions. Some, like the Swiss and Irish, became foreign mercenaries. Others, like 300,000 French Huguenots (hyu-ge-NO), moved to escape religious persecution: 40,000 of them settled in England, and 20,000 of the most skilled went to Prussia. Both the Prussian and Russian governments regularly imported specialized craftsmen. German peasants by the thousands also went east to acquire land in Hungary or Russia. And the New World enticed many. In the eighteenth century, more than 750,000 English and 100,000 Irish settlers arrived in North America, the largest national contingents of a European migration to the Americas that numbered more than 2 million people.

Cities grew rapidly in the West, the main area of commerce—both domestic and foreign—and finance. Most affected were the English towns and cities, where populations generally increased faster than those of rural areas. The scope and significance of the trend may be quickly illustrated by a few figures. London's population rose from 400,000 to over 800,000 between the Peace of Utrecht (1713) and the French Revolution (1789). Other English cities, such as Bristol, Norwich, Liverpool, Leeds, Halifax, and Birmingham, which had been country towns in the 1600s, became medium-sized cities of between 20,000 and 65,000 inhabitants. On the Continent, the population of Paris reached 750,000 by 1789, and the number of residents in Bordeaux, Nantes, Le Havre, and Marseilles (mar-SEIL-e) all increased appreciably. Farther east were other expanding cities—Hamburg, Frankfurt, Geneva, Vienna, Berlin; the last two each had more than 100,000 inhabitants in the eighteenth century. In no city did the basic services of police, health, and employment keep pace with the increase in population.

Cities, of course, were the breeding grounds of ideas and contention. There were books and newspapers, coffeehouses, sailors from foreign lands, and varied populations, exchanging views and challenging prejudices. Violent spectacles, such as animal baiting and cockfighting, provided common amusements. Urban life was not only exciting; it was also more impersonal, dangerous, and frustrating. Using every kind of trick and deceit, a large criminal element flourished in the streets. Mobs were easily formed and more easily aroused, particularly in London and Paris, both of which regularly faced riots in the eighteenth century. Unlike the relatively placid inhabitants of rural villages, city-dwellers thrived on danger, diversity, and unpredictability. One person in three in the cities was unemployed in the eighteenth century. While the unemployed men sought relief in the proliferating gin mills of London, many women had no choice but to practice prostitution to feed their children.

Oppressive Conditions for Women

Post-1648 society was especially oppressive to women, whose general prospects declined despite some slight gains among those in the upper classes. Poor widows were hit hardest, as suggested by the number starving in English workhouses. Women died, on the average, 5 years younger than men, a fact explained largely by the high proportion that died in childbirth. A significant factor was malnutrition, because poor women lacked calcium in their diets and were therefore subject to hemorrhaging. For most women among the rural and urban poor, life was a nightmare of deprivation, suffering, and struggling to survive.

This situation was particularly true for poor country women, as noted by the British writer Arthur Young, who described a French peasant woman of 28 years who appeared to be 60 or 70 (see the Document on p. 542). Capitalistic agriculture depressed farm wages, forcing farm laborers to leave the villages in search of work. Women had to stay and eke out support for the children by domestic spinning or weaving. Some went to work in the fields for lower pay and longer hours than men. As work opportunities diminished, thousands took to the roads, carrying their babies and begging for food. Many died with their children by the roadsides; others joined criminal gangs of robbers or smugglers. The hardiest and the most determined reached the cities, where the best hope for a displaced peasant woman was employment as a cook or maid with a well-to-do family.

In the cities, a poor woman's life was not much better than in the villages, however. The lucky few in household service were paid much less than men, assigned cramped quarters, fed leftovers, and frequently exploited sexually by their masters. Alternate employment was extremely limited because women were denied membership in most craft guilds. A few could find work outside the guilds, spinning, weaving, sewing, or working leather in starvation-wage sweatshops. Others took dirtier and heavier jobs in the metal trades and in the coalfields, both above and below the ground. Another option, reluctantly chosen by many women, was prostitution. This ancient profession was growing rapidly in every large city, with 50,000 known female prostitutes in London and more than 40,000 in Paris by the late 1700s. Social degradation, venereal disease, and continuous harassment marked their lives as civil authorities allowed them to operate but subjected them to periodic imprisonment.

A vast social chasm separated poor women from those of the wealthy classes; yet even at the top, another broad gulf divided the sexes. Royal and noble women exercised considerable political power, but except for numerous ruling monarchs, they operated as satellites of the men they manipulated. Among both aristocratic women and those of the wealthy middle class, many were withdrawn from meaningful work as mothers and homemakers to become social ornaments for the husbands. Legally, upper-class wives remained subordinated to their husbands in the disposition of property and rights to divorce; the double standard of marital fidelity remained supreme, both socially and legally. Indeed, despite their improved education and their artistic and literary pursuits, women were still regarded as childlike, irresponsible, and passion-ruled by such eminent eighteenth-century men as Rousseau, Frederick the Great, and Lord Chesterfield.

The Prevalence of Human Misery

A significant base for popular discontent against governments after Westphalia was an ever-prevalent misery among the ever-growing numbers of the poor. The various wars destroyed crops, ruined cities, created hordes of starving refugees, and depopulated whole provinces. Armies contributed to prevailing diseases, such as smallpox, typhus, and malaria. Lack of sanitation and the presence of horse manure on roads and streets attracted swarming flies, which spread typhoid and infantile diarrhea among thousands of children. While epidemics of plague spread throughout central Europe, rickets and tuberculosis reflected malnutrition among half the workers, who could not achieve marginal proficiency. Mortality rates were appalling: half of the children died before they reached 6 years old, one woman in five died in childbirth, and life expectancy was only about 28 years. For a large proportion of Europeans, unemployment, homelessness, grinding poverty, and hunger were inevitable. Indeed, horrible reality could be escaped only on rare affordable occasions in alcohol.

Although sometimes exciting, life in the cities was also miserable for the urban poor, who made up 20 to 40 percent of city populations. Many had come in from the country, seeking survival. Without homes, friends, or steady work, they lived as best they could, toiling at transitory menial jobs, begging, stealing, or selling themselves as prostitutes. Only a social notch higher were the apprentices and journeymen of the decaying craft guilds, who also faced real hardships. The discipline, particularly for apprentices, was difficult; hours were long; and wages were barely enough to buy food. Crowded into filthy quarters, without adequate light, air, or bathing facilities, they lived dull lives conditioned by ignorance, squalor, disease, and crime. Bad as these conditions were, they might always get worse, for as the guilds faced competition, many shops were forced to close, leaving their journeymen to become wandering artisans among the vagabonds on the roads.

Most of these pitiful derelicts were products of the century's most serious social challenge, rural poverty. Despite a general prosperity lasting until about 1770, European peasants suffered severely from ravaging armies and increasing agricultural specialization. High agricultural prices turned aristocrats into aspiring capitalists, willing to gouge their peasants in seeking greater profits. Some nobles, particularly on the Continent, revived and enforced their old manorial rights to fees and services. Others moved in an opposite direction by eliminating the peasants' medieval rights and using hired labor to work their lands. Either way, the peasants lost a substantial amount of their livelihood and were likely to become criminals, vagrants, or part of an alienated subculture. They ceased to be assets to the state—as either taxpayers or soldiers—becoming instead potentially dangerous and expensive liabilities.

Although faring better than the serfs of eastern Europe, western peasants still faced terrible conditions. Some in France were reduced from tenants to laborers when merchants bought up land to profit from rising food prices. Under Louis XV, some 30,000 rural vagrants thronged French roads. About 35 percent of the peasants who had managed to acquire land were still paying manorial fees and services to local lords in accordance with feudal law. Earlier, these exactions had hurt the peasants' pride more than their chances for survival; when the practice was stepped up during the depression of the 1780s, many lost their lands.

Responses to the plight of the urban and rural poor were crude and cruel. It was felt that the way to eliminate vagrancy was through punishment. The approach was similar to the brutal beating of military delinquents, the condemning of criminals to galley

William Hogarth cast a critical and unsparing eye on the desperate conditions of the poor in London during the eighteenth century. In *Gin Lane* (1751), he depicted the alcoholism that allowed the poor to escape momentarily the misery of their lives.

slavery, or the confinement of debtors on rotting prison ships. For the poor, similar punitive solutions were sought in the British parish workhouses and the French "beggar depots." At the end of the century, the English workhouses held 100,000 inmates, compared with 230,000 in the French depots. Both systems, like others all over Europe, perpetuated abominable living conditions while denying hope for the unfortunate victims. In England, the workhouses were favored by some large landowners, who welcomed cheap labor supplied by the state. Other taxpayers opposed the cost of improving the workhouses and tried to push vagrants into other parishes. Even a pregnant woman or one with a sick child might be given a few pennies and turned away.

Ultimately, the governments built larger workhouses for fewer parishes, attempting to spread the cost of poverty relief. Such policies destroyed the initiative of the poor and conditioned them to seek public assistance. The simmering pressure of the discontent of the multitudes could be denied for a while, but in the 1770s and 1780s across Europe, mass outbreaks of violence and finally revolution would be the price to be paid (see Chapter 18).

Protests, Riots, and Rebellions

Injustice and misery among women and the poor were obvious sources of discontent, but even more dangerous for old regimes were changing attitudes among the higher classes. A general spirit of change and hope, coupled with the chaotic confusion and inefficiency of most monarchies, aroused general feelings of dissatisfaction, particularly among members of the lower middle class and lesser nobles, who were too numerous to be absorbed into the established system. Even some favored aristocrats showed a casual indifference to royal authority and a stubborn determination to defend their privileges. Potential middle-class rebels, particularly lawyers, were well equipped to voice grievances, which they did often by the late 1700s. Although lacking education and opportunities to register direct protests, city workers and peasants sometimes did express their despair in sporadic riots and futile local uprisings.

Because their testimony must be taken from official records, often from the statements of tortured captives, no one can accurately describe peasant attitudes on the Continent at that time. They surely varied from place to place, as did the conditions. Where life was hardest, they regularly resorted to individual acts of violence, such as killing animals or burning outbuildings. Generally, they lacked long-range political objectives but could be aroused en masse by immediate threats to their well-being. Seventy-three peasant rebellions occurred in eighteenth-century Europe, notoriously in Poland (1730s), Bohemia (1775), and in Russia, the great Pugachev (poo-gah-CHOV) revolt (1773–1775). Suffering English farm laborers rioted six times between 1710 and 1772. Although generally more docile, French peasants precipitated violent

Document

Conditions Among Eighteenth-Century French Peasants

British writer Arthur Young made these observations just before the French Revolution. He saw better conditions elsewhere but was appalled at the backward state of French agriculture and the great gap in living standards between the nobility and the lower classes in the country.

SEPTEMBER 1ST. To Combourg. The country has a savage aspect; husbandry not much further advanced, at least in skill, than among the Hurons, which appears incredible amidst enclosures; the people almost as wild as their country, and their town of Combourg one of the most brutal filthy places that can be seen; mud houses, no windows, and a pavement so broken, as to impede all passengers, but ease none; yet here is a château, and inhabited. Who is this Mons. de Chateaubriand, the owner, that has nerves strung for a residence amidst such filth and poverty? Below this hideous heap of wretchedness is a fine lake, surrounded by well-wooded enclosures. Coming out of Hédé, there is a beautiful lake belonging to Mons. de Blossac, Intendant of Poitiers, with a fine accompaniment of wood. A very little cleaning would make here a delicious scenery. There is a [Château de Blossac], with four rows of trees, and nothing else to be seen from the windows in the true French style. Forbid it, taste, that this should be the house of the owner of that beautiful water; and yet this Mons. de Blossac has made at Poitiers the finest promenade in France! ...

SEPT. 5TH. To Montauban. The poor people seem poor indeed; the children terribly ragged, if possible worse clad than if with no clothes at all; as to shoes and stockings they are luxuries. A beautiful girl of six or seven years playing with a stick, and smiling under such a bundle of rags as made my heart ache to see her. They did not beg, and when I gave them anything seemed more surprised than obliged. One-third of what I have seen of this province seems uncultivated, and nearly all of it in misery....

JULY 11TH. Pass [Les] Islettes, a town (or rather collection of dirt and dung) of new features, that seem to mark, with the faces of the people, a country not French.

JULY 12TH. Walking up a long hill, to ease my mare, I was joined by a poor woman, who complained of the times, and that it was a sad country. Demanding her reasons, she said her husband had but a morsel of land, one cow, and a poor little horse, yet they had a *franchar* (42 lb.) of wheat, and three chickens, to pay as a quit-rent to one seigneur; and four *franchar* of oats, one chicken and 1 *sou* to pay to another, besides very heavy *tailles* and other taxes. She had seven children, and the cow's milk helped to make the soup. But why, instead of a horse, do not you keep another cow? Oh, her husband could not carry his produce so well without a horse; and asses are little used in the country. It was said, at present, that *something was to be done by some great folks for such poor ones, but she did not know who nor how,* but God send us better, *car les tailles et les droits nous écrasent* [because the *tailles* and other taxes are crushing us]. This woman, at no great distance, might have been taken for sixty or seventy, her figure was so bent, and her face so furrowed and hardened by labour; but she said she was only twenty-eight. An Englishman who had not travelled cannot imagine the figure made by infinitely the greater part of the countrywomen in France; it speaks, at the first sight, hard and severe labour. I am inclined to think, that they work harder than the men, and this, united with the more miserable labour of bringing a new race of slaves into the world, destroys absolutely all symmetry of person and every feminine appearance....

Questions to Consider

1. Young writes just before the French Revolution—what do you see in the first paragraph of the selection that would provoke a violent reaction?
2. Young was an agricultural reformer in England. How did he characterize the nature of the methods used by the French peasants in preparing their land?
3. What was the effect of the rural situation in France on women?
4. It is alleged that peasants have little understanding of the economic and political system in which they find themselves. Did the woman with whom Young talked on July 12 comprehend why her life was so hard?

From Arthur Young, *Travels in France,* ed. Constantia Maxwell (Cambridge: Cambridge University Press, 1929), p. 107 ff.

upheavals in 1709, 1725, 1740, 1749, and 1772. In his writings, Arthur Young recognized their surly attitudes and contempt for authority. In 1789, when they could express grievances to delegates headed for the Estates-General, they were universally bitter against feudal exactions and government taxes.

Urban workers were usually more aggressive and perhaps better informed than peasants but more confused by the complexities of their problems. Although their numbers increased with the size of cities, they became alienated from the upper classes by periodic unemployment and inflation. Rioting among workers and the idle poor of the cities was thus common, notably in London and Paris. Such outbreaks, however, were more violent than politically significant. Workers did recognize two potential enemies: the capitalist, who contracted for labor and influenced government to eliminate welfare; and the guild, which exploited the journeyman in favor of the master. To combat these enemies, workers occasionally organized in England and France. The organizations were weak, however, and their efforts usually failed for want of leadership.

Middle-class discontent, like that of some peasants, arose more from thwarted expectations than from terrible suffering. Upward mobility, from middle class to aristocracy, was a by-product of economic prosperity all over Europe, particularly in England and France. The movement took many forms—purchase of land and titles, marriage, even reward for personal services of lawyers, doctors, tutors, or governesses. This middle-class struggle for respectability was individually competitive, as long as opportunities were open. But in time, room at the top became limited, as old regimes stabilized and more of the middle class sought to climb the social ladder. At this point, ambitious middle-class outsiders became dangerously hostile to the system.

Most dissenting action came from men, but women were also represented among the malcontents. They were regularly involved in local uprisings against the high cost of bread, the introduction of machines to depress labor, and rising taxes. In 1770, a mob of Parisian women left their workplaces to protest the deportation of their vagrant children to the colonies. Such actions were not yet aimed directly against old regimes, but later (as we shall see in Chapter 18) other French and English women would go further to champion women's rights, along with the "rights of man."

More dangerous to monarchical establishments than outside opposition was aristocratic opposition from within. Gains by the nobles in Sweden, Spain, Austria, and even France increased their confidence and whetted their appetites for more power. As old regimes wavered, nobles at the top were frantically determined to maintain and improve on their positions; indeed, they professed to believe that they were more legitimate rulers than the kings. This was partly an effort to combat middle-class influence, for nobles were often heavily in debt and feared legal reforms that might require them to pay. At the same time, the majority of lesser nobles resented the court cliques; a few even dreamed of helping the middle classes change the system. Noble opinions were indeed varied, promising weakening support for royal authority but refusing cooperation with kings in curtailing privileges. On this last point, nearly all nobles were in total agreement.

Conclusion

Between the Treaty of Westphalia in 1648 and the outbreak of the French Revolution in 1789, the absolutist governments of Europe tried to impose central control—sanctioned by God— over the society, economy, church, culture, and military systems. This system of government responded to the perceived need for stability and order after more than a century of religious wars. As absolutism was the system of government in France under Louis XIV—Europe's strongest power—it was copied by almost all of the European states of the era. However, the structural weaknesses of a centralized control over a continent undergoing the revolutionary social and economic changes of the Capitalist Revolution would eventually become evident. The incapacity of the kings to impose their theoretical power led to massive corruption. The aristocracy could not or would not serve as transmitters of royal power, and across Europe, the nobles began a drive to reclaim the power they had lost to centralizing kings. Wars and the luxurious tastes of the monarchs drained the state treasuries and spread misery to the expanding populations. By the middle of the eighteenth century the absolutist system had come to be known as the *ancien régime*—the old regime—and it did not work any more.

The Dutch and the English went against the absolutist trends of the day, with differing results. The Netherlands emerged under the political, financial, military dominance of the British, while England proceeded to build a world empire. But in each case, these examples of limited government provided a different political alternative for those who had become disaffected with absolutism. When the British succeeded in ousting the Stuarts in 1688, the resulting political and theoretical doctrines established the precedent for the American Revolution a century later.

The limited central powers proved better able to ride the waves of change that swept the globe in the seventeenth and eighteenth century. Even though the political process was not marked by idealism in England, the diversity of the goals of the political elites provided a suitable framework to absorb the demographic, financial, and social changes that affected the country during the century.

The most important occurrence of the century and a half between the Treaty of Westphalia and the outbreak of the French Revolution was the Capitalist Revolution. This revolution developed so rapidly that it could hardly be controlled or even predicted. The absolutist governments tried to ride the waves of economic growth and even control them through schemes such as mercantilism. But the economic changes came so fast that, linked with a vastly expanding population, and touching all of the continents of the globe, no matter how the kings might try, they could not control the new economic pursuits that developed almost spontaneously outside of established institutions.

Suggestions for Web Browsing

You can obtain more information about topics included in this chapter at the websites listed below. See also the companion website that accompanies this text, http://www.ablongman.com/brummett, which contains an online study guide and additional resources.

Internet Modern History Sourcebook: The Early Modern World
http://www.fordham.edu/halsall/mod/modsbook03.html
Online source for numerous documents about the expanding global power of the Dutch and the British.

Trade Products in Early Modern History
http://www.bell.lib.umn.edu/Products/Products.html
University of Minnesota site chronicles the development of global trade, by the Dutch and the British in particular, as they search for a variety of products, from beaver to tulips and from coffee to tobacco.

Age of the Sun King (*L'Age d'Or*)
http://www.geocities.com/Paris/Rue/1663/index.html
Extensive site describing, with text and images, the world of France under Louis XIV.

Internet Modern History Sourcebook: The *Ancien Régime*
http://www.fordham.edu/halsall/mod/hs1000.html#ancien
Extensive online source for links about the ancien régime, *including primary documents by or about Louis XIV and Cardinal Richelieu and the enlightened despotism of Catherine the Great and Frederick II.*

Frederick the Great of Prussia
http://members.tripod.com/~Nevermore/king.html
Extensive site on the king of Prussia and his times.

The Glorious Revolution of 1688
http://www.thegloriousrevolution.com
This site includes a range of documents and images regarding the important legal and political precedents set in motion by the Glorious Revolution of 1688.

Literature and Film

Most of the novels listed here have also served as the bases of major films: Alexandre Dumas captured the drama of this period in his *The Three Musketeers* (1844), *The Man in the Iron Mask* (originally published as part of the *Vicomte de Bragelonne;* 1848–1850), and *The Count of Monte Cristo* (1844). Victor Hugo contributed *The Hunchback of Notre Dame* (1831), which takes place at the beginning of this period. Sir Walter Scott wrote *Rob Roy* (1817) and *The Pirate* (1822). A later author, Rafael Sabatini, wrote a fine swashbuckler of a book with titled *Captain Blood* (1922). Daniel Defoe captured the spirit of the English Civil War with *Memoirs of a Cavalier: Or a Military Journal of the Wars in Germany and the Wars in England from the Year 1632 to the Year 1648* (1722). He also added to the canon with *Moll Flanders* (1722). Henry Fielding's *The History of Tom Jones, a Foundling* (1749), is a rollicking view into some of the social realities in England in the eighteenth century. More recently, Nancy Mitford and Amanda Foreman have made a fine reassessment of Madame Pompadour and her world in their work, *Madame Pompadour* (New York Review of Books, 2001).

An opulent portrayal of many different aspects of eighteenth-century life is Stanley Kubrick's film masterpiece *Barry Lyndon* (1975; Hawk Films).

Suggestions for Reading

Dynamic European economic growth is strongly emphasized in Fernand Braudel, *Civilization and Capitalism, Vol. 2: The Wheels of Commerce* (Harper & Row, 1986). See also Gunnar Persson, *Pre-Industrial Economic Growth, Social Organization, and Technological Progress in Europe* (Blackwell, 1988).

For a view of the development of French absolutism to the depths of the Old Regime, see Emmanuel Le Roy Ladurie, *The Ancien Régime: A History of France, 1610–1774,* trans. Mark Greengrass (Blackwell, 1998). A general treatment of absolutism is found in John Miller, *Absolutism in Seventeenth-Century Europe* (St. Martin's Press, 1990). A revisionist views of absolutism is found in Nicholas Henshall, *The Myth of Absolutism* (Longman, 1992).

French political and social affairs are studied in Roger Mettam, *Power and Faction in Louis XIV's France* (Blackwell, 1987). Changes in the European class structure are treated in George Rude, *Europe in the Eighteenth Century: Aristocracy and the Bourgeois Challenge* (Harvard University Press, 1985), and Colin Mooers, *The Making of Bourgeois Europe* (Verso, 1991). Some obvious social threats to European monarchies are described in M. S. Anderson, *War and Society in Europe of the Old Regime, 1618–1789* (St. Martin's Press, 1988); and Frederick Krantz, *History from Below: French and English Popular Protest, 1600–1800* (Blackwell, 1988). The best overview of the effects of the age on women is Mary Wiesner, *Woman and Gender in Early Modern Europe,* 2nd ed. (Cambridge Press, 2000). Natalie Zemon Davis's *Women on the Margins: Three Seventeenth Century Lives* (Harvard University Press, 1995) recounts three European women living not only on the Continent but also in South America and North America.

On French government and classes, see Guy Chaussinand-Nogaret, *The French Nobility in the Eighteenth Century* (Cambridge University Press, 1985). On the role of eighteenth-century French women, see Joan Landes, *Women and the Public Sphere in the Age of the French Revolution* (Cornell University Press, 1988).

Jonathan I. Israel, *The Dutch Republic and the Hispanic World* (Oxford University Press, 1986), and Charles R. Boxer, *The Dutch Seaborne Empire* (Penguin, 1989), discuss the world trading empire of the Dutch. Social backgrounds are treated in Sherrin Marshall, *The Dutch Gentry, 1500–1650: Family, Faith, and Fortune* (Greenwood, 1987). On the decisive conflict with the English, see J. R. Jones, *The Anglo-Dutch Wars of the Seventeenth Century* (Addison-Wesley, 1996). Simon Schama provides a brilliant view into the seventeenth century in the Netherlands in *An Embarrassment of Riches: An Interpretation of Dutch Culture in the Golden Age* (Vintage, 1997).

On the reigns of the first two Stuart monarchs and the English civil war, see Maurice Ashley, *The English Civil War* (St. Martin's, 1990), and Derek Hirst, *Authority and Conflict in England, 1603–1658* (Harvard University Press, 1986). A recent book on the radical fringe is David Petegorsky, *Left-Wing Democracy in the English Civil War: Gerrard Winstanley and the Digger Movement* (Alan Sutton, 1997). For a broad selection of contemporary accounts of the civil war, see John Eric Adair, *By the Sword Divided: Eyewitness Accounts of the English Civil War* (Alan Sutton, 1998).

Among the best treatments of Charles II and his problems are Kenneth H. D. Haley, *Politics in the Reign of Charles II* (Blackwell, 1985). On James II and the Glorious Revolution, see John Childs, *The Army, James II, and the Glorious Revolution* (St. Martin's, 1981), and K. Merle Chacksfield, *The Glorious Revolution, 1688* (Wincanton, 1988).

CHAPTER 18

New Ideas and Their Political Consequences

The Scientific Revolution, the Enlightenment, and the French Revolutions

Outline

- Revolution in Science: Discovering the Laws of Nature
- The Age of Reason and the *Ancien Régime*
- The Failure of Monarchical Reform
- The French Revolution: The Domestic Phase, 1789–1799
- The French Revolution: The Napoleonic Phase, 1799–1815

Features

DISCOVERY THROUGH MAPS **The Heliocentric Cosmos of Copernicus**

DOCUMENT **The Widening Scope of Scientific Discovery**

SEEING CONNECTIONS **Benjamin Franklin in Paris**

DOCUMENT ***Declaration of the Rights of Man and Citizen***

DOCUMENT **Olympe de Gouges on the Rights of Women**

◀ As revolutionary justice condemned an increasing number of people to death after 1791, the guillotine provided an efficient means to behead the guilty. The advocates of using the guillotine proclaimed it to be humane because the only thing the condemned person would feel would be a "slight breeze at the back of the neck." Here, the head of Louis XVI is being shown to the crowd after his execution in January 1793.

WE SAW SOME of the long-term causes of the *ancien régime*'s failure in Chapter 17: France was unable to adapt itself to the changes brought about by capitalism; its government was unable to reform itself to deal with the misery caused by the social hardships that always occur in a time of rapid transition; finally, France's continual involvement in wars strained its economy to the breaking point. In this chapter, we will discuss an equally profound cause of the fall of the French government in 1789, new ways of thinking that challenged authority and the status quo. These new ways of thinking ranged from sixteenth-century scientists such as Copernicus to seventeenth-century intellectuals such as John Locke, men whose ideas in time would become accepted and used by the middle classes of Europe, North America, and South America. Stimulated by the ferment of new ideas, people applied the test of reason to absolutist government, the state church, mercantile economics, the Estate System, and other aspects of life and found these institutions to be unreasonable, therefore unworthy of their authority.

In European history, the French Revolution of 1789 marks the beginning of modern, mass politics on the continent. The *ancien régime* came to an end in all of its manifestations: the Estate System based on inherited privilege gave way to a social system based on economic classes; mercantilism was replaced by a market-driven economy; politics based on divine rights absolutism crumbled before the idea of political legitimacy derived from the will of the people; the dominant position the Catholic Church enjoyed as state religion was turned on its head, leaving in its wake a chastened church with no property and little political authority; in short, no part of French life was left untouched by the events of 1789.

Revolution in Science: Discovering the Laws of Nature

Why did religious authorities reject the findings of the scientific revolution, but kings such as Louis XIV embrace them?

Scientific investigations date back some five thousand years. The civilizations in ancient Mesopotamia, Egypt, China, and India all produced sophisticated astronomical observations, mathematical systems, and engineering principles. Later, in Mesoamerica and sub-Saharan Africa, the elites of the local communities charted the stars and devised complex hydraulic systems. Muslim scientists wrote learned treatises on subjects as diverse as disease and chemistry and helped transmit the numbering systems used by all countries today.

In the Western tradition, the Greeks and the Romans produced theories about the paths of the stars, the functioning of the human body, the qualities of the earth, and all of the plants and animals found on it. During the thousand years after the end of the ancient world, scholars in the church took advantage of the work of the Greeks, Romans, and Muslims to try to understand all that God created. William of Occam (c. 1295–1349), an English Franciscan, laid the foundations for later advances in scientific thinking that came to be known as *Occam's Razor.* As the great twentieth-century scientist Albert Einstein paraphrased Occam seven centuries later, "everything should be made as simple as possible, but not simpler." In other words, when trying to form a hypothesis to explain a phenomenon, the simplest and most direct explanation quite often is the best approach. Occam's Razor shaved off nonessential considerations that would form obstacles in the path of discovering natural laws.

The Revolution in Astronomy

The Polish scholar Nicolaus Copernicus (ko-PER-ni-cus; 1473–1543) wanted to affirm and perfect the old, church approved, geocentric view of the universe articulated by Ptolemy (85–165): that the sun, the planets, and the stars all circled the earth, which lay at the center of all God's creation. In preparation for his work, Copernicus had studied at the great centers of Renaissance learning—Bologna, Rome, and Padua. When he returned to Poland, however, his research led him to disprove Ptolemy's assertions, and shortly before his death, he published *On the Revolutions of the Heavenly Spheres* in Nuremberg in 1543. He restated the heliocentric theory—Aristarchus had arrived at the same conclusion in the third century B.C.E.—that postulated the sun as the center, around which the planets moved, a theory directly opposed to the traditional geocentric explanation held by the Catholic Church. The church, in the floodtide of the Counter-Reformation, attacked his findings as heretical (and later placed his book on the Roman Catholic Church's Index of Forbidden Books in 1616); Luther and Melanchton (me-LANK-ton) also ridiculed him, as did the English scientist Francis Bacon.

DOCUMENT

On the Revolutions of the Heavenly Spheres

Copernicus offered his idea as a mathematical theory. By the end of the century, however, Tycho Brahe (TEE-co BRA-hey; 1546–1601), a Danish astronomer, aided by his sister, Sophia (1556–1643), had recorded

Chronology

1450
- **1473–1543** Nicolaus Copernicus

1550
- **1564–1642** Galileo Galilei

1650
- **1690** John Locke, *An Essay Concerning Human Understanding, Second Treatise on Civil Government*

1750
- **1740–1780** Reign of Maria Theresa of Austria
- **1740–1786** Reign of Frederick II of Prussia
- **1751–1772** Denis Diderot, *Encyclopédie*
- **1762** Jean-Jacques Rousseau, *Émile, The Social Contract*
- **1762–1796** Reign of Catherine the Great of Russia
- **1780–1790** Reign of Joseph II of Austria
- **1789** Tennis Court Oath: storming of the Bastille; *Declaration of the Rights of Man* issued; women's march on Versailles
- **1791** French Constitution put in effect; National Constituent Assembly dissolved; *Declaration of Rights of Women* issued
- **1793** Louis XVI executed; "Reign of Terror"
- **1795** National Convention establishes Directory to govern France; National Convention dissolves
- **1799** Napoleon seizes power
- **1805** British navy defeats French and Spanish navies at Trafalgar
- **1807** French gain control of continent
- **1808** Overthrow of Spanish monarchy by Napoleon sets in motion Latin American revolutions
- **1812** Napoleonic forces fail in their invasion of Russia
- **1815** Napoleon defeated at Waterloo

Discovery Through Maps

The Heliocentric Cosmos of Copernicus

From the first person who walked across the mountain pass that had delimited the world to the first to see the views from satellites hovering thousands of miles above the equator, humans have drawn new maps to express their changing perspectives. Nothing made Europeans rethink their perspectives more than the discoveries of the Polish scientist Copernicus. He was not the first to postulate a sun-centered cosmic system. Among others, the Hellenistic Greeks in Alexandria had advanced the concept of the sun at the center of our planetary system with the planets revolving around it in the third century B.C.E.

Ptolemy, another Greek astronomer, disagreed and embellished on Aristotle's theory that the earth was at the center of the universe. This fit in nicely with the emerging Christian Church's theology. After all, if God created man in his image, why would God place him anywhere else but the center of the system? A tidy closed universe came to be the conventional wisdom, with the earth surrounded by crystallized rings containing the moon, sun, and planets; hovering outside the last ring were, of course, God and the angels.

Medieval observers noted obvious flaws in this explanation, but the clever thinkers of the church devised satisfactory refutations of the contradictions. In the 1490s, Nicolaus Copernicus left his home in Torun and journeyed to the Polish university town of Krakow, where he became caught up in the debate about the nature of the universe. In the next decade in Krakow and then at the University of Bologna, he pursued his study of astronomy. He returned to a post at a church in Frauenburg, where, for the next 30 years, he worked on making the church's view on the nature of the universe simpler, yet mathematically precise.

The more he worked, the less he could defend Rome's position, and finally in 1543, in a book dedicated to Pope Paul III, he advanced his hypothesis of a sun-centered (heliocentric), not human-centered (homocentric) universe. It was criticized by the church and by Martin Luther and was considered suspicious by most of the astronomers of the time. But by the end of the century, the Copernican hypothesis had been verified, and Europeans began to look to charts such as this one by Andreas Cellarius portraying the heliocentric cosmos. The universe had been turned upside down.

Questions to Consider

1. Why did Copernicus's ideas about the Cosmos spark such a wide-ranging debate? What difference did it make if the universe was seen as earth- or sun-centered?
2. What fundamental ideas in your life are being debated today, and what will be the effect on you if one of these ideas is overturned?
3. In your view, what is the nature of the relationship between science and society? Should scientists be limited by community values, or should there be an absolute freedom to find the basic laws and functions of the universe?

hundreds of observations that also pointed to flaws in the geocentric explanation. Brahe even attempted, without much success, to find a compromise between the Ptolemaic and Copernican systems by postulating that the planets moved about the sun while the latter orbited the earth. This proposition raised even more problems and therefore met with little acceptance.

Brahe's data were used by his one-time assistant, the German mathematician Johannes Kepler (yoh-HAN-nes KEP-ler; 1571–1630) to support the Copernican theory. As he worked mathematically with Brahe's records on the movement of Mars, Kepler was ultimately able to prove that the planet moved not in a circular orbit but in an ellipse. He also discovered that the paces of the planets accelerated when they approached the sun. From this he concluded that the sun might emit a magnetic force that directed the planets in their courses. The idea was not yet confirmed by a mathematical proof, but that would soon be achieved by Newton, using Kepler's hypothesis. Even in his own time, however, Kepler's laws of planetary motion almost completely undermined the Ptolemaic theory.

During the early seventeenth century, growing acceptance of the heliocentric theory precipitated an intellectual and political crisis affecting European society, particularly the Catholic Church. Medieval Catholicism had accepted Aristotle on physics and Ptolemy on astronomy. The church now saw its reputation and authority being challenged by the new ideas. Both Copernicus and Brahe had evaded the issue by purporting to deal only in mathematical speculations. Kepler and others of his time became increasingly impatient with this subterfuge. The most persistent of these scientific rebels was the Italian mathematician-physicist Galileo Galilei (1564–1642).

In 1609, Galileo made a telescope, with which he discovered mountains on the moon, sunspots, the satellites of Jupiter, and the rings of Saturn. Galileo discovered more facts to verify the Copernican theory. But, as he wrote to Kepler:

> *Up to now I have preferred not to publish, intimidated by the fortune of our teacher Copernicus, who though he will be of immortal fame to some, is yet by an infinite number (for such is the multitude of fools) laughed at and rejected.*[1]

He also knew that he was writing at a time when the church increasingly demanded obedience to its views.

DOCUMENT
Galileo to the Grand Duchess Christina

In 1616, after having published his findings and beliefs, he was forced by the church—which had originally supported his research—to promise that he would "not hold, teach, or defend" the heretical Copernican doctrines. After another publication, he was again hauled before a church court in 1633. The court found Galileo guilty

> *... of having believed and held the doctrine—which is false and contrary to the sacred and divine Scriptures—that the Sun is the center of the world and does not move from east to west and that the Earth moves and is not the center of the world; and that an opinion may be held and defended as probable after it has been declared and defined to be contrary to the Holy Scripture.*[2]

The court placed him under house arrest and effectively silenced him. After his death, he was denied burial in consecrated ground, but a century later his rehabilitation began with his reburial in holy ground and the church's permission for the publication of his works. Galileo's free pursuit of scientific truth being condemned by blind authority remained a sad episode in church history. In 1992, Pope John Paul II formally expressed his sadness at the treatment of Galileo.

By 1700, the heliocentric theory won common acceptance across Europe. The breaking down of old

▶ One of the great confrontations of *mythos* vs. *logos* came when Galileo was called before the inquisitional court of the Catholic Church, charged with possible heresy by contradicting church teachings on the nature of the universe. Galileo was found guilty, forced to deny his findings, and confined under what was essentially house arrest.

barriers of traditional authority in physiology, biology, chemistry, physics, geology, and the other sciences was made easier by the example of the astronomers. Although the struggle of *logos* over *mythos* has taken centuries, the battle continues in disputes over scientific questions such as the evolutionary development of species.

The Scientific Method

As it was developed in the seventeenth century, scientific research involved a combination of two approaches, each depending on reason, with differing applications. The *deductive* approach started with self-evident truths and moved toward complex propositions, which might be applied to practical problems. It emphasized logic and mathematical relationships. The *inductive* approach started with objective knowledge of the material world, from which proponents of induction sought to draw valid general conclusions. In the past, the two procedures had often been considered contradictory. Early European scientists were dependent on both kinds of reasoning.

René Descartes (ruh-NAY DAY-cart; 1596–1650), the French philosopher-mathematician, initiated a new critical mode of deduction. In his *Discourse on Method* (1627), Descartes rejected every accepted idea that could be doubted. He concluded that he could be certain of nothing except the facts that he was thinking and that he must, therefore, exist. From the basic proposition *"Cogito, ergo sum"* ("I think, therefore I am"), Descartes proceeded in logical steps to deduce the existence of God and the reality of both the spiritual and material worlds. He ultimately conceived of a unified and mathematically ordered universe that operated as a perfect mechanism. In Descartes's universe, supernatural processes were impossible; everything could be explained rationally, preferably in mathematical terms.

Descartes's method was furthered by discoveries in mathematics, and the method in turn popularized study of the subject. Descartes's work coincided with the first use of decimals and the compilation of logarithmic tables, which reduced, by half, the time required to solve intricate mathematical problems. Descartes himself developed analytical geometry, permitting relationships in space to be expressed in algebraic equations. Using such equations, astronomers could represent the movements of celestial bodies mathematically. Astronomers were further aided later in the century when Isaac Newton (1642–1727) in England and Gottfried Wilhelm Leibniz (LAIB-nitz; 1646–1716) in Germany independently perfected differential calculus, the mathematics of infinity, variables, and probabilities.

Another early contributor to the theory of scientific methodology was the Englishman Francis Bacon (1561–1626). He participated actively in both the tumultuous politics and intellectual debates of his time. Bacon entered Parliament after finishing his studies at Cambridge and had a successful political career, rising to the post of Lord Chancellor in 1618, before being forced to resign 1621 after admitting to accepting a bribe. At the same time, Bacon conceived of a system of thought that advocated the use of reason for interpreting human sensory experiences. His approach emphasized the use of systematically recorded facts derived from experiments to produce tentative hypotheses. When these were tested and verified by continued experiments, he believed they would ultimately reflect fundamental laws of nature. Bacon's ideas, outlined in his *Novum Organum* (1626), were the first definitive European statement of inductive principles.

The inductive approach became even more effective with the invention and perfection of scientific instruments. Both the telescope and the microscope came into use at the start of the seventeenth century. Other important inventions included the thermometer (1597), the barometer (1644), the air pump (1650), and the accurate pendulum clock (1657). With such tools, scientists were better able to study the physical world.

The Newtonian Universe

Great as the contributions of Galileo and Kepler were, their individual discoveries had not been united into one all-embracing principle that would describe the universe as a unit. Both Copernicus and Galileo—the first through mathematical speculation and the second through observation—had been dimly aware of a universal force in material nature. But the final proof was established later by Isaac Newton, who was born the year the English Civil War broke out, entered Cambridge at the time of the Restoration, and became a professor of mathematics at Cambridge University in the 1660s.

The notion of gravitation occurred to Newton in 1666, when he was only 24 and away from Cambridge because of a renewed outbreak of the plague. According to his later account, he was sitting in a contemplative mood under an apple tree when a falling apple roused him to wonder why it, and other objects, fell toward the center of the earth and not sideways or upward. A flash of insight suggested to him a drawing power in matter that was related to quantity and distance. In his *Principia* (1687)—the same year he defended the sovereign rights of Cambridge University against King James II—Newton expressed this idea precisely in a mathematical formula. The resulting law of gravitation states that all material objects attract other bodies inversely—according to the square of their distances, and directly—in proportion to the products of

Document

The Widening Scope of Scientific Discovery

In the two centuries after Copernicus advanced the heliocentric theory, European scientists laid the theoretical foundations for the study of physiology, astronomy, physics, chemistry, and biology.

- *Astronomy:* The astronomer-mathematician Pierre Laplace (1749–1827) demonstrated that apparent inconsistencies, such as comets, are also governed by mathematical laws and developed the nebular hypothesis, which maintains that our sun, once a gaseous mass, threw off the planets as it solidified and contracted.
- *Biology:* Antonie van Leeuwenhoek (1632–1723) discovered protozoa, bacteria, and human spermatozoa. Robert Hooke (1635–1703), an Englishman, described the cellular structure of plants.
- *Chemistry:* Robert Boyle (1627–1691) was the first to distinguish between chemical compounds and mixtures. On the basis of his many experiments, he devised a crude atomic theory, superseding the "four elements" and "four humors" of medieval alchemists and physicians. Boyle also investigated fire, respiration, fermentation, evaporation, and the rusting of metals. Joseph Priestley (1733–1804) isolated ammonia, discovered oxygen, and generated carbon monoxide. Along with the discovery of hydrogen (1766) by the Englishman Henry Cavendish (1731–1810), Priestley's work furnished an explanation of combustion. Antoine Lavoisier (1743–1794) proved that combustion is a chemical process involving the uniting of oxygen with the substances consumed. He also showed that respiration is another form of oxidation. Such discoveries led him to define the law of conservation: "Matter cannot be created or destroyed." Much of the credit for Lavoisier's scientific success should go to his wife, Marie-Anne (1758–1836), who assisted with all his major experiments, took notes, kept records, illustrated his books, and published her own papers. After he died on the guillotine during the French Revolution, she edited and published a compilation of his works.
- *Physics:* Galileo defined the law of falling bodies, demonstrating that their acceleration is constant, no matter what their weight or size. His experiments also revealed the law of inertia: a body at rest or in motion will remain at rest or continue moving (in a straight line at constant speed) unless affected by an external force. In addition, he showed that the path of a fired projectile follows a parabolic curve to earth, an inclination explained later by the law of gravitation. Galileo made additional notable discoveries through his studies of the pendulum, hydrostatics, and optics. His work was clarified by two professors at the University of Bologna, Maria Agnesi (1718–1799) in mathematics and Laura Bassi (1700–1778) in physics. Christiaan Huygens (1629–1695), along with Newton, developed a wave theory to explain light. Otto von Guericke (1602–1668) proved the material composition of air. His experiments showed that air could be weighed and that it could exert pressure, both properties in accordance with Newton's law.
- *Physiology:* Anatomist Andreas Vesalius (1514– 1564), in *On the Fabric of the Human Body* (1543), gave detailed drawings of the body. William Harvey (1578–1657) described the human circulatory system, tracing the flow of blood from the heart through the arteries, capillaries, and veins and back to the heart.

their masses. Hundreds of observations soon verified this principle and at the same time increased the credibility of scientific methods.

Newton had not only solved the astronomical problems defined by Kepler and Galileo but had also confirmed the necessity of combining the methods advocated by Descartes and Bacon. Although the *Principia* used mathematical proofs, these were tested by observation. Newton insisted that final conclusions must rest on solid facts; he further contended that any hypothesis, no matter how mathematically plausible, must be abandoned if not borne out by observation or experimentation.

Newton also confirmed the basic premise of modern science that all nature is governed by laws. Indeed, his own major law was applicable to the whole universe, from a speck of dust on earth to the largest star in outer space. The magnitude of this idea—the concept of universal laws—was exciting and contagious. He presented this vision as an explanation of how God worked:

> *The Deity ... endures for ever and is everywhere present, and by existing always and everywhere. He constitutes duration and space.... (He) governs all things and knows all things that are, and can be done ... Who, being in all places, is more able by His will to move the bodies within His boundless uniform sensorium, and thereby to form and reform the parts of the Universe, then we are by our will to move the parts of our body.*[3]

Within decades, his universal principles had spread throughout the Western world and had been applied in every area.

The Popularity of Science

Science, long suspect among the leaders of society and particularly the church in the sixteenth and early seventeenth centuries, had become widely accepted by 1700. Scientists were now invited to the best salons, and scientific academies gained public support as they sprang up all over Europe. The most famous were the Royal Society of London, chartered in 1662, and the French Academy of Science, founded in 1664. Most academies published journals that circulated widely. Scientists and would-be scientists carried on voluminous correspondence, developing a cosmopolitan community with its own language, values, and common beliefs.

Rising enthusiasm on the public fringes of the scientific community was matched by a fervor among national monarchs as well as hundreds of other nobles, wealthy merchants, and progressive craftsmen. Support for academies was merely one form of public endorsement. Kings endowed observatories, cities founded museums, well-to-do women helped establish botanical gardens, and learned societies sponsored well-attended lectures. Scientists became respected heroes, a stunning change in a relative short time. Giordano Bruno (gi-or-DAN-oh BRU-noh), the Italian philosopher-scientist, was burned for heresy in 1600 by the Inquisition, and Galileo was hounded by persecutors through his most productive years, but at the end of the century, Newton received a well-paying government position. He was lionized and knighted during his lifetime, and when he died in 1727, he was buried at Westminster Abbey.

The Age of Reason and the *Ancien Régime*

Why were Europe's rulers threatened by the test of reason?

On the same boat that carried Princess Mary of Holland to England in February 1689 after the Glorious Revolution (see Chapter 17), a more modest person also traveled. In his bags, John Locke carried the manuscripts of two works that he had written during his 6 years in exile in Amsterdam. Born in 1632, Locke, as a youth, had lived through all of the turmoil of the English civil war. His father was an ardent Puritan, a notary who served as a captain in the army that defended Parliament. At Oxford, Locke was interested for a while in all of the arguments of the Cromwell years, but he soon tired of the constant disputes and welcomed the calm of the Restoration. Deeply affected by the works of Descartes, he continued his studies in medicine and the development of his own philosophy.

He began to work with Lord Ashley, the count of Shaftesbury, whose unsuccessful plots against the Stuarts forced him to seek exile in Holland—the place of refuge for all Europe—and Locke went with him. Amsterdam was the center of European thought in those days, made more intellectually alive by the influx of French Huguenots, Jews, Bohemian refugees, and others. Locke pursued his studies there in an atmosphere that was violently against the Catholic Church and absolutism. He became close to William of Orange, the leader of the Dutch, and gave him a copy of a work justifying the revolt of Parliament. This work was finally published in 1690 as the *Second Treatise on Civil Government.* Its goals were to destroy absolute monarchy and to refute the theory of divine right.

Locke's *Second Treatise* supported the new English political system by grounding it on the natural laws of psychology, economics, and politics. This justification of the Glorious Revolution of 1688 became the clarion call and rationale for every revolution for the next three centuries. In passing from his studies of Descartes, medicine, and the natural world to espousing the right of revolution in the Western world—based on natural law, Locke charted the transition from the Scientific Revolution to the Enlightenment and bridged the gulfs between scientists, intellectuals, and the literate population of early modern Europe. He wrote for a more general audience, and his ideas came to be known from the Ural Mountains of Russia to the farthest tip of South America. He symbolized the age of new ideas, and it is his words, flowing through Thomas Jefferson's pen, that inspired the American Declaration of Independence of 1776.

The Age of Reason: English and Dutch Phases

In the seventeenth and eighteenth centuries, most Western thinkers understood that they lived in a new age, one that historians later called the Age of Reason. These thinkers did not have a monolithic approach to the world; rather, they reflected the particular conditions of each country in which they lived. But their principles were based on Newtonian science that dominated thinking at the start of the eighteenth century. They sought to create a science of man that would solve human problems, just as other sciences were beginning to reveal secrets of nature. At first the movement was confined to scholars, theologians, and conservative men of affairs, who opposed any threat to existing institutions. But after about 1760, as new ideas were conceived and spread in print among the middle classes, the movement generated a more radical version that logically supported the need for social and political change.

The most fundamental concepts of the Enlightenment, held by its conservative and radical proponents alike, were faith in nature and belief in human progress. Nature was seen as a complex of interacting laws governing the universe. The individual human being, as part of that system, was designed to act rationally. If free to think, the doctrine assumed, people would naturally seek happiness for themselves; reason would show them that this goal could best be attained through the well-being of others. Accordingly, both human virtue and happiness required freedom from needless restraints, including many imposed by the state and the church. Enlightenment thinkers also passionately believed in education as the path toward future improvement. Indeed, they thought society could become perfect if people were given opportunities to make free use their powers of reason.

At the beginning of the eighteenth century, a secret society including the intellectual and business elites of England, called the Masonic movement, began organizing and pleading the cause of English limited monarchy on the Continent, where France was a major rival and a wartime enemy until 1713. In Amsterdam, the Masons collaborated with French Huguenots, who themselves had fled France after Louis XIV revoked the Edict of Nantes in 1685. This latter group included Pierre Bayle (1647–1706), the French skeptic. Both French and English intellectuals fell under the influence of Baruch Spinoza (spin-O-tsah; 1632–1677), the greatest Dutch philosopher, who had been excommunicated from his Jewish community for his ideas. Spinoza, an initial follower of Descartes, taught that God exists in all of nature and in the farthest reaches of the universe: this is the underlying foundation of **Pantheism** ("All God"). The ideas of Spinoza were later used by the Anglo-Irish freethinker John Toland (1670–1722) and others to develop arguments against both state churches and the monarchies that supported them. His ideas spread slowly over the Continent via an underground press, financed by radical Dutch **Huguenots** and many antiestablishment Masonic lodges.

Spinoza's ideas complemented the most popular religious belief among participants in the Enlightenment: **Deism.** This belief involved a clear break with traditional Christianity, although most Deists accepted Jesus Christ as a great moral teacher. Deists believed in God as an impersonal force, the "master clockwinder" of the universe. Although some accepted the idea of an afterlife, Deists attached no significance to emotional faith as a means to salvation. They based all moral reliance on the individual's reason and conscience. Their common convictions also included rejection of miracles, disbelief in Christ's divinity or his virgin birth, and direct communion with God without need for church or clergy. Nature was the Deists' church, and nature's laws were their Bible. Their number included John Toland, Thomas Woolston (1679–1731), and Thomas Paine in England; Voltaire, Diderot, and d'Alembert in France; and Thomas Jefferson, Ethan Allen (1738–1789), and Elihu Palmer (1764–1806) in the English American colonies.

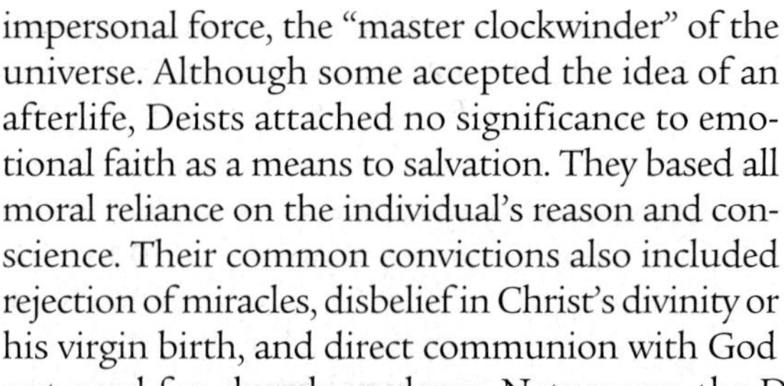

CASE STUDY

The Conflict Between Science and Religion

Rationalist leaders of the Enlightenment on both sides of the English Channel were in almost perfect agreement on one point: they championed religious freedom of conscience. In addition, most were participants in a continuing struggle against alleged abuses of organized religion. Hundreds of their writings, especially those of Voltaire and other French intellectuals, depicted churches and priests as part of a vast conspiracy aimed at perpetuating tyranny. Their crusade for separating church and state was thus particularly threatening to absolutism.

The French *Philosophes* and the Radical Enlightenment

The Enlightenment remained largely moderate as it permeated French high society. Its leading proponents were known as ***philosophes*** (fil-o-SOFS), although the term cannot be literally translated into English as "philosophers." The *philosophes* were mostly writers and intellectuals who analyzed the evils of society and sought reforms in existing institutions in accordance with the principles of right reason. Their most supportive allies were ***salonières*** (sa-lo-nee-AIRS), socially conscious and learned women such as the Marquise du Châtelet (shat-e-LAY; 1706–1749), Voltaire's mistress, who translated Newton, and Madame de Tencin (tan-SEN), whose son, Jean d'Alembert (ZHAN da-lem-BEHR; 1717–1783), was assistant editor of Diderot's *Encyclopédie.* The *salonières* regularly entertained *philosophes* in their salons, at the same time sponsoring their literary works, artistic creations, and new political ideas. By mid-century, the *salonières,* their salons, and the *philosophes* had made France once again the intellectual center of Europe.

One of the leading lights among the *philosophes* was the Baron de Montesquieu (mon-tes-KEU; 1689–1755),

Pantheism—The belief that an impersonal God is manifest in all things throughout the universe, which is governed by immutable natural laws.

Huguenots—French Protestants, many of whom fled persecution in Catholic France and resettled in England and Holland. Their views on the social contract for government influenced Enlightenment thinkers such as Locke and Rousseau.

Deism—The belief that views God as an impersonal force that created the universe and the natural laws that govern it (see also Pantheism). Deists do not believe in the supernatural or miraculous and hold reason and conscience to be the foundation of morality, not emotional faith.

philosophes—Literally, "philosophers"; writers and intellectuals in eighteenth-century France who used reason to question the political and social conditions of their time.

salonières—A group of educated, aristocratic women in eighteenth-century France who supported and sponsored Enlightenment and its leading thinkers.

a judicial official as well as a titled nobleman from near Bordeaux. Montesquieu was among the earliest critics of absolutist society. His *Persian Letters* (1721), purportedly from an Oriental traveler describing irrational European religious customs and behavior, delighted a large reading audience. Montesquieu was somewhat skeptical about the perfectibility of man through reason and he advocated the separation of powers among the executive, legislative, and judicial branches of government in his *Spirit of the Laws* (1748). He understood that a system of checks and balances would safeguard liberty by limiting the blind ambition of unreasonable people.

The bourgeois François-Marie Arouet (ar-ou-EH), better known as Voltaire (1694–1778), personified the skepticism of his century toward traditional religion and the injustices of the ***ancien régime.*** His caustic sense of humor and brilliantly written satires kept him in continuous trouble with the authorities for most of his life—including spending 11 months in the Bastille in Paris in 1717–1718. He did not change his tone, or his attitude, and he managed to anger a French noble in 1725, resulting in his exile in England from 1726 to 1729. While there, he studied Locke's writings and Newtonian science—and also developed an admiration for the English system of government. He turned out hundreds of histories, plays, pamphlets, essays, and novels, as well as an estimated correspondence of 10,000 letters, including many to Frederick the Great of Prussia and Catherine the Great of Russia. Always, he employed his wry wit in crusading for rationalism and reform of abuses. He remained a controversial figure to the end of his days, and in 1758 he built a house at Ferney on the border between Geneva and France so that he could slip into exile from one country to the other, depending on who was angry with him. Nothing more indicates the major change in opinion during the eighteenth century than that Voltaire passed from being imprisoned for his ideas and wit in his youth to becoming a major French and European celebrity as an old man.

ancien régime—Literally "old regime"; the political governing structure in Europe before the French Revolution and the reforms of the nineteenth century. Its characteristics included the divine right of monarchs and the placement of nobles and clergy above commoners.

Voltaire had many disciples, imitators, and critics among the *philosophes,* but his only rival in successfully spreading the Enlightenment was a set of books, the French *Encyclopédie,* edited by Denis Diderot (1713–1784). Begun in 1751 and completed in 1772, it contained 28 volumes and more than 70,000 articles on every conceivable subject, many of which emphasized the supremacy of the new science, decried superstition, expounded the merits of human freedom, exposed the evils of the slave trade, and denounced unfair taxes. It featured thousands of treatises on practical subjects dealing with agriculture, industry, and medicine, as well as others on art, architecture, literature, and philosophy. Authors included tradesmen and mechanics, along with professors and scientists. Such new information from the Enlightenment was a database easily used against authorities by popular journalists, who appealed first to an

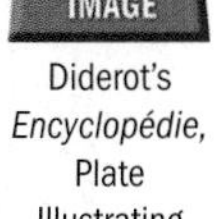

Diderot's *Encyclopédie,* Plate Illustrating Agriculture

◄ The Scottish and English may well have established the basic positions of the Enlightenment, but it was the Frenchman François-Marie Arouet, better known as Voltaire, who, by way of his travels and writings, spread the ideas of living in a world of reason throughout Europe.

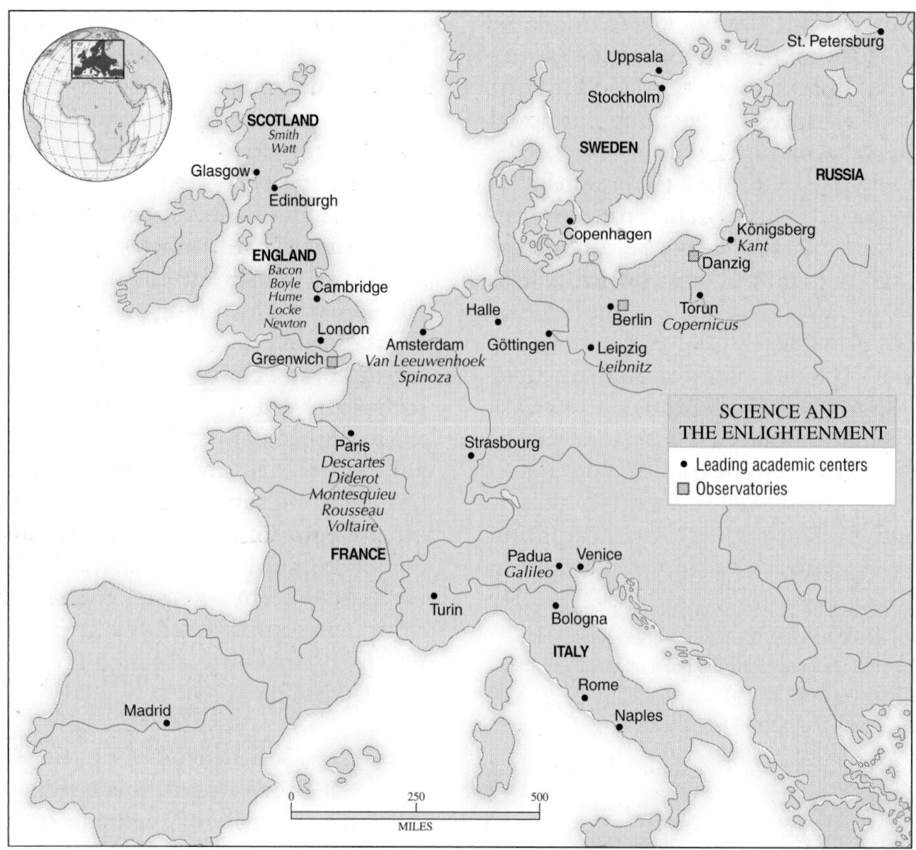

▲ Scientific advances and Enlightenment contributions came from all parts of Europe, from Königsburg in East Prussia to Glasgow in Scotland.

alienated middle class and later, in the 1780s, to an awakening world of cafés, workshops, and city streets, particularly in Paris.

Perhaps the best known *philosophe* and the forerunner of many later radicals was that eccentric proponent of Romantic rebellion, Jean-Jacques Rousseau (roos-SOH; 1712–1778). Although he believed in the general objectives of the Enlightenment, Rousseau distrusted reason and science. He gloried in human impulse and intuition, trusting emotions rather than thought, the heart rather than the mind. This emphasis was also true of his social criticism. His early rejections by polite society encouraged both contempt for old regimes and professed admiration for "noble savages," who lived completely free of law, courts, priests, and officials. In his numerous writings, Rousseau spoke passionately as a rebel against all established institutions. The most famous of his works, *The Social Contract* (1762), protested against corrupt governments. It began with the stirring manifesto: "Man is born free, but today he is everywhere in chains." In short, human beings are born with inalienable rights and the ideal state, based on contract, exists as a guarantor and protector of those rights, and not the destroyer of them—as was the case with the Old Regime.

Enlightenment Thought and Women

Few Enlightenment thinkers, however, said "woman is born free." In fact, the Enlightenment thinkers disagreed on the place of women in the natural order of things. Although a few of them advocated extending the doctrine to include females, such voices were in the minority. Nevertheless, some women, even before the issue was raised forcefully during the French Revolution, staked their claims under the widely acclaimed laws of nature.

Although she was a monarchist and a follower of Descartes rather than Locke, Mary Astell (1666–1731) claimed legal equality for women on the basis of their innate rationality in her *Serious Proposal to the Ladies* (1694). This clarion call was not repeated for decades, but its echoes were manifest in the writings of English women such as Mary Montague (mon-ta-GEU; 1689–1762), Catherine Macaulay (1731–1791), and Mary Wollstonecraft (1759–1797) during the eighteenth century. In France a number of *saloniėres,* including Madame de Puisseux (PWEE-zeuh; 1720–1798) and Madame Gaçon-Dufour (1753–1835), wrote books defending their sex. Outside the salons, between 1761 and 1775, the *Journal des Dames,* a magazine edited by women, preached freedom, progress, and women's rights.

Before the French Revolution, the question of women's status in society did not concern many leading philosophers. Rousseau represented most of them when he described the ideal woman's proper role as housekeeper, mother, and quiet comforter of her husband, who was responsible for her protection and moral instruction. A few thinkers disagreed. Both Hobbes and Locke mildly questioned the idea that women were naturally subordinate to men. D'Alembert thought female limitations resulted from women's degradation by society, and Montesquieu saw absolute monarchy as the cause for women's lack of status. But the Marquis de Condorcet (mar-KEE duh-kon-dor-SAY; 1743–1794) was the only *philosophe* who made a special plea for feminine equality. In his *Letter of a Bourgeois of New Haven* (1787), he claimed that women's rationality entitled them to full citizenship, including the right to vote and hold public office. For the most part, however, his voice went unheard.

The Economic Critique of the *Ancien Régime:* The Physiocrats and Adam Smith

Natural law, a basic concept of the Enlightenment, was applied most consistently and effectively in economic arguments against absolutism. The **physiocrats** (fee-zee-oh-KRATS), a group of economic thinkers in eighteenth-century France made effective critiques of mercantilism. Their leading spokesman was François Quesnay (kuh-NAY; 1694–1774), the personal physician to Louis XV, who also wrote for the *Encyclopédie.* Originally, Quesnay and his followers opposed the comptroller of finance Jean-Baptiste Colbert's (KOL-bair) policy of subordinating agriculture to government-controlled industry. This narrow emphasis later developed into a comprehensive theory based on natural law. Quesnay, for example, compared the circulation of money to the circulation of blood. He likened mercantilist controls to tourniquets, which shut off a life-giving flow. Quesnay also denounced the mercantilist theory of bullionism, arguing that prosperity depended on production, not gold and silver in the royal treasury. According to another physiocrat, Robert Turgot (tur-GOH; 1720–1781), selfish profit-seeking in a free market would necessarily result in the best service and the most goods for society.

The most influential advocate of the new economic theory was a leader in the Scottish Enlightenment, Adam Smith, a professor of moral philosophy at Glasgow University, who had visited France and exchanged ideas with the physiocrats. In 1776, Smith published *An Inquiry into the Nature and Causes of the Wealth of Nations,* in which he set forth his ideas. The work has since become the Bible of classical economic liberalism and capitalism, extolling the doctrine of free enterprise or **laissez-faire** (lay-SAY fehr) economics.

Smith was indebted to the physiocrats for his views on personal liberty, natural law, and the role of the state as a mere "passive policeman." He argued that increased production depended largely on division of labor and specialization. Because trade increased specialization, it also increased production. The growing volume of trade, in turn, depended on each person's being free to pursue individual self-interest. In seeking private gain, each individual was also guided by an "invisible hand," also known as the law of supply and demand, in meeting society's needs. As he wrote:

> *It is not from the benevolence of the butcher, the brewer, or the baker that we expect our dinner, but from their reward to their own interests. We address ourselves not to their humanity, but to their self-love.*

Smith regarded all economic controls, by the state or by guilds and trade unions, as injurious to trade. He scoffed at the mercantilist idea that the wealth of a nation depended on achieving a surplus of exports, amassing bullion, and crippling the economies of other countries. In Smith's view, trade should work to the benefit of all nations, which would follow if trade were free. In such a natural and free economic world, the prosperity of each nation would depend on the prosperity of all. He also saw colonies as potential economic drains on a colonial power.

The Political Critique of the Old Regime

Although proponents of the moderate Enlightenment were not revolutionaries, and most favored monarchy and an aristocratic social order, they were avid reformers. In this role, they developed a tightly organized philosophy, purportedly based on scientific principles and contradicting every argument for absolute monarchy as it generally existed in the eighteenth century. The case against absolutism, as presented by the *philosophes* and their foreign sympathizers, condemned divine right monarchy, hereditary aristocracies by birth, state churches, and mercantilism. Each was found to be irrational, unnatural, and therefore basically unsound.

---

physiocrats—A group of economic thinkers in eighteenth-century France who critiqued mercantilism.

laissez-faire—Literally "leave it alone," the economic doctrine of free enterprise and open markets advocating nonintervention by the state, more commonly, "hands off."

The thinkers in the Enlightenment saw the arbitrary policies of absolute monarchs as violations of innate rights, which are required by human nature. The best government, therefore, was the government that ruled least. This argument for human freedom was the heart of the anti-absolutist case.

According to Locke and most political theorists of the Enlightenment, government existed to maintain order, protect property, defend against foreign enemies, and protect the natural rights of its people. This idea contradicted the divine right theory, which was held by most reigning monarchs in the seventeenth and eighteenth centuries. Locke, along with many other Enlightenment thinkers including Rousseau, answered the divine right doctrine with the opposing theory of a social contract.

Locke agreed with Hobbes that the base of power was the people. But instead of seeing people as nasty and brutish, Locke saw that an existence in a free and equal society would bring out the best in human beings, as long as their property was defended and they lived in a state of reason. Locke asserted that people voluntarily came together to form governments for the protection of their basic rights, and it was the consent of the people—and that alone—that gave legitimacy to a government.

He did not invent the concept of the social contract—the Huguenots in France had discussed it a century earlier. Hobbes had used the contract idea to justify royal authority. Locke turned Hobbes's argument around in his *Second Treatise on Government,* contending that political systems were originally formed by individuals for defense of their natural rights to life, freedom, and property, against local or foreign enemies. Such individuals voluntarily ceded to government the responsibility for protecting their natural rights. In this transaction, government's authority was derived from the governed. The state was not absolute but was limited to performing the functions for which it was constituted. When its authority was used for other purposes, the contract was broken and the people had the right to overthrow it and form another government.

New Artistic Movements

The same cultural ferment that fueled the Enlightenment also drove new artistic movements. The first of these, the Baroque movement, continued the trend

▼ Vienna's Schönbrunn palace was remodeled in the Rococo style in 1749.

away from classical representations begun by Mannerism (see Chapter 14), and remained the dominant aesthetic movement throughout the eighteenth century. In Baroque art, it was not enough to simply portray an idea or a theme. Detail was juxtaposed on detail in such profusion as to create a passionate impact on the viewer. No better example can be found than that of Bernini's *The Ecstacy of St. Teresa*. The fountains Bernini created in Rome seem to flow, even without water. If Classic art was all about measure and perspective and definition; Baroque art was about emotion, uncontrolled emotion. Perhaps the best portrayal of such emotion can been experienced in Caravaggio's *The Beheading of St. John the Baptist*.

The Baroque movement had a significant impact on architecture across Europe, from its origins in Rome to Dresden, Germany (now restored to its pre–World War II glory), to the building of St. Petersburg in Russia where the tsars and tsarinas of the eighteenth century spent fortunes building Baroque palaces to impress Europe, to St. Paul's in London, and everywhere that Catholic missionaries went in the New World. Portuguese Baroque churches are especially common in Brazil. Musicians writing for the churches of the time, such as J. S. Bach in Germany and George Friedrich Handel in England, represent the high point of Baroque music.

In eighteenth-century France and Germany, variations on the Baroque movement appeared, the *Rococo* movement. In its essence, Rococo stylists sought to continue go to extremes to achieve an effect, but with more joy and frothiness. Colors tended to be lighter, themes were less monumental, and the gaiety of life in the last phase of the *ancien régime* set the standards to be followed. In architecture, Rococo influence may be found in churches in Spain, parts of the Palace at Versailles, the church at Sanssouci (the French word means "carefree," a nice Rococo touch) in Germany, and the Schönbrunn palace remodeled in the Rococo style in 1749 in Vienna.

At the end of the eighteenth century, a massive reaction to two centuries of the emotionalism of Baroque and Rococo began: *Neoclassicism*. In a back to the basics move, Neoclassic painters, sculptors, architects, and musician stripped away the excess color, exaggerated themes, and exhibitionism of the earlier movements to imitate what was perceived to be Roman and Greek art. Between 1760 and 1830, European taste underwent a major change, as can be seen in the paintings of the French artist Jacque-Louis David, the changes Tsarina Catherine II imposed on her summer palace, and in the construction of the church of the Madeleine in Paris. In music, a *Classical* movement began earlier in the eighteenth century. As with the other arts, this music was tied closely to the absolutist rulers and the royal courts of the time. Probably the most outstanding classical composers were Joseph Haydn, followed by Wolfgang Amadeus Mozart. Both men worked for the nobility and the church, two pillars of the *ancien régime* that would soon come crashing down.

The Failure of Monarchical Reform

Why were the "enlightened" despots unable to implement reforms that matched their philosophical ideals?

As old regimes faltered after the middle of the eighteenth century, an urgent need to respond to the problems of the day challenged the rulers of major European states. Neither the nobles nor the clergy, despite their high social status and political power, could provide the necessary leadership because they were committed to protecting their privileges, particularly immunity from taxation, which threatened the financial security of most countries. Responding to the literature of the Enlightenment, action by the "enlightened despots" did bring some curtailment of mercantilism, peasant exploitation, and government repression and seemed to offer a belated "best hope" for solving the problem. Events soon outran them, however, and this hope proved to be inadequate.

Frederick of Prussia

Perhaps the major figure in this "monarch's age of repentance" was Frederick II of Prussia, known as "the Great," who became a model ruler during the second half of his reign. An avowed admirer of Voltaire, Frederick, in his writings, popularized the ideal monarch as the "first servant of the state," the "father of his people," and the "last refuge of the unfortunate."[4] "Old Fritz," as his subjects called him, was slavishly committed to his principles. He left his bed at five each morning and worked until dark, reading reports, supervising, traveling, listening to complaints, and watching every aspect of government.

Under Frederick, Prussia was considered the best-governed state in Europe. Within only a few years, it recovered economically from the terrible ravages of war, largely through the state's aid in distributing seed, livestock, and tools. Frederick lessened the burdens of serfs on crown estates, imported new crops, attracted skilled immigrants, opened new lands, and tried to promote new industries, such as silk and other textiles. He codified the law and reorganized the courts, along with the civil service. Following ideas he had learned from French philosophy, he established civil equality for Catholics, abolished torture in obtaining confessions from criminals, decreed national compulsory education, and took control of the schools away from

▲ Even though Catherine II spoke of governing Russia in accordance with Enlightenment principles, the condition of the Russian peasant reached its lowest point during her reign.

the church. Until he died in 1786, Frederick worked diligently at improving Prussia.

Catherine II of Russia

Frederick's contemporary, Catherine II of Russia, was also known in her time as an enlightened despot and as "the Great." Having learned the politics of survival at the Russian court, she had conspired with palace guards to kill her erratic husband, Peter, and have herself declared tsarina in 1762. She was a ruthless Machiavellian in foreign affairs, with far more lovers than many male monarchs could boast. She also was a sensitive woman who appreciated the arts, literature, and the advantages of being considered enlightened. She corresponded with Voltaire and gave Diderot a pension. The latter even stayed at her court for a year, meeting with her daily for private discussions on intellectual subjects, including how to improve her empire.

Catherine the Great's Constitution

Catherine's reign brought considerable enlightenment and social progress to the elites of St. Petersburg society. She subsidized artists and writers, permitted publication of controversial works, established libraries, patronized galleries, and transformed the capital city with beautiful architecture. Catherine also founded hospitals and orphanages, notably those providing foundling children with improved education, one of her main interests. During the decade after 1775, she tried to start a national system of elementary and secondary schools. In that same year she began a reorganization of local government, including the cities, one of many administrative reforms that literally demilitarized civil administration in the empire by turning it over to her partners in assassination, the nobility. She secularized church land, restricted the use of torture, and won acclaim for her much publicized orders to a royal commission charged with modernizing and codifying Russian laws.

Detail of Catherine's Palace in Pushkin

Catherine's program, however, was limited in scope and significance. Almost every reform had been attempted or suggested earlier and enhanced royal authority. For example, rigid state control and political indoctrination of the curriculum were fixed in the new educational system. Local government after 1775 was controlled by aristocratic landowners, while aristocrats in the commission sabotaged the much heralded legal reforms for the general population. Such deference to the aristocracy was typical of Catherine's later internal policies following the disastrous peasant revolts of the 1770s. The nobles' hysteria forced her to issue a charter giving them freedom from taxes, release from compulsory government service, and guaranteed ownership of their serfs. The reaction thus begun was continued during the French Revolution, when Catherine reversed most of her earlier stated liberal opinions and imposed severe censorship. She even placed the statue of Voltaire, once in a place of honor, in the basement of the Tauride Palace in St. Petersburg. Her political legacy was a rigid autocracy, based on support from an aristocratic elite infected by Western liberal ideals.

Joseph of Austria

The most radical of the would-be benevolent despots was Joseph II (1780–1790), the son of Maria Theresa and her successor as Habsburg ruler of Austria. He was intelligent and well educated; indeed, Catherine considered him to be one of the reform leaders of her generation. He was also completely converted to the principles of the new philosophers. "I have made philosophy the legislator of my empire," he wrote to a friend in 1781, shortly after his accession.[5] During his whole reign, he fancied himself a royal voice of reason, fighting for human progress against ignorance, superstition, and vice.

Joseph's reign was an explosion of reform effort that threatened to destroy much of the old aristocratic Habsburg structure. He proposed to simplify Catholic services, abolish the monasteries, take over church lands, remove religion from education, and grant civil equality to Protestants and Jews. Attacking the ancient landed establishment head on, he planned to tax the nobles, abolish entail of their lands, and free the serfs. With increasing revenues, he hoped to finance national education, balance the budget, and improve opportunities for industry and trade. The whole undertaking would be consolidated and regulated under a comprehensive code of laws.

Despite their theoretical benefits, Joseph's endeavors aroused a storm of protest, lasting through the reign and bringing him practical failure. For all of his interest in progress, Joseph was a hardheaded and narrow-minded autocrat, determined to build a state on an Enlightenment model. His administrative reforms were aimed not only at higher efficiency but also at centralized government over all the multinational Habsburg territories. His attempted unification of administration seriously alienated the Hungarians and provoked revolts in the Low Countries, Bohemia, and the Tyrol. Peasants were angry because he subjected them to compulsory military service, the clergy harangued against him, and the nobles conspired to hinder the conduct of government at every level. He died in 1790, painfully aware of his unfulfilled ideals.

The French Revolution: The Domestic Phase, 1789–1799

What group played a crucial role in bringing down the ancien régime *in France?*

The last Bourbon kings in France before the Revolution, Louis XV and Louis XVI (1774–1792), did not belong in the category of enlightened despots. They responded halfheartedly to the reforming ideas discussed in the salons of Paris. Although he was almost indifferent to affairs of state and dozed through his council meetings, Louis XV oversaw the abolition of serfdom on royal lands,

MAP France, Revolution, and Europe: 1789–1815

Seeing Connections

Benjamin Franklin in Paris

Benjamin Franklin best symbolizes the connections between the Scientific Revolution, the Enlightenment, and the political revolutions of the last third of the eighteenth century. As a younger man, Franklin was a voracious reader of the works of the leading European intellectual figures of the seventeenth and eighteen centuries. His own scientific inquiries into such areas as electricity would, in his later years, earn him great prestige in Europe. During the American War of Independence, revolutionary leaders understood well that Franklin's fame for his scientific work was a great asset, and so sent him as their representative to the court of Louis XVI to seek an alliance against the British, which was signed in 1778. For the French court, Franklin was the combined Natural Man and scientific investigator. When he arrived wearing a raccoon-skin hat on his head, he was an instant success—in many ways. He cut a wide swath through French society, proposing marriage at least once, and took full advantage of the French fascination with his American-ness. He once wrote to a friend that he arrived at the French court "very plainly dressed, wearing my thin gray straight hair that peeps out under my only coiffure, a fine fur hat which comes down to my forehead almost to my spectacles. Think how this must appear among the powdered heads of Paris."[1]

[1]http://library.thinkquest.org/22254/biopenn1.htm.

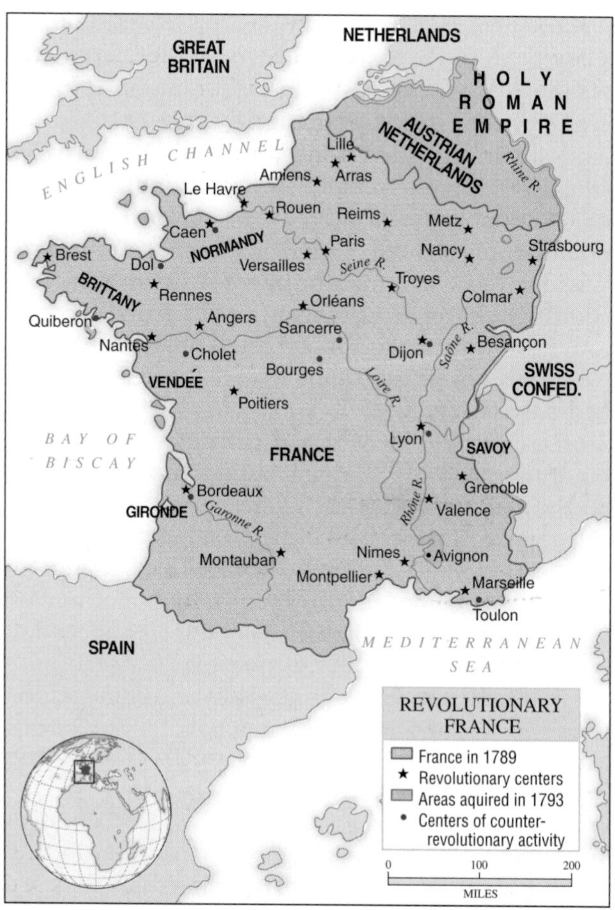

France, the model of an absolutist state and the foremost model of an "old regime," shocked and then threatened its neighbors with its thoroughgoing Revolution in the 5 years after 1789.

tried twice to tax the nobles, and attempted to curtail the special privileges of the traditional courts, particularly the most aristocratic *parlement* (par-le-MON) court of Paris. Each attempt led to years of controversy between the government and the nobles, who were part of a European-wide aristocratic effort to regain powers lost during the rise of absolutism. In each instance, Louis ultimately gave up the fight.

Louis XVI, who succeeded his grandfather in 1774, was well-meaning but poorly educated, lazy, and shy. Avoiding government business as much as he could, he spent his happiest hours in a workshop tinkering with locks or out hunting. His child bride, the frivolous Habsburg princess Marie Antoinette, furnished him with no wisdom or practical support. Although dimly aware of problems, Louis was no more successful than his grandfather. The clamor of the nobles forced him to abandon proposals for eliminating the more undeserved pensions and levying a very modest tax on all landed property to deal with France's fiscal problems. He managed in one way or another to alienate most of his subjects through his indecision and bad political judgment.

Versailles and the Estates-General: May–June 1789

Between Louis's succession in 1774 and 1789, his finance ministers faced continuously rising national deficits. The debt ultimately reached an equivalent of $6 billion (in 2006 dollars), with interest payments absorbing half of annual revenues. French financial support of the American revolutionary wars against the English brought diplomatic success, but added to the financial problems.

Because loans from abroad to cover shortfalls were becoming almost impossible to gain, the government once again in 1787 and 1788 sought help from Assemblies of Notables (prominent nobles and high churchmen). But the nobles refused to give gifts or pay taxes without audits of royal accounts and other fiscal reforms. Louis then forced the courts (*parlements*) to register new laws authorizing more taxes and loans, to little effect. The domestic crisis was intensified by poor harvests caused by spring floods in 1788, followed by devastating hailstorms in July 1788 that destroyed the second planting of grain. France endured the second coldest winter of the century in 1788–1789. Merchants holding stocks of grain drove the price of bread up to the highest level in 75 years. By the spring of 1789, the country was seething with unrest, and the government was out of money once again.

With no other recourse, Louis now bowed to the Notables and agreed to call the **Estates-General,** the nation's medieval representative assembly, which had not met since 1614. The Notables saw the Estates-General meeting as a way to gain more rights from the king in return for their support in ending the financial crisis. By blindly pursuing their narrow interests before 1789 and not helping the king, the nobles lit the fuse leading to the revolutionary explosion that destroyed their millennium-old position of superiority in French society.

During the spring of 1789, amid feverish excitement but little open hostility among the estates, electors of each order—the clergy (the First Estate); the nobles, a diverse group of which perhaps 5 percent were in the truly ancient families (the Second Estate); and the commoners (the Third Estate)—met in local

Estates-General—France's medieval representative assembly, consisting of the First Estate (the clergy), the Second Estate (the nobles), and the Third Estate (the commoners).

assemblies across the country to select representatives. A few women participated among the clergy and nobles, but the 4.3 million electors in the Third Estate were all males, aged 25 or older, who paid the head tax. Nevertheless, they included peasants, urban craftsmen, merchants, and professionals, comprising a much larger number of voters than those being able to vote in Britain.

After the delegates were elected, they compiled lists of reform proposals, the *cahiers* (kai-YEAS). The Third Estate requested a national legislature, a jury system, freedom of the press, and equitable taxes; there was no mention of overthrowing the monarchy or eliminating the aristocracy. The delegates themselves were not revolutionaries—most were moderate reformers. Of the more than 1100 delegates in the three orders, about 90 of 285 nobles were more or less sympathetic to the views of the Third Estate and 205 of 308 clergy were from nonnoble families. The 621 members of the Third Estate included 380 lawyers, 85 businessmen, and 64 landowners.

Once the Estates-General convened on May 5 at Versailles, the economic question—the issue that had led the king to call the Estates-General—was instantly forgotten. The Third Estate imposed its will on the Estates-General by insisting that voting should be by head rather than by chamber—which had traditionally been the case—because it had more members than the other two estates combined. Voting by head had already been adopted in some regional assemblies, and the principle had been requested in a large majority of the *cahiers.* This demand blocked all debate. During weeks of wrangling on this issue, some members of the clergy joined the Third Estate.

On June 17, the Third Estate declared itself the duly elected national legislature and invited members of the other estates to attend its sessions. Two days later, most of the clergy voted to accept the invitation. Then, on June 20, when members found their meeting hall closed, ostensibly to prepare for the king's upcoming address, delegates of the Third Estate moved a half-mile to an indoor tennis court (*jeu de paume;* zhu de POM-e), where they solemnly swore not to disband until they had produced a French constitution. Later, after defying a royal order to reconvene separately, they declared themselves the National Constituent Assembly of France—a group legally elected to write a constitution. The king grudgingly accepted their decision.

At this point the delegates had declared—and won—a revolution in principle. France would be placed on a constitutional basis. But the Third Estate's full understanding of the process they had set in motion,

▼ Locked out of their meeting hall on the king's orders, aroused delegates to the Estates-General, primarily members of the Third Estate, convened at a nearby indoor tennis court, where they swore the historic "Tennis Court Oath." The painting is by Jacque-Louis David.

their program, or the forces they had unleashed would develop only with time. Few members among the middle-class majority were merchants seeking free trade. Many were landowners, officeholders, or judges; many others were disappointed at not yet becoming nobles. Liberal aristocrats were willing to give up some privileges, including their manorial fees and tax immunities, in return for enlightened reforms that would improve the administration of government.

Die-hard support for the old regime was concentrated primarily among the relatively impoverished local "nobles of the sword" and the traditional peasants from remote communities. Sensing what was to come, however, there were many other nobles who chose to leave France, to become émigrés.

Suffering and Explosion in Paris and the Provinces: July–August 1789

Another factor, however, was already exerting its powerful influence. Economic depression in the late 1780s, particularly rising bread prices in the cities, prompted unrest and violence among more than 20 million French workers and peasants. This unfocused force of frustration and violence would, for the next 5 years, constantly overwhelm the plans and goals of the various governments' leaders.

Although accepting the National Constituent Assembly on June 27, Louis tried to placate the nobles by bringing 18,000 troops to the vicinity of Versailles. Middle-class members of the Assembly, nearly panicking in fear of military intervention and a bloody response, appealed for popular support. In Paris, the forces of public order were in a confused state as many of the soldiers, especially among the *gardes-françaises* (gardz fran-SAEZ), who were supposed to protect stocks of grain and weapons, refused to follow the orders of their officers. As the contradictory rumors swirled in from Versailles on the morning of July 14, Parisians broke into military storerooms and took an estimated 30,000 rifles and cannons with little or no resistance. Later that day, an estimated 100,000 Parisian shopkeepers, workers, and women demolished the Bastille—a medieval fortress converted into a prison—in Paris. The significance of the action was not in the prisoners they liberated—a small group of obscure nobles. The Bastille had served as the most visible symbol of the old regime in the city, and its fall clearly demonstrated the rapidly growing popular defiance. Paris became an independent city with its own middle-class council and its own National Guard.

Meanwhile, other urban uprisings and peasant violence in the country destroyed the remnants of the old regime and implicitly consolidated the National Constituent Assembly's position. As for the king, he had completely lost control and even comprehension of events, as can be seen by the entry he made in his journal for July 14, the day of the fall of the Bastille: *"Rien"* (ree-EN; "Nothing.").

The most dramatic action by the Assembly came on the night of August 4, 1789. By then, order had been restored in the cities, but peasants all over France were still rising against their lords—burning, pillaging, and sometimes murdering—in desperate efforts to destroy records of their manorial obligations. Faced with this violence, known as the Great Fear, the Assembly ultimately chose to grant concessions. Consequently, on that fateful night, nobles and clergy rose in the Assembly to renounce tithes, serfdom, manorial duties, feudal privileges, unequal taxes, and the sale of offices. The old regime, which had evolved over ten centuries, legally disappeared in a few hours. This was the real French Revolution.

Moderate Phase of the Revolution: August 1789–September 1791

To define its political principles and set its course, the Assembly issued the *Declaration of the Rights of Man and Citizen* on August 26 (see the Document on p. 566). Intended as a preamble to a new constitution, it proclaimed human "inalienable rights" to liberty, property, security, and resistance to oppression. It also promised free speech, press, and religion, consistent with public order. Property was declared inviolate unless required for "public safety," in which case the owner was to receive "just compensation." All (male) citizens were to be equal before the law and eligible for public office on their qualifications. Taxes were to be levied only by common consent. Other sections on civil equality and property rights indicated the document's middle-class orientation.

DOCUMENT *Declaration of the Rights of Man and the Citizen*

A climax to the summer upheaval came in October. Louis tried to delay taking official action to carry out the Assembly's decrees of August 4, and he was anxiously awaiting the arrival of a trusted regiment from Flanders. Meanwhile, angry Parisians marched and rioted in the streets. Two months later, on October 5, after the Flanders regiment had arrived, some 6000 women, many of them armed, marched to Versailles, accompanied by the National Guard under Lafayette. It was symbolic of the disconnection between Louis XVI and the events of his country that no preparation had been made to anticipate the arrival of this group. He had been out hunting, and, to his surprise, he was met by a deputation of six women who presented their demands. In the face of this confrontation, the king signed the decrees of August 4. Other women entered the hall where the Assembly was sitting, disrupted proceedings, and forced an adjournment. The next day, October 6, after

▲ The fury and force of the French Revolution came from people such as these Parisian women advancing on Versailles, October 5, 1789. They were about to bring the king, the queen, and the entire National Constituent Assembly back to Paris and the reality of the Revolution.

a mob stormed the palace and killed some guards, the king and his family returned to Paris as virtual prisoners, their carriage surrounded by women carrying pikes on which were impaled the heads of the murdered bodyguards.

Shortly after the march on Versailles, the Assembly achieved some political stability by declaring martial law, to be enforced by the sometimes dependable National Guard. During the next 2 years, the Assembly's leaders followed the Enlightenment principles and the statements of the *Declaration* in attempting to reorganize France. Because most came from the middle class, with a preponderance of lawyers and a sprinkling of nobles, they were committed to change but also determined to keep order, protect property, and further their own special interests. Thus, as they achieved their goals, they became increasingly satisfied and conservative. Good harvests and the lowering of food prices also favored them.

One thing remained constant during the revolutionary year of 1789: France was bankrupt. And this financial distress remained one of the new government's most immediate concerns. The Assembly attempted to solve the problem by seizing church properties and using them as a base for new issues of paper currency, the *assignats* (AHS-seen-yat). Some members would have gone further, but many were reluctant to abolish the state church completely, believing that it could be controlled and used to help defend property. Consequently, the Assembly decreed a "Civil Constitution of the Clergy," which made all priests salaried public servants, abolished all archbishoprics, and reduced the number of bishoprics. Monastic orders were simply dissolved. Incumbent churchmen were required to swear loyalty to the nation, but only seven bishops and half the clergy conformed. The remainder became bitterly hostile to the government and exerted great influence, particularly among the peasants.

Understandably, the Assembly's economic policies were aimed at winning middle-class support. It therefore assured payment to holders of government bonds, secured not only by impending sales of confiscated church lands but also by lands taken from nobles who had fled the country. Most of this property was sold to middle-class speculators, who resold

Document

Declaration of the Rights of Man and Citizen

This moderate middle-class document of the French Revolution was inspired by the American Declaration of Independence. Notice, however, that it differs slightly in its precise mention of property rights.

The National Assembly recognizes and declares, in the presence and under the auspices of the Supreme Being, the following rights of man and citizen.

1. Men are born and remain free and equal in rights. Social distinctions can be based only upon the common good.
2. The aim of every political association is the preservation of the natural and imprescriptible rights of man. These rights are liberty, property, security, and resistance to oppression....
3. Liberty consists in the power to do anything that does not injure others; accordingly, the exercise of the natural rights of each man has no limits except those that assure to the other members of society the enjoyment of these same rights. These limits can be determined only by law.
4. The law can forbid only such actions as are injurious to society. Nothing can be forbidden that is not forbidden by the law, and no one can be constrained to do that which it does not decree.
5. Law is the expression of the general will. All citizens have the right to take part personally, or by their representatives, in its enactment. It must be the same for all, whether it protects or punishes.
6. No man can be accused, arrested, or detained, except in the cases determined by the law and according to the forms which it has prescribed. Those who call for, expedite, execute, or cause to be executed arbitrary orders should be punished; but every citizen summoned or seized by virtue of the law ought to obey instantly....
7. The law ought to establish only punishments that are strictly and obviously necessary, and no one should be punished except by virtue of a law established and promulgated prior to the offense and legally applied.
8. Every man being presumed innocent until he has been declared guilty, if it is judged indispensable to arrest him, all severity that may not be necessary to secure his person ought to be severely suppressed by law.
9. No one should be disturbed on account of his opinions, even religious, provided their manifestation does not trouble the public order as established by law.
10. The free communication of thoughts and opinions is one of the most precious of the rights of man; every citizen can then speak, write, and print freely, save for the responsibility for the abuse of this liberty in the cases determined by law.
11. The guarantee of the rights of man and citizen necessitates a public force; this force is then instituted for the advantage of all and not for the particular use of those to whom it is entrusted.
12. For the maintenance of the public force and for the expenses of administration a general tax is indispensable; it should be equally apportioned among all the citizens according to their means.
13. All citizens have the right to ascertain, by themselves or through their representatives, the necessary amount of public taxation, to consent to it freely, to follow the use of it, and to determine the quota, the assessment, the collection, and the duration of it....
14. Society has the right to require of every public agent an account of his administration.
15. Any society in which the guarantee of the rights is not assured, or the separation of powers not determined, has no constitution.
16. Property being a sacred and inviolable right, no one can be deprived of it, unless a legally established public necessity evidently requires it, under the condition of a just and prior indemnity.

Questions to Consider

1. What themes of the Enlightenment do you see reflected in this declaration?
2. Does this document strike you as a conservative, liberal, or radical statement?
3. What role does private property play in the construction of the new society?

From Mark A. Kishlansky, ed., *Sources of the West: Readings in Western Civilization*, Vol. II, 4th ed., Longman Publishers, New York and London, pp. 115–117.

it to wealthy land-grabbers and social climbers; very little of it was ever acquired by peasants. The Assembly also abolished all internal tolls, industrial regulations, and guilds, thus throwing open to all the chance to work in the arts and crafts. It banned trade unions and decreed that wages be set by individual bargaining. Except for a few remaining controls on foreign trade, the Assembly applied the doctrines of Adam Smith and the physiocrats, substituting free competition for economic controls.

The Assembly dashed some of the high hopes held by French women. The early Revolution enlisted many, not only from the poor rioting Parisians of the shops and markets but also from those of the middle class, whose salons were political centers. Other women were already prominent in the political clubs of the era, forming women's patriotic societies and proposing female militias. In addition, some women were involved in a strong feminist movement, a cause taken up by the Friends of Truth, an organization that regularly lobbied the Assembly for free divorce, women's education, and women's civil rights. Its pleas, however, were largely ignored. Two women, Claire "Rose" Lacombe and Pauline Leon (po-LEEN LAY-on), who had struggled to survive the economic hardships of 1788, led the most important women's club, the Society of Republican Revolutionary Women. Lacombe was an actress; Leon was the daughter of a chocolate maker who tried to keep the family business going. Together, they often appeared before the Assembly, stating their case to improve women's place in society and, when war broke out, demanding the right to bear arms. The royalist Olympe de Gouges (OH-lamp duh GOOZHE) also fought for the cause through her manifestos and arguments before the assembly.(see Document, p. 568) However, it was not a promising epoch for women. The Society of Republican Revolutionary Women was shut down because of its radical leadership and programs: de Gouges, along with other women leaders, died by the guillotine in 1793.

The Assembly's Enlightenment ideology clashed with its rising conservatism on the issue of policy toward the French West Indies (see Chapter 21). News from France in 1789 brought violent uprisings on Santo Domingo and Martinique, where planters, merchants, poor whites, mulattoes, and slaves evaluated the Revolution according to their diverse interests. Planters in the Assembly differed on trade policies and colonial autonomy but concurred in their fanatic defense of slavery and their opposition to civil rights for free mulattoes. Meanwhile, mulattoes in France spread their pamphlets and petitioned the Assembly, supported by the *Amis des Noirs* (ah-MEE day nwha; "Friends of the Blacks"), whose supporters also angrily attacked slavery in the Assembly hall. The chamber was left divided and nearly impotent. It first gave the island governments complete control over their blacks and mulattoes; then, yielding to the radicals, it granted political rights to mulattoes born of free parents. This was only a temporary solution to a difficult political and social problem.

After 2 years of tedious discussions, the Assembly finally produced the Constitution of 1791, which made France a limited monarchy. It assigned the lawmaking function to the single-chambered Legislative Assembly, which would meet automatically every 2 years. Louis became a figurehead, allowed to select ministers and temporarily veto laws but denied budgetary control or the right to dismiss the legislature. He had fewer powers than the new American president, George Washington, and he could also be legally deposed. In addition, the constitution created an independent and elected judiciary and completely reorganized local government on three levels—departments, districts, and communes—with elected officials relatively free of supervision from Paris. Despite implications in the *Declaration,* only male citizens who paid a specified minimum of direct taxes acquired the vote; millions could not vote. Property qualifications were even higher for deputies to the Assembly and national officials. Women were made "passive citizens," without the vote, but marriage became a civil contract, with divorce open to both parties. Other individual rights under a new law code were guaranteed to all citizens, including Jews, according to the principles of the *Declaration.*

On September 30, 1791, the Assembly dissolved itself after mandating that no present member of the Assembly was to be eligible for election to the new legislative body, a major mistake that removed individuals—mostly moderates—with experience from the political stage. Yet, the National Constituent Assembly created an important legacy for France. It had passed more than 2000 laws that combined to end feudalism, serfdom, an irrational provincial system, conflicting courts, sale of offices, and absolute monarchy itself. It had not, however, made all citizens equal, even before the law, a point repeatedly emphasized by radical agitators and their followers among the angry street people of Paris.

The Drift Toward Radicalism: September 1791–June 1793

For more than a year before the new constitution was completed, the moderate Assembly, which wanted to protect property rights and middle-class advances, had come under the increasing pressure of radicals, who wanted to carry out fundamental political and social reforms. Despite all efforts of the National Guard, unrest in the country and mob action in the cities disturbed the uneasy peace. Particularly in Paris after the spring of 1790, radical members of the Assembly played on popular fears and suspicions, encouraged by condemnations of the Revolution from émigré nobles and foreign royalists. Tensions within France were further aggravated by secret efforts by the king and queen to enlist foreign support. In June 1791, when the king—who opposed the state loyalty oath imposed on the clergy—and his family were caught trying to flee the country, the situation deteriorated. People in favor of a republic called for Louis to be removed. Angry crowds gathered, and the Guard fired on them, killing 15 people. The resulting wave of discontent would continue to intimidate national lawmakers, shaping their policies for the next 3 years.

In this charged atmosphere, the new and inexperienced Legislative Assembly met on October 1, 1791. Its

Document

Olympe de Gouges on the Rights of Women

Olympe de Gouges's (1745–1793) father was a butcher and her mother took in washing. As a child, she had no advantage except for her beauty, which brought her marriage to a rich man close to the age of her father. She soon became a widow and had enough money to go to Paris in 1788, where she tried to enter the public debates of the time. However, because of her lack of education, she wrote badly, and was not taken seriously.

Another reason she was not taken seriously by French men was because of her radical feminist views, even though she was a royalist. Nonetheless, she wrote more than 30 pamphlets and manifestos, including the *Declaration of the Rights of Woman.* She was a courageous woman who spoke her mind, especially during the time of mass executions of the Committee of Public Safety. She soon joined the ranks of the victims and was guillotined in 1793, at the age of 48.

Man, are you capable of being just? It is a woman who poses the question; you will not deprive her of that right at least. Tell me, what gives you sovereign empire to oppress my sex? Your strength? Your talents? Observe the Creator in his wisdom; survey in all her grandeur that nature with whom you seem to want to be in harmony, and give me, if you dare, an example of this tyrannical empire.

Declaration of the Rights of Woman and the Female Citizen

For the National Assembly to decree in its last sessions, or in those of the next legislature.

Preamble Mothers, daughters, sisters [and] representatives of the nation demand to be constituted into a national assembly. Believing that ignorance, omission, or scorn for the rights of woman are the only causes of public misfortunes and of the corruption of governments, [the women] have resolved to set forth in a solemn declaration the natural, inalienable, and sacred rights of woman in order that this declaration, constantly exposed before all the members of the society, will ceaselessly remind them of their rights and duties; in order that the authoritative acts of women and the authoritative acts of men may be at any moment compared with and respectful of the purpose of all political institutions; and in order that citizens' demands, henceforth based on simple and incontestable principles, will always support the constitution, good morals, and the happiness of all. Consequently, the sex that is as superior in beauty as it is in courage during the suffering of maternity recognized and declares in the presence and under the auspices of the Supreme Being, the following Rights of Woman and of Female Citizens.

Article 1 Woman is born free and lives equal to man in her rights. Social distinctions can be based only on the common utility.

Article 2 The purpose of any political association is the conservation of the natural and imprescriptible rights of woman and man; these rights are liberty, property, security, and especially resistance to oppression.

Article 3 The principle of all sovereignty rests essentially with the nation, which is nothing but the union of woman and man; no body and no individual can exercise any authority which does not come expressly from it [the nation].

Article 4 Liberty and justice consist of restoring all that belongs to others; thus, the only limits on the exercise of the natural rights of woman are perpetual male tyranny; these limits are to be reformed by the laws of nature and reason....

Article 7 No woman is an exception: she is accused, arrested, and detained in cases determined by law. Women, like men, obey this rigorous law....

Article 11 The free communication of thoughts and opinions is one of the most precious rights of woman, since the liberty assures the recognition of children by their fathers. Any female citizen thus may say freely, I am the mother of a child which belongs to you, without being forced by a barbarous prejudice to hide the truth; [an exception may be made] to respond to the abuse of this liberty in cases determined by the law....

Article 13 For the support of the public force and the expenses of administration, the contributions of woman and man are equal; she share all the duties [*corvees*] and all the painful tasks; therefore, she must have the same share in the distribution of positions, employments, offices, honors and jobs [*industrie*]....

Article 15 The collectivity of women, joined for tax purposed to the aggregate of men, has the right to demand an accounting of his administration from any public agent....

Article 17 Property belongs to both sexes whether united or separate; for each it is an inviolable and sacred right; no on can be deprived of it, since it is the true patrimony of nature, unless the legally determined public need obviously dictates it, and then only with a just and prior indemnity.

Questions to Consider

1. What are the major differences between the *Declaration of the Rights of Man and Citizen* and the *Declaration of the Rights of Woman and the Female Citizen?*
2. What points made by Olympe de Gouges seem to you to be applicable to the drive for women's equal rights today?
3. In your opinion, why did male French revolutionaries pay so little attention to the efforts of their female counterparts?

Mark A. Kishlansky, ed., *Sources of the West: Readings in Western Civilization,* Vol. II, 4th ed., Longman Publishers, New York and London, pp. 115–117.

prospects during the fall were not promising. The sullen king continued his secret plotting with foreign supporters while a 20 percent drop in the value of *assignats,* the Revolutionary government's currency, alarmed middle-class investors. Public opinion in the cities became more radical as the popular press mounted a virulent and often vulgar campaign against Louis and the Assembly, and crowds in Paris and the port cities cursed the government. On the other side, opponents of the Revolution began to act against it. Full-scale revolts threatened to erupt among Catholic peasants in Vendée (von-DAY), Avignon (ah-veen-YON), Brittany, and Mayenne. The divisions and apprehensions in the country were naturally reflected in the Assembly.

At first, the delegates formed themselves into three groups whose location in the meeting hall provided the political vocabulary for the future: conservatives to the right of the podium, moderates in the center, and liberals to the left. In Paris in 1791, the delegates on the right supported the limited monarchy; the undecided—roughly half of the delegates—were in the center; and on the left was a diverse group split by their geographical origins—for example, the **Girondins** (ZHEE-rohn-DAN) from the southwest of the country and the **Jacobins** from Paris—and political goals, and united only by their distrust for the king and his supporters. A majority could agree only on their repudiation of the Declaration of Pillnitz (August 1791), in which the Austrian and Prussian rulers threatened military intervention if Louis XVI was not properly treated.

The Girondists exploited this foreign threat in emotional appeals that rallied the center behind a war to "save the Revolution." Debate gave way to action as the country slipped toward armed conflict during the spring of 1792. The stage was set in February, when Austria and Prussia formed an alliance, a move accented in March when the young and aggressive Francis II (1768–1835) succeeded his comparatively liberal father as Holy Roman Emperor. Louis and his queen, Marie Antoinette, were now hopeful for a war that might set them free. The Girondins savored their newfound dominance, which gave them control of the public opinion in March. The Jacobins, under Georges-Jacques Danton (1759–1794) and Maximilien Robespierre (maks-e-MIL-i-en rob-es-PEE-er; 1758–1794), argued against entering a war, noting that, in France's economic condition, war would harm the Revolution and end government economic aid for the common people.

Girondins—Radical members of the National Assembly (seated on the left) from the southwest of France.

Jacobins—Radical members of the National Assembly (seated on the left) from Paris.

There was a moment of general elation when France, nonetheless, declared war on Austria and Prussia in April. But despair soon set in when it became obvious that revolutionary enthusiasm was no match for Austrian and Prussian military discipline. There were too few trained French recruits, led by too few dependable officers—most of the noble officers had left the country. The revolutionary armies soon retreated in disorder amid mass desertions from an invasion of the Austrian Netherlands (in present-day Belgium). Only the enemy's caution and concern about a Russia advance from the east prevented a complete French disaster. Despair, however, turned to mass determination in July, when the Prussian duke of Brunswick, who commanded the invading armies, issued a threat to destroy Paris if the French royal family was harmed.

In the wake of the military collapse and the Prussian threat, the Girondist rabble-rousers in the Assembly began to lose their support and came under the attack of Danton, the Jacobin deputy prosecutor for the **Paris Commune.** Danton was an enormous brute of a man with a voice of commanding power who mesmerized angry street audiences when he denounced the king as a traitor to France and those who did not share Jacobin views as fools, or worse. On August 10, a mob of Parisians, women as well as men, broke into the palace, terrorized the royal family, massacred the Swiss guards, and looted the premises. There followed the Jacobin-directed "September Massacres," in which, under the continual pressure of the mob, the Paris Commune seized power from the Legislative Assembly, deposed the king, and executed some 2000 suspected royalists and priests who did not support the Revolution. As there was no longer a king, it was necessary to call for a new national constitutional convention with members elected by universal male suffrage to prepare the way for a new government. The Jacobin pogrom spread throughout France, even after September 22, when the new National Convention declared France a republic.

Two days earlier, a revitalized French army defeated the Prussians at Valmy, in northern France. This victory fused radicalism with nationalism as French armies began successful advances in the Austrian Netherlands, the Rhineland, and Savoy. Confirmed by their victory in November, the Convention declared universal revolutionary war by promising "fraternity to all peoples who wish to recover their liberty" and ordered inhabitants of occupied countries to accept revolutionary principles. Led by Danton, the lawyer Robespierre—a fanatical follower of Rousseau—and Jean-Paul Marat (mah-RAH; 1743–1793)—the

Paris Commune—The city government of Paris in revolutionary France.

publisher of a violent paper that consistently denounced traitors—the radical Jacobins were now riding a rising tide. But the Girondists, despite their continued enthusiasm for the war, were now the conservatives of the Convention. They had become mainly the spokesmen for wealthy middle-class provincials, who advocated clemency for the king. On this major issue, the execution of Louis XVI, the Jacobins finally triumphed by one vote—despite foreign ambassadors' bribes—and Louis was decapitated on January 21, 1793. Marie Antoinette followed her husband to the guillotine nine months later on October 16, 1793.

Early French military advances had alarmed European capitals, but the execution of Louis XVI and his queen proved to be the decisive factor in turning all of Europe against France. Britain, Austria, Prussia, Spain, the Netherlands, and Sardinia formed the First Coalition in February and March 1793. Coalition forces soon expelled French troops from the Austrian Netherlands and Germany, after which France was invaded at a half-dozen places around its borders. In the ensuing military crisis, the Convention initiated a nationwide effort to raise a new levy of 300,000 men from quotas assigned to every unit of local government. Lazare Carnot (kar-NO; 1753–1823), the Republic's minister of war, reorganized the armed forces by opening promotion to all ranks and meshing volunteers with old-line units. His efforts, along with a national patriotic response, brought a hard-won but belated stability.

As in the previous year, threats from abroad generated an internal crisis during the spring of 1793. Execution of the king spurred full-scale civil war in Brittany and the Vendée as peasant armies, led by royalist émigrés and supplied by British ships, fought regular battles against troops of the Republic. Meanwhile in Paris, worsening hunger among the poor widened the breach between Jacobins and Girondins. Again, furious mobs entered the Convention hall, protesting food prices and demanding price controls. Such a measure was pushed through the Convention in April by the *Enragés* (ahn-razh-AY), an extremist faction of the Jacobins led by the radical journalist Jacques Hébert (AY-behr; 1755–1794). When the Girondins staged uprisings in Marseilles, Lyons, Bordeaux, and Toulon, left-wing Jacobins in the Paris Commune called another armed mob into the Convention on May 31, 1793, and purged that body of any remaining Girondists. Others throughout France, wherever the Convention still retained authority, were arrested or driven into hiding.

The Jacobin Republic

The Convention was now a "rump" council of the most extreme Jacobins. Their power was secured after July 12 when Charlotte Corday (1768–1793), a young Girondist sympathizer, came to Paris from Caen and murdered Marat. He had been an adored leader of the *Enragés*, and his death infuriated the people of the street, including a contingent of revolutionary women who cursed Corday as they followed her to the guillotine. The general anti-Girondist mania brought the Convention under the domination of Robespierre, who remained in power until the late spring of 1794. During that time, revolutionary France, in a convulsion of patriotic violence, reorganized itself, suppressed internal strife, drove out foreign invaders, and catapulted the radical Jacobin party to a pinnacle of power.

The regime achieved its success largely through rigid dictatorship and terror. The 12-member **Committee of Public Safety**, headed first by Danton, and after July by Robespierre, decided security policies. Subordinate committees were established for the departments, districts, and communes. These bodies deliberately forced conformity and used neighbors to inform on neighbors and sons and daughters to testify against their parents. Suspected traitors were brought to trial before revolutionary tribunals, with most suspects receiving quick death sentences. Between September 1793 and July 1794, some 25,000 victims were dragged to public squares in carts—the famous *tumbrels* (toom-BREL)—and delivered to the guillotines. Ultimately, the **Reign of Terror,** or simply the Terror, as this period came to known, destroyed most of the revolutionaries, including the Girondists (September 1793), the Dantonists (April 1794), and Robespierre himself (July 1794).

While it lasted, the Jacobin dictatorship was remarkably efficient in its war efforts, as it mobilized all of France to fight and changed the nature of European warfare. The Convention made all males between 18 and 40 eligible for military service, a policy known as the *levée en masse* (le-VAY on MAHSS; "mass conscription"), which ultimately produced a force of 800,000, the largest standing army ever assembled in France. Its officers were promoted on merit and encouraged to exercise initiative. Soldiers were lionized in public festivals and provided with special entertainments, while 300 civilian commissars monitored morale and combat readiness. Between 1793 and 1795, these French citizen armies put down all internal rebellions and fought a series of remarkably successful campaigns against foreign invaders as well. They regained all lost French territory, annexed Belgium, and occupied other areas that extended to the Rhine, the Alps, and the Pyrenees, thus gaining in 2 years the "natural frontiers" that Louis XIV had dreamed about. By

Committee of Public Safety—A 12-member group that decided security policies for the Jacobin administration.

Reign of Terror—The period, roughly from September 1793 to July 1794, in which the Jacobin Dictatorship executed some 25,000 people by the guillotine.

1794, Prussia and Spain had left the coalition and the Netherlands had become a French ally. Only Britain, Austria, and Sardinia remained at war with France.

Despite their stated beliefs in free enterprise as an ideal, the Jacobins created a war economy, which operated under extensive controls. Government agencies conscripted labor and took over industries, directing them to produce large quantities of uniforms, arms, medical supplies, and equipment. In Paris alone, 258 forges made 1000 gun barrels a day. Reacting to bread riots and the revolutionary women's condemnation of monopolists and speculators, the Convention imposed price controls, rationing, and fixed wages while issuing currency without reference to bank reserves or market demand. The government also punished profiteers, used the property of émigrés to relieve poverty, sold land directly to peasants, and freed the peasants from all compensatory payments to their old lords.

Many other changes reflected a strange combination of reason and fanaticism. The regime prohibited all symbols of status, such as knee breeches, powdered wigs, and jewelry. It abolished titles; people had to be addressed as "citizen" or "citizeness." Streets were renamed to commemorate revolutionary events or to honor revolutionary heroes. The calendar was reformed by dividing each month into three weeks of ten days each and giving the months poetic new names; July, for example, became Thermidor (hot) to avoid referring to the tyrant Julius Caesar. The Revolution took on a semi-religious character in ceremonies and fêtes, which featured attractive young women as living symbols of reason, virtue, and duty. Along with these changes came a strong reaction against Christianity: churches were closed and religious images destroyed. For a while, "Worship of the Supreme Being" was substituted for Roman Catholicism, although, in 1794, religion became a private matter.

Colonial problems, which had confounded the National and Legislative Assemblies, were met head-on by the Jacobin Convention. The grant of citizenship to free blacks and mulattoes of the islands in 1792 had drawn the mulattoes to the government side, but their armies, enlisted by the governors, faced determined insurrection from royalists and resentful escaped slaves. Sometimes, the two anti-Convention forces were united with support from Spain or the British. In the late spring of 1793, the governor of Santo Domingo issued a decree freeing all former slaves and calling on them to join against foreign enemies. His strategy narrowly averted a British conquest. The chamber responded by freeing all slaves in French territories and giving them full citizenship rights. Later, Napoleon would reimpose slavery in the colonies, where it would last until 1848.

Unfortunately, the revolutionary women in France were not so successful. At first, they were welcomed as supporters by the radical Jacobins, until the latter gained power; then, the Jacobins regarded revolutionary women as troublemakers. In October 1793, the Convention refused to hear a group of women who wanted to protest violations of the Constitution. During the next six months, the government repressed women's societies and imprisoned their leaders. Although the Jacobin legislature denied women the vote, it did improve their education, medical care, and property rights.

Because they regulated the economy and showed concern for the lower classes, the Jacobins have often been considered as forerunners of socialism. The Constitution of 1793, which was developed by the Convention but suspended almost immediately because of the war, does not support this interpretation. It did provide public assistance for the poor and aided the unemployed in seeking work, but it also guaranteed private property, included a charter of individual liberties, confirmed the Constitution of 1791's emphasis on local autonomy, and provided for the Central Committee, appointed by the departments. The greatest difference, in comparison with the Constitution of 1791, was the right to vote, which was granted to all adult males. Although the Jacobin constitution indicated a concern for equality of opportunity, it also revealed its authors as eighteenth-century radical liberals who followed Rousseau rather than Locke.

Conservative Counter-Revolution and the End of the Terror

The summer of 1794 brought a conservative reaction against radical revolution. With French arms victorious everywhere, rigid discipline no longer seemed necessary, but Robespierre, still committed to Rousseau's "republic of virtue," was determined to continue the Terror. When he demanded voluntary submission to the "general will" as necessary for achieving social equality, justice, and brotherly love, many practical politicians among his colleagues doubted his sanity. Others wondered if they would be among those next eliminated to purify society. They therefore cooperated to condemn him in the Convention. In July 1794, his enemies sent him to the guillotine with 20 of his supporters, amid great celebration.

Robespierre's fall ended the Terror and initiated a revival of the pre-Jacobin past. In 1794, the Convention eliminated the Committee of Public Safety; the next year, it abolished the revolutionary tribunal and the radical political clubs and freed thousands of political prisoners. It also banned women from attendance in the Convention hall, an act that symbolized the return to a time when women's political influence was confined to the ballroom, the bedroom, and the salon. Indeed, as the exiled Girondists, émigré royalists, and nonconforming priests returned to France, Parisian politics moved from the streets to the drawing rooms of the elite, such as that of the former courtesan Madame Tallien (TAL-lee-en; 1773–1835), which became a center of high-society gossip and political intrigue. Outside Paris, by the summer of 1795, armed reactionary "white" terrorists roamed the countryside, seeking out and murdering former Jacobins. Everywhere, the earlier reforming zeal and patriotic fervor gave way to conservative cynicism.

Before it dissolved itself in 1795, the Convention proclaimed still another constitution and established a new political system known as the Directory, which governed France until 1799. The new government was headed by an executive council of five members (directors) appointed by the upper house of a bicameral (two-house) legislature. Assemblies of electors in each department selected deputies to the two chambers. These electors were chosen by adult male taxpayers, but the electors themselves had to be substantial property owners. Indeed, they numbered only some 20,000 in a total population of more than 25 million. Government was thus securely controlled by the upper middle classes, a condition also evident by the return to free trade.

The Directory was conspicuously conservative and antidemocratic, but it was also antiroyalist. A Bourbon restoration would have also restored church and royalist lands, which had been largely acquired by wealthy capitalists during the Revolution. Politicians who had participated in the Revolution or voted for the execution of Louis XVI had even greater reason to fear restoration of the monarchy. In pursuing this antiroyalist path at a time when royalist principles were regaining popularity, the government had to depend on the recently developed professional military establishment. More than once between 1795 and 1797, army action protected the government against royalists and radicals. The Directory also encouraged further military expansion, hoping to revive patriotic revolutionary fervor. Except for young military officers such as Napoleon Bonaparte, bureaucrats, members of the landowning middle classes, merchants in large cities, and some professionals, the majority of people in 1796 were worse off than they had been two decades before. But the Directory paid little attention to the majority of people and protected its own.

	The French Revolutions
1787–1789	Bad weather cuts down on grain harvest, drives up bread prices
August 1788	Louis XVI announces meeting of Estates-General to be held May 1789
May 5, 1789	Estates-General convenes
June 1789	Third Estate declares itself the National Assembly, Oath of the Tennis Court
July 14, 1789	Storming of the Bastille, revolution of peasantry begins
June 1791	Louis XVI and family attempt to flee Paris but are captured and returned
April 1792	France declares war on Austria
January 1793	Louis XVI executed
1793–1794	Reign of Terror
1799	Napoleon overthrows the Directory and seizes power
1804	Napoleon proclaims himself emperor of the French
September 1812	French army reaches Moscow, is trapped by Russian winter
1813	Napoleon defeated at Leipzig
June 15, 1815	Napoleon is defeated at Waterloo and exiled to island of St. Helena

The French Revolution: The Napoleonic Phase, 1799–1815

What influence did Napoleon have on French and European history?

Even as a student, Napoleon considered himself a man of destiny, and he worked hard to construct the image he wanted to project to the future. As soon as the ship carrying him to exile in St. Helena set sail in 1815, his partisans and detractors began a debate over his career that continues to the present day. Whatever the viewpoint of the participants in that debate, all agree that few people have as decisively affected their times and set in motion developments that so profoundly altered the future as did Napoleon Bonaparte.

Napoleon the Corsican

Revolutions favor the bright, the ambitious, and the lucky. Napoleon Bonaparte (1769–1821) had all three qualities in abundance. He was born on Corsica to a low-ranking Florentine noble family in 1769, the year after control of that island passed from Genoa to France. At the age of 10, he was placed by his father in the military academy at Brienne (bree-EN). Six years later, he received his officer's commission. At the beginning of the French Revolution, he was a 20-year-old officer, doomed to a mediocre future by his family's modest standing and the restrictions of the Old Regime. Ten years later, he ruled France. The Revolution gave him the opportunity to rise rapidly, to use his intelligence, ability, charm, and daring.

Napoleon arrived at the right time—a generation earlier or later, the situation would not have allowed him to gain power. He took advantage of the gutting of the old officer class by the revolutionary wars and the destruction of what was left of the older officers by the Jacobins to rise quickly to a prominent position from which he could appeal to the Directory. That self-interested group of survivors asked the Corsican to break up a right-wing uprising in October 1795. The following year, the Directory gave Napoleon command of the smallest of the three armies sent to do battle with the Austrians.

The two larger forces crossed the Rhine on their way to attack the Habsburgs while, as a diversionary move, Napoleon's forces went over the Alps into Italy. Contrary to plan, the main French armies accomplished little. Napoleon, intended to be no more than bait to lure the Austrians into Italy, crushed the Sardinians and then the Habsburg armies in a series of brilliant battles. As he marched across northern Italy, he picked off Venice and was well on the road to Vienna when the Austrians approached him to make peace. Without instructions from his government, Napoleon negotiated the Treaty of Campo Formio (FORM-ee-oh; 1797) and returned home a hero.

▲ This heroic portrait by Antoine-Jean Gros shows Napoleon at the age of 27, a time when he was leading his troops at the battle of Arcola in northern Italy in November 1796.

After considering an invasion of Britain in the first part of 1798—a cross-Channel task he deemed impossible—Napoleon set out, with the Directory's blessing, to strike at Britain's economy by attacking its colonial structure. His plan was to invade Egypt, expose the weakness of the Ottoman Empire, and from there launch an attack on India and deprive England of an important economic base. The politicians were as much impressed by this grand plan as they were relieved to get the increasingly popular Napoleon out of town. He successfully evaded the British fleet in the Mediterranean, landed in Egypt, and took Alexandria and Cairo in July. The British admiral Horatio Nelson (1758–1805), however, found the French fleet and sank it at Aboukir on August 1, 1798. Even though their supply lines and access to France were cut off, Napoleon's forces fought a number of successful battles against the Turks in Syria and Egypt.

The fact remained that the French armies were stranded in Egypt and would be forced to remain there until 1801, when a truce allowed them to come home. This development would normally be regarded as a defeat, yet when Napoleon abandoned his army in August 1799, slipped by the British fleet, and returned to Paris, he was given a frenzied, triumphant homecoming. In public appearances, he adopted a modest pose and gave addresses on the scientific accomplishments of the expedition, such as the finding of the Rosetta Stone, a discovery that provided the first clue in the deciphering of Egyptian hieroglyphics.

Napoleon, his brothers, and the Abbé Sieyès (ab-AY see-YES)—the former vicar general and author of the important 1789 pamphlet "What Is the Third Estate?"—sought to take advantage of the political dissatisfaction surrounding the Directory. Not only did the Second Coalition, led by Russia and Great Britain, threaten France from the outside, a feverish inflation ravaged the economy domestically. Various political factions courted Napoleon, whose charisma made him seem the likely savior of the country. In the meantime, he and his confederates planned their course. They launched a clumsy, though successful, coup in November 1799 and replaced the Directory with the

Consulate. The plotters shared the cynical belief that "constitutions should be short and obscure" and that democracy meant that the rulers rule and the people obey.

The takeover ended the revolutionary decade. France remained, in theory, a republic, but nearly all power rested with the 31-year-old Napoleon, who ruled as First Consul. Still another constitution was written and submitted to a vote of the people. Only half of the eligible voters went to the polls, but an overwhelming majority voted in favor of the new constitution: 3,011,007 in favor versus 1,562 against.

New Foundations

Ten years of radical change made France ready for one-man rule, but of a type much different from that exercised by the Bourbon monarchy. The events of 1789 had overturned the source of legitimate political power. Now it came not from God but from the people. The social structure of the old regime was gone and with it the privileges of hereditary and created nobility. The church no longer had financial or overt political power. The old struggles between kings and nobles, nobles and bourgeoisie, peasants and landlords, and Catholics and Protestants were replaced by the rather more universal confrontation between rich and poor.

There had been three attempts to rebuild the French system in the 10 years of revolution: the bourgeois-constitutional efforts to 1791, the radical programs to 1794, and the rule to 1799 by survivors who feared both the right and the left. Although each attempt had failed, each left valuable legacies to the new France. The first attempt established the power of the upper middle classes; the second showed the great power of the state to mobilize the population; and the third demonstrated the usefulness of employing former enemies in day-to-day politics.

Ever the pragmatic tactician, Napoleon used elements from the old regime and the various phases of the Revolution to reconstruct France. He built an autocracy far more powerful than Louis XVI's government. He took advantage of the absence of the old forms of competition to central power from the nobility and the feudal structure that had been destroyed in the name of liberty, equality, and brotherhood. He used the mercantile policies, military theories, and foreign policy goals of the old regime along with the ambitions of the middle class and the mobilization policies of the Jacobins. All he asked from those who wished to serve him was loyalty. Defrocked priests, renegade former nobles, reformed Jacobins, small businessmen, and enthusiastic soldiers all played a role. His unquestioning acceptance of the ambitious brought him popularity because 10 years of constant change had compromised most politically active people in some form of unprincipled, immoral, or illegal behavior.

Napoleon built his state on the *philosophes'* conception of a system in which all French men would be equal before the law. The Revolution destroyed the sense of personal power of a sovereign and substituted what the British historian Lord Acton would later in the nineteenth century call the "tyranny of the majority." The French state accordingly could intervene more effectively than ever before, limited only by distance and communication problems.

The mass democratic army created by the total mobilization of both people and resources was one of the best examples of the new state system. A revolutionary society had fought an ideological war under the Jacobins, and the experience changed the nature of combat forever. Because advancement and success were based on valor and victory, rather than bloodlines or privilege, the army profited from the new social structure and sought to preserve and extend it. The army best symbolized the great power of the French nation unleashed by the Revolution. Many of the economic and diplomatic problems that preceded the Revolution remained, but Napoleon's new state structure provided inspired solutions.

Taking advantage of his military supremacy, Napoleon gained breathing space for his domestic reforms by making peace with the Second Coalition by March 1802. He then set about erecting the governing structure of France, which remained virtually intact into the 1980s. He developed an administration that was effective in raising money, assembling an army, and exploiting the country's resources. His centralized government ruled through prefects, powerful agents in the provinces who had almost complete control of local affairs and were supported by a large police force. He then established a stable monetary policy based on an honest tax-collecting system, backed by up-to-date accounting procedures. The Bank of France that he created remains a model of sound finance.

Napoleon knew that the country he ruled was overwhelmingly Catholic and that national interest dictated that he come to terms with the papacy. Through the Concordat of 1801 with Pope Pius VII, the pope gained the right to approve the bishops whom the First Consul appointed to the reestablished Catholic Church. The state permitted seminaries to be reopened and paid priests' salaries. Pius regained control of the Papal States and saw his church recognized as the religion of the majority in France. The church thus resumed its position of prominence, but without its former power and wealth.

Napoleon viewed education as a way to train useful citizens to become good soldiers and bureaucrats, and he pursued the development of mass education by trying to increase the number of elementary schools, secondary schools, and special institutes for technical training. The schools were to be used to propagandize the young to serve the state through "directing political and moral opinion." Overarching the entire system was the University of France, which was more an administrative body to control education than a teaching institution. Napoleon had neither the time nor the resources to put mass education in place during his lifetime, although he did gain immediate success in training the sons—but rarely the daughters—of the newly arrived middle classes to become state functionaries.

Perhaps his greatest accomplishment came in the field of law. Building on reforms begun 10 years earlier, he assembled a talented team of lawyers to bring order to the chaotic state of French jurisprudence. At the time he took power, the country was caught in the transition from 366 separate local systems to a uniform code. By 1804, the staff had compiled a comprehensive civil law code (called the **Code Napoléon** after 1807) that was a model of precision and equality when compared to the old system. The code ensured the continuation of the gains made by the middle classes in the previous decade and emphasized religious toleration and abolition of the privileges held under the old order. Unfortunately, the code perpetuated the inferior status of women in the areas of civil rights, financial activities, and divorce. Nonetheless, it has served as the basis for law codes in many other countries.

The price France paid for these gains was rule by a police state that featured censorship, secret police, spies, and political trials, which sent hundreds to their deaths and thousands into exile. Order did prevail, however, and for the first time in a decade, it was safe to travel the country's roads. Napoleon also reduced the "representative assemblies" to meaningless rubber stamps. Liberty, equality, and brotherhood meant little in a land where the First Consul and his police could deny a person's freedom and right of association because of a perceived intellectual or political conflict.

To consolidate all of the changes, Napoleon proclaimed himself emperor in December 1804. Fifteen years after the outbreak of the Revolution, France had a new monarch. In a plebiscite, the nation approved the change by 3,572,329 to 2,579. As Napoleon took the crown in his hands from Pope Pius VII, who had come from Rome for the occasion, and crowned himself, the First French Republic came to an end.

Napoleon as Military Leader

War had been France's primary occupation since 1792, and, on the whole, it had been a profitable enterprise. The French had gained much land and money, as well as the opportunity to export the Revolution. Napoleon's reforms helped make his country even stronger in battle. At the end of 1804, Napoleon embarked on a series of campaigns designed to show France's invincibility. A key to French success was the emperor himself, who employed his own remarkable genius in leading his strong and wealthy country.

Napoleon brought intellectual strength, sensitivity to mood and opportunity, and bravery to the task of making war. He had been trained in the most advanced methods of his day, and he had better, more mobile artillery and more potent powder to blow holes through the enemy's lines. He worked well with a talented command staff, to which he gave much responsibility to wield their divisions as conditions dictated. Finally, he was the ultimate leader. Whether as lieutenant, general, First Consul, or emperor, Napoleon inspired masses of soldiers in a dramatic way. At the same time, he mobilized the home front through the use of the press and skillfully written dispatches.

Beneath this image making, the supreme commander was extremely flexible in his use of resources, always changing his tactics. He was pragmatic, moved rapidly, and lived off the land. He won the loyalty of his men by incentives and rewards, not brutal discipline. He set many military precedents, among them the use of ideological and economic warfare, as well as the rapid simultaneous movement of a large number of military columns. These columns could quickly converge on a given point with devastating results, breaking the will of the enemy. Finally, he personally led his troops into battle, exposing himself to incredible dangers with little regard for his own safety.

His nemesis was Great Britain, and during 1803 and 1804, he prepared a cross-Channel invasion. But the inability of the French navy to control the Channel and the formation of the Third Coalition (Great Britain, Russia, Austria, and Sweden) forced him to march eastward. In October 1805 Admiral Nelson and the British ended Napoleon's hopes of dominating the seas by destroying the joint French-Spanish fleet at the battle of Trafalgar (see map on p. 577).

France did far better on land, gaining mastery over the Continent by the end of 1807. Napoleon totally demoralized the Third Coalition in battles at Ulm (October 1805) and Austerlitz (December 1805). He then annihilated the Prussians, who had entered the conflict in the battles at Jena and Auerstadt (October 1806). He occupied Berlin, where he established the **Continental System,** a blockade of the Continent that was an effort to defeat Britain by depriving it of trade with the rest of Europe. Finally, in June 1807, he defeated the Russians at the battle of Friedland and

Code Napoléon—A civil law code instituted by Napoleon's administration in 1804. It formed the basis for many legal systems throughout Europe.

Continental System—An economic system Napoleon imposed on Europe to prevent countries from trading with Great Britain.

forced Tsar Alexander I to sign the Tilsit Treaty in July. This treaty, ratified on a raft anchored in the middle of the Nieman River, brought the two major land powers of Europe together in an alliance against Britain. At the beginning of 1808, Napoleon stood supreme in Europe, leading France to a dominance it had never experienced before and has not experienced since. Several of his relatives occupied the thrones of neighboring countries. The rest of the continent appeared to be mere satellites revolving around, this time, a Napoleonic sun.

Napoleon's Revolution in Europe

As he achieved his military goals, Napoleon set in motion a chain reaction of mini-revolutions that had a profound impact on the rest of the century. British sea power stood in the way of France's total domination of the Continent. Even though the British economy suffered under the impact of the Continental System (exports dropped by 20 percent, with a resultant cutback in production and rise in unemployment), the damage was not permanent. The Continental System inadvertently contributed to Britain's economic development by forcing it to industrialize quickly as it sought new markets and methods. Safe behind their wall of ships, the British turned out increasing quantities of goods as they passed through the early phases of industrialization.

Napoleon's armies carried French ideological baggage and institutional reforms across the Continent. Even though the emperor consolidated the Revolution in a conservative way in France, he broke apart his opponents' fragile social and governmental structures when he marched across the Rhine. Napoleon consciously spread the messages of liberty, equality, and brotherhood with all of the antifeudal, antiprivilege, and antirepressive themes inherent in the revolutionary triad. Where the French governed directly, they used the Code Napoléon and the reformed administrative practices.

The French presence triggered a hostile wave of nationalistic resentments. Many Europeans saw Napoleon as an imperialist, and the people he had "emancipated" began to realize that they had exchanged an old form of despotism for a new one. By posing as the champion of the Revolution, Napoleon sowed the seeds of the opposition that would work against him later, especially in Prussia. With the exception of the Poles, who had labored under Russian dominance and now served Napoleon well, the rest of Europe reacted against the French yoke.

The most significant rebellion took place in Portugal and Spain. Napoleon's entry into those countries to topple the passive Bourbons and strengthen the leaky Continental System was uncharacteristically shortsighted. The emperor had a serious fight on his hands in the Peninsular War that followed. Guerrilla uprisings soon broke out, supported by a British expeditionary force and supplies. These bloody wars tied down 200,000 to 300,000 French troops over a period of 5 years and drained the French treasury. The invasion of Spain also prompted a series of uprisings in the New World that gave birth to modern Latin American history (see Chapter 21).

The social and political changes the French triggered in Germany were equally profound. When he redrew the map of Europe after his victories, Napoleon destroyed the remnants of the Holy Roman Empire and, in so doing, erased 112 states of that ancient league. Only six of the former 50 free cities retained their status. Further, by changing the territorial arrangements of other areas, he reduced the number of German political units from more than 300 to 39. All over Germany, a wave of nationalism stirred the politically conscious population and prepared the way for the liberation movement.

Napoleon's Downfall

Opposition to Napoleon grew in both Austria and Russia. After the valiant but unsuccessful campaigns against the French in 1809, culminating in the bloody battle of Wagram, Vienna became a docile, though unreliable, ally. Napoleon's marriage to Marie Louise, the daughter of Francis I of Austria, proved to be only a tenuous tie between the French emperor and the Habsburgs. In Russia, the Tilsit Treaty had never been popular, and the economic hardships brought on by the Continental System made a break in the alliance virtually inevitable. By the end of 1810, France and Russia prepared to go to war against each other.

The emperor prepared carefully for his attack on Russia. Food supply would be a major problem for the 611,000 troops—half of them non-French—in the first and second lines of the invasion because his forces would be too large to live off the land. Furthermore, his army took with them over 200,000 animals, which required forage and water. The invasion force delayed its march until late June to ensure that the Russian plains would furnish sufficient grass to feed the animals.

The Russian campaign was both a success and a failure for Napoleon. The French did gain their objective—the city of Moscow—but the Russians refused to surrender. Shortly after the French occupied Moscow, fires broke out, destroying three-fourths of the city. After spending 33 days in the burned shell of the former capital waiting in vain for the tsar, who was 400 miles north in St. Petersburg, to agree to peace, Napoleon gave orders to retreat. He left the city on October 19. To remain would have meant having his lines cut by winter and being trapped with no supplies.

▲ Napoleon combined the military advances of the *ancien régime* and the unleashed democratic forces of the Revolution to achieve in 10 years what Louis XIV had failed to accomplish in a half century: the domination of Europe.

His isolation in Moscow would have encouraged his enemies in Paris. Leaving the city, as it turned out, condemned most of his men to death. As the remnants of Napoleon's forces marched west in October and November, they were forced to retrace virtually the same route they had used in the summer. They suffered starvation, attacks by partisans, and the continual pressure of Russian forces. Thousands perished daily, and by the end of November, only about 10,000 of the original force had made their escape from Russia.

The Empire of Napoleon in 1812

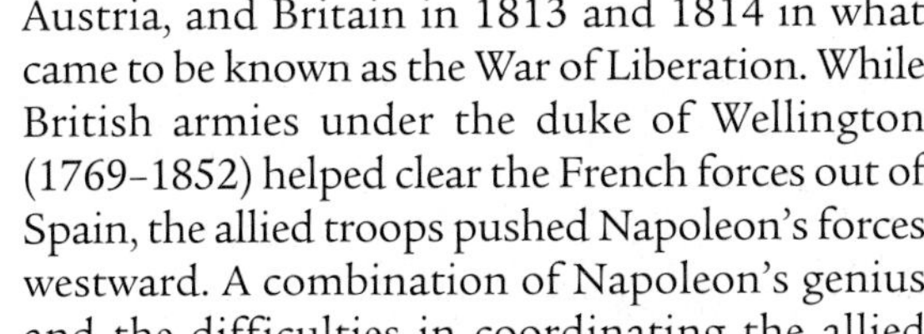

Russia, which had stood alone against the French at the beginning of 1812, was soon joined by Prussia, Austria, and Britain in 1813 and 1814 in what came to be known as the War of Liberation. While British armies under the duke of Wellington (1769–1852) helped clear the French forces out of Spain, the allied troops pushed Napoleon's forces westward. A combination of Napoleon's genius and the difficulties in coordinating the allied efforts prolonged the war, but in October 1813, the French suffered a decisive defeat at Leipzig in the Battle of the Nations, 1 year to the day after Napoleon had fled Moscow.

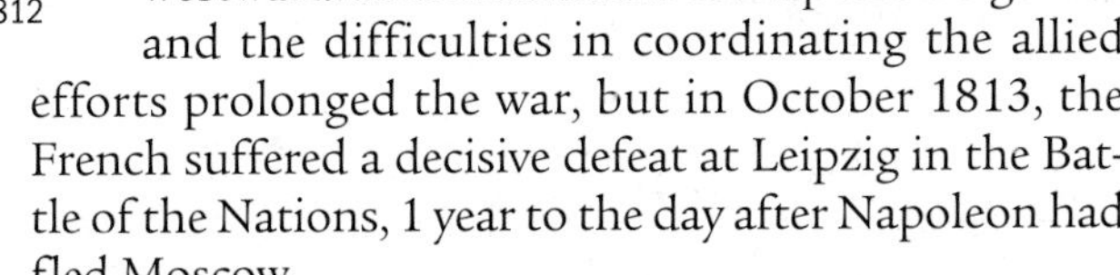

The allies sent peace offers to Napoleon, but he refused them. After Leipzig, the Napoleonic Empire rapidly disintegrated, and by the beginning of 1814, the allies had crossed the Rhine and invaded France. At the end of March, the Russians, Austrians, and Prussians took Paris. Two weeks later, Napoleon abdicated his throne, receiving in return sovereignty over Elba, a small island between Corsica and Italy.

Napoleon arrived in Elba in May and established rule over his 85-square-mile kingdom. He set up a mini-state, complete with an army, a navy, and a court. He soon exhausted the possibilities of Elba and in February and March 1815 he eluded the British fleet and returned to France to begin his campaign to regain power "within one hundred days." His former subjects, bored with the restored Bourbon Louis XVIII, gave him a tumultuous welcome. Napoleon entered Paris, raised an army of 300,000 men, and sent a message to the allies gathered to make peace at Vienna that he desired to rule France and only France. The allies, who were on the verge of breaking up their alliance, united, condemned Napoleon as an enemy of peace, and sent forces to France to put him down once and for all.

At the battle of Waterloo on June 18, 1815, the duke of Wellington, supported by Prussian troops under Field Marshall Gebhard von Blücher (fon BLOOK-er; 1749–1819), narrowly defeated Napoleon. The vanquished leader sought asylum with the British, hoping to live in exile in either England or the United States. But the allies, taking no chances, shipped him off to the bleak South Atlantic island of

St. Helena, 5000 miles from Paris. Here he set about writing his autobiography. He died of cancer in 1821 at the age of 51.

Even with the brief flurry of the One Hundred Days, Napoleon had no hope of re-creating the grandeur of his empire as it was in 1808. The reasons for this are not hard to determine. Quite simply, Napoleon was the heart and soul of the empire, and after 1808, his physical and intellectual vigor began to weaken. Administrative and military developments reflected this deterioration as Napoleon began to appoint sycophants to positions of responsibility. Further, by 1812, the middle classes, on which he depended, began suffering the economic consequences of his policies. The Continental System and continual warfare made their effects deeply felt through decreased trade and increased taxes. Even though some war contractors profited, the costs of Napoleon's ambitions began to make Frenchmen long for peace.

Outside France, the growth of nationalistic resistance on the Continent worked against the dictator, who first stimulated it by exporting the call for liberty, equality, and brotherhood. Equally important, the 25 years of French military superiority disappeared as other nations adopted and improved on the new methods of fighting. Finally, the balance-of-power principle made itself felt. France could not eternally take on the whole world.

Conclusion

Copernicus asked the fundamental questions about whether or not the earth moved, repeating a process of inquiry that in the West went back to the Greeks; similar inquiries were to be found in India, China, and Egypt. When, after extensive mathematical calculations, he established the heliocentric theory, his findings were published, to be read and challenged. As others improved on his findings and established the natural laws that defined the motion of the planets, scientific inquiries into all parts of existence became widely admired in some parts of Europe and widely attacked by Christian churches in others. The surprising discoveries of astronomers produced a new view of earth's place in the universe and led to new considerations of human beings' place on earth. If natural laws could be found to define the functioning of the universe, the logical next step taken by John Locke applied natural law theory to human society, and contributed to the eighteenth-century Age of Reason.

In France, a school of thinkers pursuing the discoveries of the Scottish and English Enlightenment, the *philosophes,* applied the test of reason to their own society, and undermined absolutism in all of its phases. The physiocrats, Adam Smith, and other early economic liberals demonstrated the futility of mercantilism. The Enlightenment's political principles substituted the social contract for divine right while emphasizing the natural human rights of political freedom and justice.

The criticisms of the *philosophes* came at a time when colonial wars had forced France to go deeper into debt and deprived the absolutist government of public support. Louis XVI's fiscal problems forced him to call the Estates-General in May 1789 and the subject of debate passed quickly from discussion of debt to considerations of social and political reform of the *ancien régime.* The old system collapsed under the weight of these considerations and, two months later, plunged France into the maelstrom of revolution from which it emerged only 10 years later, again under the control of a single leader—this time the Corsican-born Napoleon, who, thereafter, carried out his own version of the French Revolution that touched all of Europe and much of the Western world (see Chapters 21 and 23). More long-lasting than Napoleon's activities, the French Revolution furnished a precedent, a vocabulary, and a justification for revolution around the world that still remains intact.

Suggestions for Web Browsing

You can obtain more information about topics included in this chapter at the websites listed below. See also the companion website that accompanies this text, http://www.ablongman.com/brummett, which contains an online study guide and additional resources.

Galileo Project
http://es.rice.edu/ES/humsoc/Galileo/
A hypertext source of information about the life and work of Galileo Galilei and the science of his time.

Internet Modern History Sourcebook: The Scientific Revolution and the Enlightenment
http://www.fordham.edu/halsall/mod/modsbook09.html
Extensive online source for links about the Scientific Revolution and the Enlightenment, including primary documents by or about Copernicus, Kepler, Galileo, Descartes, Adam Smith, and John Locke.

Catherine the Great
http://members.tripod.com/~Nevermore/CGREAT.HTM
A treasure trove of materials on the Enlightened Empress.

Eighteenth-Century Fashion
http://www.marquise.de/en/1700/index.shtml
A virtual guided tour of European fashion during the Rococo period.

French Revolution
http://otal.umd.edu/~fraistat/romrev/frbib.html
Lists several major websites and a selected general bibliography dedicated to the French Revolution.

Marie Antoinette
http://www2.lucidcafe.com/lucidcafe/library/95nov/antoinette.html
A short biography of the queen, with related websites offering portraits, genealogy, and life at Versailles.

Napoleon
http://www.napoleonseries.org/
This site provides extensive bibliographic and general historical information about Napoleon and his times.

Military History: Napoleonic Wars (1800–1815)
http://www.cfcsc.dnd.ca/links/milhist/nap.html
Canadian Forces College site lists links on the biographies of Napoleon and Nelson, campaigns and battles, museums, naval operations, and reenactments.

The Congress of Vienna
http://members.aol.com/varnix/congress/
A good collection of documents and images from the Congress that put Europe back together again.

Literature and Film

Alexander Pope captured the spirit of the age his *Essay on Man* (1733). Jonathan Swift used satire for political criticism in *Gulliver's Travels* (1726). Voltaire's *Candide* (1759) is a fine critique of contemporary society. Daniel Defoe's *Robinson Crusoe* (1719) is a pathbreaking novel. Johann Wolfgang von Goethe's *The Sorrows of Young Werther* (1774) set the stage for modern romantic novels. See Neal Stephenson's three-volume series on the Scientific Revolution, *The Baroque Cycle,* beginning with *Quicksilver* (2003–2004).

Milos Forman's film *Amadeus* (1984; Warner) is superb. Gérard Corbiau's *Farinelli: Il Castrato* (1995; Columbia/Tristar) gives splendid insights into the society of the time. Marvin Chomsky captures eighteenth-century Russia in his film *Catherine the Great* (1995; A & E Entertainment). Sofia Coppola provides a new appreciation of *Marie Antoinette* (2006; Sony).

Two panoramic novels stand head and shoulders above the rest for this period, Charles Dickens's *A Tale of Two Cities* (1859) and Leo Tolstoy's *War and Peace* (1864–1869). There are several film versions of each. Rafael Sabatini's *Scaramouche: A Romance of the French Revolution* (1921) is a good, epic, read. Two recent historical novels deserve attention, Sandra Gulland's trilogy on *Josephine* (Touchstone, 2002) and Floyd Kemske's novel on Talleyrand, *The Third Lion* (Catbird, 1997).

Abel Gance's silent film *Napoleon* (1927; Universal) is a cinematic classic. *Danton* (1982; Home Vision Entertainment) gives a good visual context for the most radical part of the Revolution. Henry Koster casts Napoleon in a sensitive light in *Desiree* (1954).

Suggestions for Reading

A useful survey of scientific achievements during the period is A. Rupert Hall, *The Revolution in Science, 1500–1750* (Longman, 1983).

A good survey of the Enlightenment is presented in Robert Anchor, *The Enlightenment Tradition* (University of Pennsylvania Press, 1987). Steven Nadler, *Spinoza: A Life* (Cambridge University Press, 1999) is a fine biography. French and American colonial women who played roles in the Enlightenment are ably credited in Joan B. Landes, *Women and the Public Sphere in the Age of the French Revolution* (Cornell University Press, 1988).

François Furet gave a powerful reinterpretation of the whole revolutionary epoch in *The French Revolution, 1770–1814,* trans. Antonia Nevill (Blackwell, 1996). A fundamental examination of the nature of the Revolution is provided in T. C. W. Blanning, *The French Revolution: Class War or Culture Clash?* (St. Martin's Press, 1998).

On the significance of class hostilities and mob psychology, see Peter M. Jones, *The Peasantry in the French Revolution* (Cambridge University Press, 1988) and the classic George F. E. Rude, *The Crowd in the French Revolution* (Greenwood, 1986). The role of the revolutionary army is well depicted in Jean-Paul Bertaud, *The Army of the French Revolution: From Citizen Soldiers to Instrument of Power* (Princeton University Press, 1988). An important reconsideration of the 1792–1794 period is Patrice L. R. Higonnet, *Goodness Beyond Virtue: Jacobins During the French Revolution* (Harvard University Press, 1998).

Jean Tulard's *Napoleon: The Myth of the Saviour* (Weidenfeld & Nicolson, 1984) is a good study among the many on the French emperor. The military arts of the era are well described in Gunther Rothenberg, *The Art of Warfare in the Age of Napoleon* (Indiana University Press, 1978).

CHAPTER 19

Africa in the World Economy, 1650–1850

Outline

- The Atlantic Slave Trade
- The End of the Slave Trade in West Africa
- Islamic Africa
- Africans and European Settlement in Southern Africa
- African State Formation in Eastern and Northeastern Africa

Features

GLOBAL ISSUES **Slavery**

DOCUMENT **A Slave's Memoir**

DOCUMENT **Usman dan Fodio on Women and Islam**

SEEING CONNECTIONS **Moshoeshoe in European Dress**

DISCOVERY THROUGH MAPS **The Myth of the Empty Land**

◀ A portrait of Truro-Audaty, a ruler of eighteenth-century Dahomey, by Pierre Duflos, 1780.

THE MID-SEVENTEENTH to the mid-nineteenth centuries was a period of sometimes gentle and sometimes traumatic change in the states and societies of Africa. These states faced a set of challenges prompted by both external interventions and internal transformations. The internal upheavals took the forms of regional conflicts, the formation of new kingdoms, the expansion of Islam, migrations, and economic shifts from the slave trade to legitimate commerce. The external threats primarily came from the intrusion of Dutch and British settlers in southern Africa and a dramatic upswing in the Atlantic slave trade.

Europeans had also been involved for several centuries in a slave trade with Africans along the West and Central African coasts, but in the eighteenth century, as the demand increased for slaves to work on the sugar plantations in the Americas, Portuguese, British, Dutch, and French slavers bought many more slaves from African states that rarely allowed European traders to intrude in their affairs. Although the slave trade was destructive, the transatlantic trade opened up exchanges with the Americas in crops such as cassava, peanuts, and maize that benefited African agriculture and increased African populations. In the late eighteenth century, as European nations entered the industrial age, European traders began shifting away from trading for slaves to trading for commodities such as palm oil and palm kernels.

The European presence and influence in Africa was largely limited to coastal areas. However, at the southern tip of Africa, where Europeans could survive in a temperate climate, the Dutch and British established colonies. Dutch settlers primarily engaged in subsistence pastoralism; the British were interested in commercial farming. But both required land that they conquered from indigenous Africans.

The Atlantic Slave Trade

What factors contributed to the creation and the growth of the Atlantic slave trade?

Throughout the seventeenth century, Europeans became increasingly active in the Atlantic slave trade, which combined to create a huge international complex of enterprises involving the economies of four continents. The western Saharan coast was the setting for the beginning of the Atlantic slave trade in 1441, when a Portuguese sea captain kidnapped one man and one woman, who were sold into the Mediterranean slave market, to win the favor of Prince Henry. The slave trade reached its peak three centuries later as a major component in the rapidly expanding capitalism of northern Europe. Because it was conducted in partnerships between Africans and Europeans, the trade was a less obvious short-term danger to African interests than the migrating Dutch settlers in South Africa, but it posed a more serious long-term threat.

The full historical significance of the slave trade can best be understood if it is viewed in its broader setting. Europe's economy at the time derived large profits from bulk plantation commodities such as sugar, tobacco, and coffee. The most productive European plantations, which were located in the West Indies and Brazil, depended primarily on slave labor from West and Central Africa. Thus, slaving ports, such as Liverpool and Bristol in England and Bordeaux and Nantes in France, became thriving centers of a new prosperity. Related industries—such as shipbuilding, sugar refining, distilling, and textile and hardware manufacturing—also flourished. All contributed much to the development of European capitalism and ultimately to the Industrial Revolution.

Northern Europe's commercial impetus reached West Africa in the middle of the seventeenth century. The Portuguese, after losing the whole Atlantic coast to the Dutch, won back only Angola. For a while, the Dutch nearly monopolized the trade. After seizing Elmina on the Gold Coast in 1637, the Dutch West India Company was taking almost 7000 slaves a year a decade later. In the 1630s, the English also established footholds on the Gold Coast at Cormantin and Cape Castle; by 1700, they had seven other posts in the area. The French, meanwhile, acquired St. Louis on the Senegal River in the north, which allowed them to control most trade as far south as the Gambia River. In the resulting triangular competition, the Dutch faced constant pressure from their two rivals but maintained their dominance from a dozen strong Gold Coast forts.

Portuguese Travelers in Africa

By 1700, England was challenging Dutch predominance. Having defeated the Dutch at sea in the late 1600s, Britain next defeated France in the War of the Spanish Succession. At the ensuing Peace of Utrecht in 1713, Britain obtained the right to sell 4800 slaves each year in Spanish ports. Another advantage after 1751 was the British shift from a monopolistic chartered company to an association of merchants, which increased incentives by opening opportunities for individual traders. Finally, in the continuing Anglo-French colonial wars of the eighteenth century, the British fleet consistently hampered French operations. For these reasons, by 1785, the British were transporting thousands more slaves from West Africa than all of their competitors combined.

Despite this regional competition among Europeans, they conducted trade locally as a black-white partnership, largely on African terms. African rulers, who refused to grant any European nation a monopoly over the slave trade in their territories, were adept at playing one European group off another. Europeans, largely confined to their fortified coastal castles, recognized that they could easily be excluded from trade if they did not establish amicable working relationships with Africans. Hence, they learned to rely on African rulers who not only enforced their authority but also eagerly took profits from regular port fees, rents on the **barracoons** (slave stockades), and a contracted percentage on the sale of slaves.

CASE STUDY
African Empires in the Western Sudan

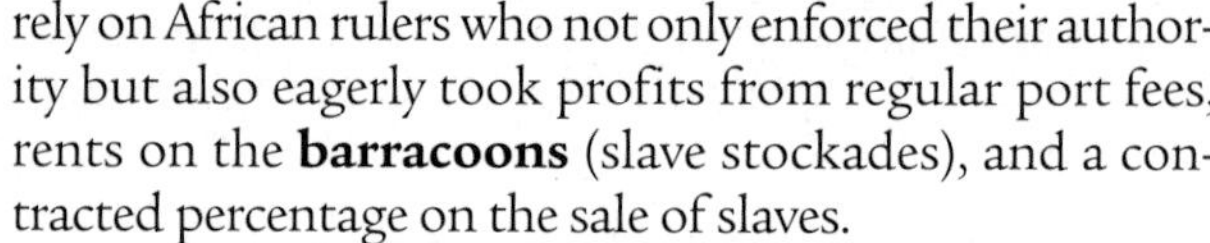

Europeans also turned to a class of Westernized blacks and Afro-Europeans who served as critical intermediaries and power brokers between Europeans and

barracoons—Slave stockades on the African coast. Barracoons were generally run by Europeans and supplied by African rulers, who leased the land for the buildings to the Europeans. Slaves were held in the stockades until shipped across the Atlantic to European colonies.

CHRONOLOGY

1550	1650	1700	1750	1800	1850
c. 1581–1663 Queen Njinga, ruler of Ndongo kingdom, Angola	**1632–1667** Reign of Ethiopian Emperor Fasilidas	**1713** British obtain right to sell slaves in Spanish ports	**1779** First Xhosa-European war in eastern Cape, South Africa	**1816** Shaka becomes king of Zulu people	**1868** Suicide of Téwodros II of Ethiopia
	1672–1727 Reign of Moroccan Sultan Mulay Ismail	**c. 1717** Death of Asante King Osei Tutu, West Africa	**1780s** Peak decade of transatlantic slave trade	**1834** Beginning of Great Trek of Afrikaners	
	1685 Portuguese invade kingdom of Kongo	**1725** Fulani Muslims launch *jihad* in Futo Jalon, West Africa		**1840** Zanzibar becomes center for Omani Arab rule	

Africans. Many adopted European dress, and a few were lionized in Europe or became Christian missionaries. Some found work as guides, clerks, or interpreters; others developed trading networks or participated actively in the slave trade. For example, Mae Aurelia Correia, the African wife of a Portuguese army captain posted to Portuguese Guinea, supplemented her husband's meager wages by venturing into the slave trade as well as by establishing peanut plantations that relied on slave labor. Most European traders were not so successful. Plagued by an unhealthy climate and surrounded by suspicious inhabitants, they led short and dreary lives in their remote posts.

Most slaves awaiting shipment in West African barracoons had been kidnapped or taken in war by other rival societies, although some were sold by their tribe or family to pay off debts, as punishment for breaking laws, or in times of famine and hunger. Only a few were seized directly by white raiders. Slaves were usually forcibly marched to the coast in gangs, chained or roped together, and worn down by poor food, lack of water, unattended illnesses, and brutal beatings. Once in the barracoons, where they might stay for several months, they were stripped and examined for physical defects by ship doctors and then displayed before captains who were looking to buy their cargoes. The bargaining was hard and complex as African traders carefully scrutinized the items exchanged for slaves. The most popular items were cloth (Indian textiles were preferred because they were durable and their colors did not run in hot climates), manufactured goods, bar iron, agricultural implements, alcohol, and firearms and gunpowder. Before some captives were loaded on slave ships, their families had the opportunity to redeem them through a payment or by substituting another slave.

About twice as many men as women were enslaved and shipped abroad. The traditional explanation for this imbalance is that men brought the highest prices in overseas markets because they could cope with the physical demands imposed on plantation laborers. But recent research has shown that women were just as likely to be assigned the harshest field work and that they fetched roughly the same prices as men. An important reason that more women slaves were kept in Africa was that they were more desired as domestic slaves in royal households, as concubines, and as agricultural laborers, and that they were less likely to resist. The British Royal African Company reinforced this imbalance by issuing a standing order to their ship captains to purchase two males for every female.

After spending time in the barracoons, slaves met a worse nightmare during the notorious **Middle Passage,** the voyage that typically took a month from Africa to Brazil and two months to the Caribbean and the United States. Slaves were separated according to age and gender. Women usually huddled together on a ship's open deck. To prevent rebellions, male slaves were chained together in pairs, in lower decks, each person allotted a space 16 inches wide by 30 inches high. Children, who made up about 10 percent of slaves, were placed in separate quarters. (See *Global Issues—Slavery* on p. 584 for more on slavery in world history from ancient times up until present day.)

Middle Passage—The collective name applied to the shipment of African slaves across the Atlantic throughout the time of the Atlantic slave trade. The voyage at sea generally took one to two months, depending on the destination, and most slaves were confined within the ship's hold. Mortality rates for the slaves ranged as high as 20 percent.

▲ A site for the slave trade since 1536, Goree Island is situated off the coast of Dakar, Senegal. Located in a holding place for slaves, the "Door of No Return" was thought to be the exit through which slaves were loaded on ships bound for the Americas, but the slaves were really placed on ships on a nearby beach. However, the Door has come to symbolize the millions of Africans who were shipped across the Atlantic, never to return to their ancestral homes.

Slavery

Why has slavery been so widespread?

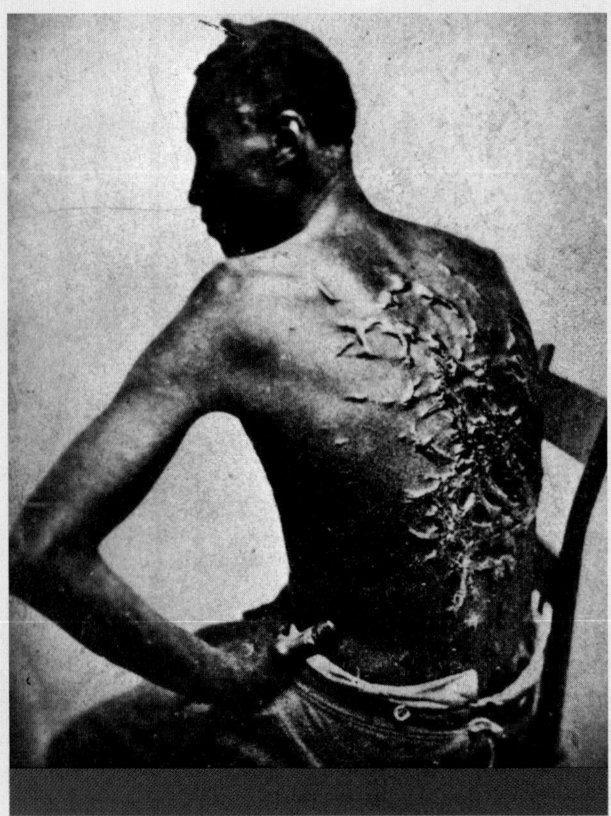

▲ Back of plantation slave whipped by his owner, Captain John Lyon, Louisiana, 1863.

Slavery—the practice of people forcing other people into servitude and treating them as property—has existed for most of recorded history. While the specific reasons why any one culture practiced slavery have varied, the simplest explanation for the existence of slavery is that, wherever and whenever it has occurred, certain people possessed the power to control other people absolutely, found it economically rewarding to do so, and faced little ethical or political opposition to their actions.

Traditionally, most slaves have been taken from outside the tribe, nation, or ethnic group that enslaved them, usually as war captives or kidnap victims. Most societies only extended social rights and protections to their own members, which made outsiders or "others" vulnerable to exploitation, particularly if they came from hostile communities. When slavery occurred within a group, those enslaved were generally singled out as punishment for criminal behavior, as debt repayment, or, as in the case of women and children, because of economic and physical vulnerability.

Most slaves have been used as agricultural workers. Agriculture was the primary source of wealth up until the nineteenth century, and the labor of slaves was needed to generate income for their masters. Slaves, however, have also served as artisans, soldiers, domestic servants, laborers, courtesans, prostitutes, and eunuchs. In certain cultures, notably the Ottoman and Arabic civilizations, slaves could rise to comparatively high stations when they showed great abilities as military leaders or administrators. In some cultures, slaves could buy their freedom or win it on the death of their masters. In others, slavery was a permanent condition, passed on from one generation to the next.

No one knows exactly when or where slavery originated. Some claim the institution is almost as old as the first *Homo sapiens*. The early Sumerians owned slaves who were usually captives taken in raids or wars. Early legal documents from the region between Mesopotamia and Egypt show the existence of debt slavery, a practice in which a person who could not repay his debt presented himself as payment. In fifth century B.C.E. Athens, one person in four was a slave, but their treatment varied widely, with some slaves considered members of the family while others were forced to perform life-threatening and physically demanding work such as mining or rowing in galleys. In ancient Rome, large numbers of slaves were taken from the various conquered peoples throughout the empire. Slave revolts were commonplace, often the result of brutal treatment in the large agricultural estates, where slaves served as both laborers and overseers. The founders of the Christian Church offered conflicting views on slavery. In the book of Colossians in the New Testament, St. Paul instructed slaves to obey their masters. Paul also urged the masters to treat their slaves as they would their brothers.

In China, war captives, criminals, and women of poor families made up the enslaved class as early as the Shang dynasty (1600–1027 B.C.E.). The archaeological record shows slaves toiling in workshops and fields, constrained by leashes and under the control of whips. Despite a long history of slavery, the Chinese showed an ethical discomfort with it. When the Emperor Wang Mang (8–23 C.E.) came to power, he forbade the buying and selling of slaves. Despite attempts to prevent slavery, the selling of indentured slaves remained a fixture of Chinese culture into the twentieth century.

Various forms of slavery have also existed in other Asian civilizations. Longstanding Hindu and Muslim legal codes justified the conditions under which bondage was lawful. Criminal activity could lead to enslavement as could being the target of a holy war. In the thirteenth and fourteenth centuries, the Mongols took so many Russian artisans as slaves that the knowledge of several crafts disappeared from Russia. Between 1400 and 1650, the Ottomans took over 200,000 mainly Orthodox Christian boys from their parents in the Balkans, converted these slaves to Islam, and trained them to be janissaries, elite infantry soldiers. Some of these slaves eventually rose to high positions within the Ottoman government.

Slavery was also practiced in the Americas. Mayan, Aztec, and Incan civilizations enslaved conquered peoples. Evidence of slavery can be found at the archaeological site at Cahokia in present-day Illinois and among the Plains Indians in the eighteenth and nineteenth centuries. When the Spanish conquistador Francisco Coronado traveled through the Pueblo towns of New Mexico in the sixteenth century, he found that people owned the slaves from present-day Kansas. Though a slave trade in the Americas predated European penetration, Europeans greatly intensified the trade after they integrated the region into their global trading networks in the sixteenth and seventeenth centuries.

Africa became the major source of slaves for both the Indian and Atlantic Ocean trades after 1300. The overseas trade grew progressively over the years as first Arabs along Africa's east coast and then later Europeans along the continent's west coast began to participate in and expand Africa's own internal slave trade. In the foreign and domestic market, slaves were paid for in cloth, tobacco, metal goods, cowrie shells, weapons, or alcohol. Both African sellers and the European and Arab buyers found the slave trade to be profitable and continually tried to tilt the advantage of transactions in their favor.

In the Atlantic trade, Portuguese, Spanish, Dutch, French, and English merchants dealt in African slaves as part of their global commerce after the fifteenth century. Portugal started the Atlantic trade, and Spain and Holland followed suit thereafter, but by the mid-seventeenth century and throughout the eighteenth century England and France assumed leading roles in the trade. Ironically, at the same time these two nations were profiting from the slave trade, they also served as seedbeds for the Enlightenment, the intellectual and political movement that led to the principles of universal human rights. Enlightenment writers such as John Locke and Voltaire made fortunes investing in companies that participated in the slave trade, just as many of the nobles and bourgeoisie of their nations did. From the sixteenth century to the nineteenth century, some twelve million Africans were shipped across the Atlantic to the Americas where most were forced to work in agriculture. Racism, specifically the belief that Africans were inherently inferior to Europeans and so deserving of enslavement, was a distinguishing characteristic of the Atlantic slave trade and slavery in the Americas.

In the Indian Ocean slave trade, Arab traders dominated from the fourteenth century through the sixteenth century. Beginning in the seventeenth century, however, the Dutch integrated the East African, South Asian, and Southeast Asian circuits of trade across the Indian Ocean, which had long been the "great highway" for eastern hemispheric migration, trade, and cultural diffusion. The Dutch transported slaves to their colonial holdings in the Netherlands East Indies (now Indonesia) and to other Indian Ocean ports. The volume of the Indian Ocean trade fluctuated between 15 and 30 percent of the Atlantic slave trade. By the end of the seventeenth century, slaves made up more than half the population of Dutch colonies and other Indian Ocean ports.

The international effort to abolish slavery is a relatively new movement that only began to take shape in Europe and its colonies in the middle of the eighteenth century. As the Enlightenment and English reform movements stressed the equality of all human beings, a growing number of people started to oppose slavery. Slaves also began to resist enslavement more vigorously. Haitian independence in 1804 represented the world's first successful slave revolt. In the United States, many freed slaves joined the abolition movement. At the same time, the development of machines and more efficient methods of production began to reduce the demand for labor in agriculture, and other economic areas. By the middle of the nineteenth century the United States and most European nations had made slavery illegal. In other parts of the world, slavery continued into the twentieth century. Today, all governments of the world condemn slavery, but traditional forms of slavery still exist in regions of Mauritania, Sudan, Myanmar, Pakistan, and Brazil. Moreover, Anti-Slavery International estimates that between 10 and 20 million people are currently subject to debt slavery the world over. Growing numbers of women and children transported across international borders and forced into prostitution or unpaid factory work also represent a new form of involuntary labor that many liken to slavery.

Questions

1. Why have so many societies kept slaves?
2. Why did the treatment of slaves vary so much from one culture to another?
3. What conditions do you think finally led to the abolition of legal slavery? What allows various forms of illegal slavery to exist today?

The treatment of slaves was abominable. White crews frequently resorted to threats of violence and lashings to control slaves. Slaves who contracted diseases were frequently thrown overboard. When slaves refused to eat, a special device, the *speculum oris,* or "mouth opener," was used to force-feed them. Some slaves jumped into the sea while being exercised. In 1694, the British captain of the *Hannibal* commented on the despondency of slaves in these conditions: "The negroes are so wilful and loth to leave their own country, that they have often leap'd out of the canoes, boats and ships, into the sea, and kept under water till they were drowned to avoid being taken up and saved by our boats. . . .[1]

Through the early seventeenth century, the cramped and unsanitary conditions and poor diets of slaves on board led to mortality rates of as many as 20 percent on each voyage. Most died from the dehydration caused by gastrointestinal illnesses such as dysentery and communicable diseases such as smallpox and fevers. With improved diets and quicker crossings, the mortality rate dropped to less than 10 percent by the end of the eighteenth century. European crews on these voyages did not fare any better. Because of diseases such as malaria and yellow fever that they contracted off the African coast, their mortality rate was almost as high as that of the slaves.

Nearly 400 slave mutinies took place during the Middle Passage. Most occurred shortly after ships left the African coast. Most of them failed, and rebels were punished with savage brutality. In 1797, women slaves on the *Thomas* rebelled a few days before the ship was due to land in Barbados. As they were exercising on deck, they seized guns from an unlocked musket closet and took control of the ship. After freeing the rest of the slaves, they were no closer to freedom because none of them knew how to sail the ship. The ship drifted for more than a month until a British warship captured the slaves and resold them into slavery.

The harsh conditions of the Middle Passage did not shake the Christian faith of slave ship captains, who stood to pocket from 2 to 5 percent of the proceeds from slaves they sold. "This day," British slave trader John Newton confided to his journal in 1752, "I have reason ... to beg a public blessing from Almighty God upon our voyage...." After four voyages, however, Newton underwent a dramatic conversion and left slaving for the ministry. His legacy is his moving hymn of atonement, "Amazing Grace."

DOCUMENT "A Defense of the Slave Trade"

The era after the Peace of Utrecht has been termed the slave century. Between 1600 and 1700, when the slave-trading companies were mostly state-chartered monopolies, some 1.5 million slaves were carried across the Atlantic. During the next century, when much more trade was being conducted by individual captains outside the forts, more than 6 million slaves were taken to the Americas. With higher prices for slaves on Caribbean sugar plantations fueling demand, the trade peaked in the 1780s when 750,000 Africans were taken from West and Central Africa.

Denmark was the first European state to end the slave trade in 1803, but it was Britain's decision to

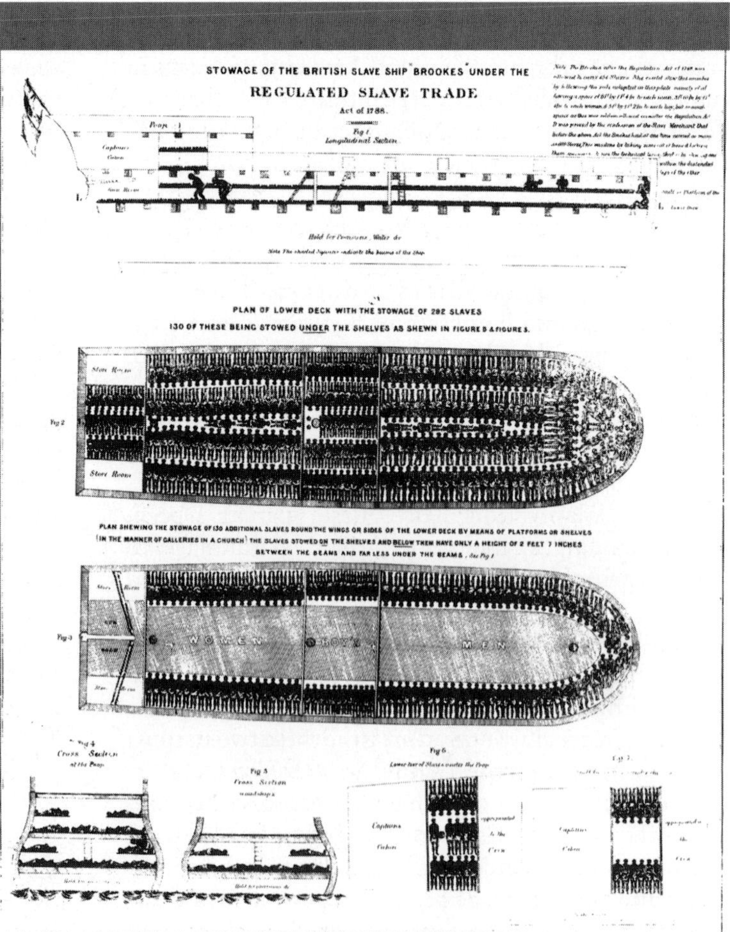

This diagram shows how slaves were packed into cargo holds for the notorious Middle Passage to the Americas. The plan was a model of efficiency, as slave traders sought to maximize profits by filling their ships up to and beyond capacity.

An African Pamphleteer Attacks Slavery

abolish the trade 4 years later that had the most far-reaching consequences. The ideals of the Enlightenment, in addition to the lobbying efforts of abolitionist movements in England, had prepared the way for this act, but even more decisive factors were the declining profitability of Britain's Caribbean plantations, a rise in the price of slaves, and pressures from British industrialists, who found it more profitable to invest in wage labor in European factories than in the sugar plantations. Although a British squadron did patrol the Atlantic after 1807, looking for slavers, the slave trade was not dramatically affected. Around that time, however, West Africans began making adjustments to their trading relations with the outside world.

There was more to the Atlantic exchange than the trafficking in human beings (p. 587). Africa's population was still expanding despite the devastation of the slave trade. New foods imported from the Americas, such as manioc (cassava), which could be grown in poor soils in forested areas and which could survive in droughts, and maize (corn), soon became staples because they could contribute many more calories to people's diets than other mainstays, such as sorghum and millet. Europeans also introduced tobacco, oranges, lemon, limes, pineapples, groundnuts (peanuts), Asian rice, and guavas to the African continent. In return, yams (sweet potatoes, which were the main provision for slaves on slave ships), sorghum, plantains, bananas, and melegueta pepper ("grains of paradise") made their way from Africa to the Americas. Groundnuts, which had come from South America, had made their way to the lower Congo region, where local people gave it the name *nguba*. After slaves from this area transplanted *nguba* to the Caribbean, peanuts were then taken to North America, where it was known as the "goober pea."

Whatever its unintended consequences, the Atlantic slave trade was a degrading experience for all the Europeans, Arabs, and Africans who participated in it. An estimated 12 million people were lost to Africa through the Atlantic slave trade over three centuries, and this number does not include the hundreds of thousands of slaves who died en route from their point of capture to the slave ports, in the cramped barracoons, and in the "floating tombs" that transported slaves to the New World.

African States and the Atlantic Slave Trade

Forms of domestic slavery were practiced in most African societies. A person could be offered into slavery as a guarantee to pay off a debt. Individuals who committed a major crime such as murder could be offered as a slave to a victim's family if it had not been adequately compensated. Slaves were a part of the household and worked with the master's family in chores and agricultural labor. The slave status did not last long, and slaves were usually freed within one to two generations. In centralized states, more demands were imposed on slaves, who lived in separate quarters and were less likely to end their bondage through **manumission.** As the demand for slaves from plantations and mines across the Atlantic escalated, African societies were confronted with the choice of whether or not to participate. Some states took advantage of the heightened demand for slaves to amass more power by investing in firearms and horses, while others devised strategies to defend themselves against slave raiders.

Mungo Park, "Slavery in Africa"

One active participant in the slave trade was the Yoruba kingdom of Oyo, situated inland on the savanna. Drawing on revenues derived from the slave trade, the Oyo *alafin* or king traded for horses from the north and assembled a cavalry that conquered the savanna region to the southwest all the way to the coast. Oyo's royal farms were tilled by slaves captured in warfare and the Sahelian slave trade, but as Oyo's rulers tapped into the Atlantic trade, surplus slaves were sold to European traders in exchange for firearms, cloth, and **cowrie shells,** which were a widespread form of currency in West Africa.

The *alafin* was not an absolute ruler. He governed with the advice of a seven-man council of state, the *oyo mesi,* and they in turn were overseen by a secret society of religious and political notables. If the *alafin* lost the backing of his counselors, they could force him to commit suicide. A turning point in Oyo's history came in the late eighteenth century when a senior counselor in the *oyo mesi* usurped the authority of the *alafin.* This bid for power set off a period of instability and internal revolts by tributary states and the Sokoto (SOH-ko-to) Caliphate that led to Oyo's collapse by the 1830s.

Of all the West African states, Dahomey (dah-HOH-may), located west of the Oyo kingdom, was particularly affected by the slave trade. Although a tributary state to Oyo for many years, Dahomey managed to maintain its autonomy, and in the mid-seventeenth century, it became a major power in its own right when its authoritarian rulers created a highly centralized state. Power revolved around the king, who passed his throne directly to his eldest son and appointed local chiefs who did not come from an established lineage. An influential figure in the palace was the queen mother, who was usually

manumission—The practice of freeing slaves from bondage. Conditions in Africa for granting freedom might include a female slave who bears a child by her master or a slave buying freedom from a master for an agreed-upon price.

cowrie shells—The cowrie, a marine gastropod, is common in the Indian Ocean, particularly around the Maldive Islands. Used as a currency in West Africa, cowrie shells were but one trade item offered by Europeans in exchange for slaves.

Document

A Slave's Memoir

Mahommah Baquaqua's account of his experiences of slavery and the slave trade is one of the few existing memoirs written by a slave. An attendant to a royal family in the Kingdom of Benin, he was kidnapped in 1845 and taken to a port on the West African coast. Although the slave trade from West Africa to Brazil had technically been illegal since 1815, slavers found ways of avoiding the British antislavery squadrons off the West African coast and took an additional 3 million Africans to Cuba and Brazil in the rest of the nineteenth century. Baquaqua was eventually sold into slavery in Brazil, but in 1847, he accompanied his owner, a ship's captain, to the United States. After the ship landed in New York City, free blacks and abolitionists encouraged him to escape and secure his freedom. Born a Muslim, Baquaqua was sponsored by Baptist missionaries in the United States and converted to Christianity.

When all were ready to go aboard, we were chained together, and tied with ropes round about our necks, and were thus drawn down to the sea shore. The ship was lying some distance off. I had never seen a ship before, and my idea of it was, that it was some object of worship of the white man. I imagined that we were all to be slaughtered, and were being led there for that purpose. I felt alarmed for my safety, and despondency had almost taken sole possession of me.

A kind of feast was made ashore that day, and those who rowed the boats were plentifully regaled with whiskey, and the slaves were given rice and other good things in abundance. I was not aware that it was to be my last feast in Africa. I did not know my destiny. Happy for me, that I did not. All I knew was, that I was a slave, chained by the neck, and that I must readily and willingly submit, come what would, which I considered was as much as I had any right to know.

At length, when we reached the beach, and stood on the sand, oh! How I wished I that the sand would open and swallow me up. My wretchedness I cannot describe. It was beyond description ... There were slaves brought hither from all parts of the country, and taken on board the ship. The first boat had reached the vessel in safety, notwithstanding the high wind and rough sea; but the last boat that ventured was upset, and all in her but one man were drowned ... The next boat that was put to sea, I was placed in; but God saw fit to spare me, perhaps for some good purpose. I was then placed in that most horrible of places.

The Slave Ship

Its horrors, ah! Who can describe. None can be so truly depict its horrors as the poor unfortunate, miserable wretch that has been confined within its portals! Oh! Friends of humanity, pity the poor African, who has been trepanned [entrapped] and sold away from friends and home, and consigned to the hold of a slave ship, to await even more horrors and miseries in a distant land ... We were thrust into the hold of the vessel in a state of nudity, the males being crammed on one side, and the females on the other; the hold was so low that we could not stand up, but were obliged to crouch upon the floor or sit down, day and night were the same to us, sleep being denied us from the confined position of our bodies, and we became desperate through suffering and fatigue.

Oh! The loathsomeness and filth of that horrible place will never be effaced from my memory; nay, as long as memory holds her seat in this distracted brain, will I remember that. My heart even at this day, sickens at the thought of it.

The only food we had during the voyage was corn soaked and boiled. I cannot tell how long we were thus confined, but it seemed a very long while. We suffered very much for want of water, but was denied all we needed. A pint a day was all that was allowed, and no more; and a great many slaves died upon the passage. There was one poor fellow so very desperate for want of water, that he attempted to snatch a knife from the while man who brought in the water, when he was taken up on deck and I never knew what became of him. I supposed he was thrown overboard.

When any of us became refractory, his flesh was cut with a knife and pepper or vinegar was rubbed in to make him peaceable (!) I suffered, and so did the rest of us, very much from sea sickness at first, but that did not cause our brutal owners any trouble. Our sufferings were our own, we had no time to share our troubles, none to care for us, or even to speak a word of comfort to us. Some were thrown overboard before breath was out of their bodies; when it was thought any would not live, they were got rid of in that way. Only twice during the voyage were we allowed to go on deck to wash ourselves—once whilst at sea, and again just before going into port.

Questions to Consider

1. What effect did the deplorable conditions on the slave ship have on the psychology of the slaves?
2. What audience was Baquaqua's biography written for, and how did that influence the content of his account?

From Robin Law and Paul Lovejoy, eds., *The Biography of Mahommah Gardo Baquaqua: His Passage from Slavery to Freedom in Africa and America* (Princeton: Markus Wiener Publishers, 2001), pp. 151-155.

chosen from a recently conquered territory. Her presence helped to integrate her people with the king; she played a pivotal role in selecting a new king.

The royal elite rigidly monopolized the slave trade and every aspect of the economy. Everyone was required to perform military service, even women, who provided an elite palace guard and who, in the early nineteenth century, served as a key regiment in major wars against Dahomey's rivals, including Oyo. As a way of balancing power with male officials, the king allo-

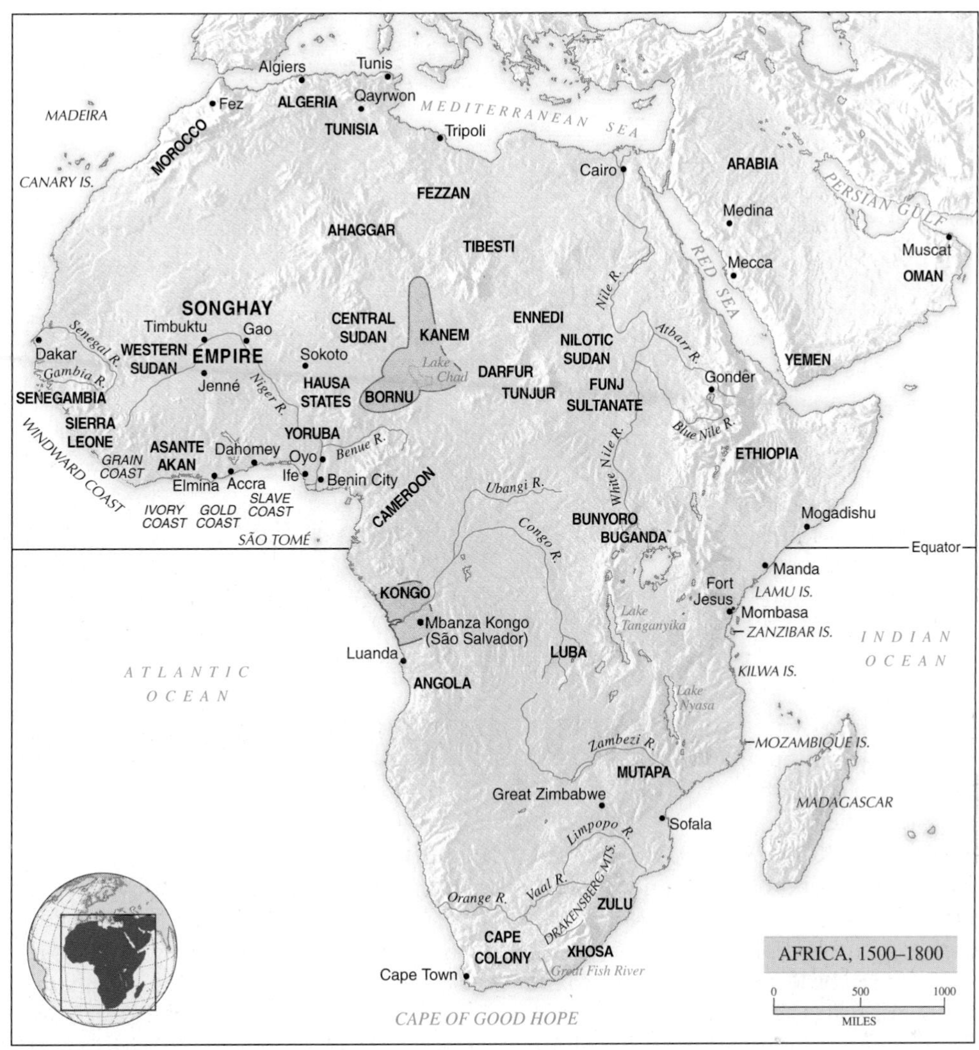

▲ From 1500 to 1800, Africans lived under a variety of political systems, ranging from small-scale societies to expansive monarchies. Dynamic kingdoms emerged in every region.

cated offices and responsibilities to the 5000 to 6000 women known as *ahosi* who served the royal court. Some were wives captured in warfare; some were wives provided by different lineages; and some were slaves. Although the legal status of female slaves was fixed, they were allowed to accumulate wealth and to assume many roles, including managing the king's resources, trading, owning private property, and serving as soldiers and ministers of state. Because of their unquestioned loyalty to the throne, female slaves were regularly appointed to the highest offices, including that of the queen mother, who did not have to be related to the king.

Another prominent regional state was Asante, a kingdom founded by Akan peoples in the gold-producing forests of the Gold Coast interior. Akan peoples had formed states based on the trade in gold, kola nuts, and slaves to the north and gold, slaves, and ivory to the Portuguese on the coast. But in the late seventeenth century, the Akan states were absorbed into the Asante kingdom, founded by *Asantehene* (king) Osei Tutu (OH-say too-too; d. 1717). Ruling from his capital at Kumasi, Osei Tutu transformed a loose confederation into a centralized state. He boosted his authority by using a consultative body, the Kotoko Council, and the Akan judicial system. He adopted the Golden Stool as the unifying symbol of Asante kingship and identity. When Osei Tutu died in battle, his successor, Opoku Ware (c. 1720–1750), extended Asante's boundaries to the savanna regions in the north and to the fringes of the forests in the south. As many as 3 million people lived within its dominion. The wars of expansion from the 1680s on were major factors in Asante's involvement in the Atlantic slave trade. Slaves captured in war or sent as tribute by conquered territories were deployed in gold mines and food-producing plantations or assimilated into families. Once the Asante kingdom began selling slaves to European traders, however, its revenues from slave sales eventually eclipsed the proceeds from the gold trade.

Queen Njinga of the Ndongo kingdom of Angola negotiated a treaty with the Portuguese in 1622. When an African had an audience before a Portuguese official, the African was normally expected to stand. Queen Njinga, however, ordered a female servant to kneel on all fours and sat on her back.

The southwest coast, from the Congo River to the Cunene River, was the largest source of slaves for the transatlantic trade. Roughly 40 percent of all slaves taken during the slave trade era came from this region. Although Dutch and British slavers were active in the area, Portuguese involvement in the Kongo kingdom's affairs was particularly intrusive. The kingdom witnessed civil strife throughout much of the seventeenth century. The Portuguese took advantage of the disorder to invade Kongo in 1685, leaving the central government in shambles and fragmenting the kingdom into ministates.

A movement to restore stability and cohesion to the kingdom was inspired by Kimpa Vita (known to the Portuguese as Doña Beatrice), a woman of noble birth. As a teenager, she claimed to have died and been reborn and to have been possessed by the spirit of St. Anthony in 1702. Her Antonian movement combined Kongo and Christian beliefs. She preached a personal religious experience that did not rely on Catholic priests, and her acolytes advocated the reunification of the kingdom under a king that she would choose. Although her message was very popular among peasants who longed for peace, it threatened Capuchin priests and royal factions vying for the kingship. After her opponents captured her, she was tried and convicted of treason and heresy and burned at the stake in 1706.

The Angolan hinterland suffered even more than the Kongo, and rulers had to maneuver constantly to protect their sovereignty. Queen Anna Njinga (c. 1581–1663) of the Ndongo kingdom was a survivor who was prepared to deal with most anyone. Succeeding her brother in 1618 in a kingdom that did not have a tradition of female sovereigns, she had to fend off hostile lineage groups that traditionally chose kings. To counter their opposition, she signed a treaty with the Portuguese in 1622 that allowed slave traders to operate in her kingdom, and she converted to Catholicism. Portuguese support was short-lived, however, and Queen Njinga, who led her troops into battle, organized a spirited resistance. She also moved east, resuscitating the nearby Matamba kingdom and taking advantage of their recognition of queens as rulers. Proceeds from slave trading gave her the resources to build up an army. When the Dutch entered Angola in 1641, she seized an opportunity to break free from the Portuguese and allied with the Dutch. However, after the Portuguese counterattacked with troops from Brazil, she negotiated another treaty with Portuguese officials in 1656 that opened her kingdom to Catholic missionaries and to Portuguese slavers in return for Portuguese recognition of her rule.

The Portuguese eventually conquered Ndongo and other kingdoms. When Brazil's sugar plantations required massive numbers of slave laborers in the 1600s, the Portuguese, operating from their coastal ports of Luanda and Benguela, turned Angola into a vast slave-hunting preserve. Armed bands of Portuguese mercenaries regularly intervened in conflicts in African kingdoms, and the kingdoms of Kasanje, Matamba, and Ovimbundu (OH-vim-BOON-doo) assisted the Portuguese by trading or raiding for slaves in remote inland areas.

Some prominent African states actively participated in the slave trade, but we also know that many African individuals and communities refused to join in and came up with defensive tactics to fend off the slavers. For instance, a community could move into thick woods or marshy areas or place villages on top of hills where they could see attackers coming from a distance. Villagers would also walk to their fields and markets in groups. Homes were made of straw that could be set alight to slow down raiders. Another approach was to build a fortified village with high walls and low entrances. This was a favored tactic in some places in Senegal, where Muslim **marabouts** (marr-eh-boo) created havens that warriors could not enter. In northern Igboland, villagers placed poisoned food, water, and wine on routes favored by slave raiders. In some cases, a community ironically had to participate in the slave trade to avoid having its members enslaved. The Balanta of Upper Guinea traded some slaves for iron so that they could produce iron weapons to defend themselves against other raiders.

The End of the Slave Trade in West Africa

What changes took place in African societies as the Atlantic slave trade came to an end?

On the West African coast, African societies were adapting to the tapering off of the Atlantic slave trade. Britain, which in the late 1700s was responsible for more than half of the slaves exported from Africa, and the United States had abolished the slave trade in 1807. Other European nations followed suit in subsequent decades. A British antislavery squadron patrolled the West and East African coasts, intercepting slave ships. Although the antislavery squadron managed to free about 160,000 slaves, it was a fraction of the overall slave trade. Between 1807 and 1888, close to 3 million more Africans were enslaved and shipped overseas, largely to sugar, coffee, and cotton plantations in Cuba and Brazil (see p. 499).

Britain and France established colonies in Sierra Leone and Gabon respectively for freed slaves. Sierra Leone's capital, Freetown, became the center for assimilating Africans from West, Central, and even East Africa. The city's **Krio** (KREE-oh), or Creole, community became a symbol in the region as an alternative to slavery. Although most Krios retained their original African languages, they learned to speak some English and developed a pidgin form of the language that came to be spoken widely along the West African coast. They applied their entrepreneurial skills and knowledge to establish an extensive coastal trading network and tap into the legitimate trade. They also created a new identity in which they began to think of themselves as Africans rather than members of individual ethnic groups or tribes.

Many Krios were Yorubas who had been sold into slavery as a result of Oyo's wars. Some were Muslims who established mosques in Freetown. Others were among the first to take advantage of mission schools and to convert to Christianity. Some became missionaries in their own right. Samuel Crowther returned to his Yoruba homeland and rose to become an Anglican church bishop.

Freed African-American slaves were settled in a territory established by the **American Colonization Society** (ACS) for former slaves who wanted to return voluntarily to Africa and for blacks captured on slave ships by the American antislavery squadron. The ACS selected a strip of territory in the Cape Mesurado area and pressured local Africans into ceding them the land. However, the black settlers who landed after 1821 had a difficult time adjusting. They were susceptible to diseases and looked down their noses at agriculture. When they declared themselves independent from the ACS and founded Liberia (from the Latin word *liber,* "free") in 1847, their population numbered only a few thousand.

The Americo-Liberians (as the settlers came to be called) patterned themselves on the United States, adopting the English language and a constitution based on the U.S. model and naming their capital Monrovia (after President James Monroe). Although their official motto was "Love of Liberty Brought Us Here," they did not extend freedom to indigenous Africans, who were regarded as uncivilized and backward. A caste system developed in which Americo-Liberians dominated politics and exploited the labor of indigenous Africans, who were not allowed to qualify for citizenship until 1904. Although Liberia's economy sputtered in the face of intense competition with European traders, and the civil service was riddled with corruption, Liberia managed to survive the European scramble for Africa and to remain an independent republic through the colonial period.

DOCUMENT
The History of Mary Prince

African societies involved in the transatlantic slave trade adjusted to its winding down in various ways. Some societies were so dependent on slave exports that they found it difficult to cope. Other societies shifted from exporting slaves to trading for more domestic slaves. The Asante kingdom in the Gold Coast acquired more domestic slaves to increase gold and kola nut production for trading with Europeans and the West African interior.

For many societies, the slave trade had been a negligible part of their overall trade, and African entrepreneurs and European merchants expanded their trading links. One African export that Europeans sought was gum arabic, extracted from acacia trees and

marabout–A Muslim holy man known for his wisdom and knowledge of the Qur'an.

Krio–A descendant of freed Jamaican slaves who were returned to settle in the Freetown area of Sierra Leone beginning in the late eighteenth century.

American Colonization Society–An organization founded in the United States in 1816 to promote the emigration of free African Americans to a settlement along the coast of West Africa that eventually was known as Liberia.

used for dyes in European textile factories. Another was palm oil, a key ingredient in candles and soap and the main lubricant for Europe's industrial machinery before the discovery of petroleum oil. Peanuts (called groundnuts) and latex were also important exports.

This shift to "legitimate" commerce did not necessarily lead to improvements or opportunities in the lives of many Africans. There was an increased demand for domestic slaves to till fields for certain products as well as porters to carry goods to the coast. Along the coast east of the Niger delta, where palm oil was a major export, palm oil production was organized on gender lines: men cut down the nuts from trees, and women extracted the oil. Although the male heads of households were the main beneficiaries of palm oil production, they gave women the proceeds from palm kernels. The demand for palm kernel oil escalated in the 1880s, when William Lever began selling Sunlight, a sweet-smelling soap made from palm kernel oil and coconut oil, to a mass market in England. Some women entrepreneurs used the profits from palm kernel sales to expand their involvement in palm oil production. However, the most important beneficiaries of the trade were not the producers but the rulers and merchants. In the Niger River delta, towns vying for control of the trade fought a series of wars.

Islamic Africa

What explains the rapid expansion of Islam in the West African Sudan in the eighteenth and nineteenth centuries?

At the end of the eighteenth century, Islam remained a vibrant force in certain regions of Africa. Muslim West Africa was beginning to experience a cultural revival and was expanding its following beyond traders and rulers. Islam was carried by a wave of religious zeal, which arose on the Senegal River and spread east across the savanna regions to Guinea and the Hausa states and to the upper Nile. In East Africa, however, Islam remained a coastal religion with limited appeal beyond the Swahili city-states.

Meanwhile, across the continent in the west, Morocco was under the control of a dynasty that established itself in 1631 and remains in power today. Sultan Mulay Ismail (1672–1727) corresponded with Louis XIV of France and sent an ambassador to the court of Charles II in England. His uncontested power was based on a large standing army, including a force of black slaves who were recruited or captured in the Sudan as children and trained for specialized tasks. The sultan proved himself an exceptionally competent administrator, a wily military commander, and a patron of the arts. Morocco's economy was based on a combination of agriculture, trade, and privateering, although its piratic activity was minor compared to that of Algiers and Tunis. Under Mulay Ismail's successors, Morocco prospered. It was not integrated into the Islamic heartlands but remained connected to them by long-standing traditions of commercial and intellectual exchange. Each year, Moroccan pilgrims and scholars made their way by land and sea to the shrines of Mecca and to the great academic institutions of the Middle East.

In the West African savanna region, Muslim states had languished as the trans-Saharan gold trade declined after 1650. The Moroccan conquest in 1591 had broken the Songhay Empire into many rival small kingdoms, but as Moroccan administrators intermarried with local people, their ties with Morocco weakened. The Moroccans themselves were displaced by the Tuaregs, another group of desert invaders, in 1737.

The region around Lake Chad was the center of one of the region's most important states, Kanem-Bornu, which became an important center of Islamic learning. The high point of Bornu's power was during the reign of *Mai* (king) Idris Aloma (c. 1542–c. 1619). After being exposed to the wider Muslim world on a pilgrimage to Mecca, he imported firearms from North Africa and employed Turkish musketeers and advisers to command his army. To lessen the possibility of revolt, which had plagued his predecessors, he placed trusted allies, rather than close relatives, in key positions around his kingdom. For over a century, Kanem-Bornu exerted a stabilizing force in the region around Lake Chad, but its power steadily waned during the eighteenth century. By that time, the Hausa city-states, notably Kano, Katsina, and Gobir, were becoming prominent, as they profited from the expanding trade in slaves now moving across the central Sahara to the Mediterranean.

In West Africa, the political map of the interior savanna dramatically changed in the eighteenth century as Fulani Muslim holy men launched a series of ***jihads*** and established new Muslim states across the region: Fulani-Tukolor kingdoms along the Senegal River in the west; the Sokoto Caliphate among the Hausa states; and the sultanates of Tunjur, Darfur, and Funj in the region south of Egypt.

In the west, Islam rapidly spread through a series of successful holy wars led by Fulani holy men who criticized the lax moralities and heretical policies of West African Muslims, particularly the rulers. The Fulani were cattle-keepers who, by the fifteenth century, had spread across the West African savanna, often pasturing their herds in regions controlled by

jihad—Literally "struggle" in Arabic; an Islamic term with broad meaning, ranging from the internal struggle of an individual to overcome sin to the external struggle of the faithful to address a social challenge or to fight against enemies and unbelievers in what is essentially a holy war.

Document

Usman dan Fodio on Women and Islam

One of the reasons Usman dan Fodio launched a *jihad* in 1804 was because of his outrage that Muslim leaders had strayed from the ideals of Islam and were not practicing the proper Muslim way of life as shown by the prophet Mohammad. In his previous writings, he had singled out the behavior of some married Muslim men towards their wives—beating them, paying attention to one wife over others, not encouraging their education, and not giving them and their children proper support. In contrast, dan Fodio provided his own wives and daughters with the opportunity to acquire education in Muslim schools. At the same time, he stressed they had to act and dress in the ways prescribed by the Muslim faith.

Most of our educated men leave their wives, their daughters, and their captives morally abandoned, like beasts, without teaching them what God prescribes should be taught them, and without instructing them in the articles of the Law which concern them. Thus, they leave them ignorant of the rules regarding ablutions, prayer, fasting, business dealings, and other duties which they have to fulfil, and which God commands that they should be taught.

Men treat these beings like household implements which become broken after long use and which are then thrown out on the dung-heap. This is an abominable crime! Alas! How can they thus shut up their wives, their daughters, and their captives, in the darkness of ignorance, while daily they impart knowledge to their students? In truth, they act out of egoism, and if they devote themselves to their pupils, that is nothing but hypocrisy and vain ostentation on their part.

Their conduct is blameworthy, for to instruct one's wives, daughters, and captives is a positive duty, while to impart knowledge to students is only a work of supererogation, and there is no doubt but that the one takes precedence over the other.

Muslim women—Do not listen to the speech of those who are misguided and who sow the seed of error in the heart of another; they deceive you when they stress obedience to God and to his Messenger (May God show him bounty and grant him salvation), and when they say that the woman finds her happiness in obedience to her husband.

They seek only their own satisfaction, and that is why they impose upon you tasks which the Law of God and that of his Prophet have never especially assigned to you. Such are—the preparation of foodstuffs, the washing of clothes, and other duties which they like to impose upon you, while they neglect to teach you what God and the Prophet have prescribed for you.

Yes, the woman owes submission to her husband, publicly as well as in intimacy, even if he is one of the humble people of the world, and to disobey him is a crime, at least so long as he does not command what God condemns; in that case she must refuse, since it is wrong for a human creature to disobey the Creator. The recompense for a woman who submits to her husband will be double, but only if she has first obeyed God and the Prophet.

Questions to Consider

1. What do Muslim teachings in general say about the proper role of women in family life and society?
2. What were dan Fodio's criticisms of the way Muslim husbands treated their wives?
3. Dan Fodio states that women must submit to their husbands. Does this contradict his encouragement of women's education?

From Thomas Hodgkin, ed., *Nigerian Perspectives: An Historical Anthology,* 2nd ed. (New York: Oxford University Press, 1975), pp. 254–255.

farming societies. In the highlands of Futa Jalon, the Fulani chafed at their Jalonke rulers' taxation and restrictions on pasture land. In 1725, they joined with Muslim traders and clerics to launch a *jihad* that by 1776 brought the area under Muslim and Fulani domination. Because of the war, slave raiding increased, and many captives were sold to work on local plantations or to European slavers at the Senegambian coast. In Futa Toro, in the middle valley of the Senegal River, other Fulani reformers joined with Tukolor Muslims to wage another *jihad*. They claimed that the Fulani elite had strayed from the Muslim faith, and they aimed to reestablish a kingdom based on Islamic law.

Their efforts inspired Fulani Muslims in the eastern Sudan—the most notable being Shehu Usman dan Fodio (1754–1817), son of a Muslim teacher and himself a scholar of some repute. When he began preaching in 1774, he stressed the fundamental principles of living a disciplined and devout Muslim life. Several decades later he began denouncing Muslim rulers in his home state of Gobir for ignoring Sharia law, for enslaving other Muslims, for tolerating what he perceived to be immoral practices such as public dancing and the playing of drums and fiddles, and for allowing the *bori* spirit possession cult to be practiced in the countryside. Because his criticisms drew the ire of Gobir's ruling elite, he and his followers followed the prophet Muhammad's example and took the Hijra, seeking a safe haven to the west. When a Hausa ruler lifted the exemption of Muslims from taxes, Usman mobilized his students, Fulani pastoralists, and Hausa peasants and declared a holy war against Hausa rulers in 1804. Usman's movement succeeded in overthrowing most of the Hausa states and unifying them into the centralized Sokoto Caliphate. This new state, with a capital at Sokoto on the lower Niger, encompassed several hundred thousand square miles.

Usman was caliph, and his brother Abdullahi and son Muhammad Bello (1781–1837) consolidated the caliphate. Usman retired in 1817 and Muhammad Bello succeeded him. Sokoto's rulers introduced a government based on Muslim administrative structures and were patrons of Muslim scholarship and schools. Although a Hausa aristocracy was replaced by a Fulani nobility, the latter allowed Hausa political and religious elites in the emirates a measure of local autonomy as long as they paid an annual tribute and recognized the caliph's political and religious authority.

Usman dan Fodio's revolution brought mixed results for women. He encouraged education among elite women and supported women who disobeyed husbands who did not educate them. His wives and daughters were educated. His daughter Nana Asmau (1793–1864), who participated in the holy war as a teenager, trained other women her age and younger to become teachers and wrote poetry that emphasized healing and counseling through reciting Qur'anic verses. However, women were generally expected to remain in seclusion and were excluded from meaningful roles in elite decision-making. The queen mother (*magajiya*) lost her power to veto decisions by male rulers and found her influence restricted to ritual matters.

The creation of the Sokoto Caliphate made little difference to the Hausa peasantry and slaves who served in households and tilled the fields of large plantations. Although elite women were freed up from agricultural production and expanded their production of indigo-dyed cloth, they were replaced in the fields by female slaves imported into the caliphate. Hausa traders maintained their prosperous links with Tripoli to the north and the Atlantic coast. Their trade items included kola nuts, grain, salt, slaves, cattle, and cloth, which made their way to countries as far away as Egypt and Brazil.

Africans and European Settlement in Southern Africa

What was the impact of European settlement on African societies in southern Africa?

Although tropical diseases such as malaria prevented Europeans from permanently settling in many parts of Africa, southern Africa had a temperate climate that made it possible for first the Dutch and then the English to establish colonies of trade and settlement in the Cape. Although the Dutch settlers later created a myth that the region south of the Limpopo River was unsettled and thus open to whoever could claim it (see p. 600), the area had been populated for many centuries by indigenous African societies with varied economies and political systems. They vigorously resisted the expansion of European settlers into the interior.

The earliest inhabitants of southern Africa were San (SAHN) hunters and gatherers and Khoikhoi (koi-koi), hunters and gatherers who had taken up sheep- and cattle-keeping. These were followed by Bantu-speaking groups that crossed the Limpopo River around the third century of the Common Era. These groups relied on mixed agriculture and herding cattle and sheep for their livelihoods. As they migrated into different parts of the region, the Bantu-speaking societies divided into two linguistic subfamilies. The Nguni (Swazi, Zulu, and Xhosa) largely settled to the east of the Drakensberg mountain range and spread down the Indian Ocean coast as far south as the Great Fish River, the point where the summer rainfall was insufficient for their agriculture. As this strip of land was hilly and well watered by rainfall coming off the ocean, Nguni families established scattered homesteads and formed small clan-based chiefdoms. Although splits in ruling families were common, as long as land was plentiful, factions could break away and form their own chiefdoms. The other Bantu-speaking group, the Sotho/Tswana (SOO-too/TSWAH-nah), populated the drier, rolling plains west of the Drakensberg Mountains. Because the grasslands were sparse, Sotho/Tswana cattle-keepers managed their scarce resources by clustering in villages and pasturing their cattle in outlying areas. Those nearest the Kalahari Desert created extensive villages, some containing as many as 10,000 to 20,000 people.

Small groups of Khoikhoi that inhabited the southwestern Cape were the first to make contact with European seafarers. In the late sixteenth century, Portuguese and English ships on the long voyage to India and Southeast Asia began making the harbor at Table Bay a regular stopover for rest and replenishment. Because they needed a reliable source of fresh meat,

Europeans depended on the Khoikhoi, who were usually willing to part with their old and sick cattle, in exchange for iron, copper, tobacco, and beads.

The English and Portuguese were followed by the Dutch East India Company, which founded a small settlement of 70 people at Table Bay in 1652. European settlers encountered a mix of African societies that had populated the region for many centuries. Because the company's primary goal was providing meat, fruits, and vegetables for its employees, its first governor, Jan van Riebeeck, had strict instructions to avoid friction and win the cooperation of the Khoikhoi. Only a few years later, however, the company made several fateful decisions that led to clashes with Khoikhoi bands.

Because their fruit and vegetable gardens did not yield enough, in 1657, the company allowed some of its soldiers to establish their own farms a short distance from the main company settlement. Dependent on its cattle trade with the Khoikhoi, the company decided to import slaves from elsewhere to work the farms. The first batches of slaves came from West and Central Africa, but, thereafter, the company turned to the Indian Ocean for most. The majority of slaves came from Mozambique and Madagascar, while the rest were brought over from India, Malaya, and Indonesia.

Over the next 150 years the Dutch colony, populated by a mix of Dutch, German, and Scandinavian settlers and Huguenot refugees fleeing persecution in France, developed a distinctive character. Company officials and personnel made up an elite at Cape Town; a second group included slaveholders whose plantations in the Cape Town vicinity produced fruit and wine; and a third group, the Boers (*boer* is the Dutch word for "farmer"; the settlers did not begin calling themselves Afrikaners until the late nineteenth century), consisted of migratory pastoralists called ***trekboers.*** By 1800, there were about 21,000 Europeans in the colony, compared to a slave population of about 25,000.

The gradual expansion of company farms into the interior alarmed the Khoikhoi, who saw their grazing lands threatened by Dutch takeover. As wars broke out with Khoikhoi groups in the Cape peninsula, the *trekboers* steadily began conquering Khoikhoi territory farther and farther from the company settlement.

Boer families lived a pastoral lifestyle, relying largely on their own resources and preferring infrequent contact with company officials in Cape Town. Boer men believed that it was their birthright to stake out farms of around 6000 acres apiece. They expected their sons to claim other farms of the same size, usually at the expense of indigenous people. By 1800, the Boers had extended the colony's boundaries 300 miles north and 500 miles east along the Indian Ocean coast.

For most of the eighteenth century, Khoikhoi and San bands resisted Boer expansion by carrying on guerrilla skirmishing. The Khoikhoi and San groups that wanted to maintain their autonomy migrated farther into the interior; others, who lost their herds, supplemented the slave population as servants or apprentices to Boers. White settlers began to refer to Dutch-speaking Khoikhoi and San, freed slaves, and mixed-race servants as "Cape Coloureds."

The Boers' first contacts with Xhosa chiefdoms were at the Great Fish River in the early 1700s. Although they initially worked out a mutually beneficial trading relationship, as more Boers moved into Xhosa territory, conflicts erupted, largely over land and cattle. The first war between the two groups broke out in 1779. Over the next century, eight more were to take place between Xhosa chiefdoms and Europeans. Unlike the small Khoikhoi and San bands, which lacked unity, Xhosa farmers outnumbered the Boers and lived in chiefdoms prepared to defend their land vigorously. Moreover, the Boers' advantage in armaments was slight. Two wars between Xhosa and Boers ended in stalemates, broken only by the entrance of the British into the Cape in 1795.

When France invaded the Netherlands in 1795, the British responded to an appeal by the Dutch royal house and colonized the Cape. Controlling the sea route around the Cape of Good Hope also allowed the British to protect the passage to India. After handing control of the Cape back to the Dutch in 1803, the British returned several years later and established a dominant presence in the Cape and southern Africa for the next century. The British were primarily interested in increased commercial ties with the Cape by expanding wine and wool production. The British relationship with European farmers who actively participated in the market economy was more amicable than that with Boer cattle-keepers, who kept their involvement in the market economy to a minimum. Throughout the nineteenth century, British strategic and economic interests would repeatedly clash with the desires of Boer pastoralists to maintain their independent lifestyle.

African State Formation

In the first decades of the nineteenth century, African societies in southeastern Africa were swept up in a period of political transformation known as the **Mfecane** ("the crushing"). Its origins can be traced to increased competition by chiefdoms for grazing land following a series of severe droughts and for control of

trekboers—Migrant farmers who moved eastward from the Cape of Good Hope in the eighteenth century.

Mfecane—A term that historians use to describe a period of heightened warfare and state formation in the early nineteenth century in southern Africa.

▲ Print of Shaka, King of the Zulus. Shaka established a major kingdom based on innovations in battle tactics and weaponry.

first the ivory and then the cattle trade with the Portuguese at Delagoa Bay. However, it was the Zulu clan, a minor chiefdom when the Mfecane began, that became the region's most formidable military power.

The Zulu owed their rise in prominence to their king, Shaka (c. 1786–1828). When he was born about 1786, his father was chief of the Zulu clan, which was later part of the Mthethwa (im-TE-twah) Confederacy ruled by Dingiswayo (DEEN-gis-WAI-yoh; c. 1770s–1816). When Shaka's father rejected his mother, Shaka was forced to spend his childhood among his mother's people. As a young man, he enrolled in one of Dingiswayo's fighting regiments. Young men of about 16 to 18 traditionally went to circumcision schools for a number of months to prepare themselves for manhood. Because Dingiswayo needed soldiers who could be called into battle on short notice, he abolished the circumcision schools and enrolled his young men directly into regiments.

Shaka soon distinguished himself as a warrior, and he rose rapidly in Dingiswayo's army. Shaka assumed the chieftaincy of the Zulu on his father's death in 1815 and became leader of the entire confederacy a few years later, after Dingiswayo was killed in a trap laid by enemies. He regrouped his followers and won over others; eventually, he vanquished his opponents. He then began constructing, primarily by cattle raiding, a major kingdom between the Phongolo and Tugela rivers that dominated southeastern Africa.

Shaka was best known for adopting new weapons and battle strategies that revolutionized warfare. He armed the Zulu army with a short stabbing spear that was not thrown but used in close fighting. He employed the *buffalo horn formation,* which allowed his soldiers to engage an opponent while the horns or flanks surrounded them. He drilled his soldiers so that they could march long distances on short notice. He also transformed his clan into a major kingdom of about 25,000 people by assimilating large numbers of war captives. He created a new hierarchy in which power was centered in his kingship and status was based not on descent but on achievement in the military regiments. He assigned his generals (*indunas*) to regimental villages around his kingdom. Groups of young women were also attached to regiments to produce food and carry out domestic chores. They eventually became the wives of the warriors, who were not allowed to marry until Shaka gave his permission.

Shaka's repeated raids for cattle and captives throughout the area proved to be his downfall, as his regiments tired of constant campaigns. Several of his half-brothers and one of his generals conspired against him and assassinated him in 1828.

During the Mfecane, refugee groups escaped Shaka's domination by migrating to other parts of the region. Some headed much farther north, adopting Shaka's fighting methods and establishing kingdoms on the Shakan model in Mozambique, Zimbabwe, Malawi, and Tanzania. Still other peoples survived by creating new kingdoms that knit together clans and refugees. One kingdom forged in this way was Moshoeshoe's Basotho kingdom.

The son of a minor chief, Moshoeshoe (moh-SWESH-shwee; c. 1786–1870) gained a reputation as a cattle raider as a young man. He succeeded his father as refugee groups began streaming into his area in the foothills of the Drakensberg. To escape their raids, in 1824 Moshoeshoe moved his small following to an impregnable, flat-topped mountain called Thaba Bosiu. Over the next several decades, he creatively built a kingdom that became one of the most powerful in the region. Moshoeshoe accumulated vast cattle herds through raiding, and he used **mafisa,** a traditional practice of lending cattle to destitute men so they could establish their own homesteads, to win their loyalty. Moshoeshoe married many times to build up

mafisa—A traditional practice among South African tribes of lending cattle to destitute men so they could establish their own homesteads.

Seeing Connections

Moshoeshoe in European Dress

Dress styles often have symbolic meanings and make important statements about social status. Moshoeshoe, the Basotho king, was photographed in 1860 while having discussions with the British governor of the Cape Colony. Although he often appears in drawings wearing a traditional garb of skins, for this and other occasions when he met British officials, he wore the formal dress of an upper-class Englishman, including an elaborate cloak and a large black top hat. Moshoeshoe's choice was deliberate. For him (and other African leaders who adopted this style), wearing formal dress conveyed a clear message that he expected to be treated equally with those with whom he was negotiating.

political alliances with neighboring chiefs and placed his sons and brothers as governors in different part of the expanding Basotho kingdom. He armed his warriors with battle-axes and formed a cavalry using ponies bred for the rugged mountain terrain.

Moshoeshoe is best remembered for his diplomatic skills. He was prepared to fight if necessary, but he preferred to negotiate wherever possible. On many occasions, he managed to salvage difficult situations by engaging in diplomacy and exploiting divisions among opponents. When a band of Ndebele warriors raided his kingdom for cattle in the late 1820s, Moshoeshoe's forces easily repulsed them. However, Moshoeshoe sent cattle to the retreating Ndebele warriors so they would not go home empty handed and provoke another raid from their ruler.

The Great Trek and British-Afrikaner Relations

As African kingdoms in southern Africa were undergoing a period of transformation, groups of Boers were preparing to escape British control by migrating into the interior of southern Africa. Prompted by the Napoleonic wars, Britain resumed control over the Cape Colony in 1806 to protect the sea lanes around the Cape of Good Hope. The British were intent on expanding commercial opportunities through wine and wool production; the Boers resented any interference with their pastoral way of life.

Relations between the two groups deteriorated in the next decades. At first the British won Boer approval for a law that tied Khoikhoi servants to white farmers, but after a humanitarian outcry from missionaries over abuses of servants, the British instituted an ordinance giving Khoikhoi farm laborers equal rights. Britain also abolished the slave trade in 1807, driving up the price of slaves, and in 1834, it emancipated the slaves. However, this action did not improve the conditions of former slaves, as most of them, unskilled and uneducated, ended up as free but servile labor on white farms. The last straw for the Boers came in 1836 when the British handed back land to Xhosa chiefdoms whose land had been conquered in a recently completed war.

To many Boers, who had very little personal capital other than their herds and found it virtually impossible to purchase land in the Cape Colony, the solution was to escape further British interference by heading

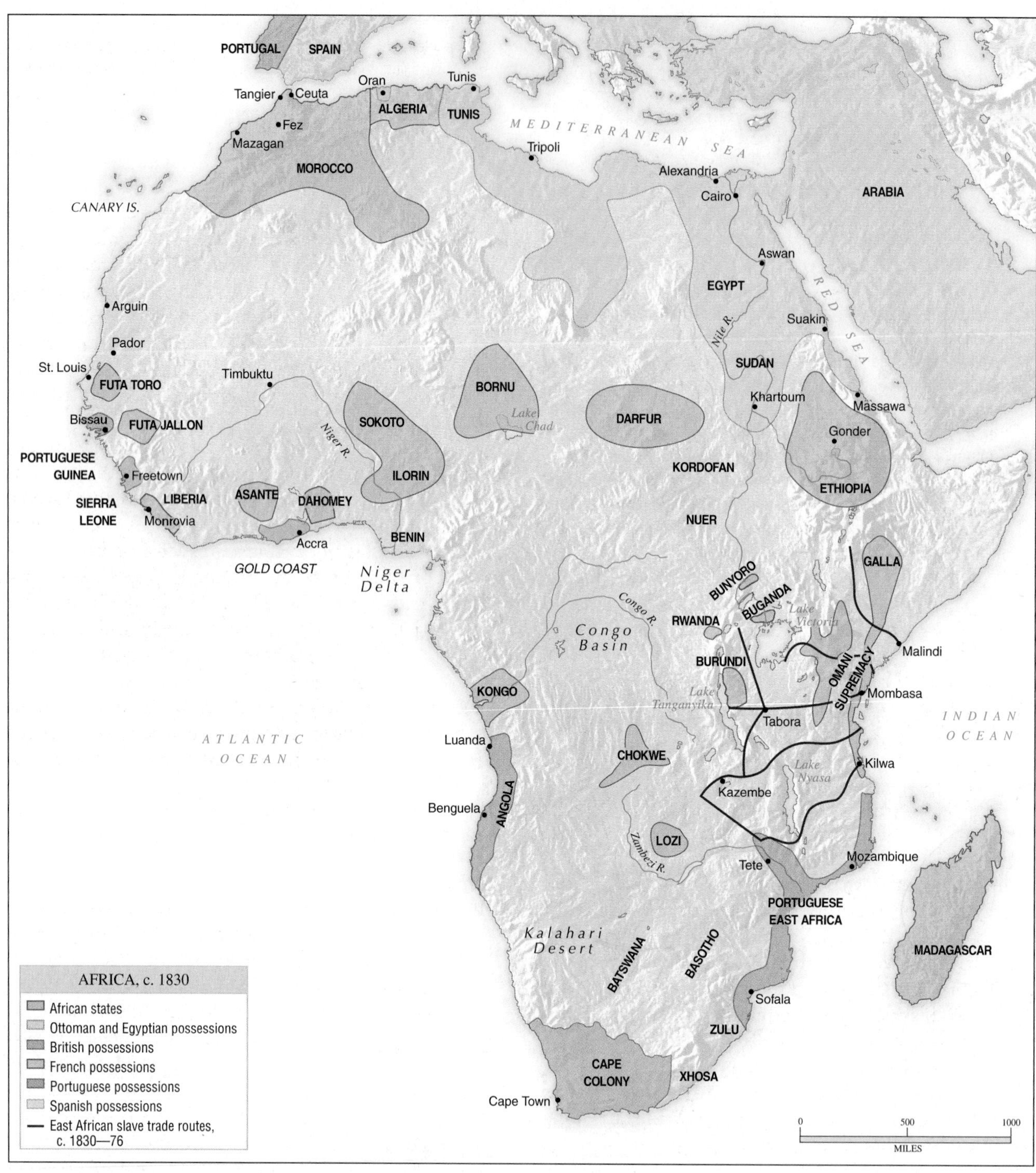

▲ Before the European conquest of Africa in the late nineteenth century, Africans in all parts of the continent were establishing new kingdoms or expanding old ones.

northeast for the high plateau, or ***veld***. In the mid-1830s, bands of migrants known as ***voortrekkers*** undertook a migration called the Great Trek in their ox-drawn wagons to lands where they could restore their way of life and maintain their domination over blacks. Each band numbered several hundred people. A total of about 15,000 *voortrekkers* eventually participated in the migration.

veld—The high plateau region within the interior of South Africa.

voortrekker—An Afrikaner farmer who migrated into the interior of South Africa in the 1830s as part of the Great Trek.

Because the Boers were pastoralists, many African rulers treated them initially as another group of cattle-keepers migrating through their lands. When *voortrekker* groups reached Moshoeshoe's kingdom, he allocated land for them to pasture their cattle temporarily. Because African societies did not have a concept of private land ownership, Moshoeshoe was not

◀ The primary transportation of *voortrekker* groups that migrated into the interior of southern Africa were light and strong wagons that were ideally suited to the rough terrain they were forced to cross. Despite their maneuverability, they could carry a surprising amount of household and other goods. This picture shows a wagon crossing a particularly difficult river.

ceding the land. However, the Boers regarded the land as their own and refused to part with it. One of Moshoeshoe's sons compared the situation to a person inviting a guest to sit down in his home and the guest taking ownership of the chair.

The *voortrekkers* established two republics: the Orange Free State and the Transvaal. For the rest of the century, they solidified their control by engaging in wars of land conquest against African kingdoms. In the meantime, the British prevented the Boers from having direct access to the Indian Ocean by extending their own settlement along the eastern coast north of the Cape and founding the colony of Natal.

African rulers such as Moshoeshoe became adept at dealing with both the Boers and the British and taking advantage of the rivalry between them. He invited French Protestant missionaries to reside in his kingdom so that he could draw on their knowledge of European life, technology, and politics. He used them as scribes to send diplomatic exchanges to British officials.

Moshoeshoe's overtures to the British were initially successful. When the British drew a boundary line between the Basotho and the Boers in 1843, they favored Moshoeshoe's claims. British policy shifted a few years later to absorb the Boer states, and Moshoeshoe saw the boundary redrawn to favor Orange Free State claims. He fought a British force to a draw in 1852, and after the British changed their policy again and withdrew from the Boer Republics in 1854, he waged two wars with the Orange Free State. The first war in 1858 ended inconclusively, but in the second, the Boers were on the verge of destroying his kingdom when Moshoeshoe successfully appealed to the British government for protection in 1868.

In 1877, British policy shifted in response to diamond discoveries in the interior of the Cape Colony.

▼ In the 1830s, bands of Afrikaners migrated from the Cape into the interior of South Africa. Through the conquest of African lands, they established two republics, the Transvaal and the Orange Free State.

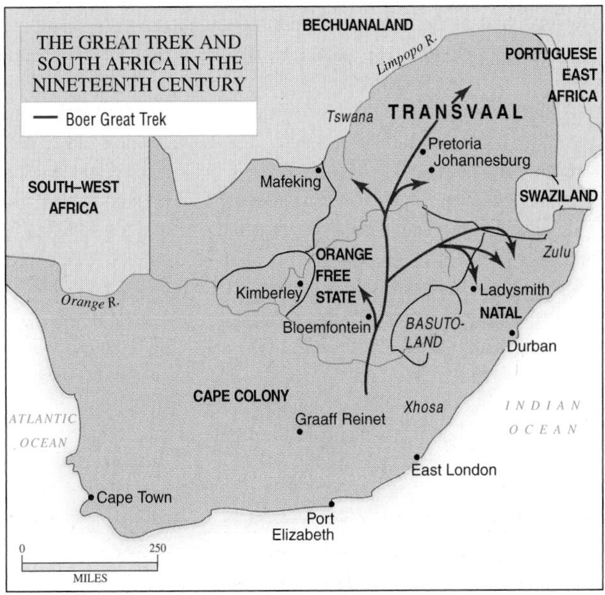

Discovery Through Maps

The Myth of the Empty Land

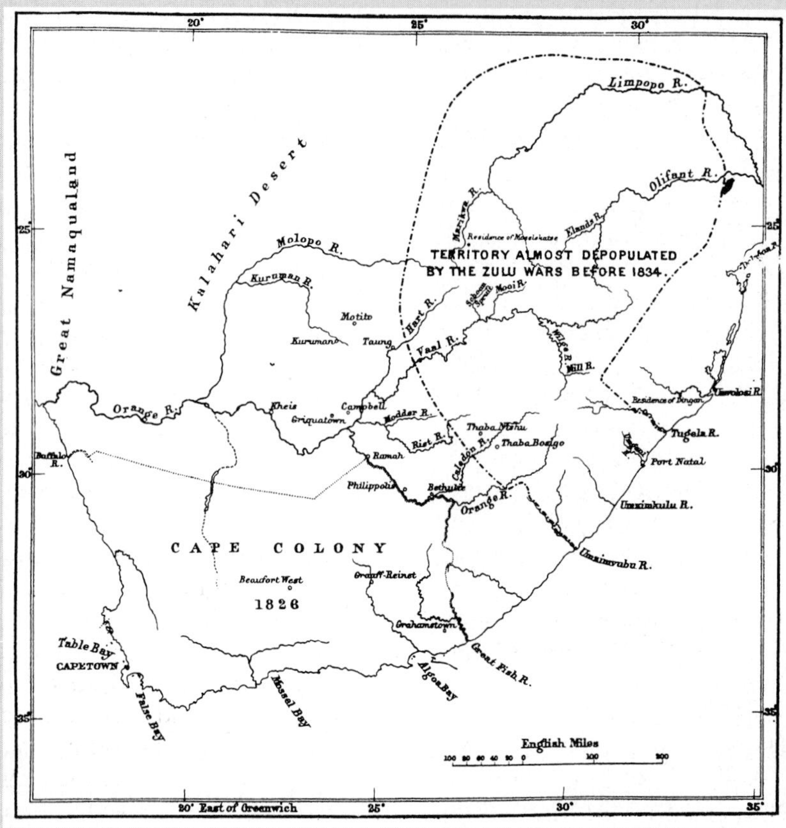

European settlement in various parts of the world was usually accompanied by the conquest of land from indigenous peoples. Because the settlers did not have a historic claim to the land, they often constructed their own versions of the past to justify their right to be there. In South Africa, one myth that white settlers created was that Dutch settlers arrived in southern Africa about the same time as Bantu-speaking peoples, the ancestors of most present-day Africans—in the mid-seventeenth century. Hence, white settlers could claim that, as they migrated from the western Cape into the interior of South Africa, they were moving into an unpopulated land that was up for grabs. Europeans could lay claim to the land, and they had just as much right to it as Africans did.

A variation of the "myth of the empty land" was based on a late nineteenth-century map drawn by George McCall Theal, a Canadian who settled in the Cape in 1861. Theal's map shows the South African interior virtually depopulated because many Africans had been displaced by the wars of the Zulu king Shaka in the 1820s and 1830s (see p. 596). Thus, the Boers who trekked into the interior in the 1830s were settling on land no longer occupied by Africans. In a speech delivered to a Cape Town audience in 1909, Theal clearly revealed his motives for the way he drew his map. "We must ... prove," he declared, "to these people [Africans] that we were no more intruders than they were, and that they enjoyed as much as they were entitled to." He added, "In reality this country was not the Bantu's originally any more than it was the white man's, because the Bantus were also immigrants ... most of their ancestors migrated to South Africa in comparatively recent times."

Theal's "myth of the empty land" became an article of faith for many white South Africans until late in the twentieth century. His interpretation was a standard feature in South African history textbooks used in both white and black schools, and South African government propaganda relied on it to justify the apartheid system to the international community.

Questions to Consider

1. The ownership of disputed land has been a thorny issue in many countries. Are there myths that settler groups have devised in other parts of the world to justify their conquests and domination of indigenous peoples and the land?
2. How accurate is the claim of Theal's map that "Zulu Wars" had depopulated the interior of South Africa before Afrikaners set out on the Great Trek?

From Christopher Saunders, *The Making of the South African Past: Major Historians on Race and Class* (Cape Town: David Philip, 1988), p. 39; Marianne Cornevin, *Apartheid Power and Historical Falsification* (Paris: UNESCO, 1980), p. 79.

Desiring to create a unified regional labor market, Lord Carnarvon, the Colonial Secretary, established a confederation of white-ruled states in the region and took over the Transvaal with little resistance from the Afrikaners (the name taken by the Boers about this time). The British attempted to win Afrikaner compliance by launching offensives against their main African rivals, the Pedi and Zulu kingdoms.

Although the Zulu had coexisted peacefully with British and Afrikaners for many decades, the British now perceived them as an obstacle to white control of the region and manufactured a war against the Zulu kingdom. They launched a propaganda war, depicting the Zulu King Cetshwayo (c. 1832–1884) as an oppressive tyrant who had lost the support of his people and threatened the stability of the region. After the British issued an ultimatum demanding that Cetshwayo disband the age regiments, the basis of his power, within 30 days, a war was inevitable.

Contrary to British expectations, Cetshwayo had the full support of his army and most of his kingdom. The war started disastrously for the British when, on January 20, 1879, the Zulu army caught a British column by surprise at Isandhlwana and overwhelmed them. A handful of British soldiers survived the battle. Cetshwayo hoped the British would end their aggression following their defeat, but they renewed their efforts and, six months later, put an end to the Zulu kingdom by carving it into 13 small pieces and exiling Cetshwayo.

This victory did not improve British relations with Transvaal Afrikaners. In 1881, they rebelled against British rule and scored a series of military successes. The British agreed to pull out of the Transvaal, although they still maintained to have a voice in its foreign affairs.

MAP
South Africa

African State Formation in Eastern and Northeastern Africa

How was eastern Africa integrated into the global economy?

During the eighteenth century, strong new kingdoms arose in the south central and eastern sections of Africa. Portuguese intervention in these regions, like that elsewhere in Africa, proved calamitous. In the seventeenth century, Portuguese settlers in Sena and Tete in the Zambezi River valley had intervened to support the *Mwene Mutapa,* or king, in a civil war within the Mutapa state; they won concessions from the king to extend trading fairs and gold-mining operations in the Zimbabwean highlands. When the *Mwene Mutapa* then attempted to curb Portuguese adventurers, they deposed him and installed a successor they could influence.

The fragmentation of the Mutapa Kingdom created a power vacuum on the Zimbabwe Plateau. Young men who lacked cattle to start their own homesteads joined the armies of wealthy patrons who were contesting for power. The most successful of these warlords was Dombo (d. 1695), who took the title *Changamire.* In the late seventeenth century, his *Rozvi* soldiers conquered the remnants of Mutapa and other kingdoms in the region. Then, Dombo's army turned its attention to the Portuguese, expelling them from the trading fairs. Thereafter, the Portuguese were allowed to trade in the interior only through African agents.

The Portuguese presence in the Zambezi River valley was restricted to the **prazos,** huge estates run by Portuguese settlers (*prazeros*) who, over time, intermarried with Africans and assimilated into local African cultures. When they failed to eke out a living from agriculture, the *prazeros* became warlords whose slave armies exacted tribute from clients and hunted elephants for the ivory trade.

In East Africa, most states remained small, except in the region west of Lake Victoria, where two kingdoms, Bunyoro and Buganda, vied for power. Bunyoro dominated a confederation based on village-based chiefdoms that paid tribute to Bunyoro and contributed regiments for cattle raids against neighboring societies. Bunyoro's economy was based on hunting, herding, and agriculture. In the late eighteenth century, those clans most likely to protect themselves against Bunyoro's raids, formed Buganda, a rival kingdom to the northwest of Lake Nyanza (later renamed Lake Victoria). Buganda's king (*kabaka*) rapidly moved his soldiers in boats on Lake Nyanza and allocated conquered lands to territorial chiefs and distributed land to lesser chiefs. Buganda's staple food was the banana, which had a high caloric yield and thrived in the rich, fertile soils bordering Lake Victoria. The banana could be produced on an annual basis, unlike the shifting cultivation practiced in most savanna regions of Africa. Because cattle did not thrive within Buganda's borders, Buganda's regiments regularly carried out cattle raids in neighboring chiefdoms to the west.

In East Africa, Islam was largely restricted to the coastal area, despite the fact that two centuries of Portuguese tyranny were brought to an end in 1698 after a 3-year siege of Fort Jesus by Omani Arabs responding to appeals of the Swahili city-states. The Portuguese retreated to their bases in southern Mozambique, but their expulsion did not bring peace and stability to the Swahili states, which fought among themselves. Pate, benefiting from immigrants from the Hadramaat who developed its trading capacity, eclipsed Kilwa as the leading Swahili state.

Oman, on the southeastern coast of the Arabian peninsula, was a major producer of dates. Oman's rulers took advantage of their new position and

prazos—Leased crown estates in the Zambezi River valley under Portuguese control.

▲ Buganda, a kingdom situated west of Lake Victoria, became a regional power in the late eighteenth century. A wide avenue led to the royal palace at its capital, Rubaga.

exported dates to East Africa in exchange for slaves for their plantations. In the late eighteenth century, the Omani ruling dynasty, the Busaids, set up a headquarters on Zanzibar and established a stranglehold over commerce along the East African coast. Non-Omani traders were excluded from trading along the coast, and Zanzibar merchants had to give the Busaids a 5 percent tax on the worth of their goods.

Zanzibar became so important to the Busaids that Sultan Sayyid Said (1791–1856), who had made trips to the island for over a decade and who had built palaces for himself and his family, transferred most of his court and government there in 1840. The sultan also welcomed a British agent of the East India Company to reside in Zanzibar and to keep the lines of communication open with the British government.

After dispatching an antislavery squadron to the Indian Ocean, the British initially established a boundary that prohibited slave trading to India, but allowed the Omanis to sustain their slave operations on the East African coast to Oman and the western Persian Gulf region. Eventually, the British began pressuring Said to give up his slave operations, and his compromise was to build up clove plantations on Zanzibar. In 1848, the British limited the slave trade to eastern Africa and its naval squadron aggressively stopped any Arab vessel thought to be transporting slaves. Zanzibar became a base for British ships and British officials dictated policy to the Omanis. Although Zanzibar did not become a British protectorate until 1890, it had long since lost its autonomy.

Throughout the nineteenth century, East and Central Africa were increasingly drawn into the world economy through long-distance trade. Gold and ivory had long been exported to China and India. Indian craftsmen especially found African ivory easier to carve into jewelry and ornaments than Indian ivory. But now ivory was in demand by European middle classes for luxury items such as combs, billiard balls, piano keys, and cutlery handles. Elephant herds paid an enormous price; 33 elephants were slaughtered for every ton of ivory exported. The scourge of slavery also ravaged the region. During the nineteenth century, several million people were enslaved. Half of them were sent to southern Arabia, Sudan, and Ethiopia, while the rest ended up on French sugar plantations on the Indian Ocean islands of Mauritius and Réunion; on Brazilian sugar plantations, whose owners found West African slaves too highly priced; and on Arab-run clove plantations on Zanzibar and nearby islands.

The long-distance trade largely consisted of ivory and slaves brought in caravans from the interior to the coast in exchange for trade beads and cotton cloth, much of it produced by American textile mills. The trade between the coast and the interior opened up new opportunities for middlemen trading groups. The Yao, Nyamwezi (nyam-WAY-zee), Afro-Portuguese, Kamba, and Swahili Arabs controlled routes in different parts of the region and recruited thousands of porters for their caravans. As Swahili merchants established trading centers such as Tabora in the interior to facilitate and oversee their networks, the Swahili language increasingly became the lingua franca along trading routes. With imported firearms and slave armies, some of the leading warlords established conquest states based on their control over the slave trade. Mirambo (1840–1884), a Nyamwezi chief, and Tippu Tip (c. 1830–1905), who was of Arab and Nyamwezi parentage, carved out domains east and west of Lake Tanganyika, respectively.

This was the era when a distinct Swahili identity developed along the coast and the maturing Swahili language, assimilating Arabic words to a greater degree into its vocabulary, produced its earliest poetry. The primary language of traders was Swahili, which spread from the coast to far into the interior.

Many African kingdoms such as Rwanda were not dependent on long-distance trade for their survival. Rwanda was composed of three main groups: the Twa, who were hunter-gatherers; the Hutu, Bantu-speaking farmers; and the Tutsi, a pastoral Nilotic people who were the last to settle in the area. Over the centuries, Tutsi clans had established a patron-client relationship with Twa and Hutu clans, but the lines between the groups were not clearly drawn. Hutu and Tutsi intermarried and shared a common language, religious beliefs, and cultural institutions, and the distinctions between Tutsi patrons and Hutu clients were often blurred.

However, in the late nineteenth century, the Nyiginya, a Tutsi clan led by King Rwabugiri, conquered other Tutsi and Hutu clans. Rwabugiri's state was highly centralized and favored the Tutsi minority, who served as administrators, tax collectors, and army commanders and controlled grazing land. Hutu chiefs were in charge of agricultural lands but tended Tutsi cattle and paid tribute to their Tutsi overlords.

While new states were rising in East Africa, the oldest African polity, the Kingdom of Ethiopia, was fragmenting. A source of trouble was the presence of Catholic missionaries. In 1607, Emperor Za-Dengel, hoping to attract more Portuguese arms and musketeers to counter his rivals from the nobility, invited Jesuit priest Pedro Pais to his court as a teacher, diplomat, and adviser. However, when Za-Dengel ignored Pais's advice and issued a proclamation banning the customary observance of the Saturday Sabbath, the nobles rose up and overthrew him. The Emperor Susneyos (soos-NAY-yohs; 1604–1632) consolidated the relationship with the Jesuits and secretly converted to Catholicism in 1612. He,

Around 1635, Emperor Fasilidas established a new capital at Gonder to unify Ethiopia's Christian north. To promote his leadership and authority, he constructed a castle with blocks of brown basalt in the center of the town.

too, subsequently forbade the observance of Saturday Sabbath as well as renouncing the Monophysite belief that Christ had both human and divine qualities. Susneyos's public conversion to Catholicism in 1622 and the zealous policies of Bishop Alphonso Mendez, head of the Jesuit mission after 1625, incurred the wrath of the Ethiopian church. Mendez tried to Catholicize the Ethiopian Orthodox faith by reordaining Ethiopian priests, reconsecrating the churches, and banning circumcision. Land was transferred from the Ethiopian church to the Catholics. A bloody rebellion forced Susneyos to reestablish the Orthodox faith in 1632. However, he had lost so much support that he abdicated. When his son, Fasilidas (fah-SIL-e-deez; 1632–1667), expelled the Jesuits several years later, a popular song captured Ethiopian sentiment:

At length the Sheep of Ethiopia free'd
From the Bold Lyons of the West ...
Rejoyce, rejoyce, Sing Hallelujahs all,
No More the Western Wolves
Our Ethiopia shall enthrall.[2]

During that era, Ethiopia's trading relationships with Europe and the Ottoman Empire declined, but slaves, coffee, and salt were still exported through the Nile valley and the Red Sea. Fasilidas founded his capital around 1635 at Gonder, a prosperous market town north of Lake Tana. The capital was situated close to the fertile agricultural lands of the Blue Nile and the juncture of three major caravan routes. Muslim traders, who dominated the trade between Ethiopia and Muslim states, lived in a separate part of town from the Christians.

During his reign, Fasilidas began reshaping the monarchy, continuing his father's policy of outmaneuvering his rivals by integrating the Muslim Oromo into his nobility. However, his policies eventually reduced Gonder's power, as the nobles expanded their personal fiefdoms around the kingdom and the Oromo asserted their autonomy. In effect, Gonder's emperors became local potentates. One exception was Iyasu II (c. 1730–1755), who ruled with the support of his astute mother, Mentewab, who was crowned queen at his coronation and served at the same time as his queen mother. Her leadership abilities were demonstrated in 1732, when a rebel faction assaulted Gonder's castle, and she presented a plan of action to the council. "If I am a woman by the manner of my creation," she candidly told her councilors, "my gifts, which I have received from God, from below [on earth] and from above [heaven], are those of a man amongst men."[3]

An Oromo, Mentewab brought many of her ethnic group into the court and the army, and she became a master at dealing with court factions and intrigues. When her son died and was succeeded by her grandson, Iyo'as, she continued to play a pivotal role in his court. One of her strategies for extending her influence was granting *gults* (land grants) and endowments to churches, which in turn legitimized her and her ruling line through their chronicles.

However, following Iyasu's reign, civil war erupted, and provincial rulers asserted their power over Gonder. The lowest point came in 1769 when Tegray's ruler, Mika'el, conspired to strangle one emperor and poison another four months later. The years between 1769 and 1855 are known as the "era of the princes" because nobles entrenched their power at the expense of a series of powerless emperors who reigned in Gonder. A royal chronicler plaintively asked: "How is it that the kingdom has become contemptible to striplings and slaves?"[4]

This state of affairs ended in the mid-nineteenth century when Kasa Haylu, a noble from western Ethiopia, began conquering various provinces and consolidating the kingdom under one ruler. In 1855, he took the name Téwodros II (tay-WHO-drohs) and was crowned emperor. His goal was to modernize Ethiopia and build up relations with European nations. He depicted himself as a latter-day Prester John, the ruler of a Christian outpost surrounded by hostile Muslim states. He made overtures to the British government for support on that basis, but to the British, Ethiopia counted for little when compared to the Ottomans and Egypt. When Téwodros grew frustrated at the absence of a British response, he took a group of Europeans hostage; the hostages included the British consul to Ethiopia. Although he was trying to win concessions by holding the prisoners, the British grew tired of his impudence and dispatched a large Anglo-Indian expeditionary force to lay siege to Téwodros at his fortress, Maqdala, in 1868. By then, his iron-fisted rule had lost him the support of most of his nobles, who refused to send soldiers. The British won a quick victory and freed the prisoners, but rather than submit to the British, Téwodros put a gun into his mouth and killed himself.

Conclusion

By the mid-nineteenth century, many parts of Africa had been integrated into the world economy to varying degrees. In the mid-seventeenth century, parts of Africa were harshly introduced to global commerce through the slave trade that wrenched millions of people from sub-Saharan Africa to service plantation economies in the Americas, North Africa, and the Middle East. Although the slave trade introduced new plants such as cassava and maize to the African continent from the Americas, the slave trade contributed little to African economic development and to the kingdoms that participated in it.

Some kingdoms such as Kongo and Oyo collapsed through their involvement in the slave trade, while many new ones were established. Islamic *jihads* created a series of Muslim kingdoms in the Sudanic region of West Africa. In southern Africa, new political states such as the Zulu and Basotho kingdoms were established during the Mfecane.

Once the plantation economy declined and the slave trade began to wind down in the nineteenth century, and as Europe's industrial economy expanded, Europeans sought new trading relationship with Africans. A legitimate trade developed in resources such as palm oil and palm kernels that could be converted into soap, lubricants, and lamp oil for the European market. However, the relationship favored Europeans as Africans sold raw resources and bought manufactured goods or finished products from non-African traders.

With the exception of southern Africa, where Dutch and British settlers seized African lands first on the coast and then in the interior, European contacts with the rest of Africa were largely limited to economic relationships in coastal areas and were controlled by Africans. However, in the last quarter of the nineteenth century, rivalries among the major powers of Europe led to a mad scramble in which European nations conquered and took direct control of almost all of Africa. The European colonizers imposed their own political boundaries and initiated economic and social changes that Africans are still coping with.

Suggestions for Web Browsing

You can obtain more information about topics included in this chapter at the websites listed below. See also the companion website that accompanies this text, http://www.ablongman.com/brummett, which contains an online study guide and additional resources.

Excerpts from Slave Narratives
http://www.vgskole.net/prosjekt/slavrute/primary.htm
This site contains over 40 first-person accounts of slavery in the Americas and African life written between 1682 and 1937.

Liberian Letters
http://etext.lib.virginia.edu/subjects/liberia/
This site features more than 50 original letters from freed American slaves in nineteenth-century Liberia to their former masters and associates in Virginia.

Cape Slavery in South Africa
http://www.museums.org.za/iziko/slavery/slavery_world.html
A presentation of aspects of slavery (slave lives, resistance, emancipation) in the Dutch Cape Colony from 1658 to 1838.

End of the Slave Trade in Africa
http://www.fordham.edu/halsall/africa/africasbook.html
Documents regarding the termination of slave trade in Africa, from the Internet African History Sourcebook.

The Atlantic Slave Trade and Life in the Americas
http://hitchcock.itc.virginia.edu/Slavery/
A thousand illustrations and photos of all aspects of the slave trade and slave life.

Literature and Film

A prominent early twentieth-century South Africa politician and journalist, Solomon Plaatje, set his novel *Mhudi* (Passagiatta Press, 1986) during the wars of the Mfecane; contemporary writer Andre Brink treated a slave uprising in the western Cape in the early nineteenth century in *A Chain of Voices* (Morrow, 1994). Beverly Mack and Jean Boyd, *The Collected Works of Nana Asma'u* (African Historical Sources, No. 9, 1998), is a collection of the poetry and other writings of the daughter of a famed West African cleric, Usman dan Fodio. Marcia Wright's *Strategies of Slaves and Women* (Lillian Barber Press, 1993) presents the life histories of nineteenth-century East and Central African women.

Suggestions for Reading

Several general studies on the transatlantic slave trade are Joseph Inikori and Stanley Engerman, eds., *The Atlantic Slave Trade* (Duke University Press, 1992), and Edward Reynolds, *Stand the Storm: A History of the Atlantic Slave Trade* (Allison and Busby, 1989). For the effects of the slave trade on Africans and Africa's engagement with Europe, see Sylviane Diouf, ed., *Fighting the Slave Trade West African Strategies* (Ohio University Press, 2003); John Thornton, *Africa and Africans in the Making of the Atlantic World, 1400–1680,* 2nd ed. (Cambridge University Press, 1998); and David Northrup, *Africa's Discovery of Europe, 1450–1850* (Oxford University Press, 2002).

Usman dan Fodio's *jihads* and the creation of the Sokoto Caliphate are treated in Mervyn Hiskett, *The Sword of Truth: The Life and Times of the Shehu Usman dan Fodio* (Northwestern University Press, 1994). The decline of the Atlantic slave trade and the expansion of trade with Europe are traced in Robin Law, *From Slave Trade to "Legitimate" Commerce: The Commercial Transition in Nineteenth-Century West Africa* (Cambridge University Press, 1996).

Long-distance trade and state formation in eastern Africa are treated in Abdul Sheriff, *Spices and Ivory in Zanzibar* (Ohio University Press, 1987), and Edward Alpers, *Ivory and Slaves in East Central Africa* (Heinemann, 1975). Ethiopia's church and state are dealt with in Donald Crummey, *Land and Society in the Christian Kingdom of Ethiopia* (University of Illinois Press, 2000).

Slavery in the Cape Colony is examined in Nigel Worden, *Slavery in Dutch South Africa* (Cambridge University Press, 1985), and Robert Shell, *Children of Bondage: A Social History of the Slave Society at the Cape of Good Hope, 1652–1838* (Wesleyan University Press, 1994).

Norman Etherington's *Great Treks: The Transformation of Southern Africa, 1815–1954* (Longman, 2001) provides overviews of the Mfecane in southern Africa. John Laband has written a comprehensive treatment of nineteenth-century Zulu history, *The Rise and Fall of the Zulu Nation* (Arms & Armour, 1997). Moshoeshoe's life is treated in biographies by Leonard Thompson, *Survival in Two Worlds: Moshoeshoe of Lesotho, 1786–1870* (Oxford University Press, 1975).

Studies of nineteenth-century South Africa include Timothy Keegan, *Colonial South Africa and the Origins of the Racial Order* (University of Virginia Press, 1996), and Jeff Peires, *The Dead Will Arise: Nongqawuse and the Great Xhosa Cattle-Killing Movement of 1856–7* (Indiana University Press, 1989).

CHAPTER 20

Asian and Middle Eastern Empires and Nations, 1650–1815

Outline

- The Ottomans in the Early Modern Era
- Muslim Politics in Iran
- Early Modern India Under the Mughals
- The Qing Dynasty Before the Opium War
- Korea in the Seventeenth and Eighteenth Centuries
- Early Modern Japan: The Tokugawa Period
- Southeast Asia: Political and Cultural Interactions
- Europeans in the New Pacific Frontiers

Features

DOCUMENT **Lady Montagu, Florence Nightingale, and the Myths of "Orient"**

SEEING CONNECTIONS **Jesuits in the Ming Court**

DOCUMENT **Lan Dingyuan, County Magistrate: Depraved Religious Sects Deceive People**

DOCUMENT **Ihara Saikaku: "The Umbrella Oracle"**

◄ *Large Perspective View of the Theatre District in Sakai-cho and Fukiya-cho* by Okumura Masanobu (1686–1764). Japan's cities were bustling centers for the arts, culture, and mercantile activities during the Tokugawa period. Artists captured the excitement of urban life in prints depicting what they called the "floating world." This street scene by Masanobu shows theaters, teahouses, restaurants, shops, and a female street vendor selling fish.

DURING THIS PERIOD, India and the Middle East faced challenges prompted by regional conflict, economic turmoil, population growth, and the military and economic ambitions of emerging European nations. In 1650, most of India and the Middle East were incorporated into agrarian empires ruled by the Ottomans, Safavids, and Mughals. These dynasties capitalized on their military successes and durable state structures to project a sense of legitimacy to their population. And yet, each faced internal challenges to central authority.

At the same time, the Portuguese, Dutch, French, and English dragged their economic and military rivalries into the Indian Ocean system. Europeans' naval weaponry militarized this important trading zone, leading to their later grab for territory. The British East India Company became a regional force in India. At the end of the period, large areas of Asia and the Middle East were still free of European political control, but their continued independence was challenged. Far from the Indian Ocean, Dutch, British, and French explorers and seekers of fortune also penetrated the Pacific Islands and Australia.

As the era began, East Asia continued to dominate Eurasian trade and production, enjoying more access to a variety of products and lower rates of abject poverty than elsewhere in the world. Until the late seventeenth century, Japan was the largest producer of silver which, together with silver from the New World, supported the world's trade system. China produced one-third of the world's economic output in 1750. Many of the world's largest cities, sustained by sophisticated banking systems and complex transportation and communication networks, were located in East Asia. In the next century, however, the Industrial Revolution gave Western nations operating in Asia and the Middle East decisive economic and military advantages.

The Ottomans in the Early Modern Era

Did attempts at modernization using European models strengthen or weaken the Ottoman Empire in the eighteenth century?

By the seventeenth century, the Muslim world stretched from the Atlantic to the Pacific. In a millennium, the spread of Islam from Arabia had indeed been phenomenal. But after 1700, Muslim rulers from Anatolia to Indonesia, like their counterparts in Africa, found it increasingly difficult to keep the European imperialists at bay. As European states expanded their military power and infringed on the routes of maritime trade from East to West, they developed new world systems of interregional trade that in part supplanted older commercial systems based in and controlled by Middle Eastern and Asian states and merchants. Control of trade in the eighteenth-century world slipped out of the hands of merchants in Istanbul, Isfahan, and Cairo. For the Ottoman sultans, who for centuries had humbled European armies and dictated the terms of trade, that ideological and economic adjustment was not easily made. Even in the great Islamic empires, economic changes, vested interests, and prolonged warfare drained state treasuries and made it difficult for traditional rulers to restructure their empires and compete with the emergent powers of Europe.

The Ottoman Empire in the Late Sixteenth Century

Ottoman Reorganization and Reform

The early seventeenth century in the Ottoman Empire was marked by a series of rebellions, one culminating in the deposition and execution of the ill-starred Sultan Osman II in 1622. Although the empire was still vast and powerful, it no longer enjoyed the stature associated with the reign of Suleiman (SU-leh-mahn) the Magnificent. Many explanations have been advanced for the weaknesses of the empire in this time period: corruption, the intrigues of harem women, and retention of princes in the harem rather than their being sent out to govern and fight in the provinces. Although these were factors, the more telling reasons were changes in the global economy (linked to late-sixteenth-century inflation and population growth), competition among the various pasha households for position and prestige, and the reorganization required when the empire reached the limits of its expansion. Economic factors fueled Ottoman rebellions when janissaries did not receive their pay, peasants fled the plots that could no longer sustain the burgeoning population, and demobilized auxiliary soldiers (with no hope of earning a living) became bandits preying on the countryside.

The Ottoman Empire was surprisingly large and surprisingly long-lived. No empire of any duration can remain static, and the institutions of the Ottomans had to change over time. As the ranks of the janissaries were inflated, as the *timar* ("fiefs") of the traditional cavalry became hereditary, and as a state based on expansion and conquest exhausted its resources fighting long wars on two fronts, the empire began to take a different form from the one it had in the days of Mehmed the Conqueror. All of these changes occurred in the context of a shift in the global economy due to transatlantic discoveries and the rise of oceanic merchant empires like those of the Dutch and the English.

Chronology

1600	1650	1700		1750	
1603–1868 Tokugawa shogunate **1606** Dutch reach Australia **1622** Ottoman Sultan Osman II deposed **1640** Tokugawa trade limited to Chinese, Koreans, Dutch **1644–1912** Qing dynasty	**1658–1707** Reign of Mughal emperor Aurangzeb in India **1662–1722** Reign of Emperor Kangxi in China **1680–1720s** Golden age of literature and arts in Tokugawa Japan	**1707–1720** Maratha and Rajput rebellions curtail Mughal power **1718–1730** Tulip Period, Ottoman Empire **1720** Müteferrika Ottoman language press founded in Istanbul **1723** Afghan invasion of Iran	**1724–1776** Reign of King Yŏngjo in Korea **1728** Vitus Bering charts Bering Strait **1736–1739** Nadir Shah becomes shah in Iran, invades India **1736–1796** Reign of Qianlong in China	**1750s** Beginning of Dutch domination in Indonesia **1752** Burmese invasion of Thailand **1757** Battle of Plassey **1759** Chinese confine European traders to Guangzhou **1768–1779** Three voyages of Captain James Cook **1771–1801** Tay Son Uprising in Vietnam **1782** Founding of Chakri dynasty in Thailand	**1788** First major British settlement in Australia **1789–1807** Reign of Selim III, Ottoman reformer **1790s** King Kamehameha unifies three main Hawaiian islands **1794** Dutch East India Company collapses **1794** Qajar dynasty emerges in Iran **1796–1804** White Lotus Uprising in China

▲ In the late seventeenth and early eighteenth centuries, the Ottomans began to lose territory on their northern frontiers. As the eighteenth century progressed, Russia emerged as a primary threat to Ottoman dominance in the region.

The Age of the Köprülü Vizirs

Mehmed IV became sultan in 1648, facing rampant inflation, a Venetian blockade of the Dardanelles, rebellion in the provinces, and a violent struggle among palace factions, including his mother, Turhan (TOOR-hahn) Sultan, and her rival, the old Valide Sultan Kösem (KOO-sem). These senior women wielded considerable influence and controlled considerable wealth in the palace system. In 1651, Turhan ended Kösem's long-term dominance of the harem by having her strangled, but Mehmed remained enmeshed in factional politics. This internal strife was compounded by a vehement struggle between groups of conservative mullahs representing the ulama (U-la-mah) and **sufis**, both of which were contending for spiritual authority and influence in the capital. By 1656, Istanbul was in a panic as the Venetians vanquished the Ottoman fleet in the Dardanelles, provincial rebels seized much of eastern Anatolia, and food supplies became scarce. In the midst of this crisis, the empire required drastic measures; it found a man willing to take such measures in the person of a 79-year-old pasha named Mehmet Köprülü (MEH-met koo-PROO-loo; 1586–1661). Köprülü is a striking example of the power that elderly members of the military-administrative class could achieve if they managed to survive the challenges of multiple military campaigns and the competition within the palace system.

sufis—Members of Islamic religious orders characterized by specific traditions of prayer and other ritual practice, some of which were controversial.

The sultan granted Mehmed Köprülü extraordinary powers. The pasha then suppressed the rebels in the provinces and broke the Venetian blockade of the Dardanelles. He used the sweeping powers granted him by the sultan to quell opposition and gain some control over the military. For two generations, Köprülü and members of his family served as reformist vizirs (veh-ZEERS), attempting to bring some power back into the hands of the central government. They launched campaigns against Austria and Poland, took Crete, and reformed taxes. They also struck thousands of men from the rolls of the janissaries, which had become bloated with nonmilitary men who collected pay but did not fight. The problems of the empire, however, were not solved; conscription had depopulated the countryside, and Russia was emerging as a major threat to the north. "Tax farms," which the government sold to finance its wars, were becoming hereditary. The empire thus entered the next century in a precarious military and economic state.

The Tulip Period

The eighteenth century for the Ottomans is framed by a period of literary and artistic florescence at its beginning and a period of concerted military reform at its end. The century began inauspiciously, with a massive revolt in the capital that deposed the sultan and brought Ahmed III (r. 1703–1730) to the throne. During his reign, the Ottomans were successful in battle against Russia but lost decisively to the Austrians. In 1718, Ibrahim Pasha became grand vizir, and under his influence, Ahmed launched a program of building, entertainments, and patronage of the arts that was later called the Tulip Period because of the fashion for extravagant gardens. Tulips were the rage, and rare varieties sold for fabulous sums. Ibrahim supervised the building of a pleasure palace for the sultan called the "Place of Happiness," a model for other palaces and their luxurious lifestyles.

▼ Images of women appeared more frequently in eighteenth-century Ottoman miniatures than in earlier Ottoman art. This late eighteenth-century work depicting childbirth in the harem also illustrates the influence of European fashions in ladies' dress styles. As the midwife delivers the child, a cradle stands by to receive it.

In the Tulip Period, Ottoman elites became great consumers of European, particularly French, styles in fashion and decor, and European artists were imported to enhance life among the elite. Yirmisekiz Chelebi Mehmed (YEER-mee-SEH-keez che-leh-bee), sent to Paris by Ibrahim, sent back reports on French zoos, gardens, women, publications, and shops, as well as on arms and military schools. It was an era when the Ottomans became highly conscious of the need to emulate Western military tactics and technology and when the fashions of the French court were admired and imitated, in part, by elite Ottoman women. The luxuries of the Tulip Period were celebrated in verse by poets, such as Nedim (d. 1730), who were experimenting with new styles: "This year, border your crimson shawl in mink, / And if the tulip cups are lacking, bring wine cups in their stead."[1] Tulips, fur-lined garments, and wine cups were all markers of elite status and wealth. Scholarship also continued to flourish under the sultan's patronage. The first Ottoman Turkish language press was founded by Ibrahim Müteferrika (EE-brah-heem MOO-teh-FEH-ree-kah) in 1720, producing maps, a dictionary, and works on science, history, and geography. The press had been opposed by some of the religious authorities but was permitted so long as it did not print books on religious subjects. The extravagance of the Tulip Period, however, did not mesh well with the conditions of economic depression and political conflict in which the empire found itself. Ahmed's reign ended as it had begun, with a violent rebellion in the capital that produced prolonged rioting and forced the sultan's abdication.

Eighteenth-Century War, Relations, and Reform

Although the empire still had its share of cultural and military successes, overall, the eighteenth century was characterized by the extension of more special commercial privileges (capitulations) to European states, loss of Ottoman territory, and a growing willingness to employ European military advisers, tactics, training methods, and technology. Travel, of Ottomans to Europe and of Europeans to the Ottoman Empire, intensified beyond the merchant activities that had for centuries connected the two regions. The Ottomans also began sending ambassadors to European courts and receiving ambassadors from more European states in return, a sign of the empire's growing weakness and need for communication. The empire had been a dominant power for centuries, and its rulers were generally persuaded of their own cultural superiority. But Ottoman military defeats prompted some Ottoman elites to consider significant military reform in order to duplicate or (they hoped) even surpass the successes

Document

Lady Montagu, Florence Nightingale, and the Myths of "Orient"

In the eighteenth and early nineteenth centuries, the Ottoman Empire stepped up its exchange of ambassadors with the states of Europe. This same time period, particularly after Napoleon's invasion of Egypt in 1798, witnessed a dramatic increase in the number of affluent European travelers who journeyed to various parts of the empire. They came not only for diplomatic and military purposes but also to seek adventure, acquire antiquities, and see the sights. Among these travelers were women of the elite classes like Lady Mary Wortley Montagu, wife of the British ambassador to Istanbul in 1716, and Florence Nightingale, who later served as a nurse in the Crimean War. Florence Nightingale traveled to Egypt in 1849–1850, nominally for her health, but actually to seek out and explore the remains of ancient Egypt and to avoid her parents' efforts to have her marry. Lady Montagu, well educated and a member of London's literary circles, came as the young and independent-minded wife of a foreign ambassador.

Like the accounts of all travelers, the letters of these women were colored by their own knowledge and expectations and by the limitations (affected, among other things, by gender and class) on what they saw and experienced of the cultures they visited. But attitude is also an important factor in the tales of travelers, and these two women were very different from one another. Both traveled in elite circles, were interested in buying up antiquities (including Egyptian mummies), and employed ethnic stereotypes; neither had much regard for the poorer classes. But while Ms. Nightingale was seeking a religious "mission," Lady Montagu was ecumenical and irreverent. While Nightingale found the Egyptians barbaric and less than human, Montagu learned Turkish, visited harems, and characterized the Ottomans as very human (and sometimes superior to the English). Nightingale seemed to prefer the architecture of Cairo to the Cairene people, while Montagu traveled veiled as a Turkish woman so that she could explore the city. Each woman suggested in her letters that she was communicating an image of the "real" Egypt or the "real" Turkey. But, in the end, Nightingale's letters convey a romantic reverence for lost antiquity combined with a horror of the Egyptian people (especially the peasants), while Montagu, writing more than a century earlier, presented a much more complex image of Ottoman beliefs and society.

You cannot conceive of the painfulness of the impression made upon one by the population here.... One goes riding out, and one really feels inclined to believe that this is the kingdom of the devil and to shudder under this glorious sun.... I cannot describe it. In Italy one felt they were children, and their dawn was coming; here one feels as if they were demons; and their sun was set ... and out of these huts come crawling creatures, half-clothed, even in this country, where it is a shame for a woman to show her face. They do not strike one as half-formed beings, who will grow up and grow more complete, but as evil degraded creatures. I have never seen misery before but I felt, "Oh, how I should like to live here! What would I give to take this field!" But here, one turns away one's face ... thanking God that one is not here to stay.

From Florence Nightingale, *Letters from Egypt: A Journey on the Nile,* 1849–1850, ed. Anthony Sattin (New York: Wiedenfeld and Nicholson, 1987), pp. 39–40.

[Letter to a Lady friend, 17 June 1717] I heartily beg your ladyships' pardon, but I really could not forbear laughing at your letter and the commissions you are pleased to honor me with. You desire me to buy you a Greek slave who is to be mistress of a thousand good qualities. The Greeks are subjects and not slaves [of the Ottoman Empire]. Those who are to be bought in that manner are either such as are taken in war or stolen by the Tartars from Russia, Circassia, or Georgia, and are such miserable, awkward, poor wretches you would not think any of them worthy to be your housemaid. The fine slaves that wait upon the great ladies or serve the pleasures of the great men are all bought at the age of eight or nine years old and educated with great care to accomplish them in singing, dancing, embroidery, etc. They are commonly Circassians and their patron never sells them except as a punishment for some great fault. If ever they grow weary of them, they either present them to a friend or give them their freedoms.

From *The Turkish Embassy Letters of Lady Mary Wortley Montagu,* ed. Malcolm Jack (London: Virago Press, 2000), pp. 103–105.

Questions to Consider

1. Lady Montagu was not an expert on slavery in the Ottoman Empire, but she did know more than her correspondents. What does her letter suggest about certain types of slavery in the empire and about English misperceptions?
2. What kinds of difference do you think it makes whether or not a traveler learns the language of the country she or he is visiting?
3. What do these letters suggest about the differences class and gender make in the ways a traveler portrays the society he or she is visiting?

of Europe. To that end, Sultan Mahmud I (r. 1730–1754) brought in the French mercenary Comte de Bonneval to help modernize the military; Mustafa III (r. 1757–1774) hired the Hungarian Baron de Tott to revamp his artillery corps and establish a military school; and Abdülhamid I (ab-dool-ha-MEED; r. 1774–1789) imported numerous foreign military advisers. All of these attempts were vehemently opposed by the janissaries, who saw them as a threat to their own status and position.

Throughout the century, the Ottomans fought intermittently with European foes and with a series of new military leaders in Iran. The government was entangled, in alliances and competing interests, with Britain, France, Austria, and Russia, all of which had designs on certain segments of Ottoman territory. The empire had already lost Hungary and Transylvania to Austria by the Peace of Carlowitz in 1699, and it surrendered to the Austrian emperor the right to intervene in the affairs of Catholics in Ottoman territory. A series of eighteenth-century wars with Russia culminated in the 1774 Treaty of Küchük Kaynarca (koo-CHOOK kai-NAHR-kah), under which the Ottomans paid a large indemnity, gave up the Crimea, allowed Russia to interfere in the affairs of Orthodox Christians in the empire, and granted Russia commercial access to the Black Sea. By granting foreign powers like Austria and Russia rights to intervene on behalf of Ottoman Christian subjects, the empire was allowing these states to undermine its sovereignty and autonomy. These concessions suggested that Christians in the empire could appeal to outside powers and circumvent the authority of Ottoman law.

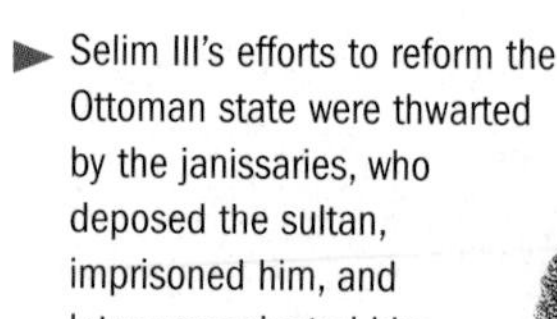

Selim III's efforts to reform the Ottoman state were thwarted by the janissaries, who deposed the sultan, imprisoned him, and later assassinated him.

Several factors demonstrate the weakness of Ottoman central control over the provinces. The semi-independent governors (*ayan*) and their private armies challenged the dictates of the palace in the provinces. In Iraq, Egypt, Tunis, Tripoli, and Algeria, Mamluk ("slave") or janissary garrisons created their own military regimes, often intermarrying with the local elites and refusing to cooperate with Ottoman decrees. A puritanical religious revival in Arabia, the **Wahhabi** (wah-HAH-bee) movement, founded by Muhammad ibn Abd al-Wahhab (1703–1792), joined forces with the Sa'ud family and seized control of Mecca in 1803, an enormous blow to Ottoman prestige. The Wahhabis were a true fundamentalist movement; they argued that Islam had to be purified and all innovations (such as Sufism) eliminated. This movement had a long-term and powerful influence on the development of Arabia.

Meanwhile, European powers also aggressively intervened in Ottoman affairs; Austria and Russia stirred up revolts in the Balkans, and in 1798, Napoleon invaded Ottoman Egypt. The Ottoman regime was powerless to stop Napoleon, requiring British assistance to defeat his forces. Although the British destroyed Napoleon's fleet and forced him to flee shortly after the invasion, the French occupation both demonstrated Ottoman weakness and left a lasting legacy of scholarship on Egypt produced by Napoleon's entourage. Their studies and images of Egypt, brought back to France, helped fuel a new European interest in travel to, and interpretation of the "Orient," its goods, and its culture.

The Reforms of Selim III

Selim III (seh-LEEM; r. 1789–1807) is often considered the first major Ottoman reformer, but his reform program was not new. Like several of his eighteenth-century predecessors, he proposed military and tax reforms as avenues to restore the empire to its past glory. Selim opened new technical schools to train officers and modernized arms production. He drastically cut the janissary rolls to get rid of noncombatants, but he mollified the traditional military corps by increasing pay and modernizing barracks. Offending the janissaries had proved disastrous for various of his predecessors. Most of Selim's efforts and resources, however, went to modernizing the navy and training a "new model" army of 23,000 men. It was a European-style infantry corps (with European-style uniforms), composed

Wahhabi– A strict, puritanical movement founded in eighteenth-century Arabia by Muhammad ibn Abd al-Wahhab that aimed to "cleanse" Islamic practice of such "innovations" as tomb visitations and Sufism.

primarily of Turkish peasants and staffed in part with French officers. Selim hoped that this new army would help restore the empire to its former position of power and be more amenable to modern techniques of warfare. But the empire was not yet ready to break the entrenched power of its traditional military forces; Selim was deposed by a janissary uprising in 1807. Eliminating the janissaries was a task that would fall to his successor, Mahmud II (r. 1807–1839). Although Selim's new army was disbanded, his reforms opened up the empire to further European influence, especially in the realm of military training.

Muslim Politics in Iran

How did Iranian relations with the Europeans change in the early modern era?

The Safavid (sah-fah-vid) Empire in Iran suffered from many of the same problems that afflicted the Ottomans, although Iran was more isolated from the conflicts of the European great powers than the Ottoman Empire was. The tribal confederations in Iran remained powerful throughout the period of Safavid rule and, after the reign of Abbas (1588–1629), increasingly challenged the central government's authority. Despite weak rulers and an Ottoman invasion of Iraq, however, the Safavid Empire remained intact and relatively secure for almost a century after Abbas died. But the eighteenth century would bring in new warlords to rule the Safavid domains and place Iran in a military squeeze between the Russians to the north, the Ottomans to the west, the Mughals to the east, and the British to the south.

The Middle East, Europe, and the World

The end of Safavid rule was initiated by an Afghan invasion in 1723 that forced Shah Husein to surrender. Although members of the Safavid family controlled parts of Iran for some years afterward, this invasion effectively ended the dynasty's rule over the region. Both the Russians and the Ottomans capitalized on Safavid distress by invading northern and western Iran. Afghan rule was not destined to last long, however. A new Turkic military commander of the Afshar tribe from eastern Iran allied himself with a Safavid prince and defeated the Afghans. By 1736, Nadir (na-DEER) Khan had defeated the Ottomans in an engagement near Tabriz and declared himself shah ("king"). This new warlord reformed the government, reorganized the army, and favored both Sunni and Shia branches of Islam, thereby alienating the Shi'ite ulama and gaining some favor with the Ottomans. By 1747, Nadir had regained lost territories, conquered western Afghanistan, plundered the Mughal capital at Delhi, and extended Iranian hegemony over the Uzbeks to the north. But his visions of unifying and ruling a Sunni and Shi'ite empire came to nothing when he was assassinated by his own men.

Iran was once again politically fragmented, but soon—between 1750 and 1779—another tribal warlord, Karim Khan Zand, emerged and gained control over most of the region. Karim Khan's reign was one of relative success and prosperity. He invaded Iraq, raided Ottoman territory, and encouraged trade relations with the British in the Persian Gulf. At his death, the country lapsed again into savage contention among tribal leaders. Zand successors ruled parts of Iran until 1794, but the Qajar (kah-jar) dynasty, which was to rule until 1924, finally managed to replace them.

As the century drew to a close, Russia, Britain, and France were all competing for Iranian trade, and Iran was drawn more directly into European power politics. An Anglo-Iranian defense and commercial treaty in 1800 encouraged the Qajar shah to expect aid against the Afghans and Russia; when this was not forthcoming, he accepted a French military mission to train his

	Middle East and South Asia
1622	Sultan Osman II deposed in an Ottoman rebellion
1637–1680	Shivaji Bhonsle, celebrated early leader of Marathas in India
1656–1691	Age of the Köprülü vizirs in the Ottoman Empire
1658–1707	Rule of Mughal emperor Aurangzeb in India
1690	British East India Company acquired land to develop base at Calcutta
1700	Mughal emperor grants British the right to trade and collect taxes in Bengal
1718–1730	Tulip Period
1723	Afghan invasion of Iran leads to end of Safavid Empire
1739	Invading army of Nadir Shah sacks Mughal capital at Delhi
1747	Durrani dynasty comes to power in Afghanistan
1765	Mughal emperor grants British administrative control over Bengal
1774	Treaty of Küchük Kaynarca after Russian defeat of Ottomans
1789–1807	Reign of the reformist Ottoman sultan Selim III
1794–1924	Qajar dynasty in Iran
1800	Anglo-Iranian defense treaty

troops. This entente collapsed when the French and Russians signed a temporary truce, demonstrating the precarious nature of alliances made with European states. The British then regained the advantage as advisers and commercial partners of the shah.

Thus Iran, like the Ottoman Empire, was increasingly drawn into the economic and military spheres of European powers, where once those same powers had come as petitioners seeking trade privileges in the Middle East. This shift in the balance of power in the late eighteenth and early nineteenth centuries did not radically alter life for the vast majority of citizens of these large agrarian empires. But it did begin to alter basic structures of economic and military organization and to produce a group of elite men who were more conversant with European ways.

Early Modern India Under the Mughals

Which domestic and international factors eroded Mughal power in the seventeenth and eighteenth centuries?

The Mughal Empire was one of the world's wealthiest and most powerful states: its rich traditions, art, and literature affected the whole Indian subcontinent. Mughal power culminated in the long reign of Aurangzeb (OR-ang-zeb; r. 1658–1707), a period marked by military and administrative success. Aurangzeb's policies, however, began to alter the imperial order, based on tolerance, established by the great Akbar (r. 1556–1605). The new emperor, who learned the entire Qur'an by heart, was a champion of Islamic orthodoxy; he saw himself as a man of great piety and patronized Islamic leaders, reversing his predecessors' balanced respect for all religions. He destroyed a number of Hindu temples and schools, although it should be noted that he did support some other Hindu temples. His attacks on some religious institutions may have had as much to do with his punishment of those temples' Hindu patrons for their presumed disloyalty as it did with anti-Hinduism. He reimposed the *jizya,* the poll tax on non-Muslims, and dismissed Hindus from government service (he cut their numbers on his staff to just 25 percent). Until about 1679, he was occupied in securing his northern frontiers, so he did not push these pro-Muslim policies vigorously at first; this changed later when he adopted a less tolerant policy.

Aurangzeb, Mughal Ruler

These abuses did not provoke mass rebellion among the Mughal subjects, who were primarily Hindu peasants, but they did make Mughal rule intolerable to many. They provoked military challenges from Hindu warlords, which, accompanied by social and economic changes, weakened Mughal rule. Several factors may have undermined the Mughals after the reign of Aurangzeb. Though some historians blame the emperor himself for failure of administration, others contend that his era was fairly successful, leading to the rise of competing forces. For instance, the Mughals rewarded the Marathas (ma-RAH-tahs), a powerful tribal confederation in the south that had ambitions to expand their territory and power, with government posts for their successes and their support. The Marathas and others soon became political and military competitors. The growth of the Mughal economy and international trade also brought in New World silver; this, together with the development of cash crops, new technologies, and new trading opportunities—all desirable developments—led to competing economic elites. The Mughals had never controlled certain areas of India, and those areas' rulers saw an opportunity to develop increasing independence from the Mughals.

The Delhi Sultanate and Mughal India

One such group was the newly rising Marathas. To fight them, Aurangzeb virtually moved his capital to a battle camp in the Deccan, staying in a tent city in the field and heading an unwieldy host of 500,000 servants, 50,000 camels, and 30,000 elephants, in addition to fighting men. By 1690, after terrible losses, he had overcome most resistance, but the south could not be permanently pacified. Time and again, the aging ruler was forced to undertake new campaigns; when he died in 1707, it was in the Deccan.

Architecture and the arts during the reign of Aurangzeb were austere and religious. Wine, song, and dance were not allowed in courtly festivals. The emperor did encourage various projects in law and theology. As in the Ottoman Empire, when revenues declined, Aurangzeb employed tax farming to provide quick government income; tax farms were farms controlled by administrators who could collect revenues from the farmers, remit most to the emperor, and use the rest to support an army. The farms enriched corrupt officials at the expense of both Hindu and Muslim peasants. Peasants had little recourse against the government although they could take their complaints to the Islamic Sharia courts. After Aurangzeb died, Mughal authority was further decentralized, and South Asia was increasingly divided among rival kingdoms. A period of civil war ensued until Muhammad Shah (r. 1719–1748) succeeded to the imperial throne. Described by one contemporary as "never without a mistress in his arms and a glass in his hand," this indolent monarch made some effort to placate Hindus, with little practical result. Local Muslim dynasties ruled in the south and in Bengal; the Sikhs (SEEKS), a sect based on a Hindu-Muslim synthesis, became autonomous in the northwest; the Hindu Rajputs (RAHJ-poots), once Mughal allies, began to break away; and the fierce Hindu Marathas,

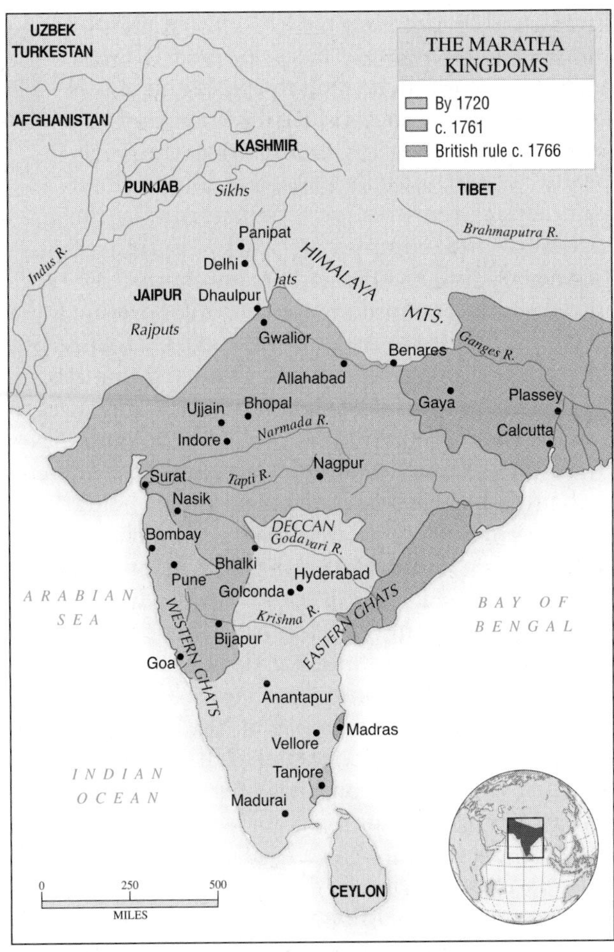

◀ The Marathas in the Deccan rebelled against Mughal rule and won many victories against the Mughal kings. In the seventeenth and eighteenth centuries, first the Marathas and then the British posed formidable challenges to Mughal sovereignty.

whom Aurangzeb had tried to subdue over a period of 30 years, extended their sway over much of central India. The impotence of the empire was most effectively demonstrated in 1739 when the army of the Iranian monarch Nadir Shah burned and looted the Mughal capital at Delhi, killing some 30,000 and carrying away the imperial Peacock Throne, which would become a centerpiece of the Iranian treasury.

Nadir Shah's invasion was but a prelude to the anarchic conditions that prevailed after Muhammad Shah's death in 1748. Mughal power met major military challenges from three directions: the Afghans in the north, the Marathas in the south, and later the British from their base in Bengal in the northeast. When Nadir Shah (r. 1736–1747) was assassinated in 1747, his Afghan troops elevated one of their commanders, Ahmad Khan (r. 1747–1773), to the position of shah. He took the title *Durr-i Durran* ("Pearl of Pearls"), after which his line was called the Durrani. Uniting the Afghans and conquering a vast territory—which comprised eastern Iran, present-day Afghanistan, the major part of Uzbek Turkestan, and much of northwestern India including Kashmir and the Punjab—he established a dynasty that would survive in Afghanistan into the twentieth century. During one campaign in India, Ahmad sacked Delhi (1756), decisively defeating the Marathas and helping to open the country to the British. At Panipat in 1761, his Afghans (employing their superior light artillery) crushed a huge Maratha army. But after Ahmad's death in 1772, the Afghans lost power in India, and his sprawling tribal state lapsed into almost continuous civil war.

The Afghans were a serious threat, but it was the Maratha Confederacy in the northwestern Deccan that had earlier emerged as the most powerful force to challenge Mughal supremacy. The first great Maratha leader was Shivaji Bhonsle (SHEE-vah-jee BONS-le; 1630?–1680). At the age of 17, Shivaji began to build a small regional state by capturing forts and passes through the Western Ghat Mountains. He seized some

▼ Mughal paintings often depicted the nobility, but some paintings also give insight into the daily life of villagers and other nonaristocratic Indians. Women carry out chores, including cooking and washing, and both men and women take part in the care of children. One little boy plays with a toy pinwheel, while another receives instruction from a teacher. At the center of the painting, a woman is having a lively discussion with a man smoking a traditional pipe. The houses are filled with jars and cooking utensils. The villagers wear beautifully dyed clothing. Until the steep economic decline in the nineteenth century, Indians, including villagers, were more prosperous than many people in other parts of the world.

territory from the kingdom of Bijapur, whose sultan sent an army under the general Afzal Khan to discipline him. Shivaji retreated to one of his hill forts, and in a famous episode, the two generals met to negotiate. Both bore arms, and in close combat Shivaji managed to disembowel Afzal Khan with a "tiger claw" (a steel weapon) concealed in the palm of his hand. Aurangzeb sent several armies to discipline Shivaji, but the Maratha chief proved illusive, raiding Mughal territory and the prosperous port of Surat on the west coast of India. When Shivaji was called to court to negotiate with the Mughal emperor, Aurangzeb publicly humiliated him. This episode set the stage for a new series of campaigns, during which Shivaji challenged the Mughal armies and extended his territory in the Deccan.

Shivaji's family had been agriculturalists, not members of the Hindu warrior or ruling caste (Kshatriya). But Shivaji was functionally a warrior nonetheless, and his rise to power illustrates the movement of a family over time from one caste group to another. To legitimize his rule, Shivaji sent to the holy Hindu city of Varanasi, where he persuaded a distinguished brahman to supply him with a Kshatriya genealogy and devise ceremonies of Hindu kingship. In these elaborate ceremonies, Shivaji offered sacrifices to the gods and received gifts from brahmans and nobles, thus reviving the notion of Hindu kingship in the subcontinent. In general, Hindu rituals were resurrected under the Marathas after long centuries of Muslim Mughal rule. After his death, Shivaji was immortalized in Maratha tales and ballads, and today he is celebrated as a hero figure by Hindu nationalists.

From the base established by Shivaji, various Marathas continued their wars of resistance against the Mughals, sometimes fragmented by civil war, sometimes losing territory or being co-opted by Mughal offers of position and wealth. Shortly after Aurangzeb's death, several Maratha leaders began to expand their territories into Malwa, Gujarat, and Rajasthan. In the second half of the eighteenth century, the Marathas gained control over central and north India, reducing the Mughal emperor to the status of puppet ruler. Elsewhere in India, Mughal power was challenged by the rise in power of tax farmers, princely rulers of territories, and provincial governors, as well as ambitious lawbreakers. In the north and east, the Mughals also came up against the forces of a new power jockeying for position in the subcontinent, the British East India Company.

The Europeans in India

As was the case in Africa, the Portuguese were the first European power to establish themselves along the coasts of South Asia and exploit the rich commerce of the subcontinent. The Dutch, French, and English followed, and by the seventeenth century, all four powers had commercial bases in India. All were attracted by the rich trade in spices and jewels and especially by the wonderful variety and volume of Indian textiles. As in Africa, the Europeans did not initially penetrate inland; their commercial ventures were dependent on the elaborate and complex networks of traders, financiers, and middlemen already conducting trade into the interior and along the routes connecting India to China, Southeast Asia, Africa, and the Middle East.

IMAGE Portuguese Church in Southern India

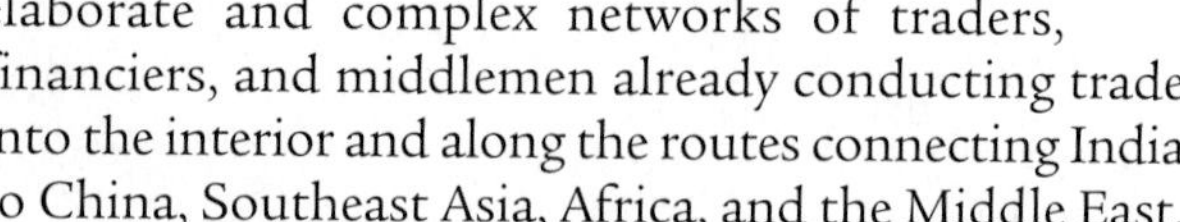

Of the European powers, the Dutch dominated in Southeast Asia, but it was the British who managed to gain ascendancy in South Asia. They established bases in India through negotiation and commercial exchange, then later extended their power and territory by force. In 1601, a group of British merchants petitioned Queen Elizabeth to grant them a monopoly over trade with "the East." Although the newly chartered East India Company (EIC) claimed a monopoly over all trade between India and Europe, what it actually acquired was a monopoly over all trade between British territory and India. The peoples of "the East," of course, had no obligation to honor such charters, but this was an era of sweeping European claims to trade and territory in various areas of the globe; the charters did give such merchant companies a legal advantage over competitors among their own countrymen.

From an early **"factory"** in Surat, the British expanded to bases in Madras, Bombay (now Mumbai, Bombay was ceded to Britain by the Portuguese as a dowry for the English King Charles II's bride), and Bengal (the territory surrounding the mouth of the Ganges river). In 1690, a Company agent acquired a piece of land in the Ganges delta that the British swiftly developed into the commercial entrepot known as Calcutta (now Kolkata). By 1700, the Company had a charter from the Mughal emperor to trade and collect taxes in the area, and by 1750, the population of Calcutta reached around 500,000. It was a major port for the Company and for Indian and independent European traders.

Calcutta provides an interesting case study for the ways (besides direct conquest) in which the British established their power in India. The Company used its bases to extend its commercial affairs inland and employed its own private army to forge alliances with local rulers. Both sides benefited (the local rulers receiving money and military assistance against their enemies from the British), although various local lords resisted British incursions. Because the balance of trade was much in favor of India, Britain sent thousands of pounds in silver to pay for its purchases. By 1800, the wealth (espe-

DOCUMENT Abu Taleb on the West and Western Influence

factory–European commercial office and warehouse in India or China, headed by a factor.

◀ The British presence in India exerted an increasing influence on the arts. This work of an Indian painter, inscribed in Persian and dated about 1760, depicts an official of the British East India Company smoking a water pipe and receiving an Indian visitor. Some British officials, like the one shown here, adopted South Asian furnishings; others adopted Indian styles of dress, food, and entertainment or married Indian women.

cially taxes) generated by the Company's activities provided a substantial portion of Britain's income.

The British East India Company in the eighteenth century provides a clear illustration of the establishment of a new world order based on seaborne circuits of trade and the extension of European imperial power beyond the port cities of Asia and Africa. Where the Dutch, British, and French established agricultural estate colonies in Africa and Southeast Asia, in South Asia they directed their attentions, at least initially, primarily to commercial establishments. There were direct links, however, between these regions, as the Indian Ocean served not only as a medium for the transport of goods to the West but also as an arena for the circulation of slaves, workers, and mariners among the burgeoning colonies of imperial Europe.

The trade conducted by the EIC is also noteworthy for its role in **mercantilism** in the eighteenth century and for its political role in the latter part of the century. By 1750, the British market was saturated with Indian calicoes and other fabrics of high quality and low cost. Low cost was possible because Indian textile workers could maintain a decent standard of living at lower wages than could their counterparts in Europe. This was due to the higher productivity of India's agriculture, which led to lower food prices in India than in Europe; workers thus needed less income to feed themselves. The cost of fabric was kept down, and resources were freed up for other types of investment. Indian textile production grew rapidly. India accounted for 25 percent of all world manufacturing in 1750 due to enormous textile sales to Europe, Asia, and the Americas. Though the British government responded to the large volume of textile imports by imposing stiff tariffs, the volume of trade remained high; the EIC carried this profitable trade.

In the second half of the century, the East India Company became increasingly involved in local politics, building its own domain in Bengal and challenging the authority of the local ruler, Siraj ud-Dawla (see-RAHJ ood-DOW-lah), who asserted his independence as Mughal power declined. In 1756, Siraj ud-Dawla retaliated by seizing Calcutta and demanding increased payments from the EIC for the privilege of trading there. The Company then sent a military force of 2000 men under Robert Clive, who crushed Siraj ud-Dawla's army in the battle of Plassey in 1757. Clive went on to defeat the French and Dutch establishments in Bengal. In 1760, the British defeated the French at Pondicherry, a decisive battle in the Seven Years' War (1756–1763). By the Treaty of Allahabad (al-LAH-ah-bahd) in 1765, the Mughal emperor granted the British administrative control of Bengal. The Company thus became one of many Indian provincial "lords." The British then extended their power inland using a combination of military force and commercial treaty. They gained hegemony over a great circuit of trade from India to China and to England, exchanging

mercantilism—Economic and political policy that regarded wealth as a measure of a nation's strength; mercantilist countries promoted companies that helped produce a favorable balance of trade.

Indian opium for Chinese tea (all the rage in England) and English silver for Indian textiles.

By the end of the century, the Mughal ruler Shah Alam II was collecting a British pension, and William Jones and other officials were cultivating British interest in Sanskrit classics (as the entourage of Napoleon cultivated scholarship in Egyptian and Arabic cultures). While the Ottoman and Iranian empires suffered military defeats and increasing economic subordination to European powers in this era, the Mughal Empire surrendered large segments of its territory, first to the Marathas and then to the British. The Mughals could only look on as the British East India Company, employing Indian armies, extended its sway over the subcontinent.

The Qing Dynasty Before the Opium War

How did the Manchu emperors make their dynasty acceptable to ethnic Chinese?

Between 1644, when the Qing rulers took Beijing, and the early decades of the nineteenth century, China was the most populous and prosperous country on earth. In 1700, China, Europe, and India each accounted for approximately 23 percent of the world's total production. In 1820, China's share had risen to about 33 percent and Europe's to about 27 percent, while India's declined to about 16 percent. China produced one-third of the world's manufactured goods in 1750, but that percentage began to decline rapidly after 1820. What historians call the "long eighteenth century"—from the late seventeenth century to the early nineteenth—was an era of splendor and growth for China. Its economy grew steadily while its literature, art, and philosophy evoked admiration from Asian and European intellectuals alike. Although impossible to predict, however, the seeds of later decline were already being sown by 1820.

The Manchus came to power after Ming loyalists called on them to help put down the rebel Li Zicheng (LEE zuh-CHUNG) in Beijing. The Manchus had developed a state north of the Great Wall in the decades before 1644. The inhabitants of Manchuria were controlled by military units called "banners," their previously tribal government was organized as a bureaucracy with laws modeled on the Ming code, and script was created to represent the spoken language. In the 1630s, Hong Taiji (TAI-jee), the son of the Manchu Nurhachi (noor-HAH-chee; 1559–1616), who had begun the process of Manchu state-building several decades earlier, proclaimed the founding of the Qing (CHING) dynasty, thereby challenging the Ming's right to rule China. Still, the Manchus seemed preferable to the rebel Chinese, and Ming loyalists like General Wu Sangui (WOO sahn-GWEH; 1612–1678) asked for Manchu assistance.

	Qing China
1644	Founding of the Qing (Manchu) dynasty
1662–1722	Reign of Kangxi
1736–1796	Reign of Qianlong
1759	Guangzhou (Canton) system established
1793	Macartney mission to China
1796–1804	White Lotus uprising

Manchu Imperial Rule

Upon coming over the Great Wall, the Manchus showed they meant to rule. They honored the Ming by giving a proper burial to the last Ming emperor but soon moved the Chinese inhabitants of Beijing to the southern part of the city while they occupied the northern part. Land was confiscated from Chinese farmers to support the Qing military banner forces. Men were required to adopt the Qing queue hairstyle as an indication of loyalty, and women were prohibited from binding their feet. The former, of course, could be enforced, while the latter, a more private practice, could be continued by Han Chinese as a covert indicator of their non-Manchu ethnicity, as women were more often indoors and their feet remained unseen.

The Manchus' first order of business was establishing military control of the Chinese realm. Emperor Shunzhi (SHOON-jih; r. 1644–1661) and his powerful successor Kangxi (KANG-shee; r. 1662–1722) conquered Ming loyalist factions in the south with the help of General Wu Sangui. When the Ming loyalists mounted armed resistance, they were brutally suppressed. One resister, Zheng Chenggong (ZHUNG cheng-GONG; 1624–1662), known to Westerners of his day as Coxinga, fled to Taiwan where he ousted the Dutch occupiers in 1662. His son held out until Kangxi's forces defeated him in 1683. The last uprising against the Qing was staged by Wu Sangui himself, but like the others, he and his followers were defeated in 1681.

Kangxi extended Qing control over an enormous realm. After defeating Chinese opponents, using Chinese troops and generals, the emperor destroyed a Russian Cossack base and signed the Treaty of Nerchinsk in 1689. This treaty both eliminated the possibility of a Russian alliance with the Mongols against the Qing dynasty and established normal relations between Russia and the Qing without imposition of a tributary relationship. In 1696 and 1697, Kangxi led troops against the Mongols and defeated them. In 1720, his armies invaded and installed a pro-Chinese Dalai Lama in Tibet. Later, during the reign of his son, the Russians recognized Chinese sovereignty over Mongolia under the Treaty of Kaikhta (1727). And, under his grandson, the Qing extended their control to Chinese Central Asia, an area with a large Muslim population permitted to retain its religion.

To underscore Qing legitimacy as a Chinese dynasty, Kangxi held a special examination in 1679 to recruit scholars to write a Ming history and other works. He patronized Zhu Xi (JOO SHEE) Confucianism. At the same time, he was fascinated by Western mathematics and sciences, and supported the Jesuits at the court. He issued an edict of religious toleration in 1692, permitting conversion to Christianity, provided Chinese converts continued to practice ancestral rites of respect. The Vatican, however, rejected Kangxi's position and sent an envoy to Beijing to assert control over Chinese Catholics. Kangxi then expelled missionaries who would not accept Chinese Christians' performance of ancestor worship.

Although the Qing tried to maintain their identity and dominance, they recognized the need to bring Chinese into the government. Paralleling the Manchu military banners, the Qing created banner forces made up of Chinese troops. In civil administration, the Qing encouraged Chinese to take exams for bureaucratic posts, most of which Chinese came to occupy. At the top levels of government, a dual administrative structure was formed in which most provinces had Chinese governors while governors-general, who were usually Manchus, ruled over two provincial governors. At the level of the top government ministers, each of the six boards had a Manchu and a Chinese minister, and half the Grand Secretaries were Chinese.

The Kangxi era was a time of creative artistic work. While many scholars took part in the compilation of the Ming history, many others refused to serve the Qing. The latter included nonconformist painters like Bada Shuren (c. 1626–1705) and philosophers like Gu Yanwu (1613–1682) whose focus on practical learning influenced later Qing philosophers.

Kangxi died an old man with 56 children. Before his death, his designated heir became cruel and mentally unstable, but Kangxi, disappointed, failed to appoint an alternative. Another son, Yongzheng (YONG-jung; r. 1723–1735), staged a coup, overthrew his incompetent brother, and ascended the throne. Like his father, Yongzheng was an effective, hard-working ruler. He established a new senior bureaucracy, the Grand Council, headed by the ministers of the six boards. He simplified the tax system and reformed the payment of local administrators so they would not be dependent on informal channels of income which opened them up to corruption. He also outlawed hereditary servitude, thus freeing members of enslaved classes.

Yongzheng's death was not followed by turmoil or a coup, as he had set up a secure system to make sure his designated heir would assume the throne. Qianlong (CHEN-LONG; r. 1736–1796, d. 1799) ushered in the most prosperous period in China's early modern history. The territorial boundaries of China extended far into Central Asia, and its wealth and productivity dwarfed those of any other country in the world.

Qianlong's capital at Beijing and numerous other cities were among the world's largest in 1800, but China was primarily agricultural. Farm production grew steadily

◀ Emperor Kangxi attempted to model himself on the ideal Chinese ruler, permitting him to consolidate Manchu power over the country during his 60-year reign.

Seeing Connections

Jesuits in the Ming Court

From the late Ming to the early Qing dynasties (approximately 1550 to 1800), Jesuit missionaries were the primary agents of cultural and scientific exchange between China and Europe. The Jesuits' stress on education and scientific knowledge greatly impressed the Chinese whose respect for learning was reflected in the requirement that rulers and administrators be highly educated. The Jesuits' appreciation of this fact is seen in their requirement that all missionaries to the Ming and Qing courts read, write, and speak Chinese. Jesuit Father Matteo Ricci, seen here on the left, had extraordinary skills in mathematics, music, astronomy, and map-making, talents admired by administrators at the highest levels of the imperial court. Ricci's respect for Chinese learning earned him many friends and a small number of converts.

On the right of the illustration is Ricci's friend, Xu Guangxi, who was baptized as "Paul Siu." Xu was the Director of the Board of Rites in the Ming court, a very high-ranking position and one responsible for making sure the proper Confucian rites were observed. Neither the Jesuits nor the court saw contradictions between Christianity and the practice of Chinese rites at that time, although the contradictions would later leave the Jesuits open to attacks by both the Chinese emperor and the pope. Xu and other Chinese officials were particularly interested in the maps of the world Ricci had, and the Chinese were first introduced to the Americas by the Jesuits' maps.

The Forbidden City, China

because of crop specialization, improved irrigation and fertilizers, and new plants from the Americas that could be grown where Chinese crops could not thrive. Silk production engaged many farmers, requiring the cultivation of mulberry trees (their leaves were the silkworms' food) as well as the careful tending of the worms. Farmers and urban folk alike had to buy food—especially farmers who planted tobacco, cotton, or mulberry trees—spurring the expansion of markets throughout the countryside. Chinese products were sold all over the realm and exported throughout the world. Chinese vessels shipped much of this trade until the end of the eighteenth century, when foreign shippers replaced them. The Chinese economy absorbed a great deal of silver from the mines of Japan and South America—that is, until the British discovered a product that the Chinese would consume in ever greater amounts and which would reverse the balance of trade by the early nineteenth century, opium.

Economic growth in the first half of the Qianlong reign was great, but its benefits were localized. Some regions did much better than others. The coastal region and towns along the Yangzi River and Pearl River delta were much more involved in local and international trade and grew much faster than inland areas. New industries led to new social arrangements such as "sisterhoods" for unmarried women or married women who worked away from their husbands' families. Sisterhoods offered lodging and support to women in silk and other kinds of production in the southeastern region of China.

Economic growth had some serious negative effects as well. Families decided to have more children than they could have had in more difficult economic times. Although individual families did not notice any ill effects of having large families—in fact, having more children to help on the farm would lead to higher family income—after several decades of population growth, China as a whole began to experience population pressure at the end of the eighteenth century, leading to migration and conflict with indigenous people living in areas to which the Chinese migrated. Population

▲ Emperor Qianlong's reign was the pinnacle of Qing success. Qianlong ruled wisely and expanded the realm until the last 25 years of his reign, when he allowed a corrupt underling to manipulate the strings of power. As a vigorous young man, depicted here at his inauguration in 1735 with his empress, Qianlong sponsored the collection of a great encyclopedia.

growth also led to depletion of resources, especially trees whose wood was used as fuel, and deforestation led to serious flooding.

Society and Culture

Eighteenth-century society was more conservative than earlier times. Laws against behaviors considered sexually deviant became much more stringent. From time to time, officials banned plays or novels for violating Confucian morality. At the same time, the government fostered education as conducive to ethical behavior, and this led to the expansion of literacy. Public governance and popular society were seen as intertwined and most efficient and ethical when locally influential families took on the responsibility for promoting the livelihoods of their nonelite neighbors. Of course, this led to meddling by puritanical officials in their neighbors' lives.

The status of women was also affected by puritanical values. Widows continued to be discouraged from remarrying, and arches commemorating "virtuous widows" (widows who did not remarry) sprang up all over China. Young girls continued to have their feet bound. On the other hand, women writers were encouraged to express their creativity in the eighteenth century. Families prided themselves on having talented daughters, and prospective bridegrooms sought out brides with poetic sensibility. Male poet Yuan Mei (yoo-AHN MAY; 1716–1797) was a particular fan of women poets, gathering a group of lively women writers around himself and declaring that they surpassed men in many ways. His detractors believed he was encouraging too much sensuality in women.

Although Confucian authorities disparaged novels, some of China's finest fiction writing was produced during the Qing dynasty. Wu Jingzi (WOO JING-zuh; 1701–1754) wrote *The Scholars*, a satire on the examination system. The best-loved novel was *The Dream of the Red Chamber* (also called *The Dream of Red Mansions* and *The Story of the Stone*) by Cao Xueqin (TSOW shweh-CHIN; 1715–1764). The novel has a large number of characters and is centered around three cousins, one boy and two girls. The three lead an idyllic upper-class life of culture and literature until the boy is forced to marry one of the girls and the other cousin dies. The male protagonist passes the exams but then abandons his declining family to seek truth in religion. The novel is an exquisite study of relationships between generations, the sexes, and masters and servants. Elite family politics are played out against the tale of family decline.

The eighteenth century came to an end with the death of the emperor Qianlong. Years earlier, however, Qianlong had become attached to a handsome, bright young bodyguard named Heshen (huh-SHEN), whom he appointed to high-ranking posts. Heshen developed

Document

Lan Dingyuan, County Magistrate: Depraved Religious Sects Deceive People

Lan Dingyuan (1680–1733) was a magistrate in a county near Guangzhou. Magistrates served at the lowest level of the Chinese bureaucracy but had wide-ranging responsibilities, including administration, collecting taxes, and enforcing laws at the local level. Educated as Confucian public servants, magistrates, like all government officials, found religious deviance from Confucianism particularly unethical. White Lotus beliefs were also threatening because of the role White Lotus adherents had played in dynastic change at the end of the Yuan dynasty several hundred years earlier. Lan Dingyuan kept notes of his trials, and here we see how he dealt with this heretical sect.

The people of Chaoyang believed in spirits and often talked about gods and Buddhas.... [L]adies of the gentry families joined together to go to the temples to worship the Buddha. In this way, heretical and depraved teachings developed and the so-called Latter Heaven sect became popular.... The sect also called itself the "White Lotus" or the "White Willow."

Zhan Yucan's wife, Lin, was thought to be the "Miraculous Lady." She claimed to possess the ability to summon wind and rain and to give orders to gods and spirits. She was the leader of the Latter Heaven sect and was assisted by her paramour, Hu Aqiu, who called himself the "Ben Peak Divine Gentleman." These two cast spells and used magic charms and waters to cure illness and to help pray for heirs. They also claimed to be able to help widows meet their deceased husbands at night.

The people of Chaoyang adored them madly; hundreds of men and women worshipped them as their masters.... [M]embers of the sect had ... already constructed a large building in the northern part of the county where they established a preaching hall and gathered several hundred followers.... I dispatched runners (office assistants to the magistrate) to apprehend the sect leaders, but the runners were afraid to offend the gods lest the soldiers of hell punish them. Besides the local officials and many of the influential families favored the sect. So they all escaped.

I, therefore, went to the place myself, pushed my way into the front room, and arrested the Divine Lady. Then I went further into the house to search for her accomplices.... It was indeed an ideal place to hide criminals.... Finally, the local rowdies as well as certain influential families, knowing they could no longer hide him, handed over Hu Aqiu (the Divine Gentleman).

In fact, these people had no special powers whatsoever, but used incense and costumes to bewilder people. The foolish people who trembled on just hearing the names of gods and spirits were impressed when they saw the Divine Lady had no fear of gods and goddesses. Hu Aqiu, who accompanied her, wore rouge, female clothing, and a wig. People believed Hu was the genuine Empress Lady of the Moon and never suspected he was a man.

When these pious women entered his bedroom and ascended to the upper chamber, they would be led to worship the Maitreya Buddha and to recite the charms of the Precious Flower sutra. The stupefying incense was burned and the women would faint and fall asleep so the leaders of the sect could do whatever they pleased.... Later members would cast spells and give the women cold water to drink to revive them. The so-called "praying for heirs" and the "meeting with a deceased husband" occurred while the women were dreaming and asleep.

The members of the Latter Heaven sect were extremely evil; even hanging their heads out on the streets would have been insufficient punishment for their crimes. However, this had been a year of bad harvest, so the villagers already had lots of worries.... Therefore, sympathetic to the people's troubles and wanting to end the matter, I destroyed the list of those involved which the culprits had divulged during the trial.

I had Lin, the "divine Lady," and Hu Aqiu beaten and put in the collar, placing them outside the court so the people could scorn them, beat them, and finally kill them.... I inquired further into the matter so that the other accomplices could repent and start a new life. I confiscated the sect's building, destroyed the concealed rooms, and converted it into a literary academy dedicated to the worship of the five great [neo-Confucian] teachers. Thus the filthy was swept away and the clean restored.

... I went to the academy to lecture or discuss literature with the people of the county.... As formal study developed, heretical beliefs ceased to exist....

Questions to Consider

1. Was the county magistrate more concerned about the criminals' sexual exploitation of women or about the rise of heretical sects?
2. How did the punishment of the criminals and the rehabilitation of the local inhabitants validate the ethical role of Confucianism in the Qing dynasty?

From Patricia Buckley Ebrey, ed., *Chinese Civilization: A Sourcebook* (New York: The Free Press, 1993), pp. 295–296.

a network of graft and corruption; however, his fall came immediately after Qianlong's death. His plundering of China's wealth was devastating. Heshen's confiscated wealth was 800 million ounces of silver, and his cronies serving in appointive posts throughout China stole millions more. When impoverished commoners joined the White Lotus religious uprising (1796–1804), government resources were not immediately available to meet the challenge. The **White Lotus movement** promised social equality among classes and a better status for women, all to be delivered by the Buddha of the future, Maitreya (mai-TRAY-ah). Eventually the movement was suppressed. At the same time, ethnic tensions arose as Chinese migrated to border regions in search of better farmland.

The next challenge came from overseas. Concerned about the rise of trade with the English and others, in 1759 the Qing sought to regulate foreign commerce by restricting it to Guangzhou (gwahng-JOH) and placing an official merchant guild in charge of dealing with Britain's official counterpart, the East India Company. For several decades, this system worked, but as England began to sell massive quantities of opium to offset its purchases of Chinese tea, China began to suffer (see Chapter 25). The world's greatest empire in 1700 would, by 1900, succumb to imperialism, famine, and civil war. China's way of relating to the world—the **tribute system**—was fundamentally at odds with Western practices of international relations. When King George III of England attempted to set up a permanent trade representative in Beijing in 1793, Qianlong rebuffed the British attempt because it did not accord with the practices of the tribute system. China did not need foreign products, Qianlong stated; moreover, Britain's representative, Lord George Macartney, failed to perform the *kowtow,* a bow of submission, to the emperor.

Korea in the Seventeenth and Eighteenth Centuries

In what ways did the late Chosŏn period defy the characterization that it was a stagnant and rigidly old-fashioned era?

The struggles against the Japanese and the Manchus in the 1590s and from the 1620s to the 1630s showed Koreans that they needed to strengthen their military. During the early seventeenth century, the Chosŏn dynasty refocused its attention on defense and strengthened its military. At the same time, serious factional struggles disrupted effective administration at Seoul. The factions were mainly concerned about power and influence, often framing their differences in terms of morality. Feuding factions disputed such issues as the proper length of the mourning period for the king's mother or the propriety of a concubine's son being designated an heir. Factionalism abated in the eighteenth century, when two strong kings ruled ably—King Yŏngjo (YONG-joh; r. 1724–1776) and his grandson King Chŏngjo (CHONG-joh; r. 1776–1800). Korea's economy, scholarship, and arts flourished during the eighteenth century.

King Yŏngjo was a patron of Confucian propriety. A scholar himself, he sponsored Confucian ceremonies and rituals. His behavior inspired the factions to cool their rivalries. He reduced one of the taxes paid by commoners and instituted land taxes on wealthy landowners. He ended the problem of homelessness. The economy developed rapidly, and the population increased by 50 percent. Though an effective and conscientious monarch, Yŏngjo committed a controversial and, to many, a cruel act; in 1762 he executed his son Sado, the designated heir, when the latter was clearly deranged and guilty of murder himself. This led to a renewal of factional divisions between the supporters and opponents of Yŏngjo. When Chŏngjo ascended the throne, he honored his executed father's spirit, thereby challenging his grandfather's actions and keeping the factionalism alive. Despite the disputes within the ruling class, however, the eighteenth century was a time of growth both economically and culturally.

Painters like Kim Hongdo (b. 1745) and Shin Yunbok (b. 1758) focused on Korean themes rather than simply following the previously dominant Chinese conventions. Kim, in particular, was known for his depictions of the everyday life of people at work or children in school. Other artists refined ceramic crafts. Writers, a number of them women, made **han'gul** (HAHN-gool) their medium of expression in the eighteenth century. Diaries, novels, and poetry written in han'gul were more expressive than the stiffer

White Lotus movement—A millenarian religious movement combining elements of Confucianism and Daoism along with its predominantly Buddhist emphasis on salvation by the Buddha of the future.

tribute system—Foreign relations system placing China in a dominant position with neighboring countries who must pay tribute to China and receive protection in return.

han'gul—An indigenous Korean script.

	Korea
1627, 1636	Manchu invasions
1724–1776	Reign of King Yŏngjo
1776–1800	Reign of King Chŏngjo
late 1600s–early 1700s	Silhak scholarship flourished

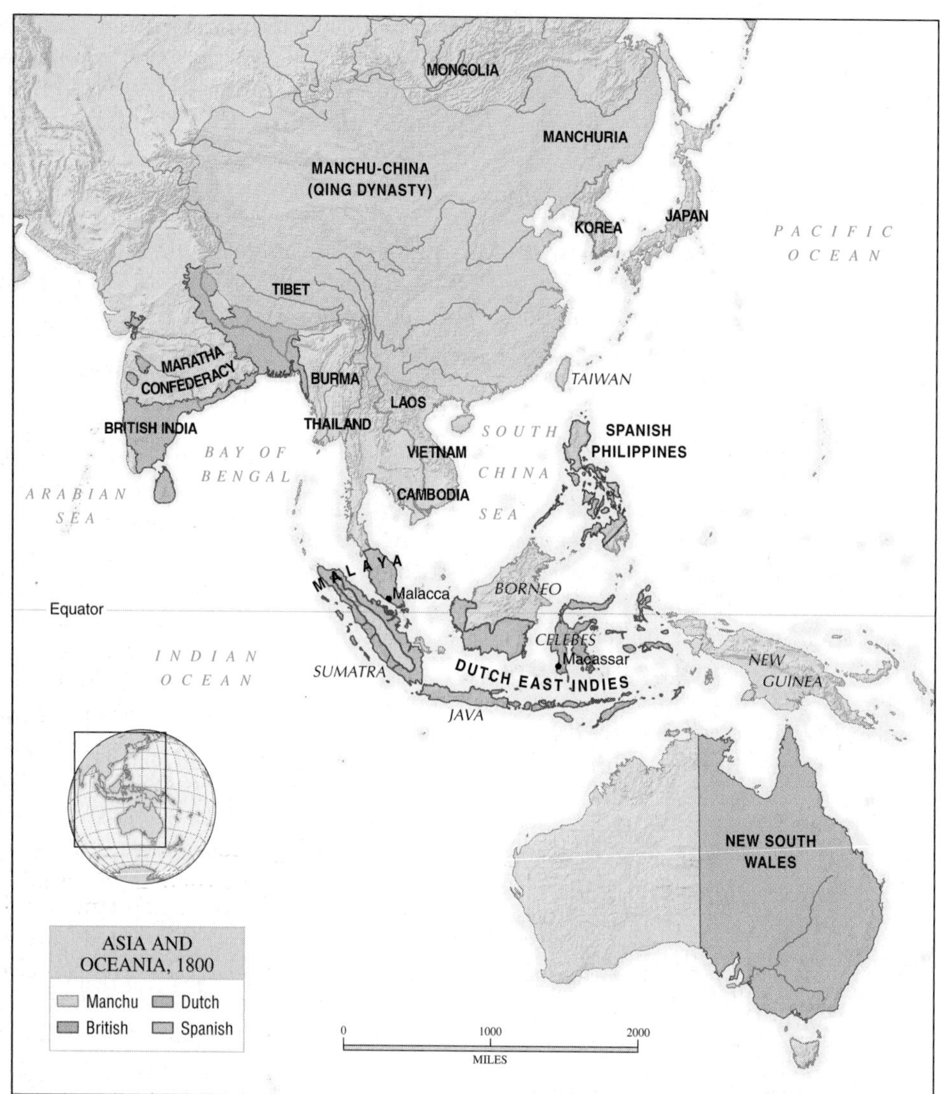

▲ Asia and Oceania, 1800. Most of Asia was still free of imperialism in 1800. The Philippines were under Spanish control, and Indonesia was under Dutch control, but British inroads into India had just begun. French domination of Vietnam and Europeans' encroachment on China would occur in the nineteenth century.

works written in the foreign language used for official government work, Chinese.

Yangban thinkers also were developing new approaches to learning. Observing that the farmers were not enjoying the wealth that accompanied economic growth, seventeenth-century scholar Yu Hyŏngwŏn (YOO HYONG-won) decided to undertake an extensive "investigation of things," the practice advocated by Zhu Xi, China's great Neo-Confucian scholar (see Chapter 10). Yu's massive work, which called for reform in government, the military, and the land system, inspired eighteenth-century scholars to undertake *silhak* (SHIL-hahk) or "practical learning." *Silhak* scholars, appalled by the plight of the peasants, advocated reforms that threatened the privileges of their fellow yangban. Some scholars who had international experience in China suggested that Koreans should emulate their Chinese counterparts who called for changes when circumstances demanded new policies. Some were impressed with Western studies they observed in China, including knowledge of astronomy, medicine, and Christianity. A few *silhak* scholars even formed an underground circle of Christians in 1754. In time, the number of adherents to the Western religion grew, and the government cracked down in bloody purges in 1801, 1811, 1849, and 1866.

Other social changes in the nineteenth century—new economic and power configurations—appeared following a century of growth. For example, many who had been slaves either bought their freedom or abandoned their owners and became a new group of laborers who worked for wages. At the ruling class level, sons of concubines were entering the government as trained specialists (clerks, accountants, and other jobs), challenging the old aristocracy. These new specialists were often concerned with social reform, and many were

Shin Yunbok, *Enjoying Lotuses While Listening to Music* (late eighteenth/early nineteenth century). Shin was one of Korea's most beloved painters. Shin's favorite themes were romantic, and he often portrayed *kisaeng* (artistic courtesans) with yangban men. The hats in this picture are the black horsehair hats that were the mark of the yangban male.

attracted to Catholicism. Even yangban disrupted the old order, especially in areas far from Seoul. At the other end of the spectrum, farmers and miners revolted on several occasions during the nineteenth century. Thus, the stage was set for the end of the Chosŏn dynasty, as Western and, later, Japanese pressure challenged the Seoul government.

Early Modern Japan: The Tokugawa Period

What developments in early modern Japan helped set the stage for modernization in the late nineteenth century?

Tokugawa Ieyasu's victory in the battle of Sekigahara in 1600, his assumption of the title of shōgun in 1603, the pacification of rowdy masterless samurai, the establishment of means of controlling the *daimyō,* and the regulation and limitation of foreign trade and contacts cemented Tokugawa rule by 1650. Japan was not yet a modern state, with its reach extending to every segment of society. But the Tokugawa shogunate did establish mechanisms to control the realm, acting as a superordinate ruler over self-regulating status groups. These statuses were the four Confucian status groups, recast for Japanese use as samurai, farmer, artisan, and merchant. In reality, the status groups were more fractured than that. Villages, cities, and towns had a variety of means of governance, depending on their relationship to their *daimyō* (for more on *daimyō,* see Chapter 13). Groups that did not fit into one of these four statuses, including those involved in the theatre or sex trades, had their own governing structure. Professional physicians and scholars could come from any status background.

The shogunate involved itself as little as possible in the day-to-day oversight of the status groups. If these groups stayed out of trouble and paid their taxes, the Tokugawa shōguns generally left them alone, sometimes issuing a warning to behave in a moral way but rarely finding reason to enforce such a decree. The one group that the Tokugawa did control was its own status group—the *daimyō*—by moving *daimyō* around for strategic placement and by the **alternate attendance system.**

The alternate attendance system required *daimyō* to spend alternate years in their domain castle and their Edo-based mansion, from which they performed attendance on the shōgun. The *daimyō*'s wives and children had to remain in Edo like hostages in fancy cages. Travel was closely controlled both to prevent clashes between the huge retinues of samurai that accompanied the *daimyō* and to make sure no firearms were being smuggled into Edo or *daimyō* wives smuggled out—signs of a possible *daimyō* plot against the shōgun. Two-thirds of the *daimyō*'s tax revenues were consumed in maintaining an elegant mansion in Edo to show off in front of their *daimyō*

alternate attendance system—Tokugawa system of controlling *daimyō* by requiring them to attend shogunal court every other year and to leave their wives and children at the shogunal court when they were away.

	Japan
1603–1868	Tokugawa shogunate
1640	Restriction of trade to Holland, Korea, China
1657	Death of Hayashi Razan, Neo-Confucian scholar; Great Edo fire
1688–1704	Genroku era, golden age of arts and literature
1730–1801	Motoori Norinaga, proponent of National Learning

neighbors, in going back and forth across the countryside every year, in feeding and housing samurai both on the road and in Edo, and in having duplicate staffs in the domain and in Edo.

The *daimyō* were technically the top rulers within their domains, with their own legal and fiscal systems. The Tokugawa collected taxes from the rice crops of their own lands, which produced about one-quarter of the realm's rice output at the beginning of the period. The *daimyō* took in taxes from their own domains. Though the *daimyō* did not have to pay regular taxes to the shogunate, they did have to respond to demands to pay for projects the shogunate desired. For example, the domain of Satsuma was ordered to build 300 wooden ships to transport rocks for Tokugawa Ieyasu's castle. The costs were high, but the economic consequences were even greater. New jobs were created for lumberjacks, sailors, shipbuilders, and suppliers of food, clothing, and lodging. The transported rocks were cut from quarries with tools made of iron, which itself had to be mined, smelted, and crafted into tools. Resources were spread around when workers used their wages to buy other goods. This is but one example of thousands in which the Tokugawa's political attempts to control the *daimyō* led to unintended economic and social growth which, in the eighteenth century, came to define Japan as a nation rather than a collection of status groups.

The Tokugawa and the World

Although later Japanese considered Japan to have been a "closed country" during the Tokugawa period, Tokugawa Ieyasu had no interest in completely cutting off trade with the Chinese, Koreans, and selected Europeans. Gold, silver, and copper were plentiful in Tokugawa mines in the seventeenth century, affording the Japanese plenty of funds to buy silk from China, herbs and medicines from Korea, and exotic plants and woods from Southeast Asia. What the shōguns did not want was Christian missionary activity, leading them to seek alternate ways of trading without bringing in missionaries.

Closed Country Edict of 1635

Although Portuguese traders hauled much of the silk and other products entering Japanese ports in the early years of the Tokugawa regime, they were soon supplanted by others, especially Korean, Chinese, and, until 1640, Japanese traders. Trade with Korea went through the island of Tsu. The volume of trade with Korea and China was huge. In one decade alone (1615–1625), a conservative estimate asserts that Japan exported 130,000–160,000 kilograms (286,000–352,000 pounds) of silver for imports from China. Japan's silver exports, entering the world monetary system through the China trade, played a significant role in global commerce until the 1680s, when the Tokugawa silver mines began to be depleted.

Soon, however, diplomatic and commercial relations became increasingly controlled. By the 1640s, relations with foreign countries were limited, and Japanese ships were no longer permitted to take part in international trade. Sailors blown off course were not allowed to come home—unless they were returning from Korea or the Ryūkyū Islands—under penalty of death.

Tokugawa policy changed because they became serious about controlling the introduction of Christianity to Japan. The Dutch, who had already driven the English out of the Japan trade by their more aggressive trade practices, next persuaded the Tokugawa to kick out the Spanish and Portuguese merchants, whom they considered too interested in promoting Christianity. The Dutch convinced the shōgun that Holland would not be interested in proselytizing. For the next two centuries, only the Chinese, Koreans, and Dutch could take part in the lucrative trade with Japan.

At the dawn of the Tokugawa era, the shōgun was worried about Buddhists as well as Christians. But by the middle of the century, Buddhism had been brought under government control. Confucian attacks on Buddhism deprived it of the intellectual vitality it had demonstrated in the medieval period. In addition, the requirement that every Japanese register as a member of a Buddhist temple to indicate rejection of Christianity, which may have appeared supportive of Buddhism, actually made the religion an instrument of Tokugawa policy. This deprived it of vitality as well. Christians were controlled more aggressively, with converts forced to renounce their religion. The Shimabara uprising, put down by the Tokugawa with Dutch assistance in 1638, was the last major Christian rebellion.

Both Korea and China were countries the Tokugawa could trust, but the relations with each of these differed greatly, as the Tokugawa rejected involvement with the Chinese tribute system that would have required Japan to subordinate itself to the Ming and later the Qing. The Tokugawa unease with the Manchu emperors may have also contributed to their lack of desire to become involved in the tribute system. The Manchu occupation of Seoul in 1627 raised fears that the Manchus would continue on to invade Japan as the Mongols had 350 years earlier. The Tokugawa even debated sending troops to aid the Koreans in repelling the Manchus; in the end, they did not. With Korea, the Tokugawa conducted foreign relations on the basis of equality. Unlike the case of Korea's relations with the Chinese court, Korean envoys to Edo did not prostrate themselves in a gesture of subordination.

At the end of the seventeenth century, Qing Emperor Kangxi lifted the century-long limits on official Chinese trade with Japan. This encouraged even greater trade between the two countries. Once the maximum official trade was reached, unlicensed trade was conducted at ports throughout western Japan. The

Dutch, worried about increased competition from the Chinese, told the Tokugawa that Kangxi was influenced by Jesuits. The shogunate began inspecting imported Chinese books for references to Christianity and decided in 1687 to restrict Chinese merchants to the tiny island of Deshima in Nagasaki Harbor, where the Dutch had been forced to live and operate since 1640. Nagasaki grew quickly as a center of trade in the late seventeenth century. In the next century, however, the volume of trade leveled off due to use of domestically produced goods instead of imports and to growing shortages in silver and other precious metals. In addition, concern about the detrimental environmental effects of mining to promote trade began to surface in the 1680s.

Economic Growth and Social Change

The seventeenth century was an era of rapid growth. Peace permitted farmers to look forward to predictable harvests. The Tokugawa and the *daimyō* regularized weights and measures. They established policies for village self-governance: they prohibited the sale of people and possession of luxury goods; and they required more fortunate villagers to help the poor, maintain roads and bridges, and organize village families into mutual-responsibility groups.

Self-governance, a prime example of the Tokugawa policy of rule by status, was at the heart of the system. Taxes were assessed on the whole-village level by local officials. The village leadership, which varied among villages from a single individual to a council of influential families, then determined each family's annual portion of the village tax bill. Villages often hid a large part of their productivity increases from the tax assessor. Not all farmers were equally able to stash away income. Some domains experienced exploitative or corrupt government or bad weather while others prospered.

Peace was not the only reason for rapid growth. Policies like the alternate attendance system and the requirement that samurai live in castle towns were also instrumental in both rural and urban growth. The *daimyō* converted the rice they received as taxes into cash in two major rice markets—Edo for domains in the east and Osaka for domains in the west. By 1720, these cities, as well as the castle towns and the old capital of Kyoto, accounted for 10 percent of the population. Edo was by then the world's largest city, with over a million inhabitants, and Kyoto and Osaka together had about 800,000. All those people needed to eat and be housed and clothed.

The alternate attendance system forced most *daimyō* to live beyond their means, so merchants extended them high-interest loans in advance of their next tax receipts. Determining rice futures as well as handling the transfer of cash from the merchant house to the *daimyō*'s Edo mansion or castle in his domain turned some of these merchants into bankers and created a system of Japan-wide financing that transcended the official fiscal independence of the *daimyō* domains. Roads, sea routes, transportation companies, and communications companies sprang up in the seventeenth and eighteenth centuries to meet the needs of the alternate attendance system, leading to economic growth unintended by the Tokugawa when they set that system up.

Money flowed into the guest houses and restaurants along the *daimyō*'s procession routes, and from there to the villages that supplied the workers in those establishments. That cash was used to buy commercial fertilizers and to develop new irrigation devices and farm tools like threshing machines. These new technologies opened new fields and permitted farm families to work more efficiently. New technologies were spread to remote villages through printed agricultural guidebooks as literacy expanded for both men and women. Urban demands for fruits, vegetables, and fibers (silk, hemp, and cotton) encouraged farm families to use some of the surplus available from their increased productivity for

Woodblock print of Mt. Fuji by Hokusai. Landscape prints flourished during the nineteenth century in Japan. Mt. Fuji, which could be clearly seen from Edo, was a favorite theme. Here, Hokusai shows a bustling rural road.

goods sold by traveling merchants. Villagers were connected to the cities in additional ways, especially as carpenters and artisans. The demand for labor drove up the cost of labor, making the large extended family of the Warring States period less efficient than the nuclear family. The old village structure, dominated by a few large families, changed to one of numerous nuclear families.

Growth of the urban economy was even more remarkable. In the medieval period, Kyoto had been the only large city. Markets had developed near Buddhist temples, but they were relatively small. Seventeenth-century castle towns gathered purveyors of goods and services to the *daimyō* and samurai; most had a population that was half commoner and half samurai. The alternate attendance system led to post-station towns every few miles along the highways, and material and artistic culture flowed easily as the samurai rotated between Edo and the small provincial towns. Although the population of the biggest cities stopped growing around 1720, regional towns continued to grow and become integrated across the various regions of Japan.

Officials were not the only ones who moved about the country. Traveling merchants brought goods to the rural areas, and maritime companies developed freight lines to haul goods cheaply. Pilgrims and sightseers, a large number of them women over the age of 40, added to the bustle and excitement of inter-urban travel. Few Japanese remained untouched by urban culture and goods by the end of the eighteenth century. The long arm of the city reached into the rural environment as well. During the building frenzy of the first few decades of the Tokugawa period, hundreds of castles and mansions, thousands of houses for samurai and merchants, and countless ships, temples, and shops depleted the resources of wood throughout Japan. Fires also ravaged the wooden cities, making lumber even more scarce. The 1657 Edo fire dwarfed all previous fires; much of the city was destroyed and 100,000 people were killed. In the eighteenth century, planners began reforestation and other environmental programs, but it took disasters like the great Edo fire to alert them to the need for environmental policies.

Economic growth, the development of cities whose culture and wealth were increasingly dominated by people of the lowest Confucian status (merchants), and the declining wealth of samurai were unintended and ironic consequences of policies undertaken to preserve a political order with the shōgun on top, the *daimyō* and samurai under control but supported by tax revenues and the right to rule, and agriculture at the center of the economy. Economic development eroded the conservative system the Tokugawa had tried to create.

When disasters occurred, such as famines in the 1730s and 1780s caused by crop failures due to unusually bad weather, the government tried a variety of reform measures in response. Most of these were conservative, seeking to reinforce Confucian morality and cutting government expenditures. During the famines of the 1730s, the shōgun Yoshimune (YOH-shee-MOO-neh; r. 1716–1745), widely respected as moral and conscientious, attempted to cut expenses, encourage agriculture, regularize taxes, standardize the diverse legal systems throughout Japan, and relax the ban on foreign technical books. He also ordered the dismissal of nearly half the court ladies to save money. With such policies, Yoshimune hoped to restore the efficiency of the past, but his policies were only temporary remedies rather than permanent solutions for the country's problems. More innovative solutions were sought in the 1780s by the shogunal advisor Tanuma Okitsugu (TAH-noo-mah OH-kee-TSOO-goo; 1719–1788), who tried to encourage foreign trade, develop the northern island of Hokkaido, open new mines, and charter new monopolies. But his reforms, which took a completely different path from Yoshimune's policies of retrenchment, were also unsuccessful in stemming the disasters brought on by the forces of nature. A few *daimyō* were able to implement economic policies in their domains that allowed their own areas not only to pull through the hard times but also to grow, but economic policies at the highest levels of the shogunate were generally unsuccessful in the middle and end of the Tokugawa period. By the middle of the nineteenth century, when the shogunate was facing American pressure to open its ports (see Chapter 25), it was the economically successful domains that were able to challenge the Tokugawa shogunate's claim of political legitimacy.

In other important ways, the system the Tokugawa intended to create was undermined by the actual behavior of the people. Samurai men were transformed by their occupations as bureaucrats and their education at state expense from warriors willing to lay down their lives for their feudal lords to diligent organization men striving to get ahead in life.

Women also challenged stereotyped notions of their behavior. Neo-Confucian ideology placed women below men in the status hierarchy, but women's roles and status varied greatly by class. Samurai women were dependent on their husbands, who received annual stipends. To continue to receive those stipends, samurai had to have male heirs, so their wives had to be tolerant of their husbands' taking of concubines or secondary wives to guarantee the family's continuity. Samurai marriages were usually arranged with little or no input from the future bride and groom. Samurai women were expected to be submissive to their husbands and their parents-in-law.

Merchant-class women were often well educated in math and literature, helped to run their families' shops, and frequently had a voice in the selection of their husbands. In fact, business owners often adopted a talented employee as a son-in-law, who then inherited and ran the business along with his wife, the daughter of the original owner. If the marriage did not work out, the hapless son-in-law might be divorced and a better match found. Merchant-class women often enjoyed the arts and culture of the cities.

Farm women's opportunities were very much determined by their families' wealth. The poorest had rough lives, with many of them forced to work as day laborers, domestic servants, or even as prostitutes in brothels located along the highways used by the *daimyō*'s processions. Middle- and upper-income farm women, however, had in some ways more opportunities than their urban counterparts. Many were educated alongside their brothers in the Buddhist temple schools that sprang up all over Japan to teach the children of the commoner classes. When they reached adolescence, village girls, like the boys in boys' associations, became members of girls' associations where they learned crafts like needlework and made important friendships. During major festivals, the boys' and girls' associations mingled, and young men and women often chose their own marriage partners based on friendships and intimate relations formed at those times. Divorce for marital incompatibility was common, and multiple marriages were not looked down upon as long as the partners were monogamous during the marriage. Farm men and women were equally important to their families' economic well-being; women planted while men reaped, and both, as well as their children, threshed the rice. Sons usually inherited, but daughters, if particularly respected by their parents or in the absence of sons, could inherit and marry a man expected to become an adopted son-in-law. Women became the skilled silk workers, bringing in cash incomes to their families. And when some farmers became entrepreneurs in the late Tokugawa period, setting up silk-reeling mills and other enterprises, teenage girls were often the wage earners for their families. Women were usually not members of the village assembly, but in some cases, they did represent their families at official events.

The official ideology concerning women was grim, but in reality most played a more important role and had greater latitude in relation to their families than that suggested in official documents. No women had "rights" in the modern sense, but neither did men.

Early Modern Scholarship and Ideology

Urbanization in the seventeenth and eighteenth centuries produced new cultural and social practices in the cities and towns. At the dawn of the seventeenth century, urban culture was samurai culture. Most scholars called Kyoto their home in the seventeenth century, but in the eighteenth, many lived in Edo as well. Many scholars were outside the four-status system; some were scholars in official posts and many of those had samurai status. But other scholars came from every type of background and earned their living as teachers, advisors, or physicians. Zhu Xi Confucianism enticed a number of scholars in the seventeenth century. Hayashi Razan (HAH-yah-shee RAH-zan; 1583–1657) and Yamazaki Ansai (YAH-mah-ZAH-kee AHN-sai; 1618–1682) both started out as Buddhist clerics but later abandoned religion for more secular Confucian learning. Hayashi's school of thought was particularly appreciated by the shogunate. Hayashi contended that the five Confucian relationships were natural and proper. The shōgun should be elevated above all others, except for the politically powerless emperor, who was to be considered, Yamazaki added, the "Heaven" from which the shōgun received the Japanese Mandate of Heaven. Thus, Zhu Xi Confucianism was blended with Shintō, the ancient Japanese indigenous religion.

Hayashi's school was considered orthodox by the shogunate, but not all scholars agreed with its point of view. Some followed the Chinese thinker Wang Yangming and called for activism in the face of social injustice. These scholars often courted banishment or other forms of punishment. Another scholar created a cult of masculinity called the "Way of the Warrior" or ***bushidō*** (BOO-shee-DOH) that elevated the samurai and shōgun as upholders of military values. Yet others, such as Ogyū Sorai (OH-gyoo so-RAI; 1666–1728) rejected Neo-Confucianism and called for a study of ancient texts themselves.

Confucianism was not the only school of thought in the Tokugawa period. Early in the period, students of history began the study of Japan's past. In the eighteenth century, an eminent literary scholar, Motoori Norinaga (MOH-toh-OH-ree NOH-ree-NAH-ga, 1730–1801) undertook a massive study of *The Tale of Genji* and other classics from the Heian and pre-Heian eras (see Chapter 10). His work, which stressed the centrality of Japan and the role of Japan's ancient Shintō gods, was not intended as political, but it inspired later scholars who advocated the restoration of the power of the emperor.

Another strand of scholarship was called "Dutch Learning." Although not specifically Dutch, this scholarship started with the translation of Dutch books—the only Western books allowed in Japan and only after 1720 at that—and expanded to encompass a wide variety of studies in medicine, geography, astronomy, shipbuilding, and other technical subjects. At the end of the eighteenth century, scholars of Dutch Learning were able to comprehend the growth of Western expansionism and, alarmed, wanted to discuss military and political subjects. But these were restricted by shogunate law.

Other important schools of thought supported the way of the merchant class. Merchants were at the

bushidō—Literally "the way of the warrior," this philosophy called on samurai to dedicate themselves unto death to their feudal lord and to live frugally and ethically.

bottom of the Confucian hierarchy, but the Kaitokudō (KAI-TOH-koo-doh) Merchant Academy in Osaka stressed the importance of commerce and the morality of merchants. In Kyoto, Ishida Baigan (EE-shee-dah BAI-gan; 1685–1744) attracted thousands of followers with his "Heart Learning," a religion based on a synthesis of Buddhism, Confucianism, and Shintō that honored merchants who were honest and frugal and carried out their trade as if it were a "calling." Respect for merchants facilitated the transition to modern economic development in the Meiji era (see Chapter 25).

Culture and Society

Non-samurai folk, with the help of creative samurai, developed a lively urban society with values that were exemplified through its arts. Arts and culture were increasingly accessible to less elite consumers as new materials and techniques, particularly printing, brought literature and visual arts into many hands.

The art prized during the late sixteenth century, such as paintings of the Kanō school, were still valued in the seventeenth century. In addition, a new aesthetic was developing among cultivated gentlemen—the polite accomplishments of skilled amateur poetry, painting, tea ceremony, music, and calligraphy—that resembled similar movements in China and Korea at the time. Less refined culture appealed to an enormous market of commoners and samurai. Sensuality was at the heart of this great cultural outpouring. Much of this culture was produced in sections of large cities like Edo, Kyoto, and Osaka, which set aside as zones of sexuality called "pleasure quarters," initially created to marginalize and control sexuality so that the samurai could focus on their duty to their *daimyō* lords. Brothels, teahouses, artists' and writers' studios, theatres, and restaurants were crammed into these zones. Although these zones were aimed at men, many women did take part, both as workers in the brothels and as audience members at plays and other artistic performances. To be sure, life for those in the brothels was not all pleasurable. The quarters were surrounded by moats and gates, and women sex workers were not permitted to leave. Sold to brothels as young girls, many experienced a tough life, despite their often elegant clothing, artistic accomplishments, and genteel bearing.

The culture of the "pleasure quarters" had its own rules, which countered Confucian sensibility and morality. For example, according to conventional belief, actors were to be looked down upon, but they were the heroes of this culture, along with the finely dressed "dandies" who prided themselves on their knowledge of song lyrics, literature, and the latest gossip from the world of the theatre. Its heroines were famous courtesans and gifted geisha (GAY-shah) or female entertainers, who were trained in the arts from an early age. The

▶ Woodblock prints, like this portrait of a courtesan and her attendants, depicted the life of workers and customers in the "floating world" of urban culture in the Tokugawa period. These prints made art readily available to a mass audience. They also helped to spread new fashions and culture beyond urban areas.

Document

Ihara Saikaku: "The Umbrella Oracle"

Ihara Saikaku embodied the lively urban culture of Japan's "floating world" in the late seventeenth century. This short story is from his 1685 collection, *Tales from the Provinces.* Japanese loved to travel throughout the Japanese islands in the Tokugawa period—foreign travel was not permitted at that time—and for those who could not get away, tales of exotic places were an enjoyable substitute. Note the urbane city-based writer's humorous treatment of country folk.

To the famous "Hanging Temple of Kannon" in the Province of Kii, someone had once presented twenty oil-paper umbrellas which ... were hung beside the temple for the use of any and all who might be caught in the rain or snow....

One day in the spring of 1649, however, a certain villager borrowed one of the umbrellas and, while he was returning home, had it blown out of his hands by a violent "divine wind." ... Borne aloft by the wind, the umbrella landed finally in the little hamlet of Anazato, far in the mountains of the island of Kyushu. The people of this village had from ancient times been completely cut off from the world ... and had never even seen an umbrella! ...

Finally, one local wise man stepped forth and proclaimed, ... "Though I hesitate to utter that August Name, this is without a doubt the God of the Sun...." All present were filled with awe.... The whole population of the village went up into the mountains and, gathering wood and rushes, built a shrine that the deity's spirit might be transferred hence from [the Great Shrine of] Ise....

At the time of the summer rains the site upon which the shrine was situated became greatly agitated, and the commotion did not cease. When the umbrella was consulted, the following oracle was delivered: "All this summer the sacred hearth has been simply filthy.... [L]et there not be a single cockroach left alive! I have also one other request. I desire you to select a beautiful young maiden as a consolation offering for me. If this is not done within seven days, . . . I will rain you all to death! ..."

The villagers were frightened out of their wits ... [T]he young maidens, weeping and wailing, strongly protested the umbrella god's cruel demand.... They had come to attach a peculiar significance to the odd shape the deity had assumed.

At this juncture, a young and beautiful widow from the village stepped forward, saying, "Since it is for the god, I will offer myself in place of the young maidens."

All night long the beautiful widow waited in the shrine, but she did not get a bit of affection. Enraged, she charged into the inner sanctum, grasped the divine umbrella firmly in her hands and screaming, "Worthless deceiver!" she tore it apart, and threw the pieces as far as she could!

Questions to Consider

1. What was Ihara Saikaku's attitude toward rural people?
2. Contrast the behavior of widows advocated in Qing China with that accepted in Tokugawa Japan.
3. How does this short story show that Japanese worshipped both Buddhist and Shintō religion?

Excerpt from Ihara Saikaku, "The Umbrella Oracle," in Donald Keene, ed., *Anthology of Japanese Literature* (New York: Grove Press, 1955), pp. 354-356.

restrictions on the freedom of these women, however, belied the exalted status they seemed to enjoy.

It was in these crowded areas of sexuality that urban culture flourished. Perhaps because so many there seemed to be tossed about by the uncertainties of life and fortune, the world of the arts came to be known as the **"floating world,"** a concept taken from Buddhism. Poets, playwrights, novelists, and woodblock artists created art meant for mass consumption. The consumer market was increasingly sophisticated, and printing and literacy exploded in the late seventeenth century. There were over 700 publishing companies in Kyoto alone around 1800. Texts and pictures alike were produced by woodblock prints and were cheap enough to be readily accessible.

Artists like poet Matsuo Bashō (1644–1694), novelist and storyteller Ihara Saikaku (1642–1693), playwright Chikamatsu Monzaemon (1653–1724), and woodblock artists Hishikawa Moronobu (1620?–1694), Katsushika Hokusai (1760–1849), and Andō Hiroshige (1797–1858) were esteemed during their own lifetimes and continued to be highly regarded for their artistic accomplishments.

Son of a minor samurai, poet Matsuo Bashō (MAH-tsoo-oh ba-SHOH) established himself as the major practitioner of a poetic form called *haikai.* But he felt constrained by the conventional haikai style, so he developed a new form called *haiku.* His own studies of Zen, Chinese literature, and medieval Japanese poetry informed his enormous poetic output. The

floating world—The urban areas in which art, literature, and prostitution flourished in early modern Japan.

haiku, a 17-syllable form, evokes mood and suggests linkages between seemingly dissimilar objects.

On a withered branch
A crow has settled—
Autumn nightfall[2]

Bashō's most popular work was his travel writing, *Narrow Road to the North,* a volume of poetry and prose recounting his long journey throughout the island of Honshō.

Bashō's contemporary, Ihara Saikaku (EE-hah-rah SAI-kah-koo), was one of many highly successful prose writers of his day. Until the last year of his life, his tales were racy stories laced with a bit of propriety. His characters revel in pleasure—popular book titles included *The Life of an Amorous Man* (published in 1682) and *The Life of an Amorous Woman* (1686)—but despite their hedonistic lifestyle, they suffer loneliness at the end of their lives. In his 1688 novel, *The Eternal Storehouse of Japan,* Saikaku focused on practical concerns of the merchant class rather than sensual pleasures, and his last book (*Worldly Mental Calculations,* 1692) was a pessimistic tale of poverty.

Theatre was most dynamic in the seventeenth and early eighteenth centuries. Nō plays from the medieval period continued to be performed but were rapidly supplanted by plays with secular themes. Many of these new plays highlighted the dilemmas of life of the merchant class, contrasting the all-too-human struggle between fulfilling one's duty and following one's heart. Two major forms predominated: *kabuki* (kah-BOO-kee), which used human actors, and *bunraku* (BOON-rah-koo), which used almost life-sized puppets and an on-stage chorus.

Kabuki was developed by a woman dancer named Okuni who brought this new form of performance to Edo in 1603. Soon female kabuki troupes were all the rage. But when these performance troupes were linked to prostitution, women actors were outlawed in 1629. Women's roles came to be performed by men and boys, just as in the English theatre in Shakespeare's day. Kabuki plays used highly sophisticated staging, with revolving stages, opulent costumes and makeup, and grandiose gestures by the actors. The actors had widely enthusiastic followers who bought prints of those they idolized.

Chikamatsu Monzaemon (CHEE-kah-MAH-tsoo mon-ZAH-eh-mon), who wrote both kabuki and puppet plays, was Japan's greatest playwright of the Tokugawa period, and arguably of all time. He preferred writing puppet plays, as kabuki actors took liberties with the lines playwrights penned. Like Shakespeare, Chikamatsu wrote both historical plays and plays with deep human emotions. The latter often focused on tragic lovers whose duty to their families or employers prevented them from marrying. The lovers had no recourse but to run away and commit double suicide, deemed a pure gesture of intense romantic love. Chikamatsu's plays, in which emotion was always balanced with duty, showed that even in the floating world hedonism had its consequences. The Tokugawa government was so appalled by the rash of love suicides that followed the performance of some of Chikamatsu's plays that it banned all plays about love suicides.

Pictorial art was intimately connected with prose and poetry in the Tokugawa period. Illuminated books combined text and images, bringing affordable art to a mass readership. Woodblock prints were the breakthrough artistic form of the late seventeenth century. Earlier in the century, erotic themes in paintings called *shunga* (SHOON-ga) or "pictures of spring" were popular, and these themes were continued when woodblock prints first developed. Hishikawa Moronobu (HEE-shee-KAH-wa MOH-roh-NOH-boo) elevated the humble print to a major art form, depicting travel scenes, handsome actors, beautiful courtesans, gardens, and the bustle of urban street life as well as erotica. His work set the standards for the *ukiyo-e* (OO-kee-yoh EH), the pictures of the "floating world" that characterize the Tokugawa period for many modern viewers. The form he developed continued to reign during the rest of the period. Katsushika Hokusai (kah-TSOO-shkah HOHK-sai) and Andō Hiroshige (an-DOH hee-ROH-shee-gheh) perfected the art of landscape prints that are still immensely popular in Japan and the rest of the world.

Southeast Asia: Political and Cultural Interactions

What role did Southeast Asia's status as an international crossroads play in its colonization by the Europeans?

The late seventeenth century was a time of turmoil on the Southeast Asian mainland. Only Laos had enjoyed sustained peace and a degree of good relations with its neighbors during the long reign of Souligna-Vongsa (soo-LIG-na-VONG-sa; r. 1633?–1694). In addition to struggles among the states of Southeast Asia, European pressure altered interstate relations. The Dutch- and English-chartered trading companies competed for commercial dominance. The Dutch pushed the English out of the Indonesian archipelago in 1623 and captured Malacca from the Portuguese in 1641. Although the Dutch were at first more interested in trade than administration, by the end of the eighteenth century the Dutch claimed administrative control of Indonesia, forcing the inhabitants to grow crops like coffee, sugar, indigo, and spices and destroying any products the Indonesians might wish to grow that could undercut Dutch profits.

The French also attempted to trade in Southeast Asia, but placed equal emphasis on missionary activity. Alexhandre de Rhodes, a Jesuit priest, spent four decades in Vietnam, converting some Vietnamese to Christianity. He is most noted for devising the Roman alphabet-based script for the Vietnamese language. Because of Vietnamese antagonism toward Christian missionary activities in the late seventeenth century, the French turned toward Thailand, where the king was more hospitable toward missionaries. But the French pushed their luck too far, attempting to capitalize on their acceptance in Thailand by sending warships and demanding special privileges. While the Thai king was away from the capital, Thai nobles pushed the French out in 1688, thereby ending French hopes in Southeast Asia until they moved into Vietnam in the nineteenth century.

The Spanish came to Southeast Asia in 1521, when Ferdinand Magellan, on his round-the-world journey, arrived (and was promptly killed) in the Philippines. Four decades later, the Spaniards established their colony there, focusing on establishing Christianity in the islands not already converted to Islam. Catholic priests dominated villages in the Philippines, acting as administrative as well as religious leaders. The Filipinos were generally allowed only religious education and were denied the learning necessary to assume self-government. Spain's presence in the Philippines allowed the triangular trade between South America, Japan, and the Philippines that permitted silver to become the basis of the great East Asian trade machine.

Meanwhile, domestic and interstate turmoil rent the Southeast Asian mainland. In 1752, Burmese leader Alaungpaya (AH-lowng-PAH-yah; r. 1752–1760) drove the Mons from the Burmese capital and continued fighting southward. In 1760, Alaungpaya entered Thai territory and destroyed the beautiful Thai city of Ayuthaya (AH-yoo-TAI-yah). The Burmese assault on Thailand was halted when the Qing threatened Burma. Burma fended off the Qing, but later Burmese attacks on Thailand proved futile as the Thais gradually gained power on the Southeast Asian mainland. At first, the Thais were hampered by factionalism. But in 1782, General Chakri (CHAHK-ree) emerged on top, assumed the royal title, and united Thailand. He extended Thai influence over Laos, Cambodia, and Malaya. The Chakri dynasty continues to reign in Thailand. The first Chakri ruler, Rama I, restored culture and religion after the Burmese sack of Ayuthaya. He convened a major Buddhist council in 1788, wrote and supervised an extensive collection of royal writings, and established a climate for lively production of prose and poetry.

Vietnam also underwent turmoil in this era. The Le dynasty, founded in 1428, had suffered defeat at the hands of the Mac dynasty (1527–1592). But in 1592, the Trinh (TRIN) helped the Le to regain the throne in the northern part of Vietnam. The Le's power did not extend to the south, where the Nguyen (noo-EN) family ruled. The Nguyen continued moving southward; by 1720, they wiped out the old Cham (Cambodian) kingdom and controlled both Saigon and Phnom Penh (PNOM PEN). Southern Vietnamese culture became a blend of Cambodian and Vietnamese traditions. Chinese institutions, so influential in the north, were less important in the south. Indigenous deities were incorporated into culture under the Nguyen. As elsewhere in Southeast Asia, the status of women was relatively high.

	Southeast Asia
1633–1694	Reign of King Souligna-Vongsa in Laos
1623	Dutch begin exclusive trade in East Indies/Indonesia
1624	Alexhandre de Rhodes arrives in Vietnam; later develops script
1752–1782	Burmese incursion into Thailand
1771–1802	Tay Son uprising ends Le dynasty in Vietnam
1782	Chakri ascends Thai throne; founds dynasty
1802–1820	Reign of Gia Long in Vietnam

By the middle of the eighteenth century, government mismanagement and excessive taxation, accompanied by natural disasters, led to great suffering among the peasants. Rebellions, the most significant of which exploded in the region of Tay Son in 1771, broke out throughout Vietnam. The Tay Son Uprising was led by three brothers and gained the support of hill people, farmers in the lowland river basins, and small-scale merchants. One of the brothers was declared emperor, and for the first time in centuries, the north and south were united. The Qing sent in 200,000 troops to support the Le, but they failed. The Trinh were driven out in the north, and the Nguyen were almost defeated in the south. But one Nguyen prince, Nguyen Anh (noo-EN AHN), fled to Thailand, and with the help of a French priest, Pigneau de Behaine (pee-NEEOH duh be-EN), Chinese merchants in Saigon, and other foreigners, Nguyen Anh reclaimed the throne. De Behaine got the French throne to agree to help the Nguyen, but the French monarchy fell in the Revolution of 1789, and when Nguyen Anh took the royal capital at Hue in 1801 only four Frenchmen were among his forces. Nevertheless, the French had gotten their feet in Vietnam's door, and later the whole country fell under French imperialism.

Nguyen Anh declared himself Emperor Gia Long (r. 1802–1820) in 1802. Gia Long and his successor Minh Mang (r. 1820–1841) restored the power of the throne, wrote a legal code modeled on that of the Qing, and set up a Chinese-style administration. They built roads and fortifications. They encouraged the arts. Poetry by both men and women flourished. The most revered writer was Nguyen Du (1765–1820), author of *The Tale of Kieu,* whose protagonist was a dutiful daughter who suffered great sexual adversity to rescue her father. Nguyen Du, a supporter of the Trinh, saw his work as paralleling his life under rulers he deemed illegitimate. Ho Xuan Huang (HO shoo-AHN hoo-AHNG), a woman poet who lived around the same time as Nguyen Du, wrote poems that called for sexual equality and mocked stuffy social norms.

Farther south, in Indonesia, the European presence was much more compelling and the native resistance much weaker, in part because thousands of migrating Chinese had diluted the Islamic values and loyalties of Muslim societies in the Malay Archipelago. By 1750, the Dutch had subordinated most native dynasties in Malaya, Java, Sumatra, and the other islands. In the process, imported plantation agriculture brought an economic revolution that conditioned much life and labor in the whole area. For more than a century, a Muslim Malay people, known in history as the Bugis (BOO-ghees), challenged Dutch supremacy. Originating on the island of Celebes, the Bugis first won fame as sea rovers and mercenary warriors, serving all sides in the competitive spice trade through the city of Macassar (mah-CAH-sar). When the Dutch took Macassar in 1667, the Bugis scattered from Borneo to the Malay Peninsula, where they concentrated at Selangor. Through conquest, intermarriage, and intrigue, they gained control of Jahore, Perak, and Kedah on the mainland while extending their influence to Borneo and Sumatra. The Bugis fought two wars against Dutch Malacca in 1756 and 1784 but were ultimately forced to accept Dutch overlordship.

While the Dutch were consolidating their control over the Indonesian islands, the British were also expanding their trade through the Malacca Straits and seeking a naval port to counter the French who still had a presence in India in the Bay of Bengal until 1760. In 1786, the British obtained Penang on the Malay coast. Later, when France made the Netherlands a satellite state during the Napoleonic era, Britain temporarily took Malacca and Java. Penang then became a rapidly expanding center of British influence in Malaya. By the nineteenth century, Dutch fortunes shifted, and they gained control of present day Indonesia.

Europeans in the New Pacific Frontiers

How did the quest for trade turn Europeans into major actors in the Pacific region?

The Europeans and Chinese became aware of the existence of islands in the southern Pacific in the fifteenth and sixteenth centuries, but historians are unsure if they were in contact with southern Pacific islanders before the 1600s. A few artifacts of Spanish and Portuguese origin from that period have been found in Australia, although the first verifiable sighting of Australia by Europeans (the Dutch) did not take place until 1606. The Dutch were lively explorers of the South Pacific and Australia in the early 1600s. In 1642 Dutchman Abel Tasman sailed from the Dutch East India Company's port at Batavia (now Jakarta, Indonesia) to Papua-New Guinea, Fiji, a land later named Nieuw Zeeland, and an island later named for him—Tasmania. The Dutch were joined by the British four decades later when Englishman William Dampier was the first Briton to sail to Australia. His diaries of his voyage to New Holland (Australia) record a wealth of information about the continent's natural history.

A European View of Asia

Almost a century passed before the Pacific islands and Australia and New Zealand were once again targeted by Western explorers. As elsewhere in the world in the late eighteenth century, France and Britain were rivals in the South Seas. In addition to official voyages of exploration, whaling ships from these counties, now joined by whalers from the infant United States, plied the waters around Australia and New Zeeland.

France made significant inroads in Polynesia and was interested in New Zealand in the late 1700s. The most significant French explorations were those of Louis de Bougainville (loo-EE duh boo-gan-VEE; 1729–1811). Bougainville visited much of southern Polynesia, the Sandwich (Hawaiian) Islands, Australia, New Guinea, and New Britain. The French suffered a setback in New Zealand, however, when they massacred 250 Maori in retaliation for killing and eating Marion de Fresne. The murdered Frenchman had committed a major violation of spiritual propriety in 1772 (de Fresne ate fish that had presumably eaten several Maori who had drowned in the area, thereby committing cannibalism, according to the Maori).

By contrast, British Captain James Cook (1729–1779), who had reached New Zealand in 1769, appeared more benign to the Maoris. The following year, Cook reached Australia and mapped portions of its east coast. In the next few decades, other British explorers sailed around Australia, confirming it was an

	Europeans in the Pacific
1728	Vitus Bering charts Bering Strait
1779	Captain Cook killed in Hawaii
1788	Botany Bay established as British penal colony in Australia
1790	Unification of Hawaiian Islands by King Kamehameha

island. In 1788, a fleet of British ships deposited 1350 people in an area near today's Sydney. Not to be outdone, several French voyages of scientific exploration reached Australia in 1788 and 1792.

European contact was devastating. Indigenous people in New Zealand and Australia, as well as many of the islands of Polynesia and Melanesia, had few defenses against the leprosy, tuberculosis, and venereal diseases brought by the Europeans. Their populations plummeted. In some cases they were replaced with Europeans. Boatloads of Irish and English convicts were exiled to Australia between 1788 and the 1850s. These convicts included many who were could not repay their debts, a punishable offense at the time. Women and children were among the transported convicts, and British authorities assumed that all would eventually contribute to a stable settler society. After serving their terms of penal servitude, convicts were free to settle where they wished. Most stayed, and together with free settlers, became the first foreign inhabitants of Australia.

In Tahiti, Tonga, and Samoa, Protestant missionaries from England and the United States quickly moved in following Captain Cook's first contacts. The missionaries' views of Polynesian chiefdoms as similar to the small monarchies or principalities with which they were familiar encouraged them to work with Polynesian leaders who also saw the advantages of collaboration. The missionaries' religion came with economic and political benefits, as it led to trade and legitimized the authority of those Polynesian leaders who worked with them. With European help, local rulers—male and female—fought to dominate their islands. Such conflict was particularly prevalent in Hawaii in the 1790s. Here, the Hawaiian chief Kamehameha (kah-MEH-hah-MEH-hah) used European ships and cannons to consolidate his rule over the three main islands.

There were also significant disadvantages to the political, economic, and religious connections with Europeans and Americans. Original cultures in Polynesia began to decline as trade goods, rum, and guns stimulated status seeking, competition for power, violence, and war. Challenged by Christian condemnation, old religions were largely abandoned. Whole communities were harmed by alcoholism, and evidence of psychological malaise, such as suicide, became prevalent.

Another striking feature of relations between Europeans and Pacific islanders was the contrast in gender roles. Male islanders, unlike European men, were used to female leadership; men were less possessive; and sexual indulgence was considered by both men and women as pleasurable but not overly significant. Some Polynesian leaders, following a successful effort by Tahitian leaders to stave off a British attack in 1767 by sending a boatload of young, attractive women to the threatening British vessels, began to send canoes filled with naked young women to approaching European vessels to pacify their crews and to acquire their trade goods. The islanders' preference for iron nails—no iron being found on the islands—resulted at times in European sailors almost dismantling their own ships to find a commodity they could readily exchange for sex. This contributed to European notions of island women as either sexually exploited, on the one hand, or excessively risqué and independent, on the other.

▲ Captain James Cook made three voyages of exploration throughout the Pacific, from the Arctic to the Antarctic. His explorations informed Europeans about many of the Pacific islands and their peoples. After his death, British illustrations depicted him in the typical image of the day, as a white man bringing "civilization" to worshipful natives. This illustration shows Hawaiians either bowing deeply or raising their arms in apparent joy and wearing little other than extensive body tattoos. Cook was killed by Hawaiians in 1779.

Except for Spanish traders and colonists in the Philippines, the North Pacific area was almost unknown to Europeans before 1550, but many came during the next two centuries. Some of this contact involved Russian ships cruising southward toward Japan from Kamchatka (kahm-CHAHT-kah); at the same time, the French and British penetrated the North Pacific from Polynesia. Captain Cook's three voyages between 1768 and 1779 went beyond the known waters of the South Pacific to Antarctica and north of Alaska to the Arctic coasts, where Cook made contact with the Russians. By the late eighteenth century, when Western ships regularly arrived at Guangzhou from Hawaii or other Polynesian islands, East Asians began to feel the Western world crowding in on them.

Russians moved out toward the Pacific in 1632, when they established Yakutsk (yah-KOOTSK) in eastern Siberia. From there, adventurers drifted down the Lena River, first reaching the Arctic and later sailing east to the open Pacific. Their discoveries were ignored until 1728, when Vitus Bering (VEE-toos BE-ring; 1680–1741), a Danish navigator sailing for Peter the Great, charted what was later named the Bering Strait, which links the Arctic and Pacific Oceans. This discovery opened the North Pacific to Russia during the eighteenth century. Meanwhile, the Russians founded Okhotsk (aw-KOTSK) on the Pacific coast opposite the Kamchatka peninsula. At Okhotsk, and at other timbered forts in Siberia, Russian governors and their Cossack soldiers exacted tribute in furs from a society of nomadic hunters. Relations between the conquerors and their subjects were not particularly friendly; indeed, local populations around the forts were often wiped out by direct violence or European diseases.

European expansion in the Pacific brought significant changes for East Asia, particularly in maritime commerce. After the middle of the eighteenth century, the British began replacing the Dutch as the major European traders, a trend climaxed by the collapse of the Dutch East India Company in 1794. At Guangzhou the number of British and American ships increased dramatically after 1790. Seeking a product that might be exchanged profitably for Chinese silk and tea, the British first concentrated on cotton and then later opium from India. When the opium trade created friction with Chinese officials, British merchants began seeking furs, particularly sea otter skins, which were obtained in the North Pacific. Hawaiian ports soon became busy centers for fitting ships and recruiting sailors. By 1815, European expansion into the Pacific had radically altered the structure of island commerce.

Conclusion

At the beginning of the nineteenth century, the Ottoman Empire continued to endure, as it would into the twentieth century with the bulk of its expansive territories, including some in Europe, intact. To the east, the Qajars consolidated their power and ruled Iran for a century, despite the territorial ambitions of Russia and Britain. The Mughals, however, had lost considerable ground to their Maratha and British rivals.

Like the recently formed Sikh state, that of the Marathas remained strong and challenged the military authority of the British in India in the first half of the nineteenth century. France had recently lost influence in Vietnam—which it would regain by the end of the nineteenth century—and was acutely aware of a revived Thailand. To Vietnam's north, China continued to be the world's largest power at the end of the eighteenth century, maintaining tributary relations with its neighbors, outproducing the rest of the world, managing great domestic growth while balancing the needs of the Manchu regime with the indigenous culture of the people, and dominating international trade. But domestic corruption, social tensions at China's boundaries due to population pressures, and creeping European imperialism began to undermine Chinese strength and wealth in the early nineteenth century. Korea, long accustomed to its subordinate status vis-à-vis China, developed its own fine arts and crafts. Its eighteenth-century monarchs ruled efficiently, and its creative scholars developed an exciting form of "practical learning" which produced reforms. Japan's vibrant urban society, as well as its growing regional wealth, developed institutions of government and society that set the stage for its dynamic modernization in the late nineteenth century. Australia, New Zealand, and the Pacific islands came under European control. Although those indigenous people who survived the onslaught of imperialism often retained some of their culture, many of these territories became settler societies with the government and culture of the metropole.

Suggestions for Web Browsing

You can obtain more information about topics included in this chapter at the websites listed below. See also the companion website that accompanies this text, http://www.ablongman.com/brummett, which contains an online study guide and additional resources.

Islam and Islamic History in Arabia and the Middle East

On the coming of the West, see
http://www.islamicity.com/education/ihame/default.asp?Destination=/education/ihame/14.asp
On the Ottomans, see
http://www.islamicity.com/education/ihame/default.asp?Destination=/education/ihame/13.asp

Internet Islamic History Sourcebook
http://www.fordham.edu/halsall/sbook1d.html
A comprehensive online source for links about Islamic history.

Internet East Asia History Sourcebook
http://www.fordham.edu/halsall/eastasia/eastasiasbook.html
An extensive online source for links about the history of East Asia, including primary documents regarding exploration, European imperialism, the legal system, and literature and arts.

Samurai Archives
http://www.samurai-archives.com/
An extensive source of links for samurai history, biographies, culture, arts, and literature.

Jesuits in the Qing Court
http://www.usfca.edu/ricci/exhibits/dragon_skies/index.htm
Detailed essay on Jesuit astronomy in Ming China.

Literature and Film

The following works provide an overview: Walter Andrews et al., trans., *Ottoman Lyric Poetry* (University of Texas, 1997); Kemal Silay, *Anthology of Turkish Literature* (Indiana University Press, 1998); *Evliya Çelebi in Bitlis,* ed. & trans. Robert Dankoff (Brill, 1990), the section on eastern Anatolia of the famous book of travels by the Ottoman raconteur Evilya Çelebi; and Sir John Chardin, *Travels in Persia 1673–1677* (Dover, 1988 reprint of 1927 edition).

The famous novel of Qing society, *Dream of the Red Chamber,* is available in various translations. See, for example, Cao Xueqin, *The Story of the Stone, The Golden Days,* trans. David Hawkes, Vol. 1 (Viking Press, 1973). For a multifaceted account of woman's place as writer during the Qing that includes representative translations of poetry, see Susan Mann, *Precious Records: Women* in *China's Long Eighteenth Century* (Stanford University Press, 1997). For an overview of the vibrant urban culture of Tokugawa Japan along with translations of some of the most famous short fiction of the Genroku era, see Howard Hibbett, *The Floating World in Japanese Fiction,* 2nd ed. (Charles E. Tuttle Co., 2002).

Japanese film directors of the mid-twentieth century doted on the Tokugawa period. Numerous excellent commercial films give an insight into seventeenth-, eighteenth, and nineteenth-century life. Kurosawa's depictions of samurai and their values may be seen in *Seven Samurai* (1954; Toho) and *Yojimbo* ("The Bodyguard," 1961; Kurosawa Production); a moving depiction of an early nineteenth-century physician is available in his *Red Beard* (1965; Kurosawa Production). Filmmaker Mizoguchi Kenzo's insightful examinations of the status and roles of Tokugawa women in *The Life of Oharu: The Life of A Woman by Saikaku* (1952; Koi Productions) are an excellent accompaniment to Ihara Saikaku's novels.

Suggestions for Reading

For background on the Ottoman Empire, see Donald Quataert, *The Ottoman Empire, 1700–1922* (Cambridge University Press, 2000); Bruce McGowan, *Economic Life in the Ottoman Empire, 1600–1800* (Cambridge University Press, 1982); Suraiya Faroqhi, *Pilgrims and Sultans: The Hajj Under the Ottomans 1517–1683* (I. B. Tauris, 1994); Fatma M. Göçek, *East Encounters West* (Oxford University Press, 1987); and David Morgan, *Medieval Persia, 1040–1797* (Longman, 1988).

On the Mughal Empire, see John Richards, Gordon Johnson, and C. A. Bayly, eds., *The Mughal Empire* (Cambridge University Press, 1996); K. N. Chaudhuri, *Asia Before Europe* (Cambridge University Press, 1990); Sushil Chaudhury, Michel Morineau, Maurice Aymard, Jacques Revel, and Immanuel Wallerstein, eds., *Merchants, Companies and Trade: Europe and Asia in the Early Modern Era* (Cambridge University Press, 1999); Susan Bayly, *Caste, Society and Politics in India from the Eighteenth Century to the Modern Age* (Cambridge University Press, 1999); Matthew Edney, *Mapping an Empire: The Geographical Construction of British India, 1765–1843* (Oxford University Press, 1999); and Om Prakash, *The Dutch East India Company and the Economy of Bengal, 1630–1720* (Princeton University Press, 1985).

Among the best general surveys of Southeast Asia in this period are D. R. Sardesai, *Southeast Asia: Past and Present* (Westview Press, 2003); and Anthony Reid, *Southeast Asia in the Early Modern Era: Trade, Power, and Belief* (Cornell University Press, 1993).

Qing China studies include Willard J. Peterson, ed., *The Cambridge History of China,* Vol. 9, part 1 (Cambridge University Press, 2001); Jonathan D. Spence, *The Search for Modern China* (W. W. Norton, 1990); and Pamela Crossley, *The Manchus* (Blackwell, 1997). R. Bin Wong, *China Transformed: Historical Change and the Limits of European Experience* (Cornell University Press, 1998), and Kenneth Pomeranz, *The Great Divergence: China, Europe, and the Making of the Modern World Economy* (Princeton University Press, 2001), place China in the world context. Jonathan Lipman, *Familiar Strangers: A History of Muslims in Northwest China* (University of Washington Press, 1998), discusses an important ethnic minority. Dorothy Ko, *Every Step a Lotus: Shoes for Bound Feet* (University of California Press, 2001) examines the meaning of foot binding in Chinese history.

Andrew C. Nahm, *Tradition and Transformation: A History of the Korean People* (Hollym International, 1988); Carter J. Eckert et al., *Korea Old and New: A History* (Harvard University Press, 1990); and Michael J. Seth, *A Concise History of Korea: From the Neolithic Period Through the Nineteenth Century* (Rowman and Littlefield, 2006), offer fine treatments of major Korean developments during the period. On the roles of Korean women, see Laurel Kendall and Mark Peterson, eds., *Korean Women* (East Rock Press, 1983).

The best overview of the Tokugawa period is Conrad Totman, *Early Modern Japan* (University of California Press, 1993). Gregory M. Pflugfelder, *Cartographies of Desire* (University of California Press, 1999), offers a unique perspective on culture in the urban "pleasure quarters." On rural social change, see Anne Walthall, *Social Protest and Popular Culture in Eighteenth-Century Japan* (University of Arizona Press, 1986), and Stephen Vlastos, *Peasant Protests and Uprisings in Tokugawa Japan* (University of California Press, 1986). For Japanese intellectual developments, see Herman Ooms, *Tokugawa Ideology* (Princeton University Press, 1989). On women, see Gail Lee Bernstein, *Recreating Japanese Women, 1600–1945* (University of California Press, 1991).

CHAPTER 21

The Americas, 1650–1825

From European Dominance to Independence

Outline

- The Iberian Colonies: 1650–1789
- The West Indies
- Breaking Away: The Creation of the United States of America
- Haiti: The First Successful Slave Revolution
- The Latin American Revolutions

Features

DISCOVERY THROUGH MAPS **The Island of California**

SEEING CONNECTIONS **Gold and Precious Stones in Brazil**

DOCUMENT **Letter from Abigail Adams**

DOCUMENT **Simón Bolívar, Proclamation to the People of Venezuela**

◀ A man of political and military genius, Toussaint Louverture led the Haitian people in their successful struggle for independence.

As we saw in Chapter 16, for the Amerindians, the European invasion at the end of the fifteenth century through the sixteenth century brought with it war, disease, and abuse leading to a two-century loss of population that killed from an estimated 80 percent of the population in Mexico and Central America to around 30 percent in North and South America. After the terrible losses of the previous two centuries, the Amerindian population began to stabilize in 1600, but the demographic mix in the Americas was far different from that found in 1500.

For the Europeans, the entry into the New World brought with it an expanding trade in new products and an increasing supply of precious metals. Greater risks for increased wealth created new challenges. The Spanish and Portuguese, during the sixteenth century, were the first to take up these challenges. They created economic systems that depended on the imports of gold and silver from the New World. But they did not develop new industries and they managed their business affairs poorly. The wealth they brought across the Atlantic flowed through their hands to the northern Europeans, who continued the new imperialism in the America. For the Europeans—northern and southern—the Americas posed the possibilities of profit and peril.

In Central and South America, the Spanish and Portuguese worked through the church to generate a new cultural synthesis, blending European, Amerindian, and African elements to produce a richness and variety not present in any of the parent cultures. Racial mixing, which created a new Latin American population and culture in the Western Hemisphere, ensured the continuity and development of this rich synthesis. The intermarriage of the Amerindians, Africans, and Europeans created a diverse society. However, the hierarchy of birth and race dominated life in the New World, as in the old.

The Iberian Colonies: 1650–1789

What effects did the Spanish and Portuguese have on their New World colonies?

As the Europeans began to exploit the riches to be found in the New World, they sponsored the immigration of their own populations and the mass importation of African slaves. In the process, the European invaders nearly destroyed the indigenous peoples' cultures and religions. They subjected most of the survivors to terrible hardships, indignities, cultural deprivations, and psychological injuries. The plight of Latin American peasants today began with Spanish and Portuguese imperial and cultural policies of the sixteenth century.

The Iberian powers carried out these policies to maintain their footholds in their massive new colonies. Spain governed an empire stretching from present-day California to Buenos Aires in the southern part of South America. Once Portugal regained its independence from Spain in 1640, it ruled the vast country of Brazil.

The Spanish Empire

Spain created an imposing administrative framework to consolidate its control of its conquests in the New World. The Spaniards faced many obstacles: distance, the lack of efficient transportation and communications links, and pockets of hostile Amerindians, among others, who did not acknowledge Spanish authority and remained ready to fight. The Spaniards built a series of fortified administrative centers such as Santa Fe in today's New Mexico in 1573 and dispatched their missionaries to convert the Indians to Christianity.

As long as the Habsburgs ruled Spain, they pursued a rule characterized by a certain decentralization that reflected the geographical and political realities of the time. When the Bourbons took the Spanish throne during the eighteenth century, there was a marked effort toward centralization, sometimes following "enlightened despots" theories described in Chapter 18. In the 1750s and 1760s, Spanish America underwent several reforms that brought colonial administration and finance more closely under the supervision of Madrid.

Society

In Spanish America, at the top of the social hierarchy were those people born in Spain called variously *peninsulares* (pay-neen-seu-LAHR-ays) or *europeos* (eu-roh-PAY-ohs). As the eighteenth century came to a close, their numbers increased significantly—to the dismay of the Creoles—to perhaps 300,000 people. They monopolized high political and church offices as well as leadership positions in business and the arts. *Europeo* women dominated local society.

One step down on the social scale came the group that competed with the *europeos* for control of the local society, the white population born in the New World—the **Creoles.** Equally conscious of the social superiority of the European-born and the competition from the ambitious mixed blood population below, they fought tenaciously to maintain their position near the top of the social pyramid. At the end of the eighteenth century, they numbered around 3 million. They possessed the **haciendas** (ah-see-END-es) and mines, positions in municipal offices and universities, and they dominated the middle clergy. The intellectual and political elites came from this group, and it was in their libraries that the works of Montesquieu, Voltaire, and Rousseau were found.

Poorer, and more numerous than the Creoles, were the people of color. These people of mixed blood—the **mestizos** (the European and Indian population), the

Creole—Along the west coast of Africa, most usually freed slaves, living in cities, who adapted themselves to Western culture. In the Americas, a person of Spanish descent born in Latin America.

hacienda—A plantation or large agricultural establishment in Spanish America.

mestizos—In Spanish America, people of Spanish and Indian ancestry.

CHRONOLOGY

1650	1675	1700	1750	1775	1800
1655 England seizes Jamaica	**1690–1760** Increased silver exports from New World to Europe	**1713** Treaty of Utrecht increases British influence in the Americas	**1750–1770** Enlightenment Administrative Reforms in Spanish Empire **1756–1773** French and Indian War **1763** Treaty of Paris sanctions British dominance in North America	**1775–1783** American Revolution **1787** Constitutional Convention **1791–1803** Haitian Revolution	**1808** Napoleon removes Spanish and Portuguese monarchs, opens generation of Latin American Revolution **1810–1821** Mexican Revolution **1823** Monroe Doctrine

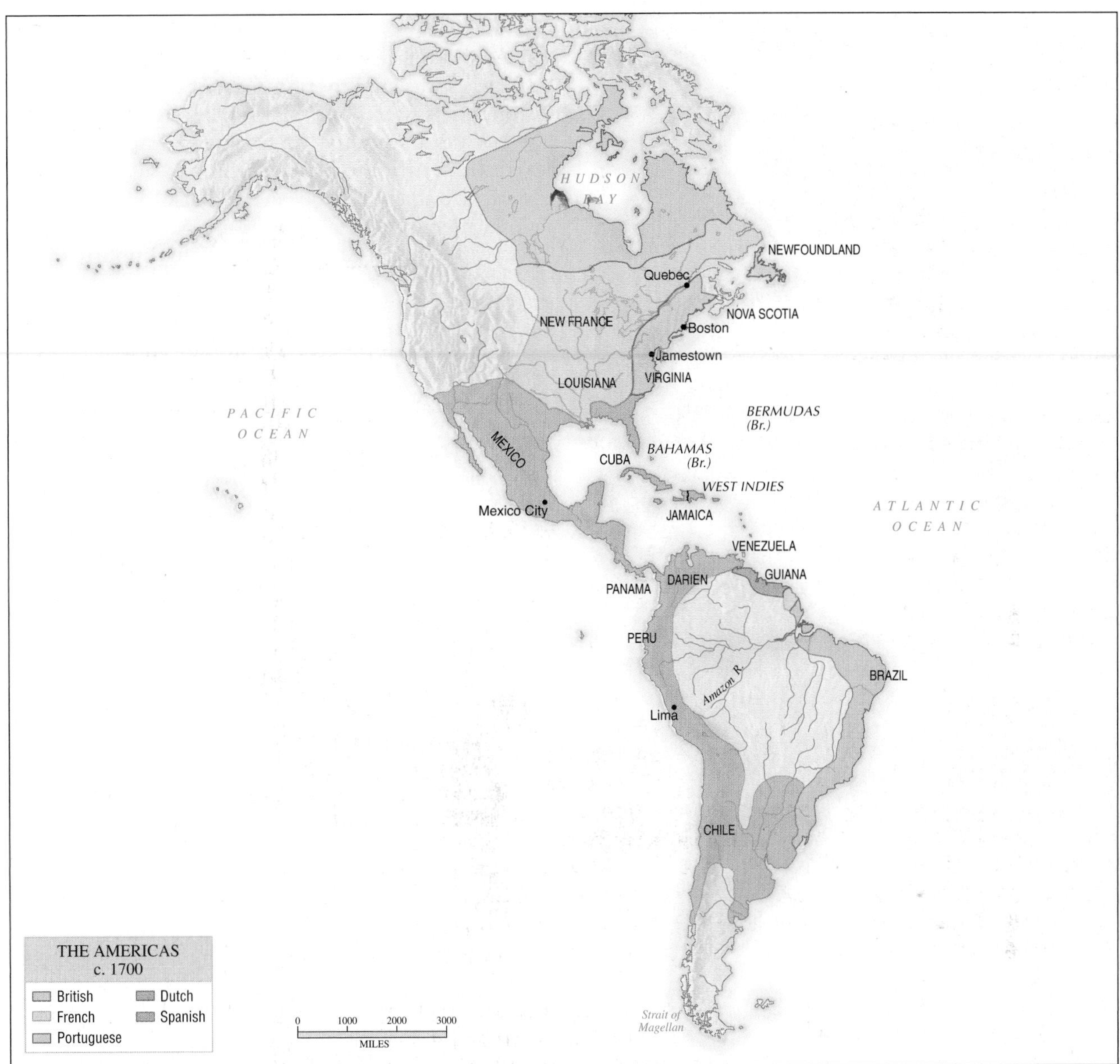

▲ After the initial wave of European explorers and conquerors had finished their work, the peoples of North and South America found themselves in the spheres of influence of the British, French, Portuguese, Dutch, and Spanish.

mulattoes (European and African), and **zambos** (Indian and African)—were the free workers, small business people, and independent farmers. A huge social and legal gap separated them from the Creoles.

Despite European immigration, importation of slaves, and emerging mixed social groups, the indigenous Indians remained the most numerous part of the population. They had legal standing and were, in principle, free. However, given their economic and social standing, the freedom brought them little advantage.

At the bottom of the social scale were the slaves, regarded as property—increasingly valuable property, as the prices of slaves soared. During the seventeenth and eighteenth centuries, the number of Africans grew rapidly in the New World. Although African slaves in the Iberian empires had a less oppressive life than those found in the English colonies they worked early on to improve their status in society. African slaves in the West Indies were among the most organized, and at the end of the eighteenth century, they fought to gain their freedom in Haiti.

Led by the Dominican and the Franciscan orders, the Spanish church labored to convert everyone in the New World to Christianity. There was an impressive

mulattoes—People of European and African ancestry.

zambos—People of Indian and African ancestry.

▲ As can be seen from the setting of the house and the quality of the clothing, this is a portrait of an upper-class family in Latin America. This mixing of population allowed the peoples of Central and South America largely to avoid the often violent racism of North America.

amount of suppleness in their approach, as they tried to reach the Indian populations in their own languages after the failure of the initial drive to make them accept the faith through the Castilian tongue. There was a classic disdain for the local civilizations and their ways of life—but also the admission that, at least in their ignorance, the Indians were not likely to have been tainted by heresy. The Spanish and Portuguese constructed churches that took the Baroque aesthetic to sometimes bizarre, but artistically impressive, extremes. The Jesuits were active at the frontiers where the Indians maintained their traditional customs, such as in Paraguay or California. They instilled a discipline that was at the same time paternalistic and severe until their order was forced to leave in 1767—they were subsequently shut down in 1773.

Economics

Spanish America in the seventeenth and eighteenth centuries was an important part of a powerful global economic system knit together by the Spanish fleet. There was an around-the-world trading system that went from Africa to India to China to the Philippines to Mexico to the Caribbean and back to Europe. Precious metals were a significant part of the cargo between Spanish America and Spain. Imported gold and, even more significant, silver affected the European economy more than all other foreign goods. Into the middle of the seventeenth century, the New World possessed the mercury mines needed to process silver.

After the Spaniards had looted Aztec and Inca treasure rooms, the gold flowing from America and Africa subsided to a comparative trickle, but 7 million tons of silver poured into Europe before 1760. Spanish prices quadrupled, and because most new bullion went to pay for imports, prices more than tripled in northern Europe. Rising inflation hurt landlords who depended on fixed rents and creditors who were paid in cheap money, but the bullion bonanza ended a centuries-long gold drain to the East, with its attendant money shortage. It also increased the profits of merchants selling on a rising market, thus greatly stimulating northern European capitalism.

Food items shipped in bulk provided the other great economic activity. After the decline of the **encomienda** (en-koh-MAY-AHN-dah) system (see Chapter 16), more and more of the production came from the plantations, the haciendas, that produced the agricultural products for domestic use and for export. The plantation was generally constructed in the form of a square with fields of sugar cane or tobacco or coffee interspersed with fields of corn and potatoes to

encomienda—Spanish institution, similar to feudalism and manorialism, that gave settlers authority over indigenous people to collect tribute or impose labor demands—at the same time, however, they had to provide protection to the Amerindians and Christianize them.

	Latin America: From Colonization to the Eve of Independence
1600–1660	Dutch move into former Portuguese- and Spanish-dominated areas
1655	Cromwell seizes island of Jamaica
1713	Treaty of Utrecht diminishes Spanish influence in Latin and South America
1690–1760	Vast increase in silver exports from Mexico and South America
1750–1770	High point of enlightened reforms in Spanish colonial government

Discovery Through Maps

The Island of California

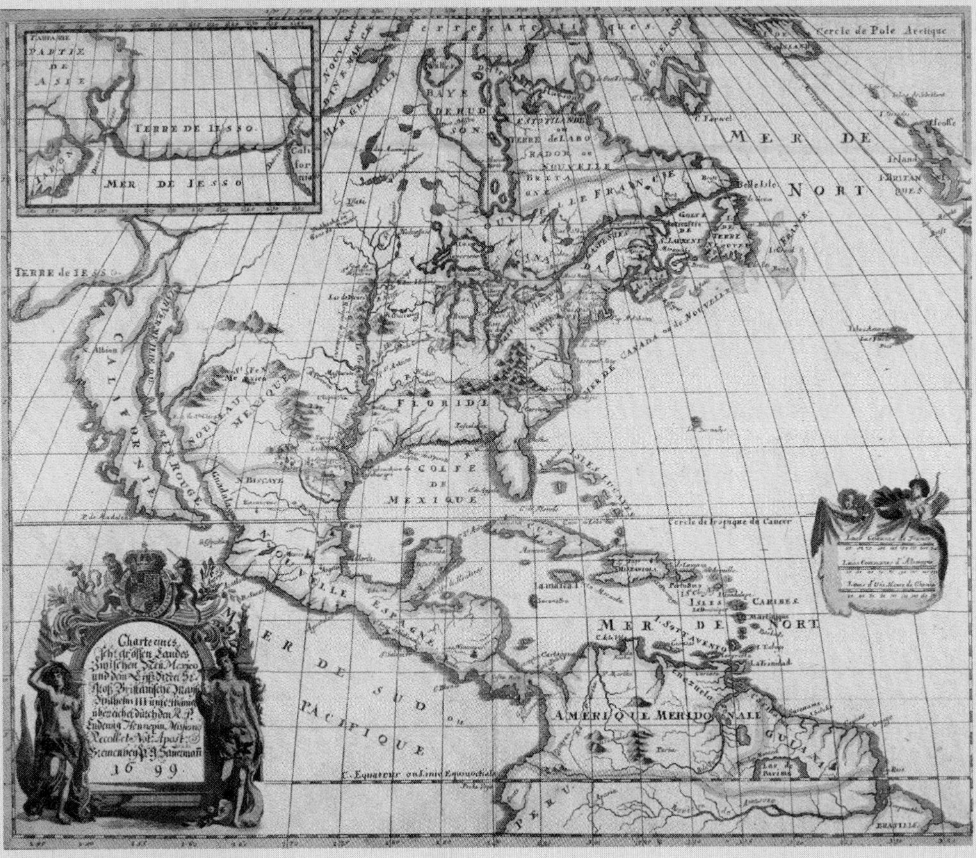

The new discovery of a very large country located in America between New Mexico and the Glacial Sea, with the necessary maps and figures and natural and moral history and the advantages to be gained there....

At Utrecht, the Merchant Guillaume Broedelet's Book Store, 1699

This late seventeenth-century map of the New World, drawn by Louis Hennepin (b. 1640), shows as an island what would later become the state of California. Hennepin's map is a collection of the observations made by French explorers up and down the Mississippi and Missouri rivers and of the charts made by seafarers in the previous century. The five Great Lakes are there, even if Lake Michigan is called Lake Illinois. Although the cartographer placed the Rio Grande in present-day Alabama, the rest of the details are quite accurate.

Hennepin seems to have consulted—either directly or indirectly—the findings of Sebastian Vizcaino's 1602 voyage in search of safe harbors for the Spanish merchant fleet crossing the Pacific from Manila. Spanish shipping drew the attentions of pirates—both those who were quasi-officially sponsored, such as Sir Francis Drake, and the merely criminal—and Vizcaino searched with not much success to find a place where they might shelter after their long crossing. He must have tired of looking, for he did not find that best of harbors—San Francisco Bay. When he came back to Mexico, however, he carried with him a wealth of information about what would become California.

The person most responsible for spreading the word that California was an island was Father Antonio Ascension, who traveled with Vizcaino. As he was summarizing his notes and preparing a report for his superiors, he depicted California as an island. Unfortunately for him, the Spanish boat carrying his report was picked off by the Dutch—at that time in the process of replacing Spain as the preeminent naval power—and the priest's findings ended up in Holland. Ascension's hypothesis of California as an island came to be accepted by Dutch cartographers, the most advanced of the time.

For the next 150 years, California appeared on maps printed around the world as an island, until cartographers at last attached it to the rest of what would become the United States.

Questions to Consider

1. Find the part of the country in which you live on Hennepin's map. How accurately is it portrayed?
2. It is often said that cartographers plagiarized shamelessly—and uncritically—in the seventeenth century. Given Hennepin's presentation of California, do you think that this is true?
3. What difficulties faced a mapmaker like Hennepin in the seventeenth century?

feed the workers. The buildings at the center were those of the master, and were usually built of brick and wood. Around them were the houses of the overseers, and then those of the slaves with their individual gardens. In the typical plantation, there were also specialized buildings used to produce the sugar or cure the tobacco or coffee, as well as a hospital. Typically, half of the slaves would be used to raise and the transport the cane, tobacco, or coffee beans to be processed, and the other half produced the finished product. Plantations were not known for their economic efficiency but rather for their wasteful practices and inefficient land use. As the soil became exhausted, progressive plantation owners introduced an agricultural rotation with crops that were not as financially rewarding as sugar, coffee, or tobacco. Other owners simply abandoned their land and went elsewhere.

Slaves suffered from tropical illnesses and from a wretched level of hygiene; on arrival from Africa, they were particularly prone to dysentery. Because of the nature of the work and the traumas of their conditions, it was rare for a slave to work beyond the age of 40. Infant mortality rates among the slave population were high, and women died frequently in childbirth because of lack of care, infection, and insufficient diet.

Brazil and the West Indies produced sugar, tobacco, or coffee. Mexico—with its Indian population's traditions—raised corn, beans, and peppers. Wines, potatoes, and oils came from South America. In all sectors, production was limited by often primitive planting and harvesting methods and by a lack of labor. The New World was not immune from the world depression that characterized the first half of the seventeenth century, and graft, smuggling, and piracy were natural results of economic distress. In the nature of the absolutist economics of the time, all business had to be done within either the Spanish or the Portuguese empire, through Seville and Cadiz, or through Lisbon. However, pirates and smugglers plagued the Iberian powers. In 1628, the Dutch captured 80 tons of silver from the Spaniards—as grave a setback as their defeat in the battle of Rocroi (rohk-KWAH) would be 15 years later. By the end of the seventeenth century, even the fiction of centralized control was abandoned. The Spanish fleet was incapable of servicing the empire, and more and more trade was carried out by the merchant vessels of the northwestern Europe—the Dutch, English, and French, who provided Spain with its markets for bulk trade while stealing its precious metals. After the Treaty of Utrecht (1713), the Spaniards lost even more influence in the region. The British gained the right under the treaty to sell slaves in Spanish America and to make a once a year visit to important ports to sell some 500 tons of their goods. The British leveraged these openings to further penetrate the Spanish markets.

▲ Finding gold and other precious metals in the New World was a challenging task for the Europeans. Even more difficult, at times, was running the gauntlet of pirates who infested the Caribbean and West Atlantic. Shown here is a Spanish galleon being boarded by pirates.

Brazil—Portugal in the New World

By the Treaty of Tordesillas (tohr-deh-SEE-yahs) (1494), the pope issued a "bull of demarcation" to divide the lands in the New World contested between Portugal and Spain. This line was drawn in such a way that the Lisbon government received the area that would come to be known as Brazil, the largest state in present-day South America. After Pedro Cabral claimed the area for Portugal, a colonial capital was founded at Salvador in 1549. The Jesuits accompanied the bureaucrats in that year: they set out to bring the local population to Christianity, just as the functionaries oversaw the establishment of the sugar cane plantations. Even when Spain absorbed Portugal in 1580, the administration of the two colonial regions remained separated for a period of 60 years.

Compared to the vast and comparatively well-organized and populated Spanish holdings, Portuguese Brazil was a loosely ruled area under the authority of a governor-general living there. After 1600, there were about 80,000 people—a mixture of perhaps one-third white and mixed-race, one-third Indian, and one-third African—in Brazil. With their lack of population and armed strength, the Portuguese in Brazil generally remained dominated by the Spaniards. Later, in the middle part of the seventeenth century, they were powerless to oppose the incursions of the French and the Dutch in Brazil. The French had already entered from the north under Henry IV in 1594. The Dutch posed a serious challenge, especially after they founded their West Indies Company in 1621. For the next 30 years, they launched a multifaceted effort toward Brazil that included smuggling and piracy combined with normal commercial relations.

Sugar remained the major enterprise of Brazil to the end of the seventeenth century. The raising of sugar cane spread from the island of Madeira to Brazil in the middle of the sixteenth century. Production went from 2,000 tons in 1560 to more than 14,000 tons in 1600. When the Dutch took the ports of Bahia and then Recife (ray-SEE-fay), they established their own sugar plantations nearby, and by 1629 there were nearly 350 sugar mills. The owners of the sugar mills typically rented the land to farmers to raise, cut, and transport the cane. Once the cane was brought to the

Seeing Connections

Gold and Precious Stones in Brazil

The English mineralogist John Mawe journeyed to South America between 1804 and 1811 for both commercial and scientific reasons. Not only did he collect precious stones and seashells for sale in England, he also traveled to the interior of Brazil for his patron, the Portuguese prince regent, with the aim of locating new diamond fields. This print, taken from his trip to Minas Gerais, Brazil, in 1809, shows Portuguese masters at their ease supervising their slaves, who are extracting diamonds from the slurry of water and mud. The slaves had to be carefully supervised to prevent them from hiding diamonds in their clothing or bodies, thus there was more or less one inspector for every two slaves. Minas Gerais (the name translates literally as "the place with a variety of mines") was found by the Portuguese to possess large deposits of gold in the second half of the sixteenth century. In the next two centuries, a veritable gold rush took place, attracting many Portuguese citizens searching for wealth and leading to the introduction of slaves from Africa, who, however, never constituted more than one-third of the labor force. In the second half of the eighteenth century, it is estimated that 80 percent of the gold and precious stones circulating in Europe arrived from Portuguese-controlled Brazil.

mills, it was processed by European technicians overseeing the work of slaves—in the 1630s, the Dutch brought in 23,000 African slaves to their part of Brazil to work in their sugar mills. Sugar production fell toward the end of the seventeenth century because of exhaustion of the soil. By that time, the Dutch had already transferred most of their sugar industry to the island of Curaçao (koo-rah-SAOW).

Once they regained their independence from Spain in 1640, the Portuguese increased the selling of slaves, principally to work in the production of sugar. They also took advantage of the Dutch wars with the British to reclaim their holdings to the north after 1654. For the rest of the seventeenth and into the eighteenth century, the Portuguese allied themselves with the English for help against the Dutch, the French, and the Spaniards. A close commercial connection was set up as the Portuguese sold their wines and sugars to England and had the protection of the British navy. Precious metals discoveries were made just as the sugar production died out in Brazil. There were 725 kilograms of gold exported in 1699, 9,000 in 1714, and 20,000 in 1725, the same year that the diamond strike occurred. The majority of the precious metals discovered at the beginning of the eighteenth century found their way to the vaults of the Bank of England. In return for these products and precious metals, British goods flooded Portugal and Brazil.

The West Indies

What made the West Indies so valuable for the European powers?

From the tip of Florida down to South America, the West Indies served as the first stop for the Europeans on their way to the New World and remain as points of contention into the twenty-first century. Columbus claimed the region for Spain on his arrival in 1492. A century later, there remained precious few of the Indian population—save for the Caribs who, by their ferocious struggles, maintained their independence. Scattered among the islands were several thousands Spaniards, a large number of mulattoes, mestizos, zambos, and African slaves.

As we saw in Chapter 16, the islands served as an essential element of the triangular trade routes between the Iberian powers, the West Indies, and North America, and they attracted all of the European maritime powers. The English staked their claims in 1620 to Saint Christopher, Barbados, Santa Lucia, St. Kitts, Nevis, Montserrat (mon-ser-RAH), Antigua (ahn-TEE-gwa), and the Bahamas. The Dutch were more interested in the islands closer to the present-day Venezuela and took Aruba, Curaçao, and Bonaire. In 1625, the French claimed part of St. Kitts, and 10 years later, they claimed Martinique, Dominique, and Guadeloupe. Because the sugar boom was just beginning, the French islands would soon become very profitable. However, fierce attacks by the Caribs limited economic development in this era before 1650. In 1655, Cromwell seized the island of Jamaica for the English, while the French picked off Tortuga and the western part of Santo Domingo.

Until the nineteenth century, the islands were the center for continual competition, and between 1648 and 1789, they often changed hands in the wake of the European wars. From their islands, the Europeans raided their neighbors' shipping and commerce, whether as filibusters—people making unauthorized war on another state—or as pirates. In addition, the French, Dutch, and English used their islands as bases to pick off Spanish shipping and to penetrate the Spanish market in the New World. Gangs of thieves in the interiors of the islands—and pirates roaming among them—took advantage of the competition among the major powers. It was a war zone, in brief, whether sparked by personal profit, national ambitions, or the desire to extend the faith as the Protestant nations fought the Catholics, and vice versa.

In the seventeenth century, the governments in Europe tried to consolidate their positions in the islands. Richelieu granted trade monopolies to merchants from La Rochelle, Nantes, and Rouen to deal in tobacco, indigo, and other goods. Colbert established the Company of the West Indies as part of his mercantilistic schemes. A significant part of his emphasis was the trade in slaves which was run out of Bordeaux, and which became the source of the wealth of many of the French bourgeoisie, including Voltaire. Curaçao became the main center for the Dutch and Jamaica for the British.

To lure people from the continent, the British and French used indentures, under which a person would agree to sign himself and his labor over to his sponsor for a certain number of years before he could become free. More than 6000 such contracts were signed in La Rochelle, France, alone—people seeking to escape debt, artisans wanting to become rich, and those simply seeking adventure. However, the British and French could not find enough people to go to their islands through the indentures and at the beginning of the eighteenth century, debt prisoners, galley slaves, and prostitutes were forcibly shipped across the Atlantic to populate the islands. Another important source of population for the islands was the Huguenots who fled France after the revocation of the Edict of Nantes in 1685. The majority of them went to the English and Dutch islands. But the most important need for labor was filled by a vast increase in the amount of African slaves brought under horrible conditions to the New World.

Slaves, by definition, were property. Nothing more, nothing less. For slave masters and their customers, family relations meant very little. If a customer needed a house slave or a field worker, the mother or father of a family was taken with little notice paid to the suffering imposed on those who remained.

Variations of the racial hierarchy in Spanish America were to be found in the West Indies. At the top of the pyramid were the Europeans, followed by those whites born in the islands, the people of color, and then the slaves. Not all slaves lived the same; they filled many different roles and did work ranging from management positions in the plantations down to common laborers. As in the Spanish world, it was a brutal life, marked by violence and racism and complicated by the inequities of the racial hierarchy. At the end of the eighteenth century, beginning in Haiti, a powerful resentment building among the lower classes would erupt.

As in Spanish America and Brazil, the plantation system prevailed, concentrating on the production of a single item, whether sugar, tobacco, coffee, or cotton. The sugar industry in the islands continued to prosper during the eighteenth century, especially in the French islands of Martinique, Guadeloupe, and part of Santo Domingo. Even though sugar was the dominant crop at the beginning of the century there, toward the end of the century, coffee came to dominate. The same tendencies could be found on the other islands.

Perhaps reflecting its economic growth, the West Indies underwent a population boom during the century. The French part of Santo Domingo went from 130,000 in 1730 to over a half million by the time of the French Revolution—and of that number, 465,000 were slaves; in Guadeloupe, in the same time, the population increased from 35,000 to 106,000, of which 89,000 were slaves. The percentage of the French economy found in the Atlantic trade went from 13 percent in 1715 to 28 percent in 1785, and the Atlantic trade played a similar role in the other economies of western Europe.

Breaking Away: The Creation of the United States of America

How did British policies and actions in its American colonies lead to the American Revolution?

During the 1600s, English settlers had come to America for several reasons: to search for religious freedom, to seek political refuge, and to better their lot in life. Soon people from other European nations arrived, and the culture began to take on an identity of its own. The North American colonies got caught up in the world struggle that was the Seven Years' War; the view from London was that they should pay higher taxes to ensure their own defense. The problem was made more severe with the accession of King George III (1760–1820), who lacked the political finesse of his two Hanoverian predecessors.

A New Consciousness

Almost from the beginning, the American colonies had gone in a direction different than that of England. Most Puritan (Calvinist) settlers in New England opposed the early Stuart kings; during the **Restoration,** a host of rebels fled to America. Many Catholics, favored by the later Stuarts and persecuted at home after the **Glorious Revolution,** came to the colonies, particularly to Maryland. By 1775, some 40 percent of the colonial population was of non-English stock, mostly from Ireland and southern Germany. After 1750, a popular party in Massachusetts opposed British ways, particularly British attempts to restrict colonial manufacturing, dictate terms for colonial foreign trade, and influence the actions of colonial legislatures.

Experience in self-government conditioned colonial development. Except for an unsuccessful attempt

Restoration—The return to the English throne in 1660 of the Stuart dynasty. The Restoration lasted during the reigns of Charles II and James II.

Glorious Revolution—A political upheaval in England during 1688 in which forces supporting the Parliament drove the Stuart dynasty from power.

at colonial domination under James II, England had steadily relaxed controls. This trend was particularly typical of relations between the colonies and the home government under the corrupt and static Whig oligarchy, whose leaders became proponents of stability as they gained power. Preoccupied by more pressing political concerns at home, they allowed the colonists relative freedom to conduct their own affairs. In contrast, radical political opinion, driven deep underground in England after 1649, ran much nearer to the surface in America, where Locke's later emphasis on the social contract appealed to a people who had created their own governments in the wilderness and who were somewhat suspicious of a distant king. By 1763, only Maryland and New Hampshire had not attained practical autonomy, and even they were well on their way to doing so when the shooting began in 1775.

Colonial political thought was shaped as much by growth and mobility as by historical circumstances. Over 2 million Europeans seeking a better life arrived in the eighteenth century. They formed a vast lower class of indentured servants, tenants, and manual workers, sharply differentiated from wealthy New England merchants or southern planters. Many other immigrants, mainly Scotch-Irish, pushed toward the frontiers and settled on free or cheap western land. Its easy availability fostered the idea of property as an individual's birthright, so that Prime Minister George Grenville's restriction on westward migration after 1763 aroused general resentment against an assumed English effort to monopolize land for a privileged aristocracy. Land speculators condemned the policy as a violation of free enterprise and, at the same time, found a common interest with craftsmen, merchants, and planters, who felt themselves dominated and exploited by British mercantilism.

Pressure from England helped bring the variety of individual complaints into a united resistance. John Adams (1735–1826), looking back on the Revolution, was well aware of this maturing American nationalism. He wrote:

> *But what do we mean by the American Revolution? Do we mean the American war? The Revolution was effected before the war commenced ... in the minds and hearts of the people.... This ... was the real American Revolution.*[1]

	The North American Evolution
1756–1763	French and Indian War
1763	Treaty of Paris increases English dominance in North America
1775–1783	American Revolution
1776	Declaration of Independence
1787	Constitutional Convention
1803	Louisiana Purchase
1823	Monroe Doctrine

The Roots of Rebellion

The North American phase of the Seven Years' War saw important combat between the British and the French from the Great Lakes up to the Gulf of St. Lawrence and along the Ohio River valley. For the most part, the Indians caught between the European competitors aligned themselves with the French, whom they saw as traders to deal with and not settlers intent on taking their lands. Owing to their superior fleet, which defeated the French navy and cut off reinforcements, the British ultimately won in the New World. The Peace of Paris of 1763 that ended the Seven Years' War gave the British control of most of North America east of the Mississippi River.

Once victory was achieved, the costs of triumph had to be paid. The Grenville program brought all the major differences between Britain and the colonies into focus. With foreign enemies out of Canada and Florida, new land beckoned colonists who no longer felt the need for British protection. They naturally abhorred new taxes and trade controls required by rising imperial costs. British troops, under the circumstances, were regarded as oppressors rather than defenders or peacekeepers. To make matters worse, a general economic depression, reflecting British postwar financial difficulties in the late 1760s, hit most colonial economies hard, particularly that of New England.

The first colonial protests came with the Grenville program, when the 1764 Sugar Act—an act to enforce British dominance over the market on imported molasses—prompted arguments against "taxation without representation" in colonial newspapers and pamphlets. These reactions were mild, however, in comparison with those following the **Stamp Act** a year later. The Stamp Act required all legal documents and other printed matter to carry a special tax stamp. Colonial assemblies in Massachusetts and New York denounced the law as "tyranny," and a "Stamp Act Congress," convening in New York, petitioned the king to repeal the law. Mob actions occurred in a number of places, but they were less effective than boycotts of English goods, imposed by a thousand colonial mer-

Stamp Act—Revenue-raising measures passed by the English Parliament in 1765 to force the colonies in North America to pay their share of defense costs.

◄ Relations between England and its colonies in North America became embittered over the issue of British imposition of trade duties on American commerce after 1763. The merchants of Boston felt these restrictions the most keenly, and on March 5, 1770, a group of protestors was fired on by British troops. Five men died, including Crispus Attucks, a freedman of color. Ironically, the same day of the deaths of these men, who later became seen as martyrs of the revolution, the Parliament in London repealed most of the offensive duties.

chants. Soon hundreds of English tradesmen were petitioning Parliament, pleading that the taxes be rescinded. Their appeal was successful in 1766, although Parliament issued a declaration affirming its absolute right to legislate for the colonies.

Having repealed the Stamp Act, Parliament almost immediately enacted other revenue measures. Charles Townshend (1725–1767), the new chancellor of the exchequer, had Parliament levy duties on imported paint, paper, lead, wine, and tea. Other laws decreed that admiralty courts, which functioned without juries, should sit in specified ports and enforce all trade regulations. In response, some Boston merchants, mainly the habitual smugglers, generated lively protests. The big wholesalers, who saw renewed boycotts of British goods as a means for reducing their overstocked warehouses, joined them. Samuel Adams (1722–1803), the main radical leader, whipped up anti-British feeling on Boston streets. This culminated on March 5, 1770, when soldiers fired into an unruly mob, killing five people. Some lesser American merchants began to waver, but nonimportation agreements had cut British imports by 50 percent and induced Parliament to repeal most duties on the very day of the Boston Massacre.

For a while, the colonies seemed angry but pacified, until Lord North (1732–1792), the king's new chief minister, persuaded Parliament to grant a two-thirds cut in duties on East India Company tea delivered to American ports. Because the company could thus undersell smugglers and legitimate tea merchants, both of these groups again resorted to political radicalism. The tea was turned away from most American ports. In what became known as the Boston Tea Party on December 16, 1773, Sam Adams's "patriots," thinly disguised as Indians, stole onto a ship and dumped its load of tea into the harbor. Parliament retaliated with the "Intolerable Acts," which closed the port of Boston, revoked the Massachusetts Charter, and provided that political offenders be tried in England.

Contentions between the home government and the colonies deteriorated into armed conflict by 1775 and complete separation by the following year. This result was not planned, hoped for, or even foreseen by the colonists. The true rebels consisted largely of the merchants, smugglers, and large landowners who were most hurt by the new British policies, supported by doctrinaire leaders of aroused city dwellers and small farmers. Although not originally committed to independence, both groups dreamed of a future America as a center of power, prosperity, and freedom.

The resulting conflagration was also a civil war, with many colonists remaining loyal to the crown. More than 20 percent of the citizenry remained loyal to Britain, and no more than one-sixth of the male population ever took up arms. Indeed, Benjamin Franklin's son was a Loyalist leader and the last royal governor of New Jersey. Most colonists were probably apolitical, intent on their own affairs, but a vocal majority of the politically minded—whether New England merchants, Virginia planters, urban intellectuals, or simple farmers—formed an angry and determined opposition. Their outlook combined Locke's political ideas with a spirit of rough frontier independence; it was also nationalistic in its dawning awareness that many English ways were foreign to American needs and values.

The Revolutionary War

By September 1774, the Boston crisis had created a revolutionary climate. Representatives of 12 colonies, meeting in the First Continental Congress at Philadelphia, denounced British tyranny, proclaimed political representation to be a natural right, and made plans for armed resistance. In April of the next year, the explosive situation around Boston finally led to a conflict between British regulars and the Massachusetts militia at nearby Lexington and Concord in which eight Americans and 293 English soldiers were killed. Those "shots heard round the world" marked the beginning of the American Revolution.

The war begun at Lexington and Concord lasted 8 years. British troops, besieged in Boston, failed to break out in June 1775 at Bunker Hill. Shortly afterward, General George Washington (1732–1799) accepted command of American forces from the recently convened Second Continental Congress. Long after the British had abandoned Boston in March 1776, his outnumbered and ill-provisioned troops fought defensive battles for survival, an ordeal climaxed at Valley Forge, in Pennsylvania, in the desolate winter of 1777–1778, when the ragged American army almost disintegrated from cold, hunger, and desertion. It was a time, in Thomas Paine's words, "to try men's souls," but it was also a time for dreams of renewed liberties and new opportunities.

The turning point of the war came in October 1777. Having occupied New York and Philadelphia, the British tried to split the country with an army moving south from Canada. Its crushing defeat at Saratoga, in upper New York, effected a diplomatic revolution. France, which had been a cautious and unofficial supplier, now entered the war on the American side and soon persuaded its Spanish ally to do the same. The Dutch followed, in a desperate effort to save their American trade. With its sea power thus countered, the British pulled their two main armies back to defensive positions in New York and Virginia. The war reached its conclusion in the southern campaigns in 1781, when French and American troops, aided by the French fleet, forced the British commander, Lord Cornwallis (1738–1805), to surrender at Yorktown, Virginia. This defeat, along with many threats abroad, caused the British to recognize the Americans' independence in the Treaty of Paris (1783).

Creating a Nation: The Logic of Locke

While the war continued, American political leaders were forming a new nation. Thomas Paine's *Common Sense,* published early in 1776 as an emotional plea for liberty, inflamed popular passions and helped convince the American Congress to break with England. In June, a congressional committee drafted a formal statement of principles. The resulting Declaration of Independence, written by Thomas Jefferson, first announced the creation of the United States. In claiming for every individual "certain unalienable rights...to life, liberty, and the pursuit of happiness," it also used typical natural law theory in a direct appeal to radical opinion.

The Declaration of Independence

An angrier radicalism, born of army wages not paid and taxes incurred among poor civilians, marked the late war years. Economic depression and other hardships created suspicions of the high-born and wealthy leaders who were so prominent in national government.

Reflections on Revolutions

This localism was evident in the **Articles of Confederation,** a national constitution finally ratified by the states in 1781. It stipulated that taxation, control of trade, and issuance of money all be left to the sovereign states, each represented by one vote in Congress. Major decisions required the assent of nine states, and amendments required unanimous agreement of all 13. Although Congress could make war and peace, maintain armies, and conduct Indian affairs, it was financially dependent on the states for these functions. The system was designed to protect liberties against a distant central government dominated by an upper class.

The 1780s, under the Articles of Confederation, brought serious postwar problems. With so much power distributed among the states, the national government was severely hampered in negotiating commercial treaties with foreign states, maintaining adequate military forces, promoting internal economic development, and maintaining domestic order. While the states contended with one another, former soldiers and impoverished civilians demanded back pay, pensions, land, and cheap paper money to pay their debts. In Massachusetts, a former army officer named Daniel Shays (1747–1825) even led a brief rebellion. George Washington and other national leaders, convinced that the prevailing disunity and disorder threatened not only property but also the new nation's very survival, urged a reconsideration of the Articles. Their efforts led to a convening of delegates from 12 state legislatures who met in Philadelphia from May to September 1787.

The Constitution of the United States

Because few radicals attended the convention, its delegates were concerned primarily with protecting property and strengthening the union. The arguments of the framers of the Constitution were expressed in a series of newspaper articles that came to be known collectively as the ***Federalist Papers.*** In these essays, people such as Alexander Hamilton and James Madison debated the future power of the United States government, its presidency, the legislature, civil rights, and the powers to be left to the states.

Almost immediately, the framers gave up amending the Articles of Confederation and began work on a new constitution. By allowing each state equal representation in the Senate, the upper house of Congress, they compromised a conflict between large and small

Articles of Confederation—The first national constitution for the United States, ratified in 1781.

Federalist Papers—Articles by, among others, Alexander Hamilton and James Madison, supporting the writing of a new constitution to replace the Articles of Confederation.

▲ The effectiveness of the work done by the Constitutional Convention can be seen by the fact that the United States still follows its provisions, only slightly amended, more than two centuries later.

states. Another divisive issue was resolved by allowing slaveholding states to count 60 percent of their slaves in the population on which their allocation of seats in the lower house of Congress would be based. With these two questions settled, the convention's work progressed rapidly.

A fundamental principle of the completed Constitution was governmental separation of powers, first proposed by the French political philosopher Montesquieu. This was revealed in the carefully defined distinction between powers granted to the national and state governments and, even more specifically, in the division of functions among the branches of the central government. Congress was to make the laws, the president was to execute them, and the courts were to interpret them. The president could veto laws passed by Congress, but the latter, by a two-thirds vote, could override a presidential veto. The Supreme Court later expanded its original charge of interpreting laws to interpreting the Constitution itself, thus acquiring the right to declare any law "unconstitutional."

In recognizing the principle of popular sovereignty, the Constitution was similar to the Articles of Confederation; it differed in its centralization of government and in its securities against disorder. Proclaiming itself the supreme law of the land, the Constitution specifically prohibited the states from coining money, levying customs duties, and conducting foreign diplomacy. The president, as chief executive, commanded the national military forces, an arrangement that could protect against popular unrest and disorder. Most of the delegates to Philadelphia favored property qualifications for voting, an idea that they abandoned only because it was politically impractical. They indicated their distrust of democracy, however, by avoiding the direct popular election of senators and presidents: Senators would be chosen by the legislature of their particular states, and the president would be chosen by a separate electoral college.

The process of ratifying the Constitution precipitated a great political debate. Congress, dominated by so-called Federalist proponents, ignored the amending provisions of the Articles and appealed directly to the states. Anti-Federalists, who opposed ratification, were alarmed but were generally overwhelmed by arguments from the wealthier, more articulate, and better-educated Federalists, who supported the Constitution. By promising written guarantees of individual liberties—the later Bill of Rights, the first ten amendments

▲ Abigail Adams personified the best qualities of the new American woman at the end of the eighteenth century. She spoke plainly, openly, and affectionately as she discussed the shape of the new nation with her husband and future president, John.

to the new Constitution—the Federalists ultimately won the required nine states, and the Constitution was formally adopted on July 2, 1788. Three years later, the first ten amendments were added, guaranteeing freedom of religion, speech, and the press and protecting the people against arbitrary government. Thus the radicals left a lasting legacy, despite the Federalist triumph.

The Constitution remains the basis of legitimacy for the continuity of the United States of America. Indeed, when a person begins work for the government of the United States—whether president or private, senator or Schedule C employee, temporary hire or beginning secretary, he or she will make an oath to "defend the Constitution of the United States."

From Theory to Reality

After winning their greatest victory, the Federalists dominated American politics for more than a decade. In 1789, George Washington was elected to the first of his two 4-year terms as president under the terms of the Constitution. His administration imposed a high tariff, chartered a national bank, paid public debts at face value, negotiated a commercial treaty with England, and, after 1794, opposed the French Revolution. Ironically, some French revolutionaries, such as the Marquis de Lafayette (1757–1834), who had helped win American independence, were bitterly denounced by American leaders a decade later.

When trade relations with the British began to improve in the 1790s, the French waged an undeclared war on American shipping, taking over 800 ships in the last 3 years of the decade. This, in addition to the undiplomatic activities of the French embassy, deeply affected the emerging party politics of the young country. Meanwhile, southern slaveholders were deeply suspicious of the French policies in their revolutionary parliaments toward slavery in their colonies in the Caribbean.

The United States benefited from one aspect of Napoleon's activities. In the seventeenth century, French explorers had laid claim to the region between the Mississippi River and the Rocky Mountains, naming it Louisiana in honor of their king. They ceded the region to the Spanish in 1763 and then took it back at the beginning of the nineteenth century. The French had never surveyed the full extent of the area and had no hope of exploiting it in the near future. As a way to block the British and the Spaniards and to make sure the port of New Orleans would remain in at least neutral hands, Napoleon sold Louisiana for $15 million to the United States in 1803. Thomas Jefferson had to take some distinctly unconstitutional steps to buy the land, but, as a result, the Louisiana Purchase doubled the land area of the new country and set a precedent for land acquisition and expansion.

Unfulfilled Dreams

The war for American rights and liberties left much unfinished business. For decades after 1783, the right to vote was restricted to propertied white male citizens. Flagrantly omitted were the common people, women, African Americans, and Native Americans, all of whom were denied full civil equality, freedom, and human justice, despite their important contributions to the American cause. The suffering of African Americans and Native Americans was particularly severe

Many blacks who had been promised their freedom during the revolutionary wars continued to be enslaved by their owners. Even laws against slavery were not always enforced. In the northern states, emancipation was often legally delayed for decades, so that in 1810, there were still more than 35,000 slaves in total in New York, New Jersey, and Pennsylvania. The conservative reaction of the 1790s, stimulated by debates in the Con-

Document

Letter from Abigail Adams

Abigail Adams, with her husband John, served as the embodiment of the American republican virtues of plain speaking, lack of ostentation, and sometimes brutal honesty. Her letter to her husband speaks to the openness and strength of their relationship. Her spelling represents the usage of the time.

Mar. 1776

I wish you would ever write me a Letter half as long as I write you; and tell me if you may where your Fleet are gone? What sort of Defence Virginia can make against our common Enemy? Whether it is so situated as to make an able Defence? Are not the Gentery Lords and the common people vassals, are they not like the uncivilized Natives Brittain represents us to be? I hope their Riffel Men who have shewen themselves very savage and even Blood thirsty; are not a specimen of the Generality of the people.

I am willing to allow the Colony great merrit for having produced a Washington but they have been shamefully duped by a Dunmore.

I have sometimes been ready to think that the passion for Liberty cannot be Eaquelly Strong in the Breasts of those who have been accustomed to deprive their fellow Creatures of theirs. Of this I am certain that it is not founded upon that generous and christian principal of doing to others as we would that others should do unto us....

I long to hear that you have declared an independancy—and by the way in the new Code of Laws which I suppose it will be necessary for you to make I desire you would Remember the Ladies, and be more generous and favourable to them than your ancestors. Do not put such unlimited power into the hands of the Husbands. Remember all Men would be tyrants if they could. If perticuliar care and attention is not paid to the Laidies we are determined to foment a Rebelion, and will not hold ourselves bound by any Laws in which we have no voice, or Representation.

That your Sex are Naturally Tyrannical is a Truth so thoroughly established as to admit of no dispute, but such of you as wish to be happy willingly give up the harsh title of Master for the more tender and endearing one of Friend. Why then, not put it out of the power of the vicious and the Lawless to use us with cruelty and indignity with impunity. Men of Sense in all Ages abhor those customs which treat us only as the vassals of your Sex. Regard us then as Beings placed by providence under your protection and in immitation of the Supreem Being make use of that power only for our happiness.

Questions to Consider

1. Why does Abigail Adams fear that the coming political changes will not benefit women?
2. What is Adams's rationale for her critique of the way men sometimes go about doing business?
3. Would Abigail Adams think her descendants living today have fulfilled her hopes for a "proper" place for women in society?

From Abigail Smith Adams, *The Book of Abigail and John: Selected Letters of the Adams Family, 1762–1784,* eds. L. H. Butterfield et al. (Cambridge, Mass.: Harvard University Press, 1975).

stitutional Convention, and the invention of the cotton gin, which gave a new impetus to cotton planting, confirmed the South's emotional commitments to slavery. American slaves after the 1790s were further from the rights of "all men" than they had been before the Revolution. This injustice was the ultimate cause for a subsequent bloody and tragic civil war.

Another abandonment of human rights affected Native Americans. Between 1700 and 1763, thousands of white settlers poured into Indian lands west of the Appalachian mountains. The result was bloody warfare, marked by atrocities on both sides. Looking to the British for protection, most of the tribes fought against Americans during the Revolution, only to have their territories put under control of their enemies in the peace of 1783. Protracted negotiations with the American government led to more surrenders and numerous treaties, all of which were broken as the flood of white land speculators and settlers moved westward. In desperation, the Indians attempted unification and a hopeless resistance. Subsequently, their Ohio federation was crushed in 1794 at the battle of Fallen Timbers; about the same time, the Cherokee union in the South collapsed. During the preceding 18 years, the Cherokees alone had lost 40,000 square miles of territory. In the same period, all Indian populations east of the Mississippi fell by more than 45 percent. By 1800, enforced living on land set aside for Indians was already promoting the disintegration of Native American cultures.

Haiti: The First Successful Slave Revolution

Why were the Haitians able to throw off French rule?

The same currents of discontent and violent frustrations seen in France in the summer of 1789 (see Chapter 18) were present in the West Indies at the same time. The middle-class intellectuals and political elites were as influenced by the Enlightenment writings as their French colleagues. And they were just as distant from the suffering of the people as were the delegates gathered at Versailles for the meeting of the Estates General. The shock waves generated by the outbreak of the French Revolution were especially deeply felt in Santo Domingo.

The French Revolution's Impact on Santo Domingo

Just as there was discontent in the French countryside over the abuses of the old regime, so too was there violent resentment of the slaves and mulattoes who sought justice from the Creoles or those who had come directly from France to control the colonial administration and the plantations in the West Indies. The free mulattoes in Haiti, the western part of the island of Santo Domingo, deeply resented the Creoles and the French, who treated them as slaves without rights. Their drive for respect and equality was supported by the slave population, who would later serve as their soldiers.

News from France in the summer of 1789 sparked violent uprisings on Santo Domingo and Martinique, especially among those who read or heard about *The Declaration of the Rights of Man and Citizen*. Those who sought satisfaction from the **National Constituent Assembly** shared increased frustrations in the next 2 years as it became evident that the Assembly's Enlightenment ideology would be set aside on the question of maintaining property, especially on the questions of slaves as property, the major issue of policy toward the French West Indies.

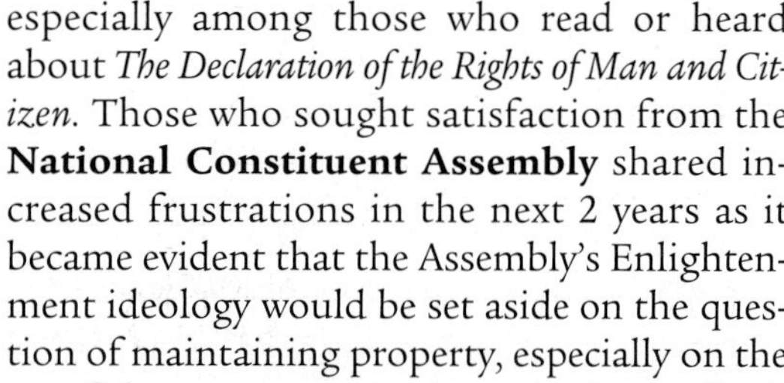

Slave Revolt in Saint Domingue, 1791

Planters in the Assembly differed on trade policies and colonial autonomy but concurred in their defense of slavery and their opposition to civil rights for free mulattoes. Meanwhile, mulattoes in France spread their pamphlets and petitioned the Assembly, supported by the *Amis des Noirs* (ah-MEE day nwah) ("Friends of the Blacks"), whose supporters also angrily attacked slavery in the Assembly hall. The chamber was left divided and nearly impotent. First, it gave the island governments complete control over their blacks and mulattoes; then, yielding to the radicals, it granted political rights to mulattoes born of free parents. Finally, it bowed to the planters and repealed this last measure in September 1791.

Toussaint Louverture and Haitian Independence

In response, Toussaint Louverture (TOO-san loo-ver-TURE; 1744–1803) and Jean-Jacques Dessalines (zhan-ZHAK DES-sal-een; 1758–1806) began a revolutionary war that would last 12 years. There had been slave uprisings during the eighteenth century, just as there had been peasant outbreaks in Europe from the Atlantic coast to the Urals. Without a coherent program and united leadership, the slaves—like the peasants—were defeated. The situation changed by the end of the century. The American Revolution also had a significant effect on the islands. The rich saw the possibility of liberation from the controls of the empire, and the poor saw the possibilities of freedom.

These visions, and the mixed messages of the French Revolution, provided the oppressed 90 percent with the unifying ideology they had lacked. In calling for support, Toussaint Louverture said, "Brothers and friends, I am Toussaint Louverture, perhaps you've heard of me. I seek vengeance. I want liberty and equality to reign in Santo Domingo. I will work to make them exist. Unite with us."[2] Combining a genius for military maneuver with a subtle understanding of the international forces at work, Louverture assembled a disciplined and victorious army.

Back in Paris, the French revolutionary assemblies continued to struggle over the policy to be adopted toward the colonies. Not only were there conflicting voices over the issue, the uprising on Santo Domingo led to a tripling of the price of sugar in Paris at the end of the summer of 1791. The authorities in the islands and in Paris began to deal in small steps with the "problem." The grant of citizenship to free blacks and mulattoes in the West Indies had drawn some mulattoes to the government side, but it was insufficient and led to insurrection uniting royalists on the island and resentful escaped slaves. This uprising complicated an already complex situation, and the Spanish and British took advantage to intervene in the French-controlled part of Santo Domingo to link up with the disaffected coalition.

Finally in the late spring of 1793, the harried governor of Santo Domingo issued a decree freeing all former slaves and calling on them to join against the foreign enemies. In February 1794, the Convention in Paris received a delegation from Santo Domingo and heard a plea for liberty from a 101-year-old former slave woman. The chamber responded by freeing all slaves in French territories and giving them full citizenship rights.

Toussaint Louverture, newly promoted by Paris to the rank of general, united all of the slave and mulatto forces into a single front and defeated the British forces. In 1797, Louverture was made commander-in-chief of the island by the French government. After noting the reactionary drift of French politics and understanding that he and his followers faced a unique opportunity, Louverture, later "governor-for-life," began moving his country from the status of colony toward independence from France.

In 1802, Napoleon ordered slavery to be reimposed in the colonies and sent a large force to Haiti to put

National Constituent Assembly—At the meeting of the Estates General in the summer of 1789, the Third Estate, joined by elements of the other two estates, declared itself to be the National Constituent Assembly, a group legally elected to write a constitution for France.

down Louverture's government and force the African population back into servitude. Given the overwhelming power of the French forces, Louverture was forced to resort to guerrilla tactics. Stymied by the resistance, the French forces called for a truce and negotiations. Louverture went in good faith to the meeting, fell into a trap, and was captured. Even though he died the next year in a prison in eastern France, his forces remained united under Dessalines. After a series of bloody battles, the Haitian army forced the French to withdraw from the island. In November 1803, Dessalines and his colleagues declared the establishment of the nation of Haiti and they proclaimed it an independent country on the first day of 1804.

The declaration of Haitian independence marked the only success of a slave revolution in history and guaranteed continued liberty to more than 500,000 people of color. Internal discord—Dessalines, the first African to head a republic, would be assassinated 2 years later—and external pressures plagued the island until the middle of the century, when it claimed its status as the Republic of Haiti.

▲ By overthrowing the Spanish king in 1808, Napoleon set in motion 20 years of independence movements in Central and South America.

The Latin American Revolutions

How did Napoleon's wars in Europe influence events across the ocean in Latin America?

Between 1789 and 1799, the French Revolution caused great excitement in Latin America. When calm returned after Napoleon imposed his power, planters, merchants, poor whites, mulattoes, and slaves evaluated the Revolution and its aftermath according to their diverse interests. Napoleon's expulsion of the Spanish and Portugal monarchs in 1808 sparked a series of complex and bloody independence movements that culminated in 1825 with most of Mexico, Central America, and South America gaining political liberty.

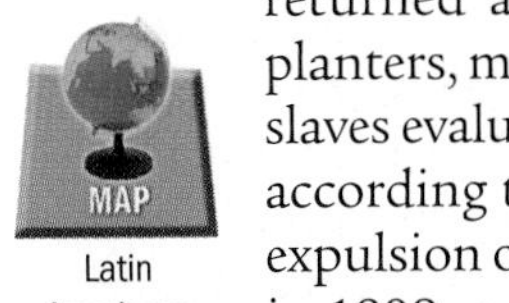

Latin Americans Obtain Independence

Revolutions in Mexico and Central and South America

Napoleon's eviction of the Spanish and Portuguese monarchs in 1808 unleashed the festering forces of discontent and ambition in Spanish and Portuguese America that had built up in the previous two centuries. Unlike the American Revolution, in which there was an argument for liberty made on the basis of a violated social contract, there was no concept of Spanish or Portuguese citizenship violated. Rather, each level of society read the signs coming from Europe in a different way. The Creoles initially dominated the independence movements, intent on gaining and strengthening their position in the liberated countries while replacing the departed Spanish and Portuguese leaders. It soon became apparent in most of the revolutions that they had little concern for the rest of society, and the mixed races, the Indians, and African slaves began to pursue their own destiny. There was not a single, unified movement toward independence in Mexico, Central America, and South America. There were several, and all were different. The only shared factor is that the fall of the three-centuries-old Spanish and Portuguese rule led to an uncertain future under American and European dominance.

Battlefields to Courtrooms: Conflict and Agency in the Americas

Just as men dominated society in Portuguese and Spain, so too did they play the major roles in the revolutions and the new governments that followed. Women were largely ignored in the major decisions during the revolutions and were rarely mentioned in the new constitutions after 1825. At the same time, they played enormous supporting roles in the revolutionary age, whether in replacing the work of men gone off to combat, providing food, nursing, raising money, or serving as spies. Some actually fought in the Túpac Amaru rebellion of 1780–1781 and in Venezuela and Mexico after 1810. When the Spanish armies defeated

Edward Thornton Tayloe's Journal

revolutionary forces in battles, they also punished the women and families involved, executing some of them alongside their husbands.

Fracture Zones and Frustrations

There were three distinct struggles for independence in Latin America: Mexico between the peasant uprising in 1810 and the conservative coup d'état in 1821; Simón Bolívar's movement to liberate the northern part of South America and part of Central America; and José de San Martín's campaign based in the southern part of South America. Each of these movements felt the impact of three key events that took place in Europe (see Chapter 18): Napoleon's eviction of Ferdinand VII in 1808; Ferdinand's return to the throne in 1814; and the Congress System's crushing of the 1820 Spanish liberal revolution.

If the Creoles—perhaps one-fifth of the population (15 percent in Peru, 20 percent in Mexico)—borrowed ideas and examples from abroad to justify their emergence into a dominant position, the other four-fifths of the people played an equally important role. In varying ways, depending on the location, the mixed races, the Indians, and slaves had begun their revolution for justice and equality—against the Creoles—in the eighteenth century. The periodic uprisings of these three groups and the success of the Haitians had frightened the Creoles, and the end of Spanish and Portuguese control gave them, also, the chance to pursue their goals. The independence movement from 1808 to 1825 in much of Latin America was as much a civil war as it was a classic European revolution.

The frustrations of the racial hierarchy fueled a massive resentment. The Creoles feared the *peninsulares,* who were becoming more and more numerous during the eighteenth century. They especially distrusted the Spanish Bourbon reforms of enlightened despotism that spoke of equality of all under a law code, a unitary state, and the recentralization of the Spanish Empire's economy. During the seventeenth and early eighteenth centuries, the Spanish government's mercantile control had weakened, allowing the Creoles to profit enormously—they could carry on their business with little regard for Spain. The reforms of the Spanish king Charles III (1759–1788) threatened the local businessmen and manufacturers by favoring Spanish made goods over those made in the New World and encouraging the production of raw materials for the "mother country."

The Creoles were also uncomfortably trapped between the presumptions of superiority of the *peninsulares* and the miserable masses. But they were far from wanting a revolution—aside from the few who had entered into commercial contact with the British. They were somewhat comfortable in the corrupt framework of the empires—they had no experience in self-government and had no desire to construct a new, multiracial society. The Creoles simply wanted what they saw as their just share of the wealth. Above all, they wanted nothing that would benefit those beneath them in the social hierarchy.

Once Napoleon made his move in 1808, there was a power vacuum that was not filled for the next 2 years. However, by 1810, in each of the regions of Mexico, Central America, and South America, the Creoles accepted the end of Spanish control and imposed their rule on the towns in which they lived. Peru remained the most faithful to the Spanish monarchy, and even though the Creoles were active in Lima, they had little impact in the countryside, where the Indians constituted a power center of their own. The Spanish did not go easily, fiercely resisting the forces of independence until 1826.

Mexico

The Mexican independence movement began earlier than any of those in Central and South America. The Mexican Creole class was smaller than that in the rest of Spanish America and far more conservative. Between 1808 and 1810, anti-Bonapartist sentiment shifted to a general rejection of the European monarchy in Creole circles throughout the viceroyalty of New Spain. But the elites were slow to mobilize their forces.

An enlightened provincial Creole priest, Miguel Hidalgo (ee-DAL-goh; 1753–1811), actually began the revolution on September 16, 1810, when he issued a call for universal freedom (the date is celebrated in Mexico today as the *Dia del Grito,* the Day of the Call). Hidalgo led his ragged army of Indians, mestizos, and idealists first to Guanajuato (gwa-ne-WAT-oh) where they carried out a great massacre, and then to the gates of Mexico City, where they stopped. Although Hidalgo was condemned by the colonial bishops and executed for treason six months after his uprising began, his cause was taken up by others, including José María Morelos (1765–1815), a radical mestizo parish priest who became an effective guerrilla leader. Unfortu-

	Independence in Latin America
1789–1803	Haitian Revolution
1804	Declaration of Haitian independence
1806–1825	Latin American Wars of Independence
1821	Spanish recognition of Mexican independence
1826	Last Spanish forces leave South America

◄ Augustin de Iturbide brought a conservative end to the Mexican revolution. He served as emperor of Mexico for ten months in 1822–1823.

nately, the popular movement fell apart because of a lack of organization and shared goals.

The Creoles in Mexico City felt threatened by the threats of Hidalgo and Morelos, and by the liberal sentiments emanating from Spain in the liberal revolution of 1820. Led by Augustin de Iturbide (au-goos-TEEN day E-toor-bee-they; 1783–1824), the conservative classes moved to take control of their own fate. In August 1821, the last Spanish viceroy recognized the independence of Mexico, whose ruling classes, unfortunately, promptly began to struggle over the constitution and the form of the new government. Iturbide, a Creole landowner and officer who had fought as a Spanish loyalist until 1816, became emperor of Mexico for a turbulent ten-month reign in 1822–1823.

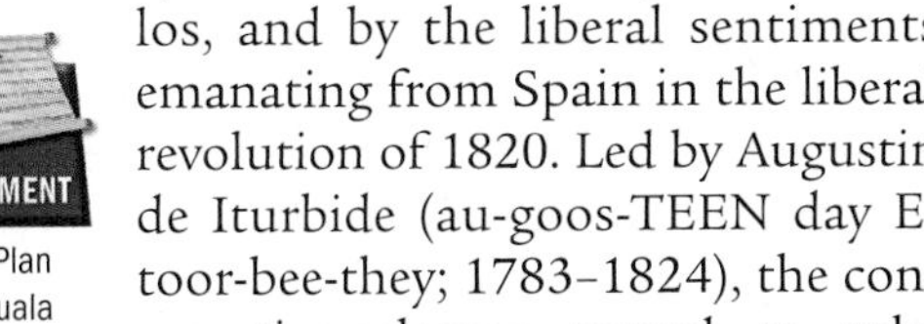

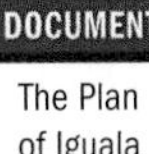

DOCUMENT

The Plan of Iguala

Simón Bolívar and the Northern Revolt

The charismatic leader who stepped into the void in the northern part of South American and Central America was Simón Bolívar (1783–1830). Born in Caracas of a rich Creole family, he was educated in Europe, where he joined the Masons. After completing his rationalist education in Paris during the last years of the **Directory,** Bolívar returned to his native Venezuela to exploit colonial resistance to the Napoleonic takeover of Spain in 1808.

IMAGE

The Great Liberator, Simón Bolívar

Bolívar, called "The Liberator," stepped into this situation by issuing a series of inflammatory and visionary messages calling for the liberation of Venezuela and Gran Colombia (modern-day Colombia, Panama, Ecuador, and Venezuela). From this base, he hoped to expand the liberation movement to include all of Spanish South America. Instead, he found himself entrapped in a multidimensional civil war involving opportunistic Creoles, fervent royalists, and frustrated and angry people of color.

Directory—The political institution that governed France from 1795 to 1799.

▼ Simón Bolívar and his army battle the Spanish at Araure in Venezuela. Although the Spanish were better trained and equipped, Bolívar led his soldiers with such personal valor that he managed to liberate four countries.

He declared an all-out war against the Spaniards in 1813, but Spanish loyalist forces frequently defeated him. He was forced to flee to Jamaica in 1815 to try to get English assistance, which was not immediately forthcoming. Then, he went to the new republic of Haiti to try to get arms and money in return for declaring an end to slavery. Despite the setbacks, he kept fighting—winning major victories in 1817—and made use of skills as an orator and as a tactician. He eventually forced the remnants of the Spanish military and administrative personnel to return to Spain.

He proposed a constitution for the newly independent regions that favored the elites of the new nations. This document was much like the one written by the French Directory, and he saw himself as something of a Caesarlike figure. He dreamed of an independent continent, with the north made up of the nation-states of Venezuela, Colombia, Ecuador, Peru, and Bolivia, but he ran afoul of liberal critics and local loyalties, and the various regions went their own ways. He went into exile in 1827 and eventually died, discouraged, in 1830.

José de San Martín and Southern Independence

Argentina, Uruguay, and Chile were liberated by the stoic, Spanish-educated officer José de San Martín (1778–1850), a man as austere and reserved as Bolívar was flashy and outgoing. San Martín, the son of Spanish aristocrats (in present-day Argentina), went to Spain to study when he was 7 years old. He served for 22 years in the Spanish army, before deciding to fight for the independence of Argentina in 1812. San Martín found a difficult political situation in the south, and determined that the key to the final defeat of Spain was to strike at the heart of their strength in Peru, the Spanish stronghold in the New World. The first step toward this goal was to prepare the way to Argentinean independence in 1816. Then, aided by his Chilean friend Bernardo O'Higgins, he liberated Chile in 1817, crossing the Andes under difficult conditions. Wherever his armies went, he liberated slaves.

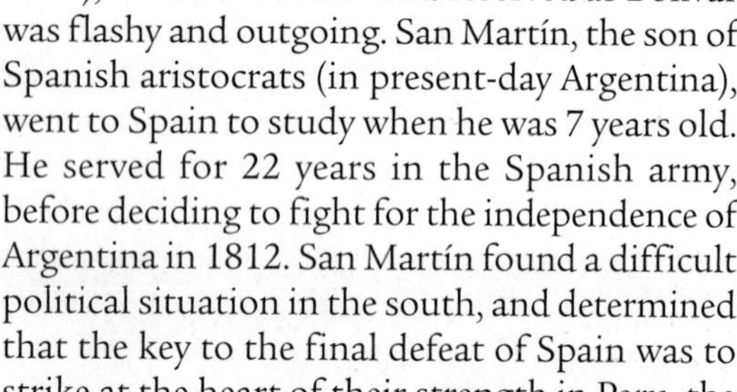

Symbolism and Contested Identities in Argentina

After 2 years of planning, San Martín launched an attack on Peru by shipping troops around Tierra del Fuego to the Pacific coast. His army took Lima, but the Spanish armies were still in the mountains. In an attempt to gain help in evicting the Spaniards, he met with Bolívar at Guayaquil (gway-ya-KEEL). The two could never forge an alliance, partly because of personality differences and partly because of San Martín's preference for a constitutional monarchy like that of Britain or of France under the Constitution of 1791. They also disagreed on military tactics. After the meeting, San Martín abandoned the struggle and went into exile. Bolívar continued the fight and bestowed a constitution on Peru in 1825, although the last Spanish forces didn't leave until 1826. San Martín spent the rest of his life in France, frustrated by his failure to achieve constitutional monarchies in the nations he liberated. Despite the disappointment, he could take some satisfaction in being viewed as the liberator of the south of the continent.

The Spanish colonies freed by San Martín may have rejected his desires for a constitutional monarchy, but the Portuguese in Brazil embraced that governmental form. King John VI of Portugal had fled his country in 1807, and for the next 14 years, he ruled the Portuguese Empire from Rio de Janeiro. Returning to Lisbon after the Portuguese revolution of 1821, the king left his son Dom Pedro as regent of Brazil. Impatient with the reactionary behavior of the Lisbon government, Pedro declared himself emperor of an independent Brazil in 1822. After a stormy interlude in which there was a struggle over the form of government and independence movements of regions wanting to break away from Brazil, Pedro stepped down in 1831 and handed the country to his son Pedro II under a regency, until he ruled in his own right as a constitutional monarch in 1840.

The Social and Economic Consequences of the Latin American Revolutions

The social and economic consequences of the Latin American revolutions were far different from those in North America and Europe. The area was much poorer and more divided. The new nations of Latin America remained the economic colonies of Europe, even if they were free. The wars of independence, the establishment of new states, and the chaotic aftermath of the time dealt a heavy blow to economic development. The conditions of the indigenous Indian population declined as the new liberal regimes confiscated the large landholdings of the religious orders, which had served to insulate the surviving Indians from direct confrontations with the Europeans' economic and technological dominance. As in every country since the Reformation in which church property was bought up by the monied classes, the local population was reorganized into a new labor force more profitable to the new owners. In Latin America, the owners simply reorganized the Indian communities into a labor force and drove the unproductive and the mestizos off the land. This movement in some countries has continued in

Document

Simón Bolívar, Proclamation to the People of Venezuela

Simón Bolívar is considered to be one of the most charismatic and ambitious men in the history of the Americas. His "Proclamation to the People of Venezuela," made on June 15, 1813, is one of his most powerful statements. It is a combination of an exhortation and an ultimatum.

SIMÓN BOLÍVAR, Liberator of Venezuela, Brigadier of the Union, General in Chief of the Northern Army

To his fellow-countrymen:

Venezuelans: An army of our brothers, sent by the Sovereign Congress of New Granada, has come to liberate you. Having expelled the oppressors from the provinces of Mérida and Trujillo, it is now among you.

We are sent to destroy the Spaniards, to protect the Americans, and to reestablish the republican governments that once formed the Confederation of Venezuela. The states defended by our arms are again governed by their former constitutions and tribunals, in full enjoyment of their liberty and independence, for our mission is designed only to break the chains of servitude which still shackle some of our towns, and not to impose laws or exercise acts of dominion to which the rules of war might entitle us.

Moved by your misfortunes, we have been unable to observe with indifference the afflictions you were forced to experience by the barbarous Spaniards, who have ravished you, plundered you, and brought you death and destruction. They have violated the sacred rights of nations. They have broken the most solemn agreements and treaties. In fact, they have committed every manner of crime, reducing the Republic of Venezuela to the most frightful desolation. Justice therefore demands vengeance, and necessity compels us to exact it. Let the monsters who infest Colombian soil, who have drenched it in blood, be cast out forever; may their punishment be equal to the enormity of their perfidy, so that we may eradicate the stain of our ignominy and demonstrate to the nations of the world that the sons of America cannot be offended with impunity.

Despite our just resentment toward the iniquitous Spaniards, our magnanimous heart still commands us to open to them for the last time a path to reconciliation and friendship; they are invited to live peacefully among us, if they will abjure their crimes, honestly change their ways, and cooperate with us in destroying the intruding Spanish government and the reestablishment of the Republic of Venezuela.

Any Spaniard who does not, by every active and effective means, work against tyranny in behalf of this just cause, will be considered and enemy and punished; as a traitor to the nation, he will inevitably by shot by a firing squad. On the other hand, a general and absolute amnesty is granted to those who come over to our army with or without their arms, as well as to those who render aid to the good citizens who are endeavoring to throw off the yoke of tyranny. Army officers and civil magistrates who proclaim the government of Venezuela and join us shall retain their posts and positions; in a word, those Spaniards who render outstanding service to the State shall be regarded and treated as Americans.

And you Americans who, by error or treachery, have been lured from the paths of justice, are informed that your brothers, deeply regretting the error of your ways, have pardoned you as we are profoundly convinced that you cannot be truly to blame, for only the blindness and ignorance in which you have been kept up to now by those responsible for your crimes could have induced you to commit them. Fear not the sword that comes to avenge you and to sever the ignoble ties with which your executioners have bound you to their own fate. You are hereby assured, with absolute impunity, of your honor, lives, and property. The single title, "Americans," shall be your safeguard and guarantee. Our arms have come to protect you, and they shall never be raised against a single one of you, our brothers.

This amnesty is extended even to the very traitors who most recently have committed felonious acts, and it shall be so religiously applied that no reason, cause, or pretext will be sufficient to oblige us to violate our offer, however extraordinary and extreme the occasion you may give to provoke our wrath.

Spaniards and Canary Islanders, you will die, though you be neutral, unless you actively espouse the cause of America's liberation. Americans, you will live, even if you have trespassed.

General Headquarters, Trujillo, June 15, 1813. The 3d [year].

SIMÓN BOLÍVAR

Questions to Consider

1. What is Bolívar's attitude toward Spain and Spaniards?
2. How does Bolívar seek to use an "amnesty" to his own advantage?
3. What form of government does Bolívar want for the region?

From Vicente Lecuna, comp., *Selected Writings of Bolívar,* trans. Lewis Bertrand (New York, The Colonial Press, 1951), pp. 31–32.

one form or another to the present day. The one great advantage gained in the independence movements was the end of slavery.

The Latin American church, led largely by *peninsulares* but staffed by the Creoles, was shattered by the national revolutions. When reconstituted with greatly reduced property and clerical personnel, the church desperately sought to win the protection of the more conservative elements in the Creole elite by opposing liberalism in any form. Since the church had been the exclusive instrument of education and social welfare before liberation, and since the ruling classes showed little interest in providing for the continuation of schools, orphanages, and relief for the lower classes, the misery of the Latin American poor grew more acute throughout the nineteenth century.

The legal and social standing of women did not benefit from political independence, controlled as it was by the often reactionary Creole class. Individual Creole women, such as Bolívar's astute mistress, Manuela Sanches, made major contributions to the revolution, but the adoption of the **Napoleonic Code** in the 1820s had the same negative impact on women's legal status in South America as it did in Europe at the same time.

It can be argued that in the wake of Napoleon's deposing the Spanish Bourbons, Latin America suffered a decline in political stability and internal economic health. The peasants and urban laborers of Indian and mixed-blood descent, the culture-shaping church, and women of all classes paid a heavy price for liberation from the Spanish and Portuguese overlords. The sole group to gain was the secular, male Creole leadership. Nevertheless, what Napoleon had destroyed was gone, and no serious attempt was made to restore the old colonial regime.

In the **Monroe Doctrine,** proclaimed in 1823, the United States let Europe know that the Western Hemisphere—including Latin America—was no longer open to colonization. For the Latin Americans, the British navy was more important for blocking the old empires from returning than was the declaration of the still young and militarily weak United States. Independence yielded the sad political results of military dictatorships that defended only the interests of the Creole class, a tendency that continued in some Latin American countries to the end of the twentieth century. Political weakness made the region the pawn of the Europeans and the North Americans.

The Americas: 1700-1900

Napoleonic Code—The comprehensive French civil law code compiled in 1804.

Monroe Doctrine—U.S. declaration in 1823 that the Western Hemisphere was no longer open to European colonization and that incursions from the Old Continent would not be welcome.

Conclusion

In the opening phases of the Capitalist Revolution in the sixteenth and early seventeenth centuries, European markets were swamped with a bewildering array of hitherto rare or unknown goods from the Americas. Potatoes, peanuts, maize (Indian corn), and tomatoes were among the new foods consumed by all levels of European society. Sugar became a common substitute for honey, and the use of cocoa, the Aztec sacred beverage, spread throughout Europe. Coffee would also soon change European social habits. Similarly, North American furs and cottons from Mexico revolutionized clothing fashions. Furnishings of rare woods from Brazil appeared more frequently in the homes of the wealthy. The use of American tobacco became almost a mania among all classes, further contributing to the booming market in Europe for goods from the Americas.

The peoples of the New World paid a heavy price for this change in European tastes and habits. Those who survived the devastating impacts of European diseases and plantation labor became caught up in a social and cultural revolution that continues to the present day. In the Iberian colonies and the West Indies, not enough of the indigenous population survived, and because of the demands of the increasing commerce, there was a labor shortage. The demand for African slaves constantly grew. In North America, despite the large numbers of European immigrants, there was a similar shortage of workers, and thousands of Africans were brought against their will to work in the middle and southern sections of the English colonies.

By the end of the eighteenth century, these currents of economic exploitation and racial injustice came to be wrapped in the arguments of the Enlightenment, which were used by different social classes to defend or advance their interests in different ways. The shock waves of European events opened the doors to revolutionary change in the Americas. In the wake of the aftereffects of the French and English wars, the English colonists of North America carried out a war that led to the creation of the United States of America. The diverse nature of the rebels found common expression in the concept of a violated social contract to justify their rebellion. To the south, the spin-offs of the French Revolution and Napoleon triggered the independence movements in Haiti and in Mexico, Central America, and South America. These movements to liberation were far more disunited and led some of the independence drives to resemble civil wars from time to time. By 1825, most of the Western Hemisphere had attained political freedom, if not stability and economic independence.

Suggestions for Web Browsing

You can obtain more information about topics included in this chapter at the websites listed below. See also the companion website that accompanies this text, http://www.ablongman.com/brummett, which contains an online study guide and additional resources.

Military History: American Revolution (1775–1783)
http://militaryhistory.about.com/od/revolutionarywa1/
This site lists links to the biographies of Washington and Paine, battles, museums, reenactments, literature, and other aspects of the era.

Women in the American Revolution
http://info-center.ccit.arizona.edu/~ws/ws200/fall97/grp11/part7.htm
This site includes a bibliography that provides insight into the role of women during the American Revolution.

Haitian History
http://www.webster.edu/~corbetre/haiti/history/history.htm
Images and background for the Haitian independence struggle are available on this site.

Simón Bolívar
http://www.geocities.com/Athens/Acropolis/7609/eng/toc.html
This site includes a collection of studies and primary sources from the life of "The Liberator."

Mexican Independence
http://www.mexonline.com/grito.htm
This site provides access to documents and studies of Mexican history.

Literature and Film

Natty Bumpo, the hero of James Fenimore Cooper's *Leatherstocking Tales*—which include *The Pioneers, The Last of the Mohicans* (1826), *The Prairie* (1827), *The Pathfinder* (1840), and *The Deerslayer* (1841)—embodies the conflict between preserving nature unspoiled and developing the land in the name of progress.

Recent films on the revolutionary events in North America are Rolland Emmerich's *The Patriot* (2000; Columbia/Tristar) and Michael Mann's *The Last of the Mohicans* (1992; Fox). PBS offers a rich range of videotapes on this era. Ken Burns' *Thomas Jefferson* (1996; TSIN-DXO-FXA) and David Sutherland's *George Washington: The Man Who Wouldn't Be King* (1992; AMEI-505-FXA) are splendid achievements. The *Africans in America* series (1998; WGBH Boston, 4 videos, AFRA-DXO-FXA) studies the Africans' fight to survive and maintain their culture from 1600 to the Civil War.

The struggle for independence brought a flood of patriotic writings, mostly poetry, although it also produced the first Spanish-American novel—*The Itching Parrot* (1816) by Mexican author José Joaquín Fernández de Lizardi (translated with an introduction by Katherine Anne Porter: Doubleday, 1942). In Argentina, the songs of gauchos gave inspiration to the poetry of Hilario Ascasubi and José Hernández. (Most translations of the works of these authors unfortunately are now out of print.)

Suggestions for Reading

A key work to understanding the contrasting motivations of imperial expansion is by Anthony Padgen, *Lords of All the World: Ideologies of Empire in Spain, Britain, and France, 1492–1830* (Yale University Press, 1998). The best survey is that by Mark A. Burkholder and Lyman L. Johnson, *Colonial Latin America* (Oxford University Press, 2003).

Robert Leckie, *George Washington's War* (HarperCollins, 1992), and Page Smith, *A New Age Now Begins: A People's History of the American Revolution,* 2 vols. (Penguin, 1989), are detailed and colorful narratives. Bernard Bailyn's *The Ideological Origins of the American Revolution* (Belknap Press, 1992) remains an essential study. Ronald Hoffman and Peter J. Albert have edited *Women in the Age of the American Revolution* (University of Virginia Press, 1989), a collection of pertinent essays on the hardships and heroics of women in the Revolution.

Leslie Bethell, ed., *The Cambridge History of Latin America,* Vol. 2 (Cambridge University Press, 1984), is encyclopedic in its coverage and superb in its research. Another useful general study of the Western Hemisphere south of the Rio Grande is D. A. Brading's *The First America: The Spanish Monarchy, Creole Patriots and the Liberal State 1492–1862* (Cambridge University Press, 1994). For studies of some of the major figures of the Latin American independence movements, see Robert Harvey's beautifully written *Liberators: Latin America's Struggle for Independence 1810–1830* (Overlook Press, 2002). See also C. L. R. James's study of the Haitian Revolution, *The Black Jacobins: Toussaint L'Ouverture and the San Domingo Revolution* (Vintage, 1989). Susan Migden Socolow's *The Women of Colonial Latin America* (Cambridge University Press, 2000) is the fundamental text on women in Central and South America.

Chapter 22

Industrialization

Social, Political, and Cultural Transformations

GREECE SERBIA Sofia Athens MONTENEGRO Belgrade

Outline

Features

◀ The early stages of industrialization required (and require) the labor of children, whether in the case of this barefoot boy at the end of the nineteenth century in a factory producing cloth or in the developing world today making clothes or shoes.

INDUSTRIALIZATION QUICKENED THE transition from a rural to an urban way of life after 1760: it produced a revolution in the way human beings live equal to that made by the Neolithic—or Agricultural—Revolution in the fifth millennium B.C.E.

Whether for cotton cloth in the eighteenth century or for computers today, industrialization produced (and produces) more goods of a higher quality at a cheaper price. Liberation from the productive limitations imposed by dependence on human and animal power is the great gift of industrialization. That gift, however, was (and is) paid for by the suffering of the first generations of workers in the factory system—whether in eighteenth and nineteenth century England or in the industrializing regions of Asia and Africa today.

As workers labored in the factories, the middle classes, the foremost advocates of capitalism and owners of the factories, became richer and more powerful. Because of their wealth and creativity, the middle classes dominated the countries of western Europe and North America during the nineteenth century. Their ascension came at the same time as the decline of the old aristocratic regimes. The middle classes recast ideology, culture, religion, and society in their own images. Through their economic power, they exported their way of life around the world.

Industrialized countries dominated the globe economically and politically by the end of the nineteenth century. The Europeans directly ruled practically all of Africa. Although China remained technically independent, it was controlled in many areas by industrialized powers. India fell directly under British rule, as did several parts of the Ottoman Empire. America expanded across the Pacific to Asia at the end of the century. Because of its reforms, only Japan was able to choose its own pace of change in the face of the industrialized European advance.

The Industrial Revolution: British Phase

Why did industrialization begin in Great Britain?

Between 1700 and 1800, partly because of the use of scientific methods to raise agricultural productivity, the percentage of English people engaged in agriculture declined from 80 to 40 percent. Because of the new methods, England had a food surplus, which meant lower prices, more food, and healthier people. At the same time, the English population almost doubled, producing more workers and consumers. A larger population meant a greater demand for goods, especially clothing. At the end of the seventeenth century, the *putting out system,* also known as the cottage industry, supplied most of the public demand for fabric. As there were not enough sheep in Britain to clothe its people in wool, the traditional fabric of choice, the demand for alternative fabrics such as cotton grew. A merchant would contract with a village to produce thread from raw cotton fibers, work that the villagers would fulfill during the autumn and winter when there was less to be done in the fields. Later the merchant would return to pay the villagers for the thread they produced and then would take it to another village where the thread would be made into cloth using traditional wooden looms operated by hand and foot. With the population explosion, however, the traditional putting out system could not keep up with the demand for cloth.

The Revolution in the Making of Cloth

Practical people seeing the need for greater output solved the basic problems of increasing production. In the many steps from raw cotton to finished cloth, there were bottlenecks—primarily in making yarn and weaving the strands together. In 1733, John Kay (1704–1764), a spinner and mechanic, patented the first of the great textile machines, the flying shuttle. This device made it possible for one person to weave wide bolts of cloth by using a spring mechanism that sent the shuttle across the loom. This invention upset the balance between the weavers of cloth and the spinners of yarn: ten spinners were now required to produce the yarn needed by one weaver.

James Hargreaves (d. 1778), a weaver and carpenter, eliminated this imbalance in 1764 with his spinning jenny, a mechanical spinning wheel that allowed the spinners to keep up with the weavers. Five years later, a barber named Richard Arkwright (1732–1792) built the water frame, which could spin many threads into yarn at the same time. Ten years after that, Samuel Crompton (1753–1827), a spinner, combined the spinning jenny and water frame into the water mule, which, with some variations, is still used today. By this time, the makers of yarn were outpacing the weavers, but in 1785, Edmund Cartwright (1743–1823) invented the power loom, which mechanized the weaving process. In two generations, what had once been a home-based craft became an industry.

Soon the demands of the new machines outran the supply of cotton. Since most of the material came from the United States, the demand exceeded the capability of the slave-based southern economy to create the supply. The best worker could not prepare more than 5 or 6 pounds of cotton per day, because removing the seeds from the cotton fibers was a time con-

	Revolution in the Making of Cotton
1733	John Kay patents flying shuttle
1764	James Hargreaves invents spinning jenny
1769	Richard Arkwright invents water frame
1779	Samuel Crompton invents water mule
1785	Edmund Cartwright invents power loom
c. 1800	Invention of cotton gin

Chronology

1780	1800	1820	1840	1860	1880
1785 Invention of general purpose steam engine **1785** Invention of power loom	**c. 1800** Invention of cotton gin **1813–1901** Life and work of Giuseppi Verdi	**1825** Repeal of the Combination Acts permits the formation of labor unions **1829** Invention of steam locomotive, George Stephenson's *Rocket* **1837–1901** Queen Victoria of the United Kingdom	**1847** Marx and Engels issue *The Communist Manifesto* **1856** Bessemer develops new process for making steel **1859** Charles Darwin publishes *On the Origin of the Species*	**1864–1876** First International **1875** German Social Democratic (Marxist) party established	**1889–1914** Second International

suming process. The American inventor Eli Whitney (1765–1825), among others, devised the cotton gin, a machine that enabled workers to increase by more than 50 times the amount of cotton they could clean each day. This device, coincidentally, played a major role in the perpetuation of slavery in the United States for another half century after its invention.

Finally, the textile industry became so large that it outgrew the possibilities of its power source: falling water. Steam came to drive the machines of industrializing Britain. In the first part of the eighteenth century, mechanic Thomas Newcomen (1663–1729) made an "atmospheric engine" in which a piston was raised by injected steam. As the steam condensed, the piston returned to its original position. Newcomen's unwieldy and inefficient device was put to use pumping water out of mines. James Watt (1736–1819), a builder of scientific instruments at the University of Glasgow, perfected Newcomen's invention. Watt's steam engine was also first used to pump water out of mines. It saved the large amounts of energy lost by the Newcomen engine and led to an increase in coal productivity. After 1785, it was also used to make cloth and drive ships and locomotives. The application of steam to weaving made it possible to expand the use of cloth-making machines to new areas, and after 1815, hand looms began to disappear from commercial textile making, replaced by the undoubted superiority of the cloth-making machines.

These inventors made their contributions in response to the need to solve particular problems of production. Their machines and the new power sources expanded productivity and transformed society in ways never before imagined.

Britain's Advantages

Industrialization began in Great Britain in the eighteenth century for a number of reasons. Although it was neither the richest nor the most populous country in western Europe, Britain possessed at virtually all

▼ Here in the Soho Engineering Works, Birmingham, England, visitors have come to observe how the steam engines invented by James Watt are made. Note the absence of modern safety equipment and standards.

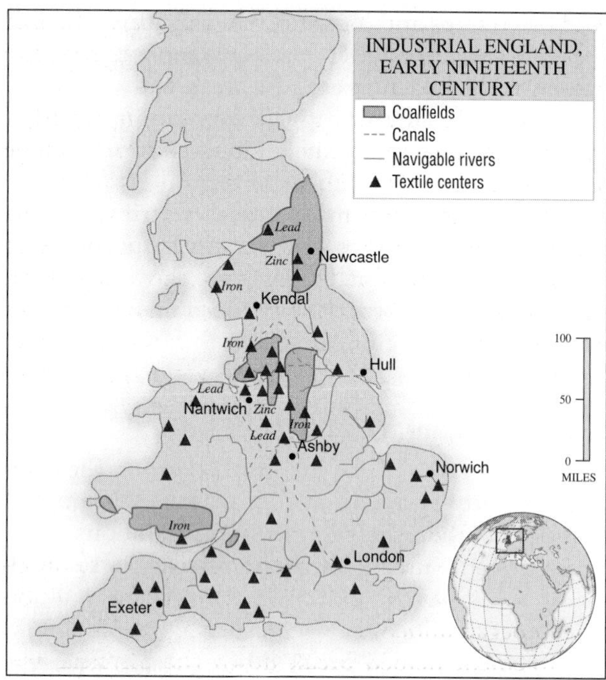

▲ English entrepreneurs established their factories at the beginning of the nineteenth century, not in the traditional population centers such as London, but out of town, close to water power and coal fields and with easy access to markets.

levels of society a hardworking, inventive, risk-taking private sector that received strong support from the government. Industrialization could not begin and grow without individual business owners who took a chance on something new. The British maintained this close tie between private initiative and creative governmental support throughout the eighteenth and nineteenth centuries.

Thanks to early governmental support of road improvements and canal construction, Britain had a better transportation network than any other country in Europe. The British also had mastery of the seas, excellent ports, and a large merchant fleet. They enjoyed the advantage of living safely on their island, away from the carnage of war, even during the Napoleonic conflicts. The chance to industrialize in stable conditions gave them the opportunity to profit from war contracts between 1792 and 1815. Finally, the Bank of England served as a solid base for economic growth by providing the money and financial stability for English businessmen.

Probably the most important factor was the relative flexibility of the British social and political systems. Members of the elite, unlike their colleagues on the Continent, pursued their wealth in the new industrial framework with great energy. At the same time, the middle classes, who had no land in the countryside and were excluded from political life until reforms in the second half of the nineteenth century, poured their enthusiasm and inventiveness into developing new businesses and technologies. The rising economic tide eventually included the workers after 1850. They benefited from gradual reforms granted to stifle any chance of revolution from below.

Napoleon's attempt to exclude the British from European markets had hurt economic growth, but it had also spurred the British to look for new manufacturing methods and markets. Once the wars were over, Britain flooded the Continent and the Americas with high-quality, inexpensive goods. No nation could compete against British efficiency.

Industrialized cotton textile production continued to increase in Britain and was supplemented by the arrival of the modern Iron Age. In 1800, Russia and Sweden had exported iron to Britain. By 1815, Britain exported more than five times as much iron as it imported. By 1848, the British produced more iron than the rest of the world combined. As in textile production, a number of inventions in iron-making appeared in response to problems. Improved refining of brittle cast iron made it more malleable and tough so that it could be used in more products. At the same time, more efficient mining processes for both coal and iron ore were used to ensure a dependable supply of raw materials.

To further help Britain dominate the metals market, in the 1850s, Henry Bessemer (1813–1898) developed a process to make steel, a harder and more malleable metal than iron, quickly and cheaply. So effective was the process that, between 1856 and 1870, the price of British steel fell to half the amount formerly charged for the best grade of iron. The drastic reduction in price due to innovations in production, a mark of industrialization, had a positive impact on all areas of the economy.

After mid-century, Britain produced more than two-thirds of the world's coal and more than half its iron and cloth. Industrial development encouraged urbanization, and by 1850, more than half of the population lived in cities and worked in industries. The British continued to enjoy the highest per capita income in the world, and the island nation stood head and shoulders above all others in terms of economic and material strength. With such a position of dominance, the United Kingdom could comfortably advocate Adam Smith's proposals for free trade.

Industrialization: The Continental Phase

How did the Industrial Revolution spread from Britain to the rest of Europe?

After mid-century, industrialization spread first to the Continent and then around the globe as British methods and techniques were imitated and then improved on.

Industrialization and Banking Changes on the Continent

The Continent faced many hurdles to economic growth after the Napoleonic wars. Obstacles to mobility, communication, and cooperation among the classes prevented the social structures there from adapting as easily to change as the British had. The farther one traveled to the south and east, the more repressive the social structure became. In many parts of the Continent, the restored nobilities reclaimed their power, but they were not intellectually, financially, or politically prepared to support industrial development. Fragmented political boundaries, geographical obstacles, and toll-takers along primary river and road systems hampered growth, especially in central Europe. In eastern Europe, the middle classes were weaker and more isolated than in the west.

Industrialization in Europe

In 1815, the initial stages of industrialization were evident in Belgium, France, and Germany. In Sweden, Russia, and Switzerland there were pockets of potential mechanized production, but these initiatives were tiny compared to industry in Britain at the same time. In 1850, only Belgium could compete with British products in its own markets. There, a combination of favorable governmental policies, good transportation, and stability brought some success.

Governments and businesses sent officials and representatives to Britain to try to discover the secrets of industrialization. The British tried to protect their advantage by banning the export of machines and processes and limiting foreign access to their factories. Industrial espionage existed then as now, however, and competitors from the Continent did uncover some secrets. Britain's success could be studied, components of its industry stolen, and its experts hired, but no other European country could combine all the factors that permitted Britain to dominate.

After mid-century, a long period of peace and improved transportation, as well as strategic government assistance, encouraged rapid economic growth in France and the German states. Population increases of 25 percent in France and nearly 40 percent in the Germanies provided a larger market and labor supply. Two generations of borrowed British technology began to be applied and improved on, but the two most important developments came in banking and in customs and toll reforms.

After 1815, aggressive new banking houses appeared across Europe, strengthened by the profits they had made by extending loans to governments during the Napoleonic wars. They understood that there was money to be made investing in new industries, such as railroads, and they worked with both governments and major capitalists. Firms such as Hope and Baring in London; the Rothschilds in Frankfurt, Paris, Vienna, and London; and numerous Swiss bankers were representative of the private financiers who had well-placed sources and contacts throughout the state and business communities.

Banking changed radically during this period to satisfy the growing demands for money. Long-range **capital** needs were met by the formation of investment banks, and new institutions were created to fill the need for short-term credit. The ultimate source of financial liquidity was the middle classes—the thousands of small investors who put their money in banks to make their own profits through interest earned. More money could be gained from the many small investors than from the few rich families who had formerly dominated banking.

The *Zollverein*

The Germans led the way in the other major development, the ***Zollverein*** (ZOHL-ver-ein), a customs union which began under Prussian leadership in 1819. This arrangement helped break down the physical and financial barriers imposed at the various state boundaries and, in the next 23 years, came to include most of central and northern Germany. Instead of the more than 300 divisions fragmenting the German states in 1800, there was a virtual free trade market, something that Britain had enjoyed since the union of Scotland and England in 1707 (and the European Union would create across the Continent at the end of the twentieth century). The significance of the *Zollverein* was that it allowed goods to circulate free of tolls and tariffs, thus reducing prices and stimulating trade.

In the second half of the 1800s, industrialization on the Continent grew rapidly, aided by the increased flow of credit and the elimination of internal barriers. Tariffs throughout the area fell to a degree not matched until after World War II and the creation of the European Common Market. Major firms, such as the German Krupp steelworks and the French silk industries, controlled portions of the European market and competed effectively with Britain throughout the world.

Agricultural and Transportation: Responses to a Growing Population

The Industrial Revolution coincided with a demographic revolution. A gradual decline in mortality rates, better medical care, more food, earlier marriages,

capital—The goods, possessions, or other items of value that constitute wealth and may be used to gain more goods, possessions, or other items of value either through production or investment.

Zollverein—A German customs union, begun under Prussian leadership in 1819, that helped break down the physical and financial barriers imposed at the various boundaries between German states. It allowed goods to circulate free of tolls and tariffs, which reduced prices and stimulated trade.

▲ The interior of the Krupp Steelworks at Essen, Germany, as painted by Otto Bollhagen. Krupp was one of the largest firms in Germany's growing industrial sector.

and better sanitary conditions contributed to the European population increase from 175 million to 435 million in the nineteenth century. The number of people grew so rapidly in Europe that although 40 million Europeans emigrated throughout the world, the Continent still showed a population increase in a single century that was greater than that of the previous 20 centuries.

This 130 percent increase between 1800 and 1910 led some observers, such as Thomas Robert Malthus (1766–1834), to forecast a tragic future of massive famine on a global scale. In his "Essay on Population" (1798), Malthus observed the limited food supply and rapidly increasing population of his day and stated that human reproduction would outrun the earth's ability to produce food. He concluded that the inevitable fate of humanity was misery and ruin, since the number of people would rise geometrically while the food supply would grow only arithmetically. What Malthus failed to anticipate was the effects of technological innovation in agriculture and transportation.

The vast increase in food production kept up with the population explosion of the nineteenth century. It is estimated that in 1815 around 60 percent of European economic output and 85 percent of the human activity were tied to agriculture. These large quantities of capital and labor were not used effectively because the agricultural advances made in the Netherlands and Britain in the seventeenth and eighteenth centuries had not spread on the Continent. However, progressive landowners gradually introduced these improved methods when they saw the money to be made by feeding the growing populations of the cities.

By the end of the nineteenth century, farmers around the world were plowing new lands and using higher-yield crops in order to compete within a global agricultural market. Industrial nations such as Britain, in which by 1900 only 10 percent of the population was engaged in farming, imported more than a fourth of their food. Even with transportation costs added on, efficient farmers in the Americas, Australia, and New Zealand could still sell their agricultural products in Europe for less than the already impoverished peasant farmers of Ireland and southern and eastern Europe.

To bring the increased food supply to the growing population and to make possible the distribution of raw materials and finished goods to the global market, industrialized countries, led by Britain, built the most complete and far-reaching transportation and communication networks ever known.

The first major leap in water transportation occurred when the Duke of Bridgewater hired the engineer James Brindley to build a 7 ½-mile-long canal from his coal mines to the city of Manchester and its warehouses and wharves. The first true commercial canal in Britain, the Bridgewater Canal, opened in 1761. The reduced transportation costs cut the price of the Duke's coal in half and gave the rest of Britain a vivid lesson in the benefits of canals. By the 1830s, nearly 4000 miles of improved rivers and canals were built, with strong governmental support, making it possible to ship most of the country's products by water. Following the British example, canal building spread through Europe and North America, and then to Egypt with the Suez Canal in 1869, and to Latin America with the Panama Canal in 1914. The first project cut the sailing time between London and Bombay, India, by nearly half; the second did away with the need to sail around South America to reach the Pacific Ocean.

Until 1815, most roads were muddy, rutted paths that were impassable during spring thaws and autumn rains. In that year a Scotsman, John McAdam (1756–1836), created the all-weather road by placing small stones in compact layers directly on the roadbed. The pressure of the traffic moving over the highway packed the stones together to give a fairly smooth surface. This practical solution cut the stagecoach time for the 160 miles from London to Sheffield from four days in the 1750s to 28 hours in 1820.

Steam-powered vessels replaced the graceful though less dependable sailing ships in ocean commerce. Clipper ships are among the most beautiful transportation devices ever built, but they cannot move without wind. Sturdy, awkward-looking steamships carried larger cargo with greater regularity and thereby

Seeing Connections

Singer Sewing Machines in Zululand

Industrialization propelled Europe into the role of world economic giant. This transformation accelerated the European colonization of the world that had begun centuries earlier. Entire continents became suppliers of raw materials for European factories, and their people were the customers for the finished goods of those factories. As a consequence, European machines came to be used the world over. This ad for Singer Sewing Machines in Zululand, present-day South Africa, shows the impact of Western industry on people in other parts of the world. In an indirect way, the spreading of machines enhanced economies in parts of Asia, Africa, and Latin America.

revolutionized world trade. The price of American wheat on the European market dropped by three-fourths in the last part of the century, to a considerable degree the result of the savings made possible by the large, reliable steamships. Transatlantic passenger and mail services were also improved by the use of steam to power seagoing vessels.

The most important element in the European arterial network was the railroad. The Englishman George Stephenson built the first steam locomotive, *Rocket,* in 1829. A year later, the first commercially profitable rail line opened between Liverpool and Manchester. By 1860, rails linked every major market in Europe and in the United States. By 1903, the Russians had pushed the Trans-Siberian Railroad to the Pacific Ocean. Railroads cheaply and efficiently carried people and large amounts of material long distances and knit countries and continents closer together. Within cities, urban rail lines and trolleys were widespread by the end of the nineteenth century; by permitting a wider diffusion of workers, these had an impressive effect on housing and business patterns. In the 1860s, London became the first city to establish subways, followed by Budapest in 1896, and Paris in 1900.

Connected with the growth of transportation networks and technological innovation were major improvements in the area of communications. Postal agreements among the various countries made cheap and dependable mail service possible. The introduction of the postage stamp and improved transportation

Economic Transformation in Europe: 1750–1850

systems brought astronomical increases in the number of letters and packages mailed after 1850. Starting in the 1840s, the electric telegraph, undersea cable, telephone, wireless telegraph, and typewriter expanded the ability to exchange ideas and information. After the transportation and communications revolutions, no longer would distance be an obstacle. The world became a smaller, if not a more unified, place.

The Workers: The Manchester Microcosm

Why did industrialization fail to bring a decent standard of living to the first generation of industrial workers?

The first generation of workers in the factory system did not initially profit from industrialization; instead, they paid a heavy price. The industrialization that began in the British Midlands in and around the city of Manchester produced wrenching social changes there and everywhere else it came into being. It drove society away from an agricultural to an urban way of life. The old system, in which peasant families worked the fields during the summer and did their cottage industry work in the winter to their own standards and at their own pace, slowly disappeared. As a result, the first generation of workers passed from a traditional agrarian society in which they might work, in total, 120 days a year in the fields, and another third of the year involved in cottage industries with the final third devoted to holidays and other moments of leisure. In the factory system, they would work 14 hours a day, six days a week, 52 weeks a year, initially with only Christmas and Good Friday as officially sanctioned holidays. After the passage of the Bank Holidays Act of 1871, Easter Monday, the last Monday in August, Boxing Day (the day after Christmas), and Whit Monday (the spring holiday after Pentecost) were added to the holiday list.

The factory was a place where, for long hours, people did repetitive tasks, using machines to process large amounts of raw materials. This was an efficient way to make a lot of high-quality goods cheaply. But the factories were often dangerous places, and the lifestyle connected to them at first had a terrible effect on the human condition.

The Factory System

In the factory system, the workers worked, and the owners made profits. The owners wanted to make the most they could from their investment and to get the most work they could from their employees. The

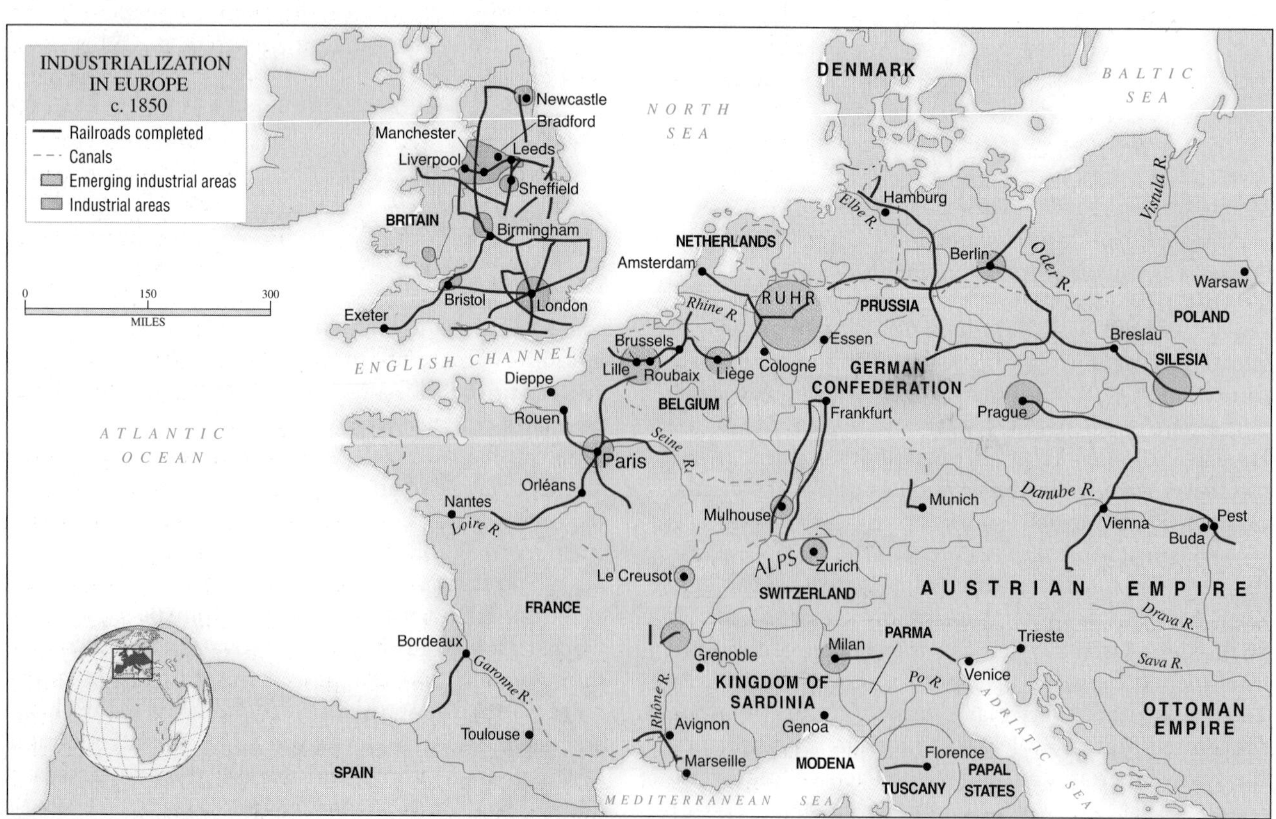

▼ By the middle of the nineteenth century, industrialization had spread across Europe, aided by the development of railroad links that brought resources to the new factories and transported their finished goods to world markets.

DOCUMENT

Industrial Society and Factory Conditions

workers, in turn, felt that they deserved more of the profits because their labor made production possible. This was a situation guaranteed to produce conflict, especially given the wretched conditions the workers faced in the first stages of industrialization.

The early English factories in Manchester and elsewhere were generally miserable places, characterized by bad lighting, poor ventilation, and dangerous machinery. Safety standards were practically nonexistent, and workers in various industries could expect to suffer serious health hazards from their work environment; for example, laborers working with lead paint developed lung problems, pewter workers fell ill to palsy, miners suffered black lung disease, and machine operators might lose fingers, hands, and even lives. Not until late in the nineteenth century did health and disability insurance come into effect. In some factories, workers who suffered accidents were deemed to be at fault; since there was little job security, a worker could be fired for almost any reason.

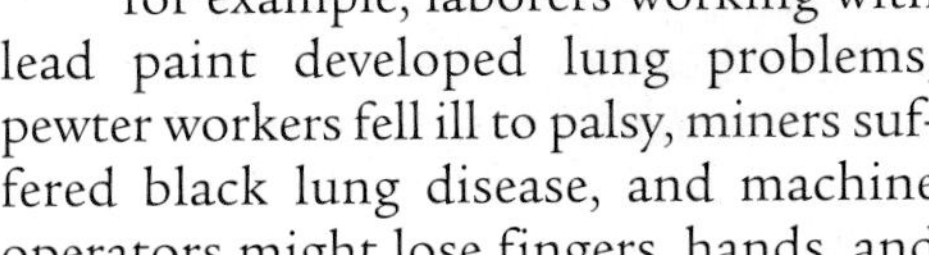

DOCUMENT

Report on Sanitary Conditions

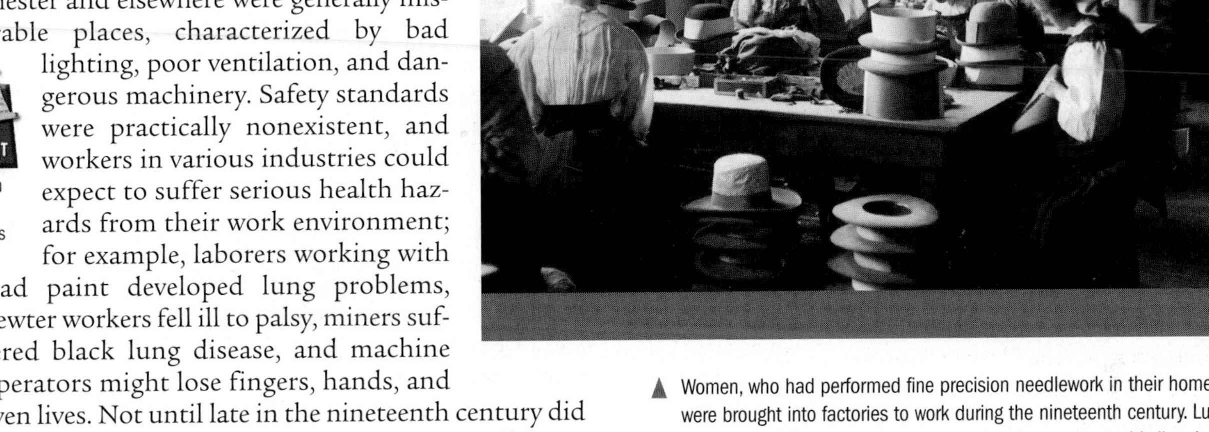

▲ Women, who had performed fine precision needlework in their homes, were brought into factories to work during the nineteenth century. Luxury items such as hats became mass produced on an assembly line, but had to be hand finished by craftswomen working 10-hour days.

Women and Child Labor

The demand for plentiful and cheap labor led to the widespread employment of women and children. As we can see in the testimony of 8-year-old Sarah Gooder before a Parliamentary Commission (see the Document *Industrialization and Children* on p. 672), girls as young as 6 years old were used to haul carts of coal in Lancashire mines, and boys and girls of 4 and 5 years of age worked in textile mills.

Women had done most of the work in the cottage industries, and according to the Occupational Distribution in the 1851 Census of Great Britain,[1] women did a substantial amount of the work during the first stage of industrialization. They made up 38.9 percent of the professions; 85.5 percent of domestic service workers; 16.6 percent of the bricks, cement, pottery, and glass workers; 20.5 percent of paper and printing workers; 49 percent of textile workers; and 54 percent of clothing manufacturers. Across the board, women were around 30 percent of the workforce. As a percentage of the total workforce in factories in 1833, women constituted almost 57 percent of the workers.

In the first half of the nineteenth century, children—boys and girls—did an important part of the work in the textile mills. Small children, under 6 years of age, were sent scurrying under the machines to gather the odd bits of thread and fabric that dropped through the cracks. Those a bit older were expert at untying the knots that occurred—but they had to be quick because the pressure built up by the blockage of the machines could cut off their fingers once the machines snapped back into operation. One source calculates that nearly 5 percent of the workers in cotton cloth in the Manchester region were less than 10 years old; more than 50 percent were under 19 years of age. Another estimate indicates that across the whole of the fabric industry, children under the age of 13 were between 10 and 20 percent of the workforce. Estimates of children working in mines range from nearly 20 to 40 percent in 1842. These numbers declined as the century progressed, but in 1881 there were still more than 30,000 boys under the age of 15 working in Lancashire mines and nearly 83,000 young girls under 15 working in textiles and dyeing.[2]

When they were not laboring, the working families in Manchester and elsewhere lived in horrid conditions. Workers took up residence near their work in the newly built slums. There were no sanitary, water, or medical services for the workers, and working families were crammed 12 and 15 individuals to a room in damp, dark cellars. There were no sewage systems and toilets were either holes in the ground or people would simply relieve themselves against the back fence. As the human waste ran into the rivers, which served as the source of drinking water, outbreaks of typhus and cholera were common. For infants and children, the

Document

Industrialization and Children

Early industrialization demanded huge sacrifices, especially from children. Despite the popularity of laissez-faire economic policy in Great Britain, Parliament began to make inquiries into the working conditions in mines and factories. They discovered that owners preferred to employ little children because their size and dexterity were especially useful in clearing up blockages in looms and in penetrating small spaces in mines. Such owners considered children as legal entities, capable of being equal partners in a legal contract.

Sarah Gooder, Aged 8 Years

I'm a trapper in the Gawber pit. It does not tire me, but I have to trap without a light and I'm scared. I go at four and sometimes half past three in the morning, and come out at five and half past. I never go to sleep. Sometimes I sing when I've light, but not in the dark; I dare not sing then. I don't like being in the pit. I am very sleepy when I go sometimes in the morning. I go to Sunday-schools and read Reading made Easy. [She knows her letters and can read little words.] They teach me to pray. [She repeated the Lord's Prayer, not very perfectly, and ran on with the following addition.] "God bless my father and mother, and sister and brother, uncles and aunts and cousins, and everybody else, and God bless me and make me a good servant. Amen. I have heard tell of Jesus many a time. I don't know why he came on earth, I'm sure, and I don't know why he died, but he had stones for his head to rest on. I would like to be at school far better than in the pit."

Questions to Consider

1. Play "devil's advocate" and construct a defense for using children in mines and factories. Take the opposite point of view and construct a critique against the use of children in industrial and mining enterprises.
2. Do you know of any instances in today's economy where children are used in the manufacturing of items used by you or your friends and family?
3. Did liberalism, as seen by John Stuart Mill and Jeremy Bentham, justify the employment of children?

From *Parliamentary Papers* (1842).

most fatal disease borne by this bad water was diarrhea. Poor diet, alcoholism, and bad air led to the prevalence of diseases such as tuberculosis among workers and reduced life spans in the industrial cities such as Manchester. Simultaneous with, and perhaps part of, the industrialization process was a dramatic increase in illegitimate births and prostitution. Up to mid-century, corresponding to the time of maximum social upheaval from industrialization, at least one-third of all births in Europe were out of wedlock.

Those who survived the first generation of industrialization escaped these desperate conditions. In England, they were replaced by a new generation of workers—immigrants from Ireland. After these workers improved their lot, they too were replaced by another wave of immigrant workers, this time from Italy.

Later generations profited from the sacrifices made by the first workers in industrialization. Factory owners began to realize that they could make more profit from an efficient factory staffed by contented and healthy workers. But the costs borne by the first generations making the transition between a family-based rural life and the anonymous cruelty of early industrial cities were immense.

Urban Crises

Industrialization prompted massive growth of European cities in the nineteenth century, as can be seen in the table below. In addition, new towns sprang up throughout the Continent and many soon reached the level of more than 100,000 inhabitants. Even in agrarian Russia, where 70 percent of the population worked on the land, there were 17 cities of more than 100,000 by the end of the century.

	Population Growth in Manchester
1717	c. 10,000
1758	c. 17,000
1801	75,381
1821	126,066
1841	235,507
1851	303,189

Between 1717 and 1751, Manchester's population expanded greatly as demands for its products increased. By 1830 there were more than 560 cotton mills in the area around the city providing work for more than 110,000 people, of which 35,000 were children.

Political leaders faced serious problems in dealing with mushrooming city growth. City leaders had the responsibility to maintain a clean environment, provide social and sanitation services, enforce the law, furnish transportation, and—most serious of all—build housing. They uniformly failed to meet the challenges of growth.

Until mid-century, human waste disposal in some parts of Paris was handled by dumping excrement into the street gutters or the Seine River. Not until Baron Georges Haussman (1809–1891) implemented urban renewal in the 1850s and 1860s did the city get an adequate garbage, water, and sewage system. Police protection remained inadequate or corrupt. Other cities shared the same problems to a greater or lesser degree. The new industrial towns that had sprung up were in even worse condition than the older urban centers.

By the end of the century, however, governments began to deal effectively with urban problems. By 1914, most major European cities began to make clean running water, central heat, adequate street lighting, urban and suburban transport, mass public education, dependable sewage systems, and minimal medical care available for their people.

The Labor Movement

The British economy suffered through a difficult time after the end of the Napoleonic wars. High unemployment struck skilled workers, especially nonmechanized loom weavers. In frustration, some of them fought back and destroyed textile machines, the symbol of the forces oppressing them. Strikes, demonstrations, and incidents such as the Peterloo Massacre on August 16, 1819, at St. Peter's Fields, in which soldiers closed down a political meeting, killing 11 and injuring hundreds, vividly expressed the workers' rage. Not until British reformers came forward in the 1820s did the laborers begin to gain some relief.

Their efforts to form labor unions received an important boost in 1825 when the Combination Acts, passed in 1799 against the formation of workers' associations, were repealed. The first unions, such as the half-million-strong Grand National Consolidated Trades Union, were weak and disorganized, split by the gulf between skilled workers and common laborers. Nonetheless, by the end of the century, the workers laid the foundations for the powerful unions that defended them.

Nineteenth-Century Urban Growth

City	Population in 1800	Population in 1910
London	831,000	4,521,000
Paris	547,000	2,888,000
Berlin	173,000	2,071,000
Vienna	247,000	2,030,000
St. Petersburg	220,000	1,907,000

Socialism and Industrialization

What is the relationship between socialism and industrialization?

Political thinkers in France and England responded to the injustices of industrial capitalism by developing the theory of **socialism.** Socialists attacked the system of laissez-faire capitalism as unplanned and unjust. They condemned the increasing concentration of wealth and called for public or worker ownership of business. The nature of the industrial system, dividing worker and owner, also raised serious problems, and socialists insisted that harmony and cooperation, not competition, should prevail.

Socialists believed that human beings are essentially good, and with the proper organization of society there would be a happy future with no wars, crimes, administration of justice, or government. In this perfectly balanced world, there would also be perfect health and happiness. Karl Marx later derisively labeled socialists who sought such a world as "Utopians."

The first prominent **Utopian socialist** was the French noble Claude Henri de Rouvroy, Comte de Saint-Simon (klod on-REE da hrouv-WHA, komt da san SI-mohn; 1760–1825). He defined a nation as "nothing but a great industrial society" and politics as "the science of production." He advocated that humanity should voluntarily place itself under the rule of the paternalistic despotism of scientists, technicians, and industrialists who would use their collective wisdom to improve the lives of the multitude of poor people.

Charles Fourier (fou-ree-AY; 1772–1837), another French Utopian, believed that the future society must be cooperative and free. He worked out a communal

socialism—An ideology proposing that the community or government have ownership of the means to create wealth.

Utopian socialism—A variant of the socialist ideology that proposes that the turning over of the means to create wealth to the community or government can be achieved peacefully.

living unit of 1620 people called a *phalanstery.* The members of the group voluntarily chose tasks that appealed to them from the work needed to ensure the phalanstery's survival. Although his plan was endorsed by many prominent people, attempts made to found cooperative Fourierist communities were unsuccessful. The famous Brook Farm colony in Massachusetts was one such short-lived experiment.

Robert Owen (1771–1858), a successful mill owner in Scotland, was a more practical Utopian socialist. His New Lanark, the site of his textile mills, was a model community. There, between 1815 and 1825, thousands of visitors saw rows of neat, well-kept workers' homes, a garbage collection system, schools for workers' children, and clean factories where workers were treated kindly and no children under age 11 were employed. In 1825, Owen moved to the vicinity of Evansville, Indiana, where he established a short-lived community at New Harmony.

Karl Marx and Communism

Karl Marx (1818–1883) took socialism from its "Utopian" to its "scientific" phase. As was the case with other creators of ideologies to aid the working classes, he came from a comparatively privileged social position, growing up in a pleasant setting in Trier, in the western part of Germany. Marx's Jewish parents converted to Protestantism so that they could participate fully in Prussian society, and then they pushed their son to become a lawyer. Instead of following his parents' wishes, he attended the University of Berlin as a doctoral candidate in philosophy and joined a circle that followed some aspects of Hegel's thought. After finishing his degree, he could not find a university position and so returned to the Rhineland, where he began writing for a local liberal newspaper. The injustices he saw around him and his reading of the French socialists Henri de Saint-Simon and Pierre-Joseph Proudhon (proo-DHON) led him to concentrate on the economic factors in history and pass from philosophical abstractions to the realities of politics and economics.

In 1845, Marx went to Paris to continue his work; there he met Friedrich Engels (1820–1895), the son of a wealthy German businessman who owned factories in England and Germany. Engels had seen firsthand how workers suffered during the first phase of industrialization when he worked at his father's plant in Manchester. In Paris, he and Marx spent ten days together sharing their ideas. The two became united in their hatred of what they saw as the inhumane nature of capitalism and spent the rest of their lives attacking it.

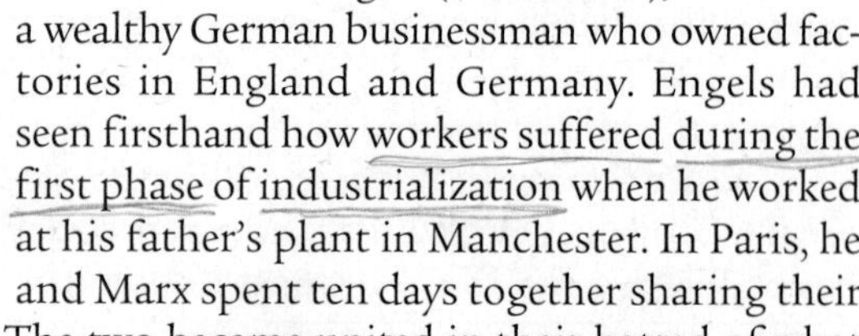

CASE STUDY

Industrial Side Effects

Marx was, from the start, the intellectually dominant partner, but Engels gave him lifelong intellectual, material, and personal support. Marx's radical ideas led to his expulsion by the French in 1845. From there, he went first to Belgium and finally to England, where he spent most of his life after 1848.

Almost every day he made his way to the British Museum, where he waged intellectual war on capitalism by doing research for his major works, especially *Das Kapital* ("Capital"; 1867–1894). At night he returned home to write, enduring difficult living conditions and the deaths of three of his children in the 1850s. He wrote prolifically, although he suffered from boils, asthma, spleen and liver problems, and eyestrain. His constant inability to handle money drove him into fits of rage against his creditors. He was increasingly intolerant of anyone who disagreed with him and became an embittered recluse; yet his vision and theories inspired reformers for the next century and a half. Marx constructed a system that gave the oppressed an explanation for their difficult position and hope for their future.

IMAGE

Karl Marx and His Daughter

A materialistic view of history shaped his approach. He wrote that economic forces drove history. He did not deny the existence or importance of spiritual or philosophical values, nor did he doubt that the occasional genius could alter the flow of events. However, the material aspects of life were much more important. Marx believed that "it is not the consciousness of men which determines their existence, but on the contrary, it is the existence which determines their consciousness." As an economic determinist, he believed that when the means of production of a given era changed, the whole social and ideological structure was transformed by the groups who controlled those means of production.

German philosopher Georg Wilhelm Friedrich Hegel (1770–1831) had written that history is made up of a number of cultural periods, each one the expression of a dominant spirit or idea. After fulfilling its purpose, a given period is replaced by a period of contradictory ideas or values. The original thesis is negated, and that negation is in turn negated once it has run its course. Marx identified the productive forces of society, not culture periods, as the key factor in history. The world is driven by class conflict between those who control the means of production and those who do not, whether master against slave in ancient Greece, patrician against plebeian in Rome, lord against serf in the Middle Ages, noble against bourgeois in early modern times, or capitalist against proletarian in the modern world. History moves in this zigzag pattern through class struggle, a reflection of the Hegelian **dialectic.** Not until the triumph of the proletariat would this pattern stop: when the workers controlled the means

DOCUMENT

The Communist Manifesto

dialectic—A process in which a thesis and an antithesis are reconciled in a synthesis.

of production, they could not logically engage in class conflict, and hence **communism** would be achieved.

The **bourgeoisie,** or the middle classes, who had erected the new capitalist society by gaining control of the means of production through organizing trade and industry, created its opposition in the proletariat, the class-conscious workers. This latter group would be, according to Marx, "the seeds of the bourgeoisie's own destruction." According to the dialectic, when the workers recognized their true power, they would overthrow the bourgeoisie. Out of this conflict would come the final act of the dialectical process, the classless society in which "each person would work according to his ability and receive according to his need." An interim dictatorship might have to occur because a number of features of the old order would remain and the proletariat would have to be protected. However, as the classless society evolved, the state would wither away.

Through his research, Marx identified a number of defects that foretold the inevitable overthrow of the bourgeoisie, among them alienation and surplus value. The factory system turned workers into cogs in the larger machine and deprived them of satisfaction in their work. In addition, Marx charged that owners did not pay workers for the value they created. A worker could, for example, produce the necessary economic value to supply one individual's needs in seven hours, but the owner would keep the worker laboring for 12 hours. The owner thereby stole the "surplus value" of five working hours from the worker, in effect robbing the worker of the fruits of his or her work.

Finally, Marx noted that in the capitalist system, the rich got richer and fewer and the poor got poorer and more numerous. This gap produced widespread discontent and increased the impetus toward revolution. Further, the masses would be unable to buy all of the goods they produced, and economic crises of overproduction and unemployment would become the rule. In time, once the bourgeois phase of dominance had run its course, the contradictions between the classes would become so great that the proletariat would rise up and take over the means of production.

Socialism and the Labor Movement

Socialist parties of all varieties helped advance the workers' movements in the second half of the nineteenth century by providing a theoretical basis and an aggressive public statement of their case. Marx, who spent his life researching and writing in the defense of the workers—even though he had precious little contact with them—organized the International Workingmen's Association, later known as the First International, in London in 1864. The First International included labor activists ranging from English trade unions to eastern European refugees to anarchists to German theorists. Not much came of the First International's efforts because of constant arguing among the factions and Marx's vindictiveness toward other major figures, such as the Russian anarchist Bakunin (ba-KOO-nin).

In the three decades after Marx's death in 1883, his theories dominated the European workers' movements, though the movements themselves were not united. The French split into three distinct socialist groups. Some British socialists were greatly influenced by the maxims of Christianity, whereas the socialist Fabian Society—among whose members were the middle-class writers George Bernard Shaw, H. G. Wells, and Sidney and Beatrice Webb—pursued a more prosaic political path. With the spread of industrialization, workers and their leaders found important support in Marx's work even in places such as Russia, where Marx had never foreseen his thoughts as having any influence.

The Social Democrats—Marxist socialists—made important gains in Germany, forcing Bismarck to make concessions (see Chapter 23). The Social Democratic Party became the largest party in the country and the strongest socialist party in Europe under the leadership of its founder, Ferdinand Lassalle. In 1871, there were two socialists in the Reichstag (the lower house of the German legislature); by 1912, the number had risen to 110.

Because of the widespread impact of Marx's ideas in the social sciences and the labor movement, the period of the Second International (1889–1914) was the most important time of his influence. A broad spectrum of thinkers among the 12 million members of the Second International claimed Marx as their

	Socialist Internationals (Labor Unions)
1864–1876	International Workingmen's Association (First International)
1889–1914	Second International, Social Democratic (non-Russian remnants remained until 1972)
1919–1943	Third International, Communist (Leninist, also known as the Comintern)
1923–1970s	Fourth International, Trotskyite (formally organized in 1938)

communism—An ideology that advocates the elimination of private property, the ownership of all goods and means of production by the community, and an elimination of conflict by the creation of a society in which each person works according to his abilities and receives according to his needs.

bourgeoisie—The middle classes, in all of their variations.

inspiration, even though they might differ in opinions about the role of the state, the functions of unions, the crisis of capitalism, the role of the proletariat, and even things he said. There was not a single, monolithic Marxist movement in Europe. Yet, despite their doctrinal differences, the Social Democrats in all countries could agree on essentials for the workers: an eight-hour day, the need to replace standing armies with militias, and a welfare state buttressed by universal suffrage.

The socialist movement strengthened Europe's labor unions, and the workers achieved substantial progress by 1914. Whether by working within the various states' legislatures or by raising the specter of revolution, the socialists helped bring about substantial reforms in the economy, labor practices, civil rights, the courts, and education. They pushed the capitalists to reform, thus, ironically, avoiding the very apocalyptic revolution forecast by Marx.

As industry became more sophisticated and centralized, so did the labor movement. Across Europe, the workers could choose anarchist, socialist, or conservative paths to follow. Some unions—the trade or craft unions—centered on a particular occupation. Some found their focus in the various productive stages of an industry, and still others, such as the English Trade Unions Congress, were nationwide and all-encompassing, wielding great power. Whatever the choice, by 1900, unions had made important advances through their solidarity in launching paralyzing strikes.

Although workers could still not negotiate on an equal basis with the owners, they had, by 1914, vastly improved their position over that endured by their grandparents. The British movement had 4 million members and was a powerful force; German unions obtained benefits for their members in a broad number of areas, from life insurance to travel. The income gap between rich and poor began to narrow. Working hours were shortened, and living conditions improved. The real wages of workers—that is, the amount of goods that their income could actually buy—increased by 50 percent in the industrial nations in the last 30 years of the nineteenth century.

The Middle Classes

Why were the middle classes interested in reform efforts and other "good works"?

Although it is difficult to give a strict definition of the middle classes, or bourgeoisie, it is easier to say who did not belong. Neither factory workers nor peasants nor the aristocracy were included. In general, the farther south and east one went in Europe, the less numerous and weaker the middle classes were.

But from the mid-eighteenth century through to the opening of World War I, they dominated Europe through their social examples, religious activities, humanitarian work, scientific accomplishment, cultural creations, and ideological work.

"Upstairs, Downstairs"

People socially closer to the laboring classes were considered the lower middle classes, whereas those near the elite formed the upper middle classes. Included in the lower middle classes were skilled artisans, bureaucrats, clerks, teachers, shopkeepers, and clergy. They realized that very little separated them from the laboring masses, and they were constantly trying to climb socially. Later in the century, they benefited most from compulsory education laws and were avid consumers of the books written by a new wave of authors, the penny-press newspapers, and state propaganda.

The upper middle classes profited the most from industrialization. It was not easy to break into this level of society, but money, taste, and aggressiveness could open the doors for the bankers, factory owners,

The English, the pioneers of the Industrial Revolution, also established the model of how "proper" middle-class people should live. This family at home embodies an ideal of social and domestic life that was copied wherever in the world a middle class came to exist.

Document

Mrs. Beeton's Book of Household Management (1861)

Mrs. Beeton's Book of Household Management was first published in 1861. It proved enormously popular; new editions were produced for over half a century. Over 2000 pages long, it covered almost every aspect of middle-class life. It was, in effect, a "guide" to successful housewifery.

The Housewife, Home Virtues, Hospitality, Good Temper, Dress and Fashion, Engaging Domestics, Wages of Servants, Visiting, Visiting Cards, Parties, Etc. Etc.

The functions of the mistress of a house resemble those of the general of an army or the manager of a great business concern. Her spirit will be seen in the whole establishment, and if she performs her duties well and intelligently, her domestics will usually follow in her path. Among the gifts that nature has bestowed on woman, few rank higher than the capacity for domestic management, for the exercise of this faculty constantly affects the happiness, comfort, and prosperity of the whole family. In this opinion we are borne out by the author of *The Vicar of Wakefield* [Oliver Goldsmith], who says: "the modest virgin, the prudent wife, and the careful matron are much more serviceable in life than petticoated philosophers, blustering heroines, or virago queans. She who makes her husband and children happy is a much greater character than ladies described in Romances whose whole occupation is to murder mankind with shafts from the quiver of their eyes."

... A woman's home should be first and foremost in her life, but if she allow household cares entirely to occupy her thoughts, she is apt to become narrow in her interests and sympathies, a condition not conducive to domestic happiness. To some overworked women but little rest or recreation may seem possible, but, generally speaking, the leisure to be enjoyed depends upon proper methods of work, punctuality, and early rising. The object of the present work is to give assistance to those who desire practical advice in the government of their home.

Hospitality should be practised; but care must be taken that the love of company, for its own sake, does not become a prevailing passion; such a habit is no longer hospitality, but dissipation. A lady, when she first undertakes the responsibility of a household, should not attempt to retain all the mere acquaintances of her youth. Her true and tried friends are treasures never to be lightly lost, but they, and the friends she will make on entering her husband's circle, and very likely by moving to a new locality, should provide her with ample society.

In conversation one should never dwell unduly on the petty annoyances and trivial disappointments of the day. Many people get into the habit of talking incessantly of the worries of their servants and children, not realizing that to many of their hearers these are uninteresting if not wearisome subjects. From one's own point of view, also, it is well not to start upon a topic without having sufficient knowledge to discuss it with intelligence. Important events, whether of joy or sorrow, should be told to friends whose sympathy or congratulation may be welcome. A wife should never allow a word about any faults of her husband to pass her lips.

Cheerfulness—We cannot too strongly insist on the vital importance of always preserving an equable good temper amidst all the little cares and worries of domestic life. Many women may be heard to declare that men cannot realize the petty anxieties of a household. But a woman must cultivate that tact and forbearance without which no man can hope to succeed in his career. The true woman combines with mere tact that subtle sympathy which makes her the loved companion and friend alike of husband, children, and all around her.

On the important subject of dress and fashion we cannot do better than quote: "Let people write, talk, lecture, satirize, as they may, it cannot be denied that, whatever is the prevailing mode in attire, let it intrinsically be ever so absurd, it will never look as ridiculous as another, which however convenient, comfortable, or even becoming is totally opposite in style to that generally worn." A lady's dress should be always suited to her circumstances, and varied for different occasions. The morning dress should be neat and simple, and suitable for the domestic duties that occupy the early part of the day. This dress should be changed before calling hours; but it is not in good taste to wear much jewelry except with an evening dress....

Questions to Consider

1. As you look at your grandmother's generation, how closely do you think her values and practices adhere to those presented by Mrs. Beeton's book?
2. What are the most important differences to be found between a woman such as that discussed by Mrs. Beeton in 1861 and women of your generation?

From Mark A. Kishlansky, ed., *Sources of the West*, Vol. 2, (New York: Longman, 2001), pp. 158-160.

lawyers, architects, doctors, high government officials, and occasionally professors, who tried. Once admitted, they gained many of the benefits of the aristocracy, such as access to the best schools. Because of their greater wealth and leisure time, they controlled politics, the press, and the universities.

The English Example

The model for all middle-class people everywhere was the British upper middle class of the Victorian era, named for Victoria (1837–1901), the long-reigning English queen. The Victorian upper middle class was riddled with contradictions. As Mrs. Beeton in her book on household management indicates, on the surface (see Document), the Victorians had little doubt about what was right and wrong, moral and immoral, proper and improper. Beneath this surface propriety, however, some members of the leading families pursued debauched lives marked by sexual excesses and drug addiction. One of the prime ministers of the era, William Gladstone, devoted considerable attention to "reforming" prostitutes. At the same time, the Victorian literary establishment concentrated on "cleaning up" Shakespeare's plays and toning down some parts of Gibbon's *Decline and Fall of the Roman Empire* so as not to corrupt the class of people in their employ: Britain had more than 2.5 million servants at the century's end—nearly a million people more than farmed the land.

The British middle classes spearheaded crusades against slavery, alcohol, pornography, and child labor, and for women's rights. Their efforts led to the passage of a series of reforms limiting the employment of young children, setting maximum working hours for teenagers, and regulating working conditions for women—even when the factory owners argued that such changes were bad for the country because they violated the freedom of contract between worker and employer. The churchgoing British upper middle class set the complex model of private excess and public virtue to be imitated by their peers around the world.

Changes in the Christian Churches

Changing times after 1760 posed serious challenges to the Christian churches. The Scientific Revolution and the Enlightenment ate away at the authority of traditional Catholicism and Protestantism. The churches were also reeling under the challenges posed by industrialization and urbanization. The demographic changes that resulted from rapid growth of cities forced the churches to respond to different audiences facing more difficult problems than those of an earlier, simpler age. As the middle class dominated the world of the nineteenth century, the churches not only coped but grew in influence by setting the limits of propriety and expressing concern for the less fortunate.

Among Christian elites, the extreme rationalism of the eighteenth century provoked strong opposition from those who found little warmth or comfort in the thoughts of a world dominated by natural laws and clockwork gods. The responses ranged from Scottish philosopher David Hume's (1711–1776) theory of skepticism to the works of the German philosopher Immanuel Kant (1724–1804), a professor at the University of Königsberg (KEN-igs-berg).

Kant was thoroughly antagonized by the materialistic extremes of the Enlightenment. Although he appreciated science and was dedicated to reason, he worked to shift philosophy back to a more sensible position without giving up much of its newly discovered rational basis. His theories, recorded primarily in the *Critique of Pure Reason* (1781), ushered in a new age of philosophical idealism. Kant agreed with John Locke on the role of the senses in acquiring knowledge of the material world, but he insisted that sensory experience had to be interpreted by the mind's internal nature. Thus, certain ideas—the mind's categories for sorting and recording experiences—were *a priori;* that is, they existed before the sensory experience occurred. Typical innate ideas of this sort were width, depth, beauty, cause, and God; all were understood yet none was learned directly through the senses. Kant concluded, as René Descartes had, that some truths were derived from material objects, not through the senses, but through pure reason. Moral and religious truths, such as God's existence, could not be proved by science, yet they were known to human beings as rational creatures. Reason, according to Kant, could go beyond the mere interpretation of physical realities.

Even more significant, during this time of political, social, and economic change, was a widespread emotional revival, stressing religion of the heart rather than the mind. A new mass movement, known as *Pietism,* reached full development in England after 1738, when the brothers John Wesley (1703–1791) and Charles Wesley (1708–1788), along with George Whitefield (1714–1770), began a crusade of popular preaching in the Church of England.

The Anglican Pietists discarded traditional formalism and stilted sermons in favor of a glowing religious fervor and hymn singing, producing a vast upsurge of emotional faith among the English lower classes. In February 1739, Whitefield preached to 200 miners from on top of a coal tip; in the following days, thousands of people arrived to hear his words. Breaking out of the ordinary venues for religion, the Wesleys and Whitefield were called "Methodists," at first a term of derision. Later the term came to be the respected and official name for the new movement. After John Wesley's death in 1791, the Methodists officially left the Anglican Church, which proved unable to respond to the needs of large numbers of its adherents, to become the most important independent religious force in England.

On the Continent, Lutheran Pietism, led by Philipp Spener (1635–1705) and Emanuel Swedenborg (1688–1772), responded to the needs of the people dissatisfied with the cold and formulaic state Lutheran church. Swedenborg's movement in Sweden began as an effort to reconcile science and revelation; after his death, it became increasingly emotional and mystical. Spener, in Germany, stressed Bible study, hymn singing, and powerful preaching. The Moravian movement sprang from this background. Under the sponsorship of Count Nicholaus von Zinzendorf (1700–1760), it spread to the frontiers of Europe and to the English colonies in America.

The **"Great Awakening,"** a tremendous emotional revival carried across the Atlantic from the European movements, was sustained by Moravians, Methodists, Baptists, and Quakers. It swept the colonial frontier areas of North America from Georgia to New England in the late eighteenth century. Women played prominent roles in this activity, organizing meetings and providing auxiliary services, running charities and providing religious instruction. Among the Quakers, women were often ministers and itinerant preachers. One was Jemima Wilkinson (1752–1819), leader of the Universal Friends; another was Ann Lee (1736–1784), who founded Shaker colonies in New York and New England.

The protestants endured and adapted, deeply affected by the ambitions and values of the ascending middle classes, especially in the rapidly growing Methodist Church in the United Kingdom and the United States. During the nineteenth century, middle-class protestant missionaries went forth as self-proclaimed messengers of the word of God. Once the Western states began competing for land around the globe, these missionaries often complemented national policy in their religious work. Buttressed by their complacent sense of speaking God's word, they felt justified in undermining the cultures of the peoples with whom they came in contact—especially if that was the price to be paid for "civilization" and the eternal salvation that came with it.

In England, the Christian Church received another powerful stimulus from the Oxford movement. At the beginning of the nineteenth century, a core of spiritual activists at Oxford University, including the future cardinal John Henry Newman (1801–1890), met to defend the church from the various secular and political forces that were besieging it. During the 1830s, the group split, some members remaining within the Anglican Church and others, including Newman, joining the Catholic Church. During the rest of the century, the Oxford movement brought new life to the church in England through its missionary work, participation in social concerns, and improvement of the intellectual level of the faith. Similar developments occurred across the Continent.

The Catholic Church faced a more difficult road, especially after the expulsion of Pope Pius IX (1846–1878) from Rome during the 1848 revolutions. This moderate pope became extraordinarily reactionary, especially after the unification of Italy. He issued the *Syllabus of Errors* in 1864. This document attacked critics who independently examined matters of faith and doctrine. In 1870, he called a general council of the church to proclaim the doctrine of papal infallibility, which states that when speaking *ex cathedra* (kuh-TAY-druh; "from the chair") on issues concerning religion and moral behavior, the pope cannot err.

Pius's successor, Leo XIII (1879–1903), a more flexible and less combative pope, helped bring the church into the modern age. In his encyclical *Rerum Novarum* (RE-rum no-VAR-um; "Concerning New

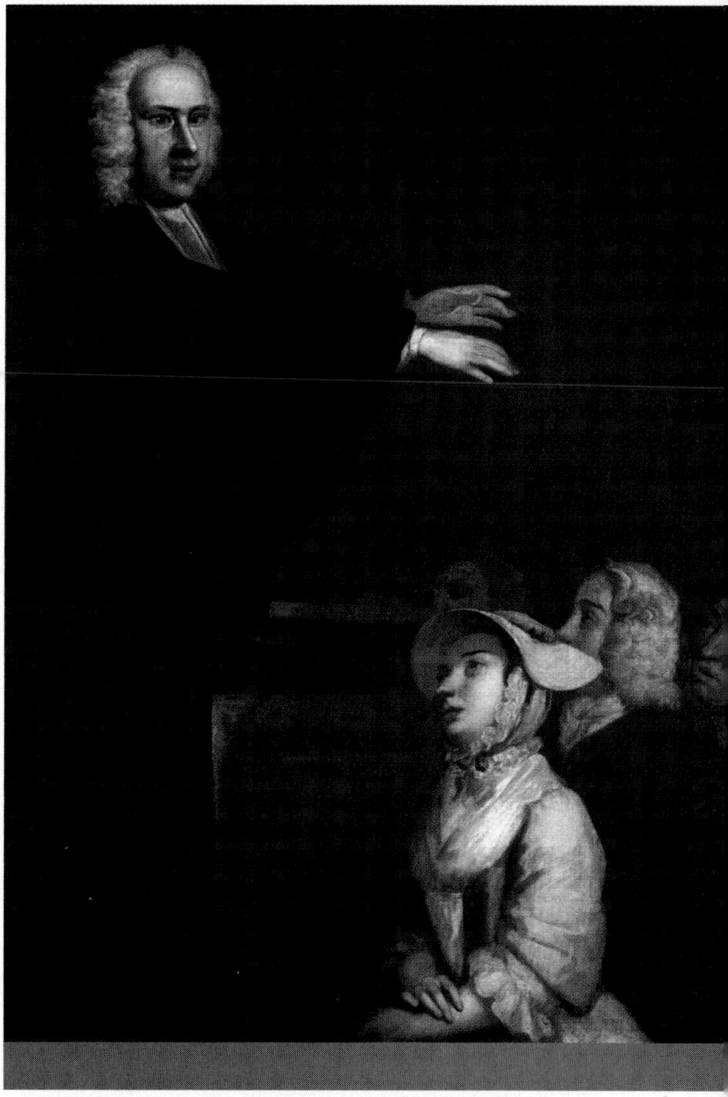

▲ Worshippers in the Church of England, the Anglican Church, in the eighteenth century expressed their faith through services of great formality, dignified language, and classical beauty. Although this may have been satisfying to the English elites, it furnished precious little comfort to the mass of Christians. New, emotional preachers such as George Whitefield went to the people, and spoke to them in an everyday language.

Great Awakening—The emotional revival of Christianity carried across the Atlantic from the European Pietist movements to the United States.

Things"), issued in 1891, Leo condemned Marxism and upheld capitalism but severely criticized the evils affecting the working classes. By pointing out some of the Christian elements of socialism, Leo placed the church on the side of the workers who were suffering the greatest ills resulting from industrialization. Leo worked to improve relations with Germany, encouraged the passage of social welfare legislation, and supported the formation of Catholic labor unions and political parties.

Humanitarian Movements

The middle classes of Europe generally embraced one of the main tenets of the Enlightenment: the concern for individual human worth. The demand for reform and the belief in human progress came to be tied to traditional Christian principles, such as human communality and God's concern for all people. Religious humanitarianism at the end of the eighteenth and throughout the nineteenth century shunned radical politics and ignored the issue of women's rights, despite the movement's strong support among women. It did, however, seek actively to relieve human suffering and ignorance among children, the urban poor, prisoners, and slaves. This combination of humanitarian objectives and Christian faith achieved remarkable results.

Notable among manifestations of the new desire to help others was the antislavery movement in England. A court case in 1774 ended slavery in that country. From then until 1807, a determined movement sought abolition of the slave trade. Its leader was William Wilberforce (1759–1833), aided by Hannah More (1745–1833) and other Anglican Evangelicals, along with many Methodists and Quakers. Wilberforce repeatedly introduced bills into the House of Commons that would have eliminated the traffic in human bodies. His efforts were rewarded in 1807 when the British trade in slaves was ended, although he and his allies had to continue the struggle for 26 more years before they could achieve abolition in the British colonies.

Religious humanitarians enforced other movements that had been pushed by the rationalist Enlightenment. For example, the movements for both legal reform and prison reform were supported by religious groups. Universal education, extolled by rationalist thinkers, also aroused interest among the denominations. The Sunday School movement, particularly in England, was a forerunner of many private and quasi-public church schools. Finally, concern for the plight of slaves, coupled with rising missionary zeal, increased popular efforts to improve conditions for indigenous peoples in European possessions overseas.

The new middle-class humanitarianism played a significant part in promoting reforms during the worst stages of industrialization. It contributed to a spirit of restlessness and discontent while encouraging independent thought, particularly as it improved education. Its successful campaign against the slave trade also struck a direct blow at the old mercantilist economies, which depended so heavily on plantation agriculture overseas. In time, the messages of the missionaries would also prove to be the most consistent force against colonialism.

Liberalism: The Middle-Class Ideology

The rising middle and commercial classes found their interests and ideals best expressed in the doctrine of **liberalism.** Liberalism affirmed the dignity of the individual and the "pursuit of happiness" as an inherent right. The ideology's roots were set firmly in the eighteenth-century soil of constitutionalism, laissez-faire economics, and representative government. Liberals thought in terms of individuals who shared basic rights, were equal before the law, and used government to gain power and carry out gradual reform. In addition, liberals believed that individuals should use their power to ensure that each person would be given the maximum amount of freedom from the state or any other external authority.

In economics, liberals followed the views of Adam Smith (1723–1790) in his *Wealth of Nations.* They believed in fair competition among individuals responding to the laws of supply and demand with a minimum of governmental regulation or interference. They agreed with Smith that society benefited more from competition among individuals motivated by their self-interest than from governmental regulation. The most intelligent and efficient individuals would gain the greatest rewards, society would prosper, and the state would be kept in its proper place, protecting life and property.

Liberals found foes from above and below as they translated their ideas into public policy, because nobles and the landed gentry still controlled most countries in Europe. Throughout the century, the middle classes fought to gain political power commensurate with their economic strength. As they were trying to increase their own influence, they sought to limit the political base of the emerging working classes. By the end of the century, the middle classes had consolidated their control over the industrialized world. This was perhaps the major political achievement of the century.

Liberals were freed from the demands of manual labor and possessed enough wealth to spend their

liberalism—An ideology founded on the freedom of the individual.

spare time in public pursuits. They had the time and leisure to work in government to control state policy to protect their own interests. They gained sufficient security that they undertook the enactment of social reforms to head off revolution. They became the dominant voices in the press and universities and gained commanding authority over public opinion. The liberals' most important contributions came in the areas of civil rights, promotion of the rule of law, government reform, and humanitarian enterprises.

The main interpreters of liberalism came from Britain, and during the first half of the century, Jeremy Bentham (1748–1832) and John Stuart Mill (1806–1873) adapted some liberal theories to modern reality. Bentham devised the concept of **utilitarianism,** or philosophical radicalism, based on the notions of utility and happiness. He connected these ideas by noting that each individual knows what is best for himself or herself and that all human institutions should be measured according to the amount of happiness they give. Bentham built on these two eighteenth-century concepts to form the "pain-and-pleasure" principle. He believed that government's function was to ensure as great a degree of individual freedom as possible, for freedom was the essential precondition of happiness. Utilitarianism in government was thus the securing of the "greatest happiness for the greatest number." If society could provide as much happiness and as little pain as possible, it would be working at maximum efficiency. Bentham recognized what later liberals would eventually espouse—that government would have to work at all levels—but he left no precise prescription as to how to proceed.

Mill spoke more to this issue. He began by noting that, in industry, the interests of the owners and workers did not necessarily coincide. He proposed the theory that government should, if necessary, pass legislation to remedy injustice, pointing out that when the actions of business owners harm the people, the state must step in to protect the citizenry. He challenged the liberal theory of minimal government interference in the economic life of the nation and pointed out that humanitarianism is more important than profit margin. He accepted the principle that maximum freedom should be permitted in business and that natural law should dictate insofar as possible the relationship of citizens.

DOCUMENT
John Stuart Mill on Enfranchisement of Women

He also pointed out that the distribution of wealth depends on the laws and customs of society and that these can be changed by human will. The rights of property and free competition, therefore, should be upheld—but within reasonable limits. Mill pointed out that the liberty of the individual is not absolute—a person has the freedom to do as he or she will as long as it does not harm another. But freedom, ultimately, has to be placed under the wider interests of society.

utilitarianism—A doctrine that desires the greatest good for the greatest number, and a balance of life in which pleasure dominates over pain.

Science, Technology, and the Second Industrial Revolution

What was the relationship between science and economics in the leading industrial states of the nineteenth century?

Until the middle of the eighteenth century, research findings generally served to satisfy the scientifically literate in the royal societies and to provoke further investigation. After 1760, however, industrialists increasingly applied the discoveries of scientists to their production. As the nineteenth century progressed, theoretical research came to have an almost immediate expression in new technologies, which led to the creation of new and profitable chemical, transportation, and electrical industries.

Medicine, Chemistry, and Physics

At the beginning of the nineteenth century, medical practices were making a slow transition away from the indiscriminate use of leeches and bleeding. In the

	Scientific Advances
1830–1833	Sir Charles Lyell's *Principles of Geology* popularizes James Hutton's concept of geological time
1847	First law of thermodynamics
1859	Darwin publishes *On the Origin of Species*
1869	Dmitri Mendeleev classifies all known elements into the periodic table
1870–1895	Louis Pasteur makes advances in bacteriology
1880–1910	Robert Koch places immunology on firm footing
1876	Dynamo perfected, based on work of Michael Faraday
1896	Pierre and Marie Curie discover radium
1900–1910	Sir Ernest Rutherford advances electron theory

▲ Marie Curie, born Manya Sklodowska in Warsaw, Poland, shared with her husband, Pierre, the 1903 Nobel Prize in physics for their work on radioactivity, a term Marie coined in 1898. She won the 1911 Nobel Prize in chemistry for her discovery of radium and polonium and isolation of pure radium. Irène Curie, Marie and Pierre's daughter, shared with her husband, Frédéric Joliot, the 1935 Nobel Prize in chemistry for their work in synthesizing new radioactive isotopes of various elements.

1840s, physicians began to use ether and chloroform to reduce pain during operations. The Scottish surgeon Joseph Lister (1827–1912) developed new antiseptic practices that made major advances against the spread of infection. By 1900, fairly sophisticated and much safer surgical procedures were available.

Probably the most important single advance came with the substantiation of the germ theory of disease by Louis Pasteur (PAS-tur; 1822–1895) and Robert Koch (1843–1910). During his search for a cure to anthrax—a disease that in the late 1870s destroyed more than 20 percent of the sheep in France—Pasteur established the principle that the injection of a mild form of disease bacterium causes the body to form antibodies that prevent the vaccinated individual from getting the severe form of the particular disease. Koch discovered the specific organisms that caused 11 diseases, including tuberculosis. The work of Pasteur and Koch placed the sciences of bacteriology and immunology on a firm footing and gave promise that the end of such deadly diseases as typhoid and smallpox might be in sight.

Modern chemistry gained its foundations during the nineteenth century, founded on the atomic theory advanced by an English Quaker schoolmaster, John Dalton (1766–1844). In 1869 Russian chemist Dmitri Mendeleev (dmeet-REE MEN-de-LE-ef; 1834–1907) drew up a "periodic table," in which he classified all known elements according to their weights and properties. From gaps in this table, chemists were able to deduce the existence of undiscovered elements. Other researchers made advances in the field of nutrition and discovered the significance of vitamins. Biochemical research threw light on the presence and function of the ductless (endocrine) glands. Chemotherapy advanced with the discovery of a chemical that could destroy the syphilis bacterium and with procedures that would lead to the discovery of sulfa drugs, penicillin, and other antibiotics.

Revolutionary strides in physics were taken in the areas of electricity and thermodynamics, the first law of which was formulated in 1847. Michael Faraday (1791–1867) prepared the way for the dynamo, a device that made possible changes in communications, the transmission of current over long distances, and the development of the electric motor. The Scottish scientist James Clerk Maxwell (1831–1879) and the German Heinrich Hertz (1857–1894) conducted basic research into the nature of electromagnetic phenomena such as light, radiant heat, and ultraviolet radiation.

Pierre Curie (1859–1906) and his wife, Marie Curie (1867–1934), made major strides toward the discovery of the X-ray and radioactivity. When they extracted radium from uranium ore in 1896, the scientific world became aware of the strength of radioactivity. Marie Curie was the first person to be awarded two Nobel Prizes, one in physics and one in chemistry.

At the beginning of the twentieth century, the British physicist Ernest Rutherford (1871–1937) helped develop electron theory. It had been postulated that the atom contains particles known as electrons. Rutherford contributed the idea that each atom has a central particle, or nucleus, that is positively charged and separate from the negatively charged electrons. These discoveries destroyed one of the foundations of traditional physics, that matter is indivisible and continuous.

Darwin

In the mid-nineteenth century, Charles Darwin (1809–1892) formulated a major scientific theory in

On the Origin of Species by Means of Natural Selection (1859). This theory of evolution, stating that all complex organisms developed from simple forms through the operation of natural causes, challenged traditionalist Christian beliefs about creation and altered views of life on earth. The theory contended that no species is fixed and changeless. Classical thinkers first stated this view, and contemporary philosophers, such as Hegel, had used the concept of evolutionary change. In the century before Darwin, other research supported the concept of change, both biological and social.

On Darwin

Darwin built on the work of Sir Charles Lyell (1797–1875) and Jean-Baptiste Lamarck (1744–1829). Lyell's three-volume *Principles of Geology* (1830–1833) confirmed the views of the Scottish geologist James Hutton (1726–1797), who stated that the earth developed through natural rather than supernatural causes. Lyell helped popularize the notion of geological time operating over a vast span of years. This understanding is essential to the acceptance of any theory of biological evolution, based as it is on changes in species over many thousands of generations. Lamarck, a naturalist, argued that every organism tends to develop new organs to adapt to the changing conditions of its environment. He theorized that these changes are transmitted by heredity to the descendants, which are thereafter changed in structural form.

Though he had originally studied medicine at Edinburgh and prepared for the ministry at Cambridge University, Darwin lost interest in both professions and became a naturalist when he was in his twenties. From 1831 to 1836 he studied the specimens he had collected while on a 5-year surveying expedition aboard the ship *Beagle,* which had sailed along the coast of South America and among the Galápagos Islands. The works of his predecessors, in addition to questions that he had about the theories presented in Malthus's "Essay on Population," helped him define his own theory. When Darwin's book finally appeared, it changed many basic scientific and social assumptions.

In his revolutionary work, Darwin constructed an explanation of how life evolves that negated the literal interpretation of the Bible taught in most Christian churches:

Species have been modified, during a long course of descent, chiefly through the natural selection of numerous successive, slight, favorable variations; aided in an important manner by the direct action of external conditions, and by variations which seem to us in our ignorance to arise spontaneously.[3]

His explanation radically affected the views of the scientific community about the origin and evolution of life on the planet. The hypothesis, in its simplified form, states that all existing plant and animal species are descended from earlier and, generally speaking, more primitive forms. The direct effects of the environment cause species to develop through the inheritance of minute differences in individual structures. As the centuries pass, the more adaptable, stronger species live on, while the weaker, less flexible species die out: the **"survival of the fittest."** Furthermore, a species may also be changed by the cumulative working of sexual selection, which Darwin regarded as the "most powerful means of changing the races of man."

After the announcement of Darwin's theories, other scientists, such as the German biologist August Weismann (VAIS-mahn; 1834–1914) and the Austrian priest Gregor Mendel (1822–1884), worked along similar lines to explore the genetic relationships among living organisms. Weismann proved that acquired characteristics cannot be inherited. Mendel's investigations into the laws of heredity, based on his experiments with the combining of different varieties of garden peas, proved especially valuable in the scientific breeding of plants and animals and demonstrated that the evolution of different species was more complex than Darwin had imagined. Based on their work, biologists hypothesized that there are what would be later called *chromosomes* that carry the characteristics of an organism. Darwin had hinted at and now further research supported the mutation theory, which states that sudden and unpredictable changes within a chromosome can be transmitted by heredity to produce new species. Scientists began to work with the very fundamental building blocks of life and established the groundwork of contemporary biotechnical research.

Technological Growth and Advances

Another reason for the Continent's economic emergence was a wide range of new technologies that took advantage of the scientific discoveries made during the century. Continental competitors, especially the Germans, began with state-of-the-art factories that allowed them to out-produce Britain, whose older factories were less productive.

Electricity

The basic change in the second phase of industrialization was the use of electricity in all aspects of life. Scientists had discovered electricity's basic principles a century earlier, but it was difficult to generate and transmit power across long distances. When the first dependable dynamo, which changed energy from mechanical into electrical form, was perfected in 1876,

---

survival of the fittest—The notion that in the evolution of species the more adaptable species live on, while the weaker, less fit die out. Later Social Darwinists came to apply this idea to human society.

it became possible to generate electricity almost anywhere. Inventors such as the American Thomas A. Edison (1847–1931) began to use the new resource in industry, transportation, entertainment, and the home. Humanity had finally found a source of power that could be transmitted and used easily. The British took the lead in applying electricity to home use. The Germans made the most advanced application of electric technology to industry.

Engines

Another fundamental change came in the use of gas and oil in the newly devised internal combustion engine. The use of steam power was limited by its appetite for huge amounts of fuel and its sheer bulk; the internal combustion engine proved to be a more fuel-efficient alternative to steam-powered engines. Gottlieb Daimler (GOT-leeb DAIM-ler; 1834–1900) perfected the internal combustion engine used in most automobiles today. In 1892, Rudolf Diesel invented the engine that bears his name. It burned fuel instead of harnessing the explosions that drove the Daimler engine.

These new developments led directly to the search for and use of petroleum and the beginning of the passenger car industry. By 1914, the production of cars was a key part of the Italian, German, French, and American economies. Automobile manufacturing called for a number of spin-off industries such as tire, ball-bearing, and windshield manufacturing—the list extends to hundreds of items. Leaving aside the passenger car's economic contribution, the world's cities and people felt the complex impact of this new form of transportation, with consequences, such as expanding the range of an individual's world and increased noise levels and pollution, that changed the character of urban areas.

Laborsaving Devices

Other new machines also changed the quality of life. Bicycles became commonplace in the 1890s, as did sewing machines, cameras, and typewriters, to name a few items. Never before had people had the ability to transform ideas almost instantly into products accessible to the average person. This was another dividend of industrialization and a symbol of a rapidly changing Europe.

Cultural Responses to the Age

What role does the culture-consuming middle class play in artistic and musical creativity?

The increasing wealth and leisure time generated by industrialization vastly enlarged the number of consumers of culture. Artists made the transition from responding to the tastes of the noble courts to the new demands of middle-class audiences attending concerts in vast new halls and viewing art in public galleries. However, these transitions were not always universally accepted. In the first part of the century, there were three major currents that dominated the cultural scene: conservatism, Romanticism, and nationalism. By the end of middle of the century another current, realism, came to fore.

Conservatism

In the nineteenth century, **conservatism** was an important cultural and political force. The reaction to the French Revolution, especially as expressed by Edmund Burke (1729–1797), provided the basis of nineteenth-century European conservatism. There were many thinkers who did not believe in the revolutionary slogan of "liberty, equality, and brotherhood." They did not believe that liberation could be gained by destroying the historically evolved traditions of the old regime. Freedom could be found only in order and be maintained solely by continual reference to precedents. A legitimate political, social, and cultural life needed the framework of tradition to survive.

The conservatives did not have faith in the individual, nor did they share the Romantics' love of pure emotion and spontaneity in life or in art. Beginning with Burke and continuing through the first part of the nineteenth century to the Frenchman Joseph de Maistre (zho-zef de MYST-ruh; 1753–1821), the Russian Nicholas Karamzin (ka-ram-ZEEM; 1766–1826), and the Spaniard Juan Donoso-Cortés (do-NO-so kor-TEZ; 1809–1853), there was a body of intellectuals who found strength, not weakness, in the church and monarchy of the old regime; danger, not liberation, in the nationalistic movements; and degradation, not exaltation, in the new Romantic art forms. The conservatives were backward-looking, finding their standards and values in the proven events of the past, not in the untried reforms and emotions of the present.

Romanticism

The Romantic movement unleashed sensitivities that played a major role in forming the literary, artistic, and musical changes of the nineteenth century. The emphasis that **Romanticism** places on the individual is apparent in the novels of Johann Wolfgang von Goethe (GEHR-te; 1749–1832) and Friedrich Schiller

---

conservatism—An intellectual movement based on a reaction to the excesses of the French Revolution.

Romanticism—An artistic movement emphasizing the importance of the individual emotional response as contrasted to the measured standards of classicism.

(1759–1805). Goethe's novel *The Sorrows of Young Werther* (1774) tells the story of a sensitive, feeling, outcast young man who kills himself with the pistol of his rival after failing to gain his true love. Schiller's play *Wilhelm Tell* (1804) describes the heroic struggle of the Swiss patriots in their drive for independence against tyranny.

Unlike the brittle wit and irony of the authors of the Enlightenment, such as Voltaire, these stories were sentimental and emotional descriptions of people, acting in response to overwhelming and impossible social or political dilemmas, who did what their hearts told them was right. It was better to experience a moving young death or to rise up against impossible odds than to look dispassionately and rationally at life.

The Romantic movement's emphasis on the individual created among some of its participants a truly picturesque lifestyle. For every Victor Hugo (1802–1885) who lived a long, full, excessive life, there were artists, writers, and musicians from London to Moscow who "burned the candle at both ends" in short, passionate, creative lives. To most Romantics, such as the poet John Keats, it was better to live briefly and intensely, according to the commandments of the heart, than to die old, fat, rich, bored, lecherous, and bourgeois.

The novel came into prominence in the eighteenth century, but it became the dominant literary form of the nineteenth. Writers such as Victor Hugo and Sir Walter Scott (1771–1832) mined the myths and legends of France and Britain, respectively, to write vastly successful works for the ever-expanding middle-class audiences. Hugo's novel, *Notre Dame de Paris* (1831), better known in English as *The Hunchback of Notre Dame,* and Scott's *Ivanhoe* (1819) detailed their nations' past so effectively that both books were imitated, and sequels and imitations continued to appear into the twentieth century. By 1850, a variety of social and psychological themes challenged the historical novel, along with the gently critical works of William Makepeace Thackeray (1811–1863), who, through deft characterizations in works such as *Vanity Fair* (1848), poked fun at the *nouveau riche* (new-VOH reesh), or "newly rich," social climbers who dominated society.

Poets responded far more pointedly to the challenges thrown down by the Napoleonic and Industrial Revolutions. In 1798 two young British poets, William Wordsworth (1770–1850) and Samuel Taylor Coleridge (1772–1834), published a volume of verse called *Lyrical Ballads.* Wordsworth wrote in the preface that poetry was "the spontaneous overflow of powerful feelings recollected in tranquility." Wordsworth sought to express "universal passions" and the "entire world of nature" through simple, unladen vocabulary. He stressed the intuitive and emotional contemplation of nature as a path to creativity. In an 1802 sonnet, he expressed his love of nature and country:

> *... Oft have I looked round*
> *With joy in Kent's green vales; but never found*
> *Myself so satisfied in heart before.*
> *Europe is yet in bonds; but let that pass*
> *Thought for another moment. Thou are free,*
> *My Country! and 'tis joy enough and pride*
> *For one hour's perfect bliss, to tread the grass*
> *Of England once again....*[4]

In *Kubla Khan* (1797) and *Rime of the Ancient Mariner* (1798), Coleridge pursued the supernatural and exotic facets of life. His vivid descriptions of distant subjects and nonrational elements of human life served as the precedent for later artists as they examined the areas of fantasy, symbolism, dream states, and the supernatural. The French poet Alphonse de Lamartine (al-FONS de la-mar-TEEN; 1790–1869) led the way in making the transition from classicism to Romanticism and had an impact across the Continent.

The British poets George Gordon, Lord Byron, (1788–1824) and Percy Bysshe Shelley (1792–1822) rebelled against the constraints of their society and expressed their contempt for the standards of their time through their lives and works. Byron gloried in the cult of freedom. When the Greeks rose up against the Turks in 1821, he joined their cause. He died of fever soon after his arrival. Shelley believed passionately that human perfectibility was possible only through complete freedom of thought and action. On the Continent, Heinrich Heine (HAI-nuh; 1797–1856), who was, like Byron, a cutting satirist, and like Shelley, a splendid lyricist, shared their romantic ideals. Heine is best remembered for his *Buch der Lieder* (book der LEE-der), songs that were put to music by Franz Schubert (1797–1828) and Felix Mendelssohn (MEN-del-son; 1809–1847).

John Keats (1795–1821) was neither social critic nor rebel; for him the worship and pursuit of beauty were of prime importance. In *Ode on a Grecian Urn* (1820), he states:

> *"Beauty is truth, truth beauty"—that is all*
> *Ye know on earth, and all ye need to know*[5]

Keats believed that the inherent beauty of an object—not some classical formula or social function—justified its existence.

Alexander Pushkin (1799–1837), Russia's greatest poet, liberated his nation's language from the foreign molds and traditions forced on it in the eighteenth century. Pushkin's work served as a transition between the classical and Romantic ages, and he helped to create a truly Russian literature, one that expressed profound depth of his love for his country.

	Greats of the Romantic Era
Literature	George Gordon, Lord Byron (1788–1824)
	Samuel Taylor Coleridge (1772–1834)
	Heinrich Heine (1797–1856)
	Victor Hugo (1802–1885)
	John Keats (1795–1821)
	Alexander Pushkin (1799–1837)
	Sir Walter Scott (1771–1832)
	Percy Bysshe Shelley (1792–1822)
	William Wordsworth (1770–1850)
Art and Architecture	John Constable (1776–1837)
	Eugène Delacroix (1798–1863)
	Joseph M. W. Turner (1775–1851)
	Eugène Viollet-le-Duc (1814–1879)
Music	Ludwig van Beethoven (1770–1827)
	Hector Berlioz (1803–1869)
	Felix Mendelssohn (1809–1847)
	Franz Schubert (1797–1828)
	Robert Schumann (1810–1856)
	Carl Maria von Weber (1786–1826)

The age of change brought new tendencies to painting as well as to other art forms. There is a great contrast between the precise draftsmanship and formal poses of the painters who worked in the classical style and the unrestrained use of color and new effects of the Romantic artists. Some artists, such as the French master Eugène Delacroix (de-la-CKWAH; 1798–1863), were met with critical resistance. His *Massacre of Chios,* a flamboyant work painted in 1824 upon receiving news of the Turks' slaying of Christians on Chios, was panned by conservative critics as the "massacre of painting."

Less flamboyant but equally part of the Romantic transition are the works of the British painter John Constable (1776–1837). Deeply influenced by Romanticism's emphasis on nature, Constable was in some respects the originator of the modern school of landscape painting. His choice of colors was revolutionary—he used greens freely in his landscape, an innovation considered radical by critics, who favored brown tones. Constable's countryman, Joseph M. W. Turner (1775–1851), sparked controversy with his use of vivid colors and dramatic perspectives that gave him the ability to portray powerful atmospheric effects.

Around 1830, Romanticism's fascination with the medieval period led to a shift from Greek and Roman architectural models to a Gothic revival, in which towers and arches became the chief characteristics. Sir Walter Scott's romances played a major role in this development, and even his house at Abbotsford was designed along Scottish baronial lines. In France, Eugène Viollet-le-Duc (vee-o-LAY-le-DOOK; 1814–1879) spearheaded the movement by writing, teaching, and restoring properties under the aegis of the Commission on Historical Monuments. For the next few decades, architecture was dominated by styles that looked back especially to the Gothic and Rococo styles, which were sometimes combined in what some consider aesthetically disastrous presentations.

Nationalism

The writers, musicians, artists, and philosophers caught up in the Romantic movement at the end of the eighteenth century and the beginning of the nineteenth rebelled against the Classicism and the cold logic of the Enlightenment. Instead, they stressed an individual's past, uniqueness, emotions, and creativity as the basis for life. The Romantics investigated history, folklore, linguistics, and myths to define their own identity. They revived the Scandinavian sagas, the French *Chanson de Roland* (shan-SOHN de ro-LAN), and the German *Nibelungen* (KNEE-be-lun-gen) stories. During a time of uncertainty, change, and stress it was both comforting and uplifting to look to the past, even an imagined one. The roots of **nationalism,** the most powerful and longest-lasting of the new ideologies, thus was to be found in Romanticism.

Unique conditions in different parts of Europe produced different variants of nationalism. However, common to them all was a populace consciously embracing a common land, language, folklore, history, enemies, and religion. These elements are the ingredients of the nation's and the individual's identity and pull the members into an indivisible unity. Nationalism can exist where there is no state structure and can thrive in a state where a minority nation is repressed. Nationalism, unlike patriotism, does not need flags and uniforms. All that is needed is a historical and emotional unity around which the members of the nation can gather, a unity that defines a shared identity and entails the total cultural and political loyalty

nationalism—A political movement based on shared land, language, folklore, history, and religion.

of the individual to the nation. (See *Global Issues—Location and Identity* on page 688 to learn about the role geography has played in nationalism and cultural identity throughout world history.)

After 1789, this new force dominated the cultural and political activities of France. The spirit of brotherhood projected by the French Revolution united the French people. On the Continent, Romantics reacted against the French and Napoleonic dominance and helped bring people together in nationalistic opposition, especially in Germany. Georg Wilhelm Friedrich Hegel built on the movement in his lectures and writings at the University of Berlin. For Hegel, history was a process of evolution in which the supremacy of primitive instincts would give way to the reign of clear reason and freedom—the "world spirit"—that would be manifested in the state. The research and writings of the Germans Johann Gottfried von Herder (1744–1803) and brothers Jacob (1785–1863) and Wilhelm Grimm (1786–1859) provided historical support and linguistic bases for the Slavic nationalist movements. Herder conceived of a world spirit, *Weltgeist* (VELT-gaist), made up of component parts of the various national spirits, *Volkgeist* (FOLK-gaist). Each of these national spirits was seen as playing an essential role in the world process, and Herder believed that the Slavs were soon to make an important contribution. The Grimm brothers' philological work aided the literary and linguistic revivals of many Slavic groups.

Romantic nationalism in Britain reacted strongly against the human costs of industrialization and the pretensions of the new merchant classes. It focused on the medieval roots of Britain, as well as on movements such as phil-hellenism (the love of ancient Greece). In France, Spain, Italy, Russia, and other parts of the Continent, the Romantic movement made important contributions to the growth of national identity. In Italy, for example, Giuseppe Mazzini (matz-zee-nee; 1805–1872) and Alessandro Manzoni (1785–1873) played important roles in the unification struggle of the country. Romantic nationalism was also found in the writings of history by Leopold von Ranke (1775–1886) in Germany, Jules Michelet (mish-e-LAY; 1798–1874) in France, Frantisek Palacky (1798–1876) in Bohemia-Moravia, and George Bancroft (1800–1891) in the United States.

Realism

Around 1850, artists and writers began responding to the new age in the realist movement. Artists, especially the French, who were among the most notable early proponents of **realism,** focused on the concrete aspects of life. This led, at the end of the century, to experiments with a range of new forms and structures in the modernist movement (see Chapter 27). At the same time that these movements were developing, a huge new group of consumers, the lower and middle classes, were becoming participants in the new mass culture. They might find little to admire in the fine arts, but through their buying power and their numbers, they would come to have a great effect on large parts of the creative community.

In literature and art, as in politics, realism replaced Romanticism after mid-century. To the realists, it was no longer enough to be true to one's instincts and emotions. Their job was to faithfully observe and graphically report all aspects of life in a dispassionate, precise manner so as to depict individuals in their proper setting. In this age of change there was much for writers and artists to portray, and a much larger public now had the leisure time and political interests to respond to their work.

The trend toward the realistic novel had been foreshadowed in the work of Honoré de Balzac (1799–1850), the author of a 90-volume tour de force, *La Comédie Humaine* (la ko-MAY-dee OO-men; *The Human Comedy*), which depicts French life in the first half of the nineteenth century. A master of characterization, Balzac described life in such detail that his work is a valuable reference on social history for present-day scholars. Gustave Flaubert (floh-BEHR; 1821–1880) was the first French realist writer. His masterpiece, *Madame Bovary* (1856), exhaustively described how the boredom of a young romantic provincial wife led her into adultery, excess, and ultimately suicide. Émile Zola (1840–1902) was the leader of the French naturalist school and a prolific author best known for his novel *Germinal* (1885). He also played a major role as the most influential author of his time by mobilizing French public opinion in 1898 to move against the injustices done to Captain Alfred Dreyfus (see Chapter 23) in his open letter to the French president, which opens *"J'accuse..."* (zha-KEUZ; "I accuse").

British novelist Charles Dickens (1812–1870) protested social conditions in his novels characterizing the everyday life of the middle classes and the poor. In such works as *Oliver Twist* (1838), *Dombey and Son* (1847–1848), and *Hard Times* (1854), he describes some of the worst excesses of industrial expansion and social injustice. Later, Thomas Hardy (1840–1928), in novels such as *Far from the Madding Crowd* (1874), dealt with the struggle—almost always a losing one—of the individual against the impersonal, pitiless forces of the natural and social environment.

American writers such as Henry James (1843–1916), Samuel Clemens, writing under the name of Mark Twain (1835–1910), and Harriet Beecher Stowe

---

realism—An art form focused on the concrete details of real life.

Location and Identity

Why do people use location to identify themselves?

▲ Two Westerners on horseback with Mount Fuji and telegraph wires in the background, woodblock print, Hiroshige Utagawa, 1873.

"East is East, and West is West, and never the twain shall meet."

Ballad of East and West, Rudyard Kipling, 1889

Though Kipling's long ballad goes on to reject that assertion, most Europeans and Americans ("West") and perhaps most Asians ("East") of his day would have accepted it. Of course, it is purely arbitrary to designate one area as "West" and one as "East" on a spherical earth rotating on a north-south axis, but historians, politicians, philosophers, generals, and clerics have all done so for millennia. People have long found ways to distinguish themselves from people in other places or even from people in their own backyard, and location has been one of the ways they have done so.

When the line-drawing seems to fail—for example, Morocco, often considered part of the Middle East, is actually west of London, and Japanese maps in the nineteenth century designated the United States as the East because it lies to Japan's east—the East then gets designated as a cultural place rather than one defined by location. But whose culture? Some would say that the culture of the rulers determines the country's identity. But this can be misleading. For instance, largely Hindu (and therefore Eastern) India did not become Middle Eastern under the Muslim Mughals or Western under British rule. Maps in the twentieth century can be equally confusing. They often painted colonies in the hues of their imperialist rulers, which seems to suggest countries could be culturally relocated by a change in rulers. Is Australia Western because its settlers mostly came from Europe, even as its leaders are currently trying to join the lucrative Asian/Eastern economic zone? Are the mostly Christian Philippines Eastern or Western?

For many centuries Europeans associated continents with the cardinal directions. Asia was East, Europe was West, and Africa was South. Later, America was sometimes considered a "new" world and therefore off the directional map, and sometimes part of the West. At first glance, continents seem to be a helpful way to divide the world into areas with some internal similarities. But the continental framework also has some inconsistencies. The Panama Canal now divides North and South America and the Suez Canal divides Africa from Eurasia. Both of those canals were dug through solid ground that had been traversed by people for millennia. And what about Eurasia? If continents have been viewed, since the eighteenth century, as "large space[s] of dry land comprehending many countries all joined together, without any separation by water,"[1] Europe and Asia are no more independent continents than the world's only "subcontinent" of India.

During the Cold War, East and West took on different meanings. The Communist anthem claimed, "The East [was] Red." A line so rigid it was called "an iron curtain" supposedly divided East from West. Many countries did not fit into those categories, however, calling themselves part of the "non-aligned movement." In time, the wealthy capitalist countries, many but not all allied with the United States, came to be called the First World; the Communist countries aligned with the Soviet Union, the Second World; and all others, including Communist China, the Third World. The Second World ended with the break-up of the Soviet Union, and the First and Third Worlds are more commonly referred to as Developed Countries and Developing Countries or by the cardinal directions North and South, with most of the old Second World countries assigned to the North. But many are uncomfortable with these terms, too.

The cardinal directions do not represent the only way that location has been used to identify people and cultures. Until the late nineteenth century, for example, Chinese rulers viewed the world as centered in China, which is reflected in the name for the Chinese realm, Central Kingdom. Chinese maps paralleled this politically inspired worldview. (Religiously inspired worldviews differed in China; India was placed at the center of maps by Chinese Buddhists.) The Chinese view explained what was essentially a power relationship in terms of the ethical virtue of the emperor. Unlike Europeans, the Chinese, who divided the world into cultured and barbarian spheres, did not ascribe these qualities to the cardinal directions East and West. Instead, distance in any direction would lessen the ethical influence of the Chinese center, which was located in the emperor's court.[2] Early modern Indian geographers centered their maps on India. One Indian geographer designated Europe, at his map's margin, as "England, France, and other hat-wearing islands."[3] Medieval Islamic mapmakers centered their world on Dar al-Islam (abode of Islam), with the holy city of Mecca at its heart. Crossing this huge stretch of territory from southern Spain to China, starting in 1325, North African adventurer Ibn Battuta found recognizable Islamic culture throughout the region.[4]

Europeans, however, were more likely to use cardinal directions to define the world's areas. These directions were conflated with cultural characteristics, most of which have been shown by historians to be inaccurate. Thus, geography became destiny—if you're in the West, you must have certain characteristics, and if you're in the East, you have a different set of cultural behaviors. This was constantly inverted as well. When those doing the defining—the "West"—decided a country had cultural characteristics that were undesirable, it could be excluded from the West or Europe by being redefined as Eastern. Even the historical insistence on calling Europe a "continent" when it met none of the usual requirements for that label was a way of setting it aside as a place with a supposedly homogenous culture, distinct from those elsewhere in Africa or the rest of Eurasia. That culture was "Western."

The ancient Greeks had divided the world they knew into three parts, which loosely corresponded to what we call Europe, Asia, and North Africa. They disagreed, however, on the boundaries between those parts. Before 500 B.C.E., the Greeks used the term "Europe" to refer to Greece and the term "Asia" for all foreign lands other than Europe. They soon expanded Europe to include the land north and west of Greece and separated "Africa" from "Asia." Later, that three-part division was given a religious underpinning when Christians asserted that God had divided the world in three parts, giving one to each son of Noah.[5] From the eleventh-century split in Christendom between a Rome-based Catholic Church and a Constantinople-based Orthodox Church, the terms *West* and *East* were increasingly used for Europe and Asia, respectively. While the East was originally a small area in the eastern Mediterranean, it grew in the popular imagination as the Europeans learned more about India and later East Asia. Seeking wealth and riches, spices and textiles, Europeans looked eastward. The East was seen as different, but not necessarily inferior.

Looking for access to the East took Columbus to a "new" world, neither Western nor Eastern but a hybrid—a "West Indies" inhabited by "Indians." In the next several centuries, European countries established relationships of imperialism over many peoples in Asia, Africa, the Americas, and Australia. But it was concerning Asians that Europeans of the nineteenth century articulated theories of Western superiority. The others were viewed as barbarians, and European dominance did not seem to need explanation. Later, as categories like "Third World" and "South" replaced "East," so-called Eastern cultural characteristics were transferred to Africa or South America.

The East came to be seen as the opposite of the West.[6] This was expressed in a series of stereotyped comparisons. For example, where the East contained countries whose people valued irrationality, the West esteemed rationality. Where the West promoted democracy, the East was run by autocratic rulers whose role derived from what was called, as late as the mid-twentieth century, an "Asiatic Mode of Production."[7] While the West was dynamic and thus had a history, Asia was stagnant and unchanging; and even if it had had a history in the murky past, scholars like Karl Marx and G. W. F. Hegel contended that it no longer did. While Europe enjoyed a temperate climate, permitting it to embark on industrialization, the East did not. Many outside of Europe or the United States also absorbed these stereotypes. In the late nineteenth century, Fukuzawa Yukichi, an advocate of modernizing Japan, accepted these supposed characteristics as natural and called on the Japanese to "leave Asia" and join the West. Though scholars have debunked all these notions as having no grounding in historical fact, they continue to influence the meanings of East and West.

A few additional categories were developed in the twentieth century. The Middle East (East of what? The Middle of what?) came into being as a category for military planning during World War II. Its boundaries are as shifting and political as those of Europe and Asia. Africa is also subjected to a number of different slicings—is North Africa separate from sub-Saharan Africa?

Locational designations, groupings by political allegiance, classification by assumed cultural characteristics, and organization by stages of economic development all influence each other. Assumed cultural characteristics today lead to the redrawing of geographic lines in places like the Balkans, where the break-up of Yugoslavia in the 1990s produced warfare over ethnically defined borders. But location may also lead to our ascribing cultural characteristics or history to a country that never even had that history. North-South and East-West are always relative categories and reflect power relations in addition to designations of cultural identity.

Questions

1. Why do people define their world geographically?
2. How are the ways in which people define locations related to politics or power?
3. Do nations' identities change when their rulers, ideology, or dominant religions change?

	Major Writers and Composers at Mid-Nineteenth Century
Literature	Honoré de Balzac (1799–1850)
	Anton Chekhov (1860–1904)
	Charles Dickens (1812–1870)
	Feodor Dostoevski (1821–1881)
	Gustave Flaubert (1821–1880)
	Thomas Hardy (1840–1928)
	Henrik Ibsen (1828–1906)
	Henry James (1843–1916)
	Harriet Beecher Stowe (1811–1896)
	Leo Tolstoy (1828–1910)
	Mark Twain (Samuel Clemens) (1835–1910)
Music	Johannes Brahms (1833–1897)
	Anton Bruckner (1824–1896)
	Frédéric Chopin (1810–1849)
	Anton Dvořák (1841–1904)
	Gustav Mahler (1860–1911)
	Modest Mussorgsky (1835–1881)
	Sergei Rachmaninov (1873–1943)
	Jean Sibelius (1865–1957)
	Bedrich Smetana (1824–1884)
	Peter Ilich Tchaikovsky (1840–1893)
	Richard Wagner (1813–1883)
	Giuseppi Verdi (1813–1901)

(1811–1896) made important contributions to the realist tradition. James tried to catch the "atmosphere of the mind" through an almost clinical examination of the most subtle details. Clemens, better known by his pseudonym, Mark Twain, used humor and accurate descriptions of the American Midwest and Far West to underscore social injustice. Stowe's detailed novel *Uncle Tom's Cabin* (1852) captured American hearts and minds and strongly bolstered the antislavery movement.

The Russian novelists Leo Tolstoy (1828–1910) and Feodor Dostoevski (dahs-tah-YEV-skee; 1821–1881) produced the most developed presentation of the realistic novel. Tolstoy stripped every shred of glory and glamour from war in *War and Peace* (1869) and gave an analytical description of the different levels of society. Dostoevski devised a chilling, detailed view of life in St. Petersburg in *Crime and Punishment* (1866), and his *Brothers Karamazov* (1880) offered a painstaking analysis of Russian life during a period of change brought about by the Great Reforms of 1861 (see Chapter 23).

Drama was deeply influenced by realism, as can be seen in the works of the Norwegian Henrik Ibsen (1828–1906), the Irishman George Bernard Shaw (1856–1950), and the Russian Anton Chekhov (1860–1904). *A Doll's House* (1879), Ibsen's understated yet tension-filled work, assailed marriage without love as immoral. Although his characters are not heroic in their dimensions, Ibsen captures the quiet desperation of normal life, and the despair that forces the heroine to leave her husband at the end of the play, in "the door slam heard 'round the world." Shaw used satire and nuance to shock the British public into reassessing conventional attitudes. Chekhov's *The Cherry Orchard* (1904) dramatized the changes wrought by emancipation of the serfs on the lives of a gentry family. Lacking obvious plot and action, the play depends on day-to-day detail to build a subtle and exhaustive social portrait.

Beethoven and His Successors

Music did not experience the shift in style from Romantic to realistic that art and literature did. Ludwig van Beethoven (1770–1827) served as a bridge between the classical and Romantic periods. However, the regularity of the minuet, the precision of the sonata, and the elegant but limited small chamber orchestra—all forms Beethoven mastered—were not sufficient to express the powerful forces of the age. A comparison of his relatively measured and restrained First Symphony with the compelling and driven Fifth or the lyrical, nature-dominated Sixth dramatically reveals the changes in the style of his compositions over the course of his career. Beethoven was the ultimate Romantic—a lover of nature, passionate champion of human rights, fighter for freedom. Beethoven spoke to the heart of humanity through his music, especially his magnificent Ninth Symphony, the "Ode to Joy."

The momentum of the forces that Beethoven set in motion carried through the entire century. Carl Maria von Weber (1786–1826), Hector Berlioz (BER-lee-oz; 1803–1869), Robert Schumann (1810–1856), along with Felix Mendelssohn and Franz Schubert (1797–1828), made major contributions to the musical repertoire of Europe by mid-century. Thereafter, Johannes Brahms (1833–1897), Anton Bruckner (1824–1896), and Gustav Mahler (1860–1911) made lyrical advances in composition and presentation. Each made unique use of the large symphony orchestra, and Brahms also composed three exquisite string quartets along with his four massive symphonies.

In addition, many composers turned to their native folk music and dances for inspiration. Beethoven had used native themes, as Schubert and Schumann did in Austria and Germany. Frédéric Chopin (SHO-pan; 1810–1849), even though he did most of his work in France, drew heavily on Polish folk themes for his mazurkas and polonaises. Jean Sibelius (si-BAI-le-us; 1865–1957) in Finland, Anton Dvořák (DVOR-ak; 1841–1904) and Bedrich Smetana (BAY-drich SME-ta-na; 1824–1884) in Bohemia-Moravia (the modern Czech Republic), and Russians Peter Ilich Tchaikovsky (chai-KOF-skee; 1840–1893), Modest Moussorgsky (1835–1881), and Sergei Rachmaninov (SER-gay rok-MAN-nee-noff; 1873–1943) all incorporated folk music in their work. This use of folk themes was both pleasingly familiar and aesthetically satisfying to audiences.

Romanticism and nationalism, with their increasing number of enthusiasts, sparked developments in opera during the century. In his fervid Germanic works, Richard Wagner (1813–1883) infused old Teutonic myths and German folklore with typically Romantic characteristics such as emphasis on the supernatural and the mystical. Wagner's cycle of musical dramas known as *Der Ring des Nibelungen* was the culmination of a long and productive career. His descendants still are involved in the management of the Festspielhaus (FEST-shpeel-hous), a theater in Bayreuth (bai-ROOT), Germany, that he designed and his admirers financed.

The greatest operatic composer of the century was Giuseppi Verdi (VEHR-dee; 1813–1901), who composed such masterpieces as *Aïda* (AI-ee-dah), *Rigoletto, Il Trovatore* (tro-va-TOR-ay), and *La Forza del Destino* (la FORT-sa del des-TI-no). His operas, along with those of Wagner, form the core of most of today's major opera house repertoires.

The music world rarely dealt with social problems or harsh realism. Its supporters were by and large the newly ascendant middle classes who had benefited from the economic growth triggered by industrialization. They used the wealth derived from their commercial prosperity to finance the building of new opera houses and symphony halls and maintain the composers and orchestras. Major soloists were the idols of their day, as they showed their virtuosity in compositions that made use of Romantic subject matter infused with sentiment and, not infrequently, showmanship such as that shown by Franz Liszt (1811–1886) in his piano concerts or Jenny Lind, the "Swedish Nightingale" (1820–1887), in her recitals. They drew capacity audiences of contented listeners.

▲ This idealized portrait of Beethoven reveals the sensitive composer who could write not only the magnificent global message of the last movement of the Ninth Symphony, but also the subtle melodies of his chamber pieces.

Impressionism in the Arts

Modernism freed painters from the need to communicate surface reality. Gustave Courbet (koor-BAY; 1819–1877) consciously dropped all useless adornments and instead boldly painted the life of the world in which he lived. He was soon surpassed by his countrymen, who became preoccupied with capturing color, light, and atmosphere. Artists such as Édouard Manet (man-AY; 1832–1882), Edgar Degas (day-GAH; 1834–1917), Claude Monet (moh-NAY; 1840–1926), Pierre-Auguste Renoir (ray-NWAH; 1841–1919), and Mary Cassatt (1845–1926) tried to catch the first impression made by a scene or an object on the eye, undistorted by intellect or any subjective attitude. They were called *impressionists* and worked in terms of light and color rather than solidity of form.

The impressionists found that they could achieve a more striking effect of light by placing one bright area of color next to another without any transitional tones. The also found that shadows could be shown not as gray but as colors complementary to those of the objects casting the shadow. At close range, an impressionist painting may seem little more than

◀ A barrage of hostility greeted Édouard Manet's *Luncheon on the Grass* (1863), which juxtaposed the frank nudity of the female model with two clothed male figures. Although the models and the setting seem realistic, Manet was in fact little concerned with subject matter; he believed that the artist's reality lies in the brush strokes and color rather than in the objects represented in the painting. This attitude later coalesced in the "art for art's sake" school of thought.

▶ A concern for the effects of light and color united the French impressionists, yet each also developed a personal style. Claude Monet was often regarded as the boldest innovator; he painted several series of paintings of the same subject, such as *Water Lilies* (1906).

splotches of unmixed colors, but at a proper distance the eye mixes the colors and allows a vibrating effect of light and emotion to emerge. The impressionists' techniques revolutionized art.

One of the weaknesses of impressionism was that it sacrificed much of the clarity of the classical tradition to gain its effects. Paul Cézanne (SAY-zahn; 1839–1903) addressed that problem. He tried to simplify all natural objects by stressing their essential geometric structure. He believed that everything in nature corresponded to the shape of a cone, cylinder, or sphere. Proceeding from this theory, he was able to get below the surface and give his objects the solidity that had eluded the impressionists, yet he kept the impressionists' striking use of color.

The expressionist Dutch artist Vincent van Gogh (1853–1890), while adapting the impressionist approach to light and color, painted using short strokes of heavy pigment to accentuate underlying forms and rhythms of his subjects. He achieved intensely emotional results, as he was willing to distort what he saw to communicate the sensations he felt. His short life of poverty and loneliness ended in insanity and suicide. Other modernist-inspired forms emerged. French artist Henri Matisse (1869–1954) painted what he felt about an object, rather than just the object itself. He had learned to simplify form partly from his study of African primitive art and the color schemes of oriental carpets.

Sculpture and Architecture

These two most substantial forms of art, sculpture and architecture, went through radical changes during the generations before and after World War I. Auguste Rodin (1840–1917) has been called the father of modern sculpture. The realistic honesty and vitality of his work made him the object of stormy controversy during his career. He shared the impressionist painters' dislike of finality in art and preferred to let the viewers' imagination play on his work. Rodin's "rough finish" technique can best be seen in his bronze works, which feature a glittering surface of light and shadow and convey a feeling of immediacy and incompleteness that emphasizes their spontaneous character.

While Rodin was making major contributions in sculpture, architects in Europe were taking advantage of new materials and technologies developed through industrialization to make major improvements in construction. With new resources and methods, architects were able to span greater distances and enclose greater areas than had hitherto been possible.

The Great Chicago Fire of 1871 may have leveled much of the city, but it had the beneficial effect of permitting new building on a large scale. A new form of structure emerged—the steel-skeleton "skyscraper," which enabled builders to erect much taller structures, thanks to engineering advances that provided safe elevators for the multistory buildings. Previously, high buildings had required immensely thick masonry walls or buttresses. Now a metal frame allowed the weight of the structure to be distributed on an entirely different principle. Also, the metal frame permitted a far more extensive use of glass than ever before.

Outstanding among the pioneers in this new approach was American architect Louis Sullivan (1856–1924), who did most of his important work in Chicago. Like others, Sullivan saw the value of the skyscraper in providing a large amount of useful space on a small plot of expensive land. He rejected all attempts to disguise the skeleton of the skyscraper behind a false front and boldly proclaimed it by a clean sweep of line. Sullivan had a far-reaching influence on the approach of choosing function over form.

In Europe, the French engineer Alexandre-Gustave Eiffel (1832–1923) planned and erected a 984-foot tower for the Paris International Exposition of 1889. Delicately formed from an iron framework, the tower rests on four masonry piers on a base 330 feet square.

Conclusion

The Western middle classes dominated and controlled the industrialization, economic transformations, and scientific advances of the nineteenth century. Their newfound wealth, harnessed to the social and legal changes resulting from the French and Napoleonic Revolutions and the reform movements in Britain and the United States, allowed them to control almost all aspects of Western political life by 1900. Both literate and numerous, they dominated religious, scientific, and cultural affairs, bringing major changes to each area. In the 99 years from the end of the Napoleonic Wars in 1815 to the outbreak of the First World War in 1914, they imposed themselves on the rest of the world through their industrial productivity, scientific and technological discoveries, and economic power.

By the mid-nineteenth century, Britain dominated the world economically, and its middle classes served as models for the elites in other societies undergoing industrialization. The British middle classes during the Victorian age were resolutely Christian and correct, conscious as they were of their dominant roles in society. They worked seriously to improve their societies through crusades against alcohol and pornography and for children and women's rights. The middle classes took the lead in changing their societies because the rapid growth of industrialized cities strained the capabilities of local and national authorities to provide utilities, education, law enforcement, and social services. However, charity often began—and remained—at home.

Using the efficiencies of liberal capitalism, the middle classes projected their influences throughout the world. They were unable to sustain their triumph, however. At the beginning of the twentieth century, the peoples in Asia and Africa would see that the Europeans—who had shown such abilities to scale intellectual mountains and spread their power around the globe—had not found the answer to the basic cultural problem of how to get along with one another.

Suggestions for Web Browsing

You can obtain more information about topics included in this chapter at the websites listed below. See also the companion website that accompanies this text, http://www.ablongman.com/brummett, which contains an online study guide and additional resources.

Industrialization
http://www.fordham.edu/halsall/mod/1794woolens.html
A fine selection of primary source documents and contemporary sketches of the first stages of industrialization.

Victorian Web
http://www.victorianweb.org/
Brown University's wonderful overview of the Victorian era in England, offering information about all aspects of Victorian life: social context, political context, economics, religion and philosophy, literature, visual arts, and science and technology.

History of Costumes: Nineteenth Century
http://www.siue.edu/COSTUMES/COSTUME15_INDEX.HTML
This site offers a lively set of images depicting how the various social classes in Europe dressed during the nineteenth century.

Plight of Women's Work in the Industrial Revolution in England and Wales
http://www.womeninworldhistory.com/lesson7.html
This site is sponsored by Women in World History Curriculum and details the working conditions, home life, and other aspects of British women working in the early 1800s.

Child Labor: British History, 1700–1900
http://www.spartacus.schoolnet.co.uk/IRchild.main.htm
Discussions and images related to child labor in Britain are presented on this site, including information about factory reformers, supporters of child labor, life in the factory, and descriptions of personal experiences.

Enter Evolution: Theory and History
http://www.ucmp.berkeley.edu/history/evolution.html
An extensive site on evolutionary theory, with brief accounts of many eighteenth-century precursors to Charles Darwin, Darwin himself, and Lamarck, Cuvier, and Malthus.

Realism in the Arts
http://martyw.best.vwh.net/Realism.html
A comprehensive collection of images by and interpretations of the realist artists.

Romantic Music
http://www.essentialsofmusic.com/eras/romantic.html
An exhaustive survey of the great romantic composers, with selections of their music.

Images of Leo Tolstoy
http://flag.blackened.net/tolstoy/
A series of sketches and photos of the great Russian writer.

Literature and Film

Romantic novelists included Sir Walter Scott (*Ivanhoe,* 1819) and Victor Hugo (*Notre Dame de Paris* [in English, *The Hunchback of Notre Dame*], 1831), whose works were so powerful that they shaped the vision of the past for their countrymen. Their work was paralleled by the poetry of William Wordsworth and Samuel Coleridge. Alphonse de Lamartine in France, Heinrich Heine in Germany, and Alexander Pushkin in Russia enjoyed similar popularity. At midcentury, Honoré de Balzac, in his collection *The Human Comedy,* and Gustave Flaubert made realistic portrayals of the contradictions of their age. In English, Charles Dickens and Samuel Clemens (Mark Twain) made similarly accurate accounts of their nation's strengths and foibles. For each of these writers and artists, there are numerous editions of their collected works.

Numerous video programs on industrialization have been produced by PBS. A compelling series discussing the middle classes at the end of the century in the United Kingdom was *Upstairs, Downstairs* (London Weekend Television, 1971–1975). The theme of marital sadness was touched on by Tolstoy in *Anna Karenina,* Gustave Flaubert in *Madame Bovary,* and Henrik Ibsen in *A Doll's House.* Fine films have been produced of each of these three, especially the Tolstoy and Bovary works.

Suggestions for Reading

For industrialization and its implications, see David S. Landes's classic, *The Unbound Prometheus: Technological Change and Industrial Development in Western Europe from 1750 to the Present* (Cambridge University Press, 2003). For the larger context of the first phase of industrialization, see Eric J. Hobsbawn's classic, *The Age of Revolution* (Vintage, 1996). For the revolutionary impact of industrialization on the American value structure, see James L. Huston, *Securing the Fruits of Labor: The American Concept of Wealth Distribution* (Louisiana State University Press, 1998). On the middle classes in the nineteenth century, see the five volumes of Peter Gay, *The Bourgeois Experience: Victoria to Freud* (Norton, 1984–1998). On J. S. Mill, see Wendy Donner, *The Liberal Self: John Stuart Mill's Moral and Political Phi-*

losophy (Cornell University Press, 1992). See also Jonathan Beecher, *Charles Fourier: The Visionary and His World* (University of California Press, 1986). Among the large number of works dealing with Karl Marx, the penetrating biography by Isaiah Berlin, *Karl Marx: His Life and Environment,* 4th ed. (Oxford University Press, 1996) is the best introduction. A recent study of change in the church in England is Frances Knight, *The Nineteenth-Century Church and English Society* (Cambridge University Press, 1996). On the complex tie between pretense and culture, see Dianne S. MacLeod, *Art and the Victorian Middle Class: Money and the Making of Cultural Identity* (Cambridge University Press, 1996). David S. Lovejoy, *Religious Enthusiasm and the Great Awakening* (Prentice Hall, 1969), captures the spirit of Pietism and religious humanitarianism. For the arts and music, see H. L. C. Jaffee, *The Nineteenth and Twentieth Centuries,* Vol. 5 in *The Dolphin History of Painting,* trans. R. E. Wolf (Thames & Hudson, 1969), and H. C. Colles, *Ideals of the Nineteenth and Twentieth Century,* Vol. 3 in *The Growth of Music* (Oxford University Press, 1956).

CHAPTER 23

Europe, 1815–1914

Political Change and Diplomatic Failure

Outline

Features

◀ Eight of Queen Victoria's nine children married into other royal houses of Europe. As these children and their spouses produced their own families, their children in turn married into still more European royal families. One survey has connected Victoria and her descendants with more than 35 royal families. As a result, most of Europe's monarchs were first or second cousins. Pictured here are Queen Victoria, her son, the future Edward VII, and the Russian Tsar Nicholas and Tsarina Alexandra—Victoria's granddaughter—with their baby, Olga.

BEFORE 1850, EUROPEAN politicians struggled to keep up with and take advantage of the economic and social transformations triggered by industrialization. They were all affected by the new ideas of liberalism, nationalism, and socialism, and their political responses ranged from democratic reform to autocratic reaction. The unbridgeable contradictions between regimes wanting to maintain the status quo and citizens inspired by the new ideas led to the continent-wide revolutions of 1848.

After the failure of the 1848 revolutions, each nation in Europe experienced a growth in centralized state power. In response to national ambitions and the popular pressures generated by mass politics, Realpolitik—realism in politics—became a prevalent theme in Europe, playing the key role in the unification movements of both Germany and Italy. By the end of the nineteenth century, there was a clear division between the nations that were the most efficient at mastering political change—Germany, France, and the United Kingdom—and other nations that struggled to stabilize their political and social infrastructures—most notably, Russia, Italy, and Austria-Hungary.

Elsewhere in the world, the peoples of Asia, Africa, and Latin America dealt with the waves of European colonization and imperialism (see Chapters 24, 25, and 26). Europeans extended their global domination through emigration—during the nineteenth century millions took part in the greatest mass movement of human beings up to that point in history. They also established colonies for economic gain through the exploitation of the natural and human resources of distant peoples. Expending most of their energies outside of their continent, the Europeans managed to avoid major wars among themselves for the greater part of the nineteenth century.

Reassembling Europe: 1815–1848

How successful were the diplomats at Vienna in negotiating a peace settlement that prevented another continental war?

The European leaders at the Congress of Vienna faced a difficult task in 1814–1815. Not only did they have to find a lasting basis for peace, they also had to restore a Europe fractured by a quarter century of wars and revolutions. The treaty they finally arrived at, plus the imperial drive to spread European hegemony around the globe, spared Europe major wars for the next century. There was one force that they did not take into consideration seriously, however, and that was the appearance of new ideologies that responded to the new economic and political realities of Europe. As vigilant as Austria and Russia were in trying to maintain the order defined at Vienna, ultimately they could not suppress the revolutionary energies sweeping the continent.

The Congress of Vienna

Once Napoleon was "safely" exiled to Elba in 1814, representatives of all the European powers except the Ottoman Empire gathered in September at Vienna. They had the imposing task of building a new political and diplomatic structure for Europe after a quarter century of wars and revolutions. The factor that had brought the British, Prussians, Austrians, and Russians together—Napoleon—was gone, and wartime unity dissolved into peacetime pursuit of self-interest.

Work went slowly during the ten-month span of the Congress of Vienna. The leaders who gathered at Vienna—Lord Castlereagh of Great Britain, Count von Hardenberg of Prussia, Prince Klemens von Metternich of Austria, Tsar Alexander I of Russia, and Prince Charles-Maurice de Talleyrand of France—met in small secret conferences to decide the future of Europe. Metternich (MET-ter-nick) came to dominate the conference, as much by his diplomatic skills as by his ability to impress on the participants the need for stability.

The Congress dealt with numerous issues: the status of France, the new political boundaries, the response to liberal and national attitudes sweeping the continent, the fate of the powers that had lost territory during the previous 25 years, and the future of dispossessed dynasties. The solutions proposed were moderate. France was allowed to return to its 1792 boundaries; however, after Napoleon's return and the One Hundred Days, the allies cut back the boundaries and imposed penalties. They virtually ignored the democratic, liberal, and nationalistic forces in favor of a more traditional solution to the upheavals of the previous 25 years.

The events since 1789 had drastically altered the map of Europe. For example, the thousand-year-old Holy Roman Empire had disappeared. In an attempt to restore some balance, the Congress followed four principles: legitimacy, encirclement of France, compensation, and balance of power. The Congress ruled that royal houses that had been expelled—such as the Bourbons in France, Spain, and Naples; the House of Savoy in Sardinia-Piedmont; and the House of Orange in the Netherlands—would be placed back on their thrones. The redrawn map of Europe resembled the 1789 configuration, except that the Holy Roman Empire remained dissolved. In its place were the 39 states of the German Confederation, dominated by Austria. The redrawing of boundaries created a protective belt of states around France to make future aggression more difficult. The principle of compensation ensured that no important power suffered a loss as the result of the Congress's work. Austria was compensated for the loss of land in the Low Countries by gaining territory in Italy and along the Adriatic. Sweden received Norway in return for permitting Russia to keep Finland.

The desire to construct an effective balance of power remained at the center of the Congress's attention. Each nation had its own idea of what constituted a proper balance, and soon the British and the Austrians found themselves arrayed against the Russians and the Prussians. Russia's ambitions in Poland almost broke up the conference because Britain feared that an enlarged Russia would threaten the balance of power. Prussia wanted all of Saxony, which justified Austria's fears of the growing Berlin-based state. As the four

Chronology

1810

1814–1815 Congress of Vienna

1819 Carlsbad Decrees in Germany; Peterloo Massacre in Great Britain

1830

1830s British reforms in Parliament; beginning of Chartist movement

1830 Paris riots against Charles X; uprisings in Belgium and Poland; Mazzini begins Young Italy Movement

1839 Belgium recognized as an independent "perpetually neutral" state

1840

1845 Potato crop failure in Ireland results in widespread famine

1847 Marx and Engels finish their *Communist Manifesto*

1848 Revolutions sweep Europe; French Second Republic proclaimed; election of Louis Napoleon

The leaders of Europe gathered at Vienna in 1814 after Napoleon went to Elba in exile; they faced the task of reconstructing the Continent after a quarter century of war and revolution. Once their common enemy had disappeared, the allies began to argue over a number of important questions. However, in the evenings, the Austrian leader Metternich arranged a series of banquets, balls, and performance to entertain the leaders and their significant others.

wartime allies split, the clever French representative Talleyrand negotiated a secret treaty binding the French, Austrians, and British to pledge mutual assistance to restrain the Russians and Prussians.

Although the Congress has been criticized for ignoring the democratic impulse in Europe, it has been praised for crafting a general settlement of a complex series of problems, especially compared to the work of the vengeful Allies at Versailles after World War I. The representatives were not totally, blindly reactionary, however; many of the changes of the previous 25 years were retained. The 40 years of general peace that followed, flawed though they may have been, are testimony to the success of Metternich and his colleagues in gaining stability. But, by ignoring the forces of change expressed in the new ideologies, the representatives at Vienna ensured the ultimate failure of the system they created.

The Congress System

The Vienna negotiators set out to coordinate their policies to maintain stability. The first proposal for postwar consultation was symbolic and quixotic. In the fall of 1815, Tsar Alexander I proposed the formation of a "Holy Alliance" to be based on "the precepts of justice, Christian charity, and peace." No one was quite sure what the tsar meant by this pact, but every ruler in Europe signed it except the British king, the Turkish sultan, and the pope. Castlereagh dismissed the Holy Alliance as "a piece of sublime mysticism and nonsense." In November 1815, Austria, Prussia, Russia, and Britain signed the Quadruple Alliance, which became the Quintuple Alliance when France joined in 1818. Under this agreement, the powers pursued their goals through what came to be known as the **Congress System,** a concert of the European powers to maintain order, peace, and stability by keeping an eye on France and maintaining the balance of power. This was the first truly functional experiment in collective security in European history.

The Congress System's dedication to the 1815 status quo was challenged in 1820 and 1821 by nationalistic and liberal revolts in Germany, Greece, Spain, Italy, and Latin America. The most violent revolutions occurred in Spain and Italy. Spanish liberals rebelled against the misgovernment of the restored Bourbon king, Ferdinand VII, and their insurrection spread to the army, which mutinied. The general uprising that followed forced the king to give in to the liberals'

Congress System—An alliance of the signatories of the Vienna settlement dedicated to maintaining the status quo in Europe after 1815.

1850	1860	1870	1880	1900	1910
1852 Louis Napoleon proclaims France's Second Empire; Georges Haussmann initiates urban renewal of Paris 1853–1856 Crimean War	1861 Kingdom of Italy proclaimed; Tsar Alexander II issues Emancipation Proclamation; start of American Civil War 1867 The *Ausgleich,* creation of the Austro-Hungarian monarchy	1870–1871 French defeat in Franco-Prussian War; Paris Commune; proclamation of the Unification of Germany	1881 Tsar Alexander II of Russia assassinated 1888 Kaiser William II becomes emperor of Germany	1905 Russian Revolution; October Manifesto issued	1914 Irish Home Rule bill passed; general strike in Italy; start of World War I

demands for a constitution and representative government. The Spaniards' success sparked rebellions in Naples and Sicily, governed by the Neapolitan Bourbon king, Ferdinand I. The Italian revolt ran much the same path as that in Spain, and with much the same result: a constitution based on the Spanish model.

Metternich arranged for the Congress allies to meet at Troppau (tro-POW) in 1820, Laibach in 1821, and Verona in 1822 to deal with the uprisings. Ferdinand I came to Laibach, supported Congress System intervention, and reneged on granting a constitution; Austrian troops invaded Italy and placed him back on his throne. In 1822, the Congress allies met to consider the Spanish problem, and the French volunteered to restore the status quo. They sent their armies in to crush the liberals. The repression of the revolts in Spain and Italy marked the high point of the Congress System's success.

Britain began its withdrawal from the Continent into "splendid isolation" in 1820, and the ardent support of British liberals for the 1821 Greek revolt against the Turks further weakened London's interest in cooperating with its former allies. When the Congress System discussed restoring the Spanish king's authority in Latin America, the British objected. Further, U.S. President James Monroe warned the Europeans in 1823 that their intervention into the Western Hemisphere would be regarded as an unfriendly act. By the middle of the decade, the Congress System had withered to an Austrian-Russian alliance in which Metternich set the agenda and the Russians acted as the policemen of European power.

The Return of the Bourbons

The restored Bourbon monarch Louis XVIII (r. 1814, 1815–1824) was an unhappy choice for the French throne. The new king, a brother of the guillotined Louis XVI, was ill equipped to lead France out of a quarter century of revolution and Napoleonic charisma. Dull and unpopular, he had been the target of a Talleyrand epigram that "the Bourbons have learned nothing and forgotten nothing." Nonetheless, he tried to hold the country together by blending elements of the revolutionary period with remnants of the Old Regime. Unfortunately, the mixture helped create the instability that plagued the country throughout the century. For 9 years, he suffered the fate of moderates trying to navigate between two extremes: the right wing assailed him for giving too much to the middle classes, and the liberals and radicals said that he had not gone far enough in his policies. Louis was succeeded by his brother, Charles X (r. 1824–1830), who cared nothing about maintaining political balance.

Charles did not accept any of the changes since 1789. In 1829 he announced that he "would rather saw wood than be a king of the English type." So out of tune was he with the times that in July 1830 he drove the usually submissive legislature to the point that it refused to support his proposed ultraroyalist ministry. When elections went badly for him, he issued a set of laws censoring the press and further limiting the already heavily restricted right to vote. These repressive acts drove liberals, radicals, and their journalist allies to revolt. They barricaded the narrow streets of Paris with overturned carts, boxes, tables, and paving stones. Fighting behind these obstacles and from rooftops, they held off the army. Three days later, a less reactionary faction took power after Charles fled across the Channel to Great Britain—the refuge for most political exiles, left or right, during the nineteenth century.

The new government represented the upper middle classes and the landed gentry and stood as a compromise between the republicans—led by the aging Marquis de Lafayette, hero of the American Revolution—and the relatively liberal monarchist supporters of the Orléans branch of the Bourbons. The new king, Louis Philippe (r. 1830–1848), who claimed the title of "citizen king," predictably supported the interests of the wealthy. Louis Philippe took great pains to present a bourgeois image of himself. He received the crown from "the people" and replaced the white Bourbon flag with the revolutionary tricolor. However, Louis Philippe's policies consistently favored the upper bourgeoisie and gentry and shut the workers and middle classes out of the political arena. Of the 32 million French citizens, only 200,000 wealthy male property owners were allowed to vote.

Workers protested that the government was ignoring their interests. Louis Philippe and his advisers were more interested in pursuing a policy of divide and conquer and ignored most suggestions for reform. Restrictive legislation was passed in 1835 to control the growing radical movement. The government kept control, but under the calm surface serious pressures were building. By 1848, France faced a serious crisis.

The French Influence in Belgium and Poland

The Paris uprising of 1830 encouraged liberals across the Continent, but only in Belgium were there any lasting results. The Vienna Congress had placed the Belgians under the Dutch crown, but this settlement ignored the cultural, economic, religious, and linguistic differences between the two people. The Belgians were primarily Catholic farmers and workers, some of whom spoke Flemish, which was related to Dutch, but most of whom spoke French. The people of the Netherlands were Dutch-speaking Protestants and, for the most part, seafarers and traders.

Belgian liberals asked the Dutch king, William I of Orange, to grant them their own administration in

▲ Eugène Delacroix's *Liberty Leading the People*, painted in 1830, presented a romantic vision of the popular demand for social reform and the violence in the streets it wrought.

August 1830. When he refused, rioting sprouted in Brussels, which the Dutch troops were unable to put down. After expelling the troops, the Belgians declared their independence and drew up a liberal constitution. William asked in vain for help from Tsar Nicholas I. The principle of legitimacy as a pretext for intervention was dead. Stalemate ensued until the summer of 1831 when the Belgian national assembly met in Brussels and chose Prince Leopold of Saxe-Coburg-Gotha (saks-KO-burg-GO-ta) as king. Eight years later, the international status of the new state was settled. Belgium was recognized as a "perpetually neutral" state.

The French rebellion had an impact in Poland, where Poles in and around Warsaw rose up in the name of liberal and national principles. After the Congress of Vienna, Poles in this region gained a special status. The area known as Congress Poland had its own constitution and substantial local autonomy. The winds of change and the repressive tendencies of Tsar Nicholas I combined to push the Poles into rebellion in the winter of 1830–1831. The rebels suffered from internal division, and the numerically and militarily superior Russians crushed them. Their major accomplishment was to tie down the Russian troops, whom Nicholas wanted to send to help the Dutch king, for six months and perhaps save the Belgian revolution.

German and Italian Nationalism

The forces of nationalism influenced central Europe from the tip of Italy through the Habsburg lands of central and eastern Europe to the Baltic Sea. Napoleon had performed a great, though unwitting, service for German and Italian nationalists by his direct governing in the area and also by revising the European map.

After 1815, the region knew the positive effects of a different style of governing and was divided into a much more rational set of political units.

Metternich had ensured that the Vienna Congress made Austria the dominant partner in the German Confederation. To preserve his country's dominance both in the Confederation and throughout the Habsburg monarchy, he knew that he had to fight continually against nationalism. The currents of Romanticism found forceful expression in the works of German poets and philosophers and in lectures in German classrooms. Nationalism and liberalism found many followers among the young. For example, a great patriotic student festival took place in October 1817 (the three-hundredth anniversary of the Reformation) at Wartburg, where Luther had taken refuge. Liberal students burned reactionary books on a great bonfire to protest their discontent with the status quo. Protests spread both openly and secretly in the *Burschenschaften* (BOUR-shen-shaft-en; "liberal societies"). Metternich moved harshly against the students. He pushed the Carlsbad Decrees (1819) through the Diet of the German Confederation. These acts dissolved student associations, censored the press, and restricted academic freedom. However, the decrees failed to stop the forces of liberalism and nationalism, which grew during the next 20 years.

Italy, which Metternich saw as a "geographical expression" and not a nation, also posed special problems. The Congress of Vienna, in accordance with the principles of legitimacy and compensation, had returned Italy to its geographical status of 1789, divided into areas dominated by the Bourbons, the Papal States, and the Austrians. This settlement ignored the fact that, in the interim, the Italians had experienced more liberty and better government than ever before. The return to the old systems was also a return to high taxes, corruption, favoritism, and banditry.

It was perhaps ironic that this fragmented, individualistic land should produce the most notable Romantic nationalist in Europe, Giuseppe Mazzini. After the Austrians put down the Italian revolutionary movements in 1820 and 1821, Mazzini began to work actively for independence. In 1830, he was implicated in an unsuccessful revolution against the Sardinian royal government and was thrown into jail for six months. Once released, he went to London and started a patriotic society that he called **Young Italy.** This organization sent appeals to students and intellectuals to form an Italian nationalist movement. The reactionaries, however, continued to resist the nationalists.

Metternich also feared nationalism in the Habsburg realm, a mosaic composed of many different nationalities, languages, and religions. If nationalism and the desire for self-rule became strong among the Magyars, Czechs, southern Slavs, and Italians, the Habsburg Empire would fall apart. Nationalism threatened the Germans, who controlled the empire yet constituted only 20 percent of its population.

By understanding the complex and combustible nature of the region in which Metternich exercised his power, his dread of democratic government and nationalism and his obsession with maintaining the status quo can be understood. Liberalism and nationalism would destroy his power. In a world that was rapidly industrializing, Metternich's power rested on a backward system. Only in Bohemia and the areas immediately around Vienna was there a middle class. The great majority of the inhabitants were peasants, either powerless serfs, as in Hungary, or impoverished tenant farmers who owed half of their time and two-thirds of their crops to the landlord. Government was autocratic, and the regional assemblies had little power and represented mainly the nobility. The social, political, and economic structures were extremely vulnerable to the winds of change that came in 1848.

Young Italy—A society created by Giuseppe Mazzini dedicated to the unification of Italy.

1848: The Revolutionary Year

What forces led to the destruction in 1848 of the international order created at the Congress of Vienna in 1815?

As it had before, France once again opened a revolutionary era, and the events there set a precedent for what was to occur throughout Europe in 1848. The overthrow of the old order came first in Paris in February and then spread to Berlin, Vienna, Prague, Buda, and Pest in March. Never before had France—or Europe—seen such a fragmented variety of political and social pressures at work at the same time. Romantics, socialists, nationalists, members of the middle class, peasants, and students could all agree that the old structure had to be abandoned, but the ideology espoused by each group envisioned a different path to

	Revolutionary Outbreaks, 1815–1848
1820–1821	The Germanies, Spain, Italy, Latin America, Greece
1825	Russia
1830	France, Belgium, Poland
1848	France, Prussia, Italy; the Habsburg monarchy: Austria, Bohemia, Hungary, Croatia, Romania

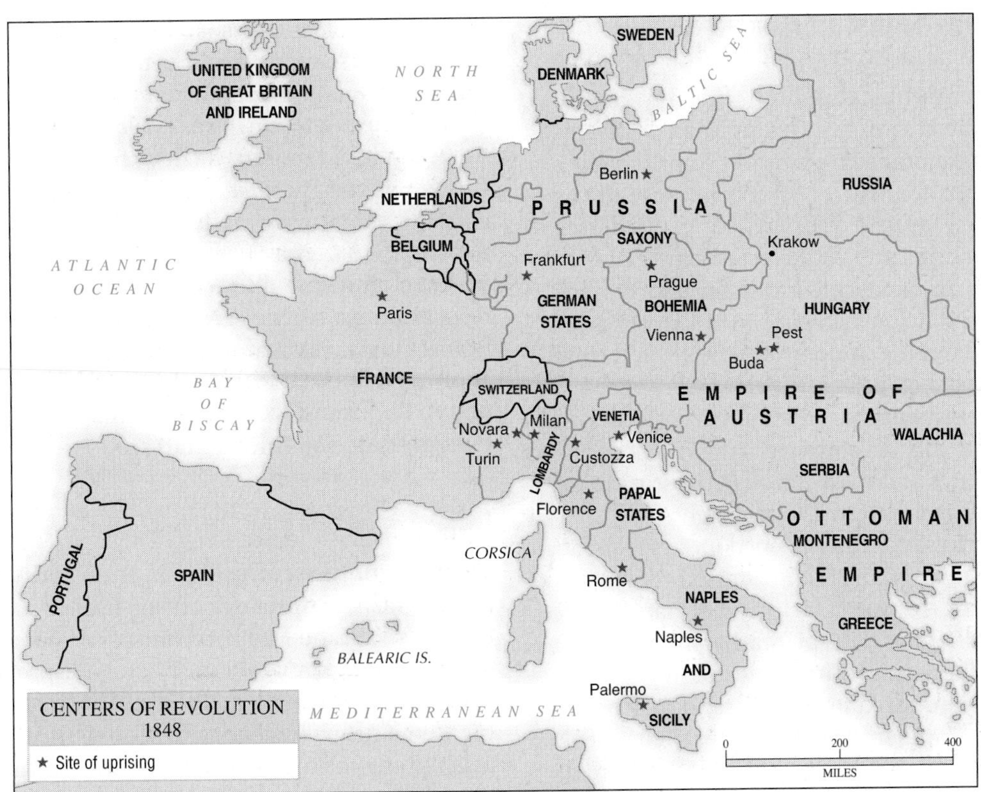

▲ The ideological seeds planted by the French Revolution swept through all of the major European continental powers except Russia in 1848. Despite initial successes, the revolutionary wave soon waned.

that goal and a separate view of what the new world should be. Louis Philippe fled Paris, Metternich abandoned Vienna, and the Prussian king, Frederick William IV, gave in. But the movements in France and elsewhere fell apart as soon as they had won because of their diversity, lack of experience, and conflicting ideological goals.

France and the Second Republic

The pressures building since 1830, strengthened by economic depression in 1846 and 1847, erupted in Paris during February 1848. Within the seemingly harmless social arena of the grand dinner party or banquet, liberals and socialists argued for electoral reforms and an end to corruption while they ate and drank at the table. When the government tried to prohibit a banquet scheduled for February 22, the opposition threw up more than 1500 barricades to block the narrow streets of Paris. Violence broke out, and republican leaders took the opportunity to set up a provisional revolutionary government and proclaimed the introduction of universal manhood suffrage. Louis Philippe fled to exile in England.

The new government, the Second Republic, had a brief (1848–1851) and dreary existence. Neither the new leaders nor the voters had any experience with representative government. The forces that united to overthrow the king soon split into moderate and radical wings. The first group wanted middle-class control within the existing social order, while the latter faction desired a social and economic revolution. By the summer the new government faced a major crisis over the issue of national workshops sponsored by the socialist Louis Blanc (BLON; 1811–1882). The workshops were to be the state's means to guarantee every laborer's "right to work." The moderate-dominated government voiced its belief in Blanc's principle of full employment, but the leaders gave the plan's administration to men who wanted to ridicule it. As a result, the workshops became a national joke. Laborers were assigned make-work jobs such as carrying dirt from one end of a park to the other on one day and then carrying it back the next.

The disbanding of the workshops incited a violent insurrection known as the June Days. The unemployed workers raised a red flag as a sign of revolution—the first time that the red flag had been used as a symbol of the proletariat. With the cry of "bread or lead," the demonstrators rebuilt the barricades and tried to overthrow the government. The bloodiest fighting Paris had seen since the Reign of Terror gave the insurgents far more lead than bread, and the movement was crushed. After that, the bourgeoisie and the workers would be on the opposite ends of the political spectrum.

Germany and the Frankfurt Assembly

The example of the French February Revolution quickly crossed the Rhine River and spread to central Europe. At public assemblies throughout Germany, patriotic liberals demanded unification. Rapid changes came with minimal casualties, largely because of the humane response of the Prussian king, Frederick William IV. When his subjects erected barricades in Berlin on March 15, he decided to make concessions rather than unleash further violence and bloodshed. He ordered the regular army troops out of Berlin and tried to make peace with his "dear Berliners" by promising a parliament, a constitution, and a united Germany. Upon learning of this development, the rulers of the other German states agreed to establish constitutional governments and guarantee basic civil rights.

The **Frankfurt Assembly** opened its first session on May 18. More than five hundred delegates attended, coming from the various German states, Austria, and Bohemia. The primarily middle-class membership of the assembly included about two hundred lawyers, one hundred professors, and many doctors and judges. Popular enthusiasm reached a peak when the assembly's president announced, "We are to create a constitution for Germany, for the whole empire." The assembly deliberated at length over the issues of just what was meant by Germany and what form of government would be best for the new empire. Some debaters wanted a united Germany to include all Germans in Central Europe, even Austria and Bohemia. Others did not want the Austrians included, for a variety of religious and political reasons. Another issue of contention was whether the new imperial crown should be given to the Habsburgs in Vienna or the Hohenzollerns in Berlin.

Germany's history changed tragically when the Assembly failed to unite and bring a liberal solution to political problems. From May to December, the Assembly wasted time in splendid debates over nonessential topics. As the participants talked endlessly, they threw away their chance to take decisive action and contributed to the failed dreams of 1848. Gradually, the conservatives recovered from the shock of the spring revolts and began to rally around their rulers, exhorting them to undo the reformers' work. In Prussia, the king regained his confidence, the army remained loyal, and the peasants showed little interest in political affairs. The Berlin liberals soon found themselves isolated, and the king was able to regain control.

Even though the antiliberal forces were at full tide, the Frankfurt Assembly continued its work. It approved the *Declaration of the Rights of the German People,* an inspiring document that articulated the progressive political and social ideals of 1848. In April 1849, the Assembly approved a constitution for a united Germany that included an emperor advised by a ministry and a legislature elected by secret ballot. Austria refused to join the new union.

When the leadership of the new German Reich ("nation") was offered to Frederick William, he refused to accept it, later declaring that he could not "pick up a crown from the gutter." After this contemptuous refusal, most of the Assembly's members returned home. Outbreaks against the conservative domination continued, but the Prussian army effectively put them down. Thousands of prominent middle-class liberals fled, many to the United States.

Frankfurt Assembly—The meeting held in 1848 to write a constitution for Germany.

Italy

The news of the revolutions in Paris and Vienna triggered a rash of uprisings on the Italian peninsula. In Sicily, Venice, and Milan, revolutionaries demanded an end to foreign domination and despotic rule. In response, King Charles Albert of Sardinia voluntarily granted a new liberal constitution. Other states, such as Tuscany, also issued constitutions. In the Papal States, meanwhile, reform had begun as early as 1846. Absolute government in Italy almost disappeared.

As in the rest of Europe, the liberal and nationalist triumphs and reforms were quickly swept away by the reactionary tide. The Austrians regained their mastery in the north of Italy in July when they defeated Charles Albert at the decisive battle of Custozza. Another defeat a year later forced him to abdicate in favor of his oldest son, Victor Emmanuel II. Austria helped restore the old rulers and systems of government in Italy to their pre-1848 conditions.

The final blow to the Italian movements came in November 1848, when Pope Pius IX, who had begun a program of reform, refused to join in the struggle against Catholic Austria for a united Italy. His subjects forced him to flee from Rome, and the papal lands were declared a republic, with Mazzini as the head. The pope's flight prompted a hostile reaction from conservative Europe, and the French sent in an army to crush the republic in July 1849. When the pope returned to Rome, he remained bitterly hostile to all liberal causes and ideas until his death in 1878.

The Habsburg Monarchy

The events of 1848 took a tragic toll in the Habsburg lands. When the news of the February uprising reached Vienna, Prague, Buda, and Pest, reformers immediately called for change. In Budapest, the nationalist liberal Lajos Kossuth (la-YOS KOS-sut; 1802–1894) attacked the Habsburg ruler's "stagnant bureaucratic system" and spoke of the "pestilential air blowing from the

Vienna charnel house and its deadening effect upon all phases of Hungarian life." He demanded parliamentary government for the whole of the empire.

In Vienna, Kossuth's speech inspired some Austrian students and workers to demonstrate in the streets. The movement soon gained the force of a rebellion, and the frightened Austrian emperor forced Metternich, the symbol of European reaction, to resign. Meanwhile, the Hungarian Diet advocated a liberal, parliamentary government under a limited Habsburg monarchy. The Vienna-controlled Danubian region, that mosaic of nationalities, appeared to be on the verge of being transformed into a federation.

Nationalities Within the Habsburg Empire

The empire's diversity soon became mirrored in a characteristic of the revolutionary movements, as the various nationalities divided among themselves. The Hungarians wrote a new constitution that was quite liberal, calling for a guarantee of civil rights, an end to serfdom, and the destruction of special privileges. In theory, all political benefits guaranteed in the constitution were to extend to all citizens of Hungary, including non-Magyar minorities. The emperor accepted these reforms and promised, in addition, a constitution for Austria. He also promised the Czechs in Bohemia the same reforms granted the Hungarians.

By summer the mood suddenly shifted. German and Czech nationalists began to quarrel, and the Magyars began to oppress the Slavic nationalities and Romanians after they in turn demanded their own political independence. Divisions among the liberal and nationalistic forces gave the conservatives in Vienna time to regroup and suggested to them the obvious tactic to regain their former dominance: divide and conquer the subject nationalities. In June, demonstrations broke out in the streets of Prague, barricades were thrown up, and fighting began. The Austrians lobbed a few shells, Prague surrendered, and any hope for an autonomous kingdom of Bohemia ended.

In Hungary, Kossuth announced that he would offer civil rights, but not national independence, to the minority nationalities under his control. In protest, the South Slavs under the Croat leader Joseph Jellachich (IO-sef ye-LA-chich; 1801–1859) attacked the Magyars, and civil war broke out. The Austrians took advantage of the situation and made Jellachich an imperial general. Following his attack against the Magyars, he was ordered to Vienna, where, in October, he forced the surrender of the liberals who controlled the capital.

By the end of the year, the weak and incapable Emperor Ferdinand I abdicated in favor of his nephew, Franz Joseph—who would rule until 1916. The Austrians began to repeal their concessions to the Hungarians, arguing that their new emperor was not bound by the acts of his predecessor. The Magyars, outraged by this maneuver, declared complete independence for their country. The Austrians, aided by 100,000 Russian troops sent by Tsar Nicholas I and the leadership of the Croatian general Jellachich, defeated the Hungarians in a bloody and one-sided struggle. In the summer of 1849, Kossuth fled the country, and the Hungarian revolution reached its tragic conclusion.

After 1848: Realpolitik and Reform

The general failures of the 1848 revolutions led to two major responses to European political needs for the next half century. On the one hand, leaders in Germany, Italy, and France pursued a Machiavellian policy

◄ The leader of the Hungarian revolutionary movement of 1848, Lajos Kossuth, gave a liberal constitution to his people but blocked the hopes of neighboring nationalities such as the Serbs, Croats, and Romanians.

of **Realpolitik** in which they felt justified in doing whatever was needed to increase the strength of their nations. In other states, such as the United Kingdom, Russia, and Austria-Hungary, political leaders tried to alter their political structures and ways of governing in order to adapt to changing times. The slow reform efforts of the London-based government would succeed in transforming the United Kingdom into a democratic state, even if women did not win the vote until after World War I and the nation remained the world's largest imperial power throughout the nineteenth century. The governments in St. Petersburg and Vienna, however, would ultimately fail in their reform efforts.

Prussia, German Unification, and the Second Reich

How did Bismarck manage to unify Germany when the surrounding states of western and eastern Europe were all opposed to unification?

After 1848, with one exception, Prussia went from strength to strength. Facing a different range of problems in a much more unified state, King Frederick William issued a constitution in 1850 that paid lip service to parliamentary democracy but kept real power in the hands of the king and the upper classes. The Berlin court wanted to form a confederation of northern German states, without Austria. This plan frightened the Austrians and made the Russians uneasy as well. A meeting of the three powers at Olmütz in 1850 forced the Prussians to withdraw their plan. Instead, the 1815 German Confederation was affirmed, with Vienna recognized as the major German power. The embittered Prussians returned to Berlin, pledging revenge for the "humiliation of Olmütz."

Realpolitik–The nineteenth-century use of Machiavelli's notion that the ends justify the means.

	Steps to German Unification
1862	Bismarck appointed prime minister
1863	Russian-Prussian accord on Poland
1864	War with Denmark
1866	War with Austria; establishment of North German Confederation
1870	War with France
1871	Proclamation of the Second German Empire (Reich) at Versailles

Despite this diplomatic setback, Prussia gained success in other areas. Berlin kept the Austrians out of the *Zollverein* (ZOLL-ver-ine), the customs union of German states, and fought off Austria's efforts to weaken it. The Prussian government, dominated by the nobles, was modern and efficient, especially when compared with that in Vienna. The Prussians extended public education to more of their citizenry than in any other European state. At the start of the 1860s a new ruler, William I (r. 1861–1888), came to power. He had a more permissive interpretation of the 1850 constitution and allowed liberals and moderates the chance to make their voices heard.

Bismarck as Prime Minister

A stalemate occurred in 1862, when King William I wanted to strengthen his army but the Chamber of Deputies would not vote to provide the necessary funds. The liberals asserted the constitutional right to approve taxes, and the king equally strongly expressed his right to build up his forces. As the king struggled with this constitutional crisis, he called Otto von Bismarck (1815–1898) home from his post as Prussian ambassador to France and made him prime minister.

Bismarck advised the king to ignore the legislature and collect the needed taxes without the Chamber's approval. Bismarck knew the necessity of armed strength in order to gain Prussia's diplomatic goals. Ironically, his later military victories would gain him the support of many of the liberals whom he had encouraged the king to defy.

Bismarck's entry on the scene in Berlin strengthened not only the king but also the hopes of all who wanted a united German state. Unification appealed to virtually all segments of German society, from the liberals to the conservatives, such as the historian Heinrich von Treitschke (HINE-reesh fon TRITE-shki), who stated, "There is only one salvation! One state, one monarchic Germany under the Hohenzollern dynasty." Berlin, through its leadership of the *Zollverein,* sponsorship of the confederation of northern German states, and efficient bureaucracy, was the obvious choice for the capital of a unified German state. With the arrival of Bismarck, the Prussians gained the necessary leadership for unification.

The prime minister was a master of the art of Realpolitik. He had the intelligence to assess the actual state of conditions, the insight to gauge the character and goals of his opponents, and the talent to move skillfully and quickly. Unlike most of his colleagues, he was an expert imagemaker, so effective that historians have used his epithet "blood and iron" to describe his career. Few statesmen have ever accomplished so much change with such a comparatively small loss of life in a controlled use of war. Bismarck was a savvy politician

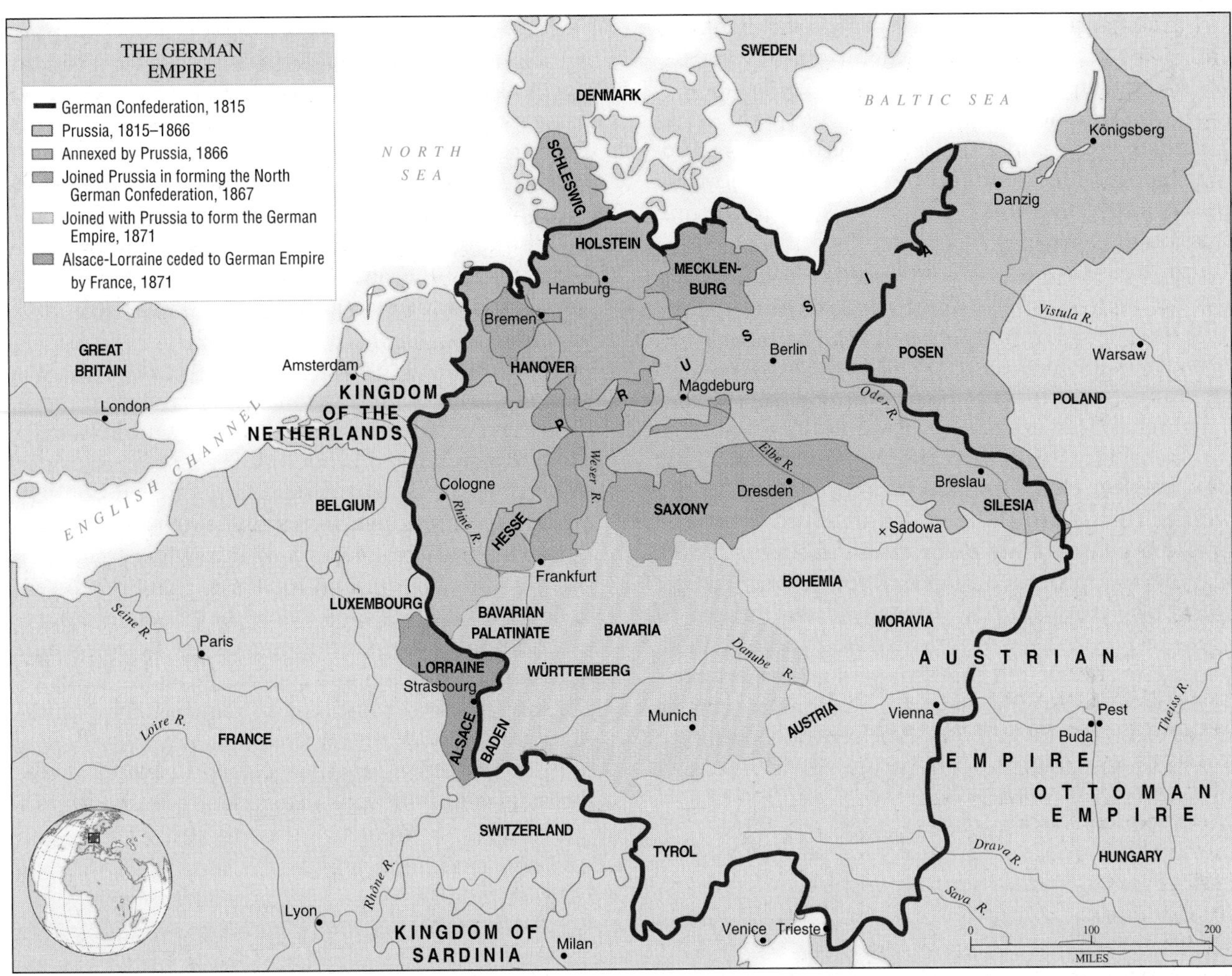

▲ The Hohenzollerns, based in Berlin, began the process of linking their widely spread territories in the seventeenth century. Napoleon contributed to a consolidated German state through his rearrangement of the map after his military conquests, and Bismarck completed the unification of Germany by 1871.

who knew that force was the final card to be played, one to be used as the servant of diplomacy and not as its master.

Some historians have attributed his successes to luck, whereas others have deemed them products of genius. An example is his approach to Russia. Bismarck knew that he would have to solidify relations with Russia, and he achieved this in 1863 by promising the Russians that he would aid them in all Polish-related problems. Giving up virtually nothing, he gained a secure eastern flank and proceeded to set up three wars that brought about German unification.

The Danish and Austrian Wars

In 1864, Bismarck invited Austria to join Prussia and wage war on Denmark. The cause of the conflict was the disputed status of two duchies, Schleswig and Holstein, bordering on Prussia and Denmark and claimed by both. The two Germanic powers overwhelmed the modest Danish forces and split the duchies: Austria took Holstein, and Schleswig went to Prussia. With his eastern and northern flanks stabilized, Bismarck set out to isolate Austria.

Italy was already hostile to the Austrians and remained so when Bismarck promised it Venetia in return for its assistance in the future war. He encouraged the French to be neutral by intimating that Prussia might support France should it seek to widen its borders. Severe domestic crises with the Hungarians absorbed Austria, which soon found itself isolated. The Prussian leader provoked war with Vienna by piously expressing alarm at the manner in which the Austrians were ruling Holstein and sending troops into the province. Austria took the bait, entered the war, and was devastated by the Prussians at the battle of Sadowa. In this Seven Weeks' War, the Prussians avenged the "humiliation of Olmütz" of 1850.

Prussia offered a moderate peace settlement that ended the old German Confederation. In its place, Bismarck formed the North German Confederation, with Austria and the southern German states excluded. Prussia annexed several territories, including Hanover, Mecklenburg, and other states north of the Main River, in this penultimate stage in the unification of Germany.

The War with France

After 1867, Bismarck turned his attention westward to France and Emperor Napoleon III (1808–1873). The French leader had allowed himself to be talked into neutrality in 1866 because he anticipated a long war between his German neighbors that would weaken them both and because he hoped to expand into the neutral state of Belgium. In August 1866, Napoleon approached Bismarck for his share of the fruits of victory, but the German leader refused to agree to French demands. Frustrated and offended, Napoleon III insisted that Prussia approve France's annexation of Luxembourg and Belgium. In a crafty move, Bismarck invited the French envoy to Berlin to put these demands into writing but still avoided giving a definite response.

Four years later, Bismarck sent the document to the British in order to gain their sympathy for the upcoming war with the French. After France's active participation in the Crimean War, there was no chance that Russia would come to Napoleon's aid. Bismarck let the Austrians know about France's cooperation with the Prussians during the 1866 war, and Italy was not about to help Napoleon III after his activities in 1859. By 1870, France was isolated. It was simply a question now of Bismarck maneuvering the French into war.

The immediate controversy centered on the succession to the Spanish throne left vacant after a revolution had overthrown the reactionary Queen Isabella. The Spaniards asked Leopold, a Hohenzollern prince, to become the constitutional king of their country. France saw this as an unacceptable extension of Prussian influence, and Leopold withdrew his candidacy. But this was not enough for Paris. The French sent their ambassador to Ems, where the Prussian king was vacationing, to gain from him a pledge that he would not again permit Leopold to seek the Spanish throne. The king refused to agree to this unreasonable request. After the interview, he directed that a message be sent to Bismarck, describing the incident. Bismarck altered the message of this Ems dispatch to give the impres-

Document

Bismarck and the Ems Dispatch

Bismarck knew how to manipulate public opinion through press leaks and doctored documents. See how he altered the Ems dispatch to achieve his goals vis-à-vis France.

I made use of the royal authorization communicated to me through Abeken, to publish the contents of the telegram; and in the presence of my two guests I reduced the telegram by striking out words, but without adding or altering, to the following form:

> After the news of the renunciation of the hereditary Prince of Hohenzollern had been officially communicated to the imperial government of France by the royal government of Spain, the French ambassador at Ems further demanded of his Majesty the King that he would authorize him to telegraph to Paris that his Majesty the King bound himself for all future time never again to give his consent if the Hohenzollerns should renew their candidature. His Majesty the King thereupon decided not to receive the French ambassador again, and sent to tell him through the aide-de-camp on duty that his Majesty had nothing further to communicate to the ambassador.

The difference in the effect of the abbreviated text of the Ems telegram as compared with that produced by the original was not the result of stronger words but of the form, which made this announcement appear decisive, while Abeken's version only would have been regarded as a fragment of a negotiation still pending, and to be continued at Berlin.

After I had read out the concentrated edition to my two guests, Moltke remarked: "Now it has a different ring; it sounded before like a parley; now it is like a flourish in answer to a challenge."

Questions to Consider

1. How does Bismarck's altering of the Ems dispatch reflect his role as a master of Realpolitik?
2. Do you think government leaders are justified in manipulating truth to gain their political actions? In your lifetime have you seen an example of this?
3. What role do governmental "leaks" such as that of the Ems dispatch play today?

From *Bismarck: The Man and the Statesman*, trans. A. J. Butler (1899).

Judged from the point of view of comparative manpower, the French and German armies appeared to be equally strong in 1870. However, the Germans took advantage of their superiority in leadership and experience to overwhelm the French in the Franco-Prussian War.

sion that the French ambassador had insulted the Prussian king and that the king had returned the insult. The rumor was leaked to the press and infuriated both the Germans and the French.

France declared war in July. The two countries' forces appeared to be evenly matched in equipment, but the Germans had a better-trained and more experienced army. In two months, the Prussians overwhelmed the French, delivering the crowning blow at the battle of Sedan, where the emperor and his army were surrounded and forced to surrender. Troops of the combined armies of the German states besieged the north of France for four months before the final French capitulation. By the Treaty of Frankfurt in 1871, France lost Alsace and a part of Lorraine to Germany and was required to pay a large indemnity. The call for revenge of France's defeat and humiliation became a major issue in French politics.

The Second German Reich

The Second Reich came into existence at a ceremony in January 1871 in the Hall of Mirrors at the Palace of Versailles. There King William I became *kaiser* ("emperor") of a federal union of 26 states with a population of 41 million. The bicameral (two-house) legislature of the new empire consisted of the **Bundesrat** (BUN-des-raht), representing the ruling houses of the various states, and the **Reichstag** (RIKE-stag), representing the people through its 397 members elected by male suffrage.

MAP
German Unity

Dominant power rested with the kaiser, who controlled military and foreign affairs and the 17 votes in the *Bundesrat* needed to veto any constitutional change. The actual head of government was the chancellor, who was appointed by the kaiser and responsible to him only. This arrangement allowed the chancellor to defy or ignore the legislature if it served his purpose. However, he had to operate within the constraints of the federal state structure, in which major powers of local government were given to the member states.

Bismarck as Chancellor

As chancellor, Otto von Bismarck built modern Germany on his belief in the inherent efficiency of a state based on one faith, one law, and one ruler. He distrusted institutions that did not fit that tripartite formula—specifically, the Catholic Church and the Socialist party. Bismarck was more constrained in domestic than in foreign affairs. It is not surprising, therefore, that he fared better in foreign matters.

The Catholic political party had sent a large bloc of representatives to the Reichstag in 1871, and these members supported the complete independence of the church from state control, denounced divorce, objected to secular education, and questioned freedom of conscience. Many Catholics strongly supported the

Bundesrat—The upper house of the bicameral German legislature after 1871.

Reichstag—The lower house of the bicameral German legislature after 1871.

Seeing Connections

French and German Rivalry

One of the more unfortunate aspects of European history is the cycle of wars fought between nation-states from the medieval era through the twentieth century. The conflicts between the Germanies and France between 1648 and 1945 illustrate this cycle well. From the seventeenth century to 1815, France usually acted aggressively toward the Germans, whether it was during the wars of Louis XIV or the brilliant campaigns of Napoleon I. By the late nineteenth century, however, the pendulum had swung, and it was the Germans who were the aggressor toward France in 1871, 1914, and 1940. Pictured here is the proclamation of the Second "Reich"—or Empire—with *König* (King) William being proclaimed *Kaiser* (Emperor) William. This ceremony took place not in Berlin, but in the Hall of Mirrors at the chateau of Versailles—the symbol of French grandeur—on January 18, 1871. Whether or not this was a calculated effort to humiliate the French, or simply taking advantage of right of conquest after the German victory in the Franco-Prussian War, the effect was the same. For the next 43 years, French politics was dominated by the desire for revenge, *la revanche.* After the armistice ending World War I was signed on November 11, 1918, in a railroad car in the forest of Compiègne, the diplomats from the new German government at Weimar were summoned to the Hall of Mirrors and forced to sign a humiliating treaty the next year. For the next 20 years, German politicians declared that their country had been forced to sign an unjust peace. When the German armies defeated France in 1940, the armistice was again signed in the same railroad car at Compiègne. Finally, leaders of both nations came to their senses after World War II and now the connection between France and Germany is symbolized by their leadership of the European Union and not by the ritual humiliation of the enemy after yet another war. Indeed, the existence of the European Union offers the hope that the cycle of wars between European nation states is finally at an end.

new dogma of papal infallibility. Within the Protestant Prussian part of Germany, Bismarck introduced anti-Catholic policies that triggered a conflict known as the *Kulturkampf* (KUL-ture-kompf; "struggle for civilization"). These so-called May Laws made it an offense for the clergy to criticize the government, regulated the educational activities of the religious orders, and expelled the Jesuits from the country. The state also required civil marriages and dictated that all priests study theology at state universities. Pope Pius IX declared these acts null and void and told loyal Catholics to refuse to obey them. Many of the chancellor's laws applied equally to Protestants, who actively protested them.

As opposition spread, Bismarck struck hard at the Catholics, imprisoning priests, confiscating church property, and closing down pulpits. When the tide did not turn in his favor, he realized that he could not afford to create millions of martyrs. Showing his shrewd sense of power, he cut his losses, retreated, and repealed most of the anti-Catholic laws.

The Social Democratic (Marxist) movement posed a greater challenge to Bismarck's rule. The party's founder, Ferdinand Lassalle (1825–1864), rejected violence as a means to gain power and instead advocated working within the existing political structure. After his death, the movement retained its nonviolent nature. The party's popularity soared when it was officially established in 1875, and its leaders pushed for true parliamentary democracy and wider-ranging social programs. In 1878, Bismarck used two attempts on the emperor's life as an excuse to launch an all-out campaign to weaken the Social Democrats, even though they had no connection with the assassination attempts. He dissolved extralegal socialist organizations, suppressed their publications, and threw their leaders in jail. Despite these measures, the socialists continued to gain support.

When he failed to weaken the socialists by direct confrontation, the chancellor changed tactics. He decided to undercut them by taking over their program. Through the 1880s, he implemented important

◀ Bismarck and the young Kaiser William II meet in 1888. The two disagreed over many issues, and in 1890, William dismissed the aged chancellor.

social legislation that provided wage earners with sickness, accident, and old-age insurance. He sponsored other laws that responded to many of the abuses workers encountered. Still, the Social Democrats continued to grow in size and influence. However, by creating the first welfare state, the pragmatic Prussian chancellor defused a potential revolution.

Kaiser William II

In 1888, William II, the grandson of the emperor, became head of the Reich. Just as Bismarck had dominated European affairs since 1862, the new emperor would play a key role until 1918. Here was a person who advocated a policy of "blood and iron," but without Bismarck's finesse. Where Bismarck knew the limits and uses of force and appreciated the nuances of public statements, William was a militarist and a bully. Serving in a modern age, the new emperor still believed in the divine right of kings and constantly reminded his entourage that "he and God" worked together for the good of the state. With such a contrast in styles, it is not surprising that William saw Bismarck not as a guide but as a threat. Once William established himself in power, he forced Bismarck to resign in March 1890.

At the beginning of the twentieth century, Germany presented a puzzling picture to the world. On the one hand, the blustering kaiser made fiery and warlike statements. He encouraged militarism and the belief that *"Alles kommt von oben"* (ALL-es kommt fon O-ben; "Everything comes down from above"). On the other hand, his thoroughly advanced country made great scientific and cultural strides. Observers of German affairs noted that one-third of the voters supported the Social Democrats, an indication of a healthy parliamentary system. A commonly held pride in Germany's accomplishments knit the country together.

More important than William's behavior was the fact that, by the beginning of the new century, the Germans competed actively in all areas with the British. Although Germany did not outproduce Britain, long-term projections showed that the island nation's growth had leveled out and that in the next generation the Reich would surpass it. The Germans dominated the world market in the chemical and electrical industries and were making strides in other areas. They boasted a more efficient organization of their industries, a higher literacy rate for their workers, better vocational training, and a more aggressive corps of businessmen. German labor unions were less combative than the British, and the government gave more support to industry than Parliament did. When the kaiser demanded a navy the equal of that of England, alarm bells went off in London.

The Decline of Austria

Why did the Austrian Empire decline in power and influence after 1867?

Conservative forces consolidated control in Vienna after 1848, but the Austrian Habsburgs operated from a weakened position. Their victory over the Hungarians brought only temporary comfort. The collapse of the liberal and nationalistic movements in the Habsburg Empire was followed by a harsh repression that did little to address the basic political problems facing Vienna. Centralizing and Germanizing tendencies stimulated nationalist sentiments in the empire. After their losses to the French and Sardinians in 1859, the Austrians considered moving toward a federal system for their lands. The Hungarians, however, demanded equality with Vienna. The government in Vienna became increasingly inept.

After the Austrians' disastrous defeat by Prussia, Franz Joseph was forced to offer the Hungarians an equal partnership with Vienna in ruling the empire. The offer was accepted, and in 1867 the constitution known as the *Ausgleich* (OUS-glike; "compromise") was enacted. This document created the **Dual Monarchy,** in which the Habsburg ruler was both the king of Hungary and the emperor of Austria—defined as the area

Dual Monarchy—The Austro-Hungarian Empire, created in 1867 by the writing of a constitution that defined the relationship between Vienna and Budapest.

▼ It fell to the Habsburgs to exercise power over the ethnic, religious, and linguistic fracture zone of southeastern Europe. Then major nationalities—especially the Hungarians—presented the Vienna-based government with severe challenges.

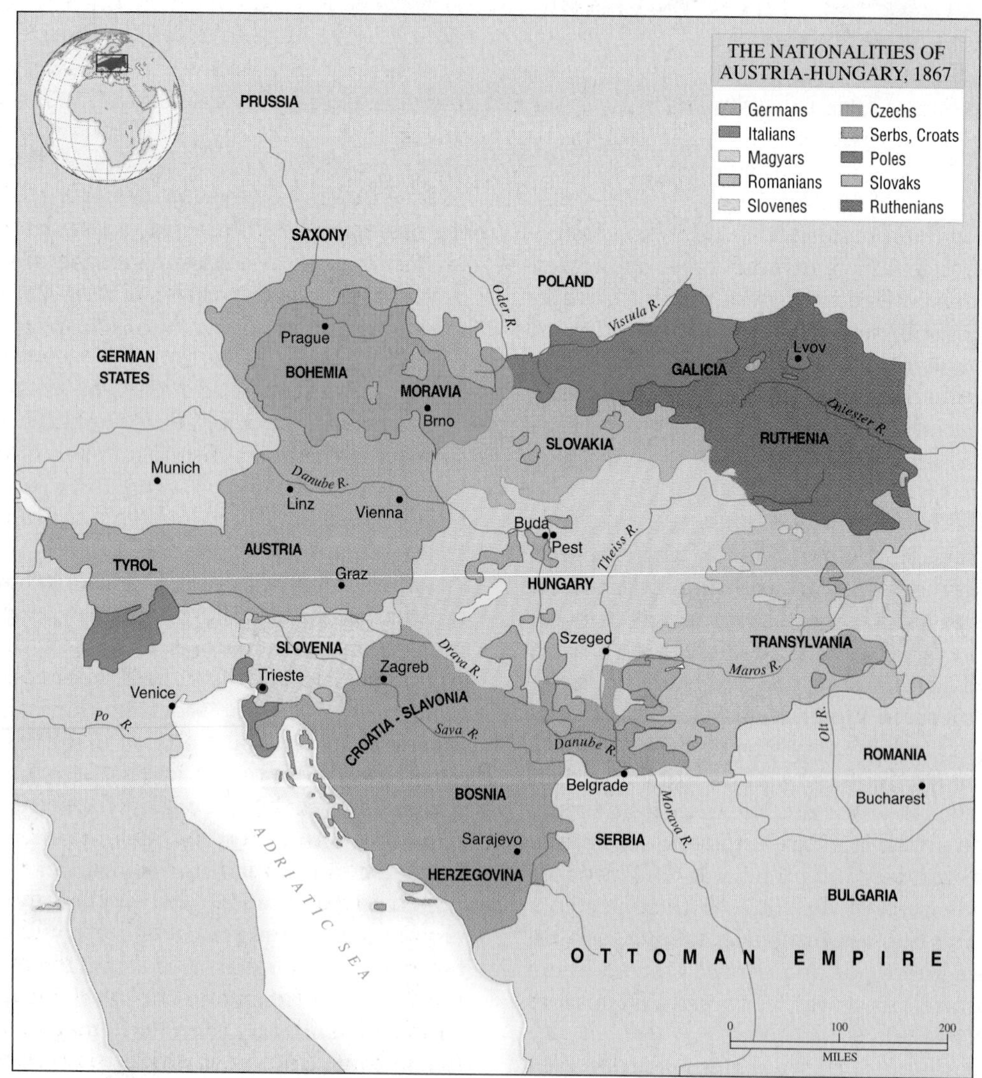

that was not part of Hungary. Each country had its own constitution, language, flag, and parliament. Ministers common to both countries handled finance, defense, and foreign affairs, but they were supervised by "delegations," which consisted of 60 members from each parliament who did not meet together, except in emergency circumstances. The *Ausgleich* was to be renegotiated every 10 years.

By the end of the century, the Dual Monarchy contained 12 million Germans, 10 million Hungarians, more than 24 million Slavs, and 4 million Romanians, among other nationalities. Although the Germans of Austria had recognized the equality of the Hungarians, the rest of the nationalities continued to live under alien rule. Now, instead of having to deal with one dominant national group, they had to cope with two. In some cases, as in the prospering, cosmopolitan, and sophisticated area of Bohemia-Moravia, the people wanted an independent state or, at the very least, more rights within the Habsburg realm. Other groups, such as the Serbs, sought the goal of joining their countrymen living in adjacent national states. The nationalities question remained an explosive problem for the authorities in Vienna and Budapest.

The functioning of the Dual Monarchy was best symbolized by the official banknotes, which were printed in eight languages on one side and in Hungarian on the other. In the Hungarian part of the Dual Monarchy, the aristocracy governed under the Kossuth constitution of 1848. The Hungarians refused to share rule with the minorities in their kingdom. A small, powerful landed oligarchy dominated the mass of backward, landless peasants. The conservative leadership carried out a virtual process of Magyarization with their minorities (imposing Hungarian culture as the desired standard) while they continually squabbled with the Austrians.

In the Austrian portion, wealthy German businessmen and the landed aristocracy dominated political life. But even with this concentration of power, the government was much more democratic, especially after 1907, when the two-house legislature was elected by universal manhood suffrage. Here, too, nationalism was a serious problem, and political parties came to be based not on principle but on nationality. Each nationality had to work with the Germans, even though it might detest them. The nationalities frequently disliked one another, and this prevented the formation of any coalitions among them. By 1914, the Austrians had extended substantial local self-government to their subject nationalities, but this concession did little to quiet discontent.

The *Ausgleich* functioned poorly, yet its defenders could still tell themselves that they were, after all, citizens of a "great empire." The Dual Monarchy occupied a strategic geographical location and had enough military strength to be very influential in the Balkans. In addition, the area had great economic potential, with Hungarian wheat, Croatian and Slovenian livestock, Czech banks and industry, and Austrian commerce. But Franz Joseph ruled over a disjointed conglomeration of peoples who shared only the pretension of being citizens of a great power.

Italy to 1914

What challenges did Cavour face in his efforts to unify Italy?

Italian Unification

After 1848, fighters for Italian unification established their base in the kingdom of Sardinia, where the young monarch, Victor Emmanuel II, refused to withdraw the liberal constitution granted by his father. The prime minister, Count Camillo Benso di Cavour (1810–1861), a liberal influenced by what he had seen in Switzerland, France, and Britain, assumed leadership of the drive to unify the peninsula. After 1852, when he became prime minister, Cavour concentrated on freeing his country from Austrian domination. He knew, however, that Sardinia needed allies to take on the Habsburgs. To that end, in 1855 Sardinia joined Britain and France in their fight against Russia in the Crimean War. This step enabled Cavour to speak at the peace conference after the war, where he stated Italy's desire for unification.

Cavour's presentation won Napoleon III's support, and the two opportunists found that they could both make gains if they could draw the Austrians into war. They agreed that if Cavour could entice the Vienna government into war, France would come to Sardinia's aid and help eject the Austrians from Lombardy and Venetia. In return, France would receive Nice and Savoy from Sardinia. The plan worked to perfection. In April 1859, Cavour lured the Austrians into declaring war. The French and Sardinians defeated them at Magenta and Solferino and drove them out of Lombardy. At the same time, revolts broke out in Tuscany, Modena, Parma, and Romagna. Napoleon was praised and proclaimed as the savior and liberator of Italy.

Upon receiving his share of the agreement, Napoleon III reversed himself and made peace with Austria before the allies could invade Venetia. The massing of Prussian troops on French borders as well as his second thoughts about the implications of a united Italy drove Napoleon to this move. The Sardinians were outraged, but they could do little but agree to a peace settlement. The agreement awarded Lombardy to Sardinia, restored the exiled rulers of Parma, Modena, Tuscany, and Romagna, and set up an Italian confederation in which Austria was included.

France's duplicity did not stop Cavour. A year later, appealing to the British, he made major changes in the peace settlement. Plebiscites were held in Tuscany, Modena, and Parma, all of which voted to join Sardinia. Even with the loss of Nice and Savoy to France, the addition of the three areas made Sardinia the dominant power in the peninsula.

The Unification of Italy, 1859–1870

IMAGE
Garibaldi Surrendering Power—British Cartoon

With the consolidation of power in the north, Giuseppe Garibaldi (1807–1882) became the major figure in the unification struggle. This follower of Mazzini, secretly financed by Cavour, led his 1000 tough adventurers, known as the Red Shirts, to conquer Sicily and Naples. He then prepared to take the Papal States. This move prompted Cavour, who feared that a march on the pope's holdings might provoke French intervention, to rush troops to Naples. He convinced Garibaldi to surrender his power to Victor Emmanuel II, thus ensuring Sardinian domination of the unification movement. By November 1860, Sardinia had annexed the former kingdom of Naples and Sicily and all the papal lands except Rome and its environs.

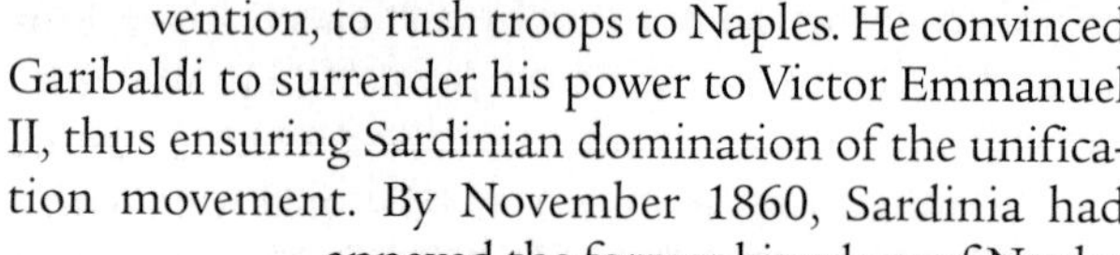

◄ Count Camillo Benso di Cavour mastered the arts of diplomatic maneuvering to create a unified Italy.

A meeting at Turin in March 1861 formally proclaimed the existence of the kingdom of Italy, a new nation of 22 million people. But Austrian control of Venetia and the pope's jurisdiction over Rome were problems that remained unsolved until after Cavour's death in 1861. Italy gained Venetia in 1866 by allying with Prussia in the Austro-Prussian war. When the Franco-Prussian war broke out in 1870, the French could do little to help the pope. Italian forces took control of Rome, and in 1871, this city became the capital of a unified Italy.

The opportunistic methods used by the Sardinians have been criticized. Cavour made no attempt to hide the true nature of his policies. He once said, "If we did for ourselves what we do for our country, what rascals we should be." He fully understood the rules of the Realpolitik game in the post-1848 state system and played it extraordinarily well.

The New Italian State

Italy faced overwhelming problems. The Italians had to deal with economic, political, and cultural differences between the northern and southern parts of the country, a lack of natural resources, and a politically inexperienced population. It also had too many people for its limited economic base.

Italy's most troubling problem, however, was the question of the papacy, which seriously weakened the state. The pope, the spiritual father of most Italians, refused to accept the incorporation of Rome into the new nation. He called himself the "prisoner of the Vatican," and encouraged—with little effect—his Italian flock not to vote. In an attempt to satisfy the pope, in 1871 the government passed the Law of Papal Guarantees, which set up the Vatican as a sovereign state and allocated the pope an annual sum of $600,000 (roughly the amount of money he had received from his previously held lands). Pius IX rejected the offer, but the state refused to repeal the law.

Despite conflicting and unstable political parties, the new Italian state carried on an impressive program of railroad building, naval construction, and attempts at social and welfare legislation. But major problems remained, especially with the peasantry in the south. Radical political parties made their presence felt after the turn of the century in the form of widespread strikes. In 1900, an anarchist assassinated King Umberto, who had taken the throne in 1878. Change proceeded slowly after that, and not until 1912, a time when there was still widespread illiteracy, did the country gain universal manhood suffrage.

The Italian leaders' ambition to make Italy a world power placed a great burden on the nation. Money spent on the army came at the expense of needed investments in education and social services. National resources were squandered in an unsuccessful attempt in 1896 and 1912 to build an empire in Africa.

Up to the beginning of World War I, Italy faced severe economic crises and labor unrest. In June 1914, a general strike spread through the central part of the peninsula. Benito Mussolini, editor of a socialist journal, played a key role in this movement. Attempts to achieve compulsory education, freedom of the press, and better working conditions did little to ease the economic hardships and high taxes that had driven thousands to emigrate to the United States. The south especially suffered, because it had not shared in the industrial gains of the northern part of the country.

France: The Second Empire and the Third Republic

Why was France unable to compete effectively with Germany during the second half of the nineteenth century?

The Second Empire

In France, the violence of the June Days moved the conservatives in the countryside and the moderates in the cities to elect Louis Napoleon, nephew of Napoleon I, to the presidency of the Second Republic in 1848. Although he had failed miserably in his attempts to overthrow the king in 1836 and 1840, he was sure that destiny intended great things for him. When he came back to Paris after the revolution, he was untainted by any involvement in the June Days and appeared to be a unifying force.

Louis Napoleon vs. General Cavaignac–British Cartoon

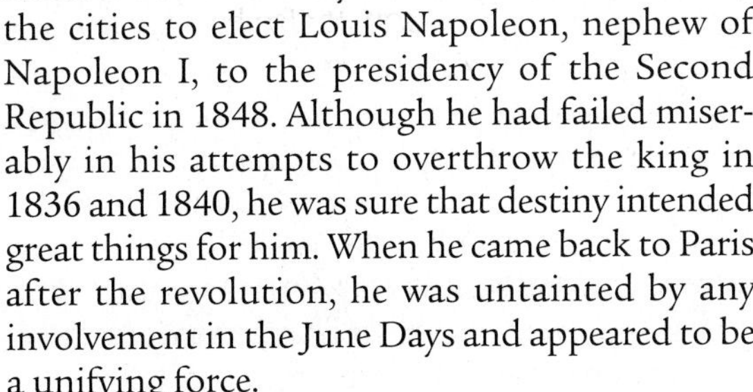

The republic's constitution gave strong powers to the president but limited the office to a single term. Louis Napoleon took advantage of the authority given him and his strong majority to fortify his position. He and his conservative allies dominated France for the next 2 years, becoming strong enough to overthrow the constitution in a coup d'état in December 1851. Louis Napoleon and his allies brutally put down the workers and peasants who opposed the coup and engineered a plebiscite that gave him virtually unanimous support. In 1852, he proclaimed himself Emperor Napoleon III, and the Second Empire replaced the Second Republic.

During its 18-year span, the Second Empire accomplished a great deal. Industrialization brought prosperity to France. Production doubled. France supported the building of the Suez Canal, and railway mileage in France increased by 500 percent. The partial legalization of labor unions and guarantee of the right to strike improved workers' conditions. Baron Georges Haussmann transformed Paris in an ambitious urban renewal that featured broad boulevards, unified architecture, modern utilities, and improved traffic flow.

The price for the order and stability needed to build this prosperity came in the form of political control. The government remained, in theory, a parliamentary regime. The emperor's agents rigged the elections to ensure a majority in the powerless legislature for the emperor. The secret police hounded opponents, both real and potential, and the state censored the press, which accordingly rarely reported bad news.

At first, the emperor brought glory to France through an interventionist and imperialist foreign policy. He continually claimed to be a man of peace, but he allied with Britain in the Crimean War, briefly supported Count Camillo Benso di Cavour in Italy, expanded French influence to ensure a foothold in Indochina, raised the French flag over Tahiti, and penetrated West Africa along the Senegal River. Foreign affairs soured for him in the 1860s when he made an ill-advised attempt to take advantage of the confusion caused by the U.S. Civil War to establish a foothold in the Americas. He placed Maximilian, a Habsburg prince, on the Mexican throne and sent 40,000 troops to support him. Mexican patriots expelled the forces, and in 1867, a firing squad executed Maximilian.

After 1866, Louis Napoleon met his match in the Prussian chancellor Otto von Bismarck (1815–1898), when his blundering ambition contributed to a quick Prussian victory over Austria. Finally, in 1870 he gambled on war against Prussia and lost. With this defeat, the Second Empire ended.

The Third Republic

The defeat of France's Second Empire at Sedan in 1870 gave birth to the Third Republic. The humiliating peace terms stripped France of part of Lorraine and all of Alsace and imposed a huge indemnity on the country. The spectacle of the Germans crowning their emperor and proclaiming the Second Reich at Versailles, the symbol of French greatness, left a bitter taste. The stark contrast between the promised grandeur of the Second Empire and the humiliation of 1871 left a legacy of domestic uncertainty and an obsession for revenge against the Germans.

Persistent class conflicts, covered over during Louis Napoleon's reign, also contributed to many years of shaky existence before the republic gained a firm footing. A new and overwhelmingly royalist national assembly was elected to construct a new, conservative government after the signing of the peace with the Germans. This, added to the shock of the defeat, touched off a revolutionary outburst that led to the Paris Commune of 1871.

Parisians had suffered such severe food shortages during the siege of the city that some had been forced to eat rats and zoo animals. When it turned out that their sacrifices had been in vain, republican and radical Parisians joined forces in part of the city to form a commune, in the tradition of the 1792 Paris Commune, to save the republic. The **Communards** advocated government control of prices, wages, and working conditions (including stopping night work in the bakeries). After several weeks of civil strife, the Commune was savagely put down. Class hatred split France further yet.

Because the two monarchist factions that constituted a majority could not agree on an acceptable candidate for the monarchy, they finally settled on a republic as the least disagreeable form of government. The National Assembly approved the new republican constitution in 1875. Under the new system, members of the influential lower house, the Chamber of Deputies, were elected by direct suffrage. There was also a senate, whose members were elected indirectly by electoral colleges in the departments. The constitution established a weak executive, elected by the legislature. The ministry exercised real power, but its authority depended on whatever coalition of parties could be assembled to form a tenuous majority in the legislature.

Communards—Parisians who lived and worked in the Paris Commune in 1871.

Boulanger and Dreyfus

The stormy tenure of the Third Republic was marked by a series of crises, including anarchist violence culminating in a series of bombings in 1893, financial scandals such as the notorious Panama Canal venture that implicated a wide range of leading figures, and lesser scandals. The two most serious threats were the Boulanger and Dreyfus affairs.

The weak and traumatized republic was both threatened and embarrassed by the public cries for vengeance uttered in 1886 by General Georges Boulanger (ZHORZH boo-lon-ZHAY; 1837–1891), the minister of war. This charismatic, warmongering figure made a series of speeches, which he ended by emotionally proclaiming, "Remember, they are waiting for us in Alsace." The considerable number of antirepublicans saw him as a man on horseback who would sweep away the republic in a coup d'état, much as Louis Napoleon had done in 1851, and bring back French grandeur. The government finally ordered Boulanger's arrest on a charge of conspiracy, and he fled the country. Later he committed suicide.

The Dreyfus case was far more serious because it polarized the entire country, divided and embittered French opinion by the anti-Semitic fervor it unleashed, and challenged the fundamental ideals of French democracy. Captain Alfred Dreyfus (1859–1935), the first Jewish officer on the French general staff, was accused in 1894 of selling military secrets to Germany.

Captain Alfred Dreyfus had to pass through this "Guard of Dishonor" each day on his way to the courtroom during his second trial in 1899.

His fellow officers tried him, found him guilty, stripped him of his commission, and condemned him to solitary confinement on Devil's Island, a dreadful convict settlement off the northeast coast of South America. Even with the case supposedly settled, military secrets continued to leak to the Germans, and subsequently a royalist, spendthrift officer named Major Esterhazy was accused, tried, and acquitted.

The case became a cause célèbre in 1898 when the French writer Émile Zola (1840–1902) wrote his famous letter *J'accuse* (zha-CUES; "I accuse"), in which he attacked the judge for knowingly allowing the guilty party to go free while Dreyfus remained in jail. The next year, Esterhazy admitted his guilt, but by that time the entire country had split into two camps. On the one side were the anti-Dreyfusards—the army, church, and royalists—on the other side were the pro-Dreyfusards—the intellectuals, socialists, and republicans. The case was once again placed under review in the military courts, and even though Esterhazy had confessed, the court continued to find Dreyfus guilty. Finally, the French president pardoned him, and in 1906, the highest civil court in France found him innocent.

The case had greater significance than just the fate of one man. Those who had worked against Dreyfus, especially the church, would pay dearly for their stand. Many republicans believed that the church, a consistent ally of the monarchists, was the natural enemy of democratic government. They demanded an end to the church's official ties to the state. In 1904 and 1905, the government closed all church schools and rescinded the **Napoleonic Concordat.** All ties between church and state were formally ended.

After weathering 40 difficult years, by 1914 the Third Republic had gained prosperity and stability. Workers had found their voice in the country as the various trade and local union groups came together in the General Confederation of Labor. Monarchists and other right-wing parties still had considerable influence, although the Dreyfus affair had weakened them.

French republicanism had wide support across the political spectrum. Most French citizens enjoyed basic democratic rights, which they exercised through the extremely complex multiparty political system of the republic. The various ministries that were constructed from the fragile coalitions came and went with bewildering rapidity. Yet France was strong and prosperous, one of only two republics among the world's great powers.

Napoleonic Concordant—Agreement signed between Napoleon and Pope Pius VII in 1801 that reestablished the Catholic Church as the religion of the majority of the French people. The church regained its prominence and role in education, but without its pre-1789 power and wealth.

The United Kingdom: Reform and Stability

What political and economic factors accounted for the stability of Britain during the nineteenth century?

The post-Napoleonic War period was the most difficult time for Britain, as the transition back to a peacetime economy and the wrenching changes caused by industrialization made their effects felt. Some traditional workers lost their jobs due to the increasing use of machines, and in response, workers smashed the machines and destroyed some factories. Violence broke out when some working-class groups and radicals pushed for rapid reforms. The worst incident took place in August 1819, in what became known as the Peterloo Massacre. In Manchester, a crowd of 60,000 gathered at St. Peter's Fields to push for parliamentary reforms. When the army was sent to disband the meeting, several people were killed and hundreds were injured.

Tory Dominance

The Tories (Conservatives), Britain's ruling party since the 1770s, were blind to the hardships of the workers. They continued to react to the long-departed excesses of the French Revolution. Instead of dealing with the misfortunes of the poor and the unemployed, they declared that the doctrine of "peace, law, order, and discipline" should be their guide. To that end, they pushed through a series of repressive acts after 1815 that suspended the Habeas Corpus Act, restricted public meetings, repressed liberal newspapers, and placed heavy fines on literature considered to be dangerous. Massive conflict between the rich and poor appeared inevitable.

Britain's political abuses were plain for all to see. Representation in the House of Commons was not at all proportional to the population. Three percent of the people dictated the election of members. The rapidly growing industrial towns such as Manchester and Birmingham—each with more than 100,000 citizens—had no representatives, while other areas, virtually without population, had them. The duke of Wellington's failure to acknowledge the need for reforms aroused the public. In the end, the "Iron Duke" and the Tories were forced to resign when members of his own party voted against Wellington in protest of the Catholic Emancipation Act of 1829, which gave Roman Catholics voting rights and the rights to serve in Parliament and most public offices. The Tories were replaced by a more liberal group, the Whigs. The drive toward self-interested changes by the upper classes had begun in the 1820s, led by Robert Peel (1788–1850) and George Canning (1770–1827). These two set in motion the British reform tradition that continued to 1914. When Wellington was voted out of office, Lord Charles Grey (1764–1845), leader of the Whig party, became head of government. In 1832, Grey pushed immediately to reform Parliament.

Self-Interested Reform

After being blocked by aristocratic interests, first in the House of Commons and then in the House of Lords, reform bills responding to these electoral abuses were finally passed. But they became law only because King William IV threatened to create enough new members of the House of Lords who would vote for the bills in order to pass them. Grey's reform bills did not bring absolute democracy, but they pointed the way toward a more equitable political system. Reformers pushed through laws that ended capital punishment for more than a hundred offenses, created a modern police force for London, recognized labor unions, and repealed old laws that kept non-Anglican Protestants from sitting in Parliament. The reform tide increased in the 1830s and 1840s. Abolitionist pressures brought about the end of slavery in the British Empire in 1833. Parliament passed laws initiating the regulation of working conditions and hours. In 1835, the Municipal Corporations Act introduced a uniform system of town government by popular elections.

Britain's government was far from being a democracy, and in the 1830s and 1840s, a strong popular movement known as **Chartism** developed. Its leaders summarized the country's needs in six demands: universal manhood suffrage, secret voting, no property qualifications for members of Parliament, payment of Parliament members so that the poor could seek election, annual elections, and equal districts. In 1839, 1842, and 1848, the Chartists presented their demands, backed by more than a million signatures on their petitions. But each time, they failed to gain their goals, and the movement declined after 1848. By the end of the century, however, all of their demands, except that for annual parliamentary elections, had been put into law.

Mirroring the ascendancy of the middle classes, economic liberalism became dominant. A policy of free trade came to be favored because, given Britain's overwhelming economic superiority, the country could best profit from that approach. The Corn Laws' protective duties on imported grain, which had favored the gentry since 1815, no longer suited the industrializing British economy. These laws had been designed to encourage exports and to protect British landowners from foreign competition. By the middle of the century, the population had grown to such an extent that British farmers could no longer feed the country, and the price of bread rose alarmingly.

The potato crop famine in Ireland in 1845 spotlighted the situation and the need for low-priced food from abroad. Repeal of the Corn Laws made possible the import of cheaper food. Soon Britain abandoned customs duties of every kind. The economy boomed under the stimulus of cheap imports of raw materials and food.

The Irish Dilemma

One dilemma escaped the solutions of well-meaning reformers, that of the British role in Ireland, which originated in the seventeenth century. The British placed large numbers of Scottish emigrants in the province of Ulster in northern Ireland, where they built a strong colony of Protestants. In the eighteenth century, the British passed a number of oppressive laws against Irish Catholics, taking what was left of their lands and restricting their political, economic, and religious freedom. Passage of the Act of Union in 1801 forced the Irish to send their representatives to the Parliament in London, not Dublin. Most of the Irish farmland at this time was controlled by parasitic landlords who leased their newly gained lands in increasingly smaller plots to more and more people. Many peasants could not pay their rent and were evicted from the land. The Irish lost both their self-government and their livelihood.

The 1845 potato famine and its aftereffects led to a tremendous decline in population. Perhaps as many as 1 million died and 1.5 million emigrated, many to the United States. Between 1841 and 1891, the population fell by more than 40 percent, from 8.8 million to less than 5 million.

For all of their suffering, the Irish gained very few concessions from London during the nineteenth century. The Catholic Emancipation Act (1829) removed legal limitations from the Irish Church and tenants received protection from being arbitrarily evicted by British landlords. The Irish Anglican Church lost its favored position when Roman Catholics were freed of the obligation to pay tax support to a church they did not attend. In the 1880s, Irish peasants were given the chance gradually to regain land that had once been theirs.

Victorian Reforms

In the mid-1800s, an alliance of the landed gentry and the middle classes worked together to dominate the British government and to keep the lower classes "in their stations." The newly ascendant middle classes believed that political reforms had gone far enough, and the Whig government of Lord Palmerston, who

---

Chartism—A movement active in the middle part of the nineteenth century that pushed British politicians to make reforms.

served as prime minister from 1855 to 1865, reflected this view. But the final third of the century would belong to the reforming politicians among the Liberals and Conservatives, who had to face the fact that the complacency of government during the "Victorian Compromise" from 1850 to 1865 could not continue. Serious problems plagued the country. Only one adult male in six was entitled to vote. Both parties felt the pressure to make the political system more representative. Both parties also knew that reform must come, and each hoped to take the credit and gain the resultant strength for extending the vote. Thanks to its wealth and adaptability, Britain built a truly democratic political structure by 1914. The state continued to support business even as it became more intimately involved in matters affecting the welfare of its citizens.

Gladstone and Disraeli

Two great statesmen, William Ewart Gladstone (1809–1898), a Liberal, and Benjamin Disraeli (1804–1881), a Conservative, dominated the first part of this period with their policies of gradual reform. They alternated as prime minister from 1867 to 1880. After Disraeli's death, Gladstone prevailed until he retired in 1894. The two leaders came from sharply contrasting backgrounds. The son of a rich Liverpool merchant, Gladstone had every advantage that wealth and good social position could give him. He entered Parliament in 1833 and quickly became one of the great orators of his day. He began as a Conservative, working in the tradition of the Tory reformer Robert Peel. Gradually he shifted his alliance to the newly formed Liberal party in the 1850s, became a strong supporter of laissez-faire economics, and worked to keep government from interfering in business. He was far more effective as a political reformer than as a social or economic one.

Disraeli had few of Gladstone's advantages. The son of a Jew who became a naturalized British subject in 1801, Disraeli was baptized an Anglican. He first made a name for himself as the author of the novel *Vivian Grey* (1826). In contrast to Gladstone, Disraeli went from liberalism to conservatism in his philosophy. He stood for office as a Conservative throughout his career and became the leader of the party.

The Liberals' turn came first. In 1866, they introduced a moderate reform bill giving city workers the vote. Some Conservatives opposed it, fearful that increasing the franchise would bring the day of revolution closer. When the proposal failed to pass, political agitation and riots rocked the country. The outbreaks evidently impressed the members of Parliament; when the Conservatives came to power in 1867, Disraeli successfully sponsored the Second Reform Bill, which added more than a million city workers to the voting rolls. The measure increased the electorate by 88 percent, although women and farm laborers were still denied the vote.

Even though the Conservatives passed the voter reform bill, the new elections in 1868 brought the Liberals back to power, and Gladstone began his so-called Glorious Ministry, which lasted until 1874. With the granting of the vote to the urban masses, it became imperative to educate their children. The Education Act of 1870 promoted the establishment of local school boards to build and maintain state schools. Private schools received governmental subsidies if they met certain minimal standards. Elementary school attendance, which was compulsory between the ages of 5 and 14, jumped from 1 to 4 million in 10 years.

Other reforms included a complete overhaul of the civil service system. Previously, in both the government and the military, appointments and promotions depended on patronage and favoritism. But in 1870, this method was replaced by open examinations. The government also improved the military by shortening enlistment terms, abolishing flogging, and stopping the sale of officers' ranks. Gladstone's government successfully revamped the justice system and introduced the secret ballot. Finally, some restrictions on labor unions' activities were removed. By 1872, the Glorious Ministry had exhausted itself, and Disraeli referred to Gladstone and his colleagues in the House of Commons as a "range of exhausted volcanoes."

Disraeli's government succeeded the Glorious Ministry in 1874, and he stated that he was going to "give the country a rest." He was no stand-pat Conservative, however. He supported an approach known as Tory democracy, which attempted to weld an alliance between the landed gentry and the workers against the middle class. Even during this "time of rest," Disraeli's government pushed through important reforms in public housing, food and drug legislation, and union rights to strike and picket peacefully.

Gladstone returned to power in 1880 and continued the stream of reforms with the Third Reform Bill, which extended the vote to agricultural workers. This act brought Britain to the verge of universal manhood suffrage. Gladstone also secured passage of the Employers' Liability Act, which gave workers rights of compensation in case of accidents on the job.

He tried to solve the Irish question, but none of the concessions made up for the lack of home rule, and the Irish patriot Charles Stewart Parnell (1846–1891) began to work actively to force the issue through Parliament. Gladstone introduced home rule bills in 1886 and 1893, but both were defeated. A home rule bill was finally passed in 1914, but by this time the Ulster Protestants strongly opposed the measure and prepared to resist their forced incorporation into Catholic Ireland. The outbreak of war with Germany postponed civil strife, but it was only a 2-year delay until the Easter Uprising of 1916. Not until 1921 did southern Ireland finally gain the status of a British dominion. The home rule bill never went into effect.

The New Liberals

Gladstone's fight for Irish home rule split his party and paved the way for a decade of Conservative rule in Britain (1895–1905). Partly because of foreign and imperial affairs, the Conservatives departed from the reformist traditions of Tory democracy. By 1905, the need for social and political reform again claimed the attention of the parties.

More than 30 percent of the adult male laborers earned what amounted to sustenance wages, just enough to survive on while employed but not enough to save any money for periods of unemployment, sickness, or family emergency. Workers demonstrated their discontent in a number of strikes. Partly in response to the workers' needs and at the prompting of British socialists, the Labour party was founded in 1900, under the leadership of J. Ramsay MacDonald (1866–1937), a self-made intellectual who had risen from humble status, and the Scottish miner Keir Hardie (1856–1915). The Liberals found themselves threatened on both their left and right flanks. They decided to abandon their laissez-faire economic concepts and embrace a bold program of social legislation. The radical Welsh lawyer David Lloyd George portrayed their program in this way: "Four spectres haunt the poor: Old Age, Accident, Sickness, and Unemployment. We are going to exorcise them."[1]

Led by Prime Minister Herbert Asquith, Lloyd George, and the young Winston Churchill, who had defected from the Conservatives, the Liberal party—with the aid of the Labour bloc—put through a broad program. It provided for old-age pensions, national employment bureaus, workers' compensation protection, and sickness, accident, and unemployment insurance. In addition, labor unions were relieved of financial responsibility for losses caused by strikes. Members of the House of Commons, until that time unpaid, were granted a modest salary. This last act allowed an individual without independent wealth to pursue a political career.

▼ Emmeline Pankhurst, in white scarf, at a rally protesting a government unresponsive to women's issues. After 1910, the women's suffrage movement turned increasingly militant.

Document

Emmeline Pankhurst, from *My Own Story*

The reform efforts of Gladstone and Disraeli did much to improve life for the average citizen in the United Kingdom in the second half of the nineteenth century: access to education, improved living conditions, and the right to vote was extended to almost all adult males. Across the political spectrum—from socialist to conservative—political leaders agreed that the time was not right for women to have the vote. At the beginning of the twentieth century, women joined the struggle to become full, functioning citizens in the United Kingdom, and leading the way were Emmeline Pankhurst and her daughters. They first tried to reason with the political establishment, and when this did not work they began to resort to illegal activities. Many of the women who worked for the vote, the suffragettes, were sentenced to long terms in prison, where some conducted hunger strikes. Most of the suffragettes stopped their activities during the First World War, and finally the right to vote was extended to women 30 years old or over who were property owners. Emmeline Pankhurst wrote of the events in her youth that propelled her, a political conservative, to work for the vote.

. . . [T]he impressions of childhood often have more to do with character and future conduct than heredity or education.... My development into an advocate of militancy was largely a sympathetic process. I have not personally suffered from the deprivations, the bitterness, and sorrow which bring so many men and women to a realization of social injustice. My childhood was protected by love and a comfortable home. Yet, while still a very young child, I began instinctively to feel that there was something lacking, even in my own home, some false conception of family relations, some incomplete ideal.

This vague feeling of mine began to shape itself into a conviction about the time my brothers and I were sent to school. The education of an English boy, then as now, was considered to be a much more serious matter than the education of the English boy's sister. My parents, especially my father, discussed the question of my brothers' education as a matter of real importance. My education and that of my sister were scarcely discussed at all. Of course we went to a carefully selected girls' school but beyond the facts that the head mistress was a gentlewoman and that all the pupils were girls of my own class, nobody seemed concerned. A girl's education at that time seemed to have for its prime object the art of "making home attractive"—presumably to migratory male relatives. It used to puzzle me to understand why I was under such a particular obligation to make home attractive to my brothers. We were on excellent terms of friendship, but it was never suggested to them as a duty that they make home attractive to me. Why not? Nobody ever seemed to know.

The answer to these puzzling questions came to me unexpectedly one night whey I lay in my little bed waiting for sleep to overtake me. It was a custom of my father and mother to make the round of our bedrooms every night before going themselves to bed. When they entered my room that night I was still awake, but for some reason I chose to feign slumber. My father bent over me, shielding the candle flame with his big hand. I cannot exactly know what thought was in his mind as he gazed down at me, but I heard him say, somewhat sadly, "What a pity she wasn't born a lad."

My first hot impulse was to sit up in bed and protest that I didn't want to be a boy. But I lay still and heard my parents' footsteps pass on toward the next child's bed. I thought about my father's remark for many days afterward, but I think I never decided that I regretted my sex. However it was made quite clear that men considered themselves superior to women, and that women apparently acquiesced in that belief....

I was fourteen years when I went to my first suffrage meeting.... The speeches interested and excited me, especially the address of the great Lydia Becker, who was the Susan B. Anthony of the English movement, a splendid character and a truly eloquent speaker. She was the secretary of the Manchester committee, and I had learned to admire her as the editor of the *Women's Suffrage Journal*, which came to my mother every week. I left the meeting a conscious and confirmed suffragist. I suppose I had always been an unconscious suffragist. With my temperament and my surroundings I could scarcely have been otherwise....

Questions to Consider

1. Do you believe that "men consider themselves superior to women...?"
2. What were the social conditions that prompted Emmeline Pankhurst to believe that she was not treated justly?
3. Do you believe that education for men is a more serious matter than education for women?

From Emmeline Pankhurst, *My Own Story* (New York: Hearst International Library, 1914; Kraus reprint, 1971), pp. 4-9. Taken from the Internet Modern History Sourcebook © Paul Halsall, October, 1994, at halsall@murray.fordham.edu

The House of Lords tried to block the Liberal reform plan by refusing to pass the 1909–1910 budget, which laid new tax burdens, including an income tax, on the richer classes in order to pay for the new programs. The Liberals and Labour fought back by directly attacking the rationale for the Lords' existence. They argued that a hereditary, irresponsible upper house was an anachronism in a democracy. The result was the Parliament Bill of 1911, which took away the Lords' power of absolute veto. Asquith announced that the king had promised to create enough new peers to pass the bill if needed (a tactic used with the 1832 Reform Bill). The Lords were forced to approve, and thereafter, they could only delay and force reconsideration of legislation.

By 1914, the evolutionary path to democracy and a modern democratic state structure had, except for women's suffrage, been largely completed. In the previous generation, some effort had been made to gain the vote for women, but to little effect. Women's suffrage was not a concern for the major parties, whose leaders for the most part felt that women's proper place was in the home. At the turn of the century, the most effective group working for women's rights was the Women's Social and Political Union (WSPU), whose members were the first to be known as "suffragettes." The founder of the group, Emmeline Pankhurst (1858–1928), first agitated, then disturbed, and then challenged the order and stability of England in the decade before World War I. Pankhurst and her colleagues traveled and worked constantly to make their case, and in 1910 the WSPU abandoned traditional rhetoric in favor of mass marches, hunger strikes, and property damage. In 1913, a young suffragette martyred herself by running in front of the king's horse at the Derby. With the outbreak of the war, the WSPU backed the national effort against the Germans, and finally in 1918, women age 30 and over were granted the vote. Ten years later, they gained equal voting rights with men.

The Dominions

Supporting the United Kingdom as allies, customers, and suppliers of raw materials were its dominions. The British dominions became self-governing without breaking their political ties to Great Britain. With the exception of South Africa, these new nations were predominantly British in stock, language, culture, and governmental traditions. In the case of Canada, however, a strong French-speaking minority in Quebec, inherited from the original French regime, persisted and preserved its French heritage. In South Africa, following a confused history of rivalry and war between the British and Dutch settlers, a shaky union was achieved (see Chapter 24). There were no complications of rival Europeans in Australia and New Zealand (see Chapter 25), which were settled by the British in the beginning and did not have to adjust to an influx of other Europeans. Both Australia and Canada attained political unity by merging a number of colonies into a single government.

Canada came into English control in 1763. London tried to ensure the loyalty of the French Canadians by issuing a royal proclamation guaranteeing the inhabitants' political rights and their freedom to worship as Roman Catholics. These guarantees were strengthened in 1774 when the British government passed the Quebec Act, called the "Magna Carta of the French Canadian race." This act reconfirmed the position of the Catholic Church and perpetuated French laws and customs. A number of developments took place during in the next century: the growth of the English-speaking population, the defeat of an attempted conquest by the United States, the grant of local self-government, and finally the confederation of Canada into a dominion. Fear of the United States, the need for a common tariff policy, and a concerted effort to develop natural resources led Canadians into confederation. A plan of union, the British North American Act, was approved by the British government and passed by Parliament in London in 1867. This act united Canada into a federal union of four provinces. The new government had some similarities to the political organization of the United States, but it adopted the British cabinet system, with its principle of ministerial responsibility. As a symbol of its connection with Great Britain, provision was made for a governor-general who was to act as the British monarch's representative to Canada.

Russia: Reform and Revolution

Why did Russia fail to successfully adapt to the political and economic transformations occurring in western Europe after 1861?

In 1815, after its victories in the Napoleonic War, Russia stood as the most powerful country in Europe. Four decades later, it was defeated in the Crimean War, fought on its own territory. It was evident to most observers, including the tsars, that Russia had neither the economic strength nor the social and political flexibility of the United Kingdom. It could not adapt successfully to the new forces of the nineteenth century. Tsar Alexander I (r. 1801–1825) saw the need for change and understood that the major obstacles to the reform of his empire were its twin foundations: serfdom and autocracy. His grandmother, Catherine II, had educated him in the liberal traditions and assumptions of the Enlightenment, and for the first 4 years of his reign, he aggressively pursued these notions. During his reign, he attempted major reforms in the areas of education, government, and social welfare. His brother Nicholas II (r. 1825–1855) understood the forces of industrialization, but the Decembrist Revolution led him to impose repressive and reactionary policies during most of his reign.

Enlightenment Dreams

Alexander's experiments with limited serf emancipation, constitutionalism, and federalism demonstrated his desire for change. The tsar was all-powerful in theory, but in reality, he depended on the nobles, who in turn gained their wealth from serfdom. Carrying out the necessary reforms would destroy the foundations of Alexander's power. The fact that his father and grandfather had been killed by nobles made him cautious. Further, it was his misfortune to rule during the Napoleonic wars, and for the first 15 years of his reign, he had to devote immense amounts of money and time to foreign affairs. His liberal reform plans were never carried through to completion, and not until the 1850s, when it was almost too late, would there be another tsar willing and able to make the fundamental social and political reforms needed to make Russia competitive in the industrializing world.

In the reactionary decade after 1815, reformers fell from favor. However, the open discussion of the need for change in the first part of Alexander's reign, the experiences of the soldiers returning from western Europe, and the activities of the expanding number of secret societies kept the dream of change alive. When Alexander failed to reform, the intensity of the reformers' discussions increased. Alexander died in December 1825, and there was confusion over which of his two brothers would succeed to the throne. The days between his death and the confirmation of his younger brother Nicholas I gave a small circle of liberal nobles and army officers the chance to advance their ill-defined demands for a constitution. The officers who led this revolt had been infected with liberal French thought. They sought to end serfdom and establish representative government and civil liberties in Russia. On December 26, these liberals led a small uprising in St. Petersburg. This **Decembrist Revolt,** as it was called, lasted less than a day and could have been put down even earlier had Nicholas been more decisive. This abortive, ill-planned attempt doomed any chance of liberal or democratic reform in Russia for 30 years.

Decembrist Revolt—This, the so-called First Russian Revolution, was a failed attempt by liberal nobles to oust Tsar Nicholas I and to introduce a constitution to their country.

Nicholas I and Russian Reaction

The Decembrist incident shook Nicholas badly, and throughout his reign, he remained opposed to liberal and revolutionary movements. To consolidate his power, he sponsored "official nationalism," whose conservative foundations were "autocracy, orthodoxy, and nationalism"—the Romanov dynasty, the Orthodox Church, and a glorification of the Russian soul. He carried out a thorough policy of censorship that included the screening of foreign visitors, publications, and even musical compositions. The government closely monitored students' activities and curricula in schools and universities. Some 150,000 "dangerous" people were exiled to Siberia. Millions of non-Russians in the empire began to experience limitations on their identities through a forced adherence to Russian customs called "Russification." These activities strengthened Nicholas's immediate control and stopped potential upheaval, but he failed to address adequately the important social and political reforms Russia so badly needed.

Despite his efforts to control intellectual and political currents, Nicholas did not succeed. Reformist activity may have been repressed, but the Russian intellectual circles were creative, tuned as they were to the works of the German philosophers and poets. In the 1840s and 1850s, a new breed of intellectuals appeared—thinkers devoted to achieving liberal and socialist political goals. Although they would not make their strength felt until after the 1860s, these thinkers, known as the **intelligentsia,** put down strong roots during Nicholas's reign. Alexander Herzen (1812–1870) and Michael Bakunin (1814–1876) were the pioneers of this peculiarly Russian movement. Herzen was a moderate socialist who advocated emancipating the serfs, liberalizing the government, and freeing the press. In 1847, he went into exile in London, where he founded his famous paper, the *Kolokol* ("Bell"), 10 years later. It was widely read in Russia, supposedly appearing mysteriously on the tsar's table. Bakunin, the father of Russian anarchism, was more radical. He believed that reform of Russia was useless and advocated terrorism. He preached that anarchy—complete freedom—was the only cure for society's ills. He too went into exile in the West.

On the Efforts of the Polish People

The Russian intellectuals debated many questions, most important of which was whether Russia should imitate all aspects of European life or pursue its own tradition of Orthodoxy and a single-centered society. The question had been posed since the reign of Peter the Great. The liberal Westerners argued that if Russia wished to survive, it had to adopt basic aspects of the West and renounce much of its own past. The Slavophiles on the other side of the dialogue renounced

intelligentsia—Intellectuals who want to use their ideas to change society.

industrial Europe and the modern West, seeing them as materialistic, pagan, and anarchic. They looked to their distant past for guidance for the future.

Nicholas was able to maintain control to the extent that the 1830 and 1848 revolutions had little influence or impact on Russia. Some aspects of industrialization were introduced—for example, the first Moscow–St. Petersburg rail line was put into operation. The government appointed commissions to examine the questions of serfdom and reform, but these extremely serious considerations were kept secret out of fear of provoking a violent reaction from the nobles or a popular uprising among the peasantry. Still, basic doubts about Russia's future remained. Dissident intellectuals, economic and social weakness, and autocratic stagnation were indicators that difficult times were in store for the country.

The Great Reforms

Russia's inept performance in the Crimean War (see p. 729) spotlighted the country's weaknesses and the need for reform. When Alexander II (r. 1855–1881) came to the throne, even the conservatives among his subjects acknowledged the need for major change. The new tsar moved quickly to transform the basis of the autocratic structure—the institution of serfdom—but ran into delay from the nobility. Alexander appointed a committee, which, after 5 years of deliberation, drew up the **Emancipation Proclamation,** issued in March 1861. By this reform, 32 million state peasants and 20 million serfs, who had no civil rights, could not own property, and owed heavy dues and services to the nobility, began the transition to land ownership and citizenship.

The government paid the landlords a handsome price for the land that was to be turned over to the peasants. In return, the peasants had to pay the government for the land over a period of 49 years by making payments through their village commune, the *mir.* The drawn-out nature of the land transfer disappointed the former serfs, who had expected a portion of the lords' lands to be turned over to them without charge. Instead, the peasants were trapped in their village communes, which received and allocated all of the land—much of it poor—and divided it among the various families and paid taxes. Even though they were granted ownership of their cottages, farm buildings, garden plots, domestic animals, and implements, the restrictions placed on the peasants by confining them to their villages constituted a serious problem. New generations of peasants increased the population, but there was no corresponding increase in their share of the land.

The emancipation of the serfs was the single most important event in the domestic history of nineteenth-century Russia. It brought about thoroughgoing reforms of the army, judiciary, municipal government, and system of local self-government. One of the most important reforms came in 1864, when local government was transformed by the *zemstvo* (ZEMST-vo) law. In the countryside, the gentry, middle classes, and peasants elected representatives to local boards (*zemstvos*). These boards collected taxes and maintained roads, asylums, hospitals, and schools. The *zemstvos* became perhaps the most successful governmental organizations in Russia.

While Alexander II pushed through the "Great Reforms," the revolutionary movement grew stronger. In the 1850s, the nihilist movement developed, questioning all old values, championing the freedom of the individual, and shocking the older generation. At first the nihilists tried to convert the aristocracy to the cause of reform. Failing there, they turned to the peasants in an almost missionary frenzy. Some idealistic young men and women joined the movement to work in the fields with the peasants, while others went to the villages as doctors and teachers to preach the message of reform. This "go to the people" campaign was known as the populist, or *narodnik* (na-ROD-nik), movement. Not surprisingly, the peasants largely ignored the outsiders' message.

Revolutionary Response

Frustrated by this rejection, the idealistic young people turned more and more to terrorism. The radical branch of the nihilists, under the influence of Bakunin's protégé Sergei Nechaev (ne-CHAI-ev; 1847–1882), pursued a program of the total destruction of the status quo, to be accomplished by the revolutionary elite. In *Revolutionary Catechism,* Nechaev stated that "everything that promotes the success of the revolution is moral and everything that hinders it is immoral." The soldiers in the battle, the revolutionaries, were "doomed men," having "no interests, no affairs, no feelings, no habits, no property, not even a name."[2] The revolution dominated all thoughts and actions of these individuals.

For the 20 years after his emancipation of the serfs, Alexander suffered under increasing revolutionary attack. It was as though the opposition saw each reform not as an improvement but as a weakness to be exploited. In Poland, the tsar had tried to reverse the Russification program of his father and in return saw the Poles revolt in 1863. Would-be assassins made a number of attempts on him, and the violence

Emancipation Proclamation—Called by some the greatest political act of the nineteenth century, the Emancipation Proclamation issued by Tsar Alexander II in March 1861 gave civil and property rights to 52 million state peasants and serfs. It also triggered a series of reforms that changed the military, law, education, and the economy.

Tsar Alexander II instituted sweeping reforms, including the abolition of Russian serfdom in 1861. For many of his subjects, however, they were too little and too late, as this satiric depicting of "The Liberator" suggests.

expanded throughout the 1870s as a number of his officials were attacked by young terrorists such as Vera Zasulich (za-SU-lich; 1851–1919). Finally, Alexander was assassinated in 1881, on the very day he had approved a proposal to call a representative assembly to consider new reforms.

Reaction and Response, 1881–1905

The slain tsar's son, Alexander III (r. 1881–1894), could see only that his father's reforms had resulted in increased opposition and, eventually, death. Consequently, he tried to turn the clock back and reinstate the policy of "autocracy, Orthodoxy, and nationalism." Under the guidance of his chief adviser, Constantine Pobedonostsev (po-bied-do-NOST-sev; 1827–1907), Alexander pursued a policy of censorship, regulation of schools and universities, and increased secret police activities. Along with renewing Russification among the minorities, he permitted the persecution of Jews, who were bullied and sometimes massacred in attacks called *pogroms.* The tsar may have been successful in driving the revolutionaries underground or executing them, and the nationalities may have been kept in their place, but under Alexander III, Russia lost 13 valuable years in its attempt to become economically and politically competitive with western Europe.

Succeeding Alexander was his son, Nicholas II (r. 1894–1917), a decent but weak man. He inherited and retained both his father's advisers and his father's policies. Larger forces overwhelmed him. Industrialization and rural overpopulation exerted a wide range of political pressures, and the autocratic structure could not cope.

Russia lacked a tradition of gradual reform and habits of compromise such as existed in England. After the assassination of Alexander II, the government increasingly used brutal force to keep order. At the same time, it did little to help the people suffering in the transition from an agrarian to an industrial society. The regime worked energetically to eliminate the opposition by placing secret agents among them, launching violent assaults, and carrying on diversionary anti-Semitic activities with bands of thugs called the Black Hundreds. By attacking the opposition, the tsarist government concentrated on the symptoms of Russia's problems—political dissent and critical, social, and economic dilemmas—rather than their causes. The tsars tried to crush all opposition movements, rather than carry out effective reform.

The Liberal party (Constitutional Democrats, or Kadets) wanted a constitutional monarchy and peaceful reform on the British model. Although limited in numbers, because of the elevated social standing of most of their members, the Kadets were a powerful voice for change in Russia.

The much more numerous Social Revolutionaries combined non-Marxist socialism with the *narodnik* tradition and simplistically called for "the whole land for the whole people." These agrarian socialists wanted to give the land to the peasants. However, they lacked a unified leadership and a well-thought-out program.

In this troubled environment, the solutions proposed by Karl Marx attracted a number of supporters. Marx himself did not believe that Russia would be a favorable laboratory for his theories. He expressed surprise when *Das Kapital* was translated into Russian in 1872 but was pleased when he learned of the broad impact of his theories. Many intellectuals looked to Marx to show them the way to a complete social, economic, and political revolution. Not until 1898, however, was there an attempt to establish a Russian Social Democratic party made up of radical intellectuals and politically active workers.

The Russians did not experience the most demanding parts of industrialization until the end of the century and then on a different basis from that of the western European countries. Russia remained an overwhelmingly agrarian society in which the state paid for building factories by using grain produced by the peasants for export on the depressed world market. However, the urban, industrial emphasis of Marx's theories sparked debate over the way in which they applied to Russia.

Lenin and the Bolsheviks

The person who would eventually apply and implement Marxist theory was Vladimir Ilich Ulyanov (VLAD-i-mir EEL-ich oo-LYAN-nov; 1870–1924), who later took the name Lenin. Born in Ulyanovsk (oo-LYAN-ovsk), formerly Simbirsk, a small city along the Volga River, Lenin grew up in the moderate and respectable circumstances provided by his father, a school administrator and teacher.

In 1887, the government arrested and executed Lenin's brother, Alexander, in St. Petersburg on charges of plotting against the life of the tsar. Shortly thereafter, Lenin began to study the writings of Marx and their potential applications to contemporary Russia. He overcame major obstacles from tsarist officials and passed his law exams at St. Petersburg University without formally attending classes. After 1893, he began to compile theories of tactics and strategy that would form the basis of the Soviet Union throughout its 73-year existence.

In 1895, a court sentenced him to exile in Siberia for his political activities. While in exile, he enjoyed complete liberty of movement in the district and could hunt, fish, swim, study, read, and keep up a large correspondence. A political ally, Nadezhda Krupskaia (na-DESH-da KRUP-ska-ia), joined him, and they were married. Later they translated Sidney and Beatrice Webb's *History of Trade Unionism* into Russian. When Lenin's exile ended in 1900, he and Krupskaia went to Switzerland, where they joined other Russian Social Democrats in exile in founding the newspaper *Iskra* ("Spark"), whose motto was "From the Spark—the conflagration."

In applying Marx to Russian conditions, Lenin found it necessary to sketch in several blank spots. Lenin's methods differed greatly from those of western European Marxists, as did his theories. Lenin advocated the formation of a small elite of professional revolutionaries, the **"vanguard of the proletariat."** These professionals, subject to strict party discipline, would anticipate the proletariat's needs and best interests and lead them through the oxymoronic theory of "democratic centralism."

The Social Democrats met in 1903 in London and split into two wings—the Bolsheviks (BOL-shuh-vik) and the Mensheviks (MEN-shuh-vik)—over the questions of the timing of the revolution and the nature of the party. (In Russian, *bolshevik* means "majority" and *menshevik* means "minority," the names stemming from a vote on party policies in 1903 when the Bolsheviks did prevail. On most occasions until the summer of 1917, however, the Bolsheviks were, in fact, in a distinct minority among the Social Democrats.) The two factions differed sharply on strategy and tactics. The Bolsheviks, following Lenin's revisionist views, were prepared to move the pace of history along through democratic centralism. The Mensheviks believed that Russian socialism should grow gradually and peacefully in accordance with Marxist principles of development and historical evolution, and they were prepared to work within a framework dominated by bourgeois political parties. They knew that their victory was inevitable, given the historical dialectic, and that the proletariat would play the lead role, assisted by the party. After their split in 1903, the two factions never reconciled.

After 1903, Lenin had little success in changing the political conditions of Russia, beyond affecting the most sophisticated part of the workers' movement. However, he continued to make significant doctrinal contributions. Lenin recommended a socialism whose weapon was violence and whose tactics allowed little long-range compromise with the bourgeoisie. However, he also saw the advantages of flexibility and encouraged temporary deviations that might serve the goals of the working class. He took little for granted and reasoned that the development of class unity to destroy the capitalists among the Russian workers might require some assistance. To that end he refined his notion of the way in which the elite party would function. In revolution, the elite party would infiltrate the government, police, and army while participating in legal workers' move-

vanguard of the proletariat—The elite revolutionary group that would anticipate the proletariat's needs and lead them through the principle of democratic centralism.

▲ An unsuccessful war against Japan, an autocratic old regime that could not respond to new conditions, and the beginning of a politically mobilized population led to the tragic events of Bloody Sunday, when the tsar's Cossack guards fired on a peaceful march of Russian workers to the Winter Palace in St. Petersburg. Artists were quick to capture the brutality of the regime in posters such as this.

ments; in government, the party would enforce its dictates on the populace with iron discipline.

Lenin looked out at the undoubted strength of the advanced technological nations and marveled at their extension of power. In *Imperialism, the Highest Stage of Capitalism* (1916), he forecast that the modern capitalist states would destroy themselves. He argued that the wages of the workers did not represent enough purchasing power to absorb the output of the capitalists' factories and that the vast amounts of capital that were accumulated could not be invested profitably in the home country. Therefore, the states would engage in an inevitable competition for markets, resources, and capital that would drive them from cutthroat competition to outright war and their ultimate destruction. At that point, he reasoned, his elite party would be ready to pick up the pieces from the blindly selfish powers.

The Revolution of 1905 and Its Aftermath

As in 1854 at Crimea, a failure in war—this time a "splendid little war" against Japan—exposed the weaknesses of the autocratic tsarist regime. Strikes and protests spread throughout the land in response to the military failure of the Russo-Japanese War during the last days of 1904. On January 22, 1905, the Cossacks opened fire on a peaceful crowd of workers who had advanced on the Winter Palace in St. Petersburg carrying a petition asking for the tsar's help. In response, a general strike broke out, with the strikers demanding a democratic republic, freedom for political prisoners, and the disarming of the police. **Soviets**—councils of workers led by the Social Democrats—appeared in the cities to direct revolutionary activities. Most business and government offices closed, and the whole machinery of Russian economic life creaked to a halt. The country was virtually paralyzed.

After a series of half-measures and stalling in response to strikes and revolutionary activities, the tsar found himself pushed to the wall. Unable to find a dictator to impose order, he was forced to issue the October Manifesto of 1905, which promised "freedom of person, conscience, assembly, and union." A national legislature, the Duma, was to be called without delay. The right to vote would be extended, and no law could be enacted without the Duma's approval. The October Manifesto split the moderate from the socialist opposition and kept Nicholas on the throne, although he was heartbroken for having made the compromise.

soviets—Councils of workers led by the Social Democrats in the 1905 Revolution.

	Russian Political Movements in 1905
Kadets	Liberals
Octobrists	Moderate liberals
Trudoviks	Populist Labor Party
Socialist Revolutionaries	Agrarian-based socialists (non-Marxists)
Bolsheviks	Revisionist democratic centralist Social Democrats (Marxists)
Mensheviks	Social Democrats, Marxist fundamentalists
Monarchist right	Supporters of the tsar
Union of Russian People	Extreme right wing, anti-Semitic and antiliberal
Jewish Bund	Marxist Jewish Workers' party

The socialists tried to start new strikes, but the opposition was now totally split apart.

Most radical forces boycotted the first Duma meeting in the spring of 1906. As a result, the Kadets became the dominant force. Even with this watered-down representation, the tsar was upset by the criticism of the government's handling of the Russo-Japanese War, treatment of minorities, handling of political prisoners, and economic policies. Claiming that the representatives "would not cooperate" with the government, Nicholas dissolved the first Duma. The Russian people turned a cold shoulder to the Kadets' appeals for support. Sensing the decline of political fervor, Nicholas appointed a law-and-order conservative, Peter Stolypin (sto-LEAP-in; 1862–1911), as prime minister. He assumed emergency powers and cracked down on the radicals.

Unlike previous tsarist appointees, Stolypin knew that changes had to be made, especially in the area of agriculture. Despite Nicholas's lack of support, Stolypin set up a process to develop a class of small farmers. He pushed through reforms that abolished all payments still owed by the peasants under the emancipation law and permitted peasants to withdraw from the commune and claim their shares of the land and other wealth as private property. He also opened lands east of the Urals to the peasants and extended financial aid from the state. He was well on the way to finding a solution to that most enduring of Russian problems, the peasant problem, before he was assassinated in 1911 by a Socialist revolutionary, who was also an agent of the secret police.

Despite its reactionary tsar and nobility, Russia took major steps toward becoming a constitutional monarchy in the years after 1905. The nation made great economic and social progress. Industrialization increased and generated new wealth. Increased political and civil rights spawned an active public life. Stolypin's death in 1911, however, deprived the country of needed leadership, and World War I gave Russia a test it could not pass.

The "Eastern Question" and the Failure of European Diplomacy to 1914

Why were the European powers unable to come to an agreement about what to do with the Ottoman Empire?

The Ottoman Empire had played a key role in European history since its creation in the fourteenth century. Until the 1750s, fear of the empire preoccupied the Austrians and the Russians. After that time, the empire went into a state of decline, and its Balkan territories became targets of opportunity for Vienna and St. Petersburg. Because of the empire's vast holdings throughout the Middle East and North Africa, the English, French, and Germans became equally involved with the fate of the Ottoman Empire. There was no easy solution to the question of what to do with the Turks—the so-called **Eastern Question**—and there was no way to partition its holdings without giving one state or another an advantageous position. During the nineteenth century, the European powers settled on a policy of propping up the sultan and maintaining the fiction of the Ottoman Empire being a great power. Unfortunately, the European states failed to devise an answer to the dilemma of what to do with the power vacuum created by the decaying Ottoman Empire and how to manage the various nations of the Balkans who began their struggles for self-determination and independence.

The Balkans Awaken

By the end of the eighteenth century, Ottoman power had substantially declined in the Balkans, just at a time when the various peoples began to experience waves of nationalism. In 1799 Sultan Selim III acknowledged the independence of the mountainous nation of Montenegro, after its long and heroic defense of its liberty. Further proof of Ottoman weakness came in 1804 when some renegade Turkish troops in Belgrade went on a rampage, disobeyed the sultan's orders, and forced the Serbian people to defend themselves. This initial act of self-protection blossomed into a rebellion that culminated in the Serbs gaining an autonomous position within the Ottoman Empire after an 11-year struggle.

Turkish weakness attracted both Russian and British interests. Russia had made a substantial advance toward the Mediterranean during the reign of Catherine II. In 1774, the Treaty of Küchük Kaynarca (kiu-CHUK kay-NAR-tsa), gave the Russians rights of navigation in Ottoman waters and the right to intervene in favor of Eastern Orthodox Christians in the Ottoman Empire. The British protested these gains, and in 1791, Prime Minister William Pitt the Younger denounced Russia for its supposed ambitions to dismember the empire. Only the common threat of Napoleon from 1798 to 1815 diverted Great Britain and Russia from their competition in the eastern Mediterranean.

The forces of nationalism in Greece took advantage of the chaotic administration of the Turks in 1821. Unlike the Serbian rebellion, the Greek revolution gained substantial outside support from philhellenic ("admiring Greeks") societies of Great

---

Eastern Question—The question of how to dispose of the declining Ottoman Empire.

Britain. Even though Metternich hoped the revolt would burn itself out, the Greeks were able to take advantage of intervention by the Great Powers to gain their independence.

During the Greek Revolt, the British feared that Russia would use the Greek independence movement as an excuse for further expansion at Turkish expense. The British intervened skillfully, and the Greeks were able to gain their independence without a major Russian advance toward the Dardanelle Straits—the control of which by the Turks blocked their access to the Mediterranean Sea and beyond. Tsar Nicholas I wanted to weaken the Ottoman Empire in order to pave the way for Russia to gain control over the Dardanelles and the Bosporus. So much did he want this expansion of his realm that he set aside his obligations to support the European balance of power. Britain became alarmed at this policy, and the upshot was an agreement in 1827 in which Britain, France, and Russia pledged themselves to secure Greek independence. Russia eventually defeated the Turks, and in 1829, the Treaty of Adrianople gave the Greeks the basis for their independence, while Serbia received autonomy. The Danubian principalities of Moldavia and Wallachia, the basis of the future state of Romania, became Russian protectorates.

By the 1830s, it became apparent that the Turks were to be an object of, rather than a participant in, European diplomacy. The sultan's government had few admirers in Europe, but the European powers agreed—at least for the present—to prop up the decaying Ottoman Empire rather than allow one nation to gain dominance in the strategic area.

In 1832, Mehemet Ali, for all intents and purposes the independent governor of Egypt, attacked the sultan, easily putting down the forces of the empire. To prevent the establishment of a new and probably stronger government at the Straits, Nicholas I sent an army to protect Constantinople. In 1833, the Treaty of Unkiar Skelessi (un-key-AR ske-less-ee) gave Russia a dominant position over the Turks.

Britain could not tolerate Russia's advantage and for the next 10 years worked diplomatically to force the tsar to renounce the treaty and sign a general agreement of Turkish independence. This diplomatic game did little to improve the Ottoman Empire's condition. In 1844, while visiting Britain, Nicholas referred to the empire as a "dying man" and proposed that the British join in a dissection of the body.

The Crimean War

The Crimean War, which lasted from 1853 to 1856, was a major turning point in the course of the Eastern Question. The immediate origins of the war were to be found in a quarrel over the management and protection of the holy places in Palestine. Napoleon III, in a move to gain support from Catholics and the military in France, upheld the Roman Catholics' right to perform the housekeeping duties. On the other side, acting under the terms of the treaty signed in Küchük Kaynarca, Nicholas stated that the Orthodox faithful should look after the holy places. From this obscure argument, the Crimean War eventually emerged, as the Great Powers all intervened in the discussions to protect their interests.

The tsar's ambassador to the Turks tried to use the dispute to improve Russia's position in the region, while the British told the sultan to stand firm against the Russians. After the Russians occupied the Danubian principalities in an attempt to show the Turks the seriousness of their demands, the Turks declared war on the Russians in October 1853. By the next summer, the French, Sardinians, and British had joined the Turks. Napoleon III saw the war as a chance to enhance his dynasty's reputation, and the Sardinians found an opportunity to gain allies in their drive for Italian unification. Under the impact of antitsarist public opinion, the British took steps to stop the Russians. The stated aim of all the allies was, of course, the defense of the sultan.

A combination of the allies' military strength and the tsarist forces' inefficiency stalemated the Russians. Austria, a former close ally of Russia, took advantage of Russia's difficulties to extend Austrian influence into the Balkans. The Russians sued for peace, and the Treaty of Paris (1856) once again attempted to resolve the Eastern Question. Rather than deal with the weakness of the Ottoman Empire, the treaty affirmed its integrity and Great Power status. The Black Sea was to be a neutral body of water, and the Dardanelle Straits were closed to foreign warships. The treaty declared that no power had the right to intervene on behalf of the sultan's Christian subjects. Russian control of the principalities was ended. The Crimean War momentarily stopped the Russian advance into the Balkans and toward the eastern Mediterranean, but the problems posed by the "sick man of Europe" remained. Further, the various Balkan nations became even more inflamed with the desire for self-rule.

The Unanswered Question

In the generation after the Crimean War, the problems posed by the disintegrating Ottoman Empire became more severe. To the north, the Russians, who could do little militarily in the Balkans during this period of intense internal reforms, broadcast the message of pan-Slavic solidarity to their "Orthodox" brothers in the Balkans. The Austrians, their appetites whetted by their part in the Crimean War, kept a wary and opportunistic eye on developments in the Balkans. British loans to the Turks cut into the Turkish tax base and led to the destruction of the indigenous Ottoman textile industry. In addition, with the completion of the Suez Canal in 1869, the eastern Mediterranean came to be even more essential to British interests. Finally, the Germans began to increase their influence in the area after 1871.

Nationalism further complicated the unresolved Eastern Question. The Bulgarians, who had been under the Turkish yoke since the fourteenth century, started their national revival in the late eighteenth century. By the 1860s, they had formed a liberation movement, which was strengthened in 1870 when the Turks gave permission to them to found the Bulgarian Exarchate, a Bulgarian wing of the Greek Orthodox faith. This permitted the Bulgarians to establish their churches wherever there were Bulgarian people, a clear invitation for the expansion of the Bulgarian nation. The Bulgarians took strength from the example of the Romanians, who, after centuries of Turkish dominance and a quarter century as a Russian protectorate, had gained their independence in 1861, largely as a result of Great Power influence. Also, during the 1860s, the Serbian leader Michael Obrenovich (o-BREN-o-vich) had worked toward a Balkan union against the Turks. Amid this maneuvering and ferment, the Turks were unable to strengthen their rule over areas theoretically under their control.

Oppression in Bulgaria and Poland

The crisis came to a head in 1875 when peasants revolted in the district of Bosnia, a Turkish-governed province populated by a religiously diverse group of Slavs. Following this insurrection, Serbia and Montenegro declared war on the Turks. In the summer of 1876, the Bulgarians revolted, but the Ottoman forces put down the rebellion. When highly emotional accounts of the Turkish massacres were published in western Europe, the incident became known as the "Bulgarian horrors" and drew British attention to the Balkans. The pan-Slav faithful in St. Petersburg and Moscow were naturally thrilled at the exploits of their "little brothers," and money and volunteers flowed southward.

The series of nationalistic uprisings in the improperly governed Ottoman provinces had captured the attention of the Great Powers, and by the end of 1875, the Eastern Question was once again the main focus of international diplomacy. The "sick man of Europe" was still strong enough to devastate the Serbs and Montenegrins in battle. The insurgents were forced to sue for peace, a move that drew Tsar Alexander II and the Russians into war with the Ottomans in 1877. After a hard-fought campaign, the Russians broke through early in 1878 and were close to achieving their final goal of taking Constantinople when the sultan sued for peace.

The resulting Treaty of San Stefano in March 1878 recognized the complete independence of Serbia and Romania from theoretical Ottoman sovereignty and reaffirmed Montenegro's independence. A large Bulgarian state was set up, nominally tributary to the Ottoman Empire but actually dominated by Russia. The Dardanelle Straits were effectively under Russian control, as the Bulgarian state would have a coast on the Aegean. The Eastern Question was almost solved by the Russians.

Britain and Austria, however, correctly perceived a major shift of the balance of power in Russia's favor, and the two of them forced a reconsideration of the San Stefano treaty at the Congress of Berlin in June and July 1878. Held under the supervision of Bismarck, the self-styled "honest broker," the congress compelled Russia to agree to a revision of Bulgaria's status. The large state created in March was broken into three parts: the northernmost section would be independent, paying tribute to the Turks, and the other two parts would be under Ottoman control. Austria got the right to "occupy and administer" the provinces of Herzegovina and Bosnia.

The congress turned back the Russian advance, stymied the national independence movement, and did little to urge Turkey to put its house in order. The Austrian gains caused great bitterness among the Serbs and Russians, a mood that added to the tension in the Balkans. The Eastern Question remained unanswered, and the Balkans remained an arena of local nationalistic conflicts that would appeal to the imperialistic designs of the Great Powers, especially the Russians and the Austro-Hungarian monarchy.

Appearances and Realities

By 1900, Europeans had many reasons to be optimistic about the future. The growth produced by the previous three generations seemed to support the sturdy belief in progress. There was a substantial amount of unity: Europe was Christian, Caucasian, capitalist, industrialized, and in command of the world. Europeans shared the same vibrant Western traditions, and even the rulers of the various states were all related to one another. As if to symbolize world changes, there were new ways to organize international communication, defuse conflicts, and maintain peace. As early as 1865, a meeting was held in Paris to coordinate the use of telegraph lines and to establish a unified rate structure. Ten years later, the Universal Postal Union was set up to handle the world's mail. To protect the rights of authors, an agreement was drawn up in 1886 for an international copyright union.

Scholars and statesmen worked to strengthen international law, the rules of warfare, and the use of arbitration. A significant example of this was the open-

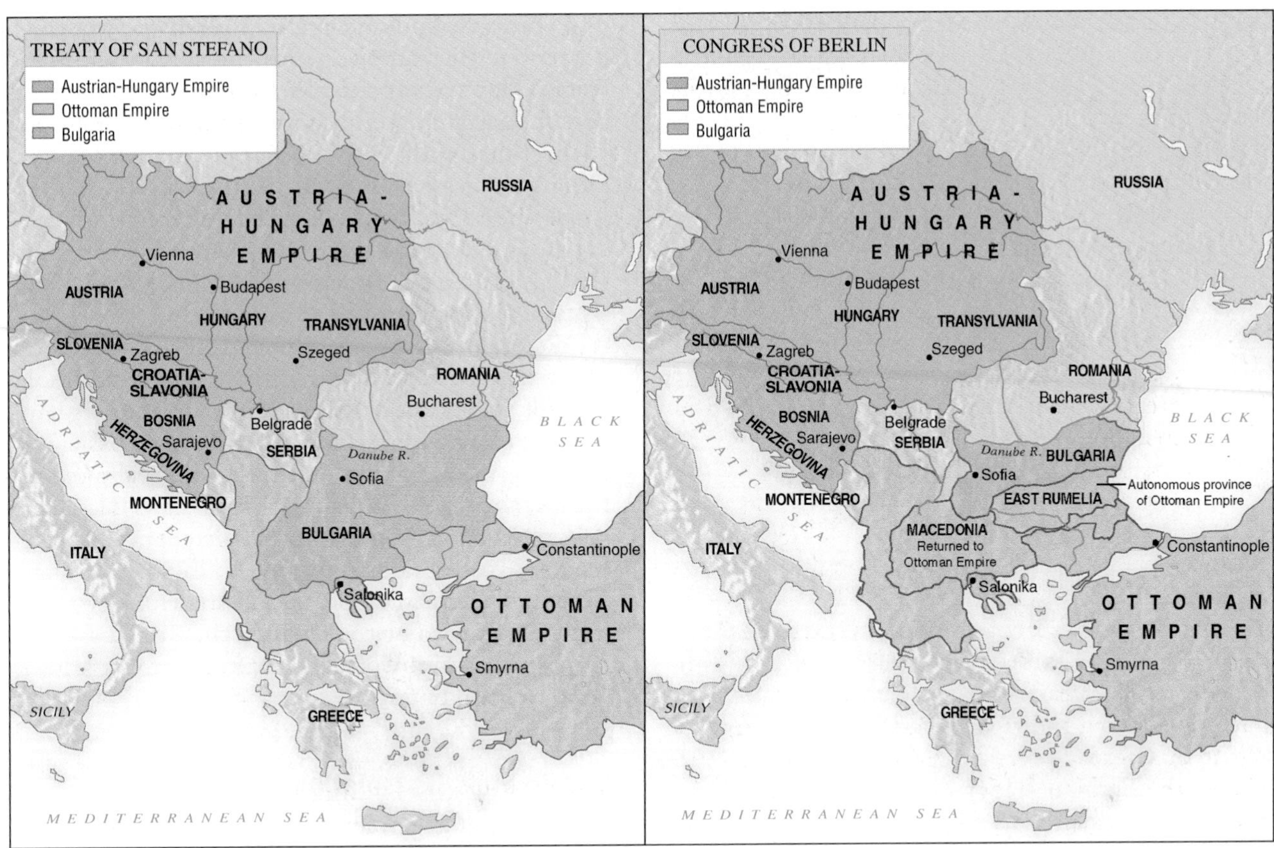

▲ In the spring of 1878, the Russians believed that they had imposed their solution to the Eastern Question through the Treaty of San Stefano. The other European powers disagreed, however, and they forced a revision of San Stefano in the Congress of Berlin a few months later. Ultimately, the Eastern Question would remain unanswered until World War I redrew the map of Europe and the Middle East.

ing of the Hague Conference in 1899. The Russian foreign minister invited the Great Powers to the Dutch city to discuss arms reduction. Although no progress was made on disarmament, the conference did reform the rules of war by improving the treatment of prisoners, outlawing the use of poisonous gas, and defining the conditions of a state of war. In addition, an international court of arbitration, the Hague Tribunal, was established, staffed by an international group of jurists. Appearance before the court was voluntary, as was acceptance of its decisions. The effectiveness of arbitration as a means to solve problems could be seen in the 10 years before the war. Various powers signed 162 treaties that pledged the signatories to arbitrate disagreements such as boundary decisions and conflicts over fishing rights.

Alfred Nobel, the Swedish manufacturer of dynamite, personified the contradictions of the age. This international producer of explosives established a peace prize two weeks before his death in November 1896. Andrew Carnegie set up the Carnegie Endowment for International Peace and built a peace palace at The Hague for international conferences. It was finished just weeks before the outbreak of World War I.

All of these developments encouraged believers in progress to envision a peaceful future. They pointed out that the wars of the nineteenth century had been generally local and short. They reasoned that if war should break out in the future, the murderous new technologies would ensure that they would not be lengthy or costly. Some social Darwinists asserted that humanity might well evolve beyond the stage of fighting wars altogether. These optimists conveniently ignored the brutal, lengthy, and costly reality of the American Civil War, in many ways the first modern, industrial war. They also ignored the reality that the European state system and military industrial complexes took on a life and momentum of their own.

The End of Bismarck's System

From 1870 to 1890, the German chancellor Otto von Bismarck dominated European diplomacy. He built a rational balance-of-power-based foreign policy devoted to the diplomatic isolation of France by depriving it of potential allies. He reasoned that the French

	Major Dates in European Alliances
1872	The Three Emperor's League (Germany, Austria-Hungary, Russia) formed
1879	Dual Alliance (Germany, Austria-Hungary) formed
1882	Triple Alliance (Germany, Austria-Hungary, Italy) formed
1890	Bismarck resigns; Reinsurance Treaty with Russia lapses
1890s	Germany decides to build fleet to compete with British navy
1894	French-Russian Alliance
1904	Britain and France conclude *Entente Cordiale*
1907	Russia joins Britain and France to form Triple Entente

would try to take revenge on Germany and regain Alsace and Lorraine, but he knew they could do little without aid from the Austrians or Russians. In 1873, Bismarck made an alliance, known as the Three Emperors' League or *Dreikaiserbund* (dri-KAI-ser-bund), with Russia and Austria-Hungary.

Conflicts between the Austrians and Russians in the Balkans soon put a strain on the league, and at the Congress of Berlin (1878) Bismarck was forced to choose between the conflicting claims of Vienna and St. Petersburg. He chose to support Austria-Hungary for a number of reasons, including fear of alienating Great Britain if he backed the Russians. In addition, he felt that he could probably dominate Austria more easily than Russia. This momentous shift paved the way for a new arrangement. In 1879, Bismarck negotiated the Dual Alliance with the Austro-Hungarian monarchy; in 1882, a new partner, Italy, joined the group, which was now called the Triple Alliance.

The choice of Austria over Russia did not mean that Bismarck abandoned his ties with the tsars. In 1881, the Three Emperors' League was renewed. Rivalries between the Dual Monarchy and Russia in the Balkans put an effective end to the arrangement, and the *Dreikaiserbund* collapsed for good in 1887. Bismarck negotiated a separate agreement with Russia called the Reinsurance Treaty, in which both sides pledged neutrality—except if Germany attacked France or Russia attacked Austria—and support of the status quo.

Under Bismarck's shrewd hand, Germany kept diplomatic control for 20 years. Bismarck chose his goals carefully and understood the states with which he worked. He made every effort to avoid challenging Britain's interests and to continue isolating France. As a result, Germany was not surrounded by enemies. The chancellor kept from alienating Russia while maintaining his ties with Austria.

In the 1890s, however, the rash actions of the new kaiser, William II, destroyed Germany's favorable position. He dismissed Bismarck in 1890, took foreign policy into his own hands, and arrogantly frittered away the diplomatic advantages the chancellor had built up. France had been attempting to escape from its isolation for some time and had begun, through its bank loans, to make important inroads into Russia even before Bismarck retired. When the kaiser allowed the Reinsurance Treaty to lapse, the Russians decided to look elsewhere. France leapt at the chance, after 20 years, to secure a strong ally. In 1894, the Triple Alliance of Germany, Italy, and Austria-Hungary found itself confronted by the Dual Alliance of Russia and France. Germany's worst fears had come to pass: it was now encircled by enemies.

Britain Ends Its Isolation

At the end of the nineteenth century, Britain found itself involved in bitter rivalries with Russia in the Balkans and in the Middle East and with France in Africa. During the Boer War, all of the Great Powers in Europe were anti-British. However, the supremacy of the British fleet helped discourage intervention. As the new century began, London became concerned that its policy of splendid isolation might need to be abandoned. In these circumstances, the most normal place for Britain to turn would be to Germany.

On the surface, nothing seemed more natural than that these two dominant European powers should adjust their national interests to avoid conflict. From the 1880s to 1901, both sides made several approaches to investigate an "understanding" between the major sea power, Britain, and the strongest land power, Germany. Tradition and dynastic relations spoke in favor of a closer tie between the two. By 1900, Berlin and London may have competed in economic and imperialistic terms, but they were far from any major strife in any either area.

The two countries could not, however, come together formally. Even though important figures on both sides could see the advantages of an alliance, strong forces worked against this development. German and British interests did not match sufficiently to permit equal gain from an alliance. The kaiser's numerous bellicose statements and clumsy actions (such as his meddling in British colonial affairs by sending a telegram to South Africa's president, Paul Kruger, in 1896) offended many British leaders. Germany's expanding influence in the Middle East and the Balkans worried the British, as did Germany's tremendous economic progress.

Most threatening for London was Germany's plan to build a fleet that would compete with Britain's. In 1900, Germany initiated a huge naval program with a 20-year timetable to create a fleet strong enough to keep Britain from interfering with German international goals. The British believed that the German program was aimed directly at them. For the island nation, the supremacy of the Royal Navy was a life-or-death matter. Since food and raw materials had to come by sea, it was crucial that the navy be able to protect British shipping.

Challenged by Germany, Britain looked elsewhere for allies. In 1904, officials from London and Paris began to settle their differences and proclaimed the *Entente Cordiale* ("friendly understanding"), setting aside a tradition of hostility dating back to the Hundred Years' War. The entente and an alliance with Japan in 1902 ended Britain's policy of diplomatic isolation and brought it into the combination that would be pitted against Germany's Triple Alliance. In 1907, London settled its problems with Russia, thereby establishing the Triple Entente. The British made no definite military commitments in the agreements with France and Russia. Theoretically they retained freedom of action, but they were now part of the alliance system.

The North African Crises

In the decade before World War I, Europe experienced a series of crises on its peripheries, none of which vitally threatened the Great Powers' survival individually. However, because of the alliance system, the incidents increased tensions and brought Europe ever closer to war.

The first serious test came in 1905 over Morocco. France sought control of this territory in order to establish a continuous line of dependencies from the Atlantic across the North African coast to Tunisia. Carefully timing their moves, the Germans arranged for the kaiser to visit the Moroccan port of Tangier, where he declared that all powers must respect the independence of the country. The French were forced to give up their immediate plans for taking over Morocco and had to agree to Germany's suggestion that an international conference be called at Algeciras (1906) to discuss the matter.

At this meeting, the Germans hoped for a split between the British and French. This did not occur. On the contrary, all but one of the nations in attendance—even Italy—supported France rather than Germany. Only Austria-Hungary remained on the kaiser's side. The conference agreed that Morocco should still enjoy its sovereignty but that France and Spain should be given certain rights to police the area.

In 1911, a second Moroccan crisis escalated tensions. When France sent an army into the disputed territory, ostensibly to maintain order, Germany responded by sending the gunboat *Panther* to the Moroccan port of Agadir. Great Britain came out with a blunt warning that all of its power was at the disposal of France in this affair. A diplomatic bargain was finally struck in which France got a free hand in Morocco and Germany gained a small area in equatorial Africa. The two rival alliances managed to avoid war over Morocco. The illusion of progress was maintained—until the alliance system reached the breaking point in the Balkans.

It was in the conduct of diplomacy that the perils of progress took their greatest toll. The vastly stronger states operated more and more under their own views of Social Darwinism, building huge defense establishments while ignoring important crises such as those around the declining Ottoman Empire. The Europeans' appetites, egos, and military forces had begun to exceed the terrain left to be taken in the world. The new mass politics, with its popular press, superpatriotic appeals, and blatant aggressiveness, could not adapt easily to the new situation. A century of grabbing territory and reprinting maps showing broader swatches of the globe in the national colors had spoiled the Western states and distorted their foreign policies. The results would bring an end to European dominance.

Conclusion

The French and Industrial Revolutions changed the Western world far beyond the comprehension of the leaders gathered at Vienna in 1814. The Congress of Vienna placed a framework of stability on Europe, while accepting many of the changes since 1789. However, it did not deal with the new political forces of liberalism, nationalism, and socialism. This soon became evident with the epidemic of revolutions in the 1820s, 1830s, and 1840s. In 1848, the legacy of the French Revolution and the process of industrialization combined to overpower the political structures of France, Germany, Italy, and the Habsburg Empire. The 1848 revolutions enjoyed brief, spectacular successes and tragic, lasting failures. The leaders of the revolutions had little or no experience, and they acted under a total infatuation with their ideals. The force of nationalism, so powerful an enemy of autocracy, soon proved to be a fragmenting force among the various liberated nationalities. These factors doomed the idealistic revolutionaries and introduced a new range of political alternatives, such as unification in Italy, the Second Empire in France, and the construction of a unified German state.

Russia and Britain avoided the revolutionary upheavals of 1848, the first through a policy of repression that failed to respond effectively to its overwhelming problems and the second because of an improving standard of living and a flexible, self-interested middle class. For the rest of the century their paths would diverge, as England would grow to establish a world empire while the Russians would struggle with reform and repression until the 1905 Revolution, which would finally bring an end to autocracy. In Europe, the German Second Reich came to be the most powerful country on the Continent and challenged the United Kingdom for commercial supremacy. The French consolidated their power after their military and diplomatic defeat in 1870. Thereafter, until 1914, despite the ramshackle nature of the Third Republic and its scandals, France had power and influence. The Italians had achieved unification under the leadership of Cavour and Sardinia, but unification did not bring miraculous improvements in the lives of the Italian people. The Habsburg Empire, after nearly twenty years of trying to deal with its fractious nationalities, redefined itself as the Dual Monarchy in 1867. It managed to hold together until the outbreak of World War I.

The European states were unable to answer the most important challenge facing them throughout the nineteenth century, and that was what to do with the Ottoman Empire—once a world power that held title to far more territory than it could effectively govern. In the political vacuum that developed in the Ottoman-dominated part of Europe—the Balkans—the subjugated nationalities began to claim their independence under their respective banners of nationalism. Crises erupted on the European peripheries of the Ottoman Empire in the 1830s, 1850s, and 1870s, and at the beginning of the twentieth century, the countries that had made so much progress domestically were failing to maintain stability internationally.

Suggestions for Web Browsing

You can obtain more information about topics included in this chapter at the websites listed below. See also the companion website that accompanies this text, http://www.ablongman.com/brummett, which contains an online study guide and additional resources.

Nationalism and Music
http://acc6.its.brooklyn.cuny.edu/~phalsall/sounds/fnlandia.mid
Through articles and sound files, this site discusses how early nineteenth-century music reflected growing nationalist feelings in Europe.

Marx-Engels Internet Archive
http://www.marxists.org/archive/marx/index.htm
An extensive site on both Karl Marx and Friedrich Engels offers biographies, a photo gallery, letters, and additional web links.

The Revolution of 1848 in France
http://history.hanover.edu/texts/fr1848.htm
This site includes original source documents from the Revolution of 1848 in France.

Revolutions of 1848
http://www.pvhs.chico.k12.ca.us/~bsilva/projects/revs/1848time.html
An extensive site that offers an overview, timeline, biographies, and essays about the revolutions of 1848.

Life of the Tsars
http://www.Alexanderpalace.org/catherinepalace/Alexander.html
This site provides access to images portraying the luxury of life for the tsars in the nineteenth century.

Benjamin Disraeli
http://projects.vassar.edu/punch/Lockwood.html
Benjamin Disraeli was a controversial figure in British history, as can be seen in the cartoon on this website. Links to William Gladstone and the political setting of the time are also found here.

Nineteenth-Century Austria and Germany
http://www.fordham.edu/halsall/mod/modsbook22.html
A rich crossroads of information about nineteenth-century Austria and Germany is offered by the Internet Modern History Source Book, which contains documents, maps, and images.

Nineteenth-Century Europe in Photos
http://academic.brooklyn.cuny.edu/history/core/pics
This website provides access to a vast array of historical images of the era.

Literature and Film

The nineteenth century was the golden age of the European novel, and across the West, there were powerful talents portraying the complexity and drama of their times. Victor Hugo's *Les Misérables* (1862) is a masterpiece of a book, the subject of both films and a stage musical. Charles Dickens captured the courage and challenge of the first part of the nineteenth century in England in books such as *Great Expectations* (1860–1861), *A Christmas Carol* (1843), *Hard Times* (1845), *Bleak House* (1852), and *David Copperfield* (1849–1850). Jane Austen's *Pride and Prejudice* (1813), *Sense and Sensibility* (1811), and other novels give an insight into upper-middle-class life and are also the bases of a number of films. The prolific Honoré de Balzac provided detailed portraits of the often cruel social practices of France after the Revolution and Napoleon. *Old Goriot* (1835), *Cousin Bette* (1846), and *Colonel Chabert* (1832) are among his more impressive works. In Russia, Nikolai Gogol skillfully captured the absurdity of the serf system in his *Dead Souls* (1842) and *The Inspector General* (1836). Ivan Turgenev accomplished the finest presentation of generational conflict in his *Fathers and Sons* (1862). Leo Tolstoy published his epochal *War and Peace* in the 1860s, followed by a number of other important works, including *Anna Karenina* (1873–1876). Perhaps the greatest Russian novelist, Fedor Dostoevski, in his finest novel, *The Brothers Karamazov* (1879–1880), described Russia under wrenching transition in the wake of the Great Reforms. His study of human behavior in *Crime and Punish-*

ment (1866) remains one of the finest psychological novels in any language. As were other great titles above, the Russian novels have been presented in several films. Herman Melville's classic, *Moby Dick* (1851), gained instant acceptance as a major contribution to world literature.

As mass education spread and literacy became more widespread, writers went in two separate directions. Poets began to imitate the symbolist work of Paul Verlaine, *Selected Poems* (Oxford University Press, 2000), and Stéphane Mallarmé, *Collected Poems* (University of California Press, 1996), or the popular and widely read works of Rudyard Kipling. See the edition of Kipling's *Kim*, ed. Edward Said (Viking, 1992) for a fine discussion of his work. Other titles by Kipling include *Just So Stories* (1902), "Rikki-Tikki-Tavi" (part of *The Jungle Book*), *The Jungle Book* (1894), and *The Man Who Would Be King* (1889), which became the subject of a fine film of the same name. A person who staked out his own route was the visionary H. G. Wells, who wrote *The Time Machine* (1895), *The Invisible Man* (1897), and *The War of the Worlds* (1898). Other writers became powerful spokesmen for justice, such as Émile Zola, who led the drive to defend Alfred Dreyfus. His *Germinal* (Viking, 1997), one in a series of 19 related novels, stands as one the most important novels at the turn of the century.

Claude Berri's *Germinal* (1994; Sony Pictures Classics) brings Zola's novel to the screen. Werner Herzog's *Fitzcarraldo* (1982; New World Pictures) portrays a man with an obsession to establish a trading network along the Amazon and to build a world-class opera house there.

Suggestions for Reading

For a general background to the period, see Eric J. Hobsbawm, *Nations and Nationalism Since 1780: Programme, Myth, and Reality* (Cambridge University Press, 1993), and Jonathan Sperber, *The European Revolution 1841–1851, New Approaches in European History* (Cambridge University Press, 1994). David Blackbourn's *The Long Nineteenth Century: A History of Germany 1780–1918* (Oxford University Press, 1998) traces the emergence of Prussia as the unifying force. Italian unification is the subject of Derek Bayles' *The Risorgimento and the Unification of Italy* (Allen & Unwin, 1982). Theodore Zeldin's superb study, *France 1848–1945,* 4 vols. (Oxford University Press, 1973–1975), provides the necessary context to understand that tempestuous century in France. A notion of the complexity of the nationalities question in eastern Europe can be found in Peter F. Sugar and Ivo John Lederer, eds., *Nationalism in Eastern Europe* (University of Washington Press, 1969). J. N. Westwood's *Endurance and Endeavor: Russian History 1812–1992* (Oxford University Press, 1993) is the best one-volume survey. A good overview of the history of the United Kingdom during this time is David Thomson's *England in the Nineteenth Century* (Penguin, 1991). Matthew S. Anderson's *The Eastern Question, 1774–1923* (St. Martin's Press, 1966) remains the best single-volume study of the issue that led to the outbreak of World War I. Joachim Remak's *The Origins of World War I, 1871–1914* (Harcourt Brace Jovanovich, 1997) is a solid analysis of Europe's diplomatic failure.

Chapter 24

Africa and the Middle East During the Age of European Imperialism

Outline

Featrues

◀ This is a woven tapestry by an Ethiopian artist depicting the Ethiopian victory over the Italians in the battle of Aduwa in early 1896.

In the eighteenth and nineteenth centuries, the states and empires of Africa and the Middle East underwent a radical restructuring; they faced internal political struggles, the transformation of the world economy, and the military, commercial, and cultural incursions of the Europeans. European states challenged the diverse, complex civilizations of Africa and the Middle East and made them targets in the competition for empire.

In sub-Saharan Africa, Africans did not have a common identity. The diversity of kingdoms and societies made a unified political response to the Europeans impossible. Their responses to European conquest ranged from accommodation to armed resistance. By World War I, most Africans found themselves living within colonies with new political boundaries arbitrarily drawn by the Europeans, without regard for the existing ethnic identities of peoples. They saw their economies restructured to meet the European demands for their crops and mineral resources. They began the painful process of adapting their cultures and religions to survive in a rapidly industrializing world.

In the Middle East, where empires already existed, politicians and intellectuals discussed ways to keep their empires strong and proposed reforms to enable them to meet the challenges of modernity. The Ottoman Empire at the beginning of the nineteenth century was still large and powerful, but by the end of the century, it had faced bankruptcy, territorial losses, and national separatist movements. The Qajar Empire in Iran was similarly weakened by foreign loans and by the military ambitions of Britain and Russia. From North Africa to central Asia, the citizens of these traditional, polyglot, multiethnic empires found themselves caught up in the great power rivalries of the new imperialists in Europe.

European Conquest of Africa

What were the motives of European colonizers for conquering most of Africa in the late nineteenth century?

In 1870, the European nations controlled only 10 percent of the continent. The two most important holdings were at Africa's geographical extremes: French-administered Algeria in the north and the Boer republics and British colonies in the south. Most of the other European holdings were small commercial ones along the West African coast. However, as their rivalries intensified, European nations embarked on a mad scramble to carve up as much of the continent as possible. By World War I, Ethiopia and Liberia were the only African states not under direct European rule.

One of the first European leaders to acquire new African territory was King Leopold II of Belgium, who had long dreamed of creating an empire modeled on Dutch holdings in Asia and the Pacific. When the Belgian government was reluctant to acquire colonies, Leopold took the initiative. In 1876 he organized the International African Association (IAA) and brought the explorer Henry Stanley (1841–1904) into his service. The association, composed of scientists and explorers from many nations, was ostensibly intended to serve humanitarian purposes. But the king had less noble motives. As he put it, he did not want to lose a golden opportunity "to secure. . .a slice of this magnificent African cake."[1] He sent Stanley to Central Africa on behalf of the association. Stanley brought along hundreds of blank treaty forms and concluded agreements with various African chiefs, few of whom understood the implications of granting sovereignty to the IAA. By 1882, the organization had laid claim to over 900,000 square miles of territory along the Congo River, an area 75 times the size of Belgium.

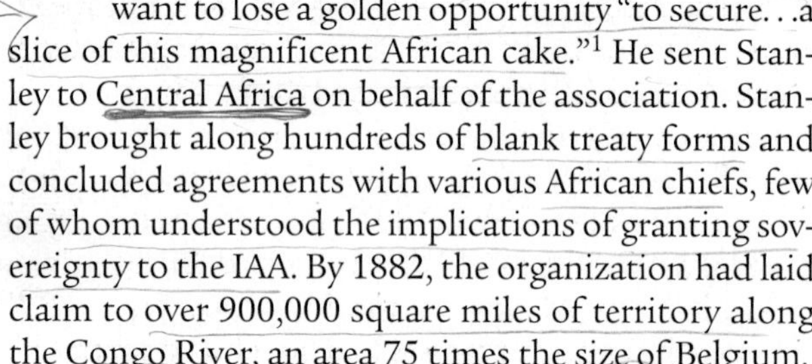

DOCUMENT

Stanley in Uganda

DOCUMENT

Mary Kingsley in Africa

Britain's occupation of Egypt (see p. 759) and Leopold's acquisition of the Congo moved Chancellor Otto von Bismarck to overcome his indifference to colonies and acquire an African empire for Germany. Beginning in February 1884, Bismarck took just a year to annex four colonies: South-West Africa, Togoland, Cameroon, and German East Africa. However, Bismarck's imperial grab was still firmly rooted in his reading of European power politics. He wanted to deflect French hostility to Germany by sparking French interest in acquiring colonies and to put Germany in a position to mediate potential disputes between France and Britain.

Africa Before the Scramble, 1876

While Bismarck was busy acquiring territory, he was also concerned about preventing clashes between colonizers. In 1884, he called the major European powers together in Berlin to discuss potential problems of unregulated African colonization. The conference paid lip service to humanitarian concerns by condemning the slave trade, prohibiting the sale of liquor and firearms in certain areas, and ensuring that European missionaries were not hindered from spreading the Christian faith. Then the European participants moved on to much more important matters.

Seeking to avoid competition for territory that could lead to conflict, they set down the ground rules by which the colonizers were to be guided in their search for colonies. They agreed that the area along the mouth of the Congo River was to be administered by Leopold of Belgium but that it was to be open to free trade and navigation. Drawing on precedents beginning in the sixteenth century, when European nations were creating sea-based empires, they decided that no nation was to stake out claims without first notifying other powers of its intention. No territory could be staked out unless it was effectively occupied, and all disputes were to be settled by arbitration. In spite of these declarations, the competitors often ignored the rules. On several occasions, war was barely avoided.

The humanitarian guidelines were generally disregarded. The methods used to acquire lands continued in many instances to involve deceiving Africans. European colonists acquired huge land grants by giv-

CHRONOLOGY

1800	1820	1840	1860	1880	1900
1801 Muhammad Ali arrives in Egypt and seizes power 1808–1839 Mahmud II, reformer, janissary corps destroyed	1821 Greek revolt against Ottoman rule 1839–1876 Ottoman *Tanzimat* reform period	1847 French finalize takeover of Algeria 1848–1896 Reign of Nasir al-Din Shah in Iran	1867 Diamonds discovered in South Africa 1869 Opening of Suez Canal 1876 First Ottoman constitutional revolution 1879 Britain seizes Khyber Pass, dominates Afghanistan	1884 European colonizers meet in Berlin to set ground rules for claiming colonies 1896 Ethiopian army defeats Italians at Aduwa 1899–1902 Anglo-Boer War	1905–1906 Beginning of Iranian constitutional revolution 1907 Britain and Russia divide Iran into spheres of influence 1908 Second Ottoman constitutional revolution

▲ Representatives of 14 nations, including the United States, met in Berlin in 1884 to set new rules to govern their "scramble for Africa." No representative from Africa was invited to participate.

ing chiefs treaties they could not read and whose contents they did not understand. In return, African chiefs were plied with bottles of gin, red handkerchiefs, and fancy red costumes. The comparison between the European treaty methods and those of the Americans in negotiations with Native American tribes is all too apparent.

The cultural differences between Africans and Europeans were especially vast regarding their conceptions of land ownership. To most African societies, land was not owned privately by individuals but was vested in their chiefs, who allocated it to their people. When chiefs allocated land or mineral rights to Europeans, they had no idea they were disposing of more than its temporary use. When the Europeans later claimed ownership of the land, Africans were indignant, claiming that they had been cheated. In 1888, Charles Rudd, a representative of Cecil Rhodes, signed a treaty with the Ndebele king, Lobengula (c. 1836–1894), in which he was given a monthly stipend and 1000 Martini-Henry rifles in exchange for a concession over minerals and metals. Lobengula was told that the treaty gave Rhodes's company the right to dig a hole in one place, but the treaty actually gave Rhodes unlimited powers.

African leaders who questioned treaty provisions were treated cavalierly. King Jaja (c. 1821–1891) of Opobo, a prosperous trading state in southeastern Nigeria, refused to sign a British treaty unless the wording of clauses on protection and free trade was altered or scrapped. The British agreed to changes, but when the British Consul invited Jaja and other chiefs to sign the treaty on a ship, they were detained and sent into exile.

The Scrambling of Africa

From the Berlin conference to World War I, European imperialists partitioned the African continent among themselves, with two exceptions—Liberia, which had been established for freed American slaves, and Ethiopia, which fended off Italian invaders. The colonizers were woefully ignorant about the geography of the areas they colonized. Europeans had knowledge of coastal areas, but nineteenth-century explorers had largely concentrated on river explorations and knew little beyond that. Thus, when European statesmen drew boundaries, they were more concerned with strategic interests and potential economic development than with existing kingdoms, ethnic identities, topography, or demography. About half the boundaries were straight lines drawn for simple convenience. As Lord Salisbury, the British prime minister, admitted: "[We] have been engaged in drawing lines upon maps where no white man's foot ever trod, we have been giving away mountains and rivers and lakes to each other, only hindered by the small impediment that we never knew exactly where the mountains and rivers and lakes were."[2]

MAP Colonization in Africa

France and Britain were by far the two leading competitors for African territory. The French vision was to create an empire linking Algeria, West Africa, and the region north of the lower Congo River. To achieve their goal, the French relied on their military to drive eastward from Senegal and northward from

Document

That Was No Brother

Europeans and Africans usually had very different perceptions of the same event. These documents recount two versions of a battle on the Congo River in the 1870s. The first comes from an African chief, Mojimba—recorded by a Catholic priest, Father Joseph Fraessle, several decades after the battle—and the second is by the famed explorer Henry Morton Stanley, written for European and American audiences.

When we heard that the man with the white flesh was journeying down the Lualaba (Lualaba-Congo) we were open-mouthed with astonishment. We stood still. All night long the drums announced the strange news—a man with white flesh! ... He must have got that from the river-kingdom. He will be one of our brothers who were drowned in that river. All life comes from the water, and in the water he has found life. Now he is coming back to us, he is coming home....

We will prepare a feast, I ordered, we will go to meet our brother and escort him into the village with rejoicing! ... We assembled the great canoes. We listened for the gong which would announce our brother's presence on the Lualaba. Presently the cry was heard: He is approaching the Lualaba. Now he enters the river! ... We swept forward, my canoe leading, the others following, with songs of joy and with dancing, to meet the first white man our eyes had beheld, and to do him honor.

But as we drew near his canoes there were loud reports, bang! bang! and fire-staves spat bits of iron at us. We were paralyzed with fright; our mouths hung wide open and we could not shut them. Things such as we had never seen, never heard of, never dreamed of—they were the work of evil spirits! Several of my men plunged into the water.... What for? Did they fly to safety? No—for others fell down also, in the canoes. Some screamed dreadfully, others were silent—they were dead, and blood flowed from little holes in their bodies. "War! That is war!" I yelled. "Go back!" The canoes sped back to our village with all the strength our spirits could impart to our arms. That was no brother! That was the worst enemy our country had ever seen.

And still those bangs went on; the long staves spat fire, pieces of iron whistled around us, fell into the water with a hissing sound, and our brothers continued to fall. We fell into our village—they came after us. We fled into the forest and flung ourselves on the ground. When we returned that evening our eyes beheld fearful things: our brothers, dead, bleeding, our village plundered and burned, and the water full of dead bodies....

Now tell me: has the white man dealt fairly by us? Oh, do not speak to me of him! You call us wicked men, but you white men are much more wicked! You think because you have guns you can take away our land and our possessions. You have sickness in your heads, for that is not justice.

From Heinrich Schiffiers, *The Quest for Africa* (New York: Putnam, 1957), pp. 196–197.

At 2 P.M. we emerged out of the shelter of the deeply wooded banks and came into a vast stream, nearly 2000 yards across at the mouth. As soon as we entered its waters, we saw a great fleet of canoes hovering about in the middle of the stream.... We pulled briskly on to gain the right bank, when looking upstream, we saw a sight that sent the blood tingling through every nerve and fiber of our bodies: a flotilla of gigantic canoes bearing down upon us, which both in size and numbers greatly exceeded anything we had seen hitherto!

Instead of aiming for the right bank, we formed a line and kept straight downriver, the boat taking position behind.... The shields were next lifted by the noncombatants, men, women and children in the bows, and along the outer lines, as well as astern, and from behind these the muskets and rifles were aimed.

We had sufficient time to take a view of the mighty force bearing down on us and to count the number of the war vessels. There were 54 of them! A monster canoe led the way, with two rows of upstanding paddles, 40 men on a side, their bodies bending and swaying in unison as with a swelling barbarous chorus they drove her down toward us....

The crashing sounds of large drums, a hundred blasts of ivory horns, and a thrilling chant from 2000 human throats did not tend to soothe our nerves or to increase our confidence.... We had no time to pray or to take sentimental looks at the savage world, or even to breathe a sad farewell to it....

The monster canoe aimed straight for my boat, as though it would run us down; but when within fifty yards off, it swerved aside and, when nearly opposite, the warriors above the manned prow let fly their spears and on either side there was a noise of rushing bodies. But every sound was soon lost in the ripping, crackling musketry. For five minutes we were so absorbed in firing that we took no note of anything else; but at the end of that time we were made aware that the enemy was reforming about 200 yards above us.

Our blood was up now. It was a murderous world, and we felt for the first time that we hated the filthy, vulturous ghouls who inhabited it. We therefore lifted our anchors and pursued them upstream along the right bank until, rounding a point, we saw their villages. We made straight for the banks and continued the fight in the village streets with those who had landed.

From Henry M. Stanley, *Through the Dark Continent*, vol. 2 (New York: Harper & Brothers, 1878), pp. 268–273.

Questions to Consider

You are a journalist covering the skirmish and you are relying on the accounts of Mojimba and Stanley for your news story.

1. What are the strengths and weaknesses of each source?
2. What would your account be? How would it differ from either source?

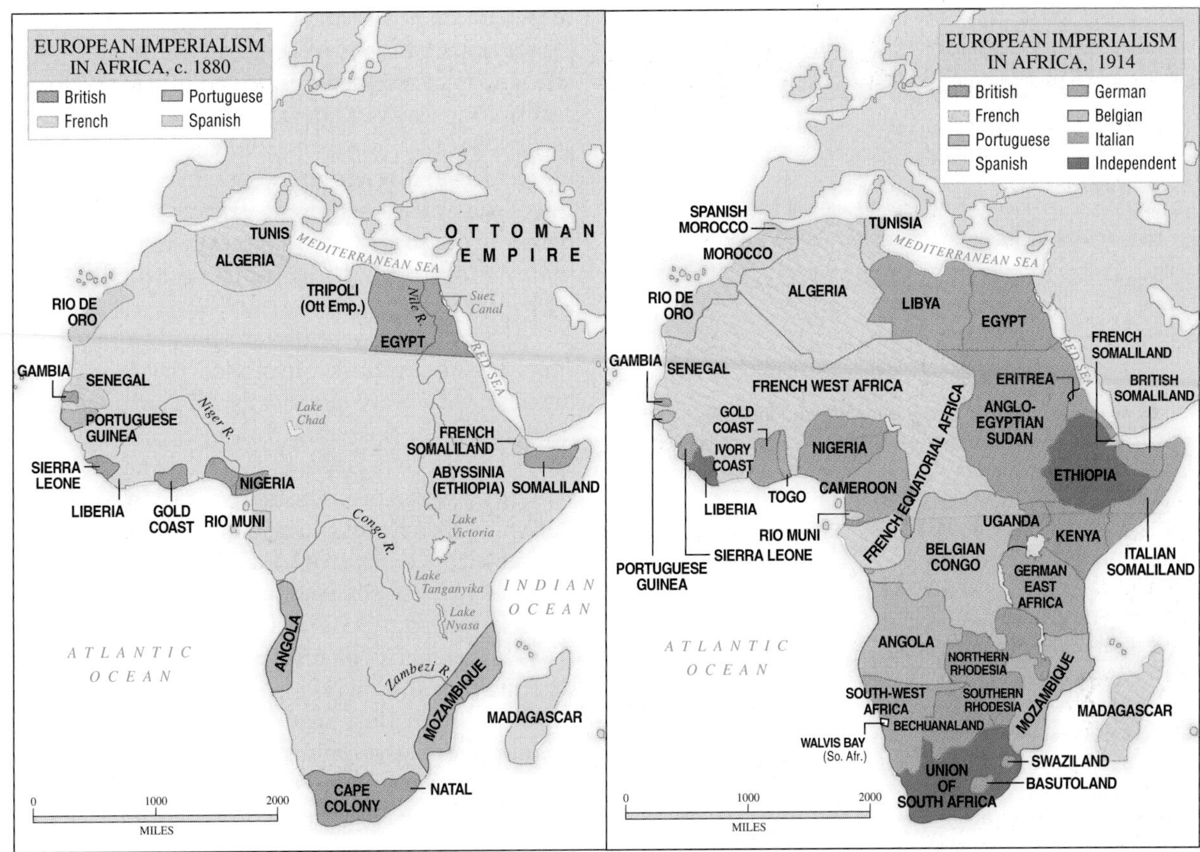

▲ Until the 1880s, only a few European countries held colonies in Africa, mostly enclaves on the coast. However, following the Berlin Conference of 1884–1885, European nations moved rapidly to conquer and partition Africa. By World War I, all of Africa, with the exception of Liberia and Ethiopia, was under European domination. Because Europeans were largely ignorant of Africa's interior regions, they drew the boundary lines of their colonies without regard for preexisting states, trading relations, or ethnic ties. This has left an enduring legacy of ethnic strife.

the lower Congo. In West Africa, the British concentrated on their coastal trading interests and carved out colonies in Gambia, Sierra Leone, the Gold Coast (Ghana), and Nigeria. But they also scooped up possessions elsewhere. In East Africa, they laid claim to Kenya and Uganda, and by 1884, they gained control over a stretch of African coast fronting on the Gulf of Aden. Because it guarded the lower approach to the Suez Canal, this protectorate (British Somaliland) was of great strategic value.

Equally important to British control of Egypt were the headwaters of the Nile, situated in the area known as the Anglo-Egyptian Sudan. The French also had their designs on the area as a bargaining chip to force the British to reconsider their exclusive control over Egypt. The French commissioned Captain Jean-Baptiste Marchand to march a force 3000 miles from central Africa to plant a French flag at Fashoda on the White Nile south of Khartoum. Several months later in July 1898, General H. H. Kitchener successfully led an Anglo-Egyptian force against Muslim forces in control of the Sudan. Then Kitchener turned his attention to Marchand, and their forces faced off nervously at Fashoda. The showdown nearly ended in war. To the British, control of the Nile was a strategic necessity. To the French, it was a matter of national prestige, but they were not prepared to go to war over it, and they withdrew Marchand.

Britain was the principal colonizer in southern Africa. British influence expanded northward from the Cape Colony largely through the personal efforts of the diamond magnate Cecil Rhodes, who dreamed of an uninterrupted corridor of British territory from the Cape of Good Hope to Cairo. When the British government hesitated to claim territory north of the Limpopo River, Rhodes took the initiative. Rhodes had heard the stories that King Solomon's mines were located there, and he thought the area had even more potential than the Witwatersrand (VIT-vah-ters-rand; "ridge of the white waters") goldfields. Lured by a mirage of gold, he poured his personal fortune into founding the British South Africa Company. In 1890, he dispatched a column of troops to settle and, if need be, conquer the area that eventually bore his name, Rhodesia.

IMAGE Cecil Rhodes Astride Africa—Cartoon

	African Societies and European Imperialism
1876	King Leopold II of Belgium founds International African Association
1879	Zulu army defeats British force at battle of Isandhlwana
1881	Muhammad Ahmad proclaims himself Mahdi in Sudan
1886	Opening of Witwatersrand gold fields
1888	Cecil Rhodes and Barney Barnato found De Beers Diamond Company
1895	Cecil Rhodes launches Jameson raid to overthrow Transvaal government
1896	Ethiopia defeats Italy at battle of Aduwa
1898	Confrontation of British and French forces at Fashoda in southern Sudan
1913	Passage of Natives Land Act in South Africa

Both Portugal and Italy had grandiose visions of empire, but they had to settle for territories the major European powers did not covet. Although the Portuguese had been involved in Africa longer than any of the other European colonizers, their ambition to unite Mozambique and Angola through a central African corridor was thwarted by Rhodes and British interests. Italy emerged from the scramble for colonies with very little territory. The Italians gained a piece of the Red Sea coast and a slice of barren and desolate land on the Indian Ocean. But these areas were of little value without the rich plateau of Ethiopia in the hinterland. However, their bid to conquer the interior was soundly rebuffed by the Ethiopian army.

European Technology and the African Response to Conquest

How did advances in technology and medicine contribute to the European conquest of Africa?

The European conquest of most of Africa was facilitated because of advances in technology and medicine. Until quinine was perfected, Europeans setting foot in Africa died in droves from illnesses such as malaria. Advances in military technology gave European armies a decisive advantage in their encounters with African forces. The gunboat allowed European armies to dominate lake and river regions, while the introduction of breechloading rifles and machine guns made it possible for European soldiers to defeat much larger African armies that possessed outmoded muskets. However, technology was not the sole reason Europeans succeeded. Because European soldiers were still susceptible to African diseases and were expensive to maintain, European armies recruited Africans to fight on their behalf. And Africans, who typically made up the vast majority of European-led units, did the bulk of the fighting.

African states were also at a disadvantage because they did not rethink outmoded battle tactics and because they were politically and ethnically fragmented. In the face of European expansion, African states sought to preserve as much of their own autonomy and sovereignty as possible. This response usually prevented them from entering into alliances with other African states to confront a common enemy.

Most African societies militarily resisted European conquest at some point, but they first weighed the costs and benefits of European rule and considered whether they should resist, make accommodations, or negotiate with Europeans. They queried European missionaries in their midst for information on the colonizers. They watched developments in neighboring states to see the results of resistance, and they sought advice on the implications of European protection. They assessed their rivalries with neighboring states and the possibility of profit from an alliance with Europeans. They also calculated whether they had the support of their own people.

Despite the disparity in firearms, African states vigorously sustained resistance to European colonizers until World War I. One of the most durable and innovative resistance leaders was Samori Touré (SA-mor-ee too-RAY; c. 1830–1900), who came from a Dyula trading family in the region of the upper Niger River in West Africa. He built up an army to protect his family's trading interests and then, between 1865 and 1875, created a powerful Islamic kingdom among the Mandinke people that stretched from Sierra Leone to the Ivory Coast. Samori's army could field over 30,000 soldiers and cavalry armed with muskets and rifles, some homemade and some imported from Freetown on the Sierra Leonean coast.

Samori's forces were a formidable opponent when they first clashed with French soldiers probing west from Senegal in 1881. However, the French superiority in weaponry eventually forced Samori to wage a scorched-earth campaign as he moved his kingdom eastward. He then had to deal with internal revolts from his new subjects and also with the British, who refused to declare a protectorate over his kingdom. Squeezed between the French and the British, he fought as long as he could before he was captured and exiled by the French in 1898.

Document

General von Trotha's Extermination Order

The colonial wars fought in Africa were a testing ground for the tactics and policies that were later used in the global wars of the twentieth century. After the Germans laid claim to southwest Africa (now the modern nation of Namibia) in 1884, they targeted the central highlands of the colony for white settlement. The Herero and Nama people who lived in that region lost their grazing lands and most of their cattle. In 1904 the Herero rebelled, killing over a hundred German settlers and traders and taking back their lands. German reinforcements counter-attacked and surrounded the Herero in a mountainous area. When they "broke out," the German commander, General Lothar von Trotha, issued an extermination order in October 1904 to kill all Herero men. The order sparked off a vigorous debate within German political and military circles. Several months later, von Trotha amended the order to state that Herero men who surrendered would be chained and branded and then put on forced labor projects. By that point, many Herero had been forced into the desert to the east, where many perished. By war's end, the Herero population had been reduced from 80,000 to 16,000 people.

I, the great general of the German troops, send this letter to the Herero People. Hereros are no longer German subjects. They have murdered, stolen, they have cut off the noses, ears, and other bodily parts of wounded soldiers and now, because of cowardice, they will fight no more. I say to the people: anyone who delivers one of the Herero captains to my station as a prisoner will receive 1000 marks. He who brings in Samuel Maherero will receive 5000 marks. All the Hereros must leave the land. If the people do not do this, then I will force them to do it with great guns. Any Herero found within the German borders with or without a gun, with or without cattle, will be shot. I shall no longer receive any women or children; I will drive them back to their people or I will shoot them. This is my decision for the Herero people.

The Great General of the Mighty Kaiser

This order is to be read to the troops at quarters with the additional statement that ... the shooting of women and children is to be understood to mean that one can shoot over them to force them to run faster. I definitely mean that this order will be carried out and that no male prisoners will be taken, but it should not degenerate into killing women and children. This will be accomplished if one shoots over their heads a couple of times. The soldiers will remain conscious of the good reputation of German soldiers.

Questions to Consider

1. What was the prevailing attitude towards the treatment of civilians in war during that era?
2. Do you believe that there is any connection between von Trotha's extermination order and Hitler's genocidal policies of the Nazi era?

From Jon Bridgman, *The Revolt of the Hereros* (Berkeley: University of California Press, 1981), pp. 127–128.

Because of their ability to inspire and unite followers, religious leaders often led the resistance to European invaders. In Sudan, Muhammad Ahmad (1844–1885), a Muslim ***shaykh*** from a village north of Khartoum, proclaimed himself a **Mahdi** ("guided one") in 1881. Muslims believe that in times of crisis, a redeemer appears whose mission it is to overthrow tyrannical and oppressive rulers and install just governments in their place. Declaring himself a successor to the prophet Muhammad, Muhammad Ahmad called on people to join him in a ***jihad*** against the unbelievers, the Egyptian-appointed administrators who were levying taxes and suppressing a profitable slave trade.

From a base 300 miles southwest of Khartoum, Mahdist forces scored numerous successes against Egyptian forces and laid siege to Khartoum in 1884. Despite last-ditch efforts by British officer Charles Gordon to negotiate with the Mahdi, the Mahdists swept into Khartoum in early 1885, killing Gordon

shaykh—Honorific title often used for the head of a tribe or village; head of a religious order.

Mahdi—One who is 'rightly guided,' i.e., by God; a divinely-guided savior expected to bring justice to the world; messiah.

jihad—Literally "struggle" in Arabic; an Islamic term with broad meaning, ranging from the internal struggle of an individual to overcome sin to the external struggle of the faithful to address a social challenge or to fight against enemies and unbelievers in what is essentially a holy war.

▲ Religious leaders played a leading role in inspiring Shona resistance against white settlers in Zimbabwe in 1896–1897. This photograph is of the spirit mediums Nehanda and Kagubi awaiting trial after they were captured.

and setting up an administration at Omdurman, across the Nile from Khartoum. The Mahdi died a short time later, but his successors founded a Muslim state that lasted until an Anglo-Egyptian force invaded the Sudan in 1898.

A Shona **spirit medium** by the name of Charwe also inspired resistance against the British South Africa Company's (BSAC) colonization of Rhodesia in the 1890s. Shona peoples believed that a person could communicate with God through a dead person's spirit. This spirit can possess a living person who becomes a spirit medium. People especially consulted mediums who were possessed by important figures of the past. These mediums were thought to be guardians of the people and able to ensure good luck in hunting, producing rainfall, and controlling diseases. In the case of Charwe, she claimed to have been possessed by the spirit of Nehanda, a woman who had lived four centuries before.

In 1896, many Shona and Ndebele rose up against the BSAC's exploitative policies. Company officials were expropriating African land, seizing their cattle, levying taxes, and forcing Africans to work on the mines. Some Shona chiefdoms were inspired to revolt by prominent spirit mediums such as Ambuya Nehanda and Kagubi, who secretly spread the message of revolt and urged people to take up arms. Their inspirational leadership sustained the Shona *Chimurenga* ("uprising") for a year. Although the Europeans were nearly expelled, they eventually defeated the rebels. Nehanda and Kagubi were captured and sentenced to hang in March 1898. But Nehanda was defiant to the end. She refused to be converted to Christianity at the last minute and she denounced the Europeans until the moment she was executed. Her prophecy that "my bones will rise" to recapture freedom was remembered by guerillas fighting in the struggle against European domination in the 1970s.[3] They, too, consulted spirit mediums, including an elderly woman who claimed she had been possessed by Nehanda's spirit.

Although African armies scored some victories against European forces, only one African state, Ethiopia, successfully repulsed European conquest. In the second half of the nineteenth century, several kings had attempted to revive a unified kingdom of Ethiopia.

Following Téwodros II's suicide in 1868 (see p. 604), his successor, Yohannes IV, tried to curb the ambitions of his principal rival, Menelik (1844–1913), the king of Shawa, who had been imprisoned by Téwodros and who had long desired to be emperor. After Yohannes sent a force to confront him, Menelik backed down and pledged his allegiance. However, Menelik took advantage of Yohannes's policy of giving provincial rulers greater autonomy and began conquering territory to Shawa's south.

After Yohannes died in a battle against the Mahdist forces in the Sudan in 1889, Menelik was crowned emperor of Ethiopia. He moved the capital to Addis Ababa ("New Flower") and began modernizing his kingdom by constructing the first railway line between Addis Ababa and the French colony of Djibouti (ji-BOO-tee), laying telephone and telegraph lines for communication with provinces, and building bridges. He continued his policy of aggressively

---

spirit medium—A religious specialist who serves as an intermediary between the living and prominent spirits.

expanding Ethiopia's boundaries, more than doubling the kingdom's size. In the end, Menelik could boast that Ethiopia was larger than it had been under any previous emperor.

At the same time, Menelik kept a wary eye on British, French, and Italian intrigues in the region. "I have no intention," he wrote Queen Victoria, "of being an indifferent spectator if the distant Powers hold the idea of dividing up Africa."[4] British and French attentions were focused elsewhere, but the Italians, who had long coveted land on the Red Sea coast, were another matter. In 1889, Italy and Ethiopia signed the Treaty of Wuchale, in which Italy recognized Menelik as emperor of Ethiopia in return for giving the Italians a free hand in an area on the Red Sea coast controlled by one of his rivals. However, the treaty's Italian version stated that Ethiopia had to conduct foreign relations through the Italians, whereas the **Amharic** version merely stated that Ethiopia could consult with Italy on foreign matters. When Menelik learned through diplomatic exchanges with Britain and France that Italy was claiming a protectorate over Ethiopia, he denounced the treaty and prepared for an eventual showdown with Italy by importing massive quantities of weapons, many of them from Italy.

When the Italians mounted an offensive in Tigré province in 1896, Menelik called on his nation to resist them: "Enemies have come who would ruin our country.... With God's help I will get rid of them."[5] Menelik's nobles rallied behind him to supply troops, and Ethiopia's army of 100,000 soldiers was more than a match for the 20,000-strong Italian army. At the battle of Aduwa, the Italian generals made a series of tactical blunders, and their force was routed. The Italians were forced to recognize Ethiopia's independence and content themselves with Eritrea, their enclave on the Red Sea coast. However, the memory of this humiliating defeat lingered in Italian minds until Benito Mussolini sought revenge decades later (see p. 938).

The Mineral Revolution in South Africa and the Anglo-Boer War

What difference did the discovery of gold and diamonds have on the relations between the British and Afrikaner and African states?

The discovery of diamonds in 1867 on the borders of the Cape Colony and the Orange Free State and of gold in 1886 in the Transvaal were to transform the whole of southern Africa economically and politically.

Amharic—Semitic language spoken by the Amhara people of central and western Ethiopia.

The Discovery of Diamonds and Gold

When the diamond fields were opened up, thousands of black and white fortune seekers flocked to the area. The mining town of Kimberley sprang up almost overnight. In the first years of the digs, there were no restrictions on who could stake claims. But in 1873, European diggers, resentful of competition from blacks, successfully lobbied British officials for a law prohibiting Africans from owning claims. This law set the tone for future laws governing who controlled mineral rights and ownership of the land.

Although Africans were excluded from owning claims, there were few restrictions on their movements and where they lived around the mines. Africans typically came to mine for three to six months and left at a time of their own choosing. This freedom changed as European mine owners sought to prevent diamond thefts and to control black workers by preventing desertion and holding down their wages. In 1885, the mine owners began erecting compounds to house black workers. Throughout their stay at a mine, black workers stayed in the compounds and were allowed out only to work in the mine. The compound system was so effective at controlling black labor that it

▼ Black South African mine workers were required to live in compounds or barracks that they shared with dozens of other miners. They slept on concrete slabs stacked around the room.

became a fixture in other mining operations throughout southern Africa.

In the early years of diamond digging, several thousand people held claims, but by the 1880s, ownership of the mines was falling into the hands of fewer and fewer people. In 1888, the two leading magnates, Cecil Rhodes (1853–1902) and Barney Barnato (1852–1897), pooled their resources to found De Beers, a company that controlled 90 percent of diamond production. Over a century later, De Beers continues to dominate the diamond industry not only in South Africa but also around the world.

In 1886, gold discoveries on the Witwatersrand sparked off another rush. The Witwatersrand gold veins were distinctive because they sloped at sharp angles beneath the earth and required shafts to be sunk at depths of up to two miles. The exorbitant costs of deep-level mining as well as of importing skilled labor, mining engineers, and the latest technology required enormous infusions of foreign capital. Profits were hard to sustain, and the main mining houses targeted black wages for cutting costs. They agreed to restrict competition for black workers by imposing ceilings on their wages and created recruiting organizations that eventually developed networks as far north as Zambia and Malawi. The result was a migrant labor system in which tens of thousands of black men came to the mines for six to nine months, while black women stayed home to raise families and look after crops. Another consequence of the mineral discoveries was the extension of railways into the interior of southern Africa.

From 1886 to the end of the century, South Africa's share of world gold production jumped from less than 1 percent to over 25 percent. The center of power in the region shifted from Cape Town to Johannesburg, renewing British interest in controlling the Transvaal. Afrikaner leaders were resolute about protecting their independence, but they feared they would be outnumbered when tens of thousands of *uitlanders* (ATE-lahn-der; "foreigners"), mainly English immigrants, flocked to the gold mines. The Transvaal's president, Paul Kruger (1825–1904), was determined that the *uitlanders* would not gain control. As a boy, he had joined in the Great Trek. As a young man, he led Boer commandos conquering African lands. As head of the Transvaal, he was passionately devoted to preserving its independence and the Afrikaners' agrarian way of life.

Kruger's main adversary was Cecil Rhodes, who in 1890 had become prime minister of the Cape Colony. An avowed imperialist, Rhodes now set his sights on bringing down Kruger's republic. He plotted with *uitlanders* in Johannesburg to stage an insurrection. In late 1895, Rhodes's private army, led by Leander Starr Jameson, invaded the Transvaal from neighboring Bechuanaland, but they were quickly captured by Afrikaner commandos. The Jameson raid had dire consequences. Rhodes was forced to resign as prime minister, Afrikaners in the Cape were alienated from the British, the Orange Free State formed an alliance with the Transvaal, and the Transvaal began modernizing its army by importing weapons from Europe.

The Anglo-Boer War

Transvaal leaders were deeply suspicious that the British had been behind Rhodes's reckless actions. Their fears were heightened when in 1897 the British selected Alfred Milner (1854–1925) as the high commissioner for South Africa. He shared Rhodes's imperialist convictions with a passion. He pressured Kruger to reduce the length of time for *uitlanders* to qualify for citizenship in the Transvaal. Although Milner thought Kruger would make significant concessions under pressure, Kruger was unwilling to meet all of Milner's demands.

The Anglo-Boer War broke out in late 1899. Most observers expected the British army to roll over the heavily outnumbered Afrikaner forces. But Afrikaner soldiers were crack shots and expert horsemen. Knowing every inch of ground on which they fought, they frequently outmaneuvered the British troops by resorting to guerrilla tactics. The British countered by conducting a scorched-earth campaign, burning Afrikaner farms and placing Afrikaner women and children and Africans who worked on their farms in unsanitary concentration camps. About 30,000 Afrikaners (half of them children) and 15,000 blacks perished in the camps from disease and starvation. Among Afrikaners, the memory of the deaths fueled animosity against the British for generations.

The Boer War and Queen Victoria—Dutch Caricature

The war attracted a host of soldiers, journalists, and adventurers such as Arthur Conan Doyle, Rudyard Kipling, and Winston Churchill. One who was lionized by the British public was General Robert Baden-Powell. During the Afrikaner siege of British troops in Mafeking, British war correspondents dubbed him the "wolf" for sneaking out at night to spy on Afrikaner positions. The youngest general in the British army, he was subsequently given command over a police unit and provided them with a motto, "Be Prepared," utilizing the initials of his last name. After his triumphant return to Britain, Baden-Powell was so alarmed by what he saw as the softness of English boys that in 1908 he founded the Boy Scouts to instill manly virtues in them. Because of his admiration for the warrior codes of the Zulu, whom he had fought against, and the Japanese *bushido* (see p. 629), he drew on their standards of bravery, discipline, obedience, honor, and resourcefulness for the scouting code of conduct.

◀ Although most black migrant workers in the gold mines were men, black women found employment in the urban areas as domestic servants and washerwomen. A Johannesburg regulation of 1899 stated that "every householder or owner of an erf [a plot of land] may keep in his backyard whatever servants he requires for domestic service."

White Rule in the Union of South Africa, 1910–1948

At the conclusion of the Anglo-Boer war in May 1902, the British could have dictated a settlement to the Afrikaners and extended full political rights to blacks, but they deferred the issue until self-government was extended to the former Afrikaner republics. Milner, the British high commissioner, set about reconstructing the devastated former Afrikaner republics, but he scored few successes. His plan for English speakers to outnumber Afrikaners failed because he could not entice many British immigrants to take up farming in South Africa, and his attempt to Anglicize Afrikaners by setting up English-language schools failed when Afrikaners formed their own independent schools.

Once Milner left South Africa in 1905 following a Liberal party electoral victory in Britain, British officials came to a political understanding with Afrikaner leaders and extended self-government to the former Afrikaner republics, the Orange Free State and the Transvaal, in 1907. The British then moved to unite their four colonies and empowered 30 Afrikaner and English delegates to draft a constitution. Only 8 years after a ruinous war, the Union of South Africa became a self-governing dominion in the British Commonwealth.

The first three prime ministers of South Africa were Afrikaners who had led the war against the British. Louis Botha (1863–1919) and Jan Smuts (1870–1950) preached reconciliation with the British, while J. B. M. Hertzog (1866–1942) promoted a separate Afrikaner nationalism. Even though the Afrikaners controlled the government and gained official recognition of their language, Afrikaans, in 1925, English speakers controlled the civil service and dominated the business sector. Despite the deep rift between Britons and Afrikaners, however, they were prepared to work together to preserve and entrench white domination over South Africa's black majority.

The all-white Parliament passed laws protecting whites and hindering the ability of Africans to advance. With the exception of a small number of African and mixed-race males in the Cape Province who could vote in elections, most blacks were excluded from any role in government. In 1936, Prime Minister Hertzog's government struck Cape Africans from the voters' roll. A 1913 law froze the land division between whites and blacks, making it extremely difficult for blacks to buy white land and vice versa. Africans, who comprised over 70 percent of the population, were restricted to reserves that made up about 7 percent of the country. Another 6 percent was later added to the reserves.

In contrast, the government addressed the plight of the numerous unskilled and uneducated whites that lived at or below subsistence level. Ninety percent of these "poor whites" were Afrikaners who, unable to compete on equal terms with blacks, had little choice but to work for pathetically low wages. The government introduced a "civilized labor" policy in the 1920s providing many poor whites with jobs on the railroads, with the post office, and in low-level civil service positions. For every white that won a job, a black had to lose one. The government also reserved supervisory and skilled jobs in the mining industry for whites only. The color bar was extended to most industries and resulted in huge wage disparities. The average wage for Europeans was just under $4 a day, while that for Africans was a little over $3 a week.

Colonial Rule in Africa

How did Europeans administer their African colonies?

The European nations had completed their conquest of African societies by World War I. They then had to figure out how to govern huge colonies with a handful of officials. In 1926 in the Ivory Coast, the French stationed one European official for every 18,000 people; in southern Nigeria, the British had one for every 70,000. The French, Belgians, Portuguese, and British pragmatically experimented with various policies of administration; whatever their approach, all of them had similar objectives: preserving law and order, quelling disturbances, and spending as little on administration as possible. Thus, the common approach was "divide and rule."

CASE STUDY

"The White Man's Burden" Across Two Centuries

The British in Nigeria

The British, through their experience with administering the Muslim Sokoto **Caliphate** in northern Nigeria, devised a policy of indirect rule, or ruling through African traditional authorities. Frederick Lugard, who had commanded the British troops that conquered the caliphate, stayed on as an administrator. An authoritarian figure who instinctively distrusted educated Africans, Lugard found that he had more in common with the conservative Muslim Fulani aristocrats who ruled the caliphate. Thus Lugard favored a policy of colonial officials ruling through indigenous political leaders—chiefs and their councils—who were allowed to continue their day-to-day rule with little interference from the British. However, chiefs were expected to observe colonial laws, carry out the directives of colonial officials, and collect taxes. Because they had difficulty balancing their ties to their subjects with their responsibility to their colonial masters, they found themselves making more and more compromises to conform to colonial rules.

Indirect rule was applied in other British African colonies, even where African societies had structures totally unlike the Sokoto Caliphate. The administrative unit for British rule was the "tribe." For the sake of efficient rule, tribes were arbitrarily created where none had previously existed. The result was an authoritarian structure that barely resembled prior systems of governance. For instance, among the Igbo peoples in southeastern Nigeria, where elders ruled small-scale societies, the British imposed chiefs and issued them warrants to legitimize their authority. The **"warrant chiefs"** provoked resentment among their subjects.

In the late 1920s, as prices for palm oil and palm kernels dropped, the household incomes of women also declined. In 1929, Igbo women, fearing they were going to be taxed, received written assurances they would not be taxed and had a warrant chief arrested for assaulting a woman. One woman in the Oloko district challenged British officials: "What have we women done to warrant our being taxed? We women are like trees which bear fruit. You should tell us the reason why women who bear seeds should be counted."[6] The women's grievances mushroomed into a widespread popular revolt against warrant chiefs and "native" administration in which women attacked jails and released prisoners. Although British troops quelled the revolt and killed 50 women, the women's efforts to reform ruling structures by appointing a council of judges to replace warrant chiefs failed because women could not serve on the courts.

"New Britains": Kenya and Rhodesia

The few Europeans who lived in French and British colonies in Africa were primarily traders, missionaries, and colonial officials who did not think of themselves as permanent settlers. Such was not the case in the British colonies of Kenya and Southern Rhodesia, where European settlers found hospitable climates and staked out extensive land claims at the expense of African societies.

Although located on the equator, a section of central Kenya is a highland area which, at 6000 to 9000 feet above sea level, has a temperate climate that Europeans could tolerate. After conquering African peoples in the region, the British government designated the highlands for white ownership only and encouraged Englishmen and white South Africans to set up farms. The first arrived in 1903; although their numbers were small, they had tremendous influence over British administrators in Nairobi, the capital city. Africans, mostly Kikuyu, who had once tilled the highlands, were classed as squatters and were allowed to farm the land as long as they were needed for labor. In the 1930s, thousands of Kikuyu squatters were expelled from white farms and forced to eke out a living in barren reserves or on the streets of Nairobi. This treatment set the stage for a major uprising after World War II.

caliphate—The territory ruled by a caliph, a leader of the Muslim community.

warrant chief—British-appointed chief who derived his authority from a warrant issued by the British.

White settlers in Rhodesia followed a similar path. After conquering Shona and Ndebele kingdoms in several wars in the 1890s, the British South Africa Company turned its attention from a quixotic search for gold to promoting agriculture. White settlers seized additional land from Africans and eventually claimed about half of the country's best land as their own. They were already a potent political force when in 1923 the BSAC gave up administrative control of the colony to the British government. That same year the British gave the largely English settlers a choice of whether they wanted to be incorporated in the Union of South Africa or become a self-governing colony. They chose the latter.

In theory, the British retained certain powers protecting the rights of the African majority. However, as the Rhodesian parliament passed one discriminatory measure after another based on South African laws, the British did not intervene. The Land Apportionment Act of 1930 divided land into black and white areas. Roads, railways, and towns were placed in the white areas; the blacks, in rural reserves, were expected to pay taxes by selling their labor to white employers. Maize and tobacco farming in white areas became profitable through generous price supports, while black farmers were forced to sell their crops at lower prices.

French and Portuguese Administration

The French had a somewhat different approach to administering their African colonies. Before the scramble for Africa, France had applied the ideals of the French Revolution to a philosophy of assimilation in which selected Africans were immersed in the French language and culture and were treated as French citizens with full political rights. This approach was possible as long as France was governing a small colony like Senegal in West Africa. But once France expanded its holdings in Africa, it was confronted with a large subject population whose cultures were still intact. The French took the attitude that most Africans could not be absorbed into French culture; thus, they relied on direct rule that featured a centralized administration. At the top were French officials; below them were layers of African "chiefs" who ruled over villages, districts, and provinces and were primarily responsible for collecting taxes, maintaining law and order, and recruiting forced labor. If a society did not have a chief, the French would select one based on education, administrative ability, and loyalty.

The Portuguese practiced another form of direct rule. Unlike other colonies in Africa, the territories of Angola and Mozambique were constitutionally part of Portugal and were treated as overseas provinces. As the Industrial Revolution in Europe had largely bypassed Portugal under the longtime rule of Antonio Salazar (1932–1968), Portugal based its economic policies on

▼ European businesses linked the expansion of their markets with the spread of European civilization "in the dark corners of the earth." This postcard for Texaco Illuminating Oils draws a direct relationship between "light" and the acquisition of Western civilization.

her African possessions' providing the mother country with cheap raw materials and foodstuffs as well as guaranteeing Portuguese manufacturers a profitable market. Colonial governors reported directly to the Salazar government, and provincial and district administrators gradually took over the collection of taxes and the recruitment of forced labor, tasks that had been previously carried out by African police and chiefs.

In theory, Portuguese officials believed that they, of all the European colonizers, had the unique ability to create a multiracial society. The reality was far different. The Portuguese created a class of *assimilados* ("assimilated people") who were supposed to be treated as equals to Portuguese citizens. To become an *assimilado,* a person had to become Christian (Roman Catholic); read, write, and speak Portuguese; and "practice a Portuguese lifestyle." The numbers of *assimilados,* however, never amounted to more than 3 percent of the African population. The rest were classed as *indigenas* ("indigenous people") and were expected to learn the "dignity of labor" by working on plantations, at public works, and in urban areas. The only way to be exempted from this forced labor system was to be classified as *assimilado* or to seek work as a migrant laborer in neighboring territories. Mozambicans annually supplied over 100,000 members of the labor force for the South African gold mines.

The Colonial Economy

Colonialism imposed a dependent economic relationship between Africa and Europe that continues to shape the economies of independent African nations. Whatever their nationality, European officials shared a common objective: to compel their colonies to produce raw materials for the world market in exchange for finished products from the mother country.

Colonial economies took two forms: colonies where European involvement was direct in the form of plantations, mines, and European settlement; and colonies where Africans with small landholdings grew cash crops such as peanuts, oil palms, cotton, rubber, sisal, coffee, and cocoa for export. Because each colony usually produced one cash crop, the colony's well-being was dependent on the price the crop fetched on the world market. The Gold Coast, for example, soon became the world's leading supplier of cocoa, which inspired a song popular in the 1950s:

> *If you want to send your children to school, it is*
> *cocoa,*
> *If you want to want to build your house, it is cocoa,*
> *If you want to marry, it is cocoa,*
> *If you want to buy cloth, it is cocoa,*
> *Whatever you want to do in this world,*
> *It is with cocoa money that you do it.*[7]

The introduction of cash crops was extremely disruptive to African agriculture. Cash crops were often grown on the best land at the expense of other crops; thus, overproduction exhausted soils and led to erosion. Colonial officials also favored the interests of African men by granting them the ownership of land on which cash crops were grown. They reaped the lion's share of any proceeds from sales, while women, who had traditionally been responsible for agriculture, were expected to shoulder the burden of tending the new crops as well as performing their normal duties.

European-run plantations and mining operations also played major roles in the colonial economy. Huge estates and mining concessions were ceded to European and American companies. The Firestone Rubber Company took advantage of minimal rents and no income taxes to establish the largest rubber plantation in the world in Liberia. The Belgian giant, Union Minière, had a virtual monopoly over the copper-rich southern Congo, and Anglo-American, a South African company, dominated diamond and gold production in southern Africa.

► Africans expressed their images of Europeans through art. In this carving, an early twentieth-century work from the Congo, a Belgian mining magnate reclines in the back seat of an automobile while the African chauffeur drives.

The worst excesses of economic exploitation were in the Congo, the Belgian monarch Leopold II's private preserve. To recoup the fortune he expended to bankroll his empire, Leopold granted extensive concessions to private companies to build railways and exploit natural and mineral resources. In 1891, he decreed that African land ownership was restricted to areas actually under cultivation. Since most Africans practiced shifting cultivation, vast tracts of land were placed under state control (*domaine privé*).

Belgian King Crushes the Congo Free State—Cartoon

Concession companies were given free rein to exploit regions, first for ivory and then, after the invention of the inflatable bicycle tire, for rubber. The drive to maximize profits encouraged the brutal treatment of Africans pressed into labor service. Leopold's private army held wives hostage to coerce husbands into meeting rubber collection quotas. First-hand reports by courageous individuals such as William Sheppard, an African-American Presbyterian missionary, and Roger Casement, a British consul, began leaking out of the "Free State" to humanitarian groups and governments about the abuses, atrocities, beatings, and killings sanctioned by Leopold's system. An American missionary reported the details from a Belgian official about the brutal work of an African policeman: "Each time the corporal goes out to get rubber, cartridges are given to him. He must bring back all not used; and for every one used, he must bring back a right hand!"[8]

Leopold's brutalities were responsible for the deaths of millions and were, as contemporary African-American historian George Washington Williams put it, a "crime against humanity."[9] The international outcry over the "Red Rubber" scandal eventually forced the Belgian government to intervene in 1908 and take over administration from Leopold. Conditions in the colony, renamed the Belgian Congo, did not improve for long under the direct administration of the government.

A vast army of migrant laborers was required to run these operations. Because African men were reluctant to leave their families and homes for extended periods, they were compelled to seek work in the towns, mines, and plantations through a head tax on all adult men that had to be paid in cash rather than in kind. Besides paying taxes, workers saved their wages to start up their own businesses back home, to acquire imported goods, and to buy cattle to pay bridewealth for marriages.

Colonialism also introduced new forms of transportation. Built on the backs of unpaid forced labor, railways were constructed from the coastal ports into the interior to extend trading networks and to facilitate the export of commodities, especially minerals. In areas where white settlers had farms, railways not only exported their products but also deliberately skirted the black reserves that supplied laborers to white farms and mines. As the ports and railway towns boomed, railways often undermined established trading networks such as the Hausa trade of northern Nigeria with Tripoli in North Africa and the caravan routes in eastern Africa. Cars and trucks also replaced human porters and animals such as donkeys and horses.

The impact of the colonial economy on different regions was uneven. Coastal areas typically benefited more from roads, railways, and economic development than the interior zones, which stagnated and became the primary sources of migrant laborers for the coast. In southern Africa, where mining was the dominant industry, South Africa became an economic powerhouse because most of the roads and railways were built in a north-south direction that steered regional trade through South Africa.

Social Change

Colonial rule opened up new avenues of social change for Africans. New roads and railways lines created new employment opportunities and the migration of workers to plantations and fast-growing urban centers. Migrant workers, soldiers, students, teachers, and civil servants were exposed to new organizations and associations, dress, music and dance styles, sports, languages, cultures, ideas, values, and faiths.

Imperial cultures had an impact on the new sports that Africans played and how they spent their leisure time. European missionaries initially introduced football (or soccer), which has become the most popular sport in Africa, to students

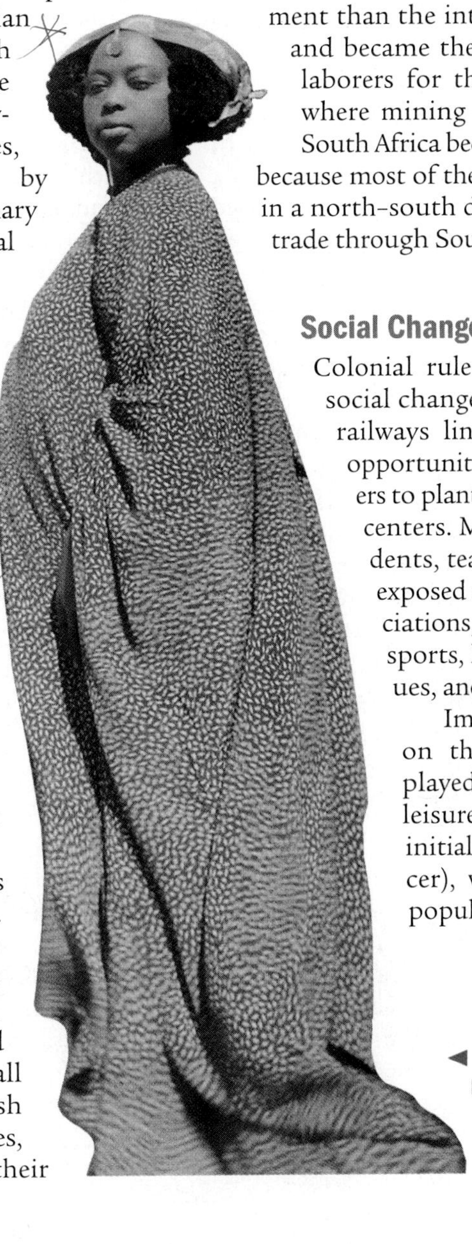

◄ "Woman in Street" by an unknown photographer from St. Louis, Senegal. St. Louis was the center of Senegal's artistic and intellectual community for many years.

at mission schools because they believed that the sport built morals and character and exposed students to Western civilization. In addition, the sport helped to attract new students. With their policy of assimilation, the French wanted to assimilate a black educated elite and develop model French citizens.

Colonial administrators, concerned about the large-scale movement of Africans, especially young men, into the urban areas and the possibilities of social disorder, introduced football to keep men content and provide an outlet for their leisure time activities. The Belgians also introduced football to its African soldiers in the Congo. Because the sport was inexpensive and simple to organize, the sport achieved a rapid popularity among both players and spectators. Colonial officials sought to control the sport by sponsoring sports bodies and leagues, but because it did not require much capital to form a team, Africans began forming their own football clubs and associations. They were among the few institutions that Africans could own and control. After World War II, football clubs became an outlet for expressing opposition to European rule. In Tanganyika, African nationalist groups utilized sporting clubs for their meetings. In Nigeria, Nnamdi Azikiwe (ah-ZEEK-way; 1903–1996), a businessman and nationalist leader who learned football as a boy on the streets of Lagos, founded a network of "Zik" Athletic Clubs across Nigeria. When he received permission from the British to take his Lagos football club on a tour around the country, he took advantage of the tour to deliver speeches attacking colonial rule after the matches.

The Growth of Christianity and Islam in Africa

Why did Islam and Christianity spread so rapidly under European rule?

The colonial era witnessed rapid expansion of both Islam and Christianity, although for contrasting reasons and in different parts of the African continent. Christianity experienced its greatest growth in the southern two-thirds of Africa; Islam spread along the northern third of the continent and in eastern coastal regions.

Missionaries and Mission Schools

Before the advent of colonial rule, Christian missionaries won few converts. Catholic missionaries who accompanied the Portuguese into Africa converted some rulers and their courts but otherwise had little influence with the general populace. In the late eighteenth and early nineteenth centuries, a fresh wave of evangelical Christianity stirred many European Protestant denominations to send missionaries to Africa and elsewhere. They believed they had an obligation to spread the Christian faith to civilize and uplift African "heathens" and to block the spread of Islam. They often saw their missions as working hand in hand with the expansion of European commerce globally.

Although some African rulers perceived the missionaries as positive assets who brought technical skills and schools, many questioned whether the missionaries were undermining their authority and restricted their activities. Thus, those who initially converted to Christianity were on the margins of African society—freed slaves, women fleeing bad marriages, famine victims, war refugees, orphans, and people accused of witchcraft.

The next wave of converts consisted of those who wanted access to technical skills and literacy offered at mission schools. Missionaries usually required their students to join their church in order to be admitted to their schools. Because most schooling was at the primary level, few students proceeded on to a handful of secondary schools. Thus high schools such as the École William Ponty in Dakar, Senegal, Achimota in the Gold Coast, and Lovedale and Adams College in South Africa attracted students from whole regions. Friendships at these schools developed into social networks that laid the foundation for anticolonial politics. Those who aspired to university education usually had to go to Europe or America before colleges such as Fort Hare in South Africa were established beginning in 1916.

Schooling affected avenues of social advancement. Age, family position, ability, and sex had traditionally determined status in African societies, but in the colonial world, whose missions, schools, civil service, and businesses required a literate elite that was fluent in European languages, education and technical skills became a main avenue to personal advancement.

African Churches

African Christians continually raised probing questions about Christian missions and Christianity. They especially challenged the attacks of European missionaries on such African cultural practices as **polygyny** and circumcision ceremonies as un-Christian and the missionaries' control of leadership and finances in the missions. Some black Christians staged their own reformation by breaking away from mission churches to form their own independent churches. In contrast to Martin Luther's rupture with the Catholic Church, most African schisms were from Protestant missions. The new African churches were carbon copies of the European mission churches but featured black leader-

polygyny—A marital practice in which a man has more than one wife.

▲ Africans who converted to Christian missions were expected not only to adopt Christianity, but also to accept many aspects of Western culture. This postcard shows an elegantly dressed wedding party of Africans at Lovedale, a famous black school in the eastern Cape that attracted students from all over southern Africa.

ship. Some of the churches adopted the name "Ethiopia" in their titles because Christianity had been established in Ethiopia long before European missionaries arrived in Africa. In 1892, Mangena Mokone (mahn-GAY-nah moh-KOH-nee), a minister near Pretoria, South Africa, left the Wesleyan Methodist Church to "to serve God in his own way" and founded the Ethiopian Church. He criticized European clergy for paying black clergy paltry wages, for continuing to segregate meetings of blacks and whites, and for refusing to allow black clergy to rise to leadership posts.

Some African church leaders drew on the Bible, with its emphasis on justice and equality, for a radical critique of colonial rule. And a few were prepared to take up arms to overthrow the Europeans. One of the most famous anticolonial rebellions was led by John Chilembwe (chee-LIM-bway), a Baptist minister from Nyasaland (currently Malawi) who had been trained at an African-American theological seminary in Virginia. In 1915, he hastily organized an uprising against British colonial rule and the recruitment of Africans to fight in East Africa during World War I. Chilembwe's intention was to "strike a blow and die" in the manner of his hero, American abolitionist John Brown. Although British troops shot and killed Chilembwe as he fled into Mozambique, his example inspired anticolonial protest in later generations.

Some black Christians Africanized Christianity by adapting Christian beliefs and rituals to African culture and religious systems. Spirit churches, for instance, were led by healer/prophets who followed African ways of treating disease and illness but invoked the Christian Holy Spirit to cure people. These healer/prophets were especially concerned with coping with diseases such as smallpox, measles, the plague, and influenza that accompanied European conquest and had a devastating impact on African peoples. When the Spanish influenza swept through Africa in late 1918, killing several million people, spirit churches emerged in its wake in many parts of Africa. A variety of Aladura ("one who prays") churches were established among the Yoruba people in Nigeria. A few of these spirit churches established close ties with American and British Pentecostal churches.

Women in the Church

Women were especially attracted to spirit churches because they offered unique ways for women to voice their spirituality and express their prophetic talents. A prominent example is the South African charismatic healer Ma' Nku, who left the Dutch Reformed Church to found her own St. John's Apostolic Church. At her central church near Johannesburg, her prayers imbued water with healing properties. So many people flocked to her that she had to install a water pump for mass healings and baptisms.

Even in churches where women were prophet leaders, men typically filled leadership roles and made decisions. However, women still found ways to carve out personalized spaces. In the Roho churches founded in the 1930s in western Kenya, women composed hymns inspired by the Holy Spirit. Their singing expressed their spirituality in a way that men could not control. In the 1930s, the Roho women sang hymns such as "We are women of war, we are women of fire" that boldly proclaimed their faith and their importance to their movement. As they marched around the countryside, they announced their approach to villages by singing their inspirational hymns.

The Spread of Islam

Despite Africa being under European rule, Islam had even greater successes in winning new converts than Christians. By World War II, an estimated half of all Africans were Muslims, most of whom were Sunni Muslims.

The initial response of Muslims to the British and the French in West Africa was either to mount overt resistance or withdraw from contact with Europeans. In Mali, Shaykh Hamallah (1883–1943) lived an isolated existence and taught only in his own mosque. Because he never expressed himself on African issues nor accepted French rule, the French believed that he was organizing resistance. After the French deported him in 1925, his followers prayed towards where he was living in exile rather than to Mecca.

Initially the colonizers took a hostile stance toward Islam. However, the British had experience in dealing with Muslim leaders in India and other colonial possessions. Once resistance died down, the British—and later the French—began courting conservative Muslim leaders who were prepared to establish peaceful relations and maintain the status quo in exchange for certain privileges. Muslim missionaries were not restricted to working within colonial boundaries, whereas their Christian counterparts were assigned to specific areas and often were not allowed to evangelize in Muslim areas. Ironically, the peace that Europeans introduced to certain areas allowed Muslims to travel freely in areas in which they had not operated before. Muslim migrant laborers who worked on plantations spread Islam, and new converts took their faith back to their home areas. Hausa and Dyula traders moved into "stranger quarters" in towns and won many new adherents to the faith. By the end of the colonial period, coastal cities such as Dakar, Freetown and Lagos had Muslim majority populations.

Muslims also took advantage of the fact that they were primarily Africans, not European, and thus were not identified with colonial rulers. They did not expect their converts to abandon their customs and cultures in the way that European Christian missionaries did. This was certainly the case of many sufi ***turuq*** (religious orders), key agents of conversion in many African regions. The Qadiriyya, founded in the twelfth century, was the oldest of the African sufi orders. It expanded its base in North Africa to northern Nigeria, where it won over the Hausa ruling elite. In Senegal in the late nineteenth century, Shaykh Ahmad Bamba (c. 1853–1927) was a religious reformer who founded a spiritual village, Touba, about a hundred miles east of Dakar, and a new sufi brotherhood, the Mourides (from the Arabic, those who are "novices seeking God"). Believing that he was preaching a *jihad* against European rule, the French exiled him three times between 1895 and 1912. When they finally allowed him to return, he was already attracting a devoted following. Bamba was prepared to reach an accommodation with colonial rule. During the First World War, he encouraged his followers to enlist in the French army and serve in Europe. But his primary concern was with spiritual matters. He instilled in the Mourides the belief that a disciplined work ethic was necessary for salvation. He called on his disciples to contribute their labor to agricultural settlements built on the edge of the desert that produced peanuts as a cash crop. The proceeds were dedicated to the spread of Mouride influence. The landless and unemployed were especially drawn to these farms. Between 1912 and 1960, the membership of the order swelled from 60,000 to 400,000.

In eastern Africa, Islam had long been restricted to the Swahili-speaking coast. However, colonial rule expanded trading networks into the interior. Africans migrating to the coastal areas came into contact with Islam for the first time. Those who converted spread Islam back to their home areas. Muslim traders also expanded their faith by taking advantage of their commercial contacts to develop a communication network that transcended boundaries. Also influential were such sufi orders as the Shadhiliya and the Qadiriyya. They utilized the Swahili language that was spoken over the region to their advantage.

Zanzibar remained a center of Islamic learning in eastern Africa. In Tanganyika, German officials relied on Muslim police and soldiers to maintain law and order and opened schools for Muslims to train them for the civil service and teaching. Because the German allied with the Ottomans in World War I, they favored Muslims. In Mozambique, however, Portuguese colonizers, who saw themselves on a crusade to spread Roman Catholicism, were hostile to the Islamic presence on the coast. Despite this persecution, Islam

turuq—The socio-religious orders associated with Sufism. Many of the Sufi orders developed their own initiation ceremonies and practices, usually carried out in conjunction with the ritual duties of Islam.

maintained a strong following. Following the Chilembwe uprising in Nyasaland, British officials worked cooperatively with Muslim chiefs who were perceived as stable leaders. In Uganda, however, where Protestants and Catholics had strong mission operations, British officials did not encourage Islam.

The Ottoman Empire Refashioned

In the nineteenth century what were the pressures for change inside and outside the Ottoman Empire?

At the beginning of the nineteenth century, the Middle East consisted primarily of two large and loosely structured empires, the Qajar Empire in Iran and the Ottoman Empire, the territories of which included Anatolia, much of the Arab Near East, and most of North Africa **(Maghrib).** The Ottoman Empire stretched from the Balkans to Sudan and from the Maghrib to Arabia, and the Ottoman sultan could still claim preeminence in the Islamic world on the basis of his status as Protector of the Holy Cities. For centuries, the Islamic world had extended well beyond the Middle Eastern heartlands. United by a common system of worship, veneration of the Qur'an and the prophet Muhammad, and adherence to Islamic law, Muslims looked to Mecca as the sacred site of pilgrimage. Every year the number of pilgrims venturing to Mecca grew. By 1900 it is estimated that more than 50,000 Indians and 20,000 Malays were making the **Hajj** each year. But the Islamic world had been politically divided since the early centuries of Islam, and Muslim states from Southeast Asia to Morocco pursued their own political agendas with little or no reference to the sovereign who controlled the Islamic heartlands.

Challenges to Ottoman Power

In the sixteenth century, the Ottoman administration had been a model of effectiveness. The Ottoman navy dominated the eastern Mediterranean, and Ottoman armies continued to expand the territories of the sultan. The balance of trade was markedly in favor of Asia, with European merchants sending precious coin to procure the goods they wanted from the Ottoman Empire, Iran, and South and Southeast Asia. By the eighteenth century, however, that balance of military and economic power had begun to shift in favor of Europe, where given states were benefiting from industrialization and new military technologies. By this point, the Ottoman Empire faced the challenges of decentralizing forces within and vigorous pressure from rivals beyond its boundaries.

Internally, central government power had been weakened by the increasing autonomy of regional governors (*ayan*) in the provinces. These notables mobilized their own provincial forces and resisted or evaded the authority of the central government in Istanbul. They gathered bands of men armed as irregular soldiers in Ottoman military campaigns to serve as their own personal armies. In North Africa the local lords had long enjoyed relative autonomy, and by the end of the eighteenth century, the Ottomans had little real power in the Maghrib.

The ranks of the janissary corps, the premier Ottoman fighting force (see Chapter 12), had also become grossly inflated. Thousands possessed papers that entitled them to collect military pay and rations even though they performed no military service; others were forced to take second jobs because inflation had drastically reduced the value of their pay. So the janissaries, once the front line of Ottoman defense, became a source of rebellion and a drain on the government treasury.

DOCUMENT

The Turkish Atrocities in Bulgaria

Indeed, the most evident signs of Ottoman weakness were in the military arena. Defeat at the hands of the Russians paved the way for the humiliating Treaty of Küchük Kaynarca (1774). Not only did the empire lose territory, but the Russians demanded the right to intervene in the affairs of the Orthodox Christian community in the empire. This concession for the first time granted a foreign state the power to meddle directly in Ottoman affairs. In 1798, Napoleon invaded Ottoman Egypt, and although his stay there was short, his easy victory illustrated the tenuousness of Ottoman control over the North African provinces.

The capitulations, treaties that granted special trade privileges to European states, also took a toll on the authority of both the Ottoman and Qajar states. In the sixteenth century, the Ottoman and Iranian sovereigns had dictated the terms of foreign trade. But as their economies weakened, they granted more and more extensive privileges to European companies, which gave states like Britain and France increasing leverage in commercial affairs. These concessions harmed the businesses of local Ottoman traders who could not compete. As the nineteenth century progressed, European states would extend their influence by granting large loans to Middle Eastern rulers. Debt loomed ever larger as a source of imperial decline.

Ottoman Reform

To counter these challenges, Sultan Selim III (r. 1789–1806) launched a series of reforms, many of

Maghrib–From an Arabic word meaning "time or place of the sunset." It refers to the western part of North Africa or the present-day countries of Algeria and Morocco.

Hajj–A pilgrimage to the holy city of Mecca that every Muslim is expected to make at least once in their lifetime. The Hajj is the fifth pillar of Islam.

The Era of Ottoman Reform	
1808–1839	Reign of Ottoman reformer Mahmud II
1839–1876	*Tanzimat,* Ottoman reform period
1876	First constitutional revolution
1876–1909	Reign of Sultan Abdülhamid II
1908	Young Turk Revolution reinstates Ottoman constitution

which were directed at his military. He created a new infantry corps composed of Turkish peasants. Selim also opened channels of communication with the European capitals by setting up embassies in London, Paris, Berlin, and Vienna. The janissaries, however, jealous of their centuries-old prominence in military life, moved rapidly to frustrate Selim's reform program. They then simply deposed the sultan. If Selim's policies fell well short of their goal, they nevertheless marked the onset of an era of Ottoman reform that would last into the early twentieth century.

A much more successful reformer was Sultan Mahmud II (1808–1839). Mahmud restored central authority in many provinces and cleared the way for military reform by destroying the janissary corps after it revolted in 1826. He then established a new European-style army, trained by Prussian and French officers. Mahmud also reformed professional education by opening medical and military schools in which the language of instruction was often French. Beyond the military sphere, Mahmud's reforms included a restructuring of the bureaucracy, the launching of an official newspaper, and the opening of a translation bureau.

Elite society now witnessed the rise of a new class of young Ottomans educated in French and at familiar with French culture. Sometimes called the "French knowers," these individuals were able to deal with their European counterparts on their own terms. Confident of their abilities and modern outlook, these same men would both challenge and reform the old Ottoman institutional order. Whereas French-style uniforms were the symbol of the new military, the frock coat became the symbol of the Europeanization of the civil bureaucracy. Mahmud II's reforms were not designed to cast off Ottoman culture and ideology but rather to create institutions, and individuals, that would enable the empire to compete with Europe and reclaim its status as a world power. There were those who resented these changes, preferring to rely on tradition and protect the status quo. But many others viewed the new schools, and the opportunities they provided, as the means for upward mobility long denied those who had stood outside of elite imperial society.

Challenging Ottoman Sovereignty in Europe

Ottoman territorial integrity was challenged in the nineteenth century by a series of separatist movements in the Balkans. The rise of nationalism in Europe and

▼ Military defeats and nationalist rebellions diminished the size of the Ottoman Empire in the nineteenth century. However, it still controlled a significant amount of territory in 1914, when the region was engulfed in the conflicts of World War I.

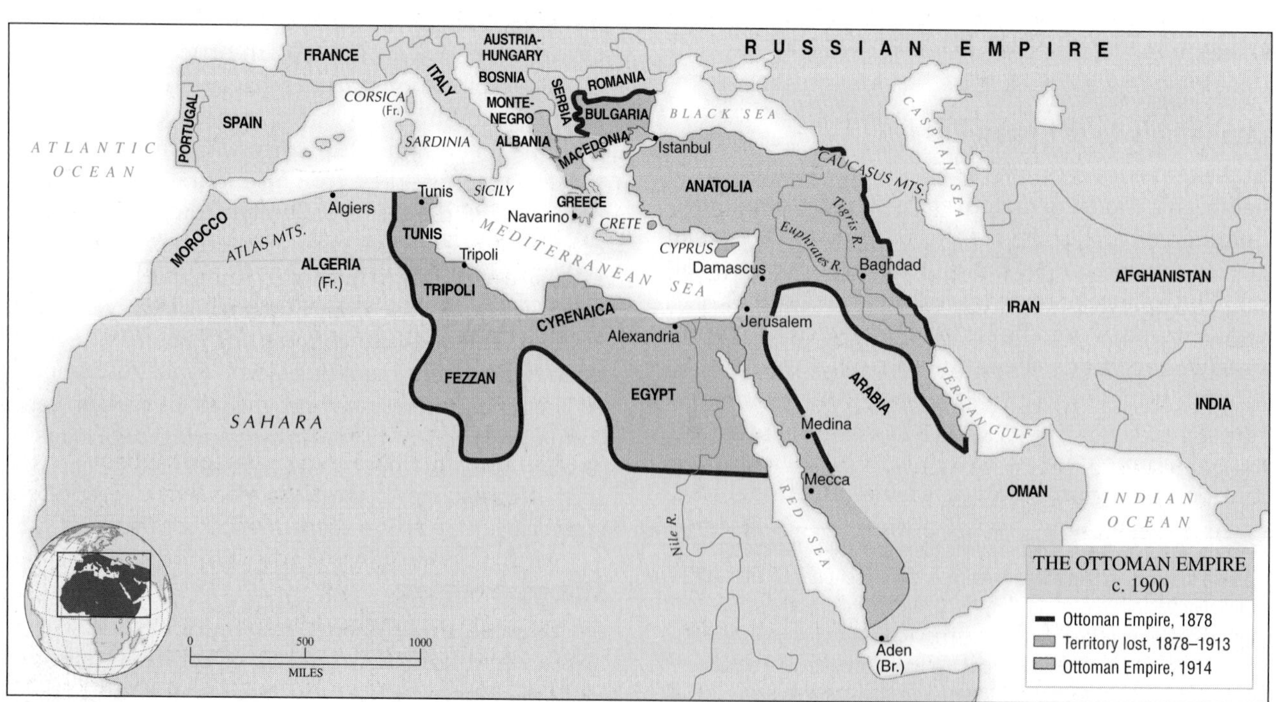

Eugène Delacroix, *Massacre at Chios* (1824). European liberals and Romantics such as Delacroix supported the Greeks in their struggle for independence from the Turks, whom they depicted as cruel oppressors.

Great Power meddling in Ottoman affairs were both factors in the emergence and evolution of these movements. The Serbs rose in revolt in 1804, followed by the Greeks in 1821, the Romanians in the 1850s, and the Bulgarians in the 1870s.

The Serbs achieved autonomy in 1830 after a long struggle. The Greek Revolt, however, more directly engaged the energies of the Great Powers, who intervened to ensure its success. The Ottomans had crushed the Greek insurrection in its early stages. But Britain, Russia, and France all viewed the rebellion in terms of what many observers of the time called the "Eastern Question." At issue was whether or not the Ottoman Empire would be dismembered, and if so, how the European states would best take advantage of its collapse (see Chapter 30). The Greek Revolt captured the imaginations of European intellectuals who were enamored of the Greek classical tradition and saw the revolt as a romantic instance of the forces of freedom triumphing over the forces of despotism. Although that romanticism had little to do with the ground-level realities of the revolt, it did fuel support for the Greeks in the cities of western Europe. Educated Europeans saw themselves as inheritors of the classical Greek traditions and ideals of liberty; conversely, they portrayed the Ottomans as backward, uncivilized, nearly as barbarians. In the end a predominantly British fleet sank the Ottoman navy at Navarino in 1827, and Britain, Russia, and France engineered a treaty to establish an independent Greece.

Russia and Britain would encounter each other again over Ottoman territory, but on opposite sides, in the Crimean War (1854–1856). Britain saved Istanbul from Russian conquest, thereby preserving the balance of power. But by the end of the nineteenth century, Europeans commonly referred to the empire as the "sick man of Europe." The reference had largely to do with the losses suffered by the Ottomans in their former Balkan provinces. The nation-states carved out of the Balkans have had a complicated history since that time. Borders have been drawn and redrawn (such as those of Yugoslavia in the twentieth century), and ethnic and religious tensions have been exacerbated, as they were in Africa and India for example, by the demands of nations contending for independence.

Egypt and the Rule of Muhammad Ali

Egypt had been a province of the Ottoman Empire since its conquest by Sultan Selim ("the Grim") in 1517. By the late eighteenth century, however, Ottoman rule was little more than nominal. The considerable resources of Egypt were, for the most part, controlled by the heads of Mamluk (see p. 227) households. In the nineteenth century, Egypt's ties to the Ottoman Empire were nearly fully severed, first by a highly successful Ottoman military commander, Muhammad Ali, then by the British, who seized Egypt as a strategic link to their colonial empire in India.

DOCUMENT A British View of Egyptian Agriculture, 1840

Muhammad Ali came to power in Egypt in the aftermath of Napoleon's invasion. The French occupation of Egypt was short-lived, although it served to stimulate European interest in Egyptian civilization. Muhammad Ali arrived in Egypt as a member of a

Seeing Connections

The Suez Canal

Completed in 1869, after many delays and massive cost overruns, the Suez Canal attracted conflicting Egyptian (nationalist) and British (imperial) claims. The British invaded Egypt in 1882, largely to consolidate control over the Canal, and so guarantee smooth passage of traders, diplomats, soldiers, and travelers to India, Britain's more distant imperial possession. Many contemporary observers marveled at the Canal as a triumph of modernity and the West's technological prowess. Little mention was made of the social and economic toll that the immense project took on ordinary Egyptians, including the many thousands who labored to dig the Canal in the first place. Long decades would pass before Egypt would lay claim to the property, and the considerable annual revenues, of the Canal.

joint British-Ottoman expedition (1801) sent to end the French occupation. He quickly established himself in power, thus filling the vacuum left by the French departure.

To consolidate power, Muhammad Ali turned first against the Mamluks (much as Mahmud II had destroyed the janissaries). He then proceeded to reorganize his military along European lines; an initial step was to recruit a new-style army made up of conscripted peasants. This was a radical change for the rural population since, traditionally, peasants had not been required to bear arms. Muhammad Ali also founded new professional schools and a government printing press, reorganized the agricultural and taxation systems of Egypt, sent men to study in France, and launched an ambitious program of industrialization. He also undermined the power of the religious establishment, the *ulama*. Unlike religious leaders elsewhere in Africa—the Mahdi of Sudan for example—the Sunni *ulama* of Egypt (and in the Ottoman Empire in general) were generally subordinate to the state. At no point were they positioned, for example, to lead *jihads* or organize political opposition.

Muhammad Ali's reforms were more extensive than those of Sultan Mahmud II, but these two contemporaries were both major symbols of Middle Eastern reform. Once Muhammad Ali consolidated his power, he moved to challenge the Ottoman state directly. Initially, he had defended Ottoman interests by defeating the **Wahhabis,** an aggressive, puritanical movement active in northern Arabia, and by taking part in the suppression of the Greek Revolt. But, in 1831, he sent his son Ibrahim to invade Ottoman provinces in Syria and Anatolia. Ibrahim's forces ultimately marched to within 150 miles of Istanbul.

Here again, Russia, Britain, and France intervened to preserve the Ottoman Empire. Muhammad Ali ultimately established an autonomous dynastic state in Egypt where his descendants occupied the throne until the 1950s. His career illustrates the weakness of the Ottoman Empire and its tenuous control over its more distant provinces. European states capitalized on the disruptions caused by Muhammad Ali to negotiate more advantageous commercial agreements with the beleaguered Ottoman state, thus undermining the economic foundations of the empire even further.

The Suez Canal

Muhammad Ali's successors pursued elements of his reform programs, with little military or economic success. Egypt benefited from the American Civil War

Wahhabis—A puritanical movement founded in Arabia by Muhammad ibn Abd al-Wahhab during the 1750s that aimed to cleanse Sunni Islam of innovations like Sufism.

when Egyptian cotton was used to replace the South's cotton exports, which were cut off when the Union blockaded southern ports. But foreign loans and the uncontrolled spending of its rulers left Egypt bankrupt by the 1870s.

The idea of a canal linking the Mediterranean to the Red Sea was hardly new. The Mamluks, rulers of pre-Ottoman Egypt, had planned such a canal but lacked the technology to accomplish it. In 1854, the Egyptian ruler, Said (1854–1863), granted a Frenchman, Ferdinand de Lesseps (d. 1894), a concession to build a canal. De Lesseps was only one among many European entrepreneurs and concessionaires flocking to Egypt seeking opportunities and commercial privileges. If occasional Egyptians gained employment from these concessionaires, many others lost out as more advanced European technologies (e.g., the telegraph, steamship, and railroads) began to replace more traditional forms of transport and communication and those who provided them. The building and completion of the canal itself radically disrupted patterns of labor as peasants were forcibly seized from their villages to provide unpaid labor digging the canal. Families were torn apart, women left their farm plots to follow and care for their drafted husbands, and thousands died in the course of the digging.

The Suez Canal was completed in 1869 under Khedive Ismail (1863–1879). Ismail was committed to the European-style transformation of his realm. But his lavish spending, particularly on his opening ceremonies for the canal, threw Egypt into a financial crisis. The opening ceremonies were a world event. Ismail commissioned the opera *Aïda* (which was not completed in time) and built special pavilions to house visiting dignitaries. His extravagance dazzled even the jaded aristocrats of Europe. The empress Eugénie of France, a notorious clotheshorse, was said to have taken 250 dresses with her to the affair.

Plagued by financial troubles, Ismail sold Egypt's shares in the canal to Britain for 4 million pounds sterling in 1875. The stock shares were snapped up by Disraeli, the astute prime minister of Great Britain, while the French dithered over whether to buy them. This sale gave Britain virtual control of this essential water link to its South Asian empire. The following year (the same year the Ottoman Empire defaulted on its loans), Egypt was unable to pay the interest on its foreign loans. Britain and France then forced Egypt to accept European control over its debts and hence its economy.

The assertion of foreign control paved the way for the British invasion of Egypt. Pressure by Britain and France led to Ismail's abdication (1879). Two years later, a military-led revolt under Ahmad Urabi (d. 1911) challenged European policies towards Egypt. Urabi also worked to limit the decision-making powers of the monarchy and create a new national assembly. Antiforeign rioting occurred in Alexandria, leading to the deaths of a number of Europeans. The British, claiming they were acting in the best interests of the Egyptian people, first attacked Alexandria then marched on Cairo. The city fell to outright British control in 1882. The British, insisting throughout that their occupation was merely temporary, administered the country until the Egyptian Revolt of 1952 and maintained control over the Suez Canal until 1956. Thus, as elsewhere in Africa, the European imperial states used a combination of economic incentive, military force, and treachery to seize control of African empires.

▲ Egypt was part of the Ottoman Empire for more than 350 years. Although the British conquered Egypt in 1882, the Ottomans still thought of it as their own territory. This Ottoman cartoon, published in Istanbul in 1908, expresses bonds of brotherhood between the Ottoman constitutionalist and the Young Egyptian nationalists who were trying to throw off British imperial rule. As the giant symbol of England leans lazily against the pyramids, the tiny Egyptians do not seem to have much of a chance.

Lord Cromer and the Dinshaway Incident

Following the British occupation, Sir Evelyn Baring, better known as Lord Cromer (d. 1917), was appointed to oversee Egypt's political and economic affairs. He set out quickly to accelerate cotton production and reorganize Egypt's finances, including the elimination of corruption. Cromer, in office from 1883 to 1907, was an able administrator who stabilized the Egyptian economy, but his harsh policies and general contempt for Egyptian culture earned him the hatred of many and helped galvanize the Egyptian nationalist movement.

Nationalist sentiments were further driven by the Dinshaway Incident (1906). The affair began innocently enough with a pigeon shoot on the part of a group of British officers. The officers, apparently unaware that the Egyptian peasants raised pigeons for food, pursued their hunt, wounding a villager of Dinshaway, a small settlement on the Nile delta. In the ensuing scuffle, two officers were wounded, one of whom later died. Determined to make an example of Dinshaway, the British punished the entire village, trying dozens of villagers and publicly hanging four of them. The incident provoked anger throughout Egypt, prompted the penning of patriotic songs, and gave force to the nationalist movement. It was clear by this point that the Egyptian populace as a whole was mobilized, on political and economic grounds, against the British occupation.

North Africa (The Maghrib)

The term "North Africa" suggests a sharp division between Mediterranean and sub-Saharan Africa. This is misleading: the two regions have long cultural, religious and commercial ties. But North Africa is grouped here with the Middle East because of its historic Arab and Islamic identity and because it was (loosely) controlled by the Ottoman Empire through the pre-modern period. North Africa, in the Ottoman period, consisted of the independent state of Morocco, ruled by the Alawi (or Filali) dynasty—which is still in power today—and three coastal states centered around, respectively, the cities of Tunis, Algiers, and Tripoli. The latter three states, established early in the Ottoman period, would dominate the western Mediterranean for some three hundred years. They were often only nominally under Ottoman control. For the most part, semiautonomous governors exercised real decision-making power, usually in uneasy cooperation with subordinate tribal leaders in their hinterlands.

Algiers, Tripoli, and, to a lesser extent, Tunis relied heavily on the revenue generated by **corsair** activity off their coasts. In the eighteenth century, they benefited from treaties with various European states willing to pay tribute and gifts in exchange for security for their merchant shipping. That shipping was part of a vast web of seaborne trade that reached from Southeast Asia and China to the American colonies. When the American colonies gained their independence from Britain, they, too, negotiated treaties with the so-called Barbary States in order to protect the lucrative American trade with North Africa. Sidi Muhammad (1757–1790) of Morocco granted the fledgling United States its first official trading privileges in 1786. The U.S. Congress authorized $40,000 for a treaty and $25,000 annual tribute for Algiers in 1790 and, shortly thereafter, provided for the building of a navy to gain leverage against the corsair state.

In the nineteenth century, however, European powers began to look to North Africa as an area ripe for conquest. Like Egypt, the Maghrib experienced European economic penetration before it suffered actual invasion. Penetration came in the form of capitulations, reflecting commercial concessions granted to European states by the Ottomans and the exploitation of North Africa as a market for European goods. The first target was Algiers. In the 1820s, the ruler, or *dey*, of Algiers sent ships to aid the Ottomans against the Greek Revolt; he also dealt with an internal revolt as Algiers's Berber tribesmen fought against his janissary troops. Pressure mounted in the meantime with growing conflicts with France over fishing rights, piracy, and debts owed by France to Algiers.

In 1827, under the pretext that the *dey* had insulted the French consul in public, France blockaded Algiers. Pursuing France's imperialist agenda, Charles X (1824–1830), the French monarch, ordered the invasion of Algiers (1830). Some seventeen years of desperate resistance followed before the French were able to consolidate control over Algiers and much of its hinterland. Only then was it incorporated as what the French thought of as an integral part of the French state.

Algiers then became a base for France to extend its influence across North Africa. Tunis, nearly independent of Ottoman rule by this point, established its own constitution in 1861. An insurrection, which united tribal and urban elements in 1864, led to the bankruptcy of Tunis in 1869. Its French, Italian, and British creditors then gained control of the Tunisian economy. Italy coveted the coastal state with its rich agricultural hinterland, but the French frustrated those ambitions by declaring Tunis a French protectorate (1881). From that point, the country's wealth was siphoned off by the French treasury, leaving much of the population in desperate poverty.

The French turned their sights on Morocco as well, playing a dominant role in that country's affairs through the second half of the century. But Germany was emerging as a significant power in the late nine-

---

corsair—Pirates operating off of the Barbary Coast of North Africa.

teenth century and cast its eye on African territory as well, including Morocco. France, however, used its established bases in North Africa and its alliance with the British to win this particular standoff. They promised the Germans territory elsewhere in Africa and took over Morocco in 1912. The French left the Moroccan dynasty in place but did not relinquish their hold on the country until 1956.

The Italians were latecomers in the scramble for Africa. Frustrated by the Ethiopians in their ambitions for northeastern Africa, they sought opportunity in North Africa. Capitalizing on the disruptions caused by the Ottoman constitutional revolution, they declared war on the Ottoman Empire in 1911 and invaded the area around Tripoli, annexing it in the face of a failed Ottoman defense. Resistance to Italian (and French) expansion was led by the Sanusiya, a Sufi order established in the region in the early 1840s. The Sanusiya had gained its influence largely by pursuing policies of Islamic reform and, by this time, enjoyed wide support in both the urban centers and rural areas. The order would later gain power in the new state of Libya when the colonial powers withdrew. The early twentieth century, however, saw North Africa, like sub-Saharan Africa, divided among the European imperial powers and incorporated into European empires.

Young Ottomans and Constitutional Reform

The challenges to Ottoman sovereignty, combined with the prospect of a newly emerging "modern" world order, prompted a period of reform known as the ***Tanzimat*** ("reorganization"), normally dated from 1839 to 1876. New professional schools were opened in the empire, the class of "French knowers" grew in size and influence, and a more modern and secular civil bureaucracy was established. The power of the *ulama* was diminished by the legal and educational reforms. As new, more secular schools opened, the *ulama* lost their monopoly on education. The government also tried to ward off separatist sentiments by emphasizing the ideology of Ottomanism, a notion that all Ottoman subjects were equal and should be committed to the preservation of the empire, regardless of ethnicity or religion. The notion, controversial in many circles, held sway at the highest levels of government from that point forward.

From the reforms of the *Tanzimat* emerged a new civil and military elite, some of whom favored elements of European culture and more democratic forms of government. The efforts of one group of intellectuals and bureaucrats, sometimes called the *Young Ottomans,* revitalized Ottoman literature and called for a new synthesis that would combine the best elements of traditional Islamic culture with European ideas and technology. These reformers debated issues of constitutional government, the adoption of European-style customs of dress and public life, and the introduction of "modern" forms of education. Much debate centered on women's rights and education.

The reformers also tackled the question of slavery. In response to British pressure on the Ottoman Empire to end the slave trade, the Young Ottomans argued that slavery in the Islamic realm differed in fundamental ways from that practiced in the European colonies and in the Americas, reliant as they were upon the Atlantic slave trade. Ottoman slavery included the elite ***kul*** system and was primarily domestic rather than agricultural. It was characterized by a predominance of female slaves (rather than the Atlantic slave trade's 2:1 male to female ratio), use of both white and black slaves, and reliance on the provisions of Islamic law. Islamic law held, for example, that the children of a female slave and her master were free and entitled to inherit.

A group of Ottoman reform-minded elites moved, in 1871, to depose Sultan Abdülaziz (1861–1876) and install Western-style constitutional government in the Ottoman Empire. But their decision was not to eliminate the monarchy, and, in fact, in the constitution they proposed, the office of sultan retained considerable authority. The reformers instead sought the creation of an elected assembly, a guarantee of freedom of the press, and equality for all Ottomans. The constitutionalists finally installed a new sultan, Abdülhamid II (1876–1909). Once in power, however, Abdülhamid, to the surprise of many observers, promptly abrogated the constitution and suspended the parliament (1878).

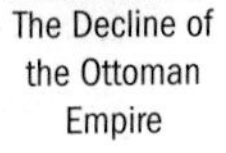

The Decline of the Ottoman Empire

Abdülhamid II and the Young Turk Revolution

Abdülhamid, paradoxically, was both reformer and autocrat. He continued many of the trends set out in the *Tanzimat* era but also dealt with political opposition harshly. He spied on political organizations, censored the press, and condemned many people to exile and imprisonment.

He also had to grapple with challenges to the Ottoman state on all fronts. Russia declared war in 1877, resulting in the loss of further Ottoman territory and the creation of a large refugee population fleeing newly acquired Russian lands. Britain occupied Egypt and the

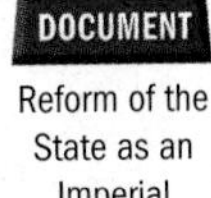

Reform of the State as an Imperial Project

Tanzimat—A period of reform (1839–1876) in the Ottoman Empire in which modern schools were opened and the influence of Muslim clerics was curtailed.

kul—Turkish term for 'slave.' It refers to the Ottoman system of training slaves for elite administrative and palace offices.

Document

A Middle Eastern Vision of the West

Middle Easterners traveled to Europe for a variety of reasons in the nineteenth century. Some went for pleasure or educational purposes; others went for medical treatments or business. As European states gained military advantages over Middle Eastern states, more Middle Eastern rulers sent diplomats to gather information on the newly prominent powers. In 1844, France bombarded Moroccan ports and forced a treaty on the Moroccan sultan, Mulay Abd ar-Rahman. The following year, interested in studying the sources of French power, Morocco sent an embassy to France. One of its members was the scholar Muhammad as-Saffar, who later recorded his impressions of French society. As a distinguished visitor, as-Saffar tended to travel in elite circles, and he certainly did not get to see all aspects of French life. But he was intensely interested in French society—from its business practices to its roads, its printing presses, and even its eating habits. Muhammad as-Saffar expressed admiration for French efficiency and military organization, recommending that his ruler imitate these traits in order to ensure Morocco's survival. He also enjoyed the spectacle of men and women dancing together at balls, although he found the French arrogant and uncharitable and their long, drawn-out dinners annoying. All in all, he was an astute observer of French culture, as these excerpts show.

The people of Paris, men and women alike, are tireless in their pursuit of wealth. They are never idle or lazy. The women are like the men in that regard, or perhaps even more so.... Even though they have all kinds of amusements and spectacles of the most marvelous kinds, they are not distracted from their work.... Nor do they excuse someone for being poor, for indeed death is easier for them than poverty, and the poor man there is seen as vile and contemptible.

Another of their characteristics is a hot-tempered and stubborn arrogance, and they challenge each other to a duel at the slightest provocation. If one of them slanders or insults another, the challenged one has no choice but to respond, lest he be branded a despicable coward for the rest of his life. Then they decide the conditions of the combat—what weapons they will fight with, how it will be done, and the place—and no one in authority interferes with them.

You should know that among the customs of these people is that they sit only in chairs and they know nothing of sitting directly on the floor.... Another of their customs is that they do not touch food with their hands, nor do they gather around a single platter.... Two people may share one pitcher but each has his own glass from which no one else may drink, for they regard that as the height of uncleanliness.... At the end of every course, the servant removes the dishes and other things, and brings fresh ones. The number of dishes piles up, because they change them at every course and no dish is ever eaten from twice. This is due to their excessive concern for cleanliness.... [T]hey linger at table for more than two hours, because it is their custom to stretch out the talk during the meal so they can overindulge in food. The Arabs say that perfect hospitality is friendliness at first sight and leisurely talk with one's table companions. But we detested the arrival of mealtimes because of the endless waiting, nor did we understand their conversation. Moreover, much of the food did not agree with us, and we got tired and irritated with the long sitting and waiting.

[At dinner as-Saffar noted the free mingling of the sexes and commented on the women's dress.] Their clothing covered their breasts, which were hidden from view, but the rest of their bosom, face and neck were bare and exposed. They cover their shoulders and upper arms in part with filmy, closefitting sleeves that do not reach the elbow. They bind their waists beneath their dresses with tight girdles which give them a very narrow middle. It is said they are trained into this [shape] from earliest childhood by means of a special mold.... In the lower part they drape their clothing in such a way that the backside is greatly exaggerated, but perhaps this is due to something they put underneath [bustles]....

Questions to Consider

1. Why do you think as-Saffar commented on French eating habits? What do you think eating habits and dress styles reveal about a people and their culture?
2. What aspects of a diplomat's life might be enjoyable? What aspects might be unpleasant?

From *Disorienting Encounters: Travels of a Moroccan Scholar in France in 1845–1856*, ed. and trans. Susan G. Miller (Berkeley: University of California Press, 1992).

island of Cyprus. Meanwhile, the empire, hampered by huge debts that it could not pay, was engaged in trying to redeem its Balkan territories. To counter these challenges, Abdülhamid worked to consolidate the authority of his office, bolster the military, and establish closer relations with an increasingly powerful Germany. Kaiser William made two state visits (1889 and 1898), including a triumphant trip to Jerusalem during which the German ruler, ever the politician, declared his undying friendship with the world's Muslims.

The sultan fostered the ideology of pan-Islam to legitimize his reign and mobilize support across the Islamic world. His rhetoric of Islamic unity and his claim to the caliphate failed to have the desired effect. More positive was the response to his project for a Hijaz railway intended to facilitate the access of *Hajj* pilgrims to the cities of Mecca and Medina. The project, supported symbolically by the collection of coins by schoolchildren, generated popular support for the sultan.

The constitutional ideal in the Ottoman Empire, however, retained its strength. Opposition to the sultan mounted as Abdülhamid entered the third decade of his reign. Outside the empire, a group of exiles clamored for the reintroduction of the constitution. Revolutionary sentiments at home grew among students, bureaucrats, and elements within the military. In 1889, a group of students in the military medical school founded a secret organization called the Committee for Union and Progress (CUP). The organization was instrumental in mobilizing opposition to the regime.

A military revolt in 1908 became the catalyst for the second Ottoman constitutional revolution, known as the Young Turk Revolution. As support for the revolt spread, the revolutionaries demanded that Abdülhamid reinstate the constitution. He acceded reluctantly to their demands. Elections followed, as did the suspension of censorship. The **Young Turks** moved quickly to curtail the powers of the sultan. The new assembly, emboldened by its hard-won authority, debated the rehabilitation of the navy, reform of the police and government, and the growing threats posed by the empire's neighbors.

The Young Turk Revolution, 1908

In April 1909, reactionary forces launched a counterrevolution in which Abdülhamid was implicated. The effort was quickly put down by the army. Abdülhamid was promptly deposed, and the CUP secured control over the Ottoman constitutional regime. Although a new sultan was installed, the revolution marked the end of Ottoman monarchical power. The new government was now firmly in the grip of a civilian elite. Discontent simmered in the Arab provinces, however, as the CUP continued the centralizing policies of Abdülhamid. But in general, the government and the remaining provinces stayed committed to the empire until World War I.

Political Opposition in the Ottoman Empire

Young Turks—The name given to a group of army officers who advocated reforming the administration and governance of the Ottoman Empire.

▼ One type of European penetration into the Ottoman Empire was the opening of textile factories in western Anatolia. The young girls and women who worked in these factories often made relatively good wages, but their work in factories raised moral issues about "unsupervised" women, much as it did in the factories of Europe. These young women workers in a silk-thread factory pose for the camera in 1878.

Young Turks march in triumph after their successful coup and overthrow of Abdülhamid II and his government. Like the sultan, the Young Turks used photography to document the events and successes of their government.

Iran and the Great Power Struggle

How did Iranian society react to the aggressive policies of Great Britain and Russia?

The Ottoman Revolution of 1908 was only one of many efforts to transform government and society in the Middle East. Factors similar to those that had prompted the Young Turk movement—an unpopular monarchy, foreign intervention, and Western-style constitutional reform—had fueled a constitutional revolution in Iran 2 years earlier. Farther east, a series of Afghan rulers struggled to retain their autonomy in the face of expansion on the part of British India and Tsarist Russia.

Qajar Rule and the Tobacco Rebellion

Iran had been ruled by the Qajar dynasty since 1794. Defeat at the hands of the Russians (1828) led the Qajar shah to concede extraterritorial rights and new commercial privileges to Russian merchants. British demands for similar concessions soon followed. As the nineteenth century progressed, the Qajars found themselves caught in a military and commercial squeeze play between Russia and Britain.

Foreign incursions reached a climax in the second half of the nineteenth century during the long reign of Nasir al-Din Shah (1848–1896). Unlike the Ottomans or Muhammad Ali, the Qajars remained dependent on the decentralized military power of tribal chiefs to defend Iran. Nasir al-Din implemented some military and educational reforms, but his government remained weak. To bolster his position, the shah negotiated loans, sold concessions to foreign investors, and brought in Russian military advisers to establish a new Cossack-style brigade.

DOCUMENT Religious Minorities in the Middle East

As Russian influence spread within the Qajar military, Britain moved to penetrate various spheres of the Iranian economy. The British completed a telegraph line from London to Iran in 1870, symbolizing their increased interest in the area. In 1890, Nasir al-Din granted a British company exclusive rights over Iran-

	The Political Transformation of Iran
1848–1896	Reign of Nasir al-Din Shah
1891	Tobacco Rebellion and boycott
1896–1906	Reign of Muzaffar al-Din Shah
1905	Constitutional revolution begins
1907–1909	Reign of Muhammad Ali Shah
1909	Constitutionalists depose Muhammad Ali Shah

ian tobacco production. The measure alienated the merchant classes, who aligned themselves with the Shi'ite religious establishment in opposition to Qajar rule and the tobacco concession. This was the Tobacco Revolt of 1891.

The Shi'ite *ulama* in Iran had never been subordinate to the state in the manner of the Sunni religious establishment in the Ottoman Empire. More like their counterparts in Africa, Iranian religious leaders constituted a powerful force for political mobilization despite the fact that influential voices among the leading clerics warned against undue involvement in politics. The alliance of merchants and *ulama* tipped the balance. A countrywide boycott of tobacco, and mounting unrest, obliged the shah to cancel the tobacco concession. The boycott not only illustrated the mobilizing power of the Shi'ite clerics, but also made clear the levels of popular discontent with an increasingly intrusive European presence.

The Iranian Constitutional Revolution

By the beginning of the twentieth century, parts of northern Iran were under the control of the Russians. Tsarist forces trained the Iranian army, put up telegraph lines, established a postal system, and developed trade. Some Iranian workers crossed into Russia to work in the Caucasus oilfields. The Russian ministry of finance even set up a bank, the Discount and Loan Bank of Iran, with branches in many parts of the nation. The bank lent the Iranian government 60 million rubles and provided 120 million rubles to Iranian merchants to enable them to buy Russian goods.

In turn, the British established the Imperial Bank of Iran in the southeastern part of the country. In 1901, Muzaffar al-Din Shah (1896–1906) granted a British subject a concession for oil rights over much of the country. The grant would lead to British control over Iranian oil that would continue into the second half of the century. Already crippled by his economic dependence on foreign powers, the shah made three costly trips to Europe during his short reign. These visits were criticized by the Iranian public as extravagant. But the shah used these visits to solicit still more foreign loans from the British, the French, and the Russians.

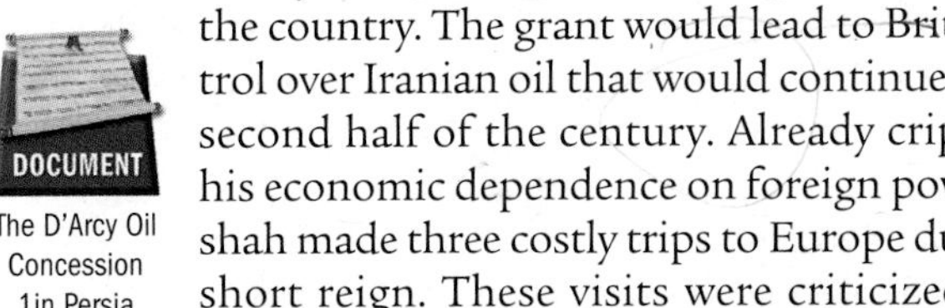

The D'Arcy Oil Concession 1in Persia

Seeking to control the sea routes between Suez and their Indian empire, the British also gained footholds in the Iranian Gulf region through treaties with a number of local *shaykhs,* including the rulers of Muscat, Oman, Bahrain, and Kuwait (1899). In 1903, the British foreign secretary issued what has been called a British Monroe Doctrine concerning this region: "I say it without hesitation, we should regard the establishment of a naval base or a fortified port in the Persian Gulf by any other power as a very grave menace to British interests, and we should certainly resist it by all means at our disposal."[10] Thus, the British won the imperialist struggle for control of the Persian Gulf just as France won the struggle for control of the coast of North Africa. Iran had no navy and could not, in any case, match British firepower.

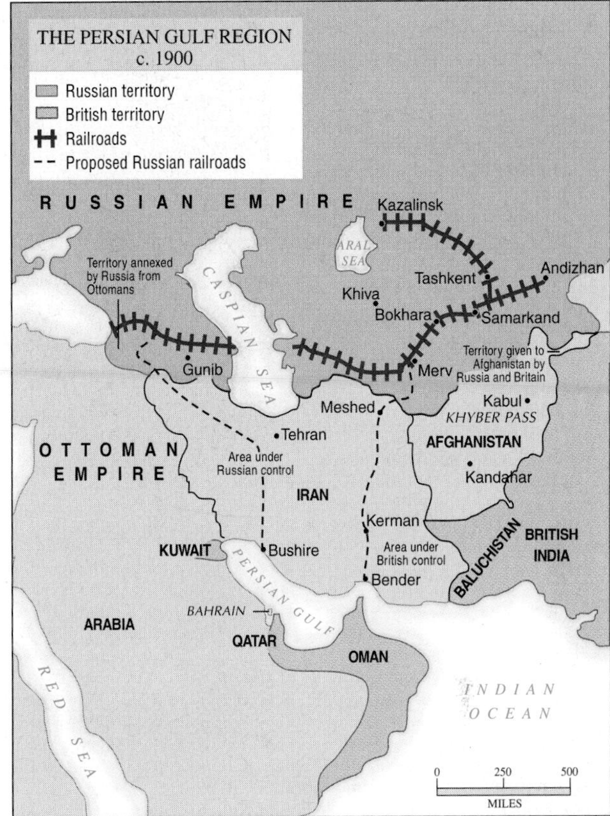

▲ By the late nineteenth century, Britain and Russia were both pressing hard to advance their interests in Persia and Afghanistan. Negotiating agreements with local rulers, Britain used the Persian Gulf region as a strategic base for its powerful fleets and as a link to its empire in India. Afghanistan became a contested buffer zone between British India and tsarist Russia.

Responding to foreign intervention, ineffectual Qajar rule, and the growing impetus for representative government, various factions within Iran mobilized a revolt beginning in 1905. The revolution began with a series of protests culminating in a general strike. Mass demonstrations, a strike led by leading clerics, and a massacre of protesters in Tehran by the Cossack brigade followed in 1906. The shah, yielding to these pressures, authorized a Constituent National Assembly. Elections were held, and new newspapers flourished in the capital. But Muzaffar al-Din died in 1906, and his successor, Muhammad Ali Shah (1907–1909), soon attempted to overturn the constitutional regime, plunging Iran into civil war. The new shah's tyranny and his use of Russian troops against

▲ The shah of Iran from 1896 to 1906, Muzaffar al-Din Shah was noted for encouraging foreign investment and accepting foreign loans. His rule was challenged by popular movements promoting representative government and, after a revolt in 1905, he authorized a Constituent National Assembly.

Iranians prompted members of the *ulama* to seek the intervention of the Ottoman sultan.

After a bitter struggle, the constitutional forces won and deposed Muhammad Ali Shah in July 1909, installing his 12-year-old son in his place. The Iranian constitutional revolution was watched closely in Istanbul and served as a prelude to the Ottoman Revolution, which followed quickly on its heels. The constitutionalists in both empires were inspired by the example of Japan, a modernizing power with a strong military. They were impressed that Japan was an Asian power (with a long history of traditional monarchy) that had successfully modernized and decisively beaten a European power, Russia, in 1905. The new Iranian and Ottoman constitutional regimes faced similar problems and were preoccupied with many of the same issues of modernization, freedom, and reform.

The Great Power Struggle for the East

As so often happens, revolution provided opportunity for territorial expansion by outside powers. European states moved quickly to extend their hold over former Ottoman lands. Between 1908 and 1913, Austria-Hungary annexed Bosnia and Herzegovina, Greece annexed Crete, and Italy—in the course of a short but difficult war—seized Tripoli and Cyrenaica (northeastern Libya). In 1912 and 1913, the Balkan nations fought two wars, which resulted in the partitioning of Macedonia. Although the Ottomans launched popular boycotts against both Austria and Italy (boycotting, for example, Italian spaghetti), they could do nothing to reverse their territorial losses.

In Iran, Russia capitalized on the revolution to seize territory in the northwest. The British and Russians signed a treaty (1907) dividing Iran into spheres of influence, with the British claiming powers of intervention in the south and Russia claiming the same powers in the north. The two states held Iran in a great pincers, with the British navy protecting its interests in the Persian Gulf and Russia's powerful armies posing a constant threat to Iranian sovereignty in the north.

Iran was not, however, the only object of this competition. Afghanistan, to its east, controlled the Khyber Pass, the most direct land route through the mountains from Russia to British-controlled India. The country had been divided previously between the Mughal and Iranian empires, but with its mountainous terrain and contending warlords, Afghanistan did not lend itself to unified rule. By the nineteenth century, the shah in Kabul, Afghanistan's capital, held tenuous sway over the tribal confederations that controlled the area.

During the first half of the nineteenth century, Iran and Afghanistan were caught up in armed conflicts with the Russians and British. In an effort to increase their influence in the area and protect India's northern frontiers, the British attempted to install their own handpicked ruler in Afghanistan. The attempt backfired, and the British were forced to retreat. A new effort, in 1879, saw the British move through the Khyber Pass into Kabul and subordinate the Afghan ruler, Yaqub Khan. Amir Abdur Rahman (1881–1901) later consolidated his power over Afghanistan though Britain retained hold on Afghanistan's foreign affairs.

Russia, meanwhile, was expanding to the southeast. Many indigenous peoples, such as the Mongols, Afghans, Turkomans, and Tatars, came within Russia's sphere of influence. Their cities—Samarkand, Tashkent, and Bokhara—became tsarist administrative centers. Russia's advance was accomplished not only by its army but also by the construction of the Trans-Caspian railway, which, at its completion in 1888, reached 1064 miles into the heart of Asia. The Orenburg-Tashkent railway, completed in 1905, stretched 1185 miles farther. A few Russian imperialists, inspired by such feats, even dreamed of sweeping across Afghanistan to take India itself. But British pressure blocked Russian designs on Afghanistan, and a British military expedition to Lhasa in 1904 countered Russian influence in Tibet.

By the terms of the Anglo-Russian entente in 1907, Russia and Britain agreed to leave Afghanistan intact. Russia agreed to deal with the sovereign of Afghanistan only through the British government. Great Britain agreed to refrain from occupying or annexing Afghanistan so long as the nation fulfilled its treaty obligations. This partnership was, however, only a marriage of convenience brought on by larger pressures in Europe. Neither side wished to alienate the other in the face of the emerging threat of Germany's war machine.

Conclusion

By 1914, European states had established control over broad regions of Africa and the Middle East. While hundreds of thousands of Africans worked in European-owned mines and plantations, many thousands of Iranians crossed into Russia to work in tsarist oilfields. While financiers in London, Berlin, and Paris skimmed the profits from the resources of Africa and Asia, European officials and diplomats dictated policy for much of the region. Although the Young Turk and Iranian revolutions brought constitutional governments to the Ottoman and Qajar empires in the Middle East, only Iran would survive the consuming conflicts of World War I. The Young Turks, engaged in rebuilding the Ottoman Empire, chose to enter the war on the German side, a decision with disastrous consequences.

Even before 1914, however, forces were at work that would end European dominance over the next half century. In sub-Saharan Africa and Egypt, nationalist movements were mobilized to throw off the European yoke. In Europe, citizens and parliamentary representatives debated the relative costs and benefits of empire and colonization. Many Europeans remained committed to Social Darwinism, the idea of a hierarchy of civilizations expressed in the notions of carrying the "white man's burden" of spreading "civilization" to the "lesser peoples." Europe's military, economic, and technological advantage over the Middle East and Africa was clear. But, as the twentieth century progressed, the so-called white man's burden would become increasingly onerous in the face of demands by subject peoples for independence and their assertion of cultural identities.

Culture and identity, of course, are never fixed; they evolve on a constant basis. From roughly 1800 to 1914, the Middle East and Africa experienced particularly intense and rapid cultural change prompted by marked transformations in economic organization and in the technologies of transportation and communication. Transformations of African and Middle Eastern societies were only compounded by the effects of political subjugation to, and economic dependency upon, the European states.

The reactions to European encroachment varied widely. The differences in response were tied, in different combinations, to social background, level of education, religious affiliation, ethnic identity, and similar factors. Some advocated the full adoption of European culture and institutional life. Others advocated resistance to all things European and a vigorous adherence to traditional patterns. More frequent were the attempts to find a middle ground, a compromise, in which elements of tradition would remain intact alongside the technological and institutional elements adapted from European culture and politics.

The assertion of European primacy over Africa and the Middle East had dramatic effects. Europeanization altered economic, political, and legal structures. Education systems, in many cases, were radically overhauled. The impact on language use, too, was dramatic: English and French became widely spoken, particularly in middle-class and wealthy urban neighborhoods. Language use went hand-in-hand with the adoption of French and British culture. But, at the same time, Western-educated Africans and Middle Easterners often turned their new-style education to the struggle for independence and a sharp critique of the colonial order.

European influence contributed to the shaping of new cultural syntheses: upper-class women in Istanbul sought out French fashions; upper-class European women dressed in "Turkish" style and consumed Orientalist art. Recently converted African Christians in sub-Saharan Africa not only embraced a new faith, but accepted the Victorian dress of the colonizers. In many ways, however, European culture was a veneer applied to powerful and far more deeply rooted indigenous traditions. In much of North Africa and the Middle East, and despite the discernible and very real impact of Westernization, Islam retained its strength. In much of sub-Saharan Africa, the colonial period ushered in the expansion of both Islam and Christianity, usually in different parts of the continent. Many African Christians, dissatisfied with the European missionaries' interpretations of Christianity, adapted the new faith to their own cultural needs and practices.

Suggestions for Web Browsing

You can obtain more information about topics included in this chapter at the websites listed below. See also the companion website that accompanies this text, http://www.ablongman.com/brummett, which contains an online study guide and additional resources.

Sultan Abdul-Hamid II Collection Photography Archives
http://memory.loc.gov/pp/ahiihtml/ahiiabt.html
This site contains nearly 2000 photographs from albums of one of the last sultans of the Ottoman Empire from 1880 to 1893.

Age of European Imperialism: The Partitioning of Africa in the Late Nineteenth Century
http://pw2.netcom.com/~giardina/colony.html
This site discusses the partitioning of Africa and includes an interesting selection of maps tracing the imperial drive in Africa.

Internet Islamic History Sourcebook: Western Intrusion, 1815–1914
http://www.fordham.edu/halsall/islam/islamsbook.html
An extensive online source for links about the history of the Middle East, including short primary documents describing nineteenth-century European imperialism and the end of the Ottoman Empire.

Literature and Film

In *The Days,* trans. Hilary Wayment, 2nd ed. (American University at Cairo Press, 2001), is a wonderful three-volume autobiography by Taha Hussein, the blind village boy who studied at al-Azhar in Cairo and became a famous scholar and author. *The Press and Poetry of Modern Persia* (Kalimat Press, 1984, reprint of 1914 edition) by Edward G. Browne is a collection of prose, poetry, cartoons, and excerpts from the press. Hasan Javadi, in *Satire in Persian Literature* (Fairleigh Dickinson University Press, 1988), offers a survey of satire divided topically, including, for example, satire on women and on religion. W. Morgan Shuster's *The Strangling of Persia* (Image Publishers, 1987, reprint of 1912 edition) is a memoir of the American financial expert brought to Iran in 1911 to manage the empire's finances. Edwin Pears, in *Forty Years in Constantinople, the Recollections of Sir Edwin Pears 1873–1915* (Books for Libraries Press, 1871, reprint of 1916 edition), gives an interesting commentary by an outsider on Ottoman affairs. *The Diary of H.M. The Shah of Persia During His Tour Through Europe in A.D. 1873*, trans. J. W. Redhouse (Mazda, 1995), is a memoir of the Iranian Shah Nasir al-Din's journey to Europe.

Chinua Achebe's trilogy—*Things Fall Apart, No Longer at Ease,* and *Arrow of God*—traces a Nigerian family through the span of the colonial period (Anchor, 1989–1994). Modikwe Dikobe's *The Marabi Dance* (Heinemann, 1984) is a novel set in a black township in South Africa in the 1930s that highlights popular culture and the urbanization of black migrant workers. Buchi Emecheta's *The Joys of Motherhood* (George Braziller, 1980) treats the difficulty of being a woman in African society and under British colonial rule.

Ethiopian filmmaker Haile Gerima's *Adwa* (1999; Mypheduh Films) chronicles the famous victory of the Ethiopians over the Italians in 1896. Senegalese filmmaker Ousmane Sembene's *Ceddo* (1977; New Yorker Films) deals with how nineteenth-century West Africans responded to external forces, such as European traders, Christian missionaries, and Muslim *jihads. Black and White in Color* (1976; Warner Home Video) is a satirical treatment of a skirmish between French and German colonials in West Africa at the outset of World War I. Based on a novel by Joyce Cary, *Mister Johnson* (1991; Artemis) is a portrait of an African clerk who faces numerous problems adjusting to his role as a civil servant under colonial administration in Nigeria. Part of an eight-part documentary series on Africa narrated by Basil Davidson, *The Magnificent African Cake* (1984; Public Media Video) covers the European scramble for Africa.

Suggestions for Reading

Studies on the European scramble for Africa include David Levering Lewis, *The Race to Fashoda: Colonialism and African Resistance* (Henry Holt, 1995). The use of technology to facilitate conquest is treated in Daniel Headrick, *The Tentacles of Progress: Technology Transfer in the Age of Imperialism, 1850–1940* (Oxford University Press, 1988).

The general subject of African resistance to European conquest is treated in Robert Rotberg and Ali Mazrui, *Protest and Power in Black Africa* (Oxford University Press, 1970), and Bruce Vandervort, *Wars of Imperial Conquest in Africa, 1830–1914* (Indiana University Press, 1998). Ethiopia's return to a centralized kingdom and its resistance to European conquest is covered in Harold Marcus, *The Life and Times of Menelik II: Ethiopia, 1844–1913* (Red Sea Press, 1995).

An excellent assessment of the Anglo-Boer War is Bill Nasson, *The South African War, 1899–1902* (Oxford University Press, 1999).

The impact of colonial rule in Africa is examined in Adu Boahen, *African Perspectives on Colonialism* (Johns Hopkins University Press, 1987). Colonialism's impact on social change is covered in Andrew Roberts, ed., *The Colonial Moment in Africa* (Cambridge University Press, 1986). Europe's image of Africa is presented in Jan Nederveen Pieterse, *White on Black: Images of Africa and Blacks in Western Popular Culture* (Yale University Press, 1992).

On the Ottoman Empire in the nineteenth century, see Roderic H. Davison, *Turkey: A Short History,* 3rd ed. (Eothen Press, 1998), for a brief, well-written survey, and see Donald Quataert, *The Ottoman Empire, 1700–1922* (Cambridge University Press, 2000), for a student-friendly survey. On the Young Turk Revolution and its political and cultural impacts, see Palmira Brummett, *Image and Imperialism in the*

Ottoman Revolutionary Press, 1908–1911 (State University of New York Press, 2000).

On the Middle East, see the relevant articles in Youssef M. Choueiri, ed., *A Companion to the History of the Middle East* (Blackwell Publishing, 2005). On the shaping of Arab nationalism, see James L. Gelvin, *Divided Loyalties: Nationalism and Mass Politics in Syria at the Close of Empire* (University of California Press, 1999). Economic issues are covered in Roger Owen, *The Middle East in the World Economy, 1800–1914* (Methuen, 1981).

L. S. Stavrianos, *The Balkans Since 1453* (Holt, Rinehart, and Winston, 1961), provides a treatment of the evolution of the Balkan states in the context of Ottoman rule. On North African politics and culture, see Ali Ahmida, *The Making of Modern Libya: State Formation, Colonization, and Resistance, 1830–1932* (State University of New York Press, 1994).

For treatments of the Qajars and the Persian constitutional revolution, see Edmond Bosworth and Carole Hellenbrand, eds., *Qajar Iran: Political, Social and Cultural Change, 1800–1925* (Mazda, 1992).

CHAPTER 25

Imperialism and Modernity in Asia and the Pacific, 1815–1914

India, Southeast Asia, China, Japan, and Oceania

Outline

- India
- Southeast Asia
- China: The Long Nineteenth Century
- Japan: Modernity and Imperialism
- Australia, New Zealand, and the Pacific Islands

Features

DOCUMENT The Great Revolt of 1857–1858

DOCUMENT Lin Zexu on the Opium Trade

SEEING CONNECTIONS Western Houses in Tokyo

DOCUMENT "The Beefeater"

◀ The arrival of Western gunboats and merchants in Asia in the nineteenth century usually initiated a period of economic and military domination. For the Japanese, the arrival of Commodore Perry in 1853 served as the beginning of a revolutionary change that made them competitors with the West by the end of the century.

As the nineteenth century opened, Asian countries confronted external pressures and, in many cases, internal turmoil. Indians remained under the centuries-old weak rule of the Mughals, but British imperialism increasingly modified their lives. The countries of the Indochinese peninsula and the islands of the Pacific and Indian oceans had been subject to European commercial influences since the sixteenth century, but more coercive forms of imperialism were soon to appear. China under the Manchus remained the world's greatest single power and economy, but it faced increasing pressure from its growing population and rapidly rising European countries.

Although most of the world's large cities were in Asia, most Asians, like people elsewhere, lived in villages. The area was, and still is, vulnerable to natural disasters such as typhoons, tidal waves, earthquakes, and droughts. Many people suffered from poor living conditions, endemic diseases, and inadequate nutrition. Yet many in Asia were materially better off than their counterparts in the West as the century opened. By the beginning of the twentieth century, however, a combination of factors—imperialism, population pressures, cultural and ethnic turmoil, and disastrous climate conditions—conspired to relegate much of Asia to colonial or semicolonial status.

Lack of political independence was by no means the only story in Asian countries. People developed new arts, culture, institutions, economic enterprises, and ways of relating to one another, which some characterized as "modernization." But by 1914, most of Asia rested under the direct or indirect control of Europe, the United States, or Japan.

India

How did British colonialism inspire a subcontinent of fractured principalities to develop a sense of nationalism?

	India: Establishment of the British Raj
1757	The battle of Plassey; the British East India Company wins control of Bengal
1820s	Indian reformers call for improvement in women's status and education and return to Golden Age of Hindu culture in reaction to British missionary activities
1857–1858	Great Revolt; its suppression ended Mughal rule and brought much of India under the British crown.
1885	Indian National Congress founded
1905	Bengal partitioned, leading to boycott

Internal struggles between the ruling Mughals and the Marathas, the Sikhs, the provincial governors, and other Indian princes offered an opportunity for the British and French to expand militarily and economically in India during the eighteenth century. The British in particular, through the British East India Company, established power in three key towns, Madras (now Chennai), Bombay (now Mumbai), and Calcutta (now Kolkata), from which they expanded their authority into the interior. By 1757, the Company was the effective ruler of Bengal, following Britain's victory at Plassey. The French and British also fought one another, and India, like North America, was part of the two European powers' world struggle for empire during the Seven Years' War. Following their victory over French forces in India in 1760, the British chipped away at India. During the next century, through absorption of the territory of local princes by conquest or trickery, integration of India's economy with that of the British Empire, and development of an Indian elite expected to be loyal to Britain, India fell increasingly under British dominance.

British traders, particularly the British East India Company, joined with British officials as rulers, assuming the dual roles of businessmen and representatives of a sovereign state. Some Indian princes accepted British domination, but others who resisted lost their land. Until 1858, administration of the subcontinent was divided into two sections: British India was ruled directly by officials sent from London, while in Indian India, the local dynasties ruled under British supervision. The British Parliament, concerned that a profit-seeking company controlled the lives of millions of people while its agents lined their pockets with graft, enacted legislation in 1773 and 1784 that gave it power to control company policies and appoint the governor-general. The governor-general was to adhere to India's "ancient uses and Institutions," but which should those be? The British rulers had Mughal precedents as well as multiple religions and cultures to consider. The British attempt to define "ancient uses and Institutions" caused them to stress differences between Hindus and Muslims as well as **caste** and hierarchy, and "traditions" defined during the colonial era contributed to religious and social tensions in the twentieth century.

DOCUMENT
Arrival of the British in the Punjab

Reform and Rebellion

British missionaries arrived in India before the end of the eighteenth century, opening schools for Indian students and propagating Christian culture. In time, a synthesis of English and Indian culture emerged, which would later fuel the fires of nationalism already sparked by indigenous Indian reformers. By 1820, Indian reformers like Ram Mohan Roy (1772–1833) called for a return to a Golden Age of Hindu culture, when women supposedly enjoyed a higher status. This justified reformers' adding their voices to those of Christian missionaries

DOCUMENT
Macaulay's "Minute on Education"

caste—Primarily among Hindus, a religious class designation inherited from one's ancestors and passed on to one's descendants.

CHRONOLOGY

1830

1839–1842 Opium War

1840

1840 Treaty of Waitangi between British and Maori

1841 New Zealand becomes Crown Colony of Britain

1842 Tahiti becomes a protectorate of France

1842 Treaty of Nanjing cedes Hong Kong to Britain

1850–1864 Taiping Rebellion

1851 Discovery of gold in Australia

1852 New Zealand parliament established

1853 Commodore Perry enters Japan

1855 Right of male political representation in Australia

1857 The Great Revolt in India

1860

1868–1912 Meiji Period in Japan

DOCUMENT
On Hindu Women and Education

and colonial officials who demanded the prohibition of ***sati*** (sah-TEE)— the burning of widows on the funeral pyres of their deceased husbands—women's seclusion in the home, and female infanticide, as well as the encouragement of girls' education and widows' remarriage. Other reforms included the suppression of banditry and murder called *thugi* (TOO-ghee, from which the English word *thug* is derived), and a multilevel, though not universally widespread, educational system.

sati —The Hindu practice of widow immolation on her husband's funeral pyre.

Believing they were "civilizing" the Indians, many of whom were already reformers, the British pushed a variety of social, technological, and economic changes onto Indian society. These included English culture (for the elite), railroads to move British products and soldiers into the hinterlands, a public works system, and a telegraph system. In the spring of 1857, a serious rebellion

DOCUMENT
The Indian Revolt

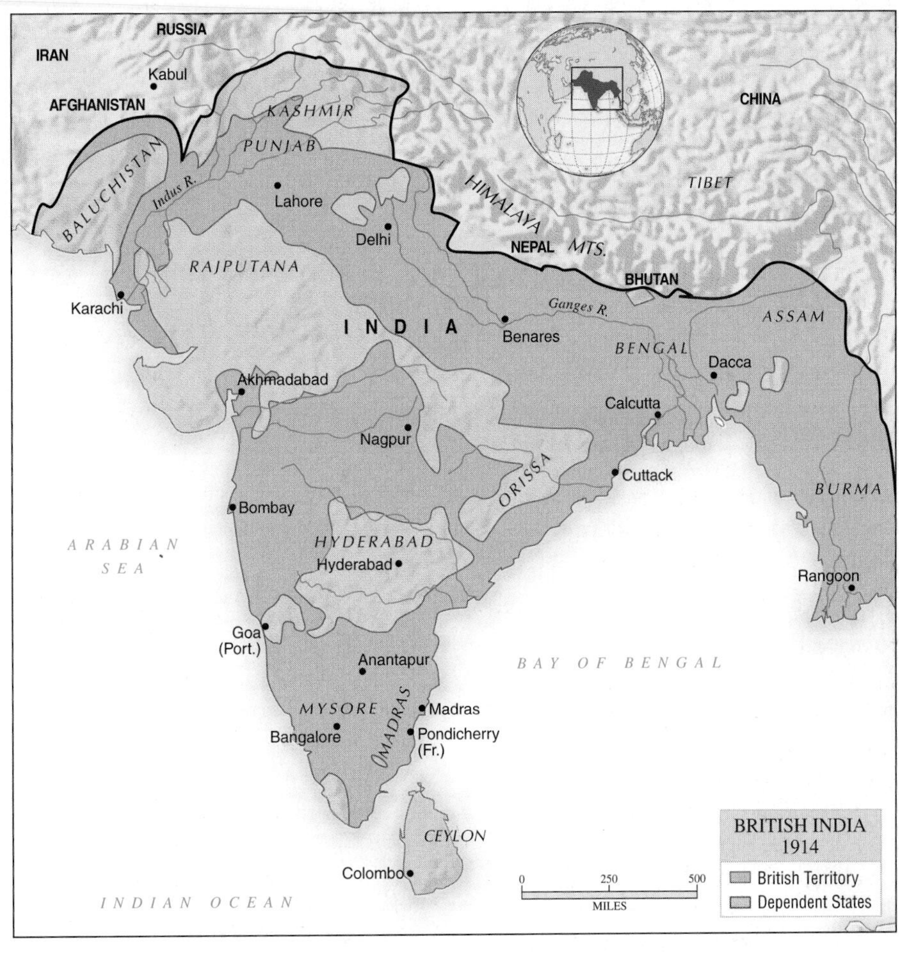

▲ By 1914, the British, on the surface at least, exercised political control over the subcontinent. At the same time, the movement for independence was gaining strength.

1880

1885 Indian National Congress founded

1893 New Zealand first country to grant women the vote

1893 Overthrow of Hawaiian monarchy

1894–1895 Sino-Japanese War

1898 Spanish-American War; United States acquires Philippines, Guam, Puerto Rico, Hawaii

1899–1900 Righteous Harmony Fists (Boxer) Rebellion; Open Door policy in China begins

1900

1901 Dominion status for Australia

1902 Anglo-Japanese Naval Treaty

1904–1905 Russo-Japanese War

1907 Dominion status for New Zealand

1910 Japan annexes Korea

▲ This drawing of a British officer of the Bengal regiment shows a British magistrate settling a court case in 1853, during the period of dual control when the British East India Company and the British government shared authority over India.

interrupted the flow of modern reforms. Indian troops, called **Sepoys** (SEE-pois), who formed the bulk of the East India Company's armed forces, started the uprising when they complained that a new cartridge issued to them was smeared with the fat of cows and pigs. This outraged both the Hindus, for whom the cow was a sacred animal, and the Muslims, who considered the pig unclean. The uprising quickly spread, embracing princes and peasants in many provinces. Many other areas remained loyal to the British or at least calm. But elsewhere there was fierce fighting on both sides; the British exterminated whole villages.

The Great Revolt of 1857–1858 marked the final collapse of the Mughals. The rebels had proclaimed the reluctant Mughal emperor as their leader. After the British put down the Great Revolt, they exiled him to Burma. The rebellion also put an end to the system of dual control under which the British government and the East India Company shared authority. Parliament eliminated the company's political role, and, after 258 years, the East India Company ended its rule.

Under the new system, the governor-general gained additional duties and a new title—viceroy. The viceroy was responsible to the Secretary of State for India in the British cabinet. In the subcontinent, the British maintained direct control of most of the high positions in government, while Indians were trained to carry out administrative responsibilities in the provincial and subordinate systems. Only on rare occasions, however, could native civil officials rise to higher positions in the bureaucracy. London reorganized the courts and law codes, along with the army and public services. The British applied odd "racial" theories to the military, claiming that some Indians were "racially" suited to military service, but others were not. English became the administrative language of the country.

India was governed by and for the British, who viewed themselves as the only people able to rule. In 1900, fully 90 percent of native men and 99 percent of native women were illiterate. Few schools existed at the village level to remedy that situation. Although the British supplied improved health standards, better water systems, and political stability, the cost was high. The masses of the rural poor paid for the government and army through taxes on beverages and salt. Moreover, India provided rich resources and vast markets for the British. By 1913, India absorbed more British exports, particularly textiles and steel, than any other

Sepoys—Indian soldiers and policemen working under contract for the British East India Company.

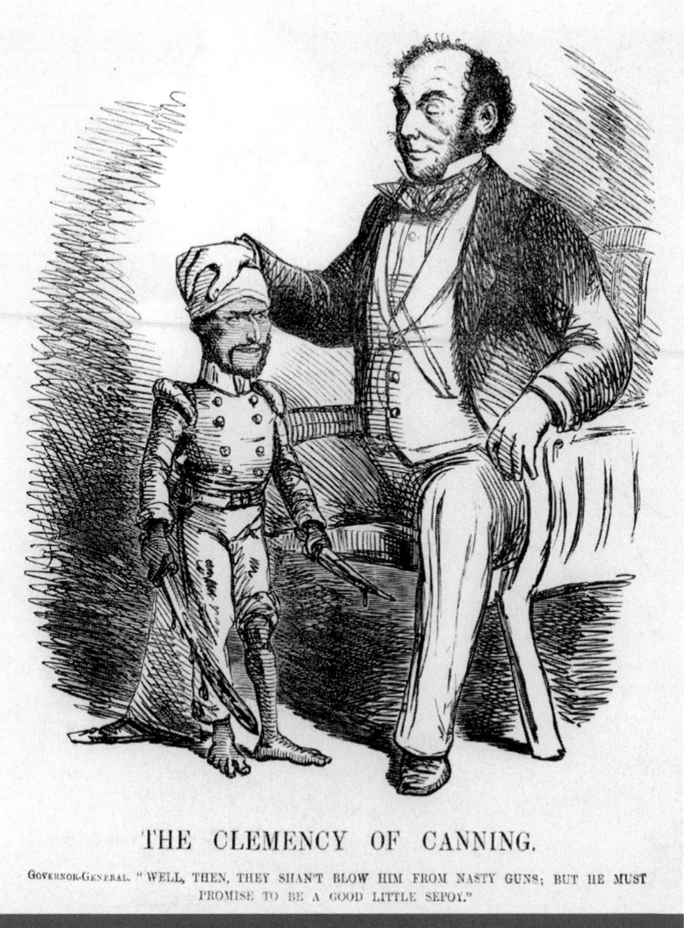

◀ A British cartoon at the time of Great Revolt shows the British Governor General treating a Sepoy soldier in a highly patronizing way. The Sepoy is depicted as a child, holding his weapons as if they were toys, and wearing tattered clothes and no shoes. The "paternal" Governor General pats him on the head and refers, in the cartoon's caption, to the brutal punishment—being blown apart by cannons—meted out to others who rebelled against colonial rule.

country. In return, India sent to England crucial raw materials such as cotton, rice, tea, and indigo.

The English language and British railroads introduced more unity to the subcontinent than it had ever known. But the imperial rulers took advantage of the subcontinent's diversity of religions, castes, and principalities (over 700 separate political units) to rule by a policy of "divide and conquer." The British, who encouraged each group to think of itself as distinct, attempted to justify their political policies and economic dominance over India by pointing out that they were improving the lives of almost 300 million people. This rationale, however, could not remove the glaring contrasts between the European and Asian ways of life in cities like Bombay, Delhi, and Calcutta.

Resentment against British rule led to the rapid growth of an Indian nationalist movement. In 1885, with the help of several Britons who had Indian political ambitions, the Indian National Congress was formed. The Anglo-Indian educational system, although it touched only a minority of the people, served as one of the most potent forces behind the new movement, as Indians embraced many of the liberal causes popular in England. Especially strong was the drive for women's equality and freedom, particularly in the areas of sexuality, disease, and prostitution. Hindu and Muslim women set up schools for girls and widows. Other reformist groups—Hindu, Muslim, and secular—inspired nationalist thinking as well. Nationalist thinking was increasingly linked to gender: boycotts of British products were a kind of consumer nationalism, and the identification of India itself with mother-goddess imagery ("Mother India") encouraged the education of women as "mothers of the nation."

DOCUMENT
An Indian Muslim Visits London

As educated Indians learned the history of the rise of self-government in England, their desire for political freedom in their own land grew. The system of British control prevented Indians from rising above a certain level, however. A pool of thousands of frustrated and unemployed educated Indian youths turned angrily against the government. At the same time, rapacious taxation, disastrous weather conditions, and bubonic plague began a decade of despair in 1896. When the British partitioned Bengal for their own administrative convenience in 1905, nationalist Indians erupted, initiating a very effective boycott of British goods. The partition was later rescinded, but it worsened Hindu-Muslim relations as each reacted differently to the partition policy.

The British responded to the ensuing nationalist violence with some changes in policy between 1907 and 1909. Although the central government's legislature remained under British control, the British allowed the various provincial legislatures to elect Indian majorities, and an Indian was seated in the executive council of the governor-general. These concessions temporarily satisfied some moderates but did

Document

The Great Revolt of 1857–1858

Raging over north and central India in 1857 and 1858, the Great Revolt, known to the British at the time as the "Sepoy Mutiny," engaged far more than the Sepoys (Indian troops under British command) alone. Indians serving the British, independent princes, reformers, and peasants joined the soldiers whom the British had counted on to be their loyal supporters. The author of this essay, Sayyid Ahmad Khan (SAI-yid AH-mahd KAHN), an Indian in service to the British who remained loyal to his employers throughout the Revolt, rejected the British assessment that the Great Revolt was the work of some disgruntled Sepoys. Rather, as he wrote, the roots went far deeper.

I believe that there was but one primary cause of the rebellion, the others being merely incidental and arising out of it. Nor is this opinion either imaginary or conjectural. It is borne out by the views entertained by wise men of past ages.... It has been universally allowed that the admittance of the people to a share in the Government under which they live, is necessary to its efficiency, prosperity, and permanence.... The Natives of India, without perhaps a single exception, blame the Government for having deprived them of their position and dignity and for keeping them down.... What! Have not [the British officers'] pride and arrogance led them to consider the Natives of India as undeserving the name of human beings?

Questions to Consider

1. According to the author, what was the primary cause of the conflict in 1857-1858?
2. Did the author believe that the Indians' love for self-government was a recent development?
3. Did the British realize the importance of respect for Indian customs, or was there an even greater ethnic divide after the Revolt?

From Barbara D. Metcalf and Thomas R. Metcalf, *A Concise History of Modern India* (Cambridge: Cambridge University Press, 2002), p. 99.

not appease the more radical protesters, who saw them as halfway measures. Nor did they address the concerns of particular communities defined by religion, class, or gender. As the twentieth century evolved, the spirit of nationalism and desire for independence became stronger. World War I and its aftermath stoked the nationalist fires.

Southeast Asia

What combination of local and international factors determined the fate of Southeast Asian countries in the face of European imperialism?

Throughout continental Southeast Asia and the islands of the Indian and Pacific Oceans, European investors established a plantation economy to grow coffee, tea, pepper, and other products demanded by the world market in the seventeenth and eighteenth centuries. They also discovered and exploited important mineral deposits. To take advantage of these resources, they attempted to limit the chronic civil war and banditry that plagued the region. In some countries, the imperialists saw their role as humanitarian and instituted limited reforms. These reforms, especially Western-style education, intensified the rise of nationalism, giving the anti-imperialist movements tools and vocabulary to challenge European domination. In the Dutch East Indies, French Indochina, and the Philippines, young intellectuals aspired to complete independence for themselves and their countries.

The Era of European Dominance

In the eighteenth and nineteenth centuries, Great Britain gained control of Ceylon (now Sri Lanka), Malaya (now Malaysia), and Burma (now Myanmar). The first colony, taken from the Dutch in 1796, later became one of the most valuable British holdings, producing such prized commodities as tea, rubber, lead, and sapphires. The Malay peninsula, with the island of Singapore at its tip, provided a vantage point from which Britain could dominate the seas surrounding southern Asia and export valuable supplies of tin and rubber. Although the Burmese struggled valiantly to hold onto national sovereignty through diplomacy and self-defense, the British conquered Burma in three wars between 1824 and 1885 and annexed it to India.

Typical of British attitudes toward Asia, one British governor of Singapore in the 1880s wrote: "I

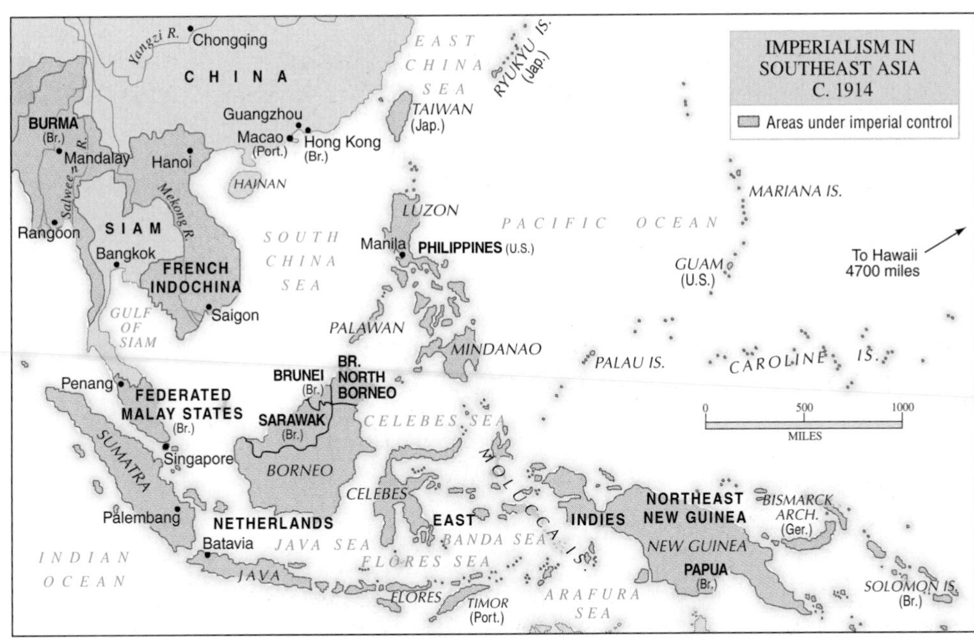

▲ At the beginning of the twentieth century, the map of Southeast Asia showed a mixture of old and new imperialism, with the Dutch still in Indonesia and the British in Brunei. But the new patterns can be seen too with the French in Vietnam, the British in Hong Kong, and the Americans in the Philippines.

doubt if Asiatics will ever learn to govern themselves; it is contrary to the genius of their race, of their history, of their religious system, that they should. Their desire is a mild, just, and firm despotism."[1]

After a century-long absence, France returned to Southeast Asia in the nineteenth century. French commercial and religious interests had been established as early as the seventeenth century, but it was not until the mid-nineteenth century that France played an imperialist role in Vietnam and Cambodia. Anti-Christian persecutions by Vietnamese monarchs in the 1850s as well as French commercial interests in Southeast Asia sparked a French war with Emperor Tu Duc (TOO DOOK), whose defeat in 1862 forced him to cede several provinces to France and to allow missionaries free reign throughout Vietnam. From that base, France expanded its influence and power through treaties, exploration, and outright annexation. France took Hanoi in 1882, governed Cochin China as a direct colony, and held Annam (central Vietnam), Tonkin, and Cambodia as protectorates that retained some degree of local control. Laos, too, was soon brought under French "protection." By the beginning of the twentieth century, France had created an empire in Indochina nearly 50 percent larger than the parent country. But due to French suppression of opposition, an independence movement quickly emerged. By the early twentieth century, Vietnamese nationalists, like their Chinese counterparts, found a model of Asian independence in Japan. During and after World War I, several types of independence movements would challenge French rule.

Thailand alone among Southeast Asian countries retained its independence. Pressed by France in Indochina on its eastern flank and Britain in Burma on its western, Thailand had two remarkable kings, Mongut (MON-goot; r. 1851–1868) and his son Chulalongkorn (CHOO-la-LONG-korn; r. 1868–1910), who successfully modernized the Thai economy and political system to ward off foreign encroachment.

Late in the sixteenth century, the Dutch had taken most of the East Indies from the Portuguese, and in 1602 the Dutch East India Company was organized to exploit the resources of the Moluccas (mo-LOO-kas) in present-day Indonesia. In 1798, the company's holdings were transferred to the Dutch crown, which forced the peasants to grow cash crops for its own benefit. In 1811, Java briefly came under British domination, and the reformist Thomas Raffles liberalized political and economic control. When the Dutch returned in 1816, the Javanese were again subjected to brutal control. The suppression of a ***jihad*** rebellion in the 1820s led the Netherlands to the point of national bankruptcy and took the lives of some 200,000 Javanese. The Dutch response was to run the islands even more brutally as a cash cow for Holland.

In the 1830s, the so-called culture system was introduced, under which one-fifth of all local land was

jihad—Religious struggle in Islam.

▲ In 1859, on the pretext of preserving Catholicism in Indochina, a French and Spanish expeditionary force stormed and captured the fortress of Saigon.

set aside to raise crops for the government. One-fifth of all the islanders' time was also required to work the lands. The production of sugar, tobacco, coffee, tea, and other products increased tremendously, ending Dutch fears of bankruptcy and financing Holland's industrial revolution. In the long run, the culture system gave the islands a prosperous means of raising crops, but its implementation deprived the people of sufficient land for their own use and often required torture to force production. Conditions began to improve in 1900 when the Dutch took the first steps to abandon the culture system, which was finally put to rest in 1917. As in other European colonies, discrimination within the education system and elsewhere gave rise to a vigorous independence movement. A Javanese revivalist movement, inspired by the feminist and nationalist ideas of Raden Adjeng Kartini (RAH-den AD-yeng kar-TEE-nee), a young woman and member of the elite, sprang up in the first decades of the twentieth century. This was followed in 1912 by the mass-based group Sarekat Islam (SAH-reh-kaht ee-SLAHM; Islamic Association), which forced the Dutch to extend limited rights to Indonesians.

The Philippines

Spanish rule of the Philippines (1571–1898) was increasingly resisted during the nineteenth century. Lay Spaniards lived mainly in the urban areas, while Catholic friars controlled the countryside, converting the masses, other than those in the Muslim areas in Mindanao, to Christianity. Resistance to racial inequality and agrarian exploitation by the friars, common since the mid-1700s, accelerated in the late nineteenth century following the rise of an educated Filipino elite. In the 1880s, when the Spanish-educated José Rizal (ho-SAY ri-ZAHL) wrote popular novels calling for reform of colonial injustices, though not for independence, the colonial authorities burned his work, repressed his family, and ultimately executed Rizal in 1896. This incited a militant independence movement. In 1897, the revolutionaries, under Emilio Aguinaldo (eh-MEE-lee-oh AH-ghee-NAHL-doh), declared the independence of the Philippines. Soon thereafter, Aguinaldo was forced into exile in Hong Kong.

At the same time, the United States had been expanding into the Pacific since the end of the Civil War, purchasing Alaska in 1867 and overthrowing the Hawaiian queen in 1893. The United States had just begun to fight Spain in the Caribbean in 1898, and to forestall a Spanish attempt to send help to Cuba from the Philippines, American Commodore George Dewey

◀ U.S. atrocities in the Philippines, depicted in an American cartoon, eventually turned U.S. public opinion against the war.

The American Anti-Imperialist League

arranged to bring Aguinaldo back to the Philippines to end Spanish rule there. But Dewey abandoned Aguinaldo, staging a mock naval battle to allow the Spaniards to save face. Then, the United States turned on the Filipinos in a brutal war, killing at least 100,000 men, women, and children and imprisoning 300,000 in barren detention camps where thousands more perished. To American soldiers who asked what to do if Filipinos were found outside the camps, one general replied, "Kill and burn.... This is no time to take prisoners.... Kill everything over ten."[2]

This radical shift in U.S. foreign policy was inspired by U.S. strategic interests in the western Pacific, Social Darwinism, the desire for Asian markets, and Christian evangelism. The 3-year war against the Philippines ended in 1902 and ushered in American colonial administration that was surprisingly liberal in light of the bloodshed and racism that had preceded it. In 1913, the legislature became predominantly local, although final authority in the most important matters was still reserved for the U.S. Congress. The Jones Act (1916) created the Commonwealth, increased local self-rule, and called for eventual independence. The Philippine tariff was shaped to favor American trade, and large amounts of capital from the United States were invested in the islands. Increased educational opportunities strengthened the desire for independence among many Filipinos. In their eyes, American government in the Philippines, no matter how efficient or humanitarian, was no substitute for self-government.

Imperialism and the White Man's Burden

China: The Long Nineteenth Century

What domestic and foreign pressures brought about China's decline from being the world's economic engine in the eighteenth century to being a failing monarchy, hobbled by unequal treaties, in the early twentieth century?

At the end of the 1800s, China's 4 million square miles held 450 million people, more than twice the number of a century earlier. The ruling dynasty was the **Qing** (CHING), established by Manchus from Manchuria, who in 1644 had superseded the Ming. Understanding that effective rule as foreigners required an appreciation of Chinese civilization, the Manchus had their subjects cooperating with them within a generation. Although the Qing Dynasty required Chinese men to wear Manchu hairstyles and forbade (unsuccessfully) the binding of Chinese women's feet, the Manchus themselves gradually adopted Chinese attitudes and habits.

MAP

Nineteenth-Century China

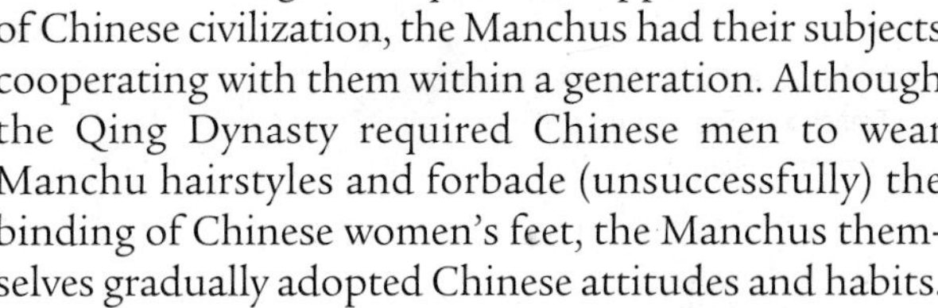

One important policy carried over from the Ming dynasty and earlier was the **tribute system** of foreign relations, which held the Chinese emperor to be morally superior and China itself to be the Central Kingdom. Subordinate states owed tribute to China in exchange for its paternalistic protection. In reality, the mutual exchange of gifts through official channels constituted a major source of regulated trade. But it also officially placed such exchanges in the context of state-to-state relations, in which China was always the dominant partner.

The reign of the Manchu emperor, Qianlong (CHEN-LONG; r. 1736–1795), was a time of great expansion. The Qing gained Central Asia, Mongolia, and Tibet. By the end of the eighteenth century, Manchu power extended even into Nepal, and the territory under the Qing control was as extensive as under any previous dynasty. Further, the Qing governed their far-flung and diverse empire with subtle and effective

Qing—Manchu dynasty (1644–1911) in China.

tribute system—China-centered foreign policy whereby subordinate countries give tribute to China and receive gifts (trade) and protection in return.

	China in the Imperialist Era
1644	Manchus establish Qing Dynasty
1759	Foreign trade restricted to Guangzhou
1793	Imperial denial of British request for permanent trade representative
1800–1840	British smuggle opium into China
1839	First Opium War, ended by Treaty of Nanjing (1842), which gives Hong Kong to the British
1850–1864	Taiping Rebellion paralyzes China, kills 20 to 30 million people
1856–1858	Second Opium War, ended by Treaty of Tianjin, which opens new ports and permits foreign missionaries to proselytize throughout China
1860	Tongzhi restoration movement
1861–1908	Rule by Cixi, the Empress Dowager
1894–1895	China's defeat in Sino-Japanese War
1895–1900	China carved into spheres of influence—areas occupied by United Kingdom, Germany, France, Japan, and Russia
1898	Hundred Days of Reform
1899–1900	Righteous Harmony Fists (Boxer) Uprising
1900	Open Door policy implemented
1911	Revolutionary overthrow of Qing Dynasty; end of monarchy in China

policies on national defense and commercial and political relations with neighboring countries within the framework of the tribute system. Their overall trade policies maintained a growing economy for their expanding population base.

Global Networks and the Challenges to Manchu Control

Evidence of some of China's problems can be found in the eighteenth-century revolts in the Taiwan, Gansu, Hunan, Guizhou (gweh-JOH), and Shandong provinces. China suppressed all of them, but clearly the Central Kingdom faced serious difficulties with its religiously and culturally diverse kingdom. Increasing challenges from the West compounded the threats to the Qing. China, with its vast resources in tea, porcelain, and silk, supplied both its own enormous market and those of Europe and Europe's colonies. From the sixteenth through the eighteenth centuries, Spanish and Portuguese, then Dutch and Japanese, and finally English and American traders called at South China's ports. After 1759, the Qing confined European trade to **"factories"** in the restricted foreigners' quarter in Guangzhou (gwahng-JOH).

By the early nineteenth century, the British East India Company controlled about 90 percent of the foreign trade at the southern port of Guangzhou. The British love for tea was behind the spectacular growth in trade. Britain's tea imports rose from 400,000 pounds in 1720 to 23 million pounds in 1800. One-tenth of Britain's government revenues derived from import taxes on tea alone. By the 1780s, 16 million ounces of silver flowed out to pay for the tea. British merchants and government officials sought ways to bring greater balance to this trade and to conduct it on terms that differed from the tribute system.

For 300 years, the Chinese had been able to regulate trade as they saw fit. Britain's rise as a world power and the expanding liberal trading regime in the Atlantic made the tribute system, under which the Manchus would neither recognize nor receive diplomatic representatives of foreign powers, seem out of date. The British sent Lord George Macartney to the Qing court in 1793 to request a permanent trade representative in Beijing. Macartney refused to perform the ceremonial kowtow (nine full-length prostrations), an important element in the tribute system. Emperor Qianlong's response to King George III summarized his view of foreign relations:

> *To send one of your nationals to stay at the Celestial Court to take care of your country's trade with China ... is not in harmony with the state system of our dynasty and will definitely not be permitted.... There is nothing we lack, as your principal envoy and others have themselves observed. We have never set such store on strange or ingenious objects, nor do we have need of any more of your country's manufactures.*[3]

Qianlong was not far off the mark. Although the Chinese did want to import large quantities of some important commodities, including raw cotton and, of course, silver to be used as currency for the huge commercial economy, there were few products unobtainable in China. China was still the world's largest economic power. That was soon to change.

Opium and Trade

Opium smoking had been introduced to China through trade with Southeast Asia in the seventeenth

factories—European office and warehouse buildings in India and China.

Document

Lin Zexu on the Opium Trade

At a time when the West struggles with the influx of illegal drugs from Asia and elsewhere, it is useful to note in the first part of the nineteenth century, the traffic flowed the other way. The British and their Western trading partners flooded China with illegal opium. A Chinese official Lin Zexu saw that the opium trade, which gave Europe such huge profits, undermined his country. He asked Queen Victoria to put a stop to it.

After a long period of commercial intercourse, there appear among the crowd of barbarians both good persons and bad, unevenly. Consequently there are those who smuggle opium to seduce the Chinese people and so cause the spread of the poison to all provinces. Such persons who only care to profit themselves, and disregard their harm to others, are not tolerated by the laws of heaven and are unanimously hated by human beings. His Majesty the Emperor, upon hearing of this, is in a towering rage. He has especially sent me, his commissioner, to come to Guangdong, and together with the governor-general and governor jointly to investigate and settle this matter.

All those people in China who sell opium or smoke opium should receive the death penalty. If we trace the crime of those barbarians who through the years have been selling opium, then the deep harm they have wrought and the great profit they have usurped should fundamentally justify their execution according to law. We take into consideration, however, the fact that the various barbarians have still known how to repent their crimes and return to their allegiance to us by taking the 20,183 chests of opium from their storeships and petitioning us, through their consular officer [superintendent of trade], Elliot, to receive it. It has been entirely destroyed and this has been faithfully reported to the Throne in several memorials by this commissioner and his colleagues.

Fortunately we have received a specially extended favor from His Majesty the Emperor, who considers that for those who voluntarily surrender there are still some circumstances to palliate their crime, and so for the time being he has magnanimously excused them from punishment. But as for those who again violate the opium prohibition, it is difficult for the law to pardon them repeatedly. Having established new regulations, we presume that the ruler of your honorable country, who takes delight in our culture and whose disposition is inclined towards us, must be able to instruct the various barbarians to observe the law with care. It is only necessary to explain to them the advantages and disadvantages and then they will know that the legal code of the Celestial Court must be absolutely obeyed with awe.

We find that your country is sixty or seventy thousand *li* [about 22,000 miles] from China. Yet there are barbarian ships that strive to come here for trade for the purpose of making a great profit. The wealth of China is used to profit the barbarians. That is to say, the great profit made by barbarians is all taken from the rightful share of China. By what right do they then in return use the poisonous drug to injure the Chinese people? Even though the barbarians may not necessarily intend to do us harm, yet in coveting profit to an extreme, they have no regard for injuring others. Let us ask, where is your conscience? I have heard that the smoking of opium is very strictly forbidden by your country; that is because the harm caused by opium is clearly understood. Since it is not permitted to do harm to your own country, then even less should you let it be passed on to the harm of other countries—how much less to China!

Questions to Consider

1. Why did the Western powers, led by the British, sell addictive drugs in China?
2. What do you think were the economic, political, and health effects of the opium trade on China?
3. What comparisons can you make between Commissioner Lin's response to the influx of foreign drugs and that of the United States today?

From Ssu-yu Teng and John K. Fairbank, eds., *China's Response to the West* (New York: Athenaeum, 1968), pp. 24–25.

century. At first, it was used for medicinal purposes, but soon it was used to alleviate the emotional and physical strains of work. Its use alarmed Qianlong, who banned its growth in China. This only made imported opium more profitable. Recognizing a great source of income to offset the drain of silver to pay for tea, the British East India Company licensed private trading ships to sell Indian opium on its behalf (the Company feared being implicated in sales of a product the Chinese government had technically prohibited in 1800). Between 1729 and 1838, imports rose from 200 to 40,000 chests per year (one chest contained 150 pounds of opium extract). Although the British were not alone in selling opium to China—Americans made handsome profits as well—the British were able to benefit from selling opium grown in their Indian colony. Soon, the balance of payments shifted, and a net outflow of silver compounded China's problems with

▲ The second opium war, also called the "Arrow War," ended with the defeat of China by the combined forces of Britain and France. Chinese diplomats, seen here arriving to negotiate the end of that war in 1858, were forced to give up much of China's sovereignty to the victors in the unequal Treaty of Tianjin.

widespread addiction and rampant criminality that accompanied the trade.

In the meantime, the empire faced other problems. Corruption spread through the army, and tax farmers defrauded the people. The central bureaucracy declined in efficiency, and the generally weak emperors were unable to meet the challenges of the time. When the East India Company lost its monopoly in 1833 following the rise of Free Trade sentiment in England, new merchant houses pressured the British government to demand more open markets. Viewing the tragedy inflicted on China, Beijing dispatched a tough, brilliant official, Lin Zexu (LIN zeh-SHOO), to Guangzhou. In the spring of 1839, Commissioner Lin confiscated and destroyed the opium. In response, the British confronted Lin's forces with 47 ships.

DOCUMENT Lin Zexu: Letter to Queen Victoria

In the war that followed, the Chinese could not match the British forces. In 1842, China agreed to the provisions of the Treaty of Nanjing. Hong Kong was ceded to Great Britain, and other ports, including Guangzhou, were opened to British residence and trade. After the Nanjing Treaty's provisions became known, the French and Americans gained the same trading rights as the British in 1844. The advantages granted the three nations by the Chinese set a precedent that would dominate China's relations with the world for the next century.

The British and French defeated China in a second opium war in 1856. By the terms of the Treaty of Tianjin (tee-un-JIN; 1858), the Chinese opened new ports to trading and allowed foreigners to travel in the interior. Christians gained the right to spread their faith and hold property, thus opening up another means of Western penetration. The United States and Russia gained the same privileges in separate treaties.

Three provisions of these treaties caused long-lasting bitterness among the Chinese: extraterritoriality, customs regulations, and "most favored nation" privileges. Extraterritoriality meant that Westerners, who argued that Chinese concepts of justice were more rigid and harsh than those in the West, had the right to be tried in their own country's consular court. China had to accept a low fixed tariff collected by Europeans, not Chinese customs officials. And the "most favored nation" privileges extended rights automatically to all Europeans (plus the United States) if any one exacted new concessions from China. For the next century, China suffered under these **unequal treaties.** This was a time of unprecedented degradation and humiliation for China.

IMAGE American Cartoon on Western Powers Carving Up China

DOCUMENT The Treaty of Nanjing

More dangerous for the Qing than the Europeans and Americans was the explosion of revolts in the north, west, and south of the country. The most serious was the Taiping (tai-PING) Rebellion, which lasted from 1850 to 1864. The uprising, fought to attain the Heavenly Kingdom of Great Peace, stemmed from widespread discontent with the social and eco-

unequal treaties—Treaties forced first on China, then on other nominally independent Asian countries, in which the United States or European countries received extraterritoriality, most favored nation privileges, and control of tariffs.

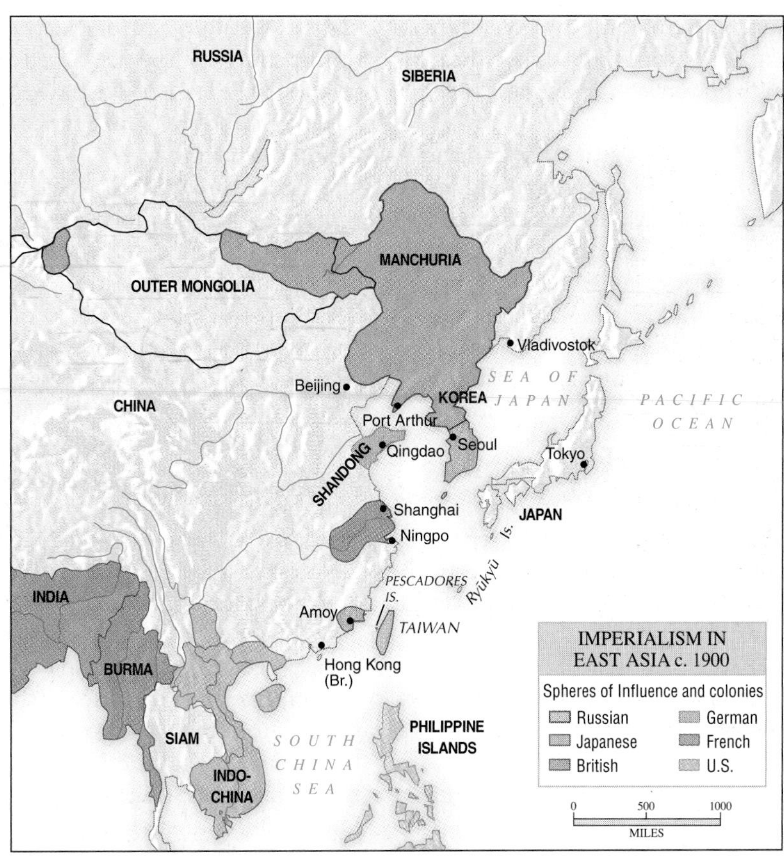

▲ Territorial impositions on East Asia were made by European and American imperialists, as well as China's modernizing neighbor, Japan.

nomic conditions of Manchu rule and the perception of a lack of authority in Beijing. The revolt began near Guangzhou, where opium addiction, unemployment, and the results of foreign penetration were felt most acutely. It centered on the plans of Hong Xiuquan (HONG shoo-CHUAHN), a man driven to desperation by consistently failing the lowest examination to gain entry into the civil service. After reading Christian tracts, he came to identify himself as a son of God, Jesus's younger brother.

He attracted numerous followers, especially from the poor. For 10 years after 1853, he and his forces controlled the southern part of China from Nanjing, and he set out to create a new society detached from the traditional Chinese fabric. Hong struck out at vice, Confucianism, private property, and landlords. He almost overthrew the central government. However, his vast movement suffered from a lack of effective coordination, giving time for provincial governors to raise new and powerful armies that eventually put down the uprising. The Taiping Rebellion was one of the most costly movements in history. It reached into 17 of China's 18 provinces. Estimates of the number of deaths range between 20 and 30 million, as the central government brutally repressed the rebels.

Qing Foreign Policy

The Chinese, whose economy was the world's largest in 1800, had been forced to compete with Westerners in military and economic terms throughout the nineteenth century. But a more serious conflict arose in the realm of civilization and values. The Chinese could note the obvious—that the West possessed technological and military superiority. The question they faced was how to adapt the strength of the West to the core of Chinese civilization in order to become able to compete effectively. In Chinese terms, this was the *ti yong* concept (*ti* = "substance"; *yong* = "use").

How the East Views the West

Combining the two elements presented the severe problem of gaining a proper balance. Those who wanted to keep the old culture opposed those who wanted to modernize the country. In 1860, the *Tongzhi* (TONG-juh) restoration movement attempted to strengthen the Manchus. Serious attempts were made to preserve Chinese culture while trying to make use of Western technology. Had these attempts at adaptation been carried out in a time of peace, perhaps the Chinese could have adjusted, but China did not enjoy the luxury of tranquility. Nevertheless, notable investments were made in cotton spinning, coal mining, and shipping as part of a "self-strengthening" movement, although low fixed tariffs prevented the Chinese from protecting infant industries.

After the external buffeting from the West and the internal uprising, the Qing dynasty limped along for another half century, led by a conservative coalition of Manchu and Chinese officials who advised the empress dowager, Cixi (tsih-SHEE), who served from 1861 until her death in 1908. Entering the court as a concubine, Cixi mastered the intricate ceremonial life and intrigue of palace politics. When the senior concubine failed to give birth to a healthy heir to the throne, Cixi bore the emperor a strong and healthy child.

Her position as mother of the heir apparent opened the door to power, and during the reigns of the next three emperors, she was a dominant power, either as sole or joint regent. She built a network of powerful allies and informers that helped her crush internal revolts and restore a measure of prestige to China during a brief period of relative tranquility from 1870 to 1895. Yet at a time when the Japanese were rapidly modernizing and foreign powers were introducing many forms of new technology in their factories, railroads, and communications, Cixi and many of her supporters, holding on to tradition and custom, failed to modernize China.

Carving Up China

During the first wars against the Europeans, the Chinese began the process of ceding territory and spheres of influence to foreigners. By 1860, as a result of the Treaty of Beijing, Russia gained the entire area north of the Amur River and founded the strategic city of Vladivostok. In 1885, France took Indochina, and Britain seized Burma. In 1887, Macao was ceded to Portugal. China was too weak to resist these encroachments on its borders. But the crowning blow came not from the Western nations but from Japan, a land the Chinese had long regarded as inferior.

Trouble had been brewing between China and Japan over the control of Korea for a decade before war broke out in 1894. The brief Sino-Japanese War resulted in a humiliating defeat for China. By the Treaty of Shimonoseki (shi-moh-noh-SEH-kee; 1895), China was forced to recognize the independence of Korea and hand over to Japan the rich Liaodong (lee-ow-DONG) peninsula (soon returned to China under Western pressure) and Taiwan.

The Chinese defeat was the signal for the renewal of aggressive actions by Western powers. Germany demanded a 99-year lease to Jiaozhou (jee-ow-JOH) Bay and was also given exclusive mining and railroad rights throughout Shandong province. Russia obtained a 25-year lease to Liaodong and gained the right to build a railroad across Manchuria, thereby dominating that vast territory. In 1898, Britain obtained the lease of Weihaiwei (WAY-hai-way), a naval base in Shandong, and France leased Guangzhou Bay in southern China.

The United States, acting not from any high-minded desires but rather from the fear that American business was being excluded from China, brought a halt, or at least a hesitation, to the process of dismemberment. In 1899, Secretary of State John Hay asked the major powers to agree to a policy of equal trading privileges. In 1900, several powers did so, and the Open Door policy was born.

The humiliation of the defeat by Japan and the dismemberment of China by the imperialist powers had incensed young Chinese intellectuals, who agitated for liberation from foreign dominance. Nationalists were to be found both in the private sector and among government officials. Individual nationalists called for social and cultural modernity to create a society able to mobilize the efforts of long marginalized people. One significant form of nationalism was the anti foot binding movement, specifically targeting the underutilized human resources of China's women. Begun in the 1890s, this movement succeeded in eliminating an almost thousand-year-old practice within a few decades.

Reformers occupied government posts as well. Enlightened and concerned patriots such as Kang Youwei (KAHNG yoo-WAY), with the support of the young emperor, Cixi's nephew, proposed a wide-ranging series of economic, social, political, and educational reforms, known as the "hundred days of reform" in the summer of 1898. Cixi and her advisers opposed the young scholars' attempts to bring about basic reforms because they threatened the interests of Cixi's supporters. She came out of retirement in 1898, imprisoned her nephew, executed several reformers, and revoked the proposed reforms. Kang and a few others fled into exile in Japan.

After the suppression of the reform movement, a group of secret societies united in an organization known as the Righteous Harmony Fists, whose members were called Boxers in the West. At first they were strongly anti-Manchu, but by 1899, the chief object of their hatred had become the foreign nations who were stripping China of land and power. The Boxers started a campaign to rid China of all "foreign devils." Many Europeans were killed, and their legations at Beijing were besieged. In August 1900, a multinational army forced its way to Beijing and released the foreign prisoners. China was forced to apologize for the murder of foreign officials and pay a large indemnity.

Treaty Ports and the Boxer Rebellion in China

By this time, even Cixi acknowledged the need for change. After 1901, she sanctioned reforms in the state examination system, education and governmental structure, and economic life. But these reforms only accelerated the demand for change. Revolutionary movements, many hatched by anti-Manchu exiles in Japan, broke out all over China. The revolution's most famous martyr, Qiu Jin (CHOO JIN), had left her husband and children, studied in Japan, and wrote widely circulated manifestos against foot binding and for women's education and other rights, all in the name of anti-Manchu nationalism. In 1912, the Republic of China was proclaimed with Sun Yat-sen as provisional president. The revolutionary Chinese leaders knew that there had to be radically different approaches taken in China to allow it to survive and compete. As one official had written in the 1890s:

> *Western nations rely on intelligence and energy to compete with one another. To come abreast of them China should plan to promote commerce and open minds; unless we change, the Westerners will be rich and we poor. We should excel in technology and the manufacture of machinery; unless we change, they will be skillful and we clumsy.... Unless we change, the Westerners will cooperate with each other and we shall stand isolated; they will be strong and we shall be weak.*[4]

Unfortunately, the Republic, which had been announced to great fanfare in 1912, was subverted by the assassination in 1913 of many democratically elected leaders and the rise of brutal warlordism.

Japan: Modernity and Imperialism

What was the meaning of "modernity" and what did the Japanese do to attain it in late nineteenth-century Japan?

At the beginning of the eighteenth century, Japan was administered from Edo (now Tokyo), the largest city in the world at that time, by the head of the Tokugawa clan, whose leader had adopted the title of **shōgun** in 1603. The Japanese emperor, in residence at Kyoto, served as a figurehead with no real function during the Tokugawa (TOH-koo-GAH-wah) period (1603–1868). The Tokugawa controlled the country through their feudal lords, the ***daimyō.*** These officials in turn governed their regions with the aid of the samurai, warriors turned bureaucrats during Japan's long centuries of peace. The samurai, about 6 percent of the population, resided in castle-towns along with merchants and artisans, who together constituted another 10 percent. Most Japanese were farmers, and it was their taxes that supported the government and its functions. The cities were lively, producing a vibrant mass urban culture of arts, theater, poetry, and novels that, in time, also influenced the increasingly literate rural population.

Domestic trade was vigorous. Samurai and *daimyō* moved across the countryside in massive annual processions to show their loyalty to the shōgun, spreading money and culture throughout the land as they traveled. Merchants moved large quantities of goods by packhorse and by ship. Men and women went on sightseeing trips and pilgrimages to temples and shrines. Japan was a realm of lively interaction in the early modern period. Its population grew from around 12 million in 1600 to 30 million in 1720, but then growth slowed. Urban expansion also slowed down in the eighteenth century, and in 1800, many innovations were taking place in rural villages and towns.

The shōgun's displeasure at the destabilizing effects of Christian missionary activities caused him to limit Japan's foreign trade to China, Korea, and the Netherlands around 1640. Knowledge of Western science entered Japan through what was called *Rangaku* (RAHN-gah-koo; "Dutch studies"). Scholars of Dutch studies, as well as Confucian scholars, began to question the competence of the shōgun as they observed the disastrous course of events in China under imperialist threat. At the same time, peasant distress intensified with poor administration and abominable weather conditions, leading to riots in the first half of the nineteenth century. The Tokugawa regime was severely challenged in the mid-nineteenth century when it was forced to confront the Western threat.

	Japan: A Modernizing State
1853–1854	Arrival of Perry; signs Treaty of Kanagawa
1868	Tokugawa overthrown; Meiji Restoration
1868–1873	Capital moved to Tokyo; universal education, universal conscription, land tax reform, factories started
1870s	"Civilization and Enlightenment"
1889	Promulgation of Meiji constitution
1890	First parliamentary elections
1895	Treaty of Shimonoseki
1902	Anglo-Japanese Treaty
1904–1905	Russo-Japanese War
1912	Death of Emperor Meiji

shōgun—Military overlord in early modern Japan.

daimyō—Japanese feudal lord before 1871.

Western Trade

Both European and American merchants and diplomats tried unsuccessfully to open relations with Japan during the first part of the nineteenth century. Americans, who had just brought California into the Union, were most eager. On July 7, 1853, four U.S. ships under the command of Matthew Perry sailed into Edo Bay and brought the issue of Japanese relations with the West into sharp focus.

DOCUMENT

A Comic Dialogue, 1855

IMAGE

Japanese Woodcut of Perry's Arrival

The four "black ships," as they were called by the Japanese, had been sent by the American government to convince the Japanese that a treaty opening trade relations between the two countries would be of mutual interest. After delivering a letter from the U.S. president, Perry departed, telling the authorities in Edo that he would return in a year for an answer. The Americans returned in February 1854, before the 1-year deadline, because they feared that the French or the Russians might gain concessions sooner from the Japanese.

The shōgun, after a period of intense debate within his country, agreed to Perry's requests. The Treaty of Kanagawa (KAH-nah-GAH-wah), the first formal agreement between Japan and a Western nation, was signed in 1854. By its terms, shipwrecked sailors were to be well treated and two ports were to be opened for provisioning ships and allowing for a limited amount of trade. European traders soon obtained similar privileges, in addition to the right of extraterritoriality. Later treaties, negotiated in 1858, established permanent trade relations and trading ports in Japan for the Americans. Like China, Japan was placed in a humiliating position by the Western powers.

The entry of the West placed a severe strain on the already weakened Japanese political structure. Antiforeign sentiment grew, even as many Japanese recognized that accommodation with the West was bound to come. European and American fleets had bombarded Kagoshima (kah-GOH-shee-mah) and Shimonoseki, two cities with many opponents of opening Japan, in 1863 and 1864, thereby convincing some of the antiforeign elements that their position was hopeless. By 1868, after a time of strife and confusion, the shōgun relinquished his power, and young Japanese reformers initiated radical changes. Edo, renamed Tokyo ("eastern capital"), became the capital of the new Japan.

The Meiji Period (1868–1912)

The new generation of Japanese leaders, most of whom were under 30 years of age and of samurai origin, did not start out with a well-developed plan. They knew they had to unite the country, so they "restored" the emperor, named Meiji (MAY-jee), as a focus for national loyalty, and they forced the *daimyō* to give up the regional autonomy they had under the Tokugawa. They moved the emperor to the old capital of the Tokugawa, Edo, and renamed the city Tokyo. They united the country politically by eliminating the feudal domains of the *daimyō,* consolidating them and renaming them prefectures. The young leaders of the **Meiji Restoration** next disbanded the old system of statuses, in which the samurai alone had ruled. Former samurai—the leaders' own class—could now enter business, and former farmers and merchants could enter government. Universal education (1872) and military conscription (1873) helped level a playing field that had been tilted in favor of the samurai. Of course, universal education was instituted primarily to create a strong modern state. And the modern military not only took away samurai privilege and regional differences by bringing the sons of the nonelite together; its main purpose was to defend the new nation against the possibility of imperialist incursions.

The new leaders felt sufficiently confident in the government's stability that half of them traveled to Europe and the United States in 1871. This group, called the Iwakura Mission for its leader, Prince Iwakura, sought to renegotiate the unequal treaties forced on them since the 1850s and to study culture, politics, national defense, factories, and schools. Every aspect of "modernity" came under the Mission's microscope. The Mission's participants returned with a sophisticated knowledge of the diversity of cultures, institutions, and technologies in the West as well as a belief that one reason for the Europeans' and Americans' international power was their more advanced level of technological development. Some returnees, like some advocates of "civilization and enlightenment," called for a rejection of things Japanese. A few even advocated replacing Japanese script with the Roman alphabet and discarding religious and artistic traditions in favor of those popular in the West. Others returned with a sense that Japan would progress as it moved along what they saw as a universal trajectory toward modernity and national strength—a trajectory, they believed, already being followed by Western nations. This belief was later developed into a form of Social Darwinism, to be discussed below. What the Iwakura Mission failed to do was persuade the Europeans and Americans that Japan was embarking on a thoroughgoing program of change and deserved greater respect.

While overseas, the Mission was informed that those left behind in Tokyo were planning to use force—

Meiji Restoration—The overthrow of the Tokugawa Shogunate and restoration of imperial rule in 1868.

Seeing Connections

Western Houses in Tokyo

During the Tokugawa period, renowned woodblock artist Andō Hiroshige produced the celebrated series on the stations of the Tōkaidō, the major road running from Edo to Kyoto. Just 7 years after the Meiji Restoration, a pupil of Hiroshige created a new series called "Famous Places on the Tōkaidō: A Record of the Process of Reform" in the style of his teacher. This pupil, who called himself Hiroshige III, recorded Japan's rapid adoption of things Western in this 1875 woodblock print entitled *Western Houses.* The houses are made of stone, a Western building material adopted by some fashionable Japanese. Outside the houses stand Western-style street lamps. Some of the male pedestrians wear Western clothing and carry Western umbrellas, symbols often used to depict a "civilized" man at that time. Rickshaws, a conveyance invented in Japan in 1868 or 1869 that blended the traditional palanquin with wheels borrowed from Western horse carriages of the time, already clog Tokyo streets. The artist used traditional woodblock techniques to produce a decidedly international-style picture of Tokyo life.

copying the gunboat diplomacy of the Americans in 1853–1854—to show Korea that Japan had changed. In particular, Japan wanted to show Korea that it had adopted the Western structure of international law that stressed national sovereignty, rejecting the Chinese tribute system that subordinated Asian nations to Chinese power. The men in Tokyo wished to have bilateral relations with Korea and to force those relations, if necessary. The overseas Iwakura Mission rushed home to squelch those plans. Many of the Tokyo group left the government in anger. Some founded liberal political movements and eventually rejoined the government. But others did not, and they became part of a movement of bitter former samurai.

Not all samurai had shared the leaders' zeal to eliminate samurai privileges. These samurai, unlike their counterparts who appreciated being freed to enter business and other occupations closed to them before, deeply resented losing their Tokugawa-era stipends and were humiliated by Japan's adoption of a conscript army. Starting in 1874, some of those samurai, now even more discontented because the government vetoed the Korean invasion, took part in rebellions. The most important of these was led by an erstwhile leader in the new government, Saigo Takamori (SAI-goh TAH-kah-MOH-ree). In 1877, Saigo led samurai into battle in Satsuma against the "dirt farmer" conscripts he disdained. The samurai were defeated in this brief civil war (called the Satsuma Rebellion) in which one-third of the 100,000 combatants died.

The positive side of the 1873 departure of many government officials was the founding of the People's Rights Movement. Former samurai joined farmers, merchants, and other advocates of Western-style civil rights for men and women to demand a constitutional system based on the **bunmei kaika** (BOON-may KAI-kah; "civilization and enlightenment") ideals—including the political theories of Jean-Jacques Rousseau and John Stuart Mill—eagerly consumed by progressive Japanese. Government leaders had abandoned some of their earlier revolutionary attitudes, so they viewed the People's Rights movement as

bunmei kaika—"Civilization and Enlightenment" ideology in Meiji Japan.

Document

"The Beefeater"

The quest for "Civilization and Enlightenment" inspired legal, social, and cultural changes in the first decades of the Meiji period. Things Japanese were considered old-fashioned, and enlightened men showed their modernity by carrying pocket watches and umbrellas, wearing some items of Western clothing, and above all, according to Kanagaki Robun (KAH-nah-GAH-kee ROH-boon), the author of this satirical monologue by an "enlightened" man, eating beef.

Excuse me, but beef is certainly a most delicious thing, isn't it? ... I wonder why we in Japan haven't eaten such a clean thing before? ... We should really be grateful that even people like ourselves can now eat beef, thanks to the fact that Japan is steadily becoming a truly civilized country.... In the West, they're free of superstitions. There it's the custom to do everything scientifically, and that's why they've invented amazing things like the steamship and the steam engine. Do you know that they engrave the plates for printing newspapers with telegraphic needles? And that they bring down wind from the sky with balloons? Aren't they wonderful inventions? Of course, there are good reasons behind these inventions. If you look at a map of the world, you'll see some countries marked "tropical," which means that's where the sun shines closest.... The king of that part of the world tried all kinds of schemes before he hit on what is called a balloon. That's a big round bag they fill with air high up in the sky. They bring the bag down and open it, causing the cooling air inside the bag to spread out all over the country. That's a great invention. On the other hand, in Russia, which is a cold country where the snow falls even in summer and the ice is so thick the people can't move, they invented the steam engine. You've got to admire them for it. I understand that they modeled the steam engine after the flaming chariot of hell, but anyway, what they do is to load a crowd of people on a wagon and light a fire in a pipe underneath. They keep feeding the fire inside the pipe with coal, so that the people riding on top can travel a great distance completely oblivious to the cold. Those people in the West can think up inventions like that, one after the other.

Questions to Consider

1. Why was being "civilized" identified with Western customs?
2. What kinds of technology seemed to be most impressive to the narrator?
3. Do you think the narrator's understanding of technology would seem strange to his contemporaries in Japan?

From Donald Keene, ed., *Modern Japanese Literature* (New York: Grove Press, 1956), pp. 31–34.

an opposition force. Nevertheless, they helped the movement in 1881 by promising a constitution and an elected **Diet** (parliament) within a decade.

After years of study of other constitutional states, Itō Hirobumi (ee-TOH HEE-ro-BOO-mee), one of the small group of elite leaders dominating the government, drafted a constitution based on conservative Prussian law. The constitution was officially approved by the Privy Council, a group close to the emperor that had been set up with the explicit purpose of approving the constitution in order to legitimate the constitutional process. The emperor then promulgated the constitution in 1889, and the first parliamentary elections were held in 1890. The electorate in those first elections was limited—by wealth and by gender—to less than 1 percent of the population.

The constitution was not a liberal document. It made the emperor sovereign and placed him in command of the military, without any oversight by the elected officials. The parliament was bicameral, with a House of Peers (nobility) and a House of Representatives (also called the Lower House). The Peers could veto any proposal passed by the Lower House. Until 1925, the Peers repeatedly rejected legislation passed by the Lower House to expand the electorate to include men of all social classes, including the poor. When wealth qualifications were finally eliminated for men, women continued to be denied the right to vote until after World War II by a House of Peers that was much more conservative than the House of Representatives.

The Meiji Constitution, 1889

Meiji Economic Development

Economic development was as important in the Meiji period as political development. The new government encouraged economic development to create a **fukoku kyōhei** (FOO-koh-koo kee-OH-hay; "rich country, strong military"). This was quite different from the official position taken by the Qing at that time. Model factories in textiles, cement, tools, and other products were set up by the Ministry of Industry in the 1870s. A

Diet—Japanese parliament.

fukoku kyōhei—"Rich country, strong army" policy of Meiji government.

reformed land tax (1873) siphoned off rural income to fund these initiatives; although this helped the industrial economy, the impact on farmers, many of whom fell into tenancy when they could not pay their taxes, was not as benign. At the same time, agricultural output did grow rapidly to feed the burgeoning population (from 30 million in 1868 to 40 million in 1900 to 73 million in 1940).

The government also rapidly built an economic infrastructure to support private industry. This included railroads, telegraph lines, ports, post offices, and schools and universities. Railroads were both the substance of and a symbol of modernity. By the dawn of the twentieth century, they reached into the hinterland, bringing national products and culture to village backwaters and drawing young men and especially women into the cities and factories. The sound of the railroad whistle was used to symbolize modernity. Schools, likewise, had an importance that went far beyond that imagined by the creators of the national educational system in the early 1870s. Even a little learning—most students did not stay in school beyond the elementary level before the 1920s—enticed people to demand greater roles in society, to yearn for what would later be called middle-class lifestyles, and to demand greater political and social rights. Though very few Japanese students were able to go to university—and women students were kept out of the prestigious government-run universities and restricted to the small number of private schools—those who did found a high level of scholarship. By the early twentieth century, Japanese scientists were making world contributions in a few areas, especially medicine.

Economic development had its negative sides, too. Because the unequal treaties prevented the Japanese from raising tariffs to support new businesses, costs were cut in other ways. Labor bore the brunt. Girls and women worked under often oppressive conditions at very low wages to produce the silk that earned Japan the foreign currency needed to import new technology. Men and women worked together in coal mines. Slum-dwellers picked garbage and did odd jobs. Tuberculosis and other diseases took their toll. Fortunately, by World War I, the worst types of labor exploitation ended, as Japan's economy took off and reforms were implemented. Unfortunately, a deep divide between the rich and the poor had also begun to emerge.

"Rich Country, Strong Army"

The other side of the slogan "rich country, strong military" was national defense. Yamagata Aritomo (YAH-mah-GAH-tah ah-ree-TOH-moh), considered the "father of the Japanese army," was also a major voice in foreign policy. His notion that Japan should have what he called a "line of sovereignty"—that is, the national boundaries of Japan and its possessions—and a "line of defense"—a buffer zone of neighboring countries into which foreign powers should not intrude—influenced Japanese policy toward Asia through World War II. But the humiliating unequal treaties with the West were Japan's biggest concern in the early Meiji period. They were finally revised when Japan flexed its muscle in the Sino-Japanese War (1894–1895), the Righteous Harmony Fists (Boxer) Uprising (1900), and the Russo-Japanese War (1904–1905). Each of these wars reflected Japan's desire for geopolitical power in northeast Asia to expand the line of defense. The West was sufficiently impressed with Japan's military strength and entrance into the colonial club to revise the treaties.

◄ Young women, like this child in a silk reeling mill, plunged their hands into pans of boiling water to remove the silk thread from cocoons. Profits from textile firms, most of whose workers were women and girls, helped fuel Japan's industrialization in the late nineteenth and early twentieth centuries.

The colonized peoples of Asia were also impressed, but for different reasons. Japan's victory over Russia indicated that it was not a failure of Asia's culture but rather of economic development that kept Asians from independence. And that, some Asian nations anticipated, could be changed. After each of these wars, Japan not only gained respect in Western eyes—the Anglo-Japanese Alliance of 1902 is one example—it also gained an empire. Imperialism was the evil twin of national defense, as Taiwan and Korea came under Japanese domination and Japan strengthened its claim on northeast Asia. But Western respect was spotty. While negotiating mutual acceptance of their colonies (the United States in the Philippines and Japan in Korea and Taiwan), the United States continued to discriminate against Japanese immigrants by passing laws to deprive them of the right to become American citizens or own land. And just as the West's acceptance of Japan was uneven, the respect colonized Asians had for Japan was also only temporary. By 1915, Japan's new imperial status made it no better than the despised Western powers in the eyes of other Asians such as the Koreans and Chinese.

Social Darwinism and the Struggle for Survival

Japan's quest for modernity was driven by fear of being left behind or even being made a colony. But that fate was avoidable, many advocates of change reckoned, because Japan could become a power and claim its place on the trajectory of progress championed in the late nineteenth century by Europeans and Americans. The ideological underpinning of that belief was Social Darwinism. At first glance, Social Darwinism seems an odd notion for an Asian country to embrace. Social Darwinism was an adaptation of Charles Darwin's theory that natural selection and survival of the fittest drove the process of biological evolution. Applied to human societies, most notably by Britain's Herbert Spencer, Social Darwinism has been called by one historian "perhaps the West's primary intellectual export in the late nineteenth century."[5] It attempted to offer a scientific explanation for income inequality and some nations' domination over others. One's fate or that of one's society was in the hands of natural forces that selected some to be on top and others to fall "naturally" behind.

These notions were widely accepted in Europe and the United States in the 1870s and 1880s and justified their imperialism and racial hierarchies. In those hierarchies, East Asians ranked below Europeans and Americans but above other people (and within countries, as in the United States, people of color, it was alleged, ranked below white people and the poor deserved to be ranked below the wealthy). Within East Asia, Japan ranked above the other countries. Japanese university professors, dazzled by Social Darwinism's seemingly scientific and thereby deceptively "progressive" nature, urged their students to work hard to elevate Japan so that it would emerge as one of the fittest in the struggle for survival.

Fukuzawa Yukichi (FOO-koo-ZAH-wah YOO-kee-chee; 1835–1901), the foremost proponent of Westernization, founder of a major university and newspaper, adviser to the government, and author of numerous books, went so far as to advocate a policy he called "leaving Asia"—that is, persuading Westerners that the rapidly modernizing Japan should not be considered part of an Asia they viewed as backward. Fukuzawa taught his Japanese students—as well as the Korean students who traveled to Japan to study with him—that Japan was following a universal, progressive trajectory of development pioneered by the Europeans. Koreans could also fend off colonialism, Fukuzawa taught, if they followed Japan's modernizing lead. Although some in Korea and, later, China agreed, many others viewed the assertion of Japanese leadership in a world ruled by Social Darwinism as patronizing.

In its more sinister form, Social Darwinism could be—and was—used to justify imperialism, Japanese as well as European and American. Yamagata Aritomo sought to expand Japan's lines of defense so Japan would not be eaten by the Western powers, but the process of becoming one of the "fittest" required that Japan gobble up others. By the turn of the century, Social Darwinism was rejected by most Japanese intellectuals, as they were disgusted that Westerners still discriminated against Japan despite its very conscious efforts to follow the European path to modernity.

Although intellectuals rejected Spencer's views that placed Europeans above the Japanese or other Asians, certain aspects of Social Darwinism did influence groups that advocated "Pan-Asianism," a notion that Japan was to lead the rest of Asia in the fight to overcome Western imperialism. Chinese revolutionaries like Sun Yat-sen worked with Japanese Pan-Asianist groups to develop Meiji-style reforms in China in the early years of the twentieth century, and anti-imperialists from India, the Philippines, Korea, and China formed the East Asia United League with Japanese Pan-Asianists to support nationalist insurgencies. These movements viewed winning the struggle for survival through national strengthening and modernity as crucial. Other than these activists, few Japanese discussed Pan-Asianism at that time. Four decades later, however, these ideas would evolve into a dangerous imperialistic notion of an East Asia under Japanese rule, playing a key role in the rise of Japanese militarism in the years preceding World War II.

End of an Era

When the Emperor Meiji died in 1912, the Japanese looked back at 45 years of breathtakingly rapid change. The clang of the railway train, a symbol of modernity, broke the pastoral calm of the countryside. Men of all classes could, in theory, enter any profession, but women still struggled for basic equality, even in marriage. The political parties came to dominate parliamentary government, but an unelected, oligarchical **gerontocracy** called the *genro* (GHEN-roh; elder statesmen) and a military responsible only to the emperor could circumvent the parliament. Factories produced consumer goods that improved the lives of people rich and poor, but labor was shackled to oppressive conditions and air and water pollution threatened those improvements in the quality of life.

Architects and city planners, writers, and artists produced a tremendous outpouring of culture. Artists used both indigenous methods (after almost two decades of rejection of pre-Meiji art at the beginning of the period) and European methods and themes. Architects built up Japan's modern cities, with their multistoried Western-style buildings. City planners built transportation systems and parks. All of these were emblems of an increasingly welcomed modernity. Writers may have affected the largest number of consumers of new culture, writing stories for publication as books and as installments in the burgeoning newspapers and magazines. Natsume Soseki (NAH-tsoo-may SOH-se-kee; 1868–1912), perhaps modern Japan's most revered prose writer, wrote of the loneliness of modernity. Yosano Akiko (YOH-sah-noh AH-kee-koh, 1878–1942), Japan's leading poet, wrote of her despair that her brother was forced to risk his life in a foreign war waged on behalf of a distant emperor.

In short, Japan was an increasingly modern country. Its poets and writers, its journalists and artists, its reformers and civil and women's rights advocates, served as the conscience of the nation. By the early twentieth century, Japan was developing as a constitutional monarchy with an overseas empire, much like its closest ally England. Although it was moving in increasingly democratic directions at home, its people continued to struggle for political rights and economic justice.

	Australia, New Zealand, and the Pacific Islands
1840	Treaty of Waitangi between British and Maori
1841	New Zealand becomes Crown Colony of Britain
1842	Tahiti becomes a protectorate of France
1851	Discovery of gold in Australia
1852	New Zealand parliament established
1855	Right of male political representation in Australia
1893	New Zealand first country to grant women the vote
1893	Overthrow of Hawaiian monarchy
1898	Spanish-American War; United States acquires Philippines, Guam, Puerto Rico, Hawaii
1901	Dominion status for Australia
1907	Dominion status for New Zealand

Australia, New Zealand, and the Pacific Islands

How were ethnic interactions and colonialism related in Oceania?

The first fleet of ships from Britain bringing 1350 convicts to Australia arrived in 1788, the year that New South Wales, a colony initially comprising New Zealand and Australia's eastern half, was founded. For the next four decades, convicts and free settlers, mainly from England and Ireland, migrated to Australia. By the mid-nineteenth century, Americans, Chinese, and other Europeans also began to migrate to the South Pacific. At the end of the century, migration took new forms—Melanesian islanders were recruited to work in Australia, Peru, French-held New Caledonia, and British-held Fiji; Indian workers were sent to Fiji; and Vietnamese found work in New Caledonia. Germans and, later, Japanese also joined the movement of foreigners to the South Pacific after their respective nations gained colonial footholds there.

Waves of migration adversely affected local populations. The combination of loss of land, introduction of diseases, and undermining of local customs and religions dealt severe blows to indigenous societies. European settlers were not entirely unhappy with that. One English missionary declared in 1856 that it was God's will that Europeans take land from people who were as "incapable of appreciating its resources as the Aborigines of Australia. The white man had indeed only carried out the intentions of the Creator."[6]

Social Darwinist thought paralleled religious justification for theft of land. Social Darwinists argued

gerontocracy—Rule by senior citizens; in this case, by elderly former cabinet members or aristocrats.

that the decimation of indigenous populations by newly introduced diseases indicated they had lost the struggle for survival of the fittest. Although some Westerners were unabashed racists who committed violence to hasten the disappearance of indigenous populations, others believed themselves humane. One New Zealand politician commented in 1856 (fortunately his prediction proved wrong in the long run): "The Maoris are dying out, and nothing can save them. Our plain duty, as good compassionate colonists, is to 'smooth down their dying pillow.' Then history will have nothing to reproach us with."[7]

Australia

Australia, while still under British jurisdiction throughout the nineteenth and part of the twentieth centuries, was able to exercise a significant degree of self-government, although political power was exclusively reserved for white settlers. Australia's government justified excluding Aborigines in several ways. Some conveniently (though incorrectly) saw the land as empty of inhabitants, others adopted the religious or Social Darwinist justifications for domination noted previously, and others defined the Aborigines who adorned themselves with paint rather than cloth as morally depraved and therefore in need of political guidance by European settlers. Immigrants from Asia were also excluded from political power. Their entrance led to a strictly defined policy of "White Australia."

Nonconvict settlers had begun to arrive from England after 1793. Explorations of the interior of the continent in the next century opened up new areas for colonists. Some, called "squatters," occupied government lands without official approval, using them to graze livestock. Squatters were later given official permission to keep their landholdings, becoming a powerful landed class.

The influx of new waves of immigrants in mid-century led to political forces that eventually undermined the squatters' power, however. The 1848 discovery of gold in California drew thousands of gold-seekers to the American West, and Californians were more easily supplied by ships from Australia than from New York. The commercial growth of Sydney spurred by the California Gold Rush came just in time for the discovery of gold in Australia in 1851. Australia's cities and towns grew overnight, with immigrants spilling in from all over the world, but especially from England, Ireland, and China.

Many of these new immigrants clashed with the administrators of the mines and demanded the right to vote and representation in the colonial parliaments. These rights were granted to males of European ancestry in 1855. Small landholders gained power as well, as the new parliamentary representatives joined them in eroding the power of the wealthy squatters. Trade unions grew in size and influence, gaining the world's first 8-hour work day in 1856. For many, Australia was a beacon of democracy and freedom.

The expansion of rights for white Australians was accompanied, however, by increasingly discriminatory attitudes toward others around the turn of the century. Both Australia and New Zealand passed legislation to keep Asians out, and both opposed Great Britain's elimination of its unequal treaties with Japan and the signing of the Anglo-Japanese Naval Treaty in 1902. Australia officially adopted a "White Australia" policy in its constitution. White Australians' focus on their national character led them to apply for dominion status, which they gained in January 1901. As in the case of New Zealand, however, full independence took several more decades, following Australia's wartime service to England. Official discrimination no longer exists in either country, but, as in many other countries in the nineteenth and early twentieth centuries, it is part of the historical record.

New Zealand

Some thoughtful colonial authorities in New Zealand reacted to Western exploitation with policies intended to prevent further harm to indigenous people. James Busby, appointed British Resident to New Zealand in 1832, convened the Maori tribes in 1835 to form a federation resembling the kingdom of Hawaii, believing that would strengthen the Maori against oppression by Western settlers. This attempt was not successful, and in 1841, fearing French designs on New Zealand, the British declared it a Crown Colony separate from the colony of New South Wales in Australia.

Before this could occur, however, the British had to address Maori claims to sovereignty in New Zealand. To that end, they negotiated the Treaty of Waitangi in February 1840. The Treaty was not signed by all Maori tribal chiefs, and the interpretations of "sovereignty" and "chieftainship" in the two versions, English and Maori, were not identical, leading to land wars between 1845 and 1872. Disputes over land increased with the discovery of gold in 1861. Although Maori were guaranteed four seats in the New Zealand parliament in 1867, this occurred 15 years after the white settler population had been given the right to self-government. Economic and cultural discrimination continued to plague the minority Maori in New Zealand, although their equality in law meant that some Maori were able to become successful. In 1893, when New Zealand became the world's first country to grant women the vote, Maori women gained that right alongside settlers and their descendants.

New Zealand earned partial independence by being declared a "dominion" (like Canada and Aus-

▲ Disputes over land ownership often erupted into war between settlers and Maori from the 1840s to the 1870s, but collaboration also took place. Here, a celebration of a flour mill built by Maori in the 1860s brought the two sides together. Maori statues surround the two leaders, Superintendent McClean and Maori chief Porokoru, and their followers. The crowd is mostly male, but some women are in attendance, too.

tralia) instead of a "colony" in 1907. After sending troops to support Britain in the Second Boer War and World War I, New Zealand gained greater independence in 1931, and the last vestiges of political subordination to Britain were removed after World War II.

The Pacific Islands

In reaction to Britain's annexation of New Zealand in 1840, the French had annexed the Marquesas. Two years later, they made Tahiti a "protectorate" (protectorate status was converted to full-scale annexation in 1881). Seeking territory for a penal colony and a space for Catholic missionaries, France made New Caledonia a protectorate in 1853. Many Melanesians in New Caledonia suffered expropriation of their property. A large number were transported to other countries as indentured workers.

France had pressured the Hawaiian king into signing an unequal treaty in 1839, demanding freedom of worship as a pretext for the treaty—by the 1830s, the Hawaiian government was largely Protestant and blocked Catholic missionaries' attempts to proselytize. This treaty was eventually revised under pressure from the United States in 1853. The increasing American presence in Hawaii in the next decades, however, did not bode well for Hawaiian independence. Following the overthrow of the Hawaiian queen in 1893 by American nationals residing in Hawaii, the U.S. government annexed Hawaii in 1898 as part of the effort to bolster its strategic position in the Pacific and support its new colony in the Philippines. Guam also became a U.S. colony that year, and eastern Samoa the following year.

Not to be outdone, the recently united Germany jumped into the imperialist game, taking the Marshalls, the Carolines, Pelau, and part of New Guinea, and later purchasing the Marianas from Spain in the wake of the Spanish loss of the Philippines to the United States in 1898. By the end of the nineteenth century, the islands of the Pacific were no longer independent.

Conclusion

With the exception of Japan and Thailand (Siam), Asia and Oceania were dominated by the West at the end of the nineteenth century. India fell under British political and economic domination but also gained tools from the imperial power to use to pursue its eventual independence. Thailand modernized its society and economy and maintained its independence in Southeast Asia, aided by the French and the British desire for a buffer state between their holdings in the region.

China suffered a distressing decline in the nineteenth century from its position as the Central Kingdom to a country in revolutionary turmoil and split into spheres of foreign influence. The Pacific islands became territories of migration and colonialism.

Japan, through the Meiji Period reforms, was able to fend off Western imperialism and compete on more or less equal terms with the West. It was able to build on conditions developed during the Tokugawa period, including a sophisticated domestic economy, a strong rural sector, a samurai ethic that stressed hard work and loyalty, a high level of literacy, and knowledge of both Western and Chinese science. Japan's "closed country" foreign relations under the Tokugawa, while detrimental in many respects, were not encumbered by a tribute system as were the foreign policies of its neighbors. Japan's leaders in the last third of the century consciously borrowed Western elements of modern economy, society, and politics. By 1945, many of these institutions would be discredited with Japan's defeat in World War II, but others set important precedents for other countries seeking to reclaim their independence during the course of the twentieth century (see Chapter 29).

Suggestions for Web Browsing

You can obtain more information about topics included in this chapter at the websites listed below. See also the companion website that accompanies this text, http://www.ablongman.com/brummett, which contains an online study guide and additional resources.

All East Asian History
http://coombs.anu.edu.au/
This site provides links to websites for numerous countries in East, Southeast, and South Asia. The site is updated frequently by a team of 40 scholars.

Images of Rural and Urban China
http://www.chinaexhibit.org/
Photos of rural China and Chinese life, 1903–1904.
http://virtualshanghai.ish-lyon.cnrs.fr/
Photos of Shanghai life.

Late Qing History
http://www.cnd.org/fairbank/qing.html
A comprehensive website for Qing history.

South and Southeast Asia
http://www.lib.berkeley.edu/SSEAL/SouthAsia/
This site has links to numerous websites with information about South and Southeast Asia.

Philippine–U.S. War
http://www.geocities.com/Athens/Crete/9782/index.htm
A comprehensive website dealing with the American–Philippine War.

Imaging Meiji, 1868–1912
http://www.ndl.go.jp/site_nippon/japane/index.html
Scenic images from Japan's National Diet Library collection.

Australian History
http://www.nla.gov.au/oz/histsite.html
A comprehensive collection of historical websites assembled by the National Library of Australia.

New Zealand History
http://www.nzhistory.net.nz/
An excellent website developed by the New Zealand Ministry for Culture and Heritage.

Literature and Film

The Indonesian writer Pramoedya Ananta Toer captures the complex fusion of Dutch and Javan cultures at the end of the nineteenth century in *This Earth of Mankind,* translated by Max Lane (Avon, 1975). For events in India in the 1850s, see V. A. Stuart, *The Sepoy Mutiny* (McBooks Press, 2001). The British experience in India drew the attentions of E. M. Forster in *A Passage to India* (Harvest Books, 1984) and M. M. Kaye in *The Far Pavilions* (St. Martins, 1997). Rudyard Kipling's *Kim* (see especially the Edward Said edition of the Penguin classics, reprinted by Viking, 1987) and *The Man Who Would Be King* (many editions) capture the flavor of the British mentality. Any novels by Japanese writer Natsume Soseki, especially *Kokoro* (Regnery Publishing, 1996), describe the pleasures and pain of modernization.

David Lean produced a classic production of the Forster novel (1984), and John Huston (1975) transferred Kipling's *The Man Who Would Be King* into a fine film. *Aa, Nomugi Pass* (1979; subtitled) is a poignant fictionalized tale of young silk workers in the Meiji period in Japan.

Suggestions for Reading

Ranajit Guha places the tie between India and Great Britain into a new perspective in his *Dominance Without Hegemony: History and Power in Colonial India* (Harvard University Press, 1998). The best concise work on Indian women's rights movements is *A History of Doing by Radha Kumar* (W. W. Norton, 1993).

For the impact of the Dutch on the region, see Anne Booth et al., *Indonesian Economic History in the Dutch Colonial Empire* (Yale University Press, 1990). An interesting analysis of Vietnam is provided in Alexander B. Woodside, *Vietnam and the Chinese Model: A Comparative Study of Vietnamese and Chinese Government in the First Half of the Nineteenth Century* (Harvard University Press, 1988).

Jonathan Spence's *In Search of Modern China* (W. W. Norton, 2001) contains a fine overview of this period. Peter Ward Fay, *The Opium War, 1840–1842* (University of North Carolina Press, 1998), is a fine study. For a study of the environmental effects of an expanding population and a traditional government, see Peter C. Purdue, *Exhausting the Earth: State and Peasant in Hunan, 1500–1850* (Harvard University Press, 1987).

For a detailed overview of Tokugawa history, including political, economic, and environmental issues, see Conrad Totman, *Early Modern Japan* (University of California Press, 1993). Gail L. Bernstein, ed., *Recreating Japanese Women, 1600–1945* (University of California, 1991) contains excellent work on women's history. Anne Walthall's *The Weak Body of a Useless Woman* (University of Chicago Press, 1998) offers an alternate view of the Meiji Restoration years. Important analyses of the Meiji era are George M. Wilson, *Patriots and Redeemers in Japan: Motives in the Meiji Restoration* (University of Chicago Press, 1992), and Carol Gluck, *Japan's Modern Myths: Ideology in the Late Meiji Period* (Princeton University Press, 1985). Excellent treatments of the longer sweep of history may be found in Andrew Gordon, *A Modern History of Japan* (Oxford University Press, 2003), and Sheldon Garon, *Molding Japanese Minds: The State in Everyday Life* (Princeton University Press, 1997).

Excellent surveys of New Zealand history include Keith Sinclair, ed., *The Oxford Illustrated History of New Zealand* (Oxford University Press, 1998), and James Belich, *Making Peoples: A History of the New Zealanders: From Polynesian Settlement to the End of the Nineteenth Century* (University of Hawaii Press, 1996). For Australia, see Donald Denoon, Philippa Mein-Smith, and Marivic Wyndham, *A History of Australia, New Zealand, and the Pacific* (Oxford University Press, 2000).

CHAPTER 26

The Americas, 1825–1914

The Challenges of Independence

Outline

- Challenges to Latin American States After Independence
- Latin America, 1875–1914
- The United States

Features

DOCUMENT **Newspaper Advertisements for Runaway Slaves in Brazil**

SEEING CONNECTIONS **The Paris of the Pampas**

DISCOVERY THROUGH MAPS **An American View of the World in the 1820s**

DOCUMENT **Susan Anthony, On Women's Right to Vote**

DOCUMENT **José Marti's Observations on the United States and Cuba**

◀ Because sugar mills in Brazil were a costly enterprise, only the wealthiest plantation owners could afford to operate one. Once a harvest came in, slaves brought the sugar cane to the mill, where it was ground to a pulp. The liquid was extracted and converted into white or brown sugar.

By 1825, most countries in the Western Hemisphere had won their independence and were beginning the challenging process of building new nations. Despite significant differences, these fledgling and often fragile states grappled with similar issues over the next century, including creating new national identities and governments; finding a proper balance between regional autonomy and central governments; coping with political instability, civil wars, and foreign interventions; dealing with indigenous peoples; ending the slave trade and slavery; attracting immigrants; and promoting trade, economic development, and industrialization.

The first to win its independence was the United States. The War of Independence laid a foundation for unity as the 13 former colonies confronted a common enemy in Great Britain and later found a constitutional formula for joining together under one government in 1789. By 1825, the United States had expanded to 24 states and nearly doubled its territory through the Louisiana Purchase. It had remained intact, while surviving a war with Great Britain and experiencing sectional tensions over slavery that would later lead to the most severe test to the republic: the American Civil War.

In contrast to the United States, the former Spanish colonies that made up most of Latin America won their independence without any expectation they would unite. From the beginning, they were unstable. Their wars of independence left a bitter legacy that was difficult to overcome. Hundreds of thousands of people died in the conflicts, hatreds and divisions remained, and civil wars were constantly a prospect. Some of the most productive areas were devastated, and communication and transportation were severely disrupted. Moreover, the colonial political cultures of autocracy and patronage were a poor foundation for new nations aspiring to become democratic republics.

Challenges to Latin American States After Independence

Why did the caudillos hold so much power in Latin American nations throughout the nineteenth century?

The successors of the great liberators that had led the independence movements throughout Latin America found it difficult to maintain control over their newly independent nations because they could not reach a consensus over how to govern and the kind of political system they desired. The **Creoles** (KREE-ols) who dominated the independence movements were inexperienced and unable to make the political compromises necessary to govern new countries. They quarreled with the **peninsulares** (Spanish-born colonists). And the groups that represented the ruling elite—landowners, church officials, mine owners, and businessmen—were at odds with one another as they vied for influence and control.

Latin Americans Obtain Independence

With the exception of Brazil (and Mexico for a year), the new countries adopted a republican form of government. Most leaders defined themselves in principle as liberals and shared the political philosophies of Locke and Montesquieu (see pp. 554–555). Liberals believed in individual rights such as freedom of speech, thought, and religion and the sanctity of property. They backed independent legislatures and judiciaries that would make governments more accountable to the people. They called for separating church and state, taking control of education from the church, and reducing the lands owned by the Catholic Church. They embraced free trade and low tariffs and allowing market forces rather than the state to manage the economy.

Opposing the liberals were the conservatives, who wanted to preserve the old order and the authoritarian structures that had been in place under colonial rule. They preferred to keep close relations between the Catholic Church and the state and did not want to diminish the church's wealth and power.

In the first half of the nineteenth century, the conservatives ultimately came to have more influence over the shaping of political systems. When faced with a choice between implementing their ideals and dealing with the harsh realities on the ground, liberals were often unprepared to give up their own privileges and instead supported state systems that resembled **enlightened despotism.**

Because governments were so fragile, many countries saw the rise of strongmen or **caudillos** (cow-DEE-ohs), who were usually prominent landowners who controlled armed gangs made up of workers on their estates. The caudillos were masters of patron-client relations and built up regional bases of support. In many ways, they operated in the same style as the Spanish administrators who preceded them.

Another challenge facing the new states was how to create a national identity in countries divided by regions, languages, and ethnic and racial diversity. In 1825, there were 15 to 18 million people in the former Spanish Empire. About three million of them were of European descent, the wealthiest and most educated population who dominated political life. That figure remained constant until the last third of the nineteenth century, when immigration from Europe increased drastically. There were about the same number of **mestizos** (mes-TEE-zohs), who scorned the Indian population but were not accepted by whites.

Creole—In the Americas, a person of Spanish descent born in Latin America; in Africa, people living in cities along the west coast, usually freed slaves, who adapted themselves to Western culture.

peninsulares—Spanish-born colonists in Latin America.

enlightened despotism—A political system in which a monarch, an autocratic ruler, or a privileged elite governs with the aim of improving the lives of their subjects.

caudillo—A military or political strongman who based his rule on personal authority and patronage.

mestizo—A person of mixed Indian and Spanish descent.

Chronology

1820	1840	1860	1880	1900
1820 Missouri Compromise adopted in United States	1840 Pedro II crowned emperor of Brazil	1861–1865 U.S. Civil War	1888 Brazil ends slavery	1910 Beginning of Mexican Revolution
1823 Monroe Doctrine issued	1846–1848 Mexican-American War	1867 French expelled from Mexico	1898 Spanish-American War	1914 Opening of Panama Canal
		1867 Federal union established in Canada		
		1879–1880 Conquest of the Desert, Argentina		
		1879–1883 Chile defeats Peru and Bolivia in the War of the Pacific		

Their numbers steadily increased, as did their ambitions. During the nineteenth century, over half of the population in most states was Indian. Deprived of the small protection once offered by the Spanish crown, they either sank into peonage or lived in semi-independence under their tribal rulers. In Brazil and most of the Caribbean islands, blacks were a large majority. Conflicts soon developed between these broad racial groups, particularly between the Creoles and the mestizos.

The social and legal status of women remained unchanged after independence, despite their participation in independence struggles as nurses, spies, couriers, hosts of political meetings in their homes, donors of financial support, and even fighters. The new civil codes were based on Spanish legal tradition that reinforced patriarchal authority in homes and in public settings. Married women had few legal rights and were subordinate to their husbands. They were expected to perform the proper role of mothers and wives. They could not be a witness in a court of law, hold office, or vote as the electorate usually consisted of literate male property owners.

▲ At the turn of the twentieth century, Latin America remained largely free of direct political control by Europe and the United States. Instead, Europe and the United States maintained an economic dominance over the region.

Economic Developments

After independence, Latin American elites were confident that once they escaped the grip of Spanish and Portuguese colonialism, they would develop not only stable political systems but healthy economies. That optimism soon faded as leadership rivalries, regional splits, civil unrest, and ideological and racial divisions frustrated economic development. The elites continued to concentrate wealth in a few hands, and they turned to the caudillos to protect their interests.

Most Latin American states suffered economic decline in the initial decades of independence. Independence wars had an adverse impact on production in silver mining in Mexico, Peru, and Bolivia; ranching in Argentina and Uruguay; plantation agriculture in Venezuela; and manufacturing in Ecuador and Mexico. There was little new investment from within Latin America as many peninsulares returned to Spain or moved to Cuba and the Catholic Church withheld its money. Landowners turned inward, preferring to remain self-sufficient rather than producing crops and goods for domestic or international markets. With little revenue coming in, governments had to borrow heavily from Europe. As a result, they had to devote much of their customs revenue and export duties to paying off external debts rather than building up infrastructure such as roads, bridges, railways, and harbors.

With little industrial development taking place, Latin American nations were integrated into Europe's industrial economy but in a subordinate position. They became providers of raw materials such as copper, tin, and hides and agricultural products such as sugar, coffee, and tobacco. Most nations relied heavily on the export of one or two products and thus were at the mercy of international prices. When the price of a product was high, their economies fared well, but when the price declined, they suffered. Latin America imported manufactured goods from Europe such as textiles and machinery, but it was slow to introduce new technologies such as the steam engine, which was only introduced in Latin America in the mid-nineteenth century. The mining and textile sectors still heavily depended on outdated technologies.

Britain was by far the leading foreign investor in Latin America until American businesses began to pour capital into countries such as Mexico in the late nineteenth century. Britain quickly recognized the newly independent states, negotiated commercial and navigation treaties, and took the place of the Spanish and Portuguese in controlling the export trade. The British economic empire was not based on formal control or direct intervention in the internal affairs of countries. Instead, British businesses concentrated their investments in key sectors of the economy such as railways and mines and used their dominance over commerce to influence the decision-making of local politicians.

Mexico

Mexico achieved independence on September 27, 1821, but at enormous cost. Hundreds of thousands of people had died in the conflicts of the previous decade. At independence, many peninsulares left taking their investment capital. Silver production declined. Over the next half century, Mexico suffered through four foreign interventions and numerous civil wars and rebellions.

Independence came as the result of a deal between a royalist, Augustin de Iturbide, and leaders of the independence struggle. Once Iturbide took control, he ruled as an emperor for a year before being ousted in a coup led by General Antonio López de Santa Anna (1794–1876). The new federal constitution was based on the principle that all Mexicans should be equal before the law. All free adult males could vote; indeed, more adult males then had the vote in Mexico than in the United States, Great Britain, or France.

However, that did not insure stability. Between 1824 and 1857, Mexico's government was a revolving door for 16 presidents, 23 provisional chief executives, and 49 national administrations. The person at the center of Mexican political life during most of these years was General Santa Anna. The son of a wealthy Spanish family in Veracruz, he served as president 11 times, the first in 1833. He shifted back and forth in his support for federalism or regional autonomy and a strong central government. Few Mexicans were neutral about him. To his supporters, he was the "Defender of the Homeland," a patriot who lost a leg to a French cannonball in 1838 and raised an army with his own money to fight the United States in 1846. To his critics, he was the "Traitor of the Nation," a figure associated with the loss of much Mexican territory. They vilified Santa Anna for his corruption and his inability to distinguish between his personal fortune and the national treasury.

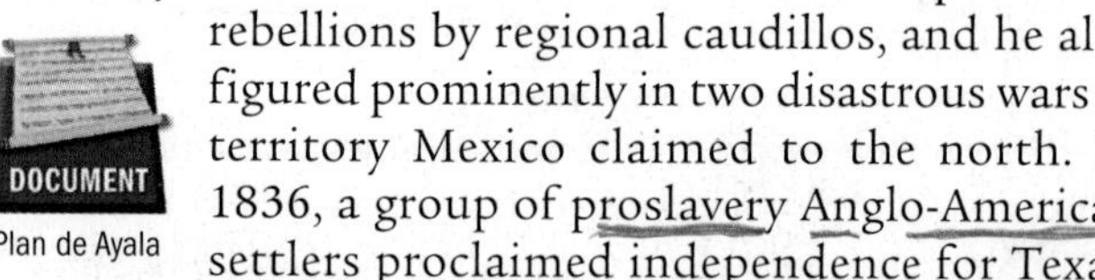

DOCUMENT

Plan de Ayala

Santa Anna attempted to establish a professional army drafted from Mexico's citizens to put down rebellions by regional caudillos, and he also figured prominently in two disastrous wars in territory Mexico claimed to the north. In 1836, a group of proslavery Anglo-American settlers proclaimed independence for Texas. Santa Anna's army defeated them at the Alamo, killing all the defenders, but lost disastrously at San Jacinto, where Santa Anna was captured and directed his officers to withdraw from Texas. Texas was eventually annexed to the United States in 1845. Although disgraced by the loss of Texas, Santa Anna made several more comebacks. In 1846, Mexico was drawn into a 2-year war with the United States that resulted in another defeat, the loss of much more land, and even greater humiliation. Santa Anna later sold southern New Mexico and Arizona to the United States for $15 million. By the time he was toppled for the last time in 1855, Mexico had lost almost half its territory to its neighbor to the north.

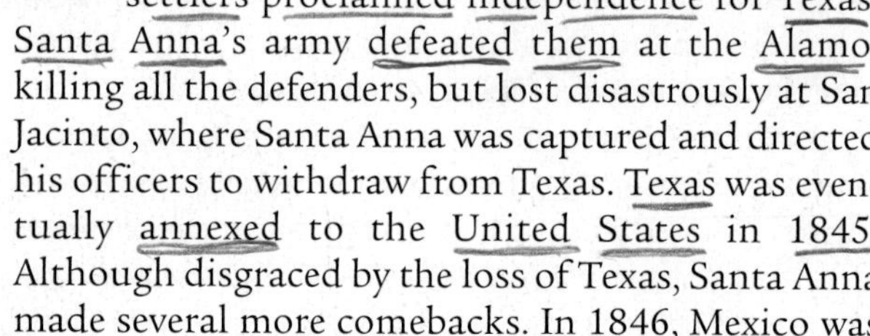

Benito Juárez (WAHR-ehz; 1806–1872), a Zapotec Indian, attempted to establish a more democratic government by implementing a sweeping program of change known as the ***Reforma.*** Juárez and his liberal supporters planned to include mestizos and Indians in political life, curtail the political and economic power of the Catholic Church by abolishing the 10 percent tithe the state collected on the church's behalf, and introduce secular education. The anti-clerical measures, however, were responsible for touching off a destructive civil war that ended in 1861 with Juárez's apparent victory.

That same year, European powers invaded when Mexico was unable to meet the payments on its debts. Although the Mexican army defeated a French army at Puebla on May 5 (Cinqo de Mayo), 1862, the French were victorious and installed a puppet regime with an Austrian Archduke Ferdinand Maximilian as emperor. Juárez mobilized resistance against the French and his forces, aided by pressure from the United States, eventually drove French troops from Mexican soil in 1867, and executed Maximilian. Juárez again set out to institute the *Reforma* and served in office until his death in 1872.

During these years, the status of women changed little. The prevailing attitude was that the proper domains of women were in the church, home, and family. In education, there was some halting progress as some lower schools were opened up for girls. Most schools were religious in nature with children praying and reciting catechisms, and women teachers had to take religious vows. Even with Juárez's reforms that established secular schools, women were expected to remain devoted wives and homemakers and were not encouraged to train for professions. It was not until the late nineteenth century that the first woman doctor graduated from college.

Argentina

Although Argentina was probably the wealthiest Spanish-speaking country in the world until the 1970s, its beginnings as an independent nation were less promising. Spanish colonizers had largely neglected the area because of its lack of minerals. However, Argentina was blessed with the bustling port

Reforma—The name for Benito Juárez's reform program that advocated restricting the powers of the Catholic Church, establishing democratic institutions, and giving more political power to mestizos.

city of Buenos Aires, whose energetic population sought to encourage European capital and commerce, and the pampas (PAM-puhs), plains that stretched for several hundred miles from Buenos Aires into the interior. The pampas, which contained rich agricultural land that was ideal for cattle ranching, were divided into large **estancias.** The ranch owners relied on the support of their clients, the gauchos (GOW-chohs), most of whom were mestizos. The independent way of life of these cowboys has been romanticized in literature and folklore.

Argentina's politics were centered around the conflict between landowners who favored a federal system that preserved their powers and the *unitarios,* the supporters of centralized government who mostly lived in Buenos Aires. However, from 1829 to 1852, Argentine politics were not controlled by either faction but by a caudillo, Juan Manuel de Rosas, a wealthy landowner and rancher who grew up on the pampas and identified with the gaucho lifestyle. Although his policies favored the ranching elite, he cultivated patron-client relationships with the lower classes and donated land and money to the poor. He had popular followings among his Indian allies and gauchos in the rural areas and blacks and mulattos in Buenos Aires. Although a slave owner himself, he courted the support of black mutual aid societies and elevated black freemen and slaves to high military ranks. His wife hosted black women on the patio of their home and his daughter attended black dances that had been banned under previous governments.

Although Rosas claimed to be a federalist, as governor of Buenos Aires province, he did not hesitate to stamp his personal authority on every aspect of political life. He kept other provinces in line by controlling the foreign relations of the whole country. He ruled with an iron fist, unleashing his armed force called *La Mazorca* (corncob) on his opponents. He paid lip service to the legislature, and he did not take the trouble to issue decrees or laws. He went so far as to require Catholic priests to wear the symbol of his followers, a red ribbon, when they conducted Mass.

In 1852, Rosas was overthrown by an uneasy alliance of Justo José de Urquiza (oor-KEE-sah), a former ally, and the *unitarios* of Buenos Aires. A constitution that proved remarkably durable was adopted in 1853. It provided for a central administration but with many powers delegated to the provinces. However, it gave power to a president to intervene in the affairs of provinces or depose provincial governors if they did not uphold the central government. Urquiza headed a confederation of interior provinces, while Buenos Aires went its own way until a war between the two resulted in a victory for Buenos Aires and the unification of the country in the 1860s.

estancia—A large estate or cattle ranch in Spanish America.

Subsequent presidents were limited to one 6-year term each. The president from 1868 to 1874 was Domingo Sarmiento (sar-MY-EN-toh). While in exile during the Rosas era, he published *Facundo* (1845), in which he contrasted the barbarism of the caudillos, which he attributed to the lack of sound government and their anarchism, with the civilized behavior found in liberal political systems. Characterizing the mestizo gauchos as the epitome of cultural backwardness, he maintained that European immigration was necessary to modernize and civilize Argentina. When he served later as Argentina's minister to Washington, D.C., during the Civil War, Sarmiento was impressed with free public American education. He acted on these ideas during his presidency, and his most important initiatives were to encourage European immigration and promote a dramatic expansion of state-sponsored education.

Another president was General Julio Roca, who led the **"Conquest of the Desert"** in 1879–1880 to expel nomadic Indian tribes in the southern pampas and neighboring Patagonia. The same year the war concluded, he was elected president. His administration's policy was to place the vanquished Indians in

Conquest of the Desert—A military campaign in 1879–1880 led by General Julio Roca against Indian tribes that opened up large areas of Patagonia and the southern pampas for settlement by large estate owners.

▼ The gauchos were romanticized in Argentina in much the same way that the cowboys were in the United States.

reservations similar to those in the United States. Their lands were parceled out as a reward to soldiers who had participated in the campaign or bought up by large landowners at cheap prices. European immigrants who lacked the resources to purchase Indian lands only found work as labor tenants on the estancias. As a consequence, Argentina never saw the development of a peasantry or experienced any pressures for land reform from below.

Brazil

The former Portuguese colony of Brazil largely escaped the violent turbulence and disorders that befell its Spanish-speaking neighbors, probably because it had achieved independence without years of warfare and because it enjoyed the continuity and legitimacy afforded by a respected monarchy.

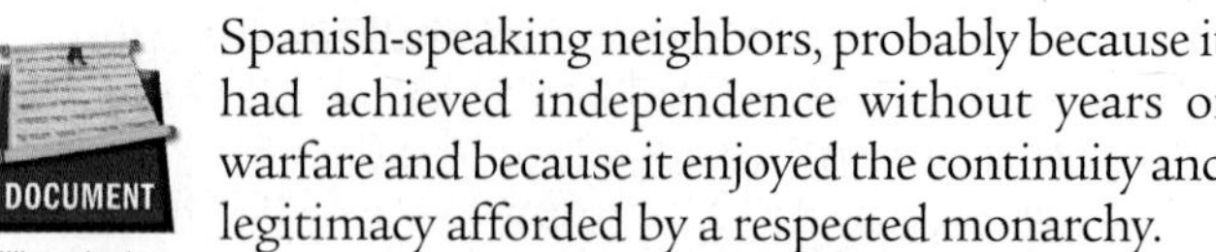

Millenarianism in Brazil

Brazil became a monarchy because the Portuguese royal family found refuge there after Napoleon's army invaded Portugal in 1807. Following an army coup in 1820, Jõao VI returned to Portugal to assume the throne. Because Brazil's landowning elite associated the idea of a republic with the violence and chaos of the French Revolution, they appealed to Jõao's son to stay behind; several years later, he was crowned Pedro I (r. 1822–1831), the first ruler of the Empire of Brazil.

Although the new constitution protected civil liberties and empowered a General Assembly elected by free adult males to make laws and control finance, the emperor retained considerable powers over church and state. He had to sign every law and decree. He could appoint cabinet ministers, military officers, and civil servants, as well as dismiss parliament. He selected bishops and could block the issuing of papal bulls. Although he rarely interfered directly in political affairs, he also benefited from rivalries within the elite, who split into two factions. The Portuguese party represented Portuguese-born conservatives who favored the monarchy, and the Brazil party consisted of liberal, southern landowners who supported reducing the power of the monarchy and protecting provincial autonomy.

A popular uprising forced Pedro I to abdicate in 1831 and join his family in Portugal, leaving his Brazilian-born 5-year-old son behind. He was placed under a regent until he assumed the throne as Pedro II in 1840. For almost the next half century, two issues—the future of slavery and the role of the monarchy—dominated his reign.

In the early years of his reign, Pedro II enjoyed considerable support from political factions and the imperial army. He was a patron of the Brazilian Historical and Cultural Society and sponsored artists and writers. He learned *Guarani* (gwah-rah-NEE), a widely spoken Indian language. However, support for him and the monarchy dramatically dropped during Brazil's destructive 5-year war with Paraguay over control of the Rio de Plata river basin, a vital transportation lifeline for Argentina and Uruguay as well as Brazil and Paraguay. Tributaries to the Rio de Plata were a crucial link for Brazil with its far western, interior provinces.

Allied with Argentina and Uruguay in a Triple Alliance, Brazil's leaders mistakenly believed it would quickly defeat Paraguay and its tyrannical leader, Francisco López and optimistically began the war in 1865 with much fanfare and patriotic fervor. As the costly war dragged on and Paraguayan forces resorted to guerilla warfare, Pedro desperately need to recruit fresh soldiers and offered freedom for slaves who joined the army. The war ended with a much larger army whose officers demanded more of a say in the government. Toward the end of the war, the emperor blundered by dismissing the liberals in the cabinet, who had a majority in the Chamber of Deputies, and replacing them with conservatives. The liberals then began agitating for reform and questioning the usefulness of the monarchy. Even the Catholic Church retreated from its support for Pedro.

Another challenge facing the emperor was how to end slavery. Most Latin American countries abolished slavery shortly after their independence, but slaves remained central to the economies of Brazil, Cuba, and Puerto Rico. Almost every type of agriculture and ranching in Brazil depended on slave labor. John Mawe, an Englishman traveling in Brazil in 1828, commented on the pervasiveness of slavery. "Slaves form the income and support of a vast number of individuals, who hire them out as people in Europe do horses and mules."[1]

	The Abolition of Slavery in the Americas
1823	Chile
1825	Costa Rica
1825	Nicaragua
1825	Mexico
1831	Bolivia
1854	Peru
1854	Venezuela
1861	Argentina
1865	United States
1886	Cuba
1888	Brazil

Document

Newspaper Advertisements for Runaway Slaves in Brazil

In nineteenth-century Brazil, slaves would commonly flee their masters, and because of the costs of replacing slaves who often had skills, slaveholders went to great lengths to recapture them. They ran newspaper advertisements describing in great detail the slaves who had fled and offering substantial rewards for their return or recapture. These descriptions offer insight into the nature of slavery and the reasons why slaves sought to escape from their masters.

$100,000 Reward

Fled on December 3 of this year from the plantation of Major Antonio de Campos Freire one of his slaves named José of the Benguella nation (though he says he is a Creole) from 25 to 30 years of age with the following characteristics: short in stature, thin, well-made body, dark color, face rather long, pale jaw, almost no beard, lips rather full, round head, and is in the habit of going abut with long hair, small eyes, long eyelashes, good teeth, nose medium large, speaks in a refined, humble, and insincere way, may have some old and small marks of punishment on his buttocks. He is a master blacksmith, also knows how to work with copper; also a master at killing ants with his bellows. He is accustomed to getting drunk and in that condition becomes violent. He took some work clothes, a poncho with a yellow lining, a firearm, a hat of rough straw; and whenever he runs away he usually claims to be free and changes his name. Whoever captures him and takes him to his master will receive 100$000 reward, in addition to expenses, which will be paid separately.

O Mercantil (Rio de Janeiro), January 13, 1845

Fled or was led astray a black girl [*moleca*] named Maria of the Cacange nation, who appears to be about 14 years of age and still does not have breasts, black color and thin, wore a dress of white calico with ribbons and pink flowers. The said girl was missing yesterday afternoon when she went to the Campo de Santa Anna to get water, and it appears that she was crying there because someone had stolen her water bucket. Whoever brings her to the Rua de Santa Anna No. 47B, upper floor, will be satisfactorily rewarded, or even someone who gives information about her so that her owner can get her back.

Diario de Rio de Janeiro, December 31, 1847

Fled from Jaraguá from the custody of Mr. Mariz on the 21st of the current month the slave Izidoro, mulatto, 18 years old, tall, long hair; at the sugar mills of Garcatorta and Villa do Norte this slave has a father and relatives; it is very possible that he went to those places; he fled with manacles on his hands and should have some marks on his feet as a result of wearing irons for some days. We appeal to anyone who captures him to deliver him in Maceió to Mr. Antonio Texeira Pinto in the Cambona, and he will be well rewarded. Maceió, December 22, 1855.

O Noticiador Alagoano (Maceió), December 30, 1855

200$000 reward to anyone who captures and brings to the Boa-Vista plantation in the district of Lorena, province of Sao Paulo, the mulatto Camillo, who ran away on the 14th of the present month and belongs to Major Manoel de Freitas Novaes.

Also will pay all expenses of the journey, etc., up to the time of delivery, the aforementioned mulatto having the following features: about 45 years of age, tall in stature, speaks with a high voice and always looks frightened, has some teeth missing in front and lettering on his forehead and on the palms of his hand which says: "Slave of Dona Fortunata," always wearing on his head a cap or handkerchief to hide the letters on his forehead. He wore trousers of woven cloth, a waistcoat of black cloth, a shirt of calico or shirt cloth, and a cloth jacket and poncho. He likes to boast that he is free. He is a master carpenter, sailor, and a coffee, cane sand hydraulic-work machinist....

All authorities and planters are asked to help capture the said slave, and not to trust the submissiveness with which he tries to deceive people of good faith in order to get away.

Diario de Rio de Janeiro, March 24, 1872

Questions to Consider

1. Do these advertisements give you any insights into why slaves fled their masters?
2. What do the advertisements tell you about how slaves acted around white people?
3. Many slaves in the southern United States escaped through the "Underground Railroad." Was there a similar network in Brazil? How do you think slaves survived in Brazil once they escaped?

From Robert Edgar Conrad, *Children of God's Fire: A Documentary History of Black Slavery in Brazil* (University Park, Pennsylvania: Pennsylvania State University Press, 1984), pp. 362–365.

Slaves labored on the *fazendas* or sugar plantations on its northeast coast, the southeastern coffee plantations, and the southern cattle ranches. Working conditions were brutal and the slave mortality rate was high. New shipments of African slaves were constantly required to replenish the labor force. As coffee production dramatically increased in the 1840s, the main port for slave imports shifted from Bahia (bah-EE-ah) in the northeast to Rio de Janeiro in the south.

The British government by this time was opposed to the slave trade and tried to prevent ships from bringing additional slaves into Brazil, but an agreement that it negotiated with Brazil to end the slave trade by 1830 had little effect. Slavers—with the open support of the Brazilian government—found ways to evade British antislavery squadrons and brought over 500,000 slaves from Africa in the 1830s and 1840s alone.

Unlike the United States, there was little division within Brazil's ruling elite about the necessity for slavery. They generally shared the view that there was no alternative to slave labor. Their justification was that African slaves were much better off in Brazil than they had been in Africa and that their living standard was better than European peasants. Pedro II freed his own slaves in 1840, but was cautious about taking on the plantation aristocracy over slavery. Even the handful of abolitionists did not argue for an immediate end to slavery. In 1850, the British government brought the issue to a head by instructing its navy to aggressively blockade the Brazilian coast and enter Brazilian waters if necessary. Faced with the choice of risking war with Britain, then the world's greatest naval power, or abolishing the trade, the emperor decreed an end to the slave trade the following year.

The institution of slavery, however, lingered on for almost more four decades. When the United States freed slaves at the end of the Civil War, Brazil was the largest slave-owning country in the world, which gave it an image as a backward country. Pedro II publicly announced his opposition to slavery, but he still feared a backlash from the slave-owning elite if he abolished it. His compromise was to begin a gradual process of ending slavery through an 1871 measure stating that children of slave mothers would no longer be defined as slaves. However, they would be bound to their mothers' owners until they reached 21.

Because of this regulation, the slave population shrank from 2.5 million in 1850 to 1 million in 1874. In the 1870s, coffee plantation owners made up for the lost labor by actively recruiting several hundred thousand European immigrants, especially from southern Europe, in the belief that they would be more productive workers and better consumers than slaves.

The attitudes of the Brazilian elite toward slavery began to shift in the 1880s because of the belief that newly arrived slaves from Africa were responsible for an outbreak of yellow fever. They were also alarmed by slave rebellions in the northeast and a series of mass escapes of slaves who began forming their own communities known as *quilombos* (kee-LOHM-bohs). On May 13, 1888, 2 years after Cuba freed its slaves, Pedro finally freed the remaining 650,000 slaves without any compensation going to slave owners. By that time, there were a growing number of Brazilians who wanted to modernize the country on many different levels and who were questioning the continued relevance of the monarchy. Military officers and republicans forced the emperor to abdicate in a virtually bloodless coup in 1889, and he and his family left for exile in Portugal.

Other Latin American Nations

Political turmoil, geographical handicaps, and racial disunity all played a part in the development of the other new nations in Latin America. Bolivia, named so hopefully for the Liberator, Simón Bolívar, underwent countless revolutions. Peru's course was almost as futile. The state of Gran Colombia dissolved by 1830, and its successors—Colombia, Venezuela, and Ecuador—were plagued by instability and civil wars. Paraguay endured a series of dictatorships, and Uruguay, created in 1828 as a buffer between Argentina and Brazil, long suffered from interventions by those two countries.

Chile also followed the model of having a strong presidency and a weak legislature. However, when President Jose Balmaceda dissolved Congress in 1890, he provoked Congress members into establishing their own government. After their forces defeated Balmaceda in a short civil war, they established a "Parliamentary Republic" that ruled Chile until 1920. However, this government was stymied by a political stalemate as it lurched from one crisis to another. An earthquake, working class unrest, and several economic depressions sapped the country until a military coup in 1924.

Central America narrowly escaped becoming part of Mexico in 1822. After a failed 15-year effort to create a Central American confederation, Guatemala, El Salvador, Honduras, Nicaragua, and Costa Rica asserted their independence. Except for Costa Rica, where whites comprised the bulk of the population, racial disunity delayed the development of national feeling. On the Caribbean island of Hispaniola, the Dominican Republic, after decades of submission to the more populous but equally underdeveloped Haiti, maintained a precarious independence. The other Caribbean islands remained under foreign dominance—British, Dutch, Spanish, or French—and served their European masters as a source of raw materials—especially coffee, sugar, and tobacco—and later as coaling stations for their steam-powered navies.

Latin America, 1875–1914

Why was Mexico the only Latin American country to undergo a revolution in the first half of the twentieth century?

Limited Political and Economic Reform

At the end of the nineteenth century, politicians who professed to be liberals were ascendant in many Latin American nations such as Mexico, where Porfirio Díaz ruled for over three decades, and Argentina, where

▲ Nitrates being mined in the Atacama Desert of northern Chile. Control of this valuable export trade could occasionally lead to war, as it did in the War of the Pacific (1879–1883), in which Chile defeated Peru and Bolivia.

General Julio Roca and a series of politicians who represented the landowning elite took command of government. More nations were experiencing political stability, but they were still controlled by large landowners.

CASE STUDY Brothers in Arms: Comparative Politics and Revolution

The liberals' influence seemed to place them in a position to open up political systems to new voices, but this was not to be. Ultimately, the liberals were more concerned with stability and order than they were to their own political ideals. Most notably, the liberals failed to live up to the principles of political accountability and free market economics. Rather than act on these principles, they expanded the powers of the executive office of government—making this office less accountable to voters and the other branches of government. Liberals also sought to break Latin America's dependence on the export of raw resources to Europe and the United States by establishing government-owned enterprises to oversee key industries such as oil and steel or raising tariffs on imported goods to protect local manufacturers.

The primary challenge to the old ruling elite, then, came not from the traditional liberals of Latin American, but from the growing urban middle class of civil servants, professionals, and shopkeepers as well as an urban working class. These new groups and classes became more assertive in political life in the later nineteenth century. In Argentina, immigrant workers brought with them the ideas of European anarchists, socialists, and communists and founded new organizations and trade unions. The middle class sought a voice in government circles and lobbied for the extension of the vote to more men. However, voting rights meant very little when elections were fraudulent or rigged. Some women also lobbied for equal rights under the law, but voting rights for women did not become a significant issue in Latin America until after World War I.

In the late nineteenth and early twentieth centuries, Latin American countries exported more crops and mineral resources in exchange for manufactured goods. A high percentage of the exports went to four leading industrializing nations: Great Britain, France, Germany, and the United States. Large-scale railway construction, often financed by foreign investors, helped fuel this expansion. Railways helped unify nations that were divided by regional loyalties and made it possible to export crops and minerals cheaply. However, as more land was opened up for cultivation, it was often at the expense of Indians whose land was either bought up or confiscated by large landowners. This was a major cause of peasant uprisings in many countries and a contributor to the Mexican Revolution of 1910.

Most Latin American economies did little to diversify their exports and create their own industries. Although the volume of exports expanded, most national economies remained tied to a few exports. Cuba, Puerto Rico, and the Dominican Republic relied on sugar; Uruguay and Argentina on wool, beef, and wheat; Chile on nitrates and copper; Bolivia on tin, Brazil on rubber, coffee and sugar; and Central American states on coffee and bananas (hence, the origin of

President Porfirio Díaz sought to stabilize and modernize Mexico, but his tenure as president from 1877-1880 and 1884-1911 was essentially a dictatorship and established the conditions for the Mexican Revolution.

the term *banana republic*). When international trade was booming, Latin American economies prospered, but inevitably, when there were downturns, they did not have the ability to cushion the blows. It was not until the 1930s that some countries such as Brazil began to promote industrialization by raising tariffs on imported manufactured goods to protect local industries. Although British capital accounted for about 60 percent of international investment by World War I, U.S. investments were rapidly expanding into Mexican mines and railways and Cuban sugar plantations.

Mexico

Mexico's political life in the last decades of the nineteenth century was dominated by Porfirio Díaz (DEE-ahs; 1830–1915), a mestizo from Oaxaca. As a military officer, he had served in numerous campaigns in Mexico's rural areas, including Cinqo de Mayo. He unsuccessfully contested several presidential elections before a coup in 1876 gave him the opportunity to take power. Elected president the following year, he ruled for all but 4 years between 1877 and 1911. A pragmatic but ruthless political manager, he was a master of patron-client relations and balancing the interests of regional caudillos with the Mexico City elite that filled his administration. Wary of the army as a potential threat to his rule, he slashed its size and brought it under state control. He relied more on an upgraded police force to keep order and rid the countryside of bandits.

Díaz's priorities were to create a stable political environment and to attract foreign investment by modernizing the legal and banking systems and business and mining codes. For advice on these matters, he consulted the *cientificos* or technocrats who wanted to modernize Mexico based on the American model. The government poured money into its schools, expanding free education to all Mexicans and encouraging literacy programs. It also constructed a hydraulic system that brought water to Mexico City.

Díaz's economic policies were enormously successful, at least up until the last years of his presidency. Under his rule, exports increased ninefold. North American investment soared from $30 million in 1883 to $1 billion in 1909, and British investment jumped from 32 million pounds in 1880 to 90 million pounds in 1910. American firms took advantage of a new mining code allowing private ownership of mines and assumed control of gold, silver, lead, copper, and zinc production. About one-third of foreign investment flowed to railway construction, which boomed during this period. By 1910, Mexico had 15,000 miles of railways compared to only 400 miles when Díaz took office. The new railways not only stimulated harbor expansions and the creation of new commercial centers and regional identities, but also helped create a national identity. In addition, it spurred the commercialization of land near railway lines as large hacienda owners expanded their land holdings often at the expense of small landowners.

The Mexican Revolution of 1910

The seeds for the Mexican Revolution were sown during the latter years of Díaz's long rule. Although his policies may have ushered in a period of unprecedented political stability and economic growth, they could not withstand a series of crises that began with a depression that hit Mexico in 1907 and a downturn in the American economy. Especially hard hit were the provinces of northern Mexico. Lower prices for Mexican exports contributed to the failure of many small businesses and massive unemployment as many workers lost their jobs in mines, farms, ranches, and textile factories. Significant strikes took place among railway and textile factory workers. Peasants deeply resented the loss of their land to commercial landowners. Food riots broke out in some cities.

More and more Mexicans were growing dissatisfied and disillusioned with the Díaz regime and were prepared for dramatic change.

Although the 80-year-old ruler had been a master of patronage and buying off competing interest groups and playing potential successors off against each other, Díaz refused to leave office of his own accord and he made no provision for a peaceful handover of power. But because of the depressed economy, he could no longer reward the beneficiaries of his rule. The *cientificos* wanted to create a national political party, while his regional caudillos were holding on to their narrow power bases.

In the election of 1910, Díaz had to fend off a strong challenge from Francisco Madero (1873–1913). Educated in Paris and the University of California at Berkeley and the son of one of Mexico's richest families, Madero courageously called for an end to Díaz's "boss rule." Although Díaz was easily reelected, he jailed Madero and numerous opposition members for refusing to recognize his regime's legitimacy. Madero moved to San Antonio, Texas, and from there, he mobilized opposition to Díaz. In late 1910, he issued the **Plan of San Luis Potosi,** which called for democracy, workers' rights, and land reform. His manifesto inspired many groups in Mexico to launch a rebellion against the Díaz regime. Madero—along with Emiliano Zapata (zah-PAH-tah; c. 1877–1923), leader of mestizos and Indians in the south, and Francisco "Pancho" Villa (VEE-yah) and Pasqual Orozco (oh-ROHS-koh), leaders with peasant, cowboy, and farm labor support in the north—carried out the first phase of the revolution. Joined by a band of 130 revolutionaries, Madero crossed the border into Mexico and, with the U.S. government turning a blind eye to his army buying weapons from American arms dealers, established a provisional government. As the rebel forces gained strength, Díaz realized his time was up and negotiated a peaceful exit. Leaving for exile in Paris, he warned: "Francisco Madero has unleashed a tiger; now let's see if he can tame it."[2]

Díaz's words were prophetic. Madero easily won a democratic election and tried to establish his own rule. But he did not reward key supporters such as Villa and Zapata, and his proposed reform of state-owned land was a failure. A Mexican bank and an American businessman ended up buying most of the land Madero had made available because the peasants did not have the resources to purchase it. Madero's military chief of staff and a former supporter of Díaz, General Victoriano Huerta, had him murdered in 1913. But Huerta's rule lasted less than a year before he was ousted by a coalition of Villa, Zapata, and Venustiano Carranza (kahr-RAHN-sah; 1859–1920).

Plan of San Luis Potosi—A manifesto issued by Francisco Madero in 1910 that called on Mexicans to overthrow the Díaz regime and supported democratic rights and land reform.

The power vacuum in Mexico City touched off a 3-year civil war that pitted Villa and Zapata against Carranza and his leading general, Álvero Obregón (OH-bray-GOHN). Although Carranza and Obregón were staunch nationalists, they were less radical than Villa and Zapata, and that won them the grudging support of the U.S. government, which supplied them with modern weapons and ammunition. The Americans had intervened before against Villa in 1916 after he staged a raid into New Mexico; they later sent in an expeditionary force under General John Pershing that ultimately aroused widespread opposition from Mexicans. Pershing's units returned to American soil a dismal failure. Carranza's forces eventually wore down the resistance of Villa and Zapata, who operated from their respective strongholds in the north and south. The cost in human life was immense. An estimated one million people died in this phase of the revolution. Indeed, few leaders of the revolution died peacefully. Zapata was assassinated in 1919, and Villa 4 years later.

Cathedral on the Zocalo, Mexico City

Despite Carranza's opposition, a constitutional convention drafted a progressive new constitution in 1917 that provided for a strong president that could not be reelected after a 6-year term, an independent judiciary, the right of the government to expropriate land, state control of all resources below the ground such as water and oil, the separation of church and state and the ending of religious education, the legalization of trade unions, an eight-hour work day, and the right of women to divorce. The latter was a major change for a country where marriage was the norm and women were expected to live contentedly in male-dominated households. Many of these provisions, however, were not implemented in the short term.

The Mexican Revolution was the first major revolution of the twentieth century, and along with the Russian Revolution of 1917, set precedents for twentieth-century revolutionary movements throughout Latin America, Africa, and Asia.

	The Mexican Revolution
1910	Madero issues Plan of San Luis Potosi
1911	Ousting of Porfirio Díaz
1913	Overthrow of Francisco Madero
1914	Overthrow of Victoriano Huerta
1917	New constitution adopted
1919	Emiliano Zapata assassinated
1923	Pancho Villa assassinated
1934	Land reform by Lazaro Cárdenas

Argentina

Argentina's political system in the late nineteenth century was authoritarian with some trappings of democracy. Liberal politicians, primarily drawn from the landowning aristocracy known as the "Oligarchy," dominated Argentina's political affairs. The 1800 individuals who owned most of the land believed in their right to run government. They made the decisions among themselves in the executive offices and regularly ignored the legislature. Elections were rife with fraud and vote buying. It was claimed that even the dead came to life to cast their ballots on election days.

Argentine politics shifted in the early twentieth century and became a struggle between the economic power of the landowning elite and the electoral clout of the growing urban working and middle classes. A decisive change in electoral politics came after a reform law was passed in 1912 that provided for universal adult suffrage for males over the age of 18, a secret ballot, and compulsory voting. The reform was designed to co-opt the growing middle class into the political system, but the Radical party that represented the middle class won the next election. Although the Radical party initially reached out for the support of the working class, they turned against labor after harshly repressing a general strike in 1919.

Many working class immigrants were drawn to socialist ideas. Anarchists and syndicalists were initially responsible for organizing among the working class, but after World War I, they lost ground to the Socialist party, which advocated bringing about change through the electoral process, and the Communist party, which focused its energies on building workers' organizations.

Between 1880 and World War I, Argentina prospered from a booming economy that grew at least 5 percent a year. Railway construction into the interior opened up production in the pampas, which contain perhaps the most fertile land in the world for growing wheat and lush grazing land for cattle and sheep. In the first half of the nineteenth century, cattle ranches primarily exported hides and beef jerky, which were mainly sold to feed slave populations in Brazil and the Caribbean. The beef industry dramatically took off with the development of steamships. The introduction of refrigerated ships around 1880 made it feasible to transport enormous quantities of fresh beef to Europe within several weeks. Two other leading exports were wool and wheat. Because the latter required many additional laborers, wheat farmers looked to the new immigrants who were pouring into the country.

▼ *Soldaderas* (sohl-dah-DEH-rahs) were female soldiers who actively participated in the armies fighting against the Díaz regime during the Mexican Revolution. Most were caregivers, collecting food, preparing meals, nursing the wounded, and washing clothes, but some took up arms and served as combatants.

Seeing Connections

The Paris of the Pampas

Argentina's affluent families were made up of landowners, businessmen, and professionals. They dominated Buenos Aires's social life, frequenting the same clubs and sending their children to elite schools. Conscious of their European identity, they followed cultural trends in Europe and patterned their dress, culture, and schools on European models. They built luxurious residences, with architecture inspired by Italian and French designs, and filled their homes with furniture imported from Europe. In the 1880s, the Argentine elite promoted the transformation of Buenos Aires's center, where most of them lived, by copying the changes that Baron Haussman implemented in Paris in the 1850s. Sections of downtown Buenos Aires were leveled and four broad avenues were constructed. Buenos Aires became known as the "Paris of the Pampas."

The intimate commercial relationship with Britain and other European countries, which lasted until after World War II, affected nearly every aspect of Argentine life. Foreign money, especially British capital, helped develop a sophisticated infrastructure; port facilities, railroads, light industry, and urban conveniences were among the most advanced in the world.

The expansion of the economy depended on a huge influx of European immigrants who settled in the rural areas, where they worked as labor tenants and wage laborers, and in Buenos Aires, where they worked in meatpacking plants, as dockworkers in the service sector, and in the civil service. Between 1870 and World War I, 3 million European immigrants—almost one-half were Italians and 32 percent were Spanish-speaking—arrived in Argentina. They made up almost one-third of Argentina's population.

The immigration policies were consciously designed to "Europeanize" the country. In Argentina and other countries such as Brazil, elites shared a common belief that Europeans immigrants were superior to people of Indian and African descent because of their work ethic and entrepreneurial skills. Many immigrants settled in Buenos Aires, which steadily grew in size. By 1936, its population was 2.5 million, which made it the third largest city in the Western Hemisphere after New York and Chicago. Despite its location on a monotonous plain beside a muddy estuary, it developed into a beautiful and vibrant city. Although buildings reflected all sorts of architectural styles, the upper class of Buenos Aires identified with Paris and promoted the construction of elegant, wide boulevards. They emulated the European gentry, living grandly in French-styled palaces and closely following Parisian fashion trends.

Conditions were very different for many of the new immigrants who also shaped the character of Buenos Aires. By 1914, they comprised two-thirds of the city's population. Most were workers who lived in slums on the city's outskirts or in dilapidated tenements around the city. They were largely single men with few prospects for finding marriageable partners. They frequented the brothels that were found in every part of the city. Prostitution was legal then and enjoyed the protection of the police and prominent politicians. From the brothels came a sensuous dance, the tango. The lyrics of tango songs reflected the immigrant men's anguish over their rootlessness and loneliness as well as their misogynistic views of "loose" women. The typical tango, as lyricist Santos Discépolo characterized it, was "a sad thought that is danced."[3]

The tango gained widespread acceptance after professional dancers and amateur bands adopted it; before World War I, it won even more respectability as it was popularized in Europe. After prostitution was banned in Argentina following the war, the tango moved from brothels to cabarets. The content of the lyrics shifted to express the confusion men felt at the growing assertiveness and independence of women. One tango song expressed this sentiment:

Before women were feminine,
now fashion has thrown all that out.
Before only the face and foot showed,
but now they show all there is to be seen.
Today all the women seem to be men,
they smoke, drink whisky, and wear pants.[4]

With the spread of radios in the 1930s, tango songs developed a mass following among women.

Brazil

The military officers who overthrew the monarchy in 1889 claimed that they were acting on behalf of all the citizens. But the officers were not social revolutionaries, and they promptly moved to increase their salaries and the army's size. Although they were the real rulers of the new United States of Brazil, they allowed the drafting of a new constitution patterned on the federalism of the United States. The constitution gave considerable autonomy to regions but also created a powerful chief executive who was elected for one term every 4 years. Congress did little to hold the president in check.

In 1894, the army removed itself from politics and the first civilian president was elected, although only 2 percent of the total population was allowed to participate in the vote. The centers of power of the First Republic (1889–1930) were São Paolo, with its coffee plantations contributing about 30 percent of Brazil's GNP, and Minas Gerais (MEE-nahs zhee-RAIS), which was dominated by large ranches. The cattle barons and coffee plantation aristocracy who ran these provinces eventually came to an understanding called the café-com-leite (coffee with milk), in which these regions alternately selected presidents.

In the late nineteenth century, Brazil's economy revolved around two products, coffee and rubber. Together they accounted for 80 percent of Brazil's exports. Brazil produced 80 percent of the world's coffee, and much of its rubber, from the Amazon River valley, went to the growing American automobile industry.

The end of slavery paved the way for opening Brazil to a steady flow of European immigrants. That fit well with the desire of Brazil's largely European elite to "whiten" the country. Between 1890 and 1930, 3 million immigrants—most of them from Italy, Portugal, and Spain—arrived in the country. Most settled in São Paolo and in other coastal cities.

The immigrants' arrival coincided with a move to modernize and clean up the larger cities such as Rio de Janeiro, whose population doubled between 1872 and 1890 to over half a million people. Telephone lines, streetcars, and water, sewage, and gas lines were introduced in the 1880s. The city's image suffered, however, because of its association with mosquitoes and yellow fever. A public health campaign was implemented to eradicate the mosquitoes, and officials set out to redesign the city. As in Buenos Aires, the upper class emulated the Parisian model and backed the building of several grand boulevards that opened up the downtown area but also destroyed working-class tenements.

The United States

Why were the North and South unable to resolve the question of slavery without going to war?

Free Land and Unfree People

A new player entered the Western political game in the nineteenth century, the former British colony of United States. The revolutionary movements in Europe during the nineteenth century fought aristocratic domination or foreign rule—or both. The nineteenth-century struggles in the United States were not quite the same. Instead, there were two major related problems. One was the annexation, settlement, and development of land occupied by Native Americans; the other was slavery. Free land and unfree people were the sources of the many political confrontations that culminated in the Civil War, the greatest struggle of nineteenth-century America.

At the conclusion of its successful revolution in 1783, the United States was not a democracy. When the constitution of the new nation was ratified, only one male in seven had the vote. Religious requirements and property qualifications ensured that only a small elite participated in government. These restrictions allowed patricians from established families in the South and men of wealth and substance in the North to control the country for nearly half a century.

Democratic Advances

The influence of the western frontier helped make America more democratic. Even before the constitu-

Discovery Through Maps

An American View of the World in the 1820s

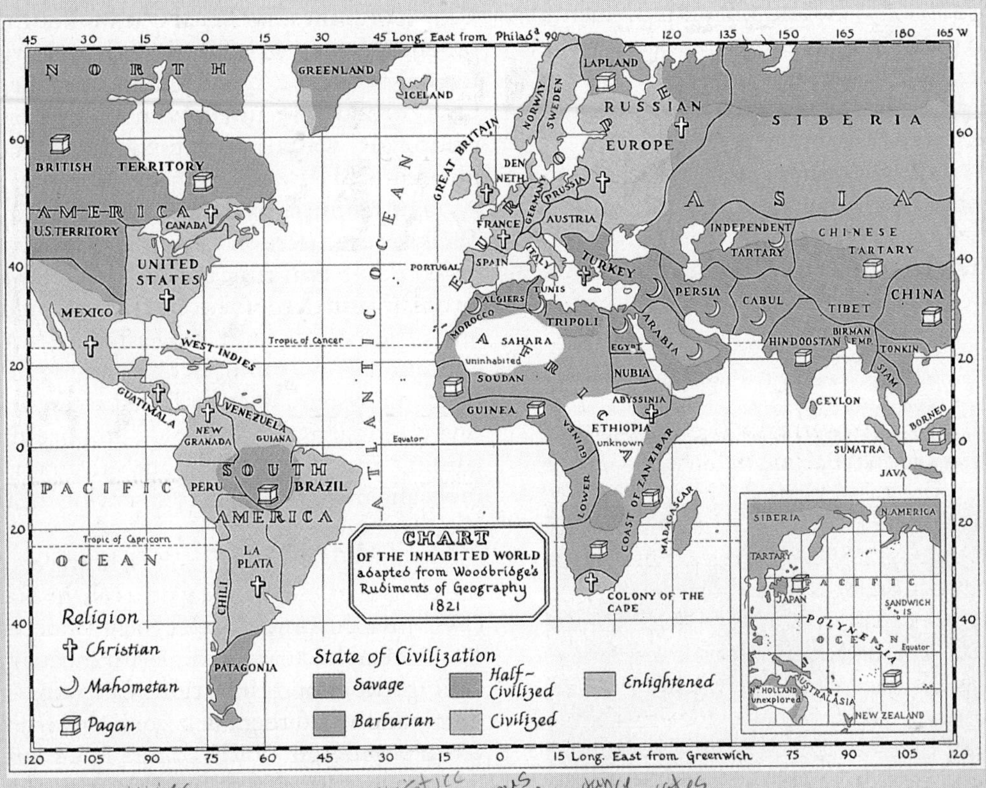

This map, adapted from *The School Atlas to Accompany Woodbridge's Rudiments of Geography* (1821), served to inform students of the status of "civilization" in the world. The color code establishes where the authors believed the various gradations of humanity were: from the "civilized" and "enlightened" to the "savage," with the "barbarians" and "half-civilized" in between. The mapmakers were apparently quite certain that regions where white-skinned Christians were to be found were civilized or at least half-civilized (though they seem to have had their doubts about adherents of Orthodox Christianity in eastern Europe). The people where Islam predominated ranged from half-civilized to barbarian. And much of China, with its four millennia of culture, was classified as barbarian, owing to its "pagan" belief systems.

A complacent arrogance permeates this map, with the area west of the 95th meridian, populated largely by Native Americans, declared to be a savage state, waiting patiently for manifest destiny to bring civilization. Much of Central and South America is admitted to being civilized—but not enlightened. Note also that the cartographer uses Philadelphia as the prime meridian—preferable, he surely thought, to the more traditional but distant Greenwich, a town in England which, after all, had invaded the United States only a decade earlier.

The map shows the dominant role played by religion in viewing the rest of the world in the first part of the nineteenth century. Later, concepts of race would dominate the American worldview, and after 1945, the world would be seen in terms of the Cold War, those areas determined to be democratic and communistic. By the end of the twentieth century, American maps emphasized industrial capacities and potential markets. After September 11, 2001, yet another shift came as the cartographers identified zones where terrorists threatened American interests. Through their emphases, cartographers tell us as much about the spirit of an age as writers and artists.

Questions to Consider

1. After studying this map, what elements do you believe moved the cartographer to identify an area as civilized?
2. When you look at the globe and consider its complexity, what elements do you use to differentiate one area from another?
3. What is the difference between being "civilized" and "enlightened"?

tion was ratified, thousands of pioneers crossed the Appalachian Mountains into the new "western country." In the West, land was to be had for the asking, and social caste did not exist—one white person was as good as another—and the indigenous Native Americans came to be seen as an irritant at the least or as a danger to be fought at the most. Vigor, courage, self-reliance, and competence counted, not birth or wealth. Ironically, throughout the nineteenth century, the West was the source of new and liberal movements that challenged the conservative ideas prevalent in the East and South, while at the same time serving as the arena for the uprooting of the Native Americans and the destruction of their way of life.

Until the War of 1812, democracy grew slowly. In 1791, Vermont had been admitted as a manhood suffrage state, in which all men could vote, and the following year, Kentucky followed suit; but Tennessee, Ohio, and Louisiana entered the Union with property and tax qualifications for the vote. After 1817, no new state entered the Union with restrictions on male suffrage except for those regarding slaves. Most appointive offices became elective and requirements for holding office were liberalized.

▼ In many regards, Andrew Jackson was the first "people's president," a national leader who looked beyond the demands of the eastern elites to the entire country. Jackson's craggy countenance projects his inner strength and independent spirit.

Andrew Jackson changed the tone and emphasis of American politics. In 1828, he was elected to the presidency following a campaign that featured the slogan "Down with the aristocrats!" He was the first president produced by the West, the first since George Washington not to have a college education, and the first to have been born in poverty. He owed his election to no congressional clique but rather to the will of the people, who idolized "Old Hickory" as their spokesman and leader.

The triumph of the democratic principle in the 1830s set the direction for political development. With Jackson's election came the idea that any man, by virtue of being an American citizen, could hold any office in the land. Governments widened educational opportunities by enlarging the public school system. With increased access to learning, class barriers became less important. The gaining and keeping of political power came more and more to be tied to satisfying the needs of the people who voted.

DOCUMENT The Seneca Falls Convention

Andrew Jackson's victories, however, symbolized the change of life for the worse for the Native Americans. After the United States gained independence, the government had tried to deal with them by placing the various tribes on reservations to control their movements and to aid them in becoming "civilized." As the white population of the United States grew, and the reservation land east of the Mississippi became more valuable, a policy of removal was implemented by leaders such as Jackson. The rationale behind the policy was that the Native Americans, being fundamentally incapable of civilization, should be pushed West into the empty lands. This policy broke the treaties signed at the end of the eighteenth century, which respected the tribes as politically sovereign peoples. Up and down the western frontier, tribes which had entertained friendly relations with the United States under treaty rights found themselves pushed out of their lands. There were tragedies such as that of the "Trail of Tears" in 1838–1839, when 16,000 Cherokees were forced to leave their homes in the southeast United States. They were rounded up in military stockades where they lived under wretched conditions, and then they were forced to walk to the present-day state of Oklahoma. More than 5000 of them died during those 2 tragic years.

But for the white population, simultaneous with the growth of democracy came the territorial expansion of the country. The Louisiana Territory, purchased from France for about $15 million in 1803 (see Chapter 21), doubled the size of the United

Document

Susan Anthony, On Women's Right to Vote

Susan B. Anthony (1820–1906), a leading campaigner for women's suffrage and abolition, summed up her beliefs in the statement: "Men, their rights and nothing more; women, their rights and nothing less." Attempting to vote in a presidential election, she was arrested on November 5, 1872, in Rochester, New York. At her trial, she argued that her act was legal because the U.S. Constitution did not restrict citizenship to males. Found guilty, she never paid the $100 fine for her offense. However, it took almost another half century before women received the vote through the adoption of the Nineteenth Amendment to the U.S. Constitution in August 1920.

Friends and fellow citizens: I stand before you tonight under indictment for the alleged crime of having voted at the last presidential election, without having a lawful right to vote. It shall be my work this evening to prove to you that in thus voting, I not only committed no crime, but, instead simply exercised my citizen's rights, guaranteed to me and all United States citizens by the National Constitution beyond the power of any State to deny....

The preamble of the Federal Constitution says:

> We the people of the United States, in order to form a more perfect union, establish justice, insure domestic tranquility, provide for the common defense, promote the general welfare, and secure the blessings of liberty to ourselves and our posterity, do ordain and establish this Constitution for the United States of America.

It was we, the people of the United States, not we, the white male citizens, nor yet we, the male citizens, but we, the whole people, who formed the Union. And we formed it, not to give the blessings of liberty, but to secure them; not to the half of ourselves and the half of our posterity, but to the whole people—women as well as men. It is downright mockery to talk to women of their enjoyment of the blessings of liberty while they are denied the use of the only means of securing them provided by this democratic republican government—the ballot....

For any state to make sex a qualification that must ever result in the disfranchisement of one entire half of the people, is to pass a bill of attainder, an ex post facto law, and is therefore a violation of the supreme law of the land. By it the blessings of liberty are forever withheld from women and their female posterity....

For them this government has no just powers derived from the consent of the government. For them this government is not a democracy; it is not a republic. It is the most odious aristocracy ever established on the face of the globe. An oligarchy of wealth, where the rich govern the poor; an oligarchy of learning, where the educated govern the ignorant, or even an oligarchy of race, where the Saxon rules the African, might be endured, but this oligarchy of sex, which makes father, brother, husband, sons, the oligarchs over the mother and sister, the wife and daughters, of every household; which ordains all men sovereigns, all women subjects—carries dissension, discord, and rebellion into every home of the nation....

The only question left to be settled now is: Are women persons? And I hardly believe any of our opponents will have the hardihood to say they are not. Being persons, then, women are citizens; and no state has a right to make any law, or to enforce any old law, that shall abridge their privileges or immunities. Hence, every discrimination against women in the constitution and laws of the several states is today null and void, precisely as is every one against Negroes.

Questions to Consider

1. Why did it take almost another half century before American women won the right to vote in 1920?
2. Compare Anthony's position on women's status in American society with Abigail Adams's views on the same subject expressed in her letter of 1776 (see p. 653).

From Ellen Dubois, ed., *The Elizabeth Cady Stanton–Susan B. Anthony Reader Correspondence, Writings, Speeches* (Boston: North-eastern University Press, 1981), pp. 152–154 and 157–158.

States. In 1844, Americans, influenced by **"manifest destiny"**—the belief that their domination of the continent was God's will—demanded "All of Oregon or none." The claim led to a boundary dispute with Great Britain over land between the Columbia River and 54°40′ north latitude. In 1846, the two countries accepted a boundary at the 49th parallel, and the Oregon Territory was settled. The annexation of Texas in 1845 was followed by war with Mexico in 1846. In the peace agreement signed 2 years later, Mexico ceded California, Texas, and the land between the two to the United States. As a result of these acquisitions, by 1860, the area of the United States was two-thirds larger than it had been in 1840.

manifest destiny—An early nineteenth-century belief voiced by clergymen in the northeast United States that God meant for white Americans to dominate the continent.

The addition of the new territories forced the issue of whether slavery should be allowed in those areas. Paralleling developments in Great Britain, abolitionists in the United States, particularly in New England, vigorously condemned slavery. Henry Clay's Missouri Compromise of 1820 permitted slavery in Missouri but forbade it in the rest of the Louisiana Purchase. This settlement satisfied both sides for only a short time.The antislavery forces grew more insistent. In the senatorial campaigns of 1858, candidate Abraham Lincoln declared:

> *A house divided against itself cannot stand. I believe this government cannot endure permanently half slave and half free. I do not expect the Union to be dissolved—I do not expect the house to fall—but I do expect it will cease to be divided. It will become all one thing, or all the other.*

By the 1850s, the North and the South had become separate societies. The North was industrial, urban, liberal, and democratic; the South was mainly agricultural, rural, conservative, and dominated by a planter aristocracy. The South strongly opposed the North's desire for higher tariffs, government aid for new rail-

Territorial Growth of the United States

1803	Louisiana Purchase (part or all of present-day Louisiana, Arkansas, Missouri, Iowa, Minnesota, North Dakota, South Dakota, Nebraska, Kansas, Oklahoma, Colorado, Wyoming, Montana)
1810–1819	Florida Cession (parts of present-day Alabama and Mississippi; all of present-day Florida)
1818	British Cession (parts of Minnesota and North Dakota)
1845	Annexation of Texas (part or all of present-day Texas, Oklahoma, Kansas, New Mexico, Colorado)
1846	Oregon Country (parts of present-day Montana, Idaho, Wyoming; all of present-day Oregon and Washington)
1848	Mexican Cession (part or all of present-day Colorado, New Mexico, Utah, Nevada, Arizona, California)
1853	Gadsden Purchase (parts of present-day New Mexico and Arizona)

▼ Taking advantage of Napoleon's sale of the Louisiana territory, a militarily weak Mexico, and an otherwise preoccupied Britain, the United States was able to attain—through financial transactions, diplomacy, and aggression—its continental limits by 1853.

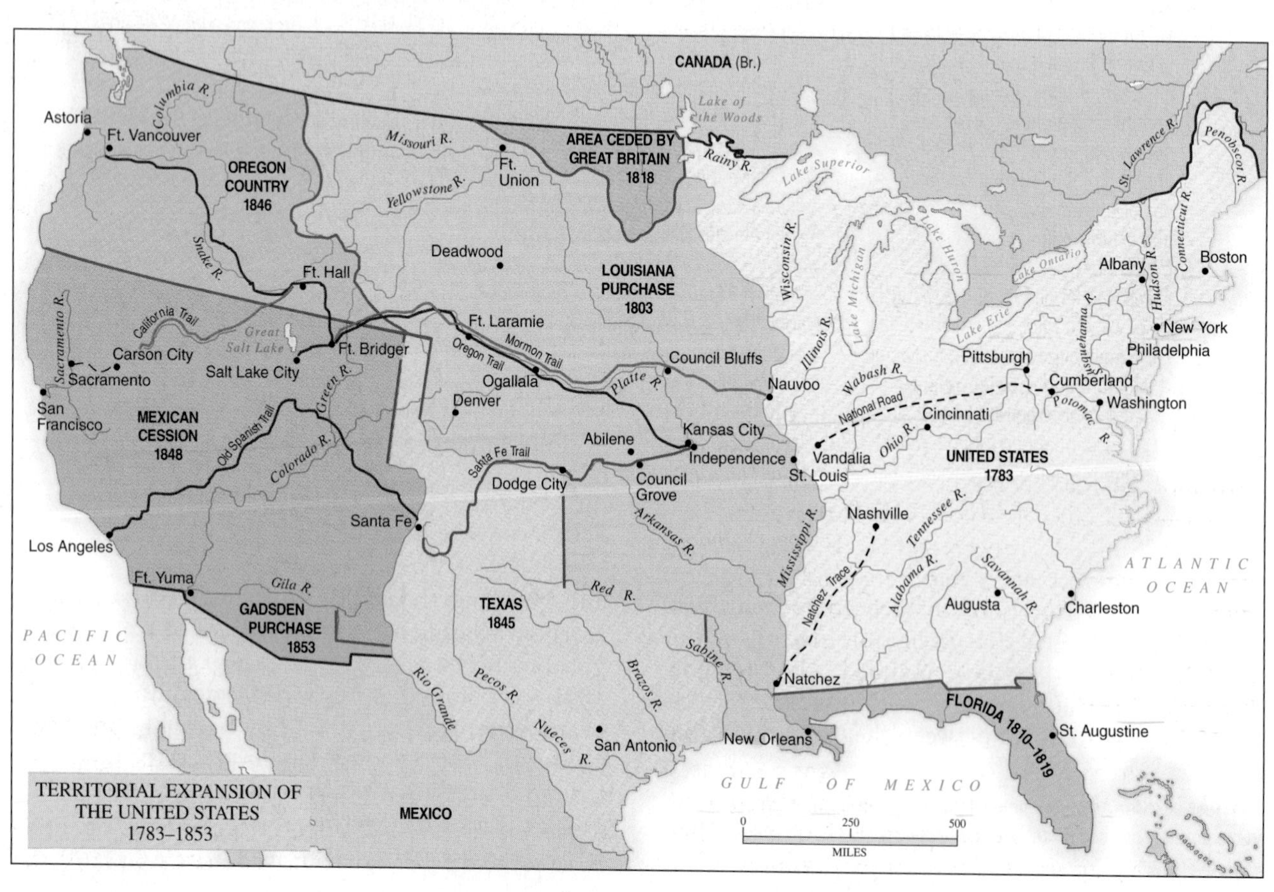

roads, and generous terms for land settlement in the West. Although these differences highlighted the very real differences and tensions separating the two regions, slavery was the driving force behind the war.

The Civil War and Its Results

Soon after Abraham Lincoln was elected as president, seven of the slaveholding southern states seceded from the Union and formed the Confederate States of America. Four more joined after the first shot of the Civil War was fired at Fort Sumter, South Carolina, on April 12, 1861, initiating the bloodiest war of American history. Four agonizing years of conflict—in which more than half a million men died and basic elements of the U.S. Constitution and law were suspended—ended when General Robert E. Lee surrendered to General Ulysses S. Grant at Appomattox Courthouse in Virginia on April 9, 1865. A few days later, the nation was stunned by the assassination of President Lincoln, who had just begun his second term.

With the final collapse of the Confederacy before the overwhelming superiority of the Union in manpower, industrial resources, and wealth, the Civil War became the grand epic of American history in its heroism, romance, and tragedy. The victorious North used military occupation to try to force the South to extend voting and property rights to the former slaves. Eventually, this so-called Reconstruction period (1865–1877) was ended by a tacit agreement between the Northern industrialists and the Southern white leaders that enabled the latter to regain political control and to deprive African Americans of their newly won rights. Later, Southerners invoked Social Darwinist arguments to justify their actions in denying full "blessings of freedom" to the former slaves.

In the century after Reconstruction, Southern politicians deprived African Americans of their voting rights by enacting state laws or employing devices such as poll taxes, literacy tests, property qualifications, and physical threats. Racial segregation in schools, restaurants, parks, and hotels was effectively applied. Laws prohibiting interracial marriage were enacted, and African Americans were generally excluded from unions. Between 1885 and 1918, more than 2500 African Americans were lynched in the United States. As second-class citizens, free but largely landless, the former slaves essentially formed a sharecropping class, mired in poverty, and deprived of educational opportunities. Not until the 1960s did the political steps occur that began to put into effect that which had been purchased in the sacrifices of the Civil War: full citizenship for African Americans.

If the causes and consequences of the American Civil War are complex, the all-important result was simple. It settled the issue of whether the United States was an indivisible sovereign nation or a collection of sovereign states. The sacrifice of hundreds of thousands of lives preserved the Union, but the mistreatment of African Americans remained.

▲ Isabella Baufree (c. 1797–1883) was born a slave in New York state and escaped her master in 1827. Taking the name Sojourner Truth, she became a prominent abolitionist. During the Civil War, she helped recruit African Americans to enlist in the Union army.

Industrialization, Abuse, and Reform

Between 1850 and 1880, the number of cities with a population of 50,000 or more doubled. The number of men employed in industry increased 50 percent. In 1865, there were 35,000 miles of railroads in the country. By 1900, this was estimated to be about 200,000—more than in all of Europe. In 1860, a little more than $1 billion was invested in manufacturing; by 1900 this figure had risen to $12 billion. The value of manufactured products increased proportionately. In 1870, the total production of iron and steel in the United States was far below that of France and Britain. Twenty years later, the United States had outstripped both and was producing about one-third of the world's iron and steel.

The North's victory was a boost for industrialization as well as a result of it, and the economic revolution in the United States that followed was more significant than the conflict itself. Railroads were built across broad prairies, and the first transcontinental line, the Union Pacific, was completed in 1869. Settlers swarmed west, breaking treaties with Native American tribes, altering the environmental balance that supported the lives of the Plains Indians, and destroying the way of life of the original inhabitants of the land.

In the age of rapid industrialism and materialistic expansion, many who pursued profits lost sight of ethical principles in business and in government. William "Boss" Tweed, the chief of the Department of Public Works for the city of New York, rewarded himself and his friends so lavishly through fraudulent contracts, payments under the table, and other corrupt activities that by 1871 he had driven the city to the brink of bankruptcy. Brought to trial, Tweed was convicted of stealing more than $200 million. Ruthless financiers such as Jay Gould and Jim Fisk tampered with the basic financial stability of the nation. The administration of President Ulysses Grant was tainted by scandals and frauds. A new rich class failed to appreciate its responsibilities to society. Corruption was a blatant feature of the new order.

For roughly a century, the gospel for the new nation of America had been rugged individualism. As in Europe, governmental interference in business was unwelcome because of the strong belief that individuals should be free to follow their own inclinations, run their own businesses, and enjoy the profits of their labors. In an expanding nation where land, jobs, and opportunity beckoned, there was little to indicate that the system would not work indefinitely. By 1880, however, the end of the frontier was in sight. Free land of good quality was scarce, and the frontier could no longer serve as a safety valve to release the economic and social pressures of an expanding population.

Between 1850 and 1900, the United States became the most powerful nation in the Western Hemisphere, increased its national wealth from $7 billion to $88 billion, established an excellent system of public education, and fostered the spread of civil liberties for its white citizens and other nations. But there were many disturbing factors in the picture. Unemployment, 10- to 12-hour workdays, child labor, and industrial accidents were common in the rapidly growing cities. Slums grew and served as breeding places for disease and crime. Strikes, often accompanied by violence, exacerbated the tension between labor and capital.

In response, the wide-ranging Progressive reform movement flourished between 1890 and 1914. This movement was rooted partly in the agrarian protests against big business sparked by the Populists of the South and the Mountain West. The Progressives effectively mobilized the middle classes to work to eliminate sweatshops, the exploitation of labor, and the abuse of natural resources.

The success of the Progressive movement was reflected in the constitutions of the new states admitted to the Union and in their introduction of the direct primary, the initiative and referendum, and the direct election of senators. All these measures tended to give the common people more effective control of the government. After the enactment of the Interstate Commerce Act in 1887, which introduced federal regulation over railroads, a steady expansion of governmental regulation of industry began.

As president of the United States from 1901 to 1909, Theodore Roosevelt launched an aggressive campaign to break up the trusts, conserve natural resources, and regulate railroads, food, and drugs. In 1913, President Woodrow Wilson started a militant campaign of reform called the "New Freedom." His administration reduced the tariff because it was too much the instrument of special economic privilege, enacted banking reform with the Federal Reserve Act of 1913, and regulated businesses in the public interest through the Clayton Antitrust Act and the establishment of the Federal Trade Commission, both in 1914.

In 1914, the United States had risen to the forefront of Western nations. The country's first census, taken in 1790, counted a population of just under 4 million; by 1910, the number was 99 million. During the nineteenth century, more than 25 million immigrants had made their way to America. Since the days of George Washington, the national wealth had increased at least a hundredfold. Once the producer of raw materials only, the United States by 1914 was producing more steel than Britain and Germany combined. A single company, United States Steel, was capitalized for $1.46 billion, a sum greater than the total estimated wealth of the country in 1790.

U.S. Foreign Policy

From the first, U.S. foreign policy pursued three goals: national security, trade, and the spread of democracy—and these goals remain largely intact today. During its first quarter century, the United States fought a brief naval war with France, became embroiled with Britain in the War of 1812, and sent two expeditions to the Mediterranean to deal with the Barbary pirates. These complications notwithstanding, Americans spent the next century developing their country. Thomas Jefferson summarized the country's foreign policy with these words: "Peace, commerce, and honest friendship with all nations—entangling alliances with none."[5]

When the country established new foreign contacts, it went across the Pacific. In 1844, the United States

▲ Theodore Roosevelt, one of the most flamboyant and effective presidents in the history of the United States, provided cartoonists at the beginning of the twentieth century with almost unlimited possibilities for caricature. Here "T. R." is afflicting the monopolists who dominated the American economy.

made its first treaty with China, opening certain ports to American trade and securing the rights of American merchants and sailors to be tried in American tribunals in China. In 1853, Commodore Matthew Perry visited Japan and, by a show of force, persuaded the Japanese to open some of their harbors to Americans. By 1854, the United States was considering the annexation of the Hawaiian Islands, and in 1867, it purchased Alaska from Russia for the amazingly low price of $7.2 million.

As productivity increased after the Civil War, the United States was forced to seek new outlets for its goods, especially now that the domestic frontier had disappeared. Foreign trade increased from $393 million in 1870 to more than $1.33 billion in 1900. During the same period, investments abroad went from almost nothing to $500 million. This economical group was instrumental in the nation's acquisition of a global empire.

The United States began building a modern navy in 1883, and by 1890, the buildup had accelerated greatly. Care was taken not to alarm the country, however, and the new ships were officially known as "seagoing coastline battleships," a handy nautical contradiction. When this naval program was initiated, the U.S. navy ranked twelfth among the powers; by 1900, it had advanced to third place. This naval strength served American foreign policy well—particularly in Asia. In 1899, U.S. Secretary of State John Hay initiated the so-called Open Door policy regarding China, an attempt to ensure equal commercial rights for traders of all nations—including, of course, the United States, a latecomer to the China trade. When Chinese patriots fought against the intrusion of foreigners in the Righteous Harmony Fists (Boxer) Rebellion, the United States again took the lead in defending its new outward-looking stance.

Growing Involvement with Latin America

Although the Monroe Doctrine of 1823 declared Latin America off-limits to European colonization, the United States did not have the political or economic power to enforce its policy for many years. Instead, throughout most of the nineteenth century, Britain, through its economic activities, continued to have the most influence in the region. American interests in Mexico and Cuba, however, increased in the mid-nineteenth century after the Mexican-American War and as American sugar interests intensified their interest in annexing Cuba to the United States. American investors also began to look to Central America in their efforts to locate a faster route from the eastern United States to the newly opened gold fields of California.

As American economic power grew in the last few decades of the nineteenth century, so too did its influence in Latin America. Both American and Latin American business elites generally profited from these arrangements. President Theodore Roosevelt oversaw the introduction of what has been called **"dollar diplomacy,"** which coordinated the activities of American foreign investors and the U.S. Department of State to obtain and protect concessions for investors. From 1890, this policy won for American businesses concessions for products such as sugar, bananas, and oil from more than a dozen Latin American republics. Between 1897 and 1914, American investment in Latin America shot up from $1.641 million to $304.3 million. Much of this investment was in minerals and oil.

The growing importance of the United States was demonstrated in a border dispute between Britain and Venezuela in 1895. When Britain delayed submitting the issue to arbitration, the U.S. State Department took the initiative and delivered a blunt note to London warning the British that refusal to accept arbitration would have grave consequences. The State Department noted U.S. dominance in the Western Hemisphere and boasted that America's geographical position protected it from European pressures. Britain was preoccupied with the Boers

dollar diplomacy—A term associated with American foreign policy of the early twentieth century that used economic power to advance foreign policy goals and American business interests.

American newspapers' coverage of the war with Spain favored the government's imperial ambitions.

MAINE EXPLOSION CAUSED BY BOMB OR TORPEDO?

Capt. Sigsbee and Consul-General Lee Are in Doubt—The World Has Sent a Special Tug, With Submarine Divers, to Havana to Find Out—Lee Asks for an Immediate Court of Inquiry—260 Men Dead.

A SUPPRESSED DESPATCH TO THE STATE DEPARTMENT THE CAPTAIN SAYS THE ACCIDENT WAS MADE POSSIBLE BY AN ENEMY.

E. C. Pendleton, Just Arrived from Havana, Says He Overheard Talk There of a Plot to Blow Up the Ship—Capt. Zalinski, the Dynamite Expert, and Other Experts Report to The World that the Wreck Was Not Accidental—Washington Officials Ready for Vigorous Action if Spanish Responsibility Can Be Shown—Divers to Be Sent Down to Make Careful Examinations.

in South Africa, the Germans in Europe, and the French in the Sudan and thus could not argue too strenuously against the message. They agreed to resolve the dispute through arbitration.

In 1902–1903, Venezuela again became the subject of American concern. A dispute between Venezuela and a coalition formed by Germany, Great Britain, and Italy provoked the three European powers into blockading the Latin American country and even firing on some of the coastal fortifications to remind the Venezuelan dictator of his obligations to some of their nationals. President Roosevelt at first stood by, watching Venezuela take its punishment. He then became suspicious of German motives and began to match threat with threat, forcing the Europeans to back down and place the issue into international arbitration.

In 1898, the United States went to war with Spain over the way the Spaniards were ruling Cuba; the mistreatment of the Cubans also affected American business interests, especially in the sugar industry. The pretext for the war came when the American battleship *Maine* was blown up in Havana's harbor with the loss of 260 crewmen. American President McKinley justified the war "in the name of humanity, in the name of civilization, and on behalf of endangered American interests." Although the U.S. military worked cooperatively with Cuban rebels to defeat Spain, the rebels did not participate in the peace negotiations that established an American protectorate ruled by the U.S. military. Reconstruction favored American business interests, but it also addressed the threat posed by yellow fever, established a system of state education, and introduced local and national government structures with adult male suffrage.

Victory in the brief, dramatic, and well-publicized Spanish-American War won the United States recognition as a world power and possession of a conglomeration of islands in the Pacific Ocean and the Caribbean. The United States annexed Puerto Rico and placed the Philippines, which were halfway around the world, under American rule. Sensitive to accusations of imperialism in Cuba, in 1903 the U.S. government offered Cuba an imperfect, closely tutored independence in which the Cubans were obliged by law to acknowledge the right of the United States to intervene for the "preservation of Cuban independence" and the "maintenance of a government adequate for the protection of life, property, and individual liberty." The United States also retained land at Guantanamo (gwahn-TAH-nah-moh) Bay where a military base was established. These and other restrictions on Cuban independence were embodied in the **Platt Amendment** (1901) to the new Cuban constitution. Over the next several decades, the United States sent in the marines on numerous occasions to put down revolts or deal with corrupt governments.

Panama also came under American influence through the United States' desire to build a canal through the isthmus. The idea to build a canal to connect the Pacific and Atlantic oceans had been discussed for several centuries, but it was not until the 1870s that Ferdinand de Lesseps, the builder of the Suez Canal, formed a company to build such a canal. The effort collapsed in 1893 because of a lack of capital. The idea of a canal was revived after the Spanish-American War when the U.S. navy took stock of the new American empire and developed the concept of a two-ocean navy.

In 1901, the British ceded to the United States the exclusive right to control any canal that might be dug through the isthmus. For $40 million, the United States bought the rights of de Lesseps's company. A lease was negotiated with Colombia, through whose territory the canal would be built, but that country's senate refused to ratify the treaty, claiming the compensation was too small. Roosevelt is reputed to have responded, "I did not intend that any set of bandits should hold up Uncle Sam." The isthmus erupted in rebellion, encouraged and

IMAGE The Panama Canal

Platt Amendment—An amendment to a congressional bill named after Senator Oliver Platt that gave the United States the authority to intervene in Cuba to maintain order and its independence, to keep land at Guantanamo Bay, and to prevent Cuba from making treaties that gave another nation power over Cuba's internal affairs.

Document

José Marti's Observations on the United States and Cuba

Born in Havana, Cuba, José Marti (1853–1895) was a major figure in the Cuban independence struggle against Spain from his youth to his death in 1895 leading a force in the second Cuban war for independence. As a young person he was deported from Cuba for his antigovernment views on several occasions and lived in Spain, Mexico, and Central America before moving to the United States in 1880. He wrote columns for Latin American newspapers on his observations of every aspect of American life, including its political culture, corruption, literature, democratic values, and the contrasts between the rich and the poor. In this letter Marti published in the *New York Evening Post* (March 25, 1899), he responded to attacks in a Philadelphia newspaper, the *Manufacturer*, on Cubans, especially those living in the United States.

This is not the occasion to discuss the question of the annexation of Cuba. It is probable that no self-respecting Cuban would like to see his country annexed to a nation where the leaders of opinion share towards him the prejudices excusable only to vulgar jingoism or rampant ignorance. No honest Cuban will stoop to be received as a moral pest for the sake of the usefulness of his land in a community, where his ability is denied, his morality insulted, and his character despised. There are some Cubans who, from honorable motives, from an ardent admiration for progress and liberty, from a prescience of their own powers under better political conditions, from an unhappy ignorance of the history and tendency of annexation, would like to see the island annexed to the United States. But those who have fought in war and learned in exile, who have built by the work of hands and mind, a virtuous home in the heart of an unfriendly community, who by their successful efforts as scientists and merchants, as railroad builders and engineers, as teachers, artists, lawyers, journalists, orators and poets, as men of alert intelligence and uncommon activity, are honored wherever their powers have been called into action and the people are just enough to understand them, those who have raised, with their less prepared elements, a town of workingmen where the United States had previously a few huts in a barren cliff, those, more numerous than the others, do not desire the annexation of Cuba to the United States. They do not need it. They admired this nation, the greatest ever built by liberty, but they dislike the evil conditions that, like women in the heart, have begun in this mighty republic, their work of destruction. They have made of the heroes of this country their own heroes, and look to the success of the American commonwealth as the crowning glory of mankind, but they cannot honestly believe that excessive individualism, reverence for wealth, and the protracted exultation of a terrible victory are preparing the United States to be the typical nation of liberty, where no opinion is to be based in greed, and no triumph or acquisition reached against charity and justice. We have the country of Lincoln as much as we have the country of Cutting.

We are not the people of destitute vagrants or immoral pigmies that the *Manufacturer* is pleased to picture nor the country of petty talkers, incapable of action, hostile to hard work, that, in a mass with the other countries of Spanish America, we are by arrogant travelers and written represented to be....

The Cubans have, according to the *Manufacturer*, "a distaste for exertion"; they are "helpless," "idle." These "helpless," "idle" men came here twenty years ago empty-handed, with very few exceptions; fought against the climate; mastered the language; lived by their honest labor some in affluence, a few in wealth, rarely in misery; they bought or built homes; they raised families and fortunes; they loved luxury, and worked for it; they were not frequently seen in the dark roads of life; proud self-sustaining, they never feared competition as to intelligence or diligence.... In Philadelphia the *Manufacturer* has a daily opportunity to see a hundred Cubans, some of them of heroic history and powerful build, who live by their work in easy comfort. In New York the Cubans are directors in prominent banks, substantial merchants, popular brokers, clerks of recognized ability, physicians with a large practice ... the "senora" went to work; from a slaveowner she became a slave, took a seat behind the counter, sang in the churches, worked button-holes by the hundred, sewed for a living, curled feathers, gave her soul to duty, withered in work her body. This is the people of "defective morals."

Questions to Consider

1. According to Marti, what are some of the strengths and weaknesses of the United States?
2. What insights do you gain from Marti's letter about the experiences of Cuban immigrants in the United States?

From Philip Foner, ed., *Our American Writings on Latin America and the Struggle for Cuban Independence by José Marti* (New York: Monthly Review Press, 1977), pp. 226–241.

▼ A hero of the Cuban independence movement, José Marti gave his life to the cause, dying in 1895, 3 years before the United States intervened in the struggle and went to war with Spain.

funded by American officials of the New Panama Canal Company. The new republic of Panama seceded from Colombia in 1903 and promptly concluded a treaty that ceded a 10-mile-wide canal zone "in perpetuity" to the United States. The canal opened in 1914, and the Canal Zone remained in effect an American colony until another treaty eventually brought American control to an end 85 years later.

Conclusion

Although all the new countries in the Americas had experienced similar stresses and strains in the nineteenth century, they entered the next century in dramatically different situations. The United States had become the preeminent industrial and political power in the Western Hemisphere and was poised to become a major player in global politics, whereas most of Latin America continued to suffer under authoritarian regimes and lagged far behind in economic development.

Through a combination of land purchases, treaties, and conquests in the nineteenth century, the United States now stretched from the Atlantic to the Pacific Ocean. The country had endured a destructive Civil War in the 1860s that nearly tore it apart, but it had subsequently enjoyed relative political stability and economic growth based on an expanding industrial sector. Women and blacks, however, were not yet sharing in the democratic ideals enshrined in the constitution nor in the full benefits of the economy. Their struggles for voting rights and equality would continue throughout the twentieth century.

The question whether democratic institutions would be implanted or dictatorial rulers would remain in place was still unresolved in most Latin American nations. In the late nineteenth century, liberal politicians appeared to be in the ascendancy. Although they gave the impression that they supported the establishment of elected, representative systems, many preferred order and stability rather than reform and change. Power continued to reside in the hands of an oligarchy of large landowners and strong executives who resisted opening up political systems to peasants, workers, the middle class, and women who were pushing for a greater voice in pubic life.

Many Latin American economies experienced steady growth in the late nineteenth century because of the strong demand for their minerals and crops in Europe and North America. Since they preferred to import manufactured goods rather than producing their own, they largely remained producers of raw materials rather than building an industrial economy.

In the coming decades, Latin American nations sharply differed over the best path to development, but they could agree on one thing—that the political independence of the early nineteenth century had not been a springboard to economic development in the twentieth century. This was a hard lesson that was learned and relearned throughout the twentieth century as colonies in Asia, the Middle East, and Africa won their freedom from European colonizers and began considering their options for economic development.

Suggestions for Web Browsing

You can obtain more information about topics included in this chapter at the websites listed below. See also the companion website that accompanies this text, http://www.ablongman.com/brummett, which contains an online study guide and additional resources.

Mexico: From Empire to Revolution
http://www.getty.edu/art/exhibitions/past/art_mexico2.html
Based on the Getty Research Collection, this website includes visual images on Mexico's history from 1857 to 1923. Included are albums, postcards, photographs, and cabinet cards. The images include leaders as well as ordinary people and railways, bridges, roads, buildings, and monuments.

Spanish-American War in Motion Pictures
http://memory.loc.gov/ammem/sawhtml/sawhome.html
This site contains 68 short films produced by the Edison Company and the Mutotope and Biograph Company during the Spanish-American War of 1898 and its aftermath. Some were based on footage shot in Cuba and the Philippines, but others were staged in New Jersey. The website highlights the importance of film for shaping American perceptions and policies towards global issues.

Excerpts from Slave Narratives
http://www.vgskole.net/prosjekt/slavrute/primary.htm
This site contains 46 first-person accounts of slavery and African life dating from 1682 to 1937.

The Lewis and Clark Expedition
http://www.peabody.harvard.edu/Lewis_and_Clark/default.html
Lewis and Clark brought back an enormous collection of material, which is housed at the Peabody Museum at Harvard.

U. S. Intervention in Latin America
http://www.smplanet.com/imperialism/teddy.html
Site offering a wide range of images, movies, and sound bites regarding intervention in Latin America, particularly the issues surrounding the Panama Canal project.

Theodore Roosevelt
http://www.theodoreroosevelt.org/
A website that touches all aspects of Roosevelt's life and work, including a fine collection of political cartoons.

The Valley of the Shadow
http://valley.vcdh.virginia.edu
Through primary sources such as letters, diaries, and newspapers, this website recounts the lives of people in Augusta County, Virginia, and Franklin County, Pennsylvania, during the American Civil War.

Literature and Film

Some of the best novels on this period examine the lives of generations of families in different settings. Isabel Allende's *House of the Spirits,* trans. Magda Bogin (G. K. Hall, 1986), traces four generations of women in twentieth-century Chile. Carlos Fuentes's *The Death of Artemio Cruz,* trans. Alfred MacAdam (Farrar, Straus and Giroux, 1991), chronicles the life of a man who was a leader of the Mexican revolution but who becomes corrupt as he becomes a leading businessman. Gabriel Garcia Márquez's *One Hundred Years of Solitude* (Perennial, 2004) examines the lives of the Buendiás family in Macondo, Colombia. Elena Poniatowska's *Until We Meet Again* (Pantheon Books, 1993) focuses on the life of a peasant woman from the Mexican Revolution to the post–World War II era. Fanny Calderón de la Barca, the English-born wife of the Spanish ambassador to Mexico in the late 1830s, provides an insightful first-person account of *Life in Mexico* (University of California Press, 1982).

The Public Broadcasting System has produced superb studies of the United States in the nineteenth century, available in VHS presentation. See the series on Lincoln (1995), Ken Burns's treatment of the Civil War (1990), and the study of the West and Lewis and Clark (2004). A searching and dramatic portrayal of the struggle for freedom among African Americans is the *Roots of Resistance—A Story of the Underground Railroad* (1995). Edward Zwick directed a stunning portrayal of African American Union troops fighting for freedom in the Civil War in *Glory* (1989; Columbia/Tristar).

In the United States, Mark Twain was a humorist who captured American life in his works, and he was joined by authors such as Theodore Dreiser, who provided strong social commentary in his book *Sister Carrie* (1900). Ida Tarbell set the foundations for investigative journalism with *The History of Standard Oil Company* (1904), a work that was widely read.

The diplomatic style of Teddy Roosevelt is captured in John Milius's *The Wind and the Lion* (Columbia, 1975). The Public Broadcasting System has produced a number of documentaries dealing with the period in the United States: *TR, The Story of Theodore Roosevelt* (1998; AMEI-999-FXA), *Not for Ourselves Alone: The Story of Elizabeth Cady Stanton and Susan B. Anthony* (1999; NFOA-DXO-FXA), and *The Richest Man in the World: Andrew Carnegie* (1997; AMEI-093-FXA).

Suggestions for Reading

An innovative comparative study of North America and the rest of the Americas is Felipe Fernandez-Armesto, *The Americas: The History of a Hemisphere* (Weidenfeld and Nicholson, 2003).

General works on Latin American history include Thomas Skidmore and Peter Smith, *Modern Latin America,* 5th ed. (Oxford University Press, 2001) and David Bushnell and Neill Macauley, *The Emergence of Latin America in the 19th Century,* 2nd ed. (Oxford University Press, 1994). Two works that critically examine the implications of Latin American independence and economic development are E. Bradford Burns, *The Poverty of Progress: Latin America in the Nineteenth Century* (University of California Press, 1980), and Jay Kinsbruner, *Independence in Spanish America: Civil Wars, Revolutions, and Underdevelopment* (University of New Mexico Press, 2000).

Specific studies on Latin American nations include Hugh Thomas, *Cuba, or the Pursuit of Freedom* (Da Capo Press, 1998); David Rock, *Argentina, 1516–1982* (I. B. Taurus, 1986); Roderick Barman, *Citizen Emperor: Pedro II and the Making of Brazil, 1825–1891* (Stanford University Press, 1999); Mark Wasserman, *Everyday Life and Politics in Nineteenth Century Mexico: Men, Women, and War* (University of New Mexico Press, 2000), Ralph Lee Woodward Jr., *Central America: A History Divided,* 3rd ed. (New York: Oxford University Press, 1999); and James Dunkerley, *Power in the Isthmus: A Political History of Central Latin America* (Verso, 1988). Latin America's economic history is examined in Stephen Haber, ed., *How Latin America Fell Behind: Essays on the Economic Histories of Brazil and Mexico, 1800–1914* (Stanford University Press, 1997).

United States history is covered in Sean Wilentz, *The Rise of Democracy: Jefferson to Lincoln* (Norton, 2005); Peter Kolchin, *American Slavery, 1619–1877,* 10th ed. (Hill and Wang, 2003); James McPherson, *Battle Cry of Freedom: the Civil War Era* (Oxford University Press, 2003); Eric Foner and Olivia Mahoney, *America's Reconstruction: People and Politics after the Civil War* (HarperPerennial, 1995); and Sean Cashman, *America in the Gilded Age: From the Death of Lincoln to the Rise of Theodore Roosevelt* (New York University Press, 1993).

CHAPTER 27

World War I and Its Economic and Political Consequences

Outline

- World War I
- The Allied Peace Settlement
- Economic Disasters
- Politics in the Democracies
- The Western Tradition in Transition: Changing Certainties

Features

DOCUMENT The Western Front: Christmas 1914

SEEING CONNECTIONS African American Recipients of the *Croix de Guerre*

DOCUMENT John Maynard Keynes on Clemenceau

GLOBAL ISSUES War and International Law

◀ At the end of the nineteenth century, wars increasingly came to be fought using sophisticated modern technology. But on the Western Front in World War I the opposing armies confronted each other from trenches separated by fifty or one hundred yards. From time to time one side or the other would try to make a breakthrough and fighting reverted to hand to hand combat, as seen here. French soldiers resisted the oncoming Germans with any weapon at hand—including stones.

Europe's global dominance was brought to an end in August 1914 by a combination of forces—militarism, rival alliances, imperialism, secret diplomacy, and bellicose nationalism. Four years later, when the armistice was signed on the western front on November 11, 1918, over 10 million soldiers from around the world lay dead on Europe's battlefields, a generation of the best and bravest. Four empires—the German, Austro-Hungarian, Russian, and Ottoman—either faded away or disappeared entirely.

No part of the world remained untouched by these upheavals. The European powers recruited soldiers from their colonies. From Senegal to India to Australia to New Zealand, hundreds of thousands of soldiers went to fight and die in the European war. The warring forces waged battles in both East and West Asia, while Asians and Africans went to work in the European countries to replace workers who had been called to the front. The world economy lost what little equilibrium it had and went into a manic cycle of inflation and depression that devastated nations around the globe between 1929 and 1932.

World War I, the "Great War"—the war that was to "make the world safe for democracy"—left a legacy of physical damage, economic disruption, and doubt that threatened the liberal advances of the nineteenth century. The horrible costs of the war made the triumph a hollow one for the democratic victors. After the initial taste for revenge had been satisfied, revulsion for war became widespread. The economic dislocation caused by inflation and depression sapped the strength of the middle classes, the traditional defenders of democracy, and paved the way for dictators.

World War I

How did European alliances make war all but inevitable?

As we saw in Chapter 23, the diplomatic structure created by Bismarck, based on a Central Power alliance with Vienna and Rome, began to come apart in the 1890s. The blustering foreign policy of the kaiser drove England, France, and Russia—three countries that had never worked together—to form the Triple Entente (on-tahnt) in 1907. The two alliances found themselves at odds over the crises in North Africa but managed to avoid going to war. The Central Powers and the Triple Entente entered into World War I in August 1914, however, because of their inability to deal with a series of conflicts in the Balkans.

The Balkan Crises

During the nineteenth century, Russia and Austria competed as they expanded their influences into the Balkan holdings of the Ottoman Empire. Throughout the last part of the nineteenth century, the two openly disagreed on the question of Macedonia, the building of railroads through the peninsula, and boundary revisions. Vienna and St. Petersburg were particularly at odds over the question of the status of Bosnia and Herzegovina (HERTS-ah-GOH-vee-nah).

The Austro-Hungarian monarchy had administered the two areas since the 1878 Congress of Berlin, much to the Russians' and Serbs' displeasure. The Russian Foreign Minister, Count Izvolskii (EEZ-vol-skee), initiated talks with Vienna in 1908 to resolve the situation. In an inexplicable move, he proposed that Russia would approve the Austro-Hungarians to annex the two areas in return for increased Black Sea rights for the Russian navy. The Austrians were pleased to annex Bosnia and Herzegovina, but the Russians never got their part of the bargain.

Serbia was outraged by the incorporation of more Slavs into the Habsburg domain and expected its Slavic, Orthodox protector, Russia, to do something about it. The Russians had been badly bruised in their war with Japan and the Revolution of 1905. Aside from making threatening noises, they could do little to block the annexation, especially in the face of Germany's support for Austria-Hungary.

After 1908, tensions remained high in the Balkans. The Austrians looked to increase their advantage, knowing they had the full backing of Germany. Serbia searched for revenge, and Russia found itself backed into a corner. After the failure of Izvolskii's efforts, the Russians had to support their Balkan allies or lose their influence.

In 1912, Serbia and its neighbors, including Greece and Bulgaria, formed an alliance with the objective of expelling the Turks from Europe. The First Balkan War began later in the year and came to a quick end with the defeat of the Turks. Each of the Balkan allies had its own particular goals in mind in fighting the Ottomans. When the Great Powers stepped in to maintain the balance, problems arose.

Serbia had fought for a seaport on the Adriatic and thought it had gained one with the defeat of the Turks. However, the Italians and Austrians blocked Serbia's access to the sea by overseeing the creation of Albania in the Treaty of London of 1913. Denied their goals, the Serbs turned on their former allies, the Bulgarians, and demanded a part of their spoils from the first war. Bulgaria refused and, emboldened by its successes in the first war, attacked its former allies, starting the Second Balkan War. The Serbs were in turn joined by the Romanians and the Turks. The Bulgarians were no match for the rest of the Balkans and signed a peace that turned over most of the territory that they had earlier gained. The Turks retained only a precarious toehold in Europe, the small pocket from Adrianople to Constantinople.

Had the Great Powers found a way to place a fence around the Balkans and allow the squabbling nations to work out their differences in isolation, the two Balkan wars of 1912 and 1913 would have had little significance. As it was, however, the combative Balkan nations added to the prevailing state of tension between the two competing alliances, whose policies clashed because of their conflicting choices of allies in the Balkans. In effect, the tail wagged the dog, as the alliances reacted to every flare-up in the turbulent peninsula.

Chronology

1905	1910			1920	1930
1908 Austria-Hungary annexes Bosnia-Herzegovina	1912 and 1913 Balkan Wars 1914 Austrian Archduke Francis Ferdinand and his wife assassinated; World War I begins	1916 Battles of Verdun and the Somme 1917 United States enters World War I; Britain pledges support for Jewish homeland in Palestine in Balfour Declaration	1918 Wilson issues Fourteen Points; Russia signs Treaty of Brest-Litovsk with Germany; armistice signed ending World War I 1919 Treaty of Versailles	1924 Dawes Plan; first Labour government in Britain 1929 U. S. stock market crashes	1930–1940 Global depression

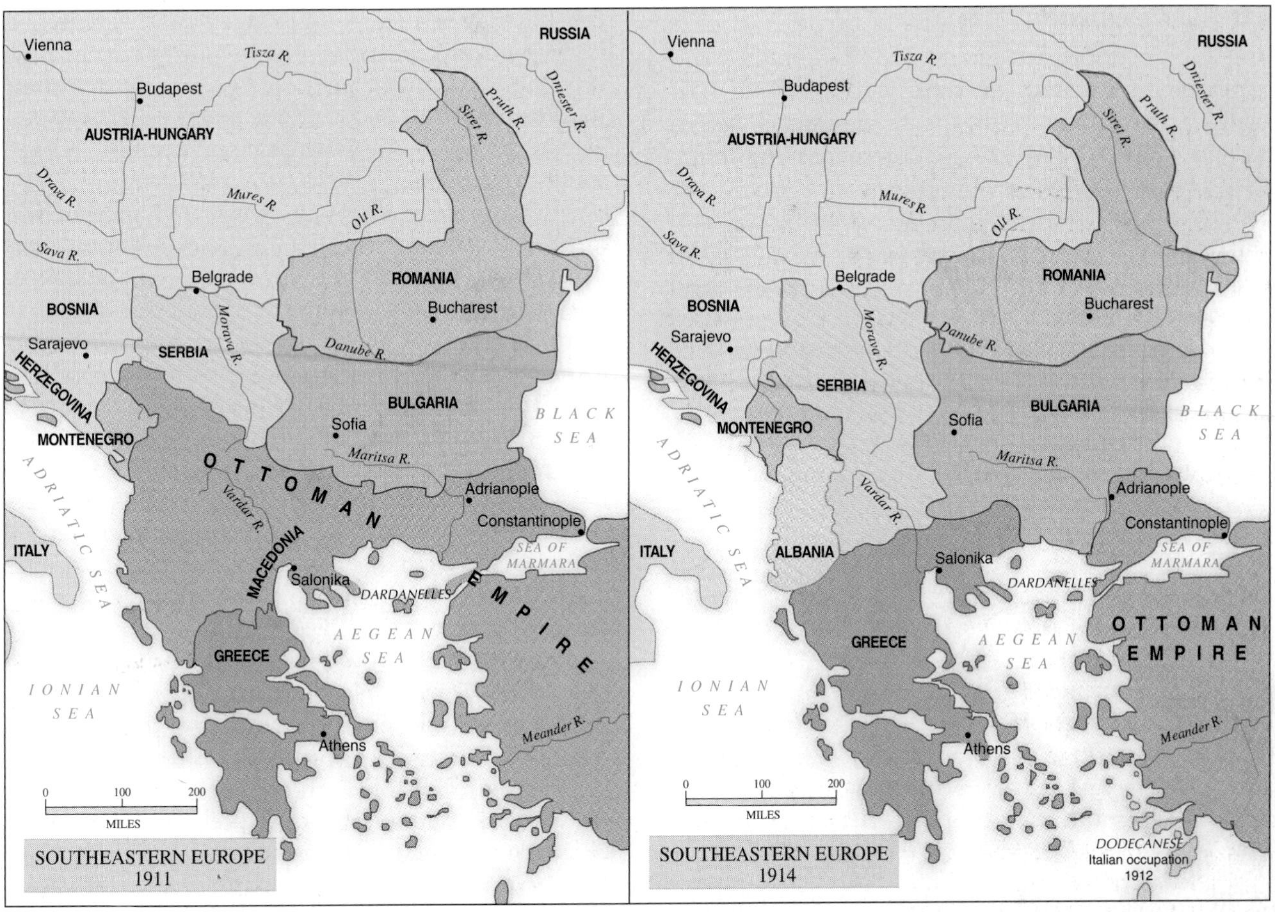

SOUTHEASTERN EUROPE 1911

SOUTHEASTERN EUROPE 1914

▲ At the end of the nineteenth century (as well as the twentieth), the Balkans were a cauldron of conflicting national memories and ambitions. In the second decade of the twentieth century, the Balkans mirrored the weakening of the Austro-Hungarian and Russian empires.

Assassination at Sarajevo

By the end of 1913, no permanent solution had been found to the Balkans' problems. Austria was more fearful than ever of Serbia's expansionist desires. Serbian ambitions had grown along with its territory, which had doubled as a result of the recent wars. The Serbian prime minister declared himself satisfied with his gains and looked forward to a direct challenge of Austria.

The spark that set off World War I was struck on June 28, 1914, with the assassination of the heir to the Austrian throne, Archduke Francis Ferdinand. The archduke and his wife were visiting the town of Sarajevo (SAHR-ah-YAY-voh) in Bosnia, which his realm had recently annexed. As they drove through the narrow streets in their huge touring car, a 19-year-old Bosnian student named Gavrilo Princip (PRIN-chip), one of seven young terrorists along the route, shot them. Princip had been inspired by propaganda advocating the creation of a greater Serbia and was assisted by Serbian officers serving in a secret organization, the Black Hand. The direct participation of the Serbian government was never proved; even so, the Belgrade authorities were likely to have been involved, at least indirectly.

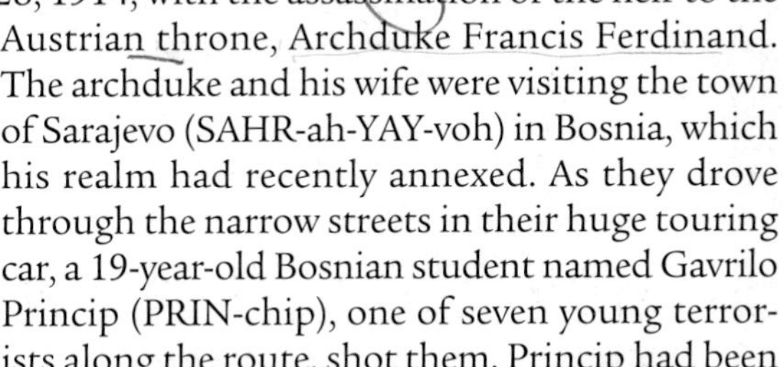

DOCUMENT

The Murder of Archduke Franz Ferdinand

The legal details of the case were lost in Vienna's rush to put an end to the problem of Serbia. Count Leopold von Berchtold (BERK-told), the foreign minister, believed that the assassination in Bosnia justified crushing the anti-Austrian propaganda and terrorism coming from the Serbs. The kaiser felt that everything possible must be done to prevent Germany's only reliable ally from being weakened, and he assured the Austrians of his full support. Berchtold received a "blank check" from Germany. Vienna wanted a quick, local Austro-Serbian war, and Germany favored quick action to forestall Russian intervention.

On July 23, the Austro-Hungarian foreign ministry presented an ultimatum to the Serbs. Expecting the list of demands to be turned down, Berchtold insisted on unconditional acceptance within 48 hours. Two days later, the Austro-Hungarian government announced that Serbia's reply, though conciliatory, was not satisfactory. The Austrians immediately mobilized their armed forces.

The Alliances' Inevitable War

The Germans began having second thoughts and urged their ally in late July to negotiate with Russia—which was anxiously following developments. Russia realized that if the Austrians succeeded in humbling the Serbs, Russia's position in the Balkans would suffer irreparably. The French, in the meantime, assured the Russians of their full cooperation and urged full support for Serbia. The British unsuccessfully advised negotiation.

Europe had reached a point of no return: the Austrians had committed themselves to the task of removing an opponent, and the Russians could not permit this removal to happen. Neither side would back down, and each had allies ready to come to its aid. Fearful that Serbia would escape from his clutches, Berchtold succeeded on July 27—in part through deception—in convincing the Habsburg emperor Franz Josef (frahnz YOH-sef) that war was the only way out. The next day, the Austro-Hungarian Empire declared war against Serbia.

As the possibility of a general European war loomed, Berlin sent several frantic telegrams to Vienna. The German ambassador was instructed to tell Berchtold that "as an ally we must refuse to be drawn into a world conflagration because Austria does not respect our advice."[1] Had the Germans spoken to their ally in such tones a month earlier, war might have been avoided. But Austria's belligerence moved the Russians to act. The tsar ordered mobilization on July 30, 1914.

▼ An illustration from *Le Journal de Paris* depicting the Serbian terrorist Gavrilo Princip assassinating Archduke Francis Ferdinand and his wife, Sophie, in Sarajevo on June 28, 1914.

Germany was caught in a dilemma that Bismarck would never have allowed. Surrounded by potential enemies, the Germans had to move decisively or face defeat. The Russian mobilization threatened them, because in the event of war on the eastern front, by treaty, there would also be war on the western front. The best plan for Berlin, one that had been worked out since the beginning of the century by the Chief of the General Staff Alfred von Schlieffen (vun SCHLEEF-en), was to launch a lightning attack against France, which could mobilize faster than Russia, crush France, and then return to meet Russia, which would be slower to mobilize. To allow Russian mobilization to proceed without action would jeopardize this plan.

The Germans set into effect their long-planned strategy to gain European dominance on July 31. They sent ultimatums to St. Petersburg and Paris insisting that the Russians stop their mobilization and demanding a pledge of neutrality from the French. Failing to receive satisfactory replies, Germany declared war on Russia on August 1 and on France two days later. On August 2, the German ambassador in Brussels delivered an ultimatum to the Belgian government announcing his country's intention to send troops through Belgium, in violation of the 1839 treaty guaranteeing Belgian neutrality. The Belgian cabinet refused to grant permission and appealed to the Triple Entente for help.

A majority of the British cabinet did not want war, but with the news of the German ultimatum to Belgium, the tide turned. Sir Edward Grey, the British foreign secretary, sent an ultimatum to Germany demanding that Belgian neutrality be respected. Germany refused, and on August 4, Great Britain declared war.

Because Germany and Austria-Hungary were not waging a defensive war, Italy declined to carry out its obligations under the Triple Alliance and for a time remained neutral. In late

▲ Threatening the generally held views of inevitable progress at the beginning of the twentieth century were the unanswered "Eastern Question" in the Balkans and the lingering conflicts over dividing up the prize of North Africa.

August, Japan joined the Allies. Turkey, fearing Russia, threw in its lot with the Central Powers—which, by the end of 1914, consisted of Germany, Austria-Hungary, Bulgaria, and Turkey.

Diplomats tried desperately to avert a general war. Through confusion, fear, and loss of sleep, the nervous strain among them was almost unbearable. Many broke down and wept when it became apparent they had failed. Grey himself noted in his autobiography that one evening, just before the outbreak of the war, he watched the streetlights being lit from his office window and remarked: "The lamps are going out all over Europe; we shall not see them lit again in our lifetime."[2]

Total War

Although the terrible struggle that racked the world from 1914 to 1918 was fought mainly in Europe, it is rightly called World War I. In the seventeenth and eighteenth centuries, European powers had competed across the globe; however, never had so many fighters and such enormous resources been brought together in a single conflict. Altogether, 27 nations became belligerents, ranging the globe from Japan to Canada and from Argentina to South Africa to Australia.

The Central Powers mobilized 21 million men. The Allies eventually called 40 million men to arms, including 12 million Russians. The two sides were more equally matched than the numbers would indicate, however. Since the Russian divisions were often poorly equipped and ineffectively used, the Allies' apparent advantage was not great. In addition, in the German army, the Central Powers boasted superb generalship and discipline. Another advantage was that the Central Powers fought from a central position and were able to transfer troops quickly and efficiently to various fronts.

The Allies had the advantages of greater resources of finance and raw materials. Britain maintained its naval dominance and could draw on its empire for support. In addition, because Germany was effectively blockaded, the United States, even though officially neutral for most of the war, served as a major source of supplies for the Allies.

The warring nations went into battle in a confident mood. Each side was sure of its strength and felt it had prepared carefully. Each nation's propaganda machine delivered reassuring messages of guaranteed victory. All expected that the war would soon be over—probably by Christmas—and concluded in a few

Document

The Western Front: Christmas 1914

More soldiers died in World War I than in any other European war until World War II. The most murderous part of that war was on the western front from the English Channel to Switzerland, where parallel long lines of trenches defined the battle zones between the Central Powers and the Allies. The two sides waged bloody battles at Verdun, the Somme, and Ypres that claimed the lives of millions of men. On both sides throughout the war, propaganda machines and churches alike dehumanized the enemy. By the end of the war, the propagandists must have achieved partial success in their efforts, as soldiers continued the murderous butchering of each other a mere 40 or 50 yards apart.

But at Christmas 1914, an unofficial truce occurred at places along the western front, during which soldiers on both sides discarded their arms, buried their dead, joined together to play a game of football, and exchanged cigarettes while chaplains on both sides carried out religious services. Historians differ on the significance of this truce, a spontaneous gesture that infuriated military leaders—who warned that "the enemy may be contemplating an attack." Paul Fussell of the University of Pennsylvania saw this event as "the last twitch of the 19th century.... By that I mean it was the last public moment in which it was assumed that people were nice, and that the Dickens view of the world was a credible view."[1] Idealists of all stripes like to view the event as a quintessential manifestation of human decency. The World War I British cartoonist Bruce Bairnsfather saw it as "the interval between rounds in a friendly boxing match," in which both sides took the chance to rest and reconnoiter before going back to killing each other.[2]

Lieutenant Johannes Niemann, 133rd Royal Saxon Regiment

We came up to take over the trenches on the front between Frelinghien and Houplines, where our Regiment and the Scottish Seaforth Highlanders were face to face. It was a cold, starry night [on December 25] and the Scots were a hundred or so metres in front of us in their trenches where, as we discovered, like us they were up to their knees in mud. My Company Commander and I savouring the unaccustomed calm, sat with our orderlies round a Christmas tree we had put in our dugout.

Suddenly, for no apparent reason, our enemies began to fire on our lines. Our soldiers had hung little Christmas trees covered with candles above our trenches and our enemies, seeing the lights, thought we were about to launch a surprise attack. But by midnight, it was calm once more.

Next morning the mist was slow to clear and my orderly threw himself into my dugout to say that both the German and the Scottish soldiers had come out of their trenches and were fraternizing along the front. I grabbed my binoculars and looking cautiously over the parapet saw the incredible sight of our soldiers exchanging cigarettes, schnapps and chocolate with the enemy. Later a Scottish soldier appeared with a football which seemed to come from nowhere and a few minutes later a real football match got underway. The Scots marked their goal mouth with their strange caps and we did the same with ours. It was far from easy to play on the frozen ground, but we continued, keeping rigorously to the rules, despite the fact that it only lasted an hour and we had no referee. A great many of the passes went wide, but all the amateur footballers, although they must have been very tired, played with huge enthusiasm.

Us Germans really roared when a gust of wind revealed that the Scots wore no drawers under their kilts—and hooted and whistled every time they caught an impudent glimpse of one posterior belonging to one of "yesterday's enemies." But after an hour's play, when our Commanding Officer heard about it, he sent an order that we must put a stop to it. A little later we drifted back to our trenches and the fraternization ended.

The game finished with a score of three goals to two in favour of Fritz against Tommy.[3]

Gunner Herbert Smith, 5th Battery, Royal Field Artillery

I went out myself on Christmas Day and exchanged some cigarettes for cigars, and this game had been going on from Christmas eve till midnight on Boxing Day without a single round being fired. The German I met had been a waiter in London and could use our language a little. He says that they didn't want to fight and I think he was telling the truth as we are not getting half so many bullets as usual. I know this statement will take a bit of believing but it is absolutely correct. Fancy a German shaking your flapper [hand shake] as though he were trying to smash your fingers, and then a few days later trying to plug you. I hardly knew what to think about it, but I fancy they are working up a big scheme so that they can give us a doing, but our chaps are prepared, and I am under the impression that they will get more than they bargained for.[4]

Questions to Consider

1. Why were the commanding officers on both sides against the Christmas truce?
2. This truce occurred in 1914, a few months into the war. Such an event never occurred again. Why?
3. Why was gunner Smith so suspicious?

[1]Paul Fussell, "The Christmas Tree—The Last Twitch," *PBS: The Great War and the Shaping of the 20th Century,* http://www.pbs.org/greatwar/historian/hist_fussell_04_xmas.html.
[2]Bruce Bairnsfather, quoted in "The Christmas Truce of 1914," http://www.worldwar1.com/heritage/xmast.html.
[3]"The Christmas Truce of 1914," http://www.worldwar1.com/heritage/xmast.html.
[4]*Ibid.*

decisive battles. They based their thinking on precedent—but they chose the wrong precedent. They assumed that the next war would be in the model of the efficient Bismarckian wars of the 1860s. Instead, the war came to resemble that of the bloody, 4-year-long American Civil War, the first industrialized war.

The First Two Years of War

All of the general staffs had been refining their war plans for years. The Germans knew that Allied naval supremacy would cut them off from needed sources abroad. They realized that they were potentially surrounded and that, according to the Schlieffen Plan, they should strike a quick knockout blow to end the war. They aimed to push the Belgians aside and drive rapidly south into France. The plan then called for the German forces to wheel west of Paris, outflank the French forces, and drive them toward Alsace-Lorraine, where they would be met by another German army. Within six weeks the French would be destroyed, caught between the western hammer and the eastern anvil. Meanwhile, a small German force would be holding the presumably slow-moving Russians on the eastern front, awaiting the arrival, via the excellent German rail system, of the victorious western forces. The plan nearly worked.

The Germans marched according to the plan until they got so close to Paris that they could see the top of the Eiffel Tower. They were hurled back by a bold French offensive through a gap that opened between their armies in the first Battle of the Marne, fought between September 5 and 12. With the assistance of a small British expeditionary force and Parisian taxi drivers who provided transportation, the French then marched north in a race with the Germans to reach and control the vital ports along the English Channel. After much desperate fighting, the enemies established battle positions that stabilized, thus creating the western front, a solid line of opposing trenches that stretched from the Channel to near the Swiss border.

For the next 4 years, this line of trenches would be the scene of a grisly **war of attrition,** as the Allies and the Central Powers launched desperate attacks, hoping to gain the decisive "breakthrough" victory that would end the war. The struggle was made all the more bloody by powerful artillery such as the German's gigantic "Big Bertha," more deadly machine guns, silent and devastating clouds of poison gas, and two new weapons: the tank and the airplane. Single battles along that line of death killed more soldiers than those lost by the North and the South combined during the 4 years of the American Civil War.

war of attrition—A war in which there are no decisive, conclusive battles. Rather, the two sides grind away at each other until one side is exhausted and gives up.

▲ Pilots of the first generation of fighter aircraft in World War I made good use of their maneuverability and fire power, as seen in this dogfight over the Western Front.

The other part of the German scheme that did not go according to plan was the unexpected speed with which the Russians mobilized. They penetrated deeply into East Prussia and overran the Austrian province of Galicia. However, confused leadership resulted in two catastrophic Russian defeats in East Prussia, and the Russians never again posed a serious threat to Germany during the rest of the war.

By the end of 1914, all sides knew that they were trapped in a new type of war, one of horrible consequences. Single battles claimed hundreds of thousands of lives, and the toll during the first few months of the conflict ran as high as 1.5 million dead and wounded.

In 1915, the British attempted a major campaign to force open the Dardanelles, closed by Turkey when it joined the Central Powers. This plan, attributed to Winston Churchill, then first lord of the admiralty, was designed to open up the sea route to Russia, which

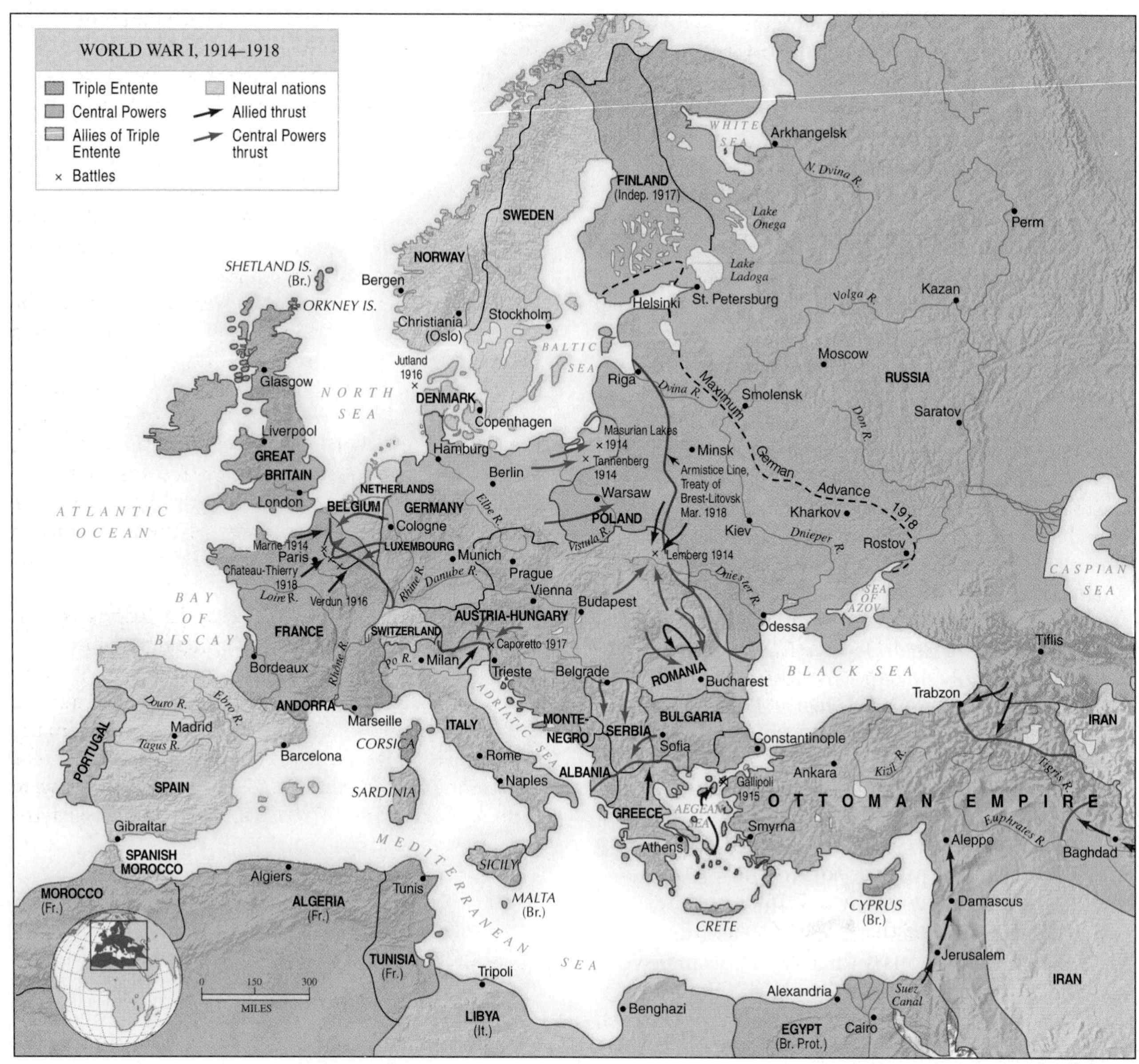

▲ The contrast between the fixed boundary between the Allies and the Central Powers, marked by trenches on the west, and the fluid lines of the eastern front are evident from this map. As much as the Central Powers were blockaded by British control of the North Sea, so too were the Russians blocked by Turkish control of the Dardanelles and the Bosporus and the Germans' control of the Baltic.

was badly in need of war supplies, and to take the pressure off the western front. After heroic and costly attacks, Allied Australian and New Zealand troops, known as Anzacs, were forced to withdraw from their landing positions on the Gallipoli (ga-LIP-po-lee) peninsula in European Turkey.

Another major Allied setback in 1915 was the defeat of the Russian forces in Poland. More than 1.2 million Russians were killed and wounded, and the Germans took nearly 900,000 prisoners. Although Russia somehow remained in the war and fought well against the Dual Monarchy, it was no longer a concern for the Germans. These defeats generated rising criticism against the tsar's government, and Russian morale deteriorated.

Serbia was the next Central Powers' victim. In September 1915, Bulgaria, still aching from its defeat in the Second Balkan War, entered the war on the side of the Central Powers. Surrounded by enemies, Serbia was helpless, and resistance was quickly crushed. The Austrians had finally gained their goal of the previous summer, but in the context of the continental tragedy, this achievement no longer seemed significant.

The Allies' only bright spot in 1915 was Italy's entry into their ranks. Italy had remained neutral in August 1914 when it had defected from the Triple Alliance, of which it had been at best a token member. Italy joined the Allies following promises made in a secret treaty in London that promised the Italians huge concessions of territory once victory had been attained.

Stalemate

The Allies' strategy on the western front was to restrict attacks to a few concentrated assaults in France, thus saving manpower and at the same time concentrating on their naval blockade. Denied badly needed imports, strategists assumed, the German war effort would be seriously weakened. Countering this tactic, the German high command under General Falkenhayn (FALK-en-hine) launched a massive offensive against the strategic fortress of Verdun (vair-DUN) in February 1916.

After their defeat in 1871 (see Chapter 23), the French had transformed Verdun into a network of 20 forts with powerful artillery, of which the fort of Douaumont (doo-OH-mon) was the most important. Verdun had repulsed the Central Powers' attack in 1914, but the Germans pulled back about 10 miles and set up lines of observation posts and logistical support. So sure were the French of the invincibility of this position that they moved some of their artillery and soldiers to other sites deemed more important. Falkenhayn began to build up his strength opposite Verdun in the late autumn of 1915, and, night after night, trains arrived loaded with men and matériel. Bad weather forced the Germans to delay their attack, but finally at 7:15 on the morning of February 21, more than 1000 German cannons along a 6-mile front fired the first of thousands of shells that descended on Verdun in a bombardment that lasted ten hours. Then the German infantry advanced, equipped with flamethrowers.

The battered and outnumbered French forces fought back bravely and, despite losing some fortified positions, denied the Germans the rapid victory they had desired. This stout resistance gave the Allies time to throw hundreds of thousands of men into the battle, which would rage into the summer and fall. Falkenhayn, who had gambled all on a quick victory, was replaced by Generals Hindenburg and Ludendorff, who decided to abandon the attack on Verdun. The French reclaimed the forts they had lost by the end of the year. The slaughter brought on by massed artillery and infantry charges between the trenches was horrible. The total loss in the battle of Verdun came to 700,000 men.

To ease the pressure against Verdun, the British army on July 1 began an offensive along the Somme River on the western front. Despite their having fired 2 million shells, the attackers' losses on the first day of the battle were catastrophic: 60 percent of the officers and 40 percent of the soldiers—60,000 men in all. Despite these awesome figures, the attacks—with the British making the first use of tanks in August—continued for three months without any substantial gains. General Haig, stymied by the tenacious German resistance, decided to stop the offensive in November. Total German casualties at the Somme were about 550,000; the British and French lost about 650,000—a staggering 1.2 million men dead or wounded.

1916 Debut of the British Tank

The only major naval engagement of the war, the battle of Jutland (May 31–June 1, 1916), reaffirmed British control of the seas. Taking enormous risks, the Germans maneuvered brilliantly. They could afford to gamble because defeat would in no way worsen their position. The British fleet, however, had to act cautiously and absorbed greater losses. Nevertheless, the Germans finally retreated to their base and remained there for the rest of the war. Only in their submarine warfare did the German navy enjoy success during the war.

On the eastern front in 1916, the Russians continued their generally successful campaigns against the Austro-Hungarian forces. But the Germans were always there to save their allies from destruction. Romania, impressed by the Russian victories, finally joined the Allies and launched an attack on the Austrians. After an initial success, the Romanians were soon knocked out of the war by a joint German-Bulgarian invasion.

The Home Front

In 1914, patriotic fervor swept each country, eliminating for a moment the barriers between domestic political opponents such as conservatives and socialist. Even the international socialist movement, whose policy it was to promote international proletarian unity over nationalism, fell victim to the rabid patriotism that infected the Continent. Workers of one country were encouraged to go out and kill workers of enemy countries in the name of the state. This was especially evident in Germany as well as in France, as the international socialist proletariat of these nations began slaughtering each other on the battlefront.

In England, the suffragette movement led by Emmeline Pankhurst stopped their work for the vote for women and joined in the war effort. By the second week of August, all of the imprisoned suffragette campaigners had been released from jail. Not all of the combatants for women's equality joined in this movement, and the Pankhurst family was split with Emmeline Pankhurst and her daughter Christabel working to encourage men to join the army while another daughter, Sylvia was against the war and refused to join the effort.

On the home front, **rationing** was instituted to ensure sufficient supplies for soldiers at the front. As men went off to fight, women took over their jobs in the workplace—the number of working women in the United Kingdom increased from 3,224,600 in 1914 to 4,114,600 in 1918—more than 700,000 of these women worked in making weapons.[3] Intensive **propaganda** campaigns encouraged civilians to buy more bonds and make more weapons. Nations unleashed a barrage of propaganda inciting total hatred of the enemy, belief in the righteousness of the cause, and unquestioned support for the war effort.

At the end of 1916, after more than two years of fighting, neither side was close to victory. Instead, the war had turned into a dreary contest of each side trying to bleed the other into submission—a far cry from the glories promised by the propaganda of 1914. War was no longer fought between armies; it was fought between states, and every citizen and office of the state participated.

rationing—A process instituted to control the distribution of resources such as food, clothing, gasoline, sugar, and so on to ensure a sufficient supply during a time of shortage or great need.

propaganda—Publicly disseminated information that has been manipulated to further one's own cause and to damage that of one's opponent.

Civil liberties suffered, and in some cases, distinguished citizens were thrown into prison for opposing the war effort. In Britain, for example, the philosopher and mathematician Bertrand Russell was imprisoned for a short time for his pacifistic views. Governments took over control of their national economies and gambled everything on a victory in which the loser would pay all the expenses incurred in the war. The various states outlawed strikes and rigidly controlled currencies and foreign trade.

At the beginning of the war, all was flag waving and enthusiasm. There was great idealism, sense of sacrifice, and love of country. At first there was no understanding of the horror, death, and disaster that comes with modern, industrialized war. The British poet Rupert Brooke caught the spirit in his poem "The Soldier":

If I should die, think only this of me:
That there's some corner of a foreign field
That is forever England. There shall be
In that rich earth a richer dust concealed;
A dust whom England bore, shaped, made aware,
Gave, once, her flowers to love, her ways to roam,
A body of England's breathing English air,
Washed by the rivers, blest by suns of home.[4]

But this early idealism, this Romantic conception of death in battle, gradually changed to one of war weariness and total futility. This growing mood is best

▼ As the men marched off to war, women left their homes to work in war-related industries. These women are working in a British munitions factory.

seen in the poetry of the young British officer and poet Wilfred Owen, himself a victim on the western front:

What passing-bells for those who die as cattle?
Only the monstrous anger of the guns ...
No mockeries for them; no prayers nor bells,
Nor any voice of mourning save the choirs, —
The shrill, demented choirs of wailing shells;
And bugles calling for them from sad shires.[5]

By the end of 1916, a deep yearning for peace dominated Europe. Sensing this mood, leaders on both sides put forth peace feelers. But these halfhearted overtures achieved nothing. Propaganda was used effectively to continue the war and support for it. The populations of the warring states were made to believe that their crusade was somehow divinely inspired. In reality, the Dual Monarchy and France fought for survival; Russia, Germany, and Italy all fought to improve their respective positions in Europe; Britain fought to save Belgium and create a renewed balance of power on the Continent.

Allied Fatigue and American Entry

In 1917, British and French military strength reached its highest point, only to fall precipitously. Allied commanders were hopeful that the long-planned breakthrough might be accomplished, but a large-scale French attack on the German lines was beaten back, with huge losses. Some French regiments mutinied rather than return to the inferno of "no-man's land" between the trenches. The British sacrificed hundreds of thousands of men without any decisive results in several massive offensives. The Allies also launched unsuccessful campaigns in Italy. Aided by the Germans, the Austrians smashed the Italian front at the battle of Caporetto (1917), an event vividly described by Ernest Hemingway in *A Farewell to Arms.* Italian resistance finally hardened, and collapse was barely averted.

The growing effectiveness of the German submarine menace deepened Allied frustration. By 1917, Allied shipping losses had reached dangerous proportions. In three months, 470 British ships fell victim to torpedoes. Britain had no more than six weeks' stores of food on hand, and the supply situation became critical for the Allies. As it turned out, the very weapon that seemed to doom their cause, the submarine, was the source of the Allies' salvation: Germany's decision to use unrestricted submarine warfare brought the United States openly into the war.

The Americans had declared their neutrality in 1914 when President Woodrow Wilson announced that the American people "must be impartial in thought as well as in action." The events of the next 2 years showed that this would not be the case.

	Steps Toward American Entry into World War I
1914	President Wilson proclaims neutrality "in thought and action"; British blockade Germany—including cable
1914–1917	Allied war bond drive
1915	German submarine sinks *Lusitania*
1916	Wilson reelected under slogan "He kept us out of war"
1916–1917	Increased German submarine activity, plots with Mexico
1917	Wilson asks Congress to declare war on Germany (April 6)

American sentiment was overwhelmingly with the Allies from the first. France's help to the colonies in the American Revolution was warmly recalled. Britain and America were closely tied by language, literature, and democratic institutions. Because Britain cut off communications between Germany and the United States, British propaganda and management of the war news dominated U.S. public opinion. Another factor predisposing the United States to the Allied cause was Germany's violation of international law in the invasion of Belgium. This buttressed the widely held view created by the kaiser's saber-rattling speeches that the Germans were undemocratic, unpredictable, and unstable.

These attitudes were reinforced by the fact that the United States had made a substantial investment in the Allied war effort. As the war progressed, it became apparent that the British blockade would permit American trade to be carried on only with the Allies. Before long, American factories and farmers were producing weapons and food solely for Great Britain and France. Industry expanded and began to enjoy a prosperity dependent on continued Allied purchases. Between 1914 and 1916, American exports to the Allies quadrupled. Allied bonds totaling about $1.5 billion were sold in the United States in 1915 and 1916. It was quite apparent to the Germans that there was little neutrality on the economic front in the United States.

What triggered the U.S. entry into the war on the Allied side was the German submarine tactics. Blockaded by the British, Germany decided to retaliate by halting all shipping to the Allies. Its submarine campaign began in February 1915, and one of the first victims was the luxury liner *Lusitania,* torpedoed with the loss of more than 1000 lives, including 100 Americans. This tragedy aroused public opinion in the United

States. In the fall of 1916, Wilson, campaigning with the slogan "He kept us out of war," was reelected to the presidency. Discovery of German plots to involve Mexico in the war against the United States and more submarine sinkings finally drove Wilson to ask Congress to declare war against Germany on April 6, 1917.

Submarine warfare and a wide range of other causes brought the president to the point of entering the war. Once in the conflict, however, he was intent on making the American sacrifice one "to make the world safe for democracy." Wilson's lofty principles caused a great surge of idealism among Americans.

Germany's Last Drive

The United States mobilized its tremendous resources of men and matériel more rapidly than the Germans had believed possible when they made their calculated risk to increase submarine warfare. Nonetheless, the Central Powers moved to try to gain a decisive victory before U.S. aid could help the Allies.

The fruitless offensives of 1917 had exhausted the British army, and the French had barely recovered from their mutinies. The eastern front collapsed with the February–March revolution in Russia. Eight months later, Lenin and the Bolsheviks took power in Russia and began to negotiate for peace. By the Treaty of Brest-Litovsk early in 1918, Russia made peace with Germany, giving up 1.3 million square miles of territory and 62 million people.

Freed from the necessity of fighting on the east, the Germans unleashed a series of major offensives against the west in the spring of 1918. During one of these attacks, a brigade of American marines symbolized the importance of U.S. support when they stopped a German charge at Château-Thierry (shah-TOH tee-ah-REE). The Germans made a final effort to knock out the French in July 1918. It was called the *Friedensturm* (FREED-en-sturm), the peace offensive. The Germans made substantial gains but did not score a decisive breakthrough. By this time the German momentum was slowing down,

MAP Europe at War: World War I, 1914–1919

Seeing Connections

African American Recipients of the *Croix de Guerre*

Around 380,000 African Americans served in the armed forces of the United States during World War I, with 200,000 of those serving on the western front in France. They were participants in President Woodrow Wilson's war to make the world safe for democracy, and yet they left a country dominated by racism and segregation in the South and Social Darwinism and racial prejudice in the North: in both parts of the country, they were often considered inferiors and were deprived, implicitly or explicitly, of the full rights of citizenship. Pictured here are nine soldiers from the 369th Infantry Regiment, also known as the "Harlem Hellfighters." Because the U.S. Army would not give African Americans official combat roles, the commander of the U.S. forces, General Pershing, assigned the unit to the French army, which had requested additional men. Almost one-third of the unit died in combat, and the French awarded the entire regiment the *Croix de Guerre* in recognition of their bravery under fire. These men and many other African American servicemen believed that they had found in France a greater degree of acceptance and tolerance than they had ever known in the United States. After the war, most of the soldiers returned home. There, having risked their lives to save democracy abroad, they would have to endure conditions in the United States that fell far short of the ideals of democracy.

and more than a million American "doughboys" had landed in France. The final German offensive was thrown back after a slight advance.

With the aid of U.S. troops, Marshal Ferdinand Foch (FOSH), the supreme Allied commander, began a counterattack. The badly beaten and continually harassed German troops fell back in rapid retreat. By the end of October, German forces had been driven out of France and Allied armies were advancing into Belgium. The war of fixed positions separated by no-man's land was over. The Allies had smashed the trench defenses and were now in open country.

By October 1, the German high command had already urged the kaiser to sue for peace, and three days later, the German chancellor sent a note to President Wilson seeking an end to hostilities. Wilson responded that peace was not possible as long as Germany was ruled by an autocratic regime. The German chancellor tried to keep the monarchy by instituting certain liberal reforms, but it was too late. Revolution broke out in many parts of Germany. The kaiser abdicated and fled to the Netherlands, and a republic was proclaimed.

While Germany was staggering under the continual pounding of Foch's armies, the German allies were suffering even greater misfortunes. Bulgaria surrendered on September 30, and Turkey a month later. Austria stopped its fighting with Italy on November 3. Nine days later, the Habsburg Empire collapsed when Emperor Charles I fled Vienna to seek sanctuary in Switzerland.

At five o'clock on the morning of November 11, 1918, in a railroad dining car in the Compiègne (kom-PIEN) Forest, the German delegates signed the peace terms presented by Marshal Foch. At eleven o'clock the same day, hostilities were halted. Everywhere except in Germany, the news was received with an outburst of joy. The world was once more at peace, confronted now with the task of binding up its wounds and removing the scars of combat. Delegates from the Allied nations were soon to meet in Paris, where the peace conference would be held.

The Allied Peace Settlement

Why was it so difficult for Allied leaders to achieve lasting peace in Europe?

In November 1918, the Allies stood triumphant, after the costliest war in history. But the Germans could also feel pleased at that moment. They had fought well, avoided being overrun, and escaped being occupied by the Allies. They could acknowledge they had lost the war but hoped that President Wilson would help them.

In February 1918, Wilson had stated that his governing principles would be that there would be no victimization of the defeated and that settlements would have to be approved by the people affected. As events transpired, however, the losers were refused seats at the peace conference. The leaders of the new German Weimar (VI-mar) Republic had no choice but to sign a dictated settlement—an act that simultaneously discredited the republic among the German people and served as the first step toward World War II.

Idealism and Realities

The destructiveness of World War I made a fair peace settlement impossible. The war had been fought on a winner-take-all basis, and now it was time for the Central Powers to pay. At the peace conference, the winning side was dominated by a French realist, a British politician, and an American idealist. The French representative was the aged premier Georges Clemenceau (KLEM-on-soh); representing Britain was the prime minister David Lloyd George; and the U.S. representative was President Woodrow Wilson. The three were joined by the Italian prime minister, Vittorio Orlando, who attended to make sure his country gained adequate compensation for its large sacrifices. These four men made most of the key decisions, even though most of the interested nations and factions in the world were represented in Paris, except for the Russians.

Clemenceau had played a colorful and important role in French politics for half a century. He had fought continuously for his political beliefs, opposing corruption, racism, and antidemocratic forces. He wanted to ensure French security in the future by pursuing restitution, reparations, and guarantees. Precise programs, not idealistic statements, would protect France.

The two English-speaking members of the Big Three represented the extremes in dealing with the Germans. Lloyd George had been reelected in December on a program of "squeezing the German lemon until the pips are squeaked." He wanted to destroy Berlin's naval, commercial, and colonial position and to ensure his own political future at home. In January 1918, President Wilson had given Congress a list known as the **Fourteen Points,** describing his plan for peace. Wilson wanted to break the world out of its tradition of armed anarchy and establish a framework for peace that would favor America's traditions of democracy and trade. At the peace conference, this shy and sensitive man communicated his beliefs with a coldness and an imperiousness that offended his colleagues.

The Great War had not been a "war to end all wars" or a war "to make the world safe for democracy." The United States had hardly been neutral in its loans and shipments of supplies to the Allies before 1917. In

Fourteen Points—President Woodrow Wilson's program to establish and maintain peace after World War I.

fact, during the war the financial and political center of balance for the world had crossed the ocean. The Americans made a rather abrupt shift from debtor to creditor status. The United States had entered the war late and had profited from it, and Wilson could afford to wear a rather more idealistic mantle.

The Europeans had paid for the war with the blood of their young and the coin of their realms. The Allies now looked forward to a healthy return on their investment. The extent of that harvest had long been mapped out in secret treaties, copies of which the Bolsheviks released for the world to see.

Open Covenants, Secret Treaties

Wilson wanted to use his Fourteen Points as the basis for a lasting peace. He wanted to place morality and justice ahead of power and revenge as considerations in international affairs. The first five points were general and guaranteed "open covenants openly arrived at," freedom of the seas in war and peace alike, removal of all economic barriers and establishment of an equality of trade among all nations, reductions in national armaments, and readjustment of all colonial claims, giving the interests of the population concerned equal weight with the claim of the government whose title was to be determined. The next eight points dealt with specific issues involving the evacuation and restoration of Allied territory, self-determination for minority nationalities, and the redrawing of European boundaries along national lines.

The fourteenth point contained the germ of the **League of Nations,** a general association of all nations whose purpose was to guarantee political independence and territorial integrity to great and small states alike. When Wilson arrived in Europe, the crowds on the streets and the victorious and the defeated nations alike greeted him as a messiah. His program had received great publicity, and its general, optimistic nature had earned him great praise.

League of Nations—International peacekeeping and humanitarian organization created in 1919 at the Paris peace conferences.

The victorious Allies came to Paris to gain the concrete rewards promised them in the various secret treaties. Under these pacts, which would not come to public knowledge until the beginning of 1919, the Allies had promised the Italians concessions that would turn the Adriatic into an Italian sea, the Russians the right to take over the Bosporus and Dardanelles Straits and Constantinople, the Romanians the right to take over large amounts of Austro-Hungarian territory, and the Japanese the right to keep the German territory of Kiaochow in China. In addition, the British and French divided what was formerly Ottoman-controlled Iraq and Syria into their respective spheres of influence. As for Palestine, on November 2, 1917, the British—with the agreement of President Wilson—in the declaration by Lord Arthur James Balfour, stated that "His Majesty's government looks favorably on the establishment of a national home for the Jewish people." Lord Balfour went on to affirm that nothing would be done that would "prejudice the civil and religious rights" of the non-Jewish communities in Palestine.

Wilson refused to consider these agreements, which many of the victors regarded as IOUs now due to be paid in return for their role in the war, but the contracting parties in the treaties would not easily set aside their deals to satisfy Wilson's ideals. Even before the beginning of formal talks—negotiations that would be unprecedented in their complexity—the Allies were split. Lloyd George and Clemenceau discovered early that Wilson had his price, and that was the League of Nations. They played on his desire for this organization to water down most of the 13 other points. They were also aware that Wilson's party had suffered a crushing defeat in the 1918 elections and that strong factions in the United States were drumming up opposition to his program.

The "Big Four" at the Versailles Peace Conference were, left to right, Prime Minister David Lloyd George of Britain, Prime Minister Vittorio Orlando of Italy, Premier Georges Clemenceau of France, and President Woodrow Wilson of the United States. Representatives from Germany were excluded from the negotiating tables. The Big Four became the Big Three when Orlando withdrew abruptly because the conference refused to give Italy all it demanded.

their identity and all its dimensions,"[3] was the most thoroughgoing attempt to destroy an entire people in history. Embracing discredited scientific theories, the Nazis identified themselves as the master race and Jews as a lower form of humanity and a threat to the purity of their own race. Their "final solution" to this problem was to kill over 6 million Jews, along with another 5 million "undesirables," including gypsies, homosexuals, handicapped people, communists, ethnic Slavs, criminals, and others.

Even before World War II was concluded, the Allies created the United Nations Commission for the Investigation of War Crimes. In 1945 and 1946, building on the Commission's work, the Allies established tribunals in Nuremberg and Tokyo to try German and Japanese leaders for violating the rules of war set forth in the Hague and Geneva conventions. The tribunal at Nuremberg represented the first international war crimes trial in history. Of the 22 men tried by the tribunal, 19 were found guilty and 11 were subsequently executed. Later, during the Tokyo tribunal, 28 Japanese leaders were tried for war crimes and seven received the death sentence.

In 1948 and 1949, the United Nations legally defined the destruction of one people by another as *genocide,* a crime against humanity:

> *"... a public policy whose intent is either (a) the extermination of a collectivity or category, usually a communal group or class, or (b) the killing of a large fraction of a collectivity or category including the families of its members, and the destruction of its social and cultural identity in most or all of its aspects."*[4]

Neither the lessons of World War II nor the precedents of Nuremberg and Tokyo, however, prevented serious violations of the rules of war, including genocide, from occurring again. During the 1970s, the communist Khmer Rouge regime set out to eliminate Cambodia's professional and middle classes, leading to the death of 1.6 million people, or 20 percent of the population. While the world condemned this outrage, the international community did nothing to punish those who had committed war crimes and crimes against humanity.

The international community was again confronted by serious war crimes and genocide in the 1990s. In 1992, after the republic of Bosnia and Herzegovina voted to secede from the crumbling Yugoslavian nation, Serbian forces began a process of population transfer and murder known as "ethnic cleansing." In places like Vukovar and Srebenica, Serbian militias rounded up and executed Bosnian men. Serbian forces also used gang rape as a weapon to terrorize Bosnian women. Croats and, to a lesser extent, Bosnian forces responded with similar outrages until the Dayton Peace Accords in 1995 brought the war to an end. Some 200,000 people were killed and 2 million people displaced in the fighting. Four years later, the Serbs repeated their policies of ethnic cleansing in Kosovo, driving nearly 800,000 Albanian residents out of the country.

While the fighting raged in the former Yugoslavia, an even greater atrocity occurred in the Central African nation of Rwanda. There, between April and August of 1994, radicalized Hutus slaughtered some 800,000 Tutsis and moderate Hutus. A Hutu elite organized the genocide, training and arming radical Hutu militias in advance, and nobody—not the old nor the young, neither women nor children—was to be spared. Instructions on how to kill the Tutsis were broadcast over the national radio stations. The killing was a preindustrial, personalized massacre, done for the large part with machetes, clubs with nails, farm tools, or even kitchen implements.[5]

While the international community was unable to prevent the atrocities committed in either the former Yugoslavia or Rwanda, in both instances it attempted to punish the perpetrators. In 1993, the United Nations Security Council established the International Criminal Tribunal for the former Yugoslavia (ICTY), based in The Hague, to try war-crimes cases. The tribunal began its work in July 1994, and a decade later it is still trying war criminals. Its most important trial to date was of ex-Yugoslav president Slobodan Milosevic, who was charged with more than 60 war crimes until he died in 2006 before he could be convicted. In 1994, the United Nations Security Council also established an International Criminal Tribunal for Rwanda (ICTR) in Arusha, Tanzania. So far it has tried nine people for genocide and another 40 are waiting to be tried.

In 1998 the United Nations celebrated the fiftieth anniversary of the Universal Declaration of Human Rights—which proclaimed the basic civil, political, social, and economic rights of all of the world's citizens. Even against the tide of atrocities cited above and more recent ongoing atrocities that have occurred elsewhere such as the Darfur region of Sudan, international law in the area of war crimes is making progress. Nongovernmental organizations (NGOs) such as Amnesty International and Human Rights Watch monitor conflicts throughout the world and issue reports identifying war crimes and crimes against humanity—while such reports carry no formal weight in international law, they do influence public opinion and can spark the international community to take action. Additionally, law schools around the world have changed their curricula to include courses on both human rights and international law and the number of lawyers working in these areas has increased.

Questions

1. Why is it so difficult to reconcile national sovereignty and international law? In your answer consider the United States' refusal to participate in the International Criminal Court.
2. What are the strengths and weaknesses that the United Nations brings to the task of enforcing international laws concerning the rules of war?
3. At what point does ethnic cleansing end and genocide begin?

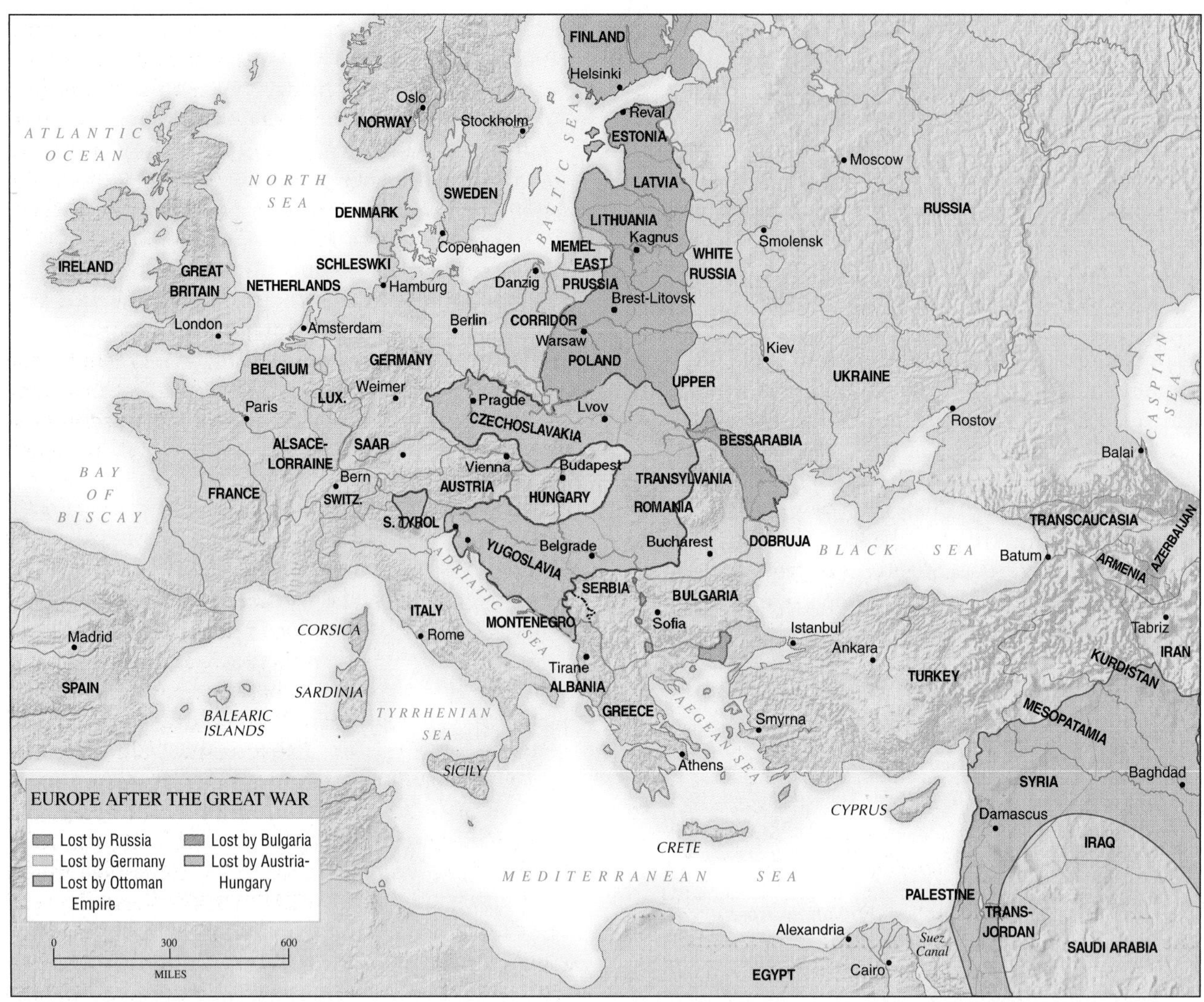

▲ In the aftermath of World War I, Europe lost four empires—the Russian, Ottoman, Austro-Hungarian, and German—and gained a number of successor states, each unhappy with its new boundaries.

Redrawing German Boundaries

After establishing the League, the diplomats got down to the business of dealing with Germany. France reclaimed Alsace-Lorraine, and plebiscites gave parts of the former German Empire to Denmark and Belgium. The French wanted to build a buffer state, made up of former German territory west of the Rhine, to be dominated by France. The Americans and the British proposed a compromise to Clemenceau, which he accepted. The territory in question would be occupied by Allied troops for a period of 5 to 15 years, and a zone extending 30 miles east of the Rhine was to be demilitarized.

In addition, the French claimed the Saar basin, a rich coal-mining area. Although they did not take outright control of the area, which reverted to League administration, they did gain ownership of the mines in compensation for the destruction of their own installations in northern France. It was agreed that after 15 years, a plebiscite—a vote of all the electorate—would be held in the area. Finally, Wilson and Lloyd George agreed that the United States and Great Britain would, by treaty, guarantee France against aggression.

In eastern Europe, the conference created the "Polish corridor," which separated East Prussia from the rest of Germany, in order to give the newly created state of Poland access to the sea. This raised grave problems, as it included territory in which there were large numbers of Germans. (The land in question had been taken from Poland by Prussia in the eighteenth century.) A portion of Silesia, north of the new state of Czechoslovakia, was also ceded to Poland, but Danzig, a German city, was placed under League jurisdiction. All in all, Germany lost 25,000 square miles inhabited by 6 million people—a fact seized on by German nationalist leaders in the 1920s.

The Mandate System and Reparations

A curious mixture of idealism and revenge determined the allocation of the German colonies and certain territories belonging to Turkey. Because outright annexation would look too much like unvarnished imperialism, it was suggested that the colonies be turned over to the League, which in turn would give them to certain of its members to administer. The colonies were to be known as **mandates,** and precautions were taken to ensure that they would be administered for the well-being and development of the inhabitants. Once a year, the mandatory powers were to present a detailed account of their administration of the territories of the League. The mandate system was a step forward in colonial administration, but Germany nevertheless was deprived of all colonies, with the excuse that it could not rule them justly or efficiently.

As the **Treaty of Versailles** (ver-SIGH) took shape, the central concept was that Germany had been responsible for the war. Article 231 of the treaty stated explicitly:

> *The Allied and Associated Governments affirm and Germany accepts the responsibility of Germany and her allies for causing all the loss and damage to which the Allied and Associated Governments and their nationals have been subjected as a consequence of the war imposed upon them by the aggression of Germany and her Allies.*

Britain and France demanded that Germany pay the total cost of the war, including pensions. The United States protested this demand, and, eventually, a compromise emerged in which, with the exception of Belgium, Germany had to pay only war damages, including those suffered by civilians, and the cost of pensions. These payments, called **reparations** (implying repair), were exacted on the ground that Germany should bear responsibility for the war.

Although the Allies agreed that Germany should pay reparations, they could not agree on how much should be paid. Some demands ran as high as $200 billion. Finally, it was decided that a committee should fix the amount; in the meantime, Germany was to begin making payments. By the time the committee report appeared in May 1921, the payments totaled nearly $2 billion. The final bill came to $32.5 billion, to be paid off by Germany by 1963.

mandates–A grant of authority from the League of Nation to a state to set up a government and other institutions in former German colonies.

Treaty of Versailles–During the peace conferences to end World War I, the actual negotiations with the various Central Powers took place at selected suburbs around Paris. The conference dealing with Germany took place at the former residence of French kings, Versailles.

reparations–Payments demanded from Germany to pay for the costs of the war.

The Allies required Germany, as part of in-kind reparations payments, to hand over most of its merchant fleet, construct new ships capable of handling 1 million tons of cargo for the Allies, and deliver vast amounts of coal, equipment, and machinery to them. The conference permitted Germany a standing army of only 100,000 men, a greatly reduced fleet, and no military aircraft. Munitions plants were to be closely supervised.

The treaty also called for the kaiser to be tried for a "supreme offense against international morality and the sanctity of treaties," thus setting a precedent for the Nuremberg tribunals after World War II. Nothing came of this demand, however. The kaiser remained in Holland, protected in his exile by the Dutch government.

Dictated Treaties

Before coming to Paris in April 1919 to receive the Treaty of Versailles, the German delegation was given no official information about its terms and thus no opportunity to debate points it found to be unjust. Allied governments stated that "Germany and its people were alone guilty." The Weimar delegation had no alternative but to sign. The continued blockade created great hardships in Germany, and the Allies threatened an invasion if the Germans did not accept the peace. The treaty was signed on June 28, the fifth anniversary of the assassination of Archduke Francis Ferdinand, in the Hall of Mirrors at Versailles, the same room where the German Empire had been proclaimed. As one American wrote, "The affair was elaborately staged and made as humiliating to the enemy as it well could be."[6]

The Allies imposed equally harsh treaties on Germany's supporters. The Treaty of St. Germain (1919) with Austria recognized the nationalist movements of the Czechs, Poles, and southern Slavs. These groups had already formed states and reduced the remnants of the former Dual Monarchy into the separate states of Austria and Hungary. Austria became a landlocked country of 32,000 square miles and 6 million people. It was forbidden to seek **Anschluss** (ON-schlus)—union with Germany. Italy acquired sections of Austria, South Tyrol, Trentino (with its 250,000 Austrian Germans), and the northeastern coast of the Adriatic, with its large numbers of Slavs.

To complete their control of the Adriatic, the Italians wanted a slice of the Dalmatian coast and the port of Fiume (fee-YOU-may). That city, however, was the natural port for the newly created state of Yugoslavia, and it had not been promised to the Italians in 1915. Wilson declared the Italian claim to be a contradiction of the principle of self-determination, and the ensuing

Anschluss–Union between Austria and Germany.

controversy almost wrecked the peace conference. The issue was not settled until 1920, when Italy renounced its claim to Dalmatia and Fiume became an independent state. Four years later it was ceded to Italy.

By the Treaty of Sèvres (SEV-ruh; 1920), the Ottoman Empire was placed on the operating table of power politics and divided among Greece, Britain, and France. An upheaval in August 1920 in Constantinople led to the emergence of the Nationalists under Mustafa Kemal, who refused to accept the treaty. Not until July 1923 did Turkey's postwar status become clear in the milder Treaty of Lausanne (loo-ZAHN), which guaranteed Turkish control of Anatolia (see Chapter 30).

Hungary (Treaty of Trianon, 1920) and Bulgaria (Treaty of Neuilly, 1919) did not fare as well as Turkey in dealing with the Allies. The Hungarians lost territory to Czechoslovakia, Yugoslavia, and Romania. Bulgaria lost access to the Aegean Sea and territory populated by nearly 1 million people, had to pay a huge indemnity, and underwent demilitarization.

The eastern European states that profited from the settlements proved to be useful allies for France in the first 15 years of the interwar period. Those that suffered were easy prey for the Nazis in the 1930s.

Evaluating the Peacemakers

The treaties ending World War I have received heavy criticism from diplomatic historians, especially when compared with the work of the Congress of Vienna. The peace that emerged brought only weariness, new disagreements, and inflation.

Russia was completely disregarded. The new Bolshevik government (see Chapter 28), in its weak position, indicated a willingness to deal with the West on the issue of prewar debts and border conflicts, if the West would extend financial aid and withdraw its expeditionary forces. The anti-Bolshevik forces in Paris did not take the offer seriously. By missing this opportunity, the Allies took a course that had tremendous consequences for "the long-term future of both the Russian and the American people and indeed of mankind generally."[7]

Many commentators have laid the genesis of World War II just one generation later at the feet of the Paris peacemakers. Other critics point out that the United States' reversion to isolationism doomed the work of the conference. Furthermore, there were never any broad plans made for European economic recovery.

Peace Treaties Ending World War

Treaty	
Versailles	Germany (1919)
St. Germaine	Austria (1919)
Neuilly	Bulgaria (1919)
Sèvres	Turkey (1920 refused; Lausanne 1923)
Trianon	Hungary (1920)

The Costs of the War

It is impossible to give a true accounting of the costs of any war because there is no way to calculate the contributions that might have been made by the individuals killed in battle. About 2 to 3 million Russians died, and more perished in the 1918–1921 civil war. Among the other major participants, almost 2 million Germans, over 1.5 million French, close to 1 million English, 500,000 Italians, 1.2 million Austro-Hungarians, and 325,000 Turks died in battle. These figures do not count the wounded, whose lives may have been shortened or altered as a result of their injuries. Furthermore, the young paid the highest price: scholars estimate that Germany and France each lost over 15 percent of their young men.

Estimates of the financial drain of the war range between $250 billion and $300 billion in early 1920s dollars. These figures do not bring home the depth of the war's impact on trade, shipping, and monetary stability. Belgium, for example, lost over 300,000 houses and thousands of factories, and 15,000 square miles of northeastern France were in ruins. How does one calculate the cost of taking the 75 million men who were mobilized away from their jobs and their homes? How can the mental carnage inflicted on the combatants and their families be measured? No balance sheet can measure the psychological toll of the conflict on the women and children who had to bear the tension of fear and loneliness for their loved ones at the front.

Political institutions felt the effects of the war in different ways. The German, Habsburg, Russian, and Ottoman empires crumbled and disappeared from the historical stage. Replacing them were uncertain republics or dictatorships. The colonial empires that remained were weakened, and indigenous nationalist movements made substantial progress.

The roots of the economic problems that plagued Europe after the war—agricultural overproduction, bureaucratic regulations, and protectionism—could be seen before 1914. Compounding these factors were the traditional challenges encountered in shifting from a wartime to a peacetime economy, especially that of demobilizing millions of soldiers and bringing them back into the labor market. Finally, the globe reeled under the blows of an influenza outbreak that ultimately killed twice as many people as the war did. The epidemic was both a tragic conclusion to the war years and a tragic first step toward the future.

Economic Disasters

In what ways did the First World War destroy global economic equilibrium?

One of the most serious problems facing the survivors of World War I was the confused and desperate situation of the world economy. Much of the direct and indirect cost of the war had been covered by borrowing, and now the bills were coming due in a world unable to pay them. The lasting results of the war touched many areas. The conflict altered global trading patterns, reduced shipping, and weakened Europe's former economic dominance. The various peace treaties multiplied the number of European boundaries, which soon became obstacles to the flow of goods, especially in the successor states of the Habsburg monarchy and in Poland. Rail and communications lines had to be reconfigured to reflect the interest of newly created states.

	Postwar Economic Events
1919–1923	Inflation (except in Britain and Czechoslovakia)
1922	Great Britain pledges to moderate debt collections
1923–1924	German hyperinflation
1924	Dawes Plan for liberalized reparations and loans for German recovery
1929	U.S. stock market crash (October 29)
1930–1940	Great Depression

The Debt Problem

During the war, a radical change had taken place in Europe's economic relationship with the United States. In 1914, the United States had been a debtor nation for the amount of $3.75 billion, owed mostly to Europe. The war totally reversed this situation. The United States lent billions of dollars and sold tons of supplies to the Allies. British blockades kept the United States from being able to deal with the Germans, precluding further profits, but by 1919 Europeans owed the United States more than $10 billion. This tremendous debt posed what economists call a transfer problem. The international obligations could be paid only by the actual transfer of gold or by the sale of goods.

Complicating the picture, Allied powers in Europe had also lent each other funds, with the British acting as the chief banker, lending more than 1.7 billion pounds sterling. When the Allies' credit dried up, they turned to the United States for financial help. Even though Britain owed huge sums to U.S. financiers, it remained a net creditor of $4 billion because of money owed it by European debtors. France, by contrast, stood as a net debtor of $3.5 billion. In addition to its own war debts, the French government suffered greatly when the Bolsheviks renounced repayment of the tsarist debt, amounting to some 12 billion francs—one-quarter of France's foreign holdings.

Some of the Allies argued that the inter-Allied debts were political, that all of them had, in effect, been poured into a common pool for victory. These people wondered how France's contribution in the lives of its young men could be figured into the equation in terms of francs, dollars, or pounds. They proposed that, with victory, all debts should be canceled. The United States, which had gone to Paris with a conciliatory spirit toward Germany in the treaty negotiations, changed its tune when dollars and cents were involved. This attitude was best expressed in a remark attributed to the American president Calvin Coolidge, who expected full repayment, when he is alleged to have said: "They hired [borrowed] the money, didn't they?" Beneath the extremes of these positions were the understandable motives of getting out of paying a huge debt or gaining from the payment of debts owed.

Weimar Germany: Debt, Reparations, and Inflation

Reparations complicated Germany's debt problem and the challenge of converting the country back to a peacetime economy. In the first 3 years after the war the German government, like other European states, spent much more than its income. This policy was masked by "floating debts ... in other words, by the printing press."[8] The mark, which had been valued at 4.2 to the dollar in 1914, went to 75 in July 1921, to 186 in January 1922, to 402 in July, and to 4000 by December of that year. The situation became so serious in the summer of 1922 that Great Britain proposed collecting no more from its debtors—Allied and German alike—than the United States collected from Britain itself. Such "statesmanship" was prompted by the fact that London had gained what it wanted from the peace settlement: Germany's navy was destroyed, Germany's merchant ships were transferred as reparations, and Germany's empire was gone. No more could be squeezed out.

Britain saw that Germany would not be able to meet its reparations payments. Without those payments, the

▲ Under the Weimar inflation in 1923, play money took on a new meaning as hyperinflation reduced German money to a value worth less than the paper it was printed on.

victors would not be able to make their own payments on the inter-Allied debts, especially debts owed to the United States. Although the United States insisted that there was no connection between the inter-Allied debts and German reparations, negotiations were carried on, and debt payment plans were set up with 13 nations. No reductions were made in principal, but in every case the interest rate was radically decreased. Still, the total amount owed came to more than $22 billion.

At the end of 1922, the Germans asked for a delay in their reparations obligations and then defaulted on some payments. In response, in January 1923, French troops, supported by Belgian and Italian contingents, marched into the rich industrial district of the Ruhr, undeterred by American and British objections. This shortsighted French move contributed nothing to the solution of Europe's problems and played into the hands of radical German politicians.

Encouraged by the Berlin government, German workers defied the French army and went on strike; many ended up in jail. The French toyed for a while with the idea of establishing a separate state in the Rhineland to act as a buffer between Germany and France. Chaotic conditions in the Ruhr encouraged the catastrophic inflation of the German currency to make up for the loss of exports and to support the striking workers. The value of the mark to the dollar went from 7200 in January 1923 to 160,000 in July to 1 million in August to 4.2 trillion in December. During the worst part of the inflation, the Reichsbank had 150 firms using 2000 presses running day and night to print banknotes. To get out of their dilemma, the Germans made an effective transition to a more stable currency by simply abandoning the old one. The French, in return, gained little benefit from their occupation of German territory.

Inflation and Its Consequences

All European nations encountered a rocky path as they attempted to gain equilibrium after the war. Britain had minimal price increases and returned to prewar levels within 2 years after the signing of the Versailles treaty. On the Continent, price and monetary stability came less easily. Only Czechoslovakia seemed to have its economic affairs well in hand.

France did not stabilize its currency until 1926, when the franc was worth 50 to the dollar (one-tenth its value in 1914). In Austria, prices rose to 14,000 times their prewar level until stability of sorts came in 1922. Hungary's prices went to 23,000 times prewar level, but this increase is dwarfed by Poland's (2.5 million times prewar level) and Russia's (4 billion times prewar level).

Inflation had massive social and political consequences, most notably in Germany. Millions of middle-class Germans, small property owners who were the hoped-for base of the new Weimar Republic, found themselves caught in the wage-price squeeze. Prices for the necessities of life rose far faster than income or savings. As mothers wheeled baby carriages full of money to bakeries to buy bread, fathers watched a lifetime of savings dwindle to insignificance. Pensioners on fixed incomes suffered doubly under this crisis. The bourgeoisie, the historical champions of liberal politics throughout Europe, suffered blows more devastating than those of war, since inflation stole not only the value of their labor but also the worth of their savings and insurance.

Where the middle classes and liberal traditions were strong, democracy could weather the inflationary storm. But in central Europe, where they were not—especially in Germany, where the inflation was worst—the cause of future totalitarianism received an immense boost. Alan Bullock, a biographer of Adolf Hitler, wrote that "the result of inflation was to undermine the foundations of German society in a way which neither the war nor the revolution of 1918 nor the Treaty of Versailles had ever done."[9]

Temporary Improvements

After 1923, the liberal application of U.S. funds brought some calm to the economic storm. Business was more difficult to conduct because protectionism became more and more the dominant trait of international trade. **Autarky,** the goal of gaining total economic self-sufficiency and freedom from reliance on any other nation, increasingly became the unstated policy of many governments.

Nonetheless, production soon reached 1913 levels, currencies began to stabilize, and the French finally recalled their troops from the Ruhr. Most significant, in September 1924, a commission under the leadership of U.S. banker Charles Dawes formulated a more liberal reparations policy in order to get the entire repayment cycle back into motion. Dawes's plan, replaced in 1929 by the Young plan (named for its principal formulator, U.S. businessman Owen Young), reduced installments and extended them over a longer period. A loan of $200 million, mostly from the United States, was floated to aid German recovery. The Berlin government resumed payments to the Allies, and the Allies paid their debt installments to the United States—which in effect received its own money back again.

Prosperity of a sort returned to Europe. As long as the circular flow of cash from the United States to Germany to the Allies to the United States continued, the international monetary system functioned. The moment the cycle broke down, the world economy headed for the rocks of **depression.** One economic historian has written:

> *In 1924–31 Germany drew some one [billion] pounds [sterling] from abroad and the irony was that Germany, in fact, received far more in loans, including loans to enable her to pay interest on earlier loans than she paid out in reparations, thus gaining in the circular flow and re-equipping her industries and her public utilities with American funds in the processes in the 1920s before repudiating her debts in the 1930s.*[10]

Danger Signs

The system broke down in 1928 and 1929 when U.S. and British creditors needed their capital for investments in their own countries. Extensions on loans, readily granted a year earlier, were refused. Even before the U.S. stock market crash between October 24 (Black Thursday) and October 29 (Black Tuesday), 1929, disaster was on the horizon.

Few people in America could admit such a possibility during the decade preceding the crash, however. The United States had become the commercial center of the world, and its policies were central to the world's financial health. The United States still had an internal market in the 1920s with a seemingly inexhaustible appetite for new products such as radios, refrigerators, electrical appliances, and automobiles. This expansion, based on consumer goods and supported by a seemingly limitless supply of natural resources, gave the impression of solid and endless growth.

Tragically, the contradictions of the postwar economic structure were making themselves felt. The cornerstones of pre-1914 prosperity—multilateral trade, the gold standard, and interchangeable currencies—were crumbling. The policies of autarky, with high tariff barriers to protect home products against foreign competition, worked against international economic health. Ironically, the United States led the way toward higher tariffs, and other nations quickly retaliated. American foreign trade declined seriously, and the volume of world trade decreased.

There were other danger signals. Europe suffered a population decline. There were 22 million fewer people in the 1920s in the western part of the Continent than had been expected. The decrease in internal markets affected trade, as did the higher external barriers. Around the globe, the agricultural sector suffered from declining prices during the 1920s. At the same time that farmers received less for their products, they had to pay more to live—a condition that negatively affected peasants in Europe and Asia and farmers and ranchers in the United States.

In the hope of reaching a wider market, farmers around the world borrowed money to expand production early in the 1920s. Temporarily, the food surplus benefited consumers, but across the world, agricultural interests suffered from overproduction. Tariff barriers prevented foodstuffs from circulating to the countries where hunger existed. By the end of the decade, people in Asia were starving while wheat farmers in Whitman County, Washington, dumped their grain into the Snake River and coffee growers in Brazil saw their product burned to fuel steam locomotives. Many farmers went bankrupt, unable to keep up with payments on these debts. The countryside preceded the cities into the economic tragedy.

The Great Crash

Because of America's central position in the world economy, any development on Wall Street, positive or negative, reverberated around the globe. The United States, with roughly 3 percent of the world's population, produced 46 percent of the globe's industrial output. The country was too shortsighted to use its

autarky—The program of total economic self-sufficiency.

depression—A time of stagnant economic activity in which high unemployment occurs.

newfound power wisely. Its financial life in the 1920s was dominated by the activities of daring and sometimes unscrupulous speculators who made the arena of high finance a precarious and exciting world of its own. The businessmen creating this world were not pursuing long-term stability. Their blind rush for profit led to America's crash, which in turn sparked a world disaster. Even before the stock market crash, Wall Street had been showing signs of distress, such as capital shortfalls, excessively large inventories, and agricultural bankruptcies. But nothing prepared financiers for the disaster that struck on October 24, 1929—Black Thursday. By noon, Wall Street was caught in a momentum of chaotic fear, and stock prices began plummeting. The end of the trading session halted the initial hemorrhage of stock values, but the damage was done.

The economist John Kenneth Galbraith has written: "On the whole, the great stock market crash can be much more readily explained than the depression that followed it."[11] Over-speculation, loose controls, dishonest investors, and a loss of confidence in the ever-upward market trend can be identified as causes for the crash. Further causes can be traced to the inequitable distribution of wealth, with the farmers and workers left out while the top 3 percent of Americans grew incredibly rich and irresponsible. Industrial overexpansion was fueled by speculators buying stock "on margin," with insufficient cash backing for the investments. In addition, the government's hands-off policies permitted massive abuses to take place unchecked.

The international impact of the crash can be explained by the involvement in the U.S. market of investors and bankers from a number of countries, the interdependent world economic structure, the peculiar Allied debt and reparations structure, the growing agricultural crisis, and the inadequate banking systems of the world.

Some economic historians believe that the cycle of highs and lows hit a particularly vicious low point in 1929. Crashes had occurred before, but never with such widespread repercussions over such a long period of time. In the United States, stock prices declined one-third overall within a few weeks, wiping out fortunes, shattering confidence in business, and destroying consumer demand. The disaster spread worldwide as American interests demanded payment on foreign loans and imports decreased. The Kredit-Anstalt (kre-DIT an-SHTALT) bank of Vienna did not have enough money to fill demands for funds from French banks and failed in 1931. This collapse set in motion a dominolike banking crisis throughout Europe. Forecasts by Washington politicians and New York financiers that the worst was over and that the world economy was fundamentally sound after a "technical readjustment" convinced nobody. There would be no easy recovery.

The World Depression

By 1932, the value of industrial shares had fallen close to 60 percent on the New York and Berlin markets. Unemployment doubled in Germany, and 25 percent of the labor force was out of work in the United States. The middle classes, which had invested in the stock market, saw their investments and savings wiped out. In nation after nation, industry declined, prices fell, banks collapsed, and economies stagnated. In the Western democracies, the depression heightened the feelings of uneasiness that had existed since 1918. In other countries, the tendency to seek authoritarian solutions became even more pronounced. Throughout the world, people feared a future marked by lowered standards of living, unemployment, and hunger.

DOCUMENT
The Great Depression

The middle classes on the Continent, which had suffered from inflation during the 1920s, became caught in a whiplash effect during the depression. Adherence to old liberal principles collapsed in the face of economic insecurity, and state control of the economies increased. Governments raised tariffs to restrict imports and reverted to command economies, an expedient usually reserved for wartime. As conditions deteriorated, fear caused most governments to look no farther than their own boundaries. Under the competing

▼ Bankrupt investor Walter Thornton attempts to sell his car for $100 following the stock market crash of October 29, 1929, "Black Tuesday."

systems of autarky, each nation tried to increase exports and decrease imports.

After almost a century of free trade, modified by a comparatively few protective duties levied during and after World War I, Great Britain finally enacted a high tariff in 1932 with provisions to protect members of its empire. In the United States, the Hawley-Smoot Tariff of 1930 increased the value-added duty to 50 percent on a wide variety of agricultural and manufactured imports.

Another technique to increase exports at the expense of others was to depreciate a nation's currency—that is, to reduce the value of its money. When Japan depreciated the yen, for example, a U.S. dollar or British pound could buy more Japanese goods. In effect, lowering the yen reduced the price of Japanese exports. In most cases, however, devaluation brought only a temporary trade advantage. Other nations could play the same game, as the United States did in 1934 when it abandoned the gold standard and reduced the amount of gold backing for the dollar by 40 percent.

The debt problem that grew out of the war worsened during the depression. In 1931, President Herbert Hoover gained a 1-year moratorium on all intergovernmental debts. The next year, European leaders meeting at Lausanne practically canceled German reparations payments in the hope that the United States would make corresponding concessions in reducing war debts. The Americans, for a variety of domestic financial and political reasons, refused to concede that there was a logical connection between reparations and war debts. As the depression deepened, the debtors could not continue their payments. France refused outright in 1932; Germany after 1933 completely stopped paying reparations; Britain and four other nations made token payments for a time and then stopped entirely in 1934. Only Finland continued to meet its schedule of payments.

Families had at least as many problems in paying their bills as the governments of the world. Factories closed down and laid off their workers. Harvests rotted in the fields as the price of wheat fell to its lowest price in 300 years and other agricultural commodities suffered similar price declines. The lives of the cacao grower along Africa's Gold Coast, the coffee grower in Brazil, and the plantation worker in the Netherlands East Indies were as affected as those of the factory worker in Pittsburgh, Lille, or Frankfurt.

The 1929 crash occurred in an economic framework still suffering from the dislocations of World War I. It began a downturn in the world economy that would not end until the world armed for another global conflict. Whether the depression ended because of World War II or whether the world would have eventually recovered on its own is a question that will always be debated. The weaknesses in American stock market operations were by and large addressed in a series of reforms.

From the major banks to the soup lines in villages, the depression had profound implications for politics. The combination of inflation and depression threatened representative government. Unemployed and starving masses were tempted to turn to dictators who promised jobs and bread. The hardships of economic stability, even in countries where the liberal tradition was strongest, led to a massive increase in state participation in the daily life of the individual.

Politics in the Democracies

What were the effects of the economic crises on democratic governments between the war?

During the interwar period, there was a loss of belief in the genius of big business and free market capitalism in most parts of the world, as business itself had to turn more and more to the powers of the state to survive. After 1918, parliamentary government—the foundation of all that the liberals of the nineteenth century had worked for—came under attack everywhere.

For the most part, only in Scandinavia—in Norway, Sweden, and Denmark—did representative government operate smoothly throughout the interwar period. Economic prosperity prevailed there throughout the 1920s, and the depression was less severe than in Britain, France, or the United States. Switzerland, the Netherlands, and Belgium also maintained relatively high standards of living and kept their governments on the democratic road. But in the 20 years after peace came to the West, Britain, France, the United States, and most of the other democracies exhibited lethargy and shortsightedness in the face of fascist aggression.

Interwar Western Society: Mass Escapism and Despair

After the devastating losses of the war and during the political and economic crises of the 1920s, the urban working and lower middle classes found escape in the popular cultural products of their countries. More leisure time and money enabled them to fill the music halls and public sporting arenas. They would rarely be found in the concert halls, art galleries, or serious bookstores. Rather, they read the penny press and dime novels, both of which featured simple vocabulary and easy-to-follow information and plots. The penny press served many functions: to inform, entertain, and sell goods. Sensationalism, whether the confessions of a "fallen woman" or the account of some adventurer, was the main attraction of dime novels. Comic strips first appeared in central Europe in the 1890s and then

▲ The German actress Marlene Dietrich became an internationally known celebrity through her performances in films such as *The Blue Angel.*

spread rapidly throughout the Western world. By the interwar period, mass culture offered relief from the bad news of the time.

A number of technological advances—coated celluloid film, improved shutter mechanisms, reliable projectors, and a safe source of illumination—were combined to introduce the cinema—motion pictures, or movies—to the world. These developments seem to have come together almost simultaneously in France, Britain, and the United States. The first public motion picture performances took place in Paris in 1895 and soon after in London and New York. Even though another 20 years passed before feature-length films were produced, movies were an immediate success, attracting an infinitely larger audience than live performances could ever reach. By the 1920s, movies had become the most popular, most universal art form of the twentieth century. From the theaters of Main Street, USA, to the private projection rooms of the Kremlin, artists such as Charlie Chaplin and Marlene Dietrich became universal favorites.

Technology touched the common people in many ways and vastly expanded leisure possibilities. Henry Ford's affordable Model T made automobiles widely accessible and opened up the world to those who cared to drive. In cities, virtually every home had electricity, which powered bright lights, refrigeration, and other conveniences. Radio brought drama, sports, and news into millions of living rooms. And the new technology vastly increased access to music.

Through radio and phonograph records millions of people discovered jazz, formerly the special preserve of black musicians and their audiences. Louis Armstrong and his trumpet and Paul Whiteman and his band became known worldwide. At the same time, Rosa Ponselle, Arturo Toscanini, and other figures from the opera and concert world became celebrities known to millions more than could ever have seen them perform in person.

The combination of increased leisure time, greater mobility, and improved communications led to the development of the modern "star" system in sports and entertainment. Sports, including football in its North American and European forms, bicycle racing, cricket, baseball, and boxing, captured the popular imagination. As times became more difficult and front-page news turned grim after World War I, the world's citizens could find some diversion in reading about their boxers—Jack Dempsey, Max Schmeling, and Georges Carpentier. In the United States, golfers and baseball stars became better known and better paid than presidents.

While the masses escaped, the elites found little hope. Among writers, Franz Kafka (1883–1924) perhaps best captured the nightmarish nature of the post–World War I world. In works such as *The Metamorphosis* and *The Trial,* he portrayed a ritualistic society in which a well-organized insanity prevails. Rational, well-meaning individuals run a constant maze from which there is no exit, only more structures.

Many sensitive artists and writers cast serious doubt on the Renaissance notion that "man is the measure of all things." Writers such as Thomas Mann (1875–1955), in his book *The Magic Mountain,* gave testimony that the Western world had gone very far off course, and the best that could be hoped for was survival. Historians worked under the profound influence of Oswald Spengler's *The Decline of the West.* The book, finished 1 year before the defeat of the Central Powers, was more widely quoted than read. In it the German historian traced the life span of cultures, from birth through maturity to death, and identified the symptoms of the West's demise. Other writers expressed a similar fascination with the death of their civilization, but perhaps more significant was that people in the West knew Spengler's name and general message. And they found the pessimistic tone justified by events.

Britain, 1919–1939

The 1920s were not a tranquil decade for Great Britain. The country endured a number of social and political crises tied to the bitter labor disputes and unemployment that disrupted the nation. Neither Liberals nor Conservatives could do much to alter the flow of events immediately after the war. From 1919 to 1922, David Lloyd George led a coalition, but it broke apart, leading to the division and decline of the Liberals. From May 1923 to January 1924, Stanley Baldwin led an unsuccessful Conservative government.

Ramsay MacDonald formed the first Labour government and became the first socialist prime minister. For ten months, he and his party pursued a program to introduce socialism slowly and within the democratic framework. His move to recognize the newly established Soviet Union (USSR) was controversial. When the London *Times* published the so-called Zinoviev (zi-NOH-vee-EF) letter, a document in which the Communist Third International supposedly laid out a program for revolution in Britain, the public backlash defeated the Labour government in the October 1924 elections.

For the next 5 years, the Conservatives under Baldwin held power. After renouncing the treaties the Labour cabinet had made with the USSR, the Conservatives set out on a generally unsuccessful and stormy tenure. Britain returned its currency to the gold standard in 1925, a policy that led indirectly to an increase in labor unrest. The government struggled through a coal strike and a general strike in which more than 2.5 million of the nation's 6 million workers walked out. Baldwin reduced taxes on business, but this move did little to remedy the deflationary effect of a return to the gold standard.

In May 1929, Labour under MacDonald won another victory. Once again, the Labourites resumed relations with the Soviet Union and attempted their measured socialist program. The effects of the depression, however, condemned MacDonald and his government to failure. In 2 years, exports and imports declined 35 percent and close to 3 million unemployed people roamed the streets. Labour could do little to address the basic causes of the disaster; in fact, no single party could. When MacDonald's government fell in 1931, it was replaced by a national coalition government dominated by the Conservatives. The coalition government initiated a recovery program featuring a balanced budget, limited social spending, and encouragement of private enterprise. By 1933, a substantial measure of prosperity had been regained, and productivity had increased by 23 percent over the 1929 level.

To achieve this comeback, some of what remained of laissez-faire policy was discarded. The government regulated the currency, levied high tariffs, gave farmers subsidies, and imposed a heavy burden of taxation. The taxes went to expanded educational and health facilities, better accident and unemployment insurance, and more adequate pensions. As for the rich, they had a large portion of their income taxed away, and what might be left at death was decimated by inheritance taxes. It was ruefully declared that the rich could hardly afford to live, much less to die.

During the 20 years between the wars, Britain's political parties lacked forward-looking programs. The parties seemed unable to measure up to the demands of a difficult new age. In the empire, demands for home rule grew during the interwar period, especially in India, Sri Lanka, Burma, and Egypt. An ominous trend was the growing antagonism between the Arab inhabitants of mandated Palestine and the Jewish Zionist immigrants. Yet these issues would not come to a crisis until after World War II.

Happier developments could be seen in the attainment of home rule by the Irish Free State (the southern part of Ireland) in 1921 and Britain's recognition in the Statute of Westminster (1931) of a new national status for the dominions (Canada, Australia, New Zealand, and South Africa). Collectively, the four states were then known as the British Commonwealth of Nations and would be held together henceforth only by loyalty to the crown and by common language, legal principles, traditions, and economic interests. For most of the dominions, democratic traditions for the white populations survived the pressures of the depression, even though they were painfully susceptible to the effects of the world slump.

Interwar France

France suffered from World War I the most of any of the democracies; loss of lives as a proportion of the population and direct property damage were enormous. More than two out of every ten French men died. Years later, the nation, which had historically experienced less rapid population growth than other European states, still felt the war's heavy losses.

Victory did not address any of France's basic political problems. The French labored under much the same political and social stagnation after 1918 as it had before 1914. The economic impact of the war and the social disruptions that occurred during and after the conflict exacerbated these conditions. A dangerous inflation plagued France and undermined its

▲ Léon Blum served as prime minister of the French Popular Front in 1936–1937, a time of diplomatic and economic upheaval.

rather shallow prosperity. The multiparty system hampered the parliamentary structure of the Third Republic, and the governments formed from shaky coalitions. The exhausted country lacked vitality and a sense of national purpose after gaining revenge against the Germans.

After 1919, the British wanted to withdraw from continental Europe to look after their imperial interests, and the United States shrank back into isolationism. Working from a dispirited domestic base, France had to bear the burden of overseeing international affairs on the Continent. Overall, with the exception of the counterproductive occupation of the Ruhr, the French carried their duties well in the 1920s. In the next decade, however, France retreated into the so-called Maginot (MAH-zhi-noh) mentality, named after the construction of the Maginot Line, a supposedly impenetrable line of fortresses to the east.

The depression struck France later than it did other countries, but in some ways the damage was greater. French leadership was no more astute than that of the other democracies before and during the depression. For a while, France managed to maintain a false prosperity from the 1920s, partly because of its large gold holdings; but by the early 1930s, it suffered much the same fate as the other countries. Tourism dried up, contributing to the already rising unemployment rate and budget deficits. In the face of these problems, the French carried the additional financial burden of rearming to face a renewed German threat.

Ministry after ministry took power, only to collapse a few months later. Citizens became impatient with the government, especially when the press exposed corruption in high places. One of the more shocking scandals was that surrounding the schemes of Alexander Stavisky, a rogue who had bribed officials and cheated French investors out of some 600 million francs. When the ministry in power in December 1933 refused to authorize an investigation after Stavisky's assumed suicide, thousands of angry citizens took to the streets of Paris in protest. In February 1934, right-wing mobs tried to storm the Chamber of Deputies.

The outcome of this affair was a new government, the National Union, a rightist coalition that endured strikes and avoided civil war for the next 2 years. France was becalmed. The leftists were unable to reorganize their forces quickly enough to gain control, and the rightists failed to deal with either domestic or foreign problems. In the spring of 1936, the leftist Popular Front took power.

This coalition, under the leadership of Léon Blum (1872–1950), won a national election and set in motion a program to bring socialist reforms to France's struggling economy. Blum's government tried to reduce the domination of the traditional ruling elite over the finances of the country on the one hand, and on the other, to work with the Communists to help block the growing fascist influences. The cooperation with the Communists caused serious problems, including the usual one of how to work with the Soviet-dominated party without being captured by it. Many French voters refused to support the Popular Front for fear that it might commit France to fight against Germany for the benefit of the Soviet Union.

In foreign affairs, the Popular Front worked closely with Great Britain and supported the work of the League of Nations. It also attempted to appease Germany, though it remained hostile to Italy. During the Spanish civil war (1936–1939), fearing civil war at home, Blum's government, along with the British, declared neutrality in the face of fascist aggression.

In this atmosphere of social, economic, and international turmoil, Blum was unable to govern successfully. Furthermore, an epidemic of sit-down strikes involving some 300,000 workers embarrassed the government. Gradually, laws introducing a 40-hour workweek, higher wages, collective bargaining, and paid vacations were enacted to satisfy many of labor's demands. In addition, the government extended its control over the Bank of France and instituted a public works program. Blum navigated as best he could, favoring the worker against monopoly and big business while avoiding the totalitarian extremes of fascism and communism. After only a year in office, however, he was forced to resign. The unfavorable trade balance, huge public debt, and unbalanced budget brought down the Popular Front government. France swung back to the right with a government that ended the 40-hour workweek and put down strikes.

The National Union and the Popular Front mirrored the widening split between the upper and lower classes. The workers believed that the Popular Front's reforms had been sabotaged and that a France ruled by a wealthy clique deserved little or no allegiance. Conversely, some business owners and financiers were horrified at the prospect of communism and openly admired Hitler's fascism. Soviet and German propagandists subtly encouraged the widening of the gulf.

As the French quarreled and France's economic strength declined, Germany—regimented and working feverishly—outstripped France in the manufacture of armaments. There were no leaders to bring France together, and the pieces were in place for the easy and tragic fall of the country to German troops at the start of World War II in the spring of 1940.

Eastern Europe

With the exception of Finland and Czechoslovakia, democratic governments fared poorly in eastern Europe in the interwar period. By 1938 most of the states retained only the false front of parliamentary forms. Real power was exercised by varying combinations of secret police, official censors, armed forces, and corrupt politicians. Except in the western parts of Czechoslovakia and among the Jewish communities, there was a welcoming attitude toward the German National Socialists (Nazis) and their programs.

Most of these countries had an unhappy legacy of oppression by powerful neighbors, minority problems, economic weakness, and peasant societies. Poland, the Baltic states, Finland, Czechoslovakia, Yugoslavia, and Albania had not existed as states before 1913. Hungary, Bulgaria, and Austria had been on the losing side in World War I and paid dearly for that alliance in the treaties ending the war. Romania, which had been among the victors, gained large amounts of land and also a number of non-Romanian minorities.

For the first decade after World War I, the small countries of eastern Europe had the opportunity to develop without undue external influence or interference. However, the exclusivist, aggressive, and perhaps paranoid nationalism that dominated each nation thwarted any possibility of regional cooperation. The peace treaties had settled few of the problems plaguing the area and instead constructed a series of arbitrary political boundaries that brought far more conflict than accord. The countries in the region all sought autarkist solutions to their economic problems by erecting huge tariff barriers, which only served to emphasize the states' weaknesses.

Among the eastern European states, Czechoslovakia, with its combination of a strong middle class, accumulation of capital, technology base, and high literacy rate, had the greatest potential for successful democratic government. Four hundred years of Austrian domination had not crushed the Czech national spirit. After the collapse of the Dual Monarchy in November 1918, the Czechs joined with the Slovaks, who had been under Hungarian domination for 1000 years, to establish a republic.

The new state possessed a literate and well-trained citizenry and a solid economic base, and it managed to avoid the roller-coaster ride of inflation in the immediate postwar period. Its solid financial institutions, advanced industry, and a small-farm-based agricultural sector made it an island of prosperity. Like the other eastern European successor states, it had serious minority problems. But of all the new states, Czechoslovakia extended the most liberal policies toward minorities. By the time of the depression, Czechoslovakia showed every indication of growing into a mature democratic country. The depression, however, heavily affected the country's export trade and hit especially hard in the textile industry, which was centered in the German-populated Sudetenland (soo-DAY-ten-land). By 1935, the economic blows had made the area ripe for Nazi agitation and infiltration.

After Czechoslovakia, Poland had the best chance of the successor states to form a democratic government. The Poles, however, had to overcome several problems: a border conflict with the Soviet Union, the dilemma of the Polish Corridor to Danzig, minority issues, and the fact that Poland had been partitioned for over a century. When the country was reunited after the war, the Poles chose to imitate the constitutional system of the French Third Republic. The multiplicity of parties, a weak executive, and the resultant succession of governments led to political paralysis until 1926, when Marshal Josef Pilsudski (1867–1935) led a military revolt against the Warsaw government.

For the next 9 years, Pilsudski imposed his generally benevolent rule on the country. After his death in 1935, a group of colonels ruled Poland, and they permitted the formation of several protofascist organizations. By the time the Poles turned back toward a more liberal government in 1938, it was too late. For 3 years they had played up to the Nazis, and now they stood isolated before Hitler's advance.

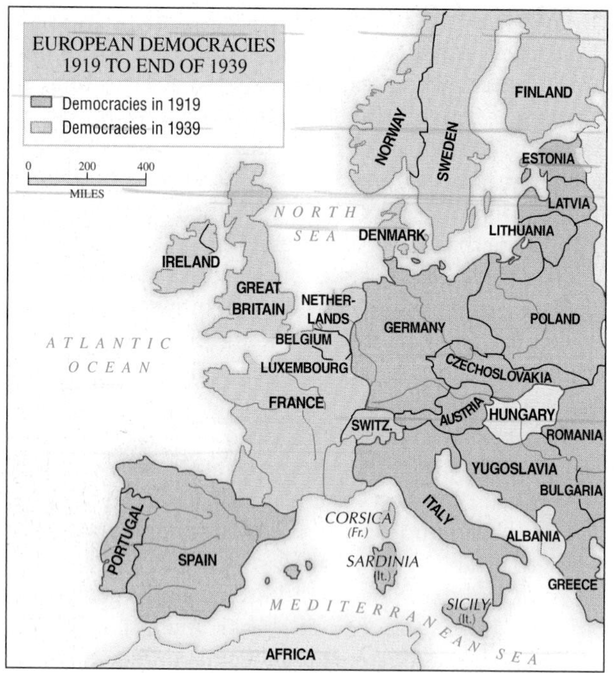

▲ Democracy waned in the uncertain years after World War I as people turned increasingly toward more authoritarian leaders whom they hoped would bring them stability and prosperity.

Problems with being trapped between powerful neighbors plagued the Baltic states of Latvia, Lithuania, and Estonia, which came into existence in 1918. The democratic governments of these countries endured much political and economic strife before they eventually gave way to dictatorial forms of government to survive with the Nazis.

The Balkan states of Yugoslavia, Albania, and Greece were buffeted by the ambitions of Italian imperialism, economic upheaval, and political corruption. Disintegration seemed a real possibility for Yugoslavia in the 1920s, but the conglomerate state stubbornly attempted to hold together the six major ethnic groups within its boundaries. King Alexander established himself as dictator in 1929 and ruled until 1934, when he was assassinated by Croatian separatists. Thereafter, the rising Nazi state drew parts of economically depressed Yugoslavia into its orbit, deeply splitting the country. By the end of the 1930s, both Greece and Albania were ruled by dictators.

Romania, another of the Balkan states, gained greatly from World War I, doubling its area and its population. Although the state had great economic potential, the government was unable to impose a stable rule during the interwar period. Severe problems with minorities and peasants and foreign control of the economy foiled the attempts of moderate politicians to rule, until, by the 1930s, fascist groups wielded a large amount of influence. In 1938, King Carol tried unsuccessfully to counter the pro-Nazi forces in Romania. Two years later, the country lost one-third of its territory and population to the Bulgarians, Russians, and Hungarians, and Carol fled to Spain.

Portugal and Spain

During the interwar period, economic problems, aristocratic privilege, and peasant misery worked against successful democratic or parliamentary government in the Iberian peninsula. After the end of World War I, Portugal endured 10 years of political indecision until Antonio de Oliveira Salazar (1889–1970), a professor of economics, became minister of finance in 1928. After helping straighten out some of the country's financial problems, Salazar became Portugal's premier and virtual dictator. He maintained Portugal's close ties with Britain while lending assistance to right-wing elements in Spain.

None of the political parties could deal adequately with Spain's problems in the 1920s. Revolts and strikes plagued the country until 1931, when the king abdicated and left the country. At the end of the year a new liberal constitution was adopted, and a republic was proclaimed. The new constitution was extremely liberal, but it had the support of neither the left nor the right. Mob violence and the threat of military coups continually harassed the republic.

By 1936, the peasants and workers were beginning to take matters into their own hands. At the same time, the military, under Generalissimo Francisco Franco, sought to pursue its own political ends. In July, the army made its move and attacked the republican government. This marked the start of a civil war in Spain, a war that in retrospect seems inevitable because of the country's indigenous social antagonisms.

The United States

The United States emerged from World War I as the strongest country in the world. But while other states looked to Washington to continue to play a political and diplomatic role in the world, the U.S. government turned inward, away from the international scene. Americans shelved Wilson's wartime idealism, ignored the League of Nations, and returned to domestic politics. At the same time, however, American businessmen played an active role in international business until 1929: not until the 1980s would a larger percentage of American financial activities take place abroad.

During the 1920s, three Republican presidents—Warren G. Harding, Calvin Coolidge, and Herbert Hoover—benefited from the well-being of the country and the generally carefree spirit of the times. Although refusing to join the League of Nations, the United

States did participate in the Washington Naval Conference in 1921–1922 to limit the race in warship construction, the Dawes and Young plans for economic stabilization, and the Kellogg-Briand pact (1928) to outlaw war.

Harding's domestic policies were marked by protectionist economics, probusiness legislation, and scandal. After Harding died suddenly in 1923, the widespread corruption of his administration was exposed. His vice president, Coolidge, easily weathered the storm and, after his 1924 election, advocated high tariffs, tax reduction, and a hands-off policy on federal regulation of business. Only nagging problems in the agricultural sphere detracted from the dazzling prosperity and honest government that marked his administration.

In the 1928 presidential elections, Herbert Hoover—a successful mining engineer who had directed Belgian relief during the war, had been present at the Versailles negotiations, and had overseen the Russian relief plan in the early 1920s—overwhelmed the governor of New York, Alfred E. Smith, the first Catholic to be nominated for president. When Hoover took office in 1929, he had the support of a Republican Congress and a nation enjoying unbounded industrial prosperity. It would be his incredibly bad luck to have to deal with and be blamed for the worst depression the United States has ever experienced.

By 1932, Americans felt the tragic blows of the Great Depression—25 percent unemployment, 30,000 business failures, numerous bank collapses, and a huge number of foreclosed mortgages. Hoover tried unprecedented measures to prop up faltering businesses with government money, devise new strategies to deal with the farm problem, and build confidence among the shaken citizenry. Yet he failed to shift the tide of the depression. Indeed, some observers note that the only force that brought an end to the crisis was the arrival of the World War II.

In the 1932 elections, Franklin D. Roosevelt, only the third Democrat elected to the presidency since 1860, defeated Hoover by assembling a coalition of labor, intellectuals, minorities, and farmers—a coalition the Democratic party could count on for nearly a half century. The country had reached a crisis point by the time Roosevelt was inaugurated in 1933, and quick action had to be taken in the face of a wave of bank closings.

Under Roosevelt's leadership, the **New Deal**—a sweeping, pragmatic, often hit-or-miss program—was developed to cope with the emergency. The New Deal's three objectives were relief, recovery, and reform. Millions of dollars flowed from the federal treasury to feed the hungry, create jobs for the unemployed through public works, and provide for the sick and elderly through such reforms as the Social Security Act. In addition, Roosevelt's administration substantially reformed the banking and investment industries, greatly increased the rights of labor unions, invested in massive public power and conservation projects, and supported families who were in danger of losing their homes or who simply needed homes.

New Deal—President Franklin D. Roosevelt's series of programs to deal with the effects of the depression.

▲ The Great Depression and the environmental disaster that accompanied it, the Dust Bowl, devastated the American economy and brought ruin to hundreds of families. Dorothea Lange's photograph of a migrant mother captured the love, strength, patience, and pain of the mothers who held those families together.

The Democrats' programs created much controversy among those who believed that they went too far toward creating a socialistic government and those who believed that they did not go far enough toward attacking the depression. Hated or loved, Roosevelt was in control, and the strength and leadership he provided were unparalleled in the interwar democracies.

Interwar Latin America

The huge wartime demand for Latin American mineral and agricultural products resulted in an economic boom that, with a minor contraction, continued on into the 1920s. However, the area's crucial weakness remained—its economic dependence on only a few products. Among Latin America's 20 republics, Brazil based its prosperity on coffee, Cuba depended on sugar, Venezuela on oil, Bolivia on tin, Mexico on oil and silver, Argentina on wheat and meat, and the various Central American countries on bananas.

Another problem was land distribution. On many large estates, conditions resembled medieval serfdom. Because the Catholic Church was a great landowner, certain members of the clergy combined with the landed interests to oppose land reforms.

During the 1920s, Mexico spearheaded the movement for social reform in Latin America. A series of governments, each claiming to be faithful to the spirit of the 1910 revolt, sought to gain more control over the vast oil properties run by foreign investors. The government solved the agrarian problem at the expense of the large landowners. These changes were accompanied by a wave of anticlericalism. Under these attacks, the Catholic Church lost much property, saw many churches destroyed, and had to work through an underground priesthood for a time.

Mexico exerted a strong influence over other Latin American countries. Between 1919 and 1929, seven nations adopted new, liberal constitutions. In addition, there were growing demands for better economic and social opportunities, a breakdown of the barriers that divided the few extremely rich from the many abysmally poor, and improvements in health, education, and the status of women. Above all, there was an increasing desire for more stable conditions.

Because of their dependence on raw-material exports, the Latin American countries suffered a serious economic crisis during the Great Depression. Largely as a result of the disaster, revolutions broke out in six South American countries in 1930.

During the 1930s, the "colossus of the north," the United States, attempted to improve its relations with Latin America and to stimulate trade. The Good Neighbor policy, originated in Hoover's administration and begun in 1933, asserted that "no state has the right to intervene in the internal or external affairs of another." Less pious, but more effective, was the $560 million worth of inter-American trade that the new policy encouraged.

Rivalries among industrialized nations for the Latin American market became intense during the 1930s. Nazi Germany concluded many barter agreements with Latin American customers and at the same time penetrated the countries politically by organizing German immigrants into pro-Nazi groups, supporting fascist politicians, and developing powerful propaganda networks. When war came, however, most of Latin America lined up with the democracies.

The Western Tradition in Transition: Changing Certainties

What transformations did Western culture and science undergo before and after World War I?

The world was in the process of change even before World War I. All of the basic definitions were changing. At the dawn of twentieth century, science made great strides, and such figures as Max Planck, Albert Einstein, Ivan Pavlov, and Sigmund Freud enlarged understanding of the universe and the individual. Even before the war, which had dealt a deathblow to the nineteenth-century legacy of optimism, these physicists and psychologists pointed out that the old foundations and beliefs on which the European world had rested needed to be rethought.

Science and Society

At the beginning of the twentieth century, the basic view of human nature changed. The Russian scientist Ivan Pavlov (1849–1936) gave the study of psychology a new impetus. In 1900, he carried out a series of experiments in which food was given to a dog at the same time that a bell was rung. After a time, the dog identified the sound of the bell with food. Henceforth, the sound of the bell alone conditioned the dog to salivate, just as if food had been presented. Pavlov demonstrated the influence of physical stimuli on an involuntary process in all animals.

The psychology of "conditioned reflexes," based on Pavlov's work, achieved wide popularity, especially in the United States, as the basis for behaviorism, which considered the human as analogous to a machine responding mechanically to stimuli. Behaviorism stressed experimentation and observational techniques and did much to create relatively valid intelligence and aptitude tests. It also served to strengthen the materialist philosophies of the period.

Probably the most famous and controversial name associated with psychology is that of Sigmund Freud (1856–1939). Placing far greater stress than any predecessor on the role of the unconscious, Freud pioneered the theory and methods of **psychoanalysis.** This theory is based on the idea that human beings are born with unconscious drives that from the very beginning seek some sort of outlet or expression. Young children often express their drives in ways that violate social conventions for proper behavior. Parents typically for-

psychoanalysis—A method of dealing with emotional problems in which the psychoanalyst encourages his patients to speak and reveal their innermost thoughts and dreams—especially dealing with events during their infancy.

bid these behaviors and punish children for performing them. As a result, many innate drives are *repressed*—pushed out of conscious awareness. Repressed drives, however, continue to demand some kind of expression. Freud believed that many repressed drives were *sublimated*, or channeled into some kind of tolerated or even highly praised behavior.

Freud was particularly interested in psychological disorders, and he treated emotional disturbances by encouraging patients to bring back to the surface deeply repressed drives and memories. By making patients aware of their unconscious feelings, Freud hoped that they would understand themselves better and be able to respond more effectively to the problems they faced. Freud used the techniques of free association and dream interpretation to explore how unconscious feelings might be related to patients' symptoms. He believed that many of his patients' symptoms resulted from repressed sexual and aggressive drives. Freud's theories have had a tremendous influence not only on the science of psychology but also on our culture as a whole, although his theories were falling out of favor as the twentieth century ended.

The old Newtonian understanding of the world changed. The scientific giant of the first half of the twentieth century, Albert Einstein (1879–1955), contended in 1905 that light is propagated through space in the form of particles, which he called *photons*. Moreover, the energy contained in any particle of matter, such as the photon, is equal to the mass of that body multiplied by the square of the velocity of light (approximately 186,300 miles per second). This theory, expressed in the equation $E = mc^2$, provided the answer to many mysteries of physics. For example, questions such as how radioactive substances like radium and uranium are able to eject particles at enormous velocities and to go on doing so for millions of years could be examined in a new light. The magnitude of energy contained in the nuclei of atoms could be revealed. Above all, $E = mc^2$ showed that mass and energy are equitable. In 1906, Einstein formulated his special theory of **relativity,** which set out a radically new approach to explain the concepts of time, space, and velocity.

Ten years later, Einstein proposed his general theory, in which he incorporated gravitation into relativity. He showed that gravitation is identical to acceleration and that light rays would be deflected in passing through a gravitational field—a prediction confirmed by observation of an eclipse in 1919 and by various experiments carried out in the American space programs in the 1960s and 1970s and the Hubble telescope in 1994. The theory of relativity has been subsequently confirmed in other ways as well. The conversion of mass into energy was dramatically demonstrated in the atomic bomb, which obtains its energy by the annihilation of part of the matter of which it is composed.

Einstein's theories upset the Newtonian views of the universe. Einstein's universe is not Newton's three-dimensional figure of length, breadth, and thickness. It is, instead, a four-dimensional space-time continuum in which time itself varies with velocity. Such a cosmic model calls for the use of non-Euclidean geometry. Einstein's theory changed scientists' attitude toward the structure and mechanics of the universe. On a broader scale, his relativistic implications penetrated many of the philosophical, moral, and aesthetic concepts of the twentieth century.

The fundamental discoveries in physics came before World War I. The British physicist Ernest Rutherford (1871–1937) advanced the theory in 1911 that each atom has a central particle, or nucleus, which is positively charged. Rutherford's argument repudiated the belief that the atom was indivisible. On the Continent, discoveries with even greater consequences were being made. German physicist Max Planck (1858–1947) studied radiant heat, which comes from the sun and is identical in nature with light. He found that the energy emitted from a vibrating electron proceeds not in a steady wave, as was traditionally believed, but discontinuously in the form of calculable "energy packages." Planck called each such package a *quantum;* thus the quantum theory was born. This jolt to traditional physics was to prove extremely valuable in the rapidly growing study of atomic physics.

Planck and Einstein investigated the infinite extent of the external

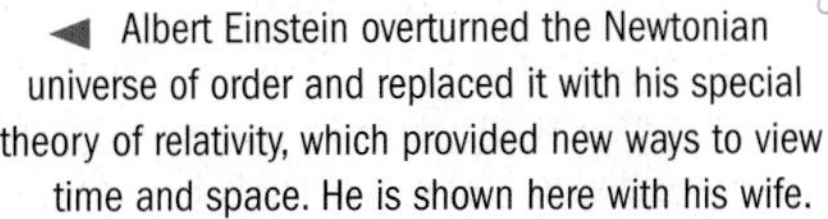

◀ Albert Einstein overturned the Newtonian universe of order and replaced it with his special theory of relativity, which provided new ways to view time and space. He is shown here with his wife.

---

relativity—A radically new approach of viewing time and motion.

universe, with a massive impact on the state of knowledge. At the same time, the equally infinite extent of the universe known as the mind also began to be studied in greater depth than ever before.

The Transformation of Literature and Music

Romanticism had broken the classical molds and opened the way for diversity in forms, styles, and themes. Romantics followed their emotions, while realists advocated a more objective way of portraying the world by stressing accuracy and precision. By the end of the nineteenth century a new movement, modernism—fragmented, disorganized, and united only in its reaction to the past—came to hold sway among Europe's writers, artists, and musicians.

By the beginning of the twentieth century, modernism freed the writer from all rules of composition and form and all obligations to communicate to a large audience. Poetry was especially affected by this new tendency. Toward the end of the century, in reaction to the demands of realism, French poets Stéphane

▼ Not only was Pablo Picasso the most prolific artist of the twentieth century, but he also taught the public, over the course of his long life, that there were many different ways to see and portray traditional subjects, as in *Les Demoiselles d'Avignon* (1907). Pablo Picasso, *Les Demoiselles d'Avignon, Paris* (June–July 1907). Acquired through the Lillie P. Bliss Bequest (333.1939). © The Museum of Modern Art/Licensed by Scala/Art Resource, NY. ©2003 Estate of Pablo Picasso/Artists Rights Society (ARS), New York.

Mallarmé (stay-FON mal-ar-MAY; 1842–1898) and Paul Verlaine (ver-LEN; 1844–1896) inaugurated the symbolist movement. Poetry rather than prose best fit the symbolists' goal of conveying ideas by suggestion rather than by precise, photographic word-pictures. In a sense, all modern literature stems from the symbolist movement. By increasing the power of the poet to reach the readers' imagination through expanded combinations of allusion, symbol, and double meaning, symbolism gave new obscurity to the written word.

Modernism affected music as it had affected poetry and art. The French composer Claude Debussy (de-BYEU-see; 1862–1918) tried in his music to imitate what he read in poetry and saw in impressionist paintings. He engaged in "tone painting" to achieve a special mood or atmosphere. This device can be heard in his "symphonic poem" *Prelude to the Afternoon of a Faun,* which shocked the musical world when it was first performed in 1894. The impressionist painters had gained their effects by juxtaposing widely different colors. The composers juxtaposed widely separate chords to create similarly brilliant, shimmering effects.

Before 1914, a number of other composers had also been rebelling strongly against lyrical Romanticism and engaged in striking experimentation. Breaking with the "major-minor" system of tonality, which had been the musical tradition since the Renaissance, some of them used several different keys simultaneously, a device known as *polytonality.* Outstanding among such composers was Igor Stravinsky (1882–1971), who was less concerned with melody than with achieving effects by means of polytonality, dissonant harmonies, and percussive rhythms. Other composers, such as the Austrian-born Arnold Schoenberg (1874–1951), experimented with atonality, the absence of any fixed key. Schoenberg developed the 12-tone system, an approach in which compositions depart from all tonality and harmonic progressions while at the same time stressing extreme dissonances. Stravinsky's and Schoenberg's music may strike the first-time listener as harsh and unpleasant, but these experiments with polytonality and atonality were symbolic of their time, when the old absolute values were crumbling—a time of clashing dissonance.

Changes in the Visual Arts

The Spanish artist Pablo Picasso (1881–1974) and others helped develop the school called **cubism.** Cubists would choose an object, then construct an abstract pattern from it, giving the opportunity to view it simultaneously from several points. Such a pattern is evident in much of Picasso's work, including the pivotal *Les Demoiselles d'Avignon* (lay day-MWAH-sels dah-veen-YON; 1907). During the interwar period, Picasso modified his cubist style and became a public figure through paintings such as *Guernica* (GWEHR-nee-kah), a mural that captures vividly the human horrors of the destruction of a small town in Spain by fascist air forces during that country's civil war. Henri Matisse (1869–1954) continued to exercise a major influence on young painters through his abstract works.

Another movement that came out of the 1920s was surrealism, led by artists such as Georgio de Chirico (KIR-e-KOH; 1888–1978) and René Magritte (mah-GREET; 1898–1967). The proponents of this approach saw the subconscious mind as the vehicle that could free people from the shackles of modern society and lead them to total creative freedom. They felt an affinity with "primitive art" and its close associations with magical and mythological themes. They exalted the irrational, the violent, and the absurd in human experience and saw World War I as proof that rationality did not exist and that, therefore, neither did artistic standards. Salvador Dalí (1904–1989) perhaps indicated his convictions about the artistic establishment and the society it represented when he gave a lecture on art while wearing a diver's helmet. Man Ray (1890–1976) and Marcel Duchamp (1887–1968) took the themes of irrationality and anti-traditionalism to their extremes in the artistic movement known as Dada.

Architecture

In the decade prior to World War I, an "international" style of architecture, which broke sharply with tradition, developed in Germany. This style, which stressed the use of various techniques from the machine age, was particularly well suited to early-twentieth-century

	Architectural Pioneers
Alexandre Gustave Eiffel (1832–1923)	Planned and built the tower that bears his name for the 1889 Paris International Exposition
Walter Gropius (1883–1969)	One of founders of the Bauhaus movement; built avant-garde exposition hall in Cologne
Louis Sullivan (1856–1924)	Chicago architect who chose function over form in his skyscrapers
Frank Lloyd Wright (1867–1959)	Greatest twentieth-century American architect

cubism—An art form that permits the portrayal of a subject from several different points of view simultaneously.

industrialization. In 1914, one of the outstanding leaders of this movement, Walter Gropius (GRO-pei-us; 1883–1969), designed an exhibition hall in Cologne that emphasized horizontal lines, used glass, exposed staircases, and did not hide its functionalism. Nearly a century later, this hall is still regarded as contemporary. Proponents of this new movement in architecture established a highly influential school of functional art and architecture, the Bauhaus, in 1918.

One of Louis Sullivan's pupils, Frank Lloyd Wright (1867–1959), originated revolutionary designs for houses. One feature of Wright's structures was the interweaving of interiors and exteriors through the use of terraces and cantilevered roofs. He felt that a building should look appropriate on its site; it should "grow out of the land." His "prairie houses," with their long, low lines, were designed to blend in with the flat land of the American Midwest. Much of what is today taken for granted in domestic architecture stems directly from Wright's experiments at the beginning of the twentieth century.

Conclusion

Germany's rapid economic growth, military buildup, ambitious foreign policy, and inability to control its Austro-Hungarian ally helped bring the normally competitive European economic arena to a crisis in the summer of 1914. By violating Belgian neutrality and declaring war on Russia and France, Germany stood as the state most responsible for the outbreak of the First World War, a fact for which it was severely punished in the Treaty of Versailles. Its actions had provided the spark to the volatile environment of the aggressive state system and set in motion 4 years in which the science, wealth, and power of Europe were concentrated on the business of destroying much of what the Continent had accomplished in the previous century.

After the war, the non-European world took advantage of the exhaustion of the colonial powers to increase their drives toward national independence. In the Middle East, Arab national ambitions had flared in 1916 into a revolt against Ottoman rule. The immigration of European Jews to Palestine led to conflict between Arabs and Jews, which was to increase as time passed. The peoples of North Africa, the Middle East, India, southeastern Asia, and Oceania were gathering strength in their battle to oust the Europeans and govern themselves. In the huge colonial area south of the Sahara, Africans were beginning to stir restlessly against European rule. Even China, tradition-bound for centuries, turned to revolution to regain the power and prestige it had lost during the era of imperialism. Although Jiang Jieshi (Chiang Kai-shek) won an internal power struggle and organized the government, the country remained poor and weak. Meanwhile, Japan embarked on its amazing technological, industrial, and military growth and became a world power.

Suggestions for Web Browsing

You can obtain more information about topics included in this chapter at the websites listed below. See also the companion website that accompanies this text, http://www.ablongman.com/brummett, which contains an online study guide and additional resources.

The Great War
http://www.pitt.edu/~pugachev/greatwar/ww1.html
This is a vast site devoted to all aspects of World War I.

World War I
http://www.worldwar1.com/
Another extensive site that offers information on all aspects of World War I.

The Great Depression
http://history.searchbeat.com/greatdepression.htm
The SearchBeat Guide to the Great Depression offers resources on the Great Depression.

Spanish Civil War
http://www.spartacus.schoolnet.co.uk/Spanish-Civil-War.htm
This extensive site includes links to maps, history, and biographies regarding the Spanish civil war.

Museo Picasso Virtual: Online Picasso Project
http://www.tamu.edu/mocl/picasso/
This extensive online project, in multiple languages, offers a tour of the life, family, travels, and works of this twentieth-century master.

Literature and Film

As noted in the chapter, this period was an incredibly rich period for novels, films, and poetry. The person who best captured the era's complexity and perversity was Franz Kafka; see a collection of his work in *The Complete Stories of Kafka* (Schocken Books, 1995). One of the finest novels about war ever written was Erich Maria Remarque's *All Quiet on the Western Front* (many editions). Alexander Solzhenitsyn's *August 1914* (Bantam, 1974) is an important piece of literature describing Russia's entry into the war. The poet T. S. Eliot captured the deceptions of the age in poems such as "The Wasteland" and "The Love Songs of J. Alfred Prufrock" (see *Collected Poems: 1909–1962,* Harcourt, 1963). Andre Gide's *Journals 1928–1939* (University of Illinois Press, 2000) give a window into the tumultuous age of the 1930s in Paris. American writers—such as F. Scott Fitzgerald—*The Great Gatsby* (1925), *This Side of Paradise* (1920), *The Beautiful and the Damned* (1922); Ernest Hemingway—*A Farewell to Arms* (1929), *For Whom the Bells Toll* (1940), *The Sun Also Rises* (1926); and Sinclair Lewis—*Main Street* (1920), *Elmer Gantry* (1927)—dealt with lost idealism and hypocrisy in their works. Films have been made of each of the American novels that are listed above, in addition to *All Quiet on the Western Front* (1930; Universal). The unofficial Christmas truce of 1914 is beautifully portrayed in Christian Carrion's *Joyeux Noel* (*Merry Christmas;* 2005).

Suggestions for Reading

The most accessible general study of the war is Martin Gilbert, *The First World War: A Complete History* (Henry Holt, 1996). Alistair Horne, *The Price of Glory: Verdun, 1916* (Penguin, 1994) deals with a key event in the war. Paul Fussell captures the brutal nature and impact of the war in *The Great War and Modern Memory,* 25th anniv. ed. (Oxford University Press, 2000). On the crisis in the French army, see Leonard V. Smith, *Between Mutiny and Obedience: The Case of the French Fifth Infantry* (Princeton University Press, 1994). See Arthur S. Link, *Wilson the Diplomatist* (Hopkins, 1957), regarding the U.S. president's participation at Paris. The responsibilities of winning the war are discussed in William Laird Kleine-Ahlbrandt, *The Burden of Victory: France, Britain, and the Enforcement of the Versailles Peace, 1919–1925* (University Press of America, 1995).

For a recent analysis of the Weimar Republic's social and economic crises, see Richard Bessel, *Germany After the First World War* (Clarendon Press, 1993). Charles P. Kindelberger, *The World in Depression, 1929–1939,* rev. ed. (University of California Press, 1986), covers the global perspective of the 1930s. Charles S. Maier surveys the social and political consequences of the difficult interwar period in *Recasting Bourgeois Europe: Stabilization in France, Germany, and Italy in the Decade After World War I* (Princeton University Press, 1988). For events in the successor states, see Joseph Rothschild, *East Central Europe Between the Two World Wars* (University of Washington Press, 1974). John Stevenson provides a good survey of British life between the wars in *Social Conditions in Britain Between the Wars* (Penguin, 1977). For developments in France in the 1930s, see John T. Marcus, *French Socialism in the Crisis Years, 1933–1936* (Praeger, 1963). For the United States, see William E. Leuchtenberg, *The FDR Years: On Roosevelt and His Legacy* (Columbia University Press, 1995).

An understanding of the interwar scene can be gained from reading some of the biographies of the participants. See, for example, Albrecht Fölsing, *Albert Einstein: A Biography,* trans. Ewald Osers (Viking, 1997); Meryle Secrest, *Frank Lloyd Wright: A Biography* (University of Chicago Press, 1998); Ian Gibson, *The Shameful Life of Salvador Dalí* (Norton, 1998); and Michael Oliver, *Stravinsky* (Phaidon, 1995). Michael Fitzgerald, *Making Modernism: Picasso and the Creation of the Market for Twentieth-Century Art* (Farrar, Straus & Giroux, 1995), details the pioneering work of Picasso in exploiting the huge market for art among the ever-increasing upper middle classes.

CHAPTER 28

The Failure of the Liberal Model and the Rise of Authoritarianism

Japan, Italy, Germany, and the USSR, 1917–1940

Outline

Features

◀ The German-Italian-Japanese alliance did not stand the test of reason from the points of view of ideology or ethnicity, but it made perfect sense geographically. The high point of this triad was 1941, and on the Atlantic and the Pacific fronts, the three nations shared a common momentum in their campaigns against the democracies. The smiling countenances of the Führer and the Japanese foreign minister indicate their confidence at that moment.

By 1900, THE liberal model developed in western Europe during the nineteenth century faced challenges. The middle-class dominated society, laissez-faire economics, and the constitutional-multiparty political system began to be criticized by the younger generation in Europe and attacked by exploited Asian and African populations in European colonies. As we saw in Chapter 27, the First World War dealt a devastating blow to the liberal system.

After the final shots of World War I were fired and the last peace treaties were signed, an uneasy 20-year period of nonwar began. The victorious Allies made their transitions from wartime to peacetime economies, and the United Kingdom, France, and the United States tried to resume their usual political pursuits. But it was impossible to return to a normal, pre-1914 life. The war's aftershocks and the destruction of global economic stability shook the deeply rooted democratic governments of the West to their core.

In countries that had more shallow democratic roots, the world war and the economic instability that followed worked against the liberal model. Japan entered a period of increasing democratization in the immediate post-1919 era, but disillusionment with international cooperation following the breakdown of the world economy in 1929 and the rising tensions on the Asian continent turned Japan toward militaristic, nondemocratic rule in the late 1930s. Italy and Germany shared a similar response to the chaotic aftermath of the war and formed new governments founded on fascism. World War I brutally weakened Russia's brief democratic movement, which had begun in 1905, and by November 1917 a communist government had taken power.

Japan: From Budding Democracy to Militarist State

What role did economic crises and challenges play in the rise of the militarists in Japan?

Japan was the rising international star in the first years of the twentieth century. A constitutional monarchy with a growing modern, industrial sector, it was one of the few Asian or African countries to escape Western imperialism. Western observers hailed Japan's entry onto the world stage. At the same time, Japan's victory in the Russo-Japanese War in 1904–1905 ushered in an era of hope to colonized people around the world. For the first time in centuries, a non-European power seemed to offer a model of liberation through modernization. Attitudes in Asia began to change by 1914, however, when Japan, under the Anglo-Japanese Naval Treaty of 1902, joined the Western powers in the war against Germany. Sensing an opportunity to stabilize China, which was wracked by instability and warlordism at the time, Japan's foreign minister issued Twenty-one Demands to the warlord of Beijing in 1915. Although most of these demands went no further than asking for economic concessions, several threatened China's sovereignty. Patriotic young Chinese were enraged, setting the stage for the deterioration of Sino-Japanese relations. As one of the victorious Allies at Versailles, Japan gained German-held territories in China and in the Pacific, exacerbating Chinese animosity. Japan had become one of the world's major democracies, part of the multilateral alliance that included the United States, Britain, France, and Italy. But its growing clash with rising Asian nationalism sowed the seeds for its unilateral approach to foreign relations that challenged and eventually destroyed Japan's fledgling democracy in the 1930s.

Post–World War I Japan

Unlike the experience for European countries, World War I was a good war for Japan. The horrors of war were never visited on Japan. On the contrary, the temporary withdrawal of European and American interests in East Asia during World War I offered Japan tremendous economic opportunities. Japan's sales to Asia and to its domestic market exploded during the war. Industrial output jumped from 1.4 billion yen in 1914 to 6.8 billion yen in 1918. Wages and prices both surged dramatically, though unfortunately for most consumers, price increases outpaced wages. Thousands of young people left the countryside following the expansion of employment opportunities in the newly emerging urban and suburban industrial workplaces. The economic benefits of World War I built on the economic growth that had begun at the time of the Russo-Japanese War (see Chapter 25).

A new middle class emerged almost overnight in the years after the war, with women joining men in new professions in Tokyo and other vibrant, modern cities. Lively cosmopolitan life, with its jazz bars, glittering department stores, mass circulation magazines, and growing access to education that introduced young people to a wealth of ideas from abroad, tied Japanese youth to international cultural currents. College men—and some women—demanded human rights, universal suffrage, and support for the still-oppressed working class. These calls for human rights and voting rights paralleled those in other countries. During and after World War I, most Japanese, even if they paid taxes, still could not vote. Taxation without representation angered small business owners and professionals, and encouraged them to join with young people, inspired by ideology and the international youth culture, to call for an expansion of voting rights to all men and women.

Although Japanese women, like most women elsewhere, did not yet have the vote, they increasingly enjoyed the cultural freedom an income could buy. "New Women" and "Modern Girls," many of them holding new middle-class jobs as schoolteachers, shop clerks, nurses, journalists, and telephone operators, strolled down Tokyo's fashionable Ginza. On Sundays, they were joined by their working-class counterparts from the textile mills who also enjoyed the freedom of urban culture, if only for one day a week, far from their parents' watchful eyes.

Emblematic of modernity, young men and women created a culture the press dubbed *ero/guro/nansensu*

Chronology

1910

1912 Mussolini becomes editor of socialist newspaper *Avanti*

1912–1931 Taishō Democracy in Japan

1915

1915 Japan issues Twenty-one Demands to China

1917 February–March Revolution overthrows Romanov dynasty; October–November Revolution overthrows provisional government; Communist rule established

1918 Treaty of Brest-Litovsk; World War I ends; revolutions in Germany

1919 Versailles treaty

1919 Weimar Constitution adopted; Weimar Republic begins

1920

1921 Mussolini elected to Chamber of Deputies, established National Fascist party

1922 Washington Conference Treaties create multilateral system for Japan, United States, United Kingdom

Japan in the Interwar Era	
1912–1931	Taishō Democracy
1915	Twenty-one Demands
1923	Tokyo earthquake
1925	Universal Manhood Suffrage Law in Japan
1931	Manchurian Incident
1937–1945	War with China
1940	Tripartite Pact (Japan, Germany, Italy)

(EH-roh GOO-roh nahn-SEN-soo; "erotic, grotesque, and nonsensical"). They read poetry by feminist poet Yosano Akiko (YOH-sah-noh AH-kee-koh); essays on democracy by highly regarded university professor Yoshino Sakuzō (YOH-shee-noh SAH-koo-zoh) and on women's liberation by feminists Ichikawa Fusae (IH-chee-KAH-wah foo-SAI) and Hiratsuka Raichō (hee-RAHTS-kah RAI-choh); novels by Tanizaki Jun'ichirō (TAH-nee-ZAH-kee JOON-ih-chee-ROH) and by Akutagawa Ryūnosuke (AHK-tah-GAH-wah ryoo-NOH-skeh), author of *Rashomon;* and saw movies and plays from Hollywood and Europe. Philosopher Bertrand Russell and birth-control advocate Margaret Sanger attracted crowds when they visited Japan.

But deep economic divisions also developed in Japan. Immediately after World War I, rampant inflation of commodity prices—by 150 percent for overall wholesale prices and by 174 percent for rice prices between 1914 and 1920—led to a nationwide outburst of what came to be called Rice Riots. The countryside stagnated while the cities grew, and rich enterprises called ***zaibatsu*** (vast conglomerates like Mitsubishi and Mitsui, with up to 600 subsidiaries) offered their workers and managers stability and good wages while other laborers toiled in fly-by-night workshops. The visible inequalities in Japan's modern society led to a host of popular movements: university students came together in groups demanding social reform for the poor; proletarian men and their liberal supporters in the Diet (parliament) struggled for, and won in 1925, votes for all men, thus removing the tax qualifications in place since 1890; feminists demanded complete social equality in the private sphere of the family and rights of equal citizenship in the public realm; tenant farmers formed unions to fend off high rents and rural social inequality; union organizers struggled for both better working conditions and human dignity and respect for workers; and reformers implemented labor reforms, such as an end to night shifts for women and children in textile mills and coal mines, encouraged by the International Labour Organization. Not all the movements of the interwar period sought to bring people together for progressive change. Some marginalized people sought camaraderie and community support through conservative organizations created by the state. After World War I, the Imperial Military Reserve Association, founded in 1910, claimed 2 million members in towns and villages throughout Japan. The Reserve Association's voluntary members were men who had passed the exam for conscription into the army but had not yet been drafted. The army, which developed this group, planned not only to keep the members ready for active duty but also to train a corps of local patriots that they could rely on to control those they viewed as political agitators. In this way, government forces co-opted some potentially disgruntled people, channeling their sentiments into state-focused directions at the same time that progressive movements drew in millions of other Japanese. The Reservist groups did not appear, in the eyes of many of their urban contemporaries in the 1920s, to be central players in popular culture. And yet they did attract millions of followers and would later assume far greater significance when Japan moved toward war in the 1930s.

It was progressive movements that captured the spirit of the 1920s, and many struggles for democratic change were successful. Even when those struggles foundered, the advocates of change saw the interwar period as a period of hope and democracy. Though

zaibatsu—Powerful, complex, multifaceted enterprises that produced many different products while building up a family-like loyalty among their middle- and upper-level managers.

1925 | **1930** | **1940**

1922 Fascists march on Rome; USSR formed

1923 Hitler's *Putsch* fails

1923 Tokyo-area earthquake kills 100,000

1924 Lenin dies

1925 Universal Manhood Suffrage, Peace Preservation Law enacted in Japan

1928 Stalin institutes first 5-year plan

1931 Manchurian Incident begins 15 years of war in Asia

1933 Hitler elected chancellor of Germany, proclaims Third Reich

1936 Anti-Comintern Pact makes allies of Germany, Italy, Japan

1936 February 26 Incident, Japan

1937 War with China, Japan

1940 Tripartite Pact

1940 Trotsky assassinated in Mexico

Many Japanese women struggled for women's rights, worked in offices and factories, and joined progressive movements in the interwar period. Later, during World War II, many would be swept up in groups working on behalf of the militarist state. Here, a group of patriotic women bows toward the imperial palace to honor the crown prince during the war.

the reign of the emperor Taishō lasted only from 1912 to 1926, many contemporaries considered the long period from 1905 till the rise of Japanese militarism at home and abroad in the 1930s as the era of *"Taishō Demokurashii"* (democracy). Japan enjoyed rather good relations with the Western powers, even though relations with China began to sour and oppressive treatment of Koreans under Japanese colonialism was replicated in the discriminatory treatment of Koreans resident in Japan. In Western eyes, Japan was one of the imperialist democracies. What was not understood in Japan, nor in the imperialist democracies of West, was that the political values of democracy and imperialism were inherently incompatible.

Japan's democratic government in the interwar period took a form different from many others at the time. Like many European governments, Japan had a constitutional monarchy. But unlike the European case, the head of the majority party in the Diet did not automatically become prime minister. Instead, an unelected group of elder statesmen, most of them aristocrats and former prime ministers, nominated the prime minister and cabinet. This changed in 1918 when the head of the majority party was asked to form a cabinet for the first time. Until right-wing terrorists frightened the elder statesmen away from nominating party leaders after 1932, elected party leaders held the dominant position in a power structure made up of elites from the Diet, the bureaucracy, the military, and big business. These party governments were not entirely democratic, however. Despite their expansion of rights and promotion of social reforms, they also passed laws that limited free expression of leftist ideas in order to undercut the attraction of socialist voices.

Citizens or Subjects?

The 1889 constitution had been hailed as a great achievement, making Japan the first constitutional government outside the West (see Chapter 25). But rights were severely constrained by the Meiji government. The electorate was limited by gender, by income, and in some cases by occupation. The number of people eligible to vote in Japan's first national election—less than 1 percent of the population—was far lower than in most other democracies of the time, although the electorates in Western democracies were also limited by gender, ethnicity and, in some cases, class. Few Japanese had rights associated with full citizenship (the vote), and many aspired to gain those rights. Indeed, the political history of the first three decades of the twentieth century is the tale of men's and women's struggles for the vote. But Japan remained a monarchy—even when many Europeans were dumping their monarchies—and no expansion of rights in a nation that considered its monarch to be the foundation of sovereignty could ever make men and women full citizens. Until the Constitution of 1947, written after World War II, removed sovereignty from the emperor and gave it the people of Japan, Japanese were not citizens but merely "subjects" of the crown.

Despite these legal limitations, optimistic Japanese acted as if popular rights could produce a new Japanese citizen in the years before the rise of militarism in the 1930s. Except for the relatively small number of socialists who challenged the existence of a monarchy, liberal advocates of human and civil rights took the monarchy for granted and focused their efforts on reforming laws and policies made by conservative prime ministers and their cabinets. Just as most failed to see a contradiction between imperialism and democracy, most also ignored the contradiction between democracy and loyalty to a monarch.

The popular movement for voting rights for all men regardless of their wealth began with Japan's first elections and culminated in the Universal Manhood Suffrage Law of 1925. Rivalries among political parties were as important as ideology in guiding Japan's parliamentary leaders toward expanding voting rights. Thinking they would gain the loyal support of new voters, party leaders gradually allowed more men to join the electorate over three and a half decades. Women would have to wait longer.

The climate of freedom after World War I energized feminists in Japan. Still shackled by Article 5 of the Public Peace Police Law that prohibited women's participation in political parties or attendance at political rallies and meetings, many sought novel ways to work for rights. Women's literary magazines like *Bluestocking,* founded by Hiratsuka Raichō in 1911, issued what later historians have called a "feminist manifesto." Hiratsuka called on women to express their literary and artistic creativity. "In the beginning," she wrote, "woman was the sun, an authentic person. Today she is the moon ... reflecting the brilliance of others." At the opposite end of the socioeconomic scale, working-class women pushed male labor leaders to include women in their unions and to recognize women's needs in the workplace.

The first feminist political organization took its name from the much talked about social phenomenon of the "New Woman." The New Women's Association, though short-lived (1919–1922), played a pioneering role. Article 5 had made it illegal for women to organize for political causes, but the NWA came together precisely to revise that law, in addition to lobbying for wives' and fiancées' right to divorce men with venereal disease. Ichikawa Fusae, who emerged as the leading suffragist in the next decade, and Oku Mumeo, who later became a leader of the feminist consumer movement, joined Hiratsuka in founding the NWA in 1919. It was Oku who persuaded the most conservative politicians that feminists, criticized by conservatives as "peculiar" and "extremely shameful," were worthy of greater civil rights when she arrived to lobby them carrying her baby on her back. If a feminist could be a loving mother, these conservatives reckoned, then maybe civil rights would not be so dangerous. Like their counterparts in other women's movements, Japanese feminists found that appealing to traditional attitudes sometimes led to the outcome for which they struggled. In the following years, women's groups, arguing that "universal suffrage" (as contemporaries dubbed the struggle for male voting rights) was incomplete without women's voting rights.

By 1931, the Women's Suffrage League (founded in 1924) and other women's groups almost succeeded in getting the right to vote at the local level. But the foreign policy disaster known as the Manchurian Incident (see p. 899) ushered in a rise in oppression, and the Women's Suffrage League and other women's groups, speaking out against militarism in the early 1930s, found their call for rights increasingly silenced. Like men in other progressive movements, women found that their demands came to be equated with the liberalism and individualism despised by right-wing elements as too "Western." Some activists were arrested and jailed. In 1925, as a counterweight to the Universal Manhood Suffrage Law, the government had passed the ironically named Peace Preservation Law. Under this law, people seen as threats to the state could be arrested, and in 1928 and 1929, 2300 leftists, students, and others were taken into custody. Among these were students in the New Man Society at the elite Tokyo Imperial University, leading the Ministry of Education to crack down on all students. Soon unions and other movements were forced by the government to abandon their more progressive demands or be sent to jail. Social movements were either co-opted by the government, went underground, or ceased to exist by the late 1930s. Terror and repression frightened many Japanese into passivity.

Interwar Foreign Policy and Economic Crises

During the 1920s, Japanese foreign policy tended to support Western-led multilateral systems, such as the Washington Conference system and the League of Nations (see Chapter 31). With the very significant exception of America's humiliation of Japan through complete prohibition of Japanese immigration to the United States in 1924 and through America's refusal to insert a racial equality clause—Japan's key demand—in the 1919 Versailles treaty, Japan was treated as a "Western" power.

On the Asian continent, meanwhile, Japanese soldiers guarding the territories through which the Japanese-held South Manchurian Railway passed became ideologues for a point of view opposed to the liberal individualism and capitalism that characterized Japan in the 1920s. They hoped to fulfill their ideological ambitions far from Tokyo's eyes. In 1928, these soldiers, based in Manchuria since Japan gained railroad rights there from Russia in 1906, assassinated the warlord of Manchuria, and, in September 1931, staged an explosion along the railroad line to look like it was done by Chinese saboteurs, using it as a pretext to start a police action again the Chinese. The 1931 event and the subsequent fighting that broke out between Japanese and Chinese forces in the next months became known as the Manchurian Incident. By 1932, the Japanese controlled Manchuria. Although some statesmen hoped to continue a cooperative policy in international affairs, others were swayed by the unilateral approach of the military stationed in Manchuria. The events of 1931 triggered continuing skirmishes between Chinese nationalist forces and the Japanese military, and in 1933, when the League of Nations condemned Japan's actions, Japan walked out, thus ending the hope that an international body like the League could guarantee world peace.

Economic distress was one reason for Japan's policy shifts from liberal internationalism to increasing militarism and a unilateral approach to foreign relations. In 1923, Tokyo had been hit by one of the largest earthquakes on record. At least 100,000 were killed, and millions were made homeless. The government lent generously to rebuild—too generously perhaps, as the loans often went unpaid, leading to bank failures in 1927. Japan had not yet recovered from that crisis when the New York Stock Exchange crashed, starting a worldwide depression in 1929. Japanese factories closed, and workers returned to their villages, leading to more violent tenant disputes when landlords took back land to allow their returning children to farm. As U.S. consumers stopped buying silk stockings, some Japanese farm families who relied on silk sales found themselves selling their daughters into prostitution. Japan started to pull out of the depression sooner than other industrial nations when its finance minister pioneered deficit financing that would, 4 years later, come to be called **Keynesianism.** Urban areas rebounded, but the countryside remained poor.

The Rise of Militarism

Right-wing fanatics, no longer confined to Manchuria, took up the cause of destitute farmers and developed an antiurban, antimodern ideology. They made several attempts to overthrow the government by assassination. Prime Minister Inukai Tsuyoshi, as well as a former finance minister and the head the Mitsui *zaibatsu,* were killed in 1932, and a major coup attempt between February 26 and February 29, 1936, killed several high-ranking government officials, bureaucrats, business leaders, and generals. After this aborted coup, called the "February 26 Incident," party-led governments were replaced by increasingly military-dominated cabinets. Urban Japanese continued to enjoy vibrant material culture until the end of the 1930s, but the rise of militarism and fears of domestic terrorism were beginning to alter their lives as early as 1931.

Although leaders in government, big business, and even the top brass of the military were far from liberal, they were despised by anticapitalist right-wing ideologues. Some of those ideologues were incensed by decisions made by generals to modernize the army. Others were upset by the government's initial reluctance to send troops to China in response to Chinese agitation against Japanese overseas business interests in the early 1930s. Many were inspired by right-wing tracts like Kita Ikki's (1883–1937) *Plan for the Reorganization of Japan,* published in 1919. Kita's pamphlet, circulated widely among right-wing young officers who took part in the February 26 Incident, rejected both capitalism and communism and called for a radical national-socialist restructuring of society under the authoritarian rule of the emperor. Although Kita had not participated in the February 26 coup himself, he was tried, convicted, and executed for having influenced those who had. The radical right-wing insurrectionists were put down, but mainstream military officers gained increasing control of the government from civilians fearful of right-wing terrorism. This affected both domestic and foreign policy, ending any hope for party-led government and accelerating the expansion of Japan's encroachment on the Asian continent.

Keynesianism—An economic theory devised by the British economist John Maynard Keynes and his followers that advocated government fiscal and monetary intervention to enhance economic activity and employment.

Konoe Fumimaro, prime minister at the beginning of the 1937 war against China, was selected because his princely heritage suggested he could manage the nation during war. He resigned in October 1941, less than two months before the attack on Pearl Harbor.

Japan's cooperation with Western democracies, especially in multilateral treaty systems and in mutual support for one another's colonial possessions—treaties with the United States, France, and England supported their common imperialism—gave way in 1936 to Japan's Anti-Comintern Pact with Nazi Germany (signed by fascist Italy in 1937), which was directed against the Soviet Union, and in 1940 to the Tripartite Pact, with the same three signatories and directed against the United States. In addition, the Japanese signed a neutrality pact with the Soviet Union in April 1941. Japan's full-scale involvement in World War II had begun in July 1937 with the war with China (see Chapters 29 and 31 for the war in China and elsewhere in Asia from 1937 to 1945). The war with the United States, begun on December 7, 1941, when Japan launched a major attack on Pearl Harbor in Hawaii, followed several years of rapidly deteriorating relations.

A European Response to Liberal Decline: Fascism

What are the basic principles of fascism?

While Japan underwent a wrenching transition from an old order after the 1860s to becoming a global power by 1919, Europeans achieved their dominant roles in the world as a result of undergoing economic and social transformations throughout the entire nineteenth century. The middle classes in England, other northwestern European states, and the United States built institutional structures based on liberal values: constitutional government, multiparty systems, laissez-faire economics, strong and active Christian churches, and the whole range of civil and political rights. The high tide of the liberal order, which had produced a comforting belief in progress, had long passed by the first decades of the twentieth century: World War I put an end to the Western world's belief in the old liberal system. In the pessimism of the 1920s, a new social and political model was embraced in many parts of Europe. A half century before Mussolini led his "March on Rome" and Hitler gained power in 1933, European thinkers had established the roots of a new political ideology: *fascism,* an ideology that rejected the liberal values and institutions of the nineteenth century and advocated the superiority of one group over all others.

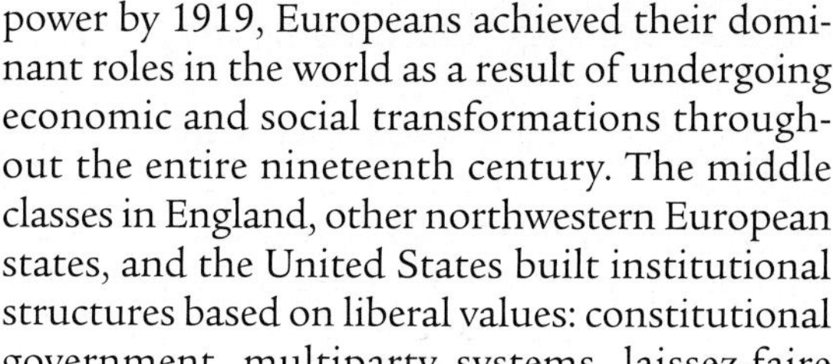

Europe in the 1920s and 1930s

"Scientific" Justifications for Superiority

European thinkers such as Joseph-Arthur de Gobineau (goh-bee-NOH; 1816–1882) devised racial hierarchies that placed their own ethnic groups at the top. Gobineau applied biological theory to politics, regarding nations as organisms. He argued that different races are innately unequal in ability and worth and that the genius of a race depended solely on heredity, not external factors. He stated a widely held belief among Europeans that white people alone were capable of cultural creativity and that intermixture with other, inferior, races would destroy that capacity to create.

Another of the bases of fascism can be found in the willful misreading of Charles Darwin's hypotheses (see Chapter 22). When simplified and distorted, the misrepresentations of his ideas were very attractive to the ascending middle classes. Darwin never dreamed of discussing human social, economic, and political activities. The popularizers of the theory of evolution, the **Social Darwinists,** applied Darwin's ideas to all aspects of life. The most popular adherent of this point of view was the English philosopher Herbert Spencer (1820–1903). By misusing Darwin's theories, he justified the superiority of northwestern Europeans—the Anglo-Saxons—over all others. Social Darwinist arguments and Gobineau's pseudoscientific theories in support of white superiority gave "scientific" justifications to blatant bigotry and provided a reassuring sanction for European domination over Asians and Africans. Spencer and Gobineau, among others, laid the foundations for modern racism.

One of the manifestations of this notion of superiority was the Anglo-Saxon movement. In Britain and Germany, writers and speakers presented the case for the superiority of northern Europeans. They stated that world leadership should naturally reside in London and Berlin because the people living there possessed the proper combination of religion, racial qualities, and culture to enable them to dictate the world's future. People as diverse as Kaiser William II and U.S. President Woodrow Wilson shared this outlook. In addition, a Pan-Germanic League was organized in Berlin in the 1890s to spread the belief in the superiority of the German race and culture. In the United States, the destruction of the way of life of the Native Americans was justified by the demands of the unstoppable tide of progress.

Modern Anti-Semitism

European expressions of cultural superiority were perhaps most clearly expressed in anti-Semitism. Systematic hostility toward the Jews in Europe can be traced as far back as the later Roman period; historians relate it to the adoption of Christianity by Constantine in the early fourth century (see Chapter 6). Later a prominent feature of medieval European society, anti-Semitism took on particular strength in the later part of the nineteenth century. The German historian Heinrich

---

Social Darwinism—A misapplication of Darwin's theories of evolution, applied to human society to justify the temporary dominance of predominantly Caucasian nations at the end of the nineteenth century.

▲ The self-proclaimed democracies may have won World War I, but they lost the peace. By the end of the 1930s, they were greatly outnumbered by fascist, authoritarian, and communist regimes.

von Treitschke (TRITE-shkee, d. 1896), giving voice to widely held opinion, said simply "the Jews are our calamity." Anti-Semitism in France played a significant role in the Dreyfus Affair (see Chapter 23). In eastern Europe and Russia, Jews suffered most forms of economic and legal discrimination, and, often with outright official support, waves of **pogroms.** The economic dislocations born of industrialization and modernization fueled anti-Jewish sentiments, as did the views expressed in such pseudoscientific tracts as the notorious *Protocols of the Elders of Zion,* a vicious document written, it appears, for use by the Russian secret police.

European Jews responded in a variety of ways including, in many cases, immigration to the United States. A second response was Zionism, a complex movement that emerged initially in intellectual and student circles in Eastern Europe and Russia. At the heart of Zionist thinking stood the demand for an autonomous homeland for the Jews. Debate raged over the best location for the Jewish state but, ultimately, the only reasonable choice for most Zionist Jews was Palestine, described in much of Jewish tradition as an ancestral home. Drawing on the ideas expressed by Leo Pinsker (d. 1891), author of *Autoemancipation* (1882), and other early Zionist theorists, Jewish groups founded settlements in Palestine. These early settlements often failed, due to lack of funding and determination as well as a mounting hostility on the part of their Palestinian Arab neighbors.

The movement gained new momentum with the involvement of Theodor Herzl (d. 1904), a Viennese playwright turned journalist, who witnessed the extent of anti-Semitic sentiments in France while covering the Dreyfus Trial in 1891. Herzl, often working at a feverish pitch, committed himself to the Zionist cause, emerging soon as its principal voice. His manifesto of 1896, *Die Judenstaat* (The Jewish State), sketched out a

pogrom—A planned massacre of defenseless people, usually Jews, at the end of the nineteenth century.

vision of a Western, liberal-democratic state in Palestine that largely brushed aside—in a fashion reminiscent of much of Western colonial thinking—the presence and attitudes of the Palestinian Arabs. Herzl's ideas also drew a harsh response from detractors in the Zionist movement and among many non-Zionist Jews. They galvanized many new supporters, however, for whom the ideas of Zionism offered great promise.

◀ Theodor Herzl founded the Zionist movement to bring to fruition the longing of the Jews of the diaspora for a homeland in the land of their ancestors, Palestine. He was driven not only by his faith but also by the rabid anti-Semitism that was resurgent in central Europe toward the end of the nineteenth century.

The End of Rationality

The Social Darwinists and racialist writers advocated the superiority of white Christian people over others. Other middle-class thinkers in the generation before World War I provided new insights that ate away at the foundations of classic Western civilization. In France Henri Bergson wrote that "vital instinct," not reason, was the most important part of creativity. In Italy, Benedetto Croce (be-ne-DET-toh KROH-chee; 1866–1952) rebelled against the positivism and rationalism of the age. At the same time that Albert Einstein began to undermine the classic Newtonian universe, Sigmund Freud questioned the whole notion of rationality. As the Social Darwinists misinterpreted the carefully reasoned hypotheses of Charles Darwin, so did opportunistic political activists begin to fill the definitional void by advocating a new kind of state based on emotion, charisma, antiliberalism, anticonservatism, antirationalism, and radical nationalism.[1]

Classic liberalism advocated freedom and equality and led to the introduction of mass democratic politics in the second half of the nineteenth century. Some European elites did not like the idea of universal manhood suffrage and the rules and restrictions of free and fair elections. Especially among younger Europeans, this resentment sparked an emotional, often irrational reaction against the values of the older generation and the desire for action—any kind of action. The writings of Friedrich Nietzsche (FREED-reesh NEET-shee; 1844–1900) calling for the dominance of an *Übermensch* (OO-ber-mensh), a "superior man" who despised the mediocrity of the bourgeoisie, became popular. In France, Georges Sorel (1847–1922), a retired engineer, stated the need for action and violence to replace parliamentary democracy from a leftist point of view. Sorel advocated the use of violence as a justifiable means to deal with the corruption of bourgeois society and to bring together like-minded people in a common crusade. To Sorel, the victims of violence paid the necessary price for progress, and their suffering was more than justified by the advances that brutality could bring.

As the end of the century approached, the notion of the bourgeois corruption and the decadence of Western civilization, especially the purported weakening of the white race, was discussed everywhere in the West. This mode of thinking was especially prevalent in Germany and Austria, and its most influential spokesman was Houston Stewart Chamberlain (1855–1927), who wrote that the blond-haired, blue-eyed "Aryan" (northern Indo-European) had a special "race soul" whose existence was threatened by Jews.

These thoughts and tendencies found fertile ground in the boredom of the middle classes. Stanley Payne writes that "quite aside from any specific political proclivity, a concern for new approaches and new values—and possibly a new style of life" was fed by this bourgeois boredom. This, plus the growth of a "youth culture," with its roots in the well-to-do middle classes, provided an audience for these ideas. "A mood of rejection of some of the dominant values of preceding generations had set in. Faith in rationalism, the positivist approach, and the worship of materialism came increasingly under fire. Hostility toward bureaucracy, the parliamentary system, and the drive for 'mere' equality often accompanied this spirit of rejection."[2] This "spirit of rejection" grew stronger after the disappointments and deceptions of the World War I, and in 1919 Benito Mussolini first used the word *fascism* to encapsulate all of these tendencies.

The Italian leader may be seen as the father of fascism, but he had no precise definition of what the movement was. Unlike communism, fascism has no basic text and takes on different forms in different countries. Robert O. Paxton, however, has established that there are certain characteristics at the core of fascism. There is

- *a sense of overwhelming crisis beyond the reach of any traditional solutions;*
- *the primacy of the group, toward which one has duties superior to every right, whether individual or universal, and the subordination of the individual to it;*
- *the belief that one's group is a victim, a sentiment that justifies any action, without legal or moral limits, against its enemies, both internal and external;*
- *dread of the group's decline under the corrosive effects of individualistic liberalism, class conflict, and alien influences;*
- *the need for a closer integration of a purer community, by consent if possible, or by exclusionary violence if necessary;*

- *the need for authority by natural chiefs (always male), culminating in a national chieftain who alone is capable of incarnating the group's historical destiny;*
- *the superiority of the leader's instincts over abstract and universal reason;*
- *the beauty of violence and the efficacy of will, when they are devoted to the group's success;*
- *the right of the chosen people to dominate others without restraint from any kind of human or divine law, right being decided by the sole criterion of the group's prowess within a Darwinian struggle.*[3]

Italy and Mussolini

How was Mussolini able to take and hold power in Italy?

After entering the war on the Allied side in 1915, the kingdom of Italy joined the peace negotiations with great expectations. The Italians had joined the Allies with the understanding that with victory they would gain Trieste, Dalmatia, Trentino, and some territory in Asia Minor. They came away from Versailles with minor gains, however, not nearly enough, in their minds, to justify the deaths of 700,000 of their soldiers.

Postwar Italy suffered social and economic damage similar to that of the other combatants. Inflation—the lira fell to one-third of its prewar value—and disrupted trade patterns hampered recovery. These ailments worsened the domestic crises the country had been struggling with before the war. There were not enough jobs for the returning soldiers, and unemployed veterans were ripe targets for the growing extremist parties. In some cities, residents refused to pay their rent in protest over poor living conditions. In the countryside, peasants took land from landlords. Everywhere, food was in short supply.

In the 4 years after the armistice, five premiers came and went, either because of their own incompetence or because of the insolubility of the problems they faced. Liberal democracy was not equal to the challenge of post–World War I government in Italy.

	Mussolini's Rise to Power
1919	Italian discontent with peace treaties
1919–1920	Gabriele D'Annunzio and his followers occupy Fiume
1919–1922	Series of ineffective governments and postwar economic crises
1922	Unsuccessful union antifascist protest; March on Rome; King Victor Emmanuel III asks Mussolini to form a government

The situation favored the appearance of a strong man, a dictator. Such a man was a blacksmith's son named Mussolini, who bore the Christian name Benito, in honor of the liberal Mexican president Benito Juárez (HWA-rez). During his youth, Benito Mussolini (1883–1945) received an education dominated by left-wing political thinkers. Even though he became editor of the influential socialist newspaper *Avanti* ("Forward") in 1912, he was far from consistent in his political views. Early on, he demonstrated his opportunistic and pragmatic nature. For example, when a majority of the Italian Socialist party called for neutrality in World War I, Mussolini came out for intervention. Party officials removed *Avanti* from his control and expelled him from the party. He then proceeded to put out his own paper, *Il Pòpolo d'Italia* (PO-po-lo dee-TAL-ee-uh; "The People of Italy"), in which he continued to call for Italian entry in the war on the Allied side.

To carry out his interventionist campaign, Mussolini organized formerly leftist groups into bands called *fasci,* a named derived from the Latin *fasces,* a bundle of rods bound around an ax, which was the symbol of authority in ancient Rome. When Italy entered the war, Mussolini volunteered for the army, saw active service at the front, and was wounded. When he returned to civilian life, he reorganized the *fasci* into the *fasci di combattimento* (FASH-ee dee kom-bat-tee-MEN-toh; "fighting groups") to attract war veterans and try to gain control of Italy.

The Path to Power

In the 1919 elections, the freest in Italy until after World War II, the Socialists capitalized on mass unemployment and hardship to become the strongest party. But the party lacked effective leadership and failed to take advantage of its position. Although the extreme right-wing groups did not elect a single candidate to the Chamber of Deputies, they pursued power in other ways.

The fiery writer and nationalist leader Gabriele D'Annunzio (ga-bree-EL-eh dan-NOON-zee-oh; 1863–1938) had occupied the disputed city of Fiume (on the Adriatic coast) with his corps of followers, in direct violation of the mandates of the Paris peace conference. This defiance of international authority appealed to the fascist movement. D'Annunzio provided lessons for the observant Mussolini, who copied many of the writer's methods and programs, especially D'Annunzio's flare for the dramatic. During his 15-month control of Fiume, D'Annunzio and his followers wore black shirts, carried daggers, and used the so-called Roman salute—raising the right arm in a rigid, ramrodlike gesture. Ironically, D'Annunzio and his band were wrong: in antiquity, slaves saluted their masters by raising their right hands; free men shook hands.

The fascists gained the backing of landowning and industrial groups, who feared the victory of Marxist socialism in Italy. Mussolini's toughs beat up opponents, broke strikes, and disrupted opposition meetings in 1919 and 1920, while the government did nothing. Despite these activities, the extreme right-wing politicians still failed to dominate the 1921 elections. Only 35 fascists, Mussolini among them, gained seats in the Chamber of Deputies; the Liberal and Democratic parties gained a plurality. Failing to succeed through the existing system, Mussolini established the National Fascist party in November.

The Liberal-Democratic government of 1922 proved as ineffective as its predecessors, and the Socialists continued to bicker among themselves. Mussolini's party, however, attracted thousands of disaffected middle-class people, cynical and opportunistic intellectuals, and workers. Frustration with the central government's incompetence, not fear of the left, fueled the fascist rise.

In August 1922, the trade unions called a general strike to protest the rise of fascism. Mussolini's forces smashed their efforts. In October, after a huge rally in Naples, 50,000 fascists swarmed into Rome, and soon thereafter, King Victor Emmanuel III invited Mussolini to form a new government. During the next month, Mussolini assembled a cabinet composed of his party members and nationalists and gained dictatorial powers to bring stability to the country. The fascists remained a distinct minority in Italy, but by gaining control of the central government, they could place their members and allies in positions of power. The October March on Rome ushered in Mussolini's 20-year reign.

Building the Fascist State

The new Italian leader followed no strict ideology as he consolidated his dictatorial rule. He threw out all the democratic procedures of the postwar years and dissolved rival political parties. He and his colleagues ruthlessly crushed free expression and banished critics of their government to prison settlements off Italy's southern coast. They censored the press and set up tribunals for the defense of the state (not the citizens). Although he retained the shell of the old system, the fascist leader established a totally new state.

Mussolini controlled all real power through the Fascist Grand Council, whose members occupied the government's ministerial posts. At one time, he personally held no fewer than eight offices. All this activity and centralization of power provided a striking contrast to the lethargy of the 4 years immediately after the war. Encouraged by the popular support for his regime, Mussolini passed a series of laws in 1925 and 1926, under which the Italian cities lost their freely elected self-governments and all units of local and provincial government were welded into a unified structure controlled from Rome.

Once he had centralized Italian political life, Mussolini pursued the development of his ideology in a pragmatic manner. In his rise to power, Mussolini lashed out against the capitalists, the church, the monarchy, and the middle classes. But he would learn to work with all of those elements in his flexible pursuit of power. He once stated in an interview, "I am all for motion."[4] Movement, not consistency and science, marked his ideology.

Early in the 1920s, Mussolini, a former atheist, began to tie the church into the structure of his new society. In 1928, he negotiated the Lateran Treaty with church representatives in order to settle the long-standing controversy between Rome and the Vatican. The new pact required compulsory religious instruction and recognized Catholicism as the state religion. Vatican City, a new state of 108 acres located within Rome itself, was declared to be fully sovereign and independent. In addition, the state promised the Vatican $91 million. Mussolini gained a measure of approval from devout Italians and the Vatican's support for his fascist government.

Mussolini's economic system, which has come to be known as *state capitalism,* aimed to abolish class conflict through cooperation between labor and capital, by state force if necessary. In communist theory, labor is the basis of society. In fascism, labor and capital are both instruments of the state. The fascists constructed a corporate state, in which

◀ Military training began early in Mussolini's fascist state. There were youth organizations for every age group over the age of 4.

Seeing Connections

Mussolini and Imperial Destiny

Benito Mussolini took advantage of the theatrical possibilities of Rome, and by implication, the Roman Empire. He identified his political program with the grandeur of Rome. He positioned himself in front of the great monuments to lend legitimacy to his ambitions. He misinterpreted history to use the extended, rigid, slightly raised, right hand salute to connect with Rome. He wrongly believed that that was the way that Romans greeted each other (only slaves used that gesture). His foreign policy implicitly sought the re-creation of the Mediterranean as *Mare Nostrum.* Without the connection with the grandeur of Rome, his movement was only a collection of unemployed toughs. With the connection, his movement was imbued with destiny.

the country was divided into *syndicates,* or corporations—13 at first, later 22. Initially, six of these came from labor and an equal number represented capital or management. The thirteenth group was established for the professions. Under state supervision, these bodies were to deal with labor disputes, guarantee adequate wage scales, control prices, and supervise working conditions. After 1926, strikes by workers and lockouts by employers were prohibited.

The pragmatic leader believed that private enterprise was the most efficient method of production: "The state intervenes in economic production only when private enterprise fails or is insufficient or when the political interests of the state are involved."[5] Mussolini liked to claim that his structure embodied a classless economic system that stood as one of fascism's greatest contributions to political theory.

Reflecting the practice of the time, the Italians sought economic self-sufficiency, especially in the areas of food supply, power resources, and foreign trade. Wheat production and hydroelectric-generating capacity both increased, but the drive for self-sufficiency was carried to an unprofitable extreme. The state, in its quest for economic independence, launched many projects to provide for a home supply of products that could be obtained much more cheaply from other nations.

State and Struggle: Mussolini's Legacy

As in the case of the other dictatorships, Mussolini's programs had some worthwhile features, including slum clearance, rural modernization, and campaigns against illiteracy and malaria. The trains *did* run on time, as Mussolini boasted, and the omnipresent Mafia was temporarily dispersed, with many of its more notable figures fleeing to the United States. But these positive achievements were more than outweighed by the ruinous war with Ethiopia (see Chapter 31), excessive military spending, and special benefits to large landowners and industrialists. In 1930, real wages remained low in comparison to the rest of industrialized Europe.

The Great Depression hit Italy later than other countries, but it lasted longer, and its effects were devastating to Mussolini's economy. The 33 percent increase in 1929 gross national product over that of 1914 was soon wiped out, and the old problems of inadequate natural resources, unfavorable balance of trade, and expanding population made the country vulnerable to economic disaster. In 1933, the number of unemployed reached 1 million and the public debt soared to an alarming level. Despite a reorganization of the nation in 1934 into 22 government-controlled corporations, a massive public works program, and agricultural reforms, Italy continued to suffer. In the 1930s, Italy's fate and future came to be closely tied to that of Germany, whose leaders embraced the ideology haphazardly begun by Mussolini.

Mussolini's fascist ideology built on the cult of the leader, *Il Duce* (eel deu-CHAY; "the Great Man") and the all-powerful corporate state. But it was Mussolini's charisma that held the movement together. The Italian dictator asserted that "life for the fascist is a continuous, ceaseless fight" and that "struggle is at the origin of all things." Mirroring the nonintellectual nature of its creator, fascism never had a text, as Marxism did. But its basis was an extreme nationalism that asserted that Italy in its present form was corrupt. Mussolini believed that it was possible to regain the nation's pure form by rejecting substantial portions of the present age: in his speeches, Mussolini referred constantly to the legacy of the Roman Empire. *Il Duce* and his followers sensed that they lived at a watershed between the tarnished old and the possible gleaming new and that it was their duty to save their nation by bringing in a new breed of man.

Mussolini's movement was antiliberal, characterized by real hatred of the bourgeoisie and all that it created in the nineteenth century. *Il Duce* encouraged a high birthrate but noted that individuals were significant only insofar as they were part of the state. Children were indoctrinated with the party line. The movement was also anticonservative, rejecting the traditional role of the monarchy and cynically using the church. Mussolini's party rejected traditional laissez-faire capitalism and the hierarchies that came with it, and, in that sense, it was socialist. Rather than waiting for the "invisible hand" to furnish the motive force of their country, Italian fascists, as good totalitarians, looked to the state to engineer life at all levels. The Italian fascists were also racists and sought to link up with like-minded people around the world. The strength of Mussolini's fascism was that it could be adapted to any ideological or cultural setting, because to be a fascist, one needed only to hate, believe, obey, and fight.

Beneath the talk of struggle and the trappings of grandeur was the reality of Italy. Mussolini was no Stalin or Hitler, and his fascism was a far milder form of totalitarianism than that seen in the USSR or Germany. The Italian people simply defused many of the potentially atrocious elements of his fascist rule. There was no class destruction or genocide in Italy. The Italians, who had endured control by the Goths, the Normans, the French, and the Austrians before unification, were survivors.

The German Tragedy

What economic and social factors contributed to the rise of Adolf Hitler?

In the first week of November 1918, as World War I came to a close, revolutions broke out all over Germany. Sailors stationed at Kiel rebelled; leftists in Munich revolted. The kaiser fled to the Netherlands after the authority of his government crumbled. On November 9, the chancellor transferred his power to Friedrich Ebert, leader of the majority party, the Social Democrats, and the new leader announced the establishment of a republic.

Violence spread quickly. The Spartacists, led by Karl Liebknecht (LEEB-knect) and Rosa Luxemburg, who formed the German Communist party at the end of 1918, wanted a complete social and political revolution. Ebert's Social Democrats favored a democratic system in which property rights would be maintained. At the beginning of 1919, the radical and moderate socialists clashed violently. Experiments in revolutionary government in Bavaria and Berlin horrified traditionalists and even the Social Democrats. In the spring, a coalition of forces, ranging from moderate socialists to right-wing bands of unemployed veterans, crushed the leftists and murdered Liebknecht and Luxemburg.

Europe Between the Wars: 1919–1939

By the end of the year, Germany had weathered the threat of a leftist revolution. Meanwhile, the moderate parties triumphed in elections to select a constitutional convention, with the Social Democrats winning the most votes. The constitution they wrote at Weimar (VI-mar) and adopted in mid-1919 created some of the problems that would plague the new government.

The liberal document provided for a president, a chancellor who was responsible to the Reichstag (RIKE-shtag), and national referenda. In addition, the constitution guaranteed the rights of labor, personal liberty, and compulsory education for everyone up to the age of 18. Once the new system was put into operation, its weaknesses were readily apparent. The multitude of parties permitted by the constitution condemned the government to function solely by shaky coalitions that often broke apart and forced the president to rule by emergency decree, thus bypassing legal constitutional procedures.

Failure of the Weimar Republic

The new Weimar Republic faced overwhelming obstacles. First, it had to live with the stigma of having accepted the Versailles treaty, with its infamous war guilt clause. The defeatist image, combined with opposition from both right- and left-wing extremists, plagued the Weimar moderates. The myth of betrayal in accepting the Versailles treaty helped Field Marshal

IMAGE
France Demands War Reparations from Germany—Cartoon

Paul von Hindenburg, a stalwart Prussian and war hero, win election to the presidency in 1925. In 1927, he formally renounced the theory of war guilt, a politically popular move but one with little effect on the obligation to pay reparations. Although these payments did not noticeably affect the standard of living after 1925, they continued to be a visible sign of defeat, especially since the money used to pay the victorious Allies had to come from foreign loans.

The Weimar government ruled during an economically chaotic period. The government caused inflation, wiped out savings, and destroyed much of the confidence of the middle class, shaking the resolve of the group on whom the fate of the republic rested. Even after 1923, when the economy took a turn for the better, perceptive observers noted that the new prosperity rested on shaky foundations.

During the five years before the onset of the Great Depression, Germany rebuilt its industrial plants with the most up-to-date equipment and techniques available, becoming the second-ranking industrial nation in the world, behind the United States. Rebuilding, however, was financed largely with foreign loans, including some $800 million from the Americans. In fact, the Germans borrowed almost twice as much money as they paid out. When the short-term loans came due, the economic bubble burst.

In addition to these economic difficulties, other problems plagued the Weimar government. Many people in Germany still idealized the authoritarian Prussian state. The German general staff and its numerous and powerful supporters were not placed under effective civilian control. Disregarding the Versailles restrictions on military growth, Germany increased its armed forces in the 1920s, in cooperation with the Soviet Union, the other European outcast. Probably more dangerous to the Weimar Republic's existence was that group of individuals described by Peter Gay as the *Vernunftrepublikaner* (ver-NUNFT-re-pub-li-kah-ner) or "rational republicans from intellectual choice rather than passionate conviction." These intellectuals, politicians, and businessmen, who should have been the strength of Weimar, "learned to live with the Republic but they never learned to love it and never believed in its future."[6]

The insecurity of the middle classes was the factor most responsible for the failure of the Weimar Republic. After the war and inflation, what professionals, white-collar workers, and skilled tradespeople feared most was being dragged down to the level of the masses. Right-wing orators played on such fears and warned that the Weimar Republic could not stop the growth of communism. After 1929, the fear and discontent of the middle classes crystallized around their children, who blamed their parents for the catastrophe of 1918 and the humiliations that followed. German youth, many of them unemployed after 1929, repudiated the Weimar Republic and sought a new savior for their country and themselves. In their rise to power, the Nazis skillfully exploited the fears and hopes of German middle-class youth.

	The Economic Cycle and the Nazis
1919	Transition to peacetime economy, massive unemployment
1920	Formation of National Socialist German Workers' (Nazi) party, drawing from out-of-work soldiers
1923	The Munich *Putsch,* massive inflation
1928	High point of economic normalization; Nazis have only 12 seats in the Reichstag
1930	Beginning of Great Depression; Nazis increase seats in Reichstag to 107
1932	Depth of Great Depression; Nazis make strong showing in July elections
1933	Social discontent caused by depression brings increased business support of Nazis; Hitler gains power with 44 percent of deputies, buttressed by Nationalist party's 8 percent

Adolf Hitler

The man who was to "save the fatherland" came from outside its borders. Adolf Hitler (1889–1945) was born in Austria, the son of a minor customs official in the Austro-Hungarian monarchy. A mediocre student and something of a loner during his school days, he went to Vienna in 1908 hoping to become an architect or an artist. When he failed to gain admission to the art institute, he abandoned pursuing a career in art.

In the cosmopolitan capital of Vienna, surrounded by a rich diversity of nationalities and religions, Hitler formed a personal political philosophy. He avidly read pamphlets written by racists who advocated the leader concept and variations of Social Darwinism. In addition, anti-Semitism was a popular political platform, and the city's mayor openly espoused it. Hitler also dabbled in pan-Germanism and Marxist socialism. The swirl of ideas and theories percolated in the brain of the impoverished and aimless young man and furnished him with the motivations and ambitions that drove him forward.

A year before World War I, Hitler moved to Munich, where he earned a meager living by selling his drawings. When the conflict erupted in 1914, he joined a German regiment and was sent to France, where he fought

During the Weimar period in Germany (1918–1933), George Grosz, in satirical paintings such as *The Pillars of Society* (1926), powerfully expressed his scorn for militarism, capitalism, the complacent middle classes, and the corrupt society of his time.
bpk, Berlin/Art Resource, NY/© Estate of George Grosz/Licensed by VAGA, New York, NY.

bravely. At the time of the armistice in 1918, he was in a hospital recovering from being blinded in a gas attack. He later said that news of Germany's defeat caused him to turn his face to the wall and weep bitterly.

Following his recovery, Hitler returned to Munich, where he was hired by city authorities to act as a special agent to investigate extremists. In the line of duty he checked on a small organization called the German Workers' party. Hitler became attracted to the group's fervently nationalistic doctrine and agreed with their antidemocratic, anticommunist, and anti-Semitic beliefs. He joined the party and soon dominated it.

In 1920, the party renamed itself the National Socialist German Workers' party, the first two syllables of which are pronounced "Nazi" in German. That same year, the party founded a newspaper to spread its views; formed a paramilitary organization from out-of-work veterans, the *Sturmabteilung* (shtirm-AB-tai-lung) or SA; and adopted a symbol, the swastika set on a red background. The swastika has been used by many cultures to express the unending cycle of life. The red background symbolized the community of German blood.

More important than the party or its symbol was Hitler, who became widely known for his remarkable powers as a speaker. His ability to arouse and move mass audiences drew large crowds in Munich. Even those who hated all that he stood for were fascinated by his performances. In the early days, he would hire a number of beer halls for his adherents and speed from one to the next delivering his emotion-filled message. He called for land reform, the nationalization of trusts, the abolition of all unearned incomes, expansion to include all German-speaking peoples in Europe, and the cancellation of the Versailles treaty. The points of his arguments were less important than the way he delivered them. As the ultimate demagogue, he could package his concepts to fit whatever audience he addressed, and his popularity soared.

In November 1923, at the depth of Germany's inflationary crisis, Hitler staged a *Putsch,* or revolt, in Munich. Poorly planned and premature, the attempt failed. Hitler was sent to prison after his arrest, and there, in comparatively luxurious conditions, he dictated his statement of principles in *Mein Kampf* ("My Struggle"). Far from a literary masterpiece, the work was both an autobiography and a long-winded exposition of Nazi philosophy and objectives.

In *Mein Kampf,* Hitler writes that history is fashioned by great races, of which the Aryan is the finest. The noblest Aryans, according to Hitler, are the Germans, who should rule the world. He charges that the Jews are the archcriminals of all time, that democracy is decadent, and that communism is criminal. He states that expansion into the Soviet Ukraine and the destruction of France are rightful courses for the Germans, who will use war and force, the proper instruments of the strong, to achieve their goals. The book, initially dismissed as the ravings of a wild man, was widely read in the 1930s. Its sales made Hitler a wealthy man.

Hitler's Chance

Hitler's first attempt to take advantage of economic disaster failed, but he would not fail the second time. After 1930, the Führer (FIU-rher; "leader") took advantage of the desperate conditions resulting from closed banks, 6 million unemployed, and people roaming the streets for food. Night after night, civil and military police battled mobs of rioting communists and Nazis. The depression was "the last ingredient in a complicated witches' brew" that led to Hitler's takeover.[7]

The depression brought on the collapse of the moderates' position in the Weimar government. In the 1930 elections, the Nazis increased their number of

▲ Adolf Hitler's ability to communicate effectively and persuasively with a majority of the German population was a major asset in his rise to power and popularity. Here he is shown (*front right*) speaking with young members of his Nazi party.

seats in the Reichstag (the German legislative assembly) from 12 to 107. As conditions grew worse, the hungry and frightened, as well as the rich and powerful, turned to Hitler. The latter groups feared the communists and saw the Führer as a useful shield against a proletarian revolution.

As the Nazi movement grew in popularity, Hitler's brilliant propaganda chief, Joseph Goebbels (GEHR-bels), used every communications device available to convert the masses to Nazism. He staged huge spectacles all over Germany in which thousands of storm troopers and the audiences themselves all became supporting players to the star of the drama, Adolf Hitler. Such controlled hysteria was more important than the message Hitler continued to repeat.

Despite Goebbels's work, Hitler lost the March 1932 presidential elections to the aged World War I hero Hindenburg. But after a strong showing by the Nazis in the July Reichstag elections, Hindenburg, following the advice of his supporters and the business community, asked Hitler to join a coalition government. The Führer refused, demanding instead the equivalent of dictatorial power.

The stalemate led to the dissolution of the Reichstag in September, and for the next two months, the government limped along until a second general election was held. This costly campaign nearly emptied the Nazis' treasury. It was also politically costly in that they lost some of their seats in the Reichstag.

Some observers believed that the Nazis had passed the crest of their power. At this critical point, however, a clique of aristocratic nationalists and powerful industrialists, fearing a leftist revolution, offered Hitler the chancellorship. In January 1933, a mixed cabinet was created with Hitler at the head. Because he did not have a clear majority in the Reichstag, Hitler called another general election for March 5.

The Nazis used all the muscle at their disposal during this campaign. They monopolized the radio broadcasts and the press, and the SA bullied and beat the voters. Many Germans became disgusted with the strong-arm methods, and the tide definitely swung against the Nazis. Hitler needed a dramatic incident to gain a clear majority in the election.

On the evening of February 27, a fire gutted the Reichstag building. The blaze had been set by a 24-year-old Dutchman, Marinus van der Lubbe, as a statement against capitalism. Apparently acting alone, van der Lubbe gave the Nazis the issue they needed to mobilize their support. Goebbels's propaganda machine went into action to blame the fire on the international communist movement. Uncharacteristically, the propaganda minister overplayed the story, and most of the outside world came to believe that the Nazis themselves had set the fire.

Hitler may not have made much profit from the incident internationally, but he did use it to win the election. The Nazis captured 44 percent of the deputies, a result which—with the 8 percent controlled by the Nationalist party—gave them a bare majority. Quickly, Hitler's forces put through the Enabling Act, which gave the Führer the right to rule by decree for the next 4 years.

Every aspect of the Weimar government was overturned, legally. The Nazis crushed all opposition parties and put aside the Weimar constitution, which was never formally abolished. Germany for the first time became a unitary national, rather than federal, state. After Hindenburg died in 1934, Hitler became both chancellor and president. As if to put the world on notice that a renewed German force was rising in central Europe, he withdrew Germany from the League of

Nations in 1933. Two years later, he introduced conscription, in defiance of the Versailles treaty.

Hitler proclaimed his regime the Third Reich, succeeding the First Reich of Otto the Great, which had lasted from 962 to 1806, and Bismarck's Second Reich, from 1871 to 1918. Hitler quickly introduced aspects of his Nazi variant of fascism, which was much more pernicious than Mussolini's. Hitler's ideology united the diverse Germans and expressed resentment against the rapid industrialization that had cut many of the people away from their traditional values. But it was primarily the racist elements of Aryan supremacy and hatred of the Jews that set Nazism apart.

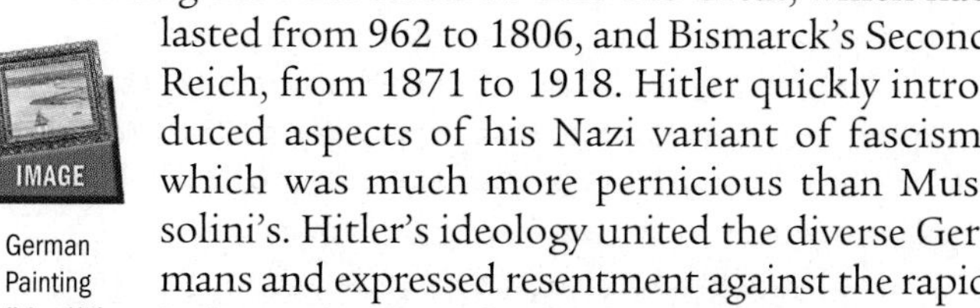
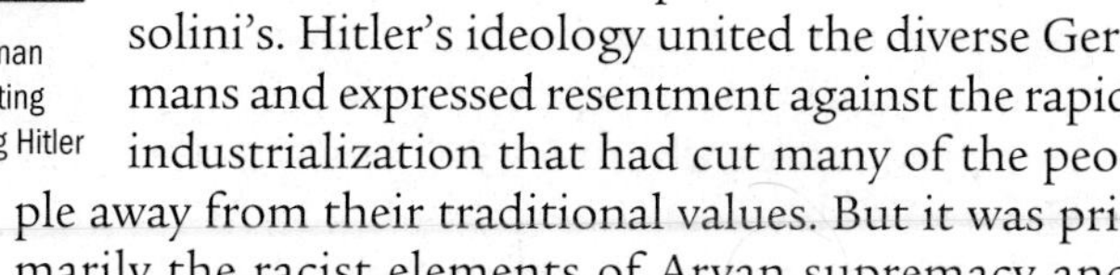
IMAGE German Painting Idolizing Hitler

War on the Jews

An essential part of the Nazi ideology was an absolute hatred of the Jews, an element of society the Nazis considered unfit to continue in the new world they envisioned. After crushing all opposition, real and potential, Hitler began to destroy the Jews. When he took power, there were only 500,000 Jews out of a population of 66 million Germans. Since 1880, the number of Jews in the population had been declining and would have continued to do so through assimilation. Hitler, however, proclaimed that Jews were everywhere, plotting to gain control of the world, and he pledged to destroy them. His beliefs reflected his own contempt for the Jews, not any demographic reality.

All Jewish officials in the government lost their jobs, Jews were forbidden to pursue their business and industrial activities, and Jewish businesses were boycotted. Non-Jews snatched up valuable properties formerly owned by Jews at bargain prices. Non-Jewish doctors and lawyers profited when Jewish professionals were forced from their practices. Hitler gained solid supporters among the business and professional classes as he pursued his racist policies. Germans willingly believed that the Jews deserved their fate as the price they had to pay for the Versailles treaty, for the harmful aspects of capitalism, and for internationalism. Half-hearted international protests failed to limit the anti-Semitic policies. Hitler had many fervent supporters both inside and outside Germany.

The Nazis set to building concentration camps; in time these would turn into death camps. In the meantime, the immediate pressures of government policies pushed many Jews into committing suicide. It has been estimated that in 1933 alone, 19,000 German citizens killed themselves and 16,000 more died from unexplained causes.

In 1935, the so-called **Nuremberg laws** came into force. Marriages between Aryans and non-Aryans were forbidden. Jews (defined as all persons with one-fourth or more Jewish blood) lost their citizenship, and anti-Semitic signs were posted in all public places. (During the 1936 Berlin Olympic Games, these notices were taken down so as not to upset visitors.) Increasingly, there was public mention of the "inferior blood" of the Jews. As the state came to need more and more money for armaments, the Jews would be made to pay. This enterprise reached a climax with vicious attacks on Jews and their businesses and synagogues on November 9, 1938, known as **Kristallnacht** (KRIS-tel-nakht; "Night of Broken Glass"). Nazi sympathizers smashed the windows of 7500 shops and burned 267 synagogues, killing 91 people in the process. The police rounded up 30,000 Jews and sent them to concentration camps. Adding insult to injury, a fine of 1 billion marks was imposed on the Jewish community in retaliation for the murder of a German diplomat in Paris.

Attacked, deprived of their citizenship and economic opportunities, and barred from public service, the Jews of Germany, who considered themselves good German citizens, bore the barbaric blows with remarkable resilience. Some, including a number of Germany's best scientific minds, were able to flee the country—a loss that may well have doomed Hitler's efforts in World War II. Most stayed. They, like the outside world, which showed little concern, did not realize that Hitler's true goal was the "Final Solution," the extermination of the Jews. His mad quest, known as the Holocaust, would lead to the deaths of more than 6 million Jews throughout all of Europe and the USSR and at least 4 million others not lucky enough to be "Aryan."

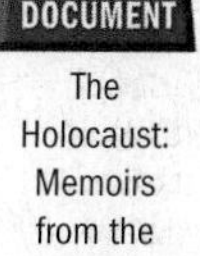
DOCUMENT The Holocaust: Memoirs from the Commandant of Auschwitz

The Nazi Impact on Culture, Church, Education, and Society

Hitler and Goebbels controlled all of the media in the totalitarian Third Reich. A Reich culture cabinet was set up to instill a single pattern of thought in literature, the press, broadcasting, drama, music, art, and the cinema. Forbidden books, including works of some of Germany's most distinguished writers, were seized and destroyed in huge bonfires. The cultural vitality of the Weimar Republic, represented by the likes of Thomas Mann, Erich Maria Remarque (re-MARK), Kurt Weill (VILE), and Bertolt Brecht (BREKHT), was replaced by the sterile social realism of the Third Reich.

Nuremberg laws—The collection of laws issued in 1935 depriving Jews in the Third Reich of most of their civil rights and dispossessing them of their legal rights and occupational possibilities.

Kristallnacht—The "night of the broken glass" when, on November 9, 1938, Nazi sympathizers smashed the windows of Jewish shops, burned synagogues, and killed 91 people. In addition, more than 30,000 Jews were sent to concentration camps and a fine of 1 billion DM was imposed on the Jewish community, all in response to the murder of a minor German diplomat in Paris.

Religion became entrapped in the dictatorial mechanism. Since Nazism elevated the state above all else, a movement was started to subordinate religion to the Hitler regime. The organized churches originally backed the Nazis warmly, until it became apparent that they were to serve the larger aim of the Aryan cause. Protestant churches suffered under the Nazi attempt to make them an arm of the state, and several dissident ministers were imprisoned. By the end of the decade, the Catholic Church, too, came under subtle but constant attack.

German universities, once renowned for their academic freedom, became agencies for propagating the racial myths of Nazism and for carrying out far-fetched experiments in human genetic engineering on selected concentration camp inmates. Only good Nazis could go to universities, and professors who did not cooperate with the regime were fired. The rich traditions of German scholarship became perverted by governmental pressure and many professors who were more than glad to collaborate with the Nazis.

▼ This painting shows a blissful Nazi family, close to nature, with the blond mother carrying out her duties of bearing and bringing up children for the Third Reich while the sturdy and caring father watches over his nursing baby.

The state used mass popular education, integrated with the German Youth movement, to drill and regiment boys and girls to be good Nazis. Boys learned, above all else, to be ready to fight and die for their Führer. The girls were prepared for their ultimate task, bearing and rearing the many babies to be needed by the Third Reich.

When they took power, the Nazis made it clear that they viewed the political and professional activity of women during the Weimar period as a sign of general decadence. Like the other authoritarian states in the 1930s, they declared that the prime role of women was to stay home and bear children—in this case, racially pure German children. As in Stalin's USSR, the state gave subsidies and other financial incentives to large families, and abortion was illegal. However, after 1937, women were first encouraged—and 6 years later, compelled—to contribute to the economy by performing whatever work the state demanded, usually in armaments factories and always at lower wages than received by men. As in Stalin's Soviet Union, the women also had to bear the burden of their housework, carrying a disproportionate share of the workload.

Economic Policies

As in Italy, fascism in Germany revolved around a form of state capitalism. In theory and practice, Nazism retained capitalism and private property. The state, however, rigidly controlled both business and labor. The Nazis dissolved labor unions and enrolled workers and employers in a new organization, the Labor Front. As in Mussolini's corporate state, the right of the workers to strike or of management to call a lockout was denied. The Nazis took compulsory dues from the workers' wages to support Nazi organizations. As a standard operating procedure, the state set up the "Strength Through Joy" movement, which provided sports events, musical festivals, plays, movies, and vacations at low cost.

The Nazis' ultimate goal was self-sufficiency—autarky—which they would try to reach through complete state control of the economy. They assumed, as the fascists did in Italy, that only the state could ensure the social harmony needed to attain the maximum productive potential for the state's benefit.

The government tried to solve the nation's very serious economic problems by confiscating valuable Jewish property, laying a huge tax load on the middle class, and increasing the national debt by one-third to provide work for the unemployed. To create jobs, the first 4-year plan, established in 1933, undertook an

Document

The New German Woman

Paula Siber served as the acting head of the National Socialist party (Nazi) Association of German Women in 1933. She established the basic guidelines for the party's expectations of what the new German woman should be. Women were not to be in the forefront, making political, economic, or military decisions. Rather, they were to be the most important actors in the creation of the new, purified national community both by giving birth to a large number of children and by passing on the essence of the German tradition to their children.

To be a woman means to be a mother, means affirming with the whole conscious force of one's soul the value of being a mother and making it a law of life. The role of motherhood assigned to woman by nature and fully endorsed by National Socialism in no way means, however, that the task of National Socialist woman within the framework of the National Community should be simply that of knowing herself to be the carrier of race and blood, and hence of the biological conservation of the people.

Over and above the duty intrinsic to her gender of conserving her race and people there is also the holy task entrusted to man and woman of enhancing and developing the inner, spiritual, and human qualities. This in the case of woman culminates in the motherhood of the soul as the highest ennoblement of any woman, whether she is married or not.

Therefore, a woman belongs at the side of a man not just as a person who brings children into the world, not just as an adornment to delight the eye, not just as a cook and cleaner. Instead woman has the holy duty to be a life companion, which means being a comrade who pursues her vocation as woman with clarity of vision and spiritual warmth....

To be a woman in the deepest and most beautiful sense of the word is the best preparation for being a mother. For the highest calling of the National Socialist woman is not just to bear children, but consciously and out of total devotion to her role and duty as mother to raise children for her people....

The mother is also the intermediary for the people and national culture ... to which she and her child belong. For she is the custodian of its culture, which she provides her child with thorough fairy-tales, legends, games, and customs in a way which is decisive for the whole relationship which he will later have to his people.... In a National Socialist Germany, the sphere of social services ... is predominantly the sphere of the woman. For woman belongs wherever social services or human care is required.

Apart from these tasks of conserving the people, educating the people, and helping the people, the final area of responsibility for the woman, one not to be undervalued, is her contribution to the national economy. Women manage 75 per cent of the total income of the people, which passes through her hands simply in running the home....

The national economy includes agriculture. It is today less possible than ever to imagine the struggle for existence and the toil involved in the economics of improving crops, refining breeds, and farming new land, activities which demand constant attention and maintenance, without the contribution of woman to agriculture in overseeing and running the farm.

Questions to Consider

1. Do you think that the Nazi party believed women to be equal in their possibilities to men?
2. What does Ms. Siber mean when she says that women are "the custodians of the [national] culture?
3. What would be your response if a national political leader issued such a statement today? Would you agree with it? Why? Would you disagree with it? Why?

From G. Kallmeyer, "The Women's Issue and Its National Socialist Solution," Wolfenbuttel, Berlin, 1933, in *Fascism: Oxford Readers,* Roger Griffin, ed. (Oxford University Press, 1995).

extensive program of public works and rearmament. The unemployed were put to work on public projects (especially in the system of superhighways, the *Autobahnen*), in munitions factories, and in the army.

Overlapping the first program, the second 4-year plan was initiated in 1936. The objective of this plan was to set up an autarkist state. In pursuit of self-sufficiency, substitute commodities—frequently inferior in quality and more costly than similar goods available on the world market—were produced by German laboratories, factories, and mills. The gross national product increased by 68 percent by 1938, but the standard of living did not rise in proportion to the higher economic growth rate. When World War II began in 1939, German industry still produced insufficient munitions, even after Hitler took over the Czech Skoda works. Germany's war economy did not hit its stride until 1942.

By then, the economic picture didn't matter. Hitler controlled Germany. How an advanced, "civilized" nation like Germany could have thrown itself willingly under this madman's control is one of history's great questions. Other nations had stronger authoritarian traditions, greater economic problems, and more extreme psychological strain. Some observers maintain that there could have been no Third Reich without this unprecedented demagoguery that found a willing audience in the troubled conditions after 1918.

Discovery Through Maps

Wishful Thinking: A Nazi Tourism Map

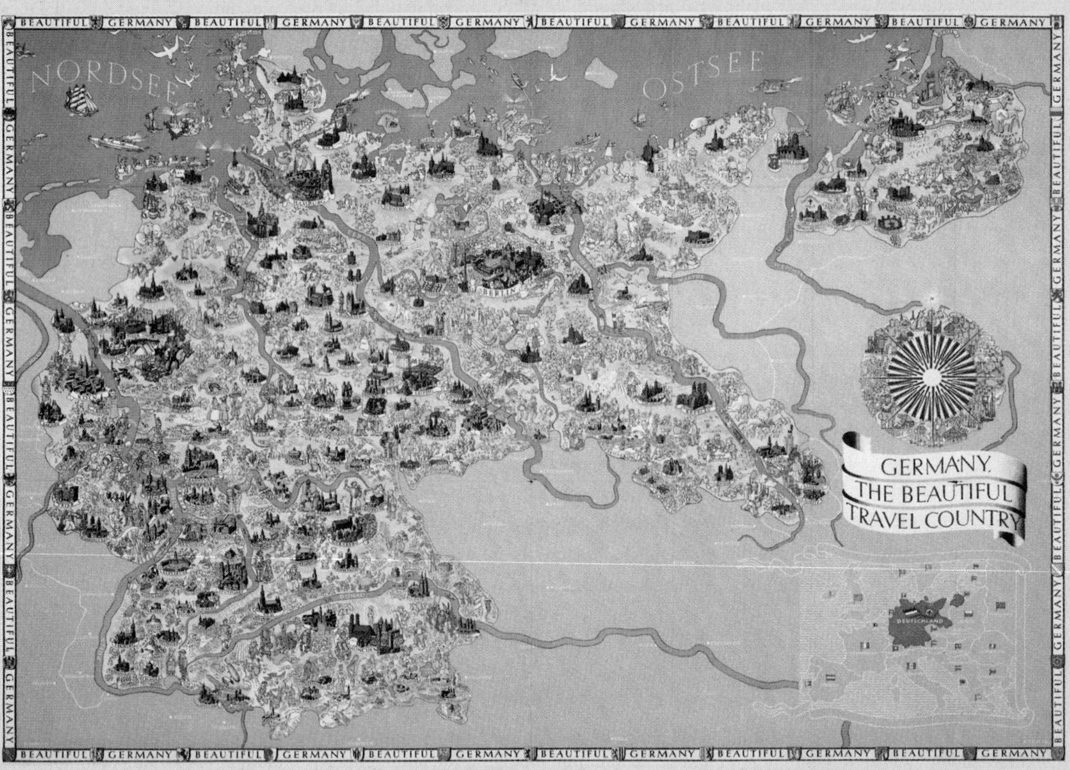

States promote tourism for a number of reasons. Tourists come, spend money, and go home—it is much like harvesting a crop, without having to do all of the difficult work. Tourists tend to be the most curious and best informed people of given society: they can have their views of a given country positively affected by their travels. Tourists go home, and if they have had a good time, they encourage others to come in sort of a multiplier effect—to visit and bring their money and their impressions.

With the exception of a few hermit regimes, most countries in the twentieth century worked hard to encourage tourists to come, for the reasons pointed out above. The Third Reich was no exception. The Reich's Tourist Information Office issued a map titled "Germany, the Beautiful Travel Country" to entice foreigners to come to the country around the time of the 1936 Olympics. It is chock full of portrayals of Germany's historic and natural sites and diverse population—except for Jews. Tourist campaigns emphasize what they take to be the positive aspects of their country, and the Third Reich did just that.

Germany, in this detail from the map, is a prosperous place under the control of the National Socialist Worker's party and the beautiful Aryan people are truly happy. There are workers shown—in gleaming new factories, picture-perfect peasant lands, sturdy fishing boats, and artisans' workshops. There are also lots of recreational activities from swimming to skiing to gamboling and gambling to hunting and bird watching. The culture of the Reich can be seen in the exhortations to visit the fine art museums, music festivals, and observe artists at work. Germany was a beautiful country to travel in, if one stayed on the proper path and didn't look too closely at what was going on.

Many people did come to Germany, and admired the work of the Nazis and their allies. English royalty, American heroes such as Charles Lindbergh, and admiring travelers from Eastern Europe all came and accepted at face value what they saw. Most tourists are like that. Not until the end of the 1930s did it become apparent that beneath the busy and happy façade, a malignant force gained strength.

Questions to Consider

1. As you look at the map, do you see it as overtly propagandistic, or as simply a solid piece of advertising? Is there a difference between the two?
2. What image does the map attempt to give the observer of Germany under the Nazis?
3. Do you notice any obvious signs of the Nazi presence, such as soldiers or images of German leaders?

Revolutions in Russia: 1917 and 1928–1939

How did the revolutions of 1917 and 1928–1939 transform Russia?

Russia entered the war in August 1914 in a buoyant and patriotic mood. It took only two months to dampen initial optimism and to expose the army's weakness and the tsarist government's corruption and inefficiency. By the middle of 1915, drastic losses (more than 2 million casualties) and food and fuel shortages lowered morale. Strikes increased among the factory workers during 1916, and the peasants, whose sons were dying in large numbers and whose desire for land reform was being ignored, became discontented. The enormous costs of Russia's participation in World War I and the incompetence of the government led in March to the first Russian Revolution of 1917, and the end of the Romanov dynasty.

The First, "Spontaneous" 1917 Revolution

A spontaneous event from below sparked the 1917 Russian Revolution. In the first part of March,[8] a strike broke out in a Petrograd factory. By March 8, sympathy strikes had virtually paralyzed the city. At the same time, a bread shortage occurred, which brought more people into the streets. Scattered fighting broke out between the strikers and protesters on one side and the police on the other. Tsar Nicholas II ordered the strikers back to work and dismissed the Duma (parliament) on March 11. His orders touched off the revolutionary crisis. The Duma refused to go home, and the strikers defied the government and held mass meetings. The next day, the army and police openly sided with the workers.

Three events that occurred between March 12 and March 15 marked the end of the old regime. On March 12, the Duma declared the formation of a provisional committee (renamed the *Provisional Government* on March 15) to serve as a caretaker administration until a Constituent Assembly could be elected to write a constitution for the future Russian republic. On the same day, Marxist socialists and Socialist Revolutionaries in Petrograd formed the **Soviet** ("council") of Workers' Deputies (renamed three days later the *Soviet of Workers' and Soldiers' Deputies*). Nicholas abdicated on March 15 in favor of his brother Michael, who turned down the throne the next day in favor of the Provisional Government. After more than three centuries in power, the Romanov dynasty ceased to rule.

For the next six months, Russia proceeded under a system that Leon Trotsky, the great Marxist theoretician and revolutionary, described as "dual power"—the Provisional Government and the Soviet. The moderates and liberals in the Provisional Government quickly produced a program of civil rights and liberties that gave Russia a springtime of freedom in 1917, the likes of which the country had never known before and would not experience again for 70 years. From the first, however, the Provisional Government was hampered by its temporary nature: it refused to take permanent action on major issues until the Constituent Assembly, elected by all Russians, could convene to write a constitution.

The Soviet was dominated by the **Menshevik** wing of the Russian Social Democratic party along with the Socialist Revolutionaries. The Mensheviks closely followed Marx's teachings and believed that a liberal, bourgeois phase of history had to run its course. Even though they had greater popular support than the Provisional Government, they refused to take power. They did not believe 1917 to be the historically proper moment, as defined by Marx's theories, and they doubted their own capacity to maintain order. After the fall of the tsar, power passed to those who could not or would not rule.

From the first, the dual power system functioned in a contradictory and ineffective way. On March 14, the Soviet issued its first law, Order No. 1, which placed the running of the army on a democratic basis, through a committee structure. Soldiers were to obey only those orders that agreed with the official position of the Soviet, which wanted peace. At the same time, the Provisional Government insisted on living up to Russia's commitments to the Allies and carrying out the war, with the hope of gaining the Bosporus, Constantinople, and the Dardanelles from the crumbling Ottoman Empire.

As the months wore on, the position of moderates in both parts of the system weakened, and all the involved parties became discredited. The Provisional Government put off calling the Constituent Assembly and thereby deferred any possibility of finding solutions to the problems Russia faced. It continued to pursue the war to "honor its commitments" and to gain the prizes promised in the secret treaties. The Provisional Government's actions, combined with the refusal of the Mensheviks to take control for ideological reasons, meant that the masses, who suffered from economic hardships or fought and died on the front lines, could find little consolation in either branch of dual power.

Soviet—A council. First used in Russia during the 1905 Revolution when the Social Democrats organized Soviets (councils) of workers.

Menshevik—The Russian Social Democrats meeting in London split into two wings in 1903—the Bolsheviks (the majority) and the Mensheviks (the minority)—reflecting from the results of a vote on party policies. The Mensheviks went on to become the most powerful branch of the Social Democrats in Russia until 1907. The Bolsheviks, led by Lenin, finally gained power in November 1917.

End of the Romanov Dynasty: The February–March Revolution of 1917

	All dates are according to the Gregorian calendar, which replaced the Julian calendar in use in Russia at the time.
March 8	Sympathy strikes paralyze city
March 11	Tsar orders strikers back to work, dismisses Duma
March 12	Army and police disobey orders; Duma declares formation of provisional committee; Socialists proclaim formation of Soviet of Workers' Deputies
March 15	Tsar Nicholas I abdicates, passes power to his brother, Michael; Duma declares formation of Provisional Government; Socialists proclaim formation of Soviet of Workers' and Soldiers' Deputies
March 16	Michael renounces authority, Provisional Government assumes power

By July, the liberals and moderates had given up the reins of power. Alexander Kerensky (1881–1970), who had been the only real revolutionary in the original cabinet, became the head of the Provisional Government. He was in an impossible situation. Leftists accused the Provisional Government of heartlessly pursuing the war, while rightists condemned it for tolerating too many leftists. In the meantime, the Soviet extended its organization throughout Russia by setting up local affiliates. Through the summer, however, the Soviets lacked the forceful leadership they needed to take control of the country.

The Second, "Bolshevik" Revolution of 1917

In 1917, Lenin returned to Russia from exile in Switzerland, intent on giving the revolution the leadership it lacked. He had spelled out his tactics and ideas in the previous decade, and his disciples in Russia, the **Bolsheviks,** had built up a core of supporters in the factories and the army. As late as December 1916, he had stated that the revolution would not occur within his lifetime. Four months later, working through Swiss contacts and with German assistance, he returned to Russia. The Germans gave him transportation and financial support in the hope that he would cause widespread chaos, forcing Russia to withdraw from the war.

Bolshevik—The branch of the Social Democratic party, led by Lenin, that governed Russia after 1917. The official name came to be the Communist party.

From the moment he stepped off the train in Petrograd on the evening of April 16, Lenin tried to control the revolution. He proposed immediately stopping the war against Germany and starting one against "social oppressors." He called for giving all power to the Soviets and nationalizing all land. He also pushed for calling all Social Democrats, of whatever persuasion, communists. Lenin badly misjudged his audience, and the Mensheviks and Social Revolutionaries rejected his program.

During the summer and fall of 1917, the Provisional Government and the Soviet continued their misgovernment. Kerensky tried to rule through a series of coalitions in which the political balance continually shifted to the left. By the middle of July, after a moderately successful offensive against the Austrians, soldiers began to desert in large numbers rather than face a useless death in World War I. The Russian front, along with the army, disintegrated. In the capital, the Mensheviks persisted in refusing to take power through the Soviet: the historical time was not right. As if to match the ineptness of dual power, the Bolsheviks made an ill-conceived attempt to take power. The move backfired, and Lenin was forced to flee in disguise to Finland.

After surviving the Bolshevik crisis, Kerensky faced a new threat from the right when General Lavr Kornilov tried to "help" the government by sending his troops to the capital. Kerensky and the Soviet interpreted this action as a right-wing counterrevolutionary move and mobilized to head it off. Kornilov's ill-advised maneuver failed, and ironically, he weakened the people he wanted to help.

Between March and October 1917, the force of the revolution ground to bits all of Russia's structures and parties, from monarchist to Menshevik. The economic system fell apart as the rhythms of planting and commerce were disrupted by the uproar. To the people caught in this chaos, the moderates' political dreams, the Mensheviks' revolutionary timing, and the Bolsheviks' schemes for the seizure of power were all totally irrelevant.

The actual revolution took place far away from the politicians and "great men." The army withered away, as mass desertions and the execution of officers became commonplace. In the countryside, the peasants began carrying out land reform on their own, expelling landowners and killing those who would not leave. In the cities, workers began to take over factories. The Russian Empire broke apart from internal conflicts, the continued pressure of war, and the rising spirits of the nationalities who had been oppressed for centuries.

Only the Bolsheviks seemed to have an answer to Russia's crisis; even their slogans, such as "Peace, Land, and Bread," reflected what was already happening. Furthermore, they had the discipline and adaptability to take advantage of events. By October 1917, the Bol-

◀ Lenin, flanked by Stalin on the left and Kalinin on the right, at Eighth Bolshevik Party Congress in 1919.

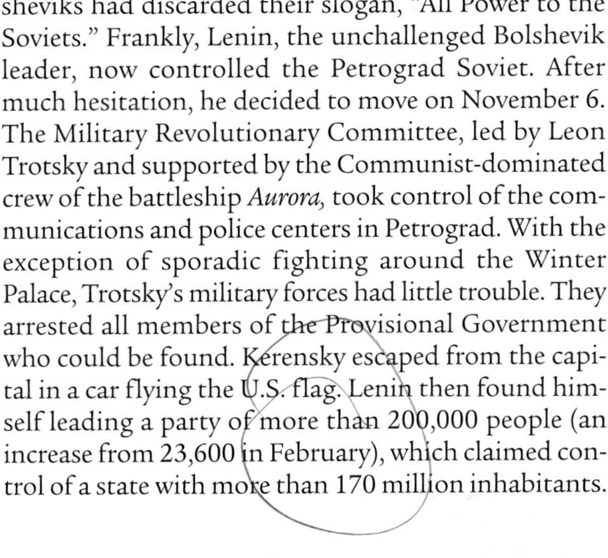

sheviks had discarded their slogan, "All Power to the Soviets." Frankly, Lenin, the unchallenged Bolshevik leader, now controlled the Petrograd Soviet. After much hesitation, he decided to move on November 6. The Military Revolutionary Committee, led by Leon Trotsky and supported by the Communist-dominated crew of the battleship *Aurora,* took control of the communications and police centers in Petrograd. With the exception of sporadic fighting around the Winter Palace, Trotsky's military forces had little trouble. They arrested all members of the Provisional Government who could be found. Kerensky escaped from the capital in a car flying the U.S. flag. Lenin then found himself leading a party of more than 200,000 people (an increase from 23,600 in February), which claimed control of a state with more than 170 million inhabitants.

Power, Allied Intervention, and Civil War

The Bolsheviks assumed power over a war-weakened, revolution-ravaged state that was in terrible condition. Lenin's takeover split the Soviet itself when the Mensheviks and the Social Revolutionaries refused to participate. Lenin had a bare majority at the Soviet's first postrevolutionary meeting. In the free elections held in December to form a Constituent Assembly, the Bolsheviks received just one-fourth of the votes. Yet such details as democratic representation did not stop Lenin. He proceeded to rule Russia. The Bolsheviks immediately put through decrees to declare peace and settle the land question. In the meantime, his cadres imposed their control over Moscow and the other cities in the country.

▼ Germany took advantage of Russian weaknesses after the 1917 revolution to deprive the revolutionary state of much of its economic base and territory. Not only did the fledgling Moscow-based communist state face intervention by the Western Allies in 1918, but it also had a war with the newly reunited Polish state over the western borderlands formerly controlled by the tsars.

Lenin then began to lay the foundations for a single-party dictatorship that endured until 1991. When the Constituent Assembly convened in Petrograd on January 18, 1918, and proved that it would not be a tool for Lenin, the Bolsheviks closed it down at bayonet point the next day. By dissolving the Constituent Assembly, Lenin crushed all remnants of the briefly flowering democracy. This decisive step sealed the fate of the Mensheviks and most other opposition leftist parties. Not for 71 years would there be contested elections, open criticism of the central power, and the possibility of a potential democratic opposition.

Almost immediately, the revolutionary government came under attack from the White forces, the Allied Expeditionary Forces, and the new Polish state. The Whites, a powerful but fragmented group of anti-Bolsheviks, responded to the overthrow of the Provisional Government and the dissolution of the Constituent Assembly by attacking the revolutionary government. The resulting Civil War would claim as many casualties in 3 years as the country had lost in World War I. The Allied Powers sent several small expeditionary armies to Russia for the stated purpose of controlling matériel they had sent to the former tsarist army. In reality, they helped the Whites.

Lenin also had to make peace with Germany, and after two months of negotiations, concluded the Treaty of Brest-Litovsk (1918). This agreement drastically reduced the territory under Russian control and made the centers of government much more exposed to attack. In reality, Lenin sacrificed territory over which he had no control and took his country out of a war it could not fight.

The Allies, still at war with Germany, feared that the Bolsheviks were in a conspiracy with the Germans, especially after the terms of the Brest-Litovsk treaty became known. They also hoped that if Lenin could be overthrown, the Whites might reopen fighting against the Central Powers. The last of the expeditionary forces, the Japanese, did not leave until 1922. War broke out between Russia and Poland over a disputed boundary.

From its new capital at Moscow, the Red (Bolshevik) government took all means to defend the Revolution. Lenin's forces reimposed the death penalty (it had been abolished in all areas—except in the Russian army at the front—by the Provisional Government) and unleashed a reign of terror. The Red Army and the Cheka (secret police) systematically destroyed the enemies of the Revolution as well as individuals who were only lukewarm in their support of the new regime. Prison camps and repressive terror harsher than any since Ivan IV dominated life in the Russian state. In July 1918, the former tsar and his family, under house arrest since the outbreak of the revolution, were herded into the cellar of the house in which they were being held and were executed. They would not receive their final burial until 1998.

After the Central Powers surrendered in November 1918, Allied intervention in Russia ceased, and the Bolsheviks concentrated their energies against the Whites. Trotsky turned the Red Army into a disciplined, centralized force. The disorganized and dispersed White opposition, whose units ranged from Siberia to the Caucasus to Europe, could not match the Red forces. Taking advantage of their shorter supply lines, ideological unity, and dislike of Allied intervention, the Bolsheviks put an end to White resistance by 1920. The Whites were united on few issues besides their hatred of the Bolsheviks. After their defeat, nearly a million of them scattered across the globe.

Theory, Reality, and the State

Lenin had no hesitation about revising Marx's doctrines to fit Russian conditions. Marx had assumed that the revolution overthrowing the bourgeoisie could take place only in an industrialized country with a well-developed and strong **proletariat.** Russia remained a peasant-dominated society, however, and Lenin from the first had to deal with the existence of a large and uncooperative peasant class. Before 1917, he had noted that the support of the peasantry would be essential for the success of the revolution. Once in power, during war communism (see p. 885), his government carried on a frontal attack against the peasantry—featuring forced collectivization and the seizure of food from the countryside. This led to the peasants' withholding food from the cities and a resultant famine. In the New Economic Policy (see p. 886), Lenin reversed these policies, and agricultural production increased.

Lenin had long opposed all democratic parliamentary procedures, especially the concept of an officially recognized opposition party. As the proletariat represented the politically conscious segment of society, and the class on which the Revolution was built, it made no sense to invent a political opposition group within it and thereby undermine the political unity of the state. Lenin advocated instead a revolutionary "dictatorship of the proletariat" under Bolshevik leadership. The new order would rule in accordance with "democratic centralism," in which the vanguard party would anticipate the best interests of the masses and rule for them.

Lenin altered certain aspects of the Marxist concept of the historical process. He accepted the view that the proletarian-socialist revolution must be preceded by a bourgeois-democratic revolution. He interpreted the March 1917 events as the first democratic revolution and his own coup d'état in November as the second, or proletarian-socialist, revolution. This approach drastically shortened the historical process by which

proletariat—In Marxist theory, the proletariat is the politically class-conscious portion of the working classes who would move to achieve the socialist revolution.

the bourgeois stage was to run its course. Lenin justified dissolving the Constituent Assembly on the grounds that a higher form of democratic principle had now been achieved, making the assembly superfluous. The November Revolution had vested all power in the Russian Republic in the people themselves, as expressed in their revolutionary committees, the soviets.

The new state acted in many spheres. In policies reminiscent of Robespierre's tenure during the French Revolution, the new government attacked the church, changed the calendar (adopting the Gregorian and rejecting the Julian system), and simplified the alphabet. The Cheka enforced ideological unity with a level of terror that set the standard for later Soviet secret police organizations.

In the first 6 years after Lenin seized power, there were three major developments relating to the Communist party, the name adopted by the Bolsheviks in 1918. First, all other parties were suppressed. Second, the function of the party was changed from that of carrying out the Revolution to that of governing the country. Third, within the party itself, a small elite group called the **Politburo,** which set policy, consolidated power in its hands. Among the members of the first Politburo were Lenin, Trotsky, and Stalin. The second major organ of the party was the Secretariat for the Central Committee, which oversaw the implementation of policy into practice.

The state itself became known as the Russian Socialist Federated Soviet Republic (RSFSR). As the Moscow-based Communist government extended its authority after the civil war, the jurisdiction of the RSFSR grew. In 1922, the Union of Soviet Socialist Republics (USSR) was formed, consisting of the four constituent socialist republics: the RSFSR, the Ukraine, White Russia (Belorussia), and Transcaucasia; the USSR would soon expand to reflect the multinational nature of the Eurasian state.

Although it appeared that the state exercised sovereign power under its president, the USSR actually was governed by the Communist party. So great did the authority of the Communist party become over the formation and administration of policy that, before Lenin's death in early 1924, it could be said that party and state were one. Consequently, whoever controlled the party—in the Soviet case, the General Secretary—controlled the state. In the new Soviet state the key person would be Joseph Stalin—who would remain the General Secretary, or *GenSec*,[9] of the party from 1922 to his death in 1953.

War Communism and the NEP

From 1918 to 1921, Lenin tried to apply undiluted Marxist principles to eliminate private ownership of

Politburo—The small, elite group of the Communist party that established policy.

▲ Russian children help carry the propaganda for Stalin's campaign for collectivization of agriculture. The banner reads, in part, "Everybody to the collective farm!" These happy faces belie the tragedy resulting from the collectivization program in which millions fell victim to slaughter or starvation.

land; nationalize banks, railways, and shipping; and restrict the money economy. This policy, known as *war communism,* was widely unpopular. The peasants, who had just attained their centuries-long goal of controlling their own land, did not like the prospects of collectivization and the surrender of their surplus grain to the state. Many workers did not want to be forced to work in factories. Former managers showed little enthusiasm for running enterprises for the state's benefit.

In the early months of 1920, the new government faced its most dangerous crisis to date. Six years of war and civil strife had left Russia exhausted. Industrial production was 13 percent of what it had been in 1914. Crop failures, poor management, and transportation breakdowns contributed to the disaster. Famine brought more than 20 million people to the brink of starvation. The government was forced to ask for help, and organizations such as Herbert Hoover's American project to bring relief to Russia helped the country through the crisis, but not before some 5 million people died.

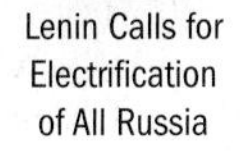

DOCUMENT

Lenin Calls for Electrification of All Russia

Internal chaos, in addition to controversy with Poland over disputed borders, further plagued Lenin's government. From 1918 to 1921, other areas of the former Russian Empire—Finland, Estonia, Latvia, Lithuania, and Bessarabia—chose to go their own way. In

February 1921, sailors at Kronstadt, formerly supporters of the regime, rebelled against the Bolsheviks and were massacred by the Red Army. Lenin said that the revolt "illuminated reality like a flash of lightning,"[10] and chose to make an ideological retreat.

War communism was a total failure. Lenin decided that it was necessary "to take one step backward in order to go two steps forward." He explained that Russia had tried to do too much too soon in attempting to change everything at once. He also noted that there had not been a firestorm of complementary communist revolutions sweeping the globe. The outbreaks in Germany and Hungary had been brutally quashed. Russia stood alone. Compromise was necessary to survive, and besides altering his diplomatic front abroad, he recommended a return to certain practices of capitalism, the so-called New Economic Policy, or NEP.

This retreat from war communism lasted until 1928 and allowed the Soviet state to get on its feet. Peasants were relieved from the wholesale appropriation of grain. After paying a fixed tax, they were permitted to sell their surplus produce in the open market. Private management could once again run firms and factories employing fewer than 20 employees. Workers in state industries received a graduated wage scale. Foreign commerce and technology were actively sought. These compromises proved to be highly beneficial, and the Soviet economy revived.

Ideological purists criticized the policy and pointed out that private businesses and the **kulaks,** as the ambitious peasants who accumulated property were called, profited greatly. Lenin's concessions and compromises gave the Communists time to regroup and recover, and the Russian people gained much-needed breathing space. Lenin emphasized the absolute necessity for the party to "control the commanding heights of the economy." The state continued to manage banking, transportation, heavy industry, and public utilities.

The NEP was Lenin's last major contribution. In broken health since surviving a would-be assassin's bullet in 1918, he worked as much as he could until his death in January 1924.

Trotsky Versus Stalin

A weakness of all dictatorships is that there is no well-defined mechanism to pass power from one leader to the next. Lenin was the one person in the party who possessed unchallenged authority and whose decrees were binding. After his death, Leon Trotsky and Joseph Stalin, rivals with conflicting policies and personalities, fought for power.

Leon Trotsky (1879–1940), born Lev Davidovich Bronstein, was a star in the political arena. He was a magnificent, charismatic orator; an energetic and magnetic leader in all areas; and a first-rate intellectual and theoretician. He turned to Marxism as a teenager and, like Lenin, had been exiled to Siberia for his revolutionary activities. He participated in the major events of Russian social democracy. Trotsky was a member of the *Iskra* (EES-craw) group of Russian exiles in Zurich, had been present in London in 1903 and opposed Lenin in the Bolshevik-Menshevik split, played a key role in the 1905 Russian Revolution, and was an essential figure in the 1917 revolutions and the civil war. His egocentricity and arrogance contrasted sharply with the shrewd and cunning nature of his less colorful but more calculating rival.

Joseph Stalin (1879–1953), born in Georgia as Joseph Vissarionovich Dzhugashvili (zhu-GOSH-vee-lee), labored for the Revolution in obscurity. While Trotsky played the star, Stalin worked behind the scenes. Trotsky was a crowd-pleasing orator; Stalin, when he spoke in Russian (his second language—Georgian was his first), was not an inspiring speaker. Admitted to a seminary to be trained for the priesthood, the young Stalin was later expelled for radical opinions. In the years before the revolutions, Stalin served the Bolsheviks by robbery to gain funds for the party's organization and propaganda activities. In all ways he faithfully supported Lenin—unlike Trotsky, who had not been a uniformly obedient disciple between 1903 and 1917. Stalin was exiled east of the Urals a number of times before he returned to Petrograd in 1917 to play an active role in the events of that year. He knew his own strengths and weaknesses. He also formed his opinion of Trotsky rather early on, characterizing him in 1907 as "beautifully useless."

After the 1917 revolutions, Stalin did much of the less glamorous organizational work of the party; he was also responsible for dealing with the various nationalities. While others in the Politburo dealt with ideological questions or fought the civil war, Stalin created a network of people—loyal to him alone—who worked in the bureaucratic apparatus and came to be known as apparatchiks (ap-pa-RAT-cheeks). With and through them, he controlled the bureaucracy. In 1922, *Pravda* ("Truth"), the official party newspaper, carried a brief announcement that the Central Committee had confirmed Stalin as General Secretary of the Secretariat, a position that became the most powerful in the Soviet Union.

After Lenin's death, Stalin moved to construct a new secular religion for the Soviet Union, Leninism, formed in 1924 and powerful for more than 60 years. The mark of faith came to be unquestioning loyalty to Lenin. The city of Petrograd, for example, was renamed Leningrad. Stalin became Lenin's St. Peter, despite Lenin's criticism of both Trotsky and Stalin in his purported last will and testament. (Although written in 1922, it was not widely published until the 1950s.)

---

kulaks—Farmers in the USSR who owned land, farm equipment, or employed laborers.

In the competition with Trotsky, Stalin won because he was the better organizer and the more skillful manipulator of people. Staying in the background, Stalin, the modest "helper," played the game of "divide and conquer" as members of the Politburo fought among themselves. By 1926, party members realized that Stalin had consolidated his position and had the full support of the party apparatus. By the end of that year, Trotsky and other opponents were removed from the Politburo. By 1929, Stalin was referred to as the "Lenin of today." Stalin's supporters occupied the key posts in both government and party, and he became the chairman of the Politburo. By 1940, he had eliminated all of the old Bolsheviks, including Trotsky, who was exiled and finally struck down by an assassin in Mexico, on Stalin's orders.

More than just an opportunist or a super-bureaucrat, Stalin had his own ideological views on the future of the country. Trotsky and others had believed, along with Lenin, that the USSR could not survive indefinitely as a socialist island in a capitalist ocean. It was the duty, they held, of Russian communists to push for revolution elsewhere. Stalin, less a theorist than a political realist, viewed the idea of a world revolution as premature. He correctly noted that Marxism had made little headway outside the USSR, despite the existence of what, from the Marxist standpoint, were advantageous conditions for revolution in Germany and Italy. Stalin called for a new policy of building up socialism in a single state. (Lenin had once hinted at that alternative in 1921.) He put an end to the NEP and began taking "two steps forward"—with brutal and far-reaching results.

Stalin's Economics: Revolution from Above, 1928–1939

Russia had begun industrialization at a late date and from the 1890s on was continuously aware of its backwardness. The drastic destruction of World War I and the civil war reversed much of the progress that had been made, and by the late 1920s, Stalin was deeply concerned with the country's economic weakness in the face of foreign invasion. He ordered a radical overhaul of the entire country and society designed to make 50 years' progress in 10.

The NEP was scrapped in 1928, and Stalin imposed collectivization of agriculture and a series of 5-year plans calling for heavy industrialization. Long working hours and a six-day workweek were instituted in an attempt to revolutionize the Soviet Union's economic structure. For the first time in history, a government controlled all significant economic activity through a central planning apparatus. This was an attempt to remove the old market-based system and replace it with new framework. To drive the entire population along, Stalin strengthened his secret police so that they could force the nation through what would be a decade of convulsive internal struggle. By 1939, Stalin had consolidated his personal dictatorship, at the cost of 10 to 20 million lives.

War on the Peasants

Stalin wanted to transform the peasants into a rural proletariat, raising food on state and collective farms, not on their own plots. He had little doctrinal help from Marx, who had not considered that the revolution he forecast could take place in a peasant-dominated society. Marx left little guidance about what to do with the peasants beyond mention of collectivized agriculture. He had assumed that capitalism would convert peasants into day laborers before the socialist revolution took place; hence farming would continue, except that now the state would own the farms.

Lenin's war communism programs had failed, yet Stalin went back to them as he drew up his guidelines to transform agriculture. The major problem he faced

▼ Joseph Vissarionovich Dzhugashvili, fourth from the right in the first row, chose to call himself Stalin ("steel") and came close to gaining totalitarian control of the USSR during the 1930s, working through his chosen men of the apparatus, the apparatchiks, pictured with him here, many of whom would remain in power for a half century.

was to convince the peasants to surrender their private lands, which they had finally received in 1917, to the state and collective farms.

Under Stalin's program, the state farms, *sovkhoz* (sof-HOHS), would be owned outright by the government, which would pay the workers' wages. The collective farms, *kolkhoz* (KOLK-hohs), would be created from land taken from the kulaks and from the peasants who would voluntarily accept the government's decree to merge their own holdings. *Kolkhoz* members would work the land under the management of a board of directors. At the end of the year, each farm's net earnings would be totaled in cash and in kind, and the members would be paid on the basis of the amount and skill of their labor.

The theoretical advantages of large-scale mechanized farming over small-scale peasant agriculture were obvious. In addition, the government intended the reforms to permit the more efficient political education of the peasants. Further, the new programs would liquidate the kulaks, successful farmers who owned more property than their neighbors and who represented a disturbing element on the socialist landscape.

The vast majority of peasants disagreed violently with Stalin's agricultural program. They did not want to give up their land. One of the party leaders, Lazar Kaganovich, noted that "women in the countryside in many cases played the most 'advanced' role in the reaction against collective farms."[11] When the peasants did not flock to the government's banners, Stalin ordered harsher methods. When the class war between the poor peasants and the kulaks did not take place, he sent the secret police and the army to the villages. The transition to collectivization was carried out under some of the most barbarous and brutal measures ever enacted by a government against its own people.

In the tragedy that followed, millions of people, especially in the Ukraine, died from direct attack, from famine, or in work camps. By a decree in February 1930, the state forced about 1 million kulaks off their land and took their possessions. Many peasants opposed these measures, slaughtering their herds and destroying their crops rather than handing them over to the state. In 1933, the number of horses was less than half the number there had been in 1928, and there were 40 percent fewer cattle and half as many sheep and goats. After 9 years of war on the peasants, however, 90 percent of the land and 100 million peasants were in the collective and state farms.

The Five-Year Plans

Stalin introduced the system of central planning in 1928. He and his advisers assumed that by centralizing all aspects of the allocation of resources and removing market forces from the economy, they could ensure a swift buildup of capital goods and heavy industries. The 5-year plans, which began in 1929, restricted the manufacture of consumer goods and abolished capitalism in the forms permitted under the NEP. Citizens were allowed to own certain types of private property, houses, furniture, clothes, and personal effects. They could not own property that could be used to make profits by hiring workers. The state was to be the only employer.

The first 5-year plan called for a 250 percent increase in overall industrial productivity. The state and police turned their entire effort to this goal. Even in the chaos that occurred—buildings were erected to house nonexistent machines, and machines were shipped to places where there were no buildings—growth did take place.

The party cited statistics to prove that the plan had been achieved in 4½ years. Whether these were accurate or not—and they have been vigorously challenged—Soviet industry and society were totally transformed. The costs were disastrous, but Stalin portrayed the Soviet Union as being in a form of war with the world, and without strength, he pointed out, the USSR would be crushed.

The second 5-year plan began in 1933 and sought to resolve some of the mistakes of the first. The government placed greater emphasis on improving the quality of industrial products and on making more consumer goods. The third plan, begun in 1938, emphasized national defense. State strategies called for industrial plants to be shifted east of the Urals, and efforts were made to develop new sources of oil and other important commodities. Gigantism was the key, as the world's largest tractor factory was built in Chelyabinsk (chel-EE-AH-binsk), greatest power station in Dnepropetrovsk (dnie-pro-PET-rovsk), and largest automobile plant in Gorki.

The plans achieved remarkable results. In 1932, Soviet authorities claimed an increase in industrial output of 334 percent over 1914 levels; 1937 output was 180 percent over that of 1932. But the high volume of production was often tied to mediocre quality, and the achievements were gained only with an enormous cost in human life and suffering and massive damage to the environment. At first the burdensome cost of importing heavy machinery, tools, equipment, and finished steel from abroad forced a subsistence scale of living on the people. These purchases were paid for by the sale of food and raw material in the world's markets at a time when the prices for such goods had fallen drastically.

In the rush to industrialize, basic aspects of Marxism were set aside. The dictatorship *of* the proletariat increasingly became the dictatorship *over* the proletariat. Another ideological casualty was the basic concept of economic egalitarianism. In 1931, Stalin declared that equality of wages was "alien and detrimental to Soviet production" and a "petit bourgeois deviation." So much propaganda was used to implant this twist that the masses came to accept the doctrine of inequality of wages as a fundamental communist principle.

Document

Stalin and State Terror

Stalin's totalitarianism brought the development of state terror to unparalleled heights as the regime victimized not only innocent people but also their families during the purges. Nadezhda Mandelstam's husband, Osip, had been rounded up in 1934 for having created a clever epigram criticizing Stalin, and he was exiled to provincial Voronezh. When the purges went into their next phase, he was rearrested in 1938 and died en route to a labor camp near Vladivostok on the Pacific coast. Nadezhda Mandelstam described the nature of the terror, and its effect on the human soul.

When I used to read about the French Revolution as a child, I often wondered whether it was possible to survive during a reign of terror. I now know beyond doubt that it is impossible. Anybody who breathes the air of terror is doomed, even if nominally he manages to save his life. Everybody is a victim—not only those who die, but also all the killers, ideologists, accomplices, and sycophants who close their eyes and wash their hands—even if they are secretly consumed with remorse at night. Every section of the population has been through the terrible sickness caused by terror, and none has so far recovered, or become fit again for normal civic life. It is an illness that is passed on to the next generation, so that the sons pay for the sins of the fathers and perhaps only the grandchildren begin to get over it—or at least it takes on a different form with them.

The principles and aims of mass terror have nothing in common with ordinary police work or with security. The only purpose of terror is intimidation. To plunge the whole country into a state of chronic fear, the number of victims must be raised to astronomical levels, and on every floor of every building there must always be several apartments from which the tenants have suddenly been taken away. The remaining inhabitants will be model citizens for the rest of their lives—this will be true for every street and every city through which the broom has swept. The only essential thing for those who rule by terror is not to overlook the new generations growing up without faith in their elders, and to keep on repeating the process in systematic fashion. Stalin ruled for a long time and saw to it that the waves of terror recurred from time to time, always on an even greater scale than before. But the champions of terror invariably leave one thing out of account—namely, that they can't kill everyone, and among their cowed, half-demented subjects there are always witnesses who survive to tell the tale.

Questions to Consider

1. Why did Stalin take writers so seriously that he persecuted and executed so many of them? How could words hurt him, he who had all of the power?
2. What does Nadezhda Mandelstam say is the goal of terror?
3. Have you ever been affected by terrorists or a terrorist act? Do you agree with Mandelstam as to the effect of terrorism on you, directly or indirectly?

From Nadezhda Mandelstam, *Hope Against Hope: A Memoir,* trans. Max Hayward.

The Great Purges

During the 1930s, Stalin consolidated his hold over the Communist party and created the political system that would last until the ascent to power of Mikhail Gorbachev in 1985. Stalin established an all-powerful, personal, dictatorial rule by doing away with all of his rivals, real and potential, in purges. He also took the opportunity to remove all scientific, cultural, and educational figures who did not fit in with his plans for the future. By 1939, Stalin had destroyed what was left of the Russian revolutionary tradition and replaced it with the rule of his people—the apparatchiks—who lived well in comparison with the rest of the Soviet population.

The long arm of the secret police gathered in thousands of Soviet citizens to face the kangaroo court and the firing squad. All six original members of the 1920 Politburo who survived Lenin were purged by Stalin. Old Bolsheviks who had been loyal comrades of Lenin, high officers of the Red Army, directors of industry, and rank-and-file party members were liquidated. Millions more were sent to forced labor camps. It has been estimated that between 5 and 6 percent of the population spent time in the pretrial prisons of the secret police.

Party discipline and fear prevented party members from turning against Stalin, who controlled the party. The world watched a series of show trials in which loyal members of the Communist party confessed to an amazing array of charges, generally tied, after 1934, to the assassination of Sergei Kirov, Leningrad party chief and one of Stalin's chief aides. Western journalists reported news of the trials to the world while the drugged, tortured, and intimidated defendants confessed to crimes they had not committed. By 1939, fully 70 percent of the members of the Central Committee elected in 1934 had been purged. Among officers in the armed forces, the purges claimed three of five army marshals, 14 of 16 army commanders, all eight admirals, 60 of 67 corps commanders, 136 of 199 divisional commanders, 221 of 397 brigade commanders, and roughly one-half of the remaining officers, or some 35,000 men. A large portion of the leadership of the USSR was destroyed.

In a sense, the purges culminated in Mexico with Trotsky's assassination in 1940. The lessons of the purges were chilling and effective. The way to succeed, to survive, was to be devotedly, unquestioningly, a follower of Joseph Stalin.

Changes in Soviet Society

In the 20 years after 1917, all aspects of Soviet society came under the control of the party. The atomization of society, a prime characteristic of dictatorial government, did not permit such secret, self-contained, and mutually trusting groups as the family to exist at ease. After the Revolution, the party dealt in contradictory terms with various aspects of social life, but, by and large, the government worked to weaken the importance of the family. Until 1936, divorces required no court proceedings, abortions were legal, women were encouraged to take jobs outside the home, and communist nurseries were set up to care for children while their mothers worked. Pressure on the family continued under Stalin, but in different ways. Children were encouraged to report to the authorities "antirevolutionary" statements made by their parents.

Women paid a heavy price for the Stalin revolutions in industry and agriculture. In the cities, they often did heavy labor, using the same tools and working the same hours men worked and suffering equally from the industrial accidents of the time. In the countryside, they carried the burden of laboring on the collective farm, doing all of the work in the home, and doing 80 percent of the work on the private plots, which provided food for the family and money from sales in the markets. Alarm spread in Moscow at the lack of population growth during the 1930s. By a law of June 27, 1936, intended to strengthen the family unit, it became harder to gain a divorce; abortions were prohibited; and to increase the birthrate, the government held out the promise of subsidies to women: the more children, the larger the subsidy. As one scholar noted in a study of these conditions, "having been mobilized for production, women would henceforth be mobilized for reproduction."[12]

The party did work to upgrade medical care, improve—for a time—the treatment of the more than one hundred national groups that made up the USSR, and extend educational opportunities. But even here political goals outweighed humanitarian objectives. Education—almost exclusively in the Russian language—existed primarily to indoctrinate non-Russian pupils with communist precepts and Russian cultural values. Religious persecution was widespread, and the strong wave of anti-Semitism seen at the end of the nineteenth century returned under Stalin. Jews were referred to as people to be suspected: "rootless cosmopolitans." Also, in their internal passports, Jews were identified by their ethnicity and not as Russians or Ukrainians. The Orthodox Church lost most of its power in education, and religious training was prohibited, except in the home.

In the first decade after the 1917 revolutions, intellectuals and artists experienced much more freedom than they would in the 1930s. The party emphasized the tenets of social realism but permitted some innovation. The Bolsheviks initially tolerated and even encouraged writers with independent leanings. Even though a large number of artists and writers fled the country after the Revolution, others, including the poets Alexander Blok (1880–1921) and Vladimir Mayakovsky (mai-ah-KOF-skee; 1893–1930), remained and continued to write. During the NEP and after, cultural life bloomed in many areas, especially the cinema, as can be seen in the works of the great director Sergei Eisenstein (1898–1948). In music, composers Sergei Prokofiev (proh-KOF-ee-yev; 1891–1953) and Dmitri Shostakovich (1906–1975) contributed works that added to the world's musical treasury, although the latter had to apologize to Stalin for the "bourgeois nature" of one of his symphonies. Once Stalin gained control, he dictated that all art, science, and thought should serve the party's program and philosophy. Artists and thinkers were to become, in Stalin's words, "engineers of the mind." Art for art's sake was counterrevolutionary. Socialist realism in its narrowest sense was to be pursued. History became a means to prove the correctness of Stalin's policies.

Conclusion

Each of the nondemocratic powers pursued its own unique path in the 20-year period between the world wars. Japan, Italy, Germany, and Russia had separate and distinct cultural, social, and political roots that gave unique qualities to their transition to nondemocratic governments. Each of the states, however, shared similar circumstances. Each faced economic upheavals, had weak traditions of liberal rule, and were easy targets for ambitious individuals or groups ready to take command. In the absence of dynamic democratic forces at home, these circumstances produced the interwar government structures of the nondemocratic states.

In Japan, the interwar period began with a push toward greater democratization and internationalism of cultural, diplomatic, and economic ties. It ended, however, with war and expansionism in Asia, isolation from and eventually war with its earlier allies, an alliance with Germany and Italy, and after a bloody war against Russia at Nomonhan in 1939, a neutrality pact with the Soviets.

For the European powers, to be sure, the fascists and the communists differed in theory: the fascists used capitalism, whereas the communists opposed it; fascism emphasized nationalism, whereas communism preached internationalism; fascism had a weak dogmatic basis, whereas communism was based on Marx's scientific socialism; and fascism made use of religion, whereas communism attacked it. But by 1939, the common interests of Berlin and Moscow were much more important than the theoretical differences. Although they may have been philosophically separate, in their policies, the states were remarkably similar—and could share foreign policy goals, as would be seen in the Nazi-Soviet pact of September 1939.

Suggestions for Web Browsing

You can obtain more information about topics included in this chapter at the websites listed below. See also the companion website that accompanies this text, http://www.ablongman.com/brummett, which contains an online study guide and additional resources.

The War Between Japan and China
http://www.fas.harvard.edu/~asiactr/sino-japanese/
Resources on the war between Japan and China, 1931–1945.

The Italian Fascist Youth Movement
http://www.library.wisc.edu/libraries/dpf/fascism/youth.html
A spectacular collection of images in the Italian Fascist Youth Movement from the University of Wisconsin's superb fascism series, Italian Life Under Fascism.

Library of Congress: Soviet Archive Exhibit
http://www.ncsa.uiuc.edu/SDG/Experimental/soviet.exhibit/soviet.archive.html
A magnificent exhibition at the Library of Congress on the Soviet years. Documents on both the foreign and domestic aspects of the USSR, with stunning evidence concerning collectivization.

A USSR Purge Trial
http://art-bin.com/art/omosc20e.html
A transcript from a purge trial. One can see the methods of Andrei Vyshinsky as he grills I. N. Smirnov.

Literature and Film

Many films produced after the war capture the suffering at the war era. Akira Kurosawa's *No Regrets for Our Youth* (1946; Home Vision Entertainment) is a moving condemnation of militarism as seen through the eyes of a brave widow of a dissident journalist; Kinoshita Keisuke's *Twenty-four Eyes* (1954; Shochiku Films) chronicles the lives and wartime deaths of the kindergarten children of one teacher. Tanizaki Jun'ichirō's novel, *The Makioka Sisters* (Vintage, 1995), written during World War II, focuses on a family with four adult sisters, each one symbolic of a different type of modern Japanese.

In Italy, the works of Curzio Malaparte capture the spirit of the interwar period and the opening of World War II. His best-known work is *Kaputt* (1944), a brilliant witness to the period. In Germany, Erich Maria Remarque's book *All Quiet on the Western Front* (1929) captured the cruelty of the First World War, and the works of Thomas Mann, such as *Buddenbrooks* (1901) and *Death in Venice* (1912), drew the wrath of the Nazis in the interwar period. Mann, the playwright Bertolt Brecht, who wrote *The Three Penny Opera* (1922) and *Mother Courage* (1939), and Remarque all found themselves on the list of unacceptable authors. The film director Leni Riefenstahl produced two cinematic triumphs for the Nazis in her *Triumph of the Will* (1934) and a documentary on the 1936 Berlin Olympics (1938).

The period 1919–1939 was a difficult time for writers and film makers in Russia, Italy, and Germany. In these authoritarian states, an arid form of Socialist Realism prevailed. In poetry, Russia suffered from the early deaths of A. A. Blok (1921) and V. V. Mayakovsky, the first a reformed noble and the second a revolutionary figure. Blok's greatest poems, "The Twelve" and "The Scythians," capture the dread and the essence of the revolution. Mayakovsky personified the avant-garde, but in his satirical plays *The Bathhouse* (1930) and *The Bedbug* (1928), he wrote two cutting critiques of the bureaucratic revolution (1930) just before he committed suicide. Anna Akmatova began her brilliant, controversial career in 1935 with her epic *The Requiem,* which was not published until 1988. At the time, Mikhail Sholokhov wrote more to the regime's liking in his novel *And Quiet Flows the Don* (1928–1940), which has a Tolstoyan sweep. Evgeny Zamyatin in *We* (1920) anticipated by 30 years George Orwell's themes in *1984*, and Mikhail Bulgakov in *The Master and Margarita* (1928–1940) gave an impression of the world of Stalinian totalitarianism. In film, the great Soviet director Sergei Eisenstein created magnificent epics with *Ivan the Terrible* (1947; Home Vision Entertainment) and *Alexander Nevsky* (1939; White Star), complete with a spectacular musical score by Prokofiev. Andrei Konchalovsky's 1991 film, *The Inner Circle/The Projectionist* (Columbia/Tristar) is a chilling, subtle look into what life among Stalin's immediate circle might have been like.

Suggestions for Reading

On Japan's politics, foreign policy, and expansion, see Louise Young, *Japan's Total Empire: Manchuria and the Culture of Wartime Imperialism* (University of California Press, 1998), and Joshua Fogel, *The Nanjing Massacre in History and Historiography* (University of California Press, 2000). See also Sheldon Garon, *Molding Japanese Minds* (Princeton University Press, 1997), and Vera Mackie, *Creating Socialist Women in Japan* (Cambridge University Press, 2002).

Essential introductions and guides to the complex world of fascism are Robert O. Paxton, *The Anatomy of Fascism* (Knopf, 2004), and Stanley G. Payne, *A History of Fascism, 1914–1945* (University of Wisconsin Press, 1995). Adrian Lyttelton's *The Seizure of Power: Fascism in Italy, 1919–1939,* 2nd ed. (Princeton University Press, 1988) remains a useful introduction. Ian Kershaw's *Hitler: 1889–1936 Hubris* (Norton, 2000) and *Hitler: 1936–1945 Nemesis* (Norton, 2001) give the best biography of the German dictator.

Orlando Figes provides an excellent perspective of Russia's inability to avoid revolution in *A People's Tragedy: The Russian Revolution, 1891–1924* (Penguin, 1998). Sheila Fitzpatrick, *The Russian Revolution, 1917–1932* (Oxford University Press, 1982), is a first-rate analysis that establishes the themes undergirding the Stalinist society that emerged in the 1930s. See also her perceptive *Everyday Stalinism: Ordinary Life in Extraordinary Times in the 1930s* (Oxford University Press, 2000). Robert Conquest details the campaign against the peasantry in *Harvest of Sorrow* (Oxford University Press, 1986). J. Arch Getty and Oleg. V. Naumov, *The Road to Terror: Stalin and the Self-Destruction of the Bolsheviks (1932–1939)* (Yale University Press, 1999) provides documents essential to understanding the purges.

CHAPTER 29

Forging New Nations in Asia, 1910–1950

Outline

- China: Revolution and Republic
- Korea: From Monarchy to Colony
- Nationalism in Southeast Asia
- India: The Drive for Independence

Features

DOCUMENT **Lu Xun and China's May Fourth Generation**

DISCOVERY THROUGH MAPS **What's in a Name? Siam or Thailand?**

DOCUMENT **Gandhi and "Truth-Force"**

SEEING CONNECTIONS **Gandhi's Non-violence and Civil Rights Around the World**

◄ The partition of India and Pakistan in 1947 was one of the greatest migrations of people in history. Hundreds of thousands perished in the transfer. Here, thousands of refugees find any space available inside and on tops of trains to move across the boundary between the two new countries.

FIFTY YEARS OF aggressive expansion by Europe, the United States and, later, Japan had spread those countries' ideas, investments, colonists, and control to much of the world. Even Asian societies that were not directly colonized were influenced by the politics, cultures, and economies of the imperialists. In the period between and immediately after the world wars many of these societies adopted the nation-state model of political organization. Japan adopted that model and, like the European and American nation-states, gained an empire.

The idea of the nation took hold among anti-imperialists throughout colonial Asia. The 1919 peace conference at Versailles promised "self determination of nations," and independence fighters throughout Asia took the victorious powers at their word. Some, inspired by the revolutionary anti-imperialist rhetoric of Marxism, embraced socialism as the path of liberation. Others, inspired by the democratic and modernist ideologies espoused by the imperialists themselves, used the language of Western liberalism. Thus, nationalist anti-imperialism of the interwar period was characterized not only by the quest to build new nations but also by a struggle between various forms of progressivism—especially socialism versus capitalism.

Both indigenous changes and global forces of modernity, as well as the economic and strategic actions of the world powers, led to the evolution of Asian states. This era witnessed a dramatic movement of people from the countryside to the city, with accompanying social and economic turmoil. The processes that gained momentum in the nineteenth century in the realms of industrialization, education, transportation, and communication remained vigorous. Independence movements, together with the blow to European imperialism dealt by the war with Japan and the Europeans' exhaustion after World War II, finally persuaded the imperialists to pull up their stakes in the decades after that war.

China: Revolution and Republic

How did cultural, political, and nationalistic forces come together to build a new nation from the ruins of a 2000-year-old imperial state?

At the dawn of the twentieth century, the Qing Dynasty maintained a tenuous grip on power. The failed Righteous Harmony Fists (Boxer) Uprising had persuaded the Empress Dowager Cixi to reform the monarchy or else lose the right to rule. Reforms in education, governance, the military, and other areas were quickly promulgated. New schools were educating 10 million boys and girls by 1910 (the government had approved girls' education in 1907, and by 1910, 1.6 million girls were already attending school). The Qing began working on a constitution in 1908. Provincial assemblies, though selected by an electorate severely limited by gender and wealth, sat for the first time in 1909. And a modern-style military, under General Yuan Shikai (yoo-AHN shuh-KAI), was commissioned.

Rather than shoring up the monarchy, however, these measures undermined it in the eyes of those who sought broader and deeper change. Similarly, the visible growth of a modern sector—with railroads, shipping companies, and banks—rather than promoting support for a modernizing state, only served to highlight its failings, as these industries were dominated by foreign investors. Protests against Russia for its occupation of Manchuria (1903) after the Righteous Harmony Fists (Boxer) Uprising and the United States for discriminatory immigration laws (1905) were additional indications of popular dissatisfaction.

	China in the Early Twentieth Century
1911	Anti-Qing Revolution
1912	Republic of China declared; Yuan Shikai comes to power
1915–1919	New Culture ("May Fourth") Era
1919	May Fourth Incident
1916–1927	Era of warlordism
1921–1925	Sun Yat-sen head of Guomindang (GMD) in southern China
1921	Founding of Chinese Communist party (CCP); members also part of GMD
1926–1927	Northern Expedition unites most of China under Jiang Jieshi and the GMD; CCP and GMD split
1928–1937	GMD forms Republic of China government at Nanjing
1931	Mao Zedong and others create Chinese Soviet Republic in Jiangxi
1934–1935	GMD forces CCP out of Jiangxi; Long March takes CCP to Shaanxi
1936	Anti-Japan united front of CCP and GMD
1937–1945	At war with Japan
1945–1949	CCP versus GMD civil war
1949	CCP victory; People's Republic of China founded

The Revolution of 1911

Many young nationalists, even while despising the dismemberment of their country, sought the tools for challenging both the foreign threat and Manchu rule in modern, and often foreign, ideas. They often were introduced to these ideas—and forged alliances with like-minded Chinese—while overseas. Japan, only a few hundred miles away from China and using a writing system many Chinese could understand, was the schoolroom for China's revolutionaries. Most of the 8000 Chinese students in Japan at the end of the Qing were men, but some were women. The most famous martyr of the Revolution of 1911, a woman who never lived to see the overthrow of the Manchus, was Qiu Jin (CHOO JIN). Qiu joined the Revolutionary Alliance *(Tongmenghui)* when she was a student in Japan, returned to China to promote revolution and feminism, and was executed for her role in an abortive coup in 1907.

More influential in the long run was Sun Yat-sen (1866–1925). Sun had studied in Hawaii and Hong Kong, founded the Revolutionary Alliance in Tokyo in

Chronology

1910	1915	1920	1930
1910 Korea becomes Japanese colony 1912 Republic of China declared	1919 Rowlett Act and Amritsar Massacre; May Fourth Incident in China; March First movement in Korea	1920 Indian National Congress launches policy of noncooperation 1921 Founding of Chinese Communist party	1930 Muslim League founded 1934–1935 The Long March: Chinese Communists escape to Shaanxi

1905, and developed what he called the "Three Principles of the People"—nationalism, democracy, and the people's livelihood. Like the thousands of their compatriots who studied revolutionary thought overseas, Qiu and Sun eagerly sought out Western ideas, especially utopian and revolutionary ideas. Some Chinese students embraced socialism, some anarchism, some liberal democracy, and some feminism.

To forestall possible foreign military intervention as the provinces peeled off from the monarchy one by one in the fall of 1911, the revolutionaries, who had formed a provisional government with Sun as president, negotiated with the Qing to abdicate and with General Yuan Shikai to step in as president until elections could be held. Full of anticipation for the new Republic of China, the 5 percent of the population eligible to vote went to the polls in February 1913. Women had struggled for the vote in 1912, modeling their tactics on Britain's militant suffragettes, but failed to achieve their goal.

The **Guomindang** (goo-aw-min-DAHNG; GMD) won the parliamentary majority, but Yuan had had a taste of power and was unwilling to step down. He crushed the pro-GMD military forces to make himself a military dictator and assassinated key political leaders, including Song Jiaoren (SONG jow-REN), leader of the GMD and framer of the new constitution. When he declared himself emperor in 1915, Yuan met an exceedingly hostile reaction. Also in 1915, Yuan had acceded to most of a series of economic and diplomatic demands by Japan, called the Twenty-one Demands, which threatened China's sovereignty and were wildly unpopular in China. His death a few months later, in 1916, plunged China into warlordism. **Warlords** were regional strongmen who controlled administrative functions in their areas and who fought with one another to expand their territory. Some were terribly brutal, and all brought about great poverty and suffering. It is small wonder that anxious Chinese patriots added the destruction of warlordism and its replacement with a unified republican form of government to their demands for liberation from foreign encroachment as national goals.

Guomindang—Chinese Nationalist party, GMD.

warlords—Military, political chieftains ruling and fighting in China, 1916–1927.

The May Fourth Generation

Liberation of a more personal sort was closely tied to national liberation. From the late nineteenth century, when **foot binding** was attacked for weakening women and thereby weakening the country, nationalists connected the self-improvement of the individual to the salvation of the nation. Self-improvement had been a basic part of Confucianism, but by the World War I/warlord era, Confucianism was beginning to be viewed as inadequate for the daunting task of total societal reform. Some turned to foreign approaches. In 1915, Chen Duxiu (CHEN doo-SHOO), Dean of Letters at Beijing University, the center of intellectual ferment, founded a new journal, *New Youth*. One of dozens of new periodicals with the word "new" in their title, *New Youth* took as its purpose the publication of radical new literature, essays, translations of political theory, and any other texts of the "New Culture" of the time.

The articles in *New Youth* were accessible to a wide readership. They were written in the totally modern vernacular language—as opposed to the classical

foot binding—Constriction of women's feet, practiced by many in China from the twelfth century to the early twentieth; its eradication was a goal of nationalists.

◄ Statesman and revolutionary leader Sun Yat-sen, the organizer of the Guomindang, is known as the father of modern China.

1935	1940	1945	
1937–1945 China at war with Japan	1941 Ho Chi Minh establishes the Viet Minh 1942 Quit India Movement	1946 Philippines gain independence from the United States 1947 Independence and Partition of India	1949 People's Republic of China founded

Document

Lu Xun and China's May Fourth Generation

The early twentieth century was a time of tremendous change and reform. Young people iconoclastically rejected Confucianism and its stultifying social constraints on their sense of personal freedom, shaking Chinese values to the core. The literary revolution of the World War I and postwar era powerfully reflects these challenges. Lu Xun's stories are emblematic of the youth movement's analysis of China's woes of their day. In his allegorical tale, "A Madman's Diary," from which this is excerpted, a young man being treated for apparent hallucinations has a sudden insight: that China, represented by his older brother (to whom the narrator should be subordinate under Confucian rules of hierarchy) is guilty of "eating people" and supporting a system, based on filial piety and other old fashioned rules, in which unsuspecting others are forced to eat people as well. No wonder the narrator seems crazy—but to Lu Xun, he is the only one who sees the truth.

I took up my chopsticks, then thought of my elder brother; I know now how my little sister died: it was all through him. My sister was only five at the time. I can still remember how lovable and pathetic she looked. My mother cried and cried, but he begged her not to cry, probably because he had eaten her himself, and so her crying made him feel ashamed.... My sister was eaten by my brother, but I don't know whether my mother realized it or not.

I think mother must have known, but when she cried she did not say so outright, probably because she thought it proper too. I remember when I was four or five years old, sitting in the cool of the hall, my brother told me that if a man's parents were ill, he should cut off a piece of his flesh and boil it for them if he wanted to be considered a good son; and mother did not contradict him. If one piece could be eaten, obviously so could the whole....

I have only just realized that I have been living all these years in a place where for four thousand years they have been eating human flesh. My brother had just taken over the charge of the house when our sister died, and he may well have used her flesh in our rice and dishes, making us eat it unwittingly....

How can a man like myself, after four thousand years of man-eating history—even though I knew nothing about it at first—ever hope to face real men?

Perhaps there are still children who have not eaten men? Save the children....

Questions to Consider

1. Why does Lu Xun use the metaphor of cannibalism for his critique of Confucianism?
2. May Fourth writers, despite their biting criticism, were optimistic about the possibility of changing the world. How does Lu Xun suggest optimism in this gruesome tale?
3. What special role do his mother and little sister play in this tale?

From Lu Hsun, *Selected Stories of Lu Hsun* (Beijing: Foreign Languages Press, 1978).

Chinese that could be read only by an elite few—advocated by the influential philosopher Hu Shi (HOO SHIH), just back from 7 years of study at Columbia and Cornell. China's most honored twentieth-century writer, Lu Xun (LOO SHOON), also used the pages of *New Youth* to publish short stories that satirized traditional culture as backward and destructive to the survival of China. The old, respected values were nothing but cannibalism, Lu wrote in his famous story, "A Madman's Diary." Equality and rights were necessary before individuals could improve themselves, and self-improvement was a requirement for national strengthening. As Chen Duxiu noted in 1915, "We must be totally aware of the incompatibility between Confucianism and the new belief, the new society, and the new state."[1]

Exciting tales of youth rejecting the past, including the previously authoritative voice of their elders, inspired young people seeking personal liberation alongside the salvation of China. New Culture ideals were widespread by May 4, 1919, when some 3000 students demonstrated violently against the decision at the Versailles peace conference in France (which ended World War I) to cede German-held territory in Shandong to Japan. Like Japan, China had joined the war on the side of the victors, sending 140,000 laborers to France. Taking seriously the heady rhetoric of American President Woodrow Wilson about "self-determination of nations," the Chinese were understandably stunned that not only did they not get back the territory taken from them as colonies or spheres of interest, but the hand of imperialism was even extended.

More than 1000 students were arrested, and the warlord of Beijing turned parts of Beijing University into a jail. But the nation's heart was with the protestors. The press, senior nationalists like Sun Yat-sen, merchants and workers, and teachers and intellectuals raised a cry for the students' release. The government released them, the cabinet fell, and China refused to sign the Treaty of Versailles. Most important, the goals and ideology of the **May Fourth** generation molded cultural politics until the 1930s—and in some ways, even beyond that time. Rallying around nationalism, freedom, science, and democracy and struggling against warlordism, imperialism, patriarchy, and the stifling grip of tradition, reformers in the next few decades sought a variety of ways to achieve those goals. Joining Lu Xun as luminaries among Chinese writers who used the pen to attack social ills were leftist writers like Mao Dun (1896–1981, whose foremost novel was *Midnight*), anarchists like Ba Jin (1904–2005, *Family*), and feminists like Ding Ling (1904–1985, *Diary of Miss Sophie*).

Nation-Building

The events of May 4, 1919, transformed the cultural revolution into a political movement. In May 1919, *New Youth* published an introduction to Marxist theory, spawning Marxist study groups. The recently established Soviet Union took interest and sent advisers to help Sun Yat-sen reorganize the Guomindang, which had been shattered by Yuan Shikai and warlord terror. Sun, because of his experience in the United States as a young man, sought American assistance, though unsuccessfully. Though the Chinese Communist party (CCP) was formed in 1921, it was just a small group within Sun's Guomindang during its early years. The Guomindang grew, attracting men like Jiang Jieshi (jee-AHNG jee-eh-SHI), also known as Chiang Kai-shek (1888–1975), head of the party's Huangpu (hoo-ahng-poo) military academy, and Zhou Enlai (JOH en-LAI; 1898–1976), the head of the academy's political education department. Both had foreign training—the anti-Communist Jiang in the Soviet Union and the Communist Zhou in France.

The new political movements had some notable successes in organizing workers in the early 1920s. Strikers protested harsh working conditions in all factories, but especially in the Chinese- and Japanese-owned mills that sprang up during and after World War I due to the cut-off of imported goods while the European countries were fighting that war. The real growth of the political movements occurred after the bloody suppression of demonstrators by British police in Shanghai's International Settlement on May 30, 1925. Sympathy strikes spread throughout China, and the Nationalists knew the time was ripe to embark on a Northern Expedition to unite the country and defeat the twin evils of warlordism and imperialism.

Sun had died in March 1925, and a struggle for dominance within the Guomindang ensued. Though Jiang had begun to arrest Communists in 1926, the two groups—the Communists and the anti-Communist Nationalists—formed a united front to carry out the Northern Expedition. This broke down, however, when the Northern Expedition reached Shanghai. In April 1927, Jiang ordered Shanghai's gangsters to kill union organizers, Communists, and even women whose modern-style bobbed (short) hair seemed to mark them as potential leftists. From then on, the Communists and Nationalists followed two paths. The Nationalists made it to Beijing in 1928, either conquering or allying with key warlords. Jiang formed a government at Nanjing (also spelled "Nanking") that was recognized by the world as the Republic of China. He never controlled all of China, however, and the Communists in particular

▼ Jiang Jieshi and his wife, Song Meiling, who was Sun Yat-sen's sister-in-law. Jiang was head of the GMD and President of the Republic of China; Song Meiling, who had gone to college in Georgia, was his liaison with the United States.

May Fourth—New Culture movement inspired by anti-imperialist uprising in 1919.

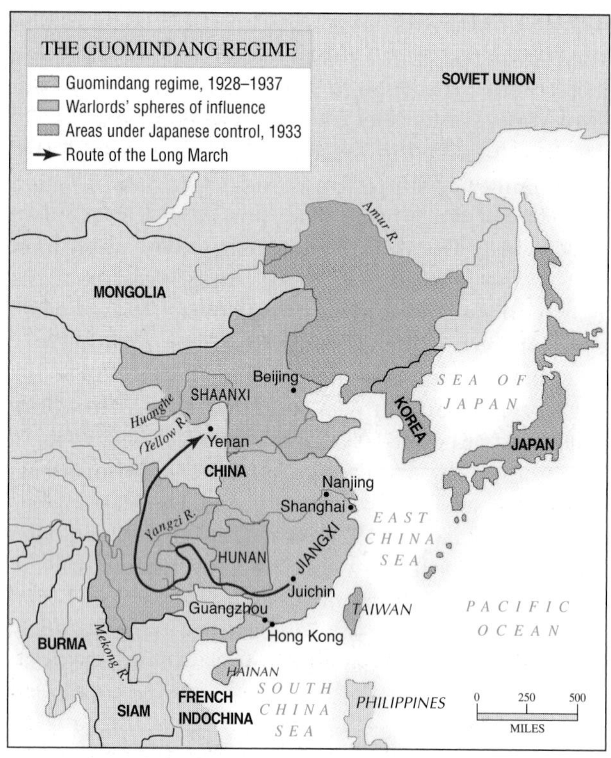

▲ The Guomindang (Nationalist) party was forced to share control of China with the warlords and the Japanese.

were able to run their own state in Jiangxi (jee-ahng-SHI) province until 1934.

Where Jiang did exercise control—the urban areas—a cosmopolitan modernity was rapidly emerging. Western-trained economists and financiers developed capitalist markets and banking. Artists and intellectuals kept up with the latest ideas from France, England, and the United States. In the coastal ports, all types of Western goods were available. Middle-class families wore Western clothing, worked in European-style buildings, and sent their children to schools that taught Western-style subjects. A professional class of engineers, architects, doctors and nurses, teachers, and city planners and bureaucrats, many trained overseas or in Chinese colleges with Western teachers, influenced the culture of Nationalist China's cities. Middle-class women gained opportunities for higher education and the rights to divorce and inherit and were promised the vote.

At the same time, a huge pool of impoverished laborers was available for the cities' factories and unskilled jobs. For Marxists, this was proof that China was on the same path to the eventual proletarian (working-class) revolution that Marx had proposed for Europe in the nineteenth century. But 80 percent of China's population lived in the countryside, and even the urban poor had close ties to rural villages. Many of the urban poor had flowed into the cities in a hopeful gamble that life would be better there.

For rural people, life in the 1920s and 1930s was miserable. Even before Chinese farmers were plunged into greater depths of poverty when the world's Great Depression destroyed the market for export products like tea and silk, farmers were oppressed by landlords who demanded excessive rent, impoverished by the pressures of population growth, and unable to coax enough food from land ruined by ecological disasters. Farmers hung on by their fingertips in good years. Bad weather, not yet diagnosed as cyclical El Niño patterns (as it would be in the 1980s), set in motion a spiral of failure. Starvation and death were part of rural life in this period.

The Guomindang, focused on the modern urban areas, did little to help the countryside. Although Marx had thought the peasants were backward and antirevolutionary, some Chinese Communists saw the distress of the rural area as an opportunity to organize. In 1921, agrarian reformer Peng Pai (PUHNG PAI; 1896–1929) tried to organize peasants against landlordism. Later, Mao Zedong (MOW zeh-DONG, also spelled "Tse-tung"; 1893–1976), a Beijing University librarian attracted to Marxist study groups in Beijing, began to focus on the potential for peasant-led revolution, an area long-neglected by traditional Marxism. In 1927, Mao took part in one of a number of peasant uprisings planned by the CCP for that year. Mao's "Autumn Harvest Uprising" failed and the peasants were severely repressed. Despite that failure, the report Mao produced following the uprising set the stage for the kind of peasant revolution he would eventually lead to victory in China two decades later. Praising violence as necessary for revolution, Mao believed that "Several hundred million peasants will rise like a mighty storm, like a hurricane, a force so swift and violent that no power, however great, will be able to hold it back."[2]

For the time being, though, the Communists hardly seemed capable of leading a mighty storm. Under attack from the Nationalist government, they set up their own government in Jiangxi province, where they established land reform and other policies while constantly fending off the Nanjing government's "annihilation campaigns." In the fall of 1934, Jiang Jieshi successfully blockaded the Communists, who were then forced out of their province and began the **Long March.** Many people, especially women and children, were left behind and suffered reprisals, but the 100,000 Communists on the Long March endured extraordinary hardships as they climbed mountains, crossed gorges, trudged through swamps, and succumbed to illness. Less than 10 percent survived the 6000-mile ordeal to arrive in October 1935 in Shaanxi (shahn-SHI) province, where the Communists remained until after World War II. Until after the death

Long March—Chinese Communist escape to Shaanxi, 1934–1935; established leadership in CCP.

of Deng Xiaoping (DUHNG show-PING) in 1997, leaders of post-1949 China all were survivors of the Long March. The other important result of the Long March was the emergence of Mao Zedong as the premier leader of the Communists.

World War II

The most significant events in China's history in the decades after the fall of the Qing were part of the struggle for national unity. Foreign relations were always important but took a back seat to domestic issues. By the 1930s, this would change, as Japan emerged as the main international player in East Asia. European imperialists continued to play a role in China's coastal areas, but the growing tensions and China's eventual war with Japan, together with internal civil war, ultimately led to the Communists' victory in 1949.

Challenged, as China was, by Western imperialism, Japan had adopted an expansive position in East Asia by the end of the nineteenth century. Taiwan was made a Japanese colony in 1895, followed by Korea in 1910. Japan's victory over Russia in the Russo-Japanese War gave it railroad rights in Manchuria in 1905. These created a Japanese presence in areas of interest to the Chinese, but Japan continued to be praised by reformist Chinese as Asia's leader until 1915. The humiliating Twenty-one Demands of that year, however, although mostly rejected, made Japan appear as aggressive as the worst imperialists—and more dangerous because of its proximity. At the end of World War I, Japan (along with the United States, Britain, France, and Canada) invaded Siberia to try to stop the Bolshevik Revolution in Russia, and Japanese troops remained in Northeast Asia until 1922. Japan's hold on Shandong (as a result of the Versailles Conference) from 1919 till 1922 was a bitter pill for Chinese to swallow. In 1922, however, relations appeared to improve, at least temporarily. The Washington Conference of 1921–1922 produced several treaties, one of which, the Nine-Power Treaty, was signed by China and Japan and guaranteed China's territorial integrity, including the return of Shandong.

At the same time, Japanese soldiers stationed in Northeast Asia were conducting a foreign policy of their own, which eventually undermined the Washington Conference treaties. Believing the warlord of Manchuria, Zhang Zuolin (JAHNG zoo-aw-LIN), whom they had supported until then because of his assistance with Japanese interests in Manchuria, was not sufficiently helpful, rogue members of the Japanese army assassinated him in 1928. Although the Japanese government eventually distanced itself from this terrorist incident, the Japanese army in Manchuria could not be controlled and carried out a much more significant incident on September 18, 1931. This Manchurian Incident led to major combat and the creation in 1932 of the state of "Manchukuo" (MAHN-joo-goo-aw), headed by the last Qing emperor, but really ruled by the Japanese army. This action was condemned by the League of Nations, but Japan simply abandoned the League in 1933.

Tensions, which often took a military form, continued between Japan and China in the next several years. In 1936, the son of the assassinated Zhang Zuolin kidnapped Jiang Jieshi, head of the Nationalist government of the Republic of China, for not moving against Japanese encroachment. Forced under the threat of death to agree to a united front with the Communists, whom he had just driven into the Shaanxi caves during the previous year's Long March, Jiang was viewed by the Japanese military as a threat to its continental ambitions. Full-scale warfare between China and Japan broke out on July 7, 1937, following an incident at a bridge outside Beijing. Thus began World War II in Asia.

By December 1937, Japanese forces had conquered Beijing, Tianjin (tee-un-JIN), and Shanghai. Chinese soldiers took a stand at Nanjing and were brutally defeated. In the

◀ Mao Zedong, Chairman of the Chinese Communist party until his death in 1976.

weeks after the defeat, as the Nationalist government decamped to the backwater town of Chongqing, Japanese soldiers went on a rampage in Nanjing so brutal that it came to be known throughout the world as the **"Rape of Nanking."** ("Nanjing" is an alternate spelling of "Nanking.") Many tens of thousands of civilians were killed, around 20,000 women were raped, and the city was ransacked. Despite brave fighting by the Nationalists in their areas and the Communists in their areas, the war dragged on. At the same time, despite the united front, Jiang continued to fight against the Communists, blockading them in 1941. U.S. President Franklin Roosevelt and British Prime Minister Winston Churchill envisioned a postwar order in which Jiang's government would play a major international role, but the continuing tensions with the Communists made that seem unlikely. After the Allied victory over Japan in 1945, civil war broke out in China (see Chapter 35). The Communists won, driving the Nationalists to Taiwan, and declared the founding of the People's Republic of China on October 1, 1949.

Korea: From Monarchy to Colony

How did Koreans attempt to build a nation while under Japanese colonial rule?

The Chosŏn dynasty (1392–1910) faced the same pressures from Western imperialists encountered by other East Asian countries in the late nineteenth century. American and French naval invasions were repulsed in 1866 and 1871. In 1876, Japan, embarking on its own program of modernization, forced a trade treaty on Korea, the Treaty of Kangwha (KAHNG-wah). In short order, unequal treaties with the United States, England, France, Germany, Russia, Italy, and Belgium opened the door to influence by Christian missionaries and trade. The Chosŏn king, Kojŏng, sent study missions to Japan and the West to decide whether to modernize Korea to save it from imperialism. Although many conservative Confucianists opposed any changes, others welcomed them, particularly young reformers who called themselves the Enlightenment Party. Calling for major changes in the style of Meiji Japan, these upper-class or **yangban** reformers, led by Kim Ok-kyun (KIM ohk-kee-OON), a former student of Japan's Fukuzawa Yukichi, who was an advocate of Westernization and modernization (see Chapter 25), attempted a coup in 1884. Japanese advisers had backed them up, but they were defeated by Chinese forces in Korea.

Tensions appeared temporarily resolved by a diplomatic agreement between the Qing and Japan that removed the bulk of those nations' forces from Korea in 1885. But China continued to meddle closely in the Korean court's foreign relations, and Korea's open ports permitted Japanese merchants to dominate trade and drive up rice prices. In 1893 and 1894, famine sparked regional uprisings, and the **Tonghak** (tong-hahk; "Eastern Learning") religious movement, suppressed in the 1860s, reemerged. Tonghak was a blend of Buddhism and folk religions, and with its respect for the downtrodden, including women, it appealed to many. King Kojŏng called in Chinese troops to put down the rebels, and under the provisions of the 1885 Sino-Japanese agreement, Japan felt compelled to send in its own troops. The Sino-Japanese War (1894–1895) was a major victory for Japan.

China withdrew from Korea, and modernizers came to the fore. The increasingly powerful Japanese pushed the Korean government to institute the Kabo Reforms (1894–1896), which called for a constitutional monarchy, modernizing schools, banking, and the military, and eliminating class distinctions. When conservatives opposed these changes, however, the Japanese instigated the murder of the conservative Queen Min, wife of King Kojŏng. Despite this extreme example of Japan's meddling in Korea's affairs, the cause of progressive change, championed by those who saw modernizing Japan as Korea's model, was not extinguished. Men and women—some educated in the Protestant schools dating from the 1880s, others educated in Japan or the West—established the Independence Club in 1896. The club's newspaper, the *Independent,* was published in han'gul, a Korean script, rather than using Chinese characters, and it celebrated Korean heroes, independence, and the need to modernize. Inspired by the nationalism of the Independence Club, Koreans flocked to meetings about progressive change, including people's rights, women's rights, and representative government. King Kojŏng banned the club and its newspaper in 1898, but both were a school for independence movements of the future, and one member would become the first president of the Republic of Korea half a century later.

Japan's victory in the Russo-Japanese War (1904–1905) expanded its role in Northeast Asia. Despite Korean protest, Japan made Korea a protectorate in 1905 and a full-scale colony in 1910. One of the first instances of Korean women organizing for national independence occurred in 1907 with the National Debt Compensation Campaign, when women activists attempted, unsuccessfully, to diminish Japan's presence through repaying Korean debts to Japan. Colonial rule

Japan's Territorial Ambitions

Rape of Nanking—Military violence by Japanese soldiers in Nanjing, December 1937; 100,000 to 200,000 Chinese killed.

yangban—Korean aristocracy in Chosŏn dynasty.

Tonghak—"Eastern Learning" movement in Korea; uprising set stage for Sino-Japanese War.

◀ During the opening years of the twentieth century, Russian forces occupied much of Manchuria and parts of Korea. Two months after the beginning of the Russo-Japanese War on February 8, 1904, Japanese soldiers marched into Seoul to evict the Russians, as represented in this painting. Under the Portsmouth treaty, negotiated by American President Theodore Roosevelt to end the war, Russia recognized Japan's paramount interest in Korea. At the same time, the United States agreed to support Japan's position in Korea in exchange for Japanese support of America's control of the Philippines.

was harsh. Koreans lost rights to join movements or speak freely, and many were deprived of rights to lands they had farmed for centuries. As in China, Korean nationalists took seriously the Wilsonian promise of self-determination of nations, and demonstrated against Japanese colonialism on March 1, 1919. Brutally repressed—thousands of Koreans were killed—what started as a peaceful demonstration set in motion a national independence movement.

Japanese colonial policy in the next decade was a reaction to the brutality of 1919. Substituting "cultural rule" for the previous "military rule," the colonial government permitted an expansion of political movements, including newspapers; organizations that studied Korean history, language, and culture; and limited political discussions about the nation. The political organization **Sin'ganhoe** (SHIN-gahn-HOH-eh) brought together Korean cultural nationalists, many of them people of wealth, and members of the Korean Communist party, many of them advocating social revolution accompanying national liberation from Japan. As in China, the two groups split. The Communists went underground or into exile but came back after the end of the colonial period in 1945, eventually becoming the government of North Korea.

The 1930s ended the period of cultural rule. As rising militarism repressed Japanese life at home, Japanese rule became increasingly harsh in Korea. Much of Korea's rice production was shipped to Japan, starving the Korean people; the language of instruction in Korea's schools was restricted to Japanese after 1934; Koreans were required to adopt Japanese surnames in 1940; several million Korean men were forced to serve in the Japanese military or work in Japanese factories and mines after 1938; and several hundred thousand Korean women and girls were forced into sexual slavery as **"comfort women"** for the Japanese military during World War II. This painful legacy of colonialism made the prospect of nation-building in the postwar era difficult—and the onset of the Cold War worsened those prospects.

Nationalism in Southeast Asia

How did Southeast Asians use Western ideas of self-governance and modernity in their struggles for independence?

The drive for independence became stronger in Southeast Asia between the two world wars. Taking advantage of the war-weakened colonialists, local leaders adapted the ideologies of the day—Wilson's "self-determination of nations," socialism, or a combination of the two—to their campaigns for freedom. The example of Japan's rise to the status of a Great Power showed that the West

---

Sin'ganhoe—Pro-independence united front movement, 1927–1931.

comfort women—Euphemism for the sexual slaves, mostly Korean women, used by the Japanese military in World War II.

had no monopoly on harnessing technology and organization to national goals.

Populations grew dramatically in Southeast Asia during the interwar and postwar periods. From 1930 to 1960, the number of people in Thailand, Malaya, and the Philippines increased more than 100 percent; in Indonesia, Burma, and Indochina the number increased more than 50 percent.

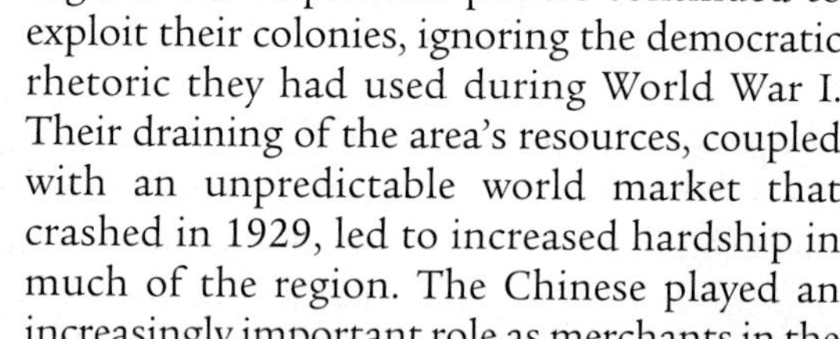

Water Buffalo in Southeast Asia

Economic trends also had great influence on most of the region. The imperialist powers continued to exploit their colonies, ignoring the democratic rhetoric they had used during World War I. Their draining of the area's resources, coupled with an unpredictable world market that crashed in 1929, led to increased hardship in much of the region. The Chinese played an increasingly important role as merchants in the local economies. In Burma, Indians played the same role. European and Chinese capital investment encouraged rapid growth in exports of minerals and forest products. In Siam (Thailand), Vietnam, and a few other countries, rice production grew more rapidly than population, and as a result those countries became rice exporters during this period.

Throughout the area, some among the elite became accustomed to Western culture as more and more young people went to the "parent countries" to be educated. The masses, however, were barely touched by this process. The result was a growing cultural and social divide between the local leadership and the people at large. Few among the imperialist powers undertook to prepare their colonies for eventual self-government, since they had no intention of letting them go.

Indochina

France's Indochinese Union—made up of three Vietnamese territories (the colony of Cochin China and protectorates of Annam and Tonkin), as well as the protectorates of Cambodia and Laos, annexed one by one between 1862 and 1893—was ruled by a French governor-general residing in Hanoi. Although the Vietnamese emperor was retained, he had little power. Indochina was run for the benefit of France. Huge landholdings came under French control, producing rice, rubber, coffee, tea, and sugar for the French market. Coal mines, also controlled by the French, shipped coal to run industries at home. Impoverished peasants from the northern part of the Indochinese Union were sent as coolie laborers to Cochin China in the south or to French Pacific colonies like Tahiti.

People and products were not only shipped out of Vietnam, but other goods were brought in, from which the French also derived revenues. Opium, salt, and wine were sold to Vietnamese consumers and taxed at very high rates.

Although most of the profits of the Indochinese colonies went to France, some Vietnamese as well as Chinese immigrants to Vietnam took part in shipping and marketing the colonies' products. In addition, a new cosmopolitan professional class, including doctors, lawyers, and teachers, emerged in Saigon (now Ho Chi Minh City). As in other East Asian colonies, it was among these urban professionals that anticolonial nationalism first stirred. Although the French espoused a goal of "civilizing" the Indochinese—that is, making them more like the French—they extended the benefits of education only to a few. But those few began to read texts by Chinese and Japanese reformers, often translations of Rousseau, Locke, and Mill. Phan Boi Chau (FAHN BOI CHOW; 1867–1940) and Phan Chu Trinh (FAN CHOO TRIN; 1872–1926) both studied in Japan, encountering Chinese and Korean revolutionaries. Others went to France and were inspired by the ideals of the French Revolution, which were utterly unfulfilled in Vietnam. One nationalist was even convicted in 1926 for the treasonous act of translating Rousseau's *Social Contract* into Vietnamese.

The urban intelligentsia in the 1920s took up the same issues that had inspired the May Fourth generation in China. To build a new Vietnam, many were saying, new social relations, including those between men and women, must be encouraged. Other radical ideas were developing in the 1920s. One hundred thousand Vietnamese had been sent to France during World War I to take the places of French workers drafted into the army. Exposed to French working-class radicalism, many later worked for the independence they believed Vietnam deserved. Ho Chi Minh (1890–1969) went to the Versailles peace conference with a petition for independence, which, like all the other non-European petitions, was denied. The Vietnamese people increasingly turned to political organizing for independence, establishing the Nationalist party of Vietnam in 1927, and the Indochinese Communist party in 1930.

Vietnamese Declaration of Independence

The French (Vichy) government continued to administer Vietnam while the Japanese military moved in between 1941 and 1945. Hoping to defeat both the Japanese and the French, Ho Chi Minh established a united front movement, the Viet Minh (League of the Independence of Vietnam) in 1941 that anticipated the end of colonialism. Ho and other Vietnamese nationalists would be surprised and disappointed when the French moved back in between 1945 and 1954.

The Philippines

The American war against Filipino independence fighters spawned an anti-imperialist movement in the United States. U.S. President McKinley had to devise a face-saving way to end the embarrassment of that colo-

◀ A Vietnamese nationalist poster dating from the end of the French colonial period. A Viet Minh supporter crushes the French soldier and his flag.

DOCUMENT
The American Anti-Imperialist League

nial war and sent U.S. officials to strike a deal with the Filipino elite. The governor-general in the war-torn Philippines, Judge (later President) William Howard Taft, allowed the elite to participate in administration at the local level while U.S. officials governed at the national level. Though an elected legislative assembly was established in 1907, it could be vetoed by the top American administrators.

By 1908, Taft feared that the expedient tactic of pacifying the Philippines' desire for self-rule by co-opting the elite was stifling the development of democracy and potentially creating an aristocratic government. Believing that a longer period of tutelage was necessary before the Filipinos could govern themselves, Taft did not support a rapid transition to independence. The U.S. position changed in 1912. Under Francis B. Harrison, appointed governor-general by President Wilson that year, the Filipinos increasingly took over administration. The **Jones Act** of 1916 became the basis for the development of constitutional government. Sergio Osmeña (SEHR-hee-oh os-MEN-yah) and Manuel Quezon (mahn-oo-EL kay-ZON), leaders of the nationalist movement, publicly advocated independence at the earliest possible time and went to the United States in 1919 to request it. The two worried privately, however, about problems with defense, currency, and free trade should the Philippines gain independence soon. The election of President Warren Harding made the question of immediate independence a moot point, as the Republican position was to take a slower approach.

The U.S. position changed radically again with the onset of the Depression in 1929. U.S. industry groups that earlier fought against independence switched to the other side as a way to keep Filipino products out of the United States. Workers wanted to deny Filipinos access to the U.S. labor market (colonial subjects were exempt from the immigration laws that kept out other Asians). These groups joined President Franklin Roosevelt in supporting liberation. The Tydings-McDuffie Act of 1934 promised complete independence within a decade, although, postponed by World War II, it was not granted until July 4, 1946.

Throughout the period of American colonialism, a sense of nationalism developed in the Philippines. Deep divisions among rich and poor worsened, but almost all Filipinos came to identify with the nation, overcoming some, though certainly not all, linguistic and ethnic divisions. Education was probably the greatest legacy of U.S. rule, with 50 percent of the population literate on the eve of World War II. Public health was also radically improved, and life expectancy jumped from 14 years in 1900 to 40 years in 1940.

Indonesia/Dutch East Indies

New schools for Indonesians, called Dutch Native Schools, trained thousands of civil servants, lawyers, doctors, and other professionals. Many of this group of educated young men, dissatisfied with traditional status hierarchies as well as with Dutch racial superiority, joined the anti-imperialist organization **Sarekat Islam** (SAH-reh-kaht ee-SLAHM) in 1912. Both anti-Dutch and anti-Chinese, Sarekat Islam claimed 2 million members by 1919. (Chinese merchants played a large role in the Indonesian economy, which was resented by nationalist Indonesians.)

Sarekat Islam's leader, Umar Said Tjokroaminoto (oo-MAHR sah-YEED tee-OH-kroh-ah-mee-NOH-toh) used a modernist form of Islam as a means of promoting Indonesian nationalism, modernization, and socialism. In 1920, the leftists in Sarekat broke away as the Partai Kommunis Indonesia (PKI, Communist

Jones Act—U.S. law passed in 1916 that promised eventual independence to Philippines.

Sarekat Islam—Indonesian independence movement, founded in 1912, also known as the Islamic Association.

party of Indonesia). The PKI grew quickly, especially among highly educated, though underemployed young men, frustrated with Dutch authoritarianism. In November 1926, the PKI proclaimed a republic and started an uprising. The Dutch cracked down, throwing 13,000 PKI members into concentration camps or forcing them into exile. That ended the PKI until the Dutch were driven out of Indonesia.

Sarekat was not much more fortunate. Though the Dutch had introduced modest political reforms in response to Sarekat's demands, the pace of change was glacially slow, only adding to the nationalists' frustration. In 1927, Achmed Sukarno (AHK-med soo-KAHR-noh; 1901–1970), Tjokroaminoto's son-in-law, established the Indonesian Nationalist party. The next year, the party adopted key elements of nationalist identity—a flag, a single national language, and a national anthem. In 1930, Sukarno was arrested by the Dutch authorities; he was released in 1931, then arrested several more times along with other nationalist leaders, and was not freed till the Japanese defeated the Dutch in 1942. Japanese forces, anxious to gain access to oil supplies in Java and Sumatra, brought Sukarno back as a local leader. With Mohammad Hatta and other anti-Dutch nationalists, Sukarno worked with Japanese forces occupying Indonesia during the war, for which he was honored by Japan's emperor in 1943. Prior to the end of the war, Sukarno's anticolonial forces, numbering approximately 2 million, were poised to fend off any Allied attempts to reclaim Indonesia. Before the Dutch could reenter Indonesia after Japan's surrender, Sukarno declared Indonesia's independence on August 17, 1945. The Dutch did return, however, and the transition to independence took several years of painful struggle.

Siam (Thailand)

In the interwar period, Siam, which changed its name to Thailand ("Land of the Free") in 1939, continued to modernize. Educational improvements, economic growth, and increased political sophistication contrasted sharply, however, with the political and administrative domination of the country by the extensive royal family. Educated, elite nonaristocrats chafed at continuing favoritism for aristocrats. In 1932, a French-trained law professor, Pridi Phanomyung (PREE-dee FAH-noh-mee-yung), led a bloodless coup d'état, and a new constitution was promulgated with the agreement of the king, turning him into a reigning, not ruling, monarch. Since then, the country has been ruled by an alliance of army and oligarchy. During the 1930s, Thailand became increasingly nationalistic, repressing Chinese merchants and limiting Chinese immigration, treating Christians as aliens, and admiring the military successes of Japan in China. In mid-1944, when it appeared Japan would lose the Pacific War, Thailand switched allegiance to the United States to preserve its independence.

Burma and Malaya

In Burma (now Myanmar), the British colonials wiped out the old social and political system. Buddhism, which had been the glue that held Burmese society together, was sidelined, especially in the Christian-oriented schools the British had established. British insults, together with anger over the presence of Indian moneylenders in Burma, fueled an independence movement. Despite their feelings about Indians in Burma, the Burmese independence movement modeled itself on the tactics practiced by the highly respected **Indian National Congress.** Buddhism, however, provided the focus for organizational activity. The Young Men's Buddhist Association, formed in 1906, organized the General Council of Burmese Associations in 1921. The General Council brought nationalism to the village level.

British promises after World War I to promote Indian self-government created a similar demand in Burma. A Buddhist-inspired uprising spread through many Burmese villages before it was crushed in 1937. Some reforms did occur. In 1937, Burma was administratively split off from India. A parliamentary system was begun with a Burmese prime minister under a British governor, who held responsibility for foreign relations, defense, and finance. The Japanese promise of independence during World War II led Burma to side with Japan against the British, but cruel behavior by the Japanese led many Burmese to join an underground resistance.

No strong nationalist movement developed in Malaya, perhaps because the large ethnic groups living there were given ample space to succeed in a pluralist society. The agricultural rights of the Malay people were not taken away, despite the formation of large, foreign-owned tin and rubber operations. The Chinese in Malaya, as elsewhere throughout Southeast Asia, were involved in commerce and allowed to expand their import-export businesses. The Indians, for the most part workers on plantations and in mines, were loyal to India as their homeland. The only serious source of tension arose among the Chinese, many of whom supported opposing sides—the Nationalists versus the Communists—in the civil war at home. And when Japan occupied the Malay Peninsula during World War II, the Chinese mounted a resistance, which led to harsh treatment of that population by the occupiers. After World War II, the British tried to disarm the anti-Japanese guerrillas. Ethnic Malays demanded independence, which Britain was reluctant to grant as

Indian National Congress—Secular independence movement in India, founded 1885.

Discovery Through Maps

What's in a Name? Siam or Thailand?

Maps nominally show the world "as it really is." But peoples, nations, and boundaries are always evolving, often very quickly. Thus, maps tend to depict the world as it used to be or as it was imagined to be. Although mapmakers may have a difficult time keeping up with the ways in which states and national identities change, there are other reasons why maps may reflect different visions of reality. Maps institutionalize points of view, ways of seeing or naming parts of the world. Should a map call a country by the name used by its own people or by the name used by those who buy the map? Older Western maps, for example, might designate the capital of China as Peking rather than Beijing. Suppose there is a political conflict in some part of the world and the contending parties call their country by two different names. Which name should the mapmaker employ? When a new government comes to power and changes the name of a state, it may take months or even years to change the name on maps, stamps, currency, and textbooks.

The frontispiece of a book published in the United States demonstrates the problems of naming and of demarcating borders in Southeast Asia. This 1941 work by Virginia Thompson is called *Thailand: The New Siam,* reflecting both the old and new names of a country in Southeast Asia. The accompanying map shows Southeast Asia in transition. The name *Siam* was officially changed to *Thailand* in 1939, but 2 years later, this mapmaker thought it wise to include both names on the map. Nor does the map reflect the political realities of the day. In 1941, the borders of Thailand were being contested. In the context of World War II, the Japanese had entered Thailand, and the Thai government was challenging the French in Cambodia. Maps also reflect the progress and losses of imperialism. Thus this map's designation "French Indo-China" shows the empire that France carved out in Southeast Asia in the nineteenth century. The sweeping title "Netherlands India" across the islands of Sumatra and Borneo suggests the long-term interests and conquests of the Dutch in this region. Compare this map to a current map of Southeast Asia (see p. 1064), and to nineteenth-century maps (see p. 777), and see how the names and borders have changed.

Questions to Consider

1. What types of identity are suggested in the names of countries?
2. Why might a people or a political group want to change the name of their country? What difficulties might they face in doing so?

long as a Communist Chinese insurgency continued. Eventually, the British handed over rule to the non-Communist Malayan Chinese Association and the United Malay National Association in 1957.

India: The Drive for Independence

What political innovations helped the disunited country of India gain its independence from Britain?

As in East Asia, World War I accelerated Indians' demands for independence—or at first, self-rule. It awakened new pride in India but at the same time set the stage for the sectarian differences that would be India's tragedy at the time of independence. When World War I began, nearly all anti-British activity in India ceased and thousands of Indian troops were mobilized to fight in World War I on the side of their colonial overlords, the British. Soon, however, the irony of Indians fighting in a struggle between civilization and barbarism—as the battle between England and its allies, on the one hand, and Germany and its allies, on the other, was characterized—was too great to swallow. In addition, India's 60 million Muslims were torn by Britain's war against the Ottoman Empire, one of the Central Powers. The large numbers of Indians who fought in Europe on the side of the British Empire were struck by the greater freedom accorded all classes of people in Europe.

South Asia

Gradual Steps Toward Self-Rule

By 1917, Indian nationalists expected immediate compensation for their loyalty in terms of more self-government. The British, however, pursued a policy stressing gradual development of self-government within the British Empire. To this end, in 1918, a British commission under the more liberal Secretary of State for India, Edwin S. Montagu, recommended a new constitution. Reforms emerged in 1919 from that commission and were codified in the Government of India Act of 1921. These provided for a system of dual government in the provinces by which certain powers were reserved to the British while the provincial legislatures were granted other, generally lesser, powers. Montagu called for an increase in Indian representation on the Imperial Legislative Council.

Taj Mahal, India

To Indian nationalists, these reforms represented only a small step toward self-rule. Indian suspicion was hardly surprising in the context of other repressive legislation passed earlier, the Rowlatt Acts, called the "Black Acts" by Indians. These laws, passed in 1919 through the Imperial Legislative Council without a single vote by an elected Indian member, denied press freedom and allowed the police and other officials extraordinary powers in searching out anti-imperialist activities. Disheartened by the limited reforms as well as the violence that followed under the Rowlatt Acts, many nationalists demanded sweeping changes. Britain, however, lacked a comprehensive plan to grant independence, and a diehard segment of British public opinion, led by the Conservative leader Winston Churchill, strongly opposed any such suggestion of the breakup of the empire.

	India on the Road to Independence
1914–1918	Indians fight for Britain in WWI
1918	Rowlatt Acts imposed
1919	Amritsar Massacre
1920	Indian National Congress launches policy of noncooperation
1930	Salt Marches
1930	Muslim League
1933	Muslim students propose new state, to be called Pakistan
1942	Quit India Movement
1947	Independence and partition

Gandhi and Civil Disobedience

The foremost nationalist leader in India was Mohandas Gandhi (moh-HAHN-das GAHN-dee; 1869–1948). Born of middle-class parents, Gandhi went to London to study law; later he went to South Africa to defend Indians there against the abuses of the planters. Gandhi's encounter with South African discrimination against "nonwhites" transformed him. In South Africa, Indians were subject to numerous legal restrictions that hampered their freedom of movement, prevented them from buying property, and imposed added taxes on them. Gandhi worked aggressively for the legal and political rights of the oppressed. He repudiated wealth, practiced ascetic self-denial, condemned violence, and advocated service to others. He launched a community *(ashram)* that served as a model for living out those principles. With Gandhi as their leader, the Indians in South Africa adopted the tactic of "civil disobedience"—they carried out various protests, refused to work, held mass demonstrations, and marched into areas where their presence was forbidden by law. Through "passive resistance" and noncooperation, Gandhi forced the government to remove some restrictions, thereby attracting worldwide attention.

Document

Gandhi and "Truth-Force"

Gandhi developed tactics of noncooperation and passive resistance as a young lawyer in South Africa and applied those methods to India's struggle upon his return home shortly after the beginning of World War I. The prospect of violence within the anti-imperialist movement concerned him deeply, and by 1920, he began to urge Indians to adopt his methods of *Satyagraha*, literally "truth-force," as superior to passive resistance. Only through complete *ahimsa* (nonviolence), coupled with a strict adherence to truth, even if truth and nonviolence did not appear to work in the short term, would the oppressed succeed. Gandhi adopted this tactic not only because it fit his spiritual orientation but also because he was pragmatic enough to know that the Indians were no match, militarily, for the British.

I have drawn the distinction between passive resistance as understood and practiced in the West and *Satyagraha* before I had evolved the doctrine of the latter to its full logical and spiritual extent. I often used "passive resistance" and "Satyagraha" as synonymous terms: but as the doctrine of Satyagraha developed, the expression "passive resistance" ceases even to be synonymous.... Moreover passive resistance does not necessarily involve complete adherence to truth under every circumstance.... Satyagraha is a weapon of the strong; it admits of no violence under any circumstance whatever; and it ever insists upon truth....

(From a letter written by Gandhi, 25 January 1920.)

In the application of Satyagraha, I discovered, in the earliest stages, that pursuit of Truth did not admit of violence being inflicted on one's opponent, but that he must be weaned from error by patience and sympathy.... And patience means self-suffering....

As an individual:

1. A satyagrahi, i.e., a civil resister, will harbour no anger.
2. He will suffer the anger of the opponent.
3. In so doing he will put up with assaults from the opponent, never retaliate; but he will not submit, out of fear of punishment or the like, to any order given in anger.
4. When any person in authority seeks to arrest a civil resister, he will voluntarily submit to the arrest, and he will not resist the attachment or removal of his own property, if any, when it is sought to be confiscated by the authorities.
5. If a civil resister has any property in his possession as a trustee, he will refuse to surrender it, even though in defending it he will lose his own life. He will, however, never retaliate.
6. Non-retaliation excludes swearing and cursing.
7. Therefore a civil resister will never insult his opponent, and therefore not take part in many of the newly coined cries which are contrary to the spirit of *ahimsa*.
8. A civil resister will not salute the Union Jack, nor will he insult it or officials, English or Indian.
9. In the course of the struggle if anyone insults an official of commits an assault upon him, a civil resister will protect such official or officials from the insult or attack even at the risk of his life.

(From *Young India*, 27 February 1930.)

Questions to Consider

1. Gandhi claimed that *Satyagraha* had nothing in common with the methods used in the struggles for freedom in the West before his time. Was he correct?
2. To what extent was this tactic secular and to what extent religious?
3. What important American leader later adapted Gandhian methods for the U.S. civil rights movement? Could they be effectively applied outside a colonial context?

25 January 1920 letter in *Collected Works of Mahatma Gandhi*, vol. 19; and 27 February 1930 article in *Collected Works of Mahatma Gandhi*, vol. 48 (New Delhi, India: Publications Division, Ministry of Information and Broadcasting, 1958–1994).

When he returned to his native land shortly after the outbreak of World War I, Gandhi was welcomed as a hero. Initially, he supported the British in the war effort, but soon he went on the offensive. A crucial factor in his decision was a journey he took in 1917 to Champaran, in Bihar in northeastern India, at the invitation of an impoverished peasant. The peasant had dogged Gandhi's steps until he persuaded him to come and see the terrible conditions of the indigo sharecroppers in his district. Gandhi already had a reputation; his visit alarmed the authorities, who threatened to jail him. But the intrepid lawyer mobilized support and launched a nonviolent campaign for reform and justice for the peasants. Gandhi viewed this episode as foundational to his movement for freedom. "What I did," he explained, "was a very ordinary thing. I declared that the British could not order me around in my own country."[3]

In India, Gandhi founded another ashram based on service, living simply, and self-reliance. He lived there off and on for the rest of his life, but his attention was increasingly turned to agitating for British withdrawal. In response to the Rowlatt Acts, Gandhi and other nationalists launched a campaign of civil disobedience. A mass strike was declared in which all work was to cease and the population was to pray and fast. Gandhi argued that moral force would triumph over physical force. How could the Rowlatt Acts, designed to punish revolutionary actions against the British, be applied, Gandhi reasoned, to those who did not engage with the government at all?

Contrary to Gandhi's plan, however, riots and violence occurred in some areas. Although the British had forbidden public gatherings, 10,000 to 20,000 men, women, and children assembled in a large walled courtyard in the sacred Sikh city of Amritsar (ahm-REET-ser) in the Punjab. In an infamous action, known as the Amritsar Massacre, the local British general, Reginald Dyer, marched armed soldiers into the courtyard and opened fire without warning on the unarmed crowd who had gathered not for political reasons but to celebrate a religious festival in April 1919. The soldiers mowed down the stampeding men, women, and children, slaughtering 379 and wounding over 1000. Dyer noted afterward that he expected to teach the Indians a lesson and do "a jolly lot of good." Days after the massacre, the general exacerbated matters by ordering that all Indians must crawl on all fours as they passed the house of a British schoolteacher who had been assaulted by some rioters. Dyer was forced to resign, but many British colonials supported the bloody suppression of the Amritsar "demonstrators." To many Indians, Dyer's actions suggested the true bottom line of Britain's rule over India.

The Amritsar Massacre and other acts of cruelty thus inflamed public opinion and prompted Gandhi and other nationalists to intensify their efforts for independence. The Indian National Congress launched a policy of noncooperation with the government in 1920, and Gandhi was arrested in 1922 and sentenced to 6 years in prison. Gandhi's imprisonment served as a symbol of Indian resistance and earned him the devotion of the Indian people. The intrepid attorney also worked for other goals besides freeing India. He sought to end the drinking of alcohol, raise the status of women, remove the stigma attached to the Depressed Classes (Untouchables), and bring about cooperation between Hindus and Muslims. These objectives challenged the fundamental social order of India and earned him many enemies.

In 1927, the Congress demanded full dominion status, the same constitutional equality enjoyed by white settler dominions like Canada and Australia. But many Muslims refused to support Congress's "Commonwealth of India" plan, as it rejected set-aside seats on the central legislative body for Muslims who, as a minority, were afraid of being excluded.

At the same time, Gandhi launched a new campaign of civil disobedience in 1930. In a well-publicized "Salt March," Gandhi led thousands of men and women to the sea, where he broke British law by panning salt. Salt was a necessity of life. Taxes on salt were a vital source of revenue for the British government in India, especially after nationalist boycotts of British cloth and alcohol cut revenues from those sources. At first, Gandhi prohibited women from participating in the **Salt Marches,** but feminist nationalism had been growing for decades, and women such as Sarojini Naidu (sah-roh-JEE-nee NAI-doo; 1879–1949), the first Indian woman elected president of the Indian National Congress, demanded a role for women. Gandhi relented, women joined the marches, and Naidu shouted, "Hail, law breaker!" as Gandhi walked into the sea to pick up a lump of salt.[4] The British authorities attacked and beat the nonviolent marchers, whose passive resistance—captured on film—presented a picture at once noble and heartrending of Indian resolve. Eighty thousand marchers, of whom 17,000 were women, were arrested. Women, on whom Gandhi also called to manufacture homespun cloth to wean India from British imports, now became a significant part of Gandhian nationalism.

The Continuing Struggle

In 1930, the British arranged a series of roundtable conferences in London. A total of 112 Indian delegates were invited, but with the exception of Gandhi and a few others, all were carefully selected by the British viceroy in India. In 1932, the British proposed the Communal Award, which sought to give special treatment to religious and social "minorities," including Muslims and the Untouchables. Although he was a lifelong supporter of the rights of the downtrodden Untouchables, Gandhi, while in jail in 1932, started a fast in opposition to this proposal, which he felt would undermine the equal treatment of all. In 1935, the British passed a new Government of India Act, which advocated a federal union to bring the British provinces and the princely states of India into a central government.

Gandhi's visit to England in the early 1930s caused a sensation, and he was in great demand for speeches and visits. As an advocate of nonviolence and self-determination, he attracted like-minded groups and leaders from all over the world. For others he was a curiosity, braving the English winter in his typical garb of loincloth, shawl, and sandals. When Gandhi was invited to visit King George V and Queen Mary for tea, the press had a field day, speculating on what he might wear to the royal occasion. Gandhi dressed in his customary fashion. Later, when someone inquired whether he had worn too little clothing, Gandhi answered with characteristic wit, "The King had enough on for both of us."[5]

The primary moving force in the independence movement was the powerful Indian National Congress, which had become the dominant party for Indian nationalists after 1935. Its membership of several million was predominantly Hindu but also

Salt Marches—Marches in 1930 led by Gandhi to protest British salt monopoly in India.

Seeing Connections

Gandhi's Nonviolence and Civil Rights Around the World

Mohandas Gandhi, seen here with a spinning wheel—a nonviolent tool to protest use of the products of imperialist Britain—developed the tactic of noncooperation and nonviolent protest to win India's independence. Although Gandhi's peaceful methods may seem most effective in the Indian context because they grew from blending the Indian concept of *ahimsa* (nonviolence) with a devotion to truth, these methods have appealed to seekers of justice beyond India's borders. An American who traveled and studied Gandhi's approach in India was Dr. Benjamin Mays, president of Morehouse College, who in turn influenced his student, Dr. Martin Luther King. King journeyed to India himself in 1959 to study Gandhian nonviolence, later making it the fundamental philosophy of his civil rights movement. Several decades later, Nelson Mandela used the Gandhi-King philosophy to transform South Africa following the end of that country's apartheid regime.

included many Muslims, not all of whom had joined the **Muslim League,** and members of other religious groups. The Congress ignored the demands of Muslims to stress communal differences, however, and focused on nationalism and getting the British out of India. Opinion varied on how to get the British out. Gandhi's opposite was Bal Gangadhar Tilak (BAHL GUN-gah-dar TEE-lahk; 1856-1920), a firebrand brahman, who, until his death in 1920, advocated Hindu supremacy and the use of violence to evict the British. His "*Svaraj* (self-rule) is my birthright, and I will have it,"[6] became a rallying cry for freedom. But soon after World War I, the Congress came under Gandhi's leadership; his personal following among the people was the chief source of the party's tremendous influence. Gandhi transformed the Congress, which had been primarily a highly educated, male, middle-class organization, into a mass movement that included the peasants. It became the spearhead of nationalist efforts to negotiate with the British for self-rule. It would dominate the Indian elections of 1937 and lead India upon achieving independence in 1947.

Another prominent leader of the Congress was Jawaharlal Nehru (ja-WAH-har-lahl NEH-roo; 1889–1964), who came from a brahman family of ancient lineage. In his youth, Nehru had all of the advantages of wealth: English tutors and enrollment in the English public school of Harrow and later Trinity College, Cambridge, where he obtained his B.A. in 1910. Two years afterward, he was admitted to the bar. On his return to India, however, he showed little interest in practicing law and gradually became completely absorbed in his country's fight for freedom.

A devoted friend and disciple of Gandhi, Nehru could not agree with the older leader's spiritual rejection of much of the modern world. At heart Nehru was a rationalist, an agnostic, an ardent believer in science,

---

Muslim League—Political organization of anti-imperialist Muslims in India, founded 1930.

▲ Jawaharlal Nehru, along with Gandhi one of the paramount leaders of Indian nationalism, later served as prime minister of independent India.

and a foe of all supernaturalism. As he himself said, "I have become a queer mixture of the East and the West, out of place everywhere, at home nowhere. Perhaps my thoughts and approach to life are more akin to what is called Western than Eastern, but India calls me."[7] Nehru expressed the sentiments of many Asians and Africans under colonial rule. They had been given a European education that alienated them from their own cultures and failed to secure for them equality with the Europeans. Nehru would later become the first prime minister of independent India. Gandhi and Nehru represented two strands of Indian nationalism. Though their visions of the ideal Indian society differed, they were in agreement that Britain must leave and allow the Indians to govern themselves.

The Hindu-Muslim Divide

As Britain's imperial control over India began to loosen, tensions between the Muslim and Hindu communities increased. Many Muslims believed that after independence they would become a powerless minority, the target of Hindu retaliation for centuries of Muslim (Mughal) rule. Some feared that the Hindu-dominated Congress party would have no place for Muslims once the British left India. Thus the conflict that emerged was a struggle for political and cultural survival.

In the early 1930s, the Muslim League, a political party, began to challenge the claim of the Indian National Congress to represent all of India. The leader of the Muslim League, Muhammad Ali Jinnah (moo-HAH-mad AH-lee JIN-nah; 1876–1948), had originally been a prominent member of the Congress party. Jinnah, once dubbed by Indian nationalists the "ambassador of Hindu-Muslim unity," became alienated by what he considered Hindu domination of the Congress and its claim to be the sole agent of Indian nationalism.

The Muslim League began to advance the "two-nation theory," and, in 1933, a group of Muslim students at Cambridge University circulated a pamphlet advocating the establishment of a new state in South Asia to be known as Pakistan. This leaflet was the opening act of what later became a bloody drama. In 1939, the Muslim League emphatically denounced any scheme of self-government of India that would mean majority Hindu rule.

DOCUMENT
Gandhi Speaks

Britain's declaration that India was at war with Germany in September 1939 rekindled angry memories of World War I when India's aid was thanked only by increased British repression. While Nehru and other Indian nationalists sympathized with Britain in its struggle against Nazi Germany, they demanded equality with Britain as a necessary condition of coming to its aid. Denied independence, Indian leaders ordered the provincial ministries of Congress to resign in protest. Muslim leaders such as Jinnah saw this as an opportunity for independent action by Muslim areas, which they had demanded of Congress for the past decade. Gandhi's entreaties to Jinnah to remain united against imperialism went unheeded. When a British delegation tried to get Gandhi to agree to allow Muslim areas to opt out of an Indian dominion to be formed after World War II, Gandhi would not budge, instead launching the **"Quit India"** movement in 1942. Other Indian nationalists created an army of the thousands of Indian soldiers the British had lost in Singapore when the Japanese captured the city. Although many Indians supported England during the war, others, later viewed as heroes of Indian nationalism, did not.

CASE STUDY
The Partition of India

In the years after World War II, Britain looked for a way out of India, but the rise of sectarian violence made them hesitant to leave. Negotiations repeatedly broke down, and in the end, India was partitioned into predominantly Hindu India and predominantly Muslim Pakistan. Bloodletting was not over, as many millions died in the 1947 transition to independence.

Quit India—Militant movement started in 1942 to eliminate British rule.

Conclusion

Between the two world wars, imperialism went on the defensive before the rise of nationalism in Asia. In the opening decades of the twentieth century, Japan, as noted in Chapters 25 and 28, served as the model of the successful Asian nation-state; it made amazing progress in industrialization and implemented a constitutional government. By 1919, the island nation had become one of the world's leading powers.

Although China was not, strictly speaking, part of the colonial world, in many ways this vast land was under the indirect influence of the Great Powers. Chinese Nationalists, led by Sun Yat-sen, overthrew the Manchu dynasty and established a republic. After years of conflict among rival factions, Jiang Jieshi consolidated power in the Guomindang regime. The nascent Chinese Communist movement, under Mao Zedong, survived World War II to go on to build a nation in the post-1949 era.

Other East Asian countries also undertook nation-building, often using the rhetoric of national strength and people's rights learned from the imperialists, to get rid of foreign domination. Koreans, Indonesians, Vietnamese, Filipinos, Burmese, and Malays all built nationalist movements on a combination of indigenous and Western thinking about independence. Many were bitterly disappointed in Western hypocrisy over the issue of self-determination of nations. In the end, World War II destroyed both Western and Japanese imperialism in East and Southeast Asia.

India also exposed colonial hypocrisy. It became a model of democratic nationalism under the leadership of Mohandas Gandhi. He preached a message of nonviolence and civil disobedience to force Britain to grant a substantial measure of self-government to the Indians. Ultimately, World War II also dissolved British imperialism in India. Though Indians had worked the longest and hardest of all nationalists to build a nation since the 1880s, however, sectarian differences tore independent South Asia apart in 1947, creating two nations, India and Pakistan.

The rise of nationalism was accomplished against a backdrop of both increasingly global diffusion of ideas and movements and increasingly inward-looking national-identity formation. While foreign ideologies and ideas informed Asians' thinking about independence, they also constituted a foil against which identity-consciousness developed. World War II, likewise, had paradoxical effects, both exposing Western dominance as a house of cards that could be toppled by the Japanese and discrediting the notion of a pan-Asian sphere led by Japan. In the end, the global reach of World War II allowed the inward-looking course of identity- and nation-building to proceed.

Suggestions for Web Browsing

You can obtain more information about topics included in this chapter at the websites listed below. See also the companion website that accompanies this text, http://www.ablongman.com/brummett, which contains an online study guide and additional resources.

History of China
http://www-chaos.umd.edu/history/toc.html
This is the table of contents for the University of Maryland's exceptionally broad coverage of sites for Chinese history, including documents, images, and explanatory texts.

Modern India
http://www.clas.ufl.edu/users/gthursby/ind/history.htm
Extensive list of history sites dedicated to India.

Gandhi
http://www.gandhimuseum.org/papers.html
An extensive collection of Gandhi's writings compiled by India's National Gandhi Museum.

Literature and Film

China's greatest fiction writers of the early twentieth century, Lu Xun and Ding Ling, portray the tensions in the struggle for justice in the modernizing state. Lu Xun's short stories are arguably the best and most accessible examples of May Fourth literature. See Lu Xun, *Diary of a Madman and Other Stories* (University of Hawaii Press, 1980). Ding Ling's short stories depict the quest for women's liberation. See Ding Ling, *I Myself Am a Woman,* ed. Tani Barlow (Beacon Press, 1989). For a satire of modernization in 1930s Vietnam, see Vu Trong Phung, *Dumb Luck* (trans. Nguyen Nguyet Cam and Peter Zinoman, University of Michigan, 2002). Gong Li's 1991 film, *Raise the Red Lantern,* depicts the struggle for autonomy of an educated young Chinese woman in a polygamous household of the 1920s.

Suggestions for Reading

For an overview of Chinese history, see Patricia Buckley Ebrey, *The Cambridge Illustrated History of China* (Cambridge, University Press, 1996) and Jonathan D. Spence, *The Search for Modern China* (W.W. Norton, 1999). Wang Zheng's *Women in the Chinese Enlightenment* (University of California Press, 1999) is an excellent study of progressive women in the interwar period.

Harry J. Benda and John A. Larkin, *The World of Southeast Asia* (Harper & Row, 1967), and D.S. Sar Desai, *Southeast Asia: Past and Present* (Westview, 1989), provide good general coverage of Southeast Asia. For Vietnam, see Hue-tam Ho Tai, *Radicalism and the Origins of the Vietnamese Revolution* (Harvard University Press, 1992). On Korea, see Carter J. Eckert, *Korea Old and New* (Harvard University Press, 1990).

Gandhi's autobiography makes fascinating reading: *Mohandas Gandhi, An Autobiography: The Story of My Experiments with Truth,* trans. M. Desai (Boston: Beacon Press, 1957). New and accessible histories of India include John Keay, *India: A History* (Grove Press, 2000) and Barbara D. Metcalf and Thomas R. Metcalf, *A Concise History of Modern India* (Cambridge University Press, 2006).

CHAPTER 30

National Movements and the Drive for Independence in the Middle East and Africa from the 1920s to 1950s

Outline

- The Middle East Divided
- The Challenge to Colonial Rule in Africa
- Pan-Africanism
- World War II and Its Aftermath
- Decolonization

Features

SEEING CONNECTIONS **The Hashimite Family**

DOCUMENT **The Color Line Belts the World**

DOCUMENT **Pass Laws and African Women in South Africa**

◀ Veiled Egyptian suffragettes demonstrate in the streets of Cairo for women's voting rights in the interwar period.

A LONG PERIOD OF aggressive expansion by the West had spread European ideas, factories, and colonial settlers throughout much of the world. Even those African and Middle Eastern societies that were not directly colonized by European states felt the dramatic influences of Western-style politics, culture, and economic life. In the period between the world wars and immediately afterward, many of these societies adopted—or had imposed on them—the nation-state model of political organization. In that same period, African and Middle Eastern peoples struggled to gain their independence.

The period between World War I and II also witnessed a dramatic movement of people from rural regions to urban centers. The result, often traumatic, was social and economic transformation. Modernization that had gained momentum in the nineteenth-century—processes of industrialization and educational reform, and the reshaping of all modes of transportation and communication—only gathered steam. New forms of political leadership emerged and with them often came radical changes in systems of government, law, economics, and social relations. Many areas of Africa and the Middle East retained age-old agrarian practices, but many others lost or abandoned traditional modes of economic organization. These transformations produced dramatic changes in the lives of individuals and families even within a single generation.

World War I and its aftershocks strengthened independence movements in Africa and the Middle East. Nationalist campaigns, present in embryonic form in most of the colonies before the war, grew rapidly in virtually all of the European possessions and mandates. India's independence movement, alongside Mohandas Gandhi's tactics of nonviolence, inspired African and Arab political leaders. Across the Middle East and Africa, nations struggled to redefine themselves and throw off the yoke of European domination.

The Middle East Divided

What impact did the outcome of World War I have on Middle Eastern politics?

World War I dramatically altered the political, cultural, and geographical configuration of the Middle East. Before the war, the Middle East was divided primarily between the Ottoman and Qajar Empires, both long-standing agrarian states. Nearly all of North Africa, by this point, however, had fallen to European colonial rule. The British had taken Egypt in 1882; France had gained control of Tunis and Algiers; and Italy had seized areas of Libya from the Ottomans in 1911. After World War I, Iran, which had remained neutral, maintained its territorial integrity. But the centuries-long rule of the Ottoman Empire in the Middle East was swept away, its territories parceled out among the war's victors, specifically Britain and France. For the interwar period, the regions of the Middle East might be divided between those that remained independent and those that fell under British or French control. The distinction would prove critical in the evolution of the modern nation-states of the region.

Europe and the Middle East After World War I

The Middle East Between the Wars	
1917	Balfour Declaration
1919	Wafd-led rebellion in Egypt
1920	Mandates set up in conquered Ottoman territory
1923	Sa'd Zaghlul becomes first prime minister of Egypt
1923–1938	Mustafa Kemal Atatürk rules the Turkish Republic
1925	Pahlavi dynasty established in Iran
1932	Ibn Sa'ud's new state named kingdom of Saudi Arabia

The War Years

The events of World War I cannot be understood without a grasp of the competition that raged between the European powers. There had long been speculation over which Ottoman territories would fall to whom—when (and if) the Ottoman state finally collapsed. The Russians coveted a warm-water port in the Mediterranean; the British wanted to retain the Suez Canal, the sea route to their Indian empire, and a strong hand in Egyptian affairs; the French had long-standing interests in the eastern Mediterranean; and the Germans sought a presence in the Middle East and territories in North Africa.

The Middle East in the 1920s

World attention was slowly drawn as well to an emerging conflict in Palestine. Although it was never a rich or strategically sensitive territory, it contained sites held sacred by Jews, Christians, and Muslims, chief among them the city of Jerusalem. Palestine had been under Ottoman rule for centuries but, in the early twentieth century, it became subject to claims by the newly emergent **Zionist** movement. The movement, which emerged initially in Russian and Eastern European Jewish circles, sought to transform Palestine into a Jewish "homeland," or, as many in the movement thought of it, reconstitute the historic Jewish state. The eventual success of the movement was to have a devastating effect on Palestinian Arab society.

Prompted by a long-standing military liaison with the Germans, and at the urging of Enver Pasha (d. 1922), the minister of war, the Ottoman Empire joined the war effort on the side of the Central Powers. The British, for their part, used Egypt as a staging point from which to conduct military operations against German and Ottoman forces. To strengthen their hand, the British pursued divergent, even contradictory diplomatic aims concerning the division of Ottoman territories. Sir Henry McMahon (d. 1949), the British high commissioner in Egypt, corresponded with Sharif Husayn of Mecca (d. 1931), head of the Hashimite family and guardian of Islam's two holy cities (Mecca and Medina). McMahon offered Husayn, in exchange for an alliance against the Ottomans, the

Zionists—Supporters of a movement to establish a Jewish homeland in Palestine.

CHRONOLOGY

1910	1920	1930	1940	1950
1912 African National Congress established in South Africa 1917 Balfour Declaration	1920 Mandates established, Treaty of Sèvres 1923 Turkish Republic recognized 1925 Pahlavi dynasty established in Iran	1933 Ibn Sa'ud grants oil concession to Standard Oil 1935 Italian invasion of Ethiopia	1945 Fifth Pan-African Congress, Manchester, England	1951 Outbreak of Mau Mau Rebellion, Kenya

support of Great Britain for an independent Arab state (under Hashimite rule). At the same time, however, Britain, France, and Russia signed the secret **Sykes-Picot Agreement** (1916), which provided for the division of Syria and Iraq between Britain and France, with Russia to receive regions of Anatolia. Palestine was to be placed under an international administration. The European powers had divided up the spoils of war even before they had won them.

Acting in part on British promises, Husayn launched a revolt against the Ottomans in 1916. His forces, Arab tribal units, were commanded by his third son, Faisal (d. 1933). The Arab Revolt, as it was known, was modest in scale; support for the Ottoman state remained high in most Arab cities. Even with its limited battlefield success, it was a drain on Ottoman military resources and a blow to Ottoman prestige. It also garnered much attention in the Western press, which crafted a romantic (and vaguely racist) account of the exploits of a British officer, T. E. Lawrence (d. 1935), or "Lawrence of Arabia" as he was known, who fought alongside the Arab forces.

Sykes-Picot Agreement—A secret agreement concluded in 1916 between Britain and France that divided the Middle East into British and French spheres of influence.

Ottoman units fought well during the war, but the empire, short of money, supplies, and ammunition, finally could not stand up to British firepower. Following the defeat of his forces in Syria (October 1918), the Ottoman sultan was forced to sign an armistice. The British allowed Faisal to enter Damascus, the capital of Greater Syria, where he quickly set out plans for an independent administration. In March 1920, the General Syrian Congress, with high hopes for the birth of a new Arab state, proclaimed Faisal king of Syria.

Faisal then traveled to the postwar Paris peace conference to plead the cause of Arab independence. He was met with great courtesy but little real interest. In April 1920, at the San Remo Conference, it was decided to

▼ After World War I, the British and French controlled Egypt, Palestine, Syria, and Iraq. Transjordan had a special status under King Abdallah.

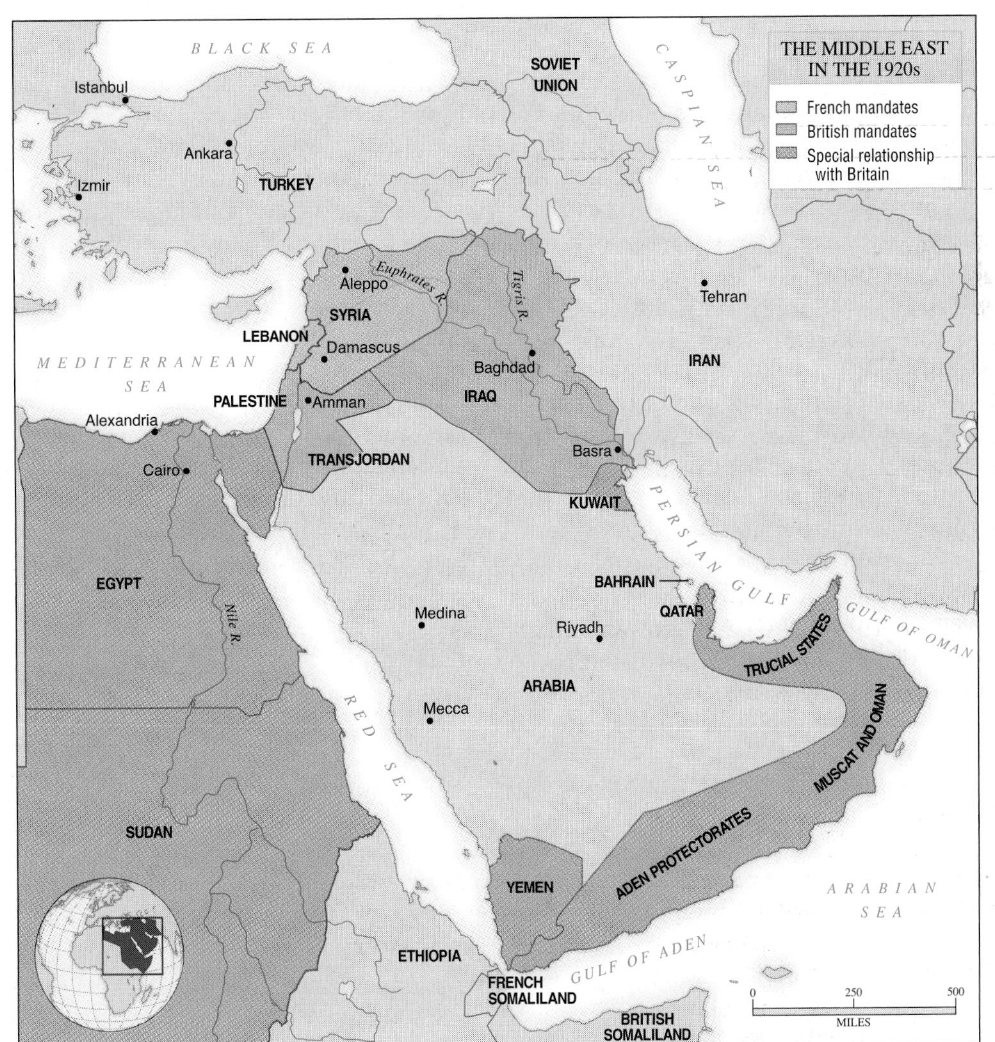

Seeing Connections

The Hashimite Family

The Hashimite family played a decisive part in Middle East politics in the interwar period. Pictured here are the sons of Sharif Husayn, the last significant Hashimite ruler of the Hijaz. Faisal (seated left), a leader of the Arab Revolt, was first named king of Syria, then king of Iraq following his ouster from Damascus by the French mandatory forces. At center is his brother Abdallah, the first king of Transjordan, to the right their brother Ali, who briefly ruled the Hijaz. Politics in the Ottoman period had often featured powerful families of this sort whose efforts left little room for the views or participation of the common people of the region. One impact of World War I—and the destruction of the once-formidable politics of empire—was to open the public arena to new broad-based movements in which students, workers, professionals and populist-style political leaders could exert influence on issues of the day. The Hashimites, in Syria and Iraq, were to see their initial fortunes in the interwar period tumble as forces for nationalism gained ground in the Middle East, particularly following the Second World War.

turn over all Arab territories formerly under Ottoman control to be administered as **mandates** by the Allied Powers. Syria and Lebanon were mandated to France; Iraq and Palestine went to Britain. Husayn's dream of a large and independent Arab state was nipped in the bud. The French, in line with the Sykes-Picot Agreement, marched into Damascus in July 1920, forcing Faisal to relinquish his newly established government.

To mollify their former allies, the British later established Faisal as king of their mandate in Iraq and set up his brother Abdallah in Amman, as ruler of a newly created territory, Transjordan. The new territory was essentially carved from the mandate of Palestine. The two episodes demonstrate the gamelike quality of the partition of the Ottoman Empire. The people of Iraq had no desire for a Hashimite king from Arabia, and there was little logic to the lines drawn around Transjordan except that it was a sparsely populated territory of little interest to either the British or the Zionist leadership, who were more concerned with the densely populated and religiously significant portions of the Palestine mandate to the west of the Jordan River. These were arrangements simply imposed on the region and its people to further British imperial interests.

The Husayn-McMahon correspondence and the Sykes-Picot Agreement were not the only significant promises made during the war. The promise with perhaps the most far-reaching impact was the **Balfour Declaration** of November 2, 1917. The efforts of Theodor Herzl and other Zionist activists (see Chapter 28) had led to the creation of the World Zionist Organization (1897) and other institutions, all geared to the establishment of a Jewish national home in Palestine. Following Herzl's death in 1904, leadership of the Zionist movement was assumed by Chaim Weizmann (d. 1952), a Russian Jew and newly minted British subject. Close ties developed between Weizmann and Arthur James Balfour (d. 1930), a former British prime minister (1902–1905) and, by now, a fervent supporter of the Zionist program. Balfour, in his capacity as British foreign secretary (1915–1919), wrote a brief letter to Lord Rothschild, a leading British Zionist and sponsor of many of the early Jewish settlements in Palestine. The letter was designed to mobilize Jewish support for Britain during World War I. It reads in part:

> *His Majesty's Government views with favour the establishment in Palestine of* a national home for the Jewish people, *and will use their best endeavors to facilitate the achievement of that object, it being clearly understood that nothing shall be done which may prejudice the civil and religious rights of* existing non-Jewish communities in Palestine *or the rights and political status enjoyed by Jews in any other country [emphasis added].*

mandates—Former territories and colonies of Germany and the Ottoman Empire that were placed under the administration of major powers such as Britain and France. The mandate system was overseen by the League of Nations.

Balfour Declaration—A statement that the British foreign minister, Arthur Balfour, issued in 1917 promising British support to Zionists for a Jewish "national home" in Palestine.

The carefully worded statement did not specify the nature of the Jewish "national home." The population of Palestine, according to British estimates, was only about 9 percent Jewish at the time, but the Balfour Declaration referred to the majority Arab population of Palestine only as "the existing non-Jewish communities." The rights and identity of the Palestinian Arab populace, in other words, were treated as secondary concerns. Zionist plans remained controversial in European and American Jewish circles, with many fearful that the establishment of a Jewish state would subject them to further discrimination in or even expulsion from their own countries. Nor was the indigenous Jewish population in Palestine necessarily in sympathy with the Zionists, who were considered by many to be European outsiders. Nevertheless, the Balfour Declaration provided a great boost to Zionist aspirations in Palestine.

World War I, and the political arrangements that followed, took a staggering toll on the peoples of the Middle East (as they did in Europe). In addition to the dead, wounded and maimed, tens of thousands of Ottoman citizens starved or fell to disease. In Armenia, long under Ottoman control, massacres by Ottoman troops, along with hunger and disease, sharply reduced the size of the Armenian population, killing upwards of a million people in what many have called the twentieth century's first act of genocide. (These events remain the subject of debate and heated controversy today.)

Over a million Turks and Greeks were uprooted from their homes in forced population transfers after the war. The Young Turk Revolution had imagined a nation with a complex multilingual, multiethnic, multireligious composition. The new map of the Middle East, instead, divided populations much along these same lines.

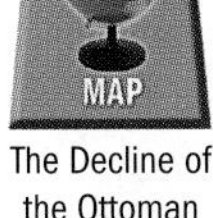

The Decline of the Ottoman Empire

Mustafa Kemal and the New Secular Model of Turkey

The intention of the Allied states—the victors in the war—was to partition former Ottoman provinces among the French, Italians, British, and Greeks. The hated capitulations, canceled by the **Young Turks,** were restored. When World War I ended, the sultan dismissed the Ottoman parliament, British warships patrolled the Bosporus and the Dardanelles, and the Greeks occupied Izmir in western Anatolia. The once great Ottoman Empire was dismembered and humiliated.

A group of Ottoman patriots, however, rallied around Mustafa Kemal (d. 1938), who, as a ranking Ottoman officer during the war, had become a hero of the Gallipoli campaign. Following the war, he had been sent by the Ottoman sultan to demobilize Turkish forces in Anatolia. Disregarding instructions, Kemal, with a group of like-minded fellow officers, reorganized their units and defied the Allies. From their base in eastern Anatolia and later, in the city of Ankara, these men formed their own government, electing Kemal as president. They upheld self-determination for all peoples, including the Turks, and proclaimed the abolition of all special rights enjoyed by foreigners in Turkey.

Kemal and his forces drove the Greeks from Izmir, thus reestablishing Turkish control over western Anatolia, and gained the support of the new Soviet Union and France. Britain, exhausted by the war, was unwilling to mobilize a major initiative to stop them. Meanwhile, Mustafa Kemal established himself in power, abolishing the sultanate and declaring Turkey a republic in 1922. The Allies agreed to a revision of the Treaty of Sèvres, and, in the Treaty of Lausanne, signed in 1923, Turkish sovereignty was formally recognized. The Turkish heartland, Anatolia, remained intact, and demands for reparations came to an end. Turkey thus emerged as an independent nation-state, escaping, in the process, the fate of the Arab provinces of the Ottoman Empire (now mandates under Britain and France).

The Six Arrows of Kemalism

Mustafa Kemal wielded tremendous authority over the new republic. He was granted, by legislative decree in 1934, the surname "Atatürk" or "Father of the Turks," a gesture meant to acknowledge his standing as the nation's "savior." His enormous prestige enabled him to dominate Turkish politics and implement a series of radical secularizing reforms. He oversaw the writing of a new, democratic constitution, but regarded autocratic rule under a single political party as a necessary stage in raising the Turkish populace to the level of education and social well-being required for proper democratic government and parliamentary rule. Committed to Westernization and secularization, he based his model of progress on the European nation-state.

Atatürk's reforms radically transformed Turkish society. He closed down the popular sufi orders, most traditional Islamic schools, and many mosques. Determined to enforce the

◄ As president of the Turkish Republic from its beginning until his death in 1938, Mustafa Kemal instituted many civil and cultural reforms. He was called Atatürk, "Father Turk."

Young Turks—The name given to a group of army officers who advocated reforming the administration and governance of the Ottoman Empire.

CASE STUDY
Soviet and Turkish Plans for Industrialization

separation of church and state, he also set aside Islamic law, replacing it with a civil code modeled on the Swiss system. Atatürk also banned the traditional male headgear, the fez, a symbol of Ottoman identity. The law on headgear was widely resented as an instance of unjust government intervention and an affront to Islamic principles. Atatürk did not dare legislate women's dress, but he did campaign actively for Western-style education and attire for women. In 1935, women were given the vote in Turkey and permitted to run for seats in the national assembly. By the time Atatürk died in 1938, Turkey was a new and different nation.

Iran in the Interwar Period

Qajar rule, despite an insistence on Iranian neutrality, barely survived World War I. The Russian occupation of northern Iran was ended by the 1917 revolution, but the British had discovered oil in western Iran shortly before the war and were determined to protect their oil concession. As a result, antiforeign sentiments developed rapidly in Iran, provoked in part by British attempts to influence decision-making in the economic and foreign policy arenas. The war exacted a harsh toll on the Iranian economy, and, in the provinces, powerful tribal leaders withdrew support for the Qajar state.

Seeing opportunity in a highly chaotic social and political environment, Reza Khan, a commander of the Cossack brigade, set out in 1921 to place himself in power. By 1925 he had succeeded, persuading the assembly to depose the Qajar shah. The shah was already in Europe, having found it expedient to follow Reza Khan's "suggestion" that he take a "vacation." Reza Khan (r. 1925–1941) thus founded a new dynasty, that of the Pahlavis. Like Mustafa Kemal in Turkey, the new shah combined a constitutional system with an authoritarian regime. He launched a program of modernizing and secularizing reforms modeled on those of Kemalist Turkey. He adopted a new legal system, thus weakening the power of the ulama, and he opened the secular Tehran University in 1935.

Iran was no longer at the mercy of foreign loans, but neither was it free of foreign intervention. The British-owned Anglo-Iranian Oil Company held a concession dating from 1901 to exploit Iranian oil. In 1933, the shah renegotiated his country's agreement with the company, but Iran still received only 20 percent of the oil revenues. To counteract British influence, the shah cultivated ties with Germany, but kept Iran neutral during World War II. Fearful of German intervention, however, Britain and Russia again used military force to intervene in Iranian affairs.

Arabia

Arabia, much like Turkey and Iran, remained independent in the aftermath of World War I. The British controlled the Persian Gulf, largely through a series of treaty arrangements with elite families along the peninsula's southern and eastern coasts. But the British saw no particular profit in trying to control the interior of the peninsula; its mostly forbidding terrain was sparsely populated, and it had no apparent strategic or natural resource value. The Hashimite family, under Sharif Husayn, was discredited because of their collaboration with the British. Despite attempts by Husayn to declare himself "caliph" after the war, his family's authority in Arabia was to come shortly to an end. Husayn's sons, somewhat more successful, were to retain authority in Transjordan and Iraq.

Sharif Husayn was finally ousted by forces led by Abd al-Aziz ibn Sa'ud (abd-al a-ZEEZ i-bin sa-UUD; d. 1953). The Sa'ud family, in alliance with the Wahhabi movement, had first emerged in the late Ottoman period in a bid to control the peninsula. Abd al-Aziz, drawing on that legacy, seized the city of Riyadh in 1902, then proceeded to unify the peninsula under Sa'udi-Wahhabi rule. Like his predecessor a century before, Ibn Sa'ud established himself as both a successful warrior and defender of the puritanical Wahhabi doctrine that aimed to purge Islam of all elements perceived by the movement as innovations (see Chapter 20).

Ibn Sa'ud's capture of the holy cities of Mecca and Medina (1925) formally ended centuries of Hashimite authority over the Hijaz. (The two sacred cities have remained ever since under Sa'udi control). Britain recognized the new king in exchange for his recognition of their special position in the Gulf. The new state was officially named the Kingdom of Saudi Arabia (1932). Ibn Sa'ud preserved traditional patterns of consultative rule and based his authority on royal decree legitimized by the consent of the Wahhabi-dominated ulama. Unlike nearly all other modern Middle Eastern states, the kingdom would have no constitution: the law of the land was the Sharia (Islamic law) as interpreted by the Hanbali legal tradition.

Saudi Arabia was impoverished but it was free, unlike most of the Arab provinces. It was a sparsely populated nation composed mostly of small, coastal commercial towns and seminomadic tribes. In 1933, Ibn Sa'ud granted a concession to the Standard Oil Company (later known as Arabian American Oil). Substantial deposits of oil were discovered in 1938. By the close of World War II, it was clear that oil was to become a significant factor in Sau'di economic life. But the full effect of these discoveries—a transformation of the lives of its people and the country's wealth—still lay over the horizon.

Egypt

During World War I, Egypt was ruled as a British protectorate, and Egyptian society was obliged to contribute militarily and economically to the war effort. The price—martial law, requisition of Egyptian labor, impoverishment of the countryside, and other developments—drove anti-British sentiments to new heights. In 1918, a group of prominent Egyptians, led by Sa'd Zaghlul (sa-AD zag-LOOL; d. 1927), formed the **Wafd** ("Delegation"). They asked Great Britain to allow them to represent Egypt at the Paris peace conference, a request that was promptly denied. Zaghlul mobilized reaction throughout Egypt: strikes, demonstrations, and walkouts culminated in a nationwide rebellion in 1919. The British responded with force but, in an attempt to calm public sentiment, the decision was taken to allow Zaghlul and others to attend the peace conference. More significant was the ability of the nationalist movement to force the British to end the protectorate.

In 1922, the British declared Egypt independent. But, as in India in roughly the same period, British measures were denounced by nationalists as half-steps. Britain, despite its stated intentions, retained control over defense, foreign affairs, the economy, the Sudan, and the Suez Canal. The capitulations remained in place, as did an overwhelming British military presence. In elections, held in 1923, the Wafd won an overwhelming victory. Sa'd Zaghlul became the first Egyptian prime minister. The *khedive,* a descendant of Muhammad Ali, assumed the title of king; Great Britain retained its dominant hand. The nature of the relationship is illustrated by the mutual defense pact that Great Britain forced on Egypt in 1936 and by its reoccupation of the country after World War II.

By this point, Egyptian society—elite and middle-class urban society in particular—was feeling the long-term effects of European influence. Graduates of Western educational institutions led the way in shaping an Egyptian women's movement. The Egyptian Feminist Union was founded in 1923. Its members threw their support to the nationalist struggle, all the while struggling for women's rights. Among their demands were women's suffrage, education for girls, and reform of personal status laws that governed marriage and polygyny. Pressures exerted by the Union led to the admission of women to the Egyptian National University in 1928. Leaders of the Union, including its founder, Huda Sha'rawi (HOO-da Shaa-ra-wee; d. 1947), dramatized their program by removing their veils on their return to Cairo from a feminist congress in Europe. At this time, the women's movement in Egypt remained mostly an urban phenomenon. Most of Egypt's population remained rural and poor, and was little affected by many of the social and political developments taking place in Cairo and Alexandria.

A second and quite different sort of movement to emerge in Egypt in this period was the **Muslim Brotherhood.** The Brotherhood was founded in 1928 by Hasan al-Banna (d. 1949), a village schoolteacher. The platform of the Muslim Brotherhood, shaped in endless meetings, sermons, and manifestos, combined condemnation of Western colonialism and secular nationalism (of the kind developed by Mustafa Kemal of Turkey) with a call for the restoration of unity and independence of Islamic society. The Brotherhood took an active role against the British presence in Egypt. But its vision of Islam contrasted sharply with that of the Western-style politicians of the Wafd *and* the very conservative, often rigid ideas of the Wahhabi movement in Arabia. The Brotherhood espoused a belief in Islam as a comprehensive way of life, one in which Islamic law governed the state as well as society. The movement developed social programs such as adult education, job training, and free clinics; it had a special attraction among the poor and became popular in both the cities and countryside. A dynamic Islamic message and a stress on Islamic values combined with social services and respect for modern technology lent the Brotherhood a powerful appeal. The group spread quickly through the Near East, with chapters founded in Syria, Palestine, Lebanon, and Iraq. The Brotherhood stands as an early and visible example of a modern **Islamist** movement, one that responded attentively to the needs of the urban poor and lower middle class and articulated a meaningful response to the often wrenching changes of "modernity."

Minarets and Mosque, Egypt

The Mandates

Unlike Egypt and the states of North Africa, the rest of the Arab world had been, at least nominally, under Ottoman control until World War I. The postwar treaties granted Britain the mandates over Iraq and Palestine (out of which Transjordan was carved) and France the mandate over Greater Syria (soon to be divided into Syria and Lebanon). One historian has called the mandate system "little more than nineteenth-century imperialism repackaged to give the appearance of self-determination."[1] Mandates were territories to be administered; their peoples, deemed incapable of self-rule, were to be governed by "more advanced" nations until such time as they were able to govern themselves. The mandate system, in part, showed the influence of Social Darwinism, a view of the world that ranked societies in hierarchical terms. The European states, needless to say, ranked at the top, with Arab, African, and Asian societies lined up beneath them.

Iraq had had no history as an independent state. Under British control, it was shaped from three Ottoman provinces (based respectively in Mosul, Baghdad, and Basra). The population of the newly formed

Wafd—An Egyptian political party founded in 1918 that challenged British rule.

Muslim Brotherhood—An organization founded in 1928 in Egypt by Hasan al-Banna. The Muslim Brotherhood promoted religious, political, and social reforms and sponsored social programs.

Islamist—Religio-political movements that advocate the establishment of government, law, and education based strictly on Islamic legal and religious tenets.

mandate was highly diverse, though Kurds predominated in the north, Shi'ite Arabs in the south and central regions, and Sunni Arabs in and around Baghdad. For the British, Iraq was a link between their strategic bases in the Persian Gulf and their oil interests in Iran. The British occupation of Iraq followed the fall of Baghdad in 1917. Shortly after the San Remo Conference, anti-British sentiments, along with resentments born of hardship suffered during the war, led to an insurrection that spread to a third of Iraq. It took British forces three months to quell the revolt.

The British then introduced the administration of the outsider, Faisal, about whom most Iraqis knew little. He was crowned king as the band played "God Save the King," an ironic statement on imported British culture. Iraq was declared a constitutional monarchy, with the British in control of Iraqi finances and military affairs. Faisal's government had considerably greater autonomy than the French allowed Syria, and in 1932, Iraq became independent. It was, however, independence with strings attached. Britain, having negotiated a 75-year lease to exploit Iraqi oil, retained air bases in the country and a close eye on foreign policy decisions. During World War II, British forces reoccupied the country, a clear reminder that Iraqi concerns were fully subject to the demands of British strategic interests.

In postwar Syria, the French adopted a "divide-and-rule" approach to governance and, to enforce their policies, established a large military presence. They divided the territories of Greater Syria in such a way as to emphasize and exacerbate religious and ethnic differences. They also tended to favor Christian communities, most especially the Maronites of Lebanon. Lebanon's population, following the division of Greater Syria, remained predominantly Arab but was divided along a variety of religious and sectarian lines. The Maronite Christians predominated in given areas, Sunni Muslims in others, and, particularly in rural areas of south and central Lebanon, Shi'ite Muslims formed a majority. Added to the mix, in areas of the Lebanese mountains, were the Druze (originally a heterodox offshoot of Shi'ite Islam). The French carved Lebanon out of the Syrian mandate in order to set up a majority Christian state that would retain close ties with France even after independence.

France kept tight control over its mandates, prompting widespread rebellion in Syria from 1925 to 1927. Syria remained without real political representation and without independence until after World War II. Conversely, in Lebanon, the French set up a constitutional regime in 1926, but election to office was based on religious affiliation, and France kept control of foreign and military affairs. When World War II began, France suspended the constitution. The French withdrew grudgingly from Syria and Lebanon only in 1943. They left Lebanon with a system of sectarian-based political representation that has plagued the nation ever since.

The Question of Palestine

The mandate for Palestine was unique from its inception. This was, in part, because of Palestine's historic standing as sacred ground for three religious traditions, and, in part, because of the contending demands made upon its territory. The British administration had now to respond to the claims of the Zionist movement, with its considerable sources of support from within the British colonial forces and at home in London, and those of the majority Palestinian Arab population, seeking independence as well as justice against the inroads of the Zionists on the lands and economic future of the territory.

The Ottoman government had tried to at least slow, if not prevent, the Zionists' acquisition of land in Palestine, but with little success. Once Palestine became a British mandate, the Jewish population was granted certain privileges—partly as an expression of British sympathy for the Zionist cause but also because the Zionists were Europeans, not "Orientals." The Zionist movement was allowed to display its own flag; Hebrew was recognized as an official language of the mandate; Jews working for the local British administration were paid more than Arabs; and the Zionist community, the ***Yishuv,*** in contrast to the Arab community, was permitted to acquire and bear arms. Many of the early Zionists were proponents of socialism, an ideology that manifested itself in the founding of communal farms called ***kibbutzim.*** It bears stressing, in this context, that the struggle between the Zionists and Palestinian Arabs was not primarily a struggle over religion (many of the Zionists were secular Jews, and the Arabs were Muslim, Christian, or secular); it was a struggle over land.

The British struggled, ultimately in vain, to balance their interests with those of the Arabs and Zionists. Unlike other mandates, Palestine never had an assembly or a constitution. Instead, the British advanced a series of abortive proposals, trying to satisfy both sides but, most often, actually favoring the Zionists. The Zionists, though often divided on ideological grounds, were far better mobilized than the Arab population, which suffered from a lack of unified leadership, little support in British circles, and a general absence of organization of its political and military resources. The most visible Arab leader was Hajj Amin al-Husayni (hajj ameen al-hu-say-NEE; d. 1974), the chief Islamic jurist of Jerusalem, and a controversial figure through much of his career.

Waves of Jewish immigration between 1919 and 1926 seemed to confirm Arab fears that the British meant to deliver Palestine into the hands of the Zionists. In 1929, Jews and Arabs clashed over activities at

Yishuv—A Hebrew word meaning "settlement" that the Zionist movement used to refer to Jewish settlers in Palestine before it became Israel.

kibbutzim—A type of agricultural settlement established by Zionist immigrants to Palestine in which land and resources are owned, and all decisions made, on a collective basis.

Jewish immigrants arriving by sea to the British-controlled mandate of Palestine in the 1930s. For Jews, immigration to Palestine represented one of the few options they had to escape rising anti-Semitism in central and eastern Europe. For the Palestinians, Jewish immigration coupled with British colonial rule represented a European effort to divest them of their land.

the Western Wall (a remnant of Solomon's Temple in Jerusalem and part of the sanctuary of the Dome of the Rock, a sacred Muslim shrine). Then, the rise of Hitler prompted a dramatic exodus of Jews fleeing Nazi Germany. Many were not Zionists, but restrictive immigration quotas in countries like the United States made Palestine a reasonable option for emigrating Jews. The enormous influx of immigrants between 1933 and 1936 further alarmed the Arab population, prompting a revolt that included demonstrations, rioting, and mass strikes. The Arab Revolt targeted Zionist settlements and British forces; it was crushed by the British within six months. The Palestinian Arab population suffered badly as a result; the losses of the revolt left the Palestinians ill-equipped to counter the rapid strides taken by the Zionist movement in the 1940s.

Throughout the 1930s, the "Palestine question" provoked heated discussion in many parts of the world. Zionists argued that Jews had a historic right to the Holy Land, that they had been promised a state by the Balfour Declaration, and that Jewish colonization constituted a "democratic and progressive" influence in the Middle East. The Palestinians responded that Palestine had been their country for over a thousand years and declared the Balfour Declaration as nonbinding since they, the local inhabitants, had not been consulted in its formulation. They asked how any people could be expected to stand idly by while outsiders, with few ties to the land, were permitted to gain control over lands, waters, and other resources, while becoming a majority in the process. For many Palestinians, the Zionists were yet another variety of European imperialism in a particularly virulent form.

With the threat of war looming in 1939, Great Britain sought to regain Arab goodwill and thereby strengthen its position in the Middle East. It issued a White Paper declaring support for the creation of a Palestinian state and limits upon Jewish land purchases and immigration. The Zionists rejected the document; Palestinian official reaction, already skeptical of all British conduct, showed guarded support. Few could foresee the developments of the Second World War and, in particular, the full extent of Nazi atrocities in Europe. The White Paper did accelerate one change in the conflict. Zionist leaders, feeling betrayed by the British, turned their energies to deepening ties with the United States. The two developments—the impact of World War II on Zionist activity and the onset of closer Zionist-U.S. ties—would transform the conflict over Palestine.

The Challenge to Colonial Rule in Africa

Were there significant differences between African protest movements challenging colonial rule before and after World War II?

By World War I, European nations had taken control of Africa and the armed resistance of Africans had ended. However, colonial rule was harsh and Africans explored other ways of voicing their many grievances—concerning forced conscription during World War I and forced labor to build roads and railways, the demand for cash crops such as cocoa and groundnuts in rural areas, competition from European businesses that undercut African entrepreneurs, excessive taxes, higher prices on goods after World War I, attacks on African cultural institutions, and discrimination against African civil servants in appointments and promotions.

Although colonial rule was built on European domination and control, the economic and social changes that colonialism stimulated—urbanization, transportation, and Western education—ironically laid the foundations for African challenges to colonial rule. Urbanization

Africa	
1912	Founding of African National Congress in South Africa
1935	Italy invades Ethiopia
1944	Formation of ANC Youth League in South Africa
1945	Fifth Pan-African Congress
1951	Beginning of Mau Mau Rebellion in Kenya

brought many Africans from different areas to cities, where they interacted and communicated with each other and developed new identities. Transportation such as buses and trains carried rural migrants back to their villages with news, fresh ideas, and different political views. Western education in government and mission schools created a literate elite that could read and write and follow discussions on nationalism and independence elsewhere in Africa and the world. This elite established dozens of newspapers (mainly in the British colonies) such as the *Lagos Weekly Record*, the *West African Pilot*, and *Imvo Zabantsundu* ("African Opinion") that vigorously criticized white rule. Literate Africans read the black press and then disseminated news and opinions to a much wider network of people.

The initial challenges to colonial rule were often based on local grievances. Protest organizations were usually based on kinship, ethnicity, or regional identities and took up issues that advanced their particular interests and improved economic conditions. However, once Africans began to recognize that their grievances were shared more widely, they explored creating organizations that reached out to larger numbers of people and ethnic groups. They began to think in terms of nationalist movements that covered a whole colony.

An urbanized educated and professional elite (lawyers, doctors, clerks in the civil service, teachers, traders, commercial farmers, and clergy) dominated the early African nationalist movements. They were well read and aware of what was happening in other parts of the world, and they borrowed their concepts of nationalism from European examples that emphasized the concept of a nation-state. European nations, however, had gone through a long process of developing national identities

▼ After colonial rule was firmly established in Africa, the only change in possessions came after World War I. Germany's four colonies were placed under the League of Nations, which established a mandate system for other colonizers to administer the territories.

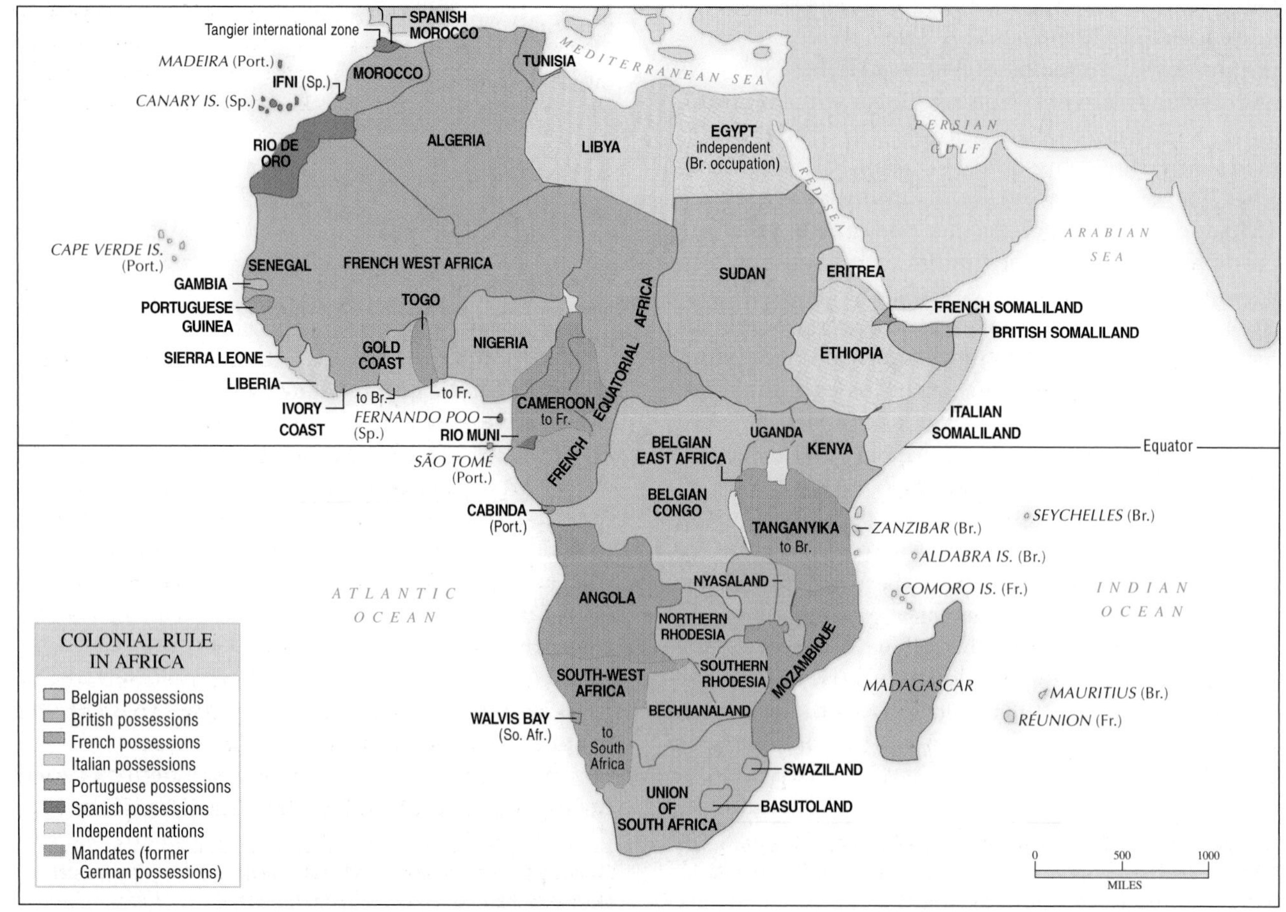

◀ The first African elected to the French Chamber of Deputies in 1914, Blaise Diagne (in bowler hat on the right) was the highest elected African official in the French colonies until after World War II.

while African colonies were arbitrarily created by European colonizers and did not have common identities.

Political movements in British colonies before World War II were moderate. They did not call for immediate independence from European colonizers but for the redress of specific grievances. Even when they criticized aspects of colonial rule, they made sure to express their loyalty to the British crown. In 1920, African professionals in the British colonies of Gold Coast (later Ghana), Gambia, Nigeria, and Sierra Leone established the **National Congress of British West Africa** (NCBWA). Its most prominent spokesperson was J. E. Casely-Hayford, a Gold Coast lawyer. The NCBWA favored using constitutional methods to achieve gradual change and protected its members' interests by calling for improved education and for new constitutions in which they would be allowed to join legislative councils that advised British officials. They wrongly thought the British would allow the councils to evolve into parliaments.

Although the challenges of elite organizations were usually restrained, some of their protests ended in violent confrontations. In Kenya, the East African Association (EAA), a largely Kikuyu organization, was formed to protest against forced labor, pass laws, high taxes, and reductions in black wages. In March 1922, its leader, Harry Thuku, was arrested in Nairobi for agitation. Demonstrators that gathered outside his jail charged the police, who then shot and killed 56 people. The EAA was banned the following year.

The Portuguese and Belgians effectively clamped down on dissent in their colonies, while the French encouraged Africans in their colonies to follow a path the French designed. One element of French policy was to assimilate a small number of Africans and give them full rights as French citizens. By 1926, about 50,000 of 13 million Africans in France's African colonies were French citizens. Most of them lived in Senegal, where four communes had elected a single deputy to the Chamber of Deputies in Paris since the nineteenth century. Europeans and Creoles had represented the communes until the 1914 election, the first time a secret ballot was used and the first time an African, Blaise Diagne (dee-AHN-yuh), was elected to the Chamber of Deputies. A former customs official, Diagne had served in French colonial outposts in the Caribbean and Southeast Asia. He remained in the Chamber of Deputies for the next two decades and was the highest elected African official in the French colonies until after World War II. He advocated racial equality and dignity for Africans, but not an end to French rule. He successfully challenged a colonial decree that severely limited the number of French citizens in the colonies but only by agreeing to recruit Africans into the French army after the outbreak of World War I.

Pan-Africanism

What was the impact of the Italian invasion of Ethiopia on black opinion around the world?

The African challenge to colonial rule was strengthened by international support from Pan-Africanism. This was a movement that grew out of the shared experiences of blacks with European domination, both in Africa and elsewhere, particularly the slave trade, racism, and colonialism. Although Pan-Africanism's primary aim was to unify and strengthen blacks, its leaders disagreed about who their main audience was. Some Pan-Africanists limited their message exclusively to Africans in sub-Saharan Africa, but others appealed more broadly to Africans throughout the continent or to blacks throughout Africa and the **African diaspora,** including the Caribbean and the Americas.

In the late nineteenth and early twentieth centuries, the leading lights of the Pan-Africanist movement were

National Congress of British West Africa—An organization founded in 1920 by African professionals in West Africa to give greater influence to educated Africans in colonial decision-making.

African diaspora—Consists of all the individuals and communities scattered around the world who claim African descent.

▲ A sociologist, W. E. B. Du Bois, was one of the founders of the National Association for the Advancement of Colored People (NAACP) in 1909 and served as the editor of its journal, *Crisis*, for many decades. He was a leading figure in the five Pan-African Congresses from 1900 to 1945.

blacks of the African diaspora such as W. E. B. Du Bois and Marcus Garvey. Born and raised in Massachusetts, Du Bois (1868–1963), an organizer of the **National Association for the Advancement of Colored People** (NAACP) and editor of its magazine, *The Crisis,* was most comfortable in intellectual circles. He asserted the right of blacks to participate in national governments and advocated the eventual self-rule of African countries. He was a prominent force behind a series of pan-African conferences held in Europe and the United States. One of the congresses, with representatives from 15 countries attending, was convened in Paris in 1919. The congress coincided with the Versailles peace conference, and Du Bois urged the gathering to place the former German colonies under an international agency, rather than under the rule of one of the victorious powers, such as Britain.

Du Bois's primary rival in the Pan-Africanist movement was Marcus Garvey (1887–1940), who emigrated from Jamaica to the United States in 1916 and founded the Universal Negro Improvement Association. A charismatic showman, Garvey won a mass following not only in the United States but also in the Caribbean, Great Britain, and many parts of Africa. Rallying his followers around the popular slogan "Africa for the Africans," he called for black self-awareness, economic self-sufficiency, and Africa's immediate independence. He founded the Black Star shipping line to repatriate blacks to Africa. His activities drew the ire of the American government, which jailed him on tax evasion charges and deported him in 1929. He spent the rest of his life in Jamaica and Britain.

An event that galvanized black opinion throughout the world was the Italian invasion of Ethiopia in 1935 (p. 938). As the only African state except Liberia that managed to avoid European colonization, Ethiopia—and its emperor, Haile Selassie (HI-le se-la-SEE)—symbolized Africa's independence and freedom. Ethiopia fell victim, however, to the expansionist designs of the Italian dictator Benito Mussolini, who sought an Italian East African empire and revenge for the Italian defeat at Aduwa in 1896.

Ethiopia's downfall had a stirring impact on black nationalists elsewhere. When Kwame Nkrumah (in-KROO-mah), a nationalist from the Gold Coast, arrived in London and heard of the invasion, he said, "At that moment it was almost as if the whole of London had declared war on me personally.... My nationalism surged to the fore."[2] Groups of blacks in the United States and Britain founded organizations to support the Ethiopian war effort and later began to take on the larger issue of European colonialism.

As World War II was drawing to a close, several hundred black delegates met in Manchester, England, for the **Fifth Pan-African Congress.** Pan-African veteran Du Bois attended, as well as the Afro-Caribbean organizers of the Manchester congress, C. L. R. James, George Padmore, and Ras Makonnen. However, the most influential participants were Africans such as Nkrumah and Kenya's Jomo Kenyatta, who pressed the congress to adopt resolutions demanding immediate freedom in Africa by any means necessary. They resolved that "if the Western world is still determined to rule mankind by force, then Africans, as a last resort, may have to appeal to force in the effort to achieve Freedom, even if force destroys them and the world."[3] Henceforth, the struggle for African independence was to be waged not in European centers of power but in Africa itself as leaders such as Nkrumah and Kenyatta returned home to lead the independence struggles in their countries.

National Association for the Advancement of Colored People (NAACP)—An organization founded in 1909 to improve the legal, educational, economic, and political lives of African Americans.

Fifth Pan-African Congress—A meeting of Pan-Africanists held in Manchester, England, in 1945 that called for the immediate independence of African colonies.

Document

The Color Line Belts the World

An ardent Pan-Africanist who was the driving force behind five Pan-Africanist Congresses held between 1900 and 1945, W. E. B. Du Bois put race at the forefront of his analysis of global politics.

We have a way in America of wanting to be "rid" of problems. It is not so much a desire to reach the best and largest solution as it is to clean the board and start a new game. For instance, most Americans are simply tired and impatient over our most sinister social problem, the Negro. They do not want to solve it, they do not want to understand it, they want to simply be done with it and hear the last of it. Of all possible attitudes this is the most dangerous, because it fails to realize the most significant fact of the opening century, viz: The Negro problem in America is but a local phase of a world problem. "The problem of the twentieth century is the problem of the Color Line." Many smile incredulously at such a proposition, but let us see.

The tendency of the great nations of the day is territorial, political and economic expansion, but in every case this has brought them in contact with darker peoples, so that we have to-day England, France, Holland, Belgium, Italy, Portugal, and the United States in close contact with brown and black peoples, and Russia and Austria in contact with the yellow. The older idea was that the whites would eventually displace the native races and inherit their lands, but this idea has been rudely shaken in the increase of American Negroes, the experience of the English in Africa, India and the West Indies, and the development of South America. The policy of expansion, then, simply means world problems of the Color Line. The question enters into European imperial politics and floods our continents from Alaska to Patagonia.

This is not all. Since 732, when Charles Martel beat back the Saracens at Tours, the white races have had the hegemony of civilization—so far so that "white" and "civilized" have become synonymous in every-day speech, and men have forgotten where civilization started. For the first time in a thousand years a great white nation has measured arms with a colored nation and been found wanting. The Russo-Japanese War has marked an epoch. The magic of the word "white" is already broken, and the Color Line in civilization has been crossed in modern times as it was in the great past. The awakening of the yellow races is certain. That the awakening of the brown and black races will follow in time, no unprejudiced student of history can doubt. Shall the awakening of these sleepy millions be in accordance with, and aided by, the great ideals of white civilization, or in spite of them and against them? This is the problem of the Color Line. Force and Fear have hitherto marked the white attitude toward darker races; shall this continue or be replaced by Freedom and Friendship?

Questions to Consider

1. As you review the events of the last century, do you agree with Du Bois that "the problem of the twentieth century is the problem of the Color Line"?
2. Du Bois asserted that that European civilization has been the dominant civilization since the battle of Tours in 732 C.E. Was he correct?
3. Was the Russo-Japanese War as significant as Du Bois believed?

From W. E. B. Du Bois, "The Color Line Belts the World," *Collier's Weekly,* 20 October 1906, p. 30, in Herbert Aptheker, ed., *Writings by W. E. B. DuBois in Periodicals Edited by Others,* Vol. 1 (Millwood, N. Y.: Kraus-Thomson Organization Limited, 1982), p. 330.

World War II and Its Aftermath

What influences did World War II have on African political thought?

World War II made a dramatic impact on the lives of many Africans whose political consciousness was raised and who began posing questions about the continuation of colonial rule. These changes stimulated new and more aggressive African nationalist movements to challenge colonizers after the war and to begin the process of ending colonial rule.

The people whose lives were most directly affected by the war were African soldiers. When Germany invaded France in May 1940, about 80,000 Africans from French colonies were serving in France. About a quarter lost their lives in the fighting, while many others were captured and sent to German prisoner-of-war camps in which they were treated poorly. The Vichy government then declared that France's colonies were neutral and that no more African soldiers would be recruited. The only African governor, Felix Ebouè (eh-BWAY), was also the lone governor to oppose this decision and support the Free French.

In the British colonies, African soldiers joined the British army in huge numbers and served as combat troops and supply carriers in many theatres of war. British West Africa contributed 167,000 soldiers; British East Africa provided 280,000 men. On the other hand, South Africa's white rulers were wary of exposing blacks to modern weapons and restricted their black units' service to laborers.

African units assisted the Allies in driving the Italians out from Somalia, Eritrea, and Ethiopia; the

Germans from North Africa and southern Europe; and the Japanese from Burma, where African troops adapted well to the tropical environment. Helping to defeat the Japanese army was significant because the Japanese had driven out the British and French from their colonies in Southeast Asia.

The experiences of African servicemen exploded the myth of European invincibility and superiority. They served as equals and interacted with white soldiers, many of whom were uneducated. They saw Europeans living in abject poverty and fighting one another. Many African servicemen, who returned home with expectations of employment and better conditions and treatment, were disillusioned by the lack of change. They took a more critical view of colonial rule and were prepared to confront it by joining nationalist parties. One returned serviceman expressed his feelings in a biting parody of Psalm 23 he submitted to a Gold Coast (Ghana) newspaper:

The European merchant is my shepherd,
And I am in want;
He maketh me to lie down in cocoa farms;
He leadeth me beside the waters of great need;
The general managers and producers frighten me.
Thou preparedst a reduction in my salary
In the presence of my creditors.
Thou anointest my income with taxes;
My expense runs over my income
And I will dwell in a rented house for ever![4]

African politicians also began questioning the motives of Britain and France for involving them in the war. The Allies claimed that they stood for democracy and racial equality in the struggle against fascism and racism. A clause of the Atlantic Charter of 1941 stated that the Allies would support "the right of all peoples to choose the form of government under which they all live."[5] Many Africans interpreted this to mean that steps would be taken to assure their independence after the war, but Churchill let it be known that he was not prepared to preside over the dissolution of the British Empire. On the other hand, President Roosevelt openly opposed imperialism and expressed his concerns for African rights. His position was critical in a postwar world in which the influence of Britain and France was greatly reduced and two nations with no African colonies, the United States and the Soviet Union, became the major global powers.

The political parties that African politicians organized after the war were of a different character than prewar organizations. They were mass parties that had full-time organizers and reached out to urban and rural people. Party leaders closely watched the independence struggle in India and Burma. Some such as Nkrumah in the Gold Coast and Kenneth Kaunda in Northern Rhodesia (Zambia) became disciples of Mohandas Gandhi and his philosophy of nonviolent civil disobedience. African politicians were direct about their goals: they wanted self-rule without delay.

In Tanzania, anticolonial protest after World War II was fuelled by unpopular British agricultural policies that were deeply resented by African peasants. Initially, protests were organized along ethnic and regional lines, but as local groups realized that a national front was necessary, they supported the founding of the Tanganyika African National Union (TANU) in 1955. TANU's leader was Julius Nyerere (nyeh-REH-reh), a Catholic teacher who had attended universities in Scotland and England. TANU effectively used the UN Trusteeship Council established to monitor colonial administration in the former mandated territories of the League of Nations. One case TANU brought to the Trusteeship Council involved 3000 African farmers in the Meru district who were losing their land to white settlers.

Urban Muslim women who joined TANU in the thousands were a key contributor to the party's growing popularity. They were not only attracted to TANU's calls for freedom from colonial rule, but also for its championing of equality in the relations between men and women and ending discrimination based on sex and religion. Many of these women belonged to music and dance groups that provided a multiethnic network for spreading TANU's message and mobilizing people to attend party rallies. They raised money for Nyerere's lobbying at the UN, composed freedom songs, and designed a TANU dress style that British officials tried to ban.

As political organizations developed in each British colony, the pace of political activities in the French colonies was tied to political developments in France. The French Constituent Assembly elected in 1945 contained five African delegates (in the total of 64 from French colonies) out of 586 delegates. The African deputies allied with the left-wing Socialists and Communists, which had a majority in the Assembly, but in 1946, conservative parties won a majority in fresh elections and adopted a new constitution that closed the door on African independence and weakened the provisions for French citizenship in the colonies.

Most African nationalist movements, even when they engaged in confrontational protests against colonial officials, did not turn to armed resistance to bring about change. In colonies such as Algeria, Southern Rhodesia, South Africa, South West Africa, and Kenya in which armed resistance developed, it was usually associated with the presence of European settlers and the expropriation of African land. In Kenya, a small community of about 60,000 white settlers was concentrated in the fertile highlands north of Nairobi, where they seized large tracks of land, especially from the Kikuyu people (see p. 748). White farmers were vocal about protecting their interests and lobbied British officials to put off any political concessions to Africans.

The Kikuyu were split into moderates, who preferred continued negotiations, and radicals, who wanted immediate action, even if it meant taking up arms. The moderates were represented by Jomo Kenyatta, who had returned home after World War II to take up the leadership of the Kenyan African Union. The radicals formed the **Land and Freedom Army** (more popularly known as Mau Mau). Its supporters went through mass oathing ceremonies in which they totally committed themselves to the movement. When their rebellion broke out in 1951, they not only attacked Europeans but also Africans who remained loyal to the British. Mau Mau fighters killed a handful of whites as well as over one thousand African loyalists who were members of the British Homeguard units. Women played prominent roles in Mau Mau not only as fighters, but also as spies, intelligence gatherers, and carriers of supplies and food to guerrillas in the forests.

▲ Langata Detention Camp, Kenya, 1954. As part of its counterinsurgency tactics, the British established detention camps such as Langata to imprison Mau Mau rebels as well as other opponents such as Jomo Kenyatta.

To quell the rebellion, the British launched a ruthless counterinsurgency campaign. They killed 10,000 Kikuyu, forcibly removed 80,000 Kikuyu households from their lands so they would not back the Mau Mau rebels, and detained 100,000 people, including Kenyatta, in jails and concentration camps. The British suspected him of masterminding Mau Mau, although he actually had no links to it. After hostilities ended in 1955, the British kept a state of emergency in effect until 1959 and did not release Kenyatta until 1961. Two years later he became the first president of an independent Kenya.

South Africa had a much larger white population than Kenya, but black South African protest was distinct from other African nationalist movements because it was not challenging a colonial ruler. Britain had pulled out from formal control when the Union of South Africa was established in 1910 and handed over power to Afrikaner and English settlers, who began passing a series of discriminatory laws.

The primary opposition to white rule was the South African Native National Congress, founded in 1912 (and renamed the **African National Congress [ANC]** in 1923) to bring Africans from all black ethnic groups together into one organization. Led by Africans educated in Christian mission schools, the ANC initially had modest goals. African leaders did not immediately call for black majority rule. They wanted blacks to be treated as equals with whites and to remove discriminatory laws. They concluded that waging armed struggle was futile, and they sought change through nonviolent constitutional means such as signing petitions, making representations to the government, and even sending delegations to the British government to pressure the South African government to change legislation. The British government, however, was deaf to all their appeals.

The ANC's first president was a Congregational minister named John Dube (1871–1946), who, while receiving his education at Oberlin College in the United States, became a disciple of the American educator Booker T. Washington and his philosophy of industrial education for advancing blacks. After returning to Natal, Dube founded his own school, Ohlange Institute, modeled on Washington's Tuskegee Institute. He also started up a Zulu/English language newspaper.

Women were not represented in the ANC's leadership, but there were prominent women activists. One was Charlotte Maxeke (1874–1939), who also had studied at Ohio's Wilberforce College in the 1890s, where she was a student of W. E. B. Du Bois. On her return to South Africa, she and her husband founded a high school, Wilberforce Institute, sponsored by the African Methodist Episcopal Church. She had an avid interest in social welfare issues and, as President of the Bantu Women's League, she led a campaign against pass laws.

With only a few thousand members, the ANC's challenge to white rule was restrained until World War II, when tens of thousands of Africans, who streamed

---

Land and Freedom Army—More popularly known as Mau Mau, this army was established by Kikuyu radicals in Kenya to attack white settlers and British colonial officials.

African National Congress (ANC)—A political organization founded in 1912 in South Africa to promote equal rights for black people and to abolish discriminatory laws and segregation.

Document

Pass Laws and African Women in South Africa

A key way in which the white minority maintained its dominance in South Africa was through pass laws that controlled where adult Africans could live, seek work, and move in white areas. In 1912, after African women in the Orange Free State province protested against these laws by organizing demonstrations and writing petitions, the government backed down and rarely enforced these laws against women. In January 1956, however, the government announced that African women had to join men and carry passes. This decision provoked tremendous resistance from black women. However, the government continued to enforce the law for another three decades.

Petition of the Native and Coloured Women of the Province of the Orange Free State

11 March, 1912

To the Right Honourable General Louis Botha, PC., M.L.A., Prime Minister of the Union of South Africa, CAPE TOWN,

Sir,

The petition of the undersigned humbly showeth:–

2. That your petitioners, as inhabitants of the said Province, are under a burden of having to carry Residential Passes in terms of Section 2 of Law 8 of 1893 (Orange Free State Statutes).

3. That this law is a source of grievance to your petitioners in that:–

(a) It renders them liable to interference by any policeman at any time, and in that way deprives them of that liberty enjoyed by their women-folk in other Provinces.

(b) It has a barbarous tendency of ignoring the consequences of marriage in respect of natives, especially the right of parents to control their children, a right which parents ought to exercise without interference from outside, and the effect of its operation upon the minds of our children is that it inculcates upon them the idea that as soon as they become liable to comply with the requirements of the law, their age of majority also commences, and, can, therefore, act independently of their parents.

(c) It is an effective means of enforcing labour and throws to pieces every element of respect to which they are entitled; and for this reason it has no claim to recognition as a just, progressive and protective law, necessary for their elevation in the scale of civilization; moreover it does not improve their social status....

Wherefore your petitioners humbly pray that the Right Honourable the Prime Minister may be pleased:–

1. To grant them immediate relief from this burdensome law by introducing a Bill in Parliament repealing it....

Lilian Ngoyi, Presidential Address to the African National Congress Women's League, Transvaal, November 1956.

... Hardly any other South Africa Law has caused so much suffering and hardship to Africans as the pass laws. Hardly any other measure has created so much suffering and racial friction and hostility between black and white. Any policeman may at any time demand to see your pass and failure to produce it for any reason means imprisonment or a fine. It makes it permissible to violate the sanctity and privacy of our homes. An African, sleeping peacefully in his house, may be woken up at night asked to produce one and failure to do so may lead to his arrest and imprisonment even though he has committed no crime whatsoever....

The pass law is the basis and cornerstone of the system of oppression and exploitation in this country. It is a device to ensure cheap labour for the mines and the farms. It is a badge of slavery in terms whereof all sorts of insults and humiliation may be committed on Africans by members of the ruling class. It is because of these reasons that the Congress has always regarded the pass laws as the principal target of the struggle for freedom.... *Only direct mass action will deter the Government and stop it from proceeding with its cruel laws*.... STRIJDOM, STOP AND THINK FOR YOU HAVE AROUSED THE WRATH OF THE WOMEN OF SOUTH AFRICA and that wrath might put you and your evil deeds out of action sooner than you expect.

Questions to Consider

1. What do we learn from these documents about the impact of passes on African women and African family life?
2. Compare the language and tone of the petition of 1913 and Lilian Ngoyi's speech 40 years later. In both cases, what do they tell you about the state and style of black protest at that time and African attitudes toward the white government?

From M. J. Daymond et al., eds., *Women Writing Africa: The Southern Region* (Witwatersrand University Press, 2003), pp. 159–161 and 242–243.

into the urban centers like Johannesburg to take up jobs, became involved in protests over housing shortages, the high costs of transportation, and pass laws. Sensing this mood of militancy, a younger generation of politicians formed a Youth League within the ANC in 1944 to push their elders to challenge white rule more aggressively. The Youth League's first president was Anton Lembede, a lawyer. He died in 1947, but other Youth Leaguers such as Nelson Mandela, Walter Sisulu, and Oliver Tambo continued to play important roles as resistance leaders for over a half century.

Opposing the ANC was a narrow form of nationalism advocated by many Afrikaners. The ANC aimed at bringing together Africans from many different ethnic groups in a common body, whereas Afrikaner nationalists focused exclusively on unifying and mobilizing

▲ A seamstress, Lilian Ngoyi (1911–1980) was an activist in the African National Congress (ANC) and the Federation of South African Women. As president of the ANC Women's League, she led a procession of 20,000 women on August 9, 1956, to the prime minister's building in Pretoria to protest the rule requiring that African women had to carry passes.

Afrikaners. In 1948, the Afrikaner-dominated National Party won the white election and began implementing the rigid system of racial separation known as **apartheid.** ANC Youth Leaguers responded by forcing a change of ANC leadership in 1949 and pressing the movement to adopt a Program of Action that advocated direct action such as strikes, boycotts, and civil disobedience. During the 1950s, as the ANC engaged in mass protests against apartheid laws, its membership swelled to over 100,000.

Decolonization

What were two of the most important factors in bringing about decolonization?

European colonizers fully expected their rule in the Middle East, North Africa, and sub-Saharan Africa to extend for the rest of the twentieth century, but events of World War II set off forces that accelerated the Arab and African nationalist challenges to colonial rule and brought freedom much sooner than expected.

apartheid—An Afrikaans word meaning "separateness," it was the policy of rigid racial segregation introduced by the National party in South Africa after 1948.

The Middle East and North Africa

Following the collapse of the Ottoman Empire, nation-states emerged across the Middle East and North Africa. Divergent political movements struggled to control these new states and their small, often badly strained economies. The discovery of oil—in Iraq, Iran, the Gulf States, and in regions of North Africa—was to transform the economic prospects of these regions but also lead to socio-economic divisions across the region. Oil, the foundation of Israel, and other factors would also lead to sustained Western intervention in regional affairs from this point forward.

In Iran, Mohammad Mosaddeq (MOS-ad-dek; d. 1967) nationalized oil, introduced liberal reforms to government, and challenged the shah so successfully that the ruler was forced to flee. Mosaddeq later was overthrown by a CIA-sponsored military coup in 1954. In Tunisia, Habib Bourguiba (ha-BEEB bor-GHEE-ba) and, in Egypt, Gamal Abdel Nasser, both secular-minded leaders, led successful national movements.

Although Algeria was an integral part of France and sent representatives to the French National Assembly, resentment against foreign control and French settlers in Algeria grew among the Muslim majority. Emboldened by the Vietnamese defeat of the French at Dienbienphu in 1954 (p. 1066), the National Liberation Front (*Front de libération nationale* or FLN) launched a rebellion against the French the same year. The fighting took its toll on both the French and Algerians, as 250,000 Algerians and 25,000 French soldiers died in 8 years of savage warfare. The war also brought down the French Fourth Republic, allowing Charles de Gaulle to assume national leadership, to negotiate an end to the conflict, and to grant Algeria independence in 1962. Most of the 2 million French residents of Algeria left the scarred and battered country for France.

The pressure of the two superpowers also hastened the end of colonization. A rare instance of the United States and the USSR working together came in the context of the Suez Crisis of 1956. The French and the English, as well as the Israelis, were eager to remove the charismatic Egyptian leader Gamal Abdel Nasser. The French were furious with him for his work in undermining their authority in North Africa. The British wanted to regain their holdings in the Suez Canal—which Nasser had nationalized—and enhance their presence in the region. The Israelis welcomed the weakening of a major Arab leader and hoped to gain the Sinai peninsula. In November 1956, without first consulting the United States, the countries attacked and defeated Egypt. The United States and the Soviet Union, working through the United Nations, forced the 3 countries to withdraw from Egypt. This was one instance, among many, in which the 2 global powers would exert influence over developments in the Middle East.

Sub-Saharan Africa

The British colony of Gold Coast set the pace for independence in sub-Saharan Africa. The British believed that the best approach for their colonies was to groom Africans for a gradual takeover of government. They introduced a constitution in 1945 that allowed for a legislative council with an African majority that was not directly elected. Several years later, a coalition of lawyers, teachers, and businessmen, many with ties to chiefs, formed the United Gold Coast Convention (UGCC) to counter the new constitution. UGCC leaders selected the recently returned Kwame Nkrumah as its organizing secretary, but he proved too radical for both the UGCC and British officials.

After Nkrumah formed a rival party, the Convention People's party (CPP), in 1949, he set out to mobilize a mass following. When his "Positive Action" campaign sparked off widespread protests, he was jailed. After his party overwhelmingly won elections in 1951 for the legislative council, the British recognized the inevitable and released Nkrumah and appointed him leader of government business. After winning several more elections, Nkrumah's party called for independence, which the British granted in 1957. The former Gold Coast colony became the new nation of Ghana.

Ghana's route to independence set a pattern for the freedom struggle in many other colonies throughout the continent. African nationalist parties won over mass followings and challenged colonial rulers, who initially resisted concessions but finally agreed to transfer power through negotiations.

However, France, Belgium, and especially Portugal were reluctant to follow Britain's lead. They still clung to the belief that their African subjects were better off under colonial rule. In 1958, President Charles de Gaulle established the French Community, in which France maintained control over economic development and the external and military affairs of its colonies. De Gaulle was so confident that France's African territories preferred to stay under French rule that he offered them a choice in a referendum of joining a French-controlled federation or independence.

▶ A passionate advocate of African unity, Kwame Nkrumah was the leader of Ghana's drive for independence from Great Britain and served as its first president from 1957 until his overthrow by the military in 1966.

The only French colony to defy de Gaulle was Guinea, where a trade union leader, Sekou Touré (SAY-koo TOO-ray), mobilized his followers to vote against continued French rule. When Guinea was granted immediate independence in 1958, the French punitively pulled out their civil servants and equipment (even ripping out telephones) and refused to offer any economic assistance. However, Guinea's independence was a turning point, and 13 other French colonies in Africa followed suit in 1960. Over the next decade, most of the other colonies gained their freedom. The exceptions were the Portuguese colonies and the white-ruled states of Rhodesia and South Africa, who resisted any transfer of power to the African majority. Independence in those territories would take much longer and would require African nationalist movements to take up arms to force change (see Chapter 33).

Conclusion

From World War I to the years after World War II, imperialism went on the defensive before the rise of nationalism in the Middle East and Africa. Independence movements against European dominance took root and flourished.

In the Islamic heartlands, one traditional empire, Qajar Iran, maintained its territorial integrity but witnessed the establishment of a new dynasty and a program of modernizing reforms. The other, the Ottoman Empire, was broken up in the aftermath of the war and divided among independent states and mandates controlled by Britain and France. Arab nationalists bitterly contested European control in the mandated areas, while Zionists, aspiring to a Jewish homeland, challenged both the British and the indigenous Arab populace for control of Palestine. The mandates in the Arab territories stood in stark contrast to the independent states of Arabia and Turkey, the latter redeemed by Mustafa Kemal Atatürk from the ruins of the Ottoman Empire. In the background of these political struggles, a new economic factor, oil, emerged as a resource that would later bring untold riches to some parts of the Middle East. But oil would not become a primary factor in global politics until after World War II.

African nationalists were not dealing with the breakup of existing empires but with challenging the European imperial presence. They sought to replace colonial rule with self-government and to bring about the political and cultural resurgence of a people whose way of life was challenged by Western imperialism. Their political activity took place at the village, regional, national and international levels, where the pan-African movement drew supporters from the black diaspora in North America, the Caribbean, and Europe. World War II, like World War I, had a dramatic impact on Africa as well as France and Britain, which came out of the war with less influence in the world. The efforts of nationalist movements gained momentum after the war and forced the French and British to consider granting independence to their colonies much sooner than they planned. During the 1950s and 1960s, most British and French colonies won their independence, thus setting the stage for the independence of the rest of Africa in the last decades of the twentieth century.

Suggestions for Web Browsing

You can obtain more information about topics included in this chapter at the websites listed below. See also the companion website that accompanies this text, http://www.ablongman.com/brummett, which contains an online study guide and additional resources.

Internet Islamic History Sourcebook: The Islamic World, 1918–1945
http://www.fordham.edu/halsall/islam/islamsbook.html#Islamic%20Nationalism
Online source for links about the history of the Middle East, 1918–1945.

Internet African History Sourcebook: The Fight for Independence
http://www.fordham.edu/halsall/africa/africasbook.html#
Online source of links about the African struggle for independence; includes sources such as the Manifesto of the Second Pan African Congress, 1922.

Historical Documents Archive African National Congress
http://www.anc.org.za/ancdocs/history/
This archive contains hundreds of documents and biographical profiles relating to the history of the African National Congress, founded in 1912 to protest segregation and white rule in South Africa.

Literature and Film

For an interesting combination of fiction and memoirs on Arab society see Siham Tergeman, *Daughter of Damascus* (University of Texas Press, 1994), and Hanna Mina, *Fragments of Memory: A Story of a Syrian Family* (University of Texas Press, 1993), an autobiographical novel, both on Syria; see also Fadia Faqir, *Pillars of Salt* (Interlink, 1997), set in Jordan. Driss Chraibi's *Mother Comes of Age* (Three Continents Press, 1994) is a wonderful autobiographical novel about a middle-aged Moroccan woman coming to terms with technological and ideological change in the World War II era. Nobel laureate Naguib Mahfouz writes of Egypt under British occupation and its struggle for independence in *Palace Walk* (Doubleday, 1990) and *Midaq Alley* (Doubleday, 1975). Abdel Rahman al-Sharqawi's *Egyptian Earth* (Saqi, 1990) is a tale of peasant life and the dilemmas of war during the 1973 Arab-Israeli war.

Two powerful African novels set in the years after World War II are Ousmane Sembene's *God's Bits of Wood* (Anchor Books, 1970), which deals with an African labor strike in West Africa, and Ngugi wa' Thiongo's *Grain of Wheat,* which focuses on the Mau Mau Rebellion in Kenya. Nelson Mandela's autobiography, *Long Walk to Freedom* (Little Brown, 1994) covers his distinguished political life in South Africa.

The Battle of Algiers (1965; Stella Productions), directed by Gillo Pontecorvo, is a feature film on Algeria's struggle for independence. *Ousmane Sembene's Camp de Thiaroye* (1988; New Yorker Films) is a fictionalized account of an actual event, the rebellion of Senegalese soldiers against the French in a camp in Senegal. *Black Man's Land,* vol. 2 (1991; Bellwether Group) is a documentary on the Mau Mau Rebellion.

Suggestions for Reading

A lucid and balanced survey of the modern Middle East is William Cleveland, *A History of the Modern Middle East* (Westview, 2000). A study of the nature of change in the Islamic world is John Voll, *Islam: Continuity and Change in the Modern World,* 2nd ed. (Syracuse, 1994). For a good introduction on the mandate for Palestine, see Charles D. Smith, *Palestine and the Arab Israeli Conflict,* 4th ed. (St. Martin's Press, 2000). On the years of World War I and the British role, see the account by David Fromkin, *A Peace to End All Peace* (Avon Books, 1988). On the history of the Jewish people, see Raymond Scheindlin, *A Short History of the Jewish People* (Oxford University Press, 1998). Ann M. Lesch, *Arab Politics in Palestine* (Cornell University Press, 1979), traces the rise of Arab nationalism in Palestine.

On the emergence of Turkey and of Mustafa Kemal Atatürk, see Feroz Ahmad, *The Making of Modern Turkey* (Routledge, 1993). On Iran in this era, see Ervand Abrahamian, *Iran Between Two Revolutions* (Princeton University Press, 1982). For a nice summary on Egypt, see Afaf Lutfi al-Sayyid Marsot, *A Short History of Modern Egypt* (Cambridge University Press, 1986). For the Iraq mandate, see Peter Sluglett, *Britain in Iraq, 1914–1932* (Ithaca Press, 1976).

African protest and nationalist movement during the colonial era are examined in the series *UNESCO General History of Africa,* Vols. 7 and 8 (University of California Press, 1985). Black protest against white rule in South Africa is examined in Vols. 1 and 2 of Thomas Karis and Gwendolen M. Carter, *From Protest to Challenge: A Documentary History of African Politics in South Africa, 1882–1964* (Hoover Institution Press, 1971). The Mau Mau Rebellion is treated in David Throup, *Economic and Social Origins of Mau Mau, 1945–1953* (Ohio University Press, 1988). The Pan-Africanist movement is assessed in Imanuel Geiss, *The Pan-African Movement* (Methuen, 1974), and the end to colonial rule is examined in David Birmingham, *Decolonization of Africa* (Ohio University Press, 1995).

CHAPTER 31

World War II

Origins and Consequences, 1919–1946

Outline

Features

◀ Although the goals of war are usually political and/or economic, they ultimately come down to human beings killing other human beings, often with great brutality. Here, Japanese soldiers perform bayonet drills on Chinese prisoners in Nanjing, late 1937 or early 1938. The Japanese were the first to unleash the aggression that culminated in World War II, a conflict that globally killed more than 48 million people.

THE "BIG FOUR," the victorious Allied states, went their separate ways after World War I. The United States refused participation in most postwar diplomatic activities but remained active in international business. Great Britain withdrew from continental Europe and looked after its own commonwealth and empire. Italy plunged into 5 years of governmental failure, leading to Mussolini's takeover. France, gravely wounded by the war, was left holding the responsibility for overseeing democratic interests in Europe.

In the first decade after the war, a few statesmen with global vision made serious attempts to control conflict through international organizations and treaties limiting arms and outlawing war. The economic disasters of the Wall Street crash and the Great Depression at the end of the 1920s, however, forced the democracies to look inward. At the same time, aggressive nations took advantage of the democracies' retreat to advance their interests: Japan invaded Manchuria and, later, China and Southeast Asia; Italy attacked Ethiopia, and Germany expanded its influence in central Europe. Burdened by domestic concerns and the memories of the losses in World War I, the representatives of the democracies tried unsuccessfully to reason with the militarists. World War II, which started in July 1937 in Asia, reached Europe in 1939.

From 1937 to 1945, the world experienced slaughter and destruction on an unprecedented scale. New and horrible technologies ravaged the globe as large bombers carried the war to civilians hundreds of miles behind what used to be known as the "front line" in Europe and Asia. While fighting his enemies, Hitler made use of industrial technology to try to exterminate the Jews in a genocide that has come to be known as the Holocaust. The Pacific theater saw all means of combat—from hand-to-hand fighting to the use of nuclear bombs.

The Troubled Calm: The West in the 1920s

Why were the European democracies unable to maintain the advantage they had gained in winning World War I?

The aftershocks of World War I overwhelmed the interwar period. The horror, expense, and exhaustion of the tragedy haunted losers and winners alike. Many of the younger generation had died, and political leadership fell to either the old or the untried. It was in this uncertain environment that the League of Nations began its work.

The League of Nations

The League's record from 1919 to 1929 was modest, neither one of total failure nor one of great triumph. Such threats to peace as disputes between Sweden and Finland and between Britain and Turkey were resolved. When a major power defied the League, however, as in the case of Italy's quarrel with Greece over Corfu, the organization could do nothing. The refusal of the United States, the world's strongest democracy, to join the League weakened its peacekeeping possibilities.

Through no fault of the League's, little progress was made in the field of disarmament; however, the League had a distinguished list of accomplishments in other areas. It supervised the exchange and repatriation of prisoners of war and saved thousands of refugees from starvation. It helped Austria, Bulgaria, and Hungary secure badly needed loans. The League also provided valuable services in administering the region of the Saar Basin and the Free City of Danzig. It investigated the existence of slavery in certain parts of the world, sought to stanch traffic in dangerous drugs, and stood ready to offer assistance when disasters brought suffering and destruction.

In the intellectual and cultural realm, the League published books and periodicals dealing with national and international problems of all kinds, and from its own radio station it broadcast important information, particularly in the field of health. Unfortunately, the League's excellent record in these areas has been obscured by its failure to maintain a lasting peace.

The French Quest for Security

Because the United States chose to play a limited role in international affairs and Great Britain returned to its traditional focus on the empire and the Commonwealth, France assumed the leadership of postwar Europe. In 1919, the French pursued a simple but difficult foreign policy goal: absolute security. Since the Napoleonic grandeur a century earlier, the French had seen their power and authority diminish while German economic and military strength had increased. Twice in 50 years, Germany had invaded France, with humiliating and horrendous results.

France spent much of the postwar decade trying to guarantee its own safety by keeping Germany weak. In the first 5 years after the armistice, the French wanted to impose maximum financial penalties on the Germans. In 1923, assisted by the Belgians, they occupied the Ruhr region in a move that had immense short- and long-range implications (see Chapter 28). Some historians have seen in this act the first step toward World War II, because it hardened the German desire for revenge. Even though the Dawes Plan eased the situation, the French attitude divided the former Allies and provided ammunition to German ultranationalists.

The rift between the French and the Germans was papered over in Locarno, Switzerland, in 1925. In the Locarno Pact, Germany, Great Britain, France, and Italy agreed to guarantee the existing frontiers along the Rhine, to establish a demilitarized zone 30 miles deep along the east bank of the Rhine, and to refrain from attacking one another. The problems along France's eastern frontier would be dealt with by inter-

Chronology

1920	1930	1935		1940	1945
1922 Germany and the USSR conclude Rapallo Pact	1931 Japan invades Manchuria	1936 Germany occupies the Rhineland; Hitler and Mussolini form the Rome-Berlin Axis; Germany and Japan sign Anti-Comintern Pact 1936–1939 Spanish civil war; Spanish Republic falls; Franco becomes dictator	1937 Japan invades China; World War II begins in Asia 1938 *Anschluss* with Austria; Munich Pact 1939 Germany and Russia sign nonaggression pact; Germany invades Poland; World War II begins in Europe	1940 France falls to the Axis 1941 Lend-Lease Act; Atlantic Charter; Japan attacks Pearl Harbor; United States enters war 1943 Russians defeat Germans at Stalingrad	1945 Germany surrenders; United States drops atomic bombs on Hiroshima and Nagasaki; Japan surrenders

Document

Erich Maria Remarque, *The Road Back*

Erich Maria Remarque, who wrote so eloquently of the horrors of war in *All Quiet on the Western Front,* compellingly expressed the despair and frustration of German veterans in *The Road Back.* In the discussion of the inflation and the bitterness of his "brother," he captures the mood that helped Hitler gain power.

Demonstrations in the streets have been called for this afternoon. Prices have been soaring everywhere for months past, and the poverty is greater even than it was during the war. Wages are insufficient to buy the bare necessities of life, and even though one may have the money it is often impossible to buy anything with it. But ever more and more gin palaces and dance halls go up, and ever more and more blatant is the profiteering and swindling.

Scattered groups of workers on strike march through the streets. Now and again there is a disturbance. A rumour is going about that troops have been concentrated at the barracks. But there is no sign of it as yet.

Here and there one hears cries and counter-cries. Somebody is haranguing at a street corner. Then suddenly everywhere is silence.

A procession of men in the faded uniforms of the front-line trenches is moving slowly toward us.

It was formed up by sections, marching in fours. Big white placards are carried before: Where is the Fatherland's gratitude?—The War Cripples are starving.

It was no good to go on assuming that a common basis for all the different groups and classes in Germany could be found. The break between them became daily wider and more irreparable. The plebiscite of the Right "against the Young Plan and the war-guilt lie" proved just as unsuccessful as those arranged in former years by the Left, but the poison of the defamatory agitation remained in the body of the community, and we watched its effects with anxiety.

In my own family the political antagonism was growing past endurance. In October Fritz had finished his apprenticeship in an old-established export house, at the precise moment when the firm went bankrupt—a minor incident compared with such events as the breakdown of the Frankfurt General Insurance Company and the Civil Servants' Bank or the enforced reorganization and amalgamation of the Deutsche Bank and the Disconto-Gesellschaft, which all happened in the course of the year and dangerously damaged the whole economic life of Germany. Yet for my brother the bankruptcy of his firm overshadowed all other happenings, since it meant that he lost his job. His three years' training was in vain—there was not a single export firm which was not forced to dismiss as many of its employees as possible.

"Yes, that's just it—millions! If it isn't my fault, whose fault is it? I tell you—your friends, the French, the English, the Americans, all those damnable nations who inflict on us one dishonorable penalty after the other—they are to blame for all this. Before the war the whole world bought German goods. My firm exported to Africa, to the German colonies. Hundreds of thousands we turned over every year. But they have robbed us of our colonies, of all our foreign markets. They have stolen the coal mines in the Saar and in Upper Silesia, they squeeze millions of marks out of our bleeding country. We'll never rise again unless we free ourselves by another war."

"Don't be foolish, Fritz. Things are bad in the whole world."

"I don't care about the world, I care only about Germany, which you and your pacifists have delivered into the hands of our enemies. I despise you, you are not worthy to call yourself a German."

Questions to Consider

1. What were some of the most important elements in the creation of German anger after World War I?
2. Whom does Fritz blame for his situation? Do you agree?
3. In Fritz's point of view, after his argument with the author, who is worthy to call himself German?

From Erich Maria Remarque, *The Road Back.*

national guarantee (although the British dominions stated their disagreement) and U.S. money. Germany received, and accepted, an invitation to join the League of Nations, a symbolic act that seemed to indicate its return to the international community. Still, the Locarno Pact addressed only Germany's western frontier and left unresolved the controversial issues of the territories of the newly formed and contentious nations of Eastern Europe.

Another well-meaning but ultimately ineffectual agreement was the **Kellogg-Briand Pact** (1928), developed by U.S. Secretary of State Frank Kellogg and French Foreign Minister Aristide Briand. This pact,

Kellogg-Briand Pact—An international treaty named after American Secretary of State Frank Kellogg and French Foreign Minister Aristide Briand that outlawed war. Sixty-two nations signed the treaty, which had little effect because there were no enforcement provisions.

eventually signed by 62 nations, outlawed war as an instrument of national policy but omitted provisions to enforce the agreement.

Soviet and German Cooperation

The Soviet Union and Germany, the two diplomatic outcasts of the 1920s, quickly forged a working relationship that was useful to both of them. The USSR had isolated itself by signing the **Treaty of Brest-Litovsk,** nationalizing foreign property, and repudiating foreign debts as well as by espousing its communist ideology internationally. Probably the greatest barrier was the ideological one, as expressed through the activities of the **Third Communist International,** or Comintern. That body, organized in 1919, was dedicated to the overthrow of capitalism throughout the world.

In the 1920s, the Comintern spread communist propaganda, established Communist parties, and infiltrated labor unions and other working-class groups throughout the world. Even after Lenin had given up hope for an immediate world revolution and started to normalize relations with the West, the Comintern encouraged radicals who had broken off from moderate socialist groups to organize Communist parties. Communists of all countries became members of the Comintern, meeting in congresses held in Moscow and setting up committees to coordinate their activities. Communist parties were different from other national political groups because they owed their allegiance to an international organization rather than to the nations in which they resided.

By 1922, the Soviet Union was pursuing a two-pronged foreign policy. One approach used the Communist parties abroad to achieve ideological goals, as in China, where the Communists worked together with Jiang Jieshi's Nationalists until 1927, when they were forced to develop an independent movement (see Chapter 29). The other approach worked through normal international channels for traditional economic and diplomatic goals, generally in Europe.

From the time Lenin left Switzerland to return to Petrograd with Berlin's assistance, the Soviet Union enjoyed a mutually advantageous relationship with Germany. At the beginning of the 1920s, the two nations ratified secret agreements allowing for joint military training enterprises. Their first major open diplomatic contact came at Rapallo, Italy, in 1922, where they renounced the concept of reparations. In the Rapallo Pact, the Germans and Russians agreed to cooperate in a number of areas.

Treaty of Brest-Litovsk—The treaty between the USSR and Germany signed in March 1918 in which peace was declared between the two countries and the USSR gave up more than a million square miles of land and more than 60 million people.

Third Communist International—The Comintern, organized in 1919, was an organization dedicated to the overthrow of capitalism.

	Soviet-German Relations, 1917–1939
1917	Germans financially support Bolsheviks
1918	Treaty of Brest-Litovsk
1919–1922	Weimar-Soviet secret joint military agreements
1922	Rapallo Pact formalizes German-Russian cooperation
1926	Rapallo Pact extended 5 years
1933–1937	Stalin unsuccessfully advocates common front against Germany
1933–1937	Hitler speaks out against USSR, signs Anti-Comintern Pact
1938–1939	Renewed secret negotiations between Moscow and Berlin
1939	USSR-German nonaggression pact

Epoch of the Aggressors

Why did Great Britain, France, and the United States not take a more vigorous stand against Japanese, Italian, and German aggression before 1939?

The awful toll taken by World War I convinced the democracies that never again should humanity have to endure such a tragedy. Multilateral efforts, especially the League of Nations, were made to prevent the kinds of alliances that were blamed for the inevitability of that war. By the mid-1930s, however, governments in Tokyo, Rome, and Berlin viewed multilateralism as weak and ineffective and saw the era as opportune for taking unilateral approaches to expansionism.

Japan Invades Manchuria, 1931

Throughout the 1920s, Japan's foreign policy was characterized by multilateral agreements and treaties. The Washington Conference system, in addition to its guarantee of Chinese sovereignty (see Chapter 29), established a balance of naval power among England, the United States, and Japan and tied Japan diplomatically to the Western democracies. At the same time, close economic ties with those countries aided trade and economic growth. When, at the end of the 1920s, rogue members of the Japanese military stationed along the Japanese-owned railroad in Manchuria tried to implement their own foreign policy in opposition to what they called Tokyo's "weak-kneed" cooperation with the West, they failed to gain much support in Japan.

But the Great Depression discredited global multilateralism in the eyes of many in Japan, making the call for a Japanese-dominated economic sphere in northeast Asia and a unilateral approach to national security increasingly attractive in the 1930s. When another group of Japanese soldiers set off a bomb on the South Manchurian Railroad on September 18, 1931, Tokyo was thrust into conflict in Manchuria, triggering military action against Nationalist Chinese forces there. A Japanese puppet state was established in Manchuria in 1932. China appealed to the League of Nations, which condemned the aggression, but Japan's withdrawal from the League in 1933 indicated the limits of its ability to guarantee world peace. Some historians consider this the beginning of what they call "Japan's 15-year war."

In 1930, the Washington Conference system had taken a hit when the Japanese prime minister was assassinated for trying to continue the cooperative policy of reductions in naval buildup after the multilateral London Conference, the follow-up to the Washington Conference. Although Japan did not have the funds to begin building up its navy in the early 1930s, by the middle of the decade, the government felt released from the arms limitations negotiated in 1922 at Washington and 1930 at London.

There was, however, no unified point of view among Japan's leaders. Many government leaders were not interested in escalating continental expansion by military means, although they were firmly committed to increasing Japanese economic penetration of China in the 1920s and 1930s.

One important link among Japanese, even those who wanted to maintain multilateral ties, was an increasing belief that Japan would have to rely on its own resources for national security. And that, in turn, led to an acceptance, at first grudging and later more enthusiastic, of Japanese military expansionism.

The Chinese Nationalists responded to Japan's creation of the Manchurian puppet state by boycotts of Japanese goods. Shanghai, which had large settlements controlled by foreign forces, most notably England but also Japan and other treaty powers, staged a particularly effective boycott in 1932. The local Japanese commandant demanded an end to the boycott, and a small skirmish broke out between Chinese and Japanese troops. The commandant took this as an insult and retaliated by bombing Chinese troops in a congested urban area. Though the Tokyo government objected to these actions and did not escalate military actions around Shanghai at that time, the United States and England expressed shock and Chinese Nationalists became determined to drive the Japanese out of Shanghai.

	Aggression and Democratic Nonresponse, 1931–1938
1931	Japanese invade Manchuria
1932	Japanese attack Shanghai
1934–1935	Italians invade Ethiopia
1935	Remilitarization of the Rhineland by Germany
1936	Spanish General Francisco Franco rebels against the government of republican Spain
1937	Japanese begin full-scale war in China
1938	German *Anschluss* with Austria; dismemberment of Czechoslovakia in the wake of the Munich Accords

At the same time, in North China, Japanese forces undertook much more aggressive action. The same forces based in Manchuria who had engineered the Manchurian Incident in 1931 decided they needed more security on the border with North China. They began a gradual but steady encroachment on Chinese territory in 1933. The Chinese Nationalist government at Nanjing, more concerned about consolidating its political control in China than about Japanese actions in the north, signed an agreement called the Tanggu (TAHNG-goo) truce establishing a demilitarized zone around Beijing and extending Japanese control to the Great Wall in May 1933. By 1935, Japanese forces in North China, hoping to create a buffer zone between the Nationalists and the Japanese state in Manchuria, pushed further into North China. Jiang Jieshi (jee-AHNG jee-eh-SHI), leader of the Nationalists, was preoccupied with the Communists, and did little to oppose the Japanese forces at first (see Chapters 28 and 29). Following the December 1936 truce between the Communists and Nationalists, China presented a united front. Jiang now joined the struggle against Japan.

In Japan, right-wing young officers had attempted to overthrow the Japanese government, which they viewed as too capitalistic, too liberal, too individualistic, and too modern. They staged a massive coup on February 26, 1936. Though these rebels were cut down by the emperor's command that they return to their barracks, as well as by the big guns of naval warships in Tokyo Bay trained on their positions, the real loser was the civilian government. After 1936, either military

▲ An abandoned Chinese baby cries out during the Japanese attack on Nanjing.

officers or defense-oriented civilians took over the reins of government in Tokyo. In June 1937, one of those civilians, Prince Konoe Fumimaro (koh-NOH-eh fu-mee-MAH-roh), became prime minister. When a small skirmish between Japanese and Chinese soldiers at Marco Polo Bridge in North China broke out on July 7, 1937, Konoe authorized full-scale war in August. Chinese bombers hit the Japanese settlement in Shanghai, and Japanese commanders swiftly retaliated, moving down the Yangzi River and reaching Nanjing by December 1937. The Japanese soldiers committed brutal carnage in Nanjing in the winter of 1937–1938 (see Chapters 28 and 29 for more about the Rape of Nanjing). Interestingly, the generals who had been the architects of the war in Manchuria were dismayed over the war in China, believing that Japan's national interests were best served by defending Korea, Manchuria, and North China against the Soviets. But Konoe did not agree. He declared that Japan would never negotiate with Jiang and the Nationalist Chinese government, and in November 1938, he declared a "New Order in East Asia."

The New Order's objectives were to expel Western interests, defined as "Anglo-American imperialism," from East Asia and establish a self-sufficient economic bloc including Japan, Manchuria, and China, "have-not" nations that had been excluded from their place in the world by the West. Three years later, Konoe attempted to give concrete form to the "New Order" policy by proclaiming a **"Greater East Asia Co-Prosperity Sphere,"** a Japanese-dominated economic zone from which Japan could procure raw materials and markets for its industry and expanding population as well as for production of munitions. The "New Order in East Asia" had its domestic counterpart in policies to promote "national spiritual mobilization," an effort to get people to conserve energy and food and to reject decadent and wasteful habits like permanent waves and fancy kimonos; the obliteration of independent unions, women's groups, and political parties and their replacement with government-run groups; and rationing and controls on scarce commodities.

As for foreign policy, Japan had few friends. The United States ended its long-time commercial treaty with Japan in 1939 to protest Japan's actions in China, setting the stage for U.S. embargoes first of iron and steel in the summer of 1940 and then of oil in the summer of 1941, following Japan's entry into southern Vietnam (with the assent of the Vichy French government). In 1936, Japan had signed its first treaty with Nazi Germany, the Anti-Comintern Pact. This was followed by a brief war against the Soviets in 1939; the **Tripartite Pact** (with Germany and Italy) against the United States in September 1940; and a neutrality pact with the Soviets in April 1941. The German invasion of the Soviet Union did more to relieve Japan of its fear of the Russians than the neutrality pact, and Japan then moved troops into southern Vietnam in preparation for operations against the Dutch East Indies (Indonesia). Dependent on U.S. oil, Japan had two options in the summer of 1941—give in to America's conditions for negotiating a return of oil shipments, which meant abandoning all the gains on the continent, or invade the oil-rich Dutch East Indies.

Italy Attacks Ethiopia

As Japan pursued continental expansionism, Italy set out to claim a prize it had failed to take in 1896—Ethiopia, one of only two independent states left in Africa. Late in 1934, fighting broke out between the Ethiopians and the Italians, and in the following year, Mussolini's forces invaded the country. Emperor Haile Selassie made a dramatic appearance before the League to appeal for help. Before he could speak, however, he had to endure the catcalls and whistles of the Italian journalists in the hall.

The League tried to arrange for arbitration. Unconvinced by the shameless Italian argument that

Greater East Asia Co-Prosperity Sphere—The projected Japanese-dominated colonial zone, most importantly including Manchuria and China, that would enable Japan to be self-sufficient economically.

Tripartite Pact—The agreement Japan signed with Germany and Italy in 1940 against the United States.

◀ Haile Selassie making a broadcast after the Italian invasion of Ethiopia.

Ethiopia, not Italy, was the aggressor, the League voted to prohibit shipment of certain goods to Italy and to deny it credit. But the effect of the sanctions was minor because oil—without which no modern army could fight—was not included in the list of prohibited articles. France and Britain gave only lukewarm support to the sanctions because they did not want to alienate Italy. The United States, which had not joined the League, and Germany, which had left it by that time, largely ignored the prohibitions. Only outraged public opinion, moved by newspaper photographs showing barefooted Ethiopians fighting the modern Italian army, drove the governments to even the pretense of action.

Using bombs, mustard gas, and tanks, the Italians advanced swiftly into Ethiopia and crushed Haile Selassie's army.

The Rhineland and the Axis

Soon after taking power, Hitler carried out the revisions the Germans wanted in the Versailles treaty. He also won his country's support by seeking revenge against the Allies. As George F. Kennan noted at the time, "The man is acting in the best traditions of German nationalism, and his conception of his own mission is perhaps clearer than that of his predecessors because it is uncomplicated by any sense of responsibility to European culture as a whole."[1] During his first 2 years in power, Hitler paid lip service to peace while increasing the tempo of rearmament. In March 1935, he negated the disarmament clauses of the Versailles treaty and a year later, reoccupied the Rhineland.

The move, which Hitler described as producing the most nerve-racking moments of his life, sent German troops marching boldly into the Rhineland in defiance of the Versailles treaty and the Locarno agreements. The Germans could not have resisted had the British and French moved in response. But London did nothing, and Paris mobilized 150,000 troops behind the **Maginot** (MAZH-ee-noh) **line** but did no more. Hitler later confessed that had the French advanced against him, "We would have had to withdraw with our tails between our legs, for the military resources at our disposal would have been totally inadequate for even a moderate resistance."[2]

In 1936, Italy and Germany formalized the friendship in the Rome-Berlin Axis, and 1 year later, Mussolini followed Hitler's lead by withdrawing from the League of Nations. Japan, the third major member of the Axis, joined forces with Germany in 1936 in the Anti-Comintern Pact. A year later, Italy also joined in that agreement, which effectively encircled the Soviet Union. Relations between Moscow and Berlin had cooled after 1934, and the Soviet Union now became the object of anticommunist rhetoric. Many right-wing leaders in the West hoped that the "Red menace" would be taken care of by Hitler and his allies.

All in all, 1936 was a banner year for Hitler. He had gained allies, pleased his own people by remilitarizing the Rhineland, learned the weakness of the democratic powers and the League, and gained international prestige from his successful staging of the Olympic Games. He also found a successful device to distract potential opponents' attention: the Spanish civil war.

The Spanish Tragedy

By 1936, the 5-year-old Spanish republic was disintegrating. It had brought neither prosperity nor stability to Spain. Reactionary forces had tried to gain control of the government while left-wing groups had resorted to terrorism. The liberal approach had failed, and in the summer of 1936, the army revolted against the legal government in Madrid.

Maginot line—A supposedly impenetrable line of fortresses constructed by France along its eastern frontier between Switzerland and Belgium in the 1920s.

General Francisco Franco (1892–1975) commanded the insurgents, who included in their ranks most of the regular army troops. Mussolini strongly backed Franco, and the rightist forces expected a quick victory. Many groups, however, stood by the republic, and they put up a strong resistance against the insurgents, stopping them at the outskirts of Madrid.

By the end of 1936, each side had gained the backing of a complicated alliance of forces. Franco had the support of the Italians, who sent large numbers of planes, troops, and weapons, and the Germans, who tested their latest military technology against the republicans. The republic gained the support of the Soviet Union, which sent arms, "advisers," and other supplies, as well as a large contingent of disorganized but idealistic antifascist fighters, including a number from Britain and the United States.

The insurgents capitalized on Soviet support for the republic, and Franco pronounced his cause to be strictly an anticommunist crusade—a cunning oversimplification of dubious validity, considering that the communists were never in control of more than a snippet of republican Spain, and that for only a few months in 1938 until Stalin decided to pull his support. While Spain bled, suffering more than 700,000 deaths, outside forces took advantage of the tragic situation for their own selfish purposes.

After the last holdout, Barcelona, fell in March 1939, the Spanish republic was no more. Franco, at the head of the new state, gained absolute power, which he held until his death in 1975. The Spanish civil war was a national catastrophe that left permanent scars on the country's people.

The Logic of Appeasement

In 1937, Neville Chamberlain (1869–1940) became Britain's prime minister. Years before he took office, the British had tried to achieve **détente** with the Germans, backed by an air force that concentrated its resources on bombers with a capacity to inflict damage on the Continent. Chamberlain tried a new strategy: a defense policy based on a fighter air force and centered solely on protecting the British Isles. He wanted to reassure Germany, acknowledge her legitimate complaints, and reach the settlement of outstanding issues peacefully by recognizing mutual interests and establishing well-defined spheres of influence. Chamberlain's name came to symbolize the policy of **appeasement,** the policy of meeting German demands and grievances without demanding firm reciprocal advantages and asking instead only for future "mutual understandings."

Chamberlain took the direction of foreign policy on his own shoulders in his attempt to explore every possibility for reaching an understanding with the dictators. He dedicated himself to an effort to ease international tensions despite snubs from those he wanted to placate and warnings from his military and foreign policy advisers. He based his policy on the most humane of motives—peace—and on the most civilized of assumptions—that Hitler could be reasonable and fair-minded. By showing good faith and by withdrawing from any possibility of being able to wage war on the Continent, Chamberlain froze himself into a position of having to avoid war at any cost. His policies were strongly supported in Britain and throughout most of the British Commonwealth.

France had shown that it would not move militarily without British backing, and under Chamberlain, the entente with France was put on the back burner, a development that hurt French resolve. The democratic world became uneasily aware of its growing weakness in comparison with the dictators. As the European balance of power shifted, the small states began to draw away from the impotent League of Nations.

The prestige of the Axis blossomed. Some nations tried to make deals with Germany and Italy, while others, including the Scandinavian countries and the Netherlands, withdrew into the shelter of neutrality and "innocent isolation." In Eastern Europe, semifascist regimes became the order of the day, as the states in that unhappy region lined up to get in Germany's good graces. In 1934, Poland had signed a nonaggression pact with Germany. In Eastern Europe, only Czechoslovakia remained loyal to Paris. Even Belgium gave up its alliance with France.

Toward Austria and the Sudetenland

When Hitler announced the military reoccupation of the Rhineland in the spring of 1936, he stated, "We have no territorial demands to make in Europe." He lied. By 1938, with the German army growing in strength and the air force becoming a powerful unit, the Führer began to implement one of his foreign policy goals—placing all the German-speaking peoples under one Reich. The first step on that path was to unite Austria and Germany in the ***Anschluss*** (ON-schleus; "joining").

In 1934 the Nazis had badly bungled an attempt to annex Austria. Two years later, softening-up operations began again, and by 1938, intense pressure had been levied against Austrian chancellor Kurt von Schuschnigg to cooperate with Berlin. After a stormy meeting with Hitler in February, Schuschnigg restated

détente—A state of reduced tensions between two countries.

appeasement—The policy of meeting German demands and grievances without demanding firm reciprocal advantages and asking instead only for future "mutual understandings."

Anschluss—The German word for "joining."

his country's desire to be independent, although concessions would be made to Germany. He called for a plebiscite in March to prove his point. Outraged at this independent action, Hitler ordered Schuschnigg to resign and to cancel the vote. Both actions were taken, but Hitler sent his forces into Austria anyway.

By March 13, 1938, a new chancellor, approved by Hitler, announced the union of Austria and Germany. After a month in which all opposition was silenced, Hitler held his own plebiscite and gained a majority of 99.75 percent in favor of union. The democratic powers did not intervene to help Austria. In fact, the British ambassador to Germany voiced no opposition to the annexation of Austria, as long as it was done in a peaceful manner.[3]

Following his success in Austria, Hitler moved on to his next objective, the annexation of the Sudetenland. This area along the western border of Czechoslovakia was populated mainly by German textile workers who had suffered economically during the depression. The Sudetenland was also the site of the extremely well-fortified Czech defenses. In September 1938, the Führer bluntly informed Chamberlain that he was determined to gain self-determination for the Sudeten Germans. He charged, falsely, that the Czechs had mistreated the German minorities. In fact, among the eastern European states, Czechoslovakia had the best record in dealing with minority nationalities. But in this affair, Britain and France consistently overlooked both the record of the Prague government and the Czech statesmen themselves.

Chamberlain persuaded French premier Édouard Daladier (da-LAD-dee-ay) that the sacrifice of Czechoslovakia would save the peace. When the French joined the British to press the Czechs to accept the Nazi demands, the Prague government had little choice but to agree. Chamberlain informed Hitler of Czechs' willingness to compromise, only to find that the German demands had increased considerably. Angered by the Führer's duplicity, Chamberlain refused to accept the new terms, which included Czech evacuation of some areas and the cession of large amounts of matériel and agricultural goods.

Munich and Democratic Betrayal

The crisis over Czechoslovakia would be the last major international issue decided only by European powers. Symbolically, it would be viewed as a failure that would affect diplomatic decisions for generations to come. On September 28, 1938, Chamberlain received a note from Hitler inviting him to attend a conference at Munich. The following day, Chamberlain flew to Germany to meet with Hitler, Mussolini, and Daladier at Nazi headquarters. They worked for 13 hours on the details of the surrender of the Sudetenland. No Czech representative was present, nor were the Soviets—outspoken allies of the Czechs—consulted.

The **Munich Conference** accepted all of Hitler's demands and, in addition, rewarded Poland and Hungary with slices of unfortunate Czechoslovakia. The tragedy for the Czechs brought relief for millions of Europeans, half-crazed with fear of war. But thoughtful individuals pondered whether this settlement would be followed by another crisis. Winston Churchill, who was then in political eclipse in Britain, solemnly warned: "Do not suppose that this is the end. This is only the beginning of the reckoning."[4]

The mounting fears of French and British statesmen were confirmed in 1939. Deprived of its military perimeter, the Czech government stood unprotected against the Nazi pressure that came in March. Hitler summoned Czech president Emil Hacha to Berlin. Subjected to all kinds of threats during an all-night session, Hacha finally capitulated and signed a document placing his country under the "protection" of Germany. His signature was a mere formality, however, for German troops were already crossing the Czech frontier. Not to be outdone, Mussolini seized Albania the following month. The two dictators then celebrated by signing a military alliance, the so-called Pact of Steel.

In response to the taking of Czechoslovakia and violation of the Munich pledges, Great Britain ended its appeasement policy and, for the first time in its history, authorized a peacetime draft. In Paris, Daladier gained special emergency powers to push forward national defense.

In the United States, isolationism reigned supreme. Between 1935 and 1937, in response to feelings of revulsion stemming from World War I, the U.S. Congress passed neutrality acts that made it unlawful for any nation at war to obtain munitions from the United States. At the same time, in response to events in Ethiopia, in Spain, and along the Rhine, President Franklin D. Roosevelt and the State Department worked quietly to alert the American people to the dangers of the world situation. In October 1937, following the escalation of Japanese warfare in China the previous July, Roosevelt pointed out that "the peace, the freedom, and the security of 90 percent of the population of the world is being jeopardized by the remaining 10 percent who are threatening a breakdown of all international order and law."[5]

The Nazi-Soviet Pact

The final step on the road to World War II was Germany's attack on Poland. The Treaty of Versailles had

Munich Conference—Conference in Munich on September 28, 1938 including Germany, Italy, France, and the United Kingdom in which the Western Allies agreed to Hitler's demands on the surrender of the Sudetenland.

▲ At the Munich Conference in September 1938, British Prime Minister Neville Chamberlain (*left*) and French Premier Édouard Daladier (next to him) capitulated to Hitler's demands regarding Czechoslovakia. Italian dictator Benito Mussolini stands to the right of Hitler.

turned over West Prussia to Poland as a corridor to the sea. Although 90 percent of the corridor's population was Polish, the Baltic city of Danzig—a free city under a League of Nations high commissioner—was nearly all German. Late in March 1939, Hitler proposed to Poland that Danzig be ceded to Germany and that the Nazis be allowed to occupy the narrow strip of land connecting Germany with East Prussia. Chamberlain, with French concurrence, warned the Nazis that "in the event of any action that clearly threatens Polish independence," the British would "at once lend the Polish government all support in their power." This was an essentially symbolic gesture, since Poland's location made any useful Western aid impossible.

In the months that followed the Allied warnings, France and Britain competed with Germany for an alliance with Russia. Stalin had closely observed the actions of the democratic powers since Hitler's rise to power. He was aware of the hope expressed in some Western conservative circles that Hitler might effectively put an end to the Soviet regime. Further, he pledged to stay out of a war between "imperialists." He had to make a closely reasoned choice between the two sets of suitors competing for Soviet partnership.

Chamberlain and Daladier had ignored Moscow at Munich, and, generally, British relations with the Communists were quite cool. Now, with the Polish question of paramount importance, the French and British approaches appeared optimistic to Stalin. In May, Vyacheslav Molotov became the Soviet foreign minister. As Molotov was negotiating publicly with the British and French, who sent negotiators not empowered to make agreements, he was also in secret contact with the highest levels in Berlin.

For centuries, Germany and Russia had shared a concern over the fate of Poland. They had been able to reach agreement at Poland's expense in the eighteenth

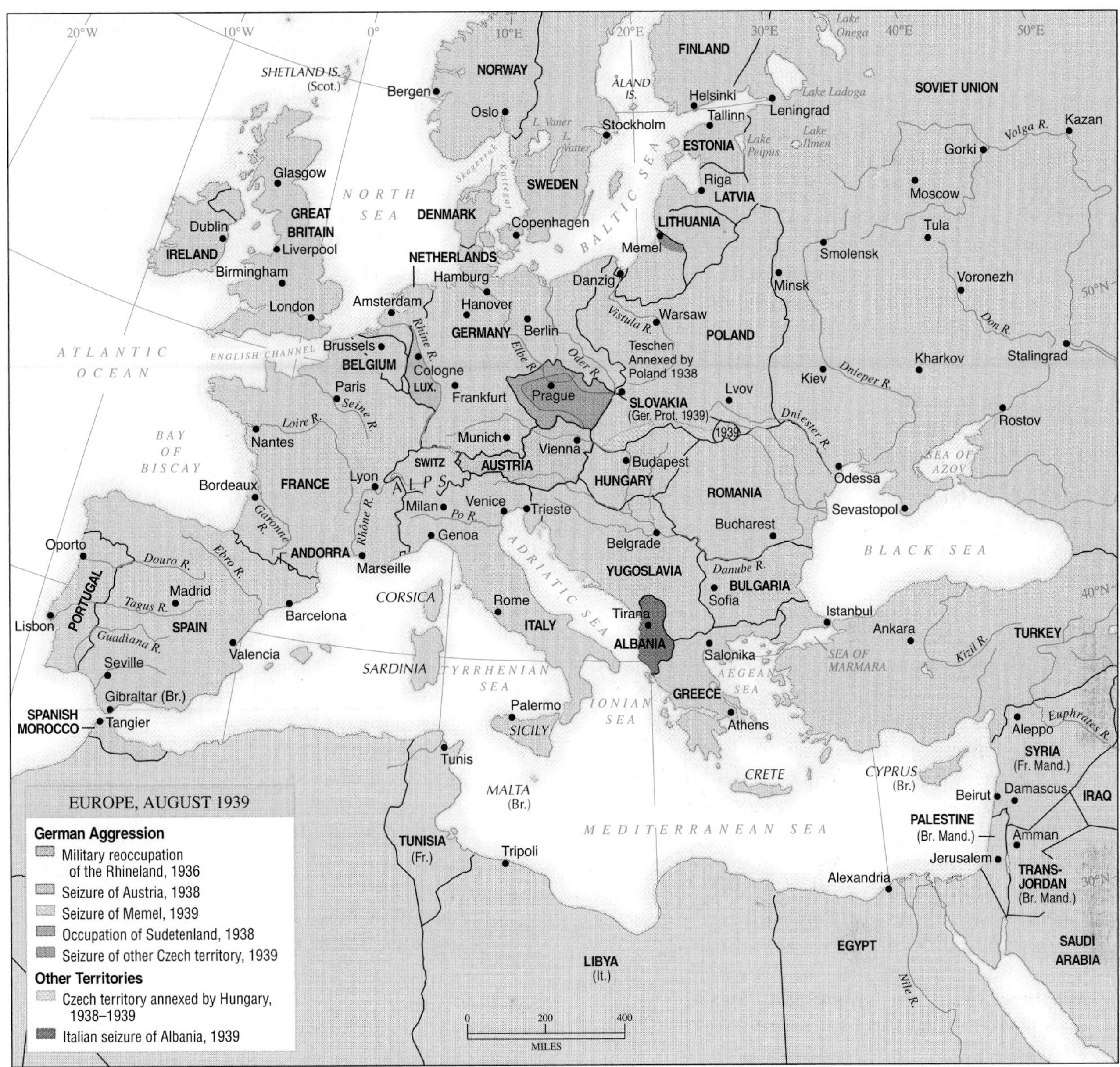

▲ The extent of Hitler's gains in expanding German hegemony by 1939 can be seen here. By using less violence than Bismarck, he took advantage of Allied weakness to become more successful than the old chancellor.

and nineteenth centuries. From late 1938 on, Moscow and Berlin pondered yet another division of the country. Negotiations between the two proceeded intensely from June through August 1939. While top-ranking German and Soviet diplomats flew between the two capitals, the lower-ranking mission sent to Moscow by Britain traveled leisurely by boat.

By 1939, Stalin had to choose wisely between the Western democracies, with their spotty record of defending their friends, and Nazi Germany, which could offer him concrete advantages in Eastern Europe. On August 21, to the world's great amazement, the Soviet Union and Germany signed a **nonaggression pact**.

Nazi-Soviet Nonaggression Pact—Diplomatic agreement in which the USSR and Germany agreed not to take up arms against each other.

In retrospect, it is not at all surprising that Stalin chose to work with the Nazis. Through this agreement, Stalin gave Hitler a free hand in the western part of Poland and the assurance of not having to fight a two-front war. After the British and French guarantees to the Poles in March, Hitler knew that his attack on Poland would precipitate a general European war. The Führer had prepared plans that called for the invasion to begin in August 1939, and thanks to the nonaggression pact, Hitler could attack without fear of Moscow's intervention. Furthermore, he did not believe that Britain and France would dare oppose him.

The nonaggression pact gave the Soviets time to build up strength while the imperialists weakened themselves in war. In addition, the USSR was secretly promised Finland, Estonia, Latvia, eastern Poland, and Bessarabia (the region principally to be found in present-day Moldova). Germany would get everything to the west, including Lithuania. The Nazis also got guarantees of valuable raw materials and grain from the Soviets. Ideological differences could be set aside for such a mutually profitable pact.

World War II

Why did the Axis powers lose World War II?

When Nazi forces crossed the Polish border early on the morning of September 1, 1939, they set off the European portion of World War II, the conflict that killed more people more efficiently than any previous war. In all areas the latest scientific and technological advances were placed in the service of a new kind of war that killed civilians as well as soldiers and sailors. New techniques and attitudes revolutionized the field of intelligence. Scientists made major advances in both codemaking and codebreaking. Intelligence-gathering no longer depended on the old cloak-and-dagger stealing of messages and secrets. Now high-altitude aerial reconnaissance aircraft, radar, the first computers, and radio intercepts allowed enemies to discover each other's plans. Among the major advances on the Allied side were the discovery of the German code mechanism and the breaking of the Japanese code. Ironically, in 1929 Secretary of State Henry Stimson had declared that "gentlemen do not read other gentlemen's mail," but this civilized attitude soon changed. In the new style of warfare, information meant victory, and the cultured assumptions of an earlier age had to be discarded.

A New Way of War

Tactics and weaponry changed greatly between the two world wars. Tanks and planes had been used in World War I, but the concept of the **blitzkrieg**—literally "lightning war," massive mobile mechanized movements and saturation bombings behind the lines—made the weapons far more lethal. The trench warfare of World War I and the concept of fixed, fortified positions, such as the Maginot line built by the French in the 1920s and 1930s, proved to be useless.

Mobility was the key—even more so than superior numbers of men and weapons. Better communications, provided by improved radio systems, increased mobility. To strike quickly, with great force, and then to exploit the advantage proved to be the main characteristics of the German successes in 1939 and 1940. The Germans broke through enemy lines by using a large number of dive-bombers and then tanks, followed by the infantry. Rarely since Napoleon had speed and concentrated force been used so effectively.

Complementing increased mobility on the ground was the expanded use of airplanes, which could spread devastating firepower across continents, hundreds of miles behind established battle lines. The new forms of war, however, sparked the inventive genius of the scientists as each technological advance elicited a response—long-range German bombers brought the need for improved radar; improved propeller-driven aircraft set off the development of jet-powered airplanes. No matter how sophisticated the aerial technology became, however, the war proved that, with the exception of nuclear weapons, air power alone could not bring an enemy to its knees.

Other innovations appeared during the war—paratroopers, advanced landing crafts, and the German flying bombs such as the V-1 and rockets such as the V-2. Aircraft carriers and amphibious forces played an important part in the war in the Pacific. The Japanese used carriers in their attack on Pearl Harbor, and the Americans used amphibious forces in "island hopping" across the Pacific.

Blitzkrieg and *Sitzkrieg*

After staging an "incident" on the morning of September 1, 1939, Nazi troops crossed the Polish frontier without a declaration of war, using the new tactics of the blitzkrieg. At the same time, the German *Luftwaffe* (air force) began to bomb Polish cities. On the morning of September 3, Chamberlain sent an ultimatum to Germany demanding that the invasion be halted. The time limit was given as 11:00 A.M. the same day. At 11:15, Chamberlain announced in a radio broadcast that Britain was now at war. France also soon declared war. After 21 years, Europe was once again immersed in war.

The world now had the chance to see the awesome speed and power of Nazi arms. The Polish forces collapsed, crushed between the German advance from the west and, two weeks later, a Soviet invasion from the east. By the end of the month, after a brave but hopeless resistance, the Poles once again saw their country partitioned between the Germans and the Russians.

Britain and France did not try to breach Germany's western defensive line, the Siegfried line along the Rhine. With their blockade and mastery of the seas, they hoped to defeat Hitler by attrition. During the

blitzkrieg—Literally "lightning war," the blitzkrieg emphasized the use of rapid mechanized mobility to overwhelm dug-in, fortified positions. The blitzkrieg was a response to the trench warfare of World War I.

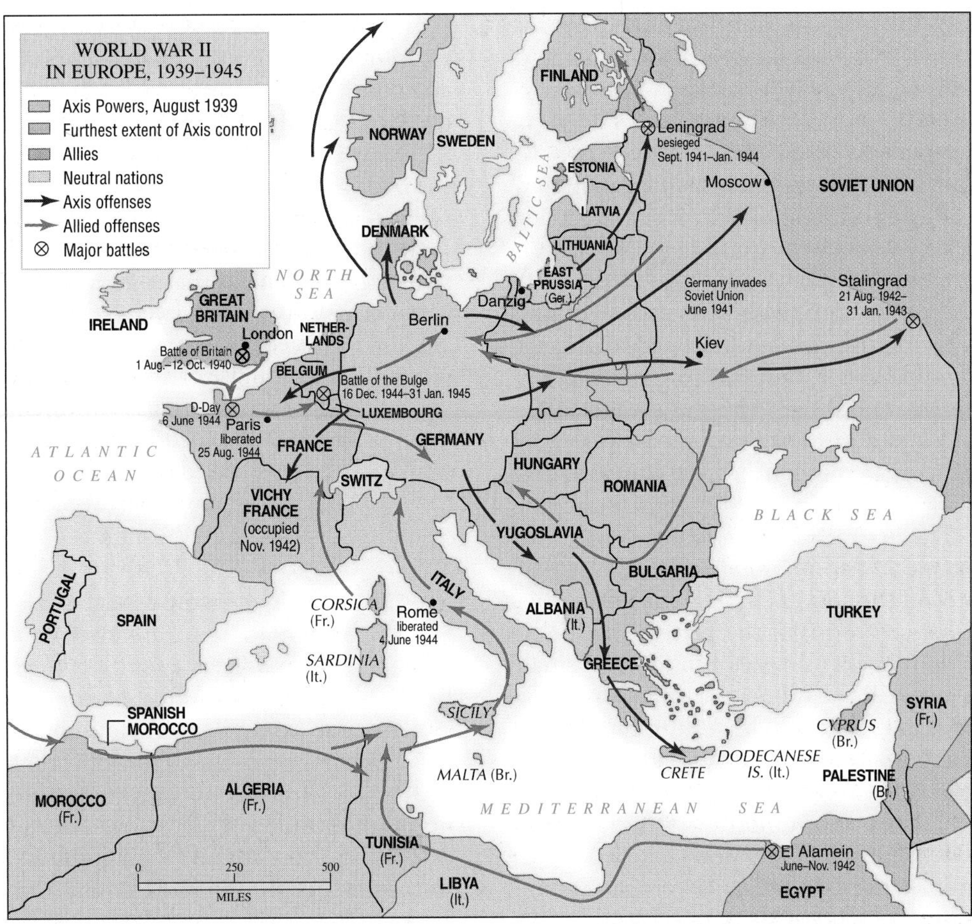

▲ Aided by the Nazi-Soviet pact of August 1939, which allowed them to concentrate their fighting on a single front, the Germans, in one of the most successful military campaigns in history, ripped through the Low Countries and France. The Maginot line of defense constructed by the French proved totally useless.

winter of 1939–1940, there was little fighting along the Franco-German frontier. The lull in action came to be referred to as the phony war, or *Sitzkrieg.*

The Soviets took advantage of the lull to attack Finland in November. This campaign revealed, to Moscow's embarrassment, the Finns' toughness and the Soviet Union's military unpreparedness in the wake of recent purges. After an unexpectedly difficult four-month-long campaign, the immense Soviet Union forced tiny Finland to cede substantial amounts of territory.

"Blood, Toil, Tears, and Sweat"

In the spring of 1940, the Nazi high command launched its attack on Western Europe. In its scope, complexity, and accomplishments, it was one of the most successful military campaigns ever carried out. In April, Nazi forces invaded Norway and Denmark. The Norwegians fought back fiercely for three weeks before being vanquished, and Denmark was taken in even less time. In the second week of May, the German armies overran the neutral Netherlands, Belgium, and Luxembourg.

The next week they went into northern France. The Germans' earlier conquests were all against forces that were militarily inferior. In France, they faced a country with more tanks, equipment, and men. However, French morale was so low and leadership so dispirited that the Germans took close to 1,800,000 prisoners with little or no resistance in the next month. German observers noted that the troops from French colonies in Africa showed more courage under fire than did their colonial masters. One German officer saw "several hundred French officers who had marched 35 kilometers without any [German] guard from a prisoner of war dispatch point to a prisoner of war transition station ... with apparently none having made their escape."[6] Accordingly, the Germans easily advanced into northern France and went all the way to the English Channel. In the process, they trapped an Anglo-French army of nearly 400,000 on the beach at Dunkirk.

The reversals in Norway and the Low Countries and the military crisis in France led to Chamberlain's resignation. Winston Churchill (1874–1965) became prime minister of Great Britain. Churchill had had uneven success in both his political and military careers. In the 1930s, his warnings against Hitler and Mussolini had been largely ignored. He was viewed as a "might-have-been; a potentially great man flawed by flashiness, irresponsibility, unreliability, and inconsistency."[7] Yet in 1940, at the age of 66, Churchill offered qualities of leadership equal to the nation's peril. For the next 5 years, he was the voice and symbol of a defiant and indomitable Britain.

Facing the prospect of the destruction of the British army at Dunkirk, Churchill refused to be publicly dismayed. Appearing before Parliament as the new prime minister, he announced, "I have nothing to offer but blood, toil, tears, and sweat." He prepared his people for a long and desperate conflict, knowing full well that only the Channel, a thin screen of fighter aircraft, and an untried device called radar protected Britain. Churchill's example inspired his people. Hitler had found his match in the area of charismatic leadership.

Hitler hesitated to quash the forces trapped at Dunkirk, thereby allowing time for hundreds of small craft protected by the Royal Air Force to evacuate across the Channel 335,000 soldiers, including more than 100,000 French troops. Military leaders had hoped that they might be able to save 30,000 of the trapped men; now they had 11 times that number. An army had been saved, though it had lost all of its heavy equipment.

After Dunkirk, the fall of France was inevitable. Eager to be in on the kill, Mussolini declared war on France on June 10. Designated as an open city by the French in order to spare its destruction, Paris fell on June 14. As the German advance continued, the members of the French government who wanted to continue resistance were voted down. Marshal Philippe Pétain (PAY-tan; 1856–1951)—the 84-year-old hero of Verdun (1916) and the French ambassador to Marshal Franco's fascist regime in Spain—became premier. He immediately asked Hitler for an armistice, and in the same dining car in which the French had imposed armistice terms on the Germans in 1918, the Nazis and French on June 22, 1940, signed another peace agreement. The Germans had gained revenge for their shame in 1918.

France was split into two zones, occupied and unoccupied. In unoccupied France, Pétain's government at Vichy was supposedly free from interference, but in reality, it became a puppet of the Nazis. France served—willingly or unwillingly—as a dependable base of economic support for the German war effort. The Third Republic, created in 1871 from the debris of defeat suffered at Germany's hands, now came to an end with a blow from the same country.

A remarkable patriot, Brigadier-General Charles de Gaulle (1890–1970), fled to London and organized the Free French Government, which adopted as its symbol the red cross of Lorraine, flown by Joan of Arc in her fight to liberate France five centuries earlier. De Gaulle worked to keep alive the idea of France as a great power and continued to aid the Allied cause in his sometimes quixotic way throughout the war.

Only Britain remained in opposition to Hitler, and the odds against the British seemed overwhelming. The Nazis planned a cross-Channel assault, while in Buckingham Palace, the queen took pistol lessons, saying, "I shall not go down like the others."[8] Britain had to pin its hopes on its navy, an army whose best equipment was still at Dunkirk, radar, and fast fighter aircraft flown by brave pilots. But Churchill's eloquence inspired his people:

> *We shall go on to the end.... We shall defend our island, whatever the cost may be, we shall fight on the beaches, we shall fight on the landing grounds, we shall fight in the fields and in the streets, we shall fight in the hills; we shall never surrender.*[9]

The Germans sent an average of 200 bombers over London every night for nearly two months in the summer and fall of 1940. They suffered heavy losses to the Royal Air Force, which profited from a combination of superior aircraft, pilots, radar sightings, and visual detection. Yet all through the fall and winter of 1940–1941, Britain continued to be racked by terrible raids. Night bombing destroyed block after block of British cities. Evacuating their children and old people to the north, going to work by day and sleeping in air raid shelters and underground stations at night, Britain's people stood firm—proof that bombing civilians would not break their will.

Mastery of Europe

During the fall and winter of 1940–1941, Hitler strengthened his position in the Balkans, but not without some difficulty. By March 1941, Hungary, Bulgaria, and Romania had joined the Axis. Hitler had to control the Hungarians and Bulgarians, who were pursuing ancient ambitions for Romanian land. In the process, Romania lost a third of its population and territory to its two neighbors. The Romanians emerged, however, as helpful allies for the Germans, and Marshal Ion Antonescu became Hitler's favorite foreign general.

Mussolini, eager to gain some glory for his forces, invaded neutral Greece in October 1940. This thrust proved a costly failure when, in December, the Greeks successfully counterattacked. The Italians met other defeats in North Africa and Ethiopia, which the British recaptured.

Partly in an attempt to pull Mussolini out of a humiliating position, the Germans, in the first four months of 1941, overran Yugoslavia and Greece. Two months of intense aerial and infantry attacks were needed to defeat the Yugoslavs and Greeks, forcing Hitler to spend considerable amounts of men and resources. But when the job was done, the Führer had secured his right flank prior to his invasion of the Soviet Union, an event for which he had prepared during the previous year.

By the spring of 1941, nearly all of Europe had come under German control. Only Portugal, Switzerland, Sweden, Ireland, Spain, and Turkey remained neutral. For the Swiss, Swedes, and Spaniards, this was a strange kind of neutrality. The Swiss played an important role as "Germany's central banker." Swiss banks absorbed the accounts of Jews who were in the concentration camps, handled transfers of German looted gold—some of which was gold later melted down from the fillings of the death camp inmates—and financed German purchases of goods from neutral countries. The Swedes permitted German troops to cross their territory for the attack on the USSR, allowed the Germans to use their railroad system, and used their navy to provide escort services for German supply ships. After the German ball-bearing factories were knocked out by Allied aircraft, replacements for that all-important commodity were found in Sweden. Spain under Franco was pro-Nazi, sending 40,000 "volunteers" to fight on the eastern front. Not all the neutrals were as blatant as the Swedes or the Swiss or as pro-German as Franco. The true neutrals were trapped in a difficult position and made the best of their situation. The others profiteered and probably prolonged the war by their activities.[10]

War with the Soviet Union

Hitler and Stalin had signed the nonaggression pact for their own specific, short-term advantages. From the first, there was tension and mistrust between the two, and neither side had any illusions about a long-lasting friendship. Stalin had hoped for a much more difficult and devastating war in the west among the "imperialists" and had not expected that Hitler would so quickly become the master of Europe.

As early as July 1940, Hitler resolved to attack the Soviets in an operation code-named "Barbarossa." In the fall of the year, he decided not to invade Britain but instead to pursue his original goal of obtaining *Lebensraum* ("living space") and resources. During 1941, British, European, and American intelligence experts told Stalin of Hitler's intentions to attack, but the Soviet dictator refused to believe the information and clung to his obligations under the nonaggression pact. Even as the Nazis were invading in June 1941, shipments of Soviet grain were headed to Germany.

Operation Barbarossa required an enormous amount of effort and resources. Along a battlefront

▼ St. Paul's Cathedral, glimpsed through the smoke and fire in the aftermath of a German bombing raid over London on December 31, 1940.

▲ An integral part of German success in World War II was the firepower and mobility of their armored divisions. Here are tanks and soldiers breaking through the Stalin line during the German invasion of the Soviet Union in 1941.

1000 miles long, 9 million men became locked in struggle. At the outset, Hitler's air force destroyed close to 900 Soviet planes—most of them on the ground, giving the *Luftwaffe* control of the skies. The Nazi tank units were unstoppable, as was the infantry. By September, the Germans had captured more than three million Soviet troops. In October, Hitler's army neared the center of Moscow (a monument today between the city's Sheremetevo Airport and the Kremlin marks the farthest advance of the German army). A month earlier, the Nazis had besieged Leningrad, beginning a 2-year struggle in which over one million civilians died. The USSR appeared to be on the verge of collapse.

When winter came earlier, and more severely, than usual, the Nazi offensive broke down. Weapons froze, troops were inadequately clothed, and heavy snows blocked the roads. The German attack halted, and in the spring of 1942, the Red Army recovered some territory. One reason that the Soviets could bounce back was the success of the 5-year plans in relocating industry behind the Urals. Another reason was the sheer bravery and tenacity of the Soviet people. In addition, the United States and Britain had begun sending supplies to the USSR.

The United States Enters the War

Following the collapse of France and during the battle of Britain, the American people had begun to understand the dangerous implications of an Axis victory. After Dunkirk, the United States sent arms to Britain, embarked on a rearmament program, and introduced a peacetime draft. The Lend-Lease Act of 1941 empowered the president to make arms available to any country whose defense was thought to be vital to the U.S. national interest. Despite ideological differences, America sent more than $11 billion worth of munitions to the Soviet Union.

To define the moral purpose and principles of the struggle, Roosevelt and Churchill drafted the Atlantic Charter in August 1941. Meeting somewhere in the Atlantic, the two pledged that "after the final destruction of Nazi tyranny," they hoped to see a peace in which "men in all the lands may live out their lives in freedom from fear and want." Although the United States had not yet declared itself at war in the fall of 1941, it was far from neutral. Yet, as late as November 1941, public opinion polls showed more than 80 percent of the American people were against becoming involved in the war in Europe.

One event, however, brought the full energies of the American people into the war against the European dictators and the Japanese militarists: the Japanese attack on Pearl Harbor on December 7, 1941, capping several years of deteriorating relations. Even though Hitler was considered the more dangerous enemy, it was Japan's expansionist policy that brought the United States into the war.

Alarmed by Tokyo's ambitions for the New Order in Asia and widely published accounts of Japanese atrocities, the United States had failed to renew the commercial treaty, frozen Japanese funds, and refused to sell Japan war matériel. Despite these measures, Japan pursued its expansion, even while attempting to negotiate an agreement with the United States to restart the flow of oil if Japan left Vietnam. In October 1941, Prime Minister Konoe resigned after failing to secure a direct meeting with U.S. President Roosevelt, and General Tōjō Hideki (1884–1948) was appointed prime minister in anticipation of a preemptive strike against the United States. On Sunday, December 7, while secretaries at the Japanese embassy in Washington were typing a translation of the final letter breaking off diplomatic relations with the United States, Japanese planes, launched from aircraft carriers, attacked the American bases at Pearl Harbor, Hawaii. The stunningly successful attack wiped out many American aircraft on the ground, crippled half of the United States' Pacific fleet, and led to almost 3300 deaths. Only the absence of aircraft carriers from Pearl Harbor saved the United States from a total disaster.

The following day, the United States declared war on Japan; Britain followed suit. The British dominions, the refugee governments of Europe, and many

Latin American nations soon joined the American and British cause. Four days later, Germany declared war on the United States. On January 2, 1942, the 26 nations that stood against Germany, Italy, and Japan solemnly pledged themselves to uphold the principles of the Atlantic Charter and declared themselves united for the duration of the war.

The Apogee of the Axis

For the nine months after Pearl Harbor, Japanese power expanded over the Pacific and into Southeast Asia. Tokyo conquered Hong Kong, Singapore, the Netherlands East Indies, Malaya, Burma, and Indochina (Vietnam). The Philippines fell when an American force surrendered at Bataan. Much of China fell under Japanese control, with the exception of interior regions around Chongqing under the Nationalists and in northwest China around Shaanxi (shahn-SHI) under the Communists.

The summer of 1942 was an agonizing period for the nations allied against the Axis. A new German offensive pushed deeper into Russia, threatening the important city of Stalingrad. The forces of the gifted German general Rommel menaced Egypt and inflicted a stinging defeat on the British army in Libya. All over the globe, the Axis powers were in the ascendancy. But their advantage was to be short-lived.

Japanese expansion in the Pacific was halted by two major American naval victories, the Coral Sea in May and Midway in June. In the first, the Americans sank more than 100,000 tons of Japanese shipping and stopped the Japanese advance toward Australia. In the second, the Americans turned back the advance toward Hawaii by devastating the Japanese carrier force. In both cases, the American forces benefited by having broken the Japanese code and intercepting key messages. After these spectacular victories, U.S. marines began the tortuous conquest of the Japanese at Guadalcanal and driving them back, island by island, while the Navy destroyed most of the Japanese merchant fleet. The destruction of shipping spelled the end of the Japanese empire, as it was dependent on raw materials from Asia.

By 1943, the main islands of Japan were cut off from their sources of raw materials and their markets. The government was forced to draft young men into the military, and older men, teenaged boys and girls, and unmarried women were drafted into the labor force. Controls over daily life—rationing of food and clothing and regimenting of films, newspapers, religion, and other aspects of civil society—destroyed civic life. In a time before instant news, the government lied to the people to retain their support while depriving them of food and necessities, telling them Japan was winning spectacular victories when, in fact, their ships lay at the bottom of the sea and thousands of soldiers were killed. Married women were told to "be fruitful and multiply for the prosperity of the nation." Millions of children were evacuated to the countryside, where those over 12 were taken from school and put to work. Colonial subjects fared even worse, as Korean and Chinese men were drafted to work in Japanese mines and factories and between 100,000 and 200,000 Korean and other Asian women were forced into sexual slavery as "comfort women" for the Japanese military.

In November 1942, British and American troops landed in North Africa, and the British defeated Axis troops at El Alamein in Egypt. By May 1943, all Axis troops in North Africa had been destroyed or captured. In July 1943, the Allied forces invaded and captured Sicily. On the twenty-fifth of that month, the whole edifice of Italian fascism collapsed when Mussolini was stripped of his office and held captive. (He was rescued by Nazi agents in September.) In the meantime, the Allies began their slow and bitter advance up the Italian boot. The new Italian government signed an armistice in September 1943, months before Rome was

▼ Sailors watch helplessly from the Ford Island seaplane ramp on the morning of December 7, 1941, as the USS *Shaw* explodes in the distance. The surprise attack shocked the United States into action. In November, public opinion polls indicated 80 percent of Americans were against involvement in foreign wars. After the U.S. declaration of war against Japan, the nation went onto a full-scale military footing.

◄ The color guard of the 30th Infantry Division marching down the Champs Elysée during the liberation of Paris.

taken in June 1944. German resistance in northern Italy continued until the end of the war.

The Russian Turning Point

The Nazis lost a great opportunity to encourage the disintegration of the Soviet Union in 1941 because they treated the peoples they encountered as ***Untermenschen,*** or subhumans. Often the Nazis, far from encountering resistance, would be treated as liberators by the villages they entered and were given the traditional gifts of bread and salt. Peasants dissolved many of the unpopular collective farms in the hope that private ownership would be restored. The separatist Ukrainians looked forward to German support for reinstituting their state. The Nazi occupation negated all of these potential advantages. The Nazis carried their mobile killing operations of genocide with them, conscripted Slavs for slave labor in Germany, and generally mistreated the population in areas that they occupied.

Hitler's campaign gave Stalin the opportunity to wrap himself in the flag of patriotism. He replaced ideological standards with those of nationalism and orthodoxy. He even went so far as to announce the end of the Comintern in 1943, an act more symbolic than real. For the first and perhaps the only time, the Communist party and the Soviet people were truly united in a joint enterprise.

The long (September 14, 1942, to February 2, 1943) and bloody battle between the Germans and the Soviets was focused on the strategic industrial city of Stalingrad on the Volga River. Hitler had fanatically sought to take the city, which, under the constant pounding of artillery, had little of importance left in it. His generals advised him to stop the attempt and retreat to a more defensible line. Hitler refused, and the German Sixth Army of 270,000 men was surrounded and finally captured in February 1943.

Along the long front, 500,000 German and affiliated troops were killed or taken prisoner. By the autumn of 1943, an army of 2.5 million Germans faced a Soviet force of 5.5 million. The initiative had definitely passed to the Allies in the European theater. The Germans lost their air dominance, and the American industrial machine was cranking up to full production. By the beginning of 1944, the Germans were being pushed out of the Soviet Union, and in August, Soviet troops accepted the surrender of Romania. Bulgaria was next to be liberated by the Soviet Union, while the Allies continued doggedly fighting their way north in Italy. But whereas the western Allies were, in their fashion, fighting the war to its military end, Stalin placed the postwar political objectives in the forefront of his advance into Europe.

An example of the Soviet use of military tactics to gain political goals could be seen in the action around Warsaw in August and September 1944 when the Red Army deferred the capture of the Polish capital to allow the Nazis to destroy potential opponents. The Polish resistance, which was centered in Warsaw and was in contact with the exile government in London, had noted the arrival of Soviet forces in Warsaw's eastern suburbs. When the Nazis prepared to evacuate the city, the resistance rose up to claim control of the capital. Since these were non-Communist Poles, Stalin's forces refused to advance to the city, choosing instead to withdraw back across the Vistula River.

During the next five months, the Soviets refused to permit the British and the Americans, who wanted to air-drop supplies to the resistance, to land and refuel in the Ukraine. Because the flight to Warsaw from London was too far to make in a round trip, the Allies could not supply the resistance. The Nazis stopped their retreat, returned to Warsaw, and totally destroyed the resistance. Soviet forces then advanced and took the

Untermenschen—Literally "subhumans." The term used by Nazi race theorists to describe non-Aryans.

Seeing Connections

Modern Civilization and Mass Killing

The twentieth century was a time when connections were made among long-held hatreds of "the other," bogus science that declared one group to be superior to another, industrialization, and efficient states. Killing large numbers of people is a difficult task in a nonindustrialized region: the radical Hutus in Rwanda slaughtered some 800,000 Tutsis and moderate Hutus by using machetes and other primitive means in 1994 and would have killed more except for the fact that they became fatigued. The Nazis had overcome those human limitations earlier. In the late 1930s and early 1940s, PhD candidates in German universities wrote theses examining the challenges involved in the destruction of large numbers of people, bureaucrats in the Ministry of Railways did a cost per person analysis of the transportation of the victims, chemists searched for the most economical and effective ways to murder people, and engineers struggled with the problems of the disposal of the bodies. A modern, civilized state mobilized all of its technical and intellectual resources to solve a problem: how to eliminate the Jews and other undesirables and to purify the Aryan race. None of this was apparent to these French mothers and their children who arrived in Auschwitz (Oswiecim) after many days freezing and starving in a freight car of the French rail system, SNCF. They emerged, dazed, into the light of day, mothers looking after their children, children wanting to play. Soon they would be stripped, their hair would be cut off, and they would be sent to "showers," and then disposed of in the ovens.

capital in January. Poland was now deprived of many of its potential postwar non-Communist leaders. When the Soviets advanced, they brought with them their own properly prepared Polish forces, both military and political, to control the country.

Axis Collapse

Following months of intense planning and days of difficult decision-making, the Allies launched a vast armada of ships that landed half a million men on the beaches of Normandy on June 6, 1944—D-Day. The Allied armies broke through the German defenses and liberated Paris at the end of August and Brussels at the beginning of September. The combined forces wheeled toward Germany. After fending off a major German offensive in the battle of the Bulge in December, the Allies were ready to march on Germany.

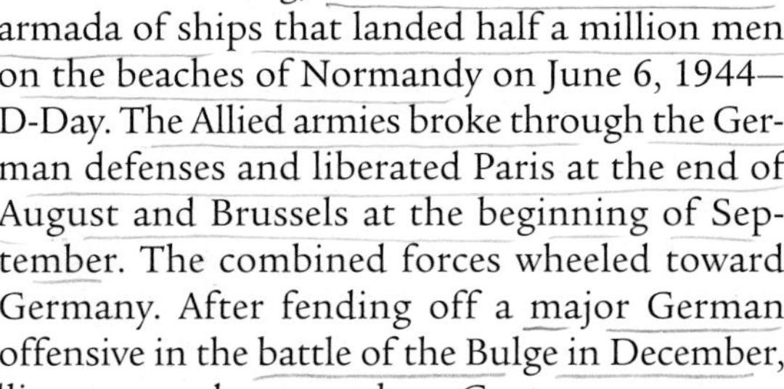

IMAGE Operation Overlord, Normandy, 1944

It took four more months for the Allies from the west and the Soviets from the east to crush the German Third Reich. By May 1, the battle of Berlin had reached a decisive point, and the Russians were about to take the city. In contrast with World War I, German civilians suffered greatly in World War II. The Allies gained total command of the skies, and for every ton of bombs that fell on English cities, more than 300 tons fell on German towns and cities; Dresden and Cologne, in particular, were essentially leveled by extensive fire-bombing.

With victory in sight, Stalin, Roosevelt, and Churchill met at Yalta in the Crimea in February 1945 to discuss the peace arrangements. They agreed that the Soviet Union should have a preponderant influence in eastern Europe, decided that Germany should be divided into four occupation zones, discussed the makeup and functioning of the United Nations (a proposed successor to the defunct League of Nations), and confirmed that the Soviets would enter the war against Japan after the defeat of Germany, which they did—two days after the atomic bomb was dropped on Hiroshima. Yalta was the high point of the alliance. After this conference, relations between the Western powers and the Soviets rapidly deteriorated.

IMAGE The "Big Three" at Yalta

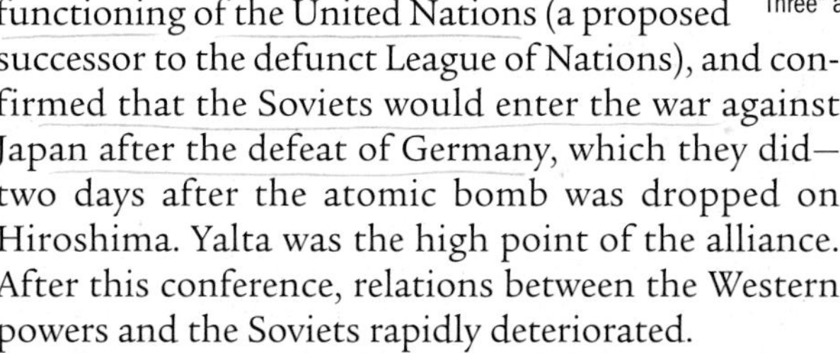

The European Axis leaders did not live to see defeat. Mussolini was seized by antifascist partisan fighters and shot to death, and his mutilated body and that of his mistress were hung by the heels in a public square in Milan on April 28, 1945. Hitler committed suicide two days later. His body and that of his mistress, Eva Braun, whom he had just married, were soaked in gasoline and set afire.

President Roosevelt also did not live to see the end of the war. He died suddenly on April 12, 1945, less than a month before the German armies capitulated. The final surrender in Europe took place in Berlin on May 8, 1945, proclaimed by the newly installed president, Harry Truman, as V-E Day, Victory in Europe Day.

The Holocaust

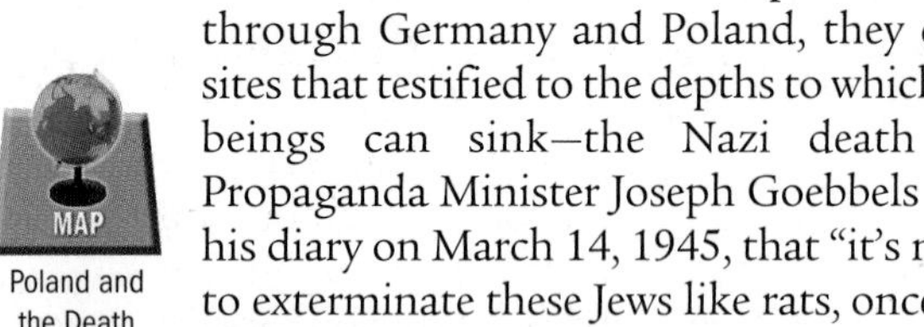

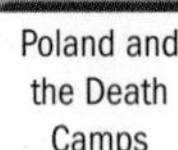

MAP

Poland and the Death Camps

As the Allied armies liberated Europe and marched through Germany and Poland, they came on sites that testified to the depths to which human beings can sink—the Nazi death camps. Propaganda Minister Joseph Goebbels wrote in his diary on March 14, 1945, that "it's necessary to exterminate these Jews like rats, once and for all. In Germany, thank God, we've taken care of that. I hope the world will follow this example."[11]

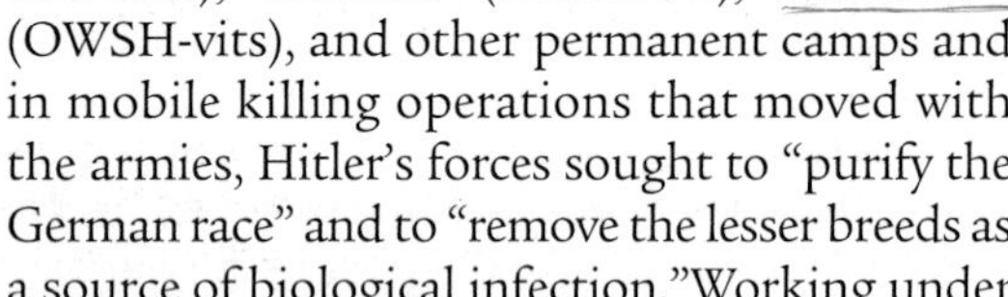

CASE STUDY

Genocide

He was only too accurate in saying that Germany had "already taken care of that." In Belsen, Buchenwald (BOO-ken-vold), Dachau (DAH-kow), Auschwitz (OWSH-vits), and other permanent camps and in mobile killing operations that moved with the armies, Hitler's forces sought to "purify the German race" and to "remove the lesser breeds as a source of biological infection." Working under the efficient efforts of the Gestapo (secret police), led by Chief Heinrich Himmler, and with the aid of hard-working Deputy Chief Reinhard Heydrich, the Nazis set out to gain the **"Final Solution"** to the Jewish question and to reduce the presence of lesser beings.

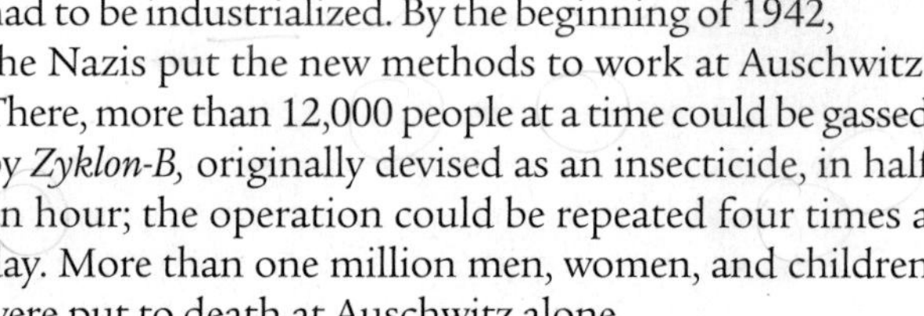

IMAGE

Memoirs "From the Commandant of Auschwitz

Although preparations had been under way for 10 years, the completed plan for the Final Solution was put into operation at the beginning of 1942. Hitler, according to an aide, Hans Frank—the head of the Government-General of Occupied Polish Territories—gave the order to "liquidate them" on December 12, 1941.[12] It was impossible to eliminate the *Untermenschen* by normal means such as a pistol shot delivered to the nape of the neck or machine gunning them. More efficiency was needed: death had to be industrialized. By the beginning of 1942, the Nazis put the new methods to work at Auschwitz. There, more than 12,000 people at a time could be gassed by *Zyklon-B,* originally devised as an insecticide, in half an hour; the operation could be repeated four times a day. More than one million men, women, and children were put to death at Auschwitz alone.

The able-bodied were forced to work until they could work no more, and then they too were gassed. Millions more died from starvation, on diets that averaged 600 to 700 calories a day.[13] Torture, medical experimentation, and executions all claimed a large toll. The victims' eyeglasses were collected, their hair

Final Solution—Term used to define the goal of the Holocaust, to eliminate all Jews from the earth.

Document

The Nazi Death Camps

Henry Friedlander gave a dispassionate description of the functioning of the Nazi death camps.

The largest killing operation took place in Auschwitz, a regular concentration camp. There Auschwitz Commandant Rudolf Hess improved the method used by Christian Wirth, substituting crystallized prussic acid—known by the trade name Zyklon B—for carbon monoxide. In September, 1941, an experimental gassing, killing about 250 ill prisoners and about 600 Russian POWs, proved the value of Zyklon B. In January, 1942, systematic killing operations, using Zyklon B, commenced with the arrival of Jewish transports from Upper Silesia. These were soon followed without interruption by transports of Jews from all occupied countries of Europe.

The Auschwitz killing center was the most modern of its kind. The SS built the camp at Birkenau, also known as Auschwitz II. There, they murdered their victims in newly constructed gas chambers and burned their bodies in crematoria constructed for this purpose. A postwar court described the killing process:

> Prussic acid fumes developed as soon as Zyklon B pellets seeped through the opening into the gas chamber and came into contact with the air. Within a few minutes, these fumes agonizingly asphyxiated the human beings in the gas chamber. During these minutes horrible scenes took place. The people who now realized that they were to die an agonizing death screamed and raged and beat their fists against the locked doors and against the walls. Since the gas spread from the floor of the gas chamber upward, small and weak people were the first to die. The others, in their death agony, climbed on top of the dead bodies on the floor, in order to get a little more air before they too painfully choked to death.

Questions to Consider

1. Why did the Nazis choose to use Zyklon B for the destruction of the Jews and others?
2. When did the systematic killing operations using Zyklon B begin?
3. Do you believe that it is possible that there will be other genocides in your lifetime? Why? Where?

From Henry Friedlander, "The Nazi Camps," in *Genocide: Critical Issues of the Holocaust,* eds. Alex Grobman and David S. Landes (Los Angeles: Simon Wiesenthal Center, 1983), pp. 222–223.

was shaved off for use in the wig trade, their gold fillings were removed as plunder, and their bodies were either burned or buried.

Thus the captured Jews, along with assorted other *Untermenschen* (Gypsies, homosexuals, petty criminals, and conquered non-Aryans), made an economic contribution on their way to extermination. The Nazis did not act alone: they were aided by anti-Semitic citizens in Poland, Romania, France, Hungary, the Baltic States, and the Soviet Union. Few of the more than three million Polish Jews survived the war, sharing the fate of those 1200 Jews killed and burned in July 1941 by their fellow Polish villagers in Jedwabne.[14] Similar devastation occurred among the Romanian Jewry.

All of this was done with bureaucratic efficiency, coldness, discipline, and professionalism. PhD candidates wrote dissertations on how to maximize the profit from the camps, industrialists competed actively for contracts to carry out the killing, and special rates were devised by the state railroad for the transportation of the doomed. Himmler believed that his new variety of knights must "make this people disappear from the face of the earth." Had this been done in a fit of insanity and madness by barbarians, it could perhaps be comprehended. But that it was done by educated bureaucrats and responsible officials from a "civilized" nation made the enterprise all the more chilling and incredible. The question of the complicity of the German people in the Holocaust continues to be debated.[15] Between 1939 and 1945 the Jewish population in Nazi-occupied Europe decreased from 9,739,200 to 3,505,800. Six million were killed in Nazi gas chambers or in executions, and another 6 million non-Jews fell victim to the Nazi slaughter.[16]

The Final Years of the Pacific War and the Atomic Bomb

Furthest Limits of Japanese Conquests

While the Allied armies finished off the Germans, the Americans continued the advance toward Japan begun in the summer of 1943, capturing on the way the islands of Tarawa, Kwajalein, and Saipan after bloody, hand-to-hand struggles on sandy beaches and in the jungles of the interior. In October 1944, with their victory in the battle of Leyte Gulf, the greatest naval engagement in history, the Allies ended the threat of the Japanese fleet.

The Allies then took Iwo Jima and Okinawa, only a few hundred miles from Japan. From these bases,

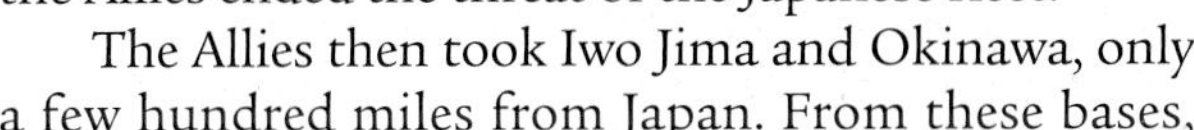

▼ For a decade after the invasion of Manchuria in 1931, the Japanese expanded their control over the region known as the "Greater East Asian Co-Prosperity Sphere." Not until the battle of Midway in June 1942 was their momentum broken.

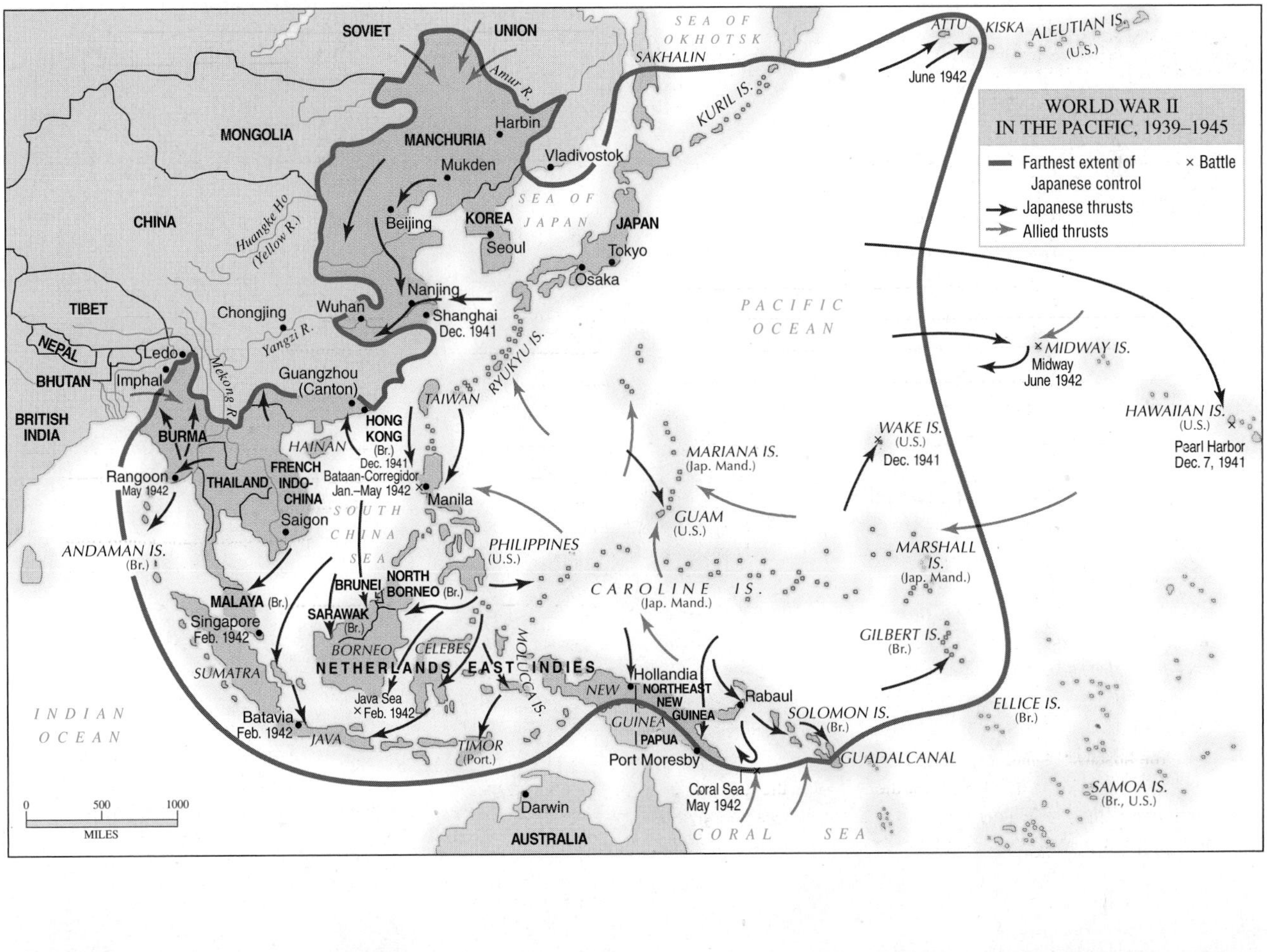

WORLD WAR II IN THE PACIFIC, 1939–1945

Farthest extent of Japanese control × Battle
Japanese thrusts
Allied thrusts

waves of American bombers rained destruction on Japanese cities. This virtually nonstop bombing claimed a huge toll of civilian casualties. One hundred Japanese cities were fire-bombed; the fire-bombing of Tokyo left at least 100,000 dead and 1.5 million families homeless in one night of incendiary attacks. The attacks on Japan's civilian population made it clear that the Japanese government had lied to its people about wartime success.

The war was devastating to non-Japanese as well, including approximately 700,000 Korean and Chinese forced laborers in Japan and several hundred thousand Chinese, Koreans, and Southeast Asians working for the Japanese occupation forces in their own countries, thousands of comfort women, and thousands of prisoners of war who received brutal treatment such as that accorded the Americans and Filipinos in the Bataan Death March in the Philippines and the Allies in the slave labor camps throughout Southeast Asia. Japan's notorious Unit 731 performed heinous medical experiments on prisoners.

In the China-Burma-India theater, the Chinese, with U.S. aid, made inroads into areas previously captured by Japan. As the Allies come closer to defeating Japan, Japan's military leadership engaged in desperation tactics, forcing several thousand young men, known as *kamikaze* ("divine wind") pilots, to fly to their deaths by crashing into American ships. Extrapolating from the death tolls in the island-hopping campaigns, American military planners projected that the casualty rate for the taking of the main island of Japan would run into the hundreds of thousands.

The final developments in the Pacific War took place in the American state of New Mexico, where by

▼ President Harry Truman's controversial decision to drop the atomic bombs on Hiroshima and Nagasaki in 1945 helped end the war in the Pacific. However, as nuclear competition between the United States and the USSR led to devices of enormously greater destructiveness than the bombs dropped in 1945, the mushroom cloud came to symbolize the reality that scientists had created weapons that could extinguish humanity. Détente between Moscow and Washington brought a period of relaxation in the 1980s and 1990s, but fears of nuclear proliferation remain.

1945, U.S. scientists, with the help of physicists who had fled central Europe to escape Hitler, invented a new and terrible weapon, the atomic bomb. After the defeat of Germany, the Japanese began to seek ways to end the war short of the "unconditional surrender" demanded by the Allies by approaching the Soviets to serve as mediators. But the Russians had already agreed to enter the war. The Potsdam Declaration, issued by U.S. President Truman and British Prime Minister Clement Atlee in July, reiterated the demand that Japan unconditionally surrender or face "utter destruction." Japanese Prime Minister Suzuki Kantarō, unwilling to abandon the emperor, which he believed would be required under unconditional surrender, decided to "silently ignore" the declaration. On August 6, an American bomber dropped an atomic bomb on the city of Hiroshima. As the mushroom-shaped cloud rose over the city, only charred ruins were left behind. An expanse of approximately 3 square miles, 60 percent of the city, was pulverized. Estimates of those killed instantly range from 78,000 to 140,000; an additional 100,000 were seriously, often mortally, wounded and 200,000 left homeless. Two days later, the Soviets declared war on Japan. The next day, August 9, a second bomb was dropped on the city of Nagasaki, killing about 70,000. Many scholars believe that the second atomic bomb was intended as a signal of American might not only to the Japanese but also to the Soviets, anticipating the tensions of the post–World War II Cold War era. Deaths from radiation sickness caused by the two bombs continued into the 1950s.

An Eyewitness to Hiroshima

On August 15, the Japanese population stood silent and dazed as they heard the emperor's high-pitched voice for the first time on the radio, telling them to "endure the unendurable." The war was over, the losses now meaningless. The surrender ceremony took place aboard the battleship *Missouri* on September 2, 1945, 14 years after Japanese forces first invaded Manchuria.

Postwar Settlements

Why were victorious allies unable to establish a lasting peace after the end of World War II?

The Japanese were left reeling from the devastation and profoundly disgusted with the war and the government that had led them into that conflict. They were ready, after defeat, to resume the democratic trends they had experienced in the 1920s, under the rule of the Allied Occupation headed by American General Douglas MacArthur.

Europeans faced the challenges of economically and politically reconstructing their countries. One-fourth of Germany's cities were in rubble, as were numerous places in Italy and central Europe. Many of the people who had escaped battle and bombing combed through the ruins to try to find food in their struggle to survive. In places like Yugoslavia, the war against the Germans and Italians and the civil wars that followed claimed 10 percent of the population and left a legacy of bitterness that would erupt in bitter conflicts 40 years later. Twenty-five million people died in the Soviet Union, and the country lost a third of its national wealth as well as the next generation of leaders—condemning the country to be ruled a generation later by leaders who were old, ill, and weak.

Europe faced two other problems at the end of the war: dealing with Nazi collaborators and resettling millions of labor slaves. In countries that had been occupied by the Germans, victorious resistance groups began to take vigilante justice against those who had worked with the invaders. Across Europe they executed thousands of collaborators. In France alone, 800 were sent to their deaths. After the war and into the mid-1990s, courts sentenced thousands more to prison terms. Eight million foreign laborers who had been exploited as slaves by the Nazis remained to be resettled. Five million of them had been sent home by the end of 1945, including many Soviet citizens who were repatriated against their will. Some of them chose suicide rather than return to Stalin's rule.

In Germany, the Allies began to carry out a selective process of denazification. Some former Nazis were sent to prison, but thousands of others remained free because of large-scale declarations of amnesty. Many ex-Nazis were employed by the scientific and intelligence services of each of the Allies. Symbolically, the most important denazification act came at the 1945–1946 trials of war criminals held at **Nuremberg.** Critics condemned the trials as an act of vengeance, "a political act by the victors against the vanquished." The prosecution declared, however, that the Nazis' crimes were so terrible that "civilization cannot tolerate their being ignored because it cannot survive their being repeated." As Telford Taylor, the American prosecutor of the German general staff, stated, "The gas chambers, mountains of corpses, human-skin lampshades, shrunken skulls, freezing experiments, and bank vaults filled with gold teeth" were the "poisoned fruit" of the tree of German militarism. Taylor brushed aside the generals' arguments that they were "just following orders." He made the point that they still had to exercise moral judgment.[17] An international panel of jurists conducted the proceedings; it condemned 12 leading Nazis to be hanged and sent 7 to prison for crimes against humanity. The panel also acquitted three high officials. Nuremberg established

Nuremberg Trials—After World War II, trials of Nazi war criminals for crimes against humanity that took place in Nuremberg, formerly the site of Hitler's mass rallies.

the precedent for War Crimes tribunals that have subsequently taken place in The Hague under the aegis of the United Nations.

Following the Yalta agreement, the Allies established four occupation zones in Germany: French, British, American, and Soviet. They divided the capital, Berlin, located in the Soviet sector, into four similar parts. The Soviets promised free access from the western zones to Berlin. Growing hostility between the Soviet Union and the United States by the end of the war blocked a comprehensive peace settlement for Germany.

Conclusion

By 1945, the victorious allies had put an end to German, Italian, and Japanese aggression. In contrast with World War I, which has spawned many historiographical controversies concerning its causes, there is no doubt that the key figure in the starting of World War II in Europe was Adolf Hitler. He was the essential link, the man whose policies and ideas welded the dictators together.

Unlike the Japanese and the Italians, whose global influence was limited by either geographical or internal problems, Hitler could build on Germany's industrial might and central location to forge a force for continental conquest. Historians vary sharply on his goals and motivations. Some see him as a politician playing the traditional game of European power politics in a most skillful way, whereas others view him as a single-minded fanatic pursuing the plans for conquest laid out in *Mein Kampf.* Between these two extremes are the scholars who believe that the Führer had thought out long-term goals but pursued them haphazardly as opportunities presented themselves.

Hitler struck the spark that set off the European conflagration. Aiding and abetting his ambitions was the obsessive desire of the democracies for peace. By 1939, the lesson had been learned that appeasement does not guarantee peace, nor does it take two equally belligerent sides to make a war.

Although Japanese militarism and expansionism were rooted in different origins—that is, aggressive imperialism compounded by a rejection of the multilateralist capitalist world order of which it had been a part for almost half a century—the linking of Japan's Asian war with the war in Europe made World War II a truly global phenomenon. The causes of war in these two theaters may not have been linked, but the outcome—the Cold War—certainly was.

Suggestions for Web Browsing

You can obtain more information about topics included in this chapter at the websites listed below. See also the companion website that accompanies this text, http://www.ablongman.com/brummett, which contains an online study guide and additional resources.

The Nanjing Massacres
http://www.gotrain.com/dan/nanking1.htm
The page attempts a full portrayal of the horrors of the Japanese taking of Nanjing.

Lycos Guide to World War II
http://www.lycos.com/wguide/network/net 969250.html
This portal provides a rich compilation of websites regarding all aspects of World War II.

Battle of Stalingrad
http://www.stalingrad.net/
This website offers rare photos of this pivotal battle of World War II.

Role of American Women in World War II
http://www.pomperaug.com/socstud/stumuseum/web/arhhome.htm
This site provides a rich repository of photos, primary interviews, and other materials detailing the role of women on the American side of the war.

D-Day
http://www.isidore-of-seville.com/d-day/
This extensive site provides information on D-Day.

The Holocaust
http://www.wiesenthal.com/
The Simon Wiesenthal Center provides a wide range of information about the Holocaust.

National Holocaust Museum
http://www.remember.org
This site provides the most exhaustive support for students searching for information on genocide and the Holocaust.

Hiroshima Archive
http://www.kyohaku.go.jp
A poignant research and educational guide for all who wish to expand their knowledge of the atomic bombing of Japan.

Literature and Film

Some major novels dealing with World War II are (all in many different editions) James Michener, *Tales of the South Pacific,* Thomas Heggen, *Mr. Roberts,* Leon Uris, *Battle Cry,* and Norman Mailer, *The Naked and the Dead.* Herman Wouk's epic *Winds of War* and *War and Remembrance* trace the war from 1939 through to the discovery of the death camps. Jerzy Kosinski's *Painted Bird* traces the path of an orphan through Poland during the war. Günter Grass's *Tin Drum* follows the Nazi progress through Danzig, and Joseph Heller captures the insanity of war in *Catch-22.* Curzio Malaparte, in *Kaputt,* traces the course of the war from the Axis side. Kenzaburo Oe's *Fire from the Ashes: Short Stories About*

Hiroshima and Nagasaki gives the reader the perspective of the victims of the first nuclear attack.

Filmmakers have presented various aspects of the war. All of the novels above have served as the basis for films. Bernhard Wicki's *The Longest Day* (1962; Fox) and Franklin J. Schaffner's *Patton* (1970; Fox) are masterpieces. Recently, Jean-Jacques Annaud captured the drama of the battle of Stalingrad in *Enemy at the Gates* (2001; Paramount). Terrence Malick's *The Thin Red Line* (1999; Fox) caught the horror of the Pacific War. Four of Steven Spielberg's most important films have dealt with various aspects of the conflict: The home front was portrayed in *1941* (1979; Universal Studios). The Japanese invasion and occupation of China were shown through the eyes of a child in *Empire of the Sun* (1987; Warner). *Schindler's List* (1993; Universal Studios) captured the tragedy of the Holocaust, and the bravery and suffering of the American GIs were presented in *Saving Private Ryan* (1998; Universal/MCA). Robert Benigni's *La Vita è Bella,* or "Life Is Beautiful" (1998; Miramax) gives a bittersweet view of Italian fascism and life in a concentration camp. Clint Eastwood has produced and directed two films on the battle of Iwo Jima—one from the American and one from the Japanese point of view: *Flags of our Fathers* and *Letters from Iwo Jima* (2006).

Suggestions for Reading

A provocative and compelling study of the twentieth century is Niall Ferguson, *The War of the World: History's Age of Hatred* (Penguin/Allen Lane). Hans Gatzke, ed., *European Diplomacy Between the Two Wars, 1919–1939* (Quadrangle, 1972), remains a useful survey. Gerhard Weinberg gives a penetrating analysis in his two books: *The Foreign Policy of Hitler's Germany: Diplomatic Revolution in Europe, 1933–1936* (University of Chicago Press, 1970) and *The Foreign Policy of Hitler's Germany, 1937–1939* (University of Chicago Press, 1980). For a study of the pressures affecting Franklin Roosevelt as he responded to the European crisis, see Barbara Rearden Farnham, *Roosevelt and the Munich Crisis: A Study of Political Decision Making* (Princeton University Press, 1997). The role of advanced technology in the Allied victory is discussed by Richard Overy, *Why the Allies Won* (W. W. Norton, 1997).

A study that reveals the multifaceted background of Chamberlain's policy is Gaines Post, *Dilemmas of Appeasement: British Deterrence and Defense, 1934–1937* (Cornell University Press, 1993). Michael Alpert provides an overview of the tragic events in Spain in *A New International History of the Spanish Civil War* (St. Martin's Press, 1998). For Hitler, see also Ian Kershaw's two-volume biography cited in Chapter 28. Albert Seaton, The *Russo-German War, 1941–1945* (Praeger, 1970), is especially strong in its analysis of Soviet strategy.

See also the study edited by Akira Iriye, *Pearl Harbor and the Coming of the Pacific War* (Bedford/St. Martins, 1999), for a series of essays and documents on the origins of the Pacific War. Yoshiaki Yashimi carried out interviews with survivors and archival research to produce *Comfort Women: Sexual Slavery in the Japanese Military During World War II* (Columbia University Press, 2001). Two indispensable studies are John Dower, *War Without Mercy: Race and Power in the Pacific War* (Pantheon Books, 1986), and Haruko Taya Cook and Theodore Cook, *Japan at War: An Oral History* (New Press, 1992).

The Nazis' genocide policies are analyzed in Raul Hilberg, *The Destruction of the European Jews* (Quadrangle, 1961). Primo Levi's *Survival in Auschwitz* (Touchstone, 1996) gives a measured view of what it was like to be inside the killing machine. Telford Taylor's memoir, *The Anatomy of the Nuremberg Trials* (Knopf, 1994), is a thorough and compelling discussion of these unprecedented hearings.

CHAPTER 32

Europe and the United States Since 1945

The Cold War and After

Outline

- The Cold War: The US and the USSR in Global Competition to 1991
- The Soviet Union and the Russian Republic
- Eastern Europe: From Soviet Control to Independence
- Western Europe
- The United States

Features

DISCOVERY THROUGH MAPS **Massive Retaliatory Power, 1954**

SEEING CONNECTIONS **JFK and Khrushchev**

GLOBAL ISSUES **The Environment**

DOCUMENT **Martin Luther King Jr., "Beyond Vietnam, A Time to Break Silence"**

◀ Early in his first administration, President Ronald Reagan referred to the Soviet Union as the "Evil Empire" and showed little interest in cooperating in any way with Moscow. After the accession of Mikhail Gorbachev, Reagan changed his attitude, and the two men worked closely to ease tensions between the two great powers.

THANKS TO EFFICIENT state structures, superior technology, effective economic systems, and powerful armies with superior firepower, Europe and its outposts dominated the globe by 1900. This domination was not to last long, however, thanks in part to chronic interstate competition among the Europeans that culminated in two disastrous world wars that exhausted if not devastated outright the traditional great powers of the West (see Chapters 27 and 31). After 1945, two countries from the peripheries of the West, the Union of Soviet Socialist Republics and the United States, competed for global control for another half century. Their ideologies presented starkly different views about the nature of politics, economics, society, and religion and the role of the individual.

This competition—coming at the same time as decolonization and the emergence of the colonial peoples to independence (see Chapters 33, 34, and 35)—never came to open war because the nuclear arsenals possessed by Moscow and Washington made the prospects of surviving such a conflict remote. Indeed, not only would nuclear war destroy the two main combatants, it would also bring utter ruin to their allies and the other nations of the world, threatening life itself on the planet. Yet the absence of open conflict did not mean that peace reigned between these rivals, who instead engaged in proxy wars and indirect conflict across the globe for more than four decades.

This time of no war/no peace was known as the Cold War, and it would divide Europe until 1989. Although the two sides concentrated millions of troops and targeted thousands of nuclear weapons against each other in Europe and beyond, the stalemate that resulted gave the Continent, whether in its Soviet Bloc or Western spheres, the longest period of peace in its modern history.

The Cold War: The US and the USSR in Global Competition to 1991

What were some of the factors that permitted the United States and the Soviet Union to avoid direct conflict during the Cold War?

August 1945 signaled a new age in world history. Within five years, the United States and the Union of Soviet Socialist Republics, the sole possessors of nuclear weapons, stood alone in their bipolar confrontation. A five-century-long epoch in world history in which the most powerful countries maintained their domination through the use of superior military technology had arrived at its final act.

The Roots of the Cold War

By the beginning of 1943, Stalin was irritated by American and British hesitation in opening the second front in Europe while his country bore the brunt of Nazi attacks. He was also upset by the lack of information from the Western Allies on their activities in North Africa and Italy. Finally, he did not think that the United States had provided enough financial support to the USSR, and he took this as a sign of insufficient appreciation for the suffering and contributions of his nation during World War II.

During the war, the Western Allies expressed their discontent at the lack of Soviet public recognition of their assistance and the USSR's unwillingness to share information. As the Russians advanced into Eastern Europe in 1944 and 1945, Washington and London noted with disapproval Stalin's imposition of pro-communist leaders in positions of power in Eastern Europe. The activities of Soviet spies in the United States and the United Kingdom also spread suspicions of Stalin and the Soviet Union.

The breakdown of wartime cooperation that led to the half century of Cold War is the subject of wide-ranging and passionate disagreement among historians. One school of interpretation accuses the United States of putting Stalin in an untenable position and of being responsible for the Cold War. Others accuse Stalin of a consistent and long-term search for the extension of communism, especially after the battle of Stalingrad; they find the Soviet Union responsible for the Cold War.

Historians who take a more centralist approach note that the United States and USSR had differed in their views on economics, politics, social organization, religion, and the role of the individual in society since the November Revolution of 1917. The Nazi invasion of Russia temporarily brought the two sides together, but fractures in the anti-Axis alliance began to appear toward the end of 1943. The decline of the traditional European powers created a power vacuum around the globe into which the forces of Moscow and Washington entered and came into competition.

No matter which view is accepted, it is clear that the devastating power of nuclear weapons ensured that the United States and the Soviet Union never directly fought each other. However, "proxy wars" fought by their client nations and their own occasional interventions cost millions of lives in the areas of Asia, Africa, and Latin America that were undergoing decolonization.

A New Capitalist Framework

Even before the defeat of the Axis in World War II, the Western allies made plans to avoid the horrendous economic crisis that had followed World War I. Forty-four nations, the core of the original membership of the United Nations, met in July 1944 at the New Hampshire resort town of Bretton Woods to put the projected peacetime world economy on a solid footing. Recalling the lessons of **protectionism** and **autarky** in the 1930s, the financial leaders devised plans to ensure a free flow of international trade.

protectionism—An economic policy of favoring domestic interests by imposing limits and tariffs on foreign trade and economic competition.

autarky—The policy of economic independence and self-sufficiency.

Chronology

1940			1950	1960
1944 Bretton Woods Conference 1945 International Monetary Fund (IMF) chartered; World Bank chartered	1947 General Agreement on Trade and Tariffs (GATT) approved 1945 Yalta Conference; Potsdam Conference; WWII ends; UN chartered; Ho Chi Minh establishes Republic of Vietnam	1947 Truman Doctrine; Marshall Plan begins 1949 NATO formed; COMECON established; Berlin blockade; People's Republic of China proclaimed	1950 European Coal and Steel Community established 1950–1953 Korean War 1956 Khrushchev begins de-Stalinization; Hungarian Revolt; Suez Crisis	1962 Cuban Missile Crisis 1963 President Kennedy assassinated 1968 Prague Spring; Soviet Bloc invasion of Czechoslovakia 1968 Martin Luther King Jr., Robert Kennedy assassinated

The **Bretton Woods Conference** created the **International Monetary Fund (IMF),** chartered in 1945, to restore the money system that had collapsed in previous decades when countries abandoned the gold standard and resorted to export-enhancing devices such as currency devaluation and protectionist measures such as tariffs and quotas. The conference intended that the IMF would oversee a system of fixed exchange rates, founded on the dollar, that could be exchanged for gold at the rate of $35 an ounce. The IMF was based on a foundation of currencies paid in by the member states. These deposits served as a world savings account from which a member state could take short-term loans to handle debt payments without having to resort to the disruptive tactics of manipulating exchange rates or devaluation.

The conference also established the International Bank for Reconstruction and Development, more commonly known as the World Bank, chartered in December 1945. In its first 10 years, the World Bank focused mostly on the rebuilding of Europe. Over the next three decades, the bank devoted the bulk of its resources to aiding states undergoing development or rebuilding.

A key development in reforming the world economy was the establishment in 1947 of the **General Agreement on Tariffs and Trade (GATT)** under U.S. leadership. Having absorbed the lessons of the protectionist and autarkic 1930s, the Allies put together an international institution to set up worldwide rules for business that would give nations the confidence to break down old barriers that blocked free trade. GATT operated through a series of meetings between nations to remove protectionist restrictions. The assurance that a nation received for entering the GATT framework was the "most favored nation" clause, which guaranteed that any trade advantage worked out in a nation-to-nation agreement would be automatically shared by all members of GATT.

Bretton Woods Conference—In July 1944, 44 nations met at the New Hampshire resort town of Bretton Woods to put the peacetime economy on a solid footing. The participants wanted to avoid the economic mistakes of the interwar period.

International Monetary Fund (IMF)—Chartered in 1945, the International Monetary Fund was created to restore the money system that had collapsed in previous decades.

General Agreement on Tariffs and Trade (GATT)—Established in 1947, the General Agreements on Tariffs and Trade sought to avoid the protectionist and autarkist errors of the interwar period and establish a framework that would permit free trade among nations.

The Soviet Alternative

The Soviet Union refused to participate in the Western plans for protecting and extending free markets. Stalin and his successors, until Gorbachev, maintained the central planning model installed in the late 1920s and implanted it in the Eastern European countries that came under their influence after the end of World War II. Under this economic system, known as **COMECON,** Moscow followed the "Socialism in One Country" theory, in which international communists had to sacrifice for the benefit of Russia. At first, the Eastern European allies—which had been, with few exceptions, dominated by the Nazis—indirectly helped pay for the reconstruction of the war-damaged Soviet Union. Then in the 1950s, Moscow attempted to organize the various socialist economies for the greater good of the socialist whole. The Soviet Union wanted each of its allied nations to specialize in producing certain items for the entire **Soviet Bloc.** This was an unpopular idea in the allied nations such as Romania, which saw itself condemned to raising corn and wheat while other countries could industrialize.

The central planning system in its USSR and Soviet Bloc versions provided for economic growth until the 1970s. New technological challenges and domestic priorities overtaxed COMECON thereafter, and the system was unable to reform itself.

COMECON—The economic bloc coordinated by the Soviet Union.

Soviet Bloc—The allies of the Soviet Union in Europe and Asia.

1970	1980	1990	2000	
1974 President Richard M. Nixon resigns 1975 Reunification of Vietnam	1985 Gorbachev declares policies of *glasnost* and *perestroika* 1989–1990 Collapse of communism in eastern Europe; reunification of Germany	1991 Unsuccessful coup against Gorbachev. End of USSR 1995 World Trade Organization (WTO) established	2001 al-Qaeda terrorist attacks in New York and Washington; U.S. invasion of Afghanistan 2002 European Union introduces the Euro	2003 U.S.-led invasion of Iraq 2004 Madrid terrorist bombings; European Union adds nine new states 2005 Terrorist bombings in London

The Cold War in Europe to 1953

From 1945 to 1948, Stalin carefully expanded his control over the region, working through his allies' domination of the various coalition governments. The Communists occupied the most powerful positions in the coalition governments; opposition parties gained largely symbolic posts. By the end of 1948, when the Americans had largely withdrawn from Europe, the governments in Warsaw, East Berlin, Prague, Budapest, Bucharest, Sofia, and Tirana operated as satellites orbiting the political center of Moscow. Stalin used the Soviet Bloc as a 400-mile-deep buffer against capitalist invasion and as a source to help the USSR rebuild. He blocked any political, economic, or cultural contact with the West. Only Yugoslavia, led by Marshal Josip Tito, remained outside of Moscow's hegemonic control.

Meanwhile, in the 3 years after 1945, the four-power agreement on the governing of Germany soon broke apart. In the fall of 1946, Britain and America merged their zones into one economic unit, which came to be known as Bizonia. The French joined that union in 1948. Germany was now split into two parts, one administered by the Western Allies and the other by the Soviets. It would remain divided until the line between the two powers—dubbed the "Iron Curtain" by Churchill in 1946—fell in 1989.

The Soviets did not return their armies to peacetime status after 1945. They challenged the West in Turkey and Iran while the Yugoslav and Albanian communist governments supported the Greek partisans against the British-sponsored government in Athens. Britain, however, was too weak to play its former dominant role in the region. The United States, as it would subsequently do throughout the globe, filled the gaps left by its wartime allies.

In 1947, President Truman responded to Soviet pressure by announcing that the United States would support any country threatened by communist aggression. He stated, "I believe that it must be the policy of the United States to support free peoples who are resisting attempted subjugation by armed minorities or by outside pressures."[1]

Soon after this proclamation of the **Truman Doctrine** in 1947, the United States sent economic and military aid to Greece and Turkey, a move traditionally held to mark the active American entry into the Cold War.

DOCUMENT
The Truman Doctrine

American diplomat George F. Kennan, in his diplomatic telegrams from Moscow, outlined the correct stance to take toward Stalin's policies, that of **containment.** In an article titled "The Sources of Soviet Conduct," written anonymously in the July 1947 issue of *Foreign Affairs,* Kennan proposed a "realistic understanding of the profound and deep-rooted difference between the United States and the Soviet Union" and the exercise of "a long-term, patient but firm and vigilant containment of Russian expansive tendencies."[2] This advice successfully shaped U.S. policy throughout Europe but later was tragically misapplied in Southeast Asia.

Truman Doctrine—The policy proclaimed in 1947 that the United States would support any country threatened by communist aggression.

containment—The doctrine proposed by George F. Kennan that stated that the best way to deal with the Soviet Union was through the exercise of a containment of Russian expansive tendencies. Kennan believed that once the forward momentum of the Soviet advance was blocked, internal contradictions would weaken the Soviet Union.

	Germany: The European Epicenter of the Cold War
1945	Russians take Berlin; Four Power Agreement on the governing of Germany; quadripartite division of Berlin
1946	Russians begin reneging on economic agreements; British and U.S. zones merged
1947	Truman Doctrine announced; start of containment strategy; Marshall Plan
1948	USSR consolidates control over Eastern Europe, blockades Berlin; French zone merges with British and U.S. zones
1949	NATO established; COMECON established; German Federal Republic (West Germany) established, Konrad Adenauer becomes chancellor; German "economic miracle" begins
1953	Workers revolt in East Germany (German Democratic Republic) over food shortage and increased working hours
1955–1961	USSR demands withdrawal of Western forces; Berlin a "free city"
1961	Khrushchev demands Western withdrawal from Berlin; construction of Berlin Wall; German Democratic Republic sealed off from West
1982–1983	Missile debate
1988	East German leaders begin censoring Russian papers
1989	East Germans flee to West through Czechoslovakia and Hungary; Berlin Wall opened up
1990	Germany reunited

Shown here in 1947 are President Harry S Truman, Undersecretary of State Robert Lovett, George F. Kennan, Director of Policy Planning at State, and Charles E. Bohlen, Special Assistant to Secretary of State George Marshall. These men were part of the team that reconfigured the foreign policy stance of the United States after World War II and could be considered as the "Godfathers of Containment."

The broad economic and political arms of containment came into play. Secretary of State George C. Marshall proposed a plan of economic aid at the Harvard commencement exercises in June 1947 to help Europe solve its postwar financial problems. Western European nations eagerly accepted the **Marshall Plan,** but the Soviet Union rejected American aid for itself and its bloc. Congress authorized the plan, known as the European Recovery Program, and within 4 years, the industrial output of the recipients climbed to 64 percent over 1947 levels and 41 percent over prewar levels. The program supplied most of the capital and technical assistance the Western European states needed for reconstruction. The Marshall Plan funds came with strict conditions: the recipients had to promise to balance their budgets, free prices, fight inflation, establish a stable currency, and eliminate protectionist trade measures. No similar aid plan was extended to Japan, although American military requisitions for the Korean War greatly helped Japan's economy to recovery after 1950.

In July 1948, after opposing a Western series of currency and economic reforms in Germany, the Soviets blocked all land and water transport to Berlin from the West. For the next ten months, the allies supplied West Berlin by air. They made over 277,000 flights to bring 2.3 million tons of food and other vital materials to the besieged city. Rather than risk war over the city, with the threat of American nuclear weapons, the Soviets removed their blockade in May 1949. In the same month, the Federal Republic of Germany came into existence, made up of the three Western allied zones. Almost immediately, the Soviet Union established the German Democratic Republic in the Soviet zone. Germany would remain divided for the next 41 years.

Marshall Plan—The U.S. plan to aid Europe in solving its postwar economic problems. The goals were not only the economic reconstruction of Europe, but also the blocking of the domestic communist movements in each country.

In the spring of 1949, the United States and its allies established the **North Atlantic Treaty Organization (NATO),** an alliance for mutual assistance. The initial members were Great Britain, France, Belgium, Luxembourg, the Netherlands, Norway, Denmark, Portugal, Italy, Iceland, the United States, and Canada. Greece and Turkey joined in 1952, followed by West Germany in 1955. At the beginning, NATO was essentially a paper organization. The Americans had withdrawn their troops from Europe and disarmed so quickly after World War II that in 1949, there was no effective force that could repel a Soviet attack. In response, military planners saw one of two solutions: either take what troops that could be scraped together and retreat behind the Pyrenees to Spain, or flee across the Channel to England. Soon, the Americans crafted their strategic response to the communists in a document known as NSC-68, which led to the creation of an immense military system and a vast expansion of the newly created Central Intelligence Agency (CIA) to counter the communist advance anywhere in the world by any means necessary.

In 1955, the Soviets created the **Warsaw Pact,** which formalized the already existing unified military command in Soviet-dominated Eastern Europe. Warsaw Pact members included, in addition to the Soviet Union, Albania, Bulgaria, Romania, Czechoslovakia, Hungary, Poland, and East Germany. The alliance lasted until 1989.

China and Korea: 1949–1953

The communist leader Mao Zedong's victory in China in 1949 (see Chapter 35) shocked the United States even more than did the communist advances in Eastern Europe in 1948. Suddenly, the global maps featured a large part of Eurasia colored in red. But few

North Atlantic Treaty Organization (NATO)—The United States and its allies constructed this alliance for mutual assistance, establishing NATO in 1949.

Warsaw Pact—The military alliance of the Soviet Bloc, established in 1955.

people in the West were prepared for what was about to happen in Korea.

After Japan's surrender in World War II, Korea had been divided at the 38th parallel into American and Soviet zones of occupation (see Chapter 35). When the occupying troops left, two hostile forces replaced them, each claiming jurisdiction over the entire country. On June 25, 1950, North Korean troops crossed the 38th parallel into South Korea. The United States immediately called for a special meeting of the **UN Security Council,** whose members demanded a cease-fire and withdrawal of the invaders. The Soviet delegate was boycotting the council at the time and was not present to veto the action.

When North Korea ignored the UN's demand, the Security Council sent troops to help the South Korean government. In what the United States termed a "police action," 3 years of costly fighting followed. United Nations forces led by the United States repelled the invaders, who were supported by the USSR and the People's Republic of China. An armistice was signed in July 1953, after Stalin's death in March and a U.S. threat to use nuclear weapons against China. Two million Koreans, north and south, perished. About half a million Chinese and over 50,000 Americans lost their lives before the armistice was signed by representatives of North Korea, China, and the United States (on behalf of the United Nations). There were no South Korean representatives present. A new border between the two parts of the country was established near the 38th parallel, and South Korea's independence was maintained. After a period of improving relations between the two Koreas, serious tensions reemerged in the early twenty-first century.

UN Security Council—The arm of the UN made up of representatives of the permanent members of the UN plus other states that serve limited terms. Its function is to maintain peace and order.

▼ The Korean War was the first in which the U.S. military forces were racially integrated.

The Khrushchev Years: 1953–1964

After World War II, Josef Stalin returned to the policies he had imposed in the 1930s—a command economy based on 5-year plans enforced by the security police. Until his death in 1953, Stalin oversaw the extension of communist governments throughout Eastern Europe and in China. Stalin came to occupy the same all-commanding position in the communist-controlled countries abroad as he did in the Soviet Union.

Red Square Military Parade, Moscow

Stalin's death in March 1953 introduced a period of collective leadership in the Soviet Union. The transition from an all-powerful despot to a clique of competing **apparatchiks** brought a change to the nature and scope of Soviet foreign policy for the 2 years after 1953. A committee initially made up of Lavrenti Beria (secret police), Georgi Malenkov (chief Stalin aide), and Vyacheslav Molotov (foreign affairs) succeeded Stalin. Within 3 years, the initial triumvirate had disappeared, elbowed aside by Nikita Sergeyevich Khrushchev (khroo-SHCHOV; 1894–1971).

Khrushchev immediately imposed his point of view that nuclear war would be suicidal for all concerned. He returned to the Leninist doctrine of **peaceful coexistence** and renounced the idea that open war between the socialist and capitalist worlds was inevitable. Peaceful coexistence ushered in momentarily better relations between Moscow and Washington and led to a summit meeting in Geneva with President Dwight D. Eisenhower in 1955. Later, the Americans refrained from interfering in the Polish and Hungarian crises that erupted in October–November 1956, and Moscow and Washington worked together during the Suez Crisis (see Chapter 33) that same year.

Khrushchev also launched a de-Stalinization campaign at home. In February 1956, at the Twentieth Party Congress, he gave a speech titled "The Crimes of the

apparatchiks—Officials working within the Stalinist bureaucracy, the party apparatus, who gained their livelihood and status from their position within the ruling structure.

peaceful coexistence—The Leninist doctrine that refutes the notion that open war between the socialist and capitalist worlds is inevitable—competition between the two systems would continue in all other areas, however.

Discovery Through Maps

Massive Retaliatory Power, 1954

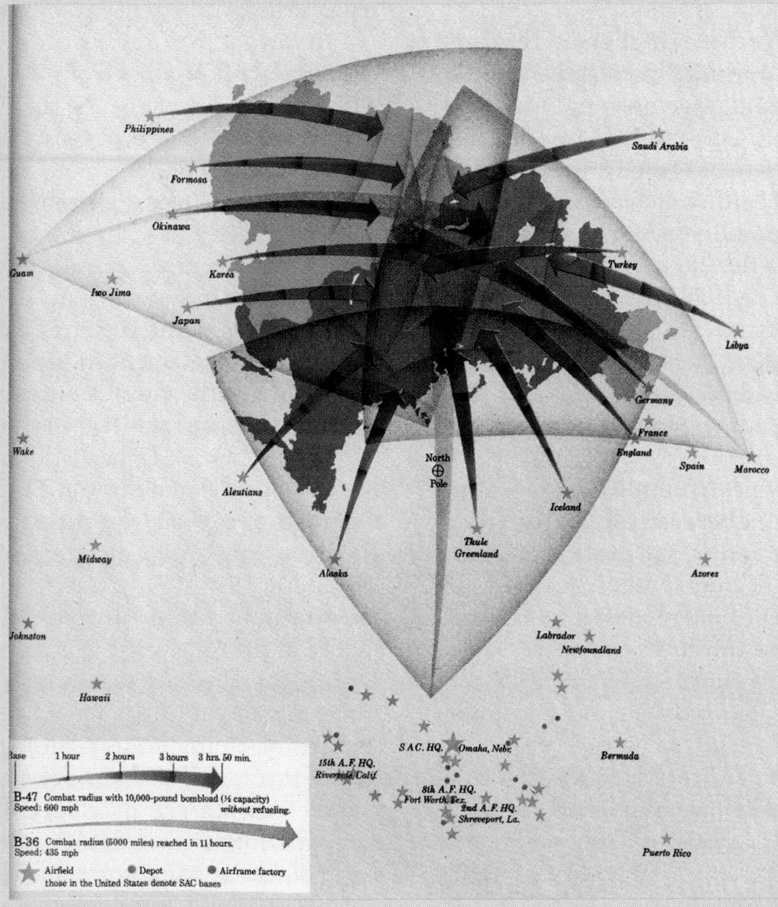

The decisive fact of life for citizens of the United States and the Soviet Union in the 1950s and 1960s was the possibility, perhaps the probability, that a cataclysmic nuclear conflict would bring an end to the human race. As open air nuclear testing spread and polluted the earth's atmosphere, Moscow and Washington pursued a race to develop delivery systems to gain an added advantage in case of war.

Students in schools practiced the maneuver of "duck and cover" to protect themselves from incoming warheads. Homeowners were encouraged to build backyard bomb shelters. Radio stations broadcast "test emergency warnings." In the northern part of the United States, volunteers scanned the skies for incoming aircraft.

This is an example of a Cold War map that was published in *Fortune* magazine in May 1954 after John Foster Dulles, the U.S. secretary of state, announced a new policy based on "massive retaliation." This map was meant to reassure Americans that the major Soviet targets were well covered and that Moscow dared not attack first.

This propaganda effort was accompanied by a program to present the Russians as evil, in order to justify the buildup of Americans arms. Only a few people were even willing to consider that similar maps were circulating in Moscow, showing American targets, and that the likeliest outcome of the retaliation strategy would be mutual destruction.

After the Cuban Missile Crisis of October 1962, the Soviet Union and the United States started a long process to lessen the possibility of a nuclear nightmare. Forty years later, George W. Bush, the president of the United States, and Vladimir Putin, the president of Russia, signed a treaty to reduce the number of their nuclear weapons by two-thirds.

Questions to Consider

1. Attack or defend the following statement: "Nuclear weapons are the only factors that have prevented a World War III."
2. In your opinion, what role did manipulation of public opinion play in justifying the U.S. arms buildup?
3. What were the advantages for the United States in their policy of "massive retaliation"?

Stalin Era." He attacked his former patron as a bloodthirsty tyrant and revealed many of the cruelties of the purges and the mistakes of World War II. He carefully heaped full responsibility on the dead dictator for the excesses of the past 25 years, removing the blame from the apparatchiks such as himself whom Stalin had placed in power. Khrushchev blamed Stalin's crimes on the dictator's "cult of the personality."

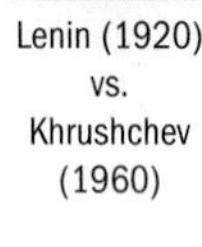

CASE STUDY Lenin (1920) vs. Khrushchev (1960)

Khrushchev's speech echoed throughout the communist world, sparking uprisings in Poland and Hungary in October and November and widening the gulf between China and the Soviet Union. Chinese-Soviet relations soured drastically after 1956, and by 1960, Khrushchev had pulled all Soviet technicians and assistance out of China. During the next decade, the split grew still wider as Mao proclaimed himself to be Khrushchev's equal in ideological affairs, and the Chinese tried to extend their own power in the developing world against both the Soviet Union and the United States by sending out the same sorts of technicians and money as the others.

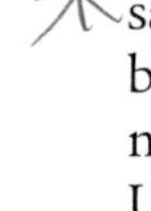

Two Soviet technological triumphs in 1957, however, escalated the tensions between the United States and the USSR. Soviet scientists put the first artificial satellite, *Sputnik,* into orbit around the earth and began building a powerful fleet of intercontinental ballistic missiles (ICBMs). These advances gave the Soviet Union the ability to land a nuclear weapon on U.S. territory in 25 minutes. The Cold War was becoming much more dangerous.

DOCUMENT Khrushchev Challenges the West to Disarm

A series of disagreements between Moscow and Washington in the late 1950s put an end to the easing of tensions achieved at the Geneva summit. A summit convened in Paris in 1960 broke up angrily when the Soviets shot down an American U-2 reconnaissance plane over Siberia. Khrushchev, sensing the presence of an ailing, lame-duck president in Eisenhower and two young, untested presidential candidates in Richard Nixon and John F. Kennedy, seized the opportunity to denounce the West and advance Soviet interests in a series of provocative moves in Asia, Latin America, and Africa. Specifically, he demanded the resignation of UN Secretary-General Dag Hammarskjold (HAM-mer-shold), whom he believed opposed the Soviet-backed side in the civil war currently raging in the Congo.

Khrushchev and Kennedy

DOCUMENT Kennedy and Cuba

In the spring of 1961, with John F. Kennedy, a young and inexperienced president, in office, Moscow continued to step up pressure around the world. In April, the failure of a U.S. attempt to land forces of Cuban exiles at the Bay of Pigs to overthrow Premier Fidel Castro gave Khrushchev a victory

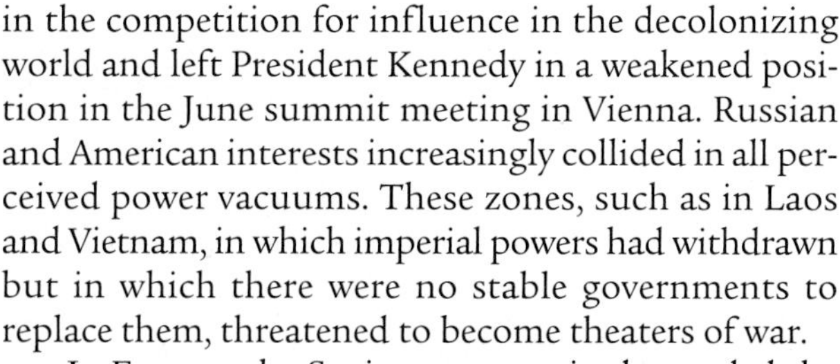

in the competition for influence in the decolonizing world and left President Kennedy in a weakened position in the June summit meeting in Vienna. Russian and American interests increasingly collided in all perceived power vacuums. These zones, such as in Laos and Vietnam, in which imperial powers had withdrawn but in which there were no stable governments to replace them, threatened to become theaters of war.

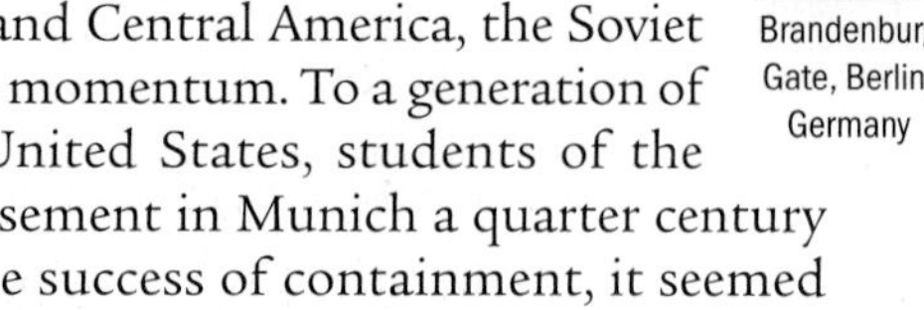

IMAGE Brandenburg Gate, Berlin, Germany

In Europe, the Soviets once again demanded the withdrawal of the allies from West Berlin. Once again, citing postwar agreements, the West refused to back down. This time, the East Germans, acting under Soviet supervision, erected a wall between the two halves of the city, thereby blocking escape routes formerly used by thousands. In Africa, Southeast Asia, and Central America, the Soviet Union seized the momentum. To a generation of leaders in the United States, students of the lessons of appeasement in Munich a quarter century earlier and of the success of containment, it seemed evident now that force had to be met with force.

In October 1962, the world came as close as it ever has to full-scale nuclear war. Three years earlier, Fidel Castro (b. 1926) had led a successful revolution against the right-wing Cuban dictator Fulgencio Batista (bah-TEES-tah; 1901–1973). Castro immediately began to transform the island into a communist state. After the failure of the American effort to overthrow him at the Bay of Pigs, the Soviets began to install intermediate range missiles in Cuba.

To the United States, these missiles were a dangerous threat to the Cold War balance of power, as they could destroy targets in one-third of the United States in five minutes. Kennedy ordered what was, in effect, a naval blockade—diplomatically referred to as a "quarantine" around Cuba—and demanded that Moscow withdraw the offensive weapons. After a few days of intense crisis in which one incident might have triggered direct military—even nuclear—action between Moscow and Washington, Khrushchev understood the seriousness of the situation. He ordered the Soviet missiles removed in exchange for assurances that the United States would respect Cuba's territory and other concessions such as the removal of American missiles in Turkey. Khrushchev was forced from office in 1964, after his retreat in Cuba and the failure of his agricultural policies. Before he left, however, he worked with the Americans to avoid future nuclear confrontations.

1962–1985: Arms Agreements, Military Parity, Vietnam, and Afghanistan

After the frightening confrontation in October 1962, the United States and the Soviet Union never again came so close to a nuclear war. They established a series of agreements that assured full communication—such as the

Seeing Connections

JFK and Khrushchev

At the Vienna Summit meeting of June 3, 1961, the two major ideological movements of the twentieth century and the two nuclear-armed superpowers came together in the persons of the Soviet general secretary of the Communist party and the American president.

Nikita S. Khrushchev, born in 1894 to a peasant family, rose in the ranks of the Soviet Communist Party under Stalin. Khrushchev and his fellow apparatchiks oversaw the industrialization and collectivization of the 1930s and World War II. After the launch of the *Sputnik* satellite in 1957, he felt emboldened to pressure first the aging U.S. president Eisenhower and then the young, inexperienced John F. Kennedy. Khrushchev had boasted that the victory of Communism was inevitable and that "we will bury you."

Kennedy, the new American president, was born in 1917 into a wealthy family, and he had all of the advantages that wealth could bring. After graduating from Harvard, he served in World War II and then entered politics, first in the House of Representatives and then in the Senate. He narrowly won the presidency in a closely fought contest with Richard M. Nixon, and in his inaugural address he stated that the United States would "... pay any price, bear any burden, meet any hardship ... in order to assure the survival and the success of liberty."

These two men from different generations and backgrounds with different dreams for the future came together in a meeting in which the fate of Berlin was at the center of discussions. The Soviet leader said that he would sign an agreement with East Germany in which Western allied access to the city would be effectively cut. The American president disagreed and refused to consider compromising the Americans' right to be in Berlin, and he implied that any limitation of the role of the United States in Berlin would be met by force. Khrushchev responded, "Force will be met by force. If the U.S. wants war, that's its problem." And then: "It's up to the U.S. to decide whether there will be war or peace." Kennedy refused to yield on Berlin and noted, "Then, Mr. Chairman, there will be a war. It will be a cold winter." The war almost came to pass, not in Germany, but in Cuba.

"hotline" between Moscow and Washington—and began to limit the growth of their nuclear arsenals. The Cuban missile crisis convinced leaders in Washington and Moscow of the need to reduce the peril of nuclear war and ushered in a 30-year process of complex negotiations dealing with all aspects of the risk of nuclear war. A limited test ban treaty was signed in August 1963, and later treaties outlawed the testing of nuclear devices in outer space, in the earth's atmosphere, or underwater. Latin America was declared a nuclear-free zone in 1968, and nonproliferation treaties followed in 1970 and 1978.

The greatest proof of the superpowers' interdependence could be found during the administration of General Secretary Leonid Brezhnev (1964–1982) in the Strategic Arms Limitation Talks (SALT I and SALT II). In these two negotiations, the United States and the USSR acknowledged, in effect, an equivalence of killing power that led to the capacity for "mutual assured destruction" (MAD). After 2 years of complicated talks, President Richard Nixon and Brezhnev signed the SALT I treaty in Moscow in the spring of 1972. This treaty limited the number of intercontinental ballistic missiles (ICBMs) that could be deployed by each side for 5 years and restricted the construction of antiballistic missile systems to two sites in each country in order to maintain MAD. SALT II, dealing with ICBMs that could be equipped with multiple independently targeted reentry vehicles (MIRVs) was eventually signed in 1979. In 1982, the Strategic Arms Reduction Talks (START) began but were interrupted in 1983 and were not renewed until Mikhail Gorbachev became the Soviet leader.

At the same time, while the superpowers carefully avoided fighting each other, they invested heavily in groups representing them in areas in the process of decolonization. Generally, each side had a proxy it financed that fought for it (see Chapters 33, 34, and 35)—few Americans or Russians died in these bloody conflicts. There were two exceptions to this rule: the United States became caught up in Vietnam in 1954–1975 (see Chapter 35) in a war that destabilized its society and economy, and after 1979, the Soviet Union became mired in a swamp of its own in Afghanistan (see Chapter 33) that had devastating consequences for its economy and society. The Russians gave enormous support to the forces opposing

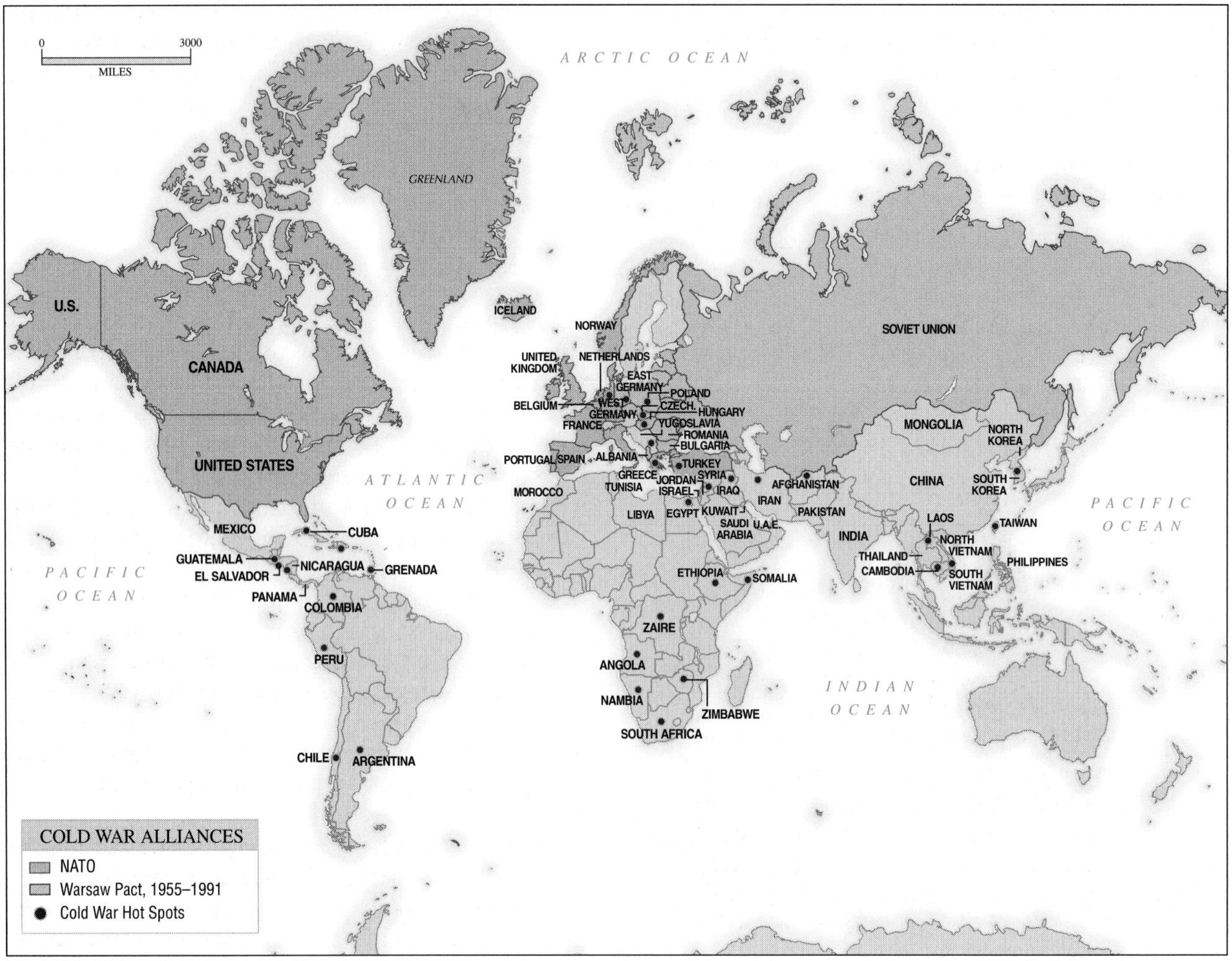

▲ Most of South America, Asia, and Africa served as arenas for Moscow and Washington's bipolar competition during the Cold War.

the United States in Vietnam; comparably, the Americans financed and trained the forces opposing the Russians in Afghanistan. Despite their massive nuclear forces, both sides failed in their interventions.

Gorbachev and the End of the Cold War

Although fewer Russians died fighting in Afghanistan than Americans did in Vietnam, the Soviet Union was ultimately less able to absorb the financial costs of its war than its rival had been. The Brezhnev years marked a long decline in the stagnant Soviet economy, which was exacerbated by the quantity of the economic resources—roughly one-third of the GDP—the state had to expend to maintain military parity with the United States. Already bogged down in a draining conflict in Afghanistan, the Soviets received additional pressure to keep pace with the Americans during the 1980s, when the President Ronald Reagan committed the United States to a new arms buildup.

It was not Brezhnev, however, who would see out the end of the Cold War, but rather one of his successors. Mikhail Gorbachev, the Soviet leader from 1985 to 1991, made major contributions in the foreign policy arena. He renounced the Brezhnev doctrine of 1968 that permitted Soviet armed intervention into fraternal socialist states. By doing so, he allowed the Soviet Bloc and its Warsaw Pact military commitments to disintegrate; in fact, they no longer existed by the end of 1989. He pulled Soviet troops out of Afghanistan in 1989 and worked to bring peace to several hot spots in Africa, including Angola. Most remarkably, he chose not to obstruct the reunification of Germany. He joined in UN resolutions condemning Iraq's takeover of Kuwait in 1990 and cooperated in the alliance's military defeat of the invading forces in 1991. In acknowledgment of his accomplishments, Gorbachev received the Nobel Peace Prize in 1990.

Gorbachev on the Need for Economic Reform

In arms control, Gorbachev brought the process to a logical conclusion. In November 1985, he met with President Reagan in Geneva to continue the discussion of arms control issues. The two powers were able to sign the Intermediate Nuclear Forces (INF) agreement in Washington in 1987. The INF accord set up the destruction of all intermediate- and shorter-range missiles within 3 years. Further, the treaty would be monitored by on-site verification, with Soviet and U.S. experts confirming the fulfillment of the treaty's provisions in each other's country. By 1989, the Cold War between the United States and the Soviet Union was finished.

The Soviet Union and the Russian Republic

Why was the USSR unable to implement reforms that would enable it to compete effectively in the post-1945 period?

USSR Postwar Policies

To achieve equality with the United States after World War II, Stalin launched a fourth 5-year plan in 1946, pushing growth in heavy industry and military goods. To increase Soviet output, he imposed double shifts on many workers. Those whose loyalty to Stalin was in the least suspect were sent to a network of camps spread from Siberia to Central Asia to the Arctic region. As they served their punishment, they contributed economically. Tragically, thousands died in the camps from overwork, inadequate food, and the bitter cold. To rebuild the devastated farming regions, Stalin returned to his collectivization policies.

Post-Cold War Russia

The dictator continued to place his supporters in all important offices, combining "the supreme command of the party with the supreme administration of the state." He made entry into the Communist party more difficult and purged many people who had slipped in through the relaxed membership standards during wartime. In the early 1950s, Stalin lashed out more ruthlessly and unpredictably than ever before, as he came to suspect everyone. His half-million-strong security police quashed any sign of dissent, criticism, or free expression. He ordered genocidal attacks on entire peoples, such as the Crimean Tatars. There were indications that the dictator was preparing a major purge that would go beyond "elite self-renewal." The purge did not occur, however, because, on March 5, 1953, Stalin died after a painful illness.

From Khrushchev to Chernenko

Stalin's death introduced a period of collective leadership in the Soviet Union. Within 3 years, the initial triumvirate had disappeared, elbowed aside by Nikita Sergeyevich Khrushchev. Unlike many of the apparatchiks, Khrushchev came from peasant stock, and he worked his way up from being a shepherd to factory worker, joining the Communist party in 1918. He rose rapidly in the 1930s, especially after pushing through the Moscow subway system, at great cost in human lives, and he became a member of the Politburo. He made no claim to being an urban intellectual; instead, he delighted in using crude and brutal language around those he considered to be pretentious people. This behavior masked the fact that he was both bright and cunning, able to spot the flaws and weaknesses in his opponents and to take advantage of both at the proper time.

One of Khrushchev's main goals was to reform agriculture. He proposed increasing incentives for the peasants and enlarging the area under production in Soviet Siberia and central Asia—the virgin lands. Between 1953 and 1958, production rose by 50 percent. Thereafter, farming in the virgin lands proved to be economically wasteful and environmentally disastrous.

▼ Stalin's chief supporters surround the bier at his funeral, March 6, 1953. Left to right, they are Vyacheslav Molotov, Kliment Voroshilov, Lavrenti Beria, Georgi Malenkov, Nikolai Bulganin, Nikita Khrushchev, Lazar Kaganovich, and Anastas Mikoyan. Khrushchev was the victor in the power struggle to succeed Stalin.

Khrushchev's de-Stalinization campaign in February 1956 at the Twentieth Party Congress had an earthquakelike effect on the international communist movement but provided "breathing space" inside the Soviet Union. By blaming all of past ills on the dead dictator, he justified the activities of the present leadership (which had all gained their places because of their slavish adherence to Stalin). Khrushchev also worked to improve the quality and quantity of consumer goods available in Soviet stores. In cultural affairs also, there was a brief relaxation in the "Socialist Realism Only" government policy toward the arts that allowed the printing and publication of important novels such as *One Day in the Life of Ivan Denisovich* (1962) by Alexander Solzhenitsyn.

Not all of his colleagues were happy with Khruschev, and in 1957, there was a failed attempt by members of the original triumvirate and their allies to remove him; thereafter, they remained vigilant. In 1964, Khrushchev resigned under pressure after the failure of his agricultural reforms and the aftermath of the Cuban Missile Crisis. Following Khrushchev's "retirement" in 1964, a classic apparatchik, Leonid Brezhnev (1906–1982), dominated the next stage of Cold War and Soviet history. Working with Aleksei Kosygin (1904–1980), he constructed an alliance with the military to deliver support that would enable the USSR to gain military parity with the United States.

From 1964 to 1974, Brezhnev and Kosygin split power. Brezhnev acted as general secretary and Kosygin as premier, overseeing sporadic reform attempts. Brezhnev later became president of the country under terms of the 1977 constitution. Serious health problems limited his effectiveness in the last years of his tenure. Politics remained based on Stalin's foundations, as modified by Khrushchev. The central planners continued to emphasize industrial growth and slowly increased the supply of consumer goods. In foreign policy, the new team pursued peaceful coexistence at the same time that they greatly strengthened the Soviet armed forces.

As the USSR gained military parity with the West, its civilian economy ground to a halt. Brezhnev was succeeded in 1982 by Yuri Andropov (1914–1984), a railway worker's son who rose to the peak of Soviet power as head of the KGB. Andropov's jobs put him at the crossroads of all information. Recognizing the disastrous condition of the USSR's infrastructure, he brought a large number of people from the provinces to work in high party positions in Moscow and set out immediately to increase output, fight corruption, and strengthen the military. He started campaigns to combat alcoholism and cheating and fired people who did not perform up to his standards. His health, however, deteriorated, and from the summer of 1983 until his announced death in February 1984, Andropov was out of public view.

The last of the Stalin protégés was Konstantin Chernenko (1912–1985), who succeeded Andropov to the posts of first secretary and president. Chernenko had ridden Brezhnev's coattails since the 1950s but had been soundly defeated by Andropov for the top job in 1982. His age and poor health signified that he would be a transition figure between the old guard and a new generation. The strain of leadership almost immediately broke Chernenko's fragile health, and even before his death in March 1985, wholesale changes were taking place in the highest levels of the Soviet government.

The economies of the Soviet Bloc states stagnated after the middle of the 1970s. By the end of the 1980s, the economic gap between the two sides forced Moscow and its allies in COMECON to seek admission to the International Monetary Fund (IMF) and to the General Agreement on Trade and Tariffs (GATT). It was apparent that the global political economy had become one of the most important factors in world relations.

Mikhail Gorbachev: *Glasnost* and *Perestroika*

After Chernenko's death in 1985, a new generation of Soviet leaders came to the fore, led by Mikhail Gorbachev (b. 1931). No less devoted to Marxism-Leninism than the former generation, the new leaders—many of whom had been placed in positions of influence by Andropov—more openly attacked the economic and social problems the USSR faced.

CASE STUDY
Gorbachev (1987) vs. Lenin (1920) and Stalin (1931)

Gorbachev moved rapidly to take power by implementing a platform based on ***glasnost*** ("openness") and ***perestroika*** ("restructuring") to try to bring new life to the Soviet system. *Glasnost* was Gorbachev's way of motivating the Soviet people to be more creative and work harder. *Perestroika* attempted to remove the structural blocks to modernization. These two themes launched the final act in the de-Stalinization campaign begun by Khrushchev in 1956.

For the first time, the party acknowledged mistakes, such as the Chernobyl nuclear disaster in April 1986. Past tragedies—especially those of the 1930s that had long been common knowledge—were now openly discussed. Gorbachev permitted unprecedented criticism of party and political leaders by the press and television. One of the unexpected results of *glasnost* was a revival of separatist movements in the various Soviet republics.

glasnost—"Openness" or "transparency." Opening the party and government structures of the Soviet Union to bring in the most progressive elements of society to reform the system.

perestroika—Literally "restructuring," a basic reform of the Soviet political and economic system.

Gorbachev originally sought to use *perestroika* to fine-tune the traditional central planning apparatus and party and state procedures, but the total failure of the Stalinist system demanded a more wide-ranging program. By 1990, the depth and severity of the Soviet Union's problems drove Gorbachev to attempt to impose a market economy, reduce the role of the Leninist "vanguard party," and alter the governmental structure.

Gorbachev invoked *glasnost* and *perestroika* to jump-start the moribund economy. Although gross domestic product figures continued to indicate that the Soviet economy was the second largest in the world, the reality was that the infrastructure was undermined by outmoded technologies, inefficient factories, a dispirited and underemployed workforce, and environmental disasters. Unlike the Chinese, who had started their economic reforms in 1978 in the countryside to ensure an adequate supply of food, Gorbachev relied on a more Leninist, democratic centralist approach and failed miserably. The Communist party, which Lenin had seen as the elite cadre that would anticipate the needs of the proletariat for the proletariat, had been turned by Stalin and his successors into an institution of privilege of, by, and for the party.

Everything went bad at once for Gorbachev. As economic conditions deteriorated, he increased concessions to party hard-liners and bureaucratic opportunists, buying time to hold power. In the spring of 1991, hundreds of thousands of people marched in the streets of Moscow to protest the premier's retreat from liberalism. Separatist protests increased in the Baltic republics of Estonia, Latvia, and Lithuania as well as in Georgia, the Ukraine, and Moldavia. Standards of living throughout the nation plummeted.

On August 19, while Gorbachev was on vacation in the Crimea, an eight-man "state emergency committee" made up of leaders of the KGB, the military, the interior department, and other offices of the central government—all appointed by Gorbachev—mounted an attempt to take power. Gorbachev's vice president announced that his leader was ill and that a state of emergency was to be imposed for six months.

The attempted coup was immediately denounced by Boris Yeltsin (1931–2007), who had been popularly elected president of the Russian Republic and who barricaded himself inside the offices of the Russian parliament building in Moscow. He instructed all army and KGB units not to obey the coup leaders' orders. The next day, 50,000 people turned out in Moscow to face down tanks sent by the central government. Larger groups mobilized in Leningrad and Kishinev. Several units of KGB and army forces refused to obey the central command's orders, and the coup began to unravel. By August 21 the crisis was over, and Yeltsin had emerged as the man of the hour.

Six days after the attempted coup, the reality of the situation became clear. Gorbachev resigned as leader of the Soviet Communist party and recommended dissolution of the Central Committee. Yeltsin claimed control of party archives and KGB records, and across the Soviet Union, in a vast revolution, the Communist party—after 74 years of almost total power—was cut off from all its vanguard roles in running the country. In addition, the party had to surrender its wealth and property to the parliaments of the various republics. Gorbachev remained as president of the Soviet Union, at least until popular elections could be held. But the USSR itself would last only four more months, ending

The Breakup of the Soviet Union

▼ On August 19, 1991, president of the Russian Republic Boris Yeltsin stands atop an armed carrier in Moscow to read a statement urging people to resist the attempted hard-line coup.

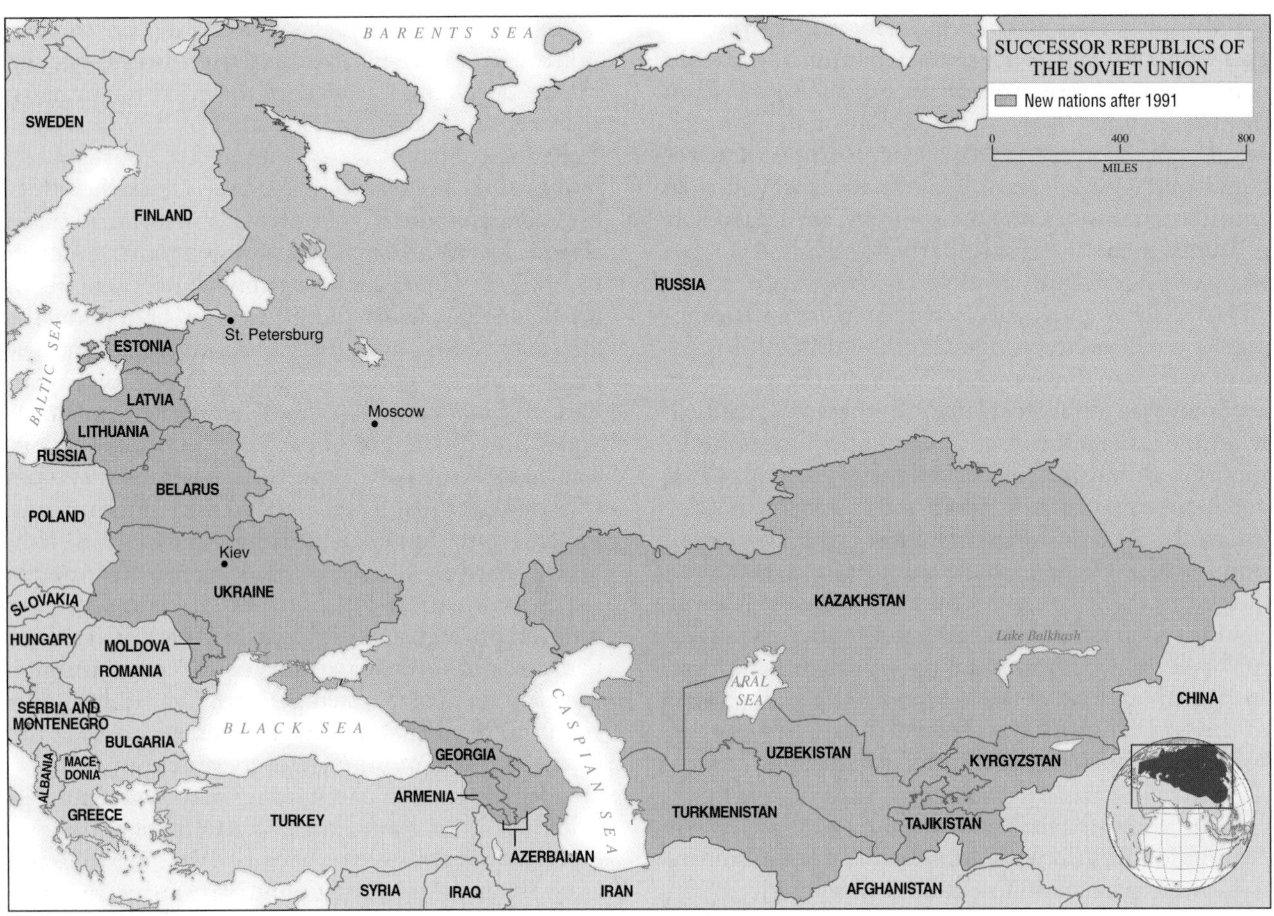

▲ The end of the Union of Soviet Socialist Republics in 1991 led to the birth of 14 new states.

its 69-year existence on December 21, 1991. It was replaced by a smaller and looser confederation, the Commonwealth of Independent States.

Boris Yeltsin and the Russian Republic

After August 1991, Boris Yeltsin was the most important Russian politician. Like other leaders at the end of a revolution, he found that a change in government did not remove the terrible problems facing Russia, such as inflation, budget deficits, and declining living standards. To deal with these problems, Yeltsin set in motion programs of privatization and the construction of a new infrastructure for international trade and commerce. There were also serious problems with ethnic minorities—especially in Chechnya.

Almost immediately, Yeltsin had to deal with opposition from the apparatchik-laden Congress of People's Deputies, elected under the old Soviet model. The Congress consistently blocked Yeltsin's attempts to implement a series of market-oriented economic reforms, such as liberalizing prices on most nonfood goods. In addition, Yeltsin faced problems from deputies who accused him of caving in to Western pressures in both domestic and foreign policy. The Russian president remained personally popular; however, this had little effect on the Congress, which continued to block his initiatives.

Yeltsin's contest with the parliament reached a stalemate in September 1993. When the Congress threatened to take much of his authority away, he responded by dissolving the Congress and calling for new elections in December. He then sent troops to surround the parliament building—the Russian White House—and told deputies that they would have to leave the building by October 4. These actions provoked widespread criticism throughout Russia, and leaders of 62 out of 89 regional councils called for Yeltsin to remove the troops.

On October 3, forces opposing the president took over the office of the mayor of Moscow and attacked the state television center. To an audience watching these events live on international television, it was remarkable that only 62 people died in the fighting. The next day, Yeltsin sent tanks and artillery against the Russian White House and battered the resisters into submission.

Yeltsin's forces and a new constitution barely carried the vote in the December elections, winning enough seats in parliament to prevent the opposition from being able to impeach the president. To maintain power in the face of an extremist coalition that was seemingly held together only by its opposition to Yeltsin, the president took a centrist course, advocating a rebirth of the Great Russian state, damping down essential programs to produce a privatized economy, and distancing himself from the West in foreign affairs—especially the extension of early NATO membership to the former Eastern European states and Western intervention in disintegrating Yugoslavia. Aided by substantial American support in financing and carrying out his campaign, Yeltsin was reelected in 1996, defeating the leader of the Communist party.

Russia's economy during the Yeltsin years proved unable to make the comparatively rapid change to a market system, as had the economies of Poland, the Czech Republic, and Hungary. The ethnic and social diversity of the continent-sized state made a "cold turkey" transition to the market system difficult. For the large majority of the Russian people, the change from a communist to a modified free market system brought no improvement to their lives. Cities such as St. Petersburg began to lose population as residents moved out to villages where they winterized huts and became full-time gardeners. For two-thirds of Russia's citizens, the quality of life declined more than 50 percent in the ten years after 1991.

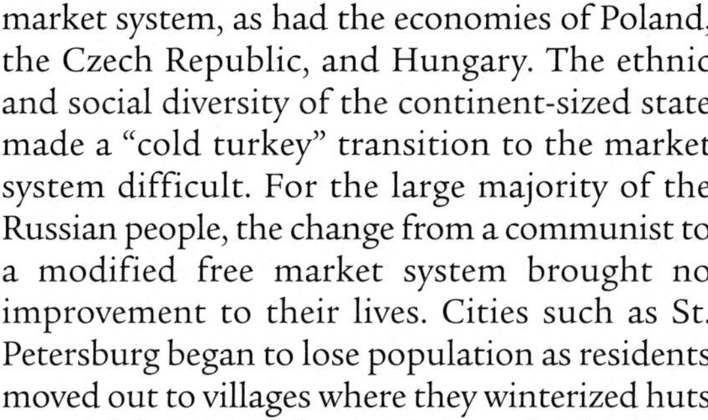

Scientists Examine Russia's Economy and Environment, 1991-1993

But for a few young, well-connected individuals, Yeltsin's haphazard privatization allowed them to gain control of Russia's basic resources of nickel, aluminum, natural gas, and oil. Russia has proven oil reserves of nearly 55 billion barrels, barely one-fifth that of Saudi Arabia, but substantial nonetheless—enough to allow Russia to be the second largest oil exporter in most years. The young capitalists, who became known as *oligarchs,* gained control of the basic resources of the country for around ten percent of their real value between 1993 and 1996. Thereafter, they took advantage of the disarray and corruption of Yeltsin's government to avoid most of the taxes they should have paid. By 2003, 17 of the world's richest men were Russian oligarchs between the ages of 36 and 54. One of them, Mikhail Khodorkovsky, who controlled Yukos Oil, was—briefly—the twenty-sixth richest person in the world.

Yeltsin's ill health and the popular perception that he was the tool of the Russian "mafia" combined to force him to step down at the end of 1999. In preparation for that event, he named Vladimir V. Putin—one of his aides, a former KGB officer in East Germany, and head of that group's successor, the Federal Security Bureau (FSB)—to be the prime minister of Russia in the summer of 1999. On the last day of the year, Yeltsin formally resigned and named Putin the acting president of Russia.

Vladimir Putin

Presidential elections in March 2000 confirmed Putin as president. He inherited the host of problems Yeltsin had not solved: massive corruption in all spheres of political life, control of major economic sectors by the "mafia" and the oligarchs, slow economic growth, the war in Chechnya, and other problems dealing with national groups within the Russian Federation. It became immediately apparent that he would be a different kind of president than Yeltsin. His major immediate goal was reassert the power of the political center in Moscow over the provinces. He used to good effect the concern over terrorist incidents in Moscow—tied to the renewed warfare in Chechnya—and his control over the most important newspapers and television stations to muster support for his position. Within the government, he began to dismiss members of the former Yeltsin team and to replace them with colleagues from the former KGB and other security agencies.

By 2004, he had broken the "mafia" and the oligarchs, imprisoning Mikhail Khodorkovsky and forcing other oligarchs to leave the country. For this, and other reasons, Putin has a popularity rating above 80 percent in Russia. He has successfully recentralized power. More efficient courts seem to be succeeding in reducing the widespread corruption that had flourished in the 1990s. There has been a large increase in tax collections. Russia's economy has stabilized, and from 2001 to 2006, the country experienced considerable economic growth.

Critics in the West still point out that Putin achieved these results by clearly undemocratic means. His party, United Russia, had a virtual monopoly on television screens in the run up to the presidential elections in March 2004, which he won by a convincing margin. By the autumn of 2006, writers and reporters who knew too much or criticized too openly were murdered by unknown assailants who were never caught or tried. Popular television stations have been silenced and commentators deemed too independent have lost their jobs. Despite this, or perhaps because of this, within Russia, the president enjoys broad support.

Russia has a long way to go. It continues to fight a demographic crisis that has men dying at an average age of 61, 15 years sooner than men in Western countries, and a lowering birthrate. Economically, President Putin has stated that Russia's goal was to equal the GDP rate of Portugal by 2015, a difficult task given that Russia's per capita GDP at the end of 2006 was $11,000 behind the Portuguese level of $20,000. Still, after the terrorist attacks on the United States, the

Russian president used his friendly relationship with the American president, George W. Bush, to make economic and foreign policy gains, especially in regard to the use of force to put down separatists along his southern frontiers. In addition, Russia supplies more than 20 percent of the natural gas consumed in western Europe, and this virtual control of a basic resource gives the Kremlin an added power in its dealing with its European neighbors.

Eastern Europe: From Soviet Control to Independence

How successful have Eastern European states been in moving from the Soviet Bloc to the European Union?

After consolidating political control over Eastern Europe by 1948, Moscow attempted to organize its allies through the trade organization COMECON. The USSR set up COMECON in 1949 as a response to the Marshall Plan and other Western projects to promote economic growth. In its first decade, the organization served Soviet postwar recovery needs. Moscow worked a reverse system of mercantilism on the region, exporting raw materials at high prices and buying back finished goods at low cost. Eastern Europe suffered greatly under this system, and nowhere could the contrast between the capitalist and communist systems be seen more dramatically than in the divided city of Berlin.

In the 1960s and 1970s, the Soviet Bloc states began to profit from buying cheap energy supplies from the USSR in return for which they could send goods they could not market to the West. Their standard of living began to improve along with their economic growth rates. By the end of the 1970s, however, COMECON faced a serious crisis. The region fell behind the rest of the world economically because of the rigidity of the centrally planned system used in the bloc economies and the restrictive bilateral nature of COMECON—everything had to go through Moscow. Prague and Budapest, for instance, could not work directly to achieve production or trade efficiency. COMECON countries faced far more barriers than the Common Market countries did. Further, each country's currency was nonconvertible; it could be spent only within that country.

Aggravating the situation was the fact that, as world energy prices fell in the latter part of the 1980s, the Eastern Europeans were trapped into paying premium prices for Soviet oil and gas. Several Eastern European states borrowed heavily from the West and invested the proceeds unwisely. Far more damaging than these purely fiscal concerns were the environmental disasters spawned by the Soviet-model centrally planned economies. Eastern Europe, as well as the former USSR, was one of the most devastatingly polluted areas in the world. Fifty years of Soviet domination were a terrible burden for the peoples of Eastern Europe.

Yugoslavia and Its Successor States

One of Stalin's major failures after 1945 was in his dealings with Marshal Josip Broz Tito of Yugoslavia. Tito had been a loyal Communist and a good Stalinist in the 1930s. During the war, he was an effective resistance leader, surviving attacks from Germans, Italians, and various right-wing factions in Yugoslavia. He had been in close contact with the Western allies and, after the war, began to receive substantial assistance from them. Tito led the liberation of Yugoslavia from the Nazis and kept the country out of Moscow's orbit.

Stalin noted Tito's independence, and from 1946 on, he sought measures to oppose him. Ethnically divided, Yugoslavia overcame its internal divisions and a 10 percent casualty rate during the war to unite behind Tito. The Yugoslav leader's national backing, geographical distance from the Soviet Union, and support from the West enabled him to stand firm against increasing Soviet meddling in his country.

Tito became the first national communist, a firm believer in Marxism who sought to apply the ideology within the context of his nation's objective conditions. This position placed him directly against Stalin, who

▶ The former Yugoslavia after 1991.

believed that communists the world over must work for the greater glory and support of the Soviet Union. Tito believed that the setting in which ideology was found had to be taken into consideration, pointing out that Lenin had to adapt Marxist doctrine to conditions in Russia. Stalin insisted that Moscow's orders and examples must be slavishly followed. In 1948, Yugoslavia was expelled from the Soviet Bloc. Successfully withstanding Stalin's pressures, including assassination attempts, Tito emerged as a key figure in the development of world communism. After Khrushchev's speech denouncing Stalin before the Twentieth Party Congress in 1956, Tito and his national communism were welcomed back into the family of socialist states

After 1948, the six republics and ten ethnic groups that formed Yugoslavia survived the pressures of national diversity, the political stresses of the bipolar world, and serious economic difficulties. Many observers doubted that the country could survive Tito's death in 1980. However, Yugoslavia remained tenuously united under its unique system of annually rotating the head of state—despite an 80 percent inflation rate and a 30 percent decline in the standard of living.

In 1991, after the collapse of communism throughout Eastern Europe, ethnic strife among Serbs and Croats and the Albanians of Kosovo finally destroyed the unity of the multinational state. Armed conflict broke out as the various constituent republics sought to break away from the Serbian-dominated coalition led by Slobodan Milosevic (SLO-bo-dahn mee-LOSH-eh-vich; 1941–2006). Slovenia (now a member of the European Union and NATO) and Croatia won their freedom in June, and Macedonia declared its independence in November 1991, followed by Bosnia-Herzegovina in December. Serbia and tiny Montenegro were all that remained in the Yugoslav "federation."

Serbs, Croats, and Bosnian Muslims fought in a continually shifting multiple-front war to claim what each side saw as its legitimate patrimony. The Bosnian Serbs, inheriting the bulk of the old Yugoslav armed forces' supplies and weapons and backed by Belgrade, gained 70 percent of Bosnia-Herzegovina and in the process became international pariahs. They carried out genocidal attacks—**"ethnic cleansing"**—on the Bosnian Muslims, who labored under an arms embargo nominally imposed by the West. In reality, the Americans tacitly permitted Islamic states to arm the Bosnians.

ethnic cleansing—The process by which a state removes—either by murder or forcing out of their homes—groups not desired. As carried out by the Belgrade government in the 1990s, some of these acts reached the level of genocide.

The Western allies made noises of protest and even got the Russians to share in the token condemnations of the Serbs, but the only tangible Western aid for the Bosnians came from a U.S. airlift, which in its first year made more sorties over the region and dumped more supplies in the general region than did the U.S. Air Force supplying Berlin in 1948. NATO forces also launched air strikes and periodically bluffed the Serbs into pulling back from Muslim enclaves such as Sarajevo and Gorazde. Truces and peace plans came and went, resolving nothing, while the West hoped that the economic sanctions against Serbia would finally yield some results. Finally the Western powers, joined by Russia, placed forces in the region, and a negotiated truce was arrived at in 1995 at the unlikely site of Dayton, Ohio. The war had led to the deaths of more than 200,000 people and forced more than 3 million to leave their homes.

A peacekeeping force led by the Americans remained in Bosnia, imposing order on the contesting forces and monitoring the activities of the Belgrade government led by Slobodan Milosevic, elected president of rump Yugoslavia in July 1997. The next year, he began to use the ethnic cleansing tactics he had used in Bosnia in the southern province of Kosovo, a province that contains the spiritual center of the Serbs, the battlefield where the Ottoman forces defeated

▼ The Serbian "ethnic cleansing" produced atrocities such as the mass murders at Srebrenica. International War Crimes Tribunal investigators uncover a mass grave as they collect evidence for use at the court in The Hague.

them in 1389. Kosovo's population was 90 percent Kosovar Albanians; after a decade of frustration, some Albanians had formed the Kosovo Liberation Army, which threatened Serb control in parts of the province. All through 1998, the Belgrade government built up its military and paramilitary presence there. Fearing a repeat of the events in Bosnia at the beginning of the decade, the Western allies in October 1998 and February–March 1999 tried to convince Milosevic to change his tactics through diplomatic means. When he did not, NATO forces began a bombing campaign at the end of March to "degrade" the Yugoslav military forces. What had been a comparative trickle of refugees and sporadic atrocities became a flood of 1 million people forced from their homes and mass murders. At the same time, the NATO bombing, which was stated to be against Milosevic and his forces and not the Yugoslav people, produced numerous civilian casualties. Thanks to the NATO coalition holding together, the energizing of Russia to support an end to the conflict, and the impact of the bombardments, peace of sorts returned to Kosovo in the middle of June. As the Yugoslavs pulled out of the province, replaced by the UN-sponsored peacekeeping forces, the reintegration of the almost 1 million Kosovars who fled the region proved to be a difficult task.

East Germany

After 1945, Eastern Europe reflected the changes that took place in the USSR. Nowhere was this more evident than in East Germany from 1945 to 1990. Following the organization of the eastern zone of Germany into the German Democratic Republic, Communist authorities broke up large private farms and expanded heavy industry. Thousands of discontented East Germans fled each week to West Germany through Berlin. In June 1953, severe food shortages coupled with new decrees establishing longer working hours touched off a workers' revolt, which was quickly put down. The westward flow of refugees continued, however, until 1961, when the Berlin Wall was constructed.

The wall stopped the exodus of people, and East Germany stabilized. For the next 28 years, the country had the highest density of armed men per square mile in the Soviet Bloc and the communist world's highest economic growth rate. The country's athletes and businesses did well in world competition, and slowly and subtly, under Erich Honecker and a new generation of bureaucrats, the German Democratic Republic improved relations with West Germany.

Gorbachev's program of liberalization threatened Honecker and his colleagues. After 1988, East German authorities stopped the circulation of Soviet periodicals that carried stories considered to be too liberal. At the same time, analysts noted the slowing economic growth rate of East Germany and the fact that the standard of living in West Germany was far higher. Old facilities, old managers, and old ideas eroded the economy of East Germany. In 1989, lack of support from Moscow and the internal contradictions of the DDR's government led to the collapse of the Berlin Wall and the end of the East German Communist party.

Poland

In Poland, as in Yugoslavia, communism acquired a national character after a slow, subtle struggle that broke open in the fall of 1956 following Khrushchev's "Crimes of the Stalin Era" speech. Polish leader Wladyslaw Gomulka (vlad-EE-slov goh-mul-KAH; 1905–1982) set out on a difficult path to satisfy both Moscow and Warsaw, Soviet power and Polish nationalism. Gomulka governed skillfully through the 1960s until 1970, when he fell victim to the pressures of economic discontent and an increasingly corrupt Communist party.

Demonstrations and strikes broke out around the country, and some, such as those at the Baltic port city of Gdansk (formerly Danzig), were bloodily repressed. Gomulka was replaced by Edward Gierek, who, throughout the 1970s, walked the same narrow line as Gomulka between satisfying Moscow and Poland. Gierek borrowed extensively from the West and made several ill-advised economic decisions. By 1980, Poland was laboring to pay the interest on a foreign debt of $28 billion, and in the summer of 1980, the delicate compromise created by Gomulka and Gierek fell apart in a series of strikes caused by increases in food prices.

A nationwide labor movement, *Solidarnosc,* or Solidarity, came into being. By October, around 10 million Poles from all segments of society had joined this movement, which stood for reform, equality, and workers' rights. In many ways, Solidarity's programs were protests against the Leninist concept of the party. It was Solidarity's proletarian base that made it so appealing to the world and so threatening to the other Marxist-Leninist leaders of the Soviet Bloc. Unfortunately, the problems that had brought down Gierek remained. A year of Solidarity-dominated government brought no solutions, only continued frustration.

When Solidarity's members pushed for their leader, Lech Walesa, to call for a national vote to establish a noncommunist government, the communist regime responded with force, in part to maintain itself and in part to avoid Soviet intervention. Martial law was declared, and security forces rounded up Solidarity's leaders. Outward shows of protest were squelched within two weeks.

Through the 1980s, Communist party morale dipped as membership fell 20 percent. Although banned, Solidarity retained the genuine affection of the Poles and the support of the Roman Catholic

Church, headed by Pope John Paul II, a former Polish cardinal. To the embarrassment of the Polish state, Lech Walesa was awarded the Nobel Peace Prize in 1983. The economic situation deteriorated as inflation increased, the standard of living plummeted, and foreign debt soared to $40 billion. The party could not solve the problems it faced, and in desperation it turned to Solidarity, which it had outlawed 8 years earlier. The June 1989 elections resulted in an overwhelming victory for the union, and in July it took its place in the Polish parliament, the Sejm (SAYM), as the first opposition party to win free elections in Eastern Europe since 1948. Solidarity won 99 out of 100 seats in the upper house and 161 seats (35 percent) in the lower house—all that were allotted to it in a preparatory roundtable.

In January 1990, Poland adopted a market economy. Even with substantial financial support from the West, the country faced rising unemployment and recession. The strains produced by the shift to a market economy tested even the Solidarity movement, which split into two wings, one led by Mazowiecki Tadeuszi (ma-zo-VIET-skee ta-dei-USH-ee), who briefly became prime minister in 1990, and one led by Lech Walesa, who eventually became the president of Poland.

Despite political roadblocks, Poland made amazing success toward privatization and market reforms. Even when Poland's former Communists, now called Social Democrats, took power in 1993, they did not reverse course. Poland stands as one of the success stories in the former Soviet Bloc, with a thriving stock market and a successful market economy. From 1993 to 2004, foreign investment in Poland has more than doubled, and by 2006, the per capita gross domestic product reached nearly $13,000—still only one-third of that of Western industrialized countries, but higher than many other former Soviet Bloc nations.

Admission into the North Atlantic Treaty Organization in 1999 and the European Union in 2004 confirmed Poland's progress from Soviet Bloc state to full-fledged member of the European community. The transition remains a difficult one for the Poles, however, as an unemployment rate close to 20 percent continues to bedevil the country in 2007, racism and anti-Semitism have become problems, and conservative elements within the nation have opposed EU policy positions on issues such as abortion and the teaching of evolution in schools.

Czechoslovakia and the Czech and Slovak Republics

After the fall of the democratic government in 1948, the Czechoslovak Communist party, the most Stalinist of the European parties, imposed harsh control for 20 years. In the spring of 1968, however, the country's liberal traditions came into the open. Under the influence of Marxist moderates, a new form of communism—"socialism with a human face"—was put into effect by the Slovak leader Alexander Dubcek (DOOB-chek; 1921–1992). As in Yugoslavia under Tito, the Czechoslovaks chose not to rebel against Moscow but rather to adapt communism to their own conditions. But in August 1968, the Soviet Union and four Soviet Bloc allies invaded Prague with more than 500,000 troops. Within 20 hours, the liberal regime, which advocated policies strikingly similar to those supported by Gorbachev 20 years later, was overthrown. The Soviets captured Dubcek and took him to Moscow to confront Brezhnev.

The Soviets took their action against Czechoslovakia pursuant to the so-called Brezhnev Doctrine, under which Communist states were obliged to aid their fraternal colleagues against "aggression," even when the fraternal colleague does not ask for aid, in order to safeguard the communal gains of the socialist movement. The Soviet-led forces crushed the Czechoslovak reforms to "protect the progress of socialism."

Events in East Germany precipitated the October 1989 events in Prague, when a pro-democracy meeting by over 10,000 demonstrators was savagely broken up by the police. Protests in November met similar results. Still the Czechoslovaks were not deterred. In the "Velvet Revolution" of November 1989, some 200,000 demonstrators in Prague demanded free elections and the resignation of the Communist leaders. The wave of change from Moscow initiated by Mikhail Gorbachev after 1985 was unable to adapt to the new conditions, and dissidents, including president-to-be Vaclav Havel (VAT-swof HAV-el; b. 1936), who in January 1989 had been thrown in jail for human rights protests, found themselves running the country by December of that year. Symbolic of the new freedom, Dubcek came out of internal exile, and in the June 1990 elections, Havel was confirmed as president. As in the other Eastern European states, however, the high spirits of the 1989 revolution were soon replaced by the sober realities of repairing the effects of two generations of Communist rule.

Serious political problems and Slovak separatist demands drove Czechoslovakia to split into its constituent parts, the Czech Republic and the Slovak Republic, on January 1, 1993. The Czech Republic suffered little from the dissolution of the 65-year-old federation, but the Slovaks suffered for the next few years from economic decline and political instability under the rule of the former Communist hard-liner Vladimir Meciar (vlad-DEE-mir MECH-ee-ar; b. 1942). Thirteen years later, Slovakia achieved a remarkable economic growth with a GDP per capita of more than $16,000, but with an unemployment rate of 12 percent. The Czech Republic's economic growth faltered briefly in the 1990s but rebounded in the first part of the new century. Confirming their post-Soviet-era orientation toward the West, the Czech Republic entered NATO in 1999 and the European Union in 2004; Slovakia joined both organizations in 2004.

Hungary

After the Stalin purges, the Hungarian Communist party became increasingly inept until October 23, 1956. Fed by excitement over events in Poland, the discontent with Soviet dominance erupted into revolution. For a week, a popular government existed, and Russian troops withdrew from Budapest. When the new government announced its intentions to leave the Warsaw Pact and become a neutral state, Soviet forces returned and crushed the rebellion. More than 200,000 refugees fled to the West.

Over the next 30 years, Janos Kadar (YA-nosh ka-DAR; 1912–1989) oversaw an initially bloody repression of the revolution and the execution of Hungarian premier Imre Nagy (EEM-re NAHZH; 1896–1958). Later, Kadar led a subtle pursuit of a Hungarian variant of communism. In the process, the Hungarians gained a higher standard of living than the Soviets, an active intellectual life, and a range of economic reforms. In the mid-1980s, however, the Hungarian economic system, which encouraged more private initiative and decentralization, ran into difficulties. Hungary's foreign debt and inflation both increased. Gorbachev encouraged the Hungarians to pursue their reforms, sometimes at the discomfort of Kadar, who was gently moved from power in 1987. The next year, the Hungarians continued the westernization of their economy by approving of the installation of a capitalist-style MBA program in Budapest at the International Management Center.

In 1989, the Hungarians dismantled the barriers, fences, and minefields between themselves and the Austrians. Hungary imposed the first income tax and value-added tax in Eastern Europe, allowed 100 percent foreign ownership of Hungarian firms, opened a stock market, and set up institutions to teach Western management methods to Hungarian businessmen. The economy remains competitive, with a $16,300 GDP per capita, but government officials say that it will take 10 years before Hungary can reach Western European standards of living.

By March 1990, Hungary had installed a multiparty system and was holding free elections, which led to the installation of a right-of-center government led by Joszef Antall and the overwhelming repudiation of the Communists. The next 4 years proved to be frustrating to the Hungarians, however. Substantial Western investment came in, but the suffering among the poorer population in the country increased.

Tragically, in this area stripped of Jews by the Holocaust, anti-Semitism reemerged as a political force. Anti-Gypsy feelings also intensified. Elections in 1994 resulted in a victory for the Social Democrats, who promised to maintain the free market reforms while extending social justice. Although they fulfilled these promises, a rise in organized crime and growing doubts about the Social Democrats' competence led back to a right-of-center government in the summer of 1998 under the young Viktor Orban. Despite substantial foreign debt, Hungary has exhibited impressive governmental and social stability and entered NATO in 1999 as the third nation from the former Soviet Bloc to join. Tensions remain with its neighbors, however, as Orban's government in 2001 attempted to gain special status for Hungarians living in Romania, Slovakia, and Serbia. The Social Democrats regained control of the government in 2002 when Peter Medgyessy (PAY-ter MEDZH-yes-si; b. 1942) became prime minister. Medgyessy led Hungary into the European Union in 2004, after which he was succeeded by another socialist leader, Ferenc Gyurcsani (DZHIUR-chan-ee; b. 1961).

Bulgaria

Bulgaria proved to be a loyal ally of Moscow after 1945, and its standard of living greatly improved. The Bulgarian economy averaged a growth rate of close to 3 percent a year and became increasingly diversified. Todor Zhivkov (TOE-dor ZHIV-kov; 1911–1998) skillfully followed the Soviet lead and showed flexibility in responding to the early Gorbachev programs, especially the agricultural reforms. Until the autumn of 1989, the party appeared to be conservative and nationalist, as shown in its campaign against the country's Turkish minority (nearly 8 percent of the population) to deprive them of their heritage.

The wave of freedom hit Bulgaria at the end of 1989. Zhivkov was ousted in a party-led coup and replaced by Peter Mladenov (PAY-ter MLO-day-nov; 1936–2000). It seemed in the free elections in May 1990 that Mladenov and his allies would be the only party group to make the transition and maintain power in Eastern Europe. But even he was thrown out in July, when his role as orchestrator of the Zhivkov coup was noted, and the noncommunist philosopher Zhelyu Zhelev (ZHEL-iu ZHE-lev; 1935–) became president.

The Bulgarians avoided making the hard economic choices needed to reform their country, and at the end of 1996, they experienced a virtual economic collapse. Inflation soared, wiping out savings and driving prices up. At the same time, the government proved unable to pay the interest on the foreign debt. The International Monetary Fund imposed an austerity program on Bulgaria that caused widespread distress. Local mafias prospered, conducting black market trade with the various factions during the Yugoslav conflict and serving as a conduit for the international drug trade between Afghanistan and Europe. As if in despair, the country voted in 2001 to elect its former king, Simeon II, as prime minister of the country until 2005.

Slow progress has been achieved recently, but crime and the black market remain as important elements in the national economy. Bulgaria became a part of NATO in 2004 and entered the European Union in 2007.

Romania

After the 1960s, Romania under Nicolae Ceausescu (chow-SESH-koo; 1918–1989) was the most independent of the Warsaw Pact countries in foreign policy. Domestically, the country labored under one of the most hard-line and corrupt regimes in the Soviet Bloc, a regime whose economic policies of self-sufficiency plunged the standard of living to unprecedented depths. Ceausescu achieved his goal to become free of foreign debts by the summer of 1989, but at a cruel cost in human suffering.

Ceausescu, accused by critics of desiring to achieve "socialism in one family," developed the cult of the personality to new heights. While imposing severe economic hardship on the nation, he built grandiose monuments to himself. Protected by his omnipresent secret police, the *Securitate,* he seemed untouchable. But the 1989 wave of democracy spread even to Romania by December, which was the only country to experience widespread violence during that revolutionary year. Ceausescu and his wife were taken into custody and executed, thus bringing their dreadful regime to an end.

The Romanian pattern of political corruption continued, and Ion Iliescu (yo-ON ee-ly-ES-koo; 1930–) manipulated the elections of May 1990 to keep power. Later in the summer, the National Salvation Front made shameless use of miners and former *Securitate* officials to terrorize its critics. An uneasy equilibrium was attained, but little progress was made to heal the devastating wounds inflicted by the Ceausescu regime. Under Iliescu, the Leninist heritage remained strong in Romania, whose authoritarianism had a chilling effect on the pluralistic tendencies in the region.

Finally in 1996, the neo-Communists lost power when Emil Constantinescu (aei-MEEL kon-stan-tee-NES-koo; b. 1939) became president. The country faced many of the same problems as neighboring Bulgaria—the need to privatize inefficient state industries, to introduce efficient management methods, and to gain some sort of control over the rampant corruption that plagued and plagues its economy. Many Romanians placed high and unrealistic hopes on being invited to join NATO in the 1990s.

When that did not happen, there was a backlash against the West among a segment of the population who support the neo-fascist politics of Vadim Tudor. In the 2000 elections, however, Iliescu again returned to power as the Romanians chose to go with a familiar face. Finally in 2004, Traian Basescu (TRY-yon ba-SESH-koo; b. 1951) became president, ending the reign of the socialists. Romania entered NATO in 2004 and the European Union in 2007. Despite the corruption that characterizes business relations in the country, foreigners invested in the automotive sector (France), oil and gas (Russia), and telecommunications (Greece). The GDP per capita has reached nearly $8200, but with the flight of technicians and young people abroad, it will be difficult to maintain a long-term trend of economic progress.

Albania

Albania under Enver Hoxha (HOD-zha; 1908–1985) worked closely with the Soviet Union until 1956. After Khrushchev's denunciation of Stalin, the country switched its allegiance to the Chinese until 1978. For the next decade Albania—the poorest and most backward country in Europe—went its own way in seeming isolation, only reluctantly entering into trade, diplomatic, and sports relations with other nations. Yet even Albania was not immune to the unrest sweeping Eastern Europe in 1989.

In the summer of 1990, people desperate to escape the country flocked into foreign embassies, and soon some 40,000 Albanians had fled to Italy and Greece. Democratic elections were held in March 1991, but even there, the Albanians marched to their own tune, as the Communists carried two-thirds of the vote. Two years later, the Democratic party won an overwhelming victory. Albania remained the poorest and most backward country in Europe throughout the 1990s.

Tragically, the economically inexperienced Albanians flocked to "get rich quick" pyramid schemes that collapsed in December 1996, when those who were in first started to pull out their money. Civil order collapsed in the country as factions gained control of the army's weapons and the country dissolved into regions controlled by local strongmen. European intervention led by the Italians brought order, but then Albanians living in Yugoslavian provinces began to rebel against their Belgrade overlords. In 2007, Albania remains a fragmented nation and a potential tinderbox, overwhelmed by the hundreds of thousands of Kosovar Albanians seeking refuge there and its role as a conduit of illegal goods and prostitution into Western Europe. Its weak economy—GDP per capita of $4900 in 2006—forces thousands of its young to seek work elsewhere in Italy, Switzerland, and Austria, legally or illegally.

Western Europe

What factors contributed to the creation of the European Union?

The most significant development in postwar Western Europe was the progress toward integration. The desire for cooperation came from the lessons learned during World War II, taught by visionaries such as the French statesmen Jean Monnet and Robert Schumann. Benefiting from the Marshall plan and protected by the U.S. nuclear umbrella, European leaders could escape from the centuries-old cycle of European wars. In 1950, Monnet and Schumann put forth a program to create the European Coal and Steel Community to coordinate the supply of those two essential industrial commodities in West Germany, France, Italy, Belgium, the Netherlands, and Luxembourg. Five years later, the European Atomic Energy Community was created.

The same six nations that participated in these supranational organizations in 1957 established the **European Economic Community (EEC),** the Common Market. The organization's goal was to build enduring foundations for the closer union between European peoples. To that end, it reduced tariffs among its members and created a great free-trade union that became the fastest-growing market in the Western world. In 1992, after the Treaty of Maastricht was approved by the member states, the Common Market became the European Union. In May 2004, the number of states participating in the European Union grew to 25, with other nations waiting to be admitted.

DOCUMENT

A Common Market and European Integration

Economic Growth and the Dilemma of Legal and Illegal Immigration

Europe became a single market, the European Union (EU), at the end of 1992, with the approval of the Treaty of Maastricht, an act similar to the 1707 Act of Union between England and Scotland, the Constitution of the United States, and the North German *Zollverein* (TSOHL-fer-ain) in the first part of the nineteenth century. Reaching the goal of "Europe 1992" was not easy. Serious controversies over agricultural policy, banking policies, and tax differences had to be overcome. The European leaders worked hard to reassure the rest of the world that their 12-nation market would not be protectionist while they put together the more than 300 directives that would form the laws for the commercial union.

European Economic Community (EEC)—A free-trade union among West Germany, France, Italy, Belgium, the Netherlands, and Luxembourg created in 1957. This initial group served as the basis for the enlarged European Union.

The program entailed opening up the 12 nations' boundaries so that there would be no restriction to the movement of goods and people and establishing a "social dimension" to define the "rights of ordinary people in the great market and to help the poorer among them." There was also a more difficult drive toward economic and monetary unity, including a single European currency and central bank. One indication of the EU's success was the introduction of the currency, the Euro, across most of Europe in January 2002. Economic union also included single standards on electricity, pipeline pressures, safety, and health.

IMAGE

European Money Before the Euro

Another response to the Common Market's success has been a massive influx of foreigners into the region. These included emigrants from Turkey who came to Germany and Scandinavia as *Gastarbeiter* (gahst-ahr-bait-er; "guest workers"), North Africans who came to France and Spain, people from the Balkans who entered Italy, and a wide variety of workers from the former imperial holdings who came to Europe to pursue their futures. Given the comparatively low birthrate of Europeans, countries such as Germany are encouraging the continuation of legal immigration. Engineers and computer technicians from Turkey and the Balkan states are being encouraged to move to Germany to fill the gaps in the nation's workforce as more and more German workers take early retirement.

A more difficult problem is that of illegal immigrants. The wealth of the European Union has attracted a large number of people entering illegally from Ukraine and Moldova and other countries of the former Soviet Bloc. Smuggling people from China and Africa is a high-profit enterprise for unscrupulous individuals who place their customers in difficult conditions to get them into the European area. Those who succeed in making it to a European city generally find themselves crowded into substandard public housing in industrial suburbs surrounding the city center. Because of their illegal status, the jobs they can find are badly paid with no benefits. Unemployment runs as high as 30 percent among illegal immigrants in countries like France and Germany—where unemployment among citizens is already higher than 9 percent. They also suffer from the disdain of the local population, attacks from right-wing parties such as the National Front in France and the Neo-Nazis in Germany and Austria, and a lack of hope. It is from the ranks of such migrants that terrorist networks such al-Qaeda draw recruits and organized crime networks find a receptive audience.

Despite these problems, and in response to the Common Market's successes, other trade zones have been established: NAFTA, which linked Canada, Mexico, and the United States; and the Asia Pacific Eco-

▲ The European Union and NATO are in the process of expanding toward the east. As of 2007, the states of Europe were arrayed in the European Union, NATO, and the Euro common currency zone, and several states in the east are awaiting admission to one or all three groups.

nomic Cooperation (APEC), which included the Pacific Rim states of Australia, Brunei, Canada, China, Hong Kong, Indonesia, Japan, South Korea, Malaysia, New Zealand, the Philippines, Singapore, Taiwan, and the United States.

The United Kingdom

Britain emerged from World War II at the height of its prestige in the twentieth century, but the glow of victory and the glory earned by its sacrifices served only to conceal the nation's dismal condition. The country was in a state of near bankruptcy. As a result of the war, its investments had drastically declined and huge bills had been run up for the support of British armies overseas. In addition, increases in welfare benefits drained the economy until the 1990s.

After 1945, the London government could not reinstate the delicately balanced formula under which Britain had paid for massive imports of food and raw materials through exports and income from foreign investments, banking, and insurance. The British people, who had paid dearly to defeat the Axis Powers, did not produce the necessary export surplus to restore Britain's wealth. Over the next 40 years, they would watch their vanquished enemies become wealthy while they struggled with aging industrial facilities and extremely costly welfare programs.

The Conservatives dominated British politics for the half century after the end of the war, with interludes of Labour rule. Since the late 1990s, the Labour party has controlled Parliament. Generally, the Conservatives under leaders such as Harold Macmillan (1957–1963) and Margaret Thatcher (1979–1990) opposed nationalization of industry, encouraged private enterprise, and favored a reduced social welfare program. Until 1995, Labour supported nationalization of industry and a thorough welfare state. Prime Minister Tony Blair, elected to office in 1997, changed those basic positions after he gained control of the Labour party. He effectively neutralized its radical element and took a centrist path, which pleased British business. In presenting socialism with a capitalist face, Blair set a trend in European politics that was followed by Lionel Jospin in France and Gerhard Schroeder in Germany. Notably achievements in Blair's first term included negotiations to end the long-running conflict in North Ireland and the devolution of regional power to legislative assemblies in Scotland and Wales. The success of Blair's approach could be seen in his overwhelming victory for a second term in 2001 and again for a third term in 2005 and his survival, albeit with greatly diminished prestige, in the face of powerful opposition to his policies on Iraq and higher education.

By the middle of 2007, Blair's former finance minister, Gordon Brown, had replaced Blair as head of the Labour Party and as prime minister. Although the nation continues to enjoy a strong economic sector, it confronts a number of challenges. Britain's transportation infrastructure remains in need of overhaul. A rising Scottish National Party has promised to seek a referendum on Scotland's status in the United Kingdom if elected to power. Finally, the county's participation in the invasions of Afghanistan and Iraq, particularly the latter, has made the United Kingdom a target for Islamic terrorism, as tragically demonstrated by the July 2005 terror attacks in London and a number subsequent terror plots that have been averted by Britain's security services.

▶ Margaret Thatcher was the first woman to head a major British party (the Conservative party) and the first woman to serve as prime minister of Great Britain, a post she held for 11 years.

France: Grandeur and Reality

Although most of France agreed to do the "rational" thing and capitulate to the Nazis in June 1940, Charles de Gaulle urged the government to move to North Africa and continue the struggle. During the war, he personified France as a Great Power rather than a humiliated Nazi victim.

After the liberation of Paris in August 1944, de Gaulle was proclaimed provisional president, and for 14 months he was a virtual dictator by consent. Elections held in October 1945 confirmed that the people wanted a new constitution. Sharp differences, however, developed between de Gaulle and members of the government. The general resigned in January 1946, and in the fall of that year, the Fourth Republic was established.

The Fourth Republic struggled along under the same problems that had beset Third Republic until 12 years later, when it collapsed over the issue of Algeria. Revolt against the French colonial government there began in 1954 and for the next 8 years drained French resources. The French population in Algeria, more than a million people, insisted that Algeria remain French. Army leaders supported them, and plots were started to overthrow the government in Paris. Facing the prospect of a civil war, the ineffectual French government, which had been referred to as a "regime of mediocrity and chloroform," resigned in 1958, naming de Gaulle as president. His new government was granted full power for six months.

De Gaulle returned to Paris and oversaw the drafting of a new constitution, this for the Fifth French Republic. The new code was overwhelmingly approved by referendum in September 1958. De Gaulle was named president for 7 years and proceeded to make this office the most important in the government. In both the Third and Fourth Republics, the legislature had been dominant, but now the president and cabinet held supreme power. During a crisis, the executive could assume nearly total power. De Gaulle once commented, "The assemblies debate, the ministers govern, the constituent council thinks, the president of the Republic decides."

De Gaulle ended the Algerian war and shrugged off assassination plots and armed revolts. For the next 7 years, he worked to make France the dominant power in Europe, a third force free of either U.S. or Soviet domination. To this end, he persisted in making France an independent nuclear power. In 1966, he withdrew French military forces from active participation in NATO, although France remained a consultative member of the alliance. Above all, de Gaulle was opposed to membership in any supranational agency. For this reason, although he tolerated the Common Market, he blocked any attempts to transform it into a political union. Even though he wielded great influence internationally, at home his position weakened.

A serious upheaval of university students and workers' strikes in 1968 further diminished de Gaulle's authority. A national referendum had been called to reorganize the government on a regional basis. De Gaulle unnecessarily made it a vote of confidence. When the referendum failed, he resigned his office and retired to his country estate, where he died 18 months later.

His successor was Georges Pompidou (ZHORZ-HE pom-pee-DOO; 1911–1974), an able administrator who gave evidence of vision in his leadership. When Pompidou died unexpectedly in 1974, the country elected Valéry Giscard d'Estaing (ZHEES-car des-TANG) as president. The new president initiated a series of important reforms relating to urban growth, real estate, and divorce. He also favored lowering the voting age to 18. Despite the generally high quality of leadership in France, the country was afflicted by the international economic difficulties relating to the energy crisis and American financial woes after 1973. Problems of inflation and housing shortages helped the rise to power of the Communist and Socialist parties, whose active participation in the wartime resistance had increased their popularity. The strength of the left continued to grow in the face of economic problems and discontent with Giscard's personal rule. In May 1981, Socialist leader François Mitterrand was elected president, and 20 years of right-of-center government came to an end.

Mitterrand set out to reverse two centuries of French tradition by decentralizing the governmental apparatus installed by Napoleon. In addition, he pursued a program to nationalize some of France's largest business and banking enterprises. Mitterrand's honeymoon did not last long, as the parties to his right began to practice stalling tactics in the Assembly to block his programs. Mitterrand had to deal with the economic problems of slow industrial growth, inflation, and unemployment, and he found these as resistant to solution as Giscard did.

Mitterrand died in 1996 and was succeeded by the centrist leader Jacques Chirac. Despite serious charges of corruption, he remained as president for 11 years. During his presidency, he worked with a prime ministers of his own party and then with Socialists—in an awkward system known as cohabitation—and finally, in the spring of 2002, Chirac overcame a serious challenge from the extreme right wing to be reelected for a 5-year term with a powerful majority in the National Assembly. Chirac gained temporary popular support in 2003 and 2004 with his opposition to the American campaign in Iraq. However, the deeper, underlying social and economic problems in France remained. After the events of September 11, 2001, the French were reminded of their own problems with terrorism throughout the 1990s, as immigrants in the Muslim-dominated suburbs of Marseille celebrated the attacks in America and tensions grew between French and Arab citizens of the Republic leading to riots in the Paris suburbs in 2005. Increasing incidents of anti-Semitic and Islamophobic activities further added to the feeling of unease. In 2007, Nicolas Sarkozy (b. 1955) succeeded to the presidency, the first French president born after the Second World War.

Germany: Recovery to Reunification

West Germany to 1989

The most dramatic postwar European transformation has been that of West Germany. Recovering from the death, disaster, and destruction of World War II, the Bonn government accomplished political and economic miracles. When the Soviet Bloc disintegrated in 1989, the Bonn government moved rapidly to extend economic aid and work for reunification. By October 1990, unification had been accomplished, justifying the dreams of postwar Germany's most important leader, Konrad Adenauer, who led his country from the status of despised outcast to that of valued Western ally.

Adenauer's one driving obsession was to get his people to work. Taking advantage of the tensions of the Cold War, he succeeded admirably. Under the force of his autocratic and sometimes domineering leadership, the Germans rebuilt their destroyed cities and factories using some $3 billion in Marshall Plan assistance. As early as 1955, West German national production exceeded prewar figures, with only 53 percent of former German territory. Providing the initial economic guidance for this recovery was Adenauer's minister of economics, Ludwig Erhard, a professional economist and a firm believer in laissez-faire economics. Germany's economic growth was accompanied by little inflation, practically no unemployment, and few labor problems.

Adenauer's achievements in foreign affairs were as remarkable as his leadership in domestic affairs. The Federal Republic of Germany gained full sovereignty in 1955. At that same time, West Germany was admitted into the NATO alliance. Adenauer decided to align closely with the West and cultivated close ties with the United States. In 1963, he signed a treaty of friendship with France, ending a century-long period of hostility. Adenauer expressed his attitude toward foreign affairs when he said, "Today I regard myself primarily as a European and only in second place as a German." It was natural that he brought his nation into Europe's new institutions, the European Coal and Steel Community and the Common Market. Adenauer's great frustration in foreign affairs was his failure to achieve the reunification of Germany.

Conservatives continued to control German politics after 1963 and Adenauer's retirement until 1969 with the victory of the Social Democratic party. This moderate, nondoctrinaire socialist party was led by Willy Brandt, who became chancellor. Brandt was very active in setting West Germany's foreign policy. He was instrumental in getting Britain into the Common Market, and he tried to improve relations with Eastern Europe and the Soviet Union through *Ostpolitik,* a policy of cooperation with Warsaw Pact nations. In journeys to both Moscow and Warsaw in 1970, he negotiated a treaty with the USSR renouncing the use of force and an agreement with Poland recognizing its western border along the Oder and Neisse rivers. A treaty was also signed with East Germany for improving contacts and reducing tensions. These negotiations and others paved the way for the entry of the two Germanies into the United Nations.

Brandt's concentration on foreign affairs led to the appearance of neglect of domestic issues such as inflation and rising unemployment. Important segments of German public opinion attacked him on the policy of *Ostpolitik*. After a spy scandal rocked the government, Brandt resigned in the spring of 1974. Helmut Schmidt, who succeeded him, paid closer attention to domestic affairs. Under Schmidt's leadership Germany continued its strong economic growth in the wake of the oil embargo. In the late 1970s, Schmidt asked the United States to counter the Soviet placement of SS-20 intermediate-range missiles by placing intermediate-range ballistic missiles in Europe, thereby setting off a debate that did not end until 1983. Schmidt faced both the disapproval of antinuclear demonstrators, who did not want the missiles, and the displeasure of conservatives in his country and the United States concerning German economic ties with the Soviet Union. In the autumn of 1982, political power passed again to the Christian Democratic party, now led by Helmut Kohl.

Helmut Kohl's party proved to be a staunch supporter of the United States, in particular of its program to place U.S. intermediate-range missiles in Europe. In the face of strident Soviet protests, Kohl, aided by French president François Mitterand, guided a bill through the West German parliament in November 1983 to deploy the missiles. After that success and a strong victory in 1987, Kohl—despite his reputation as a plodding politician—came to play a strong role in European affairs and in relations with the Soviet Union. In the course of his tenure, Kohl changed with the times to deal with environmental issues brought forcefully to the public forum by the environmentally focused Green party. (See *Global Issues—The Environment* on page 986 for more on the role environment has played in world history.)

Unification

In September 1989, East Germans, looking for a better life, again fled by the thousands to the West, this time through Hungary and Czechoslovakia. This exodus, followed by Gorbachev's visit to Berlin in October, helped precipitate a crisis, bringing hundreds of thousands of protesters to the streets of Berlin. Erich Honecker was removed as East Germany's leader in October, and on November 9, the Berlin Wall was breached. Once that symbolic act took place, both East and West Germans began to call for a unified Germany. Press exposés revealed corruption and scandals among the Communist elite. In the East German elections of March 1990, pro-Western parties won overwhelmingly. By October, Germany was reunited, with the first free all-German elections since Hitler took power. By 2000, Berlin was once again the capital of a united Germany.

Helmut Kohl masterfully took advantage of the breakdown of the German Democratic Republic to claim the issue of reunification for himself and his party. In the next 5 years, Kohl devoted most of his time and his country's money to integrating the former German Democratic Republic into the new German state. He had to privatize inefficient East German firms, draw investment from the West, and convince the former communist state to participate fully in the German democracy. A distrust and disdain sprang up between the two parts of the country, the East and the West: the West found the Easterners (*Ossis*) to be lazy and not sufficiently grateful, while the East saw the Westerners (*Wessis*) to be arrogant and cold.

By the end of 1994, Kohl had confounded critics who had contempt for his intellect and thought him politically naive. He overcame all the opposition for election, and his three-party coalition once again enabled him to remain chancellor. The cost of incorporating East Germany into the republic continued to be immense and has led to a high unemployment rate, centered in the east, which will need at least another decade to catch up with its neighbors to the west. Yet after a brief downswing, German industries have reformed themselves and are reclaiming parts of the world market, especially in automobiles, that they lost in the 1980s. None of this resurgence helped Kohl in the September 1998 elections, however, as his center-right coalition was replaced by a center-left coalition headed by the moderate Socialist Gerhard Schroeder.

The charismatic and colorful Schroeder was initially aided by a scandal stemming from an illegal use of funds by Kohl and his Christian Democratic party. His coalition with the Greens and other liberal parties withstood the challenges posed by the NATO bombing of Yugoslavia during the Kosovo conflict at the end of the decade, and Schroeder moved to have his country take a more prominent military and diplomatic place in the world, including vigorously opposing the U.S.-led attack against Iraq. Economic problems remained, however, as Germany continued a recession that started in 2004 and carried an unemployment rate that approached 10 percent. These problems threatened the Social Democrat's hold on power, and the chancellor's attempts to reform the social security system provoked revolts within his own ranks. In the 2005 elections, the Social Democratic government was replaced by a coalition government led by the conservative prime minister Angela Merkel.

Italy: Political Instability, Economic Growth

Following the end of Mussolini's regime, Italy voted by a narrow margin to end the monarchy. A new constitution, adopted in 1947, provided for a premier and a ministry responsible to the legislature. The Christian Democratic party—strongly Catholic, pro-Western, and anticommunist—was the leading middle-of-the-road group. Its spokesman and leader was Alcide de Gasperi (al-CHEE-da da gas-SPAR-ee), whose ministry governed the country from 1947 to 1953. Like Adenauer, de Gasperi was a strong adherent of democracy and supported European unity. Italy joined NATO in 1949 and the Common Market in 1957.

In little more than a decade, the Italian economy changed from predominantly agricultural to industrial. For a time, in the late 1950s and early 1960s, industry advanced faster in Italy than in any other part of Europe. In 1960, the output of manufacturing tripled pre-1939 levels, and in 1961, steel production exceeded 1 million tons. By the end of the 1970s, Italy ranked among the world's leaders in high-tech industry, fashion, furniture design, and banking. Most economic development occurred in northern Italy around the thriving cities of Turin, Milan, and Bologna. However, since then, the economy has stagnated.

Southern Italy did not progress as rapidly. Too many people, too few schools, inadequate roads, and inefficient, fragmented farms worked by poor peasants were among the problems besetting the area. The government offered help in the form of subsidies, tax concessions, and programs for flood control and better highways, but southern Italy remained a challenging problem.

If the Italian economy was a source of optimism, politics was another story. After de Gasperi's retirement in 1953, politics became increasingly characterized by a series of cabinet crises, shaky coalitions, and government turnovers. Between the end of World War II and the end of the century, Italy had more than fifty governments, few of which have addressed the real problems facing the nation.

Widespread corruption and inefficiency in the Christian Democratic-dominated system were exposed in a series of trials that reached to the highest levels of Italian society and government in the 1990s. Exposure of the nationwide network of corruption in 1992 sent some of the most powerful Italian leaders to jail, where some committed suicide. Revulsion provoked by the widespread corruption led in 1993 to a reform of the political system from that of a senate based on a proportional system of representation to a scheme in which power went to the group claiming the majority of votes. In 1994, a national election to form the new parliament resulted in victory for the charismatic television businessman, soccer team owner, and right-winger Silvio Berlusconi. Berlusconi's *Forza Italia* ("Let's Go, Italy") coalition included openly fascist politicians. Predictably, within six months, Berlusconi's government itself was embroiled in crisis and ended in December. In 1998, the man himself was sentenced to 2 years in prison for corruption. But because of the appeals process and his political power, he avoided going to jail.

The businesslike government of Romano Prodi (1996–1998) stabilized the Italian economy and politics, and Italy was one of the first European countries to meet the standards for entry into the Euro monetary system. He was replaced in 2001 by the scandal-ridden Berlusconi, who managed to escape his legal problems to become an ardent upholder of Prodi's status quo. The swashbuckling Berlusconi kept power by the sheer force of his personality and his control of most of the televised media in Italy, even maintaining his position while supporting the unpopular American involvement in Iraq. In 2006, he finally was forced out of office, replaced once again by the Socialist leader Romano Prodi, who after a brief honeymoon became increasingly unpopular as he had no solution to the serious economic problems faced by Italy.

Portugal

Portugal was an incredibly corrupt monarchy until 1910. The country then became a republic, but its record of internal turmoil continued. Between 1910 and 1930, there were 21 popular uprisings and 43 cabinets. Toward the end of that period, the army ousted

The Environment

Why has concern for the environment grown so much in recent decades?

▲ If in the coming century global warming were to cause significant melting of the ice sheets of Antarctica and Greenland (shown here), sea levels around the world could rise by as much as 20 to 40 feet with devastating consequences for those living in low-lying coastal areas.

Exaggerating the importance of the earth's environment would be hard to do. The environment has played a pivotal role not merely in the rise and fall of civilizations, but also more profoundly in the evolution of humans and, indeed, every other life form on the plant. It can rightly be said that the earth's environment is the very crucible of life itself. In recognizing this we should also acknowledge that the environment is not a simple static entity but instead is a highly complex dynamic system. Over the course of the earth's existence, its environment has varied dramatically. During the earth's early history, the environment was so harsh and alien from what it is today that it could not sustain life. The comparatively temperate, oxygen- and water-rich environment we are familiar with now did not arise spontaneously, but rather resulted from the interaction of inorganic and organic processes occurring over more than four billion years. Indeed, it was the genesis and proliferation of life itself on the planet—most notably, that of photosynthetic, oxygen-producing organisms—that helped transform the earth's environment, over the eons, into what it is today.

One might expect the environment to remain forever as friendly to life as it is now, but concerns are growing that humanity is changing the environment in profoundly harmful ways, even hastening the day when life on the planet, at least certain forms of it, will no longer be sustainable. Some, in fact, fear that humanity is near or has already crossed the "tipping point" from which it will be impossible to reverse worldwide environmental devastation. These concerns and others have recently led the physicist Stephen Hawking to suggest that humanity should seek out new worlds in which to live before the earth becomes uninhabitable.[1] To the skeptic, such an assertion may ring of catastrophism, but no reasonable person today could claim that the rapid growth of human populations, the runaway consumption of natural resources, and globalized industrial activity have not dramatically changed the earth's environment, often in harmful ways.

A number of specific environmental challenges confront the world today, including the pollution of the air, water, and soil; deforestation, desertification, and the destruction of ecosystems; the widespread extinctions of plant and animal species; the changing chemistry of the oceans; ozone depletion; and global warming. The last issue—the increase in the planet's temperatures due to release of heat-trapping greenhouse gases into the atmosphere—has received the most prominent attention in recent years because of its potentially devastating, worldwide impact. Not many years ago, skeptical pro-business political leaders such as Oklahoma Senator James Inhofe were declaring that global warming was "the greatest hoax ever perpetrated on the American people," yet the number of scientific bodies suggesting otherwise has only grown with each passing year. In 2007, after years in which many of the world's governments and businesses had pressured scientists to take a more skeptical stance toward global warming, the UN Intergovernmental Panel on Climate Change (IPCC) reported that "warming of the [world's] climate system was unequivocal" and that that human activity was very likely responsible (with 90 percent certainty) for most of the observed warming. Now the debate has largely shifted away from whether or not humanity is responsible for global warming to argu-

[1] Stephen Hawking, Interview, BBC, November 30, 2006.

ments about its future severity, the extent of its negative consequences, and what, if anything, the world's nations can or should do to halt or limit the warming.

If only a few of predicted negative consequences of global warming occur in the coming century, we and the other life forms on the planet face difficult times ahead. Probable destructive outcomes include the accelerated extinction of animals and plants, which cannot rapidly adapt to climate change; extended droughts and greater desertification, particularly in the tropical regions of the developing world; stronger storms generated by warmer oceans; the spread of endemic tropical diseases to temperate regions; and the melting of the ice sheets in Greenland and Antarctica and the subsequent rise in sea levels. The last outcome posses the largest question mark. In 2001, the IPCC estimated a sea level rise between 3.5 inches and 2 feet by 2100, but this is generally considered to be a conservative estimate and does not factor in natural feedback mechanisms that may be triggered by warming, principally the release of methane trapped in ice crystals within the ocean or in the melting peat bog permafrost of Siberia. Some more dire climate models point to dramatic temperature increases in the world's high latitudes in the coming century and the rapid melting of major ice sheets. Such an occurrence could potentially raise sea levels by as much as 20 to 40 feet, which is not so fantastic as it might sound if one considers that the total volume of water frozen as ice in Greenland and Antarctica, if melted, is sufficient to rise the world's sea level by more than 400 feet. Even a modest rise in sea levels by 10 feet would likely displace hundreds of millions of people living in low-lying coastal regions. The results of such a displacement—entirely aside from other aspects of global warming—would likely create massive economic disruption, agricultural losses, social and political chaos, and potentially even war.

Since the modern global economy is so heavily dependent on the burning of carbon-based fossil fuels, the principal source of greenhouse gases, finding a practical and economically feasible solution to global warming has not been easy. Indeed, proposed solutions so far have been piecemeal, largely consisting of the voluntary reduction (but not cessation) of carbon-based emissions and increased funding for alternative forms of energy. To date, the Kyoto Protocol, the broadest international effort to address global warming, has been endorsed by most industrial nations but faces opposition from other nations such as the United States and Australia, which fear potential adverse affects on their economies.

History suggests that a grim outcome could wait humanity in the future unless we are able to halt our environmentally destructive activities—be they the release of greenhouse gases, pollution, or otherwise—and replace them with more sustainable practices. In his 2005 book *Collapse: How Societies Choose to Fail or Succeed*, UCLA professor Jared Diamond identified a number of past civilizations, including the Norse of Greenland, the Polynesians of Easter Island, and the Maya of Central America, that ultimately failed, at least in part, because they could not or would not adopt environmentally sustainable practices. Whereas in the past, individual civilizations might collapse as a result of poor environmental management, today we live in a globalized world in which all of the earth's nations are economically—and environmentally—tied together. Environmental problems are no longer merely regional in scope, but are now global. For example, the Amazonian rainforest plays an essential role in the recycling of the world's fresh water and air and is also an important regulator of the earth's climate. As such, threats to the Amazonian rainforest are not just Brazilian or even South American concerns, but world concerns.

Today, just a partial survey of the environmental challenges confronting humanity might be sufficient enough to provoke pessimism about the future of the earth, but there are reasons for hope. Historically, public awareness of environmental challenges, frequently spurred by the efforts of trailblazing figures, has often been the first step in finding practical solutions to those challenges. More than 100 years ago, the pioneering efforts of John Muir and others helped generate early environmental awareness in the United States at a time when the economic exploitation of natural resources and public land was largely unregulated; this awareness eventually led to the creation of the National Parks system and early conservations efforts. In 1962, the publication of Rachel Carson's *Silent Spring*—considered to mark the beginning of the modern environmental movement by many—warned of the perils of pollution, fostering so much public outcry that the U.S. government ultimately banned the widely-used pesticide DDT and other toxic chemicals. More recently, concern generated by the world's scientific community regarding the destruction of the earth's ozone layer led to a worldwide international effort, embodied in the Montreal Protocol, to ban all ozone depleting substances such as chlorofluorocarbons (CFCs)—an notable example of mutual global cooperation on the environment that former U.N. Secretary-General Kofi Annan labeled "Perhaps the single most successful international agreement to date...."

These examples and others suggest that humanity has the capacity to change in order to meet the challenge of environmental threats. Whether it will use that capacity for change wisely in the future remains to be seen.

Questions

1. Why should people be concerned about the earth's environment?
2. What do you consider to be the biggest single environmental challenge confronting the world today? Why do you feel this way?
3. What sacrifices would you be willing to make to help preserve the earth's environment?

the politicians and took control of the government. In 1932, the generals called on Antonio de Oliveira Salazar to run the country. This former economics professor, a fervent and austere Catholic, shunned social life and was content to live on a very small salary. He devoted all of his time to running an authoritarian government. The press was censored, and education—in a country in which two-thirds of the population was illiterate—was neglected. Some economic improvement did take place, but the people, who were frozen out of politics, remained poor. In 1955, a 5-year program to stimulate the economy was launched, but its gains were canceled out by population increases and the huge costs resulting from wars in Portugal's African colonies.

Salazar retired in 1968 because of ill health, and 6 years later, a group of junior army officers overthrew the government. Serious divisions appeared between the moderate liberal factions and the Communists. In the summer of 1976, however, elections confirmed the victory of the moderate Socialists. A new constitution was enacted, establishing a democratic system. The government faced difficult economic problems—600,000 refugees from Portuguese Africa had to be absorbed, fueling high unemployment and runaway inflation. After the 1974 revolution, workers had seized many businesses, large farms, and hotels. In most instances, private ownership had to be restored under efficient management. During the 1980s, political and economic stability returned to the country, led in the latter part of the decade by Mario Soares (SWA-rush), ruling through a Socialist coalition. Compared with the northern Europe, Portugal remained poor, but it has stabilized its economy with a 3 percent inflation rate and increased literacy rates. In the new millennium, it also has maintained its substantial cultural and financial influence in Brazil.

Conservatives and socialists alternated after Soares, and presently the stable, economically growing country of Portugal is led by the socialist Prime Minister José Sócrates.

Spain

In the four decades after World War II, Spain passed from the Franco dictatorship to a rapidly industrializing, modern European state. Franco ruled over an almost ruined country after taking control in 1939. Many of Spain's most talented and productive people had fled, and 700,000 people had died in the civil war. So horrible was the conflict and so great the losses that Franco gained a grudging toleration from the majority of the exhausted population. Those who did not cooperate faced his secret police.

Cold War tensions eased Spain's reentry into the community of nations in the 1950s. The United States resumed diplomatic relations, and Spain became a member of the UN in 1955. The following year, the Pact of Madrid provided naval and air bases for the Americans, in return for which Spain received more than $2 billion a year in aid. In the 1960s and 1970s, the widespread poverty and backwardness that had long characterized Spain began to diminish. Inspired by the Portuguese Revolution of 1974, workers and students began to demonstrate and show their unrest. In the summer of 1975, Franco died. He had named Prince Juan Carlos as his successor, thereby indicating his wish that the monarchy be restored.

The young king was crowned in November 1975, and in his speech of acceptance he promised to represent all Spaniards, recognizing that the people were asking for "profound improvements." In 1976, the reformed government announced amnesty for political prisoners, freedom of assembly, and more rights for labor unions. An orderly general election took place in the spring of 1977. Post-Franco Spain began its parliamentary-monarchy phase with impressive stability. Underneath, deep ideological divisions remained, which decreased over time. The major crisis came in February 1981, when radical elements of the army invaded the parliament building to attempt a coup. Juan Carlos put his life on the line by going to parliament and intervening to block the overthrow attempt. It immediately became apparent that there was no support for the coup among the public at large, and the attempt was brushed aside.

In May 1982, Spain joined NATO—still a controversial decision—and later that year, elected Felipe Gonzales of the Socialist party to run the country. Gonzales brought Spain into the Common Market and worked hard to diversify the country's economy. He strengthened his position in the 1986 elections, and by 1990 he was governing a country attractive to investors in high-tech industries. Gonzales's party became complacent in their years in power and lost the 1996 elections to the Conservatives led by José Maria Aznar, who imposed a strict program of fiscal responsibility on the country.

A major challenge to Spain remains the Basque separatist movement, ETA, in the northwestern part of the country. Bombings and assassinations were a weekly event throughout the country at the beginning of the century, as the separatists successfully resisted international efforts to penetrate their ranks and destroy them. The terrorist bombings of the Madrid rail system in March 2004—by Islamic militants purportedly seeking to punish Spain for its participation in the occupation of Iraq—and the Aznar government's initial attempt to blame the atrocity on ETA led to the return of the Socialists to power under the leadership of José Luis Rodriguez-Zapatero.

Greece

Greece, since its modern creation in 1821, has rarely enjoyed political stability. From that year until 1945, there were 15 different types of government with 176 premiers, who, obviously, averaged less than one year each in office. Inefficiency in government, economic backwardness, and political crises have continued to plague Greece since 1945. In the Greek civil war (1946–1949), pro-Western forces, who controlled only the major cities, turned back a powerful Communist surge for power and reestablished the monarchy. Greek politicians ignored the complex economic issues affecting the peasants, preferring instead to attempt to regain various islands and territories controlled by Greeks in the long-distant past known as *irredentas* (ir-re-DENT-as). In the spring of 1967, a group of army colonels seized power. A dictatorship was established that jailed many political figures and harshly punished any criticism of its rule. Many Greeks fled into exile. The military junta made a serious miscalculation in 1974 when it connived to increase Greek authority on Cyprus, a move that led to a Turkish invasion of the island. This blunder led to the junta's downfall.

Thereafter, the Greeks created a republic, complete with a new constitution. They applied for membership in the Common Market in 1975 and were admitted in 1981. In its application, the government stated that its desire to join the European Economic Community was "based on our earnest desire to consolidate democracy in Greece within the broader democratic institutions of the European Community to which Greece belongs." Since that time, Greek leaders have maintained their democratic traditions. In November 1981, the Socialist party, led by Andreas Papandreou (AN-dre-as pa-pan-DRAY-oo), gained power and held it through 1989. He led his party back to power 4 years later. Papandreou ran on pledges to evict U.S. forces from Greek bases and to move Greek foreign policy away from its Western orientation. In the middle of the decade, Papandreou followed traditional Greek tendencies as he worked to reclaim land lost to Turkey in the past 500 years and to mobilize the nation by actively opposing the independence of the former Yugoslav republic of Macedonia on political, economic, and historical grounds.

Yet the Greeks remained active participants in NATO and the Common Market. Like Portugal, Greece is, by European standards, a poor country with a stagnant economy and an inflation rate of 18 percent. In the 1989 elections, these factors—plus scandals surrounding Papandreou's personal life—led to the defeat of the Socialists and the forming of an unlikely coalition made up of the Communist and Conservative parties, which enjoyed a short tenure in power. As the decade came to an end, the Greek prime minister, Costas Simitis (1996–2004), walked a political tightrope between nationalist expectations, fired up by the conflicts in Yugoslavia to his north and the need for sound fiscal policies. The difficult relationship with Turkey, which has plagued the country for most of its existence, remains at the forefront of Greek consciousness, along with problems of domestic terrorism. The Greeks temporarily put all of that behind them as they successfully hosted the 2004 Olympic games.

The United States

What factors contributed to make the United States the world's dominant power?

As we have seen, the United States devoted a large part of its attention to the pursuit of the Cold War for most of the half century after the end of World War II. It had emerged from World War II with its landscape unscathed and its economy the most powerful in the world. And this wealth enabled the United States over the next 40 years to assume vast responsibilities such as the Marshall Plan and the maintenance of a global military presence.

The United States in World History: A Chronological Perspective

Domestically, until 1981, both Democratic and Republic administrations based their policies firmly on the legacy of Franklin D. Roosevelt's New Deal. Politicians who opposed the Roosevelt programs suffered decisive defeats. In addition, the major parties after 1965 generally lent their support to the emerging civil rights movement that finally removed the legal restrictions to equal citizenship for the African-American population and extended the possibility of equal treatment for women. However, starting in the 1980s, conservative leaders began questioning various aspects of the New Deal legacy.

Postwar Leadership

In addition to his foreign policy accomplishments after 1945, Harry S Truman, who served as president from 1945 to 1953, continued to crusade for the rights of the "common man" and against the "fat cats" as he extended the New Deal to include his Fair Deal. Truman reached out to the African-American population as he integrated the armed forces and extended federal programs to this formerly ignored group. He also oversaw the full extension of the GI bill to all former servicemen and servicewomen—white and black.

Republican Dwight David Eisenhower, the former supreme commander of Allied forces in Europe, was twice elected to the presidency with overwhelming victories. He continued, with somewhat less enthusiasm, to oversee the growth of federal programs and the beginnings of racial integration in public schools. Eisenhower's appointment of judges such as Earl Warren to the Supreme Court established a liberal core of judges that would make its mark felt in the civil rights decisions during the 1960s.

Eisenhower's successor, the Democrat John F. Kennedy, was elected president in 1961 and promised a "New Frontier" spirit for America. Although he spoke out for programs to aid the poor and minorities, he was unable to push his programs through a generally hostile, southern-controlled Congress. He captured the nation's idealism, especially with the formation of the Peace Corps, but his assassination in November 1963 cut his presidency short.

The Crisis of the Presidency

Kennedy's vice president, Lyndon B. Johnson, picked up the burden of the slain chief executive and completed a series of major domestic reforms. Johnson could claim credit for the **Civil Rights Act of 1964,** the War on Poverty, Medicare, important environmental legislation, and the creation of the Department of Housing and Urban Development. However, major problems such as environmental pollution, decay of the inner cities, and minority discontent—the crisis of rising expectations—remained unsolved.

In foreign affairs, the increasingly unpopular Vietnam conflict (see Chapter 35) plagued Johnson's presidency. The war alone cost more than $30 billion annually, and this outlay, along with expensive domestic programs, fueled the inflation that would come in the 1970s. Congress was hesitant to provide the funds needed to improve conditions for minorities and the inner cities while at the same time conducting a costly war. These priorities angered many Americans, spurring the development of a powerful protest movement beginning with university students and spreading to average citizens. A majority of Americans found themselves in deep and serious opposition to their government's policies. The ensuing political turmoil turned especially ugly in 1968 with the assassinations of civil rights leader Martin Luther King Jr. (see the Document *Martin Luther King Jr., "Beyond Vietnam: A Time to Break Silence"*) and of Senator Robert F. Kennedy, brother of the former president, who was close to gaining the Democratic presidential nomination after Johnson had withdrawn from the primary contest.

The fragmentation of the Democratic opposition led to the 1968 election by a razor-thin margin of Republican Richard M. Nixon. Nixon had served as Eisenhower's vice president for two terms before being narrowly defeated by John Kennedy in 1960. Nixon, reelected by a landslide in 1972, shifted toward a more pragmatic philosophy of government. To fight inflation, caused in part by the costs of the Vietnam War and social programs, the administration, for the first and only time after World War II, imposed a wage and price freeze from August to November 1971 and wage and price controls from November 1971 to January 1973. These measures helped reduce the rate of inflation to about 3 percent. But when the administration returned to a free market policy at the end of April 1974, prices began to rise. The oil embargo imposed by the **OPEC** nations to protest American support of Israel contributed to a rise in the inflation rate to 12 percent and a 6 percent unemployment rate.

During this time, the Nixon administration also concentrated on foreign affairs—especially matters related to ending the war in Vietnam, keeping peace in the Middle East, opening relations with China (see Chapter 35), and maintaining détente with the Soviet Union. In each area, Nixon and his chief adviser, Henry Kissinger, compiled a substantial record of success. This record, however, was overshadowed by scandal.

Nixon's vice president, Spiro T. Agnew, resigned under the weight of charges of bribery, extortion, and kickbacks dating from his time as governor of Maryland. (Under the Twenty-fifth Amendment to the U.S. Constitution, passed just 6 years earlier, Nixon appointed a new vice president, Gerald R. Ford.) A far more serious scandal during Nixon's administration involved several men connected with his 1972 reelection campaign who were arrested and charged with burglarizing the Democratic party's campaign headquarters at the Watergate, an apartment and hotel complex in Washington, D.C. Citing "presidential confidentiality," Nixon withheld information concerning these activities from a special prosecutor, a grand jury, and the public. When lengthy televised hearings led to the conviction of his closest associates, Nixon lost the confidence of most of the nation. The Judiciary Committee of the House of Representatives voted in July 1974 to recommend impeachment. Repudiated and disgraced, Nixon resigned in August. His handpicked successor, Gerald Ford, later granted Nixon a full pardon.

The Limited Presidency

Economic problems—including high inflation that reduced the value of the dollar and high unemployment—continued to plague the nation. In 1976, Ford ran against the relatively unknown Jimmy Carter, former governor of Georgia. Carter campaigned on promises to restore trust in government, extend social programs, and improve economic conditions. Carter

Civil Rights Act of 1964—Legislation that imposed equal voting rights, outlawed racial discrimination, and continued to demand desegregation at all levels of society, among other reforms.

OPEC—Organization of Petroleum Exporting Countries created in 1960 by several petroleum-producing states to gain control over their oil output and pricing.

Document

Martin Luther King Jr., "Beyond Vietnam: A Time to Break Silence"

One of the most powerful moral voices of the postwar United States was the Reverend Dr. Martin Luther King Jr. He knew his own flaws, and also those of the country in which he lived. As he overcame his own limits, he worked to make his country a place truly more moral, just, kind, and caring. He gave voice to the demands and needs of African Americans that helped achieve the Civil Rights Acts of the 1960s that gave, for the first time, equal citizenship rights to all Americans. In this speech at Riverside Church in New York City in 1967, he addressed the moral dilemma posed by the war in Vietnam.

I have come to this magnificent house of worship tonight because my conscience leaves me no other choice. I join with you in this meeting because I am in deepest agreement with the aims and work of the organization which has brought us together: Clergy and Laymen Concerned about Vietnam. The recent statement of your executive committee are the sentiments of my own heart and I found myself in full accord when I read its opening lines: "A time comes when silence is betrayal." That time has come for us in relation to Vietnam....

Since I am a preacher by trade, I suppose it is not surprising that I have seven major reasons for bringing Vietnam into the field of my moral vision. There is at the outset a very obvious and almost facile connection between the war in Vietnam and the struggle I, and others, have been waging in America. A few years ago there was a shining moment in that struggle. It seemed as if there was a real promise of hope for the poor—both black and white—through the poverty program. There were experiments, hopes, new beginnings. Then came the buildup in Vietnam and I watched the program broken and eviscerated as if it were some idle political plaything of a society gone mad on war, and I knew that America would never invest the necessary funds or energies in rehabilitation of its poor so long as adventures like Vietnam continued to draw men and skills and money like some demonic destructive suction tube. So I was increasingly compelled to see the war as an enemy of the poor and to attack it as such.

Perhaps the more tragic recognition of reality took place when it became clear to me that the war was doing far more than devastating the hopes of the poor at home. It was sending their sons and their brothers and their husbands to fight and to die in extraordinarily high proportions relative to the rest of the population. We were taking the black young men who had been crippled by our society and sending them eight thousand miles away to guarantee liberties in Southeast Asia which they had not found in southwest Georgia and East Harlem. So we have been repeatedly faced with the cruel irony of watching Negro and white boys on TV screens as they kill and die together for a nation that has been unable to seat them together in the same schools. So we watch them in brutal solidarity burning the huts of a poor village, but we realize that they would never live on the same block in Detroit. I could not be silent in the face of such cruel manipulation of the poor.

My third reason moves to an even deeper level of awareness, for it grows out of my experience in the ghettoes of the North over the last three years—especially the last three summers. As I have walked among the desperate, rejected and angry young men I have told them that Molotov cocktails and rifles would not solve their problems. I have tried to offer them my deepest compassion while maintaining my conviction that social change comes most meaningfully through nonviolent action. But they asked—and rightly so—what about Vietnam? They asked if our own nation wasn't using massive doses of violence to solve its problems, to bring about the changes it wanted. Their questions hit home, and I knew that I could never again raise my voice against the violence of the oppressed in the ghettos without having first spoken clearly to the greatest purveyor of violence in the world today—my own government. For the sake of those boys, for the sake of this government, for the sake of hundreds of thousands trembling under our violence, I cannot be silent....

Questions to Consider

1. What are Dr. King's arguments against the American involvement in Vietnam?
2. Is Dr. King's argument a political or a moral one?

From Rev. Martin Luther King Jr., "Beyond Vietnam: A Time to Break Silence," April 4, 1967, http://www.hartford-hwp.com/archives/45a/058.html.

won the close election, becoming the first president from the Deep South since before the Civil War.

Carter inherited the same problems as his predecessors and incurred some new ones. To deal with the crisis in the Middle East, he brought the leaders of Egypt and Israel together at the presidential retreat in Camp David, Maryland (see Chapter 33). He continued to pursue limitations on nuclear arms. But for many observers, his greatest accomplishment was that he made human rights considerations an operative part of American foreign policy. Domestically, Carter attempted to enact an extremely ambitious program of social and economic benefits while maintaining sufficient military strength. Not surprisingly, spending increased despite the goal of a balanced budget.

Rising fuel prices and declining per capita output exacerbated the economic difficulties. American helplessness and frustration grew when Iranian militants captured 53 hostages during a takeover of the U.S. embassy in Tehran (see Chapter 33). The combination of economic problems, the foreign policy crisis surrounding the Soviet invasion of Afghanistan, and the hostage dilemma led to Carter's defeat in November 1980 by Ronald Reagan, former actor and governor of California. As a final snub to Carter, the Iranians released the American hostages just as Reagan took the oath of office in January 1981.

Reagan won the presidency by an overwhelming margin in 1980 and again in 1984, and he promised to set about reversing a half century of increasing federal involvement in American life by making drastic cuts in federal programs. These cuts were part of his "New Federalism" program, also known as "Reaganomics." The president believed that he could cut personal and business taxes and increase military spending at the same time. The assumption underlying the policy was that the budget cuts and tax cuts would simultaneously cure inflation and bring about economic growth. The tax cuts were not matched by reduced federal spending, however. The percentage of gross domestic product spent by government increased during Reagan's first term. By the time he left office in 1988, the federal deficit had soared to unprecedented heights spurred primarily by increased defense costs.

Reagan faced a number of foreign policy challenges in the Middle East and North Africa. A bombing in October 1983 killed 241 marines Reagan had sent to Lebanon in 1982 to act as part of an international peacekeeping force. This attack forced Reagan to withdraw U.S. troops from the region. Relations with Israel cooled when Israeli forces bombed an Iraqi nuclear facility, annexed the Golan Heights (wrested from Syria in 1967), and invaded Lebanon. The aggressive policies of Libyan leader Muammar al-Qadhafi (mu-am-MAR al-ga-DHA-fi) led to conflicts with the United States, which triggered U.S. air attacks on Libya in the spring of 1986. In another controversial move, Reagan sent U.S. naval forces to the Persian Gulf when war between Iran and Iraq threatened to disrupt international oil shipments.

Festering social and economic problems in Latin America erupted into revolutionary movements in El Salvador and Nicaragua. The Reagan administration sent in military advisers and millions of dollars to support the factions it considered "democratic." When Congress withdrew support for the rebels known as the Contras, who were fighting the leftist Sandinista government of Nicaragua, officials in the Reagan administration conspired to carry out illegal maneuvers, including selling weapons to supposed moderates in Iran and then diverting the proceeds to the Nicaraguan rebels. The "Iran-Contra affair" cast a pall over the last 2 years of the administration and led to felony convictions for high-ranking Reagan aides.

The Republicans maintained their hold on the White House with the election of George H. W. Bush in 1988. The new president failed to maintain the Reagan momentum in extending American influence favorably to affect the development of democracy and free markets in the Soviet Union. Bush instead drew back, choosing to be "prudent" and to consult closely with allies and opponents alike to maintain stability during the enormous changes occurring in Eastern Europe and the Soviet Union during 1989.

Bush's major success in foreign policy was his leadership of the anti-Iraq coalition during the Persian Gulf War in 1990 and 1991, mounted after Iraq invaded and annexed neighboring Kuwait. Deftly working through the United Nations and mobilizing a powerful coalition, Bush effectively stymied the Iraq government diplomatically and then sent U.S. troops to lead the UN coalition forces in a massive bombing campaign against Iraq. A 100-hour ground offensive ultimately drove Saddam Hussein's Iraqi forces out of Kuwait. The coalition constructed by Bush did not go on to Baghdad, however, because of the terms under which the coalition was assembled. Also, Bush and his advisers understood that the taking of Baghdad would spark an insurgency in Iraq. This in turn would be followed by a probable Kurdish drive for an independent state, which would threaten the interests of Iran, Turkey, and Syria. Finally, there was the fear that a power vacuum in Iraq would allow the Shi'ite Iranian regime to expand its power into southern Iraq.

Bush's administration faced worsening economic problems: a growing budget deficit, productivity declines, balance-of-trade problems, the failure of many savings and loan institutions, and the fear of recession. Makeshift solutions to foreign opportunities, the deficit crisis, and other pressing domestic problems contributed to the president's decline in public opinion polls.

Nagging economic problems helped ensure the 1992 victory of Bill Clinton, who used a succinct catchphrase to keep his campaign staff focused: "It's the economy, stupid!" In his first 2 years in office, the former Arkansas governor attempted to take the Democratic party to a more centrist position, responding to conditions in the bond market more than to his presumed constituency of labor, the poor, and the disaffected. Despite successes such as gaining U.S. acceptance of the **North American Free Trade Agreement (NAFTA),** the cloud of earlier personal improprieties

North American Free Trade Agreement (NAFTA)—North American Free Trade Agreement, agreed to by Canada, the United States, and Mexico and put into effect in 1994. NAFTA created a free-trade zone in North America and removed obstacles to cross-border investment.

and inadequate staff work gave the Clinton administration an image of muddling inefficiency in both domestic and foreign affairs, and that perception contributed to a sweeping Republican victory in the 1994 midterm elections, giving the GOP control of both houses of Congress.

Clinton and his advisers learned their lessons from that defeat and moved increasingly to the political center. In the 1996 elections, he ran on a program that was ideologically to the right of George H. W. Bush's positions in 1992 and easily defeated the Republican candidate, former Senate leader Robert Dole. Clinton benefited from the booming economy, which resulted from a basic overhaul of American management and manufacturing techniques, and the generally peaceful world situation.

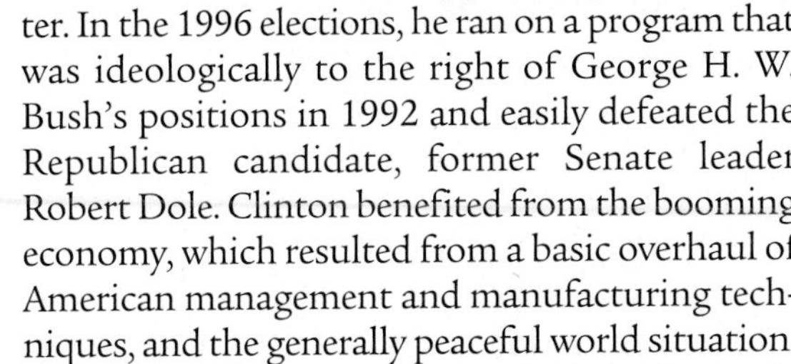

Rabin and Arafat Shake Hands at the White House, 1993

In his second term, Clinton worked continuously to find a solution to the Israeli-Palestinian crisis. He used the prestige of his presidency to try to bring the two peoples together, personally intervening in conferences in the United States and overseas to try to produce a joint agreement on such thorny issues as the status of Jerusalem and an independent Palestinian state. He also placed the United States fully into the complex questions revolving around the ethnic cleansing activities of the Yugoslav state in Bosnia, Croatia, and Kosovo. That he did not find a solution to these difficult problems is a reflection more on the nature of ethnic conflicts than on the efforts of his administration.

A tawdry scandal plagued the president throughout 1998; after finally admitting to improper behavior and lying to the American people, Clinton was impeached by the House of Representatives and his case was sent to the Senate for trial. But the economy continued to be strong and no Americans were dying in foreign wars; perhaps that is why the public seemed more embarrassed than embittered by the entire spectacle and greeted his acquittal by the Senate in 1999 with a collective yawn.

The New Century: Electoral Crisis and Terrorism

The United States greeted the new millennium with a sense of optimism. There was an unprecedented, if uneven, growth in wealth, and the stock markets leapt from one record high to another, riding on the back of companies dealing in the new computer based technologies, the so-called dot-coms. Public opinion focused blithely on the imagined triumphs and tragedies of athletes, actors and actresses, and politicians. As the country became richer, it became less and less concerned with the rest of the world, and the major television networks and newspapers, with few exceptions, reduced their coverage of international affairs.

The 2000 presidential campaign between Vice President Albert Gore and the governor of Texas, George W. Bush, a son of the forty-first president, served to excite more jokes than serious attention. The near dead heat in the November elections was followed by more than a month of recounts in the state of Florida and the juridical jousting of attorneys for the Republican and Democratic parties. In December, the Supreme Court severed the Gordian knot of challenges with a decision that effectively handed the presidency to George Bush. Subsequent surveys showed that Bush would have won the state of Florida had the recounts been permitted, and by taking Florida he would have won the Electoral College. In any event, he finished more than half a million votes behind Albert Gore in the popular vote.

President Bush's team effectively oversaw three months of successes for the Republican program before the balance of power swung to the Democratic side in the Senate in the wake of a change-of-party decision by a Republican senator. At the same time, the stock market began a rather severe decline, as the dot-coms experienced the evaporation of their value. This event was heralded by Wall Street observers as a long overdue market correction. In fact, it was the beginning of a recession. In foreign policy, the Bush team dealt with challenges such as the emergency landing of an American surveillance aircraft in China, began a substantial change in relations with Russia, and irritated its allies through a series of unilateral withdrawals from major international accords.

In the morning of September 11, 2001, the benign contentment and even boredom that characterized public discourse came to an abrupt end when four passenger jets belonging to U.S. airlines were hijacked by al-Qaeda terrorists acting on orders from Osama bin Laden (see Chapter 33). In a skillfully orchestrated set of maneuvers, hijacked jumbo jets, fully loaded with enough fuel to make a transcontinental flight, crashed into the two World Trade Center towers in New York. The combination of the impact of the Boeing jumbos and the heat generated by the burning jet fuel brought down the twin towers, killing nearly 3000 people. Two other airliners attempted kamikaze-type attacks on Washington, D.C. One crashed into the Pentagon, cutting a huge gash in the five-sided building. Another plane also targeted the White House or the Capitol. It crashed in Pennsylvania after passengers fought back and thwarted the hijackers' plans.

These events, seen live on TV across the globe, had a traumatic effect on the United States that was matched only, perhaps, by the effects of the Japanese attacks on Pearl Harbor in 1941. The images of the collapsing buildings, their inhabitants jumping to their deaths from the top floors, and the bravery of fire, police, and emergency personnel as well as ordinary citizens, galvanized the United States into a unity and purpose not seen in generations.

George W. Bush proclaimed a global assault against terrorism in all of its forms and struck at and

▲ At 8:46 A.M. (Eastern Daylight Time) on September 11, 2001, hijacked American Airlines Flight 11 from Boston crashed into the north tower of the World Trade Center. Seventeen minutes later, hijacked United Airlines Flight 175, also from Boston, shown here, crashed into the south tower. These two events launched the United States of America into a new millennium and a new world.

destroyed the Taliban regime in Afghanistan, a state that had served as the host and protector of Osama bin Laden and al-Qaeda. Public opinion polls gave the president overwhelming support for whatever he wanted to do, and the House and Senate voted through authority to pursue the terrorists wherever necessary. At the same time, new legislation, the **Patriot Act,** was passed by the House and Senate and signed into law by the president. This act gave the government unprecedented authority to delve into the personal lives of Americans and to limit certain civil rights. In addition, a new agency was created, the Homeland Security Office, that was supposed to coordinate police and information gathering activities at all levels to block terrorist attacks.

Patriot Act—The USA Patriot Act was signed into law in October 2001. Its goals can be seen by its official title: "The uniting and strengthening [of] America by providing appropriate tools required to intercept and obstruct terrorism (USA Patriot Act) of 2001."

After removing Taliban control in Afghanistan, President Bush and his advisers turned their attention to Iraq, where they deemed that Saddam Hussein had close relations with al-Qaeda and possessed concealed stores of chemical and biological weapons, or **weapons of mass destruction.** After a year of trying to gain international cooperation through the United Nations, the Americans and their British allies constructed a coalition of small powers and struck at Iraq in a preemptive attack in the spring of 2003. They quickly defeated Saddam Hussein and his forces militarily, but there appeared to be no well-conceived plan for the postwar period. The vacuum created by the removal of Saddam's Ba'th party by the allies led to all manner of looting and violence. In January 2007, even though a democratically elected Iraqi government was in place, nearly 150,000 American soldiers remained in Iraq, unable to stop an Iraqi insurgency—aided by anti-American forces coming in from outside and accompanied by murderous attacks between Sunnis and Shi'ites.

weapons of mass destruction—Chemical, biological, and nuclear weapons whose capacity to inflict massive casualties far outstrips conventional weapons.

The 2003 U.S. invasion and occupation of Iraq have divided America politically and cost the country much blood and treasure. By July 2007, more than 3600 Americans, including Marine Gunnery Sergeant Philip Jordan—whose casket is shown being carried from Holy Family Church in Enfield, Connecticut—have died in Iraq. Ten times that number have been seriously injured. Left behind are those who have lost their loved ones.

Bush's "go-it-alone" policies toward Iraq had negated all of the pro-American sentiment that had developed in Europe and around the world after September 11, 2001. After it became apparent that there were no weapons of mass destruction in Iraq and no peace following the invasion, polling data indicated that sentiments toward the United States across the globe had fallen to an all-time low. Domestically, President Bush lost the wave of high public support he had had after September 11. By the summer of 2004, public approval of his handling of the war on terrorism had declined, and a majority of Americans questioned the war and occupation of Iraq. The absence of proof of a close Iraqi tie with al-Qaeda combined with the failure to discover weapons of mass destruction in Iraq led many Americans to become cynical about the Bush administration's involvement in the Middle East. In addition, federal investigations indicated a state of passivity and unpreparedness on the eve of September 11th attacks and grave failures in the intelligence community.

In the November elections, the intensity of the passions of the supporters for each candidate and the unprecedented efforts to mobilize voters produced the highest turnout in recent elections. In 2004, George W. Bush again won a close victory in the Electoral College, but unlike in the 2000 election, he gained a sizable majority in the popular vote. Thus armed with what he termed "political capital," the president set out to implement an ambitious, if controversial, program in domestic and international affairs.

President Bush's reelection, however, would represent the last time he enjoyed support from a majority of the nation. Thereafter the worsening situation and rising U.S. casualties in Iraq would compel greater numbers of Americans to question the administration's rationale for invading the Middle Eastern country and sustaining its occupation. Along with growing public opposition to the war, a series of domestic scandals further eroded support for the Bush administration and Republican party. Confirming the shift in the public's mood, the 2006 midterm elections saw the Democrats regain control of both the House and Senate from the Republicans. By the end of 2007, Democrats were making preparations to retake the White House in the 2008 presidential elections. However, even if the Democrats regain the presidency and withdraw U.S. forces from Iraq, the political instability in that country and the rest of the Middle West and a resurgent Taliban in Afghanistan are likely to remain pressing U.S. foreign policy challenges for years to come.

Conclusion

The Union of Soviet Socialist Republics and the United States of America had been divided conceptually and philosophically since November 1917. Their brief period of cooperation in order to defeat Nazi Germany was the exception rather than the rule. After World War II, the two nations, led by Harry S Truman and Josef Stalin, became the world's sole superpowers, and they set forth on an epic global competition, only avoiding open war with one another due to the mutual threat of nuclear annihilation.

With the exception of the Cuban missile crisis in 1962, their struggle finally came down to the question of economic efficiency. The West's economy had always been more productive than that of the Soviet Bloc. The USSR and its allies suffered drastic damage during World War II, and it took the better part of the next decade to recover to even the prewar levels. The communist nations' centrally planned economic system worked reasonably well when focused on a single, well-defined goal: military buildup. However, after the mid-1970s, the West presented challenges beyond those of a military nature. Citizens of the Warsaw Pact, who had constantly lagged behind the citizens in the NATO alliance in terms of standards of living and quality of life, began to demand improvements. In response, the Soviet Bloc leaders were forced to reform, and the rigid centrally planned system was ill-equipped to produce the needed changes.

This economic failure contributed to the breakup of the Warsaw Pact, the end of the Cold War, and the end of the USSR itself. In 1989, the Soviet Union and the eastern bloc disintegrated under a tide of revolutionary change. Nearly two decades later, the results were varied. Some former Soviet republics, such as Latvia and Lithuania, entered the European Union after gaining their independence. Those such as Ukraine and Moldava faced corruption and ethnic conflict. In general, except for the top 10 percent of the population, the Russians endured a general decline in the quality of life but seemed to be adapting to their new system of democracy under Putin.

The United States, experiencing its longest-running economic growth cycle, still faces the challenges of making its pluralistic system work and preserving its basic civil liberties in the face of the terrorist attacks of September 11, 2001. Its investments in antiterrorist campaigns and the Iraq and Afghan wars have led to a federal budget deficit of close to $500 billion and a dependence on imported capital, to the tune of $1 billion a day. If Europe can continue to work out the old problems of political and cultural particularism, its economic union holds the promise that in the twenty-first century, as in the nineteenth, economic power will return to the Europeans. Its success will depend on its being able to integrate the states of Eastern Europe and successfully assimilate new immigrants into their political culture.

Suggestions for Web Browsing

You can obtain more information about topics included in this chapter at the websites listed below. See also the companion website that accompanies this text, http://www.ablongman.com/brummett, which contains an online study guide and additional resources.

Cold War International History Project
http://wwics.si.edu/index.cfm?topic_id=1409&fuseaction=topics.home
This website offers a wide range of scholarly discussions of the conflict.

National Security Archive
http://www.gwu.edu/~nsarchiv/
This online project provides up-to-date revelations of Cold War events based on newly opened archives.

National Security Agency Venona Project
http://www.nsa.gov/venona/index.cfm
The National Security Agency's Central Security Service provides an in-depth account of the U.S. infiltration of Soviet cryptology, revealing the extent of the USSR's attempt to penetrate the highest levels of the American national security apparatus.

National Security Agency Cuban Missile Crisis
http://www.nsa.gov/publications/publi00033.cfm
This site reveals the importance of spies and spy planes in the incident that almost led to a nuclear confrontation.

Cable News Network's Series on the Cold War
http://www.cnn.com/SPECIALS/cold.war/
The CNN series offers a wide range of interviews with participants and never-seen-before photographs.

Brookings Institution's U.S. Nuclear Weapons Study Project
http://www.brook.edu/fp/projects/nucwcost/weapons.htm
This site contains documents covering the assumptions that nuclear weapons brought "more bang for the buck."

Russia: How Has Change Affected the Former USSR?
http://www.learner.org/exhibits/russia/
This site, sponsored by the Annenberg/CPB Project Exhibits Collection, details the enormous changes that have taken place in the former Soviet Union since 1991.

NATO Official Home Page
http://www.nato.int
Official documents for the rapidly changing European scene.

The European Union
http://www.eurunion.org
Information on events within the European Union.

Literature and Film

Jean Larteguy detailed the frustration of the French in their withdrawal from their colonial world in *The Centurions* (Paperback, 1961). The best chronicler of the deceptions and deceit of post-1945 world is John Le Carré in a series ranging from the 1960s into the new century with titles such as

The Spy Who Came in from the Cold; Smiley's People; The Little Drummer Girl; Tinker, Tailor, Soldier, Spy; A Perfect Spy; A Small Town in Germany; The Honourable Schoolboy; The Russia House; and *The Looking Glass War.*

Gillo Pontecorvo's *Battle of Algiers* (1966; Rhino Video) is the ultimate film about a war of national liberation. The Australian Peter Weir's *The Year of Living Dangerously* (1983; Warner) presents the complexities of transitions in Indonesia. Stanley Kubrick captured the insanity of the nuclear age in *Dr. Strangelove or How I Learned to Stop Worrying and Love the Bomb* (1964; Columbia/Tristar).

America's involvement in Vietnam attracted the best efforts of Oliver Stone in *Platoon* (1986; MGM/UA), Francis Ford Coppola in *Apocalypse Now* (1979; Paramount), and Michael Cimino in *The Deer Hunter* (1978; Universal Studios). The CNN series on the Cold War is marked by frank interviews with most of the surviving players. PBS has produced a number of programs dealing with the epoch, such as *The Marshall Plan: Against the Odds* (MPAO-DXO-FXA); *Spy in the Sky* (AMEI-809-FXA), a study of the use of surveillance aircraft in the early years of the Cold War; and several documentaries in the NOVA series. The BBC's presentation of John Le Carré's *Tinker, Tailor, Soldier, Spy* (1979), starring Alec Guinness, was a triumph.

Thomas Wolfe's novels and essays—for example, *The Bonfire of the Vanities* (1987) and *Radical Chic & Mau-Mauing the Flak Catchers* (1970)—cast a cynical eye on the realities of the 1960s and 1970s. Neal Stephenson's *Snow Crash* (1992) opened up new horizons in the writing of science fiction. The novels and short stories of John Updike and Norman Mailer show as much about their evolution as that of the country. Marguerite Duras dealt with love in a difficult time in *The Lover* (1984) and *Hiroshima Mon Amour* (1959).

In film, the Italian Frederico Fellini dealt with the insanities of the nuclear age in *La Dolce Vita* (1960; Republic) and *Amarcord* (1974; Home Vision Entertainment), a portrayal of growing up in fascist Italy, which had a contemporary relevance. In France, François Truffaut led a new wave of French filmmakers with films such as *Jules et Jim* (1962; Fox Lorber) and the film version of Ray Bradbury's *Fahrenheit 451* (1966; Universal). Oliver Stone provided a compelling, particularist viewpoint of America in *JFK* (1991; Warner), *Nixon* (1995; Warner), *Wall Street* (1987; Twentieth Century Fox), *Born on the Fourth of July* (1989; Universal), and *World Trade Center* (2006; Paramount).

Sam Mendes held a magnifying glass up against the tensions and fractures of American families in *American Beauty* (1999; Universal/MCA). Spike Lee's *Malcolm X* (1992; Warner) traced a leader's saga. Michael Wadleigh's *Woodstock* (1970; Warner) caught a movement's life at its apogee. Joel Schumacher's *St. Elmo's Fire* (1985; Columbia/Tristar) provides a window into the lives of an idealistic generation's process of coming to terms. Gary Ross's *Pleasantville* (1998; New Line) is a time warp into the conformity of the 1950s. Alan J. Pakula's *All the President's Men* (1976; Warner) examines the reporters who brought down a president. Barry Levinson's *Wag the Dog* (1997; New Line) lays bare the role of spin doctors in American political life. Woody Allen's *Annie Hall* (1977; MGM/UA) sparred with the concept of romantic love.

Suggestions for Reading

The origins of the Cold War remain a major issue of debate among historians. Perhaps the best overview on the historiographical conflict is Louis J. Halle, *The Cold War as History* (HarperCollins, 1994). John Lewis Gaddis's magisterial study *The Cold War* (Penguin 2005) is the best and most accessible study of the half century of competition. Robert L. Beisner has written an important biography of one of the most important American secretaries of state in *Dean Acheson: A Life in the Cold War* (Oxford, 2006) A solid summary of the Vietnam war is Marilyn Young, *The Vietnam Wars, 1945–1990* (HarperCollins, 1994). Stephen White, *Gorbachev and After* (Cambridge University Press, 1991), gives a solid account of the dénouement of the Gorbachev revolution. Easily the wisest coverage of the collapse of communism in Eastern Europe is Gale Stokes, *The Walls Came Tumbling Down* (Oxford University Press, 1993). William E. Odom's authoritative *The Collapse of the Soviet Military* (Yale University Press, 1999) is essential to understanding the dilemmas facing Gorbachev. J. L. H. Keep's *Last of the Empires: A History of the Soviet Union 1945–1991* (Oxford University Press, 1995) is a fine study of the factors bringing an end to the USSR.

The resurgence of Western Europe is dealt with in Tony Judt, *Postwar: A History of Europe Since 1945* (Penguin, 2005). Roger Cohen, *Hearts Grown Brutal: Sagas of Sarajevo* (Random House, 1998), captures the human tragedy of the Yugoslav crises. For a new compilation of articles on the political situation in Russia after 1991, see Michael McFaul, Nikolai Petrov, and Andrei Ryabov, eds., *Between Dictatorship and Democracy: Russian Post-Communist Political Reform* (Carnegie Endowment for International Peace, 2004).

CHAPTER 33

The Middle East and Africa Since 1945

The Struggle for Survival

Outline

- The Middle East: Religion and Politics
- Africa: The Search for National Identities

Features

DISCOVERY THROUGH MAPS **Borders and Identities: The UN Partition Plan**

SEEING CONNECTIONS **Ayatollah Khomeini**

GLOBAL ISSUES **Terrorism**

DOCUMENT **The Village That Has "Eaten Itself Limb by Limb"**

◀ Long lines of people wait to vote in Soweto, as South Africa holds its first election open to all of its citizens in 1994.

THE MIDDLE EAST and Africa comprise new countries that were created after 1945. These new nation-states arose following the collapse of European colonial rule. During the Cold War, the two regions were subject to intense competition between Washington and Moscow. Middle Eastern and African leaders, in some cases, learned to manipulate the superpower rivalry to their own advantage; others attempted to do so with far less success. In addition to the Cold War, new forms of political leadership, population pressure, health crises, external debt, and economic dependence were major factors in the evolution of Middle Eastern and African nations in the second half of the twentieth century.

At the turn of the twenty-first century, many nations of the developing world, including most of Africa, remained trapped by poverty, overpopulation, and the indifference of the developed world. More than 92 percent of the world's population lived in areas where annual per capita GDP (gross domestic product) scarcely exceeded $3000. Different factors—in various combinations from one region to the next—accounted for this widespread stagnation, among them: corrupt leadership, the dominance of a peasant subsistence economy, the residual effects of colonialism, the lack of capital, substandard education, rising fuel prices, inflation, inadequate health care, environmental degradation, and overpopulation.

Millions of people have left depressed rural areas for densely populated urban megacenters that are plagued by crumbling infrastructure, air and water pollution, crime, and joblessness. The end of the Cold War and the increased threat of terrorism, however, have signaled a worldwide reconfiguring of economies, governments, allegiances, and identity politics. Whether the nations of the Middle East and Africa will benefit or suffer from rapidly evolving global circumstances remains to be seen.

The Middle East: Religion and Politics

Why have Islamist movements become popular in so many Muslim countries?

Four major developments conditioned the evolution of the Middle East in the second half of the twentieth century: the struggle over Palestine (known also as the Arab-Israeli Conflict), decolonization, the exploitation of oil resources, and the Cold War. (The latter three factors, it is important to note, also characterized regions of Africa and Latin America.) Toward the end of the century, a fifth development, the rise in popularity and activity of **Islamist** movements, has challenged the established, largely secular regimes of the Middle East and North Africa. World attention was drawn to the region, and the politics of Islamic activism, by the attacks on the World Trade Center (September 11, 2001) and the related bombings in Madrid (March 11, 2004) and London (July 7, 2005), all of which are purported to have been carried out by cells attached to or inspired by the radical Islamist group al-Qaeda.

Decolonization was a gradual and often wrenching process. Although certain Arab states were granted independence in the interwar period, the mandate powers, Britain and France, retained a significant military and economic presence in the region. During World War II, England reoccupied Iraq and used Egypt as a staging ground for its war effort. Only in the generation after the war did the nation-states of the Middle East gain full independence.

In the meantime, the arrival of waves of European Jews seeking refuge in Palestine after the war, Zionist mobilization (which aimed at the establishment of a Jewish state in Palestine), and Great Power political alignments led to the creation of the state of Israel in 1948. This touched off a bitter conflict between the new Jewish state and its Arab neighbors, who viewed Israel as illegitimate and a symbol of continued European imperialism in the region.

In the aftermath of the creation of Israel, a determined group of Egyptian army officers decided to free Egypt from the last vestiges of British control. Gamal Abdel Nasser (d. 1970), a colonel in the Egyptian army and a veteran of the first Arab-Israeli war in Palestine in 1948, organized the revolution that overthrew King Faruq in 1952. He proceeded to remake Egypt into a republic in 1953 and challenged British control over the Suez Canal. Nasser became a hero of Arab nationalism and the Non-Aligned Movement, winning wide support in the context of the Cold War by attempting to find middle ground between American and Soviet demands. Nasser, in overly ambitious fashion, imagined Egypt in a predominant role in Arab, African, and pan-Islamic affairs. His bold program to modernize Egyptian society and its stagnant economy stumbled badly, as did an experiment to merge Egypt and Syria into a single state (the United Arab Republic, 1958–1961). Egypt and Israel formed two of the central poles around which the Arab-Israeli conflict was to revolve in the decades to come.

The Modern Middle East

The Arab-Israeli Conflict

In 1947, plagued by war weariness, a battered economy at home, and a campaign of terror waged by Zionist forces in Palestine, Great Britain referred the question of the Palestine mandate to the United Nations. The resulting plan recommended the partition of Palestine into two parts, one Jewish, one Arab, with a separate enclave containing Jerusalem, Bethlehem, and other religiously sensitive sites. The Palestinian Arabs rejected the plan immediately, noting, among other matters, that although they constituted over 65% of the population at that time and could rightfully claim deep historic ties to the land of Palestine, the plan accorded them only 45% of the land. The Zionist leadership gave reluctant support to the plan since it provided the Jews with statehood and open immigration. As with its precipitous withdrawal from (and partition of) India about the same time, Britain responded to the deteriorating situ-

Islamist—Religio-political movements that advocate the establishment of government, law, and education based strictly on Islamic legal and religious tenets.

CHRONOLOGY

1940	1950	1960	1970		1980
1948 State of Israel proclaimed; National party wins white election in South Africa and institutes apartheid	1957 Ghana becomes first sub-Saharan nation to gain independence; Suez Canal Crisis	1960 Eighteen African nations gain independence; OPEC founded 1967 Arab-Israeli War; Israel occupies Jerusalem, the West Bank, Gaza, the Golan Heights, and the Sinai	1973 Yom Kippur War; Arab oil embargo; energy crisis in West 1975 Lebanese civil war begins	1976 Soweto uprising in South Africa 1979 Iranian Revolution; start of Iran-Iraq War; Israel-Egypt peace treaty	1980 Zimbabwe institutes black majority rule 1981 Egyptian President Sadat assassinated by Islamists

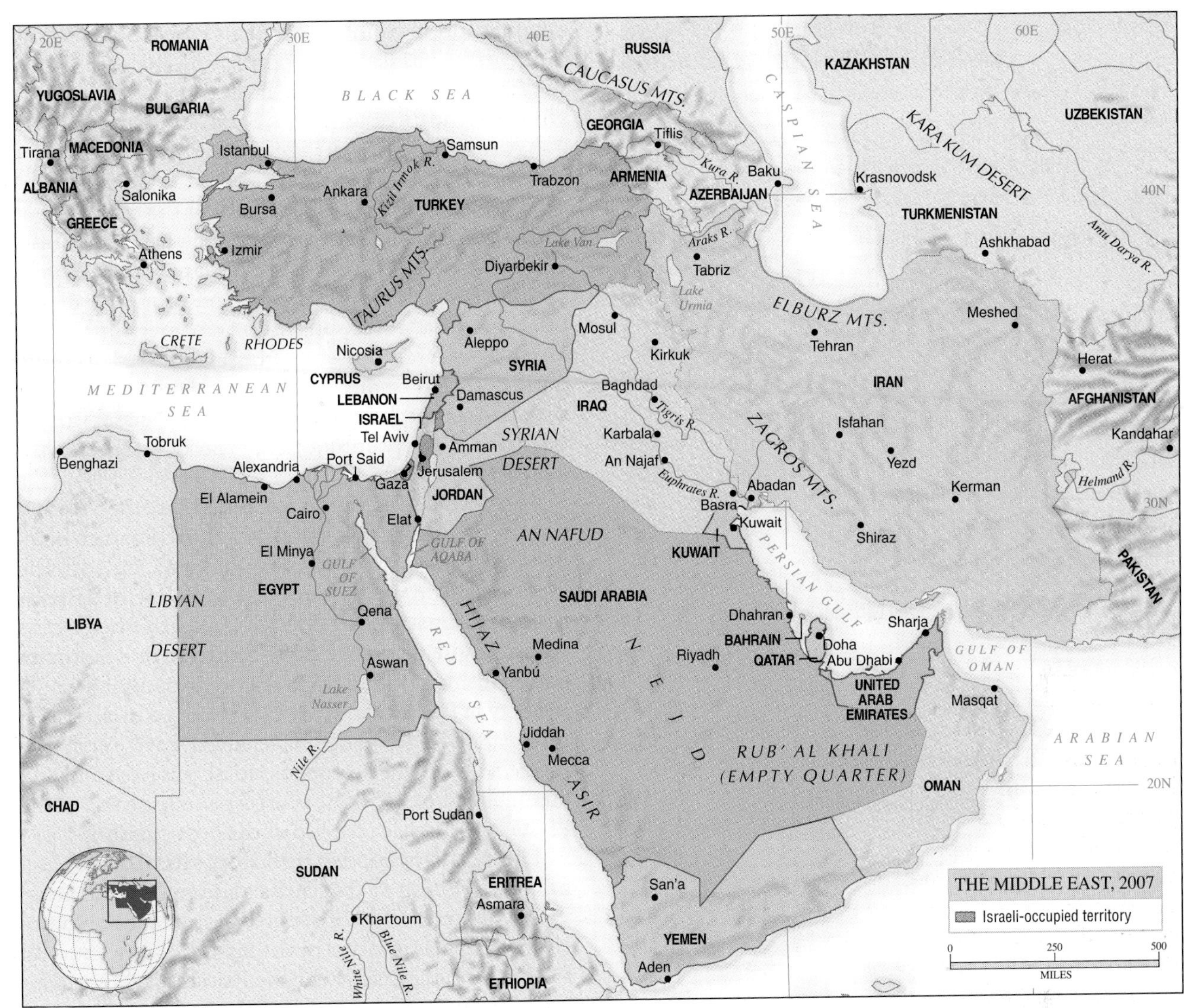

▲ All the national borders of the Middle East have been drawn after World War I. National identities have evolved since that time and regional allegiances have taken on a variety of configurations.

ation in Palestine by announcing the end of the mandate. In the ensuing chaos and civil war, disciplined and well-organized Zionist forces outfought Palestinian units, backed by small armies sent into Palestine by neighboring Arab states, including Egypt. David Ben Gurion (d. 1973), Israel's first prime minister, proclaimed the independent state of Israel on May 14, 1948.

Conscious of its hostile surroundings, the fledgling Jewish state took steps to become militarily, economically, and politically robust. The success of these efforts became quite evident in 1956 when Nasser nationalized the Suez Canal. Joined by Britain and France, Israel retaliated by sending forces to seize the

1990 | **2000**

1987 Start of first *intifada* as Palestinians in West Bank and Gaza revolt against Israeli occupation

1989 Death of Ayatollah Khomeini

1990 Iraq invades Kuwait; start of Gulf War

1991 Start of Algerian civil war

1993 Israel and PLO sign Oslo Peace Accords

1994 Nelson Mandela elected president of South Africa; Rwandan genocide

1995 Israeli Prime Minister Rabin assassinated by Jewish ultra nationalist

1995 Islamic party wins election in Turkey

1996 Start of Congo Wars

1999 President Mugabe's ruling party begins seizing white-owned farms in Zimbabwe

2000 Second *intifada* begins

2003 U.S. invasion of Iraq; start of Darfur conflict in Sudan

2005 Israel withdraws from Gaza Strip; Ellen Sirleaf Johnson elected president of Liberia

2006 Israeli-Hizballah clashes devastate Lebanon

	The Arab-Israeli Conflict
1948	State of Israel proclaimed; Arab states attack
1956	Israel joins Britain and France in war on Egypt for control of Suez Canal
1964	Palestine Liberation Organization (PLO) founded
1967	Israel wins Arab-Israeli war (Six-Day War), occupies conquered territories; UN Resolution 242
1973	Egypt and Syria attack Israel (Yom Kippur War)
1977	Egyptian President Anwar Sadat talks peace in Jerusalem
1978	Camp David Accords
1982	Israel invades Lebanon
1993	Israel and Palestinians negotiate limited autonomy for the Palestinians
2001	Ariel Sharon becomes prime minister of Israel; new Palestinian intifada
2005	Israel withdraws from the Gaza Strip

Canal. Despite initial successes, international pressure applied by the United States, the USSR, and the United Nations forced Israel and the two European states to withdraw. Israel's successful partnership with the old colonial powers was a slap in the face to the Arab states, still smarting from their failure to prevent the establishment of Israel in 1948. The Suez Crisis, as it was known, was nonetheless a triumph for Nasser in the Arab world, where widespread opinion held that he had stood up forcefully to the Western powers.

Hostilities resumed by the mid-1960s. Nasser had involved Egypt in a civil war in Yemen (1962–1965). The effort quickly went sour, with large numbers of Egyptian casualties and few political gains to show the Egyptian people. The issues of Palestinian rights and statehood, the security of the state of Israel, and free access to the Suez Canal continued to be contested, monopolizing the attention of policy-makers in the region, as well as decision-makers in Moscow and Washington. In the early summer of 1967, regional tensions escalated rapidly. Nasser, led to believe that Israel was planning for war, took steps to challenge the Jewish state, including the withdrawal of UN peace-keeping forces from the Sinai and a blockade of the Gulf of Aqaba, Israel's access to the Red Sea. Israel retaliated, and within 72 hours, completely overwhelmed the forces of Egypt, Syria, and Jordan.

A cease-fire was arranged after only six days of fighting. Israel, with surprising speed, had seized from Egypt the Sinai peninsula, including the east bank of the Suez Canal and Gaza; the tactically sensitive Golan Heights from Syria; and, from Jordan, East Jerusalem and the West Bank (of the Jordan River). The defeat was a humiliation for all three Arab governments. In an emotional radio address, Nasser tendered his resignation, only to be met by a massive display of popular insistence that he remain in office. Nasser subsequently led Egypt into a costly war of attrition with Israel (1969–1970).

Meanwhile, the Palestinians, less than impressed by the efforts of the Arab states, began to organize independently in an effort to confront Israel, on both the diplomatic and military fronts. The **Palestine Liberation Organization (PLO)** was first established by the **Arab League** in 1964, in an effort to stem Palestinian nationalism. It was an umbrella organization in which a variety of Palestinian groups, of many political stripes, took part. The defeat of 1967 enabled a new, more radical generation of Palestinians, notably Yasser Arafat (d. 2004)—head of Fatah, the largest single group in the PLO—to assume leadership of the organization.

In this first period of its history, the PLO sought a military solution to the conflict and refused all recognition of Israel. Efforts by the Palestinian forces were given particular impetus by the Six-Day War, a triumph for Israel but a disaster for the Palestinians. The conquest of the Occupied Territories created new waves of refugees and placed Israel in control of a large and resentful Arab population. Israel now had three sorts of residents. Israeli Jews enjoyed full rights as citizens of the Jewish state. Israeli Arabs (Muslim and Christian), though also citizens, were burdened by second-class social and political standing. The Palestinian Arab population, noncitizens, were now under full military occupation and subject to the policies (and whims) of the Israeli state.

The UN Security Council responded to the war with UN Resolution 242, which recognized Israel's right to exist but ordered the return of the Occupied Territories. Arguing that they were essential to the security of Israel and that they constituted an integral part of the historic Jewish homeland, Israeli leaders refused to surrender the territories. Instead, they

Palestine Liberation Organization (PLO)—A group founded in 1964 whose goal was to establish an independent state of Palestine.

Arab League—An organization of 21 Arab states formed in 1945 to coordinate policies on economic affairs, communication, social and health issues, and international affairs.

Discovery Through Maps

Borders and Identities: The UN Partition Plan

The borders of new nations can be planned and mapped, but those plans and maps are often radically different from ground-level realities. The United Nations' partition plan for the British mandate of Palestine is a case in point. After World War II, the Zionists in Palestine began to push aggressively for the establishment of a Jewish state. Violence in the mandate, created out of the Ottoman Empire by the treaties of World War I, escalated between 1944 and 1947. Then Britain's foreign secretary, Ernest Bevin, reflecting Britain's loss of control in the area, referred the "Palestine Question" to the United Nations. The UN created a special committee in 1947 that proposed the end of the mandate and its partition into one Arab and one Jewish state, with Jerusalem as a special internationalized city. The proposal was accepted by Zionist leaders and rejected by Arab leaders. After hard lobbying by U.S. President Harry Truman, the partition plan passed in the UN General Assembly. But the plan, shown on this map, never became a reality. Britain's planned withdrawal from Palestine caused a panic in the mandate. Zionist forces seized the initiative, gained control of Palestine, and proclaimed an Israeli state on May 14, 1948.

The drawing of borders in the Middle East for mandates after World War I, and later for nation-states, often did not take into account the identities or wishes of the people living there. But the drawing of these borders ultimately did create new national identities, like those of Israelis and Jordanians, residents of newly created states. Others, like the Palestinians, were dispossessed by the new boundary lines and began a struggle for their own nations and "national" identities. The UN partition plan for Palestine was designed by a committee that spent only five weeks in the mandate. It had to take into account the political, religious, and strategic interests and demands of many competing parties outside of Palestine. The resulting map was an awkward patchwork of divided territories. Over fifty years later, the ultimate shape of the map of Israel is still contested.

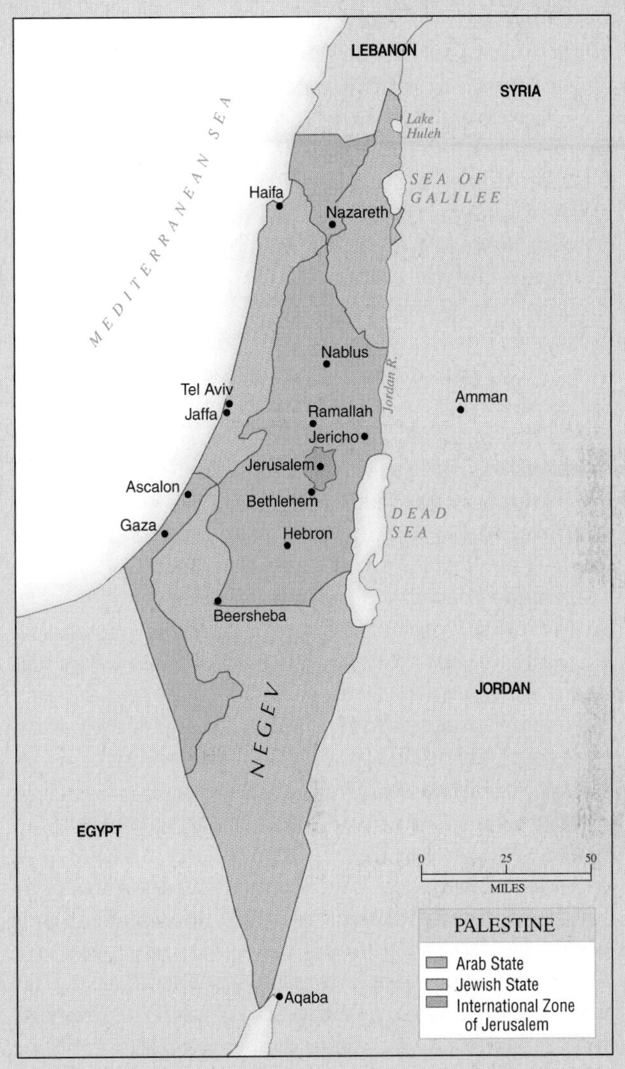

Questions to Consider

1. Look at a series of maps of this region beginning in 1900; how frequently have the boundaries changed?
2. The mandate for Palestine was a small territory and not rich. Why did so many groups and states have an interest in what happened there?
3. What factors prevented the creation of a Palestinian state out of the mandate for Palestine?

launched a program of Jewish settlements designed to consolidate Israeli control over the newly conquered lands; many observers dubbed them "facts on the ground." Given that the Occupied Territories had been seized by force, the settlements stood in full violation of international law. The occupied lands thus became the centerpiece of an ongoing struggle between Israel, the Palestinians, and the surrounding Arab states.

After 1967, the PLO worked to organize resistance to Israel. It supported political activities; constructed schools, clinics, and housing for Palestinian refugees; established work programs; and conducted military and guerrilla training. Tensions mounted as attacks by Palestinian guerrillas were met with Israeli counterattacks. An Israeli policy of disproportionate retaliation only fueled tensions in the region. The Soviet Union emerged as a major supplier of arms, aid, and technicians to the Arab states, including Syria and Egypt. The United States provided arms and aid to its Arab allies, notably Jordan and Saudi Arabia, but committed itself as well to the security of Israel, investing billions of dollars a year in the Jewish state in the form of economic and military assistance. That support was a reflection of American perceptions that Israel, as a "Western" democratic state founded by European immigrants, was a natural ally, but it also reflected the support of many Americans for the Judeo-Christian tradition and biblical promises of the Jews' return to Zion.

Nasser's sudden death (September, 1970) provided an opening for new diplomatic initiatives. Nasser's successor, Anwar Sadat (1970–1981), offered to swap peace with Israel for the return of the Sinai to Egypt. The initiative failed. Determined to force Israel's hand, Syria and Egypt launched a coordinated attack in October 1973. For the first few days, the Arabs held the initiative, but Israeli forces counterattacked, crossing the Suez Canal into Egypt and driving to within 25 miles of Damascus, the Syrian capital. In some of the most concentrated armored combat since World War II, thousands of lives were lost and thousands of tanks and aircraft destroyed.

During the fighting, the United States organized a large airlift of arms to Israel, and the Soviets responded with troop movements. Soviet and American leaders, however, averted a possible showdown through consultations. A UN-sponsored cease-fire was then arranged. In January 1974, Egypt and Israel signed a pact, providing for mutual troop withdrawals, the return of the east bank of the canal to Egypt, a UN buffer zone, and an exchange of prisoners. Fighting continued for a time longer between Israel and Syria in the strategic Golan Heights area.

The Yom Kippur War and its spin-offs were costly for the Middle East. Israel spent $5 billion and suffered 5000 casualties in addition to an ever-increasing rate of inflation generated by war expenses. Arab casualties were more than five times the Israeli losses. But whereas the Israelis came to a sober realization of their demographic and financial limitations, the Egyptians came out of the war with improved morale.

The Politics of Oil

Cold War rivalries and the conflict over Palestine were but two areas in which developments in the Middle East assumed global significance. A third was oil. By the 1950s, oil production was having a profound impact on the economic and social outlook of the region. Oil had first been exploited by the British in Iran early in the twentieth century. In 1933, Ibn Sa'ud, sovereign of the newly constituted kingdom of Saudi Arabia, granted an oil concession to Standard Oil Company (which was later nationalized and became known as Arabian American Oil Company or ARAMCO). Bahrain began exporting oil in 1934 and became the first Gulf state to develop an oil-based economy. Oil was soon discovered in Arabia and in the kingdom of Kuwait (a British protectorate from the end of World War I until 1961).

The Saudi-ARAMCO "50/50" Agreement

Saudi Arabia, Kuwait, and the other Gulf states now control at least 50 percent of the world's proven oil reserves. But major production did not gear up until after World War II, and foreign companies tended to control the revenues and organization of Middle Eastern oil resources in the 1950s. Their dominance began to change in 1960 when the Organization of Petroleum Exporting Countries (OPEC) was founded by Iran, Iraq, Kuwait, Saudi Arabia, and Venezuela to gain control over oil production and pricing. For each of these states, oil offered global influence. Oil also meant an influx of foreign workers for the petroleum-producing states: Western technical workers, South Asian laborers, and workers from neighboring Middle Eastern states seeking higher wages. These workers were part of a global process of labor migration that intensified in the second half of the twentieth century, affecting Africa and Latin America as well as the Middle East. Foreign technical workers enjoyed excellent wages and a high standard of living, but foreign domestics often worked under conditions reminiscent of slave labor. Neither group was well integrated into their host Middle Eastern societies.

In 1973, OPEC's Arab member states deployed oil as a weapon in the aftermath of the Yom Kippur War. Saudi Arabia placed an embargo on oil shipments to the United States, and the Arab oil-producing states cut production, creating panic in the industrialized world and long lines at gas pumps. The embargo symbolized a new balance in systems of world power. It harshly affected the Japanese and the Western Europeans, who respectively received 82 and 72 percent of their oil from the Middle East.

The United States, which imported only 11 percent of its oil supplies from the Middle East, nevertheless suffered substantial disruption in its economic activity, and a shocked American public began to rail against Saudi "oil *shaykhs*." The embargo was lifted in 1974, but the industrialized nations had been forced into a greater appreciation of oil as a world-class weapon wielded by states that otherwise had little leverage in world affairs. Oil prices have fluctuated since then, with sharp rises in recent years. OPEC has used its control over price and production levels to gain for its member states a greater voice in global markets and politics. Indeed, OPEC serves as a model for newly independent oil-producing nations among the one-time Soviet republics that hope to use current and projected oil resources as leverage on the world economic and political stage.

Egyptian-Israeli Détente

In late November 1977, President Anwar Sadat initiated a dramatic shift in regional affairs when he flew to Jerusalem to conduct peace talks with Israeli leaders. Sadat faced serious problems at home, brought on by a faltering economy and a rapidly increasing population. Social and economic pressures, including runaway inflation, culminated in serious "bread riots" across Egypt in 1977. Many observers understand Sadat's initiatives towards Israel as an attempt to resolve Egypt's internal crises by easing its military expenditures and turning a new diplomatic face to the world.

The United States strongly supported Sadat's peace overtures. President Jimmy Carter (1977–1981) invited Sadat and Israel's prime minister, Menachem Begin (d. 1992), to meet at Camp David, outside Washington, in September 1978. Following intense negotiations, the three leaders produced a framework for peace, in which, among other steps, Israel agreed to return the Sinai peninsula to Egypt. The parties failed to reach agreement on the status of the West Bank and Gaza, by then home to a populace of over 1 million Palestinians. It was proposed that negotiations should begin to create an elected self-governing authority for the Palestinians and to end Israeli military rule over the Occupied Territories. The Camp David Accords recognized that the Palestinian question was inextricably linked to the question of Middle East peace. Nonetheless, while Egypt and Israel have maintained a sometimes precarious relationship, the Palestinian question—now some three decades later—has yet to be resolved. The final status of Jerusalem, the West Bank and Gaza, and the future of Jewish settlements in the territories remain critical issues.

For their efforts, Sadat and Begin received the Nobel Peace Prize in 1978. The Sinai peninsula was returned to Egypt, and the Suez Canal opened to Israeli ships. In 1980, the two nations opened their borders to each other, exchanged ambassadors, and began air service between the countries. Sadat was condemned, however, by much of the Arab world, in particular by Palestinians, who viewed his efforts as a betrayal of their cause. Egypt was voted out of the Arab League, losing its dominant position in the region. Egypt did become a major recipient of U.S. foreign aid, thus tying the regime ever closer to Washington and to U.S. policy towards the Middle East.

The Evolution of Turkey

The postwar states of the Middle East have evolved in a number of different ways. Saudi Arabia, Iraq, and other oil-producing states grew wealthy; other, often smaller states, such as Syria and Jordan, without abundant natural resources, struggled to sustain economic development. Most established different sorts of secular government; others, like Saudi Arabia, retained the Sharia (Islamic law) as the basis of law, education, and domestic politics. In the Cold War competition between the United States and the Soviet Union, Middle Eastern states chose sides, cultivated alliances, or tried to remain aloof.

Unlike much of the Middle East, Turkey escaped the fate of falling under Western colonial rule after World War I. Its attainment of independence early in the century and the success of Atatürk's sweeping secularizing reforms made Turkey a model for those who envisioned Western-style, secular government as the proper course for national development.

Turkey's first multiparty elections were held in 1946. In 1950, the opposition Democrat party won a substantial majority of the vote. One of its first acts was to legalize the call to prayer in Arabic, reverting to a traditional practice once outlawed by Atatürk. Over time other elements of Atatürk's secularizing program came into question, reflecting the social and religious sentiments of much of the Turkish populace, for whom Islam remains a vital source of identity and meaning. Despite these changes, however, Atatürk remains a dominant figure in the Turkish public imagination, his Western-style, secular policies broadly supported within the Turkish military and by much of elite society.

Following World War II, Turkish and Iranian sovereignty were threatened by Soviet expansionism, which led both states to develop strong relations with the United States. From the late 1940s on, the United States, seeing Turkey and Iran as strategic bulwarks against the Soviet Union, devoted large amounts of military and economic aid to the regimes of both states. Turkey permitted the Americans to establish military bases on its territory and expanded its own armed forces with U.S. training and aid.

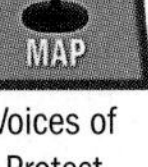

Voices of Protest

Since the 1950s, Turkey has retained its secular, democratic, multiparty government, although coups in 1960, 1971, and 1980 each brought interludes of military rule. Turkish society, in this period, struggled with a series of challenges ranging from devastating inflation and currency devaluation to an undeclared civil war with elements of its Kurdish population in the eastern provinces to new political challenges mounted by Islamist parties. Turkish governments also grappled with questions related to the massacre of Armenians following World War I; charges of genocide have been consistently rebuffed by Turkish leaders and the highly influential Turkish military command.

In the 1990s, Turkey elected its first female prime minister, Tansu Ciller (1993–1996). Charges of

▲ Tansu Ciller greets supporters in Istanbul in 1998. Although this photo shows the prime minister dressed conservatively in a headscarf, Ciller was educated in the United States and, like many Turkish women, routinely wears "Western"-style professional clothing. The headscarf in Turkey has, however, become a symbol of women's right to choose their dress and their identity.

corruption and elitism leveled at her administration are thought to have boosted the popularity of Islamist candidates. A key figure at the time was Necmettin Erbakan, head of the Refah party. The politics of this period reflect the divergent strains of modern Turkish politics. The Refah party, which promised a series of Islamic reforms, won substantial victories in 1994 in the major centers of Istanbul and Ankara. A populist party, with its appeal to Islamic values and vigorous social programs, it struck a sympathetic chord, especially among the urban poor, many of them recent migrants to Turkey's growing urban centers. Refah, winner of the 1995 national elections by a slim margin, established a fragile coalition government with Erbakan as prime minister (1996–1997). But the military, interpreting Refah's successes as a threat to Turkey's secular traditions, maneuvered to oust Erbakan, and in 1998 the Turkish High Court outlawed the Refah party.

In 2002, the moderate Islamist Justice and Development party won a two-thirds majority in parliament. The party's head, Recep Erdogan, who had been jailed in 1999 on charges of inciting pro-Islamist sentiments (for reading lines of religious verse at a rally), was chosen prime minister. Erdogan's popularity had much to do with his many achievements as mayor of Istanbul (1994–1999). This time the military refrained from direct involvement in the political process. Erdogan has worked to better relations with Greece and sought to have Turkey admitted as a full member of the European Union, a difficult, ongoing process. His government also presided over a parliamentary vote, in 2003, denying the United States access to Turkey's military bases at the onset of the invasion of Iraq.

The Iranian Revolution

Iran, the object of British and Russian competition in the nineteenth and early twentieth centuries, became a source of contention between the United States and the Soviet Union after World War II. Shah Mohammad Reza Pahlavi (d. 1980) ascended the Iranian throne in 1941 after the Allies forced his father to abdicate for supporting Germany in World War II. After the war, he asked foreign troops to withdraw from Iran. But the continued presence of Soviet troops on his borders, the aggressive activities of the Iranian Communist party (Tudeh), and a shared interest in exploiting Iranian oil moved the shah increasingly into the U.S. camp as the Cold War accelerated. The United States became Iran's principal source of foreign economic, military, and diplomatic support.

The young shah came to power in the midst of considerable unrest within Iran. Powerful interests were chafing under the monarchy and the continued control of Iranian oil by Britain. They found a hero in Mohammad Mosaddeq (MOS-ad-dek; d. 1967), a member of the traditional landed class (see Chapter 30). Elected prime minister in 1951, Mosaddeq led a broad coalition movement in advocating liberalizing reforms and nationalization of Iranian oil. His program directly challenged the shah, who fled the country. The United States, committed to the shah as a Cold War ally, viewed Mosaddeq as a threat. It boycotted Iranian oil, used the CIA to support a military coup that overthrew Mosaddeq in 1954, and helped restore the shah to power. For the next 25 years, Iran rested firmly within the orbit of the United States as a valuable source of oil and bulwark against Soviet expansion. In return, the Americans supplied Iran with massive military aid and strong support in the international diplomatic arena. Mosaddeq remained under house arrest and became a symbol of Iranian resistance to both Western imperialism and kingly authority.

The shah attempted a rapid modernization of his country, but his so-called White Revolution, to his many detractors, threatened the integrity of Iranian culture. The shah imagined himself a benevolent father, dragging an unwilling and ignorant Iran into the twentieth century. But many Iranians came to view him as a brutal dictator and a Western pawn.

To stem the growing opposition to his regime, the shah relied increasingly on intimidation and repression. The armed forces and secret police (SAVAK) carried out arrests, torture, and assassinations. The storm broke in January 1978, when armed forces fired on a demonstration of religious students in the northern city of

Seeing Connections

Ayatollah Khomeini

Grand Ayatollah Sayyid Ruhollah Mosavi Khomeini (1900–1989) emerged in the early 1960s as a leading critic of the Iranian monarchy headed by Shah Mohammad Reza Pahlavi (d. 1980). Khomeini's harsh response to land reforms proposed by the shah in 1963 led the Iranian government to exile Khomeini. Offered sanctuary in Iraq, where he remained for nearly 14 years, Khomeini denounced monarchy as an un-Islamic form of government and argued for an overhaul of Iranian political society. In his book, *Islamic Government,* published in 1971, he argued that the *ulama* should move beyond their traditional role as religious and legal authorities and assume a central part in government and politics. This radical new interpretation of the role of the religious establishment would guide the creation of the Islamic Republic, the government established in Iran following the Islamic Revolution of 1979 (see discussion in this chapter on pp. 1007–1008). Khomeini would never hold elected office, but would exert sweeping authority over the newly established Islamic regime as the official head of state and as the final arbiter of legal and political decision-making.

Qom. Many were killed and wounded, and, as word spread, strikes and demonstrations erupted across Iran. The army and secret police proved helpless in the face of the revolt. In January 1979, the shah once again fled the country, seeking asylum in the United States, then in Panama, and finally in Egypt, where he died in 1980.

The revolution had been waged by a coalition of forces, all dedicated to toppling the monarchy. That task accomplished, the coalition quickly collapsed. A new regime, led by radical Shi'ite clergy, used its organizational apparatus to gain ascendancy. The diffuse and widespread revolution found its leader in Ayatollah Ruhollah Khomeini (d. 1989), a high-ranking member of the Shi'ite religious establishment. Khomeini had been in exile since 1963 for speaking out against the shah. From Iraq, and later from Paris, he had carried on an incessant propaganda effort directed at the shah's "godless and materialistic" rule. Khomeini's rhetoric struck a sympathetic chord among Iranians offended by the shah's anti-Islamic reforms, ostentatious lifestyle, and "selling out" of Iran's resources to the West.

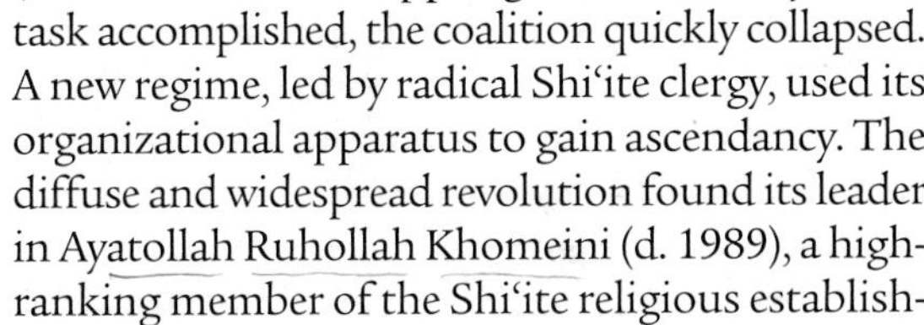

Ayatollah Khomeini

When the shah was finally forced out, Khomeini returned in triumph to Iran where, by popular mandate, he took up the reins of power. The monarchy was abolished, and Iran became a republic with a single-house parliament (the Islamic Consultative Assembly). The new regime embraced a stern, puritanical program. Western music on radio and television, "provocative" bathing suits, liquor, and a broad range of other items deemed "un-Islamic" were all banned. Consolidating his power after the revolution, the Ayatollah retained Iran's constitutional government but based it firmly on the Sharia (Islamic law). He then changed the curriculum and textbooks of Iran's schools to reflect the ideology of the new regime. The implementation of sexual segregation in the schools and the mandatory reveiling of women in public provoked a reexamination of, and considerable debate about, the status (and proper place) of women in society.

Khomeini, dubbing the United States the "Great Satan," condemned U.S. policy towards Iran. The United States, in his view, was not only closely associated with the abusive rule of the shah, but it also stood as the very symbol of imperialism, materialism, and godlessness. He encouraged the expression of anti-American sentiments, largely in an effort to consolidate the power of the new regime. In November 1979, a group of young Iranians seized the U.S. embassy, holding 53 hostages for over a year. This act and other consequences of the revolution alienated Iran from its previously warm relations with Western powers, who were fearful of the implications of Islamic rule and of the potential for destabilization of the Middle East.

Iran's regional neighbors were also alarmed at Khomeini's rise to power, fearing the prospect of the spread of Islamic-style revolution. In September 1980, in the aftermath of the Islamic Revolution, Saddam Hussein (d. 2006), the Iraqi dictator, hoping for a speedy victory over a weakened Iran, ordered an attack on Iranian airfields and oil refineries. The attack provoked a war that devastated the Iranian economy, already severely disrupted by the revolution. The financial drain of the war helped force the Iranians to release the U.S. hostages in return for the United States' release of Iranian assets frozen in response to the hostage taking.

The Iran-Iraq war dragged on for nearly a decade until, exhausted, the two sides reached an armistice in 1989. The conflict had taken on the dynamics of a war of attrition in which both sides suffered enormous losses. The Iranians employed all of their resources, including 12- and 13-year-old boys used to clear minefields, in attacks against the well-ensconced but smaller Iraqi army. Iraqi forces, for their part, violated well-established international rules of combat by using chemical weapons, not only against Iranian troops but also in a vicious campaign against northern Kurdish villages within Iraq as well.

Khomeini died in June 1989, but the idea of Islamic revolution lived on. Iran became a touchstone for Muslims across the globe disenchanted with secularism and interested in new forms of politics that might combine representative government with Islamic models of culture and law. Sunni Muslim movements, though wary of the Shi'ite elements in the Iranian model, were nevertheless inspired by the ability of Khomeini's movement to wrest power over a central Muslim state.

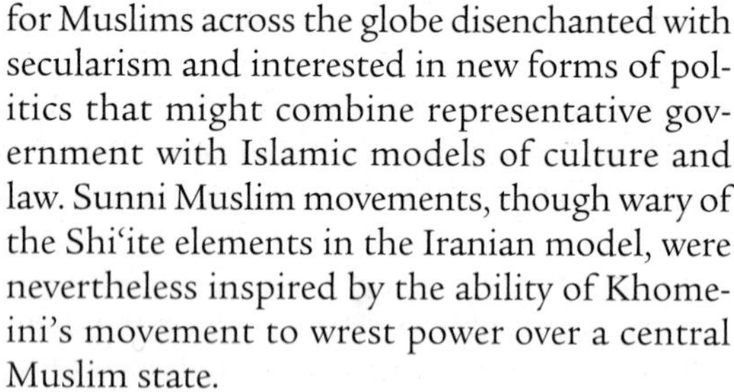

Ayatollah Khomeini's Vision of Islamic Government

Within Iran, as in Turkey after the death of Atatürk, a period of adjustment was inevitable. While the new Islamic government better reflected the religious and cultural beliefs of many Iranians, a government controlled by the **mullahs** (Muslim clerics) proved to be too conservative, too restrictive, or too religious for many segments of the society. Iran also has a very youthful population; in 1991, 44.3 percent were under age 15 and 71 percent under age 30. In 1997, with strong support from young people, women, and intellectuals, Mohammad Khatami (a moderate member of the religious establishment) was elected president by a nearly 70 percent vote. Khatami advocated a less restrictive interpretation of Islamic law, fewer restrictions on the media, and a warming of relations with the West. His election (and reelection in 2001), in which women voters played a prominent role, reflects the struggle within Iran over the social and political interpretation of the 1979 revolution.

As Khatami pushed for further liberalization and reform in government, Iranian journalists and filmmakers tested the limits of censorship with a vibrant and satirical press and film industry. Meanwhile, the enormous Iranian student population—male and female alike—experimented with its own forms of political opposition by demonstrating for more freedoms and pushing back the veil required by law for women in public places. However, these reformist advances were dealt a severe blow in the parliamentary election of 2004, when the Council of Guardians, which screens candidates, disqualified over 2000 reformists from participating in the election. As a result, those opposed to reform won an overwhelming victory. Opponents of reform gained further ground with the election, in 2005, of Mahmoud Ahmadinejad, former mayor of Tehran, to the Iranian presidency. A fierce critic of U.S. policies towards the Middle East, Ahmadinejad has made opposition to Israel and the promotion of Iran's nuclear program centerpieces of his leadership to date, pushing his country into renewed confrontation with the United States.

Toward a New Balance

During the first part of the 1980s, Egypt remained ostracized from the Arab world because of its détente with Israel. In October 1981, a small group of Islamic militants assassinated Sadat while he was reviewing a military parade. Shortly before his death, he had ordered a crackdown on the **Muslim Brotherhood** and other Islamist movements that opposed his reconciliation with Israel and Egypt's secular policies.

Sadat's successor, Hosni Mubarak, pledged to continue Sadat's commitments and welcomed U.S. military and economic support. During the 1980s, Mubarak improved Egypt's relations with other moderate Arab states as he struggled with his country's overwhelming economic problems, brought on by a mushrooming population along the Nile and chronic problems of corruption within the authoritarian

mullahs—Islamic clerics.

Muslim Brotherhood—An organization founded in 1928 in Egypt by Hasan al-Banna. The Muslim Brotherhood promoted religious, political, and social reforms and sponsored social programs.

regime. Mubarak solidified his position, maintained Sadat's foreign policies, and has proved remarkably durable after 20 years in office and significant challenges from Islamist factions.

The Israeli-Palestinian conflict again drew world attention in the late 1980s with the onset of the first Palestinian ***intifada*** ("uprising"). A popular uprising, the *intifada* was the expression of long-standing frustrations by the inhabitants of the West Bank and Gaza with the heavy-handed policies of the Israeli administration, and in particular, the steady expansion of Jewish settlements in both territories. The uprising, in large part, took the form of civil disobedience, with Palestinians demonstrating, striking, refusing to pay taxes, and boycotting Israeli goods. Israel sought to crush the uprising: over the first 4 years of the uprising, Israeli troops killed over one thousand Palestinians, wounding and jailing countless of thousands of others. Local Palestinian leadership, despite these losses, was galvanized. Pressure built upon the PLO leadership, now in exile in Tunisia after being driven from Lebanon. Arafat and his aides developed a series of steps aimed at coaxing Israel to talks over security and the creation of an independent Palestinian state. Events elsewhere in the Middle East finally led Israel's leadership to consider serious negotiations.

Soon after the Iran-Iraq war ended, Saddam Hussein launched another military offensive. In August 1990, Iraqi troops invaded and overran the oil-rich nation of Kuwait. This aggressive act, and its implied threat to Saudi Arabia, produced an immediate response. The fear that if Iraq took the Saudi oilfields, it would control one-third of the global oil reserves moved the UN Security Council to impose a series of strict sanctions on Baghdad. The Soviet Union and the United States, both former patrons of Hussein, lined up in opposition to the Iraqi dictator.

intifada—In Arabic, "shaking off." The name given to two separate Palestinian uprisings against Israel in the occupied West Bank and Gaza Strip, the first between 1987–1993 and the second from 2000 through the publication date of this text.

For a six-month period, the UN, led by a coalition assembled by the United States, increased pressure on Iraq. The Iraqi leader received the support of the PLO and Jordan, but much of the Arab world viewed his aggression with fear and anger. When the program of economic sanctions failed to drive Iraq from Kuwait, an American-led 26-nation coalition (including Egypt, Saudi Arabia, Syria, Turkey, France, Italy, and the United Kingdom) attacked Iraq in January 1991. A month later, coalition forces launched a land offensive that, in 100 hours, evicted Iraq's soldiers from Kuwait and left the coalition in possession of one-fifth of Iraq. This smashing of Iraq's forces represented a post–Cold War reconfiguration of Middle Eastern alliances. It was clear that each nation-state in the Middle East was pursuing its own agenda and that pro-U.S. or pro-Soviet designations were no longer adequate to explain Middle Eastern policy.

The Gulf War, in other words, led to a reshaping of the Middle East's political map. Support by the PLO leadership for Saddam Hussein had badly weakened it, with financial support withdrawn by Saudi Arabia and other Gulf states, and worldwide condemnation for its stance. Israel, seeking to exploit the PLO's weakness and out of fear of the spread of radical Islam, agreed finally to negotiate with the PLO. Talks led, in September 1993, to a meeting of Yassir Arafat and then Israeli Prime Minister Yitzhak Rabin (d. 1995) in Washington. The two leaders signed the Oslo Peace Accords, an agreement to turn designated areas of the Occupied Territories over to Palestinian control in return for guarantees of peace for Israel.

DOCUMENT
Israel-PLO Declaration

The agreement set up a 5-year-long framework of limited autonomy for the Palestinians in Jericho and the Gaza Strip and continuing negotiations for a permanent solution. The newly created Palestinian Authority assumed control over certain designated areas. In the context of Israel-Palestinian talks, in 1994, Jordan signed a peace treaty with Israel that normalized relations between the two states. Despite hopes for progress on the Israeli-Palestinian front, a lasting settlement remained out of reach. Prime Minister Rabin was assassinated by an Israeli right-wing extremist in 1995, who vehemently opposed the Oslo Peace Accords; and many Palestinians became disillusioned with their limited gains under the new arrangements. The Israeli government refused (and continues

◄ Israeli Prime Minister Yitzak Rabin, standing beside U.S. President Bill Clinton, shakes hands with Palestinian Liberation Organization leader Yasser Arafat during the signing of the Oslo Peace Accords in Washington, D.C., in 1993.

to refuse) to halt its program of constructing Jewish settlements (which have increased in number by 60 percent since 1993) in the Occupied Territories and has stepped up its annexation of Palestinian lands around Jerusalem. Suicide bombings by Palestinian factions across Israel helped derail peace negotiations.

Frustrated by the failure to achieve peace and security, Israelis in 2001 elected the aging warhorse Ariel Sharon as prime minister. A war hero, Likud party stalwart, ardent proponent of Israeli settlement in the Occupied Territories, and principal engineer of the invasion of Lebanon, Sharon promised Israel security and strong leadership. To the Palestinians, however, Sharon, whom they hold responsible for the 1982 massacres at the refugee camps in Lebanon, was a symbol of Israeli intransigence and their dashed hopes for statehood. Arafat's control over the Palestinian Authority was in the meantime weakened by infighting and corruption. Buoyed by new strength at the ballot box, and by its growing military capability, the Islamist movement, Hamas, founded in the Occupied Territories in the 1980s, challenged Arafat's leadership directly. In elections held 2 years after Arafat's death in late 2004, Hamas and allied Islamist groups captured a majority of seats in the Palestinian legislature.

The ongoing conflict in Israel and Palestine, however, was soon to be overshadowed by a new war in Iraq. Despite his country's defeat in the Gulf War and U.S led-efforts to constrain and oust his regime, Saddam Hussein retained his stubborn hold on power. Following the ouster of his forces from Kuwait, Hussein had brutally suppressed uprisings by Shi'ite groups in the south of Iraq and by Kurds in the north. Hundreds of thousands of Kurds had fled and become refugees. Saddam Hussein proved to be a survivor. For over a decade after the Gulf War, he successfully resisted postwar, UN-mandated weapons inspections and maintained a tight grasp on Iraqi politics. The suffering of ordinary Iraqis under a prolonged international boycott, which Saddam Hussein exacerbated by appropriating oil revenues intended to buy food, was terrible.

Things were soon to get worse for the Iraqis. In 2002, after the United States overthrew the Taliban regime in Afghanistan for its support of al-Qaeda, the Islamist group responsible for the terror attacks of September 11, 2001, it focused its attention on Iraq. Claiming—erroneously in the view of most observers across the globe—that the Hussein regime was a threat to regional and global stability because of its weapons of mass destruction and its support for international terrorism, the administration of President George W. Bush pushed ahead without a UN mandate to organize a U.S.-dominated coalition to topple Hussein. That goal was achieved in rapid fashion in 2003—Hussein, captured late that year, was eventually executed by the new Iraqi government in 2006. The campaign, however, split America's traditional allies, with Britain, Spain, Italy, and Japan supporting the United States, and France, Germany, and Canada refusing to participate. More ominously, within months of the invasion, what had been naively planned as a trouble-free occupation and smooth transition to Iraqi-led democratic government instead exploded into a full-blown insurgency against the U.S.-led forces. A coalition of Islamist, secular nationalist, and pro-Hussein elements, the insurgency targeted the foreign troops but

▼ Israel has been erecting a controversial security fence between Israel and Palestine's West Bank. Israel claims the fence is necessary to prevent Palestinian terrorists from entering Israel and killing civilians, but Palestinian officials maintain that Israel is expanding its borders by building parts of the fence on Palestinian land.

also the Iraqi government that assumed power following elections held in 2005. In 2006, the situation grew even more violent and chaotic after the bombing of a historic Shi'ite shrine pushed the country into a civil war pitting Shi'ite and Sunni forces against one another. Staggering levels of violence across the center of the country into the early part of 2007 have raised serious questions over the long-term prospects of Iraq as a unified state and hopes for regional stability.

Islamist Factions

After three generations of independence, many in the Middle East have become thoroughly disillusioned with the promises of Western-style secular nationalism. Their hopes for prosperity and freedom under long-standing regimes have often failed to materialize. Their frustrations have found expression, in many cases, in support for Islamist movements. These movements, which assert the central role of Islam in culture, politics, and law, are not a new phenomenon (and they are not limited to the Middle East). They have their roots in the Islamic reform movements—the Muslim Brotherhood, for example—of the nineteenth and early twentieth centuries. But Islamist factions have been given impetus in recent decades by the success of the Iranian Revolution, the struggles of Hamas and Hizballah against Israel, the economic failures of secular regimes, and the corruption of moral and family values widely associated with globalization and the spread of Western-style cultural patterns.

In the context of widespread poverty and political strife, Islamist movements have gained broad support across the Middle East. These movements span a range of ideological and political positions. They may advocate a return to "traditional" piety and communal values, a rejection of Western consumerism and cultural imperialism, a more significant role for Islam in schools and government, or a collapse of secular rule altogether. Often they augment their political base of support by providing social services such as adult education, health care, job training, and relief services. The assassination of Sadat in Egypt and the victories of the Refah party in Turkey are indicators of the success of Islamist politics among broad segments of the Middle Eastern populace. So too is the emergence of Hizballah in Lebanon. The organization gained much support in its determined resistance to the invasion of Israeli forces into Lebanon in 2006. A particularly militant variant of Islamism came dramatically to world attention in 2001 when members of al-Qaeda—a clandestine international terrorist organization financed by the wealthy Saudi national Osama bin Laden—launched an attack on the World Trade Center in New York and the Pentagon in Washington, D.C. Bin Laden, born to a wealthy Saudi business family, adopted a form of militant Islam (that most Muslims reject) as a young man and joined other Muslim volunteers fighting a holy war against Soviet troops occupying Afghanistan in the 1980s. From his bases in Afghanistan (see Chapter 32) and elsewhere, he trained young men to die as "martyrs" in attacks against nations he considered "enemies of Islam." Originally, bin Laden's primary target was Saudi Arabia, whose ruling regime he criticized for impiety, corruption, and allowing U.S. troops on Saudi soil during the Gulf War. But, increasingly, the United States, as the world's superpower and the backer of both the Saudi regime and Israel, became his primary target. Most Muslims, including the leadership of many more moderate Islamist groups, have denounced al-Qaeda's activities as both un-Islamic and criminal. Bin Laden's argument that the United States is an intrusive and greedy imperial power, bent on imposing its will on the Middle East and Islamic worlds, has nonetheless tapped into long-standing currents of resentment. (See *Global Issues—Terrorism* on page 1012 for more on terrorism in world history.)

Governments in the Middle East fear Bin Laden's repressive and extremist interpretation of Islam, a puritanical and violent interpretation that rejects their legitimacy and preaches their overthrow. Most regimes in the Middle East remain committed to secular rule, as do many ordinary Middle Easterners. But the successes of Islamist movements in the region are in large measure a reflection of a worldwide process of self-examination among peoples suffering from economic deprivation and repressive government, critical of the systems imposed during the period of Western imperial dominance, and interested in incorporating their own cultural traditions and values more directly into the institutions of government, education, and law.

Africa: The Search for National Identities

What was the legacy of European colonialism in Africa?

In 1945, there were just four independent African nations; at the end of the century, there were 53 sovereign states. The critical years were from the mid-1950s to the end of the 1960s, when dozens of African states won their independence. Africa's postindependence leaders generally embraced Kwame Nkrumah's dictum to "seek ye first the political kingdom." They were optimistic that once they had thrown off the shackles of colonial rule, they could build viable nation-states and tackle the poverty and underdevelopment that gripped the continent. But their optimism was short-lived as they underestimated the long-term impact of the colonial legacy and the fragility of their new states. The disillusionment of many Africans with their newly independent states is captured in the lament of Joshua Nkomo, a veteran leader

Terrorism

What is terrorism exactly and who properly fits the label of terrorist?

▲ An illustration of a terrorist bombing by anarchists and Russian nihilists on the Avenue de la Republique in Paris, from *Le Petit Journal*, February 1905.

Terrorism—few words today are charged with more impact and emotion. This wasn't always the case, but since the September 11, 2001 al-Qaeda terror attacks on New York and Washington, D.C., and the controversial War on Terror subsequently led by the United States, terrorism has grown to become one of the preeminent issues of our times. While we are all aware of the negative connotations of terrorism and the bloody images of mayhem associated with it, beyond these a deeper understanding often seems lacking. What specifically is terrorism, and who properly fits the definition of terrorist?

In attempting to answer these questions we must first acknowledge the difficulty of doing so. There are, in fact, numerous definitions of terrorism. A recent study by terrorism expert Walter Laqueur found nearly 100 different definitions of the word in English. The United States Department of State defines terrorism as "Premeditated, politically motivated violence perpetrated against noncombatant targets by subnational groups or clandestine agents." Another description, perhaps more useful for our examination of the term in its historical context, is "the use or threatened use of violence to intimidate individuals, groups, or states in order to achieve political aims." The operative principle of the latter definition is that *any* entity can engage in terrorism, be they subnational groups, clandestine agents, or states and their various institutions. It should also be recognized that both definitions imply that terrorism is a military tactic and not an ideological movement. According to either of these definitions, it should be apparent that terrorism is an old phenomenon that likely dates back to the origin of civilization, if not earlier. As but one early example of state-directed terrorism, Assyrian kings in ancient Mesopotamia employed a policy they officially described as "calculated frightfulness" to intimidate unruly subjects. Innocent victims were publicly flayed, impaled, and tortured in order to terrorize the population to which they belonged and to bring about its submission to Assyrian authority.

Activities today associated with terrorism, particularly attacks on noncombatants and the use of fear to manipulate civilian populations, have clearly been with us for some time, but the term terrorism itself is relatively modern. It is thought to originate from the French Revolution, specifically the revolutionary government under the Jacobins, known as the Reign of Terror. The Terror, as it was more simply known, marked a radical turn for the Revolution and the widespread use of the guillotine in mass executions. In 1794, the Jacobin revolutionary leader Maximillian Robespierre stated "Terror is nothing other than justice, prompt, severe, inflexible; it is therefore an emanation of virtue." Robespierre and other Jacobin members of the Committee of Public Safety employed agents known as "terrorists" to enforce the emergency laws they enacted to protect the revolutionary state.

Thus, "terrorism" and "terrorist" first entered usage in the English language in close association with violence perpetrated by government—albeit revolutionary government. It was only later in the nineteenth century that these terms began to assume their more modern connotations. During this time, political revolutionaries in Europe—nationalists, socialists, anarchists, and others—began waging sometimes violent campaigns against the governments in many nations. Though their actions might involve assassination and bombings against government, military, and business targets, the revolutionaries rarely directed their attacks specifically at civilian populations. Nevertheless, European governments and their civilian supporters began characterizing the revolutionaries as terrorists and their actions as terrorism. In the twentieth century, European governments used the same terminology to describe the nationalist revolutionaries and guerillas in their Asian and African colonies. During the postcolonial era that followed, Western nations usually reserved the terms terrorist and terrorism for the antigovernment violence of ethnic nationalists, leftist revolutionaries, or, in recent years, Islamic militants.

Of course, while all nations of the world publically condemn terrorism, definitions of what actually constitutes terrorist activity vary from culture to culture and nation to nation. One does not need to embrace moral relativity to recognize a kernal of truth in the old saw "one man's terrorist is another's freedom fighter." This isn't to suggest that everyone taking up arms against an oppressive regime is a terrorist or that, conversely, anyone wantonly killing civilians in the name of a political cause is a freedom fighter; rather, it is merely to acknowledge the role that subjectivity—be it informed by culture, religion, nationality, ideology, or ethnicity—plays in shaping our views about the legitimacy of violence. In noting this, we should also point out that a number of so-called former terrorists have gone on to become respected political leaders of international standing, including the Israeli Prime Ministers Menachim Begin and Yitzhak Shamir, the Palestinian leader Yasser Arafat, the South African President Nelson Mandela, and many others.

Today, those who engage in terrorism are often described as acting in an immoral, unjustified manner, without regard for human life or the "laws of war." They are also usually pictured as acting independently of states and their military forces (although many so-called terrorist groups are in fact sponsored by states and receive military training from them). While the term terrorist is always used in a negative fashion, few labeled as such would admit to the charge but instead would likely describes themselves in a more positive light using terms such as revolutionary, freedom fighter, martyr, militant, guerilla, or *jihadi,* to list only a few.

Another hallmark of contemporary terrorism is that many associate it with asymmetrical warfare, viewing it primarily as a tactic employed by the weak against the strong, usually individuals or groups with limited resources fighting against well-organized and powerful states. Certainly most modern instances of terrorism seem to conform to this generalization, including the al-Qaeda and affiliated terror attacks in East Africa, the United States, Bali, Spain, England, and elsewhere; the Chechnyan separatists attacks against a Moscow theater and primary school in Beslan; suicide bombings by Palestinian militants in Israel; insurgent attacks in Iraq; even Timothy McVeigh's bombing of the Federal Building in Oklahoma City. Despite such trends, however, we should recall that according to our broader definition of terrorism, the strong are also capable of waging campaigns of terror against the weak. History is littered with examples of this. The policies of conquest used by the Roman empire against the Germanic tribes involved wholesale slaughter of innocent noncombatants to dishearten and demoralize their opposition. The Aztecs were in part thought to have practiced human sacrifice on a massive scale in an effort to terrorize subject peoples into capitulating to their rule. China's Manchu dynasty in the nineteenth century employed state-sponsored brutality against civilians as part of its attempts to control the empire. Some might even argue that the Allied bombing campaigns against German and Japanese cities during World War II, including the U.S. atomic bombing of Hiroshima and Nagasaki, constituted forms of terrorism in that they were indiscriminately directed at enemy civilian populations. In more recent times, the Sudanese government has employed Arab militias, the *janjaweed,* to terrorize the African tribes of Darfur. Ostensibly, international law today is supposed to prevent state directed terror of this sort, but it has only been marginally successful in doing so (see also *Global Issues—War and International Law* on page 838).

As far as terrorism by subnational groups goes, perhaps the most worrying trend in recent years has been the rise of "super terrorism," that is, terrorism that aspires to much larger acts of carnage than did earlier forms. Today, modern weaponry and technology enable what author Thomas Friedman calls the "super-empowered angry man" to bring about destruction on a massive scale. If, in the past, terrorists might plan a single attack killing dozens, today's terrorist, particularly those affiliated with or inspired by al-Qaeda, aim to perpetrate multiple attacks killing hundreds if not thousands. If one day in the future, as many predict, terrorists are able to deploy chemical, biological, or even nuclear weapons in an attack, the results are likely to be truly catastrophic. A particularly dreaded form of contemporary terrorism is suicide bombing. While this form of attack is now closely associated with Islamic militants, it was actually Tamil separatists in Sri Lanka who first developed this tactic in the 1980s (the suicide mission, moreover, has had a long history in warfare). And because of the worldwide speed of communications, most clearly embodied in the Internet, every terrorist act can now be quickly brought to a global audience, spreading fear around the world.

The optimist might hope to see a day when terrorism ends; others might take a more skeptical view of human nature and conclude that terrorism is here to stay. It remains for all of us interested in the past, however, to learn useful lessons from this military tactic as best we can, and so as to become better able to understand the complexities of today's conflicts.

Questions

1. Do you think there are any instances in which terrorism is justified? Explain your answer.
2. How would you distinguish between terrorism and legitimate forms of antigovernment violence?
3. Do you think it is possible to defeat terrorism militarily? Explain your answer.

	Africa
1957	Independence of Ghana
1963	Creation of Organization of African Unity (OAU)
1975	Intervention of US and USSR in Angolan Civil War
1976	Soweto uprising in South Africa
1990	Release of Nelson Mandela from prison
1991	Start of Algerian civil war
1994	Nelson Mandela elected as president of South Africa after first free election; genocide in Rwanda
1996	Congo Wars begin
1999	Election of Olesegun Obasanjo as President of Nigeria
2003	Darfur conflict begins
2005	Ellen Sirleaf Johnson elected president of Liberia

of the freedom struggle in Zimbabwe: "The hardest lesson of my life has come to me late. It is that a nation can win freedom without the people becoming free."[2]

One of the most pressing problems the new states faced was how to build and maintain national unity among different and sometimes antagonistic religious, cultural, regional, and ethnic groups. In most cases, the new African states were not the product of a long historical process such as took place in Europe. Most African boundaries were arbitrary creations of the colonizers and had little relation to the people who lived there. Nigeria, for example, was known as the "linguistic crossroads of Africa" because it encompassed hundreds of diverse ethnic groups, all competing for a share of national resources. When African countries founded the **Organization of African Unity (OAU)** in 1963, however, they decided to maintain existing boundaries rather than to open up conflicts by redrawing them.

In most newly independent countries, the men who led the freedom struggle took over the reins of power. However, politicians had little experience with running governments, political parties were immature, and civil cultures were weak. The authoritarian governing styles of colonial rulers shaped the outlooks of many politicians, who did not tolerate opposition parties. A democratic culture did not take root, and power became increasingly concentrated in the hands of executive presidents who often proclaimed themselves "president for life." There was little difference between a president's pronouncements and official policy.

Civilian leaders in many African countries did not last long, however, because their armies frequently staged coups against the governments. African armies are generally small, but they have the means to topple civilian governments with ease. Soldiers usually justified a coup by portraying themselves as guardians of the public interest who were saving their country from corrupt and inefficient politicians. As in Nigeria, they also intervened to protect regional interests. More than half of all African states experienced military takeovers in the past half century. Between 1952 and 1985, 54 coups took place. A common cycle was for the military to stage a coup, return to the barracks in favor of civilians, and then intervene again.

Botswana is one of the few African states to sustain a multiparty system, despite living for many decades in the shadow of neighboring white regimes. One party, the Botswana Democratic party (BDP), has governed since independence in 1966. Despite the fact that opposition parties garnered almost 50 percent of the vote in the 2004 national elections, the BDP won about 80 percent of the seats in the National Assembly.

Since the end of the Cold War in the late 1980s, a second wave of independence swept through Africa. Grassroots organizers and civic associations around the continent stepped up their calls for democratic government, and some promising steps have been made toward implanting democratic rule. Since the late 1980s, Africa has witnessed dozens of elections. Some of them have installed genuine democratic governments, while in others, one party has dominated elections or autocratic rulers and military officers have rigged elections to stay in power.

Religion also has played a major role in new African states. Both Islam and Christianity achieved rapid growth over the last century. In most African countries, Christians and Muslims coexist peacefully, but in Nigeria and Sudan, religious rivalries have been divisive. The Sudan experienced a long civil war because its central government, dominated by Muslims who largely live in the north of the country, discriminated against southerners who are either Christians or practitioners of indigenous African religious beliefs. In 2004, the Sudanese government and the Sudan People's Liberation Army ended the conflict after signing a power-sharing agreement.

Another critical part of the colonial inheritance was that independent African nations were saddled with underdeveloped economies that were closely tied to their former colonial rulers. In the 1960s, African countries depended on primary products such as minerals and crops for about 80 percent of their exports.

Organization of African Unity (OAU)—An organization founded in 1963 to promote African unity and economic cooperation between member states and to advance Africa in science and technology, defense and security, and education and culture. It had 53 members and was replaced in 2002 by the African Union.

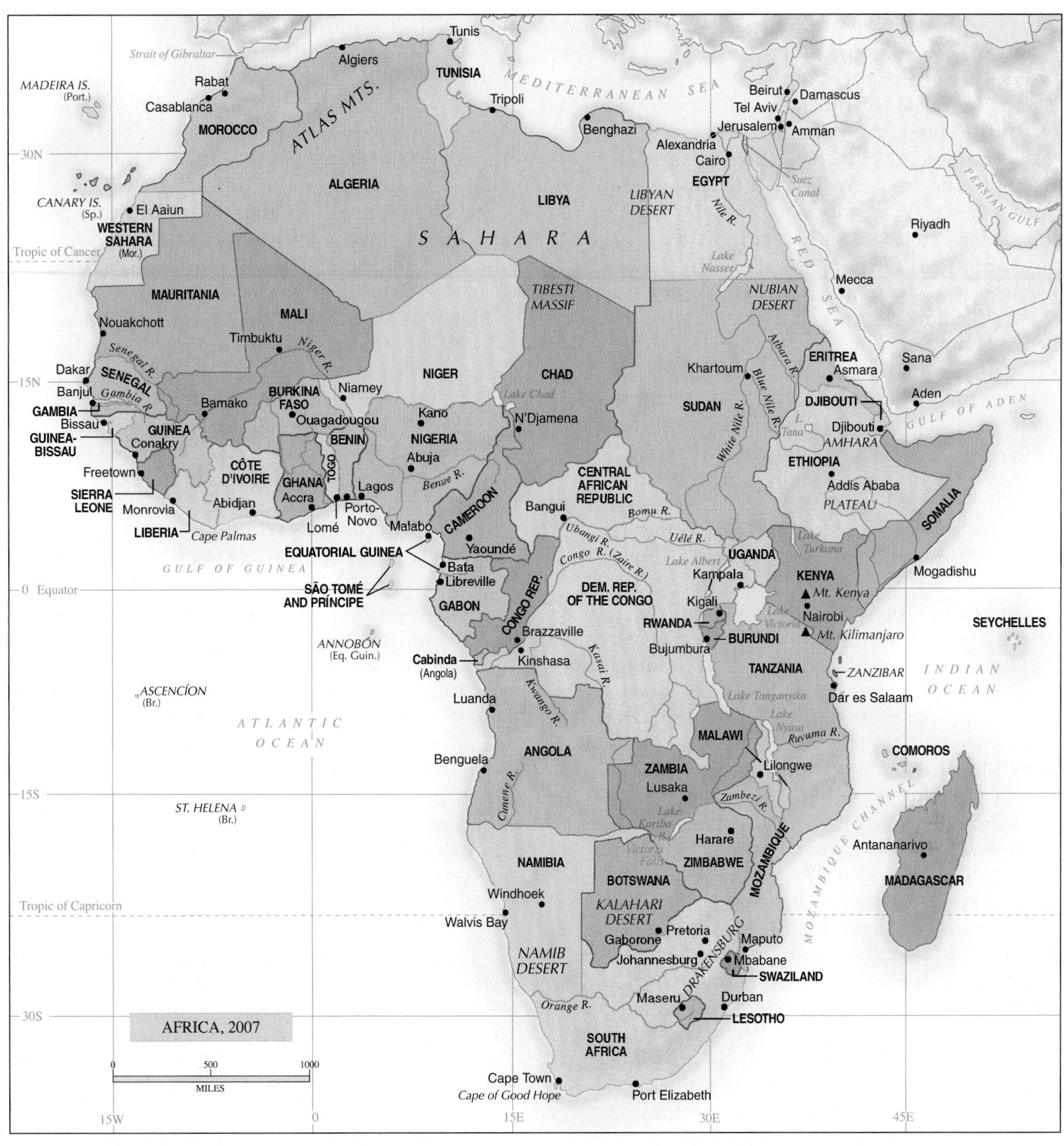

▲ When African nations gained their independence, they maintained the boundaries drawn by European colonizers in the late nineteenth century. Eritrea, which won its independence from Ethiopia in 1993 after a long war, is the only African nation to secede successfully from an existing country.

That dependence has not changed appreciably since then. Thus the health of African economies is still largely dependent on the prices their raw materials receive in world commodity markets.

Some African nations, such as Kenya and the Ivory Coast, adopted the view that the capitalist path was the correct path to development and prosperity. They modeled their policies after Western Europe and the United States, encouraged foreign investment and private businesses, and promoted rapid industrialization.

Other African leaders took the attitude that African economies, because of their marginal position in the global economy, were doomed to perpetual underdevelopment and poverty. They tried to break their states' dependency on the West by adopting socialism and developing close relations with the Soviet Union or China. African socialism typically meant state ownership of public enterprises, mines and industries, and banks and insurance companies, but socialist policies came in many varieties. Some states, such as Ethiopia, Angola, and Mozambique, practiced an orthodox brand of Marxism, while others, such as Tanzania, experimented with a socialism based on African communal values.

Regardless of the path taken, most African economies have not prospered. The nations of Africa import more goods than they export, they have to import food to feed their own citizens, they have not attracted significant amounts of foreign assistance or investment, and they have been plagued by enormous debts to lending institutions. Presently, African states devote about four times as much funding to repaying debts as they do to providing health services. The net result is that most African states have GDPs smaller than the endowments of top Ivy League universities. Thirty-two of the 47 countries classified by the World Bank as "least developed" are in Africa. Currently, sub-Saharan Africa's share of world trade is 2 percent and 1 percent of global gross domestic product (GDP). Almost 75 percent of all people in sub-Saharan Africa live on less than $2 per day.

In the first decades after independence, most African states retained close ties with their former colonial rulers economically and politically, leading some observers to charge that independence was really another form of colonialism, or **neocolonialism.** Of the former colonizers, France retained a unique status in its former colonies. French culture and language persisted among African elites, and France maintained its financial, technical, and military links. The French military intervened on several dozen occasions to rescue African leaders under fire from their own people. Francophone (French-speaking) African leaders usually paid more attention to their ties with France than to those with the OAU.

By the 1980s, African states were shackled with enormous debts, declining standards of living, and sluggish economies. GDP growth rates in the 1980s averaged only 2.1 percent per year, while the population growth rate increased to 3.1 percent per year. As a result, since the mid-1980s, African governments shifted their ties with their former colonial rulers to international lending agencies such as the World Bank and the International Monetary Fund (IMF).

The World Bank and IMF cure for ailing African economies was **Structural Adjustment Programs (SAPs)** that compelled African governments to promote market economies, liberalize foreign investment codes, and sell off state-owned enterprises to the private sector. More than two-thirds of African countries adopted SAPs, but the cure was often been worse than the illness. The conditions for loans—currency devaluations, an end to the subsidies of staple foods, and wage freezes—imposed enormous pressures on governments to carry out highly unpopular policies that have provoked protests. Some countries and individuals benefited from SAPs, but many others suffered. Women and children were hurt the most by these policies as various government support programs for food staples, education, and health care were ended.

World Bank-Supported Day Care

The most interesting economic development in recent years has been the blossoming of a new "Silk Road" between African nations and Asia and increased investment by India and China in African countries. Although the European Union and the United States remain Africa's leading trade partners, by 2006, some 27 percent of Africa's exports were flowing to Asia, a figure that seems likely to grow in the future.

The gravest challenge confronting many nations in sub-Saharan Africa is the AIDS (acquired immunodeficiency syndrome) pandemic; the disease infected an estimated 34 million Africans and killed 12 million in the last 20 years of the twentieth century. During that period, about 11 million children were orphaned. According to 2005 statistics from the UN AIDS program, roughly 10 percent of the world's population lives in sub-Saharan Africa, but it accounts for an estimated 60 percent of the people living with HIV/AIDS worldwide.

AIDS has particularly been devastating in southern Africa, where life expectancy has dramatically declined. In Botswana, life expectancy dropped from 60 years in 1985 to 38 years in 2003. AIDS spread rapidly in the region because thousands of migrant laborers move from urban to rural areas, condoms have not been extensively used, people are already infected with other sexually transmitted diseases or have weak immune systems because of malnourishment, and AIDS sufferers are socially ostracized if their condition becomes publicly known, which encourages denial or secrecy. AIDS has adversely affected every aspect of African life, ranging from agriculture, where farmers stricken with AIDS can no longer till their fields, to the commercial sector, where businesses have to train many more workers because a certain percentage of the staff are out with AIDS-related illnesses, and to African governments, which find it very difficult for their health care systems and providers to cope with the staggering cost of treating so many AIDS patients. Although cheaper generic drugs have more recently made it possible for more countries to provide their citizens with the antiretrovirals needed to suppress AIDS, most citizens

neocolonialism—The control exerted by developed nations over developing nations, usually former colonies that are still dependent on their former colonizers in economic and/or cultural areas, even though they are politically independent.

Structural Adjustment Programs (SAPs)—Economic policies such as selling off state-owned enterprises and devaluing currencies that countries must follow to qualify for new World Bank and International Monetary Fund loans and to make loan repayments on existing debt owed to commercial banks and the World Bank.

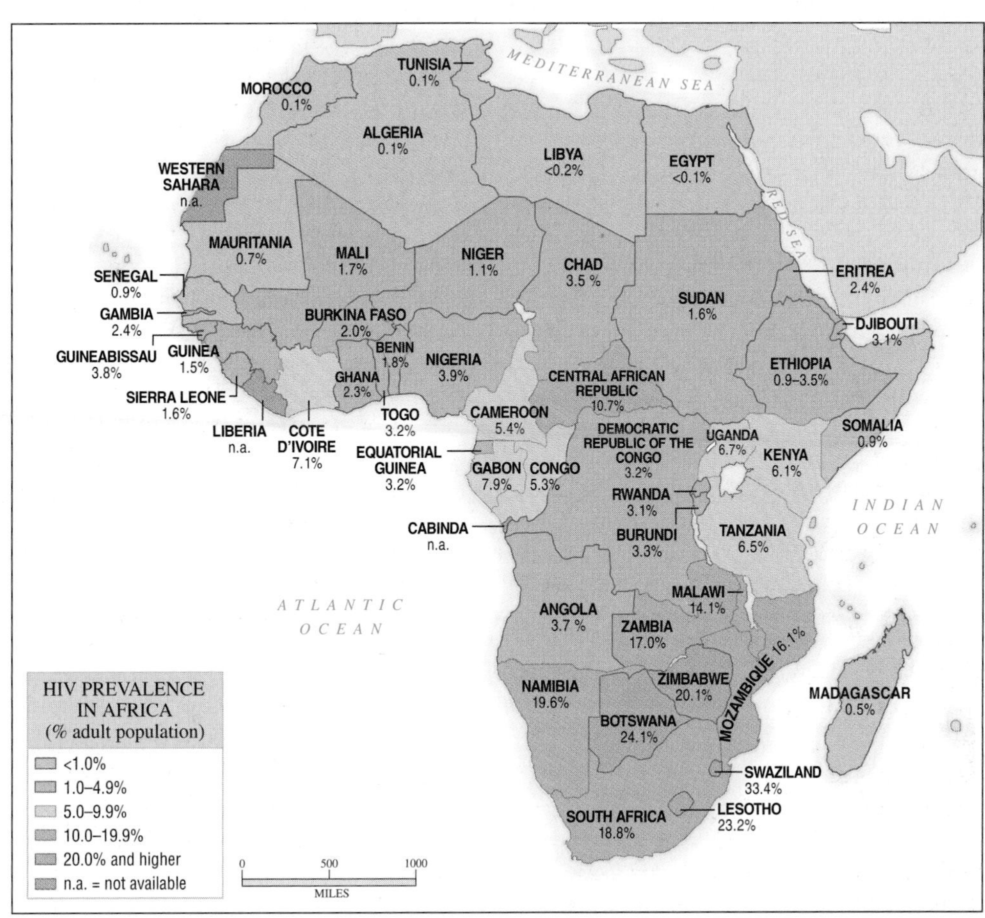

▲ The spread of AIDS over the last two decades has hit the hardest in the continent of Africa. This map shows the estimated percentages of those infected with the HIV virus in African countries in 2005.

cannot afford or gain access to the drugs. For instance, in South Africa, only 15 percent of the people who needed antiretrovirals in mid-2005 were receiving them.

North Africa

France's two protectorates in North Africa, Tunisia and Morocco, gained independence in a relatively peaceful way in 1956. In sharp contrast stands the transfer of autonomy to Algeria, which went through a bitter civil war between the French government and settlers, on the one hand, and the **Front for National Liberation (FLN),** on the other. For the first three decades following Algeria's independence in 1962, the FLN ruled together with the armed forces. Abundant oil and natural gas reserves attracted foreign investment and sustained a dramatic expansion of agriculture and industry. In the 1980s, a sluggish economy and social unrest forced the government to introduce political reforms and hold the first multiparty elections for local government in 1990. When elections were held in 1992, the Islamic Salvation Front (FIS) won an unexpected victory over the FLN. However, the military intervened, voided the elections' results, and banned the FIS. In the civil war that followed during the 1990s, over a hundred thousand people lost their lives in bitter fighting between radical Islamists and the government before an understanding was reached to open up the political process. In 1999, an election was boycotted by the main opposition parties, but in 2004, 40 political parties contested the election, which saw Abdelazic Bouteflika reelected president with 85 percent of the popular vote. Recent Islamist terror attacks in Algeria and neighboring Morocco, however, suggest that the political situation in this region is far from fully stabilized.

"The Wretched of the Earth"

Libya made the transition from Italian colony to independent nation in 1951 following a period of French-British supervision. Inspired by Nasser's revolution in Egypt, a group of young army officers led by Colonel Muammar al-Qadhafi (gha-DAH-fee) overthrew the monarchy in 1969. As "leader of the revolution," Qadhafi has remained Libya's head of state,

Front for National Liberation (FLN)—A political organization established in 1954 that led the Algerian struggle for independence from France.

Document

The Village That Has "Eaten Itself Limb by Limb"

In 2000, the global estimate for HIV/AIDS deaths was 3 million. HIV/AIDS deaths number about 20,000 annually in North America; the figure for sub-Saharan Africa is 2.4 million. This is the equivalent of two World Trade Center/Pentagon tragedies every day. Besides its toll on human life, HIV/AIDS has left a profound mark on social and economic life and has become a major threat to human security. The following newspaper article comments on the impact of HIV/AIDS on a village in Zimbabwe.

In Charumbira village in Masvingo province, Zimbabwe, Wednesday is a sacred day. According to custom, it is the chief's chosen day and no one is allowed to work in the fields or dig—unless it is a grave that's being dug up. All women are to remain at home while the men gather under a barren fig tree to discuss matters arising in the village.

However, this custom has changed over the past two years. Now every Wednesday, 200 to 300 widows meet under the fig tree, to learn how to live with the HIV/AIDS virus.

The widows, whose husbands began dying of HIV/AIDS in the late 1980s, have now come together to form a support group that will help them to cope with the impact of HIV/AIDS. The group has been further divided into smaller groups of 30 to 40 women who meet regularly and visit each other to share their experiences or pay visits to the sick. The groups also help children with food and money for school, in families where both parents have died.

Each group chooses three or four people to go for training, and on their return to impart their newly acquired knowledge about HIV/AIDS and how to live with it.

Although many women in the village have not been tested for HIV/AIDS, most believe they are HIV-positive. Miriro Mukeda (30), whose husband died a few weeks ago, believes she is also infected. "I was still sleeping with Jacob when he fell sick, and unless there is some miracle, there is no doubt that I am infected with AIDS as well."

Another widow, Susan Charumbira (44), who lost her husband 12 years ago, says villagers have been avoiding talking about AIDS. The cause of death is left to speculation. "People never wanted to talk about it, but my husband was HIV-positive, and I don't know how I have lived to this day. I thought I was going to die, and so was my child, who was then only one and half years. It is difficult to believe he is now finishing high school. However, I am getting sickly these days," she says, touching blisters on her face.

According to Maget Madenga, also a widow, and one of the leaders and founders of the support group, the idea of a support group started in 1994, but could not take off because many widows feared to be associated with AIDS and they refused to join. "It was only two years ago, that women started facing financial problems in sending children to school and feeding them, that started turning to support groups."

AIDS has destroyed the economic base of the village and provoked changes in its social fabric. Mupazi Tsveta (76), one of the village elders, has lost four sons to the pandemic and now has to care for their four widows and children.

"The village has eaten itself limb by limb and it is now hanging on the balance," he says. "Once the women start to die there will be no village to talk about anymore."

"It is difficult to establish how many people have succumbed to the pandemic in Charumbira." Tsveta stretches out his fingers, only to lose count after a few names, and all he can say is, "*Pasi radya* [the land has swallowed up countless villagers]."

Chief Fortune Charumbira says all men who were between the ages of 20 and 45 in 1990 have now died and most of them have left children and wives.

A survey done by a local secondary school, Mudavanhu, shows that at least 18 students in a class of more than 40 pupils have no fathers. "It was after we saw an increasing number of very bright pupils dropping out of school, missing lessons and losing concentration that we decided to look into the matter," says deputy principal Reason Tsvakiwa.

Tsvakiwa says HIV/AIDS is causing major disruptions in school. Children can no longer afford to pay school fees and as a result the school has resorted to fundraising to keep operations running.

"Being a teacher has become more than classroom work. We have to ensure the school has minimum resources to continue operating. Sometimes teachers contribute from their own salaries to help children who come to school on an empty stomach."

Questions to Consider

1. What impact is HIV/AIDS having on family and social structure in this village?
2. What does this article tell you about the challenge of combating HIV/AIDS in rural areas?

From Scotch Tagwiyeri, "The Village That Has 'Eaten Itself Limb by Limb,'" *Weekly Mail and Guardian* (Johannesburg, South Africa), March 12, 2001.

promoting a model of governance known as *jamahiriya* (ja-MAA-he-REE-ya; "rule of the masses"), an eccentric mix of socialist and Islamic ideas. Seeking to frustrate the formation of political parties and parliamentary democracy, Qadhafi established a government based on people's committees and popular congresses. In 1977, Libya proclaimed itself the Socialist People's Libyan Arab Jamahiriya.

Oil revenues have been the main source of Libya's economic growth, financing industrial development and paying for social programs, housing, health care, and education for many of its citizens. Qadhafi's regime nationalized all foreign-owned property, but declining oil prices led to the opening up of the private sector in the 1990s.

Libya's oil wealth allowed Qadhafi to promote an idiosyncratic foreign policy based on pan-Arab nationalism and support for revolutionary movements such as the PLO. Libya's intervention in Middle Eastern and African affairs led to confrontations with Western European nations and the United States, which accused Libya of sponsoring international terrorism. When Libyan agents were implicated after bombs exploded on a Pan American Airlines flight over Lockerbie, Scotland, and a French UTA flight over Niger, the UN imposed a trade and international flight embargo on Libya. The embargo was lifted in 1999 after Libya handed over the accused bombers of the Pan American flight for a trial in the Netherlands, where one was convicted. After the United States ousted Saddam Hussein's regime in Iraq in 2003, Qadhafi declared his opposition to terrorist groups and committed Libya to give up its nascent nuclear weapons program. Libya has been rewarded with diplomatic recognition from European states as well as the United States in 2006.

Middle Africa

Ghana was the first nation south of the Sahara to gain independence. In 1957, Kwame Nkrumah (c. 1909–1972), its prime minister, was the idol of African nationalists for championing African unity, and his newly freed nation was the symbol of freedom and democracy in Africa. But in the year after taking power, Nkrumah began to muzzle the press and imprison the opposition. In 1964, he made Ghana a one-party state. As he developed into an outright dictator, he embarked on ruinous economic policies such as a showy hydroelectric dam and support of a large military establishment. Nkrumah's controlled press called him the "Great Redeemer" and "His Messianic Majesty," while his economy slid downhill under the weight of extravagant spending and corruption.

Kwame Nkrumah on African Unity

Kwame Nkrumah

When it gained independence in 1960, Nigeria, Africa's most populous nation, offered the greatest promise of a prosperous and stable future among all new African states. It had several thousand well-trained civil servants, more than 500 doctors, an equal number of lawyers, a substantial body of engineers and urban professionals, and vibrant universities. It was endowed with a variety of important natural resources, especially oil.

Between 1962 and 1966, however, a series of crises—disputed elections, corruption, and crime waves—undermined the government's stability. In 1966, military officers seized control of the country in a bloody coup. The following year, Ibo groups in southeastern Nigeria seceded and proclaimed the independent Republic of Biafra (bee-AH-frah). The Nigerian government launched military offensives as well as an economic blockade against the rebel state. Hundreds of thousands, especially children, died of starvation. In 1970, Biafra surrendered and was reincorporated into Nigeria.

After 13 years of military rule, civilian government was restored in 1979, along with a new constitution patterned after that of the United States. Designed to prevent a return of the ethnic and regional feuds that had wrecked the first republic, the new constitution created a federal system providing for the allocation of powers between a central and 19 state governments. However, following a sharp drop in petroleum prices, the military intervened again in 1983 and banned all political parties.

In the early 1990s, it appeared that the military was preparing to hand over power to civilians. But after newspaper publisher Moshood Abiola (ah-bee-OH-lah) was elected president in 1993, the governing military council declared the election results null and void, and jailed Abiola. Following the deaths in 1998 of Abiola in prison and of military strongman Sani Abacha, military leaders allowed elections and a return to civilian rule. In the 1999 and 2003 elections, Olesegun Obasanjo (oh-bah-SAHN-joh) was elected and reelected president. As an army general, Obasanjo had served as head of state under a military government from 1976 to 1979, but he had distinguished himself then by advocating the return of government to civilians. Obasanjo's major task is creating national unity in the face of regional, ethnic, and religious rivalries and ensuring that oil revenues are distributed more evenly around the country. The sharing of revenues has been a major grievance of protesters in the oil-rich Niger Delta region.

By contrast, the Democratic Republic of the Congo, a country as large as Western Europe but lacking any ethnic or political unity, has made halting progress toward creating a stable political environment. In 1959, the Belgian colonizers, in the face of general protest and serious rioting, promised independence. When self-government came the next year, 120 political parties representing regional and ethnic interests contested elections. The new government of Patrice Lumumba, a fiery nationalist, lacked unity and stability. A civil war broke out almost immediately, and Katanga province, which produced 70 percent of the country's mineral wealth, seceded. After Lumumba was murdered in 1961 at the instigation of the Belgian government, the new Congolese government appealed to UN peacekeeping forces to intervene to restore order and quell the Katanga secession, which they did by 1964.

The government still lacked coherence, and the army commander, General Joseph Mobutu Sese Seko (1930–1997), staged a coup in 1965. He renamed the

▲ Ellen Johnson-Sirleaf, the President of the Republic of Liberia and modern Africa's first woman head of state, delivers a speech before the Deputies of the European Parliament in Strasbourg, France, September 2006.

country Zaïre, but his style of rule mirrored that of King Leopold of Belgium a century earlier. Mobutu was a "kleptocrat": He and his elite bilked the mineral-rich country of billions of dollars while leaving their people with one of the lowest per capita incomes in the world. Mobutu cleverly played Cold War politics and won support from the West by portraying himself as a bulwark against communism. When the Cold War ended, Mobutu made halfhearted attempts at negotiating with opposition groups for a democratic constitution. His regime was finally toppled in 1997 by an insurgency led by Laurent Kabila, who was supported by several neighboring states. Kabila, who restored Congo as the country's name, spent most of his energy dealing with the subsequent war to hold the politically fragmented nation together and protect its resources from neighboring states, principally Uganda and Rwanda. The war, though given little attention in Western media, resulted in the huge population displacements and the estimated deaths of 3.8 million people, mostly through starvation and disease, making it one of the deadliest conflicts since World War II. Kabila was assassinated in 2000. His son, Joseph, who succeeded him and was elected president in 2006, faces the same problems of ending the civil war and maintaining national unity.

Northeastern Africa, known as the Horn of Africa, consisted of Ethiopia, Somalia, and several small states. It became geopolitically significant after 1945 because of its proximity to the sea lanes of the Red Sea and the Persian Gulf. After Emperor Haile Selassie (1892–1975) returned to Ethiopia following the expulsion of the Italians in 1941, he kept the anachronistic feudal system largely in place. In the 1960s, in the face of student and ethnic protests, the emperor failed to move decisively on land reform or reduce the dominance of his Amhara ethnic group in government. The crisis that led to his downfall began with a famine in 1973 that killed an estimated 200,000 people. Blame was pinned on his government for mismanaging drought relief, and strikes, student unrest, and scandal among the royal family all combined to bring success to a military coup that dethroned the emperor in 1974.

The new military rulers were bitterly divided among moderates and radicals. Following 3 years of disputes, the radicals, led by Mengistu Haile Meriam (b. 1937), seized control. Their governing council, the *Dergue* (committee), immediately set to abolishing the country's feudal system, transforming Ethiopia into a socialist state with a Stalinist one-party system. The council nationalized businesses and land, introduced collective farms, censored the media, imprisoned opponents, and executed at least 10,000 opponents.

In the late 1970s, the Dergue also became bogged down in protracted wars with Eritrean and Tigrean guerrillas, who were fighting for independence in provinces bordering each other. When Eritrea won its independence in 1993, it was the first case in which an African state successfully seceded from another.

Tigrean rebels toppled the Mengistu regime in 1991 and have governed the country since then. Ethiopia and Eritrea engaged in two brief but bloody wars after 1998 over an unresolved border dispute. Although a cease-fire is in effect, relations between the two countries remain tense.

In Somalia, where clan rivalries dominated national politics, Siad Barré (b. 1919) maintained himself and his Maréhan clan in power for several decades by manipulating clan rivalries. However, insurgencies, droughts, and refugees contributed to the collapse of the Barré regime in 1991, and a civil war between clans broke out. Food shortages in the rural areas of southern Somalia led to some 300,000 dying of starvation. Televised pictures of dead and dying infants moved the international community to action, and in 1992 a UN peacekeeping force intervened to facilitate food relief.

What started out as a humanitarian crusade, however, ended in disaster when the UN force attempted to disarm warring Somali factions and stabilize the situation. A number of UN and American troops lost their lives attempting to disarm the soldiers of one of the clan leaders, Mohammed Aydeed. The American contingent of the UN force was withdrawn in 1994 and the remaining UN forces a year later. Unity talks between clan leaders faltered and no faction or coalition was able to form a cohesive central government.

One of the most tragic events in recent African history was the 1994 Rwandan genocide that saw Hutu extremists massacre Tutsis and moderate Hutus. This tragedy had been in the making during the colonial era. German and Belgian colonial officials had reinforced Tutsi dominance over the Hutus by favoring Tutsi chiefs, replacing Hutu chiefs with Tutsi chiefs, and compelling the Hutu to provide forced labor for the colonial economy. Catholic missionaries compounded the problem by favoring Tutsis and excluding Hutus in their schools.

Antagonisms between the Hutus and the Tutsis intensified. Before Rwanda's independence in 1962, the Tutsi monarchy was deposed and some Hutus took vengeance and massacred thousands of Tutsis. After independence, the Hutu majority took power and excluded Tutsis from political life and discriminated against them. Many Tutsis fled into exile in neighboring states. After 1972, the dominant figure in Hutu politics was a military officer, Juvenal Habyarimana (hah-byah-ree-MAH-nah; 1936–1994), who seized power in a military coup in 1972 but who won elections from 1983 on.

In 1990, a Tutsi-led rebel force invaded Rwanda from Uganda, sparking off a civil war that forced thousands of refugees to flee the country. Habyarimana and the rebels negotiated a transitional government, but in April 1994, as Habyarimana and the president of Burundi were returning from peace talks, a rocket from an unknown source shot down their plane, killing them both. Hutu extremists who opposed Habyarimana's negotiations with the Tutsi rebels blamed his death on a Tutsi conspiracy. They methodically incited violence against the Tutsis. Mobilizing Hutu militia groups, known as ***interahamwe*** (in-ter-ah-HAHM-way), and the presidential guard, they launched a reign of terror against Tutsis and any Hutu moderates who opposed them. Although the killers wielded simple weapons—machetes, clubs with nails, and farm tools—they were able to slaughter 10 percent of Rwanda's population within the space of 90 days. By the end of their genocidal campaign, they had killed 800,000 people and forced more than 2 million refugees into exile. In the chaos, the Tutsi-led rebels seized power and ousted the Hutu-dominated regime. Many Tutsi and Hutu refugees eventually returned to Rwanda, and since 1994, the Tutsi-led government of Paul Kagame has been trying both to bring the genocide's primary instigators to justice and reconcile the country's ethnic factions.

Sadly, the genocide in Rwanda has not been the last such tragedy in Africa. When fighting erupted between the Sudanese government and several rebel groups in the Darfur region of western Sudan in 2003, the government sent in its troops and Arab militias called the ***janjaweed*** (jahn-jah-WEED; literally "evil horsemen") to eradicate the opposition and drive the so-called black population from its land. Since then, an estimated 450,000 people have died and 2.5 million have become refugees in neighboring countries, mainly Chad, which is now being drawn into the conflict.

Southern Africa

In southern Africa in the 1950s and 1960s, white-ruled regimes resisted the calls for black majority rule, and African nationalist movements turned to armed struggle to bring about change. Self-governing white regimes in Rhodesia and South Africa dug in their heels and defied the "winds of change" to the north. Portugal clung to its African colonies because they were profitable and enhanced Portugal's prestige in the world and because large numbers of Portuguese, especially the rural poor, had emigrated to the African colonies after World War II. Frustrated by the lack of political change, African nationalist movements launched wars of liberation in the Portuguese colonies in the early 1960s. By 1970, Portugal was committing over 40 percent of its budget and more than 150,000 soldiers to the African insurgencies. A decisive moment came in April 1974 when the Portuguese military, weary of the protracted African wars, revolted against the dictatorship that had ruled Portugal for nearly 50 years. The new military junta quickly concluded settlements with African political movements in Angola, Mozambique, and Guinea-Bissau. The last two gained independence with little difficulty as power was transferred to the leading party.

Freedom for Angola was complicated by superpower rivalries and three Angolan political parties contesting for power. Following the granting of independence in 1975, the parties were supposed to share power in a unity government, but bloody strife broke out between them. The United States covertly assisted the National Union for the Total Independence of Angola (UNITA), while the Soviet Union and

interahamwe—Literally, "those who work together"; Hutu militia groups that helped carry about the Rwandan genocide against the minority Tutsi and moderate Hutus.

janjaweed—Literally, "evil horsemen"; Arab militias used by the Sudanese government in Darfur to fight against rebellious tribes and to terrorize and kill the local population, driving them from their land.

Cuba backed the Movement for the Popular Liberation of Angola (MPLA). When the South African military invaded in support of UNITA, the Cubans sent troops to aid the MPLA. The South Africans pulled back their forces, but a civil war continued between UNITA and the MPLA and their external backers for the next two decades until UNITA's leader, Jonas Savimbi, was killed in 2002. Savimbi's death created the possibility of stability, although the future of this oil-rich country is unclear.

Zimbabwe, the successor to Rhodesia, also suffered a painful war. In the 1960s, some 250,000 whites owned about half the land and ruled more than 5 million Africans. In 1965, the white minority proclaimed its independence from Great Britain, which responded by declaring that it would not recognize Rhodesia's independence until full political rights had been granted to the African majority. Britain did not send troops to end the rebellion, but neither a trade embargo imposed by Britain nor economic sanctions levied by the UN could force the whites to give up power. In the early 1970s, Britain and Rhodesia negotiated an agreement that would have allowed whites to maintain power indefinitely. But the agreement foundered because African nationalists were virtually unanimous in their opposition to it.

In the mid-1960s, African nationalists launched a guerrilla war to overthrow white rule. A decade later the war intensified. Zambia and newly independent Mozambique allowed guerrillas to infiltrate into Rhodesia, while South African troops joined Rhodesian forces in search-and-destroy missions, often crossing the borders into neighboring countries. In 1978, when the Rhodesian government struck a bargain with several black leaders that placed blacks in political leadership but protected white privilege and landholdings, African movements led by Joshua Nkomo (1917–1999) and Robert Mugabe (b. 1924) boycotted the elections and continued the war. After Britain brought all the parties together for fresh negotiations and brokered a settlement, new elections were held in April 1980, and Mugabe's party won a decisive victory.

Mugabe was elected president of the nation, renamed Zimbabwe, and in four subsequent elections, he entrenched himself and his political party in firm command of the government. Mugabe changed his ideology from Marxist socialism to market socialism, and he promoted pragmatic reforms rather than a radical transformation of the economy and society. The most sensitive issue was the continued control of a small number of white farmers over the best land. In the first decade of his rule, Mugabe's government bought some white farms that were usually handed over to his political party's elite. However, beginning in 1999, as Mugabe lost support among urban Africans and war veterans of the freedom struggle, he tried to appeal to rural Africans by unleashing bands of thugs to seize white farms. Ostensibly, these farms were to be distributed to the landless poor, but frequently the richest and most profitable of them went to the elite of Mugabe's party. The resulting chaos and an accompanying regional drought devastated the country's agricultural sector, which had formerly been among the most productive and profitable in Africa. Along with involving his country in the Congo War, which further drained the government's financial resources, in 2005 Mugabe launched Operation Murambatsvina (moo-rahm-bah-CHEE-nah; "Sweep Away the Rubbish") to demolish squatter settlements around urban areas and drive the poor away from the cities. As a result of Mugabe's policies, Zimbabwe's economy plummeted and millions of Zimbabweans fled to neighboring states. More Zimbabweans, in fact, now live in Johannesburg, South Africa, than in any Zimbabwean city except for the capital, Harare. By 2007, with the economy crippled by hyperinflation, Mugabe's regime teetered on the verge of collapse.

South Africa was the dominant actor in the region, and its white minority defied the winds of change the longest. In 1948, the Afrikaner-dominated National party won a surprise victory in white elections and began implementing its policies of rigid racial separation known as

▶ Robert Mugabe has been Zimbabwe's only president since its independence in 1980. Although he has stated that he will step down as president in 2008, his policies since the mid-1990s have contributed to a sharp decline in Zimbabwe's economy.

apartheid (ah-PART-hate). Parliament passed hundreds of new laws entrenching inequality. The Population Registration Act separated South Africans according to arbitrary racial classifications. The Group Areas Act segregated residential and business areas in cities along racial lines.

The cornerstone of apartheid was its program of territorial segregation, based on the historical fiction that all racial groups belonged to distinct nations and that Africans belonged to ten "autonomous" states known as **Bantustans,** or homelands. These bogus states, carved out of land of little value to white South Africans, were, not surprisingly, poor and underdeveloped, forcing a constant exodus of blacks from them to find employment on white farms and in urban areas as migrant workers. Those who could not find work and housing and meet other requirements were classed as illegal immigrants and shipped back to the homelands. Millions of people, almost all of them black, were forcibly moved from their homes to achieve the apartheid vision.

In the 1960s, the Bantustans were offered self-governing status and, in the mid-1970s, full independence. Four homelands accepted it, but because recognition meant conceding that Africans were no longer citizens of South Africa, no country outside South Africa recognized their independence. In the 1970s, the government began experimenting with piecemeal reforms to prolong white domination into the next century. Laws were repealed prohibiting sexual relations and marriages across the color line and segregating racial groups in public places. In 1984, a new constitution established a tricameral parliament that featured legislative bodies for whites, Indians, and Coloureds (people of mixed-race ancestry) but pointedly left out Africans. The reforms, however, came too late to satisfy most blacks.

Black political groups had waged nonviolent protest campaigns for many decades. Thus, when new laws required African women to start carrying passes, 20,000 anti-apartheid women of all races marched on the prime minister's offices in Pretoria in 1956 to present petitions. They sang a song composed for the occasion that became an anthem for women's groups: "Now you have touched the women ... You have struck a rock. You have dislodged a boulder. You will be crushed."[3] As these and other protests persisted, the government banned the African National Congress (ANC) and the Pan-Africanist Congress in 1960. Their members responded by forming guerilla wings and waging armed struggle. The government ruthlessly clamped down on the opposition, wielding new laws that allowed detention without trial. Many opposition leaders such as Nelson Mandela (b. 1918) were imprisoned for lengthy jail terms, and others were forced into exile to organize resistance from bases in African states to the north.

Resistance was dampened for a few years until black workers and students renewed the protest. In 1976, black students rebelled against the government's education policies, which prevented most blacks from acquiring skills. When police and soldiers clamped down on their protests, thousands of youths left the country to take up the armed struggle. When the ANC and PAC renewed their guerrilla activities in 1980, South Africa launched a campaign of destabilization against southern African countries that supported them. To bring regional states into line, the South African government applied a variety of economic pressures, unleashed cross-border raids against ANC bases in neighboring states, and supported antigovernment guerrillas in Angola, Mozambique, and Lesotho. The cost of the wars and economic destabilization to southern African countries has been estimated at close to $1 billion.

A White Journalist on Apartheid

apartheid—An Afrikaans word meaning "separateness," it was the policy of rigid racial segregation introduced by the National party in South Africa after 1948.

Bantustans—An official name that the South African government gave in the 1950s to land reserves occupied by the Africans. These reserves comprised about 13 percent of the country's total land. The government later changed the name to "homelands."

◄ Nelson Mandela and Frederik W. de Klerk led the negotiations that brought about an end to white majority rule and elections in South Africa in 1994. Mandela was elected president, and de Klerk served for 3 years as a deputy vice president.

By the late 1980s, South Africa was under pressure on a number of fronts to end apartheid. International economic, arms, and sporting sanctions were taking a toll on the country. The economy was stagnating, new government programs were at a standstill, and repression of anti-apartheid activists was not silencing opposition. Moreover, time and demographics were on the side of the black majority, whose members were gaining clout in trade unions and the economy. Without a decisive break from its apartheid past, long-term prospects for change without considerable bloodshed looked remote.

President F. W. de Klerk (b. 1936) made a bold move in early 1990 by legalizing all banned political parties and freeing Mandela, the symbolic leader of many South African blacks. De Klerk, who had not been known as a reformer, and Mandela, the inveterate foe of apartheid, were unlikely partners. However, they and their negotiating teams began the arduous process of dismantling apartheid and preparing the way for the writing of a new constitution. They had to contend with ultra-right-wing whites and secret government hit squads that sought to polarize the country as well as conservative blacks who wanted to prevent an ANC government.

Although thousands died in fighting leading up to the elections of April 1994, amazingly, the elections proceeded with few problems. The ANC decisively won the election, and Mandela was inaugurated as president, with de Klerk serving as a vice president (he stepped down in 1997). A crisis that a decade earlier seemed destined for a tragic end had been resolved through compromise and democratic elections. Mandela's government concentrated on healing the divisions between whites and blacks and tackling apartheid's legacy of inequality in housing, health care, land redistribution, education, and water resources. Mandela stepped down after one term in office, and in the 1999 and 2004 elections the ANC and President Thabo Mbeki easily stayed in power.

Despite Mbeki's general popularity, he has come in for strong criticism, both internationally and at home, for his government's slow response to the AIDs crisis. South Africa has one of the highest percentages of HIV-positive people in the world, but Mbeki's government only began to address the disease seriously in 2003 when it introduced a government-subsidized treatment program.

Conclusion

All the countries of the Middle East and Africa, from the richest to poorest, have been affected by decolonization, the Cold War, the technological revolution, and shifts in the global economic system. All of them entered the modern era in a period of European dominance that often provoked violent rebellion. Many now face major economic and demographic issues that find expression in political instability. After World War II, the creation of new nation-states as imperial powers withdrew from territories such as Palestine and Nigeria created massive refugee problems or inflamed ethnoreligious tensions in ways that have significantly shaped—and continue to shape—the destinies of nations of the Middle East and Africa.

In the Middle East, the politics of oil have reconfigured global economic relations and split the region dramatically into haves and have-nots. Cold War divisions of the political space no longer split the region into pro-U.S., pro-Soviet, and "neutral" states; rather, new configurations of allegiance based on economics, ideology, and strategic interest (including varied relationships to Israel) are still emerging. Meanwhile, conflicts over the right to self-determination and the degree to which Islam will play a role in shaping national identity, law, and government have taken center stage as the political and social reverberations of the Israeli-Palestinian struggle and the Iraq War affect the entire region and as Islamist movements (through both peaceful and violent means) move to more directly challenge the legitimacy of secular governments.

African nations succeeded in gaining their independence from European colonizers and white-settler regimes in southern Africa. However, these new nations have been plagued by a host of problems in their quest for stability, including regional, religious, and ethnic factionalism, dictators and military coups, Cold War rivalries, lack of trained administrators, and weak physical infrastructures. From the 1990s to the present, high HIV/AIDS rates ravaged many African countries, killing millions of people. In addition, despite abundant natural resources, most African countries are economically underdeveloped and have high rates of poverty. Despite the challenges of independence, a growing number of African nations have introduced democratic political systems and policies that have improved their economic performance.

Suggestions for Web Browsing

You can obtain more information about topics included in this chapter at the websites listed below. See also the companion website that accompanies this text, http://www.ablongman.com/brummett, which contains an online study guide and additional resources.

Internet Islamic History Sourcebook: The Islamic World Since 1945
http://www.fordham.edu/halsall/islam/islamsbook.html#
Extensive online source for links about the history of the Middle East since 1945, including country studies, international affairs, and the Israel-Palestine conflict.

Internet African History Sourcebook: Modern Africa
http://www.fordham.edu/halsall/africa/africasbook.html#
Detailed online source for links about the history of Africa since 1945, including primary documents regarding country studies, continuing imperialism, international affairs, and gender and sexuality.

Literature and Film

Elias Khoury, *The Kingdom of Strangers* (University of Arkansas Press, 1996), is a rich interweaving of stories set in war-ravaged Lebanon and Palestine. Samar Attar, *Lina: Portrait of a Damascene Girl* (Three Continents, 1994), is a memoir of life and family in the Syrian capital seen through the eyes of a young girl. Gholam-Hossein Sa'edi, *Fear and Trembling* (Three Continents, 1984), is a critique of politics, society, and Westernization by one of Iran's premier literati.

Yusuf Al-Qa'id, *War in the Land of Egypt* (Interlink, 1998), is an interesting and antiwar presentation of the effects of the 1973 war on an Egyptian village. Samad Behrangi, *The Little Black Fish and Other Stories,* 2nd ed. (Three Continents, 1987), tells tales of the poor, set in Tehran and in Iranian villages under the shah's rule. Shusha Guppy, *The Blindfold Horse: Memories of a Persian Childhood* (Beacon, 1988), is the memoir of an elite young woman growing up in an increasingly Westernized Iran.

Chinua Achebe's *A Man of the People* (Anchor, 1989) is a biting social commentary on the personal and political corruption of independent African leaders. Mariama Ba's *So Long a Letter* (Heinemann, 1989) treats the struggles of a middle-aged woman in a Muslim society after her former husband dies. Set in the apartheid era of South Africa, Andre Brink's *A Dry White Season* (HarperCollins, 1979) deals with a conservative Afrikaner teacher coming to terms with the brutalities of white oppression and the challenges of black resistance. Tsitsi Dangaremba's *Nervous Conditions,* 3rd ed. (Seal Press, 2002) is the story of a young African woman seeking education in white-dominated Zimbabwe in the 1960s.

A Veiled Revolution (1982; Icarus Films), directed by Marilyn Gaunt, presents the voices of Egyptian women in the 1970s on the issue of veiling. *The Palestinian People Do Have Rights* (1979; Icarus Films), is a UN documentary on the plight of the Palestinian people after the creation of the state of Israel. *But You Speak Such Good English* (1999; 30 Bird Productions), directed by Marjan Safinia, is a short and humorous documentary on Iranian expatriates and their children growing up in London.

The main character in *Mapantsula* (1988; California Newsreel) is an African gangster faced with the painful choice of becoming a police informant or supporting the freedom struggle in South Africa. *Xala* (1975; California Newsreel) is Ousmane Sembene's satirical portrayal of the African elite in Senegal. *Lumumba* (2001; Zeitgeist Video) recounts the rise of nationalist leader Patrice Lumumba to become Congo's first president in 1960 and his assassination a year later. Two documentaries treat recent African events: *Hopes on the Horizon* (2001; Blackside) examines African struggles for democracy in the 1990s, and *Mandela's Fight for Freedom* (1995; Discovery Networks) covers South Africa's transition from apartheid in the 1980s to the first democratic election in 1994.

Suggestions for Reading

A good survey of the Middle East in the late twentieth century is William Cleveland, *A History of the Modern Middle East* (Westview, 2001). The best survey of the Arab-Israeli conflict is Charles D. Smith, *Palestine and the Arab-Israeli Conflict,* 4th ed. (St. Martin's Press, 2000). On the United Nations' original partition plan, see Walter Laqueur and Barry Rubin, eds., *The Israeli-Arab Reader: A Documentary History of the Middle East Conflict,* 5th ed. (Penguin, 1995).

An insightful book on Iran is Said Arjomand, *The Turban for the Crown: The Islamic Revolution in Iran* (Oxford University Press, 1988). On Turkey, see Feroz Ahmad, *The Making of Modern Turkey* (Routledge, 1993). Daniel Yergin, *The Prize* (Touchstone Press, 1991), is a beautifully written and acutely analytical study of the impact of oil on politics and diplomacy in the world.

A general study on contemporary African political and economic development is Paul Nugent, *Africa Since Independence* (Palgrave Macmillan, 2004).

Recent developments in specific African countries are covered in Kinfe Abraham, *Ethiopia* (Red Sea Press, 1994), and Paul Beckett and Crawford Young, *Dilemmas of Democracy in Nigeria* (University of Rochester Press, 1997). Rwanda's genocide is examined in Fergal Keane, *Season of Blood: A Rwandan Journey* (Viking, 1995).

Afrikaner politics and the construction of the apartheid system are covered in Dan O'Meara, *Forty Lost Years: The Apartheid State and the Politics of the National Party, 1948–1994* (Ohio University Press, 1996). The African challenge to apartheid is treated in Thomas Karis and Gail Gerhart, *From Protest to Challenge: A Documentary History of African Politics in South Africa,* Vols. 3 and 5 (Indiana University Press, 1997). The ending of apartheid and the transition to democratic rule in South Africa is covered in Allister Sparks, *Tomorrow Is Another Country: The Inside Story of South Africa's Road to Change* (University of Chicago Press, 1996)

CHAPTER 34

Latin America Since 1910

Reform, Repression, and Revolution

Outline

- Latin America: 1910–1945
- The Perils of the Postwar Era
- South America
- The Caribbean
- Mexico
- Central America

Features

DOCUMENT **President Hugo Chávez's 2006 Address to the UN General Assembly**

DOCUMENT **Evita Speaks**

SEEING CONNECTIONS **Lucha Libre**

◀ One of Mexico's greatest muralists, José Clemente Orozco, painted *The Epic of American Civilization* at the Baker Library, Dartmouth College, from 1932 to 1934. The several dozen panels cover the history of the Americas from the migration of the Aztecs into central Mexico to modern society. This panel, entitled *Hispano America,* depicts the struggle between progress and idealism and corruption and greed. The central figure in the mural is Emiliano Zapata, the rebel leader of the Mexican revolution, who stands for Latin American idealism against capitalist greed and imperialism. Behind him stands an American general who is preparing to stab Zapata in the back. Below Zapata are corrupt politicians and soldiers who are greedily grasping for money.

COVERING THE REGIONS of Central America, South America, and the Caribbean, Latin America owes its name to the French who, in the mid-nineteenth century, coined the term to express what they believed was their common Latin identity with Portuguese and Spanish speakers in the New World—and, more pragmatically, to promote cultural and economic ties between them. Although French hopes were never realized, the name stuck.

The 26 nations that make up contemporary Latin America range from Haiti, which has one of the world's lowest per capita incomes, to Brazil, the world's eighth largest economy; from Chile, which elected its first woman president in 2006, to Cuba, which has had but one ruler since 1959; from Belize, which only gained its independence from the United Kingdom in 1981, to French Guiana, which is not an independent nation at all but rather an overseas department of France and as such officially part of the European Union.

Although Latin American nations represent enormous diversity in languages and cultures, they all sought answers to common problems throughout the twentieth century. How would the ruling elites who had long dominated Latin American nations respond to the new ideologies and organizations created by the influx of European immigrants or the massive movement of people from rural to urban areas? How would Latin American nations break their dependence on exporting raw materials and diversify their economies? How would Latin Americans cope with the authoritarian regimes that became prevalent during the Cold War era? And how would they address the glaring socio-economic inequalities within their societies?

Latin America, 1910–1945

What social and economic changes did Latin America undergo in the first half of the twentieth century?

In the first half of the twentieth century, Latin America underwent a profound social and economic transition, as its countries made the leap from a largely agricultural economy to an urban industrial economy. This transition was necessary because there were few jobs and little open land in the rural areas, conditions that drove people to the cities in large numbers. The transition also represented an effort to break the pattern of economic dependency established during the colonial era, when Latin American nations exported agricultural products or mineral resources in exchange for finished goods from Europe or the United States. The shift to an urban industrial economy was, in fact, but one of a variety of strategies—others included exporting primary products, import substitution, and directing trade into regional partnerships—that Latin American nations employed in the effort to diversify their economies.

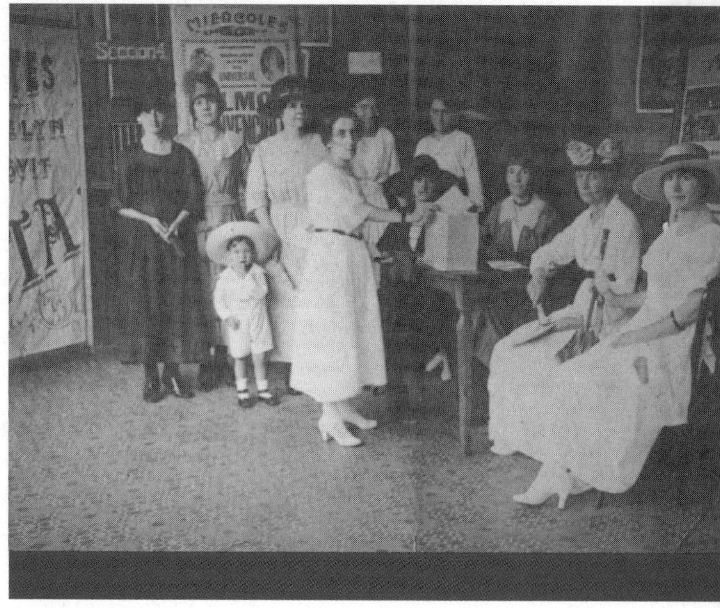

▲ Argentine suffragists casting symbolic ballots in the 1920s—women would not earn equal voting rights with men until 1947.

Limited Political Reforms

The expanding urban centers of Latin America became fertile ground for the new political movements sweeping Europe in the late nineteenth and early twentieth centuries. The growing middle and working classes of the cities pressed for political change and established new parties. New immigrants, largely from Europe, were sympathetic to radical ideologies such as socialism, Marxism, and anarchism. But as in the nineteenth century, the upper classes of Latin America resisted opening up their nation's political systems because they feared losing their social and economic privileges. They joined hands with the military and conservative members of the middle class to maintain the political status quo.

The initial political battles of early twentieth century Latin America, however, were not primarily focused on the sweeping transformation of politics or society, but rather on simply expanding the franchise to all men, not just those who owned land. Following World War I, the women's suffrage movement also gained momentum, especially after women in the United States won the right to vote in 1920. Latin American women's organizations had previously worked on social reforms such as improving working, sanitary, and health conditions, expanding access to education, and changing civil codes so that women had the right to divorce, to control their earnings, and to enter into contractual agreements. After World War I, their energies focused on securing the vote.

In the late 1920s and early 1930s, a handful of states introduced the vote for women but often for reasons having little to do with advancing women's interests. In Ecuador (1929), a conservative ruling elite

Chronology

1920

1929 Women gain vote in Ecuador

1930

1937 Getúlio Vargas establishes the *Estado Novo* in Brazil

1938 Lazaro Cárdenas expropriates foreign oil companies in Mexico

1940

1948 Juan Perón elected president of Argentina; founding of Organization of American States (OAS)

1950

1959 Cuban Revolution

1960

1960 United States establishes Alliance for Progress; Brasília becomes capital of Brazil

1960–1996 Civil war in Guatemala

1962 Cuban Missile Crisis

1964–present Colombian civil war

1968 Mexico City hosts Olympic games; Mexican government violently suppresses student protests

	The Enfranchisement of Women in the Americas
1920	United States
1929	Ecuador
1932	Brazil and Puerto Rico
1934	Cuba
1945	Dominican Republic and Panama
1946	Venezuela
1947	Argentina
1948	Chile
1952	Mexico
1955	Nicaragua and Peru

adopted the vote as a way to broaden its support in the face of continued threats from radical military officers who had staged a coup in 1925. In Uruguay, another ruling elite, threatened by the prospect of new male immigrants winning the vote, extended the vote to women in 1932 because they thought they would be much more conservative and more likely to preserve the status quo.

Economic Woes and Military Interventions

Despite these voting reforms, many Latin American countries were still vulnerable to military interventions because of their history of autocracy and their weak economies. When Brazil's coffee industry slumped in the 1920s because of overproduction and a steep dip in the international price of coffee, the country had to take on a large foreign debt. After the Wall Street crash of 1929, the demand for coffee dropped even further and the price tumbled from 22.5 to 8 cents a pound. With the economy in tatters, the Brazilian military intervened, claiming that it had to save the country from the misrule of civilians.

In Argentina, a faltering economy during the Great Depression prompted the military, which had stayed aloof from politics, to stage a coup in September 1930. The military, which had become an independent institution with no loyalty to any political party, tried to establish a broad-based political party to run the country. After the military proved to be no more effective than civilian politicians, popularly elected politicians regained control of the government for a brief time before the military intervened once again in 1943.

Mexico After the Revolution

Although many Latin American countries experienced social unrest and rebellions, Mexico was the only country to undergo a revolution (see pp. 806–807) until Cuba in 1959. After defeating his rivals in a bitter civil war, Venustiano Carranza became the first of three successive presidents from Sonora province in northern Mexico. All were substantial landowners and were reluctant to carry out the revolution's goals. Subsequent presidents did little to advance the goals of the revolution until Lazaro Cárdenas held the presidency from 1934 to 1940. He opened up 44 million acres of land to peasants by using the **ejido,** a traditional Indian institution that held land communally for all the people in a community; 800,000 peasants benefited from the land reform.

Cárdenas nationalized railroads in 1937 and established a state monopoly over oil the following year. When companies appealed to the Roosevelt administration, which was promoting a "Good Neighbor" policy, to intervene, it worked out a compromise

---

ejido—The system of communal ownership of land that was practiced by Indian societies before the arrival of the Spanish.

1970	1980	1990		2000	
1973 Chilean President Salvador Allende ousted by military coup 1976–1983 Argentina's military dictatorship wages "Dirty War" against dissident citizens 1979 Sandinistas overthrow Somoza dictatorship in Nicaragua	1980–1992 Civil war in El Salvador 1982 Falklands/Malvinas War between Argentina and United Kingdom 1983 United States invades Grenada 1989 United States invades Panama	1990 Augusto Pinochet steps down as president of Chile (remains head of military until 1998) 1993 The North American Free Trade Agreement (NAFTA) signed between the United States, Mexico, and Canada	1998 Hugo Chávez elected president of Venezuela 1999 United States transfers sovereignty of Canal Zone back to Panama; Argentine economic crisis begins	2000 Vicente Fox elected president of Mexico, ending more than 70 years of one-party rule 2003 Luis Ignácio Lula da Silva elected president of Brazil; Chile signs free-trade agreement with United States	2005 Evo Morales elected president of Bolivia, the first indigenous head of state in 470 years

in which the Mexican government compensated the oil companies for their losses. Cárdenas also strengthened his party's political machinery. He established a principle that called for a president to step down after his 6-year term was over and allowed him to choose a successor in consultation with party bosses. Cárdenas renamed the party the *Partido de la Revolución Mexicana* or Mexican Revolutionary Party (PRM). Renamed the **Party of Revolutionary Institutions (PRI)** in 1946, this party dominated Mexican political life for the rest of the century.

	Latin American Politics at the Turn of the Century: The Shift Leftward
1998	Leftist Hugo Chávez elected president of Venezuela (reelected in 2000 and 2006)
2000	Conservative Vicente Fox elected president of Mexico, ending more than 70 years of one-party rule
2003	Leftist Luis Ignácio Lula da Silva elected president of Brazil (reelected in 2006); leftist Néstor Kirchner elected president of Argentina
2005	Leftist Evo Morales elected president of Bolivia, the first indigenous head of state in 470 years
2006	Socialist Michelle Bachelet elected president of Chile, becoming her nation's first female head of state; conservative Felipe Calderón narrowly defeats leftist Andrés Manuel López Obrador in Mexican presidential election; leftist Daniel Ortega elected president of Nicaragua

The Perils of the Postwar Era

What has been the impact of external debt on the economies of Latin American countries since the mid-1970s?

Modern Latin America

After World War II, Latin American and Caribbean nations shared many of the problems experienced by the developing countries of the world outside Europe. Formerly competitive economies—such as those of Argentina, Mexico, and Brazil—fell far behind rapidly advancing areas, such as Japan, South Korea, Taiwan, and Singapore. Whether in countries of primarily European stock (Argentina, Uruguay, Chile, and Costa Rica), those of mainly mixed Indian-Spanish background (Peru, Bolivia, Ecuador, Mexico, and most of the Central American countries), or racially diverse societies such as Brazil and Venezuela, Latin America faced serious challenges.

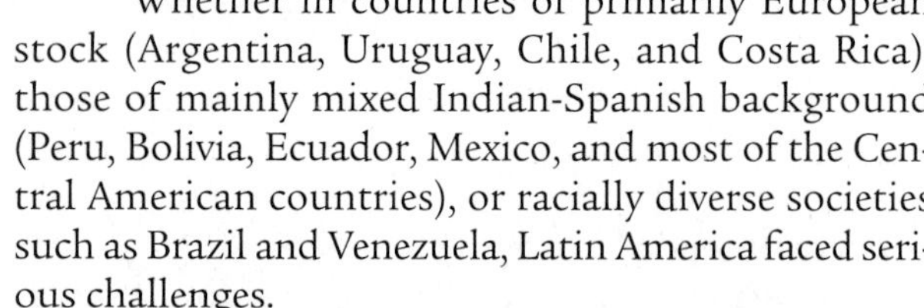

Party of Revolutionary Institutions (PRI)—The political party founded in 1929 that dominated Mexican political life until the end of the twentieth century.

From Authoritarianism to Democracy

The years after 1945 witnessed many economic challenges and much political instability and social unrest throughout Latin America. For example, until opposition party candidate Vicente Fox was elected president in Mexico in 2000, a single party, the PRI, had ruled the country since 1929. The Mexican example was far from the exception. In fact, after 1950, most of the Latin American countries with continuously elected governments were typically those dominated by a single major party.

The political situation in Latin America at this time was greatly exacerbated by the Cold War (see Chapter 32). The major clashes were between leftist movements and militaries, which generally served the interests of Latin American elites who feared leftist policies such as the

▶ The election of Vicente Fox as Mexico's president in 2000 brought an end to the dominance of the *Partido Revolucionaro Institucional* (PRI) in Mexican politics for the most of the twentieth century.

Document

President Hugo Chávez's 2006 Address to the UN General Assembly

Venezuela's president, Hugo Chávez, has been using his country's oil wealth to win support in Latin America and develop closer ties with oil-producing nations. He has been a strident critic of U.S. foreign policy. In September 2006, he delivered a speech at the United Nations General Assembly in New York attacking American president George W. Bush and the U.S. government. But one of his goals, promoting Venezuela for a 2-year term on the United Nations Security Council, was unsuccessful.

The hegemonic pretensions of the American empire are placing at risk the very survival of the human species. We continue to warn you about this danger and we appeal to the people of the United States and the world to halt this threat, which is like a sword hanging over our heads....

Yesterday the devil came here. Right here. [crosses himself] And it smells of sulfur still today.

Yesterday, ladies and gentlemen, from this rostrum, the president of the United States, the gentleman to whom I refer as the devil, came here, talking as if he owned the world. Truly. As the owner of the world....

The president of the United States, yesterday, said to us, right here, in this room, and I'm quoting, "Anywhere you look, you hear extremists telling you can escape from poverty and recover your dignity through violence, terror, and martyrdom."...

The imperialists see extremists everywhere. It's not that we are extremists. It's that the world is waking up. It's waking up all over. And people are standing up.

I have the feeling, dear world dictator, that you are going to live the rest of your days as a nightmare because the rest of us are standing up, all those who are rising up against American imperialism, who are shouting for equality, for respect, for the sovereignty of nations....

Yes, you can call us extremists, but we are rising up against the empire, against the model of domination.

The president then—and this he said himself, he said: "I have come to speak directly to the populations in the Middle East, to tell them that my country wants peace."...

And you can wonder, just as the president of the United States addresses those peoples of the world, what would those peoples of the world tell him if they were given the floor? What would they have to say?

And I think I have some inkling of what the peoples of the south, the oppressed people think. They would say, "Yankee imperialist, go home." I think that is what those people would say if they were given the microphone and if they could speak with one voice to the American imperialists.

Questions to Consider

1. Who are the "peoples of the south" that Chávez refers to? Does Chávez accurately state what their views of United States' foreign policy are?
2. What audience around the world was Chávez appealing to in his speech?
3. If you had the opportunity to respond to Chávez's speech, what would you say?

www.informationclearinghouse.info/article15041.htm

redistribution of land and wealth. Between 1950 and 1966, militaries intervened to overthrow 14 governments. Dictatorial rule was imposed on more than half the Latin American population, and opposition groups were squashed. As a consequence, guerilla insurgencies emerged and protracted civil wars were fought, mostly in Central America and the Andean nations of South America. However, only in Nicaragua and Cuba did revolutionary movements take control of governments. In the 1980s, most military regimes, after repeated failures at managing economies and the ending of the Cold War, began handing over the reins of government to civilian politicians and allowed multiparty democratic systems to develop.

In recent years, numerous elections have been held throughout the region, a dozen in 2005 and 2006 alone. Although some countries have maintained conservative parties in power, a recent trend has been the election of left-leaning parties and leaders. The most notable example is in Venezuela, where Hugo Chávez, a former military officer who led a failed coup in 1992, first won election in 1998 and was reelected again in 2000 and 2006. He has used Venezuela's considerable oil resources to win followers by funding social programs and to wield influence in global politics. An outspoken critic of the U.S. government, he has cultivated close relations with Fidel Castro's Cuban government and other enemies of the

United States (see the Document *President Hugo Chávez's 2006 Address to the UN General Assembly*).

The Few Haves and the Many Have Nots

Latin America has the most uneven distribution of wealth in the world, and the gap between rich and poor has increased in recent decades. The largely failed efforts at economic liberalization during the 1980s and 1990s have only exacerbated matters further, as the real value of workers' wages has continued to decline over this period. Educational, health, and sanitation services are inadequate, and literacy rates remain low. Life expectancy for Latin American males is around 55 years—17 years less than in the United States and Canada. The population increases by about 2 percent yearly. By 2005, the population of Latin America and the Caribbean topped 561 million. Of those, 150 million still live on less than $2 a day.

Because agricultural productivity is inefficient and low, millions of people have moved from the rural areas to urban centers. Seventy-seven percent of the people of Latin America and the Caribbean currently live in urban areas. Mexico City, São Paulo, Rio de Janeiro, and Buenos Aires, four of the world's largest cities, boast populations from between 10 to 20 million people. Squatter settlements or *barriadas* on the edges of large cities house hundreds of thousands amid filth, disease, hunger, and crime. A great majority of the poor are blacks and mestizos.

Before and after World War II, the principal economic strategy of Latin American nations was import substitution, a policy that aimed at reducing reliance on European and American goods and producing their own manufactured goods to trade with other Latin American nations. This strategy faltered, however, because it did not create many jobs and because there were too many poor people to create a large enough consumer market for locally produced goods. In addition, the economic health of many Latin American states continued to depend on the world market prices for one or two leading exports such as copper, wheat, and coffee. In the 1960s, as the international prices for these products declined, economies stagnated.

Pope John Paul II Address

Since the 1970s, Latin American states have also been saddled with crippling foreign debts. With the fivefold rise in the price of oil following the 1973 Arab-Israel war and another jump in 1979, governments turned to international banks for loans as a way of stimulating their economies and to compensate for the losses of state-owned businesses. The debt owed international banks rose from $27.6 billion in 1970 to $231 billion in 1980 and to $755 billion dollars in 1990. Many Latin American states found it very difficult to pay off the interest on the debt, let alone the debt itself. Many of those that agreed to structural adjustment programs of the **International Monetary Fund (IMF)** made some progress in paying or restructuring debt repayments. For some Latin American countries, the debt forced them to improve transportation and communications and make their economies more attractive to foreign investment, but for others such as Argentina, which experienced a severe economic crisis as recently as 1999 to 2003, the debt led to enormous economic hardships and political instability.

Narcoeconomics and the Drug Wars

In the past few decades, another major problem has been the international drug trade and money-laundering schemes. Colombia, followed by Mexico, Peru, and Bolivia, have been the major producers of cocaine and heroin, and Central American and Caribbean nations are important transit points for shipping drugs to North America, Europe, and Asia. The coca bush and opium poppy grow wild, especially in the foothills of the Andes Mountains. Small farmers in less-developed areas are reluctant to give up their production because they provide important sources of income for which there are no alternatives.

The drug trade has presented a major challenge to the stability of governments because it creates a parallel economy—or **narcoeconomy**—that is not under their control, and because it leads to lawlessness. Guerrilla groups, paramilitary units, and drug cartels finance themselves on its profits. Bribery and corruption have undermined the police, soldiers, judges, and politicians. Drug lords have targeted judges, politicians, and journalists who oppose them for assassination. In Colombia, the government declared war on the drug cartels centered in the cities of Medellín and Cali, but even after the cartels' leaders were jailed or killed, others leaders sprouted up in their place or other cartels materialized elsewhere.

The United States, in cooperation with Latin American governments, has poured money into the war on drugs, particularly in Colombia, through subsidizing government security forces, seizing illegal drug shipments, paying for the spraying of herbicides to kill plants such as the coca bush, and convincing growers to shift from coca or opium to alternative crops. Despite these measures, the war on drugs has not made a dent in the volume of drugs entering the United States, nor has it provided small growers with enough of an incentive to stop cultivating drug plants. In Colombia, for instance, small growers were encouraged to produce coffee, but the price of coffee slumped in 2001 and Vietnam

International Monetary Fund (IMF)—Chartered in 1945, the International Monetary Fund was created to restore the money system that had collapsed in previous decades.

narcoeconomy—A regional or national economy whose foundation rests on the production and trade of illegal drugs.

▲ Although most Latin American nations won their independence in the nineteenth century, they have struggled to free themselves of authoritarian regimes and to pursue economic stability and growth in the shadow of the United States, which has long dominated the region.

increased its coffee production, causing some growers returned to coca production to earn an income.

The Yankee Factor

In the immediate aftermath of World War II, Latin America was not significant to American policymakers, who focused their attention on rebuilding the economies of Europe and Japan. However, as American fears of the spread of Soviet influence escalated, the United States began to pay more attention, because it wanted to keep Latin American nations in its orbit.

The **Organization of American States (OAS)** was created in 1948 to bring 35 North and South American countries together for foreign policy consultations. The United States pressured Latin American states to abolish their Communist parties and break off diplomatic relations with the Soviet Union. All except Mexico, Argentina, and Uruguay did so. The United States also signed bilateral defense pacts with governments that forged closer ties between the American military and Latin American military elites. Finally, the United States assisted in overthrowing regimes whose policies were perceived to be threatening American interests. In 1954, the CIA aided in ousting Guatemala's president, Jacobo Arbenz, because his land reform policies were opposed by the **United Fruit Company,** an American corporation and Guatemala's largest landowner.

Organization of the American States (OAS)—An organization composed of North and South American states originally founded as the International Union of American Republics. It changed its name to the OAS in 1948 and now has 35 members. Its primary objectives are to promote peace and security, representative democracy, conflict resolution, and economic development among member states.

	Latin America During the Cold War: Civil Wars, Coups, and Invasions
1959	Cuban Revolution
1960–1996	Civil war in Guatemala
1962	Cuban Missile Crisis
1964–present	Colombian civil war
1968	Mexican government violently suppresses student protests
1973	Military coup overthrows Chilean President Salvador Allende
1976–1983	Argentina's military dictatorship wages "Dirty War" against dissident citizens
1979	Sandinistas overthrow Somoza dictatorship in Nicaragua
1980–1992	Civil war in El Salvador
1982	Falklands/Malvinas War between Argentina and United Kingdom
1983	United States invades Grenada
1989	United States invades Panama
1990	Augusto Pinochet steps down as president of Chile

▲ U.S. soldiers patrolling the streets of Panama City in the wake of Operation Just Cause, an invasion President George Bush launched in December 1989 to remove Manuel Noriega as president of Panama.

Following the Cuban Revolution of 1959 (see p. 1041), the American government quickly became alarmed after Fidel Castro's regime moved sharply to the left, aligning itself with the Soviet Union. When the American-sponsored invasion at Cuba's Bay of Pigs failed in 1961, President John F. Kennedy initiated the **Alliance for Progress** to improve the quality of life and strengthen democratic institutions in Latin American nations. The United States pledged $20 billion, to

United Fruit Company—An American-based company established in 1898 that became a major producer of tropical fruits such as bananas and pineapples and had significant economic interests in Central American countries.

Alliance for Progress—A U.S. government assistance program initiated in 1961 by President John F. Kennedy aimed at improving relations between the United States and Latin American nations by promoting democratic government and economic development and addressing economic inequalities.

be matched by the other members of the alliance, but the alliance failed by 1970 as little economic growth took place. The United States supported counterinsurgency campaigns against leftist guerillas and backed anticommunist military regimes that took over in many Latin American countries.

One long-standing source of discord between the United States and Latin America was removed in 1978 when the U.S. Senate approved the treaty that returned sovereignty of the Panama Canal Zone to the Republic of Panama in 1999, while safeguarding American interests in the area. This agreement, negotiated over a period of 14 years under four American presidents, was a sign to some that the United States was eager to improve relations with its neighbors to the south.

South America

Why have South American nations politically shifted to the left in recent years?

In the period after World War II, many countries in South America followed a similar pattern. Civilian governments were overthrown by military elites, who blamed civilian politicians for economic failures and corruption. In the last two decades, however, most states have made the transition from military to civilian rule, although the new democracies remain fragile.

◀ Football (known in the United States as soccer) is the world's most popular sport. Here, Ronaldo, the famous striker, holds aloft the winner's trophy after his Brazilian team defeated Germany to win the World Cup in 2002. The victory marked the fifth time Brazil had claimed the World Cup trophy, the most of any nation in the world.

Brazil

Brazil is the world's fifth largest and South America's largest country, comprising almost half of the continent's land surface. Although Brazil's plantations historically had been the mainstay of its economy, their contributions to Brazil's **gross domestic product (GDP)** have declined to about one-third. Boasting the eighth largest economy in the world, Brazil is the world's largest producer of coffee and exports a range of tropical products such as bananas, cacao, black pepper, and palm oils.

Although Brazil maintained democratic rule in the decades after World War II, its military loomed in the background and often served as a power broker. The delicate balance between civilian politicians and the military broke down during the presidency of João Goulart (1961–1964). A populist, Goulart's policies appealed to the left but alienated some of Brazil's most powerful groups: large landowners, who resisted Goulart's land reform for peasants, and senior military officers, who opposed his proposal to create a trade union for soldiers. In 1964, the military ousted Goulart and, clamping down on dissent, recognized only two parties—one representing the government and the other the opposition. The military also suppressed a guerrilla movement active between 1969 and 1973. Although the regime's economic policies encouraged rapid economic growth from 1968 to 1974, the "Brazilian miracle" faded by 1980 as inflation reached more than 100 percent and foreign debt escalated. In 1982, the foreign debt reached $87 billion, the highest in the world at the time.

Chico Mendes on the Rain Forest

A return to civilian rule in 1985 did not stabilize the economy. Inflation ran out of control, reaching 1585 percent in 1991 and almost 2500 percent in 1993. President Fernando Cardoso, elected in 1994 and reelected in 1998, curbed inflation by linking a new currency, the *real,* to the U.S. dollar, and grappled with huge budget deficits and currency devaluations, which slowed economic growth. An economic downturn in 2001 was partly caused by an energy crisis. Brazil has lessened its imports of gasoline considerably by tapping into new

Brazil's Constitution of 1988

gross domestic product (GDP)—A way of measuring the size of a country's economy. It is the sum of the market of value of all final goods and services produced in a country in a specific time period.

▲ The wife of Argentine president Juan Perón, Eva Perón became a charismatic political force in her own right. Popularly known as Evita, she developed a strong following among women and the working class, whose issues she championed. Here, she speaks to workers at a rally in Buenos Aires in 1952, the year she died.

offshore oil fields and by processing sugarcane and cassava and converting them into ethanol.

Cardoso's successor, Luis Ignácio Lula da Silva (popularly known as Lula), was elected president in 2003. A labor leader and head of the Workers' party, the largest leftist party in Latin America, President Lula has blended conservative economic policies with progressive social policies, striving to boost the economy while also increasing the minimum wage and expanding social welfare programs for the poor. Despite a number of corruption scandals that rocked his party and administration, Lula was comfortably elected to a second term in the 2006 elections.

Argentina

Argentina's political system following World War II was dominated by military-civilian rivalries and by the personality and policies of Juan Perón (pay-ROHN; 1895–1974), a middle-aged army colonel who won the 1946 election. His most loyal following came from urban workers, whose wages he increased, and especially from working-class women who migrated from the rural areas into Buenos Aires in the 1930s and 1940s and made up half of the workforce in the textile, garment, and chemical industries. He won their support through laws that provided for the right to divorce and for wives to have equality with husbands in a marriage and equal authority over their children.

DOCUMENT Perón and Postwar Populism

Perón's charismatic second wife, Eva (popularly known as Evita), was one of those recent urban immigrants, and although she was rejected by Argentina's social elite because of her humble origins, she was popular with the poor and the middle class and earned international recognition for her glamour and beauty (see the Document *Evita Speaks*). In the 1952 election, women gave Juan Perón a resounding 64 percent of their votes.

Perón also favored state control of the economy and developed the industrial sector at the expense of rural areas, where beef and wheat had been traditional mainstays of the economy. His clashes with the Catholic Church, however, brought about his downfall. He alienated Catholic leaders by legalizing divorce and placing church schools under state control. In 1955, the military removed him from power.

Although Perón was in exile and military officers ran government, his Perónist followers continued to influence Argentina's political life. Perón returned from Spain to recapture the presidency in 1973 elections. After his death a year later, his third wife Isabel succeeded him, but she did not have the same flair for politics. After the military expelled her in 1976, they took brutal steps to stifle dissent. During the so-called Dirty War (*Guerra Sucia*) from 1976 to 1983, an estimated 30,000 dissident civilians "disappeared" after being picked up by security squads. **The Mothers of the Plaza del Mayo** sought information on the fate of their missing relatives and children by carrying on a lengthy vigil at the plaza in front of the presidential palace.

In 1982, the military junta made a major blunder by asserting a long-standing claim to the Falkland Islands (called the *Malvinas* by Argentina), a British possession. After invading the islands, the Argentine army was easily defeated by the British in a 70-day war. As a consequence, the discredited Argentine military restored the government to civilian hands.

The election of a Perónist, Carlos Menem, to the presidency in 1989 marked the first time since 1928 that a transfer was made from one sitting president to another without military interference. Menem, however, had to placate the military by issuing pardons to former members of the military junta implicated in human rights abuses during the Dirty War.

The Mothers of the Plaza del Mayo—A group of Argentine mothers who began demonstrating in 1977 every Thursday at the Plaza del Mayo in front of the presidential palace. They were challenging the military government to explain what happened to their children who disappeared at the hands of the government.

Document

Evita Speaks

Born in 1919 in a small rural Argentine town, Maria Eva Duarte left for Buenos Aires at age 15. She eventually found steady work as an actress in theatre and radio programs. She met Juan Perón, then a cabinet minister, in 1943 and they were married in 1945. Although she assumed the role of "President's Lady" after he became president the following year, she was shunned by the elites in society because of her humble background. She reinvented herself, taking on a new identity as Evita, whose loyalty was to the poor rather than the rich. She established the Eva Perón Foundation to support charitable work and actively promoted women's rights issues. She headed the Perónist Women's party, which established centers that provided many services for women—day care, free legal and medical advice, and meeting halls. In the 1952 election, women gave Perón a resounding 64 percent of their votes. After contracting cancer, Eva Perón died in 1952, and her husband was forced to step down as president 3 years later.

I might have been a president's wife like the others.

It is a simple and agreeable role: a holiday job, the task of receiving honors, of decking oneself out to go through the motions prescribed by social dictates. It is all very similar to what I was able to do previously, and I think more or less successfully, in the theater and in the cinema.

As for the hostility of the oligarchy, I can only smile.

And I wonder: why would the oligarchy have been able to reject me?

Because of my humble origin? Because of my artistic career?

But has that class of person ever bothered about these things here—or in any part of the world—when it was a case of the wife of a President?

The oligarchy has never been hostile to anyone who could be useful to it. Power and money were never bad antecedents to a genuine oligarch.

The truth is different. I, who had learned from Perón to choose unusual paths, did not wish to follow the old pattern of wife of the President.

Also, anyone who knows me a bit—I don't mean now, but from before, when I was a "simple Argentine girl"—knows that I could never have enacted the cold comedy of oligarchical drawing rooms.

I was not born for that. On the contrary, there was always in my soul an open repugnance for that kind of acting.

But also, I was not only the wife of the President of the Republic, I was also the wife of the Leader of the Argentines.

I had to have a double personality to correspond with Perón's double personality. One Eve Perón, wife of the President, whose work is simple and agreeable, a holiday job of receiving honors, of gala performances; the other, "Evita," wife of the Leader of a people who have placed all their faith in him, all their hope and all their love.

Questions to Consider

1. How did Eva Perón challenge the traditional role of a wife and political wife in Argentine society?
2. Eva Perón has achieved international recognition through Andrew Lloyd Webber's opera, *Evita*. How is she portrayed in that production?

Eva Perón, *My Mission in Life* (New York: Vantage Press, 1953), p. 60.

Menem also addressed economic problems by adopting **neoliberal** policies of privatizing state-owned corporations and linking a new Argentine currency, the *peso,* to the American dollar. His policies brought economic stability in the short run. Inflation, which had reached 150 percent per year at the beginning of his term of office, dramatically dropped to 4 percent by 1994, and the GDP grew at a healthy rate.

In 1997, the impact of a general economic slowdown throughout Latin America and a revaluation of the U.S. dollar finally pushed the fragile Argentine economy into recession, as the unemployment rate climbed to 14 percent. The country's economic crisis grew significantly worse in 1999, with the GDP dropping by 4 percent. In 2001, de la Rúa's administration was unable to make payments on its $132 billion debt to foreign and domestic creditors and the *peso* underwent an 80 percent devaluation. As a result, there was a run on the banks as Argentines sought to withdraw their savings and covert their *pesos* to dollars before they lost any more value. Riots broke out in the streets of Buenos Aires, and the crime rate across the nation soared. By October 2002, some 57 percent of the population was officially living under the poverty line due to the devaluation of the *peso.* In the face of the deepening economic crisis, de la Rúa resigned and was quickly followed by four other presidents. The last of

neoliberalism—Refers to free-market economic policies usually associated with the World Bank and International Monetary Fund. These include promoting free trade, limiting government involvement in the economy, privatizing government enterprises, and cutting government social welfare programs.

these, Néstor Kirchner, became president in 2003. He only brought about an end to the economic crisis by instituting an austerity program that included limiting government spending, devaluing the *peso,* and refinancing the country's foreign debt. Although Argentina's GDP has grown at a surprisingly strong rate since 2003, its economy still confronts a number of long-term challenges.

Chile

In the post–World War II period, Chile sustained a healthy democratic system with a number of political parties vying in elections. The Christian Democrats, who controlled government in the 1960s, promoted moderate reforms to give more land to peasants and attempted to gain more ownership of the copper industry, which was dominated by American corporations and accounted for about 80 percent of Chile's exports in the early 1970s.

The 1970 presidential election was a closely contested race with three parties splitting most of the vote. Although the Communist-Socialist candidate, Salvador Allende (al-YIN-day), took office with only 36 percent of the vote, he immediately implemented a socialist agenda, redistributing landholdings and nationalizing important sectors of the economy: the copper, steel, and coal industries and 60 percent of private banks. His policies prompted strong opposition from the business sector, especially from U.S. interests. Allende's rule came to a bloody end in a 1973 coup. Military leaders, with covert financial assistance from the CIA, ousted the president, who died—by his own hand—when the army laid siege to the presidential palace.

The new regime, led by General Augusto Pinochet (PEE-noh-SHAY), dissolved the congress, suspended the constitution, banned all political parties, and clamped down on opposition groups. Pinochet's free-market policies—reducing tariffs, government subsidies, and the size of the civil service—appealed to property and business owners. On several occasions, he called plebiscites to endorse his continued rule, but in 1988, the political opposition united to mobilize voters to vote no to continued military rule.

When moderate politician Patricio Aylwin took office in 1989, he had to carry out a difficult balancing act—investigating human rights abuses under the military regime while placating the military, which was headed by Pinochet until 1998. A Commission for Truth and Reconciliation was established to record the experiences of the several thousand people killed by the military under Pinochet's rule and to compensate families of victims. The commission, however, did not have the authority to prosecute the guilty. Hence, Pinochet, who was implicated in the killings, was not put on trial, and he continued to wield influence even after he finally stepped down as head of the military. In 1998, Pinochet was arrested in the United Kingdom at the request of Spanish authorities who held him accountable for crimes against Spanish citizens in Chile in 1973. Pinochet was eventually allowed to return to Chile and was given immunity to prosecution since he retained a seat for life in the Chilean Senate (that he gave up in 2002). The Chilean government eventually sought to prosecute Pinochet for his crimes, but the former leader's age and apparent illness hindered their efforts and Pinochet died in 2006 before he could ever be convicted.

The conservative economic policies of Aylwin and his successor, Edwardo Frei Ruiz-Tagle, focused on reducing the international debt and attracting foreign investment. Chile's economy grew at 6.7 percent per annum from 1990 to 1998, but it slowed to less than 1 percent in 1999. In 2000, a Socialist politician, Ricardo Lagos, was elected president. An economist trained at Duke University, he maintained market-oriented policies while devoting more resources to social programs and addressing social inequities. His successor, Michelle Bachelet, who was detained, tortured, and exiled during Pinochet's rule in the mid-1970s, has maintained these policies. Bachelet's election in 2006 made her the nation's first female head of state.

Peru

After World War II, Peru's governments alternated between civilian administrations and military dictatorships. Until 1968, the American Popular Revolutionary Alliance (APRA), which was opposed to the military and the economic elite, dominated government, but in 1968, mid-level military officers seized power. Aiming to steer the country on a course between capitalism and socialism, they introduced major reforms. They expanded the government's control over the economy, nationalizing banks, telecommunications, and railways and redistributing half the country's arable land to 375,000 rural families.

In 1980, the military permitted elections, but newly formed guerilla groups, including the leftist Tupac Amáru Revolutionary Movement (MRTA) and the Maoist *Sendero Luminoso* or Shining Path, challenged the new government. Drawing significant support from students and peasants, Shining Path stood out because half its leaders were women. It advocated violent revolution and waged a brutal campaign, assassinating government officials and financing its operations by taxing drug traffickers in areas it controlled. An estimated 70,000 people died in the conflict.

By the early 1990s, the government was on the brink of collapse when it regained the initiative under Alberto Fujimori, the son of Japanese immigrants to Peru. Elected president in 1990, he suspended the constitution several years later and gave the military increased powers to combat the guerillas. In 1992, Shining Path's insurgency was dealt a major blow when its leader, Abimael Guzman, who is currently serving a life sentence, and other key leaders were captured. Although Fujimori is credited with rebuilding the economy, his autocratic rule contributed to his downfall. In 2000, amid some major corruption scandals, he fled the country to avoid arrest. He is presently living in Chile, although the Peruvian government is trying to extradite him.

In 2006, APRA's Alan Garcia won election against Ollanta Humala, an ally of Venezuela's Hugo Chávez. Peru is the world's second largest coca producer, and Garcia has been given emergency powers to combat drug traffickers.

Bolivia

The military largely controlled Bolivia's governments throughout the 1960s and 1970s, but there were internal rivalries between left-wing and right-wing officers. In 1980, Argentina's military sponsored a military coup in Bolivia that installed officers who were closely tied to narcotics traffickers. Even though a civilian government took over in 1982, subsequent administrations have had to confront the drug trade, since Bolivia is the third largest coca grower in the world. From 1997 to 2001, for example, the government of Hugo Bánzer introduced free-market reforms and, with U.S. government assistance, began destroying the coca crops. Despite some early success is disrupting coca production in Bolivia or at least pushing it to other Andean nations, because little emphasis was given to finding alternative crops to sustain the former coca growers, many peasant farmers have returned to coca growing in recent years.

Although indigenous Indians make up 60 percent of Bolivia's citizens, up until very recently they have held little political power in the nation. Indeed, when an Indian, Evo Morales, a former coca grower, was elected as Bolivian president in 2006, it marked the first time since the Spanish conquest, nearly five hundred years earlier, that an Indian had led the nation's government. Allied with Venezuela's Hugo Chávez, Morales has led Bolivia sharply to the left, placing the energy industry under state control. He has also advocated large-scale land redistribution as a means of addressing the fact that some 50,000 families, most of them of European ancestry, still own 90 percent of the nation's land.

Columbia

With the exception of military rule from 1953 to 1958, Colombia has been ruled by civilian administrations since World War II. In the late 1950s, Colombia's primary political parties, the Liberals and Conservatives, formed a coalition to share power in the cabinet and to alternate presidents. That arrangement held until 1983, when the Conservatives refused to participate in the coalition after a Liberal, Virgilio Barco, was elected president. The Liberals maintained power until 2002, when Alvaro Uribe, an independent candidate and former Liberal, was elected president.

Since the 1960s, Colombia has been caught up in violence from many quarters. In the 1960s, leftist guerillas formed the Revolutionary Armed Forces of Colombia (FARC) and the National Liberation Army (ELN). Despite negotiations with the government in the late 1990s, they continue to wage war. Another source of violence has been drug trafficking, which escalated in the 1970s when drug cartels based in Medellin and Cali took control of the production and smuggling of cocaine. The cartels produce an estimated 90 percent of the cocaine that currently reaches the United States. They have waged "narcoterrorism" against the Colombian government by bribing state officials and kidnapping and assassinating politicians. The cartels also pay protection money to FARC in coca-growing regions controlled by the guerilla group. A third source of violence is right-wing paramilitary groups that were initially established by large landowners for their protection against leftist guerillas. In recent years, these paramilitary groups have become linked to the drug cartels, as well as to the police and army.

In 2000, the United States initiated Plan Colombia to back the Columbian government in its war against the drug cartels. The plan provides financial assistance to upgrade the Columbian security forces and judicial system and to aid the government in destroying coca fields. President Uribe has waged an aggressive security campaign against guerillas and drug cartels, and although the level of kidnappings and murders has declined in recent years, Columbia is not yet a stable country.

Venezuela

Over the first half of the twentieth century, Venezuela was ruled by authoritarian regimes. In 1957, protests forced Venezuela's military dictator Pérez Jiménez to flee. Two parties, Democratic Action (DA) and the Committee of Independent Electoral Organization (COPEI), agreed to share power and to prevent any more dictators from coming to power. Eventually, they controlled appointments to the civil service, the military, and judiciary. This agreement worked well for them for the next two decades until fluctuations in the price of oil set off economic crises.

Venezuela's oil industry began in the late nineteenth century, and the sale of oil on the world markets generates a high percentage of government revenues. After taking control of the petroleum industry in 1970, the Venezuelan government became a founding member of the Organization of Oil Exporting Countries (OPEC). Venezuela's economy boomed when the price of oil was high, but it experienced a crisis in the late 1970s when oil prices plummeted and the government was forced to take on large debts to external lenders.

In the 1980s, the alliance of DA and COPEI was more concerned about preserving its privileged position than addressing needs of the country's citizens, many of which were poor. Official corruption became rampant. And in the late 1980s, when the government adopted neoliberal economic measures recommended by the International Monetary Fund, independent political movements developed. One source of opposition was a group of junior officers led by Lieutenant-Colonel Hugo Chávez, who staged a failed coup in 1992. Chávez served a jail term, but after he was pardoned and prohibited from further military service, he directed his energies into electoral politics. His criticisms of neoliberal economic policies made him extremely popular among the poor. In 1998, he stood for president as the candidate of the Fifth Republic Movement. Identifying himself with Simón Bólivar, the father of Venezuela's independence, he promised a "Bolivarian revolution," which would rewrite the constitution, reorganize state institutions, and redistribute the nation's wealth to the poor. First elected with 56 percent of the vote, he was reelected in 2002 and 2006, although a high percentage of citizens abstained from voting in those elections.

Of mixed Indian and European ancestry, Chávez's populist policies won him the support of the poor—most of whom are black and Indian—who comprise 60 percent of the population. However, Chávez's policies also created a hostile opposition, especially among the Venezuelan Workers Confederation (CTV) and the independent media. In April 2002, he was briefly overthrown in a coup with the encouragement of the U.S. government, but 48 hours later, following huge demonstrations from his supporters and mounting international criticism, palace guards loyal to Chávez overthrew the new junta. Subsequently, he survived a referendum calling for his ouster and a three-month general strike organized by CTV in late 2002 that effectively shut down the petroleum industry.

Chávez has reoriented Venezuela's foreign policy. He supported creating an integrated Latin America to realize Bólivar's original vision of a united South America, reducing Venezuela's economic dependence on the United States, improving relations with other oil-producing nations, and developing good relations with OPEC. He has been a close ally of Fidel Castro's Cuba and a vociferous critic of U.S. foreign policy, opposing the U.S. invasions of Afghanistan and Iraq.

Chavez's political goals are tied to Venezuela's abundant oil revenues, which give the government clout domestically and internationally. Venezuela is the world's sixth largest oil producer, and the petroleum industry generates about 80 percent of government revenues. Venezuela supplies about 10 percent of the U.S. oil supplies, and the U.S. market takes nearly 60 percent of Venezuelan oil.

The Caribbean

How did Caribbean nations address their economic challenges in the late twentieth century?

In the Caribbean, the British successfully ushered in independence in the West Indies—Jamaica, Trinidad and Tobago, Barbados, and numerous other colonies became sovereign nations. Although most of these states have maintained multiparty systems, they remain economically weak because of their lack of capital and their reliance on exporting a few crops or minerals. Twelve nations of the Caribbean encourage regional integration through the **Caribbean Community and Common Market (Caricom),** established in 1973, but most Caribbean states still send the bulk of their exports to the United States and Canada. A key source of revenue is tourists from Latin America and North America, but because so few jobs have been created, there has been a massive emigration of people to the United States and other countries.

Jamaica

Jamaica, which gained its independence in 1962, has a more varied economy than most Caribbean nations. Although the sugar industry has declined, tourism, citrus fruits, and bauxite exports have become the mainstays of its economy. However, the unemployment rate has consistently remained at between 20 to 30 percent.

Since independence in 1962, Jamaica's main political rivalry has been between the Jamaican Labour party (JLP) and the People's National Party (PNP). The PNP's most prominent leader, Michael Manley, served as president over two periods. In his first term (1972–1980) he preached "democratic socialism" and advocated a strong role for the state in the economy. He was also a prominent spokesman for Third World causes. Manley was succeeded by the JLP's Edward Seaga, whose policies were more sympathetic to private enterprise and who favored U.S. interests. As Jamaica's economy faltered, however, Manley was reelected in 1989 as a moderate and an advocate of free-market policies. Since he retired because of poor health in 1992, his successor, Percival Patterson, has maintained the PNP in power.

Caribbean Community and Common Market (Caricom)—An organization founded in 1973 to serve as a forum for promoting democracy and human rights and to encourage multilateral discussions on issues of common concern such as trade, regional security, and transport. It has 15 members.

Cuba

Cuba's modern history has been dominated by its revolution of 1959. Before the revolution, Cuba had been controlled by a former army sergeant, Fulgencio Batista, who had ruled on his own or through civilian presidents since 1934. Cuba's economy largely depended on sugar exports and American investment, and Cuba's capital, Havana, was a haven for American tourists (and gangsters), lured by the tropical climate and gambling casinos.

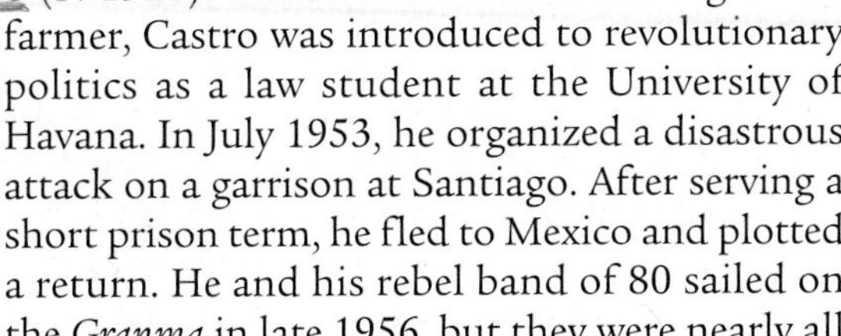

Castro Defends the Revolution

Cuba's revolutionary movement was led by Fidel Castro (b. 1926). The son of a well-to-do sugarcane farmer, Castro was introduced to revolutionary politics as a law student at the University of Havana. In July 1953, he organized a disastrous attack on a garrison at Santiago. After serving a short prison term, he fled to Mexico and plotted a return. He and his rebel band of 80 sailed on the *Granma* in late 1956, but they were nearly all killed when they landed in Oriente province. Castro and a small band of rebels escaped to the Sierra Maestra Mountains in southeast Cuba, from which they waged a guerrilla war. With popular support for Castro's movement growing and Batista's National Guard collapsing, Batista abruptly fled after his annual party on New Year's Eve, 1958. Castro's rebels marched unopposed into Havana.

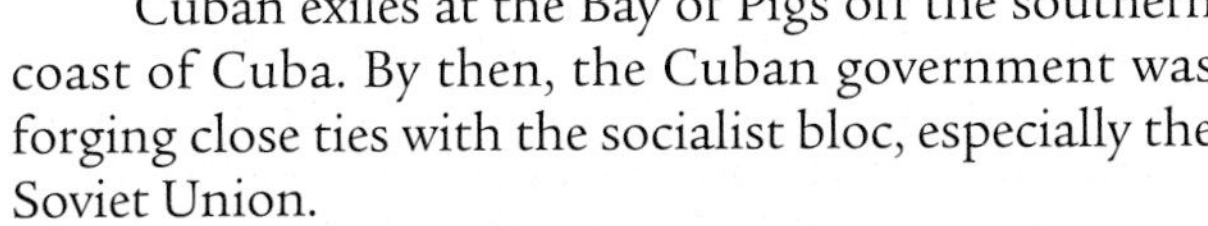

The Cold War and Cuba

Although he billed himself as a nationalist reformer when he took power, Castro moved sharply to the left in 1960 and proclaimed the revolution socialist the following year. His rhetoric became stridently anti-American. Shortly after John F. Kennedy became the U.S. president in 1961, the United States supported an ill-fated invasion by Cuban exiles at the Bay of Pigs off the southern coast of Cuba. By then, the Cuban government was forging close ties with the socialist bloc, especially the Soviet Union.

Castro's policies were dogmatically socialist. He built up the Communist party and jailed thousands of opponents, including former comrades. His government created a command economy in which the government controlled most sectors of the economy. It seized American property and nationalized businesses. It also addressed social problems and launched successful campaigns to eradicate illiteracy and to provide basic health care to the lower classes. Educational and health standards rose appreciably, as did living conditions among the peasants, who constituted the great majority of the population. The professional and middle classes, however, suffered losses in both living standards and personal liberties, and many hundreds of thousands fled to the United States.

After the U.S. government imposed a rigid trade embargo on Cuba, Cuba was drawn even closer to the Soviet Bloc and exported much of its sugar crop in exchange for oil, food, and other subsidies. In 1975, some 16 members of the OAS voted to end the embargo, and the United States intimated a desire for détente. This last possibility was made virtually impossible after thousands of Cuban troops and advisers were dispatched to support pro-Soviet regimes in Angola, Mozambique, and Ethiopia.

Torres and Liberation Theology

By the mid-1990s, global political changes had created new challenges for Castro. Cuba's role overseas ended with peace talks in Angola. Russia could no longer afford the luxury of propping up Castro's faltering economy and virtually abandoned him. Defying predictions that his regime would quickly collapse, Castro sustained his rule by modifying certain of his policies. He invited Pope John Paul II to pay a state visit in 1998 and allowed Christmas to be celebrated as a public holiday for the first time in three decades. He attracted foreign exchange by creating space for some private enterprise, especially in the area of attracting foreign tourism, although that did not benefit many Cubans. He eased the impact of the American economic boycott against Cuba by permitting Cuban exiles to send money to their families in Cuba and improving trade ties with Latin American, Caribbean, and European nations.

Although the American government has generally taken a hard-line stance toward Cuba, there have been slight differences from one administration to another. In the late 1990s, the Clinton administration eased restrictions on humanitarian assistance and medicines being sent to Cuba. However, George W. Bush's administration resumed tightening the embargo after 2000. Castro has remained in power longer than any other leader in the Western Hemisphere since Emperor Pedro II of Brazil, but in 2006, complications stemming from intestinal surgery greatly weakened his health, forcing him to transfer his

Venezuelan President Hugo Chávez portrays himself as carrying on the revolutionary ideals of Cuban President Fidel Castro. In January 2007, Chávez visited the ailing Castro in his hospital room in Havana, Cuba.

authority to his brother Raúl. By the middle of 2007, Castro's health appeared to be improving, but he had not yet formally reassumed his role at the nation's leader and what happens to Cuba after he and Raúl finally leave the scene remains an open question.

Haiti

One of the world's poorest countries, Haiti passed through a series of military rulers and dictators after World War II. In 1957, François Duvalier, popularly known as "Papa Doc," seized power. He used the police, military and secret police, known as the *Tontons Macoutes,* to terrorize opponents. Declaring himself president for life, he looted the state treasury for his personal enrichment. After his death in 1971, his son, Jean-Claude or "Baby Doc," served as president until he was forced out of office and fled the country in 1986.

There have been many obstacles to creating democratic institutions in Haiti. In February 1991, Jean-Bertrand Aristide, a Catholic priest, was elected president. Seven months later, the army expelled him. In response, the UN imposed an oil and arms embargo on the country, which led to a compromise under which Aristide would be allowed back in the country. When the compromise collapsed, a wave of reprisals and random murders swept the country and led to the frantic exodus of thousands of Haitians by sea to the United States and elsewhere. These voyages were often made in boats that were overloaded and poorly equipped for journeys across the open sea, leading to the drowning of many refugees. By autumn 1994, after the coup leaders refused to give in to international demands for Aristide's return, the United States and its Caribbean allies negotiated the departure of the coup leaders and restored Aristide to power—but only after he agreed not to run for reelection.

After Aristide's party's candidate, René Préval, succeeded him as president in 1996, Aristide grew dissatisfied with Préval's performance and formed his own political party, *La Fanmi Lavalas.* In 2000, Aristide captured the presidency in elections boycotted by the opposition parties. After a rebellion against him erupted in 2004, Aristide was forced to leave the country. In 2006, with Aristide still in exile, Préval once again was elected to a 5-year term. However, with Haiti's unemployment rate at 70 percent and a per capita annual income of $250, Préval's government has to cope with a challenging situation.

Mexico

Why has Mexico generally been more stable politically than other Latin American nations since 1945?

With a population of around 100 million people, Mexico is the largest Spanish-speaking country and the fourteenth largest country in the world, and it has the twelfth largest world economy. From 1950 to 1995, the number of people living in urban centers shot up from 10 million to 69 million.

Mexico's political life for most of the twentieth century was dominated by the PRI. Although the PRI's roots were in the Mexican revolution of the early twentieth century, in the post–World War II years, revolutionary fervor dimmed and the party cooperated with business interests and framed policies that favored the middle class and urbanized citizens. Until the 1980s, the primary political competition was between factions of the PRI. The sitting president, chosen every 6 years, had enormous powers because he handpicked his successor and nominated party officials.

The PRI's near monopoly over the political system began to weaken in the 1980s. One factor was a major earthquake that struck Mexico City in 1985, killing an estimated 7000 people. The PRI was blamed for not conducting an aggressive rescue mission and for allowing violations of construction regulations.

PRI rule was also shaken by economic problems. Despite oil discoveries in the Gulf of Mexico in the 1970s that generated $13 billion in earnings in 1981 and made Mexico the sixth largest petroleum exporter in the world, Mexico's economy could not overcome a slump in oil prices in 1981. By 1982, Mexico's debt amounted to $90 billion, and it was unable to repay its creditors. It had to be bailed out by the U.S. government and international financial institutions. Although Mexico's economy eventually recovered, another debt crisis was narrowly averted in 1994. The Mexican government was also discredited by the widespread corruption of its top politicians.

The 1993 signing of the **North American Free Trade Agreement (NAFTA)** between Mexico, the United States, and Canada has had a major impact on the Mexican economy. Responding to the development of the European Union and the possibility of a unified Asian market, the United States pushed for the creation of NAFTA, which went into effect on January 1, 1994. Since NAFTA was implemented, the Mexican economy has been tied even closer to the United States. In 2001, almost 90 percent of Mexican exports went to the United States, which supplied Mexico with two-thirds of its imports. Cheaper American agricultural products have flooded the Mexican market, driving the smaller Mexican farms out of business. Moreover, a hoped-for boom in Mexico's industrial sector that was to follow in the wake of NAFTA never fully materialized as cheaper labor markets in China and elsewhere in Asia siphoned off foreign capital investment in Mexican industry.

North American Free Trade Agreement (NAFTA)—An agreement signed by Canada, the United States, and Mexico and put into effect in 1995, which created a free-trade zone in North America and removed obstacles to cross-border movement.

Seeing Connections

Lucha Libre

Professional wrestling has attracted a devoted following around the world. In Mexico, where it was imported from the United States in the 1930s, it took the name *lucha libre* (literally "free fight") and became the most widely attended spectator sport after soccer. The most popular wrestler of the 1930s in Mexico was Rodolfo Huerta, whose ring name was El Santo and who wore a trademark mask. He represented wrestlers known as *técnicos,* who honored the rules and did not cheat to win. Their rivals were *los rudos,* the bullies who invariably ignored the rules and bribed referees to come out on top. In the end, the only way the *técnicos* could even the odds was by seeking outside help or bending the rules. Although this melodrama was (and still is) played out in a wrestling ring, it came to symbolize the larger arena of Mexican politics where the little guys fought against the odds and took on the corrupt establishment who fixed the system. The photograph here was taken in Mexico City's *zocalo* (town square) during protests against the 2006 presidential election results. The man in the wrestler's mask speaking on a cell phone stands before a poster of Andrés Manuel López Obrador, the leftist presidential candidate who claimed voter fraud by his opponent's party cost him the election.

The inability of the Mexican economy to create enough jobs for its citizens has forced some six million Mexicans to cross illegally into the United States in search of work. U.S. efforts to tighten its southern border in the wake of the September 11, 2001, terrorist attacks have made illegal entry into the country from Mexico more difficult, forcing many migrants away from more heavily guarded urban areas along the border into the open desert. Hundreds of these migrants die each year in the Sonoran Desert, succumbing to heat exhaustion before they can reach safety. The issue of illegal immigration and migrant workers has strained relations between Mexico and the United States in recent years. President George W. Bush has proposed overhauling his government's immigration policies and instituting a temporary worker program, but such legislation faces significant opposition in the U.S. Congress, and by 2007 it had not yet been drafted into law.

In Chiapas, a southern state with widespread poverty, the government faced an insurrection by the Zapatista Army of National Liberation (EZLN), which launched its rebellion on January 1, 1994, the same day the NAFTA treaty went into effect. Inspired by the Mexican Revolutionary hero Emiliano Zapata (see p. 807), the Zapatista leadership hoped to spur a new revolution that would sweep the nation; however, few Mexicans wanted to plunge the nation into the chaos and violence that would accompany a new revolution. The fighting itself between the Zapatistas and the Mexican Army was brief and one-sided, but the rebellion itself only officially ended after peace talks in 1996.

In 1997, the PRI lost its absolute majority of Mexico's congress to opposition parties for the first time in over fifty years. Then, in the 2000 presidential election, Vicente Fox, the candidate for an opposition coalition Alliance for Change, defeated the PRI's Francisco Labastida, earning 44 percent of the popular vote to Labastida's 37 percent. Fox's election was historic because it marked the first time that a candidate of the PRI had lost a national election in its 70-year history. Fox, a former Coca-Cola executive with a conservative, pro-business agenda, sought to reform the Mexican government and economy, but PRI control of the congress thwarted many of his reforms. Although he was generally popular with the Mexican people, Fox's 6 years in office brought little real change to the country.

In 2006, the National Action party's Felipe Calderón narrowly defeated the Party Democratic Revolution's Andrés Manuel López Obrador in a bitterly contested presidential election that required a two-month recount. Obrador, a leftist and popular former mayor of Mexico City, alleged voter fraud by the National Action party and insisted that he had won the presidency. Official confirmation of Calderón's victory by the federal electoral tribunal indicated that he had won the election by less than 1 percent of the vote (or fewer than 250,000 votes). Obrador, however, refused to accept the tribunal's ruling and established a parallel government, which though it held no formal power functioned in symbolic opposition to the Calderón government. Polls have shown that most Mexicans support the outcome of the election and oppose Obrador's post-election actions, but the leftist candidate appears to have tapped a deep vein of popular discontent among Mexico's poor and underprivileged.

Central America

What effect did the Cold War have on the countries of Central America?

In contrast to Mexico's relative political stability, most Central American states underwent long periods of turmoil, if not outright civil war, during the Cold War era, as leftist guerrilla movements challenged oligarchies that controlled most of the land and political systems.

Nicaragua

In Nicaragua, three generations of dictators from the Somoza family ruled the country from 1937 to 1979 before Anastasio Somoza had to resign in the face of a popular uprising and the collapse of his national guard. The successor government was an uneasy coalition between representatives of business and the guerrilla movement, the Sandinista National Liberation Front (named after a guerrilla leader of the 1930s, César Sandino).

In 1984, the Sandinista leader Daniel Ortega won an election and began implementing socialist policies. However, he was staunchly opposed by the Reagan administration, which imposed an embargo on Nicaragua in 1985 and began funneling support to a counterrevolutionary group called the Contras. A peace accord was signed in 1987, and national elections were held in 1990. The National Opposition Union, a coalition of anti-Sandinista parties, won that election and subsequent ones as the Liberal Constitution party. Despite charges of government corruption and a slumping economy, the ruling party candidate Enrique Bolaños won the presidency in 2001, beating back a vigorous challenge from Ortega. However, Ortega, who had softened his leftist ideology and publicly embraced Christianity, won the 2006 election with a former leader of the Contras serving as his vice presidential running mate.

El Salvador

El Salvador also struggled through a bloody civil war in the 1970s and 1980s. The war erupted when Napoleon Duarte, who won the election in 1972, was denied the presidency. The military took on leftist guerrillas of the Farabundo Marti National Liberation Front (FMLN). Right-wing death squads and the guerrillas brought terror to the countryside. The warfare ended in 1991 when the government signed a peace agreement with the FMLN. A right-of-center party, the National Republican party, has ruled the country since then. To escape the bloodshed and chaos of the war, hundreds of thousands of Salvadoran immigrants left for the United States. They send back over a billion dollars a year in remittances to their families in El Salvador.

Guatemala

Political stability also eluded Guatemala until recently. In 1954, President Jacobo Arbenz was overthrown by a coup sponsored by the CIA and Guatemala's landowning elite, after Arbenz expropriated land owned by the United Fruit Company, producer of Chiquita bananas. Successor regimes served the interests of the business elite. In the early 1960s, discontented army officers inspired by the Cuban revolution established a guerilla movement, the Rebel Armed Forces. Over the next three decades, the government, the Rebel Armed Forces, and other guerilla movements fought a protracted civil war in which an estimated 200,000 people lost their lives or disappeared. The conflict largely pitted poor rural Mayans against the urban mestizo elite that controlled the government and military and owned most of the country's land. The worst period of fighting came in the mid-1980s, when General Efrain Rios Montt's security forces unleashed death squads that waged a ruthless war on rural populations. Since a peace accord was signed in 1996, Guatemala has been relatively stable. In 2003, Óscar Berger, head of a coalition of political parties, was elected president.

Costa Rica

Costa Rica stands out in Central America for its stable political system and diverse economy. Its economy exports coffee, bananas, beef, and microchips, but its largest earner of foreign exchange is its ecotourism industry, which is built around its lush tropical forests. One reason why Costa Rica has avoided the civil wars that have plagued its neighbors is because its constitution prohibits a standing army. Although Costa Rica has regularly seen peaceful transfer of powers from one political party to another, its image was damaged in recent years by accusations of corruption against two former presidents, Miguel Ángel and Rafael Ángel, who are currently awaiting trial. In 2003, the Costa Rican constitution was amended to permit a president to run for a second term. That allowed Oscar Arias, who had been president in the late 1980s and had won the Nobel Peace Prize for helping to bring an end to civil wars in Nicaragua and El Salvador, to win a closely contested election in 2006.

Conclusion

Unlike African countries following colonial rule, Latin American states have not had to create new national identities in the twentieth century, but they have still faced daunting challenges in achieving political stability and economic prosperity. From the 1950s to the 1980s, many Latin American governments were burdened with the repressive rule of dictators and military regimes and were weakened by a succession of civil wars. But these military regimes proved incapable of managing modern economies, and they alienated their people with their repressive policies. The end of the Cold War, however, lessened the ability of the Soviet Union and the United States to intervene in the affairs of Latin American nations. Since then, there have been promising moves towards democracy throughout the region.

Despite the political gains, economic weakness, coupled with the drug trade in some countries, has continued to plague Latin American countries. The failure of neoliberal economic policies to improve the lives of average citizens during the 1980s and 1990s has led to a broad political movement to the left in recent years. Growing poverty and the widening gap between rich and poor, however, remain threats to regional stability. Although some Latin American states have attempted to develop their own self-sustaining economies, the region's accumulation of debt and its continuing reliance on the export of agricultural products and natural resources have not dramatically shifted its economic vulnerability and dependence on international creditors.

Suggestions for Web Browsing

Internet Modern History Sourcebook: Latin America
http://www.fordham.edu/halsall/mod/modsbook55.html#
A detailed online source for documents regarding specific countries, common themes and issues, and indigenous peoples.

Castro Speech Database
http://lanic.utexas.edu/la/cb/cuba/castro.html
A repository of thousands of Fidel Castro's speeches delivered between 1959 and 1996.

National Security Archive: Sources of Latin America
http://www.gwu.edu/~nsarchIV/NSAEBB/#Latin20America
An archive of declassified U.S. government documents on American policy in Latin America.

Literature and Film

Gabriel Garcia Marquez's *One Hundred Years of Solitude* (Perennial, 2004) deals with a century of life in a small town. Octavio Paz's *Labyrinth of Solitude* (Viking Penguin, 1985) addresses the creation of Mexican identity in the twentieth century and relations between Mexicans of Native American and European ancestry. Isabel Allende's *House of the Spirits* (Alfred A. Knopf, 1986) portrays the life history of a poor woman who rises to wealth and influence.

A Cuban-produced film, *Memories of Underdevelopment* (1973; New Yorker Films), is an honest portrait of a well-off young man who grapples with the implications of the Cuban revolution. *La Historia Oficial* (1985; Fox Lorber, *The Official Story*) is an Argentine film about a family who learns that their adopted child was taken from a "disappeared" family. *The Buena Vista Social Club* (1999; Artisan Entertainment) is a documentary on Cuban popular music of the 1940s and 1950s featuring legendary performers. *The Motorcycle Diaries* (2004; Universal Music and Video Distribution) tells the story of a journey Ernesto "Che" Guevara and a friend took by motorcycle across South America in 1952 and the evolution of Guevara's political awareness.

Suggestions for Reading

General studies on Latin America include Leslie Bethell, ed., *Latin America: Economy and Society Since 1930* (Cambridge University Press, 1998) and Robert Gwynne and Cristobal Kay, eds., *Latin America Transformed: Globalization and Modernity* (Arnold, 2004). In the 1990s, scholars focused on the transition from military to civilian governments. Among the key studies is John Peeler, *Building Democracy in Latin America* (Lynne Rienner, 1999). Francesca Miller's *Latin American Women and Social Justice* (University Press of New England, 1991) examines women in organized social movements. Jacqueline Barnitz, *Twentieth-Century Art of Latin America* (University of Texas Press, 2001) is a good chronological survey of the most important styles and artists from Mexico, Cuba, and South America in the last century.

A general study on Mexican politics is Roderic Al Camp, *Mexico: Politics in Mexico,* 2nd ed. (Oxford University Press, 1996). A specific study on Brazil is Javier Martinez-Lara, *Building Democracy in Brazil: The Politics of Constitutional Change, 1985–1995* (St. Martin's Press, 1996). An assessment of the Cuban revolution is Marifeli Pérez-Stable, *The Cuban Revolution: Origins, Course, and Legacy* (Oxford University Press, 2003).

American foreign policy toward Latin America is examined in Lars Schoultz, *Beneath the United States: A History of U.S. Policy Toward Latin America* (Harvard University Press, 1998).

CHAPTER 35

Asia and the South Pacific Since 1945

Political, Economic, and Social Revolutions

Outline

- The People's Republic of China
- Japan: From Defeat to Dominance to Doubt
- Korea: A Nation Divided
- Southeast Asia
- The Subcontinent
- Australia, New Zealand, and the Pacific Islands

Features

DOCUMENT **Mao on Communism in China**

DOCUMENT **Kōra Rumiko, "When the War Ended"**

SEEING CONNECTIONS **The Transistor**

DOCUMENT **Benazir Bhutto at Harvard**

◀ Students at Beijing's Central Academy of Fine Arts erected a 10-meter-high statue they called the "Goddess of Democracy" during the 1989 demonstrations in Tiananmen Square. Made of papier maché and metal, the statue was placed so that it confronted the giant portrait of Mao in the square. The statue, which inspired thousands of Chinese young people to demand greater democratic rights, was destroyed in the violent suppression of the demonstrators on June 4, 1989, by the People's Liberation Army.

POSTWAR ASIA'S SURVIVORS faced a complex range of concerns—decolonization, the Cold War, the rise of new technologies, and the need to come to terms with the legacy of the war, as well as the development of nations based on nationalist thought incubated in the previous decades.

Nation-building was not painless. Wars of independence took place against the backdrop of the Cold War, turning some into proxy wars for the United States and the Soviet Union while inflicting great carnage on the former colonies. In many cases, retribution along ideological or ethnic lines continued for some decades. In 1945, few could imagine that the devastated lands of East Asia and the religiously divided lands of South Asia would reassert themselves as pivotal players in the global economy by the end of the twentieth century.

Asia's nations are linked to the rest of the world through military, environmental, and economic globalization. An economic crisis in East Asia in 1997 spread virus-like across the Eurasian landmass. Real viruses also know no boundaries—avian flu has spread rapidly across Eurasia with the migration of birds. Hollywood has had a profound effect on Asian filmmakers, and at the same time, India's "Bollywood" is starting to find a bigger share of the market in the West. Chinese and Japanese films routinely find large Western audiences, and Japanese "anime" (AH-nee-may) cartoons influence youth culture everywhere.

In the geopolitical realm, international terror organizations as well as international movements for human rights cross boundaries from Asia to Europe to North America. The December 2004 tsunami affected countries throughout the region and led to a global humanitarian relief effort. Politics and economics in Asia matter deeply to countries at great distances from Asia.

The People's Republic of China

Why has China shifted course so frequently in its post-1949 quest for political integration and economic growth?

Announcing that the "Chinese people have now stood up," Mao Zedong proclaimed the founding of the People's Republic of China on October 1, 1949. Decades of war and revolution were then to give way to nation-building. But the trajectory of China's nation-building in the next half century was anything but smooth. Moving from land reform and industrial reconstruction, to collectivization and communization, and later to increasing market incentives, economic development made frequent changes in course. In the realm of foreign policy, China shifted from a close relationship with the Soviet Union and a bitter enmity with the United States to a rupture of relations with the former and a rebuilding of ties with the latter. And China's approach to human rights in free expression, artistic license, women's rights, and other social and cultural areas often changed direction.

	China
1949	Founding of People's Republic of China
1950–1952	Land Reform program
1950	Marriage reform
1956–1957	Hundred Flowers campaign
1958–1961	Great Leap Forward
1960–1989	Sino-Soviet rupture in relations
1966–1976	Cultural Revolution
1972	Nixon goes to China
1976	Death of Mao, arrest of Gang of Four
1978	Deng Xiaoping introduces Four Modernizations
1989	Tiananmen Square demonstrations
1997	Hong Kong reverts to China

The Communist Victory

Between 1927 and 1937, the Nationalist, or Guomindang (GWAW-min-dang), government of Jiang Jieshi (jee-AHNG jeh-SHEE; also known as Chiang Kai-shek) had initiated useful reforms in the areas under its control. The Japanese war in China prevented the expansion of those policies to the rest of the country. At the end of World War II, Jiang insisted that Japanese forces surrender only to the Nationalists. But the Soviets, who had declared war on Japan in the last week of the Pacific War, held Jiang's forces out of Manchuria while the Russians plundered Japanese investments there. In the meantime, Mao Zedong's Communist forces moved into Manchuria. The Nationalists appeared to be much stronger than the Communists, having larger numbers of troops and a government recognized by the rest of the world. Jiang sent 500,000 Nationalist troops to Manchuria.

The tensions between the Communists and Nationalists threatened to reopen the civil war in China, and United States President Harry S Truman sent the U.S. army chief of staff, General George C. Marshall, to China to mediate between the two sides. Newly appointed as American secretary of state, Marshall returned home in January 1947, his mission a failure. In his final report, he blasted extremists on both sides for failing to make peace.

Jiang felt confident in his rejection of the American's advice. His armies swiftly moved to capture Communist strongholds. In July 1947, however, the tide of war had changed. Jiang's assassination of Nationalist critics, the Guomindang's brutal suppression of the Taiwanese, and the failure of the economy eroded support for the Nationalist government. By the end of 1947, the Nationalist forces went into retreat, and in 1948 the Nationalist presence in Manchuria collapsed. The complete defeat of Jiang's armies occurred in 1949

Chronology

1940	1950	1960	1970	
1947 India and Pakistan become independent 1949 People's Republic of China established; Republic of Indonesia formed	1950–1953 Korean War 1952 U.S. Occupation of Japan ends; Japanese obtain political independence 1958 Mao initiates Great Leap Forward	mid-1960s to mid-1970s China's Cultural Revolution 1968 Suharto becomes Indonesian head of state	1971 Civil war in East Pakistan leads to war between Pakistan and India; Bangladesh formed out of East Pakistan	1978–1985 Deng Xiaoping introduces market reforms to China 1979 Soviet invasion of Afghanistan

when Mao's "People's Liberation Army" captured the major cities in China. Mao proclaimed the establishment of the People's Republic of China (PRC) on October 1, 1949, and by the middle of 1950, Mao ruled all of mainland China's 550,000,000 people. Jiang's Nationalists fled to the island of Taiwan.

Right-wing Americans, influenced by the anticommunist demagoguery of Wisconsin Senator Joseph McCarthy, charged that liberals and "fellow travelers" (anyone who espoused social aims similar to those of the communists) had lost China.[1] In fact, American military aid to China during World War II totaled $845 million; from 1945 to 1949, it came to slightly more than $2 billion. It is extremely doubtful whether additional American military aid to China would have changed the final outcome of the civil war.

The period from 1949 to 1952 in China was one of consolidation of the Communists' power and structuring of the new state. Mao Zedong's administration extended to Manchuria, Inner Mongolia, and Chinese Turkestan. In 1950, his armies moved into Tibet. The Beijing government continued to seek to regain the traditional holdings of the Qing Dynasty, including the lands gained by Russia during the nineteenth century. Such a policy caused serious problems not only for the Soviet Union but also for Vietnam, Burma, and India.

Relations with the United States deteriorated during this period and were put on a Cold War footing until the 1970s. The United States supported Jiang in his struggle against the Communists, and relations further declined with the outbreak of the Korean War in June 1950. The United States began to give massive economic and military aid to the Nationalists on Taiwan, and when U.S. forces in Korea moved toward the Chinese border, China entered the Korean War. U.S.-China relations hardened into complete opposition for the next two decades.

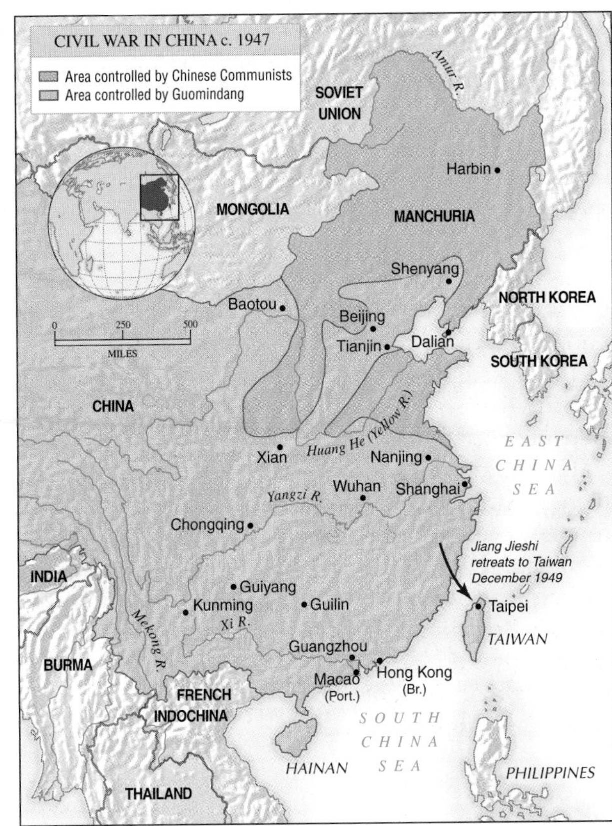

▲ In 1947, Mao's Communist forces were engaged in a civil war with the Nationalist government's army.

Mao's Government

After 1949, Mao used his version of Marxism to change the whole order of Chinese society from its traditional patterns. He concentrated power in the Chinese Communist party (CCP), which was led by the party's **Central Committee.** Though democratic forces were at first tolerated, they were soon subsumed under the power of the CCP. The day-to-day work of the Central Committee fell to a smaller Politburo, headed by Mao, who was also Chairman of the CCP and head of the government of the PRC.

The new government brought both inflation and corruption under control. Mao's interest in rural

Central Committee—Body of approximately three hundred members elected by CCP National Congress held every 5 years. The Central Committee selects the ruling Politburo.

1980

1984 Indira Gandhi assassinated

1988 Benazir Bhutto becomes first woman elected to lead Pakistan

1989 Tiananmen Square Massacre in China

1990

1998 Hindu nationalist BJP wins Indian elections

2000

2001 China enters WTO

2001 United States invades Afghanistan, ousting the Taliban regime

2002 East Timor gains independence from Indonesia

2004 Congress party wins elections in India

2004 Indonesian earthquake triggers catastrophic tsunami

Document

Mao on Communism in China

Mao Zedong adapted Marxism to China. After paying tribute to the Soviet Union in a speech delivered in 1949, he stated his goals for the future.

Communists the world over are wiser than the bourgeoisie, they understand the laws governing the existence and development of things, they understand dialectics and they can see farther. The bourgeoisie does not welcome this truth because it does not want to be overthrown.

As everyone knows, our Party passed through these twenty-eight years not in peace but amid hardships, for we had to fight enemies, both foreign and domestic, both inside and outside the Party. We thank Marx, Engels, Lenin, and Stalin for giving us a weapon. This weapon is not a machine-gun, but Marxism-Leninism....

The Russians made the October Revolution and created the world's first socialist state. Under the leadership of Lenin and Stalin, the revolutionary energy of the great proletariat and labouring people of Russia, hitherto latent and unseen by foreigners, suddenly erupted like a volcano, and the Chinese and all mankind began to see the Russians in a new light. Then, and only then, did the Chinese enter an entirely new era in their thinking and their life. They found Marxism-Leninism, the universally applicable truth, and the face of China began to change....

There are bourgeois republics in foreign lands, but China cannot have a bourgeois republic because she is a country suffering under imperialist oppression. The only way is through a people's republic led by the working class....

Twenty-four years have passed since Sun Yat-sen's death, and the Chinese revolution, led by the Communist Party of China, has made tremendous advances in both theory and practice and has radically changed the face of China. Up to now the principal and fundamental experience the Chinese people have gained is twofold:

1. Internally, arouse the masses of the people. That is, unite the working class, the peasantry, the urban petty bourgeoisie and the national bourgeoisie, form a domestic united front under the leadership of the working class, and advance from this to the establishment of a state which is a people's democratic dictatorship under the leadership of the working class and based on the alliance of workers and peasants.
2. Externally, unite in a common struggle with those nations of the world which treat us as equals and unite with the peoples of all countries. That is, ally ourselves with the Soviet Union, with the People's Democracies and with the proletariat and the broad masses of the people in all other countries, and form an international united front.

To sum up our experience and concentrate it into one point, it is: the people's democratic dictatorship under the leadership of the working class (through the Communist Party) and based upon the alliance of workers and peasants. This dictatorship must unite as one with the international revolutionary forces. This is our formula, our principal experience, our main programme....

The Communist Party of the Soviet Union is our best teacher and we must learn from it. The situation both at home and abroad is in our favor, we can rely fully on the weapon of the people's democratic dictatorship, unite the people throughout the country, the reactionaries excepted, and advance steadily to our goal.

Questions to Consider

1. How was Mao's application of communism different from that of the leaders of the Soviet Union?
2. Why are the communists wiser than the bourgeoisie, according to Mao?
3. What is a "democratic dictatorship"? Is this an oxymoron, or a viable concept?

From Mao Zedong, "In Commemoration of the 28th Anniversary of the Communist Party of China, June 30, 1949," in *Selected Works*, Vol. 5 (New York: International Publishers, n.d.), pp. 411–423.

reform dated back to the 1920s, so he turned his attention early on to the plight of the countryside. Since more than 70 percent of farmland was owned by 10 percent of the landlords, the government encouraged angry landless peasants to confiscate large holdings and redistribute them. This process included violent actions against large landlords, including the killing of many of them, but it was supported by the bulk of the formerly land-poor peasants. Owning their own land, farmers increased productivity and allowed for a surplus that would be shifted to industrial development. The land-to-the-tiller policy was a successful policy. But it was not to last.

Mao Zedong's interpretation of Marxism was different from most other Marxists' views. Marx had stated that people's ideology was strongly influenced by their class identity, but Mao believed that individuals could change their ideology much more quickly. Wanting to move to a more Communist state, Mao believed he could change people's outlook overnight by changing their material circumstances. As peasants became small holders with the land reform of 1950–1952, they could be encouraged to embrace communism, he figured, by moving first, in 1953, to "mutual aid teams" that allowed farmers to pool their machinery and resources, then, from 1955 to 1957, to full **collectivization** of farms. Nearly all farmers were made members of rural collectives in which all labor, farm equipment, and land were controlled by the state.

Mao made plans for the industrial sector as well. A Soviet-style 5-year plan for economic development in industry was initiated in 1953. The Russians sent machinery and thousands of advisers. The Chinese made impressive advances in heavy industry, and the success of the first plan led to a second 5-year plan. But Mao was distressed that the industrial sector had outpaced the agrarian sector. Mao also expressed concern about inequalities between average workers and the privileged party bureaucrats. Thus, in 1956 and 1957, he urged intellectuals and others to speak out against bureaucratic corruption. Dubbed the **"Hundred Flowers"** campaign, Mao's efforts were at first ignored by frightened intellectuals. Later, promised freedom of speech, many spoke out. Mao cracked down severely, purging hundreds of thousands from their jobs, jailing countless others, and destroying the fledgling literary and artistic worlds. When Mao announced his **Great Leap Forward** in 1958, no intellectuals dared to criticize its obvious shortcomings.

Mao launched the Great Leap Forward with a huge propaganda campaign and galvanized millions of urban and rural workers into a frenzied effort to tremendously increase the production of steel, electricity, and coal. Thousands of small backyard furnaces sprang up to produce steel. The Chinese boldly predicted that they would surpass British industrial capacity in 15 years.

In the countryside, Mao installed "people's communes." The state created some 26,000 of these units, each averaging 5,000 households, or about 25,000 people. The heads of the communes collected taxes and ran schools, child care centers, dormitories, communal kitchens, and even cemeteries. Mao tried to convert farmers into a rural proletariat paid in wages. Until the late 1970s, almost all land, dwellings, and livestock were effectively owned by the communes. Among the few benefits of the otherwise failed policy of the creation of the communes were improvements in distribution of medical care and literacy.

The Great Leap Forward ultimately proved disastrous for China. Central planners erred in allocating resources and capital, and farm production dropped dangerously. The steel and iron produced in the rural backyard furnaces turned out to be unusable. Farmers were often left without the tools to produce the food they and the urban population required. From 1959 to 1961, Chinese industry lacked essential raw materials, and millions of people went without adequate food. Between 1960 and 1962, a combination of bad weather and chaos bequeathed by the failure of the Great Leap resulted in malnutrition and the death of between 16 and 30 million people. At the same time that the Great Leap was failing, the Soviet Union withdrew its technological and financial support. Indeed, this marked the beginning of a Sino-Soviet split that rivaled the Cold War tensions as a threat to world peace. Soviet Premier Khrushchev's attack on Stalin in 1956 was taken by Mao as an implicit criticism of himself; the Soviets' refusal to help China take back Taiwan and the Soviets' support of India, which had given refuge to Tibet's Dalai Lama and others fleeing Chinese suppression in Tibet, sealed the break. A three-power Cold War scenario—Russia, China, and the United States—emerged, complicating international affairs and promoting deadly proxy wars around the world for the next three decades. Faced with these crises, Mao, who had championed the Great Leap Forward, was bypassed by more pragmatic leaders in the Communist Party, especially Liu Shaoqi (lee-OO show-CHEE) and Zhou Enlai (JOH en-LAI).

The Cultural Revolution and International Recognition

By the early 1960s, an ideological schism had widened between Mao and the longtime comrades who signaled the rejection of his more rigid ideology by referring to Mao as an "ancestor"—revered and even worshipped but ignored in everyday life. Moderates advocated gradual social change and economic development, while radicals like Mao sought to pursue the drastic restructuring of Chinese society. Mao believed that many in the Communist party had lost their revolutionary zeal.

When a historical play written by a government official was taken as a thinly veiled criticism of Mao, the revered ancestor struck back, calling on young people and supporters in the army to attack the party leadership for their conservatism. High school and college students fell under the spell of utopian Maoism, forming themselves into bands called **Red Guards,** determined to wipe out what they considered old fashioned art, ideas, and even the old guard of the CCP. Top leaders like Liu Shaoqi were arrested—he later died in prison—universities were closed, and scholarship ceased. Young people replicated the fabled "Long March" and went down to the countryside to live among the farmers, many of whom resented having to take care of city

---

collectivization—Merging of previously privately held farms into one large unit owned jointly and farmed collectively.

Hundred Flowers—Movement urging intellectuals to speak out against corruption, first encouraged and later repressed by Mao.

Great Leap Forward—1958-1961 attempt to equalize output of industrial and agricultural sectors by forming rural communes, requiring all to work, and providing extensive social services. Its failure led to starvation.

Red Guards—During the Cultural Revolution, school-age youth inspired by Mao to attack vestiges of pre-1949 Chinese life and culture.

▲ From 1966 to 1969, schools in the PRC closed down as students, waving books of Mao's quotations or carrying his image, demonstrated throughout the country as Red Guards of the Cultural Revolution.

slickers. Placing political purity above economic growth and applying Maoist ideas from *Quotations from Chairman Mao* (nicknamed the "Little Red Book"), the Red Guards hampered production and research. Their rallies and demonstrations disrupted the entire educational system. "Redness" (ideological purity) was favored over technical expertise. Only nuclear research was spared the attacks of the anti-intellectual Red Guards; guarded by the People's Liberation Army (PLA), the nuclear labs were a protected space.

The effects of these events, called the **Cultural Revolution,** were dire. By 1967, industrial production had plummeted and basic education and most research had ceased; some areas of the country were approaching anarchy. Eventually, Mao called on the PLA to bring the Red Guards under control, restore order, and put an end to the excesses of the Cultural Revolution.

Premier Zhou Enlai (1898–1976), Mao's longtime associate, gradually helped to restore the country's industrial productivity. The return to political stability was more difficult, but Zhou managed to hold the country together while rival factions intrigued for power. Zhou removed China from diplomatic isolation. He responded to an initiative by the Nixon administration in 1971 and moved closer to the United States, motivated perhaps by the armed border clashes with the Soviet Union that had begun to occur along the Amur River. In 1971, the United Nations voted to seat the PRC rather than the Nationalist government of Taiwan. The American policy shift signaled to other nations, such as Japan and some NATO countries, that the United States would not object to the restoration of diplomatic relations with the PRC. The United States recognized the PRC and withdrew diplomatic recognition of Taiwan in 1979. In addition, China sought to develop its industrial capacity through the use of foreign technology and to bring in foreign currency through both an expanded banking system based in the British crown colony of Hong Kong and the development of a tourist industry.

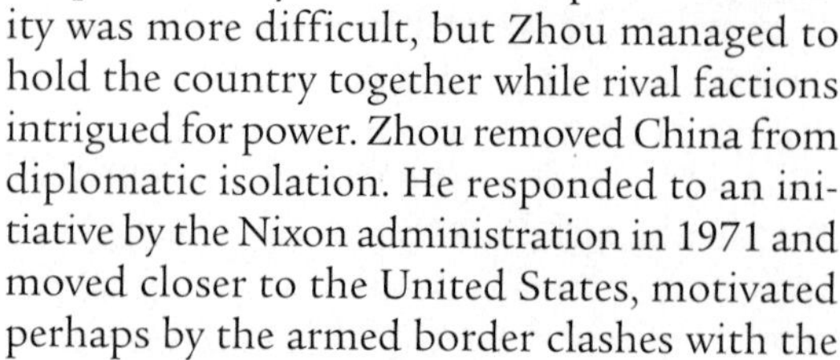

The Shanghai Communiqué, 1972

Deng Xiaoping's Pragmatic Reforms

After Zhou and Mao died in 1976, politicians jockeyed for control with varying intensity. Leading the most militant faction, known as the **Gang of Four,** was Mao's widow, Jiang Qing (jee-AHNG CHING; 1914–1991), who was overthrown, disgraced, and brought to a televised show trial in 1980. Jiang, as one of the leading ideologues of the Cultural Revolution, was blamed for its excesses. The trial of the Gang of Four deflected blame for the Cultural Revolution to a few people, thereby paving the way for the advent of a more moderate, pragmatic group of officials led by Deng Xiaoping (DUHNG show-PING).

Deng was a political survivor whose roots in the party went back to the 1920s. He endured political exile and the Cultural Revolution to introduce his variant of reform Marxism, in which the party kept control of the "commanding heights" of the economy. Aided by his moderate chief lieutenants, Hu Yaobang (HOO yow-BAHNG) and Zhao Ziyang (JOW zee-YAHNG), Deng introduced a series of economic reforms called the **Four Modernizations** (agriculture, industry, science, and defense). The first major move to introduce a more market-oriented economy came in the countryside in 1978. The party allowed greater personal profit for farmers, and this resulted in a vast increase in productivity. In 1982, communes were stripped of their political authority and replaced by cities, towns, and villages. The incentive-based plan gave China a grain surplus in

Cultural Revolution—Maoist movement, 1966–1976, to destroy traditional culture and modern "bourgeois" culture; founded on utopian, revolutionary dreams.

Gang of Four—Four of the many leaders of the Cultural Revolution who were blamed for the failures and brutality of that movement. The group included Mao's widow.

Four Modernizations—Vigorous program designed by Deng Xiaoping to reject vestiges of the Cultural Revolution by embracing Western methods in military, science, industry, and agriculture.

6 of the next 7 years. With an increased food supply and a contented rural population, Deng in 1985 encouraged the introduction of market incentives in the cities, with the goal of gaining similar economic gains there. To foster more rapid development, Deng permitted the entry of Western experts and technology, a process called the "Open Door Policy." Western, especially American, influence grew in the cities in China during the 1980s, along with foreign trade and an influx of other foreigners.

The government continued to keep the cost of medicine low and supplemented wages with accident insurance, medical coverage, day care centers, and maternity benefits. The standard of living in China improved, but the removal of price controls on food and other staple items led to inflation. The standard of living in China remained far below the standards in industrialized countries.

The educational system changed drastically under the Communists. In the 1930s, only 20 percent of the people had been literate. By 2007, the figure had risen to 90 percent. Across China, a crash program of schooling was initiated, and schools with work-study programs for those unable to attend school full-time were established. Thousands of Chinese students went abroad to study, including some 200,000 to the United States.

Deng had worked for economic liberalization but failed to sponsor similar reform on the political front. Students and workers began to express discontent with inflation, corruption, and a lack of democracy. In December 1978, a young worker was arrested for calling for a fifth "Modernization"—democracy. The newly liberalizing state did not know how to deal with ideological diversity. Greater opportunities for expression alternated with periods of crackdowns in the next decade. New ideas flowed into China in the 1980s—music from Japan, movies from Hong Kong, and literature from around the world. By the end of the 1980s, even relations with Russia were improving. As the world's media were gathering in Beijing to witness the historic restoration of ties between the Soviet Union and China in the spring of 1989, students were carrying out massive demonstrations for democratization. The protest reached a climax in May and June when thousands of demonstrators calling for democracy occupied the ceremonial center of modern China, Tiananmen Square in Beijing. Both the students and the government were aware of the historic timing of their demonstrations—May 4, 1989, was the seventieth anniversary of the May Fourth Movement that also started with demonstrations in Tiananmen Square. The whole world was watching.

The party split over how to deal with the protesters and their supporters, sometimes numbering 1 million. Zhao advocated accommodation, but the hard-line prime minister, Li Peng (LEE PUHNG), called for a crackdown. By the end of May, the students had won the enthusiastic support of the workers and citizens of Beijing, Shanghai, and Chengdu. In June, the People's Liberation Army, using tanks and machine guns, cleared the square and the surrounding area of the student demonstrators. More than 3000 people were killed in the massacre.

Premier Zhao Ziyang, who had counseled a moderate approach to the demonstrators, was forced from office. Jiang Zemin (jee-AHNG zuh-MIN; b. 1926), who replaced him, continued economic liberalization and international ties but also continued a policy of strict political controls.

China in the 1990s and Beyond

During the 1990s, China's export trade expanded dramatically, and foreign economic interests increased their activities in China. Economic ties between the Chinese and the United States grew rapidly, and China enjoyed most favored nation trading status with the United States. It maintains a high level of trade with Europe and Japan but of even greater importance are its ties with Taiwan and Singapore. Inflationary pressures resulting from rapid economic growth threatened to create major social problems for the

◄ Despite astounding economic modernization over the past 20 years, China remains a country of startling contrasts. Here, the very latest in electronic goods are transported by a traditional three-wheel bicycle.

Chinese Communist leadership. At the same time, the Chinese continued to construct enterprise zones along the coast in which the most modern technology was used by Chinese businesses working closely with world banking and commercial interests for joint profits. Beijing joined the World Trade Organization (WTO) in 2000.

Culture blossomed in the 1990s and 2000s. Rock stars delighted Chinese audiences; public intellectuals founded journals on a variety of subjects from fashion to environmentalism; painters used techniques from a variety of traditions and showed their works around the world; architects created new urban cityscapes. Chinese filmmakers gained an international audience of millions, even as many filmmakers had to fight censorship. Chinese artists worked throughout Asia, Europe, North America, and Australia, enriching cultural styles wherever they went.

The Communist party remained fairly strong, counting around 52 million members in 1992, even though fewer than 10 percent of those applying for party membership were admitted. When Deng Xiaoping died in 1997, China had weathered the transition in leadership. It became a world power by the early twenty-first century, a full member of the World Trade Organization, and a regional leader.

There is a great disparity, however, in the benefits of the new, market economy between those living along the special economic zones on the Pacific coast and those living in the interior. Among the 1.25 billion Chinese are those who, living in cities such as Guangzhou, have profited from participating in the globalized economy.

Opportunities for women remain a major issue in China. The 1950 Marriage Law was a significant advance for Chinese women, offering them legal freedom within marriage. Men as well as women earned rights to land under the land reform policies of 1950–1952. The Great Leap Forward, for all its economic disasters, enhanced women's equality by expanding their opportunities to earn money, even though women did not earn equal pay for equal work. Slogans such as "Women Hold Up Half the Sky" suggested the goal of gender equality during the Cultural Revolution.

And yet women were not treated equally, despite laws and policies. Ding Ling (see Chapter 29) was persecuted for demanding that the PRC recognize gender as a category as important as class. When Deng Xiaoping instituted the Four Modernizations in 1978, he called for limiting family size to one child per family in order to enhance economic growth.The burden of implementing population control fell on wives. Pressured by their families to produce sons—sons were greatly favored over daughters—wives were often punished for giving birth to daughters. Baby girls were at times abandoned or killed, and their families thought they could try again to have a boy. Infanticide was illegal, but some families tried to circumvent the law. As a result, China today faces the twin crises of female infanticide and of too many boys. Many men will never marry and the government fears the consequences of an explosion in the population of adolescent boys. The one-child policy has been relaxed, and two children are permitted in rural areas and unlimited children in ethnic minority areas, but overall, the sex ratio remains greatly unbalanced. China's fertility rate (1.7 children per woman) is below replacement level but considerably higher than the fertility rates in richer East Asian countries.

DOCUMENT China's One-Child Family Policy

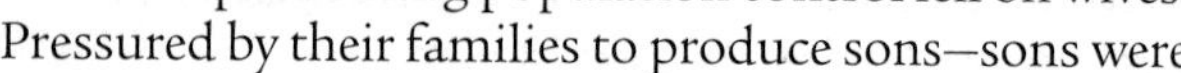

Jiang Zemin stepped down as General Secretary of the CCP in 2002, and his replacement, Hu Jintao (HOO jin-TOW; b. 1942), seems to take a similar approach to the development of a market economy while maintaining political controls. Economic liberalization has helped society become somewhat more liberal. Some tensions common to industrial societies have begun to be felt, however. The water has also become dangerously polluted, the air so dirty that a permanent haze envelopes the cities, and deforestation so pervasive that desertification has spread in the northwest. China will have to rigorously address these problems as its economy grows.

China in the coming years faces several major challenges, including reducing the disparities in income between coastal and interior areas; deciding how to deal with the ethnic minorities, especially in Tibet and in the northwest provinces where the Uigurs want an autonomous status; responding to environmental degradation; widening democratic opportunities in a globalizing society; and expanding and equalizing the rights of women, from infancy through education, employment, marriage, motherhood, and old age.

China has taken steps to underscore its regional great power status. Following the tsunami that devastated Southeast Asia and the Indian Ocean world, China made its largest donations to date. Though far smaller than donations from Japan, the United States, and some other countries, the $60 million sent by China was a mark of both generosity and international standing by a nation that was once one of the world's largest aid recipients. The world will have an opportunity to gauge China's ability to address its problems in 2008 when the Summer Olympic Games take place in Beijing. Just as Japan in the 1960s and Korea in the 1980s, China will use the Games to highlight its growth and emergence as a major player on the international stage.

Japan: From Defeat to Dominance to Doubt

Did postwar Japanese prefer growth at any cost over protection of the environment, women's rights, consumer benefits, and improvements in the workplace?

On August 28, 1945, just three weeks after atomic bombs were dropped on Hiroshima and Nagasaki, an advance party of 150 Americans, the lead group of a substantial army of occupation, landed in Japan. Supreme Commander General Douglas MacArthur soon arrived to preside over Japan's transition from one military authority to another. The Japanese had successfully recast their infrastructure during the Meiji Restoration. They would make another massive—and successful—adjustment after 1945.

Postwar Japan

The Americans were convinced that a program of demilitarization and democratization would create a new Japan. Many believed that Japan would become a peaceful agrarian country. Little did the Americans, very few of whom had any knowledge of Japan, imagine that the program of change was just what Japan needed to emerge in two decades as one of the great economic powers. Japan's democratic movements and quest for modernity in the years before the war had already accustomed many to the kinds of values and institutions necessary for rapid reconstruction. Despite the beliefs of the members of the U.S. Occupation, democracy and individualism, though suppressed during the war, were not unfamiliar concepts to many Japanese. Significantly, defeat itself opened up an opportunity to start afresh. Social inequalities were leveled when rich and poor alike were homeless and without food. When Japan rebuilt, it built from the bottom up. Until the last two decades, class differences in postwar Japan were far smaller than those in other industrialized countries. The devastation of the war had another effect: disillusioned with their own wartime leaders, the Japanese offered no resistance to the Occupation.

	Japan
1945–1952	American Occupation of Japan
1947	Reverse course in Occupation
1955	Formation of Liberal Democratic party
1960	Demonstrations against U.S.-Japan Security Treaty
1970s–1980s	Trade tensions with United States
1989–1990	Beginning of recession

The Occupation—nominally international but in reality dominated by the Americans—cut Japan's territorial possessions back to the four main islands. Korea and Taiwan were decolonized, and Manchuria and other areas were removed from Japanese control. Millions of soldiers, sailors, and colonists, some of them with no home in Japan, were forced to return to the home islands. Others were taken prisoner by the Russians and died in Siberian gulags. The military was demobilized, reservist organizations disbanded, and key wartime military and civilian leaders were placed on trial. Japanese Prime Minister Tōjō Hideki (TOH-joh hee-DEH-kee) and six of his colleagues were executed. Two hundred thousand governmental and business leaders were blocked from resuming their jobs, though many were able to go back to work when the Americans left in 1952. For a while, industries were dismantled for reparations, particularly by the Russians in Northeast Asia, but this practice was soon stopped.

Unlike the case of Europe, the Americans did not pay for the rebuilding of Japan's industrial infrastructure. In the first winter after the end of the war, Japan faced massive starvation and disease. The Americans did supply food and medicines, but most people still had to resort to the black market to survive.

One of the first public policies changed was civil rights for women. The feminist activists of the prewar era lost no time appealing for women's rights to the prime minister. Knowing that the Occupation would soon demand those rights, he granted them to the feminist petitioners. Women voted for the first time in the elections of April 1946. In the next few months, a new constitution was written, ostensibly by the Japanese, but in reality by a committee of Americans, one of whom was a 21-year-old young woman, Beate Sirota (Gordon). The constitution was promulgated in 1947 and modified the Meiji-era document in several important ways: the people rather than the emperor were sovereign; two fully elected houses of Parliament were the governing body at the national level; the Supreme Court had the right of judicial review; all rights were made absolute, not reversible as in the Meiji document; and **Article IX** renounced war as a way to settle international disputes.

The Constitution of Japan, 1947

Social changes included a new educational system based on the American pattern of decentralized public

Article IX—Article in Japan's 1947 constitution outlawing war and the use of force as a way to resolve international tensions.

schools, with textbooks rewritten to delete references to militant nationalism. Almost all schools were open to boys and girls, and both sexes could attend universities. Admission was to be based on merit, but in later years, merit came to be measured by passing exams based on extensive memory work. Another important social change was the constitutional guarantee of equal rights for men and women; although they are often ignored in practice, the constitution may be used to demand rights in a court of law. Labor unions were once more permitted to exist. In February 1947, however, Cold War fears of a Communist victory in nearby China led the Americans to outlaw a planned general strike that they believed would slow Japan's economic recovery. The era of unbridled democratization came to an end in what contemporaries called the "reverse course."

To be sure, democratic changes did continue even after February 1947. Two key areas of economic change also had social implications. Perhaps most important, especially in the creation of a conservative rural electorate, was land reform. As in China, land was taken from rich landlords and given to poor tenant farmers. But the process was much more benign, and wartime agricultural policies had already begun the shift in ownership of land. The other major change was the forced dismantling of the large industrial combines known as *zaibatsu.* The Americans believed that small enterprises would foster competition, improve economic growth, and ensure fairness. By 1947, the "trust-busting" policy was seen as slowing economic recovery and was stopped. In time, many of the large firms regrouped, but in new ways that avoided breaking the laws against economic concentration.

Recovery was also slowed by devastating inflation. The Occupation instituted a policy of deflation, which threw many workers out of their already tenu-

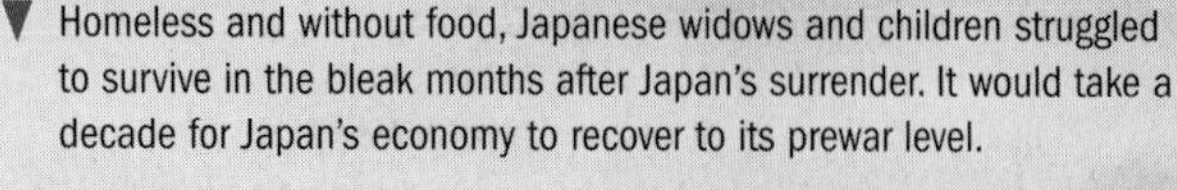

▼ Homeless and without food, Japanese widows and children struggled to survive in the bleak months after Japan's surrender. It would take a decade for Japan's economy to recover to its prewar level.

Document

Kōra Rumiko, "When the War Ended"

Feminist poet Kōra Rumiko (b. 1932) grew up during the bitter days of World War II and the U.S. Occupation. Her poetry reflects her profound commitment to pacifism and to justice for women in Asia. Her work is a constant reminder not to forget the victims of war. Kōra was not alone in this position—Japanese feminism in the late twentieth century was closely linked to pacifism, environmentalism, and the plight of Asian women exploited during the war as "comfort women" and after the war by Japanese and other foreign enterprises seeking cheap labor. This poem stresses her fundamental belief in women's nurturing maternal role, criticizing Japan's wartime leaders for denying women and men their basic human rights.

When the war ended
the men came home.
At last, the cry of babies
was heard abundant throughout our cities
and villages,
The stream of life of the young children
promised to fill the dreadful void left by the
dead.
But in this country there are some women
who will never mother children,
the women who lost the men they were to
marry,
the women who lost the men who were to
be their lovers
before they even knew their names.
And in this country there are some men
who will never father children,
the men whose white bones lie rotting in
the South Seas,
the men who lie not beside the warm flesh
of their wife
but in the cold earth of a foreign land.
Those who ordered them to die
father children, carry on the bloodline,
surrounded by the warmth of family, they
smile.
But the dead look on
in the spaces between the highrises
they reflect on the meaning of their death.
Why did we kill and why did we die?
A wind blows down from the heights of futility
an infinite anger.

Questions to Consider

1. At whom is the "infinite anger" in the last line of the poem directed?
2. Why were the men's bones left to rot in the South Seas?
3. The poet is known as a feminist. Do you think this poem can be seen as a feminist work?

From Sandra Buckley, *Broken Silence: Voices from Japanese Feminism* (Berkeley, CA: University of California Press, 1997), pp. 127-128.

ous jobs. The real recovery came when the Americans began to place orders for equipment to be used in the Korean War.

As a result of the Cold War in Europe and the Communist invasion of South Korea in 1950, Japan became the United States' principal ally in the Pacific. Despite Soviet opposition and without the participation of the USSR, a peace treaty was signed in 1951 and went into effect the next year, giving Japan full political independence. A security pact between Japan and the United States allowed the Americans to station troops in Japan. The Socialist party and the Japanese peace movement continued to protest against that pact as damaging to Japan's national sovereignty in subsequent years.

Political and Social Change

Conservatives have consistently, with brief interruptions, controlled the Japanese government. In 1955, responding to a merger of two Socialist parties, two conservative parties merged to form the Liberal Democratic party, which was friendly to big business, favored modest rearmament, and backed the alliance with the United States. Allied with professional civil servants and business interests, it was sufficiently strong to endure periodic charges of corruption for the next 38 years. The Socialist party, the major opposition, demanded retention of Article IX, opposed the 1952 security pact with the United States, and favored neutrality in foreign affairs. The small Communist party was vocal but weak. In the first half of the postwar era, rural voters tended to vote for conservative candidates, while most urban areas had Socialist mayors. Many people voted for their local candidate less for reasons of ideology and more because the candidate had a record of getting things done for his (or, rarely, her) constituency.

Rapid urbanization and industrialization posed enormous social challenges. Rural areas lost population, and at the same time, city populations—and consequent environmental problems—skyrocketed. With more than 23 million people, the Tokyo metropolitan region became one of the largest urban areas in the world. The cities of Tokyo, Osaka, and Nagoya occupied only 1 percent of the country's land area but contained over one-fourth of the country's population.

In a headlong rush to rebuild, pollution affected Japan more seriously than any other industrial country in the 1960s. Prime Minister Ikeda Hayato (EE-kay-dah HAH-yah-toh) promised the Japanese people that he would double per capita income within a decade. The Japanese were dispirited by the government's parliamentary maneuvering and strong-arm reaction to demonstrations against the renewal of the U.S.-Japan Security Treaty in 1960, and to regain popular support, the prime minister focused on satisfying consumer needs. Within 7 years, the GDP had doubled and Japanese enjoyed televisions, cars, and more comfortable, though still cramped, homes. Factories churned out these products, refineries produced oil, and mining dug up hillsides. By 1970, industrial waste produced deadly mercury poisoning, and the air was so foul that authorities told Tokyo children to stay indoors and not breathe the air. In 1970, the Japanese people had had enough. At what price should middle-class lifestyles be bought? In the early 1970s, Japan therefore took the international lead in overcoming pollution, producing less polluting cars, requiring antipollution devices on smokestacks, and requiring recycling at home.

Urban living also caused traditional values and attitudes to change. Parental authority and family ties weakened as young married couples, forsaking the traditional three-generation household, set up their own homes. The stresses and strains of urbanization were reflected in student riots and in the appearance, for the first time in Japanese history, of juvenile delinquency. International influences—seen in fashions, television, sports, and beauty contests and heard in rock music—became embedded in Japanese culture. Today, high fashion and popular culture alike are as likely, if not more so, to originate in Japan as in Europe or the United States.

The early 1950s were a time of intense labor strife and union clashes with industrial management. But by the 1960s, as the economy was booming, labor became more complacent. A cooperative spirit developed between labor and management as long as jobs were plentiful. Male workers worked long hours, and in exchange, were promised lifetime career security. Industrial concerns seemed to be characterized by a kind of harmony. Contrary to popular stereotypes, this harmony was not innate in Japanese society. It was created by government and company policies after World War II, when women were told to go back to the home to make way for returning soldiers. The "New Life Movement" developed by companies and the government promoted long work days for men and roles as nurturing wives and mothers for women. In reality, large numbers of women continued to work outside the home, although the image that they did not served to depress their wages and their ability to advance in the workplace.

By the late 1960s, however, young people were becoming more interested in meeting the individual needs of their families and began to question unstinting dedication to their companies. Men increasingly claimed they wanted to spend more time with their families, and women workers faced an exhausting double shift of work and child care. These trends paralleled the questioning of growth at the expense of the environment or personal health in the 1970s. And they certainly accelerated in the 1990s when corporations themselves went back on the promise of job security as Japan faced economic recession. Guaranteed lifetime employment came increasingly under challenge. Corporate paternalism had to be discarded to satisfy the demands of efficiency. Slowly but surely, the communalism that had dominated Japanese life weakened under the impact of economic and cultural individualism.

Perhaps the greatest changes were those affecting women. Before World War II, many Japanese women were part of the workforce, especially young women. The poor worked in textiles, domestic service, farming, or the sex trades, and middle-class women worked in offices, department stores, nursing, and teaching. But no women had full civil rights. There was an active movement for women's civil rights, but like other movements, it was suppressed in the 1930s. After 1945, women gained the right to own property, sue for divorce, pursue educational opportunities, and vote. Despite the existence of these rights, women still faced an uphill battle toward equality. Women were socially expected to shoulder the entire burden of taking care of the home, leaving little opportunity to obtain workplace equality.

A revived feminist movement in the 1970s represented a coalition of new feminist activists and prewar women's rights activists like Ichikawa Fusae. They mounted a series of legal challenges to continuing gender inequality. This led to the passage of the Equal Employment Opportunity Law in 1985 and family care leave laws in the 1990s. In addition, convenience foods and other home aids have made it somewhat easier for women to enter the workforce. By 2002, women constituted 50 percent of the nation's workforce—although an even thicker glass ceiling prevailed in Japan than in other industrialized countries, preventing women from reaching top management positions. More than 30 percent of women high school graduates attended postsecondary institutions.

Politics has been even harder for women to break into than the upper echelons of business. Japan has fewer women members of parliament than most advanced industrial countries. Feminists speak out

Seeing Connections
The Transistor

Japan's jump into the electronic age started with the simple little transistor. A device developed by Bell Labs in New Jersey in 1947 to amplify phone signals more effectively than the vacuum tubes used until then, the transistor soon was put to other uses, primarily in computers for the U.S. military and semiconductors for the new computer companies just getting started in California's Silicon Valley. A German company placed the transistor in a radio in 1953, and a small U.S. company did the same, but it was the acquisition of the transistor by a small company in Tokyo, later named Sony, that started the consumer electronics revolution. In destitute postwar Japan, scientist Ibuka Masaru persuaded the Ministry of Finance to let him use $50,000, a huge fee for Japan at the time, to pay for the license for the transistor. For Bell Labs, on the other hand, this represented just a small part of the cost of producing the new technology—but no one could have foreseen Sony's success with the transistor. In 1955, Ibuka was joined by Morita Akio in mass-producing transistor radios for Sony. By 1957, Sony began to dominate the American market, using that success to enter the television and calculator markets.

about continuing inequalities. But what may be most telling is the extraordinarily low birthrate. Japanese society still places barriers on mothers' full participation in the workforce. Schools assume mothers will be home during the day, and companies hesitate to hire mothers for fear of absenteeism. So, many women who may want to have children never marry, and those who do marry have one or no children. Japan's birthrate, one of the world's lowest, is far below replacement level. Unless present trends change, 2006 will have marked the beginning of a long-term decline in Japan's population.

Economic Dominance and Doubt

Japan's developmental trajectory from the early postwar years shows a shift from anxiety about survival, to growth at all costs, to responsible balancing of health and other human needs with wealth, and finally to worrying about the outsourcing of jobs and the rise of serious global competition. Japan encountered serious obstacles in its path to economic development. Farmland is scarce, and Japan is self-sufficient only in rice. It has to import much of its other food for its population (126 million in 2001) and most of the raw materials for its industries. The start of the Korean War in 1950 gave Japan an initial boost, as American forces spent lavishly. In 1950, the GDP was $10 billion. The 1973 oil embargo and subsequent price increases hit Japan hard. Inflation skyrocketed, economic growth plunged, and for a while, the balance of trade was negative. Japan's business managers made the necessary adjustments for recovery.

By the end of the 1970s, the Japanese built half the world's tonnage in shipping and had become the world's biggest producer of motorcycles, bicycles, transistor radios, and sewing machines. The Japanese soon outpaced the United States in automobile production and drove the American domestic television industry virtually out of business. After the October 1987 U.S. stock market slide, Tokyo temporarily became the world financial center, as it dominated banking.

In the late 1980s, the Japanese began to watch uneasily as South Korea, Taiwan, Hong Kong, and Singapore, using the Japanese formula of a strong and disciplined workforce and efficient use of new technology, became effective competitors in the world market. Japan has been eclipsed in labor-intensive industries like ship-building and small electronics in particular. South Korea has launched a direct challenge to Japan in the high-technology and automotive markets.

Recession in Japan was not as serious as in some Asian countries in the late 1980s, but it hit hard after 1991 because of the overinflated prices for stocks and real estate in the 1980s. A vastly overpriced real estate market called a "bubble" (at one time, the listed real estate value for the Tokyo area alone exceeded the real estate value of the entire United States); a weakening management structure, with a parade of industrial chiefs solemnly apologizing for running their firms into ruin and atoning by resigning from their companies; and a disastrous series of bad loans that ruined several large banks brought the nation to the brink of a financial crash. The Asian financial crisis compounded those problems. Japan's annualized GDP fell 5.3 percent in the first three months of 1998—and that in a part of the globe that saw the annualized GDP of South Korea, Malaysia, Thailand, and Indonesia fall by 20 percent in 1997. The yen continued to decline against the dollar into 2002. As Japan entered another recession, observers held their breath to see if the Japanese government would take the necessary steps to put its financial structure in shape.[2] But the Japanese economy remained one of the world's strongest. Japan's per capita GDP in 2006 was $33,100, compared with $43,000 in the United States. In recent years, the recession has ended, and the yen has recovered against the dollar.

Although the Japanese economy may not be the model it once seemed, Japanese culture and the arts are now at the forefront. Japanese arts and letters began to reclaim their place on the world stage in the decades after World War II. Writers like Nobel Prize winners Kawabata Yasunari (KAH-wah BAH-tah YAH-soo-NAH-ree, 1899–1972) and Ōe Kenzaburō (OH-ay KEN-zah-boo-ROH, b. 1935) joined filmmakers like Akira Kurosawa (AH-kee-rah KOO-roh-SAH-wah, 1910–1998) in earning international acclaim. In recent years, Japanese popular culture, especially in new fields like anime, sets the standard for postmodern youth culture. Japanese architects' buildings are found throughout the world. Writers such as Murakami Haruki (MOO-rah-KAH-mee HAH-roo-kee, b. 1949) and Yoshimoto Banana (YOH-shee-MOH-toh bah-NAH-nah; b. 1964) and other young women and men are the pop writers of the current generation. Filmmaker Miyazaki Hayao (MEE-yah-ZAH-kee hah-YAH-oh, b. 1941), creator of blockbuster animated films like *Spirited Away* (2001), has a worldwide audience. The works of these artists are part of a global culture that need not be interpreted as Japanese.

Korea: A Nation Divided

Will economic and political differences continue to outweigh the Korean desire for reunification?

After Japan's surrender on August 15, 1945, Koreans, who had been anticipating liberation from foreign rule, were deeply disappointed. Japanese colonial rule was replaced by American occupation in the south and by Soviet in the north. The Soviet Union, which had maintained neutrality with Japan throughout World War II, entered the war after the United States had dropped the atomic bomb on Hiroshima. In the next days, Russian forces moved into Northeast Asia—Manchuria and Korea had been under Japanese control—and when the Japanese surrendered, the Russians joined the Americans in accepting that surrender. Koreans, eagerly awaiting independence, felt betrayed. The departing Japanese occupying force actually hand-picked its successor. They chose the populist (but non-communist) Yŏ Un-hyŏng (YOH oon-hee-ONG; 1885–1947), who negotiated a treaty ensuring that the Japanese would not be part of any Korean peacekeeping. The new leader set up the Committee for the Preparation of Korean Independence (CPKI) in Seoul, which attempted to make itself into a national government. Local self-governance committees sprang up throughout Korea, ready to take up local administration as the Japanese departed. The CPKI convened a meeting of representatives of these committees in September 1945.

The Politics of Decolonization, Occupation, and Division

The CPKI proclaimed the formation of the Korean People's Republic on September 6, 1945. Its agenda was decolonization. In addition to land reform that would take land away from the Japanese and those who had collaborated with them, to nationalizing such major industries as mining and railways, and to estab-

	Korea
1948	North Korea and South Korea created
1950–1953	Korean War
1961–1979	Pak Chŏnghŏi rules as president
1980–1988	Chŏn Tuwhan as president
1988	Seoul Olympics, beginning of democratization
1994	Death of Kim Ilsŏng; rule by his son Kim Jongil

lishing labor laws to protect adult and child labor, the CPKI worked to remove from civilian administration those Koreans who had benefited from Japanese colonial power or who had held positions in the colonial government. This government was rejected by both the American and Soviet occupying forces, who divided Korea at the 38th parallel and proclaimed that Korea would be under American and Soviet "trusteeships" until it could govern itself.

The U.S. government of occupation outlawed the Korean People's Republic and set up another foreign government of occupation, the United States Army Military Government in Korea (USAMGIK). Koreans were bitterly disappointed not only by the loss of self-government so soon after they had gained it, but also by the fact that the U.S. forces gave positions of authority to those the Koreans considered collaborators with the Japanese colonialists. Over 80 percent of police officers in the Korean National Police in October 1945 had worked for the Japanese Government General as police officers, the most detested arm of the state.

The following February, in P'yŏngyang (pee-ong-YAHNG) in the Soviet sector, the guerrilla fighter General Kim Ilsŏng (KIM il-SONG; also spelled "Il-Sung") was proclaimed head of the Interim People's Committee. In the south, U.S. authorities established a Republic of Korea (ROK) in August 1948. The Americans chose the anticommunist Syngman Rhee, an octogenarian who had been involved in anticolonial actions at the dawn of the Japanese occupation in the early twentieth century, as the first president of the ROK. In response, the Soviets proclaimed Kim Ilsŏng to be premier of the Democratic People's Republic of Korea (DPRK), which the Soviets created. Then, in late 1948, the Soviet Union ended its occupation of Korea, and during the following spring, American troops ended their occupation south of the 38th parallel. Both governments—the ROK and the DPRK—claimed jurisdiction over the entire country.

Within 2 years, the two new governments were embroiled in a Korean civil war that lasted from 1950 to 1953 (the war is technically not over, as only an armistice has been signed). This war led to the devastation of a people barely beginning to recover from colonial rule. During those 3 years, families were divided, and over 2 million Koreans were killed, wounded, kidnapped, or declared missing. The destruction of industrial infrastructure and housing by incendiary bombing, along with the numbers of refugees in camps, can be measured, but the psychological damage caused by this warfare is just beginning to be understood.

Cold War tensions produced conflicting views of the start of the war, although archival findings support the view that northern forces, encouraged by the Soviet Union, crossed the 38th parallel into South Korea on June 25, 1950. Washington immediately called for a special meeting of the UN Security Council, whose members demanded a cease-fire and withdrawal of the invaders. The Soviet delegate was boycotting the council at the time and was not present to veto the action. When North Korea ignored the UN's demand, the Security Council sent troops, led by General Douglas MacArthur who had recently been directing the U.S. Occupation of Japan, to help the South Korean government. Three years of costly fighting followed, in what the UN termed a "police action." Led by the United States, United Nations forces, which suffered over 140,000 casualties, repelled the northern forces, who were supported by the USSR and later the People's Republic of China. After Stalin's death in March 1953 and a U.S. threat to use nuclear weapons against China, an armistice was signed in July 1953. A new border between the two parts of the country was established near the 38th parallel.

North Korea and South Korea

Since its inception, North Korea has been a familial dictatorship of General Kim Ilsŏng until his death in 1994, followed by his son Kim Jongil (also spelled Kim Jong-il). The general and his son perfected the art of the cult of the personality in their dictatorships. North Korea is the last of the totalitarian states built on a Stalinist model of constant mobilization against external enemies and of continuous economic mismanagement. Despite its investments in long-range nuclear missiles and nuclear research, North Korea cannot feed itself. Only international food aid has stopped a massive famine. Although the state has achieved full literacy among its population, it restricts contact with outside ideas and influences. There are elections, but there is only one party, the Korean Workers party—no opposition parties are tolerated.

The record of this regime, aside from impressive mass demonstrations of love for the regime for the benefit of visiting foreigners and constant mobilization, has been escalating economic failure. The centrally planned economy is in a state of near collapse from lack of investment in needed infrastructure. The collapse of communist governments in Eastern Europe and Russia meant that North Korean goods no longer had a market; thus North Korea's "self-reliance" policy crumbled. The size of North Korea's economy is now just 5 percent of South Korea's. Half of the gross national product is spent on the military, while the country faces malnutrition and declining standards of living. The per capita GDP in North Korea in 2006 was $1,800; the GDP for South Korea, $24,200. The government has vacillated in its economic policies; for a while, it allowed small-scale farmers to market some of their own produce but returned to a more controlled market and rationing of grains in 2005. The regime even restricted humanitarian aid in December 2005, despite the famine that gripped the country for years.

South Korea has had an entirely different experience since the 1953 armistice. The first years of the postwar ROK were marked by poverty, homelessness, and a failed economy. Foreign aid kept South Koreans from starving. The South Korean government of the 1950s was characterized by favoritism and corruption. President Syngman Rhee maintained control with the aid of the National Security Law of 1948, which allowed for the imprisonment of tens of thousands of suspected communists. His 1959 extension of the National Security Law outlawed all criticism of his regime. The following year, however, Rhee met his downfall. Popular dissatisfaction with the president was expressed in massive demonstrations by university and high school students. After over one hundred students were killed by police firing point-blank into their crowd, Rhee had no choice but to resign. He was followed by the democratically elected Chang Myŏng (CHAHNG mee-ONG), who was overthrown by a military coup in 1961.

The Pak Chŏnghŏi (PAHK chuhng-hoo-EE; also spelled "Park Chung Hee") era of military rule followed. The "Korean-style democracy," of Pak's junta, lasting from 1961 until 1979, contained no democratic elements. In 1961, South Korea was placed under martial law, and the Korean Central Intelligence Agency (KCIA) was established. By the time martial law was ended in 1963, the KCIA system of domestic and international surveillance was well established. Once order had been established, Pak's priority was economic growth. To that end, he rounded up "illicit profiteers" and adopted a practice from the Chinese Cultural Revolution—convicted businessmen were paraded through the streets, with signs that said, "I am a corrupt swine," "I ate the people," and other denunciations. He also instituted "Export Day," which celebrated family, filial piety, and loyalty. Although one key phrase was "treat employees like family," Pak's success had more to do with industrial planning under the direction of the central Economic Planning Board, a concept borrowed from the colonial Japanese in Manchuria and from postwar Japan.

In the 1970s and 1980s, South Korea underwent a rapid economic growth, labeled an "economic miracle" by several observers. The nation earned an important portion of international trade in the areas of shipbuilding, automobiles, computers, and insurance. Pak supported the economic dominance of **chaebŏl** (JEH-bul)—industrial/banking/marketing combines. These chaebŏl had close ties to the government. Pak's export-oriented approach was not invulnerable to the ups and downs of the global trading cycle, however. In 1972, the combination of recession and depression preceded the declaration of a state of emergency. Pak suspended the constitution and banned all political parties and exercise of civil liberties. In place of the freedoms he had suspended, Pak called for a "revitalizing" (*yushin*) including the new ***"yushin* constitution."** The new order, an obvious dictatorship, was followed by arbitrary arrests, forced confessions under torture, and detentions in prison. Neither politicians, religious leaders, professors, nor students escaped punishment. In response to Pak's repressions, a student movement, supported by intellectuals, workers, and ordinary housewives, gained in momentum. By 1979, demonstrations by students and workers were out of control, and the Pak dictatorship was brought to a violent end. After arguing about political means of bringing dissent under control, Pak's KCIA director shot and killed Pak.

South Korea Enters the U.S. Auto Market

Jockeying for power following Pak's assassination led to victory of yet another junta under General Chŏn Tuhwan (CHON doo-WAHN; also spelled "Chun Doo-hwan," b. 1931), more state repression, and another round of demonstrations. The 1980 Gwangju (GWAHNG-joo, also spelled Kwangju) uprising began with student demonstrations against martial law and led to an insurrection during which Gwangju citizens seized weapons in order to drive out paratroopers responsible for atrocities. Within little more than a week, up to 2000 people had been killed. The leading opposition leader, Kim Taejung (KIM DEH-joong; also spelled "Kim Dae Jung," b. 1925), was sentenced to death. Under Chŏn there were some reforms such as the abolition of a curfew existing since the Korean War and of school uniforms that had been introduced by the Japanese colonial government. However, the pattern of state repression, including torture and violent popular unrest, continued.

The people's, or *minjung*, movement, which began to take shape in the early 1970s, was a leading force in political activism. The movement provided an organizational force not only for intellectuals, students, and workers, who had already been active, but also for members of the new white-collar class. Chŏn, who was to become the most hated leader in postwar South Korean history, responded by throwing journalists, civil servants, labor organizers, teachers, and all others suspected of sedition into "purification camps" where they were starved and beaten. The "Korean Model" of economic success was based on such state control, but by the mid-1980s, the Chŏn regime was challenged by

chaebŏl—Korean economic conglomerates similar to Japanese *zaibatsu* before World War II.

***yushin* constitution**—Constitution written by Pak's government in 1972 that guaranteed Pak a permanent position as the president. Pak was assassinated in 1979, and the *yushin* constitution was replaced in 1980.

◀ The Japanese military's sexual exploitation of Korean women as "comfort women" during World War II continues to influence Korea's relations with Japan. Two former Korean "comfort women" protest against proposed textbooks for Japanese middle-school children that give little coverage to wartime atrocities.

labor unrest, and many Korean youths were committing suicide as a form of protest.

In 1987, a year before the Olympics were set to open in Seoul, Chŏn provoked another crisis by selecting a successor—and a general at that. Rioting ensued, but it was pacified by the desire to show the world that Korea could handle a massive undertaking like the Olympics. Repression abated as No Tae'u (NOH TEH-oo; also spelled "Roh Tae-woo," b. 1932) the new president, calmed dissent. Greater economic and social liberalization accompanied the growth of personal income and Koreans' increasing identification as part of the middle class. In 1993, Kim Yŏngsam (KIM yong-SAHM; also spelled "Kim Young-sam," b. 1927) became South Korea's first civilian president in 30 years. He had former presidents No and Chŏn arrested for corruption and attempted many democratic reforms, but the Asian economic crisis hit during his last year in office. Kim Taejung, once sentenced to death, was elected president in 1997. Kim Taejung was hampered by a strongly entrenched opposition and the continuing Asian economic disaster. International bailouts were necessary to keep South Korea afloat. In addition, relations with Japan—with whom Korea hosted the World Cup of Football (soccer) in the summer of 2002—remained rocky. Korean women who had been abused as "comfort women" by Japanese troops during World War II gained neither an apology nor compensation for their suffering. Japanese textbooks minimizing atrocities during the war have also caused outrage in Korea. Kim Taejung nevertheless continued to try to improve relations.

One long-term problem, relations between the South and North, began to be addressed. Kim Taejung and Kim Jongil began talks to open contacts between Seoul and Pyŏngyang in 2000 as part of South Korea's **"Sunshine Policy,"** for which the South Korean president won the Nobel Peace Prize. After that, there were family visits and improved relations. In 2003, however, the North declared it had nuclear weapons capability, precipitating a worsening of diplomatic relations. The ROK government under current president Roh Moo Hyun (ROH MOO hee-OON) would like to continue improving relations, a difficult task in light of North Korea's nuclear ambitions.

DOCUMENT
North-South Korean Accord

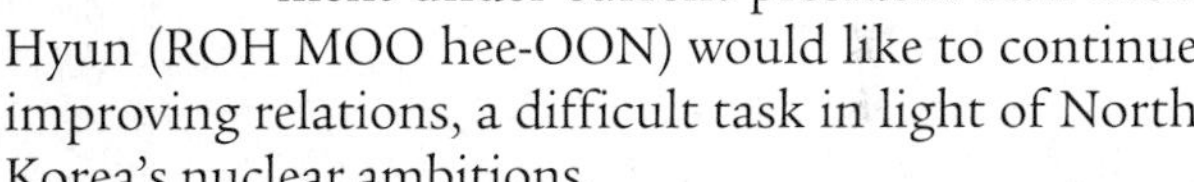

South Korea faces a number of crucial issues in the future, including its relations with the North, the need to improve the status of women, and the recovery, after 60 years, from the humiliation of colonialism.

Southeast Asia

What were the roles of nationalism, ethnicity, ideology, and religion in the building of Southeast Asian nations in the post-World War II era?

One of the first indications that the whole structure of European imperialism would quickly collapse came in the late 1940s when Indonesian nationalists demanded a complete break with the Netherlands and forces for independence began their drive for freedom in Indochina.

MAP
Modern Southeast Asia

Indonesia

Immediately after Japan's surrender, independence fighters Achmed Sukarno and Mohammed Hatta proclaimed Indonesia's independence on August 17, 1945. But the Dutch would not leave, and the United States and Great Britain initially supported the return of the Dutch. An ugly war against the Dutch colonial masters then broke out. Finally in 1949, through UN mediation,

---

Sunshine Policy—South Korean investment in North Korea, encouragement of visits by South Koreans to northern family members; President Kim Taejung received the Nobel Peace Prize for the Sunshine Policy.

▲ The states of East and Southeast Asia wield considerable influence in world politics and economies.

the Netherlands East Indies formally became the Republic of Indonesia, achieving nationhood at roughly the same time as the states of India and Israel. Although it is the biggest and potentially richest nation in Southeast Asia, Indonesia has enjoyed little tranquility since it gained independence.

Indonesia, whose population of 245 million makes it the fourth largest country in the world, is 87 percent Muslim but encompasses a mixture of many cultures on more than 3000 islands, ranging from hunter-gatherers to urban professionals and intellectuals. Complicating the situation is the prominence of the Chinese minority. Chinese Indonesians, making up less than 3 percent of Indonesia's population, control two-thirds of the nation's economy. Anti-Chinese riots and plots against the central government in Java have arisen in various places.

For the first 15 years after independence, Indonesia experienced inflation, food shortages, and declining exports. Its population increased while its economy declined. A large portion of the blame for this situation rested with Indonesia's flamboyant president, Achmed Sukarno. He contracted huge Russian loans for arms, fought a costly guerrilla campaign against Malaysia, confiscated foreign businesses, and wasted money on expensive, flashy enterprises. Sukarno had come to power as a prominent leader in the preindependence nationalist movement. After experimenting with what he called "guided democracy" in the 1950s, Sukarno assumed dictatorial power in 1959 and declared himself president for life in 1963.

Muslim students in Indonesia triggered the events that led to Sukarno's downfall. After an attempted communist coup in 1965, they launched attacks on Indonesians they believed to have communist connections. The Chinese minority was targeted, and 500,000 to 750,000 people were executed or killed during several months of lawlessness. The army's chief of staff, General T. N. J. Suharto, who put down the coup, became effective head of state and in March 1968 officially became president.

Suharto initially installed a more Western-oriented government and, in return, received substantial American aid for the country. He rehabilitated the Indonesian economy by continuing Sukarno's "guided democracy" and developed highly successful literacy programs. But over the next 25 years, Suharto's military regime engaged in several violent incidents. In 1971 and again in 1974, there were serious racial outbursts during which thousands of students went on rampages, looting and damaging Chinese shops and homes. The Indonesians invaded East Timor, the Portuguese half of one of its islands, in 1975 and initiated a savage occupation that led to the death of over 200,000 people. During the 1970s, some 30,000 political dissidents were imprisoned, while rampant corruption dominated government, the civil service, and business. Enormous wealth remained concentrated in the hands of a few individuals.

The end of Suharto's regime was reminiscent of its beginning. Indonesia shared in a radical slowdown of East Asian economies that began in 1997. As economic discontent simmered, mass demonstrations of Indonesian students turned violent. The students demanded democratization, an end to government corruption, new elections, and the ouster of Suharto. As in the earlier crises, violence was both random and directed at the economically privileged Chinese minority. Terrified shopkeepers painted notices on the fronts of their buildings saying they were "good Muslims" or Hindus, in other words, not Chinese. In 1998, in the midst of mass protests and widespread looting and burning, Suharto was forced to step down. The Indonesian students celebrated his resignation as a victory over autocracy. Since 1998, Indonesia has had four presidents, including Megawati Sukarnoputri, daughter of Sukarno. In 2004, Susilo Bambang Yudhoyono was elected president.

A series of national liberation movements, combined with the downturn in the economy, placed huge challenges to the leadership of this important country. The territory of East Timor conducted an August 1999 plebiscite in which 98 percent of the people voted; 80 percent opted for independence. A group of quasi-independent militias took issues into their own hands and began a campaign of terror against the people of East Timor. The resulting murders and rapes moved the international community, acting through the United Nations, to send a force to restore calm.

The tragic success of the East Timorese prompted other groups in the 17,000-island archipelago to seek greater autonomy or outright independence. Rebel groups in the Aceh (AH-cheh) province of Sumatra challenged Jakarta for years. Along with the suffering caused by the insurgency and the central government's harsh efforts to suppress it, Aceh was the site of additional sorrow in December 2004, when the Asian tsunami devastated Aceh, wiping out numerous towns and villages—at least 100,000 were killed and $4 billion of damage was done by the tsunami. The following year, the Aceh rebels, their mood perhaps altered by the tsunami and the aid that followed in its wake, reached a peace agreement with the Indonesian government. In May 2006, another massive earthquake rocked Java, causing $3 billion in damages. Natural disasters and domestic turmoil have hit Indonesian society and economy very hard. Its per capital GDP was just $3600 in 2006.

	Indonesia and Malaysia
1949	Independence of Indonesia
1950s	Sukarno's "guided democracy" policy in Indonesia
1963	Independence of Malaysia
1965	Anti-Sukarno coup; rise of Suharto in Indonesia
1981	Mahathir assumes power in Malaysia
1998	Suharto forced out; democratic elections instituted in Indonesia

Malaysia

Created out of former British holdings, the Federation of Malaysia was admitted into the British Commonwealth in 1957. In 1963, it became independent and immediately faced Sukarno-sponsored guerrilla attacks. As in Indonesia, a major problem in Malaysia was the country's racial mix and the resulting hostilities. The largest group (45 percent of the population) is Malay and Muslim, but the mainly Buddhist Chinese (35 percent) hold the majority of the wealth, and what they do not control is owned largely by the small Hindu Indian minority (10 percent). In the late 1960s and early 1970s, Malays attacked the other two groups, and ethnoreligious conflicts continue to plague the region.

Political organizations are structured around ethnicity: the dominant United Malays National Organization (UMNO); the Malayan Chinese Association (MCA); and the Malayan Indian Congress (MIC). The three formed the Alliance party, which held power until 1969. Thereafter, sectarian riots tore them apart, and UMNO demanded precedence. After 1989, the Alliance was reconstituted.

Mohamad Mahathir (moh-HAH-mahd MAH-hahteer), prime minister from 1981 to 2003, attempted to impose calm on the ethnic conflicts and maintain a fiscal balance. He called on Malaysians to "Look East"—that is, to Japan and not to the United States or Europe.

However, at the end of the 1990s, the Asian economic crash deeply affected Malaysia as it did other Asian countries. Since then, the Islamic majority of the country—most of the world's Muslims live in South and Southeast Asia, not the Middle East—has attempted to increase its influence in the country in ways ranging from the use of Islamic law in the regions it controls to the requirement that women wear the veil. Malaysia and Indonesia, like other countries in the region, are working out the dynamics of democratic versus theocratic rule in the contexts of rapidly changing economics and ethnoreligious tensions of long standing. Malaysia's economy has rebounded since the late 1990s crash, and per capital GDP today stands at about $13,000. Nevertheless, the government under Prime Minister Abdullah bin Ahmad Badawi (ahb-DOO-la bin AH-mad bah-DAH-wee) faces continuing problems, including a high birth rate, trafficking in women and children, and some disputes over territory with its neighbors.

Thailand

Intellectuals and others in Thailand have struggled to create a truly democratic society for almost a century, while affluence and a benevolent monarchy have moderated the demands for rule by elected officials.

From the era of the nineteenth century's reforming King Chulalongkorn through the reign of his successors, monarchs have been esteemed by the public and, in return, have tried to maintain a balance of authority among the National Assembly, the educated bureaucracy, and a military that has often been modern in its outlook. Following World War II—when Thailand supported Japan—the National Assembly attempted to rule by a coalition of civilian interests. But the governing coalition was fragile, and after eight cabinets and five prime ministers in just 2 years, the military in 1947 staged the first of more than 30 coups they would carry out in the next 40 years. After each coup, King Bhumibol would give his approval, and the new coalition, usually led by military men, would begin their rule with high favorability ratings, soon to plummet as promises of progressive reform and clean government were broken time and again.

After a return to a democratically elected prime minister in 1988, the military staged a coup in 1991 that was roundly denounced by Thai intellectuals. Democracy began to creep back in during the 1990s, but the collapse of Thailand's economy during the Asian economic crisis slowed these efforts.

Vietnam

Japanese forces moved into Vietnam, Laos, and Cambodia in July 1941. Though they maintained a military presence until the last months of the war, they did not assume any role in civil administration, which remained in French hands. The emperor remained in place in Annam and Tonkin. Meanwhile, Ho Chi Minh contacted Americans to collaborate against the Japanese. Unknown to Vietnamese independence fighters, the United States was not prepared to back up Ho when he declared Vietnam's independence in September 1945. Rather, the United States and its World War II allies agreed to let China accept Japan's surrender in the northern part of Vietnam and Britain to accept it in the southern part. Soon the French reasserted control over the hapless Vietnamese.

	Vietnam
1945–1954	Anticolonial war against France
1954	Geneva Conference; founding of Republic of Vietnam (South Vietnam)
1960	Creation of National Liberation Front
1964	Gulf of Tonkin Incident, escalation of U.S. war in Vietnam
1973	Withdrawal of U.S. forces
1975	Reunification of Vietnam
1994	United States and Vietnam restore diplomatic relations

Fighting a losing war with Vietnamese who wanted their country's independence, the French set up Bao Dai as the monarch of Vietnam. Ho Chi Minh's Democratic Republic of Vietnam (DRV) was recognized by the Soviet Union and the PRC in 1948, and the United States decided that Vietnam was now part of the Cold War. The United States threw its support to France, offering massive funding and other forms of aid. In March 1954, Vietnamese forces, now increasingly Communist, decisively defeated France at Dienbienphu. France called for an international meeting to end its colonial occupation of Vietnam. The conference at Geneva, Switzerland, was attended by Britain, the USSR, France, China, the DRV, and Laos and Cambodia. The United States attended as an observer so that it need not feel bound to accept the terms of the conference. The conference called for a cease-fire at the 17th parallel and elections within 2 years. France left Vietnam, but elections never took place. The temporary armistice line hardened into a long-lasting boundary between two countries, the DRV (North Vietnam) and the Republic of Vietnam (South Vietnam).

The United States then supported a succession of leaders in the South as Vietnam became a pawn in the Cold War. On a more-or-less belligerent footing, liberties were suppressed, though a democratic artistic culture did begin to emerge for a while in the South. In the North, Ho Chi Minh suppressed those he deemed "class enemies."

The ruler of South Vietnam, Ngo Dinh Diem (NOH DIN zee-EM) favored his family members, Catholics, and sycophants and ignored the pressing problems of the countryside. Buddhist reformers, as well as secular, leftist opponents of the regime who came together in the National Liberation Front (NLF), stepped up pressure against Diem. Viewing the struggle in Vietnam as part of the global communist threat, President Kennedy sent 11,000 troops to Vietnam. In the next decade, the number of U.S. troops reached 543,000, and large amounts of modern munitions—including aircraft, defoliants, and bombs—were used against the NLF, now joined by North Vietnamese forces. The Soviets and the PRC helped to supply the communist forces. Life in both the North and the South was brutal. Recognizing the United States could not win, President Nixon negotiated an end to the U.S. involvement in 1973. In 1975, Northern forces moved into the South and defeated the South Vietnamese state. The first years of a reunited Vietnam were focused on rebuilding the chemically polluted, mercilessly bombed-out country. At the same time, bitter reprisals against southerners began. Many fled, especially those who were ethnically Chinese. By 1986, exhausted, the Vietnamese Communist party adopted a program of economic liberalization similar to China's Four Modernizations.

The communist government in Hanoi embarked on a policy of maintaining its ideological base and political stability while opening to the world economic community. But ideology began to erode, and the communist government periodically shifted from greater openness to greater repression. Vietnam also lost technological and economic assistance with the end of the USSR in 1991. The Asian financial crisis at the end of the 1990s temporarily stalled economic growth, but since 2000, Vietnam has returned to a pattern of improvement. In March of that year, William Cohen, the U.S. secretary of defense at that time, led a high-level delegation to Vietnam to discuss the question of American prisoners of war and those declared missing in action during the war. Discussions also extended to commercial contacts and possible limited military cooperation. Ties with the United States have improved greatly. In addition to formal diplomatic relations achieved under President Clinton, President George W. Bush normalized trade relations in 2002. Vietnam's economy is rapidly growing, but per capita GDP still hovers around $3100 (in 2006). Continuing problems include outbreaks of avian flu. In addition, freedom of expression is not universally guaranteed, although artists have increasing latitude to express themselves. In 2006, Nguyen Minh Triet became president and Nguyen Tan Dung, prime minister.

Cambodia

After the Khmer Rouge genocidal attacks on the urban classes that led to the deaths of over 2 million people from 1975 to 1979, Cambodia has made slow but steady progress. The UN-sponsored elections in 1993 brought back something close to a normal political life under the Cambodian monarch King Norodom Sihanouk (NOR-oh-dom SEE-hah-nook)—who reigned from 1953 to 2004—and Prime Minister Hun Sen. Sihanouk's son Sihamoni (SEE-ha-MOH-nee) follows in his father's footsteps. The country has regained some of its former tourist trade, and it is this that led to annual economic improvements until 1997, when the Asian financial crisis made its effects felt. In 1998, the remnants of the Khmer Rouge surrendered and another successful election was held. For the first time in 30 years, the country enjoyed living in a state of peace, but its GDP remains low, at $2600 per capita in 2006. Sex trafficking in girls and women is a serious problem. Like its neighbors, Cambodia has experienced outbreaks of avian flu.

Myanmar (Burma)

Myanmar (Burma) has been run by a military junta since 1991. It is principally known for its extremely profitable trade in illegal drugs and a high rate of AIDS—some 500,000 out of the 41 million population. Economic indices become less than dependable in the face of the extremely active black market operating in the country, but 2006 figures indicate a per capita GDP of $1800. The Nobel Peace Prize Laureate Aung San Suu Kyi (OWNG SAN SOO KEE), who has struggled for democracy in her country, has been under house arrest for much of the time since 1991. Myanmar is the world's second largest producer of opium.

The Philippines

The Philippines since World War II have had a complex relationship with the United States. For almost half a century, the United States ruled the Philippines as a colony. In 1946, the country became politically independent—though militarily and economically dominated by the United States for the next 20 years. Wealthy families dominated the democratically elected government, postponing the necessary changes to overcome poverty, rural landlessness, and underdevelopment. While Manila and other cities became showcases of modernity, other sectors lagged. When Ferdinand Marcos and his wife Imelda took power in 1965, he instituted a policy he called "constitutional authoritarianism." His authoritarian rule was hardened in 1972 when he declared martial law. Unfortunately, U.S. presidents, fearful of the spread of communism, supported the Marcos dictatorship. His wife was put in charge of building Manila, and in the process the two Marcoses plundered the Philippines economy, while ruling with an iron fist. Communist and Islamic insurgencies developed under this repression. Finally, in the 1980s, even business interests in the Philippines were alienated from the Marcoses, and together with religious interests, the poor, the intellectuals, and brave people throughout the islands, they ousted Marcos.

Marcos was forced from office in 1986 by the "People Power" election of Corazon Aquino, widow of the heroic opposition leader murdered by Marcos's forces in 1983. The built-up resentment against Marcos and his U.S. backers as well as volcanic eruptions led to the Americans' closing their last base in the Philippines in 1992. Since then, the country has made considerable economic progress. Throughout the 1990s, the Philippines maintained a favorable balance of trade. Politically, factionalism within the government led to the unseating of Joseph Estrada, who was elected in 1998, in 2001. More than 100,000 of his opponents demonstrated in the streets for his removal from office on the grounds of massive corruption. When the leaders of the armed forces joined them, Estrada left office, to be succeeded by his vice president, Gloria Macapagal Arroyo, who was reelected president in 2004.

◄ Philippine President Gloria Macapagal Arroyo addresses her people as she arrives at the presidential palace for the first time in January 2001.

The Subcontinent

What role did ethnicity and religion play in the formation of new nations in South Asia after 1947?

In the Indian subcontinent, the western thrust of the Japanese armies in World War II and the appeal of Subhas Chandra Bose's alliance with Japan against Britain induced the British government to negotiate with Indian nationalist leaders. In 1942, Britain offered India independence and the option of joining the British Commonwealth when the war ended. But Gandhi called this a "postdated cheque on a failing bank" and called for a forceful "Quit India" movement. During and immediately after the war, tensions between the Muslim and Hindu populations in India, which had been compounded by the British administration, were inflamed. The minority Muslim population was fearful that when the British withdrew, it would be targeted and dominated by the Hindu majority.

Partition

When World War II ended and it became apparent that the British would indeed leave India, the shape the new state would take was vigorously contested. The Indian National Congress, founded in 1885 and the primary Indian nationalist organization, had had great success in the 1936–1937 elections and took the lead in negotiations for independence with the British government. Congress included many Muslim members, but in the late 1930s the Muslim League, guided by onetime Congress member Muhammad Ali Jinnah, began to agitate vigorously for separate Muslim seats, though not at first for a separate Muslim state. Muslims constituted one-fifth of the population of the subcontinent, and many Muslims feared majority Hindu rule. Gandhi had envisioned an independent India where all communal groups shared in governance and lived in harmony. But India had a long history of ethnic hostilities dating to the medieval era.

Indian Declaration of Independence

Gandhi: Against the Partition of India

This religious animosity and mistrust, the presence of armed, demobilized World War II soldiers in the countryside, and the insecurity produced by negotiations over the future nature of the Indian state resulted in communal violence and chaos in some provinces as the British prepared to leave India. Jinnah sought strength for his vision of "Pakistan"—a collection of Muslim-majority provinces within a unified India and equal voice for Muslims and Hindus. This would weaken the central government while strengthening the provinces.

Jinnah, the "Father" of Pakistan

Jawaharlal Nehru, the leader of the Congress party, rejected this proposal in favor of a strong central state that would encourage economic development. Talks broke down, and violent riots broke out. Thousands were killed as Hindus, Muslims, and now Sikhs took to the streets. The Muslim League decided to support a separate state.

Lord Mountbatten arrived in India as British viceroy in March 1947 to help settle the turmoil but promptly determined that the date for British withdrawal should be moved up. Although the Muslim League's demand for a separate state called Pakistan did not represent the wishes of all Muslims, Mountbatten was persuaded that India must be partitioned along religious lines. Accordingly, when the British withdrew, they divided the subcontinent into Hindu and Muslim sectors. On August 12, 1947, they handed over the reins of government to two new sovereign states, India and Pakistan. India was a huge nation comprising most of the subcontinent. The new Muslim state of Pakistan consisted, awkwardly, of two chunks of land separated by 1000 miles of Indian territory. Although Jinnah was not satisfied with the land allocated to the new state, he had little choice but to accept the British division. As it turned out, however, the borders drawn in 1947 would not be final.

The Tandon Family at Partition

Defining the boundaries of the new states was not easily accomplished. For one thing, the British had not directly ruled all of India. Nearly 600 Indian princes were governing about 40 percent of the subcontinent in autonomous or semiautonomous states. These principalities, based primarily on timeworn landlord-client relations and peasant labor, had to be incorporated into the new political entities. The boundary lines of the two new nations, which took months to formalize, also sacrificed existing economic, ethnic, and linguistic affinities in order to ensure religious divisions. Partition radically disrupted long-standing patterns of commerce, social relations, and people's day-to-day lives. As occurred with the drawing of new national boundaries in the Middle East, families were separated—some members residing in one state, while others nearby resided in another.

As the boundaries were drawn, many Indians, fearful of discrimination and communal violence, left their homes: Muslims to migrate or flee to Pakistan and Hindus to the new state of India. Millions became refugees. Hundreds of thousands died in the relocation process or in the riots, killings, and panic produced by the hastily imposed partition. This terrible slaughter is engraved in the memories of the citizens of the two nations and has contributed to the continuation of communal violence. One example of the chaos and instability created out of this ill-conceived slashing of new national boundaries is the princely state of Jammu and Kashmir. Jammu and Kashmir had an overwhelmingly Muslim population but a Hindu ruler who had submitted to the British crown; furthermore, it was located in the wide swath of contested borderlands between the two proposed states. Although Kashmir was ultimately allocated to the new state of India, that allocation has been contested on and off ever since partition. Kashmir remains a critical source of conflict in the tense relationship between India and Pakistan. Following the shedding of much blood over Kashmir, serious negotiations between India and Pakistan began in 2004.

DOCUMENT
Women in Karimpur, India

Partition had additional painful consequences. Thousands of women were raped and kidnapped, to be distributed as spoils of war. The two governments attempted to right this wrong by repatriating these women to their "rightful" country. But their former families often did not want them back and many of the women themselves had made new families, so the problem could not be easily resolved. Another painful outcome was the murder of Mahatma Gandhi on January 30, 1948, by a Hindu nationalist. In subsequent years, violent Hindu nationalism would challenge India's democracy.

India: The World's Largest Democracy

After independence, India's parliament functioned with little friction. This success was due to the efforts of a cadre of very skilled and capable men in the Congress party (see Chapter 29). One of them was Jawaharlal Nehru, the country's first prime minister, who held that office from 1947 to 1964 and was an Anglophile of sorts and an ardent devotee of democratic government. Nehru asserted the power of strong central government while trying to manage the decentralizing tendencies of his large, polyglot, multiethnic state. He sought to maintain close relations with both the Soviet Union and China, often to the discomfort of the United States. Relations with China, however, were compromised by a border conflict that led to a major military action in the first part of the 1960s and acted as a drain on India's economy. Nehru, along with Egypt's President Nasser and Yugoslavian President Tito, was a founder of the **Nonaligned Nations Movement,** which aimed to avoid commitment to either the United States or the Soviet Union in the context of the Cold War. Through this movement, states like India hoped to assert their autonomy and to have a real voice in world affairs.

Nehru's daughter, Indira Gandhi (no relation to Mohandas Gandhi), was elected prime minister in

---

Nonaligned Nations Movement—Organization of approximately 100 countries not formally allied with a major power bloc. Founded in 1961, the movement struggles to find relevance in a post–Cold War era.

India After Independence	
1947	Independence from Britain
1947–1964	Jawaharlal Nehru, prime minister
1966	Indira Gandhi, Nehru's daughter, becomes prime minister
1971	India defeats Pakistan; Bangladesh formed
1975	Indira Gandhi declares emergency, assumes dictatorial powers
1977	Moraji Desai, prime minister
1979	Indira Gandhi reelected
1984	Gandhi assassinated; son Rajiv succeeds her
1991	Rajiv Gandhi assassinated
1998	Bharatiya Janata (BJP), Hindu nationalist party, wins elections
2004	Congress under Sonia Gandhi's leadership wins elections; Manmohan Singh becomes prime minister

1966. The Congress party hoped to use her, as Nehru's daughter and a well-loved and highly visible public figure, to guarantee its position of power. But she proved to be less malleable than Congress leaders had expected and moved to consolidate her own power and achieve a new political stability for India. Her popularity reached a peak with the defeat of Pakistan in a 1971 war that led to the creation of the country of Bangladesh out of East Pakistan. From 1972 to 1974, however, India's mildly socialist economy was battered by serious crop failures, food riots, strikes, and student unrest. In the face of mounting opposition, and claiming to act in defense of national unity, Gandhi declared a state of emergency in June 1975 and took over direct control of the government. She jailed 10,000 of her critics, imposed press censorship, and suspended fundamental civil rights.

With the opposition muzzled, the people were exhorted to "work more and talk less." After a year, the new order claimed numerous gains, advances in productivity, a drop in inflation, curbs in the black market, and more widespread birth control measures to alleviate India's population pressures. Although Gandhi declared that her drastic measures were only temporary, some critics observed that she was trying to move "from dictatorship to dynasty."

Although India achieved a certain economic success and political prominence under Indira Gandhi, it also faced serious ethnic and communal conflicts. In the south and in Sri Lanka, the culturally and linguistically distinct Tamils agitated for independence. In the north, the religiously and linguistically distinct Sikhs, who constitute a majority in the state of Punjab, also entertained separatist aspirations.

The Sikh religion dates to the early sixteenth century, when the mystic Nanak founded a monotheistic creed that was influenced by both Hinduism and Islam. The Sikhs, whose territories were divided in the 1947 partition, had a golden temple in their sacred city of Amritsar. When Sikh extremists took over and occupied the temple in 1984, Gandhi sent in the army to blast them out. This reckless act was considered a desecration of the Sikh temple and led to an explosion of rioting and violence. In October of that year Gandhi was assassinated by members of her Sikh bodyguard.

Indira Gandhi was succeeded by her son Rajiv, a former pilot and political novice who soon showed a surprising degree of confidence and competence in governing the world's largest democracy, with more than 800 million citizens. Rajiv consolidated his political position and moved India toward a more Westernized, capitalist orientation. Still, the country's widespread poverty, exploding population, and internal divisions, especially the long-standing Kashmir border dispute with Pakistan and the continued challenges of Sikh and Tamil separatism, posed significant problems for Gandhi's administration. He was defeated in elections at the end of 1989 and replaced by V. P. Singh of the National Front party, which proved unable to consolidate its power. In 1991, new elections returned the Congress party to power, but not before Rajiv Gandhi was assassinated by a Tamil separatist.

After independence, the Indian government had pursued Mohandas Gandhi's ideal of self-sufficiency. It insisted on indigenous control of the economy and emphasized developing the production of consumer goods at home rather than relying on imports. It demanded 51 percent Indian control of foreign companies on its soil, even refusing to let the Coca-Cola Company operate in India unless it shared its secret formula. In these efforts, India was relatively successful, developing many locally produced goods. During the first half of the 1990s, however, Indian leaders abandoned many of the socialist foundations of their economic structure and introduced various aspects of the capitalist market economy. Analysts had pointed out during the 1980s that India possessed the largest essentially untapped middle-class market in the world. With the entry of market forces into the country, the Indian economy expanded. The countryside had gained self-sufficiency in the 1970s and 1980s. Now it was the turn of the cities and the business community to become major players in the international economy.

In 1995, P. V. Narasimha Rao was the only prime minister not in the bloodline of the Nehru-Gandhi dynasty to have lasted through the first half of a parliamentary term. Working with his finance minister, Manmohan Singh, and enjoying the total support of the business community, he continued to pursue market reforms. India's economy continued to grow under the changes in the central government in the 1990s.

As the large cities of India developed an upwardly mobile and cosmopolitan middle class, those same cities have seen their infrastructures overwhelmed by population growth, in-migration from the countryside, and air pollution produced by industrialization and the increasing numbers of the middle classes who own motorized vehicles. Delhi and Mumbai, for example, are crammed with squatters' huts that have become permanent settlements. Large swathes of huts, in places like public parks and along railroad tracks, are periodically bulldozed. Thousands of residents then either promptly rebuild them or are forced into the streets to search for living space elsewhere. Although municipal governments try to regulate the movement of trucks, the large numbers of diesel-powered vehicles create air pollution that has increased the incidence of respiratory and heart disease, even among the young.

The communal hostilities inflamed by partition have not ended half a century after independence. The constitution of India aimed to make all citizens equal before the law. All Indians were entitled to receive an education in their own language and in the language of the state, Hindi. But caste, class, and communal differences (as elsewhere in the world) were not so readily eradicated. Upper-caste Hindus resisted privileges, such as guaranteed slots in university and civil service positions, given by the government to the members of the Untouchable caste. In response, the **Untouchables,** taking the name *Dalits* ("the oppressed"), organized politically.

Modern South Asia

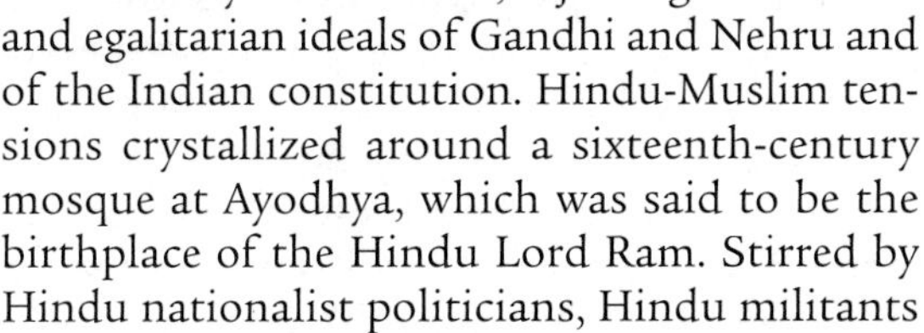

In the 1980s, Hindu parties mobilized to make India an indelibly Hindu state, rejecting the secular and egalitarian ideals of Gandhi and Nehru and of the Indian constitution. Hindu-Muslim tensions crystallized around a sixteenth-century mosque at Ayodhya, which was said to be the birthplace of the Hindu Lord Ram. Stirred by Hindu nationalist politicians, Hindu militants tore the mosque down by hand in 1992, prompting further intercommunal violence. In the 1996 elections, the Hindu nationalist Bharatiya Janata party (bah-RAH-tee-ya jah-NAH-tah; BJP), representing business and entrepreneurial interests, won 186 seats in parliament, up from only two seats in 1984. In 1998, the BJP won the Indian elections, prompting new fears that Muslims, Sikhs, and other minorities would suffer under Hindu rule. Shortly after coming to power, the BJP enhanced its popularity among Indians and sent a message of warning to China and Pakistan when it set off a series of nuclear bomb tests. In so doing, India initially alienated its Western allies but staked its claim as a major power for the next century. Prime Minister Vajpayee (Vahj-PAH-yee) of the BJP, however, began to move toward better relations with Pakistan, especially over the issue of Kashmir, and supported modern high-tech development in the years before the BJP's defeat at the polls in 2004. The Congress party was returned to power with Manmohan Singh (mahn-MOH-hahn SING) as prime minister, and though it promised greater assistance to the poor, who were left behind as the Indian economy boomed in recent years, the trend of increasing internationalization and economic growth is likely to continue.

Untouchables—Persons outside the four *varnas,* historically employed in leatherwork, burials, and similar occupations.

Pakistan

Pakistan's two distant parts had religion in common but not language or culture. When Jinnah, the primary voice for the creation of Pakistan and its constitutional government, died in 1948, the artificially constructed state splintered as each region pursued its own local agenda. Meanwhile, Pakistan had to contend with challenges on its borders with India and Afghanistan. In a broader frame, Pakistan joined U.S.-backed alliances to contain the Soviet Union and, in return, benefited from U.S. aid.

In 1958, General Mohammad Ayub Khan came to power. His regime gave Pakistan reasonable stability and some relief from corrupt politicians, and under his tutelage, the country made economic progress. Ten years later, however, pent-up dissatisfaction against corruption in the government led to a new military dictatorship under General Yahya Khan. Regionalism continued to be a major problem. The more prosperous West Pakistan dominated and exploited East Pakistan, and the East's grievances escalated into riots and threats of secession.

The Pakistani government sent troops into East Pakistan in 1971 in response to an uprising. This attack and the depredations committed by the troops caused an influx of East Pakistani refugees into India. India intervened on behalf of East Pakistan, defeating the central government's forces and encouraging the region to break away. In 1972, East Pakistan became the new state of Bangladesh. Bangladesh, covering an area not much larger than the state of Arkansas, was an instantaneous economic disaster with twice the population density of Japan. The Bangladeshi population in 2000 was approximately 130 million (about half the population of the United States), while the per capita GNP was a mere $260. Like Indonesia, Bangladesh is home to a significant percentage of the

Document

Benazir Bhutto at Harvard

Benazir Bhutto became Pakistan's first female prime minister in 1988. She came from an elite Muslim family and had led a life of wealth and privilege. Her father, elected president by popular mandate in 1970, was executed in 1979 by the military dictator Zia ul-Haq (1977–1988). In Pakistan, Benazir Bhutto's election held the promise of a new era of democracy and progress. In the West, she was viewed as a leader likely to modernize, Westernize, and ally her nation with the United States. She had, after all, attended Radcliffe College, Harvard University. Bhutto's memoirs provide interesting insight into the Western-style education many prominent South Asians received; they also suggest the dilemma of being a "foreign" student abroad during an era of political turmoil for both Pakistan and the United States.

I was born in Karachi on June 21, 1953.... In our house education was a top priority. Like his father before him, my father wanted to make examples of us, the next generation of educated and progressive Pakistanis. At three I was sent to Lady Jennings Nursery School, then at five to one of the top schools in Karachi, the Convent of Jesus and Mary. Instruction at CJM was in English, the language we spoke at home more often than my parents' native languages of Sindhi and Persian or the national language, Urdu. And though the Irish nuns who taught there divided the older students into houses with inspirational names like "Discipline," "Courtesy," "Endeavor," and "Service," they made no effort to convert us to Christianity....

There was no question in my family that my sister and I would be given the same opportunities in life as our brothers. Nor was there in Islam. We learned at an early age that it was men's interpretation of our religion that restricted women's opportunities, not our religion itself....

[Bhutto's father was determined that she study abroad (he himself had studied at Berkeley) and at the age of sixteen she was admitted to Radcliffe.]

... "Pak-i-stan? Where's Pak-i-stan?" My new classmates had asked me when I first arrived at Radcliffe. "Pakistan is the largest Muslim country in the world," I replied, sounding like a handout from our embassy. "There are two wings of Pakistan separated by India." "Oh, India," came the relieved response, "You're next to India." I smarted every time I heard the reference to India, with whom we had had two bitter wars. Pakistan was supposed to be one of America's strongest allies.... Yet Americans seemed completely unaware of the existence of my country.

[In 1970, Bhutto's father was elected president, and the union between East and West Pakistan began to break down. In March 1971 the Pakistani army attacked the East Pakistani rebels.] Looting. Rape. Kidnappings. Murder. Whereas no one had cared about Pakistan when I arrived at Harvard, now everyone did. And the condemnation of my country was universal. At first I refused to believe the accounts of the Western press of atrocities being committed by our army in what the East Bengal rebels were now calling Bangladesh. According to the government-controlled Pakistani papers my parents sent me every week, the brief rebellion had been quelled. What were these charges then, that Dacca had been burned to the ground and firing squads sent into the university to execute students, teachers, poets, novelists, doctors and lawyers? I shook my head in disbelief.... I found security in the official jingoistic line in our part of the world that the reports in the Western press were "exaggerated" and a "Zionist Plot" against an Islamic state. My classmates at Harvard were harder to convince. "Your army is barbaric," the accusations would come.... "You people are fascist dictators."... "We are fighting an Indian-backed insurgency," I'd lash back. "We are fighting to hold our country together, just as you did during your own Civil War." How many times since have I asked God to forgive me for my ignorance. I didn't see then that the democratic mandate for Pakistan had been grossly violated. The majority province of East Pakistan was basically treated as a colony by the minority West.... Eighty percent of government jobs were filled by people from the West. The central government had even declared Urdu our national language, a language few in East Pakistan understood, further handicapping the Bengalis in competing for jobs in government or education.... I was too young and naïve at Harvard to understand that the Pakistani army was capable of committing the same atrocities as any army let loose in a civilian population. The psychology can be deadly, as it was when U.S. forces massacred innocent civilians in My Lai [Vietnam] in 1968.

Questions to Consider

1. Bhutto's memoir was published in 1989. How might that affect her portrayal of herself, her father, and her country and its conflicts?
2. Why would an elite Muslim family send its children to an English-language missionary school in Pakistan and to college in the United States?
3. What does this excerpt suggest about the ways a foreigner like Bhutto could and could not adjust to college in the United States?

From *Benazir Bhutto, Daughter of Destiny* (New York: Simon and Schuster, 1989), pp. 45–46, 54–55, 58–64.

world's Muslims; the number of Bangladeshi pilgrims journeying to Mecca every year is second only to the number of Indonesians.

A civilian government was established in Pakistan in 1970, led by Zulkifar Ali Bhutto (1928–1979), a populist leader who had been educated at universities in Oxford and Berkeley. Throughout the 1970s, Pakistan's economic problems persisted, along with its domestic instability. Bhutto was overthrown in 1977 by General Mohammad Zia ul-Haq (ZEE-ah ool-HAHK), who had him executed in 1979. In 1979, the Iranian Revolution and the Soviet invasion of

Afghanistan enhanced the importance of Pakistan's Cold War alliance with the West.

In 1985, Zia ul-Haq lifted martial law; he was killed in 1988 in a plane crash. Bhutto's daughter Benazir, the first woman elected to govern a Muslim nation, succeeded him at the age of 35. She remained in office for 20 months, but her power was circumscribed. Under pressure from the army, she was dismissed after accusations of incompetence and corruption. She returned to prominence in the early 1990s and serves as an example of both the strength of political dynasties in South Asia and the ability of well-placed Muslim women to hold positions of great power. In the fall of 1999, the military under General Parvez Musharraf (PAR-vez moo-SHAR-ruf) again seized power in Pakistan, demonstrating the continued power of the military in politics and popular discontent with its civilian governments.

Like India, Pakistan continues to grapple with the problems of high population growth and uneven economic development. Relations between India and Pakistan remain tense, especially over the issue of Kashmir. In 1998 India asserted its sovereignty and defied Western nations by conducting nuclear tests. Pakistan replied shortly thereafter by exploding its own nuclear bombs, claiming that it had no choice in the face of the Indian nuclear threat. While the United Nations and established nuclear powers like the United States condemned these tests as the beginning of another nuclear arms race, citizens of Pakistan and India celebrated their respective states' tests as symbols of national power and autonomy.

▲ Nuclear tests by India and Pakistan in 1998 prompted the launching of this hot-air protest balloon, which sails past the Taj Mahal in Agra, northern India.

The Pakistan-Afghanistan Connection

Along with the development of nuclear weapons and the long-standing conflict with India over Kashmir, the flood of Afghan refugees in the aftermath of the 1979 Soviet invasion created serious turmoil for Pakistan in both its domestic and its foreign affairs. Afghanistan, like India, had been forced to assert its independence in the context of British dominance in the region. After it gained independence in 1919, Afghanistan established a special relationship with the Soviet Union that would endure throughout much of the twentieth century. As the Cold War evolved in the 1950s and 1960s, Afghanistan became a significant client of the Soviets, while the United States cultivated Pakistan as a bulwark against Soviet expansion. The two Asian nations, however, shared many similarities. Like the boundaries between India and Pakistan, what became the boundary between Afghanistan and Pakistan had been rather arbitrarily drawn by the British. There was nothing "natural" about this national boundary; it split ethnolinguistically similar communities and caused chronic friction between the two nations. Nonetheless, Pakistan and Afghanistan shared Islam as their majority religion along with many ethnic and cultural connections. When the Soviets invaded Afghanistan in 1979, millions of Afghan refugees flooded into Pakistan, disrupting its politics and economy. As the Soviet occupation dragged on, despite significant Afghan resistance, those refugees became semipermanent residents of Pakistan.

Both Pakistan and the United States supported Afghan resistance against the Soviet occupation. Arabs from the Middle East also traveled to Afghanistan to assist in what they deemed a "holy war" against the Soviets. Among them was a young Saudi millionaire named Osama bin Laden, who would later launch the clandestine, international terrorist network known as al-Qaeda. Ultimately, the Afghan resistance was successful, and the Soviets began to withdraw from Afghanistan in 1988. But that withdrawal sparked a vicious civil war in Afghanistan as various factions struggled for dominance. The violence of the occupation was succeeded by the violence of civil war for the Afghan people, and a new force called the Taliban emerged to dominate Afghan politics. The Taliban ("students") were a core group of very conservative Muslim clerics and theology students who had been trained in the madrasahs (Islamic schools) of Afghanistan and Pakistan. These men, preaching "law and order" and an ultraconservative vision of Islam, mobilized followers and secured support from Pakistan. They managed to seize military control of the bulk of Afghan territory. There they established an order of sorts, and then implemented a repressive Islamic government that included the banning of music and alcohol and the sequestering of women in their homes (forbidden to attend school or work).

The Taliban regime was considered a threat by its neighbors, Iran and the newly independent Central Asian Republics; Pakistan was one of its few supporters. Ultimately, the Taliban leadership entered into an alliance with Osama bin Laden, from whom they received funding and to whom they provided sanctuary. When, in September 2001, bin Laden masterminded the attacks on the World Trade Center and the Pentagon, the United States demanded that the Taliban hand him over. They refused. The United States secured the support of Pakistan (which abandoned its former clients, the Taliban) and launched a concerted air attack on Afghanistan. The Taliban were toppled from power, and Pakistan took a leading role in helping to negotiate the establishment of a new Afghan regime. But General Musharraf's support for the U.S. war effort was not popular among many of Pakistan's people, and the Afghan war provoked new hostilities between Pakistan and India, especially after an Islamic militant group based in Pakistan sent gunmen to attack the Indian parliament in December 2001. As 2002 began, troops were massed on both sides of the India-Pakistan border; those tensions have abated and India and Pakistan began negotiating improved relations in 2004. The new regime in Afghanistan remains in a precarious position, however, trying to establish some stability in a country devastated by war and by factional politics. Although there were successful elections in 2004, Taliban and other forces continue to play a role outside the capital at Kabul.

Australia, New Zealand, and the Pacific Islands

Why are wealth and political stability distributed so unevenly throughout Oceania?

Active members of APEC, the 21-member association for Asia-Pacific Economic Cooperation, Australia and New Zealand increasingly orient themselves toward Asia and the expanding markets there. Their former linkages with Britain through the Commonwealth of Nations ended with Britain joined the European Union. Australia acts as a regional power when neighboring islands experience turmoil. Yet, great disparities exist between the larger countries of New Zealand and Australia, on the one hand, and the tiny island countries on the other. The former emerged as nations early in the twentieth century from their status as settler colonies, whereas the latter became independent of colonial control by Europeans, Americans, and Japanese only after World War II.

Australia

Australia's previously monocultural national character changed dramatically after World War II. Waves of immigrants from new areas of the world—at first non-British Europeans but by the 1960s and 1970s, also Asians and others—transformed society. The arts and culture gained major international standing; Australian filmmakers and musicians are now at the top of the charts in popularity and awards around the world. Cosmopolitan attitudes in the arts were accompanied by increasingly progressive actions in politics and society. The Aboriginal rights movement earned improved status for indigenous Australians, and state and local governments have issued formal apologies for past discrimination and indignities.

On the political scene, Robert Menzies remained in power as prime minister from 1949 to 1966 (he had briefly held that post from 1939 to 1941 as well). Several other conservative governments ruled before the Labour party's Gough Whitlam became prime minister in 1972. Whitlam pushed through a number of reforms but alienated many voters. The governor-general, the representative of the British monarchy to Australia, demanded Whitlam's resignation. This created a constitutional crisis—that is, was Australia fully independent or was it, at some level, still a British subject? Since the 1970s, there has been strong sentiment that Australia should be a fully independent republic, but a lack of consensus about the form a republic should take has stalled that change.

New Zealand

New Zealand's relationship with Great Britain—since 1907 it had been a dominion—was radically altered after World War II. Strategically, New Zealand aligned itself with Australia and the United States in the 1951 ANZUS pact, recognizing the declining position of England after the war. (The United States withdrew its commitment to New Zealand when the latter banned nuclear weapons and nuclear-powered warships in 1985.) When England joined the European Economic Community in 1973, New Zealand's farm and dairy products lost their preferential treatment in the British market. This led to a major shift in New Zealand's primary trading partners from the United Kingdom to Australia, the United States, Japan, China, and Germany. New Zealand is an active member of the Asia Pacific Economic Cooperation (APEC) forum. The 1986 Constitution Act removed the legality of the British Parliament's passage of laws that applied to New Zealand. The British monarch remains as head of state (now called a "realm" rather than a "dominion"), but for all intents and purposes New Zealand is an independent country.

Four out of five New Zealanders are of European descent—mostly English and Irish—but the country is increasingly multicultural. Asians, Polynesians, and others have joined the Europeans and indigenous Maori in populating the islands in recent decades. The previous attitude of British superiority has been replaced with a policy of relatively open immigration. In 1985, the Maori gained a legal framework for restitution for violations of the Treaty of Waitangi. New Zealand is progressive in other ways as well. Until August 2006, the top government officials in New Zealand were all women: Prime Minister Helen Clark, Speaker of the House of Representatives Margaret Wilson, Chief Justice Sian Elias, and Governor-General Silvia Cartwright. New Zealand is a world leader in environmental protection and human rights. The country has top international rankings in political and civil rights as well as literacy, and the lowest level of corruption.

The Pacific Islands

Since gaining independence in the past several decades, many Pacific islands have struggled with problems created outside their region. Global warming, caused by carbon-based emissions in the developed and developing world, have begun to raise sea levels and threaten to do so much more dramatically in the decades to come. Tiny countries dependent on tourism, like the Marshall Islands, have now lost a large part of their beaches. Even more ominously, the Samoan fishing industry has suffered, and seawater has crept into underground fresh water aquifers, destroying crops on Kiribati. Worst of all, villages and even whole islands in Kiribati, Vanuatu, and Papua New Guinea have sunk beneath the waves.

Another problem with origins outside the islands is the epidemic of obesity. As many as 75 percent of the people of Nauru, Samoa, American Samoa, the Cook Islands, Tonga, and French Polynesia are obese—the world's highest levels of obesity. Traditional foods have been abandoned for the canned meats, soft drinks, sugar, and flour marketed by overseas companies. The rise in obesity and other dietary problems has, in turn, led to an explosion of diabetes and heart disease among Pacific islanders. Clean water and medical care are in short supply, exacerbating health problems in many of the island countries.

At the same time, several of the tiny island nations also face domestic turmoil. Fiji has struggled with ethnic rivalries between native Fijians and descendants of Indian laborers brought to the island nation by the British in the last century. Two military coups in 1987, one in 2000, and another in 2006 have undermined the fragile democracy there. Since 1998, the Solomon Islands have been rocked by civil strife due to rivalries for land. Hundreds of people have been killed and thousands made homeless. More than 50 percent of the population is under 15 years of age. In the Solomon Islands fewer than 70 percent of school-age children attend school, and fewer than that finish elementary school—a lower percentage than in any of the

▼ Aotea Square in Auckland, New Zealand, contains numerous architectural and sculptural elements, including a 1911 wooden Town Hall, used today for concerts, and a *waharoa* (gateway), sculpted by contemporary Maori artist Selwyn Muru. *Aotea* is a shortened form of Aotearoa, the Maori name for New Zealand.

other Pacific islands. In early 2007, an earthquake-generated tsunami hit the Solomon Islands, displacing many thousands and disrupting the economy.

Conclusion

In the second half of the twentieth century, Asia remained a theater of conflicts, including those in Afghanistan, Kashmir, the Korean peninsula, Vietnam, and Indonesia. There is a complex set of reasons for these regions becoming centers of violence. These countries hold the world's fastest-growing populations, its most essential resources, and the most politically explosive situations stemming from either politics or ideology. All of these countries, from richest to poorest, have been deeply affected by decolonization, the Cold War and its conclusion, and the technological revolution. All of them entered the modern era in a period of European, American, and Japanese dominance that often provoked violent encounters. Many face major economic and demographic issues that find expression in political instability. The drawing of new nation-state boundaries after World War II as imperial powers withdrew from territories like India, Korea, maritime Southeast Asia, and Indochina created massive refugee problems and inflamed ethnoreligious tensions in ways that have significantly shaped—and continue to shape—the destinies of nations in Asia.

China fought its own ideological battles before entering a period of rapid modernization after 1978. Japan emerged from the radioactive ruins of World War II to become the second largest economy in the world. South Korea, Singapore, Hong Kong, and Taiwan constructed their own economic miracles to become major players in the global economy. Indonesia and Malaysia freed themselves from the yoke of European dominance and enjoyed substantial economic progress. However, independence unleashed powerful ethnic and religious antagonisms, many of which remain unresolved. The countries of Indochina—Vietnam, Laos, and Cambodia—slowly emerged out of the generation of wars after 1945 but faced a long and difficult road to equal the progress made by other Asian nations. Myanmar (Burma) is mired in repression and poverty, whereas Thailand, continental Asia's only country to escape the clutches of imperialism, enjoys a relatively good standard of living under a benevolent monarchy despite repeated military coups.

After the British withdrew from the subcontinent, India and Pakistan entered a half century of frequently bitter competition. Hindu nationalism has joined the more secular political movements of the past and has, at times, triggered communal violence in India, the second most populous nation in the world. International and domestic Islamic movements affect the development of policies in Pakistan.

Australia and New Zealand are continuing to be transformed as multicultural states due to immigration of people from around the world and the expansion of equality and rights for indigenous peoples. Both are leading producers of international culture and are intimately linked to global networks of trade and culture. Several of the Pacific islands continue to face postcolonial domestic turmoil. All struggle with rising sea levels that threaten to inundate them as well as severe health problems caused by worsening diet and lack of access to medical care.

Suggestions for Web Browsing

You can obtain more information about topics included in this chapter at the websites listed below. See also the companion website that accompanies this text, http://www.ablongman.com/brummett, which contains an online study guide and additional resources.

Internet East Asia History Sourcebook: China Since World War II
http://www.fordham.edu/halsall/eastasia/eastasiasbook.html#
An extensive online source for links about the history of China after 1949.

History: People's Republic of China
http://www.hartford-hwp.com/archives/55/index-b.html
This site features numerous recent articles about economic, political, and social events in China.

Changing Relationships Between the United States and Japan
http://www.mofa.go.jp/region/n-america/us/
The relationship between the United States and Japan is a rapidly changing one. This Japanese Ministry of Foreign Affairs site provides both information and the opportunity for interchange.

Postwar Japan
http://www.lib.duke.edu/ias/eac/histwww.htm#postwar
An excellent collection assembled by the Duke University library.

Itihaas: Chronology—Independent India
http://sify.com/itihaas/independent_india/index.php
An in-depth chronology of independence; most entries include subsites with text and images.

Korea
http://www.koreasociety.org
Resources for all levels of historical study. The guide for teachers is especially informative.

Southeast Asia
http://www.ocf.berkeley.edu/~sdenney
An extensive collection of documents on Vietnam, Laos, and Cambodia.

Literature and Film

In *Wild Swans: Three Daughters of China* (Doubleday, 1991) Jung Chang gives an autobiographical account of the Cultural Revolution. *White Badge, A Novel of Korea,* by Ahn Junghyo (Soho Press, 1989), relates the story of Korean soldiers who fought in the Vietnam War on the U.S. side. The book was made into a fine movie in 1992, directed by Ji-yeong Jeong. *The Rainy Spell and Other Korean Stories,* rev. ed. (M. E. Sharpe, 1997), trans. Suh Ji-moon, includes a wonderful translation of Yun Hung-gil's title story. *The Sacred Willow* (Oxford University Press, 2000), by Duong Van Mai Elliott, describes four generations in the life of a Vietnamese family. *When Heaven & Earth Changed Places* (Plume, 1993), by Le Ly Hayslip with Jay Wurts, describes a peasant girl growing up in Vietnam, Vietnamese-G.I. relationships, and her journey to America.

Difficult Daughters (Penguin, 1998), by Manju Kapur, is an intriguing exploration of gender relations and women's place. Bapsi Sidwa, in *Cracking India* (Milkweed, 1991), presents the story, at once terrifying and funny, of family relations (especially in the Parsi minority community) and the communal violence that ensued in the aftermath of Partition. Arundhati Roy's *The God of Small Things* (HarperCollins, 1998) is a literary tour de force set amid the Syriac Christian community of Kerala in the last decades of the twentieth century. The author captures many facets of contemporary Indian cultural and social life.

The Oxford Book of Japanese Short Stories, ed. Theodore W. Goosen (Oxford University Press, 2002), is an excellent collection of contemporary Japanese prose writing. The film *Ikiru* (1952; Toho), directed by Japanese master Akira Kurosawa, is the moving portrayal of a gentle civil servant after World War II. *The Blue Kite* (1993; Beijing Film Studio) allows a wonderful look at how political changes can even touch the smallest of lives; it is also harshly critical, in a subdued sort of way, of what happened in China during the 1950s and 1960s.

In *Two Daughters* (1961; Columbia), the celebrated director Satyajit Ray relates a tale of poverty, kindness, and abuse in the village, and marriage customs in the city. In Ray's trilogy *Pather Panchali, Aparajito,* and *The World of Apu* (1955–1959; Columbia), he details the life of a young man in the village, his struggles in college, marriage, and decision to become a writer.

New Zealand's multicultural society is highlighted in Toa Fraser's award-winning movie, *No. 2* (2006), about a Fijian family in New Zealand. Australia's Nobel Prize winner, Patrick White, wrote many novels and short stories, including the fine book *The Twyborn Affair* (Vintage Press, 1979), set in London, France, and Australia's Snowy Mountains, that traces gender, colonial, and class identities.

Suggestions for Reading

An excellent survey of the first decades of the People's Republic of China is *Mao's China and After: A History of the People's Republic,* by Maurice Meisner (Free Press, 1986). A useful local study of one village through war and revolution is *Chinese Village, Socialist State,* by Edward Friedman, Paul Pickowicz, Mark Selden, and Kay Ann Johnson (Yale University Press, 1991). William A. Joseph, Christine Wong, and David Zweig, *New Perspectives on the Cultural Revolution* (Harvard University Press, 1991), offers an incisive treatment of that cataclysmic era. Merle Goldman and Roderick MacFarquhar, eds., *The Paradox of China's Post-Mao Reforms* (Harvard University Press, 1999), is an excellent treatment of the last three decades. The lives of women in the post-Mao decade are cogently treated by Gail Hershatter and Emily Honig in *Personal Voices: Chinese Women in the 1980s* (Stanford University Press, 1988).

The best book on the immediate postwar era in Japan is John Dower, *Embracing Defeat: Japan in the Wake of World War II* (W. W. Norton, 1999). *Postwar Japan as History,* ed. Andrew Gordon (University of California Press, 1993), is a fine collection of essays on a wide range of topics. For an insightful examination of the meaning of late twentieth-century history, see Norma Field, *In the Realm of a Dying Emperor: A Portrait of Japan at Century's End* (Pantheon Books, 1991).

For a comprehensive collection of excellent articles on Southeast Asia, see Nicholas Tarling, *The Cambridge History of Southeast Asia: Nineteenth and Twentieth Centuries* (Cambridge University Press, 1992). On the Philippines, see Jose Arcilla, *An Introduction to Philippine History,* 4th ed. (Ateneo de Manila Press, 1999), and Stanley Karnow, *In Our Image: America's Empire in the Philippines* (Ballantine Books, 1990). Women in Southeast Asia and other Asian countries are treated in Louise Edwards and Mina Roces, eds., *Women in Asia: Tradition, Modernity and Globilisation* (University of Michigan Press, 2000).

Robert Dujarric has edited a solid study dealing with the complexities of bringing North and South Korea together in *Korean Unification and After: U.S. Policy Toward a Unified Korea* (Hudson Institute, 2000). The role of Korean women in national definition is studied in Elaine H. Kim and Chungmoo Choi, eds., *Dangerous Women: Gender and Korean Nationalism* (Routledge, 1997).

Some valuable surveys of modern India include Stanley Wolpert, *A New History of India,* 7th ed. (Oxford University Press, 2004); Sugata Bose and Ayesha Jalal, *Modern South Asia: History, Culture, and Political Economy* (Routledge, 1998); and Barbara D. Metcalf and Thomas R. Metcalf, *A Concise History of India* (Cambridge University Press, 2001). On Afghanistan, see Ahmed Rashid, *Taliban* (Yale University Press, 2000). On Australia and New Zealand, see Donald Denoon, Philippa Mein-Smith, and Marivic Wyndham, *A History of Australia, New Zealand, and the Pacific* (Blackwell, 2000).

Chapter 36

Into the Twenty-first Century
An Uncertain Future

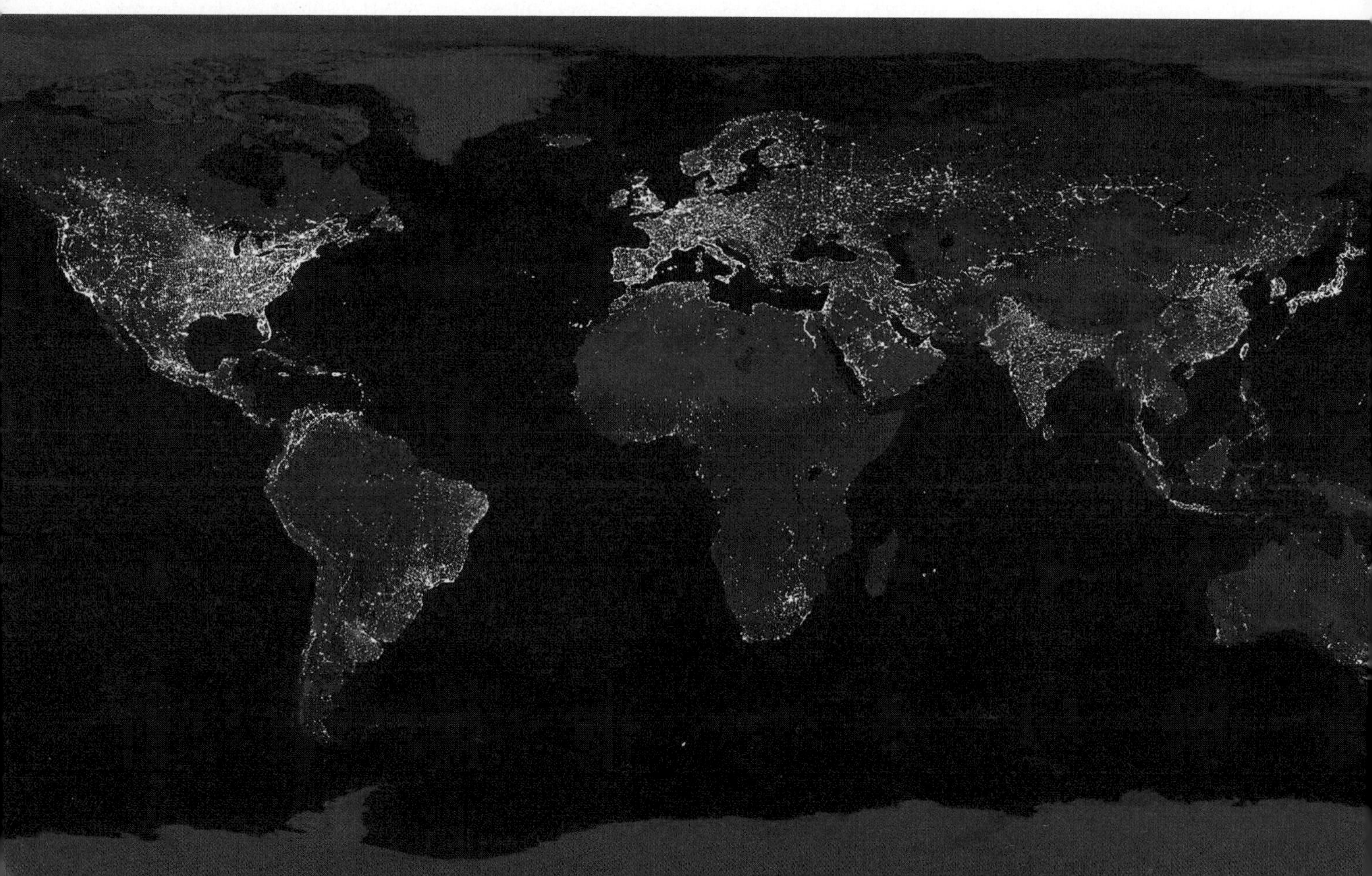

Outline

- Economics: The Tension Between Dollars and Sense
- The Promises and Perils of Technology
- People on the Move in a Changing World
- Toward a World Culture
- Looming Challenges
- Reasons for Hope

Features

DOCUMENT **Muhammad Yunus's Acceptance Speech for the 2006 Nobel Peace Prize**

GLOBAL ISSUES **Marriage**

SEEING CONNECTIONS **The Earth**

DOCUMENT **Wangari Maathai, *A Matter of Life or Death***

◀ This beautiful composite satellite photograph of the earth at night was taken by NASA in 2000. Thanks to computer enhancement of electronic illumination, the photo makes a useful tool for identifying the distribution of power consumption (and hence wealth) across the globe. Brightly illuminated Europe and the large dark expanse of Africa makes this photograph unintentionally conform to old imperial stereotypes. Note also the Korean peninsula, in particular the abject dark of the north and brightness of the south. As an exercise in contrasts, compare this photograph with the map on page 1084.

UNCERTAINTY ABOUT THE future hovers over the world as it moves into the new millennium. A number of seemingly insoluble challenges confront humanity. These include global warming, environmental degradation, the increased scarcity of natural resources (especially water), overpopulation in the world's poorest regions, growing inequality, the spread of new and more virulent diseases, the proliferation of nuclear weapons, terrorism, and the rising tension between the West and the Islamic world. And yet all is not bleak. The spread of democratic government, the continued economic miracle in other Asian countries, and the promise of further breakthroughs in science, technology, and medicine suggest that the twenty-first century is not without promise.

To better evaluate the challenges and prospects that will shape our future, we should consider some of the global trends that have developed since World War II. The second half of the twentieth century saw the beginning of a revolution in the way people live. With the development of more effective birth control, women, first in the West and then elsewhere, entered the workplace in large numbers, altering both global economics and the nature of family life. Major advances in technology changed the way people work and use their free time, while improvements in medicine and food production have significantly raised life expectancies. Human rights have also expanded in policy and practice since the 1948 adoption of the Universal Declaration of Human Rights by the United Nations.

Positive developments such as these, however, have not been shared by all of the world's six billion people. Perhaps the biggest challenge confronting humanity in the twenty-first century, then, is finding a way to narrow the widening gap between the world's "haves" and increasingly numerous "have-nots."

Economics: The Tension Between Dollars and Sense

How has globalization both benefited and endangered the world?

As the twenty-first century began, it was evident that global interdependence placed pressures on private citizens and political leaders. On the one hand there was the struggle by individuals, most of them in non-Western countries, to maintain their cultures and values in the face of rapid **globalization**—economic, social, and cultural—dominated by North American, Western European, and Northeast Asian economic powers. On the other hand, national leaders everywhere found themselves more and more at the mercy of international currents over which they had little control: globalization, terrorism, global warming, and pollution. The Internet, satellite television, and cell phones joined traditional media such as radio and newspapers to inundate people on all continents with a flood of information. There were a few individuals isolated from the swiftly rising tide of interdependence. But there were no political leaders who could claim to be in control of events.

The World Economy and Globalization

After 1945, the world experienced unprecedented economic growth and development and increasing interdependence, which after the fall of the Soviet Union came to be known increasingly as globalization—a common market for the globe, although the term encompasses culture and ideology as well. But trade flows changed. The international monetary system of exchange rates pegged to the dollar and the fixed price of gold lasted until 1971, when trade imbalances led to enormous gold outflows from the United States to rising manufacturing powers in Europe and Japan. President Richard Nixon dealt a fatal blow to the Bretton Woods system (see p. 961) by severing the link between gold and the dollar. His move opened the way for "floating rates," the determination of exchange rates by market mechanisms that further reduced the control of nation-states over their economies.

This policy change aided—and encouraged the creation of—multinational firms, headquartered in one country but with operations throughout the world. By shifting operations and investments, they could take advantage of exchange rate differences to reduce cost. In addition, the dispersed nature of multinational corporations gave them greater freedom from national laws and regulations. Decisions made by companies, then, also played a role in diminishing the global political system of nation-states. In response, countries whose economies depended on the export of raw materials began to band together in an attempt to control the price of their goods, because the price of their goods determined the value of their currency. Collaborative efforts by raw material exporting countries had varying degrees of success. The most successful was the Organization of Petroleum Exporting Countries **(OPEC)**.

The oil embargo of the 1970s imposed by OPEC, many of whose members were Middle Eastern countries, originally was intended to punish the nations that supported Israel in the 1973 Arab-Israeli war but dealt a serious blow to the economies of the major oil importing nations. Quadrupling their prices, the OPEC nations gained in wealth at the expense of their international customers. Rich oil-importing countries faced gas shortages and simultaneous inflation and

---

globalization—The ongoing development of extensive worldwide patterns of economic relationships, social integration, and cultural connections across geographic and political boundaries.

OPEC—Organization of Petroleum Exporting Countries, created in 1960 by several petroleum-producing states to gain control over their oil output and pricing.

Chronology

1940

1940s First electronic computers invented

1940s–1960s Green Revolution boosts agricultural production throughout developing world

1945 International Monetary Fund (IMF) and World Bank chartered; United States drops atomic bombs on Hiroshima and Nagasaki

1947 General Agreement on Trade and Tariffs (GATT)

1948 United Nations adoption of Universal Declaration of Human Rights

1950

1953 James Watson and Francis Crick discover molecular structure of DNA

1957 European Economic Community founded; Soviets launch first satellite, *Sputnik*

1960

1961 Soviet cosmonaut Yuri Gagarin makes first manned space flight; world's population reaches 3 billion

1962 Rachel Carson's *Silent Spring*

1963 First artificial heart patented

1969 *Apollo 11* mission lands U.S. astronauts on the moon

1970

1970 First Earth Day celebration

1974 World's population reaches 4 billion

1977 *Apple II*, the world's first home computer, introduced

	Global Economic Milestones
1944	Bretton Woods Conference plans peacetime economy
1945	International Monetary Fund (IMF) and World Bank chartered
1947	General Agreement on Trade and Tariffs (GATT)
1957	European Economic Community founded
1973–1974	OPEC oil crisis
1989	Asia-Pacific Economic Cooperation (APEC) forum established
1992	European Union (EU) established
1993	The North American Free Trade Agreement (NAFTA) signed
1995	World Trade Organization (WTO) established
1997–1998	Asian economic crisis
2002	European Union introduces the euro

recession; some, like Japan, reacted by diversifying their energy supply to eliminate dependency on Middle Eastern suppliers. Poor oil-importing nations were hit much harder. They borrowed on international markets to finance their oil purchases. Banks in the United States, Europe, and Japan made substantial loans to countries in Eastern Europe, Latin America, and Africa—whose total debt by the end of the 1970s topped $1.3 trillion. Brazil's debt was nearly $100 billion; Mexico's was close to $90 billion. To ensure their survival, nations such as Brazil, Hungary, and Poland allowed World Bank personnel following the theories of Milton Friedman (1912–2006) to impose regulations on their domestic economic policy. In return for loans, they made unprecedented sacrifices of national sovereignty to an international body. In time, the adverse effects of these loans came to be felt far beyond the poor nations' borders. Nonpayment by the debtor nations threatened to topple the world's banking structure as it became apparent that these poor nations could not repay their loans. The debt crisis of the 1980s stressed the capacities of the **International Monetary Fund (IMF)** to the limit. Debts continued to be rescheduled, but the largest debtors showed an ever-declining ability to pay. In January 2002, Argentina faced a severe economic and political crisis—it went through four governments in two weeks—as it was unable to pay even the interest on its foreign debts and faced harsh solutions to stabilize its economy (see Chapter 34).

This situation, and the multination recessions of 1978–1985 and 1998–2001, had different effects on different parts of the globe. Unemployment soared in many countries, especially in the less-developed countries, some of which were also plagued with rising population rates. In the United States, the recession in the early 1980s contributed to huge trade deficits and federal budget deficits. In 1985, the United States was the first nation to recover from the global recession largely by generating a huge national debt and borrowing heavily from foreigners. A creditor since 1917, the United States became a debtor nation under the Reagan administration and continues to depend on borrowing a billion dollars a day from abroad, mainly from Japan and China, to maintain its economy. Consumer spending keeps the American economy going, with the consumers themselves generating considerable personal debts. Some economists believe that if the housing market seriously declines, consumers stop spending, or foreign countries refuse to buy any more U.S. debt, the fragility of the American economy will become evident, with disastrous results. Others argue

International Monetary Fund (IMF)—Chartered in 1945, the International Monetary Fund was created to restore the money system that had collapsed in previous decades.

1980

1981 HIV/AIDS virus first identified

1983 Internet first established

1986 Chernobyl nuclear disaster

1987 World's population reaches 5 billion

1989 Asia-Pacific Economic Cooperation (APEC) forum established

1990

1992 European Union (EU) established

1995 World Trade Organization (WTO) established

1997 Birth of first cloned sheep, "Dolly"

1999 World's population reaches 6 billion

2000

2000 International Space Station put into operation

2001 Al-Qaeda terrorist attacks in New York and Washington

2002 European Union introduces the euro

2003 Human Genome Project finishes sequencing complete set of human genes

2005 Asian tsunami kills over 250,000; first face transplant performed

2007 UN reports human activity is most probable source of global warming that the current level of national debt, while not insignificant, is sustainable as a percentage of the U.S. **gross domestic product (GDP),** and as such is comparable to the rate of debt maintained by other industrialized states such as France and Canada.

Although it faces stiff foreign competition from East Asian and European nations, the U.S. economy is still dominant in a number of key sectors such as advanced technology, computers, software, aircraft, and arms. In more traditional industries, such as steel production and automobile manufacturing, the United States has ceded its place at the top to other nations. In 2007, this was demonstrated when Toyota surpassed General Motors as the largest producer of automobiles in the world. In earlier times, such a shift would have been bad news for the U.S. economy, but new industries have surpassed traditional ones. Symbolic of the times, at the beginning of 2007, Google, the Internet search engine firm, had a market capitalization of $155 billion, more than eight times that of General Motors.[1]

Since 2000, Russia has benefited from the market for its oil and gas and the increase in the prices for these commodities. By 2007 the country had paid off virtually all of its foreign debts and was poised to wield far more political power in Europe through its importance as an energy supplier than it had in the last decade of the Soviet Union. An extremely rich, if small, upper class has absorbed most of the profits, while the bottom 70 percent of the Russian population live at a lower standard of living than they possessed under communism.

Given the turbulence of the previous half century, however, the foundation established at Bretton Woods allowed the industrially developed countries of the world to avoid the devastating inflation and depression that marked the 1920s and 1930s. The long-running Uruguay Round of the **General Agreement on Tariffs and Trade (GATT)** talks, in which 116 states worked to update the GATT rules, ended successfully in December 1993. This led to the establishment of the **World Trade Organization (WTO),** a streamlined approach to continuing the fight against trade barriers that had been successfully waged by GATT since World War II. In 2001, the WTO admitted China into its ranks. The interdependence of the world economy means that economic shocks and downturns in one location have ripple effects and can cause problems elsewhere. The Bretton Woods philosophy dedicated to maintaining the free market remains, even though several countries practice preferential subsidies of various segments of their economies, such as agriculture.

Migrant Workers and Outsourcing

Globalization involves the free flow of capital and resources across national boundaries. It also brings with it the flow—free or otherwise—of workers to areas of booming economic activity. Sometimes this movement is internal, as in the Chinese migration from the rural interior to the cities of its eastern seaboard. At other times, the movement is across national borders, as in the migration, legal and illegal, from the Middle East and Africa into the European Union, from Mexico and Latin America into the United States, or from Southeast Asia into the Middle East and Australia.

Extralegal immigration can be voluntary—as when individuals and families seek better economic conditions outside their home countries—or involuntary. The latter takes the form of slavery, a human tragedy of huge proportions. Exact numbers of modern-day slaves are not known, but it is estimated that as many as 12 million slaves worldwide, mostly girls and women forced into domestic work or prostitution, make up part of today's global movement of workers.

Outsourcing is a contrasting feature of globalization. In this case, rather than workers flowing to where the work is, the work flows to where the cheap workers are. Under traditional free-market competition between nations, work, of course, has always been known to move to where it enjoys more competitive advantages; for example, although the United States is still a major steel manufacturer, its once dominant position in the world market was surpassed first by Japan and later by China, where steel production was either more efficient (Japan) or cheaper (China). This traditional form of economic movement involves shifting entire industries to new nations, where new companies control them. In contrast, under outsourcing, large, often multinational corporations either move business activity from one country in which they operate to another where the costs of such activity are cheaper, or they farm out the activity to foreign subcontractors, again at lower cost.

Whatever form it takes, outsourcing has hurt mid-wage workers in the United States, Europe, and Japan who have seen their jobs move abroad. IBM moved many positions overseas, and the German car maker

---

gross domestic product (GDP)– The total market value of the goods and services produced by the residents of a nation in a given period of time, such as a year.

General Agreement on Tariffs and Trade (GATT)–Established in 1947, the General Agreements on Tariffs and Trade sought to avoid the protectionist and autarkist errors of the interwar period and establish a framework that would permit free trade among nations.

World Trade Organization (WTO)–The successor organization to GATT (the General Agreement on Trades and Tariffs), established in 1995. As with its predecessor, the organization carried on the fight against trade barriers.

outsourcing– The practice of subcontracting work and jobs to foreign countries, usually for lower wages.

Volkswagen transferred some of its automobile production to Puebla, Mexico, where labor costs are much cheaper than they are in Germany. Toy-maker Lego is also moving most of its production from Denmark to the Czech Republic and Mexico. American, Japanese, and Taiwanese corporations outsource much production to the People's Republic of China.

Outsourcing has struck seriously at several European countries, with structural unemployment—that is, people out of work for a period longer than 12 months—growing. In Italy, the figure has risen to 58 percent of the workforce, while in Greece it is 55 percent. At the other end of the scale in Europe is Denmark, the developed country that has made the most progress in adapting itself to the new age, creating more jobs through its fluid labor market than it loses to outsourcing.

Within Europe, Ireland has profited the most from outsourcing, as many corporations are eager to locate their European operations to a place with high educational standards, an English-speaking working class, and favorable governmental conditions. Ireland remains a magnet for young people from the European Union to come and find work. It is not just industrial jobs that are being transferred from one country to the next—service jobs are also increasingly relocating to other countries, as positions in such diverse fields as accounting, reading MRIs, insurance claim processing, and tax preparation have left the United States for India and other English-speaking countries. Software programmers based in the United States are paid ten times as much as similarly skilled workers in India, so corporations clearly benefit from the skilled but lower-paid workforce available in other countries.

Women in the Workplace

Economic interdependence, technological advances that have reduced the demands on physical labor, and the need for more workers have all contributed to bring women into the modern workforce in larger numbers than ever before. Of course, women have always worked, but between the Neolithic Revolution and the Industrial Revolution, most of this work for the vast majority of the world's women has consisted of production of goods in the household and on the farm. The trend toward women earning wages outside of the home in factories and other business began in Europe, the United States, and Japan during the Industrial Revolution and accelerated during World War I and World War II, when, with so many working-age males enlisted in the armed services, women were encouraged to take men's places in factories and elsewhere temporarily in order to meet the wartime production demands placed on industry.

The entry of women into the workplace has brought about fundamental changes in the traditional family, redefining social roles assigned to men and women and how they went about bringing up children. These changes differed by country, social class, and ethnicity. Among American middle-class families, despite this change, women were still generally expected to do the bulk of certain types of work such as cleaning and cooking within the home, although gendering of domestic labor would see other activities such as yard work and home repairs fall to men. Even though modern laborsaving devices permitted housework to be done in one-tenth the time it had taken in the past, the burdens of wage earning and housework placed great demands on women's time. The advances in the equality of women with men were not the same everywhere.

Today, at any given time in the developed world, between 60 and 80 percent of women between the ages of 25 and 54 work outside of the home. Still, even though almost one-half of the paid labor force in industrialized countries is made up of women, they earn much less than men. In the United States, women are paid, on average, 73 cents for every dollar a man makes doing the same work. The so-called **glass ceiling,** limiting women's upward mobility, is still in place for most women in the developed world; only a very small—but increasing—percentage of women make it into senior management positions in government and in business. A recent survey, however, has found that in Western Europe and North America, most women would want to work "whether or not they needed the money." The same survey found that close to 60 percent of working women in Europe contributed more of the family income—with French women leading the way. The revolutionary change in women's status is nicely illustrated by a Gallup poll taken some 60 years ago. At that time, 82 percent of people in the United States, both men and women, believed that "a married woman should not earn money if her husband was capable of supporting her."[2]

One of the most profound changes in women's lives in many countries is their role as mothers. Except for the United States, almost all advanced industrialized countries—and even some countries in earlier stages of industrial development—have birthrates that are below the replacement level needed to maintain a stable population. Women who want to develop their careers make individual decisions that, taken together, have enormous effects on the politics and economies of their societies. Wealthy countries like Japan and Korea in Northeast Asia and Italy, Spain, and Germany

glass ceiling—The unacknowledged discriminatory limitation to women's and minorities' professional advancement to leadership positions.

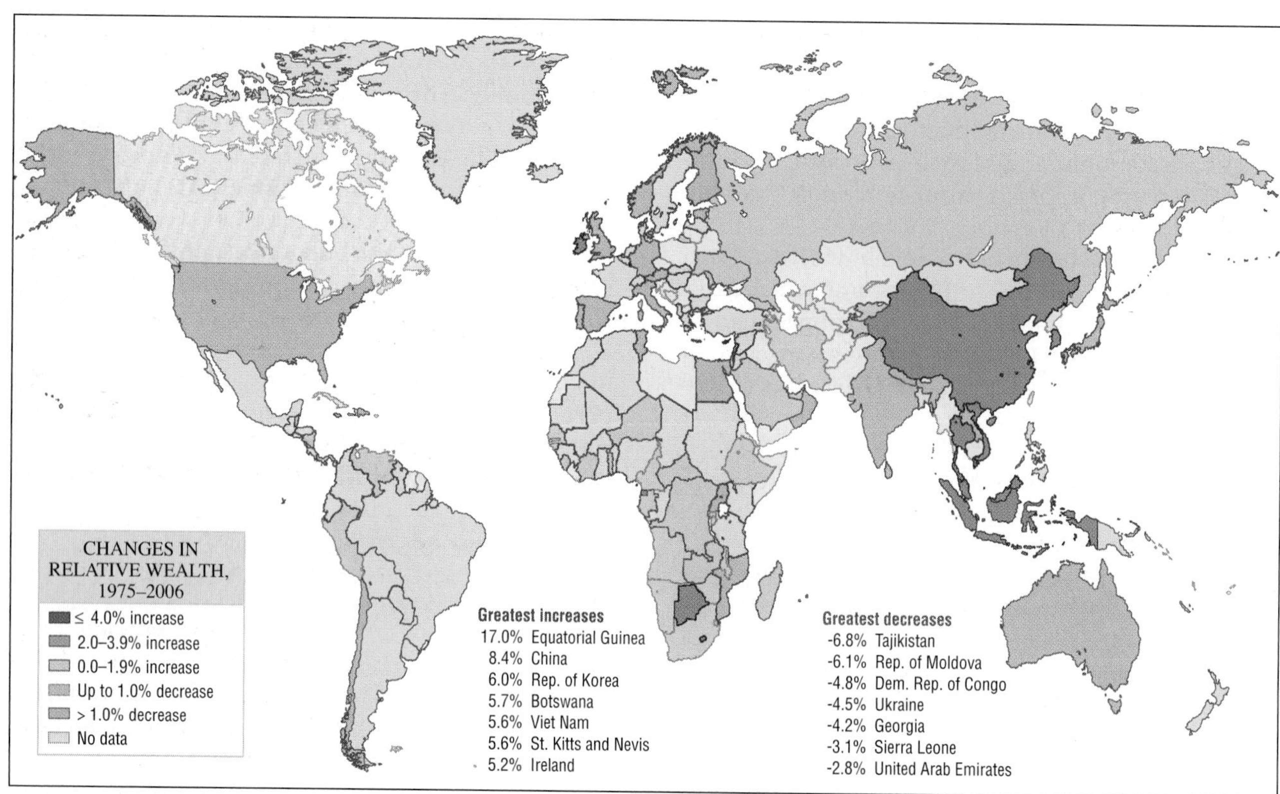

▲ Proportion of worldwide economic growth between 1975 and 2006.

in Europe are joined by developing countries like Thailand that have total fertility rates that fail to keep up with the growth of their elderly, retired populations. In 2006, Japan's population actually began to decline, and its leaders worry about the nation's ability to support its social security system and its diminishing global importance if its population, as expected, is reduced by half in the next century.

Income Inequality

The movement of jobs from developed nations to the developing world, either by outsourcing or through more traditional free market shifts in industry, may harm workers in developed nations such as the United States and Germany, but it also benefits workers in the developing nations where these jobs go. According to the World Bank, the number of people living on less than one dollar a day declined from 40 percent of the world's population in 1981 to 21 percent in 2001. Even with the trickling down from a growing world economy, however, three billion of the globe's six billion plus people live on less than $2 a day. The gap between rich and poor remains immense, but the shifts in the world job markets are not all negative and have prompted some positive changes in developing countries, most notably China and India, which collectively possess one-third of the world's population. These nations have expanding economies and growing middle classes.

Nevertheless, the world's very rich have become richer. During the same time, the middle classes of the developed world have seen their income stagnate or even recede in the face of inflation. Since 2000, the income of a typical middle-class American has gone up only by 1 percent, not enough to keep up with inflation.[3] Over a longer term, "the typical [American] worker earns only 10 percent more in real terms than he did 25 years ago." Although this problem is considerably worse in a developing country such as Brazil than it is in the United States, it is still a worrying trend, especially when one considers the crucial role the middle classes play in democratic states.

Agriculture: A Key to Poverty in the Developing World

The vast majority of the poor developing countries in the world depend on agriculture as a major source of their revenues. Since there is little chance, in the short term, that these countries can compete successfully against the developed world in the industrial and postindustrial marketplace, one hope for reducing poverty in such countries is to grant them free-trade access for their agricultural products in developed nations. Although this idea appears promising, it faces significant obstacles. Nations such as the United States and Japan, as well as those within the European Union, have been reluctant to stop subsidizing their agricultural sectors and/or shielding them from free-market competition with tariffs or from import restrictions on genetically modified crops, because farmers represent an important part of their constituency, and agriculture, because of its foundational role in providing for citizens' well-being, is often viewed in protective cultural or even national security contexts. Some countries have understandable concerns that free movement of farm products may unleash unintended global environmental hazards. This is a key example of the simultaneous benefit and harm of globalization.

So it is that the Malian cotton farmer has to compete with the cotton farmers in the United States, who use the most advanced methods of factory farming to harvest their crops, which are further subsidized to the tune of $4 billion, producing $3 billion worth of cotton that is then dumped on the world market. Similarly, the European Union supports its sugar beet growers with subsidies to help them compete on the world market. To make a pound of beet sugar in Europe costs around 26 cents, while in Brazil it only costs about 5 cents. Yet, with the government subsidies, European sugar sells cheaper than the Brazilian sugar in certain markets.

The Doha Round of the World Trade Organization begun in 2001was supposed to address these questions, but political pressures have made a settlement impossible. Poorer developed countries are unlikely to make economic progress if their agricultural sectors continue to face competition from the subsidized agricultural products from the developed world.

Microfinance: A New Solution to an Old Problem

For the six decades after the end of World War II, the problems of global poverty were approached by major private organizations or governments loaning large amounts of money to states or organizations that were in need of help. However, between the cashing of the check and the delivery of aid to the poorest people, there was a substantial amount of money lost. Overhead costs in the granting states or organizations took an important percentage of the money as did comparable costs in the receiving states and organizations. On top of this, corruption in developing countries often redirected the grant money to the overseas bank accounts of political leaders more interested in enriching themselves than helping their people. The aid money that finally trickled down to the people often was squandered through wasteful practices and poor financial management.

In the 1970s, however, a new approach to financial aid for the poor came into being: microfinance. In this form of lending, poor people received small loans directly from a bank to invest in their economic activities–be it making clothes, farming, or small scale tool manufacture. Initially, the loans distributed to the poor averaged about one hundred dollars with very low interest. The repayment rate was close to one hundred percent and in villages across countries like Bangladesh, family enterprises began to make money, build financial surpluses, and make further investments. The Bangladeshi Muhammad Yunus was one of the pioneers of microfinance. He made his first loan in 1974, and then established the Grameen Bank shortly thereafter. In recognition of his efforts to alleviate poverty in the developing world, he received the Nobel Prize in 2006 (see Document–Muhammad Yunus, Acceptance Speech for the 2006 Nobel Peace Prize on p. 1086).

▲ Microfinance pioneer, Grameen Bank founder, and 2006 Nobel Peace Prize winner Muhammad Yunus discussing the startup of a rural mobile phone business with rural Bangladeshi women.

The Promises and Perils of Technology

How can technological innovations simultaneously make lives easier and more challenging?

As we saw in Chapters 1 and 22, two great changes in the past, the Neolithic Revolution and the Industrial Revolution, brought about fundamental transformations in the ways people lived. Since 1945, humanity has been undergoing another such revolution brought about by technology. Computers and robotics have changed the ways people in developed countries and developing countries live, relate to one another, and spend their leisure time.

Technological Revolutions

Propelling the developed world's economic growth was the exceedingly fruitful work of its inventors, scientists, and engineers. Atomic energy continued to present the double-sided prospect of unlimited energy and great danger, with the latter revealed

Document

Muhammad Yunus, Acceptance Speech for the 2006 Nobel Peace Prize

Born in 1940, the Bangladeshi Muhammad Yunus studied economics at Vanderbilt University, where he earned his doctorate in 1969. Had it not been for the outbreak of the Bangladeshi War of Liberation in 1971, he might have gone on to have a distinguished academic career in the United States. But once his nation became free, he abandoned his life as a professor to work in helping construct his new state. The overwhelming fact of mass poverty blocked Bangladesh's entry into the world economy, and after studying the problem from every conceivable angle, he developed the concept of microfinance—loaning small amounts of money to very poor people. His approach to economic development earned him the Nobel Prize in 2006.

By giving us this prize, the Norwegian Nobel Committee has given important support to the proposition that peace is inextricably linked to poverty. Poverty is a threat to peace. World's income distribution gives a very telling story. Ninety-four percent of the world income goes to 40 percent of the population while sixty percent of people live on only 6 percent of world income. Half of the world population lives on two dollars a day. Over one billion people live on less than a dollar a day. This is no formula for peace...

Peace should be understood in a human way—in a broad social, political and economic way. Peace is threatened by unjust economic, social and political order, absence of democracy, environmental degradation and absence of human rights.

Poverty is the absence of all human rights. The frustrations, hostility, and anger generated by abject poverty cannot sustain peace in any society. For building stable peace we must find ways to provide opportunities for people to live decent lives.

The creation of opportunities for the majority of people—the poor—is at the heart of the work that we have dedicated ourselves to during the past 30 years.

I became involved in the poverty issue not as a policymaker or a researcher. I became involved because poverty was all around me, and I could not turn away from it. In 1974, I found it difficult to teach elegant theories of economics in the university classroom, in the backdrop of a terrible famine in Bangladesh. Suddenly, I felt the emptiness of those theories in the face of crushing hunger and poverty. I wanted to do something immediate to help people around me, even if it was just one human being, to get through another day with a little more ease. That brought me face to face with poor people's struggle to find the tiniest amounts of money to support their efforts to eke out a living. I was shocked to discover a woman in the village, borrowing less than a dollar from the money-lender, on the condition that he would have the exclusive right to buy all she produces at the price he decides. This, to me, was a way of recruiting slave labor.

I decided to make a list of the victims of this money-lending "business" in the village next door to our campus.

When my list was done, it had the names of 42 victims who borrowed a total amount of US $27. I offered US $27 from my own pocket to get these victims out of the clutches of those money-lenders. The excitement that was created among the people by this small action got me further involved in it. If I could make so many people so happy with such a tiny amount of money, why not do more of it?

That is what I have been trying to do ever since. The first thing I did was to try to persuade the bank located in the campus to lend money to the poor. But that did not work. The bank said that the poor were not creditworthy. After all my efforts, over several months, failed, I offered to become a guarantor for the loans to the poor. I was stunned by the result. The poor paid back their loans, on time, every time! But still I kept confronting difficulties in expanding the program through the existing banks. That was when I decided to create a separate bank for the poor, and in 1983, I finally succeeded in doing that. I named it Grameen Bank or Village bank.

Today, Grameen Bank gives loans to nearly 7 million poor people, 97 percent of whom are women, in 73,000 villages in Bangladesh. Grameen Bank gives collateral-free income generating, housing, student and micro-enterprise loans to the poor families and offers a host of attractive savings, pension funds and insurance products for its members. Since it introduced them in 1984, housing loans have been used to construct 640,000 houses. The legal ownership of these houses belongs to the women themselves. We focused on women because we found giving loans to women always brought more benefits to the family.

In a cumulative way the bank has given out loans totaling about $6 billion. The repayment rate is 99 percent. Grameen Bank routinely makes profit. Financially, it is self-reliant and has not taken donor money since 1995. Deposits and own resources of Grameen Bank today amount to 143 percent of all outstanding loans. According to Grameen Bank's internal survey, 58 percent of our borrowers have crossed the poverty line...

Questions to Consider

1. According to Mr. Yunus, what is the relationship between poverty and peace?
2. How does Mr. Yunus define poverty?
3. Why does Mr. Yunus's bank make most of its loans to women?

http://nobelprize.org/nobel_prizes/peace/laureates/2006/yunus-lecture-en.html

dramatically in the disastrous 1986 reactor meltdown at Chernobyl (cher-NOH-bul) in the Soviet Union. Advances in biology and biochemistry produced a similar mixed picture.

In 1953, James D. Watson and Francis H. C. Crick, building on the work of Rosalind Franklin, revealed a model of the structure of the DNA (deoxyribonucleic acid) molecule, the basic genetic building block of all living things. Research stemming from their work brought new insights into processes of heredity and led to the possibility of shaping the future of numerous species. Like the problems associated with nuclear technology, scientific advances that permit the altering of genes pose profound social and ethical issues. The new research promises to help cure maladies ranging from Alzheimer's disease to Parkinson's disease to various birth defects, but some of the procedures to make this progress involve using stem cells taken from embryonic fetal tissue, violating the moral codes of certain religions.

The cloning of animals, including the sheep "Dolly," who suffered from premature arthritis, and the possibility of cloning human beings pose serious challenges to governments and spiritual leaders alike. Other spin-offs from advances made in the use of DNA have come in the American criminal justice system, where the use of DNA evidence in judicial appeals has led to the reversal of death penalties levied on innocent people.

Genetically modified organisms (GMOs) are increasingly used with undoubted short-term results of improved production and a greater capacity of crops to resist parasites and drought, offering hope that the world will be able to feed itself with fewer pesticides as its population continues to grow. But many have concerns about the unpredictable long-term impacts of tampering with the genetic codes of plants and animals, especially as genes that can have adverse effects on consumers, such as those that trigger allergies, are introduced into the gene pool.

The potential for automation in industry was vastly enhanced by the development of the silicon chip, a complex miniature electric circuit etched onto a tiny wafer of silicon crystal. One type of chip, the microprocessor, could serve as the "brain" of a computer. Besides being able to carry out computing functions in a small space, no larger than a thumbnail, it was much cheaper than earlier vacuum-tube technology and much safer and more reliable.

Microtechnology and its growing cousin nanotechnology, which operates on scales too small for the naked eye to see, have radically transformed communications and information technology, not to mention the nature and extent of human economic activity. In the space of 20 years, the personal computer went from a minimally functional novelty item for technophiles in the late 1970s to an essential communications and information device as common as the television by the late 1990s, especially in the elite and middle-class homes of the developed world. Among the poor of the developed

▲ In more and more applications such as this automotive assembly line, robots are being used to replace human laborers in work.

	Scientific and Technological Milestones
1940s	First electronic computers invented
1953	James Watson and Francis Crick discover molecular structure of DNA
1957	Soviets launch first satellite, *Sputnik 1*
1961	Soviet cosmonaut Yuri Gagarin makes first manned space flight
1963	First artificial heart patented
1969	*Apollo 11* mission lands U.S. astronauts on the moon
1977	*Apple II*, the world's first home computer, introduced
1983	Internet established
1997	Birth of first cloned sheep, "Dolly"
2000	International Space Station put into operation
2003	Human Genome Project finishes sequencing complete set of human genes
2005	First face transplant performed

world, and throughout the developing world, access to computers has been much less ubiquitous.

Greatly expanding the utility of the computer has been the Internet, which was only established in 1983, and in little more than 10 years has linked billions of people together into a vast transnational cyberspace community. Again, while access to the Internet is taken for granted throughout most of the developed world, this isn't the case in most developing countries, where even if access is available, it will still be limited to those with higher incomes who are literate in one of the world's major languages—English, by far, being the most prominent language used on the Internet.

For individuals, everything from financial planning to training to basic communications can now be done on computers and over the Internet. For businesses, inventories can be more effectively monitored, and financial operations have been simplified. These new systems have led to the increased use of robotics in assembly lines, which are cheaper and more effective than humans for carrying out repetitive work.

By the beginning of the twenty-first century, all parts of the world were industrializing. There were major petrochemical complexes in the Middle East, automated steel mills in India, computer factories in Brazil, and sophisticated hydroelectric installations in Africa. All around the Pacific Rim, nations big and small experienced technological transformation. India benefited from all aspects of the international use of computers: a large part of the new developments in software took place there. A vast network of highways, pipelines, railways, shipping and air lanes, fiber-optic cables, and communications satellites united the world. All of these served the needs of multinational firms and publicly owned enterprises.

Technology, in turn, transformed agriculture and diet. Food canning and refrigeration, together with the bulk transport of grains, permitted the shipping of perishable goods to all parts of the world. Food production first expanded in the developing world in the 1940s through the 1960s, in what was known as the **Green Revolution.** Although these advances in agriculture have benefited many people, there have also been unforeseen consequences of the Green Revolution, including the pollution of the land through heavy application of pesticides, the poisoning of waterways through excessive use of fertilizers, and the desertification of vast tracts of previously fertile land by the redirecting of water to massive irrigation projects. Food production in the developed world, in turn, has been further boosted in recent years by the introduction of genetically modified crops, the use of new managerial methods, and the consolidation of operations under large-scale agribusinesses, with machines steadily reducing the number of workers doing menial labor.

Green Revolution—An aggressive effort by scientists in the mid- to late twentieth century to dramatically increase agricultural production by developing new strains of crops, particularly grains, that often require high amounts of water, plant nutrients, and pesticides.

The Ethics of Information Technology

Technology is a tool, lacking in any moral value of its own, but it can be easily misused, and even when used with the best of intentions, it transforms the world, giving critical advantages to those situated to use it most efficiently and leaving those who are not at a disadvantage. Not surprisingly, then, the use of new technologies raises a number of ethical issues.

One area that has received much attention lately is the Internet, specifically the free flow of information it facilitates. Although freedom of speech is viewed as a basic civil right in most developed nations, this isn't the case in some other places. Is it acceptable for U.S. companies such as Google and Yahoo to aid the Chinese government in censoring and controlling the Internet within China to gain access to that nation's lucrative markets?

Of course, as the Chinese government has found out, getting big Western companies to comply with their demands is one thing, completely controlling the flow of information over the Internet is another. Indeed, the Internet has greatly facilitated the continued existence of political dialogue in repressive societies like China and Iran. Just as multinational corporations challenge the sovereignty of nation-states, the Internet creates global communities that transcend the community of the nation.

But the Internet facilitates the flow of all information, whether it is worthy of our attention or not. Consider the examples of hate speech and pornography. Most nations, developed or otherwise, place restrictions on these, and yet the open architecture of the Internet makes bypassing such restrictions child's play. Unfortunately, although the Internet has become an invaluable tool for individuals seeking to circumvent political repression as well as for researchers, scientists, professors, and other professionals, it has also become nearly as useful for criminal gangs, con artists, sexual predators, and, perhaps most worrying, terrorists. Indeed, radicals, from Islamic militants to neo-Nazis, have used the Internet to spread their views around the world, employing it effectively for communications, propaganda, and recruitment.

Privacy is another area of ethical concern. Many feel that our right to privacy has become a victim of new technologies, with the rise of surveillance cameras, phone and computer taps, GPS tracking, Internet espionage, identity theft, and electronic credit card and bank fraud. Others also lament such problems, but they suggest that they are merely the price we have to pay for living in a high-tech society.

Businesses now regularly use software to keep track of consumers' buying habits and to predict future purchases. Internet companies such as Amazon, for example, suggest books to their users that align with their past purchase and search criteria. Similarly, politics has been changed forever by new polling techniques that rely on computers and the Internet. In the United States, social, economic, and political analysis of the country by each zip code is now a feature of modern campaigning. Political campaigns rely on the Internet to get their message to the potential voters. The extensive use of the Internet in 2007 by French presidential candidate Ségolène Royal and American candidate Hillary Rodham Clinton suggests that the Internet will transform women's access to political roles.

The flip side of intrusions into our private space is that these new technologies also empower the average person to participate in media culture and news collection like never before. The pairing of the digital camera with the cell phone has turned each of us into a potential photojournalist and major media networks now regularly air video clips taken by people who have been on hand to witness accidents and disasters. Politically active citizens post candidates' comments to YouTube, thereby molding the political message.

The New Communities of Cyberspace and Virtual Reality

In the past, the primary meeting place for people was the village center or marketplace. For thousands of years, people would gather in such locations to hear news, discuss politics, exchange ideas, pass along rumors, spread lies, evaluate potential mates, purchase goods, and arrange business deals. Now, although this model still holds true in parts of the world, it has largely been supplanted by the advent of popular media.

People around the world, of course, have been getting their news and information from newspapers, radio, and TV for decades now (centuries in the case of print journalism). The Internet has joined this mix within the last 20 years, but what sets it apart from the other media formats is its open access and interactivity. This has made the Internet not only a format where people can get information, but also one in which they can conduct business and interact socially. The result has been the rise of online communities.

One such community is represented by Wikipedia, the free online encyclopedia whose users write and maintain its entries (currently at over 1.7 million for its English site). Any user, with certain restrictions, can write entries and edit the entries of others. Such a system would seem to open Wikipedia up to considerable error, but self-policing by the site's users is surprisingly successful at reducing such errors or at least calling disputed facts to everyone's attention. Indeed, some authorities believe the site's science entries are as accurate as those written in traditional encyclopedias.

MySpace and FaceBook represent online communities pitched primarily to young people. These sites are geared toward social networking and interest in music and popular culture. Users of these sites compose profile pages for themselves (or the personas whom they wish to appear as) that can include multimedia presentations with music, photographs, and video.

YouTube, another online community, permits users to upload video clips to its site and share them with other users. The site, which was started in 2005, has quickly emerged as the world's largest library of video clips. As an indication of how quickly the site has swept the world, shortly after the former Iraqi dictator Saddam Hussein was executed in December 2006, clips of his hanging found their way onto the site. So too did clips of insurgent attacks on U.S. troops in Iraq and Afghanistan.

The online marketplace eBay has changed the nature of commerce, attracting millions of users around the world to buy and sell goods at what can only be described as a global garage sale. Other online communities have grown up around gambling and computer games. These communities allow users from around the world to enter virtual environments in which they can sit at a poker table and compete against others in a game of Texas Hold 'Em or enter a fantasy realm where they and fellow users wield swords and cast spells against trolls and dragons. Such communities are not without their critics. For example, some suggest that it is much easier to develop a gambling problem via cyberspace than it is in a casino. With computer games, which appeal most strongly to teenage boys, some fear that addictive gaming can lead to social isolation. A few gamers may face even more serious consequences. In 2004, a Chinese computer game addict was reported to have died of heart failure after 20 straight hours of continuous gaming.

Recent innovations such as podcasting, webcams, weblogs (blogs), and videologs (vlogs) have only increased the interactive appeal of online communities, which promise to grow larger and more complex in the future.

New Technology in the Developing World

As far as the cultural and economic impact of new communications technology goes, there is no doubt that cell telephones have made the biggest difference to populations in the developing world. Without the need to string expensive copper wire across the landscapes, cellular phone service is now available in impoverished areas such as sub-Saharan Africa, where around 15 percent of the people now have cell phones.

The economic benefit has been significant. With these communications devices, rural traders are now better informed about market conditions and have a better sense when and at what price to sell their products. If the $100 windup-powered laptop computers developed by MIT can be distributed to students in developing nations, poor people in rural parts of Africa and elsewhere will be wired to the rest of the world, gaining access to an ocean of information that to this point they have largely been denied.

People on the Move in a Changing World

What forces are driving people to migrate in larger numbers than ever before?

We do not know exactly why the first humans left their East African homeland eons ago, but it was probably for the same reasons that people leave their homes today—in search of food, security, and opportunity. The numbers of people on the move today, however, are unprecedented in their scale. Most of the people moving today are economic migrants leaving behind the poor developing world for job opportunities in the prosperous developed world, where declining birthrates and aging host populations have become the norm. These two trends—the migration of the world's poor and contracting populations in rich nations—are poised to radically transform the world in the twenty-first century.

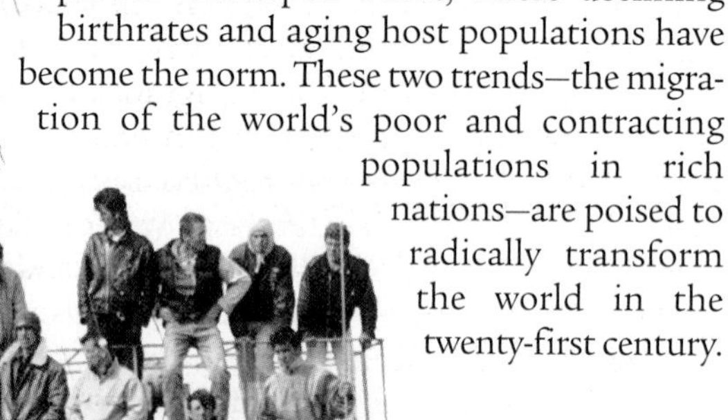

◄ Illegal immigration into the United States and the economically prosperous nations of the European Union has become a serious political and economic issue with long-term cultural and demographic consequences. Shown here is a boat full of Albanian migrants and refugees being turned away at Italian port of Brindisi in 1997.

Economic Migration

The imbalance of a world in which one-fourth of the population is rich and three-fourths are poor has produced a movement of people that has surpassed even the great migrations of the nineteenth century. Those who migrate abroad, especially the young between 18 and 34, deprive their home countries of their talent and labor, while at the same they help to sustain their home economies through the **remittances** they often send back to family members left behind. Their example and growing dependency on remittances in their home countries only serve to lure more young people to migrate abroad.

In the developed world, poor migrants, who often enter developed nations illegally, boost the local economy by providing cheap sources of labor. In some countries, they make use of the social welfare systems and other public services, placing strain on limited resources. Immigrants often come from profoundly different cultural and political backgrounds than those of their new host nations, which can lead to considerable tension between the migrants and established populations. In Europe, for example, many recent Muslim immigrants from North Africa and the Middle East have not yet successfully assimilated European values and cultural norms. Certain cultural practices such as polygamy, honor killing, and female genital mutilation conducted by small numbers of these migrants have alarmed many Europeans and helped to fuel a rise in anti-immigrant sentiment and **Islamophobia.** Even the use of headscarves and other forms of "veiling" by Muslim women has raised objections. In 2004, France banned the use of headscarves and other prominent religious symbols in schools and government facilities. Muslim immigrants, often those from rural and more conservative segments of society, express dismay over what they perceive to be the promiscuity, hedonism, racism, materialism, and godlessness of modern European society.

Even the children of migrants who have grown up in Europe and largely assimilated its culture are often treated as outsiders by established populations. Their sense of disenfranchisement and alienation

remittances—Money sent from one place or person to another, usually from an immigrant or guest worker in a developed country back to relatives left behind in a developing country.

Islamophobia—Fear of or prejudice against Muslims or Islamic culture.

has prompted some to turn to radical interpretations of Islam or to engage in criminal activity. In 2005, riots in Paris and other French cities by young migrants and citizens of North African descent were the result of just such sentiment, as are the rise of homegrown terror cells in Britain.

Tensions between local populations and immigrants have a long history. Local populations have often attacked economic migrants. For example, in the past quarter century, East Africans and Fijians have both denied rights and, in some cases, murdered immigrants from India, whose culture they disdained. In the 1960s, Chinese living in Indonesia, whose generally middle-class status and cultural differences distinguished them from their neighbors, were brutally attacked. Economic migration is usually a hopeful gamble for the migrant, but often cultural differences between immigrants and their host country, as well as racial and religious discrimination, make immigration a painful and difficult process.

Responses to Immigration

The challenges of migration have been addressed in a variety of ways. The United Kingdom pioneered a multicultural model that resembled the ethnic enclaves that emerged in the United States in the nineteenth century. A former colonial empire, Britain has a large variety of ethnic groups among its immigrants. The British allowed immigrants to form their own communities within the nation provided they adhere to the laws of the state. Prior to the September 11, 2001, terrorist attacks in New York and Washington, D.C., this model was generally considered to be the most successful in Europe. During the 1990s, however, Britain's welcoming attitude toward political refugees and dissidents permitted a small core of Islamic extremists who had fled or were driven from their home countries to settle in the country. They, in turn, set about radicalizing immigrant and British-born Muslims, particularly in lower-middle-class or poorer neighborhoods. Britain's participation in the invasions of Afghanistan and, in particular, Iraq fueled the spread of radical teaching in British Muslim communities. Following the July 7, 2005, suicide bombing attacks on the London transportation system by British-born Muslims and the disruption of a large number of other terrorist plots, the situation in Britain has become more strained. For all of the recent trouble, however, larger percentages of Muslim immigrants have managed to integrate into British society than have done so in other European countries. And, of course, Muslims make up only one element of an increasingly multicultural Britain.

The benign neglect model attempted by the Scandinavians and the Dutch sought to integrate the immigrants into host nations without demanding assimilation into the local language, manners, and mores, but it has not been particularly successful and has largely resulted in the ghettoization of immigrant communities, who with few employment opportunities subsist largely on government aid.

Germany, beginning in the 1960s, welcomed large numbers of Turks as "guest workers" in an effort to deal with labor shortages following the Second World War. This was done under the assumption that the migrants would return home after a few years of work. This did not happen, however, as many male workers took up permanent residence in the country and then moved their families and new wives from Turkey to Germany. Although Germany has not been subject to terrorist attacks like those perpetrated by small minorities of Muslim migrants elsewhere in Europe, tensions have arisen over questions of immigration and assimilation by Turks and others from developing countries (Muslims and non-Muslims alike). Ethnic conflict does occur, particularly in the former East Germany, where depressed economic conditions have fuelled the rise of neo-Nazi and skinhead groups among ethnic Germans who are opposed to the presence of foreigners in Germany.

France has an idealistic notion that all of its citizens are equal in the French Republic. As such, its government does not even keep track of the ethnic statistics of citizens and new immigrants. In principle this may be a noble concept, but in practice there is considerable discrimination against immigrants and their French-born descendants in France. This discrimination is not part of the French legal code, but it is engrained in French attitudes and greatly constrains the economic, educational, and political opportunities open to immigrants. Because the French government is relatively generous with the economic and housing benefits it extends to its citizens, its model for dealing with immigration appeared reasonably stable until the end of the twentieth century. By this time, immigrant communities in the suburbs of major French cities had witnessed rising levels of unemployment, failure in schools, and discrimination, all of which has led to higher rates of criminal activity, and in some quarters, militancy, including Islamic radicalism.

Japan has handled the need for cheap immigrant labor in distinct ways. The plummeting of birthrates and the reluctance of Japanese to do menial but necessary work has led to the introduction of two new sorts of immigrants. For the past three decades, young women from poorer countries in East Asia have been brought in to marry Japanese farmers unable to find brides among rural Japanese women, many of whom leave for more exciting lives in the cities. The larger source of immigrants is South American-born descendants of Japanese who had migrated to Peru, Brazil, and other countries in the past century. Hoping to avoid cultural problems, the Japanese government figured that Japanese-Brazilians or Japanese-Peruvians would quickly blend into Japanese society. But they are not Japanese, and as soon as they arrived, they set up Portuguese and Spanish newspapers and community and cultural centers. A South American–style "Carnival" has recently become an important local celebration.

Since the 1950s immigration into the United States from Mexico, the Caribbean, and Central America has dramatically increased, with migrants responding to the regional economics that created few job opportunities in their home countries and just the opposite in the United States. During the 1990s, immigration from these regions and elsewhere led to ten million people moving to the United States, many of them undocumented or illegal immigrants. In 2007, illegal immigration in particular became a point of active debate, with some arguing these immigrants drained the country's resources and services and others arguing that the immigrants' net contributions to the economy exceeded any costs they incurred. The White House and Congress attempted to draft new legislation on immigration, but struggled to find a compromise solution that would be agreeable to Republicans, who generally favored tighter immigration controls, and Democrats, who wanted to create a path to citizenship for the illegal immigrants already living in the country.

Rural Flight to Megacities

Migration from the developing world to the developed world continues to grow, but it isn't the only form of migration underway in the world today. Those who remain behind in the developing countries often participate in rural-urban migration. This massive population transfer from the country to the city has led to the creation of megacities such as São Paolo, Mexico City, Lagos, and Shanghai. These cities, with populations as large as 23 million people, are often surrounded by miles and miles of shanties whose residents live without clean water, medical and police services, or schools.

In the Nigerian city of Lagos, only 0.4 percent of people have a toilet connected to a sewer system. As a result, the abundant human sewage dumped into alleyways and ditches has contaminated the groundwater from which most of the drinking water is taken. There are few jobs for poor and uneducated men in the city, and for women the situation is often worse, leaving prostitution as one of the few ways they can eke out an existence. In the absence of minimal law enforcement, gangs impose control over individual shanty neighborhoods. Air pollution remains a constant problem, as do waterborne diseases. In 1950, the population of Lagos was around 300,000, and in a little more than fifty years, it has climbed to between 12 and 13 million. If growth trends continue, by 2015 it will be one of the world's five largest cities, with a population of around 20 million. The filthiness of Lagos was a major reason why the Nigerian government abandoned it as capital in 1991 and began building a new capital city at Abuja.

Around one billion people—almost half of the developing world's urban population—live in slums. UN reports indicate that in the next 20 years, the global urban population will double from 2.5 to 5 billion—mostly in developing countries without the resources or expertise to deal with the myriad problems accompanying rapid urbanization.[4]

Worse, the median age in these megacities is between 15 and 18, which is to say that 50 percent of the people there are young, with no real hope of a

▼ The Ajeromi slum of Lagos, Nigeria. In Africa, Latin America, and Asia, a constant rural to urban migration has led to the creation of "mega-cities" such as Lagos. These agglomerations can number up to 23 million people and have generally grown so quickly and are so poor that they have limited water and sewage systems, roads and sidewalks, and education and police services.

decent life, yet they are exposed to popular media that seductively depicts the comforts of life in the developed world. Such conditions are likely only to fuel further migration to the developed world and political instability in the developing world.

What the Future Holds

A common truism says that demography is destiny. This cliché may not be entirely accurate, but basic population trends are indicative of future political realities. For example, the ethnic makeup of the Kosovo region of the former Yugoslavia featured a substantial Serbian majority in 1940. Yet by 2000, the Serbian population had become a small minority and Albanians the vast majority. In another example, the Muslim population in Israel and the Occupied Territories is growing at a faster rate than the Jewish population, and so when Prime Minister Ariel Sharon unilaterally disengaged from the Gaza Strip in 2005, he did so less in a gesture at achieving peace with the Palestinians than in recognizing demographic realities confronting his nation.

In recent years, policymakers in the developed world have begun to express concern about the graying of their populations. By 2050, the population of the European Union will be 440 million, and the average age of that population will be 53—and a sizable segment of the population in retirement will be receiving government pensions supported by the tax revenue generated by less than one worker per retiree. The economic strains on the European social system will be intolerable. In contrast, the United States is projected to have a population somewhere between 400 and 550 million by 2050, with the average age a comparatively young 37.5. Yet even in the United States, declining numbers of tax-paying workers relative to retirees will make it challenging for the government to find the revenue to pay social security benefits to its many retirees. Already the economic system of nations such as Germany and Italy cannot function without a constant inflow of foreign labor from Eastern Europe and the Middle East.

Although birthrates have declined in both Western Europe and the United States in the last 50 years, the average life expectancy has risen over the same period. People in these nations can expect to live into their late 70s on average, if not longer. All East Asian nations, with the exception of the Philippines, Laos, Cambodia, and Myanmar, have birthrates well below replacement level. Japan has the world's longest life span (86 for women, 79 for men). In other nations, this isn't the case. Russia's overall population is declining thanks to a low birthrate and a high death rate—the average man dies now at 59, 4 years younger than 10 years ago, and the average woman dies at 72. Such a short life expectancy, while dramatic, pales before the staggering life expectancies in parts of sub-Saharan Africa beset by the AIDS epidemic. In Botswana, for example, AIDS has driven the average death age for men to 34 years—down from 60 before the AIDS epidemic struck.

Toward a World Culture

Is the rise of world culture a good thing, a bad thing, or something else?

The global economy now features multinational corporations, world brands (McDonald's, Sony, Coca-Cola, Nestlé, Starbucks, Adidas, etc.), universally accepted music (hip hop is favored by urban youths the world over), films from Hollywood and Bollywood, and the ubiquitous wardrobe of blue jeans, t-shirts, athletic shoes, and baseball caps among the world's young men and many of its young women. These are but a few signs that a truly global culture and way of life is being created.

Another feature of this global transformation in culture is represented by the rise of an international professional class, a movement that was already underway even before American, European, and Asian corporations began outsourcing work and exporting their corporate cultures around the world. The first members of this international professional class, in fact, were the children of elites throughout the developing world who were sent to American and European universities after World War II and returned home having assimilated at least some of the values of the West's professional classes.

Gender and Family

One particularly significant aspect of the growth of world culture is the changing ideas about gender, family, and sexuality that have transformed the globe since the advent of widely available birth control and the entry of women into the global economy in the years following World War II. Under Mao Zedong, the Chinese communist government used the slogan "Women Hold Up Half the Sky" to push for greater equality for Chinese women. Their efforts and the efforts of others elsewhere have had mixed results over the years, but economic necessity would seem to guarantee that women won't be leaving the workforce anytime soon. In fact, in Europe and America—as well as in Japan and the Philippines—women are beginning to be elected in significant numbers in regional and local government and in national legislative assemblies, even if not yet in numbers reflecting their proportion of the population. After 30 years of organized work by groups such as the National Organization for Women (NOW), women are becoming the dominant political force in the United

States, even though an Equal Rights Amendment was never ratified.

The middle-class family in the United States and Western Europe experienced a fundamental redefinition in the decades following World War II. If one believes the 1950s American television series *Father Knows Best,* the immediate postwar years represented the golden age of the traditional family. According to this TV program, such a family consisted of a genial and patriarchal working father, an attentive and loving housewife, two or three adorable but mischievous children, a dog, a house in the suburbs, and one, maybe even two, automobiles. This iconic presentation did not reflect the reality of most Americans at the time, but it made up part of the popular mythology of the United States. By the end of the twentieth century, the idea that love had to be the basis of marriage led to divorce rates in Europe and parts of the United States that reached 50 percent of all marriages. Single-parent families had become more reflective of reality. Economic demands and the liberation of women from traditional roles meant that working mothers could be found in most families, single-parent or otherwise. Increasing numbers of men chose to perform domestic work and care for their children while their wives worked.

As the global economy produces more and more changes, the institution of the family is undergoing redefinition. In 1998 and 1999, for example, the French instituted laws allowing nontraditional couples—homosexuals or unmarried men and women living together—to have the same legal rights as traditional married couples. In 2001, Holland became the first nation in the world to legalize same-sex marriage outright. Belgium followed suit in 2003, Spain and Canada in 2005, and South Africa in 2006. The state of Massachusetts in the United States legalized same-sex marriage in 2004, but this legislation provoked considerable opposition from conservative elements of society, and many U.S. states have refused to recognize same-sex marriages performed in Massachusetts. The controversial and emotional debate about the nature of the family and the roles of men and women in the new global society shows no signs of being resolved. (See *Global Issues—Marriage* on page 1096 for more on attitudes toward marriage throughout world history.)

Reactions Against World Culture

Some see the advent of global culture as **cultural imperialism,** that is, an imposition of culture by way of economic, political, and military dominance. This is true of the French, in particular, who resent that Anglo-Saxon influence—currently manifested in the form of American hegemony—has supplanted their own influence in the world and want to devise French alternatives to Google, CNN, and GPS satellites. Many in the developing world also considers the penetration of outside influence—Anglo-Saxon, French, Japanese, or otherwise—into their own culture as a threat to their identity, forgetting perhaps that all cultures, even their own, consist of layered influences from multiple sources.

Of course, the spread of global culture does not favor all equally by any means. The world's most dominant nations, principally the United States, exert the most influence on the evolution of global culture, whereas other, smaller nations and communities have much less say, if any, in the shape of that culture. Moreover, the rise of global culture advocates certain ways of life over others, with the result that it threatens the existence of smaller, more localized cultures and languages. Of course, the spread of dominant cultures at the expense of smaller cultures did not begin with globalization, but rather thousands of years ago with the advent of regional civilizations in the Near East, Mediterranean, India, and China. Globalization merely represents the most recent, world-encompassing stage of a long historical process, not that this fact is much consolation to the many peoples whose age-old cultural identities, languages, and beliefs are under threat by globalization.

The question is whether the twenty-first century will see the creation of a truly international civilization, or if some of the examples mentioned merely represent part of a cruel façade. Globalization has certainly provided fine rewards to the efficient and the well positioned. For those who are on the other end of the equation, however, globalization has only deepened the divide between the "haves" and "have-nots," while spreading media technology that allows the "have nots" to see just how well the "haves" live. The winners in globalization do live in an increasingly universal culture—their children attend similar schools, dress remarkably alike, listen to the same music, see the same films, and share many of the same political feelings. The remainder of humanity does not. Some of these "have nots" respond to their inequality by embracing dangerous ideologies, supporting local rulers—however corrupt or oppressive they may be—against their foreign enemies, seen by many as the developed world, or even more specifically, the United States.

In reaction against globalization, many of the world's poor are returning to their cultural roots with an aggressive zeal that bodes ill for the future. Some experts refer to this fragmentation of society as the return of tribalism. The classic definitions of identity—language, religion, myth, history, land—remain as

---

cultural imperialism—The practice of promoting the culture of one nation in another nation; usually the former is a large and powerful nation and the latter is a smaller, less affluent one.

strong as ever and are clung to more earnestly in the face of globalization. Ironically, the tools of globalization and Western-style modernity, especially the Internet, have played a central role in creating a worldwide, transnational "community" defined by the local, tribal aspects of identity. One can see this in the political chaos and violence consuming so much of the Middle East and Africa in recent decades.

As is true of other regions of the developing world, the Middle East and North Africa have experienced deep levels of economic and social inequality along with persistent political oppression. The *Arab Human Development Report,* which was written by Arab scholars and published by the United Nations Development Program, first in 1999 and again in 2002, 2003, and 2004, produced sobering statistics. According to these studies (and their findings have been challenged), much of the Arab world ranks far behind the rest of the developing world on the Human Development Index. The reports, for example, are highly critical of the state of education in the Arab world and identify three critical features lacking in its nations: freedom, knowledge, and equality for women. With regard to knowledge, the reports argue, by way of example, that Spain translates more books into Spanish in 1 year than all the Arabic-speaking world has in many centuries. Female illiteracy in the Arab world is the highest in any region of the world outside of sub-Saharan Africa. Compounding the situation and suggesting that even greater challenges lie ahead in the future, the Arab world has the world's youngest population—in 2002, 38 percent of Arabs were younger than 14.

Many observers in the Arab world—including those who espouse a radical Islamic agenda, among them the members of al-Qaeda and other related groups—point to different combinations of factors. Criticism of the corruption and undemocratic rule of most Arab governments figures high on most lists. Many also point to deep-seated cultural stagnation, brought on by persistently low levels of investment in education. Those with a clearly religious agenda also point to a perceived falling away from the "true" teachings of Islam by the people. Most observers, to different degrees, also point to the interference of the United States and other Western powers in the economic and political affairs of the region in the post–World War II period. A major source of bitterness has been the strong support shown by Western governments, the United States in particular, for the state of Israel. Many blame that support for Israel's often callous policies toward the Palestinian people, particularly those of the West Bank and Gaza (territories seized by Israel in the 1967 war). No less palpable is anger over Western support for the autocratic regimes of the region. In recent years, the U.S.-led invasion of Iraq and Israeli actions against the Palestinians have only served to fuel even greater anti-American, anti-Israeli, and anti-Western sentiment. The problem of the United States and Israel aside, Western secular culture is troubling to many in the Arab world, as are its social values, which, at least in more conservative eyes, undermine traditional family structures by extending new educational and economic opportunities to women.

In much of the Arab world, as in many other developing regions of the globe, the rise of an ultramodern, highly technological, and globalized culture raises questions about the long-term prospects of local communities. There are many people, in both developed and developing nations, who are convinced that local cultures will have to adapt quickly to avoid extinction. And as the gulf between the rich and the poor grows larger as a result of globalization, so too will the gulf between the cultures of the "haves" and the "have-nots."

▼ A crumbling Coca-Cola billboard in Managua, Nicaragua. Multinational companies such as Coca Cola (United States), Nestlé (Switzerland), and Sony (Japan) have turned the globe into a market for their products. For some, the actions of these companies represent both a damaging economic intrusion and an unwanted cultural infiltration into the developing world.

Looming Challenges

How might the world overcome the many challenges it faces in the future?

The challenges facing humanity in the twenty-first century are vast and imposing. This chapter has already examined some of these challenges in its explorations of economics, technology, demographics, and world culture, but there are many others, too.

Weapons Proliferation

The world thankfully managed to avoid nuclear Armageddon during the Cold War, but most of the nuclear weapons built by United States and the former

Global Issues

Marriage

Why have attitudes toward marriage changed so profoundly in the modern era?

▲ A same-sex marriage ritual in the Netherlands.

So universal all mankind,
In nothing else, is of one mind.
For in what stupid age, or nation,
Was marriage ever out of fashion?

Samuel Butler, *Hudibras*,
Part III, Canto 1 (1663–1678)

While marriage may never have been out of fashion, it has frequently taken forms that today's Americans would not recognize. Humans have never been "of one mind" about marriage which, like other human institutions, has a long and diverse history.

Until modern times, marriages have been used to cement political and economic alliances with scant concern for the partners' emotions or sexual feelings. Traditionally, relatives, often parents, arranged marriages. During much of human history, preserving the family and its property and developing a productive unit of men, women, and children were more important goals for marriage than creating a love-based emotional support system, which is the goal of most marriages in the West today. If in the past love drew a couple together in defiance of family interests, as in Shakespeare's *Romeo and Juliet*, only heartbreak and disaster could ensue. In some societies, love ideally developed after marriage—many in India today also view post-nuptial love as ideal. Conversely, in China prior to the twentieth century, growing affection between a husband and wife might qualify as grounds for divorce if it threatened the extended family's interests. The Roman philosopher Seneca's contention that "Nothing is more impure than to love one's wife as if she were a mistress" resonated in European thought for more than 1500 years. Our ancestors, however, were not loveless automatons. Some societies limited freedom of choice, but others required consent to marry. Over 1000 years ago, Japanese aristocrats had romantic relations with multiple partners before selecting a spouse. A thousand years before that, Romans had encouraged consent, though economic pressure and subservience to parental or political power often limited one's options. Our ancestors were also familiar with romantic love. Passion was celebrated in poetry and song. In classical Japan, works like *The Tale of Genji* praised marital and premarital romance.

Because of the singular importance of reproduction for the continuity of humanity, most societies have attempted to control sexuality through the state, religion, or custom. Marriage was the principal tool to regulate sexuality, serving state power through marriage alliances and, even more importantly, families' reproductive and economic needs. Marriage could be a relationship between one husband and more than one wife, *polygamy,* as practiced in early Judaism, Islam, nineteenth-century Mormonism, pre-modern China, and parts of Africa. Marriage could also involve one wife with several husbands, *polyandry,* as occurred in Tibet. Other more rare forms of marriage include sequential marriages of a widow to brothers, as practiced in ancient Judaism, and the marriage of female husbands to female wives, as practiced in some African societies.

In Paleolithic societies, marriage involved one husband and one wife who each provided gender specific labor . When food-gathering patterns shifted to hunting with weapons, women with small children focused on gathering fruits, berries, grains and other plant foods. But food supplies were unpredictable, so fostering relationships with other families on whom one could rely was an important reason for marriage. Many societies developed the custom of *bride wealth*—payments to the bride's family—or *bride service*—a prospective husband's labor for his wife's family—as a marker of that reliability.

While economic considerations and social calculation have figured prominently in marriage, they have not been the only factors determining who could marry whom. Prohibitions against incest, religious restrictions, class and caste boundaries, a preference for heterosexual pairing, and racism have also limited marriage partners. What exactly constitutes incest has varied from culture to culture, but all societies have had at least some form of injunction against marriage between members of the same family. Some religions prohibited marriage to partners of different faiths, although this provision could sometimes be overcome through the partner's conversion. Other societies limited marriages to members of the same social class or caste. In early modern Japan, commoners were not allowed to marry samurai and farmers could not marry city-folk, although these restrictions were often ignored. In India, marriages between Hindus were—and, in many cases, still are—supposed to be between members of the same castes. Attitudes toward same-sex and interracial marriage have historically varied. Same-sex marriage has not been very common, even in societies that tolerated homosexuality, because of the reproductive obligations associated with marriage. In ancient Rome, male same-sex marriages were accepted until 342 C.E., and in some Native American cultures same-sex partners who performed heterosexual gender roles were accepted. Some African marriage systems allow a woman to be a husband to a woman who bears children for the former's lineage. Today, a number of European and South American countries, South Africa, Canada, and a few U.S. states permit same-sex unions of various sorts.

Marriages between whites and members of other races, principally blacks, were long prohibited in many places in the United States. Many laws against interracial marriage were repealed in the 1950s, but it was not until 1967 that the Supreme Court, in overturning the arrest of interracial couple Richard and Mildred Loving, declared that marriage was "one of the 'basic civil rights of man.'"

How did marriage evolve from an institution to link families, consolidate property, and produce heirs to a basic civil right? To understand how this came about, we need to examine the course of marriage in Western culture. Married couples appeared frequently in the Hebrew Bible, where procreation within marriage was a divine commandment. The New Testament took a different view of marriage. The Gospels mention few couples other than Mary and Joseph. The early Christians elevated celibacy above marriage, believing celibacy would allow men and women to exercise self-control to pursue salvation. Sex even within marriage was "carnal pleasure," and that was blameworthy. Jesus condemned divorce, and thus divorce was prohibited to Christians.

From the fourth century C.E., the Catholic Church assumed the right to regulate marriages in Western Europe. But initially the Church inserted itself only in marriages of the clergy and the elite; and clerical marriage was prohibited only in the late eleventh century.

As for commoners, in 1231, the Church required the posting of *banns*—announcement of a couple's intent to marry—and in the next few centuries decreed that marriages must be performed with witnesses at the door of a church. In the sixteenth century, the Church ruled that priests were necessary to validate a marriage. At the same time, despite such injunctions, the Church also accepted a statement of intent to marry, even without witnesses or clergy, as a valid marriage. In 1563, the Council of Trent added that parents' blessing was not required to validate a marriage. With these provisions, Europeans were well on their way to redefining marriage as a love bond.

Martin Luther encouraged Protestant clergy to wed and serve as models of companionate marriage to their parishioners. Nevertheless, many of Luther's contemporaries were unable to marry due to poverty. In the 1500s in northern Europe, up to half of all adults were unmarried. The median marriage age for English women between 1500 and 1700 was 26. By the late 1700s, the rise of wage labor made young people more independent of their parents, and the age of marriage began to drop. At the same time, the notion of rights and revolution led some women to state that just as monarchs should not tyrannize their people, husbands should not be little monarchs in the family. The stage was now set for the explosion of love in Victorian marriages.

Victorians replaced the economic partnership concept of marriage with the notion of the husband as breadwinner and the wife as the angel in the household, raising her children in a pious atmosphere. This model carried over into the twentieth century. As young people based marriage primarily on love, the age of marriage plummeted—50 percent of all women married before the age of 20 in 1965—and by the 1970s, divorce due to marital incompatibility had became common. Was this a sign of the end of marriage? Perhaps not. In recent years the U.S. divorce rate began to decline, accompanying the rise in the age of first marriage due to higher levels of women's education and workforce participation. Increasing length of marriage as well as the notion that marriage should supply individuals' primary emotional and sexual satisfaction has made marriage a fundamental human right in the contemporary West. But as we have seen, this idea is by no means universal or transhistorical.

Questions

1. Why were marriages based on love seen as immoral in many eras and societies?
2. Some scholars contend that marriage is the foundational relationship of human society. Do you agree or disagree?
3. Should contemporary marriages follow single models set by law and local customs in each country today?

Soviet Union are still in existence today and serve as the foundation of both American and Russian military might. Some nations have used this fact and the weapons possessed by the other members of the nuclear club—which currently includes Britain, France, China, Israel, India, Pakistan, and now most probably North Korea—as justification for seeking nuclear weapons of their own.

In recent decades, a nuclear black market has evolved in which some states who have or are seeking nuclear weapons trade nuclear technology and materials. The Pakistani nuclear scientist A. Q. Kahn and elements of the Pakistani state were essential in the spread of nuclear technology to North Korea and Libya, and while the North African state has subsequently given up its nuclear programs, the North Koreans have gone on to develop nuclear weapons. In the past few years, Iran has also shown a commitment to the development of its nuclear capacity. Perhaps more worrisome even than so-called rogue states acquiring nuclear weapons is the idea of such technology falling into the hands of **nonstate actors** such as terrorist groups or organized crime.

Not as evident, but equally murderous, is how far research into biological and chemical warfare has progressed in the past half century. Germ warfare has been present for thousands of years, at least in primitive forms, but with new technology and methods of transporting diseases, modern nations are equipped to spread death through anthrax, botulism, tularemia, plague, smallpox, and hemorrhagic fever. Chemical weapons, first invented and used by European states during World War I, have been most recently deployed by Iraq during its war with Iran in the 1980s. The most prevalent form of chemical weapon today is nerve gas. Again, the thought of nonstate actors securing either biological or chemical weapons chills the blood. Most security analysts suggest it is not a matter of *if* but rather *when* a widespread attack using chemical weapons will occur.

	Population Growth and the Environment
1940s–1960s	Green Revolution boosts agricultural production throughout developing world, feeding population growth
1961	World's population reaches 3 billion
1962	Rachel Carson's *Silent Spring* published
1970	First Earth Day celebration
1974	World's population reaches 4 billion
1986	Chernobyl nuclear disaster spreads radiation throughout the USSR and Eastern Europe
1987	World's population reaches 5 billion
1999	World's population reaches 6 billion
2007	UN reports human activity is most probable source of global warming

Environmental Threats

During the twentieth century, each of the world's developed nations took measures to protect its own country's environment and to conserve its natural resources, but their record with regard to the planet's overall environment, particularly in the areas of global warming and resource consumption, has not been nearly as good. In fact, it is developed nations that are most responsible for two of the three greatest environmental challenges confronting the world. The first is the burning of fossil fuels, which is the primary source of the greenhouse gases responsible for global warming. The second challenge is the great demand for the world's natural resources exhibited by the economies of developed nations, which is responsible for a vast range of environmentally harmful activities ranging from the cutting down of tropical hardwood forests to the water and air pollution caused by mining operations. The third of the world's great environmental challenges is overpopulation in the developing world, which fuels yet more resource consumption and pollution.

As a consequence of the environmental challenges confronting the world, the tropical rain forests of Africa, Southeast Asia, and South America are being destroyed at a rapid rate. The deforestation of the Amazonian basin, which holds the vast majority of the world's tropical rain forest and most of its biodiversity, is of particular concern to environmental scientists because of this region's role in recycling the world's fresh air and water. Overpopulation is a major factor in deforestation in the Amazon and the rest of the developing world, as each year added population pressures compel greater numbers of people to cut down trees to create more open land for farming and ranching or simply to acquire firewood for home heating and cooking. Deforestation removes an important climate moderator from the environment, often leading to climate change, drought, and desertification.

Another area of great environmental concern is the world's oceans, where alarming changes have been occurring in recent years. During the 1950s and 1960s,

nonstate actors—Nongovernmental organizations, some armed and some unarmed, that play a role in international relations; unarmed nonprofit groups often have humanitarian goals, while armed groups are often criminal or terrorist organizations.

the oceans were touted as a source of virtually unlimited stocks of fish that would sustain the world's population indefinitely. This hasn't proved to be the case, as factory fishing fleets plying the seas have decimated fishing stocks, threatening the existence of whole species. Perhaps even more worrisome is that pollution and global warming are altering the chemical composition of the oceans, making the water cloudier and more acidic and facilitating the spread of toxic algae blooms, all of which put greater pressures on the oceans' fish and other living organisms.

What is happening to the oceans is only part of the world's water concerns; in fact, a more urgent matter for much of the world's poor is the scarcity of fresh water, which is under threat from overpopulation, pollution, and desertification. Many of the world's poor people have to go to great lengths to obtain water. That water is often not fit for drinking and so requires boiling to kill the bacteria in it; this in turn leads to more deforestation as the poor seek out more firewood. Even more greenhouse gases are then released into the earth's atmosphere.

Pollution is a growing problem. The 1972 UN Conference on the Human Environment produced no serious negotiations on this issue, but at least it did publicly acknowledge for the first time that the problem of pollution knows no national boundaries. Since that time, a number of international congresses and conventions have discussed the problems of global pollution. Of course, for every victory in the war against pollution, from local campaigns to clean up polluted lakes and rivers, to new technologies designed to reduce carbons emissions in automobiles—there are additional setbacks in other areas.

The threat to the earth's ozone layer, which not too long ago was viewed as the world's biggest single environmental issue, appears to have largely subsided, but it has been replaced by an even more pressing challenge: global warming. This long-term challenge is caused by the release of greenhouse gases into the atmosphere, mostly through the burning of fossil fuels, which in turn (acting like the glass windows of a greenhouse) trap more of the sun's heat energy within the atmosphere. The effects of this process take years to be felt, but they have accelerated in recent decades, and not surprisingly, most of the world's hottest years on record have all occurred within the last 10 years.

In 2007, a panel of world scientists brought together by the UN finally reported that human activity is the most probable source of global warning, after decades in which many of the world's governments had pressured their scientists to take a more skeptical stance toward the problem. Tentative steps to control the process of global warming, such as the Kyoto Protocol, have gained broad international support, although some key major producers of global pollution, such as the United States and Australia, have resisted taking these steps, fearing the effect they will have on their economies.

▼ Children wearing wrestling masks play near the La Oroya refinery and metals processing plant in the central Andean region of Peru. Government regulations control pollution in the developed world, but in developing nations such as Peru government controls are lax and industries can largely get away with releasing toxic materials into the air, water, and soil

Reasons for Hope

Why should we have any optimism about the future?

Despite the many challenges confronting the world in the twenty-first century, there are a number of positive trends today that should give us hope for the future. First, it should be recognized that there are more people living longer and healthier lives on the planet today than at any other time in the world's history. Although AIDS and other diseases old and new continue to pose threats to human well-being, modern medicine has cured or pushed back a range of ailments that killed or maimed great numbers of people in the past, including polio, smallpox, measles, typhus, and cholera. Even existing scourges such AIDS and malaria may be overcome in the coming years as medical researchers move closer to developing vaccines to prevent each disease.

We have already discussed some of the positive changes in the lives of women, but there are health benefits that need to be considered, too. Thanks to improved sanitary standards and better diet, fewer women, excepting the world's abject poor, die in childbirth. During the twentieth century, in fact, the life span of women the world over increased more dramatically than that of men, who, in general, engaged in riskier occupations and led unhealthier lifestyles.

Seeing Connections

The Earth

Throughout this book, we have emphasized the "connectedness" of the peoples of the world, and we have discussed examples of human interactions ranging from the magnificent to the tragic. Now, in the third millennium, we face a situation in which we deal not with discrete groups of humans interacting with each other, but with the whole human community facing a definite challenge to our collective future.

Four centuries ago, John Donne (1572–1631), in his *Meditations XVII,* philosophically understood this connection, and wrote:

> *... No man is an island, entire of itself... any man's death diminishes me, because I am involved in mankind; and therefore never send to know for whom the bell tolls; it tolls for thee.*

Donne's words have been used by all manner of people, from preachers to politicians to writers such as Ernest Hemingway, to stress the "connectedness" of us all. But, until William Anders, the *Apollo 8* Lunar Lander pilot, took this photo in 1968, no one had actually *seen* the globe for what it is—a fragile blue jewel of a planet surrounded by cold, infinite space. All of a sudden, humanity's notion of its tiny home in the universal scale of things and the uniqueness of our blue planet became evident.

As we enter the twenty-first century, scientists such as Stephen Hawking advocate speeding up space exploration in order to find another planet to serve as a "lifeboat" to save humanity. He fears that the abuse of our beautiful planet and its exquisite balance will continue. One of the most effective educators dealing with this question, the former U.S. vice president Al Gore, has been trying to convince American political and industrial leaders for the past 20 years of the dangers of global warming. In his documentary film, *An Inconvenient Truth,* he used the images taken by the *Apollo 8* crew.

The question we must ask is simply this: does global warming, which seems linked to increased human-generated CO_2, serve as the bell's tolling for the future of humanity? Or, because as Donne wrote, we are all "involved in mankind," will we try to save our planet? The answer is ours to give.

Today, in the developed world, women live from 4 to 7 years longer than men.

Hunger and famine still occur in the world, but not on the scale they did in the past. In a matter of decades, the Green Revolution, despite its problems, has turned India and China, two countries containing the world's highest populations and traditional sites of some of the world's worst famines, from food importers to food exporters. Indeed, outside of the poorest nations of Africa, the problem of hunger in the world now is less one of inadequate food production than it is the result of extreme poverty and warfare. Although there are a number of challenges associated with genetically modified crops, it seems likely that the application of science and technology to food production will continue to ensure that the world will not confront the great food shortages of the past.

Some view the pervasive spread of media technology negatively, but it has played a crucial role in shaping a global conscience among the people of the world. Coverage of the 2005 Asian tsunami by international media prompted unprecedented donations to aid organizations involved in the relief effort, not only from the governments of the developed world, but also privately from its citizens. As part of the evolution of a truly global conscience, prominent business and entertainment personalities have taken up the challenges of dealing with the world's problems through concrete actions. Bill Gates, Warren Buffett, Richard Branson, Bob Geldof, Bono, the late Princess Diana, Madonna, and Angelina Jolie are but a few of the people who have made this commitment with their time and resources, contributing millions of dollars of their own money and perhaps more importantly generating

Document

Wangari Maathai, *A Matter of Life or Death*

A conservationist and environmental activist, Dr. Wangari Maathai (b. 1940) founded the Green Belt Movement in Kenya in 1977. Her movement's primary objective is to increase Kenya's forest cover from 2 to 10 percent of its land surface by planting 30 million indigenous trees with the aim of improving air quality, combating soil erosion, and creating sustainable jobs for thousands of people in rural areas. Awarded the Nobel Peace Prize in 2004, she has now taken her movement international with a goal of planting 30 billion trees worldwide.

In many developing countries environmental problems are relegated to the periphery because they do not appear to be as urgent as other issues. However, a clearer understanding of environmental issues shows that they are a matter of life and death and should be a priority.

We cannot survive without clean drinking water, food and pure air. Environmental concerns are not a luxury in Africa....

The experience we have had in the Green Belt Movement for the last 30 years shows that it is possible to mobilize millions of individual citizens in every country to plant trees, prevent soil loss, harvest rainwater, and practice less destructive forms of agriculture.

Deforestation is on the increase across Africa. The UN recommends forest cover of at least 10 percent, but in Kenya it is less than 2 percent. Reforestation and conservation programs are two ways in which Africa can help face the huge challenge of climate change.

It is important to educate citizens on the need to protect trees, especially indigenous mountain forests, which are sources of water and biological diversity. Through the Green Belt Movement we have learned that when local communities understand the link between trees and their own livelihoods, they are more likely to protect them....

Political leadership is important and that is why we call on all governments to come on board. However, it is also important to get citizens involved because in the end, it will be citizens who force their governments to make tangible commitments.

The Green Belt Movement can help by enlarging our tree planting campaigns. This is not an excuse for developed countries to continue their emissions. Carbon offsetting is a mechanism that is needed to support work in developing countries and assist the developed countries to reduce their carbon emissions.

Forests play a major role as carbon sinks. We must assist people and governments to rehabilitate and protect the standing trees and vegetation. We need incentives including employment opportunities in forestry.

I believe the Billion Tree Campaign is wonderful because everyone can get involved—individuals, institutions, corporations, and governments. It's time for everyone to take action and support initiatives that can make a difference.

Questions to Consider

1. Why does Wangari Maathai believe that Africa will be hit the hardest by climate change?
2. In Maathai's view, what is the benefit of ordinary citizens participating in the movement to improve the environment?
3. What has been the impact of deforestation on developing countries?

From Wangari Maathai, "A Matter of Life or Death," *Guardian*, November 13, 2006. Available online at http://politics.guardian.co.uk/development/comment/0,,1946852,00.html.

public awareness of critical issues. Despite the criticism leveled against it by many on both the right and the left, the United Nations remains the principal international organization responsible for responding to the needs of the suffering around the globe.

The twentieth century was a bloody one, distinguished by two of the deadliest wars in human history and attempts to use modern technology in the service of exterminating whole populations. The pernicious scourge of war, sadly, remains with us in the twenty-first century. Still, if the United States and the Soviet Union could use reason and self-interest to avoid igniting a nuclear war between themselves, and if the nations of Europe, which have been warring with one another incessantly for more than a thousand years, can achieve the lasting peace that has reigned between them since 1945, the promise of a broader world peace may one day be achievable.

Finally, there are even some reasons to be optimistic about the earth's environment. If the international community of nations could come together and mutually agree to restrict the chlorofluorocarbons (CFCs) and other ozone-depleting chemicals that were threatening the ozone layer in recent decades, it seems within reason to expect that these nations, despite their present disagreements, can work together to find practical and economically feasible solutions to global warming in the coming years. The rise of environmental consciousness in the developing world, particularly the Green Belt Movement (see Document, Wangari Maathai, *A Matter of Life or Death*), offers hope that current rates of deforestation and desertification can be checked if not reversed.

Conclusion

In closing this last chapter of our book, we turn our attention away from the past and its many tragedies and triumphs, look beyond the uncertainty of the present and the near future, and imagine the world at the turn of the next century. What will the earth be like in 2100? Will humanity have found solutions to pressing challenges such as global warming, environmental degradation, resource depletion, overpopulation, economic inequality, disease, nuclear weapons, terrorism, and intercultural conflict? Will the average man or woman living in Africa, the Americas, Asia, Europe, and elsewhere consider the world to be a better place in 2100 than it was 100 years earlier during our own time?

While it is impossible to answer these questions with certainty, it seems very likely that humanity will need to learn to work together collectively in the coming years if it is to avoid tragedies equal to or greater than those of the twentieth century. This will require that the world's nations set aside their immediate and individual interests long enough to address the planet's long-term and collective interests. Indeed, more than any previous era, the twenty-first century will demand that we recognize the connections between local and global issues. With the accelerating tempo of developments in business, communication, transportation, and technology, each nation of the world will be brought into even closer contact with other nations in the future.

If economic and political events that happen in even the most remote corners of the world affect each of us individually today, such interdependence will be even greater in 2100. In fact, the political and social leaders of tomorrow may need to think in terms of a global constituency, not merely a national constituency. While we all hope that the leaders, thinkers, scientists, artists, and other great men and women of the twenty-first century will find ways to overcome the many challenges confronting the planet, the task of finding solutions isn't only up to them. Each of us will also play a role in determining what the world of tomorrow looks like. If you question how you as a single individual can bring about positive change, remember that interdependence means that the acts everyone takes, even small ones, affect others elsewhere in the world. A popular catchphrase of the environmental movement in the 1990s was "Think globally, act locally." This catchphrase carries special resonance for the twenty-first century—and not just for environmental issues. As the examples of Muhammad Yunus and Wangari Maathai showed in this chapter, small actions taken at a local level can have profoundly beneficial effects. They can even grow—like microfinance and Green Belt Movement—to become worldwide movements.

Suggestions for Web Browsing

You can obtain more information about topics included in this chapter at the websites listed below. See also the companion website that accompanies this text, http://www.ablongman.com/brummett, which contains an online study guide and additional resources.

UN Millennium Development Goals
http://www.un.org/millenniumgoals/
This site presents the eight development goals that the world's nations have agreed to meet by 2015.

Intergovernmental Panel on Climate Change
http://www.ipcc.ch/
There is a panel of international scientists established by the WMO and UNEP to study global warming. In 2007, the panel released its fourth and most recent report of climate change, which is outlined at this site.

The Green Belt Movement
http://www.greenbeltmovement.org/
The official website of the Green Belt Movement and its founder, the 2004 Nobel Peace Prize Laureate, Professor Wangari Maathai.

Wikipedia
http://en.wikipedia.org/wiki/Main_Page
Wikipedia is the free online encyclopedia composed by its users.

Literature and Film

The globalization of culture has allowed writers and filmmakers around the world to find audiences in societies beyond their shores. They have dealt with a wide range of topics that have become increasingly important in the twenty-first century, including the benefits and perils of modern technologies, reactions to changes in gender roles, environmental crises and disasters, cultural interactions, and economic inequalities. Chilling views of the future are featured in science fiction works like Ray Bradbury's classic *Fahrenheit 451* (1951), which deals with the implications of thought control through the destruction of the written word; Canadian novelist Margaret Atwood's *The Handmaid's Tale* (1998), which portrays a reactionary future in which women are denied all rights and made into reproductive machines; and African-American writer Octavia Butler's *Patternist* series of novels that highlight racial and gender tensions. Other important science fiction works include the cyberpunk, postmodern *Snow Crash* by American writer Neal Stephenson (1992) and *Solaris* by Polish writer Stanslaw Lem. Gender and cultural tensions (including those that involve modernization and the West) are addressed by the Nobel Prize winner Orhan Pamuk in *Snow* (published in Turkish in 2002, in English in 2004); by Nuruddin Farah in *Gifts* (Somalia, 1999); by Kuwana

Hausley in *The Red Moon* (Kenya, 2004); and by Tsitsi Dangarembga in *Nervous Conditions* (Zimbabwe, 2004).

Migration, identity, human rights, and intercultural relations are treated by Shouleh Vatanabadi and Mohammad Mehdi Khorrami in their anthology of modern Iranian short stories, *Another Sea, Another Shore: Stories of Iranian Migration* (Interlink Publishing Group, 2003). In *Strangers in the House: Coming of Age in Occupied Palestine,* Raja Shehadeh, a West Bank Palestinian lawyer and human rights activist, pens an eloquent memoir of living under occupation. Alaa Al Aswany's *The Yacoubian Building* (Harper Perennial, 2006), a widely read and controversial novel in Egypt, weaves together the lives of ordinary Caireans, residents of a once ultramodern, now rundown apartment building. *Welcome to Our Hillbrow* by Phaswane Mpe (South Africa, 2001) discusses the South African psyche in postapartheid South Africa, as well as xenophobia, powerlessness, crime and violence, rural prejudice, poverty, and HIV/AIDS.

Science fiction has been a staple of filmmaking for the past century, and it has treated many of the same subjects as prose works. Chris Marker's *La Jetée* (*The Jetty*; 1962, France) deals with Paris in the aftermath of World War III; Stanley Kubrick's pathbreaking *2001: A Space Odyssey* (1968) moves seamlessly from the dawn of the earth's existence through the year 2001, when human space travelers interact with the postmodern HAL, a computer; and Mexican filmmaker Alfonso Cuaròn's *Children of Men* (2006) addresses the issue of women's reproduction. Davis Guggenheim's Oscar-winning documentary *An Inconvenient Truth* follows Al Gore's speaking tours as he warns viewers about global warming.

Films that treat the difficulties of migration and ethnic clashes include Mexican filmmaker Sergio Arau's comedy *A Day Without a Mexican* (2004), the award-winning documentaries *Lost Boys of Sudan* (2004; directed by Megan Mylan), *Who Killed Vincent Chin?* (1987; directed by Renee Tajima and Christine Choy), and *Uprooted: Refugees from the Global Economy* (2001; directed by Sasha Khokha, Ulla Nilsen, Jon Fromer, and Francisco Herrera).

Hany Abu-Assad's *Paradise Now* (2005) follows the last hours of two suicide bombers in the West Bank. The film generated much controversy for its careful portrayal of the lead characters. Ilan Ziv's *The Junction* (2004) uses the deaths of two men, a Palestinian farmer and an Israeli soldier, to raise pointed questions about Palestinian-Israeli relations. *Al Jazeera, Voice of Arabia* (2003), directed by Tewfik Hakem, is a documentary on al-Jazeera, the Qatar-based media outlet, much criticized in the United States and Europe for its coverage but a popular news source in the Arab world. Shi'ite ritual and the political turmoil of post-Saddam Iraq is the subject of Katia Jarjoura's *The Road to Kerbala* (2005). *Al-Qaeda's New Front* (2005) examines the rise of Islamic extremism in modern Europe. Important recent African films include Abderrahmane Sissako's *Bamako* (2006), which discusses Africa's economic plight in the context of a young couple's troubled marriage; Zeze Gamboa's *The Hero* (2005), a tale of a disabled soldier returning home after 20 years fighting in Angola's civil war; and Senegalese director Ousmane Sembene's *Faat Kine* (2001), which focuses on women in postcolonial society. The documentary *Black Gold* (2006), directed by Marc Francis and Nick Francis, discusses the politics of coffee.

Suggestions for Reading

Scholarly works on the environment include Rachel Carson's pioneering work, *Silent Spring* (Houghton Mifflin, 1962); John R. McNeill, *Something New Under the Sun: An Environmental History of the Twentieth-Century World* (W. W. Norton, 2001); Al Gore, *An Inconvenient Truth: The Planetary Emergency of Global Warming and What We Can Do About It* (Rodale Books, 2006); Nobel Prize winner Wangari Maathai, *The Green Belt Movement: Sharing the Approach and the Experience* (Lantern Books, 2003); and Jared Diamond, *Collapse: How Societies Choose to Fail or Succeed* (Viking Books, 2005) that links environmental change to the success or failure of civilizations.

Social and political approaches to the successes and failures of civilizations include Paul Kennedy, *The Rise and Fall of the Great Powers* (Random House, 1987); Thomas Friedman, *The World Is Flat: A Brief History of the Twenty-first Century* (Farrar, Straus, and Giroux, 2005); and Samuel P. Huntington, *The Clash of Civilizations and the Remaking of World Order* (Simon and Schuster, 1996).

Classic analyses of women's rights in the West—Simone de Beauvoir's *The Second Sex* (Vintage, 1989) and Betty Friedan's *The Feminine Mystique* (W. W. Norton, 1963)—are joined by numerous recent books, including Estelle Freedman, *No Turning Back: The History of Feminism and the Future of Women* (Ballantine, 2002). Poverty is treated by Mike Davis, *Planet of Slums* (Verso, 2006) and Muhammad Yunus, *Banker to the Poor: Micro-Lending and the Battle Against World Poverty* (Public Affairs, 1999).

The often-misunderstood doctrine of *jihad* and its role in modern Islamic society and thought are discussed in Gabriele Marranci's *Jihad Beyond Islam* (Berg Publishing, 2006). Amira Hass's *Drinking the Sea at Gaza: Days and Nights in a Land Under Siege* (Metropolitan Books, 1999) is a fine account of life in occupied Gaza in the late 1990s. John Bowen's *Why the French Don't Like Headscarves: Islam, the State, and Public Space* (Princeton University Press, 2006) looks at the issues surrounding the rising presence of Islam in contemporary France.

New media create new identities. Video games are a global phenomenon that both build communities and allow individuals to create their own identities. For theoretical and historical treatments of video gaming, see Mark J. P. Wolf and Bernard Perron, *The Video Game Theory Reader* (Routledge, 2003), and Noah Wardrip-Fruin and Pat Harrigan, eds., *First Person: New Media as Story, Performance, and Game,* (MIT Press, 2004). The essays in Dale F. Eickelman and Jon W. Anderson, eds., *New Media in the Muslim World: The Emerging Public Sphere,* 2nd ed. (Indiana University Press, 2003) look at the impact of all forms of media, including the Internet, on contemporary Islamic societies.

Photo Credits

Chapter 12

p. 364: Stapleton Collection/Corbis; p. 367: The British Library (Or.5736.f.172v); p. 370: "Suleyman the Magnificent," mid-16th cent. The Metropolitan Museum of Art, Rogers Fund, 1938. (38.149.1) Photograph © 1986 The Metropolitan Museum of Art.; p. 371: Weltkarte des piri Reis, 1513. Istanbul, Topkapi. Serail-Museum/akg-images; p. 372: Rare Books Division, Department of Rare Books and Special Collections. Princeton University Library; p. 373: "Portrait of a Sufi," 16th century. The Metropolitan Museum of Art, The Cora Timken Burnett Collection of Persian Miniatures and Other Persian Art Objects, Bequest of Cora Timken Burnett, 1956 (57.51.27) Photograph © 1989 The Metropolitan Museum of Art; p. 377: Roger Wood/Corbis; p. 378: Folio from the "Haft Awrang" of Jammi Iran, 1556–1565. Freer Gallery of Art, Smithsonian Institution, Washington, D.C. Purchase (F1946.12.59a); p. 381: Angelo Hornak/Corbis; p. 382: J. Vidler/SuperStock; p. 383: Abu'l Hasan, "Allegorical Representation of Emperor Jahangir and Shah 'Abbas of Persia," South Asian, Mughal, c.1618. From the St. Petersburg Album. Full color and gold on paper; 23.8 x 15.4 cm. Freer Gallery of Art, Smithsonian Institution, Washington, D.C.; Purchase (F1945.9a); p. 385: "Birth of a Prince" from an illustrated manuscript of the Jahangir-nama, Bishndas (Attributed to), Northern India, Mughal, c.1620. Museum of Fine Arts, Boston, Francis Bartlett donation of 1912 and Picture Fund (14.657)

Chapter 13

p. 388: Craig Lovell/Corbis; p. 392: "Portrait of Hung-Wu." Collection of the National Palace Museum, Taipei. Photograph by Wan-go H.C. Weng; p. 393: By permission of The British Library, Maps Library Reproductions (Maps 33.c.13); p. 394: Tu Shen, "The Tribute Giraffe with Attendant", Philadelphia Museum of Art: gift of John T. Dorrance, 1977 (1977-42-1); p. 396, top: Burstein Collection/Corbis; p. 396, bottom: National Palace Museum, Taipei, Taiwan, Republic of China; p. 401, top: Courtesy, The Trustees of the Victoria and Albert Museum, Photograph by Ian Thomas; p. 401, bottom: Courtesy, The Trustees of the Victoria and Albert Museum, Photograph by Ian Thomas; p. 406: Mike Yamashita/Corbis; p. 407: Michael Maslan Historic Photographs/Corbis; p. 409: Michael Freeman/Corbis

Chapter 14

p. 414: Vatican Museums and Galleries, Vatican City, Italy/Bridgeman Art Library; p. 418: Asian Art & Archaeology/Corbis; p. 421: Scala/Art Resource, NY; p. 422: Erich Lessing/Art Resource, NY; p. 424: Scala/Art Resource, NY; p. 425, top: Erich Lessing/Art Resource, NY; p. 425, bottom: Scala/Art Resource, NY; p. 426: Bibliotheque de l'Institute de France, Paris/Art Resource, NY; p. 427: Erich Lessing/Art Resource, NY; p. 428, left: Scala/Art Resource, NY; p. 428, right: Summerfield Press/Corbis; p. 430: Archivo Iconografico, SA/Corbis; p. 431, left: akg-images; p. 431, right: National Gallery, London (NG 186); p. 432, left: Historical Picture Archive/Corbis; p. 432, right: Scala/Art Resource, NY; p. 433: Reunion des Musees Nationaux/Art Resource, NY; p. 438: Lucas Cranach the Younger, "Martin Luther and the Wittenberg Reformers," c. 1543. Toledo Museum of Art (1926.55) Purchased with funds from the Libbey Endowment, Gift of Edward Drummond Libbey; p. 441: Erich Lessing/Art Resource, NY; p. 447: Archivo Iconografico, SA/Corbis; p. 449: Scala/Art Resource, NY

Chapter 15

p. 452: Corbis; p. 454: Giraudon/Bridgeman/Art Resource, NY; p. 456: Corbis; p. 458: Austrian Archives: Haus-, Hof- und Staatsarchiv, Vienna/Corbis; p. 459: National Gallery Budapest/Dagli Orti/The Art Archive; p. 461: Scala/Art Resource, NY; p. 468: Wallach Collection, New York Public Library, Astor, Lenox and Tilden Foundations; p. 470: Musees de la Ville de Strasbourg; p. 472: Barry Lewis/Corbis; p. 473: Archivo Iconografico, SA/Corbis; p. 475: The Art Archive/Corbis; p. 476: The Art Archive/Corbis

Chapter 16

p. 480: British Museum, London, UK/Bridgeman Art Library; p. 483: National Maritime Museum, Greenwich (HC0705); p. 484: Bettmann/Corbis; p. 486: Museo de Arte Antiga Lisbon/Dagli Orti/The Art Archive; p. 488: Werner Forman/Art Resource, NY; p. 489: Library of Congress; p. 493: Bibliotheque Nationale de France, Paris; p. 495: The Trustees of the British Museum (1950AM22 1); p. 496: Library of Congress; p. 497: akg-images; p. 502: Bodleian Library, Oxford University; p. 506: Library of Congress; p. 507: Bettmann/Corbis

Chapter 17

p. 510: Krause, Johansen/Archivo Iconografico, SA/Corbis; p. 513: Archivo Iconografico, SA/Corbis; p. 515: Reunion des Musees Nationaux/Art Resource, NY; p. 517: Bettmann/Corbis; p. 518: Archivo Iconografico, SA/Corbis; p. 523: Bildarchiv Preussischer Kulturbesitz/Art Resource, NY; p. 525: Bettmann/Corbis; p. 533: Rijksmuseum, Amsterdam; p. 534: Stapleton Collection/Corbis; p. 536: Corbis; p. 538: Corbis

Chapter 18

p. 546: Giraudon/Art Resource, NY; p. 549: By permission of the British Library (Maps C.6.c.3. bet 22 & 23); p. 550: Stefano Bianchetti/Corbis; p. 555: Bettmann/Corbis; p. 558: Murat Taner/Zafer/Corbis; p. 560: Sovfoto; p. 561: Bettmann/Corbis; p. 563: Giraudon/Art Resource, NY; p. 565: Giraudon/Art Resource, NY; p. 573: Erich Lessing/Art Resource, NY

Chapter 19

p. 580: Stapleton Collection/Corbis; p. 583: Kenneth Martin/Landov; p. 584: Bettmann/Corbis; p. 586: Library of Congress; p. 590: Jean-Loup Charmet/Bridgeman Picture Library; p. 596: Panos Pictures; p. 597: South African Library of Capetown/Panos Pictures; p. 599: Mary Evans Picture Library; p. 602: Peter Newark's Pictures; p. 603: Caroline Penn/Corbis

Chapter 20

p. 606: Museum of Fine Arts, Boston. William Sturgis Bigelow Collection, 11.19687. Photograph © 2004 Museum of Fine Arts, Boston.; p. 610: "Birth in the Harem," late 18th century. Los Angeles County Museum of Art, The Edward Binney, 3rd Collection of Turkish Art. Photograph © 2005 Museum Associates/Los Angeles County Museum of Art; p. 612: Mary Evans Picture Library; p. 615: Burstein Collection/Corbis; p. 617: Victoria & Albert Museum, London/Art Resource, NY; p. 619: Pierre Colombel/Corbis; p. 620: Photography Courtesy Peabody Essex Museum (Neg #19184); p. 621: "Giuseppe Castiglione, Italian (worked in China), 1688–1766. "Inauguration Portraits of Emperor Qianlong, the Empress, and the Eleven Imperial Consorts," 1736. Hand-scroll, ink and color on silk, 52.9 x 688.3 cm. © The Cleveland Museum of Art. John L. Severance Fund, 1969.31; p. 625:; p. Pleynet/Art Resource, NY; p. 627: Erich Lessing/Art Resource, NY; p. 630: Isoda Korysai, "Hinagata Wakana Hatsumoyo" series, c. 1775. Collection of the Newark Museum, Louis V. Ledoux Collection. The Newark Museum/Art Resource, NY; p. 635: Bettmann/Corbis

Chapter 21

p. 638: Gianni Dagli Orti/Corbis; p. 642: Museo de America; p. 643: University of Minnesota, James Ford Bell Library; p. 644: Bettmann/Corbis; p. 645: Corbis; p. 647: Bettmann/Corbis; p. 648: Bettmann/Corbis; p. 651: Architect of the Capitol; p. 652: The Granger Collection; p. 657: Organization of American Studies (2)

Chapter 22

p. 662: Corbis; p. 665: The Granger Collection; p. 668: Historisches Archiv Fried, Krupp AG.; p. 669: Library of Congress; p. 671: Hulton-Deutsch Collection/Corbis; p. 676: Culver Pictures, Inc.; p. 679: Francis G. Mayer/Corbis; p. 682: Hulton-Deutsch Collection/Corbis; p. 688: Asian Art & Archaeology, Inc./Corbis; p. 691: akg-images; p. 692, top: Erich Lessing/Art Resource; p. 692, bottom: Claude Monet, French, 1840–1926, Water Lilies, 1906, oil on canvas, 34 1/2 x 36 1/2 in. (87.6 x 92.7 cm.), Mr. And Mrs. Martin A. Ryerson Collection, 1933.1157 Reproduction, The Art Institute of Chicago

Chapter 23

p. 696: Bettmann/Corbis; p. 699: Bettmann/Corbis; p. 701: Erich Lessing/Art Resource, NY; p. 705: Corbis; p. 709: Gianni Dagli Orti/Corbis; p. 710: Art Resource, NY; p. 711: Hulton Archive/Getty Images; p. 714: Mansell Collection/Time Life Pictures/Getty Images; p. 716: Bibliotheque Nationale de France, Paris; p. 720: Courtesy, The Museum of London (#11274); p. 725: Hulton-Deutsch Collection, Corbis; p. 727: Swim Ink 2, LLC/Corbis

Chapter 24

p. 736: The British Museum; p. 739: Culver Pictures, Inc.; p. 744: National Archives, Zimbabwe; p. 745: Corbis; p. 747: Museum Africa; p. 749: Courtesy of the author; p. 750: Werner Forman/Art Resource, NY; p. 751: Revue Noire; p. 753: Courtesy of the author; p. 757: Erich Lessing/Art Resource, NY; p. 758: Mary Evans Picture Library; p. 759: Ottoman Gazette Kalem; p. 763: Roger-Viollet/Getty Images; p. 764: Brown Brothers; p. 766: Reunion des Musees Nationaux/Art Resource, NY

Chapter 25

p. 770: The Mariners' Museum; p. 774: The Granger Collection; p. 775: Hulton Archive/Corbis; p. 778: The Granger Collection; p. 779: General Research Division, The New York Public Library, Astor, Lenox and Tilden Foundation; p. 782: Historical Picture Archive/Corbis; p. 787: Asian Art & Archaeology, Inc./Corbis; p. 789: akg-images; p. 793: Corbis

Chapter 26

p. 796: Giraudon/Art Resource, NY; p. 801: Bettmann/Corbis; p. 805: Mary Evans Picture Library; p. 806: Bettmann/Corbis; p. 808: Corbis; p. 809: Archivo General de la Nacion, Buenos Aires, Argentina; p. 812: Ralph E. W. Earl, "Portrait of

General Andrew Jackson, President of the United States." Memphis Brooks Museum of Art, Memphis, TN; The Memphis Park Commission Purchase, 46.2; p. 815: Bettmann/Corbis; p. 817: The British Museum; p. 818: Collection of the New York Historical Society, negative number 43054; p. 820: Bettmann/Corbis

Chapter 27

p. 822: Hulton-Deutsch Collection/Corbis; p. 826: Leonard de Selva/Corbis; p. 829: Corbis; p. 832: Imperial War Museum; p. 834: Corbis; p. 836: Brown Brothers; p. 838: Gideon Mendel/Corbis; p. 844: Hulton-Deutsch/Corbis; p. 846: Bettmann/Corbis; p. 848: Bettmann/Corbis; p. 850: Hulton Archive/ Getty Images; p. 853: Library of Congress; p. 855: Underwood & Underwood/Corbis; p. 856: The Museum of Modern Art/Scala/Art Resource, NY

Chapter 28

p. 860: Bettmann/Corbis; p. 864: Bettmann/Corbis; p. 866: Bettmann/Corbis; p. 869: The Granger Collection; p. 871: Hulton-Deutsch Collection/Corbis; p. 872: Stefane Bianchetti/Corbis; p. 875: Bildarchiv Preussischer Kulturbesitz/Art Resource, NY/© Estate of George Grosz/Licensed by VAGA, New York, NY; p. 876: Robertstock.com; p. 880: Petersham Book Loft; p. 883: Bettmann/Corbis; p. 885: Sovfoto; p. 887: Sovfoto

Chapter 29

p. 892: Bettmann/Corbis; p. 895: Bettmann/Corbis; p. 897: ENA/Popperfoto/ Robertstock/Retrofile; p. 899: akg-images; p. 901: Leonardo de Selva/Corbis; p. 903: Photos12.com; p. 910: AP/Wide World Photos

Chapter 30

p. 912: Corbis; p. 916: Corbis; p. 917: Hulton Archive/Getty Images; p. 921: Hulton-Deutsch Collection/Corbis; p. 923: Keystone Press Agency/Zuma; p. 924: Bettmann/Corbis; p. 927: Topham, London/The Image Works; p. 929: Bailey's African History Archives; p. 930: Hulton Archive/Getty Images

Chapter 31

p. 932: Bettmann/Corbis; p. 938: NARA; p. 939: Hulton-Deutsch Collection/ Corbis; p. 942: Corbis; p. 947: Hulton Archive/Getty Images; p. 948: Corbis; p. 949: National Park Service/epa/Corbis; p. 950: akg-images; p. 951: Bettmann/Corbis; p. 954: Roger Ressmeyer/Corbis

Chapter 32

p. 958: Corbis; p. 963: Bettmann/Corbis; p. 964: Corbis; p. 967: Corbis; p. 969: Sovfoto; p. 971: TASS/Sovfoto; p. 975: AP/Wide World Photos; p. 982: Peter Jordan; p. 994: Robert Clark/Aurora Pictures; p. 995: Reuters/Corbis

Chapter 33

p. 998: AP/Wide World Photos; p. 1006: AP/Wide World Photos; p. 1007: Bettmann/Corbis; p. 1009: Reuters/Corbis; p. 1010: Reinhard Krause/Reuters/ Corbis; p. 1012: Stefano Bianchetti/Corbis; p. 1020: Christophe Karaba/epa/Corbis; p. 1022: Reuters/Corbis; p. 1023: Corbis

Chapter 34

p. 1026: Commissioned by the Trustees of Dartmouth College, Hanover, New Hampshire/Hood Museum of Art.; p. 1028: Archivo Generale de la Nacion, Buenos Aires, Argentina; p. 1034: Steve Starr/Corbis; p. 1035: Stephane Mantey/Tempsport/Corbis; p. 1036: Bettmann/Corbis; p. 1041: Estudio Revolution/Handout/epa/Corbis; p. 1043: David de la Paz/EFE/Corbis

Chapter 35

p. 1046: Peter Turnley/Corbis; p. 1052: Bettmann/Corbis; p. 1053: Time Life Pictures/Getty Images; p. 1056: Corbis; p. 1059: Bettmann/Corbis; p. 1063: Reuters/Corbis; p. 1068: AFP/Getty Images; p. 1073: "Greenpeace Action Against Indian Nuclear Test," Taj Mahal, Agra, India. GREENPEACE/Morgan; p. 1075: Macduff Everton/Corbis

Chapter 36

p. 1078: Corbis; p. 1086: Karen Kasmauski/Corbis; p. 1087: Charles O'Rear/ Corbis; p. 1090: AP/Wide World Photos; p. 1091: Gideon Mendel/ActionAid/ Corbis; p. 1094: Hollandse-Hoogte/Corbis; p. 1096: Carl and Ann Purcell/Corbis; p. 1098: Reuters/Corbis; p. 1099: Bettmann/Corbis

Text Credits

Chapter 12

p. 384: Pages xxii-xxi, 219, 368, 376, 441", from The Jahangirnama, edited by Wheeler Thackston, translated by Wheeler Thackston. Copyright © 1999 by Smithsonian Institution. Used by permission of Oxford University Press, Inc.

Chapter 13

p. 398: Reprinted with the permission of The Free Press, a Division of Simon & Schuster Adult Publishing Group, from Chinese Civilization: A Sourcebook, Second Edition by Patricia Buckley Ebrey. Copyright © 1993 by Patricia Buckley Ebrey. All rights reserved; p. 405: From Kan'ami Kiyotsugu, "Sotoba Komachi" from Anthology of Japanese Literature, edited by Donald Keene. Copyright © 1955 by Grove Press, Inc. Used by permission of Grove/Atlantic, Inc; p. 410: From Ma Huan,Ying-yai Sheng-lai: The Overall Survey of the Ocean's Shores (1433), trans. Feng Ch'eng Chun, intro. by J.V.G. Mills, 1970. Used by permission of David Higham Associates Ltd.

Chapter 14

p. 442: From A Tudor Tapestry by Derek Wilson, published by William Heinemann Ltd. Reprinted by permission of The Random House Group Ltd.

Chapter 16

p. 491: From The Rise and Fall of Swahili States by Chapurukha M. Kusimba, 1999. Used by permission of Rowman & Littlefield Publishers, Inc; From Basil Davidson, African Past. Copyright © 1964 by Basil Davidson. Reprinted by permission of Curtis Brown, Ltd.

Chapter 17

p. 542: Arthur Young and Constantia Maxwell, Travels in France. (New York: Cambridge University Press, 1929) p. 107; p. 519: (PENDING) From "Catherine II on Life in St. Petersburg in 1750" from The Memoirs of Catherine the Great trans. by Moura Budberg, 1961, pp. 136-140.

Chapter 18

p. 568: From The Burgundian Code: Book of Constitutions of Law of Gundobad, Additional Enactments (Sources of Medieval History) trans. by Katherine Fischer Drew, Edward Peters. Copyright © 1972. Reprinted by permission of the University of Pennsylvania Press.

Chapter 19

p. 588: From The Biography of Mahommah Gardo Baquaqua His Passage from Slavery to Freedom in Africa and America, by Robin Law and Paul Lovejoy, eds. Copyright © 2001 by Markus Wiener Publishers, Princeton, NJ. Reprinted by permission.

Chapter 20

p. 622: Reprinted with the permission of The Free Press, a Division of Simon & Schuster Adult Publishing Group, from Chinese Civilization: A Sourcebook, Second Edition by Patricia Buckley Ebrey. Copyright © 1993 by Patricia Buckley Ebrey. All rights reserved; p. 631: Excerpt from Ihara Saikaku, "The Umbrella Oracle" from Anthology of Japanese Literature, edited by Donald Keene. Copyright © 1955 by Grove Press, Inc. Used by permission of Grove/Atlantic, Inc.

Chapter 24

p. 743: Jon M. Bridgman, The Revolt of the Hereros. Berkeley: University of California Press, 1981, pp. 127-128; p. 762: From Disorienting Encounters: Travels of a Moroccan Scholar in France in 1845–1856, ed. and trans. Susan G. Miller. Copyright © 1992 The Regents of the University of California. Reprinted by permission of the University of California Press.

Chapter 25

p. 776: Barbara D. Metcalf and Thomas R. Metcalf, A Concise History of India. (Cambridge: Cambridge University Press, 2002), p. 99.

Chapter 26

p. 803: From Robert Edgar Conrad, Children of God's Fire: A Documentary History of Black Slavery in Brazil. (University Park, Pennsylvania: Pennsylvania State University Press, 1984), pp. 362-365; p. 819: From Philip Foner, ed., Our American Writings on Latin America and the Struggle for Cuban Independence by José Marti. Copyright © 1977 by Monthly Review Press. Reprinted by permission of Monthly Review Foundation.

Chapter 27

p. 828: (PENDING) "The Western Front Christmas 1914", "An Artilleryman Remembers" by Gunner Herbert Smith, 5th Battery, Royal Field Artillery; (PENDING) "The Western Front Christmas 1914", "The German View of Events-including the Football Match" by Lieutenant Johannes Niemann, 133rd Royal Saxon Regiment.

Chapter 28

p. 879: G. Kallmeyer, "The Women's Issue and Its National Socialist Solution," Wolfenbuttel, Berlin, 1933, as in Fascism: Oxford Readers, Roger Griffin, ed., Oxford University Press, 1995; p. 889: Reprinted with the permission of Scribner, an imprint of Simon & Schuster Adult Publishing Group, from Hope Against Hope: A Memoir by Nadezhda Mandelstam, translated from the Russian by Max Hayward. English Translation copyright © 1970 by Atheneum Publishers. All rights reserved.

Chapter 30

p. 928: (PENDING) From "Petition of the Native and Coloured Women of the Province of The Orange Free State" March 11, 1912; (PENDING) From "Lilian Ngoyi, Presidential Address to the African National Congress Women's League, Transvaal", South Africa 1956.

Chapter 31

p. 935: From The Road Back by Erich Maria Remarque. Copyright © 1931 by A. G. Ullstein; copyright renewed © 1958 by Erich Maria Remarque. All Rights Reserved. Reprinted by permission; p. 952: From Henry Friedlander, "The Nazi Camps," in Genocide: Critical Issues of the Holocaust, ed. Alex Grobman and David S. Landes. (Los Angeles: Simon Wiesenthal Center, 1983), pp. 222-223.

Chapter 32

p. 991: "Time to Break Silence" by Dr. Martin Luther King, Jr. Copyright 1967 Martin Luther King Jr.; copyright renewed 1995 Coretta Scott King. Reprinted by arrangement with The Heirs to the Estate of Martin Luther King Jr., c/o Writers House as agent for the proprietor New York, NY.

Chapter 33

p. 1018: From Scotch Tagwiyeri, "The village that has 'eaten itself limb by limb" first published in Daily Mail and Guardian, March 9 to 15, 2001. (Johannesburg, South Africa). Reprinted by permission.

Chapter 34

p. 1031: (PENDING) "President Hugo Chavez's 2006 Address to the U. N. General Assembly"; p. 103: (PENDING) From My Mission in Life by Eva Peron trans. by Ethel Cherry, 1953, p. 60.

Chapter 35

p. 1057: From Broken Silence: Voices from Japanese Feminism by Sandra Buckley. Copyright © 1997 The Regents of the University of California. Reprinted by permission of the University of California Press.

Chapter 36

p. 1085: "Muhammad Yunus, Acceptance Speech for the 2006 Nobel Peace Prize." © The Nobel Foundation 2006. Reprinted by permission; p. 1100: From "A Matter of Life or Death" by Wangari Maathai as appeared in Guardian Unlimited, November 13, 2006. Copyright Guardian News & Media Ltd 2006. Reprinted by permission of Guardian Unlimited.

Notes

Chapter 12

1. Vincent A. Smith, *Akbar, the Great Mogul,* 2nd ed. (Mystic, Conn.: Verry, 1966), p. 522.
2. Zahiruddin Muhammad Babur, *Baburnama,* trans. and ed. Wheeler Thackston (New York: Oxford University Press, 1996), pp. 350–351.
3. Babur, p. 351.
4. Quoted in Bamber Gascoigne, *The Great Moghuls* (New York: Harper & Row, 1971), p. 128.

Chapter 13

1. Quoted in Stephen Turnbull, *The Samurai: A Military History* (London: Routledge Curzan, 1996), p. 180.
2. Quoted in Anthony Reid, *Southeast Asia in the Early Modern Era,* (Ithaca, NY: Cornell University Press, 1993), p. 79.

Chapter 14

1. Copyrighted by Pall Halsall, March 1996, from http://www.fordham.edu/halsall/source/witches.html.
2. http://www.thecaveonlinecom/APEH/reformdocument.
3. Quoted in Roland Bainton, *Here I Stand: A Life of Martin Luther* (New York: Abingdon Cokesbury, 1950), p. 54.
4. Quoted in Heiko A. Oberman, *Luther, Between God and the Devil* (New Haven, Conn.: Yale University Press, 1982) p. 190; see also pp. 187–188.
5. From Henry Bettenson, ed., *Documents of the Christian Church* (New York: Oxford University Press, 1963), pp. 280–283.
6. Quoted in Harold Grim, *The Reformation Era* (New York: Macmillan, 1968), p. 17.
7. From "Institutes of the Christian Religion," in Harry J. Carroll et al., eds., *The Development of Civilization* (Glenview, Ill.: Scott, Foresman, 1970), pp. 91–93.
8. From Lowell H. Zuck, ed., *Christianity and Revolution* (Philadelphia: Temple University Press, 1975), pp. 95–97.

Chapter 15

1. Charles Tilly, ed., *The Formation of the National States in Western Europe* (Princeton, N.J.: Princeton University Press, 1975), p. 42.
2. See Charles Tilly, *Coercion, Capital, and European States, AD 990–1992* (Oxford: Blackwell, 1992).
3. See K. Bosl, A. Gieysztor, F. Graus, M. M. Postan, F. Seibt, *Eastern and Western Europe in the Middle Ages,* ed. Geoffrey Barraclough (London: Thames and Hudson, 1970).
4. Wallace T. MacCaffrey, *Elizabeth I, War and Politics 1558–1603* (Princeton, N.J.: Princeton University Press, 1992), p. 6.
5. Peter F. Sugar, *Southeastern Europe Under Ottoman Rule: 1354–1804,* Vol. 5 of Peter F. Sugar and Donald W. Treadgold, eds., *A History of East Central Europe* (Seattle and London: University of Washington Press, 1977), pp. 55–59, 273–274.
6. Peter F. Sugar, *Southeastern Europe Under Ottoman Rule: 1354–1804,* Vol. 5 of Peter F. Sugar and Donald W. Treadgold, eds., *A History of East Central Europe* (Seattle and London: University of Washington Press, 1977), pp. 55–59, 273–274.

Chapter 16

1. Quoted in David Killingray, *A Plague of Europeans* (New York: Penguin, 1973), p. 20.
2. Quoted in Robert Rotberg, *A Political History of Tropical Africa* (New York: Harcourt Brace, 1965), pp. 85–86.
3. Quoted in John Middleton, *The World of the Swahili: An African Mercantile Civilization* (New Haven, Conn.: Yale University Press, 1992), pp. 46–47.

Chapter 17

1. Quoted in F. Tyler, *The Modern World* (New York: Farrar & Rinehart, 1939), p. 186.
2. Quoted in Robert B. Asprey, *Frederick the Great: The Magnificent Enigma* (New York: Ticknor & Fields, 1986).
3. See the superb book by Simon Schama, *The Embarrassment of Riches: An Interpretation of Dutch Culture in the Golden Age* (New York: Vintage, 1997).
4. Quoted in Pierre Gaxotte, *Frederick the Great* (London: Bell, 1941), p. 357.

Chapter 18

1. Quoted in Stillman Drake, *Galileo at Work* (Chicago: University of Chicago Press, 1978), p. 41.
2. Giorgio de Santillan, *The Crime of Galileo* (Chicago: University of Chicago Press, 1955), p. 310.
3. Quoted in Stephen F. Mason, *A History of Sciences* (New York: Collier Books, 1962), p. 206.
4. Quoted in James Harvey Robinson and Charles A. Beard, *Readings in European History,* Vol. 1 (Boston: Ginn and Co., 1908), pp. 202–205.
5. Quoted in E. Neville Williams, *The Ancient Régime in Europe* (New York: Harper & Row, 1970), p. 424.

Chapter 19

1. Hilary Beckles, *Natural Rebels: A Social History* (New Brunswick, N.J.: Rutgers University Press, 1989), p. 155.
2. Richard Pankhurst, *The Ethiopians* (London: Blackwell Publishers, 1998), p. 109.
3. Donald Crummey, *Land and Society in the Christian Kingdom of Ethiopia from the Thirteenth to the Twentieth Century* (Oxford: James Currey, 2000), p. 95.
4. Crummey, p. 131.

Chapter 20

1. From Walter Andrews et al., trans., *Ottoman Lyric Poetry* (Austin: University of Texas Press, 1997), p. 137.
2. Matsuo Bashō, cited in Harold G. Henderson, *An Introduction to Haiku* (New York: Doubleday, 1958), p. 18.

Chapter 21

1. Quoted in Clinton L. Rossiter, *The First American Revolution* (New York: Harcourt Brace, 1956), prefatory note.
2. Quoted in Madison Smartt Bell, *Master of the Crossroads* (New York: Pantheon, 2000).

Chapter 22

1. R. B. Mitchell, *Abstract of British Historical Statistics,* (Cambridge: Cambridge University Press, 1962), p. 60, as cited by Joyce Burnett, "Women Workers in the British Industrial Revolution," http://eh.net/encyclopedia/article/burnette:women.workers.britain.
2. Carolyn Tuttle, *Child Labor During the British Industrial Revolution,* http://eh.net/encyclopedia/article/tuttle.labor.child.britain.
3. Charles Darwin "The Origin of Species," in *Introduction to Contemporary Civilization in the West,* Vol. 2 (New York: Columbia University Press, 1955), pp. 453–454.
4. William Wordsworth, "Composed in the Valley Near Dover on the Day of Landing," in *Selected Poetry of William Wordsworth* (New York: Modern Library, 1950).
5. From John Keats, "Ode on a Grecian Urn," from *Poems* (1820).

Chapter 23

1. Quoted in F. Owen, *Tempestuous Journey: Lloyd George, His Life and Times* (London: Hutchinson), p. 186.
2. Quoted in Basil Dmystryshyn, ed., *Imperial Russia: A Source Book, 1700–1917* (New York: Holt, Rinehart, and Winston, 1967), p. 241.

Chapter 24

1. Adam Hochschild, *King Leopold's Ghost* (New York: Houghton Mifflin Co., 1998), p. 58.
2. *London Times,* Aug. 7, 1890.
3. David Lan, *Guns and Rain: Guerrillas and Spirit Mediums in Zimbabwe* (Berkeley: University of California Press, 1985), p. 6.
4. Adu Boahen, *Africa Under Colonial Domination, 1880–1935,* UNESCO General History of Africa, Vol. VII (Berkeley: University of California Press, 1985), p. 4.
5. Harold Marcus, *The Life and Times of Menelik II Ethiopia 1844–1913* (Oxford: Clarendon, 1975), p. 160.
6. Nina Mba, *Nigerian Women Mobilized: Women's Political Activity in Southern Nigeria, 1900–1945* (Berkeley, Calif.: Institute of International Studies, 1982), p. 76.
7. Quoted in William Tordoff, *Government and Politics in Africa,* 3rd ed. (Indiana University Press, 1997), p. 39.
8. Patrick Manning, *Francophone Sub-Saharan Africa, 1880–1985* (Cambridge: Cambridge University Press, 1988), p. 45.
9. Hochschild, *King Leopold's Ghost,* p. 112.
10. Quoted in N. D. Harris, *Europe and the East* (Boston: Houghton Mifflin, 1926) p. 285.

Chapter 25

1. Frederick Weed, quoted in D. R. Sar Desai, *Southeast Asia: Past and Present* (Boulder, Colo.: Westview Press, 1989), p. 101.
2. General Jacob F. Smith, quoted in Sar Desai, p. 149.
3. Quoted in Franz H. Michael and George E. Taylor, *The Far East in the Modern World* (New York: Holt, Rinehart and Winston, 1956), p. 122.
4. Quoted in Ch'u Chai and Winberg Chai, *The Changing Society of China* (New York: Mentor Books, 1962), p. 189.
5. Julia Adeny Thomas, "Naturalizing Nationhood: Ideology and Practice in Early Twentieth-Century Japan," in Sharon A. Minichiello, ed., *Japan's Competing Modernities* (Honolulu: University of Hawaii Press, 1998), p. 117.
6. Presbyterian minister Dunmore Lang, quoted in Donald Denoon and Philippa Mein-Smith, eds., *A History of Australia, New Zealand and the Pacific* (Oxford: Blackwell Publishers, 2000), p. 120.
7. Isaac Featherston, quoted in Denoon and Mein-Smith, p. 80.

Chapter 26

1. Robert Conrad, *The Destruction of Brazilian Slavery, 1850–1888* (Berkeley, Calif.: University of California Press, 1972), p. 11.
2. Michael C. Meyer and William H. Beezley, eds., *Oxford History of Mexico* (Oxford: Oxford University Press, 2000), p. 403.
3. Peter Standish, ed., *Dictionary of Twentieth Century Hispanic Culture of South Africa* (New York: Gale Research, 1995), p. 265.
4. Donald Castro, "Women in the World of the Tango," in Gertrude Yeager, ed., *Confronting Change, Challenging Tradition: Women in Latin American History* (Wilmington, Del.: Scholarly Resources, 1994), p. 68.
5. Quoted in Foster Rhea Dulles, *America's Rise to World Power, 1898–1954* (New York: Harper & Row, 1955), p. 4.

Chapter 27

1. Quoted by C. J. H. Hayes, *A Political and Cultural History of Modern Europe,* Vol. 2 (New York: Macmillan, 1939), p. 572.
2. Edward Grey, Viscount of Fallodon, *25 Years,* Vol. 2 (New York: Stokes, 1925), p. 20.
3. "Women and the First World War," http://www.spartacus.schoolnet.co.uk.
4. "The Soldier," in *The Collected Poems of Rupert Brooke* (New York: Dodd, Mead, 1915).
5. "Anthem for a Doomed Youth," in *The Collected Poems of Wilfred Owen.* Copyright © 1963 by Chatto & Windus, Ltd., 1946. Reprinted by permission of New Directions Publishing Corporation and Chatto & Windus on behalf of the estate of Wilfred Owen.
6. Quoted in R. J. Sontag, *European Diplomatic History, 1871–1932* (New York: Century, 1933), p. 392.
7. George F. Kennan, *The Decision to Intervene* (Princeton, N.J.: Princeton University Press, 1958), p. 471.
8. A. J. Ryder, *Twentieth-Century Germany: From Bismarck to Brandt* (New York: Columbia University Press, 1973), p. 216.
9. Alan Bullock, *Hitler: A Study in Tyranny* (New York: Harper Torchbooks, 1964), p. 91.
10. Sidney Pollard, *European Economic Integration, 1815–1970* (New York: Harcourt Brace Jovanovich, 1974), p. 138.
11. John Kenneth Galbraith, *The Great Crash, 1929* (Boston: Houghton Mifflin, 1961), p. 173.

Chapter 28

1. Roger Griffin, *Fascism: An Oxford Reader* (Oxford: Oxford University Press, 1995), pp. 4–9.
2. Stanley G. Payne, *A History of Fascism, 1914–1945* (Madison: University of Wisconsin Press, 1995), ch. 1.
3. Robert O. Paxton, *The Anatomy of Fascism* (London: Penguin Books, 2004), pp. 219–220.
4. Benito Mussolini, *Fascism: Doctrine and Institutions* (New York: Fertig, 1968), p. 38.
5. Elizabeth Wiskemann, *Fascism in Italy: Its Development and Influence* (New York: St. Martin's Press, 1969), p. 23.
6. Peter Gay, *Weimar Culture* (New York: Harper Torchbooks, 1968), p. 23.
7. David S. Landes, *The Unbound Prometheus: Technological Change and Industrial Development in Western Europe from 1750 to the Present* (Cambridge: Cambridge University Press, 1969), p. 398.
8. After 1917, the Communist authorities adopted the Western-style, Gregorian calendar. In the calendar in use at that time, however, the Julian calendar, the first Russian Revolution took place in February.
9. In the 69 years of the USSR's existence, there were only seven general secretaries: Stalin, Nikita Khrushchev (1953–1964), Leonid Brezhnev (1964–1982), Yuri Andropov (1982–1984), Konstantin Chernenko (1984–1985), Mikhail Gorbachev (1985–1991), and the acting GenSec who served for five days during the abortive coup attempt from August 24 to August 29, 1991, Vladimir Ivashko.
10. J. N. Westwood, *Endurance and Endeavour: Russian History, 1812–1986* (Oxford: Oxford University Press, 1987), p. 276.
11. Lynne Viola, "Bab'i i Bunty and the Peasant Worker's Protest During Collectivization," in Beatrice Farnsworth and Lynne Viola, eds., *Russian Peasant Women* (Oxford: Oxford University Press, 1992), pp. 191, 198.
12. Roberta Manning, "Women in the Soviet Countryside on the Eve of World War II, 1935–1940," in Farnsworth and Viola, *Russian Peasant Women,* pp. 206–207.

Chapter 29

1. Chen Duxiu, inaugural issue of *New Youth*, 1915, cited in Patricia Buckley Ebrey, *The Cambridge Illustrated History of China* (Cambridge, University Press, 1996) p. 270.
2. Mao Tse-tung, "Report on an Investigation of a Peasant Movement in Hunan," in *Selected Works of Mao Tse-tung* (Beijing: Foreign Languages Press, 1967), Vol. 1.
3. Louis Fischer, *The Life of Mahatma Gandhi* (New York: Collier Books, 1966), p. 159.
4. Sarojini Naidu, cited in Stanley Wolpert, *A New History of India*, 6th ed. (New York: Oxford University Press, 2000), p. 315.
5. Fischer, p. 285.
6. Tilak, cited in Wolpert, p. 261.
7. Jawaharlal Nehru, *Toward Freedom* (New York: Day, 1942), p. 353.

Chapter 30

1. William Cleveland, *A History of the Modern Middle East* (Boulder, Colo.: Westview Press, 1994), p. 155.
2. Kwame Nkrumah, *Ghana: The Autobiography of Kwame Nkrumah* (London: Nelson, 1957), p. 27.
3. Ali Mazrui and Michael Tidy, *Nationalism and New States in Africa* (London: Heinemann, 1984), p. 22.
4. Basil Davidson, *Modern Africa: A Social and Political History,* 2nd ed. (New York: Longman, 1989), p. 66.
5. Michael Crowder, *West Africa Under Colonial Rule* (London: Hutchinson and Co., 1968), p. 482.

Chapter 31

1. George F. Kennan, *Memoirs* (New York: Bantam Books, 1969), p. 122.
2. John Toland, *Adolf Hitler* (New York: Ballantine Books, 1977), pp. 522, 529.
3. Francis L. Loewenheim, *Peace or Appeasement* (Boston: Houghton Mifflin, 1965), pp. 2, 4.
4. Robert Keith Middlemas, *Strategy of Appeasement: The British Government and Germany, 1937–1939* (Chicago: Quadrangle Books, 1972), p. 177.
5. Winston L. S. Churchill, *Blood, Sweat, and Tears* (New York: Putnam, 1941), p. 66.
6. Franklin D. Roosevelt, "Address at Chicago, October 5, 1937," in *The Literature of the United States,* eds. W. Blair, T. Hornberger, and R. Stewart, Vol. 2 (Chicago: Scott, Foresman, 1955), p. 831.
7. Niall Ferguson, *The War of the World* (London: Penguin/Allen Lane, 2006), p. 388.
8. S. E. Ayling, *Portraits of Power* (New York: Barnes & Noble, 1963), p. 159.
9. Nigel Nicolson, ed., *Harold Nicolson: The War Years, 1939–1945* (New York: Atheneum, 1967), p. 100.
10. Churchill, *Blood, Sweat, and Tears,* p. 297.
11. James Risen, "U.S. Details 6 Neutral Countries' Role in Aiding Nazis," *New York Times,* June 21, 1998.
12. *Last Letters from Stalingrad,* trans. Franz Schneider and Charles Gullas (New York: Signet Books, 1965), p. 20.
13. Quoted in John Vinocur, "Goebbels in Published 1945 Diary Blames Goering for Nazi's Collapse," *New York Times,* Jan. 3, 1978.
14. Ferguson, *The War of the World,* p. 446.
15. For important testimony about life in Auschwitz, see Primo Levi, *Survival in Auschwitz* (New York: Touchstone Books/Simon and Schuster, 1996).
16. For a summation of this story, see Jan T. Gross, "Neighbors," *New Yorker,* March 12, 1991, pp. 64–77. For fuller coverage, see *Gross's Neighbors: The Destruction of the Jewish Community in Jedwabne, Poland* (Princeton, N.J.: Princeton University Press, 1991).
17. See Daniel Jonah Goldhagen, *Hitler's Willing Executioners: Ordinary Germans and the Holocaust* (New York: Knopf, 1996). The most outspoken criticism of Goldhagen's thesis is to be found in Norman G. Finkelstein and Ruth Bettina Birn, *A Nation on Trial: The Goldhagen Thesis and Historical Truth* (New York: Henry Holt, 1998).
18. Raul Hilberg, *The Destruction of the European Jews* (Chicago: Quadrangle Books, 1961); Maurice Crouzet, *Histoire Générale des Civilisations,* Vol. 7 (Paris: Presses Universitaires de France, 1957), pp. 358–359.
19. "Obituary, Telford Taylor," *The Economist,* May 30, 1998, p. 95.

Chapter 32

1. From U.S. Congress, *Congressional Record,* 80th Congress, 1st Session, Vol. 93 (Washington, D.C.: U.S. Government Printing Office, 1947), p. 1981.
2. Quoted in David Rees, *The Age of Containment* (New York: St. Martin's Press, 1967), p. 23.

Chapter 33

1. Samad Behrangi, *The Little Black Fish and Other Stories,* trans. Eric and Mary Hooglund (Washington, D.C.: Three Continents Press, 1982), p. 37.
2. Joshua Nkomo, *The Story of My Life* (New York: Methuen, 1984), p. 245.
3. Elizabeth Schmidt, *"Now You Have Touched the Women": African Women's Resistance to the Pass Laws in South Africa, 1950–1960,* Notes and Documents 6/83. (New York: United Nations Centre Against Apartheid, March, 1983), p. 19.

Chapter 35

1. Richard Rovere, *Senator Joe McCarthy* (London: Methuen, 1959), p. 24.
2. "As Japan Goes... ," *The Economist,* June 20, 1998.

Chapter 36

1. "Business...," *The Economist,* November 24, 2006, p. 7.
2. Bill Emmott, "Freedom's Journey," *The Economist,* September 18, 1999 (special supplement), pp. 10, 11, 37, 38.
3. "The Rich and the Poor and the Growing Gap Between Them," *The Economist,* June 17, 2006, pp. 24-26.
4. George Packer, "The Megacity," *New Yorker,* November 13, 2006, pp. 62–75.

INDEX

Note: Page numbers followed by letters *i* and *m* indicate illustrations and maps, respectively. Boldface page numbers indicate key terms.

C

D

F

G

H

K

M

N

S

T

U

X

Y

Contemporary Political Map of the World
ALASKA (U.S.)
CANADA
GREENLAND (KALAALLIT NUNAAT) (Den.)
ICELAND
IRELAND
UNITED STATES
AZORES (Port.)
ATLANTIC OCEAN
CANARY IS. (Sp.)
WESTERN SAHARA (Mor.)
MEXICO
BAHAMAS
DOMINICAN REPUBLIC
HAITI
CUBA
JAMAICA
BELIZE
GUATEMALA
HONDURAS
EL SALVADOR
NICARAGUA
COSTA RICA
PANAMA
PUERTO RICO (U.S.)
ST. KITTS AND NEVIS
ANTIGUA AND BARBUDA
GUADELOUPE (Fr.)
DOMINICA
MARTINIQUE (Fr.)
ST. VINCENT AND THE GRENADINES
ST. LUCIA
BARBADOS
GRENADA
TRINIDAD AND TOBAGO
GUYANA
SURINAME
FRENCH GUIANA (Fr.)
VENEZUELA
COLOMBIA
ECUADOR
GALÁPAGOS IS. (Ec.)
CAPE VERDE
SENEGAL
THE GAMBIA
GUINEA-BISSAU
GUINEA
SIERRA LEONE
LIBERIA
HAWAII (U.S.)
PACIFIC OCEAN
BRAZIL
PERU
BOLIVIA
PARAGUAY
CHILE
URUGUAY
ARGENTINA
FALKLAND IS. (U.K.)
WESTERN SAMOA
AMERICAN SAMOA (U.S.)
TONGA
FRENCH POLYNESIA (Fr.)
0 1,500 3,000 Miles
0 1,500 3,000 Kilometers
Tropic of Cancer
Tropic of Capricorn
0° Equator

20°E
40°E
60°E
80°E
100°E
120°E
140°E
160°E
CTIC OCEAN
SWEDEN
FINLAND
RUSSIA
ESTONIA
LATVIA
LITH.
RUS.
POLAND
BELARUS
CZ. REP.
SLVK.
UKRAINE
AUS.
HUNG.
MOLDOVA
ROMANIA
CRO.
YUGO.
B.–H.
BULGARIA
ITALY
ALB.
MAC.
GREECE
GEORGIA
ARMENIA
TURKEY
AZERBAIJAN
KAZAKHSTAN
MONGOLIA
UZBEKISTAN
KYRGYZSTAN
TURKMENISTAN
TAJIKISTAN
N. KOREA
S. KOREA
JAPAN
CHINA
PACIFIC OCEAN
TUNISIA
MALTA
CYPRUS
SYRIA
LEB.
ISRAEL
IRAQ
IRAN
AFGHANISTAN
PAKISTAN
JORDAN
KUWAIT
BAHRAIN
NEPAL
BHUTAN
LIBYA
EGYPT
SAUDI ARABIA
QATAR
UNITED ARAB EMIRATES
OMAN
BANGLADESH
INDIA
MYANMAR (BURMA)
LAOS
TAIWAN
Hong Kong
Macao (Port.)
VIETNAM
CHAD
SUDAN
ERITREA
YEMEN
DJIBOUTI
THAILAND
CAMBODIA
PHILIPPINES
NORTHERN MARIANA IS. (U.S.)
GUAM (U.S.)
MARSHALL IS.
CENTRAL AFRICAN REP.
ETHIOPIA
SOMALIA
MALDIVES
SRI LANKA
BRUNEI
MALAYSIA
PALAU
FEDERATED STATES OF MICRONESIA
CAMEROON
GABON
CONGO
RWANDA
UGANDA
KENYA
DEM. REP. OF THE CONGO
BURUNDI
TANZANIA
SINGAPORE
NAURU
KIRIBATI
COMOROS
MAYOTTE (Fr.)
SEYCHELLES
INDONESIA
PAPUA NEW GUINEA
TUVALU
SOLOMON IS.
ANGOLA
ZAMBIA
MALAWI
INDIAN OCEAN
VANUATU
FIJI
ZIMBABWE
MADAGASCAR
NAMIBIA
BOTSWANA
MOZAMBIQUE
RÉUNION (Fr.)
MAURITIUS
NEW CALEDONIA (Fr.)
AUSTRALIA
SWAZILAND
SOUTH AFRICA
LESOTHO
NEW ZEALAND
ANTARCTICA